Legislative Process

ASPEN PUBLISHERS

Legislative Process

Third Edition

Abner J. Mikva

Former Visiting Professor of Law
University of Chicago
Former Counsel to the President
of the United States
Former Chief Judge, United States
Court of Appeals, D.C. Circuit
Former United States Representative
State of Illinois

Eric Lane

Eric J. Schmertz Distinguished
Professor of Public Law
and Public Service
Hofstra University

 Wolters Kluwer
Law & Business

AUSTIN   BOSTON   CHICAGO   NEW YORK   THE NETHERLANDS

Aspen Publishers
Attn: Permissions Department
76 Ninth Avenue, 7th Floor
New York, NY   10011-5201

To contact Customer Care, e-mail customer.care@aspenpublishers.com, call 1-800-234-1660, fax 1-800-901-9075, or mail correspondence to:

Aspen Publishers
Attn: Order Department
PO Box 990
Frederick, MD 21705

Printed in the United States of America.

1 2 3 4 5 6 7 8 9 0

ISBN 978-0-7355-7662-9

CIP or ISSN

Library of Congress Cataloging-in-Publication Data

Mikva, Abner J.
    Legislative process / Abner J. Mikva, Eric Lane. — 3rd ed.
        p.   cm.
    Includes bibliographical references and index.
    ISBN 978-0-7355-7662-9
    1. Legislation — United States.   2. Legislative power — United States.   3. Statutes — United States.   4. Law — United States — Interpretation and construction.   5. Representative government and representation — United States.   I. Lane, Eric, 1943-   II. Title.

KF4945.M55 2009
328.73'077 — dc22

                                                                          2009007700

About Wolters Kluwer Law & Business

Wolters Kluwer Law & Business is a leading provider of research information and workflow solutions in key specialty areas. The strengths of the individual brands of Aspen Publishers, CCH, Kluwer Law International and Loislaw are aligned within Wolters Kluwer Law & Business to provide comprehensive, in-depth solutions and expert-authored content for the legal, professional and education markets.

CCH was founded in 1913 and has served more than four generations of business professionals and their clients. The CCH products in the Wolters Kluwer Law & Business group are highly regarded electronic and print resources for legal, securities, antitrust and trade regulation, government contracting, banking, pension, payroll, employment and labor, and healthcare reimbursement and compliance professionals.

Aspen Publishers is a leading information provider for attorneys, business professionals and law students. Written by preeminent authorities, Aspen products offer analytical and practical information in a range of specialty practice areas from securities law and intellectual property to mergers and acquisitions and pension/benefits. Aspen's trusted legal education resources provide professors and students with high-quality, up-to-date and effective resources for successful instruction and study in all areas of the law.

Kluwer Law International supplies the global business community with comprehensive English-language international legal information. Legal practitioners, corporate counsel and business executives around the world rely on the Kluwer Law International journals, loose-leafs, books and electronic products for authoritative information in many areas of international legal practice.

Loislaw is a premier provider of digitized legal content to small law firm practitioners of various specializations. Loislaw provides attorneys with the ability to quickly and efficiently find the necessary legal information they need, when and where they need it, by facilitating access to primary law as well as state-specific law, records, forms and treatises.

Wolters Kluwer Law & Business, a unit of Wolters Kluwer, is headquartered in New York and Riverwoods, Illinois. Wolters Kluwer is a leading multinational publisher and information services company.

To Edward H. Levi, my law school teacher and friend, who made me think about the legislative process, but who bears no responsibility for the thoughts.

—Abner J. Mikva

In memory of my father, Jesse Lane, an intellectual and advocate, who instilled in me a cautious trust in representative government.

To my wife, Joyce Talmadge, whose love and encouragement nurtured my efforts and whose incisiveness helped limit their excesses.

To my mother, Louise Lane, for her inspiring energy and curiosity.

And to the other members of my family, Adam, Josh, Deborah, Larry, Jane, Arthur, Rick, Taryn, Courtney, and Travis, for being such important parts of my life.

—Eric Lane

Summary of Contents

Contents

PART I   Introduction: Legislatures and Statutes

1

CHAPTER 1   The Age of Statutes

3

CHAPTER 2 The Anatomy and Publication of   45
Statutes

PART III The Legitimizing Characteristics of American Legislatures   269

CHAPTER 6 Representativeness — The Electorate   271

CHAPTER 7   Representativeness — Elections, Qualifications, Representative Duties   351

PART IV   Establishing the Meaning of a Statute   671

CHAPTER 10   The Interpretation of Statutes   673

Preface to the Third Edition

Seven years have elapsed since the publication of our second edition. During those years the United States has fallen victim to domestic terrorist attacks, engaged in two wars abroad and a global war against terrorism, watched its economy fall to a point lower than most of us have ever known, and, on the hopeful side, elected its first African-American President. Congress' institutional role during this period not only has been overshadowed by the executive, but has also, to a degree, deteriorated. Congressional scholars Thomas E. Mann and Norman J. Ornstein have labeled it "the broken branch," in reference to Congress' all but total abrogation of its constitutional obligation to check a President's drive toward war. Beyond that, a number of scandals involving lobbyists further challenged Congress' legitimacy. In this new edition we address these issues through an increased focus on legislative oversight and executive privilege, and a look at the Honest Leadership and Open Government Act of 2007.

This edition also updates the law in a number of areas. For example, Davis v. Bandemer is replaced with Vieth v. Jubelirer, as the Court continues to evidence uncertainty about the justiciability of gerrymandering. We also take a look at Wisconsin v. City of New York for an update on the census, sampling, and statistical tools for redistricting. Finally, we address developments in campaign finance reform—this time through an exploration of the Bipartisan Campaign Reform Act of 2002 and McConnell v. FEC.

At the suggestion of a number of law professors we also have made an organizational change to the text. For the last edition we had moved our introductory chapter on statutory interpretation to the front of the book, for some long-forgotten reason that seemed to make sense at the time. In practice it didn't. So we have moved that chapter back to Part IV of the book.

These changes reflect our continuing and unwavering commitment to providing both teacher and student with a broad range of material that allows them to fully explore and evaluate the legislative process. And, through this exploration and evaluation, we hope to spur more direct involvement by lawyers in the legislative process and in its never-ending need for improvement.

We are pleased to acknowledge those who have helped with this edition. Dean Nora Demleitner and the Hofstra Law School have provided generous support for this effort. A number of students also proved generous with their time, enthusiasm, and energy. Mimi Alinikoff, Ella Govshtein, Gariel Nahoum, and Joshua Wolf all explored sections of the book for possible updates and, where needed, researched and drafted proposals. These proposals then went through an iterative editing process. At the end of that process, some of their writing remained intact. In that sense, they all deserve credit for some portions of the new text, but only we bear responsibility for its substance and expression.

A.J.M.

E.L.

February 2009

Preface to the Second Edition

The law has changed or been clarified with respect to many of the topics we addressed in the first edition in 1995. For example, the United States Supreme Court has limited Congress' Commerce Clause jurisdiction, added an equal protection screen over its voting rights jurisprudence, and placed political party spending under the protection of the First Amendment. It has also found federal term limits, scarlet letter initiative, and a balanced budget statute unconstitutional. Additionally, Congress has enacted a new lobbying act and, as this edition is being published, is struggling to restructure the regulation of campaign finance. These changes and more have been incorporated into the second edition.

The second edition includes one substantial organizational change. We have rewritten and relocated our introduction to statutory interpretation from Chapter 10 to Chapter 3. We made this change first because of the chapter's introductory nature and second because many of the cases we use to illustrate various aspects of the legislative process involve statutory interpretation. The earlier placement of the primer will make those cases easier to understand.

These changes reflect our unaltered commitment to providing teachers and students with a broad range of materials that will allow them to fully explore and evaluate the legislative process. And, through this exploration and evaluation, we hope to spur more direct involvement by lawyers in the legislative process and its never ending need for improvement.

We are pleased to acknowledge and thank those who have helped with this edition. Dean David Yellen and former dean, now president, Stuart Rabinowitz have provided generous support for this effort. A number of students have also participated. Melissa A. Siegel has been the mainstay of this effort, doing not only research, but the grinding work of indexing the text. Others whose aid has proved invaluable are Angel M. Anton,

Laurie Berberich, Nicole Maglio, June D. Reiter, and Allison J. Weisman. Finally, the people at Aspen also improved this effort.

A.J.M.
E.L.

February 2002

Preface to the First Edition

This book is about American legislative institutions and the processes they employ to consider and enact legislation. There are close to 40,000 legislative bodies in the United States: two for the nation, ninety-nine for the states (Nebraska has a unicameral legislature), and the remainder for the multitude of counties, cities, towns, villages, and other municipalities that demark this country's political landscape.

Each year these legislative bodies pass thousands of laws that regulate or affect our lives. Through their processes, substantially similar in every legislature, these representative bodies imprint on our lawmaking the emblems of this country's democracy: the establishment of a legislative agenda by measuring and sifting infinite individual and group demands; the slowness, deliberateness, and often redundancy of the process, all aimed at protecting against legislative intemperance (but which also lead to inefficiencies); and the representation of diverse views and moderation of these views through compromises.

This cascade of legislative activity has effected a significant change in the practice of law. Thousands of lawyers are now involved in the consideration of legislation as legislators, legislative staff, and lobbyists. Many more spend their time interpreting and applying these statutes in government agencies and in private practice. And finally, the work of the courts has followed this change, as they have been called on increasingly to settle conflicting interpretations of statutory language. Consequently, there has been an evolving recognition on the part of most law schools that the education of law students must include an awareness of the significance of statutory lawmaking and a critical understanding of legislative institutions and their processes.

Each of us has taught courses in the legislative process using a variety of different materials. We have found that the best way to make students privy to the legislative process is through the extensive use of primary legislative materials. We do not abjure cases, however. We use them to explore the judicial role in the legislative process. In the best of the common law tradition, cases are about judicial thinking and judicial processes, not about legislative thinking and legislative processes.

This book is a product of our teaching experiences as well as our respective experiences participating directly in the legislative process. Using materials such as bills, committee reports, legislative rules, debates, statutes, constitutional provisions and cases, and other legislative authorities, we hope to provide teachers and students with a range of materials that will allow them to fully explore and evaluate the legislative process in its various contexts.

While much of the material deals with the United States Congress, the many similarities between the congressional process and the processes of other American legislative bodies, as well as the considerable materials from and references to these other processes, expose the student to all of the varieties of the legislative species.

Notwithstanding our criticisms in this book of the failings and imperfections of the legislative process, it would be disingenuous of us not to acknowledge our admiration for the legislative process as the model of government closest to the ideals of representative democracy We hope that by writing this book we share an informed enthusiasm with teachers and students and spur some of them to direct engagement with the process and its needed improvements.

A.J.M.
E.L.

About the Authors

ABNER J. MIKVA

Abner J. Mikva was a visiting professor at the University of Chicago Law School. He has served as Counsel to the President of the United States (1994-1995), judge on the United States Courts of Appeals for the District of Columbia Circuit (1979-1994), and as chief judge of the D.C. Circuit (1991-1994). Before coming to the bench, he served as a Congressman for five terms and, prior to that, as a member of the Illinois House of Representatives. He also served as a law clerk to Supreme Court Justice Sherman Minton.

ERIC LANE

Eric Lane is the Eric J. Schmertz Distinguished Professor of Public Law and Public Service at Hofstra University School of Law, where he has been teaching since 1976. He also serves as the Senior Fellow at Brennan Center for Justice. He has also served as Counsel to the Speaker of the New York City Council, Counsel to the New York State Temporary Commission on Constitutional Revision (1993-1995), as Chair of the New York City Task Force on Charter Implementation (1990), as Executive Director/Counsel to the New York City Charter Revision Commission (1986-1989), and as Chief Counsel to the New York State Senate Minority (1981-1986).

Legislative Process

PART *I*

Introduction: Legislatures and Statutes

PART I
Introduction: Legislatures
and Statutes

CHAPTER *1*

The Age of Statutes

We live in an age of statutes. Since the early part of the twentieth century, the nation's legislatures have served as the dominant institutions for determining public policy and translating it into law. Legal historian J. Willard Hurst observed in Dealing with Statutes 1 (1982):

> More than constitutional law or common law, legislation and interpretation of legislation by lawyers, executive and administrative officers, and judges provide the bases for those parts of legal order which enter most broadly into people's everyday lives as well as into grand designs of public policy. Statute law directly embodies governing standards and rules for major sectors of life in society. . . .

Through statutes, today's legislatures:

- redistribute enormous amounts of wealth for the benefit of the poor, the ill, the aged, the unemployed, and the disabled, to name a few;
- regulate the market by prohibiting trusts, requiring minimum wages, controlling wages and prices, setting trade policy, favoring certain interests through tax incentives, setting the borrowing limit, and authorizing huge expenditures;
- protect the health and safety of workers;
- promote peaceful labor relations;
- support huge transportation systems;
- maintain and ultimately govern school systems;
- regulate the environment;
- address race, sex, disability, and age discrimination in the political process and the workplace;

- protect against risk in consumer products;
- require fairness and reduce commercialization in broadcasting;
- define property rights;
- create standards of acceptable individual behavior;
- define and regulate familial relations; and,
- where appropriate, create administrative agencies and authorize the expenditure of enormous amounts of money for the administration of programs.

These purposes are effected by many thousands of statutes passed each year by Congress and state and local legislatures throughout the country.

Legislative activity during this period of time has been so dramatic that one scholar has characterized it as "a rights revolution," which "has renovated the original constitutional framework and the system of government under which the nation operated for most of its history." Cass Sunstein, After the Rights Revolution 12-13 (1990). Another has stated:

> Law making in our time depends on legislation, and our primary reliance on statutory law is being increasingly recognized. . . .
>
> The New Deal Legislation of the 1930's not only applied legislation to the solution of the economic, social, and ultimately legal problems of its times, but it also changed the very nature of the legislative product. The ascendancy of legislation resulted not only in a far greater legislative output, but also in the development of massive programmatic legislation, unique in its character and different in kind from the narrow, limited statutes that had preceded it. . . . [T]he new legislative approach, here referred to as programmatic legislation, imposes a responsibility for legal training which develops to the fullest the ability to use legislation as the way to solve today's legal problems.

Frank P. Grad, The Ascendancy of Legislation: Legal Problem Solving in Our Time, 9 Dalhousie L.J. 228, 228 (1985).

This chapter addresses the lawmaking efforts and powers of legislative bodies. It provides an introduction to the study of the legislative process: first, by noting the breadth of modern legislative activity; second, by broadly describing, from a historical perspective, the rise of statutes as the nation's primary source of law and the conditions that contributed to this rise; third, by highlighting some of the most important elements of the legislative process and briefly comparing them with some aspects of the judicial process; and, fourth, by briefly exploring the constitutional grants of powers to legislatures.

Legislation is not abstract. (This is a point we will stress continuously throughout the book.) It is the consensus product of the collective decisions of elected representatives about the dimensions of particular problems and their sense of the appropriateness of various solutions. These decisions are never made in calm settings. They are usually arrived at in highly pressurized environments, in which numerous groups compete for the protection or advancement of different and opposing interests. These pressures are tempered and molded into legislation by a complex, broad, instrumental, and unending legislative process that also includes elections and judicial decisions. This process, particularly at the federal and state levels, is the subject of this book.

A.   DEMAND FOR STATUTES: A BRIEF HISTORICAL EXPLORATION

1.   The Ascendancy of Statutory Law

In America, legislatures were established as the first branches of the federal and state governments. It is not by accident that the Framers of the U.S. Constitution and most state constitutions devoted the first articles to the legislative branch and granted exclusive lawmaking powers to these bodies. Also not by accident, it is only Congress and the state legislatures that, of all the branches of government, play a role in the amendment of the federal and state constitutions. According to the historian Gordon Wood:

> Putting the magistracy in its place may have set the cornerstones of the new state constitutions, but it hardly completed the business of building free governments. For the legislatures remained to be constructed, and no one doubted that the legislature was the most important part of any government. "It is in their legislatures," declared a Rhode Islander, echoing Locke and all good Whigs, "that the members of a commonwealth are united and combined together into one coherent, living body. This is the soul that gives form, life and unity to the commonwealth." In fact, the Revolution had begun precisely because the English, by "declaring themselves invested with power to legislate for us in all cases whatsoever," had threatened the Americans' very existence as a free people. To legislate was to make law, and "as a good government is an empire of laws," said John Adams, "The first question is, how shall the laws be made?"

Gordon S. Wood, The Creation of the American Republic, 1776-1787, 162 (1969).

The possession of power does not assure its exercise, and, for much of their earlier history, the nation's legislative bodies remained relatively quiet.

> In the first three quarters of the nineteenth century the performance of Congress and the state legislatures showed relatively limited and unskillful use of their endowments. The bulk of the statute books consisted of highly

particularized measures; statutes of broad policy or general reach were relatively few and reflected little bold programming or implementation.

J. Willard Hurst, Dealing with Statutes 10 (1982). Such legislative quiescence was relative to the needs of the times and should not mask the statutory efforts of Congress and state legislatures to establish new governments, after the ratification of the Constitution, and to promote economic growth. See generally Lawrence M. Friedman, A History of American Law (1985); Morton Horwitz, The Transformation of American Law (1977); J. Willard Hurst, Dealing with Statutes (1982); James C. Sundquist, The Decline and Resurgence of Congress (1981).

One consequence of legislative inactivity was a significant level of judicial lawmaking activity. During this "common law" period, "judges became our preferred problem-solvers" (Grant Gilmore, The Ages of American Law 35-36 (1977)), and a "vast majority of regulatory functions were undertaken by the common law courts, which elaborated the basic principles of property, tort, and contract. Public and private interactions were controlled largely through these principles." Cass Sunstein, After the Rights Revolution 16 (1990). See generally Morton Horwitz, The Transformation of American Law (1977).

What explains such legislative inactivity? Certainly the traditional mistrust of government and the resulting structural checks on its activities stood against active legislatures. It is useful, as Professor Sunstein points out, "to understand the system as designed largely to protect rights against government." Cass Sunstein, After the Rights Revolution 17 (1990). The elements of the design are the various forms of checks and balances found in both federal and state constitutions. Included among these elements are provisions mandating the separation of powers, providing for bicameral legislatures and the veto, and establishing the federal system. Many of these provisions were intended to curb perceived popular despotism reflected in the acts of many state legislatures during the period immediately preceding the adoption of the Constitution. See Gordon S. Wood, The Creation of the American Republic, 1776-1787, 403-13 (1969). Later, popular mistrust of state legislative activities became so substantial that various state constitutions were amended to limit the scope of state legislative activity. Discussion of such checks and balances occurs throughout this book.

But neither tradition nor structure alone can explain legislative inactivity. Legislative activity is built on demand for change; if legislative bodies are inactive, it is largely because politically recognized demands by politically recognized people are not being made. Professor Hurst captures this concisely: "[c]ontemporary society more readily accepted lawmaking by judges because people so often saw problems as calling for relatively limited adjustment of one-to-one confrontations—between buyer and seller, mortgagor and mortgagee, tortfeasor and victim, husband and wife."

J. Willard Hurst, Dealing with Statutes 12 (1982). As discussed in Section C of this chapter, early legislative activity reflected this same perception of problems, as legislative bodies spent considerable time resolving problems of individual persons, such as granting divorces.

The ascendancy of legislatures to their present position in the legal order was the result of a change in the attitude described by Hurst. Individual confrontations increasingly gave way to group confrontations, which needed a different arena for their resolution. While it is impossible to capture with detail the myriad of forces and events that led to this result, consider the three following descriptions.

Lawrence M. Friedman, A History of American Law, 338-39 (2d ed. 1985): Between 1850 and 1900, the population swelled; the cities grew enormously; the Far West was settled; the country became a major industrial power; transportation and communication vastly improved; overseas expansion began. New inventions and new techniques made life easier and healthier; at the same time, the social order became immeasurably more complex, and perhaps more difficult for the average person to grasp. New social cleavages developed. The North-South cleavage was bandaged over in the 1860s and 1870s. The black man was put back in a subordinate place. When the blood of the Civil War dried, the Gilded Age began. This was the factory age, the age of money, the age of the robber barons, of capital and labor at war. And the frontier died. The pioneer, the frontier individualist, had been the American culture hero, free, self-reliant, unencumbered by the weakness that inhered in the cities. The frontier had been a symbol of an open society; opportunity was as unlimited as the sky. In 1893, Frederick Jackson Turner wrote his famous essay, "The Significance of the Frontier in American History." He traced the influence of the frontier on American character and institutions; but as he wrote the essay, Turner also announced that the frontier was dead.

What really passed was not the frontier, but the idea of the frontier. This inner sense, this *perception* of change, was perhaps one of the most important influences on American law. Between 1776 and the Civil War, dominant public opinion exuberantly believed in growth, believed that resources were virtually unlimited, that there would be room and wealth for all. The theme of American law before 1850 was the release of energy, in Willard Hurst's phrase. Develop the land; grow rich; a rising tide raises all boats. By 1900, if one can speak about so slippery a thing as dominant public opinion, that opinion saw a narrowing sky, a dead frontier, life as a struggle for position, competition as a zero-sum game, the economy as a pie to be divided, not a ladder stretching out beyond the horizon. By 1900 the theme was: Hold the line.

Many trends, developments, and movements provide at least indirect evidence of some such basic change in legal culture. One piece of evidence was the increasing propensity of Americans to join together in organized interest groups. The United States became a "nation of joiners." De Tocqueville had already noted in his travels a magnificent flowering of clubs and societies in America. "Americans," he wrote, "of all ages, all stations in life, and all types of disposition are forever forming associations ... religious, moral, serious, futile, very general and very limited, immensely large and very minute." But organization in the last half of the 19th century was more than a matter of clubs and societies. Noticeably, groupings developed that centered around economic interests — labor unions, industrial combines, farmers' organizations, occupational associations. These interest groups jockeyed for position and power in society. They molded, dominated, shaped American law.

Kermit L. Hall, The Magic Mirror 267 (1989): The Depression, which lasted from 1929 to 1941, was an economic plague so sweeping that it altered expectations about the proper relationship of law to society, of government to the governed. The white middle class had historically provided the bedrock support for the legal culture, but it experienced perhaps the most wrenching changes. That economic calamity should befall poor blacks and whites made sense in light of the laissez-faire individualism associated with the late nineteenth and early twentieth centuries, but that prosperous and hardworking citizens should be flung into unemployment and uselessness was something else altogether. The Great Depression sorely tested old assumptions, which held that voluntary rather than governmental regulation was best, that economic well-being flowed from personal virtue, and that government had a limited role in promoting the collective social welfare. The New Deal, which President Franklin D. Roosevelt initiated in 1933, stood for the proposition that lawmakers should provide a social and economic security net to catch the victims of an impersonal industrial order.

Roscoe Pound, Law in Books and Law in Action, 44 Am. L. Rev. 12, 26-27, 30 (1910): Of the defects in our American administration of justice with which fault is found today, the more serious are reducible ultimately to two general propositions: (1) over-individualism in our doctrines and rules, an over-individualist conception of justice; and (2) over-reliance upon the machinery of justice and too much of the mechanical in the administration and application of rules and doctrines. ... The former expresses the feeling of the self-reliant man that, as a free moral agent, he is to make his own bargains and determine upon his own acts and control his own property, accepting the responsibility that goes with such power, subjecting himself to liability for the consequence of his free choice, but exempt from interference in making his choice. The latter expresses the feeling of the same self-reliant man that neither the state, nor its representative, the magistrate, is competent to judge him better than his own conscience; that he is not to be judged by the discretion of men, but by the inflexible rule of the law. . . . Each is a phase, therefore, of the extreme individualism which is one of the chief characteristics of the common law. . . .

When in a period of collectivist thinking and social legislation, courts and lawyers assume that the only permissible way of thinking or of law-making is limited and defined by individualism of the old type, when, while men are seeking to promote the ends of society through social control, jurists lay it down that the only method of human discipline is "to leave each man to work out in freedom his own happiness or freedom," conflict is inevitable.

The three preceding passages describe how, after the Civil War, America grew to be enormous, crowded, diverse, and economically complex. Resources became limited and opportunities were reduced. Individual efforts alone, at least for an extraordinarily large percentage of the population, no longer seemed to suffice. Organization of interests became essential for their protection and advancement. In this environment of limitation, competition between such organizations or groups for resources and opportunities became endemic. "Organization was a law of life, not merely because life was so complicated, but also because life seemed to be a competitive struggle, jungle warfare over limited resources. . . ." Lawrence M. Friedman, A History of American Law 339 (2d ed. 1985).

Interest group confrontations alone, though, do not explain the heightened increases in statute making. The role of an institution is determined, to a large extent, by its processes. The demands resulting from the changes in American society after the Civil War were, at best, too overwhelming and too immediate for the narrowly focused, "slow, unsystematic, and organic quality of common law change." Guido Calabresi, A Common Law for the Age of Statutes 5 (1982).

Also, by this period, the pragmatic judicial reasoning that had characterized the early half of the nineteenth century had given way to a more mechanical approach to decisionmaking that was far less tolerant of change (as were the judges who applied it).

American Legal Realism xii (William W. Fisher III et al. eds., 1993): Before the Civil War, an American court confronted with a difficult case typically made a conscious effort to adopt a rule and reach a decision that simultaneously advanced "public policy" (for example, by creating incentives for economic development) and secured "justice" (for example, by ensuring that no morally innocent parties suffered net economic injury or were subjected to obligations to which they had not voluntarily agreed). After the war, this frankly consequentialist style of analysis fell into disfavor. Invocations of precedent — efforts to follow rules or interpretations announced in prior judicial decisions—became more common. When no prior decision seemed directly applicable, a court often would attempt to extract from the rulings made in a group of loosely related prior cases a general principle (the more abstract and encompassing the better) that could be brought to bear on the case before it. Lawyers and judges arguing in this vein did not ignore policy considerations altogether, but tended to invoke them only when selecting the "first principles" from which they could then generate particular rules to deal with particular problems. By 1900, these and a host of related changes had produced a style of legal analysis dramatically different from the mode of reasoning that had been paradigmatic in 1850.

The legislative process, on the other hand, proved a magnet for such disputes. "Legislation bulked larger in social regulation when more numerous and varied interests began to press claims for attention, and when politically effective opinion sensed a need to bring more factors into policy calculations. In that context both petitioners and lawmakers began to realize the process implications of the open door jurisdiction of the legislative branch in contrast to the narrower avenues of access to judicial lawmaking." J. Willard Hurst, Dealing with Statutes 12 (1982) (footnote omitted).

Frank P. Grad, The Ascendancy of Legislation: Legal Problem Solving in Our Time, 9 Dalhousie L.J. 228, 233-34 (1985): The sentiment against statutory law of the 1890's recognized a unique characteristic of legislation — its capacity for making major changes in the existing social order. Common law is private law. Legislation opens the fields of public law. No judicial decision on a workplace injury can have as far-reaching effects as the legislative establishment of a workers' compensation system. . . . [C]ase law is limited by the nature of the case that gave rise to the decision, and even landmark cases will not have an impact beyond a fairly limited legal field. The decision of a case may have significant and direct impact on the law, but it is not likely to have any such direct impact on the social order. The legislation to establish workers' compensation had an impact on employer-employee relations which was not only different in degree, but different in kind from the impact of even the most significant decisions in individual cases on employer liability for workplace accidents. A case establishing a pharmacist's liability for improperly labelling a medication, however influential in the law of product liability, is quite different in its impact from a comprehensive food and drug act, which sets labelling requirements prospectively.

Central to understanding legislative ascendancy is recognizing how the "open-door jurisdiction" of the legislative process so easily accommodates group demands. The elements of this jurisdiction are the broad lawmaking powers of legislative bodies and the relative ease with which groups can access such bodies. The broad lawmaking powers of legislatures are discussed in this chapter. The characteristics of the legislative process, such as accessibility, are the subject of Part III of this book.

2. The Rise of Statutes: The Bench and Bar

Above, we briefly explored the history of legislative activity from its modest beginnings to its dominant modern-day position. The initial response of both the bench and the bar to the beginnings of statutory primacy was considerably hostile. They were committed to the substance and processes of the judge-made law of their time. Statutes brought change. This change was substantively unwelcome, occurred outside of the control of the traditional legal establishment, and offended the perceived characteristics of judge-made law: certainty, stability, calmness, and logic. This negative reaction is characterized in the following passages.

Roscoe Pound, Common Law and Legislation, 21 Harv. L. Rev. 383-84 (1908): Not the least notable characteristics of American law today are the excessive output of legislation in all our jurisdictions and the indifference, if not contempt, with which that output is regarded by courts and lawyers. Text-writers who scrupulously gather up from every remote corner the most obsolete decisions and cite all of them, seldom cite any statutes except those landmarks which have become a part of our American common law, or, if they do refer to legislation, do so through the judicial decisions which apply it. The courts, likewise, incline to ignore important legislation; not merely deciding it to be declaratory, but sometimes assuming silently that it is declaratory without adducing any reasons, citing prior judicial decisions and making no mention of the statute. . . . It is fashionable to point out the deficiencies of legislation and to declare that there are things that legislators cannot do try how they will. It is fashionable to preach the superiority of judge-made law.

American Legal Realism xi (William W. Fisher III et al. eds., 1993): . . . [I]ts best-known manifestation was a series of decisions by appellate courts that strengthened the positions of business corporations in their struggles with workers and consumers. For example, federal and state courts invented new legal remedies (such as the labor injunction) and new common law doctrines (such as the rule that union organizers may be held liable for interfering with employers' "contractual relations") that assisted businesses in their efforts to prevent strikes and other forms of collective action by their employees. Early legislative efforts to discourage the formation or to control the behavior of monopolies were construed narrowly by most courts. Last, but not least, many appellate courts around the turn of the century interpreted the "due process" clause of the Fourteenth Amendment — and similar clauses in the state constitutions — in favor of sharply restricting the ability of the state legislatures to interfere with property or with employers' "freedom to contract."

Jerome Frank, Courts on Trial 292 (1950): [W]hen legislatures [change] the rules, our courts, until quite recently, resented it, treated statutes as intrusions and therefore to be so interpreted as to do the least possible to alter the judge-made rules. "Here," the judges felt, "is a stable body of rules which create legal certainty. We ourselves seldom change any of them and then only after the most careful consideration. But the legislature makes new rules, frequently without adequate consideration, which upset legal certainty. The legislatures do their work capriciously, superficially, on the basis of the limited subjective impressions of a few members of a legislative committee. Why should we greatly respect such shoddy products?"

This explicitly hostile attitude toward statutes and the legislative process moderated over time. The legal establishment changed, with growing numbers of its members more sympathetic to social legislation, more familiar with legislative activity, and more skeptical about the "objectivity" of judge-made law. Such skepticism, as exemplified by the comments of Justice Holmes set forth below, was nurtured by a growing number of judges and scholars, known generally as the Legal Realists, who engaged in an "effort to define and discredit classical legal theory and practice and to offer in their place a more philosophically and politically enlightened jurisprudence." Introduction to American Legal Realism xiii-xiv (William W. Fisher III et al. eds., 1993). For a broad collection of their writings, see American Legal Realism (William W. Fisher III et al. eds., 1993).

Oliver Wendell Holmes, The Path of the Law, Collected Legal Papers 167, 180-81 (1920): The fallacy to which I refer is the notion that the only force at work in the development of the law is logic. . . .

This mode of thinking is entirely natural. The training of lawyers is a training in logic. The processes of analogy, discrimination, and deduction are those in which they are most at home. The language of judicial decision is mainly the language of logic. And the logical method and form flatter the longing for certainty and for repose which is in every human mind. But certainty generally is illusion, and repose is not the destiny of man. Behind the logical form lies a judgment as to the relative worth and importance of competing legislative grounds, often an inarticulate and unconscious judgment, it is true, and yet the very root and nerve of the whole proceeding. You can give any conclusion a logical form. You always can imply a condition in a contract. But why do you imply it? It is because of some belief as to the practice of the community or of a class, or because of some opinion as to policy, or, in short, because of some attitude of yours upon a matter not capable of exact quantitative measurement, and therefore not capable of founding exact logical conclusions. Such matters really are battle grounds where the means do not exist for determinations that shall be good for all time, and where the decision can do no more than embody the preference of a given body in a given time and place.

Yet, notwithstanding the significance of statutes as the primary source of law and the requirement that practicing lawyers possess legislative skills to participate both in the making of statutes and their application, many in the legal profession and legal education system maintain an uneasy attitude toward statutes and the processes by which they are created. This phenomenon is well described in the following comments of Professor Williams.

Robert F. Williams, Statutory Law in Legal Education: Still Second Class After All These Years
35 Mercer L. Rev. 803, 813-16, 828-29, 835 (1984)

In recent years few lawyers would have disputed the statement: "The primary instrument of ordered social change is legislation." This is simply not a controversial proposition, and the change has taken place since the case method was developed. The common law could not deal adequately with the modern, complex industrial/welfare state. . . .

Legal educators, of course, control the content of the law school curriculum. As we have seen, a few legal educators early in this century began to see the folly of ignoring statutes, or what Freund called reliance on the judicial point of view in the study of law.

In 1917, at the same time Ernst Freund was making that point, Thomas Reed Powell told the Association of American Law Schools:

> Professional law study deals only casually and indirectly with the improvement of the law. Though such improvement must be accomplished largely through legislation, our law schools have thus far given but slight attention to the law that legislatures *have made or ought to make*. Both the field and the mechanics of legislative law making seem to have been regarded as outside the pale of professional law training. This neglect has doubtless been a factor in producing the attitude toward legislation which is characteristic of so many lawyers. There seems to be a widespread notion that statutes are wanton interferences with the legal natural order.

In the same forum in 1933, Arthur Vanderbilt said:

It seems to me that we must do something to inculcate in our students a
different attitude toward statute law. They readily become so enamored of
case law that they have not only somewhat of a contempt for the legislative
output but, what is more serious, little facility for coping with it.

Willard Hurst observed in 1941 that "legislation still has to win its place
in most law schools as a separate focus of the curriculum." In the same year
David Cavers said: "Legislation is not a newcomer to our law school curricula, but its recognition has generally been more symbolic than actual." In
1944, Karl Llewellyn, speaking on behalf of the Association of American
Law Schools Curriculum Committee, pointed out the need for skills training in the application of statutes. Esther Brown's 1948 study of legal education, as well as Albert Harno's 1953 study, were critical of the neglect in
the area of statutory law. Also in 1953, Frank Horack concluded: "A proper
course in legislation is no luxury in the curriculum; it is a necessity if the
general practitioner is to be well trained."

In 1949, Harry Jones characterized the failure of law schools to train
students in legislation as a "record of neglected opportunity." A 1969
Ford Foundation report and a 1977 American Bar Foundation study,
both specifically on law school teaching of legislation, concluded that the
responses of law schools were deficient.

Despite this well reasoned and sustained call for action by influential
legal educators during a time when developments in the "real world"
supported their position, the performance of most law schools still must
be characterized as a "neglected opportunity." . . .

Relatively few law students will become legislators. But the education of
the potential legislator is just as important as that of the potential judge. The
dominance of lawyers in the legislative branch, and in government in
general, is well known. The reason, however, for providing adequate training in statutes is not that law graduates will become legislators, but rather
that statutes will be important in their law practice.

A practicing lawyer in modern times needs legislative skills, if not for the
development and drafting of statutes, at least for their application. . . .

The lawyer's predictive function on behalf of clients can be as important
in legislative development of the law as in judicial development. Because
traditional legal education and legal materials have not prepared most
lawyers adequately for this function, legislative developments often take
lawyers and clients by surprise. Frank Horack said that "[t]he development
of legislative policy follows as predictable a system as does the judicial
opinion." This predictive skill can be developed only by better understanding of the process by which statutes are created and adopted.

A lawyer trained by the case method (even in statutory interpretation)
with either real or hypothetical facts always given, may have difficulty

predicting the effect of proposed or newly-enacted legislation. He must conjure up hypothetical facts, and the reasoning process is basically deductive instead of inductive. This type of "issue recognition" is the opposite of regular law practice (or law school) in which the client gives the lawyer facts and the lawyer picks out the legal issues. Here, by contrast, the lawyer is given the legal rule, and he must create fact situations in which the rule might apply to the client. These are two very different mental operations.

Lawyers may be called upon to represent clients directly before the legislature and its committees. More and more professional, community, public interest, and small trade association groups are seeking legislative representation. Even legal services lawyers now are representing clients in the legislative process. In addition, lawyers have an obligation to advise clients of relevant statutory developments as they are taking place. Finally, on the other side, there are some unique problems in representing policy-making persons or bodies. . . .

Another ramification of thinking like a common-law lawyer is distrust of law created in a *political*, group struggle process instead of a process of "legal reasoning." A common assumption is that legislative bodies do not respond to rational argument but only to the influence of power and, therefore, that rational argument need not be developed nor attempted. This view does not leave much room for thinking like a lawyer.

Although most law professors and lawyers currently acknowledge the political content of judicial decisions, at least the legal profession maintains a virtual monopoly over the judiciary. Lawyers speak the same language. Certainly the same cannot be said for the legislature. Legal training is not a required qualification for legislative service. Entrance into the legal profession brings with it a heightened social class not necessarily obtained by non-lawyer legislators. When was the last time a bar association went on record for increased *legislative* salaries?

One recent manifestation of the "distrust of law created in a *political*, group struggle process instead of a process of 'legal reasoning,'" referred to above by Professor Williams, is the popularity among some legal scholars of what is known as *public choice theory*. "Public choice theory is a hybrid: the application of the economist's methods to the political scientist's subject." Daniel A. Farber and Philip P. Frickey, Law and Public Choice 1 (1991). Applying these methods to the legislature, public choice theorists render a negative picture of the legislative process and posit an enhanced remedial role for the court. A description of the public choice model follows.

Richard A. Posner, The Problems of Jurisprudence 354-55 (1993):
[L]egislators are rational maximizers of their satisfactions just like everyone

else. Thus nothing they do is motivated by the public interest as such. But they want to be elected and reelected, and they need money to wage an effective campaign. This money is more likely to be forthcoming from well-organized groups than from unorganized individuals. The rational individual knows that his contribution is unlikely to make a difference; for this reason and also because voters in most elections are voting for candidates rather than policies, which further weakens the link between casting one's vote and obtaining one's preferred policy, the rational individual will have little incentive to invest time and effort in deciding whom to vote for. Only an organized group of individuals . . . will be able to overcome the informational and free-rider problems that plague collective action. But such a group will not organize and act effectively unless its members have much to gain or much to lose from specific policies, as tobacco farmers, for example, have much to gain from federal subsidies for growing tobacco and much to lose from the withdrawal of those subsidies. The basic tactic of an interest group is to trade the votes of its members and its financial support to candidates in exchange for an implied promise of favorable legislation. Such legislation will normally take the form of a statute transferring wealth from unorganized taxpayers (for example, consumers) to the interest group. If the target were another interest group, the legislative transfer might be effectively opposed. The unorganized are unlikely to mount effective opposition, and it is their wealth, therefore, that typically is transferred to interest groups.

As a model of legislative activity, the public choice description is, at best, incomplete. This is discussed in the comments below. One of the commentators, Nobel Laureate Professor James Buchanan, is one of the theory's constructors. Some aspects of public choice theory are revisited in Chapters 6 and 7.

Geoffrey Brennan and James M. Buchanan, Is Public Choice Immoral? The Case for the "Nobel" Lie, 74 Va. L. Rev. 179, 180 (1988): Also, as we have argued, there may be good reason to believe that *homo economicus* [wealth-maximizing egotists] may be descriptively somewhat less relevant in the political setting than in economic markets. The more appropriate use of the *homo economicus* construction is to further the normative exercise of investigating the incentive structures embodied in various institutional forms rather than the descriptive exercise of providing predictions as to the likely outcomes of political interactions.

Daniel A. Farber and Philip P. Frickey, The Jurisprudence of Public Choice, 65 Tex. L. Rev. 873, 891-900 (1987): The core of the economic models is a revised view of legislative behavior. In place of their prior assumption that legislators voted to promote their view of the public interest, economists now postulate that legislators are motivated solely by self-interest. In particular, legislators must maximize their likelihood of reelection. A legislator who is not reelected loses all the other possible benefits flowing from office.

The issue, then, is what legislators must do to win reelection. Economic models can be classified into two groups, depending on their answer to this question.

Models in the first group assume that legislators attempt to maximize their appeal to their constituents. These constituents, in turn, vote according to their own economic self-interest. Thus, these models suggest that legislative votes should be highly predictable on the basis of the economic interests of constituents.

Models in the second group emphasize the role of special interest groups. To the extent that voters lack perfect information about a legislator's conduct, his financial backing, publicity, and endorsements become more important. These forms of support, as well as other possible benefits, are provided by organized interest groups, which thereby acquire the ability to affect legislative action. . . .

The "free rider" problem suggests that it should be nearly impossible to organize large groups of individuals to seek broadly dispersed public goods. Instead, political activity should be dominated by small groups of individuals seeking to benefit themselves, usually at the public expense. The easiest groups to organize presumably would consist of a few individuals or firms seeking government benefits that are financed by the general public. Thus . . . politics should be dominated by "rent seeking" special interest groups.

The two kinds of economic models of legislation have in common their rejection of ideology as a significant factor in the political process. They assume that ideology, defined simply as individual beliefs about the public interest, influences neither voters nor legislators. Thus, the heart of the economic approach is the assumption that self-interest is the exclusive causal agent in politics.

These models identify some important political realities. Clearly, legislators with more affluent constituents often vote differently from those with blue-collar or unemployed constituents, and those from agricultural districts often vote differently from those from manufacturing centers. These differences are consistent with the assumption that legislators represent their constituents' economic interests. Moreover, as the political science literature indicates, special interest groups play a major role in the legislative process. . . .

Some crucial features of the political world, however, do not conform with the economic models. Most notably, the models do not account for popular voting. Elections provide a classic example of the incentives to free ride. Given the number of voters, the chance that an individual vote will change the outcome is virtually nonexistent. Because voting is costly in terms of time and inconvenience, no economically rational person would vote, yet millions of people do. A theory that cannot even account for people going to the polls, let alone explain how they vote once they are there, can hardly claim to provide a complete theory of politics. . . .

The economic models clearly overlook important aspects of the political process. Nevertheless, a theory that makes unrealistic assumptions also may prove highly useful in making predictions. Even a physicist, when seeking to describe a complex physical system, often will make simplifying assumptions that are known to be, at best, approximations. The basic assumptions of micro-economic theory are notoriously unrealistic, but most economists believe that the predictions are sufficiently accurate to justify the continued use of the assumptions. In short, the ultimate test of an economic model is its predictive ability.

The economic theory of legislation, however, does not perform well empirically, despite the common assumption to the contrary in the legal literature. Most of the empirical evidence supporting the economic theory of legislation is, in fact, quite unconvincing.

Two types of evidence are commonly cited to support the economic theory. The first consists of studies demonstrating that some particular law favors a discrete economic group. For example, environmental regulation may benefit firms owning large plants more than those owning small plants; this finding has been cited as proving that even legislation apparently in the public interest is really the product of special interests. Such evidence, however, is unpersuasive. First, a finding of differential impact often can be effectively challenged. Researchers disagree, for example, over whether trucking regulation benefitted owners, drivers, or both. If economists cannot determine the economic impact of legislation after its implementation, interest groups evaluating proposed legislation presumably suffer far greater uncertainties. Second, demonstrating that a law benefits a certain group does not establish that passage of the law was due to the group's efforts. In other words, evidence of a law's differential economic impact does not disprove the influence of ideological forces.

The other type of empirical study attempts to meet this criticism by using the economic model to predict the votes of individual legislators. Typically, the researcher identifies several rough measures of a law's economic effects on constituents or campaign contributors. The researcher then looks for a statistical correlation between the votes of individual legislators and these economic impacts. In general, as predicted by the economic model, these studies find positive relationships between legislative behavior and economic variables. The results fail to establish, however, that economic factors are more important than noneconomic ones.

Other studies have focused on noneconomic factors. Such research indicates that ideology, usually measured by the annual ratings given by the Americans for Democratic Action (ADA), is a better predictor of legislator behavior than economics. Even on purely economic matters, ideology is a strong predictor of legislators' votes. For example, in analyzing votes on natural gas deregulation legislation, Mitchell found that over ninety percent of the votes, 361 out of 399, could be predicted simply by whether a congressman's ADA score was greater than forty-five percent.

Given this evidence of the importance of noneconomic factors, validation of the purely economic model requires proof that it performs better than models that include noneconomic factors. The economic model has not done well in such tests. Studies that examine both economic and ideological influences generally conclude that ADA scores are a substantial factor in predicting legislators' votes. Models that include both ideological and economic factors outperform purely economic models, even when predicting votes on strictly economic legislation.

One response to these studies is that ADA scores themselves reflect the views of legislators' constituencies. Hence, an ADA score may measure indirectly the composition of a legislator's district, rather than the legislator's own political view. This argument, although clever, turns out to be ill-founded. To test its validity, several researchers developed a technique of "cleansing" ADA scores of their association with constituent makeup. The cleansed scores were still significantly related to legislative votes. . . .

Indeed, the cleansed score results may well underestimate the importance of ideology. The statistical method essentially assumes that whenever a legislator's ideology correlates with the interests of his constituency, his votes are attributable solely to the constituency's economic interests. It is plausible, however, that the economic makeup of the constituency contributes to constituency ideology, which in turn relates to the choice of legislator, so that constituency economic interest may have little direct effect on legislators' votes. If, as seems likely, the truth lies somewhere between the economic model and this purer ideological model, ideology may play at least as great a role in the political process as economics.

A less grandiose version of the economic theory would simply postulate (1) that reelection is an important motive of legislators; (2) that constituent and contributor interests thus influence legislators; and (3) that small, easily organized interest groups have an influence disproportionate to the size of their membership. In short, the model could be used to identify tendencies within the political system, but not to explain all of politics.

Abner J. Mikva, Foreword to Symposium on the Theory of Public Choice, 74 Va. L. Rev. 167, 168-70 (1988): I would offer a more plebeian defense of the public persona against the public choice calumny. I have known a lot of public people over the years. Some undoubtedly fit the cynical description of "rent-seekers," but most have not. . . . I have spent much time talking to politicians, watching them work, trying to figure out what they would do and why. I was wrong as often as I was right in my predictions. My quarter-century of empirical research persuades me that the quantification of a public person's behavior for the purpose of predicting future behavior is even less useful than most other quantifications of human behavior. . . .

What I am suggesting . . . is that the motivations of politicians are far too mixed to be understood through the generalizations that . . . public choice theorists formulate about political behavior. Most of the public choice theorists . . . have eschewed holding public office, running for public office, or even talking to politicians. It is hardly surprising, then, that their descriptions of public officers are so skewed. . . .

My chief objection to the use of the public choice analysis is that it claims to be scientific and therefore infallible. . . . The public choice theorists, adopting the economists' lingo, start equations by saying "everything else being equal"; but of course nothing else *is* equal in the political arena, and as such the models just aren't very useful. In fact, the claims for accuracy despite the lack of real empirical data put the public choice theorists in the league of the blind man who felt the trunk of the elephant and proclaimed the animal to be a tree.

NOTES AND QUESTIONS

1. *The lessons of history.* What were the changes in American society that led to the ascendancy of legislatures and statutes in the legal landscape, and how did these changes favor legislative primacy?

2. *Institutional differences.* One of the points made by the above materials is that institutional differences between the legislative and judicial branches of government favored legislative ascendancy in the context of changing societal demands. What are those differences, and how do you think they contributed to the ascendancy (for example, elected decision makers versus appointed decision makers)?

3. *Resistance by the bench and bar.* Some of the most intense opposition to the modern legislative role has come from the legal establishment. A number of reasons have been offered to explain this resistance. What are they, and how would you evaluate them?

For the most part this resistance has been unsystematic. What differentiates the public choice theorists from their earlier counterparts is the positing of a theoretical basis for their disenchantment. What is their theoretical basis, and what are its criticisms? How would you evaluate them all?

Despite recognition of public choice theory's shortcomings in analyzing the legislative process, it maintains a beachhead in legal scholarship, partially because it identifies some problems in the legislative process. For example, it is evident that campaign fundraising is an issue that deserves considerable attention as part of any study of the legislative process. (See Chapter 7, Section C.2.) But these academic insights are not significant enough to support the level of interest. (Nor are they unique to public choice theorists.) Other explanations also have currency. First, the legislative process is complex, and public choice theory simplifies it.

Second, it provides a basis for criticism of the legislative process by a profession that continues to remain uncomfortable with legislative supremacy in policy making. Third, public choice theory provides a basis for criticism of the legislative product — statutes — through discrediting the processes by which they are made. Interestingly, most proponents of public choice theory are politically conservative and uneasy with legislative efforts at redistribution and regulation.

B.   THE LEGISLATIVE PROCESS: AN INTRODUCTION

In outline, the process by which legislation is enacted is elementary and familiar. Legislators are elected. Legislators introduce proposed laws in the form of a bill. The bill is sent to a committee and, if adopted by the committee, with or without amendments, it may reach the floor of the legislature. If it is passed there, the bill is sent to the other legislative house (the federal and all state governments except Nebraska have bicameral legislatures) where the same process occurs. If the bill, in the identical form passed by the first house, is passed by the second house, it is sent to the executive. The executive can then either approve the bill (and it becomes law) or veto the bill. If vetoed, the bill is sent back to the legislature, which can override the veto by a supermajority.

The above description of the legislative process, while accurate, is not revealing. It misses the complex structures and processes through which a statute is really shaped. As President, then Professor, Woodrow Wilson wrote:

> Like a vast picture thronged with figures of equal prominence and crowded with elaborate and obtrusive details, Congress is hard to see satisfactorily and appreciatively at a single view and from a single stand-point. Its complicated forms and diversified structure confuse the vision, and conceal the system which underlies its composition. It is too complex to be understood without an effort, without a careful and systematic process of analysis.

Woodrow Wilson, Congressional Government 57 (Johns Hopkins Univ. Press ed., 1981).

The following description of New York State's legislative process illustrates President Wilson's observation. Missing from this description is any reference to the role played by the executive in the enactment process, which is discussed in Section B3 of this chapter. The New York State process described below is one of the nation's least deliberative, particularly because of the traditional dormancy of their committee system. See Eric Lane, Albany's Travesty of Democracy, City Journal 490 (Spring 1997). A description of most other states' legislative processes would show even more complication and diversification.

TABLE 1-1
How a Bill Becomes a Law in New York

1. Idea for a bill is submitted to Bill Drafting Commission, where it is translated into formal language.
2. Then the bill is introduced, assigned the number it will be known by, and then printed.
3. Bill assigned to appropriate committee for discussion and analysis. If a majority of members on the committee support it, the bill is reported to the floor. If not, it is said to have "died in committee."
4. All bills requiring an expenditure of state funds must first be sent to the Ways and Means Committee. They make sure the state can afford the cost of the bill. These bills won't reach the floor for a vote unless Ways and Means okays the expenditure. Similarly, bills which impose criminal and civil sanctions must go before the Codes Committee.
5. Final version of the bill is printed — must be on members' desks for at least 3 days before being voted on.
6. Bill reaches floor for debate and vote.
7. Once a bill passes the Assembly, it is sent on to the Senate, where it goes through a similar process. If both houses pass a bill, it is then sent to the Governor for his or her signature.
8. The Governor can sign a bill, veto it, or give it "pocket approval" (when the Governor fails to act on a bill within 10 days of receiving it, it is automatically approved). If the Governor vetoes a bill, it can still become a law, if a 2/3 majority of both houses votes in favor of the bill. This is known as an override.
9. Bill, once signed by the Governor, becomes law.

Eric Lane, Legislative Process and Its Judicial Renderings
48 U. Pitt. L. Rev. 639, 645-50 (1987)

[Introduction of Legislation]

Ideas for the introduction of bills spring from many sources, including constituents, lobbyists, representatives of other governmental agencies, as well as from the legislator's own perception of district and state problems needing legislative response. The decision to propose legislation is related of course to the demand level, the legislator's own interest in and concern about the subject, and his or her own level of legislative industriousness. The more complicated a legislative solution appears to be, the fewer the number of members willing to undertake it.

[Drafting Legislation]

In most cases, once the decision to introduce legislation has been made, the outline of a legislative response will be drafted. That response generally will be a joint effort of the legislator, legislative staff and, in many cases, interest groups which favor the measure. . . . [T]his legislative outline will [in many jurisdictions] then be forwarded to a bill drafter. . . .

The bill drafter is responsible for transforming the proposed solution into bill language, bill form, and to fit its provision within the existing body of statutory law. A draft bill is then produced and returned to the requesting legislator for review. The main purpose of this review is to make sure that the bill drafter has properly translated the legislator's ideas. Revisions, if needed, are then made and the bill is introduced. . . .

Many bills, however, follow different paths to introduction. A member will sometimes introduce a bill provided by the executive or an outside group. On other occasions, depending on the significance of the problem to the particular legislator and the sophistication of the legislator's staff, the bill will be drafted by the legislator and his or her staff. In certain instances bills will also be drafted by the staff [of a relevant committee or] of the conference to which the legislator belongs. This latter category always includes the session's most controversial bills and also frequently involves bills on issues on which the [committee or] conference staff has developed particular expertise. . . .

[Committees]

Once a bill has been introduced, it is referred to a committee where the vast majority of bills are gratefully allowed to die. For example, of the 9,624 bills introduced in the New York State Senate in 1986, only 1,852 bills passed the Senate, while only 265 bills were actually signed into law. One reason for this disparity is that in New York, unlike some other states, a member may introduce an unlimited number of bills. Consequently, legislators will introduce legislation in response to almost any demand from constituents, lobbyists or other interest groups. The introduction of legislation, thus, is frequently not a commitment to pursuing passage of a new law or even airing a proposal, but rather a tactic for reducing pressure from these groups.

[Majority Building]

Once a "serious" bill is referred to a committee, two overlapping processes begin, revision and majority building. The revision process, in its most limited sense, is the process by which a bill is reviewed by committee members, staff and conference staff to ensure that the legislative idea is properly expressed. This process continues even after a bill has been reported from the committee to the legislative calendar. Not infrequently, a bill will pass through several prints prior to the actual vote on it. A bill will also undergo revisions in the process of building a majority as provisions are changed to secure the number of votes needed for passage. [In New York, the committee process is actually now controlled by the leadership of the majority in each house. This control is exercised by control over the committee staff who are hired almost exclusively by the leadership. See Eric Lane, Albany's Travesty of Democracy, City Journal 490 (Spring 1997).]

[Non-Controversial Bills]

The process of building a majority in the New York State Legislature is relatively easy for most bills. In New York, as in all other states, the legislature has jurisdiction over numerous local matters such as alienating public property, creating municipal water districts, and other, similar matters. As a result, a large number of bills are not controversial and they occasion no particular contention. These local bills generally pass the legislature with near unanimity, and with very little individual legislative attention other than that of the sponsor. Legislative staff members, however, will generally review those bills to verify their clarity and provide summaries of their contents to the conference members. Local bills tend to generate little litigation.

Bills other than local bills may also be non-controversial. Whether a bill is non-controversial or controversial depends not on the significance of a bill's content, but on the intensity and diversity of the legislative viewpoints which swirl around its contents. For example, a corporate take-over bill enacted in 1985, the contents of which had potentially profound effects on the New York economy, sailed through the legislative process virtually without comment. As with local bills, the absence of legislative contention concerning potentially significant legislation means that the bill will receive less legislative attention, although a significant bill will generate extensive staff-prepared briefing papers.

[Controversial Bills]

While bills for which it is difficult to build a majority are far fewer in number, they take up the largest part of legislative time. These are controversial bills, which, to repeat, are not defined by their content but by the intensity and diversity of the legislative viewpoints with which they are received. The intensity and variety of legislative viewpoints that a bill generates are of course fueled by a mixture of influences, including individual and party policy, political predilections, and constituency and interest group pressures. The more intense and diverse the viewpoints and hence the more controversial a bill is, the more the legislative body will focus on the particular subject of the bill and strain to void that irritant. During this period of strain, legislative politics is at its most robust and fragile and "essential techniques of politics in real life persuasion, exchange of services, rewards and benefits, alliances and deals" take place. In addition, during this time the legislative process exercises its most moderating influence on those with inconsistent viewpoints, as compromises are forged to win votes and reduce adverse pressures. While this process frequently does not allow for an individual drafter to explore every implication of a bill, the foreseeable implications are generally examined in the intense exchanges which occur among interested parties, through which the ultimate legislation is fashioned.

[Party Conferences]

Majorities are most frequently built before a bill is ready for formal legislative action. In the New York State Legislature, majority building generally occurs in private nonrecorded conferences, where legislative leaders express their views on bills, staff are given an opportunity to fully brief the legislators on the provisions of each controversial bill, members most openly discuss the policies and politics of each bill, and conference negotiators are given their instructions. The more controversial a bill becomes, the more it will be discussed in conference and the less freedom negotiators will have in making an agreement. . . .

Legislative conferences also bring together members of the same party for intra-party trading. Inter-party trading and discussions with lobbyists, of course, occur outside the conference, although the results of this trading are brought inside by the actions of the particular legislator with respect to controversial legislation.

[Floor Debates]

Since most majorities are built behind the scenes, it is rare for a floor debate to influence the outcome of a bill, particularly a controversial one. As a result, most statements on the floor do not relate to the deliberative process, but to the public relations process. In other words, members do not speak substantively to their colleagues in floor debate, but politically to their constituents and interest groups. Occasionally, however, there will be an actual floor debate in which an analysis of the bill is undertaken. This debate will almost always involve the bill's sponsor and presents one of the few publicly accessible moments of actual legislative deliberation or exposition. . . .

[The Legislative Decision]

While the decision to support or oppose a non-controversial bill is rather simple, grounded to a large extent in personal affinities and leadership cues, the decision on a controversial bill is more complex. The more controversial a bill, the more the typical legislator's decision will be the product of his or her independent cognitive process. This process of deciding whether to support or oppose a controversial bill will include the legislator's own understanding of a bill based on a reading of it, a reading of staff-prepared memoranda, and discussion with colleagues and lobbyists. . . . Once a bill is understood, numerous factors are weighed in determining whether to vote for its enactment. They include the legislator's judgment on the merits of the bill, the views of his or her constituents, any impact on the chances of reelection, views of lobbyists and colleagues, conference and leadership views of editorial boards, campaign fund raising opportunities, opportunities for amending the proposed legislation, and opportunities for trading for the support of his or her own legislation or for other legislative favors. It is impossible to determine in any given case the weight of any of these factors, since they depend to a large extent on the continuing intensity of each and on the current needs of the legislator.

Despite this complexity, as President Wilson noted, a "careful and systematic" exploration can reveal a clear picture of the legislative process. A note on compromise, the essential step in the legislative process, a comparison between the legislative and judicial decisionmaking processes, and some observations about the executive role in the legislative process introduces our effort at this exploration.

1.   Compromise: The Heart of the Legislative Process

Throughout the book, reference will be made to the act of compromising or to various legislative compromises. The need to compromise in a legislative body is the heart of the legislative process. Bills, for the most part, cannot become laws without compromise. This is a consequence of majority decisionmaking, particularly in a heterogeneous society, with an open and deliberative legislative process. For a bill to become law, it must, constitutionally, win the majority of votes in each house of a legislature, or more votes, if the executive veto power is exercised. It must also, in most cases, first win the votes of a variety of legislative committees before it can ever reach the legislative floor. To win a committee majority, a house majority, and a majority of each house, a bill must be acceptable to a substantial number of legislators, many of whom have different views of the problem and solution the bill addresses.

Compromise is also a consequence of meeting in assembly. As legislators become increasingly familiar with each other, they become more and more familiar and comfortable with each others' views and interests. In short, they come to appreciate other policy views and interests. This latter point was made by a former Speaker of the New York State Assembly, Stanley Fink, in an interview, in which he described his first year in office. "I went to Albany as a New York City representative, to pursue an urban agenda. But through formal and informal interactions with my colleagues across the state, I began to recognize and appreciate the views and interests of representatives from other areas. The result of this education, was that my advocacy for urban interests was frequently tempered by my understanding of its impact on the interest of others."

The importance of compromise to the process places a premium on the political skills of its participants. While rational argument remains an important currency, the ability to negotiate and moderate views in the context of such negotiation is equally important. The moderation of policy preference is viewed in the legislative process as a virtue, if such moderation leads to legislative progress. In the legislature "half a loaf" is better than none.

2. A Comparison of Legislative and Judicial Processes

As part of the brief history in Section A of this chapter, attention was partially focused on the relationship between the legislative and judicial branches of government. As the legislative branch ascended, the judicial branch descended in terms of its lawmaking significance. A cause of this shift was the suitability of the legislative process (and unsuitability of the judicial process) to accommodate societal changes.

What elements of the legislative process made it more suitable to accommodate change than the judicial process?

Consider the description of the legislative process by Professor Lane set forth earlier in this section. How does it compare with the judicial decision-making process?

3. The Executive as Legislator

The focus of this book is primarily on the legislative process as performed by legislators in a legislative body. But no discussion of the legislative process should fail to note the central and pervasive role played by the president and the states' governors in the consideration of legislation. So significant has this role been at times that one political scientist has written (perhaps overstated) about the President and Congress: "The legislature is

TABLE 1-2
Comparison Between Decisional Process in Legislatures and Courts

Legislatures	*Courts*
1. Broad authority to regulate future behavior and redistribute wealth. Legislatures make law.	1. Decisions bound by statutes or, for the most part, precedent. Courts find law.
2. Open access, no rules of standing.	2. Rules of jurisdiction and standing limit parties.
3. Broad fact-finding capacity, no formal rules of evidence, generally no requirement that statutes be supported by factual basis.	3. Decision must be based on facts presented pursuant to rules of evidence.
4. Statutes, for the most part, aimed at prospective behavior.	4. Decisions apply to past behavior.
5. Decisional process is mostly public, usually with active media coverage.	5. Decisional process is secret.
6. Floor debates, committee reports, speeches, media coverage all explain law.	6. Opinion must speak for itself; judges not allowed to explain or interpret decision.
7. Legislatures are proactive, and timing is in their discretion.	7. Courts are reactive and timing is not of choice.
8. Decisions are reached through democratic, political process; policy preferences expected.	8. Decisions appear to be reached through logic; policy preferences discouraged.
9. Legislatures look at broad, relatively general problems.	9. Courts look, mostly, at the case before them.

not the dominant influence in the legislative process. The President is more influential. He leads and Congress controls. Leadership in this context means two things: to initiate the legislative process, that is to perform its early stages, and to impel it, or to continuously drive its process forward." Arthur Maas, Congress and the Common Good, 10 (1983). This role for the nation's governmental executive is not portrayed through a literal reading of the U.S. or state constitutions. The veto power (see Chapter 9, Section C) enjoyed by the President and all of the states' executives (except North Carolina), of course, provides some executive leverage. A veto changes the vote needed to pass legislation and creates a different political dynamic in which legislation is considered. The threat of veto opens legislative doors to executive participation in many cases in which he or she would not otherwise be welcome. But it is not the veto alone that accounts for such widespread executive participation. Nor is it the provision in the Constitution and similar ones in state constitutions that require the executive to report on the state of the union and recommend measures as the executive considers necessary (see, for example, Article II, §3 of the U.S. Constitution). Although this provision provides the constitutional imprimatur for the President's State of the Union message and an active executive legislative role, the energy for executive action flows from living in an age of statutes and the consequential political process in which the executive, as the nation's or state's leader, is seen by the public as the most important initiator of legislation. This is underscored by election campaigns, which generally revolve around ideas for legislation. The Voting Rights Act of 1965, discussed in detail in Chapter 6, was a presidential initiative and probably would not have become law without the executive efforts to mobilize the nation in its support.

NOTES AND QUESTIONS

1. *The comparisons between legislative and judicial processes.* For most students of the legislative process, there is little value in comparing the legislative process with the judicial decisionmaking process. For the law student, doing so is important because of the overshadowing emphasis on judicial process in the law school curriculum. As the above materials indicate, there are numerous points of comparison and various ways to express those comparisons.

Concerning legislative and judicial decisionmaking, first, what factors do you think legislators weigh in deciding whether to support a bill, and what factors do you think judges weigh in making a judicial decision? How would you evaluate those factors? The factors that influence legislative decision making are discussed in Chapter 7, Section D.

Second, it is true that appellate courts are consensual decision makers because a judgment must be based on a majority of the judges who hear the case, but the process is different. What differences do you think there are between arriving at a judicial consensual decision and a legislative decision?

2. *Legislative compromise.* The legislative compromise has not been without its critics. For example, public choice theorists, drawing from some political scientists, frequently characterize compromises as "deals" that undermine the "public interest." See Chapter 1, pages 15-22. This same sentiment is often offered in support of initiative and referendum proposals. See Chapter 9, Section F.

C. THE LAWMAKING POWERS OF LEGISLATURES

This section provides a brief survey of the lawmaking power of Congress and state legislatures. The detailed study of this topic (at least of Congress' power) is the subject of constitutional law texts.

The lawmaking power of the nation's legislative bodies is found in the federal and state constitutions. For Congress, authority for legislative activity flows from Article I, §1 of the Constitution, which vests in it all federal legislative power, and from specific constitutional grants of power, found primarily in Article I, §8, which defines the vested power. This formal listing of congressional lawmaking power has remained unchanged since the ratification of the Constitution, except for the additions of specific grants of powers found in a series of Constitutional Amendments: the three post–Civil War Amendments (XIII, XIV, and XV) and the Sixteenth Amendment, which authorized the imposition of the income tax.

For state legislatures, lawmaking authority has been cast, most usually, in plenary terms (that is, terms granting all of a state's lawmaking power to its legislature). While such grants of power have remained constant, many states have amended their constitutions to prohibit or impede the enactment of "special" legislation, to limit the power of the purse, and, through the addition of procedural rules, to make the legislative process more accessible and deliberative. Many of these amendments were adopted during the latter half of the nineteenth century in response to real and perceived legislative corruption and in response to the redistributive efforts of legislative bodies, which were increasingly comprised of and influenced by new immigrants. State legislative power is also limited by Article I, §10 of the Constitution, which prohibits the states from enacting bills of attainders and ex post facto laws and from impairing "the obligation of contracts."

1.   Congress and Its Specific Grants of Power

The Constitution of the United States

Article 1

SECTION 1. All legislative Powers herein granted shall be vested in a Congress of the United States, which shall consist of a Senate and a House of Representatives. . . .

SECTION 8. The Congress shall have Power To lay and collect Taxes, Duties, Imposts and Excises, to pay the Debts and provide for the common Defence and general Welfare of the United States; but all Duties, Imposts and Excises shall be uniform throughout the United States;

To borrow Money on the credit of the United States;

To regulate Commerce with foreign Nations, and among the several States, and with the Indian Tribes;

To establish an uniform Rule of Naturalization, and uniform Laws on the subject of Bankruptcies throughout the United States;

To coin Money, regulate the Value thereof, and of foreign Coin, and fix the Standard of Weights and Measures;

To provide for the Punishment of counterfeiting the Securities and current Coin of the United States;

To establish Post Offices and post Roads;

To promote the Progress of Science and useful Arts, by securing for limited Times to Authors and Inventors the exclusive Right to their respective Writings and Discoveries;

To constitute Tribunals inferior to the supreme Court;

To define and punish Piracies and Felonies committed on the high Seas, and Offenses against the Law of Nations;

To declare War, grant Letters of Marque and Reprisal, and make Rules concerning Captures on Land and Water;

To raise and support Armies, but no Appropriation of Money to that Use shall be for a longer Term than two Years;

To provide and maintain a Navy;

To make Rules for the Government and Regulation of the land and naval Forces;

To provide for calling forth the Militia to execute the Laws of the Union, suppress Insurrections and repel Invasions;

To provide for organizing, arming, and disciplining the Militia, and for governing such Part of them as may be employed in the Service of the United States, reserving to the States respectively, the Appointment of the Officers, and the Authority of training the Militia according to the discipline prescribed by Congress;

To exercise exclusive Legislation in all Cases whatsoever, over such District (not exceeding ten Miles square) as may, by Cession of particular States, and the Acceptance of Congress, become the Seat of the Government of the United States, and to exercise like Authority over all Places purchased by the Consent of the Legislature of the State in which the Same shall be, for the Erection of Forts, Magazines, Arsenals, dock-Yards and other needful Buildings;—And

To make all Laws which shall be necessary and proper for carrying into Execution the foregoing Powers, and all other Powers vested by this Constitution in the Government of the United States, or in any Department or Officer thereof.

Other powers of Congress include the power to alter state regulation concerning congressional elections (Article I, §4), the power to establish inferior courts (Article III, §1), the power to make regulations for the nation's territories and property (Article IV, §3), and the implementing powers found in Amendments XIII, XIV, XV, XIX, XXIII, XXIV, and XXVI.

The use of particular grants of power for Congress, along with the Tenth Amendment, originally appeared to make the federal government one of limited power in a federal system that protected the political integrity of states.

> The Constitution, in granting congressional power, thus simultaneously limits it: *an act of Congress is invalid unless it is affirmatively authorized under the Constitution.* State actions, in contrast, are valid as a matter of federal constitutional law unless *prohibited,* explicitly or implicitly, by the Constitution. The Tenth Amendment makes the doctrine of enumerated powers an explicit part of the Constitution.

Laurence H. Tribe, American Constitutional Law 298 (1988) (footnotes omitted, emphasis in original). This concept of limited federal government has been almost entirely eroded by congressional response to demands for "national" solutions to a host of issues that were not known or not contemplated as "federal" at the time the Constitution was adopted.

Section A sets forth a brief history of the growth of legislative activity. Central to that growth were the increasing collective demands for regulation and the redistribution of resources. In this process, formal distinctions between federal and state legislative jurisdictions were of little significance. Simply put, if Congress determined there was a need for a national solution to a problem, it would craft a solution, notwithstanding any perceived constitutional weakness. The constitutional language circumscribing congressional lawmaking facilitated these efforts. Particularly susceptible to broad construction were such constitutional generalities as "general welfare," "to regulate commerce," and "necessary and proper."

The Supreme Court has, at least, historically acquiesced to Congress' own construction of its lawmaking powers. The legal historian J. Willard Hurst puts it nicely: "Judicial review has its drama. That this may exaggerate its long-run influence was most strikingly shown between 1934 and 1937. In that period the Supreme Court first asserted, then renounced, the greatest degree of control over legislative policy that judges have ever claimed in the United States." J. Willard Hurst, The Growth of American Law, The Law Makers 28 (1950).

Despite numerous challenges to Congress' definition of its jurisdiction, the courts have supported congressional construction. For example, regarding the "general welfare" clause, the Court, after more than a century of debate over whether this clause was limited to taxation and appropriation for implementing the enumerated powers, has held that "the power of Congress to authorize expenditure of public money for public purposes is not limited by the direct grants of legislative power found in the Constitution." United States v. Butler, 297 U.S. 1, 66 (1935). Similarly, in an early test to the necessary and proper clause, the Supreme Court held:

> We admit . . . that the powers of the government are limited, and that its limits are not to be transcended. But we think the sound construction of the constitution must allow to the national legislature that discretion, with

respect to the means by which the powers it confers are to be carried into execution, which will enable that body to perform the high duties assigned to it in the manner most beneficial to the people.

McCulloch v. Maryland, 17 U.S. 316, 421 (1819). See also Buckley v. Valeo, 424 U.S. 1 (1976). And with respect to the interstate commerce clause, the Court has reasoned: "The activities that are beyond the reach of Congress are 'those which are completely within a particular State, which do not affect other states, and with which it is not necessary to interfere, for the purpose of executing some of the general powers of government.'" Katzenbach v. McClung, 379 U.S. 294, 302 (1964) (quoting Gibbons v. Ogden, 22 U.S. 1, 195 (1824)).

But this acquiescence, to a large extent, has reflected a national consensus over legislative outcomes. During the last ten years, there has been an unraveling of such consensus as the cry for more state autonomy and, selectively, a more limited federal government has attracted serious political support. The tension produced by this advocacy has spilled over into the Supreme Court, where Justices appointed by Presidents who have advocated a narrower role for state government have clashed with Justices who have advocated a broader federal role. This conflict has resulted in a number of 5-4 Supreme Court decisions that have restricted Congress' reach. Among these cases United States v. Morrison, 120 S. Ct. 1740 (2000) (holding unconstitutional the Violence Against Women Act of 1994), is the most important because of the limitation it places on Congress' view of its own authority under the commerce clause. Five years earlier, in a less clear commerce clause decision, United States v. Lopez, 514 U.S. 549 (1995), the Court struck down the Gun-Free School Zones Act of 1990.

In City of Boerne v. Flores, 521 U.S. 507 (1997), the Court (6-3) struck down the Religious Freedom Restoration Act of 1993, holding that Congress' authority to enforce against state action the constitutional right to the free exercise of religion under the XIV Amendment is not broad enough to support legislation found to be an unreasonable intrusion into traditional state authority to regulate the behavior of a state's citizens. Similarly, in Florida Prepaid Postsecondary Education Expense Board v. College Savings Bank, 119 S. Ct. 2199 (1999), the Court, after declaring that legislation pursuant to §5 of the XIV Amendment can abrogate state sovereign immunity, held such an abrogation in the Patent and Plant Variety Protection Remedy Clarification Act unconstitutional because Congress had failed to identify a historical pattern of states infringing on patents or of states failing to provide adequate remedies for such infringements. Also, in a companion case, College Savings Bank v. Florida Prepaid Postsecondary Education Expense Board, 119 S. Ct. 2219 (1999), the Court held that the Trademark Remedy Clarification Act could not limit state sovereign immunity because the business activities protected by the Act were not protected property rights under the XIV Amendment. In another XIV Amendment case,

Kimel v. Florida Board of Regents, 120 S. Ct. 631 (2000), the Court held that §5 of the XIV Amendment could not sustain a clear abrogation of states' XI Amendment immunity in the Age Discrimination in Employment Act of 1967. And in a later XI Amendment case, Board of Trustees of the University of Alabama v. Garrett, 531 U.S. 356 (2001), the Court held that state employees could not sue state employers for violations of the Americans with Disabilities Act of 1990.

Finally, in Printz v. United States, 521 U.S. 898 (1997), the Court declared §922(s)(2) of the Brady Handgun Prevention Act to be an unconstitutional violation of states' rights under "the system of dual sovereignty." The provision commanded the chief law enforcement officer of local jurisdictions to conduct, on an interim basis, background checks on handgun purchasers.

Excepted from this formulation of historical judicial acquiescence to legislative definition are the external limitations on the authority of Congress that are found in the Bill of Rights and elsewhere in the Constitution. The terms of these provisions have not been left to legislative definition alone but have been, at least starting in the latter half of the twentieth century, watched over by the courts. Legislative bodies normally effect majority norms screened through the legislative process, and, on occasion, do not adequately protect individual rights asserted against prominent majority views. This role has been assumed by the courts. As legislatures have grown more active, court dockets have reflected more and more challenges to the scope and interpretation of statutes measured against the limitations incorporated in bills of rights.

2. The Plenary Powers of State Legislatures

> The legislative power is vested in a General Assembly consisting of a Senate and House of Representatives. . . .

This provision, extracted from the Constitution of the State of Illinois (Article 4, §1), is typical of the plenary grants of power vested in state legislatures. In some states, such as California, this power is shared directly with the people through the power of referendum and initiative. Referenda and initiatives are discussed in Chapter 9, Section F. The use of the term "plenary" to characterize state legislative power differentiates such power from the (now theoretically) limited grants vested in Congress. State legislatures are not affirmatively limited to legislating on particular subjects; their acts are valid unless they are otherwise prohibited by the federal or state constitutions. "The legislature may pass any law not expressly prohibited by the constitution, and it possesses every power not delegated to another department or to the Federal government, or not denied to it by the Federal or State constitutions." People v. Metropolitan Sanitary District of Greater Chicago, 150 N.E.2d 361, 367 (Ill. 1958).

Historically, state constitutions contained few prohibitions on legislative power, with bills of rights being the most prevalent exception. The definition of lawmaking was left to the legislative process. While demands for broad policy enactments awaited post–Civil War society, the almost unlimited jurisdiction of state legislatures attracted many applicants, individual and corporate, for statutes creating particular rights and obligations. On a regular basis, legislatures would, for example, grant divorces, pardon convicted felons, and grant particular franchises. So egregious did this activity become that a number of state constitutions were amended in the latter half of the nineteenth century to prohibit such activity or to make it more difficult. See generally Lawrence M. Friedman, A History of American Law 346-62 (2d ed. 1985). A prominent example of such constitutionally imposed limitations is found in the 1870 amendment to the Illinois Constitution:

ARTICLE 4, SECTION 22. The general assembly shall not pass local or special laws in any of the following enumerated cases, that is to say: for —
Granting divorces;
Changing the names of persons or places;
Laying out, opening, altering and working roads or highways;
Vacating roads, town plats, streets, alleys and public grounds;
Locating or changing county seats;
Regulating county and township affairs;
Regulating the practice in courts of justice;
Regulating the jurisdiction and duties of justices of the peace, police magistrates and constables;
Providing for change of venue in civil and criminal cases;
Incorporating cities, towns or villages, or changing or amending the charter of any town, city or village;
Providing for the election of members of the board of supervisors in townships, incorporated towns or cities;
Summoning and impaneling grand or petit juries;
Providing for the management of common schools;
Regulating the rate of interest on money;
The opening and conducting of any election, or designating the place of voting;
The sale or mortgage of real estate belonging to minors or others under disability;
The protection of game or fish;
Chartering or licensing ferries or toll bridges;
Remitting fines, penalties or forfeitures;
Creating, increasing or decreasing-fees, percentage or allowances of public officers, during the term for which said officers are elected or appointed;
Changing the law of descent;
Granting to any corporation, association or individual the right to lay down railroad tracks, or amending existing charters for such purpose;

> Granting to any corporation, association or individual any special or
> exclusive privilege, immunity or franchise whatever.
>   In all other cases where a general law can be made applicable, no special
> law shall be enacted.

The restrictions placed on special and local legislation did not limit or
interfere with general lawmaking powers.

> So far as constitutional limitations on special and local laws were effective,
> they increased rather than reduced the importance of the legislature. After
> 1870 the typical legislature was under constant pressure of detail and
> particular interests. Any device that offered some protection from these dis-
> tractions could hardly do other than add to the legislature's potential
> capacity to take the lead in making important policy.

J. Willard Hurst, the Growth of American Law, The Law Makers 30 (1950).
And at the end of the nineteenth century, state legislatures did become
laboratories for meeting the demands of emerging new groups.

> The states' historic police powers furnished the constitutional support for
> legislative efforts to regulate industrialization. . . . Through the last quarter
> of the nineteenth century, the states were the center of regulatory activity,
> limiting corporate enterprise, throwing up a shield of protective legislation
> for women and child laborers, and pioneering the development of bureaus
> and independent regulatory commissions. . . .

Kermit L. Hall, The Magic Mirror 197 (1989).
These efforts of state legislatures did not initially meet with judicial
approval; see Section A.2 of this chapter and, for example, Lochner v.
New York, 198 U.S. 45 (1905) (declaring unconstitutional a New York statute establishing a 60-hour work week), but state lawmaking ultimately
became almost as free of judicial interference as federal lawmaking has
been.

J. Willard Hurst, The Growth of American Law, The Law Makers
31-32 (1950)

Judges had far more effect than constitution makers on state legislative
power; the record of their influence was the judge-made constitutional
law of the due process and equal protection clauses of the Fourteenth
Amendment. Perhaps the courts would not have needed the vague principles of that amendment to rationalize their veto. In the 1850's state courts
began to say that legislation was subject to general principles of right and
justice, fixed by natural law or perhaps by that "law of the land" which
some state constitutions invoked as a measure of lawful government
action. [For a modern rendition of this view, see Judge Posner in dissent

in United States v. Marshall, excerpted in Chapter 11 at page 769.] Our English constitutional inheritance gave to the concepts under which judicial review operated the prestige of safeguards to the liberty of the subject. Time made clear the fact behind the new symbols offered by the Fourteenth Amendment: judges asserted their power to limit the efforts of late-nineteenth-century legislatures to regulate the conduct of business and to redress the balance of power between social or economic classes or interests. Few judicial rulings under the Fourteenth Amendment prior to the 1930's protected the civil liberties of the individual against legislative invasion. In part, of course, this was because legislatures were not yet interesting themselves in much that concerned civil liberties. But this fact only emphasizes that in their constitutional decisions the courts were setting their judgment against that of the legislature in the main field of late-nineteenth-century controversy — the relation of economic power to other values in the society.

In three particularly basic respects judges set marked limits to the legislature's right to fix public policy: (1) the prohibition of minimum wage legislation; (2) the strict definition of the category of business so "affected with a public interest" that its charges and practices might be regulated; (3) the frustration of statutory protection for labor's right to organize.

The courts never lost all sense of the caution needed to handle social issues that ran this deep. Even in their broadest assertions of power, the judges kept open the means to accommodate judicial review to necessary change. They regularly conceded that statutes must be presumed constitutional; constitutionality was to be judged only as a particular case required it, and then in the light of the existing social justification for what the legislature had done. Through the sounding adjectives of the opinions gradually emerged the simpler concept: that the basic issues of due process and equal protection were whether reasonable men could find that the facts showed a public interest in a given regulation, and that the regulation might be thought a reasonable means to effect the public interest.

This more pragmatic approach reflected the powerful pull of the facts and of public opinion toward more government intervention in the economy. The judges exerted their veto at its fullest between about 1875 and 1905. In that period they drastically limited the legislature's power over the economy. However, by 1910 the courts were on the defensive; by then — though now increasingly under executive leadership — the legislature was in the ascendant. The surest evidence of the undertow of events came in 1912 when that naive opportunist, Theodore Roosevelt, made national issues of the proposals for the recall of judges and of judicial decisions. Power was in the balance in the 1920's. The depression '30s demanded affirmative government action in economic affairs. This cast the issue decisively in favor of legislative power as against the judicial veto, on the state as well as the national front. The Supreme Court of the

United States set the tone for the handling of due process and equal protection questions the country over. It dramatized the turning point when, in the October term, 1935, it reaffirmed by a 5-to-4 vote that the due process clause forbade legislative fixing of minimum wages for women, and then in the October term, 1936, again by 5 to 4 overruled this and the previous rulings, to sustain such regulation. By 1950 it appeared that within the predictable future there was little likelihood that any legislation regulating economic affairs would be held unconstitutional.

Today, state lawmaking efforts are extensive. Almost every issue of national concern has a state parallel, and a number of subjects — for example, family relationships, probate issues, and criminal behavior — are primarily matters of state concern. The legislative process responds to demand, and such demand cannot be long stayed by legislators' references to the abstract principles of federal supremacy or states' rights.

> When people or groups demand central control, they do not want big government as such. Few people care (and why should they?) whether government is big or not at any level. They care about results. Arguments about centralism and decentralism have little political appeal, in themselves. They are surrogates for something else. Southerners who used to preach states' rights were not really professing a political theory. They had a shopping list of interests and demands, and they knew which stores carried the goods.

Lawrence M. Friedman, A History of American Law 659 (2d ed. 1985). Sometimes, corresponding state legislation is specifically invited by federal legislation. Other times, state activity is perceived to be in conflict with federal jurisdiction. This has forced the courts to address issues arising from a federal system of government. Despite a somewhat complex jurisprudence, the basic rule has been to favor federal power.

3. *Power of the Purse*

Of all lawmaking powers, the power of the purse is the most important. This is easy to understand. "Money," wrote Alexander Hamilton, "is, with propriety, considered as the vital principle of the body politic; as that which sustains its life and motion, and enables it to perform its most essential functions." The Federalist No. 30, at 188 (Jacob E. Cooke ed., 1961). To which James Madison added, speaking particularly about the House of Representatives, "[t]his power over the purse, may in fact be regarded as the most compleat and effectual weapon with which any constitution can arm the immediate representatives of the people, for obtaining a redress of every grievance, and for carrying into effect every just and salutary measure." The Federalist No. 58, at 394 (Jacob E. Cooke ed., 1961). One telling example of Madison's observation relates to Congress' power over the nation's war activities. The Constitution grants Congress the power to declare war (Article I, §8), but the meaning and exercise of this power have been the subjects of considerable contest between Congress and the President. For a short round-up of the issues, see Louis Fisher, The Politics of Shared Power, ch. 6 (3d ed. 1993).

Congress, nevertheless, can exercise effective control over the executive on this issue through the power of the purse. On this point, Judge Mikva has written, concerning events that occurred during his tenure as a member of Congress:

> I am reminded here of the close, in the mid-1970's, of the Vietnam War. For years — arguably, for decades — Congress abdicated its responsibility to resist this costly and futile foreign venture. But when the legislature finally became convinced that the war in Vietnam had to stop, it worked its will through its budgetary power. In 1974 and again in 1975, Congress refused to appropriate the more than one-half billion dollars requested by the President to continue the war effort. The denial effectively forced the cessation of hostilities; Congress had seized the initiative in exactly the manner contemplated by the founders. Had Congress not possessed this plenary power — had the President retained any authority to raise, appropriate, or divert funds — this catastrophic war would certainly have continued. For the source of almost all congressional power — the spine and bite of legislative authority — lies in Congress' control of the nation's purse. If ever Congress loosens its hold on this source of power or if ever the President wrests it away, then, to quote the late Senator Frank Church, "the American Republic will go the way of Rome." The delicate balance created by the Framers will have been destroyed.

Abner J. Mikva, Congress: The Purse, The Purpose, and the Power, 21 Ga. L. Rev. 1, 4 (1986).

The power of the purse is actually three powers: the power to tax, the power to borrow, and the power to spend. The federal government and most states, by constitution, operate on annual budget cycles, which means they must exercise these powers annually. No other legislative decisions, over the long run, have more impact. As a consequence, enormous amounts of legislative time and energy are directed toward the process through which this power is exercised.

a.   The Power to Tax

Of the powers of the purse, the power to tax is the most awesome and essential. The power not only "involves the power to destroy" but also:

> is essential to the very existence of government, and may be legitimately exercised on the objects to which it is applicable, to the utmost extent to which the government may choose to carry it. The only security against the abuse of this power is found in the structure of government itself.

> In imposing a tax the legislature acts upon its constituents. This is in general a sufficient security against erroneous and oppressive taxation.

McCulloch v. Maryland, 17 U.S. 316, 428 (1819). The prescience of this insight is particularly clear to anyone who has ever participated in attempting to adopt legislation that increases taxes. Taxing is not an endeavor for timid souls, particularly those whose tenure must be reaffirmed by the taxed every two years or so. Former Congressman Barber Conable captures it well by quoting Samuel Johnson "[t]o tax and be loved . . . are not given to mortal man." Barber B. Conable, Jr., Congress and the Income Tax 110 (1989). But, notwithstanding such timidity to tax, the age of statutes is also an age in which the costs of government have increased dramatically to pay for and administer its statutory landmarks. This explains the decision of the House of Representatives in 1995 to amend its Rules to require a three-fifths majority for increasing tax rates. See Chapter 5, pages 266-267.

For Congress, the power to tax is found in Article I, §8 of the Constitution: "The Congress shall have Power To lay and collect Taxes, Duties, Imposts and Excises to pay the Debts and provide for the common Defence and general Welfare of the United States," and in the XVI Amendment, ratified in 1913, which grants Congress the "power to lay and collect taxes on incomes, from whatever source derived, without apportionment among the several States, and without regard to any census or enumeration."

The power to tax is also the power to regulate. The imposition of a tax is the imposition of an additional cost on the activity or event being taxed. Sometimes the regulation, and not the revenue, is the goal of the tax. Tariffs are one example. Their purpose is the protection of particular industries and only secondarily (if at all) the production of revenue. Taxing the sale of otherwise prohibited drugs is another example. The goal is to provide another means for the prosecution of drug offenses.

For states, the power to tax is part of the general grant of legislative power found in most state constitutions. Amendments to many state constitutions, particularly during the latter part of the nineteenth century, added various limitations on the exercise of this power. Included among these restrictions were provisions requiring uniform taxation and prohibiting graduated taxes. These are discussed in detail in texts on state and local government. See, for example, D. Mandelker et al., State and Local Government in a Federal System (3d ed. 1990).

The federal Constitution also contains some express limitations on state taxation powers. These include Article I, §10, which prohibits the states from imposing imposts or duties on imports or exports. In recent years, the federal courts have used the commerce clause of the Constitution to limit the breadth of state power, as states have searched for more and more sources of revenues. See, for example, Robert A. Sedler, The Negative Commerce Clause as a Restriction on State Regulation and Taxation, 31 Wayne L. Rev. 885 (1985).

b. The Power to Borrow

The power to borrow money is an indispensable power of government. Traditionally, governments have borrowed for long-term capital projects, the benefits of which are intended to be realized over future years, and for wars, the costs of which are frequently in excess of available revenues. Governments also borrow for needs caused by unpredicted declines in anticipated revenues or unanticipated increases in the costs of particular programs. Since the 1930s, the federal government has also viewed borrowing and spending as a method for stimulating the economy.

Congress has unfettered constitutional authority to borrow. Article I, §8 grants to Congress the authority "to borrow Money on the credit of the United States." This grant is limited only by the government's obligation to repay its debts. See Perry v. United States, 294 U.S. 330 (1935); Lynch v. United States, 292 U.S. 571 (1933); Sinking-Fund Cases, 99 U.S. 700 (1878). Since the 1930s, and particularly since 1980, Congress has used this power liberally.

Borrowing is not free; interest payments are its most obvious costs. Increasing levels of interest payments are the cause of legislative nightmares. The concept is simple: Interest must be paid from either existing revenues or new ones. This means programs must be cut, taxes must be increased, or, as was the case for most of the 1980s, more money must be borrowed.

From time to time, Congress has attempted to come to terms with this problem. Each year it adopts debt-ceiling legislation. Such legislation is basically meaningless because it is adopted after it is determined how much borrowing is necessary to support the programs Congress wants to fund. Congress also has attempted to resolve the deficit issue through some complicated legislation. An example of this legislation is the Deficit Reduction Act of 1994 discussed in Chapter 3 on page 83. But such acts, while creating tensions between Congress' spending inclinations (spurred by the public demand for programs) and its chronic anti-taxing attitude (spurred by significance of antitax votes in the election process), have a difficult time withstanding legislative desires to meet programmatic demands. This helps to explain the popularity of various proposed balanced budget amendments to the United States and state constitutions.

State borrowing has not proceeded as unhampered by legal obstacles as has the borrowing by the federal government. Fear of both public corruption and democratization resulted in sweeping changes to most state constitutions during the latter half of the nineteenth century. Included among those changes were various substantive and procedural limitations on state borrowing. See generally Lawrence M. Friedman, A History of American Law (2d ed. 1985); J. Willard Hurst, The Growth of American Law, The Law Makers (1950); William J. Keefe, The Functions and Powers of the State Legislature, in State Legislatures in American Politics 37 (Alexander

Heard ed., 1966). The need for borrowing has proved to be an overriding force, pushing state legislatures to devise various schemes to escape such inflexible restraints.

A New York example makes this point. The New York State Constitution (Art. VII, §11) requires certain state debt authorizations to be subject to referendum before such debt can be incurred. Pursuant to this provision, the New York State legislature adopted a statute (Chapter 850 of the laws of 1981) authorizing borrowing, subject to referendum, for prison construction.

After a heated political campaign over the referendum, mostly over the costs of prison programs, it was defeated. Notwithstanding this defeat, in 1983 the New York State legislature adopted legislation to authorize a state public authority, the Urban Development Corporation, to effect the same purpose as the referendum. This statutory authorization was challenged in the New York courts by one of the opponents of the referendum. New York State Coalition for Criminal Justice, Inc. v. Coughlin, 479 N.Y.S.2d 850, *aff'd*, 485 N.Y.S.2d 247 (1984). "[W]here, as here, we are called upon to deal with an intricate scheme for public financing or for public expenditures designed to meet a public interest, the court must proceed in its review with much caution. It is the Legislature which is mandated to make policy decisions in such areas and the court may not invalidate its decisions, enacted into law, out of a mere preference for a different or more restrained approach." (Internal citations omitted.) Id. at 854-55.

c. **The Power to Spend**

The federal power to spend is lodged exclusively in Congress by Article I, §9, clause 7 of the Constitution. "No Money shall be drawn from the Treasury, but in Consequence of Appropriations made by Law. . . ." State constitutions generally follow this model but frequently set forth detailed procedures for budget adoption. The reason for government spending needs little elaboration. The products of the nation's legislatures during this age of statutes have been expensive. Money is spent for programs, and *more* money is spent for the administration of these programs. While all legislators are against spending too much money, the definition of "too much" is always hazy, and such reluctance rarely becomes a philosophical objection to spending money that directly benefits the legislators' constituents. Spending occurs in one of two forms: either through general programs such as Social Security, or through specific projects or programs in a particular legislator's district. The latter items of spending, done by almost all legislative bodies, are known as "member items," "member initiatives," or, pejoratively, "pork barrel." The growth of spending over the last century has been so considerable that enormous legislative effort has been devoted to creating various procedural and substantive obstacles to its continuation.

There are no constitutional limits on Congress' power to spend, although considerable political debate occurs on the cost and virtue of various programs. At the beginning of the Republic, considerable debate occurred over the permissible scope of congressional spending. Article I, §8, clause 1 of the Constitution provides that "[t]he Congress shall have Power To lay and collect Taxes . . . to pay the Debts and provide for the common Defence and general Welfare of the United States." The meaning of the general welfare provision was the subject of considerable historical debate. Hamilton argued that it provided an independent source of authority for spending. Madison saw it as limited by the enumerated powers. Congressional activity over the decades following the debate supported the Hamiltonian view, but not without considerable dissent. The debate seems to have been formally settled in favor of Hamilton by several decisions that challenged the spending programs of the New Deal. See, for example, Helvering v. Davis, 301 U.S. 619 (1937); Steward Machine Co. v. Davis, 301 U.S. 548 (1937); United States v. Butler, 297 U.S. 1 (1935).

NOTES AND QUESTIONS

1. *The breadth of legislative power.* The federal Constitution provides certain enumerated legislative powers to Congress. The notion was to maintain a limited federal government. It is difficult to characterize today's federal government as limited. What are the factors that contributed to this situation?

2. *The definition of the enumerated powers.* Consider the general language of the enumerated powers on which congressional activity is based. In the material above, emphasis was placed on judicial acquiescence to congressional definition of the meaning of several of the grants of power. Could it have been otherwise? Could the Court have determined that certain acts were not "necessary and proper" or that certain expenditures were not in the "general welfare"? What standards would they have used? Is this an appropriate judicial role? In Helvering v. Davis, 301 U.S. 619 (1937), the Court upheld, under the general welfare clause, the expenditure of federal tax dollars for an old-age pension program under the Social Security Act. "The line must still be drawn between one welfare and another, between the particular and the general. The discretion belongs to Congress unless the choice is clearly wrong, a display of arbitrary power, not an exercise of judgment." Id. at 640, per Cardozo, J. See also Steward Machine Co. v. Davis, 301 U.S. 548 (1937). What do you think this answer means? Can you give an example of a legislative choice that is "clearly wrong" in this context?

3. *Federal-state legislative competition.* As the materials make clear, congressional activity has not diminished state legislative activity. It, too, has grown. This, on occasion, has led to competition between the federal

government and state governments on how to resolve a particular problem. Under the federal Constitution, federal law is the supreme law of the land, and any state law in conflict with it must bend. This is one aspect of the complicated federal preemption doctrine. See Laurence H. Tribe, American Constitutional Law 481-97 (2d ed. 1988).

CHAPTER **2**

The Anatomy and Publication of Statutes

A law enacted by a legislature is most commonly known as a statute. It may also be called a public law or a chapter law. Until it is enacted, the document in which the proposed law is set forth is usually called a bill.

Excerpts from two statutes ("acts") are included in this chapter. Their subject is voting rights. The first statute is the "Voting Rights Act of 1965," and the second is the "Voting Rights Amendments of 1982." The second statute amended provisions of the first statute as well as certain amendments to the first statute made between 1965 and 1982. These statutes are both very significant because they reflect great changes in the nation's view of political representation. Both are part of what Professor Sunstein has characterized as the "rights revolution." (See Chapter 1, page 4.) In this chapter, however, our focus is not the policies advanced by these statutes; these are addressed in Chapter 5. (We also study these statutes again later when we discuss the enactment process in Chapter 3, policy in Chapter 4, lobbying in Chapter 7, and the judicial application of statutes to particular fact patterns in Chapter 12.)

In this chapter we read the two Voting Rights Acts as exemplars of statutes. Our goal is to introduce you to the conventions of statutes: their language, form, and elements. By elements we refer to the title and enacting clause, found in every statute, and to various generic provisions that are common to most statutes. Examples of generic provisions are findings, definitions, sanctions, severability clauses, and effective dates. In this chapter, we also explore the publication of statutes and each publication's evidentiary value.

It is hard to read a statute. The language is predominantly general, bordering on abstract. It reveals no story, no characters, no drama — just a dry recitation of rights and obligations. Sometimes provisions are in conflict or are unclear or vague. About this, two thoughts must be borne in mind. First, legislatures never exercise power in the abstract. They are always responding to situations that are perceived of as problems needing legislative resolution. Although usually not expressly revealed by the language, there is always an underlying story. And sometimes, as with the Voting Rights Act of 1965 and with the Voting Rights Amendments of 1982, the story can be quite dramatic. Second, statutes are also the products of compromise. For a bill to become a statute, it must receive the support of at least a majority of the whole number of the representatives of each legislative house. In the House of Representatives, for example, this would mean 218 of 435 votes. Frequently these representatives have different ideas about the nature of the problems about which they are legislating and different views of how to resolve them. For a bill to go forward in this environment, compromise is required. Some of these compromises result in proposed provisions being omitted from a statute; some result in changes in existing language; some result in additional (sometimes redundant, sometimes conflicting) language or provisions; and some result in clear statutory language purposefully being made unclear.

A Problem

While reading the following statutory excerpts, think about the particular problems being addressed by each of the provisions and about the compromises that may have been struck to effect their enactment. Also, because lawyers never read statutes without a problem in mind, consider the following problem while you plow your way through the statutes.

A hypothetical state, call it X, elects its lower house legislators from multimember districts. In X this means that each lower house district (there are 20) is represented by four house members. The voters in these districts can vote for four candidates for the lower house. (On the other hand, state senators are elected on the basis of single-member districts of which there are 30.) In 10 of the lower house districts, African-Americans make up 35 percent of the voting age population. No African-American has ever been elected from any of these districts. On rare occasions, candidates supported by African-Americans have been elected.

The Attorney General of the United States wants your advice on whether this representational scheme violates the Voting Rights Act of 1965, and, if so, what remedies are available.

A. THE VOTING RIGHTS ACT OF 1965 AND ITS 1982 AMENDMENTS

The Voting Rights Act of 1965
Pub. L. No. 89-110

An Act

[Title]

To enforce the fifteenth amendment to the Constitution of the United States, and for other purposes.

[Enactment Clause and Short Title]

Be it enacted by the Senate and House of Representatives of the United States of America in Congress assembled, That this Act shall be known as the "Voting Rights Act of 1965." . . .

[Changes in Law]

SEC. 2. No voting qualification or prerequisite to voting, or standard, practice, or procedure shall be imposed or applied by any State or political subdivision to deny or abridge the right of any citizen of the United States to vote on account of race or color.

SEC. 3. (a) Whenever the Attorney General institutes a proceeding under any statute to enforce the guarantees of the fifteenth amendment in any State or political subdivision the court shall authorize the appointment of Federal examiners by the United States Civil Service Commission in accordance with section 6 to serve for such period of time and for such political subdivisions the court shall determine is appropriate to enforce the guarantees of the fifteenth amendment (1) as part of any interlocutory order if the court determines that the appointment of such examiners is necessary to enforce such guarantees or (2) as part of any final judgment if the court finds that violations of the fifteenth amendment justifying equitable relief have occurred in such State or subdivision: *Provided*, That the court need not authorize the appointment of examiners if any incidents of denial or abridgment of the right to vote on account of race or color (1) have been few in number and have been promptly and effectively corrected by State or local action, (2) the continuing effect of such incidents has been eliminated, and (3) there is no reasonable probability of their recurrence in the future.

(b) If in a proceeding instituted by the Attorney General under any statute to enforce the guarantees of the fifteenth amendment in any State or political subdivision the court finds that a test or device has been used for the purpose or with the effect of denying or abridging the right of any citizen of the United States to vote on account of race or color, it shall suspend the use of tests and devices in such State or political subdivisions as the court shall determine is appropriate and for such period as it deems necessary. . . .

SEC. 4. (a) To assure that the right of citizens of the United States to vote is not denied or abridged on account of race or color, no citizen shall be denied the right to vote in any Federal, State, or local election because of his failure to comply with any test or device in any State with respect to which the determinations have been made under subsection (b) or in any political subdivision with respect to which such determinations have been made as a separate unit, unless the United States District Court for the District of Columbia in an action for a declaratory judgment brought by such State or subdivision against the United States has determined that no such test or device has been used during the five years preceding the filing of the action for the purpose or with the effect of denying or abridging the right to vote on account of race or color: *Provided*, That no such declaratory judgment shall issue with respect to any plaintiff for a period of five years after the entry of a final judgment of any court of the United States, other than the denial of a declaratory judgment under this section, whether entered prior to or after the enactment of this Act, determining that denials or abridgments of the right to vote on account of race or color through the use of such tests or devices have occurred anywhere in the territory of such plaintiff.

An action pursuant to this subsection shall be heard and determined by a court of three judges in accordance with the provisions of section 2284 of title 28 of the United States Code and any appeal shall lie to the Supreme Court. The court shall retain jurisdiction of any action pursuant to this subsection for five years after judgment and shall reopen the action upon motion of the Attorney General alleging that a test or device has been used for the purpose or with the effect of denying or abridging the right to vote on account of race or color.

If the Attorney General determines that he has no reason to believe that any such test or device has been used during the five years preceding the filing of the action for the purpose or with the effect of denying or abridging the right to vote on account of race or color he shall consent to the entry of such judgment.

(b) The provisions of subsection (a) shall apply in any State or in any political subdivision of a state which (1) the Attorney General determines maintained on November 1, 1964, any test or device, and with respect to which (2) the Director of the Census determines that less than 50 per centum of the persons of voting age residing therein were registered on

November 1, 1964, or that less than 50 per centum of such persons voted in the presidential election of November 1964.

A determination or certification of the Attorney General or of the Director of the Census under this section or under section 6 or section 13 [omitted] shall not be reviewable in any court and shall be effective upon publication in the Federal Register.

(c) The phrase "test or device" shall mean any requirement that a person as a prerequisite for voting or registration for voting (1) demonstrate the ability to read, write, understand, or interpret any matter, (2) demonstrate any educational achievement or his knowledge of any particular subject, (3) possess good moral character, or (4) prove his qualifications by the voucher of registered voters or members of any other class.

(d) For purposes of this section no State or political subdivision shall be determined to have engaged in the use of tests or devices for the purpose or with the effect of denying or abridging the right to vote on account of race or color if (1) incidents of such use have been few in number and have been promptly and effectively corrected by State or local action, (2) the continuing effect of such incidents has been eliminated, and (3) there is no reasonable probability of their recurrence in the future. . . .

Sec. 5. Whenever a State or political subdivision with respect to which the prohibitions set forth in section 4(a) are in effect shall enact or seek to administer any voting qualification or prerequisite to voting, or standard, practice or procedure with respect to voting different from that in force or effect on November 1, 1964, such State or subdivision may institute an action in the United States District Court for the District of Columbia for a declaratory judgment that such qualification, prerequisite, standard, practice, or procedure does not have the purpose and will not have the effect of denying or abridging the right to vote on account of race or color, and unless and until the court enters such judgment no person shall be denied the right to vote for failure to comply with such qualification, prerequisite, standard, practice, or procedure: *Provided,* That such qualification, prerequisite, standard, practice, or procedure may be enforced without such proceeding if the qualification, prerequisite, standard, practice, or procedure has been submitted by the chief legal officer or other appropriate official of such State or subdivision to the Attorney General and the Attorney General has not interposed an objection within sixty days after such submission, except that neither the Attorney General's failure to object nor a declaratory judgment entered under this section shall bar a subsequent action to enjoin enforcement of such qualification, prerequisite, standard, practice, or procedure. Any action under this section shall be heard and determined by a court of three judges in accordance with the provisions of section 2284 of title 28 of the United States Code and any appeal shall lie to the Supreme Court. . . .

Sec. 6. Whenever (a) a court has authorized the appointment of examiners pursuant to the provisions of section 3(a), or (b) unless a declaratory judgment has been rendered under section 4(a), the Attorney General certifies with respect to any political subdivision named in, or included within the scope of, determinations made under section 4(b) that (1) he has received complaints in writing from twenty or more residents of such political subdivision alleging that they have been denied the right to vote under color of law on account of race or color, and that he believes such complaints to be meritorious, or (2) that in his judgment (considering, among other factors, whether the ratio of nonwhite persons to white persons registered to vote within such subdivision appears to him to be reasonably attributable to violations of the fifteenth amendment or whether substantial evidence exists that bona fide efforts are being made within such subdivision to comply with the fifteenth amendment), the appointment of examiners is otherwise necessary to enforce the guarantees of the fifteenth amendment, the Civil Service Commission shall appoint as many examiners for such subdivision as it may deem appropriate to prepare and maintain lists of persons eligible to vote in Federal, State, and local elections. . . .

SEC. 7. (a) The examiners for each political subdivision shall, at such places as the Civil Service Commission shall by regulation designate, examine applicants concerning their qualifications for voting. An application to an examiner shall be in such form as the Commission may require and shall contain allegations that the applicant is not otherwise registered to vote.

(b) Any person whom the examiner finds, in accordance with instructions received under section 9(b) [omitted], to have the qualifications prescribed by State law not inconsistent with the Constitution and laws of the United States shall promptly be placed on a list of eligible voters. . . .

[Legislative Findings]

SEC. 10. (a) The Congress finds that the requirement of the payment of a poll tax as a precondition to voting (i) precludes persons of limited means from voting or imposes unreasonable financial hardship upon such persons as a precondition to their exercise of the franchise, (ii) does not bear a reasonable relationship to any legitimate State interest in the conduct of elections, and (iii) in some areas has the purpose or effect of denying persons the right to vote because of race or color. Upon the basis of these findings, Congress declares that the constitutional right of citizens to vote is denied or abridged in some areas by the requirement of the payment of a poll tax as a precondition to voting.

(b) In the exercise of the powers of Congress under section 5 of the fourteenth amendment and section 2 of the fifteenth amendment, the Attorney General is authorized and directed to institute forthwith in the name of the United States such actions, including actions against States or political subdivisions, for declaratory judgment or injunctive relief against the enforcement of any requirement of the payment of a poll tax as a precondition to voting, or substitute therefor enacted after November 1,

1964, as will be necessary to implement the declaration of subsection (a) and the purposes of this section. . . .

SEC. 11. (a) No person acting under color of law shall fail or refuse to permit any person to vote who is entitled to vote under any provision of this Act or is otherwise qualified to vote, or willfully fail or refuse to tabulate, count, and report such person's vote.

(b) No person, whether acting under color of law or otherwise, shall intimidate, threaten, or coerce, or attempt to intimidate, threaten, or coerce any person for urging or aiding any person to vote or attempt to vote, or intimidate, threaten, or coerce any person for exercising any powers or duties under section 3(a), 6, 8 [omitted], 9 [omitted], 10, or 12(e) [omitted].

(c) Whoever knowingly or willfully gives false information as to his name, address, or period of residence in the voting district for the purpose of establishing his eligibility to register or vote, or conspires with another individual for the purpose of encouraging his false registration to vote or illegal voting, or pays or offers to pay or accepts payment either for registration to vote or for voting shall be fined not more than $10,000 or imprisoned not more than five years, or both: *Provided, however,* That this provision shall be applicable only to general, special, or primary elections held solely or in part for the purpose of selecting or electing any candidate for the office of President, Vice President, presidential elector, Member of the United States Senate, Member of the United States House of Representatives, or Delegates or Commissioners from the territories or possessions, or Resident Commissioner of the Commonwealth of Puerto Rico.

(d) Whoever, in any matter within the jurisdiction of an examiner or hearing officer knowingly and willfully falsifies or conceals a material fact, or makes any false, fictitious, or fraudulent statements or representations, or makes or uses any false writing or document knowing the same to contain any false, fictitious or fraudulent statement or entry, shall be fined not more than $10,000 or imprisoned not more than five years, or both.

SEC. 12. (a) Whoever shall deprive or attempt to deprive any person of any right secured by section 2, 3, 4, 5, 7 or 10 or shall violate section 11(a) or (b), shall be fined not more than $5,000, or imprisoned not more than five years, or both. . . .

(f) The district courts of the United States shall have jurisdiction of proceedings instituted pursuant to this section and shall exercise the same without regard to whether a person asserting rights under the provisions of this Act shall have exhausted any administrative or other remedies that may be provided by law. . . .

SEC. 14. . . . (b) No court other than the District Court for the District of Columbia or a court of appeals in any proceeding under section 9 [omitted] shall have jurisdiction to issue any declaratory judgment pursuant to section 4 or section 5 or any restraining order or temporary or permanent injunction against the execution or enforcement of any provision of this Act or any action of any Federal officer or employee pursuant hereto. . . .

[Authorization]

SEC. 18. There are hereby authorized to be appropriated such sums as are necessary to carry out the provisions of this Act.

[Severability Clause]

SEC. 19. If any provision of this Act or the application thereof to any person or circumstances is held invalid, the remainder of the Act and application of the provision to other persons not similarly situated or to other circumstances shall not be affected thereby.

After your initial analysis of the problem, the Voting Rights Act of 1965 is amended by the 1982 Act. (It was actually amended several times earlier, as will be discussed in Chapter 4.) The Attorney General also wants your judgment as to whether the amendment changes your initial view and why.

Voting Rights Act Amendments of 1982
Pub. L. No. 97-205

An Act

[Title]

To amend the Voting Rights Act of 1965 to extend the effect of certain provisions, and for other purposes.

[Enactment Clause and Short Title]

Be it enacted by the Senate and House of Representatives of the United States of America in Congress assembled, That this act may be cited as the "Voting Rights Act Amendments of 1982." . . .

[Amendment by Reference]

SEC. 2. (a) Subsection (a) of section 4 of the Voting Rights Act of 1965 is amended by striking out "seventeen years" each place it appears and inserting in lieu thereof "nineteen years."

(b) Effective on and after August 5, 1984, subsection (a) of section 4 of the Voting Rights Act of 1965 is amended —

(1) by inserting "(1)" after "(a)";

(2) by inserting "or in any political subdivision of such State (as such subdivision existed on the date such determinations were made with respect to such State), though such determinations were not made with respect to such subdivision as a separate unit," before "or in any political subdivision with respect to which" each place it appears;

(3) by striking out "in an action for a declaratory judgment" the first place it appears and all that follows through "color through the use of such tests or devices have occurred anywhere in the territory of such plaintiff.", and inserting in lieu thereof "issues a declaratory judgment under this section.";. . . .

(4) by striking out "in an action for a declaratory judgment" the second place it appears and all that follows through "§4(f)(2) through the use of tests or devices have occurred anywhere in the territory of such plaintiff.", and inserting in lieu thereof the following: "issues a declaratory judgment under this section. A declaratory judgment under this section shall issue only if such court determines that during the ten years preceding the filing of the action, and during the pendency of such action —

(A) no such test or device has been used within such State or political subdivision for the purpose or with the effect of denying or abridging the right to vote on account of race or color or (in the case of a State or subdivision seeking a declaratory judgment under the second sentence of this subsection) in contravention of the guarantees of subsection (f)(2);

(B) no final judgment of any court of the United States, other than the denial of declaratory judgment under this section, has determined that denials or abridgements of the right to vote on account of race or color have occurred anywhere in the territory of such State or political subdivision or (in the case of a State or subdivision seeking a declaratory judgment under the second sentence of this subsection) that denials or abridgement of the right to vote in contravention of the guarantees of subsection (f)(2) have occurred anywhere in the territory of such State or subdivision and no consent decree, settlement, or agreement has been entered into resulting in any abandonment of a voting practice challenged on such grounds; and no declaratory judgment under this section shall be entered during the pendency of an action commenced before the filing of an action under this section and alleging such denials or abridgements of the right to vote;

(C) no Federal examiners under this Act have been assigned to such State or political subdivision;

(D) such State or political subdivision and all governmental units within its territory have complied with section 5 of this Act. . . .

(E) the Attorney General has not interposed any objection (that has not been overturned by a final judgment of a court) and no declaratory judgment has been denied under section 5, with respect to any submission by or on behalf of the plaintiff or any governmental unit within its territory under section 5, and no such submissions or declaratory judgment actions are pending. . . ."

[Amendment by Reenactment]

SEC. 3. Section 2 of the Voting Rights Act of 1965 is amended to read as follows:

"SEC. 2. (a) No voting qualifications or prerequisite to voting or standard, practice, or procedure shall be imposed or applied by any State or political subdivision in a manner which results in a denial or abridgement of the right of any citizen of the United States to vote on account of race or color, or in contravention of the guarantees set forth in section 4(f)(2), as provided in subsection (b).

(b) A violation of subsection (a) is established if, based on the totality of circumstances, it is shown that the political processes leading to nomination or election in the State or political subdivision are not equally open to participation by members of a class of citizens protected by subsection (a) in that its members have less opportunity than other members of the electorate to participate in the political process and to elect representatives of their choice. The extent to which members of a protected class have been elected to office in the State or political subdivision is one circumstance which may be considered: *Provided*, That nothing in this section establishes a right to have members of a protected class elected in numbers equal to their proportion in the population." . . .

[Effective Date]

SEC. 6. Except as otherwise provided in this Act, the amendments made by this Act shall take effect on the date of the enactment of this Act.

Approved June 29, 1992.

NOTES AND QUESTIONS

1. *Advice to the attorney general.* What is your advice to the attorney general?

2. *Effects and compromises.* What does each of the excerpted provisions of these statutes accomplish? What problem do they each resolve? Can you identify any compromises in the statute or any provision that might be the consequence of compromise? Why may it be important to find the compromises that underlie the provisions of a statute?

3. *Compare and contrast.* How do these statutes compare to judicial decisions? What can we learn about the legislative and judicial functions from such a comparison?

B.   THE CONVENTIONS OF STATUTES

1.   Who Drafts a Statute?

While a bill may often have a single author, a statute usually has many, each of whom has initial views on the subject somewhat different from those of the original bill drafter. To enact legislation in a representative democracy, a bill must be supported by a majority of each house of the legislature and by the executive, or, in the case of an executive veto, by a greater than simple (super) majority in each legislative house. Gaining such support most often requires compromises on particular points with legislators or other interested parties. These compromises are frequently effected through the acceptance of language in bill draft form. Language may be supplied by legislators, legislative staff, representatives of the executive branch, lobbyists, and, where they exist, professional bill drafting services. An example of a bill drafting service is the Office of the Legislative Counsel of the House of Representatives. Its purpose is to "advise and assist the House of Representatives, and its committees and Members, in the achievement of a clear, faithful, and coherent expression of legislative policies." 2 U.S.C. §281a. Its function is to provide technical drafting support, on a nonpartisan basis, to committees and members of the House of Representatives.

To give you an idea of the participatory nature of the bill drafting process, consider the experience of Professor Lane when he served as counsel to the New York State Senate Minority. Professor Lane was charged with preparing a bill to provide public transportation in the City of New York for people who were without access to public transportation because of a disability. The initial version of the bill, as drafted by Professor Lane, was then introduced by the minority leader in the Senate. A working group of Democratic Senators and staff members, and, to a lesser extent, the New York State Legislative Bill Drafting Commission as well as several lobbyists for the groups representing these people, then began to thoroughly dissect and examine the bill.

As it made its way through the enactment process, the bill underwent a series of changes. Changes were proposed through critiques of the bill's substance and by submission of newly drafted statutory language, designed to replace or amend the initial draft bill. Those proffering such new statutory language were not only other legislators, but included the office of the Governor's Counsel, the Metropolitan Transportation

Authority (the agency in charge of New York City's subways and buses), the City of New York, the Eastern Paralyzed Veterans Association, and various lobbyists representing the elderly. These amendments ranged from simple clarifications to significant substantive changes. Many of the suggested language changes were adopted — some because, in the view of the sponsor, the proposed changes improved the language of the bill, some because they improved the substance of the bill, and some because they improved the likelihood of the bill's passage.

2. General Form of a Statute

A statute starts with a designation — for example, Public Law 89-110 and Public Law 97-205 in the case of the two voting rights statutes excerpted above. Each two-year term of Congress is identified chronologically, and, similarly, each bill enacted into law during that term is assigned a number that reflects the chronological order in which it has been enacted. The Voting Rights Act of 1965 is the 110th public law enacted by the 89th Congress (1964-1965), thus 89-110. The Voting Rights Amendments of 1982 is the 205th law enacted by the 97th Congress (1981-1982), and so 97-205.

The designation is followed by a title and enacting clause and the body of the statute. Within the body, the modern format (with some ordering differences among commentators) sets forth the following parts in the following order: a short title, any purpose and findings, any definitions, the change in law, details, exceptions to the change, agency mandates, sanctions, severability clauses, and effective dates. Professor Dickerson informs this structure with several guidelines:

1. General provisions normally come before special provisions.
2. More important provisions normally come before less important provisions.
3. More frequently used provisions normally come before less frequently used provisions (i.e., the usual should come before the unusual).
4. Permanent provisions normally come before temporary provisions.
5. Technical "housekeeping" provisions, such as effective date provisions, normally come at the end.

Reed Dickerson, The Fundamentals of Legal Drafting 90 (2d ed. 1986).

As you can see from the voting rights statutes, not every statute includes all of these parts (they are not always needed or desired) nor do they follow this exact order. A good example of a statute that follows this outline (except for the absence of a severability clause) is the National Voter Registration Act of 1993, which in outline form is as follows:

Section 1.   Short Title
Section 2.   Findings and Purposes
Section 3.   Definitions
Section 4.   National Procedures for Voter Registration for Elections for Federal Office
Sections 5-8.   [Details and Exceptions]
Sections 9-10.   [Mandates to Agencies]
Section 11.   Civil Enforcement and Private Right of Action
Section 12.   Criminal Penalties
Section 13.   Effective Date

Notice also that there is one significant difference in form between the two voting rights statutes. The first statute, the Voting Rights Act of 1965, is freestanding or new. This does not mean that the subject matter of this statute has not been the subject matter of prior law, but that this statute does not expressly amend existing statutes. It may, however, implicitly amend or repeal provisions of existing statutes if there are existing statutory provisions in conflict with its provisions.

The second statute is by its terms, an amendment to existing law. It contains two separate approaches to amendment. The first is exemplified by §2 of the Voting Rights Acts Amendments of 1982. This is an amendment by *reference.* An amendment by reference is one in which the amending statute effects the change in the existing statute by explicitly referring to that statute's title and then directing that certain words or phrases be added or omitted. As you can understand from reading §2 of the Voting Rights Act Amendments of 1982, this approach to amendment is extremely hard to follow, both for legislators trying to follow the process and for the public trying to understand the law. Without a side-by-side comparison between the amendment and the provision of law being amended, the reader cannot understand the effects of the amendment.

The second approach to statutory amendment is exemplified by §3 of this statute, which amends §2 of the Voting Rights Act of 1965. This is an amendment by *reenactment or restatement.* It is, as you can tell, much easier to follow, as it shows all of the changes to the law. Because of this virtue of ease in comprehension, the reenactment-restatement method is required by the constitutions of most states. Using this form, "a citizen or legislator [will] not be required to search out other statutes which are amended to know the law on the subject treated in the new statute." Washington Education Ass'n v. State, 604 P.2d 950, 952 (Wash. 1980). For example, Article 4, §9 of the California Constitution provides: "A statute may not be amended by reference to its title. A section of a statute may not be amended unless the section is re-enacted as amended." One disadvantage to this approach is that it does not show what has been changed without comparison with the provision that has been amended. A practice that is followed in many jurisdictions to resolve this problem is to strike out the text that is being omitted and either redline or underscore the text that is being added (underscoring is used here). Following this model, the 1982 amendment to §2 of the Voting Rights Act of 1965 would be reflected in the statute as follows (this example only addresses a small part of the amendment):

> SEC. 1. Sec. 2 of the Voting Rights Act of 1965 is amended as follows:
> "SEC. 2. No voting qualification or prerequisite to voting, or standard, practice, or procedure shall be imposed or applied by any State or political subdivision ~~to deny or abridge~~ <u>in a manner which results in a denial or abridgement</u> of the right of any citizen of the United States to vote on account of race or color. . . ."

The reference to the Voting Rights Act of 1965 in the amendments can also be misleading. For example, §2 of the Voting Rights Act of 1965 did not contain the "or in contravention of the guarantees set forth in section 4(f)(2). . . ." That provision was added by the 1975 amendments to the Voting Rights Act of 1965.

3.   Title of a Statute

Every statute has an official title. On the federal level this is customary, except for the titles of appropriation bills, which are required by statute. 1 U.S.C. §105 (1988). In most states, titles are required by constitution. In some states, such as New York, titles are required only by legislative rule. The titles of the two voting rights statutes set forth above are "An Act to enforce the fifteenth amendment to the Constitution of the United States, and for other purposes" and "An Act to amend the Voting Rights Act of 1965 to extend the effect of certain provisions, and for other purposes." These titles, known as long titles, are descriptive in that they attempt to describe the statute's purpose. For purposes of easier reference, legislatures sometimes, as part of the act itself, give statutes short titles. Each of these statutes (but not all statutes) has a short title, "The Voting Rights Act of 1965," and "The Voting Rights Act Amendments of 1982."

In legislative practice, titles provide notice to legislators and to the public of the substance of pending legislation. (See Chapter 8 for a discussion of notice of legislative activity.) It is the bill title that usually appears on the agendas for legislative committee meetings and legislative floor action. For this reason titles ought to be informative.

> Modern authorities on bill drafting assert that — excluding titles so general as to be meaningless — the best title is one which is brief and kept in general terms, not one which is an abstract of all the incidental provisions of the bill.

If the title expresses the general object or purpose of the bill, all matters fairly and reasonably connected therewith and all measures which will or may facilitate the accomplishment of such object or purpose are properly incorporated into the act and are germane to the title.

New York State Legislative Bill Drafting Commission, Bill Drafting Manual 12 (n.d.).

How do the titles of the two voting rights statutes conform to this prescription?

Consider similarly the following title for an omnibus tax bill from New York. This is just the first of three pages:

CHAPTER 57 OF THE LAWS OF 1992

AN ACT to amend the tax law, in relation to retaining in 1993 the state personal income tax rates and standard deduction amounts in effect during the 1992 tax year and providing for the personal income tax rates, household credit and standard deduction amounts for tax years beginning after 1993; to amend article 30 of the tax law and chapter 17 of title 11 of the administrative code of the city of New York, in relation to retaining in 1993 the tax rate tables, household credit and standard deduction amounts in effect in the 1992 tax year and providing for tax rate tables, household credit and standard deduction amounts for tax years beginning after 1993 under the New York city personal income tax on residents; to appeal section 18 of chapter 55 of the laws of 1992 amending the tax law and other laws relating to taxes, in relation to withholding; to amend the tax law, in relation to extending certain business surcharge taxes and the current rate applicable to the minimum taxable income base under article 9-A thereof; to amend the tax law, in relation to the rate adjustment calculations under the petroleum business tax imposed by article 13-A thereof and to the disposition of revenues therefrom; to amend the tax law, in relation to the estimated provisions of the state franchise and certain business taxes, to conform to estimated tax provisions recently enacted for federal purposes; to amend the tax law, in relation to increasing the rates of taxes on cigarettes and tobacco products imposed by article 20 of such law; to amend the tax law, in relation to the deposit and disposition of certain revenues in the metropolitan mass transportation operating assistance fund and the general fund and repealing certain provisions upon expiration thereof; to amend the vehicle and traffic law, in relation to reducing regional design plate fees; to amend the tax law, in relation to amending the definition of consideration and original purchase price and restructuring certain penalties imposed with respect to the tax on gains derived from certain real property transfers; the uncoupling from certain federal income tax provisions in the calculation of the franchise tax on entire net income of insurance corporations; to amend the abandoned property law, in relation to security deposits held by title insurers and agents; to amend chapter 41 of the laws of 1990, relating to authorizing and directing the transfer of hazardous waste remedial fund industry fee transfer account balances and receipts to the general fund and the state finance law, in relation to industry fee surcharges and the calculations relating thereto; to amend the state finance law, in relation to the establishment of a New York state passenger facility charge fund. . . .

As noted earlier, in many states, titles are the subject of constitutional or statutory provisions. The formalization of title requirements is related to a decline in the reading of bills to the assembled legislative body. Historically, because of the high rate of illiteracy, each bill in almost every legislative body was read three times by the clerk before a vote was taken. Usually these readings had to be accomplished on different days. As this practice changed, the importance of titles as notice of the subject matter of bills began to grow. As one scholar has written:

> The bill was read to the legislators instead of being printed to be personally read by them. Whether the presumption that they would all know the contents because the clerk laboriously read the measure aloud on three separate occasions, was justified, may be subject to doubt. It was assuredly a better method than putting written or printed copies in the hands of the members would have been at that time, for illiteracy was no disgrace and many of even those who could read would find it a much easier task to listen than to spell through the clumsy wording of a law. Then too the bills were fewer in number, the questions were easier to comprehend and required less complex phrasing than now. . . . The reading of the bill was the only way the member had of becoming acquainted with its contents. . . . [T]he fact that the bill was read made it unimportant whether the title was exact or whether the bill had any title at all.
>
> The same indifference continued after the bills had come to be printed and after the reading of the bills, which actually took place in the assembly, had degenerated into a perfunctory reading of the title by the clerk. . . . The theory was, that since the bills were printed and at the hand of the member, he must be presumed to know their content, just as he was when the bills were read in open session. The presumption was probably contrary to fact in both cases, but it became especially so when, with the growth of larger governmental problems, the number, length and complexity of bills increased. The member seldom read the bills unless the titles indicated a subject in which he was interested and he paid no attention when they were read by title during the sessions.
>
> The result was a complete change in the importance of the heading itself. . . .
>
> In practice it is the only means used by the legislator to determine whether he is interested in the subject-matter or not. He relies on the general debate of the open session or on party caucuses, or conversation with his friends in the legislature, to put him in touch with the principle involved. Under such conditions it becomes of the greatest importance that the title should be accurate. Otherwise a harmless-looking title may cover a vicious bill; it may be made the sheep's clothing for a legislative wolf.

Charles L. Jones, Statute Law Making in the United States 62-64 (1912). For a complete listing of information on title requirements, see Inside the Legislative Process 52-53 (National Conference of State Legislators 1991).

Title requirements have had considerable costs associated with them. Mainly they have given rise to considerable litigation that sometimes has resulted in otherwise valid legislation being declared unconstitutional.

This has caused a number of states to revisit their title requirements. Illinois, for example, amended its Constitution in 1970 to eliminate title requirements. In 1986, Texas amended its Constitution to provide (for your practice, we present this in bill form):

> ART. 3, SEC. 35. (a) No bill . . . shall contain more than one subject, ~~which shall be expressed in its title. But if any subject shall be embraced in any act, which shall not be expressed in the title, such act shall be void only as to so much thereof, as shall not be so expressed.~~
> (b) The rules of procedure of each house shall require that the subject of each bill be expressed in its title in a manner that gives the legislature and the public reasonable notice of that subject. The legislature is solely responsible for determining compliance with the rule.
> (c) A law, including a law enacted before the effective date of this subsection, may not be held void on the basis of an insufficient title.

Titles are often used as a basis to refer bills to appropriate legislative committees. As the assignment of the bill to a committee may be the most important decision over the fate of the bill (see Chapter 5), titles are sometimes written in a manner calculated to assure that a favorable committee (in situations in which alternatives are possible) will consider the bill. A good example of this is provided by Judge Mikva. He recalls that, while he was serving in Congress in 1969, he was told about the existence of a detention camp, located in the United States and intended for "subversives." This camp had been established pursuant to the Emergency Detention Act of 1950. Concerned about the continuations of the policies expressed in this Act, Mikva decided he would attempt to repeal the legislation and discovered that a group of Japanese-Americans had been similarly attempting such a repeal, reflecting the experience of the internment camps during World War II. See Korematsu v. United States, 323 U.S. 214 (1944). Unfortunately, the bill being promoted by the Japanese-Americans had been languishing in the House Committee on Internal Security, an unfriendly committee; it had been sent there as a result of its title, "[a] bill to repeal the Emergency Detention Act of 1950." As part of the strategy that finally led to the repeal of this 1950 statute, the bill was reintroduced with a new title, "[a] bill to amend title 18, United States Code, to prohibit the establishment of emergency detention camps. . . ." This bill was sent to the Judiciary Committee, which had jurisdiction over title 18 amendments and was a sympathetic committee. The bill was favorably reported to the House and later became law. The referral of bills to committee is discussed in more detail in Chapter 5.

One final word on titles. Recall that they come *before* the enactment clause. They are not part of the body of the statute. This can be of significance in the interpretation of statutes. See, for example, Church of the Holy Trinity v. United States, Chapter 11, page 744.

4. Enacting Clause

The statute's title precedes an enacting clause that reads, in the case of the two statutes above, "[b]e it enacted by the Senate and House of Representatives of the United States of America in Congress assembled." The purpose of an enacting clause is to provide formal notice that what follows is uniquely important. It also serves to distinguish a bill from other forms of legislative communications, such as resolutions. (Resolutions, except in certain cases when signed by the President, are communications that deal with matters within the prerogative of one or both houses. They do not have the force of law.) The federal enacting clause is prescribed by statute (1 U.S.C. §101). State enacting clauses are frequently prescribed by constitutional provisions. For example, Article IV, §8 of the Illinois State Constitution provides: "[t]he enacting clause of this State shall be: 'Be it enacted by the People of the State of Illinois, represented in the General Assembly.'" The enacting clause provision is usually considered mandatory, and its absence (a rare occurrence) invalidates a statute. See, for example, People v. Dettenthaler, 77 N.W. 450 (Mich. 1898). In some legislatures, the method for killing bills is to move to strike the enacting clause.

5. Number of Subjects in a Statute

Statutes may contain a variety of distinct subjects. Such legislation is frequently known as omnibus legislation. Its goal is generally to forge support for each subject of the legislation by tying the many subjects together. In other words, a legislator will support the omnibus bill because he or she supports some part of it. This practice is sometimes referred to as logrolling, but logrolling is a broader practice that more traditionally includes the promise of one legislator (A) to support the legislation of a second legislator (B) in return for legislator B's promise to support the legislation of A. Omnibus legislation is also used to provide a shield to legislators by allowing them to argue that they supported unpopular provisions of a bill in order to enact popular provisions. Such legislation is also used, on occasion, to force executive approval of disfavored legislation by combining it with legislation favored by the executive. This leaves the executive with an all-or-nothing choice in deciding whether to exercise the veto, and accounts for the inclusion of the line item veto in some state constitutions. See Chapter 9, Section C.3.

How many subjects are addressed by each of the voting rights statutes?

In over 40 states there are constitutional requirements, known as *single subject rules*, that restrict statutes to single subjects. Typical of a single subject rule is Article 4, §8 of the California Constitution: "[a] statute shall embrace but one subject. . . ." The primary purpose of single subject restrictions is to prohibit omnibus legislation.

> The primary and universally recognized purpose of the one-subject rule is to prevent log-rolling in the enactment of laws — the practice of several minorities combining their several proposals as different provisions of a single bill and thus consolidating their votes so that a majority is obtained for the omnibus bill where perhaps no single proposal of each minority could have obtained majority approval separately. . . .
>
> Another purpose served by the one-subject rule is to facilitate orderly legislative procedure. By limiting each bill to a single subject, the issues presented by each bill can be better grasped and more intelligently discussed. Also, limiting each bill to one subject means that extraneous matters may not be introduced into consideration of the bill by proposing amendments not germane to the subject under consideration.

Millard H. Rudd, "No Law Shall Embrace More Than One Subject," 42 Minn. L. Rev. 389, 391 (1958). Do you think that the single subject rule accomplishes its purposes? Certainly it does not restrict vote trading on separate bills. Moreover, the definition of a single subject is elusive. How would you define it? Do you think the New York tax bill noted on page 59 of this chapter covers a single subject?

Consider the following problem. During his tenure as a member of the Illinois State Legislature, Judge Mikva encountered a bill that had as its subject the creation of a number of commissions. Assume the bill's title read: "A bill for the establishment of certain commissions." Among the commissions listed in the bill was a Fair Employment Practices Commission that Mikva had proposed and also several that Mikva opposed. Illinois has a single subject rule. Article 4, §8 of the Illinois Constitution provides that "[b]ills, except for appropriations and for the codification, revision or rearrangement of laws, shall be confined to one subject." Off and on during his tenure, Mikva had used this provision to argue in opposition to legislation that had been cobbled together by the legislative leadership. He wanted to be loyal to his position on the single subject rule. Do you think maintaining that position requires a "no" vote on this particular legislation? In the end, Mikva supported the legislation.

The problem above illustrates a tension that sometimes occurs between the imperatives of the legislative process — enacting laws — and those of externally imposed rules of legislative procedure. While Mikva was a supporter of the single subject rule, much of his opposition to earlier omnibus legislation had been based on the merits of the legislation he opposed, rather than on the bill's form. Being confronted with legislation that contained provisions important to him raised a different question that made him read the rule as broadly as possible. Nor have courts, except in extreme cases, compelled narrower readings. There has been a uniform and principled reluctance on the part of courts throughout the country to overturn statutes on such a basis. For a detailed exploration of these points, see Millard H. Rudd, "No Law Shall Embrace More Than One Subject," 42 Minn. L. Rev. 389 (1958).

6. Statutory Findings and Statements of Purpose

Sometimes statutes provide details about the concerns that led to their enactment. Section 10(a) of the Voting Rights Act of 1965 contains such a legislative finding. Consider the following excerpts from the Americans with Disabilities Act of 1990:

SEC. 2. FINDINGS AND PURPOSES

(a) FINDINGS. — The Congress finds that —

(1) Some 43,000,000 Americans have one or more physical or mental disabilities, and this number is increasing as the population as a whole is growing older; . . .

(3) discrimination against individuals with disabilities persists in such critical areas as employment, housing, public accommodations, education, transportation, communication, recreation, institutionalization, health services, voting, and access to public services;

(4) unlike individuals who have experienced discrimination on the basis of race, color, sex, national origin, religion, or age, individuals who have experienced discrimination on the basis of disability have often had no legal recourse to redress such discrimination;

(5) individuals with disabilities continually encounter various forms of discrimination, including outright intentional exclusion, the discriminatory effects of architectural, transportation, and communication barriers, overprotective rules and policies, failure to make modifications to existing facilities and practices, exclusionary qualification standards and criteria, segregation, and relegation to lesser services, programs, activities, benefits, jobs, or other opportunities; . . .

(7) individuals with disabilities are a discrete and insular minority who have been faced with restrictions and limitations, subjected to a history of purposeful unequal treatment, and relegated to a position of political powerlessness in our society, based on characteristics that are beyond the control of such individuals and resulting from stereotypic assumptions not truly indicative of the individual ability of such individuals to participate in, and contribute to, society. . . .

Pub. L. No. 101-336.

What is the purpose of including such provisions within the statute? What is their effect? In Sutton v. United Air Lines, 119 S. Ct. 2139 (1999), the Court was asked to resolve whether corrective measures should be considered in determining whether an individual was disabled under the ADA. In holding that an airline's standard that all pilot applicants have a minimum requirement of uncorrected visual acuity of 20/100 did not discriminate against myopic job applicants because they could fully correct their visual impairments, the Court used the purpose and findings clause of the ADA to resolve the question:

> Finally, and critically, findings enacted as part of the ADA require the conclusion that Congress did not intend to bring under the statute's protection all those whose uncorrected conditions amount to disabilities. Congress found that "some 43,000,000 Americans have one or more physical or mental disabilities, and this number is increasing as the population as a whole is growing older." §12101(a)(1). This figure is inconsistent with the definition of disability pressed by petitioners.

Id. at 2147.

Assume someone, adversely affected by the statute, thought he or she could prove that 20 million and not 43 million Americans "have one or more physical or mental disabilities." Could this be a basis for challenging the statute?

7. Definitions

Statutes frequently contain definitions. An example is §4(c) of the Voting Rights Act of 1965, which sets forth a definition of "test or device." Through definitions, a legislative body can give a word or phrase any meaning it chooses. Definitions are used in a statute to limit the common meaning of certain words or phrases, or to make sure that certain words and phrases are given a particular meaning. The addition of a definition section to a statute may be only a matter of purposely clear drafting (the use of the term "test or device" in the Voting Rights Act of 1965), but it also may be the result of legislative compromises (such as defining employers as those who employ more than 25 persons in the Civil Rights Act of 1964) or a desire to limit the discretion of administrative agencies or the courts. In fact, statutory definitions, after statutory sanctions, can be the most important part of a statute.

In contrast, common language of statutes should not be statutorily defined. "A term that is familiar, clear, and used in its dictionary sense should never be formally defined (unless there are special circumstances that call for reassurance to the reader) — it would be unnecessary and might create doubts about the meaning of other familiar words in the bill." Lawrence E. Filson, The Legislative Drafter's Desk Reference 120 (1992).

8. Remedies and Sanctions

Statutes often contain remedies and sanctions, allowing the government and private individuals to bring lawsuits and authorizing or requiring imprisonment, fines, damages, and injunctions for statutory violations. These are among the most important provisions in a statute and are frequently the focus of legislative debate. For example, who would have opposed the Voting Rights Act of 1965 if it had simply provided that "no voting qualification . . . shall be imposed or applied . . . by any state . . . to deny or abridge the right of any citizen . . . to vote on account of race or color"? What are the remedies and sanctions contained in the excerpted portions of the Voting Rights Act of 1965?

9. Severability Clauses

Section 19 of the Voting Rights Act of 1965 is a *severability clause.* Such clauses are included without thought in almost all statutes. The idea behind severability clauses is to make clear to the courts that it is the legislative intent to preserve as much of the statute as possible in case part of it is invalidated. In some instances, a better approach to statutory drafting may be to include an *inseverability clause.* An inseverability clause is one that specifically ties certain provisions together. If one of these provisions, then, is invalidated by the courts, the other provisions would also be invalidated by statutory command. Use of this approach would protect important legislative compromises from being undermined. An example of such a clause is found in S.3 of 1994, a bill amending the Federal Election Campaign Act Amendments of 1974. The bill failed to pass the House of Representatives. It provided:

> (c) Effect of Invalidity on Other Provisions of Act. — If section 501, 502, or 503 of title V of FECA (as added by this section), or any part thereof, is held to be invalid, all provisions of, and amendments made by, this Act shall be treated as invalid.

Judge Mikva, when in Congress, explored the use of an inseverability clause as a remedy for the problem created by the Supreme Court's decision in Immigration & Naturalization Service v. Chadha, 462 U.S. 919 (1983) (Chapter 9, page 563). In *Chadha,* the Court struck down Congress' power to veto a regulation of an administrative agency, except through the enactment of a statute. Mikva and others considered, as one solution to the problem they saw left by the decision, adding to an agency appropriation bill a provision containing a legislative veto and an inseverability clause. For example, added to an appropriation bill for purchase of parkland would be a congressional right to veto the locations. These would be tied together by an inseverability clause that would invalidate the appropriation if the veto provision was successfully challenged. In the end, the approach was abandoned for various political and policy reasons.

10. Effective Date of a Statute

Among the most important provisions of any statute is its effective date. For the legislator, choosing an effective date raises two questions: When should the statute go into effect? What does "go into effect" mean? The Voting Rights Act of 1965 contains no effective date. The Voting Rights Act Amendments of 1982 provide that they should take effect immediately. What is the effective date of the Voting Rights Act of 1965?

Many state constitutions and statutes regulate the effective dates of statutes. For example, Article 4, §7 of the California Constitution provides that "a statute enacted at a regular session shall go into effect on January 1 next following a 90-day period from the date of enactment of the statute." This provision also provides for certain exceptions to this rule. A more lenient version is found in the Illinois Constitution, Article 4, §10, which provides that:

> [t]he General Assembly shall provide by law for a uniform effective date for laws passed prior to July 1 of a calendar year. The General Assembly may provide for a different effective date in any law passed prior to July 1. A bill passed after June 30 shall not become effective prior to July 1 of the next calendar year unless the General Assembly by the vote of three-fifths of the members elected to each house provides for an earlier effective date.

What do you think accounts for the different treatment of bills passed before July 1 and bills passed after June 30? Section 43 of the Legislative Law of New York provides that "[e]very law unless a different time shall be described therein shall take effect on the twentieth day after it shall have become law." How does this approach compare to those of California and Illinois?

Sometimes statutory provisions setting forth the effective date of a statute do not inform as to the timing of the statute's applicability. For example, the Civil Rights Act of 1991 provides that its provision should take effect immediately, but, as discussed below, questions remain as to whether it should be applied to discriminatory actions that took place before its enactment (retroactively) or only to such acts that occur after its enactment (prospectively). Statutes, except for those establishing crimes, may be applied retroactively, and whether they are or are not depends on the language of the statute and its interpretation. The interpretation of statutes is discussed in Part IV of this book.

The choice of an effective date for a statute is frequently one of the most hotly contested points in the consideration of a piece of legislation. Consider the following example provided by Judge Mikva from his days as a member of the Illinois legislature. A child had fallen through the rotted railing of a common stairway on the third floor of an apartment building and had died. Under the terms of the lease, the tenant had waived liability for the landlord's negligence. Such lease provisions were strictly enforced under Illinois law. Mikva introduced a bill declaring such lease provisions to be against public policy. For his effective date he wanted to provide that the statute should be applicable to all existing leases and to all claims then pending or which thereafter may arise under existing or prior existing leases, except as otherwise barred by any statute of limitations. In other words, Mikva wanted to cover every accident, not yet subject to a final judgment, except if it were too late to commence the action because of the statute of limitations. That would also mean that if a claim had been appealed and was before the Illinois Supreme Court, the court would apply the new statute. While there was a great deal of support for the bill's policy goal, Mikva's effective date caused considerable dispute. Some argued for covering existing leases but only for accidents that occur after the date the statute is enacted; while others argued for affecting only new leases.

What are the merits of each argument?

In the end, to gain enough support to pass the bill, Mikva accepted a compromise that obscured the bill's effective date. It definitely did not cover the accident that led to the introduction of the legislation, but whether it applied to accidents that already had occurred but had not yet been fully litigated was left to the courts to decide.

Such disputes over the effective date of a statute are not easily resolved. Consider the Civil Rights Act of 1991, which was noted at the beginning of this section. This bill was intended to resolve problems created by several Supreme Court decisions that Congress believed had too severely restricted the reach of Title VII (Employment Discrimination) of the Civil Rights Act of 1964. Among the major issues was the effective date. This was of particular import because the bill contained new provisions on compensatory and punitive damages.

One group of the bill's supporters, led in the Senate by Senator Kennedy, wanted the bill to apply retroactively to cover discriminatory actions that predated the enactment date of the statute. Another group, led by Senators Danforth and Dole, argued for prospective application only covering discriminatory actions that postdated the statute. This was a make-or-break issue for each group, and the failure to resolve it might have led to legislative inaction or the defeat of any bill. As enacted, §402 of this statute provides that "this Act and the amendments made by this Act shall take effect upon enactment."

Who prevailed in this dispute? Consider the following remarks:

> *Senator Danforth:* My review of Supreme Court case law supports my reading that in the absence of an explicit provision to the contrary, no new legislation is applied retroactively. Rather, new statutes are to be given prospective application only, unless Congress explicitly directs otherwise, which we have not done in this instance. 137 Cong. Rec. S. 15472 (daily ed. Oct. 30, 1991).

> *Senator Kennedy:* I would ... like to state ... my understanding with regard to the bill's effective date. It will be up to the courts to determine the extent to which the bill will apply to cases and claims that are pending on the date of enactment. Ordinarily, courts in such cases apply newly enacted procedures and remedies to pending cases. ... And where a new rule is merely a restoration of a prior rule that has been changed by the courts, the newly restored rule is often applied retroactively. 137 Cong. Rec. S. 15485 (daily ed. Oct. 30, 1991).
>
> *Senate Staff Member:*   You have to decide if there are votes there to support this type of enactment, and we didn't have the votes on the left. ... The deal was cut to make the (language of) the statute fairly clear and then to leave it to the courts to pound out the issues.

Dispute over Retroactivity of Civil Rights Act Stems from Legislative History, Hill Staffer Says, 14 Daily Lab. Rep. A-13 (1992). How the courts treated this problem is found in Landgraf v. USI Film Prods., excerpted in Chapter 12 at page 869.

11. Private and Local Statutes

Statutes are not always of a general nature. Sometimes they address the interests of an individual or a small group of people. These are known as private statutes or, in most states when such legislation is directed toward a particular locality within the state, as local statutes. The legislative granting of a corporate charter or franchise (discussed in Chapter 1, Section C.2) are examples of private statutes. Similarly, Congress' enactment of laws that allow named individuals to immigrate to the United States or enjoin the deportation of particular individuals are private statutes. Congress and state legislatures also enact private legislation to resolve various types of individual claims. Such statutes may include waiving a statute of limitation for a particular individual, waiving the requirement of refunds for an unauthorized payment of funds for services actually performed, or awarding damages in tort claims. In this last group, Congress has, for example, voted settlements in several cases flowing from the government's experiments involving hallucinogenic drugs during the 1950s.

There is an equity impulse behind most private legislation. The usual situation is a unique problem for which no other institution can or will provide a remedy. Consider the following New York bill that was introduced after a particular governmental agency decision had been upheld by New York State's highest court. See In re O'Rourke v. Kirby, 54 N.Y.2d 8 (1981).

STATE OF NEW YORK

Senate — Assembly

January 20, 1982

AN ACT in relation to requiring the Suffolk county department of social services to return one Stephanie Petzold, a six and one-half year old child, to her former foster parent, Mrs. Veronica O'Rourke, and to direct such department to permit the adoption of Stephanie Petzold by Mrs. O'Rourke.

The People of the State of New York, represented in Senate and Assembly, do enact as follows:

SECTION 1. The legislature hereby finds and declares that Stephanie Petzold is a six and one-half year old child who has been removed from the only home and mother figure she has ever known and been placed by the Suffolk county department of social services with a total stranger, perhaps only to be returned to the "limbo" of foster care again. Stephanie's natural mother is deceased and her natural father unknown, not being named on her birth certificate nor ever attempting to contact Stephanie.

The recommended time period established by the legislature for placement of a child with a foster parent, in this case Mrs. Veronica O'Rourke of 36 Wooded Way, Calverton, New York, has been recently reduced from two years to eighteen months in recognition of the fact that prolonged care and custody by a foster parent gives rise to a presumption that the "best interest" of the child is served by remaining with the foster parent. Suffolk county department of social services has allowed Stephanie to remain with Mrs. O'Rourke for six consecutive years.

Mrs. O'Rourke has claimed that Stephanie will experience permanent psychological harm if she is removed from her custody and she has shown, through expert testimony, that Stephanie identifies with her as "psychological parent." Stephanie deserves and requires stability of continuity in parenting.

SECTION 2. Notwithstanding the provisions of any law, rule, regulation or order to the contrary, the legislature hereby directs the Suffolk county department of social services to return Stephanie Petzold to the care and custody of Mrs. Veronica O'Rourke, her former foster parent of more than six years and residing at 36 Wooded Way, Calverton, New York, and to supply any necessary assistance to lessen any disorientation which Stephanie may experience, and to assist both Mrs. Petzold and Mrs. O'Rourke in compensating for any physical or emotional problem from which Stephanie may suffer.

SECTION 3. The Suffolk county department of social services is hereby directed to allow Mrs. Veronica O'Rourke, upon proper application under article seven of the domestic relations law, to adopt Stephanie Petzold as her child.

SECTION 4. This act shall take effect immediately.

This bill passed the New York State Assembly and was sent to the Senate, where many senators supported it. It did not become law. During the period between introduction and adoption in the Assembly, a large majority of senators began to question the wisdom of such an act and finally stopped its passage. Assume that this bill had been enacted.

Would it violate a provision of the New York State Constitution that provides that the judicial power of the state shall reside in the state's judiciary branch?

A state's authority to enact such private legislation is found in its plenary legislative power, although in many states such power has been restricted to prohibit certain types of private bills. See Chapter 1, Section C.2. Which of Congress' enumerated powers authorizes such private legislation? Article I, §8 of the Constitution grants Congress the power to pay the debts of the United States, and such debts have been interpreted as including debts based on what Congress considers to be an equitable obligation of the nation. See United States v. Realty Co., 163 U.S. 427 (1896).

In many jurisdictions, private and local bills are treated differently from general legislation. In Congress, for example, there is separate consideration of this type of legislation on fixed days during the month.

C. PUBLICATION OF STATUTES, CODIFICATION, AND EVIDENCE OF LAW

If you are searching for a particular provision of either the Voting Rights Act of 1965 or its 1982 amendments, where should you look? For most law students, lawyers, professors, and, indeed, judges, the answer would be the United States Code (or state codes for provisions of state statutes). Assume that you found a particular provision of the Voting Rights Act in the code and during a litigation over the code, your adversary offered a different version of that provision that he had found in something called either an enrolled bill or slip law. Which provision would prevail? The answer to this question requires an exploration of publication of statutes and the rules that govern their prioritization.

1. Enrolled Bills

An *enrolled bill* is one that has passed both houses of a legislative body (except in Nebraska, which, like local legislatures, has one house) in identical form. The bill is then presented to the President or governor. The enrolling process, presided over by the enrolling clerk of the house in which the bill originated, is intended to make sure that the bill presented to the executive is a bill that has passed the houses of the legislature in identical form.

In Congress, as in most state processes, enrolling entails super-imposing on the bill that first passed the originating house any subsequent amendments that both legislative houses have adopted. For example, assume that a bill passes the House of Representatives. This bill, signed by the Clerk of the House as having passed the House on a particular date (known then as an *engrossed bill*), is sent to the Senate. Assume that, in the Senate, amendment 1 and amendment 2 to the House bill are adopted. At this point, neither house has passed an identical bill. The bill with the two amendments, signed by the Secretary of the Senate, is then sent back to the House of Representatives. In the House, amendment 1 is adopted, but amendment 2 is not. Neither house has yet passed identical bills. The two versions of the bill (the Senate version with amendments 1 and 2, the House version with amendment 1) are now sent to a conference committee in an attempt to resolve the dispute. (The conference committee is selected by the House Speaker and the presiding officer of the Senate. Conferees are usually members of the substantive committee that reported the legislation and are recommended by the committee chair and ranking minority member.) The conference committee reports a compromise on amendment 2, as set forth in a conference report. That compromise is sent to both houses; if both houses adopt the compromise (known as a *conference report*), identical bills have been enacted. At this point, it is the task of the House enrolling clerk (because the bill originated in the House) to take the bill that first passed the House (the engrossed bill) and add to it amendment 1 and the compromised amendment 2. This enrolled bill is then printed, in Congress on parchment paper, signed by the presiding officer of each house (the Speaker of the House of Representatives, the President *Pro Tem* of the Senate, or other designated representatives or senators), and then presented to the President.

The enrolled bill evidences the legislative enactment, and in most cases is conclusive evidence of the law. The President and the governors of some states are allowed to veto items in an appropriation bill. (In Washington, parts of a nonappropriation bill may also be vetoed.) In cases in which an item veto is exercised, the remainder (the nonvetoed portion) of the bill becomes law. The enrolled bill, then, is the bill approved by the governor, which is different from the bill first presented to him.

2.   Slip Laws

An enrolled federal bill that becomes law, either by executive action (signature), by executive inaction (pocket approval), or by legislative override of an executive veto, is sent by the executive or, in the case of enactment by override, by the appropriate legislative official to the Archives of the United States, where the original is officially stored pursuant to 1 U.S.C. §106a. Most states require that enrolled bills be filed with their secretary of state. For example, New Jersey requires that enacted (enrolled) bills be delivered:

> to the Secretary of State, to be filed in his office, in such order that the laws . . . of each sitting of the Legislature shall be kept separately, according

to the year in which they shall be passed, and not delivered to any person whatsoever, but safely kept by the Secretary of State in his office, and not suffered to be taken or removed therefrom on any pretext whatsoever.

N.J. Stat. Ann. §1:2-5 (West 1992). Enrolled bills are generally not accessible, and few legislators or staff members have ever seen one.

The first official publication of a new federal law is referred to as a *slip law*. The slip law is simply the enrolled bill after it has become law (by executive approval, by executive inaction, or by legislative override of an executive veto). The Voting Rights Act of 1965, excerpted in this chapter, is an example of a federal slip law. A slip law contains the text of the new statute, the date of enactment, and (since 1976) a citation to the volume of the Statutes at Large in which it will appear. Federal slip laws also contain marginal notes referring to any statute mentioned in the text, (since 1974) the United States Code classification of the statute or provisions of the statute, and a legislative history of the statute, with references to the Congressional Record. Federal slip laws are prepared by the Office of the Federal Register in the National Archives and Records Administration and are attainable through the Government Printing Office. They are also found in the United States Code Service (ASCUS) advance service, the United States Code Congressional and Administrative News (U.S.C.C.A.N.), and through various electronic services.

State slip laws, sometimes known as *chapter laws* or *pamphlet laws*, are generally less accessible. Some states officially publish copies of individual statutes, but many do not. But in almost all states, private publishers publish copies of newly enacted laws as part of their advance sheets service.

3. Slip Law Collections — Statutes at Large, Session Laws, and Others

At the end of each legislative session (equal to one year), the slip laws enacted during that session are collected sequentially by public law number or chapter number and published as *session laws*. The collection of federal slip laws is known as the *Statutes at Large*. The Statutes at Large are required to be published at the end of each legislative session of Congress by the Archivist of the United States and to contain "all the laws . . . enacted during each regular session of Congress." 1 U.S.C. §112. States have similar publications. For example, §44 of the Legislative Law of New York (McKinney's 1991) requires the annual publication of the session laws, arranged by chapter numbers. Session laws are also unofficially published by private publishers. For a listing of the session law publications in each state, see the latest edition of The Bluebook, A Uniform System of Citation.

4.   Codes

When you are searching for an applicable statute or reading provisions of a statute in a case, an article, or a brief, it is most likely that your reference point will be the United States Code, the United States Code Annotated, one of the 50 state annotated codes, or the codes (annotated or not), of the multitude of national municipalities. Codes are the consolidation and systematic arrangement (*codification*) by subject matter of a particular jurisdiction's statutes. *Annotated* refers to the inclusion of various references to cases interpreting statutory provisions, law review articles discussing the particular statute or provision, and other references or cross-references.

The United States Code is the consolidation and codification of the Statutes at Large or slip laws. Every state has a code, all of which are listed in The Bluebook, A Uniform System of Citation.

The need for codes is evident. They give life to statutory law. The Statutes at Large or similar collections moreover are not useful for determining those laws in force at a given time or applicable to a particular subject. For example, assume you are asked to determine what, if any, federal statutory law is applicable to a decision by a national bank in a rural community to sell insurance to its customers or to strangers. (We use this example because its facts are the basis of the case discussed on page 76.) Assume further that codes do not exist. How would you perform this research? Your most systematic choice would be to start with the first volume of the Statutes at Large and work forward to the most recent volume to find any applicable statute or statutory provision (in the case of omnibus statutes, those that cover more than one subject). You would then check whether that statute or provision had been repealed or amended by later statutes or provisions, until you arrived at what in your view is the present law. Such a task would be overwhelming. Codification solves this problem.

The United States Code contains the public laws of the United States organized by title (topic). The code is prepared and published, pursuant to 2 U.S.C. §285b, by the Office of the Law Revision Counsel of the House of Representatives. The responsibility of this office is:

> (1) To prepare, and to submit to Congress, one title at a time a complete compilation, restatement, and revision of the general and permanent laws of the United States which conforms to the understood policy, intent, and purpose of the Congress in the original enactment, with such amendments and corrections as will remove ambiguities, contradictions, and other imperfections both of substance and of form, separately stated, with a view to the enactment of each title as positive law on a title by title basis. . . .
>
> (3) To prepare and publish periodically a new edition of the United States Code (including those titles which are not yet enacted into positive law as well as those titles which have been so enacted), with annual cumulative supplements reflecting newly enacted laws.

(4) To classify newly enacted provisions of law to their proper positions in the code where titles involved have not yet been enacted into positive law.

(5) To prepare and submit periodically such revisions in the titles of the code which have been enacted into positive law as may be necessary to keep such titles current.

The process the codifiers follow is to choose subject titles, arrange the statutes under these titles, remove statutes or provisions that have been repealed or amended, and generally clean up confusion without varying from congressional policy, intent, or purpose. Such codification also requires a renumbering of included statutes or provisions. For example, the sections of the National Voter Registration Act of 1993 are found in 42 U.S.C. §§1973gg-1973gg-10. The titles are then individually submitted to the House Judiciary Committee to begin the enactment process. As of 1998, Congress had adopted 22 of the original 50 titles. No new title has been adopted since this time. One important reason for this "lag" is the political nature of Congress or of any legislative body. To ask legislators to enact a code is to ask them to affirm, or be accountable for, the work of past legislatures. Such an action could not be taken in a vacuum. No interested legislator or group would simply enact a code of existing law without considering the substantive and political merits of that law. This means that, from a legislative perspective, a bill to enact an unenacted code may be treated no differently than any other bill: competing for attention and subject to current political and policy views.

Many important provisions of a statute may not be codified. Provisions setting forth the statute's purposes or findings, its effective date, and its severability or nonseverability are usually omitted from the codes (but found in their notes). Provisions such as the last two just named address the effectiveness or operation of the statute but not its substance and therefore are usually omitted. Provisions setting forth legislative findings or purposes, while adding a unique meaning to a particular statute, are not codified because they are particular to the individual statute, not to the body of law as a whole. On the occasion that a code is enacted, a purpose section sometimes is included in the enacted code. This is particularly true when the enacted code is not simply the codification of existing law but a legislative attempt to enact a new statute to replace all of the existing law, for example, the Bankruptcy Act of 1994.

5.   Evidence of the Law — Of Codes, Slip Laws, Enrolled Bills, and Journal Entries

A statute, as described earlier, is the product of the legislative enactment process. A code is the systematic collection of statutes by subject matter. For the most part, codes are unenacted. Such codes are, at most, prima facie evidence of the law, but not conclusive evidence of the law. This point, although rarely considered by most students of the law, should be evident. The work of the codifiers in creating and maintaining a code requires judgment concerning the impact of subsequent statutes on prior ones. Errors are sometimes made in the reading and transcribing of slip law sections or in the exercise of judgment about the applicability of particular statutes. Unenacted codes are simply the opinion of codifiers, whether public or private, as to the effect a subsequent statute has had on an earlier one. For example, did it repeal or amend an earlier decision? That is why Title 1, §204 of the United States Code provides:

> (a) **United States Code.** — The matter set forth in the edition of the Code of Laws of the United States current at any time shall, together with the then current supplement, if any, establish *prima facie* [emphasis added] the laws of the United States, general and permanent in their nature, in force on the day preceding the commencement of the session following the last session the legislation of which is included: *Provided, however,* That whenever titles of such Code shall have been enacted into positive law the text thereof shall be legal evidence of the laws therein contained, in all the courts of the United States, the several States, and the Territories and insular possessions of the United States. [first emphasis added]

Incidentally, Title 1 of the United States Code is one of the titles enacted into positive law. It was so enacted in 1947 by Public Law No. 61-278, entitled "An Act to codify and enact into positive law, Title 1 of the United States Code, entitled 'General Provisions.'"

The significance of the prima facie evidentiary status of an unenacted code provision is illustrated by a Supreme Court decision involving the same regulatory scheme about banks and the sale of insurance used as an example on page 74. In National Bank of Oregon v. Insurance Agents, 508 U.S. 439 (1993), the issue was whether a national bank with a branch in a small community through which it sold insurance could sell insurance outside of that community. The answer to the question hinged on whether Congress had repealed the statute on which the bank claimed authority was based. The Statutes at Large contained a 1916 statute that authorized such sales of insurance by banks (39 Stat. 753), and this statute was codified in Title 12 (unenacted) of the United States Code as §92, until 1952. In 1952, the codifiers removed §92 with an explanatory note that this section had been repealed by a 1918 statute. In attempting to unravel the complicated history that led to the codifiers' decision, the Court wrote:

> Though the appearance of a provision in the current edition of the United States Code is "prima facie" evidence that the provision has the force of laws, 1 U.S.C. §204(a), it is the Statutes at Large that provides the legal evidence of laws, 1 U.S.C. §112, and despite its omission from the Code section 92 remains on the books if the Statutes at Large so dictate.

Id. at 448. United States Code §112 provides that "[t]he United States Statutes at Large shall be legal evidence of laws . . . in all courts of the United States, the several states, and the territories and insular possessions of the United States." Similar provisions are found in state statutes.

Despite the above statutes, questions still arise as to the evidentiary conclusiveness of a slip law or enrolled bill. Sometimes in the enrollment process errors occur that result in differences between the bill enacted by the legislature and the bill presented to the executive. See, for example, Harris v. Shanahan, discussed at page 78. Such errors raise constitutional questions about the validity of the statute. In Field v. Clark, 143 U.S. 649 (1891), importers of various cloth materials challenged a tariff act that impacted their business. They claimed that the act was constitutionally a nullity because "a section of the bill, as it finally passed, was not in the bill authenticated by the signatures of the presiding officers of the respective houses of Congress, and approved by the President." Id. at 669. In other words, the appellant argued that the enrolled bill was, in fact, not passed by Congress. The evidence they offered to support this view comprised of entries from legislative journals and committee reports. In rendering its decision in favor of the tariff acts, the Court announced what is known as the *enrolled bill rule:*

> In regard to certain matters, the Constitution expressly requires that they shall be entered on the journal. To what extent the validity of legislative action may be affected by the failure to have those matters entered on the journal, we need not inquire. No such question is presented for determination. But it is clear that, in respect to the particular mode in which, or with what fullness, shall be kept the proceedings of either house relating to matters not expressly required to be entered on the journals; whether bills, orders, resolutions, reports and amendments shall be entered at large on the journal, or only referred to and designated by their titles or by numbers; these and like matters were left to the discretion of the respective houses of Congress. Nor does any clause of that instrument, either expressly or by necessary implication, prescribe the mode in which the fact of the original passage of a bill by the House of Representatives and the Senate shall be authenticated, or preclude Congress from adopting any mode to that end which its wisdom suggests. . . .
>
> The signing by the Speaker of the House of Representatives, and by the President of the Senate, in open session, of an enrolled bill, is an official attestation by the two houses of such bill as one that has passed Congress. It is a declaration by the two houses, through their presiding officers, to the President, that a bill, thus attested, has received, in due form, the sanction of the legislative branch of the government, and that it is delivered to him in obedience to the constitutional requirement that all bills which pass Congress shall be presented to him. And when a bill, thus attested, receives his approval, and is deposited in the public archives, its authentication as a bill that has passed Congress should be deemed complete and unimpeachable. . . .

It is admitted that an enrolled act, thus authenticated, is sufficient evidence of itself — nothing to the contrary appearing upon its face — that it passed Congress. But the contention is, that it cannot be regarded as a law of the United States if the journal of either house fails to show that it passed in the precise form in which it was signed by the presiding officers of the two houses, and approved by the President. It is said that, under any other view, it becomes possible for the Speaker of the House of Representatives and the President of the Senate to impose upon the people as a law a bill that was never passed by Congress. But this possibility is too remote to be seriously considered in the present inquiry. It suggests a deliberate conspiracy. . . . Judicial action based upon such a suggestion is forbidden by the respect due to a coordinate branch of the government. The evils that may result from the recognition of the principle that an enrolled act, in the custody of the Secretary of State, attested by the signatures of the presiding officers of the two houses of Congress, and the approval of the President, is conclusive evidence that it was passed by Congress, according to the forms of the Constitution, would be far less than those that would certainly result from a rule making the validity of Congressional enactments depend upon the manner in which the journals of the respective houses are kept by the subordinate officers charged with the duty of keeping them. . . .

Id. at 671-73.

This rule is not universally followed. A number of states have rules that allow references, in certain instances, to legislative journals and sometimes other documents to contradict the enrolled bill as evidenced by the slip or session law. Legislative journals, discussed in Chapter 8, Section B, are constitutionally required journals of legislative proceedings. These rules effectively make the slip law or session law presumptive, not conclusive, evidence of the law, notwithstanding state statutes declaring session laws conclusive. For example, in Harris v. Shanahan, excerpted in Chapter 11, page 790, the enrolling clerk omitted from an enrolled bill a provision that had been included in the bill that had passed the legislature. The court impeached the enrolled bill on the basis of legislative journals, after stating the general rule that an enrolled bill can only be impeached if truthful legislative journals show beyond all doubt that the bill enrolled and signed by the governor was not the bill passed by the legislature.

The jurisprudence on such rules is too varied to be easily catalogued. As the reporters for the National Conference of State Legislatures have observed:

1. There does not appear to be agreement between the states concerning whether to rely on the journal record or the enrolled bill record to determine whether a bill has been duly passed and what the provisions of the bill are when there are conflicts in the records.
2. It appears that the enrolled bill as certified on the bill itself by the presiding officers and the legislative officers of both houses is more likely to be correct than the record maintained by the journal clerk.

The state constitutions contain provisions concerning the journal and the records that must be kept and some have rules concerning the enrollment of bills. These requirements vary widely from state to state. It is sometimes difficult to reconcile the different rules for even one state and apparently impossible to reconcile law on the subject generally. It appears that the law in each state must be arrived at from a consideration of the constitution, court decisions and rules of that state.

National Conference of State Legislatures, Mason's Manual of Legislative Procedure 481 (1989).

CHAPTER 3
The Structures and Processes of American Legislatures

A. THE STRUCTURE OF AMERICAN LEGISLATURES

In basic outline, Congress and all of this nation's state legislatures are similarly structured. Congress and all of the state legislatures, except for Nebraska, are divided into two houses. For purposes of this section, we will generically refer to the most populous house of a state legislature as the "House," and to the least populous house as the "Senate" (although they may have different names in different states). (Bicameralism is discussed in Chapter 9, Section B.) Each legislative house is organized by political party affiliations, through party caucuses, and by committees. Each house also has its own leadership structure. There is also a staff structure that includes administrative, professional, and political staffs. In this section we introduce these units of organization and explore, generally, the roles played by each. Reference to these units will be made throughout this chapter and the book. Within each house there also may be a number of more informal, interest-related groups such as the Democratic Study Group of the House of Representatives and the Congressional Black Caucus. While these groups will not be covered in the following discussion, at any given moment they may exercise critical power in the legislative process. For example, because of their numbers and unified commitment to certain issues, the Congressional Black Caucus played a very important role in the formulation and adoption of President Clinton's 1993 deficit reduction program. See Kitty Cunningham, Black Caucus Flexes Muscle on Budget — And More, 51 Cong. Q. 1711 (July 3, 1993).

1. Party Organization

The party system is the most significant organizational unit in Congress and in many state legislatures. Legislators run for office as Democrats or Republicans and, once in the legislature, organize themselves according to these labels. In each house of Congress and in each house of most state legislatures, each party has a *caucus* (often referred to as a *conference*) made up of all legislators of that party. The U.S. House of Representatives, for example, consists of the Democratic Caucus and the Republican Conference. Likewise, the U.S. Senate consists of the Democratic and Republican Conferences. These formal organizations meet regularly in most jurisdictions, and adopt and operate under their own caucus bylaws and customs.

The caucuses also establish committees to aid in the performance of their functions. For example, the Democratic Caucus of the U.S. House of Representatives (for the 103d Congress, 1993-1994) had the Democratic Personnel Committee (patronage), the Democratic Steering and Policy Committee (legislative scheduling and committee assignments), and the Democratic Congressional Campaign Committee (campaign support for House seats). The Republican Conference of the House had the National Republican Congressional Committee (campaign support), the Republican Committee on Committees (committee appointments), the Republican Policy Committee (legislative strategy), and the Republican Research Committee (development of policy alternatives).

Although the legislative caucuses bear the names of national and state political parties, to a substantial extent they exist separately from these parties. National and state parties are dominated by presidential and gubernatorial politics and achieve power through successful executive elections. Winning executive elections requires each single party in the two-party system to choose among the party's many disparate views in order to create a platform on which to run. If the national or state party elects an executive, that executive will appoint the leader of the national or state party and totally control its efforts. The executive's programs will become the national or state party's programs. Power for legislative caucuses comes from having as large a membership as possible. As is discussed below, the majority party dominates the legislative process, and the larger the majority the greater this domination. This creates, within the legislative caucus, a distaste for ideological choices that might drive members from its ranks.

These different approaches for gaining power cause tension between legislative caucuses (parties) and their national and state counterparts. Frequently this leads to considerable friction between a particular executive and the legislative caucuses of the executive's party. Although there are very successful efforts to create unified positions between executives and the caucuses of their party, often this unity can only be accomplished through significant policy compromises by the executive. A clear example is the experience of President Clinton in his first year in office (1993). Elected on, among other things, his program of deficit reduction through tax increases and spending cuts, a program joined by almost all Democratic legislative candidates, his bill proposals for advancing his ideas were the subject of substantial amendment by the Democratic caucus in each house of Congress before a program was enacted. For example, his broad energy (BTU) tax was replaced with a gasoline tax; his tax on social security income was downwardly modified; Medicare spending cuts were added to his proposal; and his food stamp program was reduced. This process contrasts sharply with the process, followed in most other democracies. In those countries, policy making is the purview of the prime minister and his cabinet, who are members of the legislature and leaders of the majority party. Legislation is adopted as introduced, party membership determines voting, and the failure to carry a measure can topple a government.

The legislative party system serves two functions: legislative governance and legislative consensus building or policy making. As an institution of governance "[t]he party [caucus] system governs the elections of . . . [legislative] leaders, the allocation of staff and financial resources, the determination of the chairmen of committees and subcommittees, the daily flow of legislative activities, and even the actual seating of members both in the committee rooms and on the floor." Abner J. Mikva and Patti B. Saris, The American Congress 67 (1983). We will examine this role when we discuss the leadership system in Section A.2, the structure of committees in Section A.3, and staff in Section A.4 of this chapter.

As a consensus builder, the caucus serves as a forum for policy and political debate:

> Each party [caucus] serves to unify [the disparate ideas of its members]. In particular, the . . . caucus functions primarily to create alliances, agreements, and compromises to form the basis for policy and action. When the caucus is strong and its leadership powerful, the caucus is usually successful in hammering out critical differences behind-the-scenes, providing thereby a powerful front to the opposite party on the floor of the chamber. Without this forum for ironing out differences within the party (a forum that is not always successful), frequent free-for-alls would occur on the floor with each member following his own political conscience and needs.

Abner J. Mikva and Patti B. Saris, The American Congress 79 (1983). This unifying role is particularly important given this country's two-party system, in which legislators in one party may hold a variety of conflicting points of view. In fact, to some extent, almost every view on every issue is represented in each party. Individuals choose to become Democrats or Republicans for a wide variety of reasons. Sometimes it has to do with support for particular legislative positions, but more likely these choices are determined by broader perceptions of the party's views of defining events (the Vietnam War) or perceptions (pro-labor, pro-business) or by family tradition or culture or opportunity. Democratic and Republican legislators, for example, may be for or against government regulation of abortion; for or against more aid to the poor; for or against higher or lower taxes; for or against more regulation of industry to protect the environment; or, for or against free trade treaties. Such disparate interests and views must be melded to advance legislation.

In studying the functions of legislative caucuses, a distinction must be made between the majority and minority caucus of each house. In an institution that operates by majority vote, the majority will have more power. In a house with a strong majority (both a factor of number of members and cohesiveness), the majority caucus will control both governance of its house's process and the substance of the legislation it produces. It is a general rule of legislative practice that, in any legislative house, a majority of the majority party (although it is not a majority of the whole house) can block the consideration of legislation. This means that even if a bill is reported from a committee (and all committees have a majority of members from the majority caucus), it must gain the support of a majority of the members of the majority caucus before it can be considered or adopted by the house that caucus controls. In New York, for example, in order to maintain party discipline, the practice in both legislative houses (at least from 1981 through 1993) is to "lay aside" or "table" a bill that is on the floor if it appears that the bill will not receive the votes of a majority of the majority caucus.

What do you think about this rule?

The stronger (more unified and more numerous) the majority caucus, the more reactive the minority caucus becomes. For instance, over the last several decades in the U.S. Senate, a large number of minority party members (under Senate rules that increase minority strength, for example, filibusters and non-germane amendments (see Chapter 5)) assure a meaningful role for the minority caucus in governance and policy making. In the House of Representatives, on the other hand, the small minority caucus spends most of its time deciding whether or not to support, oppose, or offer amendments to legislation that the majority is scheduling for final consideration.

Even the weakest minority caucus has some bargaining power. The control of a legislative house depends on cooperation from the minority caucus. A determined minority caucus, through proactive use of the legislative rules and liberal use of amendments, can "ensnarl the process procedurally and impede progress." Abner J. Mikva and Patti B. Saris, The American Congress 94 (1983).

Not every bill before every caucus requires a caucus consensus in support or opposition. Sometimes the function of a caucus is simply to provide an explanatory briefing on the substance of particular bills, with no concern for reaching a caucus view. This may reflect a weak caucus (one in which it is impossible to forge a consensus), but it also may reflect a decision by the caucus that there is no reason to try to forge a consensus on the bill, or that to attempt to forge a party view would be damaging to the party. For example, there may be no interest in forging a consensus over technical amendments to regulatory legislation, or there may be no possible way of forging a consensus over death penalty or abortion legislation or other issues that trigger intense personal and political responses.

Arriving at a caucus consensus does not mean that all members of the caucus will support the caucus position. Some legislators, depending upon the issue, simply will not agree. There are no formal rules for dealing with such deviation. As indicated earlier in this section, caucuses are not ideological but pragmatic institutions that encourage as broad a membership as possible. The creation of rules about voting would work against this model. And while there is a substantial correlation between caucus membership and voting on bills over which competing caucuses are in conflict, supporting a position not followed by a majority of the members of the caucus will most frequently go unquestioned, particularly when the deviation from the caucus view is justified on the basis of constituent needs. But on occasion, greater premiums are placed on party loyalty. This occurs when a caucus, usually at the initiation of its leadership, decides that a particular bill is of unusual significance to its interests. The bill, in effect, is made a "party" bill. There is usually no formal determination of such status, but its recognition flows from caucus debate.

In 1993, for example, the Democratic Caucus of the House of Representatives decided to support a compromised version of President Clinton's deficit reduction plan that contained a number of items that many members of the caucus believed would have an extremely negative impact on their districts. At a caucus meeting, the caucus leadership told the members that the bill was very important for the new administration and for the Democratic caucus because it would address the deficit problem and because it would demonstrate that a Democratic President and Democratic Congress could work together to enact important legislation. The caucus members were also told that the administration had made a number of compromises to satisfy the concerns of various members of the caucus. According to a report in the Congressional Quarterly, "[f]reshmen in particular were warned that leaders can impose political exile on renegades." Beth Donovan, Democrats May Punish Chairmen Who Defied Clinton on Vote, Cong. Q. 1411 (June 5, 1993). The bill passed the House 219 to 213, with a number of Democrats in opposition. Among this number were 11 subcommittee chairs. A number of members of the caucus, led by some of the freshmen who had supported the party position against their own political interests, petitioned the caucus to strip these eleven of their subcommittee chairs.

In the end the caucus took no direct action against the eleven. In reporting this result, the Speaker indicated that the caucus view was that maintaining a leadership position should not depend on a single vote. Such a view emphasizes the point made earlier about the practical, non-ideological nature of legislative caucuses and the importance of constituent views to a legislator. Two comments, following the caucus meeting that considered the charges against the subcommittee chairs, underscore this point. From Jimmy Hayes, chairman of a Science, Space and Technology subcommittee on the practical nature of caucuses: "If you decide there are two Democratic parties, one that can have subcommittee chairs and one that can't, I might decide I don't like either." And from Bill Sarpalius, who chairs a Small Business subcommittee, on the view of constituents: "I do not need a few liberals . . . to decide for me what is the correct vote for my congressional district." Beth Donovan, Maverick Chairmen Forgiven as Clinton Reworks Bill, 51 Cong. Q. 1451 (June 12, 1993). On the other hand, consistent variance from consensus positions may make it difficult for a legislator to gain or maintain a prominent caucus role. One example of this is provided by Charles Tiefer: "In the 1980s, the Democratic leadership made party loyalty (of reelected Members seeking transfer [to different committees]) a critical consideration, rewarding with choice assignments those who had voted with the leadership on key votes such as the 1981 budget and tax votes." Charles Tiefer, Congressional Practice and Procedure 96 (1989).

2. *Legislative Leadership*

Among the most important decisions that a legislative caucus makes is the choice of its leadership. The ability of a legislature to respond to problems perceived as needing legislative response depends on the existence of some formal leadership to administer the legislative process and meld disparate views toward a solution that will be acceptable to a majority of the legislators. "The constitutional requirement of a majority vote in both houses to pass legislation hardly explains the machinations necessary to usher a bill successfully through the legislative labyrinth. Without leadership, mere support of a bill by a majority of the . . . rank and file would be virtually meaningless." Abner J. Mikva and Patti B. Saris, The American Congress 85 (1983).

For the most part, leadership structures in Congress and in most state legislatures are similar. The most populous house (the House) has a speaker, and the least populous house (the Senate) has a president. In the U.S. Senate and in the senates of many state legislatures, the vice president and lieutenant governors serve as presidents of the Senate. Usually they have very limited powers: to preside over the body and to cast votes in case of a tie. In these bodies, legislative leadership is usually provided by the majority leader, as in the U.S. Senate, or by a temporary president (president pro tem). In some states, lieutenant governors play a more active role in the process, for example, participating in committee assignments and scheduling the consideration of legislation. Finally, in some states there is no lieutenant governor, or the lieutenant governor is assigned no legislative tasks at all. See generally Alan Rosenthal, Legislative Life 150 (1981). Speakers and temporary presidents are the only members of the legislative leadership chosen by their respective houses. All other positions are chosen by legislative caucuses. They include, with some variation from legislature to legislature, a majority leader, assistant majority leaders, minority leaders and assistant minority leaders, and majority and minority whips and assistant whips.

The tasks of legislative leadership are multitudinous. The following description about congressional leadership applies to both state and local legislatures. "Leaders help to organize orderly consideration of legislative proposals, promote party support for or against legislation, attempt to reconcile differences that threaten to disrupt the chambers, plan strategy on important legislation, consult with the [executive], and publicize legislative achievements." Walter J. Oleszek, Congressional Procedures and Policy Process 28 (1989). They also are the focal point for asserting legislative prerogative against incursions from either the executive or legislative branch of government. In the following sections of this chapter and throughout the following chapters, you will encounter illustrations of the exercise of leadership power.

To effect these tasks, legislative leaders are granted various powers by legislative rules and tradition. Among these are, for example, the choice of committee chairs, appointments to committees, scheduling of legislation, and the referrals of bills to particular committees. The distribution of these powers among the legislative leadership, party caucuses, and committee chairs has shifted, historically, as reformers have responded to excesses of either centralized or decentralized power. The ebbs and flows of power among these power bases are described in the following passage.

Abner J. Mikva and Patti B. Saris, The American Congress
90-93 (1983)

Throughout the nineteenth century, the House leadership experimented with different procedures to cope with the rapidly increasing size of its membership. With the decline of the party caucus under Andrew Jackson, who used the veto and popular opinion to reassert the power of the president, an effective means for disciplining members and promoting efficient and expeditious passage of legislation was lacking. To fill the vacuum left by the declining party structure, over the course of the nineteenth century the speaker accumulated greater and greater powers. The speaker obtained the power to choose not only committee chairmen but also committee membership. . . .

Speaker Thomas B. Reed, elected in 1889, probably did more than any one else to buttress the powers of the House leadership. At the time, the major procedural barrier facing the House was the "disappearing quorum." By this technique, a minority of the House could thwart any legislative effort by refusing to answer "present," thereby preventing the quorum necessary to conduct business. Reed . . . ordered the clerk to record those present who refused to be counted as part of the quorum. . . . [A]n appeal on the procedural point was tabled and a new procedural precedent was established. Indeed, the problem of defining a "quorum" was so serious that a challenge to legislation, based on the absence of a quorum, actually reached the Supreme Court, which upheld the Reed position. [United States v. Ballin, discussed on page 104 of this chapter.] . . .

Reed's successor, Joseph G. "Uncle Joe" Cannon, . . . increased the powers of the speaker to a point never before known. . . . With these powers he stopped legislation that he did not support even though it was supported by a majority of his party; he provoked the rank-and-file membership of the House to revolt.

Cannon's source of power was his appointment and control of committee chairmanships and membership. . . . His grip on the committee system was so extensive that many committees actually sought his approval before drafting legislation. . . . As chair of the Rules Committee [the House gatekeeper, see Chapter 5] Cannon's power was almost complete, for he could prevent any legislation from coming to a floor vote.

. . . [Finally, after Cannon continued to block legislation favored by President Theodore Roosevelt,] Roosevelt, able to muster a majority of the Congress behind his progressive policies, provoked a revolt against Cannon, which substantially weakened the power of the speaker for future generations. Of the many changes the insurgents managed to obtain in the following congresses, the most prominent was the "Calendar Wednesday" rule, permitting a committee chairman to call up a bill reported out of his committee for floor consideration even without the approval of the Speaker or the Rules Committee.

In 1909 . . . [t]he Speaker was . . . stripped of his exclusive power to make committee assignments. Instead, at the commencement of each Congress, the members of each committee and the chairmen were elected by the party caucuses and confirmed by the whole House. Finally, with the decline of the speaker, the party caucus reemerged in a short-lived burst of energy. However, the seniority system, which reached full bloom in the 1920s, ensured that for more than fifty years the congressional committees would be the real source of power in Congress.

During the 1960s and 1970s congressmen with seniority held the powerful positions of committee chairmen. As increasing numbers of liberal and younger rank-and-file congressmen were elected to office, the demand grew to replace older chairmen with younger members, or at least to limit their influence. Liberals turned to the speaker as the counterpoint to the conservative committee seniors. Numerous measures during this period, in particular the Legislative Reorganization Act of 1970, enhanced the office of the speaker. Under the short-lived "21-day rule," the speaker was given the power to permit a committee chairman to bring a bill to the House floor if the Rules Committee failed to act within a 21-day time period. Most important, the Democratic party caucus was revived as an instrument for forcing committee chairmen to abide by the wishes of the congressional rank and file.

The caucus, turning to the speaker as an ally, created a new Democratic Steering and Policy Committee to assist him in developing party and legislative priorities. The membership of the Steering and Policy Committee was designed to reflect the geographical make-up of the Democratic majority. Although the country was divided into "zones" for the purpose of electing almost half of the committee, the speaker retained substantial input into the committee's membership. The elected leadership of the House . . . and several of the key committee chairmen were voting members. . . . In addition, the speaker was allowed to designate six members of the committee. . . .

Finally, the caucus beefed up the speaker's power over appointment to committees. Prior to 1974, the Democratic members of the Ways and Means Committee had . . . appointed freshman congressmen to committee slots. This function was switched to the Steering and Policy Committee. . . . The Speaker was then entrusted with the power to nominate the Democratic members of the Rules Committee subject to caucus ratification.

———————————

For a fully detailed discussion of congressional leadership, see Charles Tiefer, Congressional Practice and Procedure, Chapters 4 and 7 (1989).

As the above observations point out, sometimes leadership can grow too strong. Of course, how strong is "too strong" is a matter of perspective. The most important perspective is that of the members who elect the leadership. But there are other points of view as expressed below by one of the authors:

Eric Lane, *Albany's Travesty of Democracy*
City J. 49 (Spring 1997)

New York's Legislature taxes, spends, and regulates more energetically than almost any other state's. During its most recent session, completed last summer, it enacted more than 700 laws and appropriated over $60 billion, drawing on the $33 billion that it raised in direct taxes and on vast sums of federal aid. These decisions profoundly affect life in the entire state. In New York City alone, the Legislature lays down the law for everything from the sales tax and Medicaid, to police pensions and governance of the public schools.

But activist government should not be mistaken for democratic government—and Albany is anything but democratic. Yes, New Yorkers cast their votes for State Assembly and Senate, but when the vast majority of their representatives arrive at the Capitol, they don't legislate; they meekly follow the instructions of their legislative leaders. It is no exaggeration to say that the speaker of the Assembly and the majority leader of the Senate *are* the legislative branch in Albany. They pick the issues, close the deals, and—ultimately—make the laws. A newspaper photo from a few years back furnishes the perfect emblem for this system. In it, the majority leader of the Senate stands behind a member of his party who had just voted no on a bill that the leadership had sponsored. The leader's thumb is turned up—an order to the clerk to reverse the erring senator's vote. . . .

Consider the Legislature's moribund committee system. In healthy legislative bodies—in Congress or other state legislatures or even the New York City Council—committees do much of the heavy lifting. They introduce legislation, debate it, amend it in markup sessions, hear the opinions of outside experts and the public, and issue committee reports describing their intent and reasoning to fellow members and to the executive agencies and courts that will have to interpret their handiwork. Although party leaders sometimes coordinate such committee work from above, committee chairmen and members usually act independently, even defiantly; they are power centers in their own right.

Such a division of labor, and authority, is largely unknown in Albany. As a former legislative staffer has neatly summarized the Legislature's committee life: "Nothing ever happens. A leadership-created agenda is followed and bills are voted on, always favorably. No debates or markup sessions are held, no amendments permitted. Nothing except votes are recorded." Needless to say, these meetings produce no committee reports, since there is, quite literally, nothing to report. And committee members make no effort to benefit from the knowledge of outsiders who might shed light on matters before the Legislature: former comptroller Ned Regan reports that during his 14 years as New York State's own chief financial officer, no committee ever asked him to testify, despite his repeated offers to do so.

As if to prove that committees in Albany are mere window dressing, leaders in both houses drop all pretense of needing them during the last month of each year's session, when the Legislature traditionally turns to the really important items on its agenda. Committees stop meeting altogether, and the leadership's top staff members take over as gatekeepers, with suppliant legislators lined up outside their doors in hopes of getting bills onto the legislative floor. I once asked the counsel to several former speakers how legislation gets on the docket in the Assembly: "Don't you guys have a rules committee?" Without missing a beat, he replied, "I'm it."

3. *Committee Structure*

Committees are the working arms of legislatures. Woodrow Wilson's observation about Congress in 1885 remains broadly applicable to Congress and many state legislatures today. "[I]t is not so far from the truth to say that Congress in session is Congress on public exhibition whilst Congress in its Committee Rooms is Congress at work." Woodrow Wilson, Congressional Government 69 (Johns Hopkins ed. 1981). There are various forms of legislative committees — for example, standing, select, and joint — but here our focus is the standing committee. These are the permanent committees that have the authority to consider and report bills and conduct oversight investigations. Committee functions and processes are the subject of Chapter 4.

The number of standing committees and subcommittees, their jurisdiction, and size of their membership and party ratio (number of majority party and minority party members as a percentage of the whole number of members) is usually established by the rules of each chamber, although in the House of Representatives, for example, the number of members for each committee and party ratio is determined by the Speaker in consultation with the minority leader. The number of members on a committee is the product of a number of factors, most significantly the demand for seats on particular committees by members of the majority caucus. In most cases, the party ratio relates to percentage of members each party has in the particular chamber, although this may vary. For example, in 1975, to challenge the growing coalition of conservative Democrats and Republicans on various committees, the Democratic Caucus voted to increase the number of Democrats on each committee beyond their customary formula to allow for the appointment of noncoalition Democrats. In 1981 the Republicans unsuccessfully challenged this action in the courts. Vander Jagt v. O'Neill, 699 F.2d 1166 (D.C. Cir. 1983). On what basis do you think that this challenge was denied?

Appointments to committee are generally recommended by caucus committees (for example, the Policy and Steering Committee of the Democratic Caucus of the House of Representatives), in consultation with legislative leadership, and approved by each respective caucus. In most legislative bodies, such as Congress, they are then "elected" by their respective houses. In both houses of Congress and in most state legislatures there is an unwritten "property right" rule that reelected members can maintain (with seniority) the committee assignments they had in the previous legislative term, unless they ask for a transfer. The significance of committees to legislative work means that there can be considerable competition for open seats. Members see committees as a way to help their constituents, further their reelection goals, join the party leadership, and further their policy agendas. The assignments to open committee seats are determined by a number of factors, including seniority, caucus loyalty, leadership loyalty, political needs, and geography. The choice of committee chairs and of ranking minority members is also subject to the approval of the respective legislative caucuses. The standing committees of Congress as of 2007 are set forth in Table 3-1. The jurisdictions of these congressional committees are found in the respective rules of each legislative house.

Congress, unlike state legislatures, has an extensive subcommittee system that has been spawned over the last half of the twentieth century. Subcommittees in Congress are the product of a number of factors including workloads that involve greater concentrations of expertise and focus, the ambition of more members for more involvement in the legislative action, and a desire on the part of some members, historically, to circumvent the power of certain committee chairs. For the most part, the number of subcommittees, their jurisdiction, their size, party ratio, and membership are determined by the members of the parent committee, acting through committed political caucuses. Competition for subcommittee positions can be fierce.

At the beginning of each Congress, each committee of the House and Senate holds an organizational session. These sessions are preceded by some of the least visible and most intense political maneuvers, as members assess their interests in the assignment of themselves and others to subcommittees and

TABLE 3-1
Standing Committees, House and Senate (2007)

House	Senate
Agriculture	Agriculture, Nutrition, and Forestry
Appropriations	Appropriations
Armed Services	Armed Services
Budget	Banking, Housing, and Urban Affairs
Education and Labor	
Energy and Commerce	Budget
Financial Services	Commerce, Science, and Transportation
Foreign Affairs	Energy and Natural Resources
Homeland Security	Environment and Public Works
House Administration	Finance
Judiciary	Foreign Relations
Natural Resources	Health, Education, Labor and Pensions
Oversight and Government Reform	
Rules	
	Homeland Security and Governmental Affairs
Science and Technology	
Small Business	Indian Affairs
Standards of Official Conduct	Judiciary
Transportation and Infrastructure	Rules and Administration
Veterans' Affairs	Small Business and Entrepreneurship
Ways and Means	Veterans' Affairs

the choice of subcommittee chairs. Both for the Members and for legislation, organization can have great significance. For example, in any session, one Judiciary Committee subcommittee may handle vital legislation concerning civil rights, another may handle vital legislation of economic interest to well-heeled lobbies handling issues such as video copyright legislation, and a third may only handle matters of peripheral interest. Which Members end up on which subcommittees determines both the balance of power on that legislation, and the Members' ability to promote their policy goals, serve their constituencies, and raise campaign contributions from interest groups.

Charles Tiefer, Congressional Practice and Procedure 106-07 (1989). The expansion of the subcommittee system, particularly in the House, has been the subject of considerable criticism. The thrust of this criticism is that the establishment of subcommittees on the congressional scale seriously decentralizes power, making the enactment of legislation more difficult than it would be without the subcommittees. For these critics, each sub-committee becomes an additional obstacle in the legislative process that a bill must overcome in order to be enacted into law. We address the structural difficulties to statutory enactment in Chapter 8.

4. *Legislative Staff*

Many thousands of people work for legislative bodies. Basically they fall into several categories: administrative; clerical; political (the personal staffs of legislators); and policy (committee staff and staff of such support organizations as the Congressional Research Service). In Congress and most state legislatures, a growth of staff has accompanied the growth of legislative activities discussed in Chapter 1. The staff of Congress dwarfs that of any state legislature, but among state legislatures, the number of staff members varies. See generally Alan Rosenthal, Legislative Life (1981).

Of particular significance is the role played by the policy staff in the lawmaking process. In Congress in 1930, approximately 1,400 people worked for representatives and senators as well as congressional committees. In 1947 and 1960, there were approximately 2,400 and 6,000 congressional staff members, respectively. "Today more than 22,000 individuals work for the United States Congress. This includes Representatives' and Senators' personal and committee staffs, a police force, and a maintenance force, along with the staff who work for the Congressional support agencies — the Congressional Research Service (CRS), a division of the Library of Congress; the Congressional Budget Office (CBO); and the General Accounting Office (GAO)." American Association for Geriatric Psychiatry, Legislative and Regulatory Agenda 2007-2008, app. E at 27 (2007-2008). The impact these staff members have on the legislative process has been the subject of considerable concern and debate. Particular aspects of this debate will be discussed in Chapter 4 with respect to staff role in the preparation of committee reports. This particular topic will also be addressed in Part IV of this book with respect to the probative value of committee reports in the interpretation of statutes. In the passage that follows, the role of policy staff in the legislative process, particularly in Congress, is discussed more generally.

Abner J. Mikva and Patti B. Saris, The American Congress
186-90 (1983)

In Unelected Representatives, Michael S. Malbin classified committee staffs into three categories. First, he described the passive, bipartisan staff, which serves as neutral expert. Typified by the Joint Committee on Taxation, the passive staff limits (at least theoretically) its role to evaluating proposed legislation and suggesting alternatives to achieve the same substantive goal. The second kind of staff is the purely technical staff, which provides the figures and data necessary to develop legislation, such as the staff of the Armed Services Committee. Finally, there is the entrepreneurial staff, which aggressively asserts a committee's legislative priorities, tries to grab jurisdiction from other committees, and dominates policy formation. Malbin classifies the staffs of most standing committees as entrepreneurial, and it is with respect to this kind of committee staff that Malbin addresses most of his attention.

Malbin asks a basic question: Does an entrepreneurial committee staff conflict with the needs of the legislative institution as a whole? On balance, Malbin answers that question in the affirmative. Although he concedes that large staffs may be essential for Congress' efforts to keep track of the bureaucracy, he criticizes highly personalized staffs who devote their loyalty to individual members, not to Congress as an institution and not to the leadership. In a chapter pointedly entitled "Congressional Staffs and the Future of Representative Government," Malbin reluctantly concedes the importance of staff, especially given the heavy congressional workload:

> If we take Congress' workloads as given and focus on negotiations, we see that the staffs, acting as surrogate for their "bosses," do as creditable a job of representing their interests as any attorney would for a client in a parallel situation outside Congress. With loyal surrogate lawyers carrying out their wishes, the members are able to follow more issues than they could if they had to attend all meetings personally. Institutionally, this means that both the members as individuals and Congress as a whole are able to manage a heavier workload with the staffs than would be possible without them. To some extent, therefore, the staffs seem to help Congress do its work.
>
> But, as we have seen, the surrogate-lawyers are generally expected to be more than just passive representatives of their clients: they are also expected to go out and drum up new business. The increased use of personalized

entrepreneurial staffs has helped Congress retain its position as a key initiator of federal policy, despite the growing power of the executive branch. The relationship between this use of entrepreneurial staff and Congress' power seems almost obvious. Most other national legislatures depend on their cabinets for almost all policy initiatives. Congress is not so passive today, thanks largely to its staff.

The system of individualized staff control seems also to be responsible for much of the oversight that gets accomplished outside of the General Accounting Office. Having a substantial number of staff people with appropriate investigative authority seems a necessary condition for congressional oversight of the executive branch and the independent regulatory commissions. . . . Thus, the movement away from a system of collegial nonpartisan committee staffing to a more personalized one has been associated with an increase in congressional oversight activities, largely because a personalized system lets chairmen have activist staff entrepreneurs, and chairmen who use entrepreneurial staffs tend to be more interested in maintaining their independence from the executive branch.

After conceding the weighty advantages afforded by an "entrepreneurial" staff, Malbin proceeds to give the "gloomier" side, arguing that the overuse of staff destroys legislative deliberation:

> For a process of legislative deliberation to function reasonably well, at least three distinct requirements must be satisfied. The members need accurate information, they need time to think about that information, and they need to talk to each other about the factual, political, and moral implications of the policies they are considering. The new use of staff undercuts each of these.

Malbin launches three arguments against the use of "entrepreneurial staff." First, he argues that such a staff provides distorted or "partial" information. Because the entrepreneurial staff generates an increase in the number of hearings and amendments, Malbin argues that each legislator becomes so overextended that he cannot personally become involved in legislative decision making. Finally, Malbin points out that legislative deliberation has been replaced by "staff negotiations." Malbin concludes that a nonpartisan, neutral staff serves Congress better than does the entrepreneurial staff because it does not inject itself into policy making. By restoring the deliberative function to the members themselves, Congress will better serve the national interest because the members will then concentrate on only those issues of most importance to their constituencies. It is only because of the existence of a legislative staff, he argues, that members have the resources to spread themselves so broadly over so many issues and to distance themselves from the logrolling so important to forging a national consensus in a nation as diverse as the United States.

Malbin has a point. The examples are legion of the excessive powers and authority exerted by staff. After the passage of the Regulatory Flexibility Act of 1980, which reduced the impact of regulations on small business, one staff member said no senator had read the legislation—and he was right. Furthermore, in a related piece of legislation, the staffs of the Governmental Affairs and Judiciary committees were entrusted by their respective leaders to hammer out a compromise; the subsequent product is another example of legislation not by committee, but by staff. More often than not, committee staffs write committee reports, which are never read by any committee member, but nonetheless become critical legislative history. Some committee staffs have extracted policy promises from nominees, both judicial and executive, by threatening to slow down the confirmation process. Likewise, staff members threaten to "kill" a bill unless it is modified to meet their members' alleged concerns, even on issues to which members are not committed or did not even know about. With a good poker face, staff members—through promises, threats, and cajoling—often accomplish policy objectives without the members' awareness. Frequently, a Senate staff member places a "hold" on legislation without the members' advance knowledge. And finally, many members vote on amendments after a thirty-second briefing or a three-line memo from the staff. Of course, the power of a staff varies with the different management style of different members. Some members delegate tremendous authority to their staffs; others use staff in a very limited, controlled fashion.

Despite the problems of an entrepreneurial staff, so well articulated by Malbin, the benefits of an aggressive, personalized staff exceed the costs both from the perspective of the member and the Congress as an institution. As Malbin himself would concede, without an aggressive staff it is unlikely that Congress would be able to maintain its role as an assertive policy initiator and vigorous overseer of the executive branch. Although Malbin cites the Federalist Papers to support his thesis that staff impedes the deliberative process, the most fundamental thesis of the Federalist Papers militates toward the opposite result:

> But the great security against a gradual concentration of the several powers in the same department, consists in giving to those who administer each department the necessary constitutional means and personal motives to resist encroachments of the others. . . . Ambition must be made to counter ambition. The interest of the man must be connected with the constitutional rights of the place.

[Federalist No. 51.] Without staff, the ambitions of each member, each committee, and the Congress as a whole would not be well served, and the ambitions of the legislative branch could not possibly counter the equally strident ambitions of a much better staffed executive branch. Thus, the doctrine of checks and balances would not work without an aggressive staff.

Moreover, the Malbin thesis is a bit overstated. Members do participate to a large degree in deliberations on the major issues that affect their local and national constituencies. Anyone who has spent a large amount of time on the floor, in party caucuses, and in committee mark-ups realizes that the issues aired publicly represent a distillation of all the issues upon which the staff failed to forge consensus. Therefore, the members themselves work out the big policy differences, whether through compromise or floor votes. As the clerk reads the endless quorum calls during a legislative fight in the Senate, clusters of senators huddle in a corner trying to work out the details of an amendment. Sometimes staff members are there to help, but the decisions are made by the elected representatives. In the Democratic party caucus over Reagan's budget reductions, the fights were often acerbic, but the members themselves — not the staff who were barred from the room — worked out the compromise on amendments that was acceptable to all: school lunch funds would be fought for, legal services would not. Even in the committee, where an entrepreneurial staff can exercise the most clout, the members themselves must resolve the major controversies on issues of enough concern to generate public attention. The staff may have considerable leverage over marginal issues, but it does not extend to the major concerns of constituents. The arm twisting and peer-group pressure necessary to enact any piece of controversial legislation remain the prerogative of the members — much as some staff would like to think otherwise. Consequently, leaving the details of legislation to the staff is not harmful but rational, sane, and effective, for then the members are free to "wheel and deal" on the big issues.

A closing thought: An overly aggressive entrepreneurial committee staff can be harmful from one institutional viewpoint. It places inordinate power in the hands of committees at the expense of a more centralized policy coordination by the party leadership. It is hardly surprising that the role of the leadership in both the House and the Senate is so minimal in developing coordinated strategies and policies when one considers that the party leadership has a smaller staff than that possessed by even the smallest committee. Perhaps a staff of experts loyal to the party leadership and more aggressive on behalf of the party would enable Congress to act more efficiently, promptly, and effectively in sorting out legislative priorities. The problem of party strength and coordination is particularly acute when the party affiliation of the leadership differs from that of the president. With a more centralized, party-oriented staff to complement, not supplant, committee staffs, it is possible that the Congress could serve as a more effective counterpoint to the president.

B.   LEGISLATIVE RULES AND THEIR ENFORCEMENT

Every house of every legislature and most legislative caucuses and committees operate under a set of procedural rules. These rules govern everything from the form of a bill, to the method of its introduction, to the manner by which a bill is considered at every step in the legislative process, to the votes necessary to enact legislation. You have already learned about a variety of these rules in earlier sections.

Some of these rules are found in the federal and state constitutions. Of these constitutions, the U.S. Constitution contains the fewest requirements for processing bills. Article I, §5 designates a majority of each house of Congress as a quorum for doing business, mandates a journal, and provides for recorded votes in certain circumstances. Article I, §7 contains the veto process. State constitutions are filled with considerably more procedural detail.

Most legislative procedural rules are part of the standing rules of legislative bodies. These are enacted under grants of power found in the federal and all state constitutions. These grants are all similar to Article I, §5 of the U.S. Constitution, which provides: "Each House may determine the Rules of its Proceedings." The rules of a particular house are usually published and available. The rules of the House of Representatives are found in a document known as the Constitution, Jefferson's Manual, and the Rules of the House of Representatives; the rules of the Senate are found in a document known as Senate Manual Containing the Standing Rules, Orders, Laws, and Resolutions Affecting the Business of the U.S. Senate. They are available from the Government Printing Office. Committee and caucus rules, if written, are less accessible and must be requested from the particular caucus or committee.

The use of the term "rule" can prove confusing, particularly with respect to the practices of the U.S. House of Representatives. In the House, almost every bill that is reported to the floor for consideration is accompanied by its own "rule," adopted by the Rules Committee, that governs the manner in which the particular bill will be debated. These "rules" are not part of the standing rules of the House, although the rule that there be a unique governing rule for each bill is. The Rules Committee and its rules are discussed in Chapter 5.

Rules bring procedural order to the legislative process and offer protection to minority interests. They "determine the ways in which collective decisions are made, and they constitute the context in which individual members pursue their policy and political objectives and attempt to maximize their legislative achievement." Stanley Bach, The Nature of Congressional Rules, 5 J.L. & Pol'y 725, 726 (1989). So significant is the need for rules that Thomas Jefferson, who prepared a Manual of Parliamentary Practice for his own use as President of the Senate during his vice presidency, considered the existence of legislative rules to be equally as or more important than their substance:

> [T]he only weapon by which the minority can defend themselves against similar attempts [improper measures] from those in power are the forms and rules of proceeding which have been adopted as they were found necessary, from time to time, and are become the law of the House, by a strict adherence to which the weaker party can only be protected from those irregularities and abuses which these forms were intended to check, and which the wantonness of power is but too often apt to suggest to large and successful majorities.

And whether these forms be in all cases the most rational or not is really not so great importance. It is much more material that there should be a rule to go by, than what that rule is; that there may be a uniformity of proceeding in business not subject to the caprice of the Speaker or captiousness of the members. It is very material that order, decency, and regularity be preserved in a dignified public body.

Constitution, Jefferson's Manual, and the Rules of the House of Representatives, H. Doc. No. 248, 100th Cong., 2d Sess. 117-18 (1988).

Legislative rules serve a variety of functions. The key ones among them, according to the political scientist Walter J. Oleszek, "are to provide stability, legitimize decisions, divide responsibilities, reduce conflict and distribute power." Walter J. Oleszek, Congressional Procedures and the Policy Process 6 (2007). Additionally, legislative rules provide opportunities for members of the minority caucus or individual legislators to protect themselves against legislative excesses by majorities. In the following passages, these functions of legislative rules are discussed.

Charles Tiefer, *Congressional Practice and Procedure*
5-6 (1989)

The scale of Congress' business, the need for public acceptance of its legitimacy, the requirement that the same Members do business with each other year after year, provide potent incentives for order.

Most important of all, procedural order solves a fundamental problem in the American political system. While the national parties organize national politics, individual Members follow their states' and districts' interests and their own perspectives, rather than the party line. In other words, the United States has a "weak" party system. Thus, although the majority party leadership must run the chambers, frequently the opposition, not the majority party leadership, has an actual voting majority on particular propositions. In either chamber, a conservative coalition of southern Democrats and Republicans often outvotes the "national" Democratic leadership; conversely, moderate coalitions, or for that matter regional or issue-specific coalitions, may outvote any leadership.

Congressional procedure provides stability despite this weak party system. Very simply, both sides, or all sides, can win occasionally, without the government falling, because congressional procedure provides for easy alternation in success. Congressional procedure favors certain powerful institutions that play functional roles within the Congress; in fact that procedure gives those institutions much of their strength — institutions like the party leadership, the committees, and the managers of bills. At the same time, orderly procedure provides safety valves for successful opposition coalitions. Such safety valves include offering of Senate nongermane amendments, getting amendments adopted in either chamber, Senate "holds," filibusters, committee discharge, defeat of House special rules, and defeating bills on final passage.

Thus, the majority party leadership can set an agenda for the chamber without falling over defeats; the opposition can resist and win, at times, without being oppressed. Congressional procedure keeps a dynamic balance, with majority advantages and yet minority rights, powers of control and yet tolerance of resistance, preservation of past patterns and yet responsiveness to change. The heart of congressional procedure consists of the various procedures by which the majority's powers — agenda control and bill management — balance against the legitimate means for opposition resistance.

Moreover, this dynamic balance legitimates the government, and its new laws. It legitimates the government because the source of legitimacy in our democracy is, firstly, the will of the majority, and the Congress' procedures allow the representatives of the majority to work their will — to do what the people want. At the same time; the system consists of many and varied obstacles and screens. Before a majority in each chamber passes a bill; both the majority, and the bill, must run a veritable marathon — through committees, past the party-controlled gates to the floor, across the battlefield of floor consideration and the many techniques for stalling, changing, or killing bills.

In the end, the majority which backs a bill can differ substantially from the one which backed it originally. The bill may get larger in scope, or more modest; more or less expensive; more or less pointed in its ideology; more or less helpful to a particular region or to interest groups. As the bill changes, so does the coalition which supports it. Thus not only is the bill as finally passed the will of the majority, but the majority which passes it has itself metamorphosed during the consideration process, making it the current expression of a vast array of competing political considerations and hence an eminently legitimate expression of the current political balance.

If the enactment process is to legitimize both the passage of new laws and the retention of old ones, it must satisfy expectations on all sides of fair play — both in techniques of control, and techniques of resistance — and must meet standards by which both sides judge whether those expectations are being fulfilled. Although both chambers know their leaders are partisan, both chambers expect rulings from the Chair with objectivity and neutrality. Each chamber has written rules supplemented by precedents and practices which it expects its Chair to follow. Each chamber has an expert and neutral Parliamentarian to hold those rulings together despite their often confused and heated context.

Despite Jefferson's emphasis on the need for rules as rules, the substance of the rules is inexorably related to legislative productivity and to the policies that are enacted into law.

Walter J. Oleszek, *Congressional Procedures and the Policy Process*
12-13 (2007)

Legislative procedures and policy making are inextricably linked in at least four ways. First, procedures affect policy outcomes. Congress processes legislation by complex rules and procedures that permeate the institution. Some matters are only gently brushed by the rules, while others become locked in their grip. Major civil rights legislation, for example, failed for decades to win congressional approval because southern senators used their chamber's rules and procedures to kill or modify such measures.

Congressional procedures are employed to define, restrict, or expand the policy options available to members during floor debate. They may prevent consideration of certain issues or presage policy outcomes. Such structured procedures enhance the policy influence of certain members, committees, or party leaders; facilitate expeditious treatment of issues; grant priority to some policy alternatives but not others; and determine, in general, the overall character of policy decisions.

A second point is that very often policy decisions are expressed as procedural moves. House Republican leader Robert H. Michel, Ill., frustrated with his party's minority status for more than three decades and the majority party's procedural control of that body, highlighted the procedure-substance linkage.

> Procedure hasn't simply become more important than substance — it has, through a strange alchemy, *become* the substance of our deliberations. Who rules House procedures rules the House — and to a great degree, rules the kind and scope of political debate in this country.

Or as John D. Dingell, D-Mich., the chairman of the House Energy and Commerce Committee, phrased it, "If you let me write the procedure, and I let you write the substance, I'll [beat] you every time." . . .

Third, the nature of the policy can determine the use of certain procedures. The House and Senate generally consider noncontroversial measures under expeditious procedures, whereas controversial proposals normally involve lengthy deliberation. . . .

Finally, policy outcomes are more likely to be influenced by members with procedural expertise. Members who are skilled parliamentarians are better prepared to gain approval of their proposals than those who are only vaguely familiar with the rules. . . .

Members who know the rules will always have the potential to shape legislation to their ends and to become key figures in coalitions trying to pass or defeat legislation. Those who do not understand the rules reduce their proficiency and influence as legislators. . . .

Procedural Rules in State Constitutions

Compared to the federal Constitution, which requires little, many state constitutions are noteworthy for the extensive procedural detail they contain. The Constitution of the State of Texas is perhaps the most extreme. Consider the following provisions from the Texas Constitution:

ART. 3, §5(a) The Legislature shall meet every two years at such time as may be provided by law and at other times when convened by the Governor.

(b) When convened in regular Session, the first thirty days thereof shall be devoted to the introduction of bills and resolutions, acting upon emergency appropriations, passing upon the confirmation of the recess appointees of the Governor and such emergency matters as may be submitted by the Governor in special messages to the Legislature. During the succeeding thirty days of the regular session of the Legislature the various committees of each House shall hold hearings to consider all bills and resolutions and other matters then pending; and such emergency matters as may be submitted by the Governor. During the remainder of the session the Legislature shall act upon such bills and resolutions as may be then pending and upon such emergency matters as may be submitted by the Governor in special messages to the Legislature. (c) Notwithstanding Subsection (b), either House may determine its order of business by an affirmative vote of four-fifths of its membership. . . .

ART. 3, §34. After a bill has been considered and defeated by either House of the Legislature, no bill containing the same substance, shall be passed into a law during the same session. . . .

ART. 3, §37. No bill shall be considered, unless it has been first referred to a committee and reported thereon, and no bill shall be passed which has not been presented and referred to and reported from a committee at least three days before the final adjournment of the Legislature.

Such constitutional detailing of legislative procedures attests to the public view that legislatively adopted rules (the preexisting rules) were resulting in "bad" legislation. As one scholar has observed:

By contrast, the legislative articles of virtually all state constitutions contain a wide range of limitations on state legislative processes. Generally, these *procedural* limitations did not appear in the first state constitutions. Instead, they were adopted throughout the nineteenth century in response to perceived state legislative abuses. One observer during that era noted that "[o]ne of the most marked features of all recent State constitutions is the distrust shown of the Legislature." Last-minute consideration of important measures, logrolling, mixing substantive provisions in omnibus bills, low visibility and hasty enactment of important, and sometimes corrupt, legislation, and the attachment of unrelated provisions to bills in the amendment process — to name a few of these abuses — led to the adoption of constitutional provisions restricting the legislative process. These constitutional provisions seek generally to require a more open and deliberative state legislative process, one that addresses the merits of legislature proposals in an orderly and rational manner.

Georgia's famous Yazoo land scandal, where a virtual giveaway of land was authorized in a bill "smuggled" through the legislature, led to the requirement that a bill contain a title disclosing its subject. Other familiar examples of state constitutional limitations on the legislature include the requirement that a bill contain only matters on a "single subject"; that all bills be referred to committee; that the vote on a bill be reflected in a legislature's journal; that no bill be altered during its passage through either House so as to change its original purpose; and that appropriations bills contain provisions on no other subject. These procedural restrictions must be distinguished from the common *substantive* limits on state legislation, such as those prohibiting statutes limiting wrongful death recoveries or mandating a certain type of civil service system, and from the general limits contained in state bills of rights.

Robert F. Williams, State Constitutional Limits on Legislative Procedure: Legislative Compliance and Judicial Enforcement, 48 U. Pitt. L. Rev. 797, 798-99 (1987). The inclusion of such procedural detail in state constitutions has been the subject of criticism. Professor Frank Grad, for example, has written:

> While it may be appropriate to settle constitutionally and inflexibly such essential matters of representative government as the kind of majority required to pass a law, or the vote required to override a veto by the governor, the constitutional requirement of three readings of a bill is clearly obsolete, and requirements governing the style to be followed in a bill, or limiting a bill to a single subject, have caused considerable damage through invalidation of noncomplying laws on technical grounds.

Frank Grad, The State Constitution: Its Function and Form for Our Time, 54 Va. L. Rev. 928, 963 (1968). For a fuller exploration of these criticisms, see Robert F. Williams, State Constitutional Law Processes, 24 Wm. & Mary L. Rev. 169 (1983).

What do you think of Professor Grad's criticism? While for the most part it has not been heeded by the states, the examples of Illinois and Texas amending their constitutions with respect to their title provisions, described in Chapter 2, Section B.3, demonstrates some agreement with him.

The Enforcement of Legislative Rules

For the most part legislative bodies enforce their own rules. If rules become too restraining in a particular situation, most legislative bodies "are free to set aside most rules, or create temporary rules, by unanimous consent, and they do so daily. . . . Whatever procedures are being followed by the House or Senate, whatever legislative rules are in effect, its members retain the power to enforce them or not, as they choose." Stanley Bach, The Nature of Congressional Rules, 5 J.L. & Pol'y 725, 737-39 (1989). Sometimes, however, disputes over legislative rules reach the courts. For example, United States v. Ballin, referred to in the passage from Mikva and Saris, The American Congress, on page 88 of this chapter, was a challenge to a ruling of the House of Representatives on the meaning of the constitutional term "quorum." Also, Vander Jagt v. O'Neill, referred to on page 91 of this chapter, was a challenge to the ratio of Democrats to Republicans on certain committees of the House of Representatives. In both of these cases the Court upheld the procedure under question. In fact, though, there are few procedural challenges to federal statutes because of the absence of any significant procedural details in the U.S. Constitution.

State courts, because of the inclusion of procedural detail in state constitutions, have been far more active as forums for determining the validity of legislative procedures. See generally Robert F. Williams, State Constitutional Limits on Legislative Procedure: Legislative Compliance and Judicial Enforcement, 48 U. Pitt. L. Rev. 797 (1987). The following two cases exemplify this. In one case the legislative rule is overturned, and in the other it is upheld. Consider carefully the differences between the two cases. They contain discussions of a range of approaches to the issue of judicial enforcement. Internal citations have been omitted except where particularly relevant.

King v. Cuomo
81 N.Y.2d 247 (1993)

Bellacosa, J.:

The bicameral "recall" practice used by the Legislature to reacquire Assembly Bill No. 9592-A of 1990 from the Governor's desk is not authorized by Article IV, §7 of the New York State Constitution. The Constitution prescribes the respective powers of the Executive and the Legislative Branches as to how a passed bill becomes a law or is rejected. . . . [T]he challenged procedure should be declared unconstitutional, but only prospectively.

Assembly Bill No. 9592-A, entitled "AN ACT to amend the agriculture and markets law, in relation to siting of solid waste management-resource recovery facilities within agricultural districts," was passed by the

Assembly and the Senate on June 28, 1990 and June 29, 1990, respectively. It was formally sent to the Governor on July 19, 1990. The next day, according to the official journals of the Legislature, the Assembly adopted a resolution, with which the Senate concurred, requesting that the Governor return the bill to the Legislature. The Executive Chamber accommodated the request on the same day. . . .

I

Preliminarily, the State defendants argue that the Judicial Branch may not review the constitutionality of this recall practice, as it would be an intrusion on the inviolate roles of the separate law-making Branches. We conclude that the courts do not trespass "into the wholly internal affairs of the Legislature" (Heimbach v. State of New York, 452 N.E.2d 1264, *appeal dismissed*, 464 U.S. 956) when they review and enforce a clear and unambiguous constitutional regimen of this nature. In Heimbach v. State of New York (supra), by sharp contrast, the internal procedural issue involved how the Clerk of the Senate recorded and certified a roll call of votes. . . . Our precedents are firm that the "courts will always be available to resolve disputes concerning the scope of that authority which is granted by the Constitution to the other two branches of the government." That is precisely what is being done here.

The internal rules of the Assembly and the Senate, which reflect and even purport to create the recall practice, are entitled to respect. However, those rules cannot immunize or withdraw the subsisting question of constitutional law-making power from judicial review. Since the authority of the Legislature is "wholly derived from and dependent upon the Constitution," the discrete rules of the two houses do not constitute organic law and may not substitute for or substantially alter the plain and precise terms of that primary source of governing authority. The rule-making authority of Article III, §9 prescribes that "each house shall determine the rules of its *own proceedings*" (emphasis added). Contrary to the assertion of the dissent, that authorization cannot justify rules which extend beyond the Legislature's "own proceedings" and are inextricably intertwined with *proceedings* pending entirely before the Executive. These rules substantially affect Executive *proceedings* after the Legislature's proceedings, with respect to a passed bill, have formally ended by transmittal of the passed bill to the Governor's desk.

The challenged recall practice significantly unbalances the law-making options of the Legislature and the Executive beyond those set forth in the Constitution. By modifying the nondelegable obligations and options reposed in the Executive, the practice compromises the central law-making rubrics by adding an expedient and uncharted bypass. The Legislature must be guided and governed in this particular function by the Constitution, not by a self-generated additive.

II

Article IV, §7 of the State Constitution prescribes how a bill becomes a law and explicitly allocates the distribution of authority and powers between the Executive and Legislative Branches. The key provision grants law-making authority from the People as follows:

> every bill which shall have passed the senate and assembly shall, before it becomes a law, be presented to the governor; *if he approves, he shall sign it; but if not, he shall return it with his objections* to the house in which it shall have originated . . . *if any bill shall not be returned by the governor within ten days* (Sundays excepted) after it shall have been presented to him, *the same shall be a law in like manner as if he had signed it* [emphasis added].

The description of the process is a model of civic simplicity: (1) Approval; (2) Rejection by Veto; or (3) Approval by Inaction. The Constitution thus expressly creates three routes by which a passed bill may become a law by gubernatorial action or inaction or be rejected by veto.

The putative authority of the Legislature to recall a passed bill once it has been formally transmitted to the Governor "is not found in the constitution" (People v. Devlin, 33 N.Y. 269, 277). We conclude, therefore, that the practice is not allowed under the Constitution. To permit the Legislature to use its general rule-making powers, pertaining to in-house procedures, to create this substantive authority is untenable. As this Court stated in *Devlin*, "when both houses have . . . finally passed a bill, and sent it to the governor, *they have exhausted their powers* upon it." That expression and principle apply with equal force here, even though in *Devlin* the recall was attempted by only one house rather than both. . . .

When language of a constitutional provision is plain and unambiguous, full effect should be given "to the intention of the framers . . . as indicated by the language employed" and approved by the People. . . .

The New York Legislature's long-standing recall practice has little more than time and expediency to sustain it. However, the end cannot justify the means, and the Legislature, even with the Executive's acquiescence, cannot place itself outside the express mandate of the Constitution. We do not believe that supplementation of the Constitution in this fashion is a manifestation of the will of the People. Rather, it may be seen as a substitution of the People's will expressed directly in the Constitution. . . .

The recall practice unbalances the constitutional law-making equation, which expressly shifts power solely to the Executive upon passage of a bill by both houses and its transmittal to the Executive. By the ultra vires recall method, the Legislature significantly suspends and interrupts the mandated regimen and modifies the distribution of authority and the complementing roles of the two law-making Branches. It thus undermines the constitutionally proclaimed, deliberative process upon which all People are on notice and may rely. Realistically and practically, it varies the roles set forth with such careful and plain precision in the constitutional charter. The limbo status to which a passed bill is thus consigned withdraws from or allows evasion of the assigned power granted only to the Executive to approve or veto a passed bill or to allow it to go into effect after ten days of inaction. . . .

Additionally, the recall practice "affords interest groups another opportunity to amend or kill certain bills," shielded from the public scrutiny which accompanies the initial consideration and passage of a bill. This "does not promote public confidence in the legislature as an institution" because "it is difficult for citizens to determine the location in the legislative process of a bill that may be of great importance to them." Since only "insiders" are likely to know or be able to discover the private arrangements between the Legislature and Executive when the recall method is employed, open government would suffer a significant setback if the courts were to countenance this long-standing practice.

In sum, the practice undermines the integrity of the law-making process as well as the underlying rationale for the demarcation of authority and power in this process. Requiring that the Legislature adhere to this constitutional mandate is not some hypertechnical insistence of form over substance, but rather ensures that the central law-making function remains reliable, consistent and exposed to civic scrutiny and involvement.

We are satisfied also that legitimate correction of mere technical oversights or errors in passed bills may be accomplished by chapter amendments, through messages of necessity and other available mechanisms. It is no justification for an extraconstitutional practice that it is well intended and efficient, for the day may come when it is not so altruistically exercised. . . .

III

The particular remedy and relief appropriate to this case is a critically distinct issue. Appellants seek an order compelling the Secretary of State to execute a certificate that Assembly Bill No. 9592-A became law on or about July 30, 1990. Though the recall practice is not constitutionally authorized, neither is the mandamus relief warranted.

Despite the removal of the subject bill from the Governor's desk, logic and sound public policy do not compel or persuade us to treat the bill in this case as having been on the Executive's desk for the requisite 10 days, within the meaning of Article IV, §7. Also, the bill in question lapsed when the 1990 session of the Legislature ended, and resuscitation by judicial decree in the fashion requested would be a disproportionate remedy and would "wreak more havoc in society than society's interest in stability will tolerate." Prospective application of a new constitutional rule is not uncommon where it would have a "broad, unsettling effect." . . .

SMITH, Judge (dissenting in part):

... I agree with the majority's conclusion on the latter issue that the bill was not on the Governor's desk for the requisite 10 days and, thus, did not become a law "in like manner as if he [governor] had signed it" (N.Y. Const., art. IV, §7). However, I disagree with the majority's conclusion, as to the primary issue, that the power of the Legislature to recall a bill that has been presented to the Governor "is not found in the constitution" and, therefore, does not exist. ...

Contrary to the majority's position, the recall procedure utilized by the Legislature does not "undermine ... the integrity of the law-making process." Rather, it exemplifies the constitutionally authorized power of the Legislature to "determine the rules of its own proceedings" (N.Y. Const., art. III, §9). In Heimbach v. State of New York (59 N.Y.2d 891, 893), this Court stated that "based upon our respect for the basic polity of separation of powers and the proper exercise of judicial restraint, we will not intrude into the wholly internal affairs of the Legislature." Here, the Legislature had in place internal rules for recalling bills which had been presented to the Governor, prior to their becoming law. Pursuant to Rules of the Assembly, Rule II, §4(d), the Assembly prepared a printed form "JC-14" to commence recall procedures regarding Assembly Bill No. 9592-A. Using its internal procedures, the Senate concurred with the Assembly resolution to recall the bill. Again using internal rules, the Assembly forwarded the request for recall to the Governor, who, as he had done many times in the past, immediately complied with the request. There is nothing before the Court to indicate that the actions by the Legislature in recalling Assembly Bill No. 9592-A from the Governor the day after it was sent to him constituted anything other than "the wholly internal affairs of the Legislature," into which we should not intrude.

The majority's argument that since the power of the Legislature to recall a bill which has been presented to the Governor is not expressly found in the Constitution it does not exist must fail. Article IV, §7 of the State Constitution, entitled "Action by governor on legislative bills; reconsideration after veto," addresses the action by the Governor on legislative bills and what gubernatorial action results in a bill becoming a law. The only reference to legislative action is in regard to reconsideration of a bill after veto by the Governor. Thus, no inference of any kind can be drawn from the omission from article IV, §7 of a provision expressly granting recall powers to the Legislature. ...

Here, the bill was recalled by concurrent resolution of the Assembly and Senate and agreement by the Governor, not by a one-house recall as was the case in *Devlin* (supra). In addition, [Assembly R]ule II, §4(d), and [Senate R]ule VI, §9, specifically address the Legislature's internal procedures for recalling bills. Furthermore, the long-standing practice of recalling bills from the Governor, through concurrent resolution of the Assembly and Senate dates back to 1865. Thus, it cannot be said that the power of the

Legislature to recall bills from the Governor is not grounded in the internal rules of the Legislature or in custom.

Moreover, nothing in the language of the Constitution indicates that the act of recalling a bill once it had been presented to the Governor for approval or objection, violates the Constitution. To the contrary, the State Constitution vests in the Assembly and the Senate the power to "determine the rules of its own proceedings" (N.Y. Const., art. III, §9).

Heimbach v. State of New York
454 N.Y.S.2d 993 (1982)

TITONE, JP, GIBBONS, WEINSTEIN, GULOTTA and THOMPSON, JJ., concur. PER CURIAM.

Chapter 485 of the Laws of 1981 (Senate Bill 1905; Assembly Bill 9059) increases by one quarter of 1% the sales and compensating use tax of the State within the Metropolitan Commuter Transportation District (MCTD). . . .

As recorded in the Journal of the Senate, Senate Bill 1905 was passed by that body with the minimum number [31] of affirmative votes required by the State Constitution (N.Y. Const., art. III, §14). The voting procedure employed is known as the "fast" roll call, and one of the affirmative votes recorded is that of Senator Howard Nolan. It is not disputed that when the vote was taken, Senator Nolan was a patient in the hospital being prepared for elective surgery. The bill was certified as passed on July 8, 1981 by the Speaker of the Assembly and the Acting President of the Senate. It was approved by the Governor on July 11, 1981 and became effective on September 1, 1981. . . .

Initially, we observe that while "in general the courts will not interfere with the internal procedural aspects of the legislative process, judicial review may be undertaken to determine whether the Legislature has complied with constitutional prescriptions as to legislative procedures."

Howard Nolan, who has been a member of the State Senate since January 1, 1975, was scheduled to undergo elective surgery on July 9, 1981. On the morning of July 8, 1981, he entered the Senate chamber and had himself designated as present by the Clerk of the Senate. Later in the day, he left the Senate, without informing the clerk, first going home and then to the hospital. . . . During the early morning hours of July 9, while Senator Nolan was in the hospital, a vote was taken on Assembly Bill 9059 (Senate Bill 1905) by means of the "fast" roll call. According to the entry in the Senate Journal, the Senate voted 31 to 26 in favor of the bill, with three Senators "excused." The vote of Senator Nolan is included among the 31 "Aye" votes, which is the minimum number of votes required for passage.

Our State Constitution requires that no bill "shall . . . be passed or become a law, except by the assent of a majority of the members elected to each branch of the legislature" (N.Y. Const., art. III, §14), but the Constitution has prescribed no method of determining the assent of a majority. Section 9 of article III of the Constitution vests in each house of the Legislature the power to determine the rules of its own proceedings. In the exercise of that power, the Senate has adopted rules VIII (§6) and IX (§1) which provide:

SENATE RULE VIII, PASSAGE OF BILLS

§6. Final Passage . . . b. The question on the final passage of every bill shall be taken immediately after the third reading and without debate. On the final passage of every bill and concurrent resolution a fast roll call shall be taken by the Secretary calling the names of five Senators, two of whom shall be the Temporary President and the Minority Leader, provided however, that each Senator's name shall be called on a slow roll call if requested by five Senators. Each roll call, including the names of the Senators who were absent, shall be entered on the journal. Upon each roll call vote, the Secretary shall announce the names of the Senators voting in the negative and the names of the Senators who were absent. Such roll calls shall be available for public inspection upon request in the office of the Journal Clerk. When a bill or concurrent resolution does not receive the number of votes required by the Constitution to pass it, it shall be declared lost, except in cases provided for by subdivision d of section two of Rule IX hereof.

SENATE RULE IX, SENATORS

SECTION 1. ATTENDANCE AND VOTE

a. Every Senator shall be present within the Senate Chamber during the sessions of the Senate, unless duly excused or necessarily prevented, and shall vote on each question for which a vote is required stated from the Chair unless excused by the Senate, or unless he has a direct personal or pecuniary interest in the event of such question. If any Senator refuses to vote, unless he be excused by the Senate, or unless he be interested, such refusal shall be deemed a contempt.

The Senate voting procedures are described by Senate Minority Leader Manfred Ohrenstein as follows:

4. To vote for the passage of a bill a senator must be present on the day the particular vote is taken. Presence is established under the senate rules and customs by a senator's physical entry into the chamber at some point during a session day. However, . . . a senator's *presence in fact* as opposed to his above described *designated* presence is not necessary for his vote to be cast, in most cases.

5. Under the rules of the senate, voting on the final passage of bills may take place under one of two methods — a fast or slow roll call (Rule VIII, §6). On a fast roll call, a vote is taken by calling the names of five senators, including the Temporary President, the Minority Leader and three others

usually the first and last two senators on the alphabetically arranged senate roll call list. What is particularly important to note under the fast roll call method of voting is that under a long established senate custom, a senator who has had his presence designated by the clerk of the senate, as described in "4" above, need not be in the chamber to have his or her vote counted in the affirmative. In other words, a senator who has had himself or herself marked present will be deemed to be voted in the affirmative on any particular vote even if in fact he or she is in his or her office or elsewhere at the time the vote occurs. To vote in the negative, however, a senator must be in the chamber and indicate a negative vote by a show of hand.

6. This practice is not followed in a slow roll call. Here, after five senators have stood to request this voting process, each of the sixty senator's [*sic*] names are called, and only those members answering "aye" or "nay" to their names are recorded as having voted. Those members not responding when their names are called are recorded as having not voted on the measure despite the fact that they may have already been designated present for that day's senate session (see Rule VIII, Sec. 6). . . .

11. Under the rules of the senate a senator who has not had himself designated as present (see paragraph 4 above) is recorded as absent on every roll call vote unless such absence has been excused by the senate. Once a senator is present as described above he or she is voted on each fast roll call vote, present in fact or not, unless excused by the senate (Rule IX, Sec. 1). The normal practice for excusing a senator who has had himself designated as present and then who wants to leave is for that member or another member to rise and request of the senate to excuse him or her from voting on further items, which such excuse is generally accepted by the majority without objection. In the case of excusing someone who has not had himself designated as present, the clerk is generally notified of the requested excused absence by my staff at the end of a session and the senate approves it or hot on the following day when it approves the preceeding [*sic*] day's journal.

According to the intervenor, Senator Anderson, 97.9% (1,954 of a total of 1,995) of all bills voted on in 1981 "passed on a fast roll call vote."

Senator Nolan stated in his affidavit in support of plaintiffs' motion for summary judgment on the third cause of action, that "for at least the past seven years while I have been a member of the New York State Senate, it has been the custom, and still is the custom in the Senate on the Minority side, to arrange for an excused appearance through the office of the Minority Leader, i.e., Senator Manfred Ohrenstein. I have used this procedure on several occasions in the past and have never questioned the same, relying on tradition and custom." In "accordance with custom," he claims that he informed Senator Ohrenstein in person, the previous week, that he was entering the hospital the night of July 8 to undergo elective surgery. After he left the Senate on July 8, he received a telephone call at home from Senator Ohrenstein's Administrative Assistant who informed him that there would probably be a vote later that evening on the subject package of bills and that his presence was needed because the vote on several of the bills was likely to be close. In Senator Nolan's words:

> Senator Ohrenstein came to the phone and I reminded him of our conversation of the previous week, which he acknowledged and said that he had forgotten about the fact that I was entering the hospital. I also reminded him that I had told him previously that I would not help his cause in any event, as I would have voted against all of the proposed taxing measures if I were present, and would probably speak against some of them, which was obviously a position contrary to that of the Democratic leadership in the Senate. Senator Ohrenstein acknowledged my previous conversation concerning my hospitalization, wished me good luck, and personally assured me that I would be marked "excused because of being in the hospital" for any votes taken that evening or on the following day.

Senator Ohrenstein responded:

> The crux of plaintiff's [*sic*] argument however appears to revolve around Senator Nolan's allegations that he attempted to have his designation as "present" converted to an excused absence by making this request of me by telephone sometime in the evening of July 8, 1981. . . . [From] a legal perspective, assuming the accuracy of Senator Nolan's recollection, any request to be excused that he might have made of me does not in any way insure that such designation would be forthcoming. Moreover, there is no legal obligation on my part to even convey his request to the senate, although as a matter of senate courtesy and leadership responsibility, any such reasonable request would generally be honored. In other words, I could choose not to ask that a senator be excused, in which case if a senator was not able to have himself or herself excused in the manner described above he or she would be considered absent for votes if he or she had not checked in and as voting in the affirmative on fast roll calls if he or she had checked in. . . .
>
> I acknowledge that Senator Nolan called me on the evening of July 8, 1981 to discuss his pending hospitalization. I have however no recollection whatsoever of any request that he be excused. Moreover, even had this request been made, as alleged, it would have had no effect on the casting of Senator Nolan's votes. The reason for this is that at that time I was under the clear impression that Senator Nolan was absent that day and therefore not voting on any issue. Thus, even if I had knowledge of this request it would have only meant to me that he wanted his absence to be considered an excused absence and not that he wanted his status as "present" to be converted to the status of "excused absence." At best, then, my staff would have informed the journal clerk of the request at the end of the session — after the vote complained of had occurred.

Noting that of "the eight bills relating to the MTA six . . . were passed by fast roll call and two . . . by slow roll call," Senator Ohrenstein asserted that "Senator Nolan who was not in the chamber at the time was properly recorded in the affirmative on the six (6) fast roll call votes and as not voting (slash through his name) on the two slow roll calls." . . .

Before Special Term, the plaintiffs admitted that:

> For purposes of this motion, it will be conceded that for Senators in presence and making up part of the quorum which allows the Senate to proceed in the first place, a failure or refusal to vote for whatever reason, including perhaps an abstention will be deemed as a vote in favor of the measure before the Senate. A Senate Rule of custom so provides.

The plaintiffs contended, however, that such was not the case here, since Senator Nolan was not in presence and did not make up part of the quorum which allowed the Senate to act on the bill in the first place.

The Constitution provides that "[a] majority of each house shall constitute a quorum to do business" (N.Y Const., art. III, §9). The Senate rules require every Senator to be "present and to "vote" (Rule IX, §1). Section 2 of Rule IX pertinently provides:

§2. QUORUM.

a. A majority of all the Senators elected shall constitute a quorum to do business. In case a less number than a quorum of the Senate shall convene, those present are authorized to send the Sergeant-at-Arms, or any other person, for the absent Senators. . . .

f. If at any time during the session of the Senate a question shall be raised by any Senator as to the presence of a quorum, the Presiding Officer shall forthwith direct the Secretary to call the roll, and shall announce the result, and such proceeding shall be without debate; but no Senator while speaking shall be interrupted by any other Senator raising the question of a lack of a quorum, and the question as to the presence of a quorum shall not be raised oftener than once in every hour unless the lack of a quorum shall be disclosed upon a roll call of the ayes and nays.

g. Whenever upon a roll call any Senator who is upon the floor of the Senate Chamber refuses to make response when his name is called, it shall be the duty of the Presiding Officer, either upon his own motion or upon the suggestion of any Senator, to request the Senator so remaining silent to respond to his name, and if such Senator fails to do so, the fact of such request and refusal shall be entered in the journal, and such Senator shall be counted as present for the purpose of constituting a quorum.

The rules provide no means for determining when a Senator is "present" or "upon the floor of the Senate Chamber."

The Senate rules generally do not set forth basic parliamentary rules and details. When the Legislature has not adopted rules for a particular subject or purpose, it "is governed by the generally accepted rules of parliamentary procedure which flow from general principles of common law." Under recognized principles of parliamentary law, where "it appears that a quorum was present at a certain time, and it does not appear that after that time there was an adjournment, it will be presumed that the quorum continued to be present." By long-standing custom, a Senator's presence is established by his actual entry into the chamber at some point during a session day and having himself marked present by the Clerk of the Senate. Thereafter, his presence is presumed to continue unless he requests that he be excused or informs the Clerk of his departure.

The Senate rules and custom are a reasonable and practical interpretation of the constitutional requirement. As the plaintiffs concede in their brief, under general principles of parliamentary law there is a presumption that Senators present in the Chamber and not recorded as voting are presumed to have voted in the affirmative. . . .

As represented at oral argument by the plaintiffs, the gravamen of their complaint with respect to the third cause of action is that the Senate rules and custom were not observed in that Senator Ohrenstein failed to have Senator Nolan marked "excused because of being in the hospital" for any votes taken on the evening of July 8 or on the following day.

While there is a dispute as to the content of their conversation, it is agreed that Senator Ohrenstein had a telephone conversation with Senator Nolan at his home the evening of July 8. For the purposes of this argument, we assume, as Senator Nolan contends, that there has been an unwritten custom in the Senate for a member to arrange for an excused appearance through the office of the Minority Leader, Senator Ohrenstein, that Senator Nolan informed Senator Ohrenstein that he had registered with the clerk on July 8, and that Senator Ohrenstein agreed to arrange to have him marked "excused" but neglected to do so.

Courts may not "impeach the validity of [a] law, by showing that in its enactment some form or proceeding had not been properly followed or adopted by the legislature, the supreme law maker." "[R]espect for the basic policy of distribution of powers in our State government, and the exercise of a proper restraint on the part of the judiciary in responding to invitations to intervene in the internal affairs of the Legislature as a co-ordinate branch of government [are most important]—'it is not the province of the courts to direct the legislature how to do its work.' (People ex rel. Hatch v. Reardon, 184 N.Y. 431, 442.)" Judicial review of every internal dispute between the members of the Legislature "would frustrate the legislative process and violate" the constitutional principle of separation of powers. . . .

NOTES AND QUESTIONS

1. *Compare and contrast.* Based on these two cases, what standard will the New York courts apply in determining whether a particular legislative practice is consistent with constitutional mandates?

2. *Applying the standard.* The recall process discussed in the *King* decision was, for the most part, an alternative to the veto process. It gave a bill's sponsor the opportunity to pull back from the governor's desk legislation that the governor said he would otherwise veto. This would allow continued negotiation on a particular bill outside of the veto framework. Of course, the sponsor could refuse the recall request and chance the veto. The sponsor's decision would be influenced by both the substantive complaint of the executive and by the politics of the situation.

One truism about legislatures is that if an invalidated practice is necessary to effect legislative goals it will be revised in some other form. One way in which the legislature could circumvent the strictures of *King* is to establish an informal arrangement with the executive by which after bills pass both houses they would be held in the particular house in which they were first passed for executive review prior to presentation to the governor. During this period, the governor could informally review these bills and suggest the ones he might veto, if not change. The legislature could then amend the bill or pass an amendatory bill that could be presented to the governor at the same time that the original bill was submitted. Of course, the legislature would have to be in session to accomplish this maneuver. What would happen if a bill's sponsor refused to allow her bill to be amended and the legislative leaders did not want to force the governor to veto it? Could the one responsible for sending it to the governor (the leader of house in which the bill was first passed) simply let it die by refusing to present it? The only relevant New York provision of law is Article IV, §7, which provides: "Every bill which shall have passed the senate and assembly shall, before it becomes a law, be presented to the governor. . . ." Under this provision, the New York State Court of Appeals in the Matter of Campaign for Fiscal Equity, Inc. v. Marino, 661 N.E.2d 1372 (1995), found that legislative leaders could not withhold bills that had passed both houses from the governor. What do you think of the court's reading of New York's presentment clause? One virtue of this decision, without concern for its constitutional logic, is that it does limit the power of the legislative leadership in New York's intensely leadership-dominated legislature and requires, consistent with *King*, a more open and public process. As the Court stated: "To hold otherwise would be to sanction a practice where one house or one or two persons, as leaders of the Legislature, could nullify the express vote and will of the People's representatives."

3. *To enforce or not to enforce.* The jurisprudence on the enforcement of state constitutional process limitations has been inconsistent — at least with respect to constitutional practices not inescapably in violation of a particular constitutional command.

> State courts have developed a surprisingly wide range of approaches to enforcing restriction on legislative procedure under circumstances where an act does not violate procedural limitations on its face. Even within single jurisdictions, one can detect inconsistent doctrines and a lack of continuity

over time. These widely varying judicial doctrines reflect what are essentially political decisions, made in the context of adjudicating actual controversies, concerning the extent of judicial enforcement of state constitutional norms.

The range of approaches can be viewed as a continuum. At one end of the continuum is the "enrolled bill rule." . . . This is marked by judicial passivity and complete deference to the legislative enactment. At the other end is the "extrinsic evidence rule," characterized by judicial activism and recognition of the written constitution as a binding source of law.

Robert F. Williams, State Constitutional Limits on Legislative Procedure: Legislative Compliance and Judicial Enforcement, 48 U. Pitt. L. Rev. 797, 816 (1987). The enrolled bill and extrinsic evidence rule are discussed in some detail in Chapter 2, pages 71-72. Where in the Williams observation do the *King* and *Heimbach* decisions fit?

4. *Due process of legislative lawmaking.* The above cases raise the question of how far a court should and can go in determining the processes followed by legislatures. Consider Professor Lane's observations about the New York State Legislature on page 89 and the following comments of retired justice (now Professor) Hans A. Linde of the Oregon Supreme Court. What level of court involvement would you support?

Hans A. Linde, Due Process of Lawmaking
55 Neb. L. Rev. 197, 238-45 (1976)

"Process" as Process. The question before us is not what substantive rights may be found elsewhere within or outside of the Constitution, but what pertinence the due process clause may have for lawmaking when the constitution-makers, at the time of the fourteenth amendment as much as the time of the fifth, gave the term "due process" no more than a procedural connotation. To extend it from procedure to substance was an aberration of the 1890s. As Professor Bickel reminded us, neither Justice Brandeis nor Justice-to-be Frankfurter thought us intellectually bound to this, nor need we be bound to rely only on due process to hold the states to the privileges and immunities of the Federal Bill of Rights. Of course, precedent being what it is, I am not now speaking of how to brief your first constitutional case. But since we are engaged in an excursion into constitutional theory, let us examine the implications if we had followed Brandeis and returned "due process of law" to its procedural meaning. What might "due process of law" mean in lawmaking?

The obvious answer is that government is not to take life, liberty, or property under color of laws that were not made according to a legitimate lawmaking process. There is nothing very obscure in this reading of "due process." . . .

Of course, reading "process" to mean "process" requires us to decide which lawmaking processes are legitimate and which are not. Even if the answers are not always self-evident, at least this reading poses the right questions. This is so not simply because we follow the procedural meaning of "due process"; they are the right questions because the answers make sense as constitutional directives for the conduct of government. . . .

For keep in mind that the manner in which our governments make law is itself governed by law. The legitimacy of government — its composition, selection, and procedures — occupies a large part of the federal and state constitutions and, in the case of local governments, is grounded in statutes and charters. Laws govern even lawmaking by the people themselves. Some of these laws define the legitimacy of lawmaking institutions, for example the number of their members, their qualifications, their election, the length of their term in office. Others define the prerequisites of law-making procedure; for instance, the central concept of enactment by a majority of a legal quorum, or sometimes a larger number; passage of the same text by two separate houses; the assent of an independent executive or reenactment after consideration of his objections. What is not fixed in constitutions and statutes is often spelled out in the rules of the lawmaking body itself. Bribery, the classic threat to the integrity of government, is universally outlawed by statute or constitution. The Court has spoken of the *"due"* functioning of the legislative process under the speech and debate clause.

Two things are striking about this body of rules for the law-making process. One is that over the years its successive authors have measured the process, explicitly or implicitly, by the standard of its legitimacy — the basic constitutional standard of democratic accountability or, if you will, of a republican form of government. That is not a universal practice in the world. The architects of our system have identified what from time to time they have perceived as prerequisites of legitimate lawmaking and as threats to its achievement, they have debated alternative solutions both in institutional and in procedural forms, and they have known how to state these solutions with considerable precision and detail. The second striking thing is that these rules of the lawmaking process, with some exceptions, are followed as a matter of course, unquestioningly, not with a constant weighing of possible sanctions for their violation. We would not say this with equal confidence about daily practice in the processes of criminal and administrative law. In short, due process in lawmaking in many, if not all, respects is a very concrete, well understood set of institutional procedures.

This conscious and deliberate legitimization of the lawmaking process has never come to an end, frozen in the forms of 1789 or of 1868. The constituency entitled to select and to retire its lawmakers has been progressively enlarged by the fifteenth, the nineteenth, the twenty-fourth and the twenty-sixth amendments. Some states, such as my own State of Oregon, found means to enforce equal apportionment of legislative representatives before the Supreme Court extended this political equality to all states. In the 19th century, the reaction to legislative recklessness, ignorance, logrolling, and corruption led to constitutional strictures on the forms and procedures of enactment, some of which we now find inappropriate. A number of states turned to the popular referendum as a safeguard. Waves of reform have been aimed at local institutions and processes, with good reason. Not all of these efforts have proved wise, and contradictory views have prevailed in different states; but the impulse to secure responsible government has not run its course.

Indeed, we presently live in a period of the most intense attention to the lawmaking process since the burgeoning of new legislation and administrative regulation thirty years ago led to the Congressional Reorganization and Administrative Procedure Acts of 1946. By the Legislative Reorganization Act of 1970 and its sequels, Congress has opened many previously closed proceedings to public scrutiny, required members to cast recorded votes, and surrounded committee hearings and committee action with new safeguards of notice and rights of minority participation. It has equipped itself with procedures and professional staff intended to allow both majority and minority members to deal rationally with such problems as the economic impact of the budget and the consequences of technological changes if they so choose. Environmental impact statements are required for agency proposals to Congress as well as for administrative actions. Many states have seen the same efforts to strengthen the institutional capacities of lawmaking bodies and also their accountability, through new laws regarding open meetings, open records and conflicts of interest. Some require that every bill carry an estimate of its cost.

Of course, our lawmaking process is not about to become perfectly responsible, perfectly accountable, perfectly democratic, even if these ideals did not conceal unresolved contradictions. The point is, rather, that the process everywhere is governed by rules, that these rules are purposefully made and from time to time changed, and that most of them are sufficiently concrete so that participants and observers alike will recognize when a legislative body is following the due process of lawmaking and when it is not. There is generally no reason to doubt what process is called for. If a legislative body fails to reapportion itself when required, if it stops the clock in order to enact bills after the constitutional deadline, if absent members are counted as part of a quorum or as having voted, if impractical requirements for reading bills are ignored, the participants know that they are not complying with the constitution or can readily be reminded of it by anyone. The same is true of legislative procedures governed by rules other than a constitution, and of local lawmaking bodies. Those who cut procedural corners will argue practical justifications; they will deny culpability if no substantive injustice results, and the fact that improperly made laws are not invalidated no doubt encourages this pragmatic view; however, they will not claim ignorance of the rules.

The problem with due process in lawmaking lies in the consequences of its violation. When a law is promulgated without compliance with the rules of legitimate lawmaking, is it not a law? Remarkably, we have no coherent national doctrine on this fundamental question. Judicial views on allowing a law to be attacked for faulty enactment differ from state to state and with the nature of the asserted fault; most courts and commentators find it improper to question legislative adherence to lawful procedures. This reluctance is often phrased as a problem of proof, or of respect between coordinate branches, but these are rationalizations. Neither problem keeps courts from insisting on such adherence by executive officers or by local lawmakers, and those who oppose judicial review of faulty lawmaking on evidentiary grounds will equally oppose it on uncontested pleadings or stipulations. Fear of legislative resentment at judicial interference is not borne out by experience where procedural review exists, any more than it was after the Supreme Court told Congress that it had used faulty procedure in unseating Representative Adam Clayton Powell. It is far more cause for resentment to invalidate the substance of a policy that the politically accountable branches and their constituents support than to invalidate a lawmaking procedure that can be repeated correctly, yet we take substantive judicial review for granted. Strikingly, the reverse view of propriety prevails in a number of nations where courts have never been empowered to set aside policies legitimately enacted into law but do have power to test the process of legitimate enactment.

In any event these are problems of judicial review, and in our present theoretical excursion they are secondary to what the Constitution demands of lawmakers. We do not assume that a law has been constitutionally made merely because a court will not set it aside, nor does the Supreme Court, despite Holmes's dictum that law is only the prophecy of what courts will do. Other participants than courts have the opportunity, and the obligation, to insist on legality in lawmaking. When an objection is raised on a significant point of procedure in the Congress, the presiding officer and the members are obliged to address the point as one of legal principle, and they quite generally do so. A governor or a President ought to veto, on constitutional grounds, a bill that he knows to have been adopted in violation of a constitutionally required procedure, even though the courts would not question its enactment. If an attorney general advises prosecutors not to enforce a law enacted with the clocks stopped after a constitutional deadline, he acts to maintain due process despite the fact that a conviction under the law would be sustained. Congress itself prefers to treat an improperly made act as never having become law even though the courts might not do so. It is not mere theory to distinguish between constitutional law and judicial review.

The Problem of Relief. Yet the question of the consequences of noncompliance remains an obstacle to simply equating due process and compliance with prescribed rules for lawmaking. For the due process clauses do not command compliance with legitimate procedure in the abstract; they state that no person shall be deprived of life, liberty, or property without such compliance. The guarantee runs in favor of the individual. But courts will not relieve individuals of the application of a law on every showing that it was improperly enacted. They are reluctant to visit the past sins of its legislative fathers on an otherwise inoffensive statute, especially when to do so seems a windfall for an undeserving but resourceful litigant. It is not unlike the problem of letting the criminal go because the constable blundered, only, in the case of a statute, the consequences are far wider. This, and not problems of proof or institutional deference, is the practical reason to withhold judicial review. But to deny an injured party relief from an improperly made law means either that courts will tolerate violations of due process of law, or else that every breach of the prescribed process does not fall short of due process in the constitutional sense.

The second of these will seem the more appealing solution, as it has been for the judicial view of due process in criminal and in administrative law. It sacrifices reading due process of laws to require adherence to law, and instead calls for deciding which standards of the lawmaking process are essential to a valid enactment and which are not. Due process of lawmaking will include some but not all of the rules governing the particular lawmaking body; it will also provide a constitutional standard below which no lawmaking process may fall. Of course, courts, as they have done in the past, can continue to insist directly on compliance with rules beyond the demands of due process where this is the practice. Examples of this are rules governing the subject and titles of bills or the reading of proposed ordinances at properly convened meetings. What the due process clauses add to such rules is the claim to protection against injury to private life, liberty, or property, beyond the injury to the societal interest in legitimate government; and fourteenth amendment due process can add a federal floor under lawmaking processes in the states.

NOTES AND QUESTIONS

1. *The goal of legislative due process.* Traditional due process protects an individual's right to be heard through creating minimum procedures that government must follow when life, liberty, or property interests are being impacted. What is the goal of legislative due process?

2. *Determining the process due.* Determining the process due is a judicial function. Is Professor Linde suggesting that the judicial branch has the authority to impose minimum procedural rules on the legislative process? If not, how is his vision of due process to be enforced? If so, doesn't this raise serious separation of power questions?

3. *Applying Professor Linde's theory.* Assume you were a New York State judge devoted to the teachings of Professor Linde. How would these teachings inform your position in both King v. Cuomo and Heinbach v. State of New York?

PART *II*
The Exercise of the Lawmaking Power

CHAPTER *4*

The Functions and Procedures of Legislative Committees

In Chapter 3, we examined the structure of committees in the context of describing the organization of legislatures. In Chapter 5, we will observe the referral of both H.R. 6400 and S. 1564 to the judiciary committee of each chamber. We will also watch their return from each committee to the legislative chamber. S. 1564 will be reported with proposed amendments, but without committee recommendations with respect to the bill or its amendments. H.R. 6400 will be reported with amendments in the nature of a substitute. The amendments will be recommended by the House committee. In the case of H.R. 6400, we will also observe that, before it reaches the House floor for debate, it will have to pass through two additional committees: the Committee on Rules and the Committee of the Whole House on the State of the Union. In this chapter, our focus is on the functions of committees and the procedures they follow in the consideration of legislation.

A. THE FUNCTIONS OF LEGISLATIVE COMMITTEES

Committees are the locus of most legislative activity. To understand the legislative process, one has to understand the functions and procedures of legislative committees. All bills are assigned to committees, and most never leave them. It is usually the committee that decides whether a particular problem, raised by a bill, merits formal legislative attention and whether the solution posed by the bill is appropriate for formal legislative consideration. These decisions are usually discretionary. A committee may simply ignore a bill by failing to consider it. Or, a committee may substantially rewrite a bill so that the amended version provides an entirely different solution than did the original one. "Committees decide with respect to legislation what will be buried, what will barely come out of committee, and what will come out with a favored likelihood of enactment." Charles Tiefer, Congressional Practice and Procedure 57-58 (1989).

That committees are so significant to the legislative process is not surprising. It is through committees (and subcommittees) that legislatures are able to effectuate the levels of expertise, specialization, and participation necessary to satisfy the vast demands on their resources. As one of the authors has previously written about Congress:

> Standing committees provide Congress with the expertise necessary to deal with national problems. Most House and Senate members choose to work on a particular committee as a way to affect national policy. To become experts, they frequently hire staff experienced in the committee's policy area.
>
> To take the lead in policy innovation, expertise is critical. As one study pointed out, the fragmented and decentralized policy-making structure of Congress facilitates, rather than inhibits, policy information. For example in the Senate Health Care Subcommittee, staffed by doctors and health-care professionals, Chairman Edward Kennedy developed comprehensive health care legislation and focused national attention on the need for a national comprehensive health-care program. . . .
>
> Without expertise, a committee could not effectively oversee the executive branch agency within its jurisdiction. . . .
>
> Because of the committee system, executive branch initiatives can be evaluated and criticized. As one longtime professional staff member pointed out, committees sometimes change elements of a presidential package to let the president know that they are "in the driver's seat." Without committee expertise, Congress would most certainly play a role subordinate to the better staffed executive branch. . . .
>
> Because of committee expertise, most presidential legislative packages are not rubber stamped, not even when the Congress is controlled by the president's own party. . . .
>
> The committee system allows Congress to function. Without a clearly defined separation of responsibilities, Congress could not process the hundreds of bills, resolutions, and nominations that it considers every year, nor could it adequately oversee the executive branch. Each committee oversees a specific function in the executive branch. . . . Some committees . . . are composed of numerous sub-committees, each responsible for a particular agency. To effectively watchdog more than 100 federal agencies, specialized committees are the only answer.
>
> In addition, committees provide on-the-job training for new members. In the smaller, friendlier, less formal confines of a committee room, a member can begin to understand the legislative process, parliamentary procedures, and collegial niceties. . . .
>
> Finally, committees block ill-advised, inadequate legislation. . . . Before legislation hits the floor for debate, committee experts criticize it, revise it,

and fully explore the merits of the proposal. In addition, committees prevent extremely controversial legislation from reaching the floor when the majority party is trying to achieve other priorities.

Abner J. Mikva and Patti B. Saris, The American Congress, 142-43 (1983).

Representational Imbalance

This reliance on committees raises issues about the representative nature of legislative committees. Committees are almost always unrepresentative, to varying degrees, of the parent chamber. No committee is an exact reflection of the interest mix of its parent body, and many are quite different. For example, Professor Fenno, in his study of congressional committees, shows that the Interior Committee of the House, during his period of study, had a pro-development, western bias that was inconsistent with the more conservationist view of the House itself. Richard F. Fenno, Jr., Congressmen in Committees (1973). Such imbalances reflect the relationship between the jurisdiction of the committees and goals of individual legislators. For example, during the period of Fenno's study, the jurisdiction of the Interior Committee included projects affecting irrigation, mines, national parks, and the like.

Each of the members on this committee believed that service to their constituents was their primary legislative goal. Such service would be performed by advancing projects favored by their constituents, who were most frequently in favor of the development of land resources. It would have been far less likely that representatives who opposed such projects would have joined this committee. Their experience on the committee would have been extremely negative (voting no on projects) and would have been hard to translate into a meaningful reelection theme. Most representatives would prefer to battle such projects on the floor of the legislative chamber, reserving committee time for more affirmative efforts.

The unrepresentativeness of legislative committees is far less of a concern when committees report legislation than when they kill it. The reporting of legislation means that it can be subject to the will of the chamber; the killing of legislation usually means that it will not be considered by the chamber. In reporting legislation, committees are often aware of their unrepresentativeness and attempt to compensate for it:

> Interior members must get their bills passed if they are to reap electoral benefits. But their regional unrepresentativeness threatens such passage. Therefore they cultivate House confidence by the careful, orderly processing of bills, the minimization of partisanship, the emphasis on specialized expertise, the stress on Committee independence of the executive, the internal effort to conciliate non-Western members of the Committee, and the external effort to portray subsequent Committee decisions as national in outlook.

Richard F. Fenno, Jr., Congressmen in Committees 259-60 (1973).

In killing legislation, committees, if they are particularly unrepresentative, may be frustrating the representative interests of the remainder of the parent chamber. On this point Mikva and Saris comment:

> But the very system essential to promoting congressional leverage over policy formation is also the nemesis of an effective, politically responsive Congress. As they developed in this century, committees often function as feuding, jealous fiefdoms, which by rule, tradition, and generally accepted norm, have virtually unlimited power to control the outcome of legislation within their bailiwicks. Thus a committee chairman sometimes bottles up legislation even though it is widely supported by a majority of congressmen. Introduction of legislation that is not supported by a committee chairman or at least by a powerful committee member of the majority party is, to use a common expression on the Hill, like dropping a rock to the bottom of a very deep ocean. It will never again emerge.

Mikva and Saris, The American Congress 24 (1983). This singular power of a committee to kill legislation has led to the development of a number of practices and rules for circumventing committee power.

Circumventing Committee Power

In Chapter 5 you will see a battle in the Senate over the restrictions on committee consideration of S. 1564 (the Voting Rights Act of 1965). These restrictions were part of a strategy by proponents of voting rights legislation to assure senate consideration of a voting rights bill, despite the hostility of the chairperson of the relevant committee to such legislation. This was an unusual approach because it undermined the committee's authority, even before the committee had demonstrated an unwillingness to "move" the legislation. A more typical method for addressing such a problem would be for the legislative leadership to refer the bill to a friendlier committee (if one existed and it had overlapping jurisdiction) or for the legislative chamber to support a motion for discharge.

The rules of most legislative bodies provide for some method of discharging a bill from a committee without that committee's support. These discharge procedures are, in theory, escape valves for the pressure created by popularly supported legislation that is being bottled up in a committee. The procedures can be quite elaborate, as is evidenced by Rule XV of the Rules of the House of Representatives:

2. Discharge Motions, second and fourth Mondays . . .
    (b) (1) A Member may present to the Clerk a motion in writing to discharge —
        (A) a committee from consideration of a public bill or public resolution that has been referred to it for 30 legislative days; or

(B) the Committee on Rules from consideration of a resolution that has been referred to it for seven legislative days and that proposes a special order of business for the consideration of a public bill or public resolution that has been reported by a standing committee for 30 legislative days.

(2) Only one motion may be presented for a bill or resolution. . . .

(c) A motion presented under paragraph (b) shall be placed in the custody of the Clerk, who shall arrange a convenient place for the signatures of Members. A signature may be withdrawn by a Member in writing at any time before a motion is entered on the Journal. . . . When a majority of the total membership of the House shall have signed the motion, it shall be entered on the Journal, published with the signatures thereto in the Record, and referred to the Calendar of Motions to Discharge Committees.

(d) (1) On the second and fourth Mondays of a month (except during the last six days of a session of Congress), immediately after the Pledge of Allegiance to the Flag, a motion to discharge that has been on the calendar for at least seven legislative days shall be privileged if called up by a Member whose signature appears thereon. . . . Privileged motions to discharge shall have precedence in the order of their entry on the Journal.

(2) When a motion to discharge is called up, the bill or resolution to which it relates shall be read by title only. The motion is debatable for 20 minutes, one-half in favor of the motion and one-half in opposition thereto.

(e) (1) If a motion prevails to discharge the Committee on Rules from consideration of a resolution, the House shall immediately consider the resolution. . . . If the resolution is adopted, the House shall immediately proceed to its execution.

(2) If a motion prevails to discharge a standing committee from consideration of a public bill or public resolution, a motion that the House proceed to the immediate consideration of such bill or resolution shall be privileged if offered by a Member whose signature appeared on the motion to discharge. The motion to proceed is not debatable. If the motion to proceed is adopted, the bill or resolution shall be considered immediately under the general rules of the House.

There are considerable pressures against the use of motions to discharge (as there are against efforts to undermine committee authority). Supporters of such motions, in fact, are second-guessing the decisions of their colleagues on the committee and may be similarly second-guessing in the future. For this reason, motions to discharge rarely succeed. Consider the following passage about Congress:

> Since the revision of the rule in the 1920s and 1930s, its use has been divided into roughly two eras. The first, from the late 1930s to the early 1970s, consisted largely of efforts by Liberals to free legislation bottled up by the conservative coalition domination of the Rules Committee and the committee chairs. This era began in 1937 when the newly-established conservative coalition denied a special rule to the bill to establish a national

minimum wage and maximum number of hours. Liberals responded by achieving an incredible record of "requir[ing] only two and one-half hours to obtain the 218 signatures" for the petition to discharge a special rule for the bill, and the bill became law. During the following 35 years, liberals obtained sufficient signatures to force release of bills on lynching in the 1930s, civil rights and federal pay increases in 1960, civil rights again in 1964, home rule for the District of Columbia in 1965, and the Equal Rights Amendment in 1970. Yet overall, successful enactment through discharge was rare.

By the 1970s, as previously discussed, the House broke the power of the Rules Committee and of the committee chairs to block the majority party agenda. This began a second era of use of the discharge rule consisting largely of use by the minority party, with conservative Democratic assistance, to release bills bottled up by the majority leadership. This era's beginning may be set in 1971, when conservatives discharged a constitutional amendment regarding school prayer from the Judiciary Committee, followed in 1979 and 1982 by discharge from the same committee of constitutional amendments regarding busing and a balanced budget. All three constitutional amendments failed on the House floor. In contrast to the failure of those "social agenda" bills, discharge won success for some economic measures during this era: a 1980 antitrust exemption for soft-drink bottlers, and a 1983 repeal of withholding of taxes on interest and dividends.

In 1982, the House Democratic Caucus proposed raising the number of petition signatories needed to discharge a constitutional amendment from half of the House to two-thirds. That proposal represented a reaction against the 1982 discharge of the balanced budget amendment, regarded by the House leadership as an Administration attempt to embarrass Democrats on the eve of election. Initially, on December 8, 1982, the House Democratic Caucus adopted the proposal, but the leadership withdrew the proposal the following month.

Charles Tiefer, Congressional Practice and Procedure 317-20 (1989).

In 1993, another change was made in the House rules relating to the discharge of bills held in committee. Under prior rules, the names of members who signed discharge petitions were kept secret until the threshold of 218 signatures was reached. This process, according to those who pushed the reform, allowed members to pretend to be sponsoring legislation while, in fact, not pushing for its reporting from committee. The new rules make the names public from the beginning. While this arcane process may seem to be of little consequence, the reform was pushed by several editorials in the Wall Street Journal and became an important agenda item for a number of government reform groups, particularly that of Ross Perot's United We Stand. The consequences of this reform remain to be seen.

The use of a discharge procedure may have other goals. Consider the following experience of one of the authors, Professor Lane, from his tenure as Counsel to the Minority of the New York State Senate. As an election strategy, dozens of such motions were made to politically embarrass the Senate majority. Politically popular (but sometimes slightly irresponsible) bills were introduced by members of the minority and, as a matter of course, assigned to committees. For many reasons, these bills were not favored by the Republican majority in the Senate and had no hope of being reported from committee for floor action. A motion to discharge was prepared for each such bill, and each motion to discharge was discussed on the floor as if it were the bill itself. Inevitably these motions were defeated by the majority to ensure party discipline and to protect the committee system. At the next election, these votes were used to argue that the majority members had voted against the bills themselves. Could this happen under Rule XV of the Rules of the House of Representatives? Under the then Rules of the New York State Senate, a member could move to discharge a bill from a committee on three days' written notice. To have prevailed, the motion must have received the support of a majority of all of the members (not just of those present) of the Senate.

B.   CONSIDERATION OF LEGISLATION BY COMMITTEES

1.   *Gathering Information and Creating a Record: Committee Hearings*

One of the most significant decisions a committee (or subcommittee) makes is to hold a hearing. This decision, in most cases, determines a committee's policy priorities and commits a considerable amount of its resources. "At both the full and subcommittee level, hearings are seldom a paragon of spontaneity. They are carefully mapped out and scripted in advance." Abner J. Mikva and Patti B. Saris, The American Congress 210 (1983). There are two types of hearings: legislative and oversight. "In a legislative hearing, the focus is on a particular bill or bills. . . . In an oversight hearing, the focus is on the functioning of some federal program or agency — its efficiency, obedience to statutory mandate, or new policies — or some private sector problem." Charles Tiefer, Congressional Practice and Procedure 149 (1989). The hearings on the Voting Rights Act of 1965 were legislative hearings. There the focus was on proposed voting rights legislation. An example of an oversight hearing is the activities of the House Committee on Intelligence, which are explored later in this chapter.

The overall function of a committee hearing is to create a public record on which to base legislative activity. There is no legal requirement for such a public record nor even for the holding of a hearing on a bill. Members gain information about problems and proposed solutions, including the political alliances and ramifications of both (who thinks what and who will bear the costs), from numerous sources in many different ways, with hearings being only one of many inputs. Indeed, this is one of the reasons that many committee hearings, particularly legislative hearings, are poorly attended by members of the legislature. But hearings can be enormously important beyond their value of informing legislators about a proposed bill. First, they focus public attention on a particular subject. Second, they serve as a public record for why a legislature acted in a particular fashion. This record may have implications for subsequent judicial action, particularly if the court is examining challenged legislation through the equal protection lens and is looking for a predicate for its enactment. Third, they provide a forum at which the public can evaluate the significance of the subject under review. Fourth, they establish a forum at which legislators can be evaluated. And finally, they provide a formal opportunity for interested parties to be heard on a particular bill.

For the most part, witnesses at hearings are not "average citizens," but representatives of the executive branch (particularly for oversight hearings) and of various organizations and associations who are interested in the proposed legislation. This observation is affirmed by a survey, prepared by the United States Senate:

> Witnesses fall into several categories summarized in a Senate survey of 8,500 witnesses testifying in one year. Of these, 2,500 were from the Executive Branch. Some 1,800 came from business generally — companies, trade associations, banks, industrial research firms, law firms and professional associations. About 700 came from state governments, and about 500 were from unions, public interest and consumer groups, and nonprofit institutions. Another 600 were academics, consultants, or from nonprofit research groups. That left only 2,400 either from miscellaneous institutions or unaffiliated — the "citizen witnesses." . . .
>
> Another study concluded that of roughly 10,000 to 12,000 witnesses in House hearings in 1974, only 1,200 were citizen witnesses. Clearly, testifying is the activity of representatives of the executive and interested institutions much more than of individual citizens.

Charles A. Tiefer, Congressional Practice and Procedure 156 (1989).

The Use of Compulsory Process and the Rights of Witnesses

In most instances, witnesses are eager or at least willing to appear before committee. But on occasion, people are unwilling to testify or produce the documents requested. In these instances, the committee may decide to require such testimony or documents through the issuance of a subpoena. In the following case, Watkins v. United States, the Court addresses many of the legal issues surrounding the legislative use of compulsory process. This is an abnormal case because of the extreme nature of the legislative activity in question. But it brings into sharp focus the potential conflicts that may arise when a legislative body turns to compulsory process to secure information. This issue is raised again in the materials on executive privilege, starting on page 142 of this chapter. Internal citations have been omitted, except where particularly relevant.

Watkins v. United States
354 U.S. 178 (1957)

CHIEF JUSTICE WARREN delivered the opinion of the Court. . . .

Petitioner was prosecuted for refusing to make certain disclosures which he asserted to be beyond the authority of the committee to demand. The controversy thus rests upon fundamental principles of the power of the Congress and the limitations upon that power. We approach the questions presented with conscious awareness of the far-reaching ramifications that can follow from a decision of this nature.

On April 29, 1954, petitioner appeared as a witness in compliance with a subpoena issued by a Subcommittee of the Committee on Un-American Activities of the House of Representatives. . . .

[At the hearing,] counsel for the Committee . . . began to read . . . [a] list of names to petitioner. Petitioner stated that he did not know several of the persons. Of those whom he did know, he refused to tell whether he knew them to have been members of the Communist Party. He explained to the Subcommittee why he took such a position:

> I am not going to plead the fifth amendment, but I refuse to answer certain questions that I believe are outside the proper scope of your committee's activities. I will answer any questions which this committee puts to me about myself. I will also answer questions about those persons whom I knew to be members of the Communist Party and whom I believe still are. I will not, however, answer any questions with respect to others with whom I associated in the past. I do not believe that any law in this country requires me to testify about persons who may in the past have been Communist Party members or otherwise engaged in Communist Party activity but who to my best knowledge and belief have long since removed themselves from the Communist movement.
>
> I do not believe that such questions are relevant to the work of this committee nor do I believe that this committee has the right to undertake the public exposure of persons because of their past activities. I may be wrong, and the committee may have this power, but until and unless a court of law so holds and directs me to answer, I most firmly refuse to discuss the political activities of my past associates.

The Chairman of the Committee submitted a report of petitioner's refusal to answer questions to the House of Representatives. The House directed the Speaker to certify the Committee's report to the United States Attorney for initiation of criminal prosecution. A seven-count indictment was returned. Petitioner waived his right to jury trial and was found guilty on all counts by the court. . . .

We start with several basic premises on which there is general agreement. The power of the Congress to conduct investigations is inherent in the legislative process. That power is broad. It encompasses inquiries concerning the administration of existing laws as well as proposed or possibly needed statutes. It includes surveys of defects in our social, economic or political system for the purpose of enabling the Congress to remedy them. It comprehends probes into departments of the Federal Government to expose corruption, inefficiency or waste. But, broad as is this power of inquiry, it is not unlimited. There is no general authority to expose the private affairs of individuals without justification in terms of the functions of the Congress. . . . Nor is the Congress a law enforcement or trial agency. These are functions of the executive and judicial departments of government. No inquiry is an end in itself; it must be related to, and in furtherance of, a legitimate task of the Congress. Investigations conducted solely for the personal aggrandizement of the investigators or to "punish" those investigated are indefensible.

It is unquestionably the duty of all citizens to cooperate with the Congress in its efforts to obtain the facts needed for intelligent legislative action. It is their unremitting obligation to respond to subpoenas, to respect the dignity of the Congress and its committees and to testify fully with respect to matters within the province of proper investigation. This, of course, assumes that the constitutional rights of witnesses will be respected by the Congress as they are in a court of justice. The Bill of Rights is applicable to investigations as to all forms of governmental action. Witnesses cannot be compelled to give evidence against themselves. They cannot be subjected to unreasonable search and seizure. Nor can the First Amendment freedoms of speech, press, religion, or political belief and association be abridged. . . .

Clearly, an investigation is subject to the command that the Congress shall make no law abridging freedom of speech or press or assembly. While it is true that there is no statute to be reviewed, and that an investigation is not a law, nevertheless an investigation is part of law-making. It is justified solely as an adjunct to the legislative process. The First Amendment may be invoked against infringement of the protected freedoms by law or by lawmaking.

Abuses of the investigative process may imperceptibly lead to abridgment of protected freedoms. The mere summoning of a witness and compelling him to testify, against his will, about his beliefs, expressions or associations is a measure of governmental interference. And when those forced revelations concern matters that are unorthodox, unpopular, or even hateful to the general public, the reaction in the life of the witness may be disastrous. This effect is even more harsh when it is past beliefs, expressions or associations that are disclosed and judged by current standards rather than those contemporary with the matters exposed. Nor does the witness alone suffer the consequences. Those who are identified by witnesses and thereby placed in the same glare of publicity are equally subject to public stigma, scorn and obloquy. Beyond that, there is the more subtle and immeasurable effect upon those who tend to adhere to the most orthodox and uncontroversial views and associations in order to avoid a similar fate at some future time. That this impact is partly the result of nongovernmental activity by private persons cannot relieve the investigators of their responsibility for initiating the reaction. . . .

Accommodation of the congressional need for particular information with the individual and personal interest in privacy is an arduous and delicate task for any court. We do not underestimate the difficulties that would attend such an undertaking. It is manifest that despite the adverse effects which follow upon compelled disclosure of private matters, not all such inquiries are barred. . . . [A]n investigation into individual affairs is invalid if unrelated to any legislative purpose. . . .

Petitioner has earnestly suggested that . . . there was no public purpose served in his interrogation. . . . The sole purpose of the inquiry, he contends, was to bring down upon himself and others the violence of public reaction because of their past beliefs, expressions and associations. . . .

We have no doubt that there is no congressional power to expose for the sake of exposure. The public is, of course, entitled to be informed concerning the workings of its government. That cannot be inflated into a general power to expose where the predominant result can only be an invasion of the private rights of individuals. But a solution to our problem is not to be found in testing the motives of committee members for this purpose. Such is not our function. Their motives alone would not vitiate an investigation which had been instituted by a House of Congress if that assembly's legislative purpose is being served.

Petitioner's contentions do point to a situation of particular significance from the standpoint of the constitutional limitations upon congressional investigations. The theory of a committee inquiry is that the committee members are serving as the representatives of the parent assembly in collecting information for a legislative purpose. Their function is to act as the eyes and ears of the Congress in obtaining facts upon which the full legislature can act. To carry out this mission, committees and subcommittees, sometimes one Congressman, are endowed with the full power of the Congress to compel testimony. In this case, only two men exercised that authority in demanding information over petitioner's protest.

An essential premise in this situation is that the House or Senate shall have instructed the committee members on what they are to do with the power delegated to them. It is the responsibility of the Congress, in the first instance, to insure that compulsory process is used only in furtherance of a legislative purpose. That requires that the instructions to an investigating committee spell out that group's jurisdiction and purpose with sufficient particularity. Those instructions are embodied in the authorizing resolution. That document is the committee's charter. Broadly drafted and loosely worded, however, such resolutions can leave tremendous latitude to the discretion of the investigators. The more vague the committee's charter is, the greater becomes the possibility that the committee's specific actions are not in conformity with the will of the parent House of Congress.

The authorizing resolution of the Un-American Activities Committee was adopted in 1938 when a select committee, under the chairmanship of Representative Dies, was created. Several years later, the Committee was made a standing organ of the House with the same mandate. It defines the Committee's authority as follows:

> The Committee on Un-American Activities, as a whole or by subcommittee, is authorized to make from time to time investigations of (1) the extent, character, and objects of un-American propaganda activities in the United States, (2) the diffusion within the United States of subversive and un-American propaganda that is instigated from foreign countries or of a domestic origin and attacks the principle of the form of government as guaranteed by our Constitution, and (3) all other questions in relation thereto that would aid Congress in any necessary remedial legislation.

It would be difficult to imagine a less explicit authorizing resolution. Who can define the meaning of "un-American"? What is that single, solitary "principle of the form of government as guaranteed by our Constitution"? There is no need to dwell upon the language, however. At one time, perhaps, the resolution might have been read narrowly to confine the Committee to the subject of propaganda. The events that have transpired in the fifteen years before the interrogation of petitioner make such a construction impossible at this date. . . .

Unquestionably the Committee conceived of its task in the grand view of its name. Un-American activities were its target, no matter how or where manifested. . . .

Combining the language of the resolution with the construction it has been given, it is evident that the preliminary control of the Committee exercised by the House of Representatives is slight or non-existent. No one could reasonably deduce from the charter the kind of investigation that the Committee was directed to make. As a result, we are asked to engage in a process of retroactive rationalization. Looking backward from the events that transpired, we are asked to uphold the Committee's actions unless it appears that they were clearly not authorized by the charter. As a corollary to this inverse approach, the Government urges that we must view the matter hospitably to the power of the Congress — that if there is any legislative purpose which might have been furthered by the kind of disclosure sought, the witness must be punished for withholding it. No doubt every reasonable indulgence of legality must be accorded to the actions of a coordinate branch of our Government. But such deference cannot yield to an unnecessary and unreasonable dissipation of precious constitutional freedoms.

The Government contends that the public interest at the core of the investigations of the Un-American Activities Committee is the need by the Congress to be informed of efforts to overthrow the Government by force and violence so that adequate legislative safeguards can be erected. From this core, however, the Committee can radiate outward infinitely to any topic thought to be related in some way to armed insurrection. The outer reaches of this domain are known only by the content of "un-American activities." . . .

The consequences that flow from this situation are manifold. . . . The Committee is allowed, in essence, to define its own authority, to choose the direction and focus of its activities. In deciding what to do with the power that has been conferred upon them, members of the Committee may act pursuant to motives that seem to them to be the highest. Their decisions, nevertheless, can lead to ruthless exposure of private lives in order to gather data that is neither desired by the Congress nor useful to it. Yet it is impossible in this circumstance, with constitutional freedoms in jeopardy, to declare that the Committee has ranged beyond the area committed to it by its parent assembly because the boundaries are so nebulous.

More important and more fundamental than that, however, it insulates the House that has authorized the investigation from the witnesses who are subjected to the sanctions of compulsory process. There is a wide gulf between the responsibility for the use of investigative power and the actual exercise of that power. This is an especially vital consideration in assuring respect for constitutional liberties. Protected freedoms should not be placed in danger in the absence of a clear determination by the House or the Senate that a particular inquiry is justified by a specific legislative need.

It is, of course, not the function of this Court to prescribe rigid rules for the Congress to follow in drafting resolutions establishing investigating committees. That is a matter peculiarly within the realm of the legislature, and its decisions will be accepted by the courts up to the point where their own duty to enforce the constitutionally protected rights of individuals is affected. An excessively broad charter, like that of the House Un-American Activities Committee, places the courts in an untenable position if they are to strike a balance between the public need for a particular interrogation and the right of citizens to carry on their affairs free from unnecessary governmental interference. It is impossible in such a situation to ascertain whether any legislative purpose justifies the disclosures sought and, if so, the importance of that information to the Congress in furtherance of its legislative function. The reason no court can make this critical judgment is that the House of Representatives itself has never made it. Only the legislative assembly initiating an investigation can assay the relative necessity of specific disclosures.

Absence of the qualitative consideration of petitioner's questioning by the House of Representatives aggravates a serious problem, revealed in this case, in the relationship of congressional investigating committees and the witnesses who appear before them. Plainly these committees are restricted to the missions delegated to them, i.e., to acquire certain data to be used by the House or the Senate in coping with a problem that falls within its legislative sphere. No witness can be compelled to make disclosures on matters outside that area. This is a jurisdictional concept of pertinency drawn from the nature of a congressional committee's source of authority. . . . When the definition of jurisdictional pertinency is as uncertain and wavering as in the case of the Un-American Activities Committee, it becomes extremely difficult for the Committee to limit its inquiries to statutory pertinency.

Since World War II, the Congress has practically abandoned its original practice of utilizing the coercive sanction of contempt proceedings at the bar of the House. . . . The Congress has instead invoked the aid of the federal judicial system in protecting itself against contumacious conduct. It has become customary to refer these matters to the United States Attorneys for prosecution under criminal law.

The appropriate statute is found in 2 U.S.C. §192. It provides:

> Every person who having been summoned as a witness by the authority of either House of Congress to give testimony or to produce papers upon any matter under inquiry before either House, or any joint committee established by a joint or concurrent resolution of the two Houses of Congress, or any committee of either House of Congress, willfully makes default, or who, having appeared, refuses to answer any question pertinent to the question under inquiry, shall be deemed guilty of a misdemeanor. . . .

The problem attains proportion when viewed from the standpoint of the witness who appears before a congressional committee. He must decide at the time the questions are propounded whether or not to answer. . . .

It is obvious that a person compelled to make this choice is entitled to have knowledge of the subject to which the interrogation is deemed pertinent. That knowledge must be available with the same degree of explicitness and clarity that the Due Process Clause requires in the expression of any element of a criminal offense. . . . There are several sources that can outline the "question under inquiry" in such a way that the rules against vagueness are satisfied. The authorizing resolution, the remarks of the chairman or members of the committee, or even the nature of the proceedings themselves, might sometimes make the topic clear. This case demonstrates, however, that these sources often leave the matter in grave doubt. . . .

We are mindful of the complexities of modern government and the ample scope that must be left to the Congress as the sole constitutional depository of legislative power. Equally mindful are we of the indispensable function, in the exercise of that power, of congressional investigations. The conclusions we have reached in this case will not prevent the Congress, through its committees, from obtaining any information it needs for the proper fulfillment of its role in our scheme of government. The legislature is free to determine the kinds of data that should be collected. It is only those investigations that are conducted by use of compulsory process that give rise to a need to protect the rights of individuals against illegal encroachment. That protection can be readily achieved through procedures which prevent the separation of power from responsibility and which provide the constitutional requisites of fairness for witnesses. A measure of added care on the part of the House and the Senate in authorizing the use of compulsory process and by their committees in exercising that power would suffice . . .

JUSTICE CLARK, dissenting.

As I see it the chief fault in the majority opinion is its mischievous curbing of the informing function of the Congress. While I am not versed in its procedures, my experience in the Executive Branch of the Government leads me to believe that the requirements laid down in the opinion for the operation of the committee system of inquiry are both unnecessary and unworkable. It is my purpose to first discuss this phase of the opinion and then record my views on the merits of Watkins' case.

I

It may be that at times the House Committee on Un-American Activities has, as the Court says, "conceived of its task in the grand view of its name." And, perhaps, as the Court indicates, the rules of conduct placed upon the Committee by the House admit of individual abuse and unfairness. But that is none of our affair. So long as the object of a legislative inquiry is legitimate and the questions propounded are pertinent thereto, it is not for the courts to interfere with the committee system of inquiry. To hold otherwise would be an infringement on the power given the Congress to inform itself, and thus a trespass upon the fundamental American principle of separation of powers. The majority has substituted the judiciary as the grand inquisitor and supervisor of congressional investigations. It has never been so.

II

Legislative committees to inquire into facts or conditions for assurance of the public welfare or to determine the need for legislative action have grown in importance with the complexity of government. The investigation that gave rise to this prosecution is of the latter type. Since many matters requiring statutory action lie in the domain of the specialist or are unknown without testimony from informed witnesses, the need for information has brought about legislative inquiries that have used the compulsion of the subpoena to lay bare needed facts and a statute . . . here involved, to punish recalcitrant witnesses. . . .

The Court indicates that in this case the source of the trouble lies in the "tremendous latitude" given the Un-American Activities Committee in the Legislative Reorganization Act. It finds that the Committee "is allowed, in essence, to define its own authority, [and] to choose the direction and focus of its activities." This, of course, is largely true of all committees within their respective spheres. And, while it is necessary that the "charter," as the opinion calls the enabling resolution, "spell out [its] jurisdiction and purpose," that must necessarily be in more or less general terms. . . .

Permanent or standing committees of both Houses have been given power in exceedingly broad terms. For example, the Committees on the Armed Services have jurisdiction over "Common defense generally"; the Committees on Interstate and Foreign Commerce have jurisdiction over "Interstate and Foreign commerce generally"; and the Committees on Appropriation have jurisdiction over "Appropriation of the revenue for the support of the Government." Perhaps even more important for purposes of comparison are the broad authorizations given to select or special committees established by the Congress from time to time. Such committees have been "authorized and directed" to make full and complete studies "of whether organized crime utilizes the facilities of interstate commerce or otherwise operates in interstate commerce"; "of . . . all lobbying activities intended to influence, encourage, promote, or retard legislation"; "to determine the extent to which current literature . . . containing immoral, [or] obscene . . . matter, or placing improper emphasis on crime . . . are being made available to the people of the United States . . ."; and "of the extent to which criminal or other improper practices . . . are, or have been, engaged in the field of labor-management relations . . . to the detriment of the interests of the public. . . ." [Emphasis omitted.] Surely these authorizations permit the committees even more "tremendous latitude" than the "charter" of the Un-American Activities Committee. Yet no one has suggested that the powers granted were too broad. To restrain and limit the breadth of investigative power of this Committee necessitates the similar handling of all other committees. The resulting restraint imposed on the committee system appears to cripple the system beyond workability. . . .

One needs only to read the newspapers to know that the Congress could gather little "data" unless its committees had, unfettered, the power of subpoena. . . . The Court generalizes on this crucial problem saying "added care on the part of the House and the Senate in authorizing the use of compulsory process and by their committees in exercising that power would suffice." It does not say how this "added care" could be applied in practice; however, there are many implications since the opinion warns that "procedures which prevent the separation of power from responsibility" would be necessary along with "constitutional requisites of fairness for witnesses." The "power" and "responsibility" for the investigations are, of course, in the House where the proceeding is initiated. But the investigating job itself can only be done through the use of committees. They must have the "power" to force compliance with their requirements. If the rule requires that this power be retained in the full House then investigations will be so cumbrous that their conduct will be a practical impossibility. . . .

While ambiguity prevents exactness (and there is "vice in vagueness," the majority reminds), the sweep of the opinion seems to be that "preliminary control" of the Committee must be exercised. The Court says a witness' protected freedoms cannot "be placed in danger in the absence of a clear determination by the House or the Senate that a particular inquiry is justified by a specific legislative need." Frankly I do not see how any such procedure as "preliminary control" can be effected in either House of the Congress. What will be controlled preliminarily? The plans of the investigation, the necessity of calling certain witnesses, the questions to be asked, the details of subpoenas duces tecum, etc.? As it is now, Congress is hard pressed to find sufficient time to fully debate and adopt all needed legislation. . . .

IV

I think the Committee here was acting entirely within its scope and that the purpose of its inquiry was set out with "undisputable clarity." In the first place, the authorizing language of the Reorganization Act must be read as a whole, not dissected. It authorized investigation into subversive activity, its extent, character, objects, and diffusion. While the language might have been more explicit than using such words as "un-American," or phrases like "principle of the form of government," still these are fairly well understood terms. We must construe them to give them meaning if we can. . . . The fact that the Committee has often been attacked has caused close scrutiny of its acts by the House as a whole and the House has repeatedly given the Committee its approval. "Power" and "responsibility" have not been separated. But the record in this case does not stop here. It shows that at the hearings involving Watkins, the Chairman made statements explaining the functions of the Committee. And, furthermore, Watkins' action at the hearing clearly reveals that he was well acquainted with the purpose of the hearing. It was to investigate Communist infiltration into his union. This certainly falls within the grant of authority from the Reorganization Act and the House has had ample opportunity to limit the investigative scope of the Committee if it feels that the Committee has exceeded its legitimate bounds.

The Court makes much of petitioner's claim of "exposure for exposure's sake" and strikes at the purposes of the Committee through this catch phrase. But we are bound to accept as the purpose of the Committee that stated in the Reorganization Act together with the statements of the Chairman at the hearings involved here. Nothing was said of exposure. . . . The Court indicates that the questions propounded were asked for exposure's sake and had no pertinency to the inquiry. It appears to me that they were entirely pertinent to the announced purpose of the Committee's inquiry. Undoubtedly Congress has the power to inquire into the subjects of communism and the Communist Party. As a corollary of the congressional power to inquire into such subject matter, the Congress, through its committees, can legitimately seek to identify individual members of the Party. . . .

V

The Court condemns the long-established and long-recognized committee system of inquiry of the House because it raises serious questions concerning the protection it affords to constitutional rights. It concludes that compelling a witness to reveal his "beliefs, expressions or associations" impinges upon First Amendment rights. The system of inquiry, it says, must "insure that the Congress does not unjustifiably encroach upon an individual's right to privacy nor abridge his liberty of speech, press, religion or assembly." In effect the Court honors Watkins' claim of a "right to silence" which brings all inquiries, as we know, to a "dead end." I do not see how any First Amendment rights were endangered here. There is nothing in the First Amendment that provides the guarantees Watkins claims. . . . Watkins was asked whether he knew named individuals and whether they were Communists. He refused to answer on the ground that his rights were being abridged. What he was actually seeking to do was to protect his former associates, not himself, from embarrassment. He had already admitted his own involvement. He sought to vindicate the rights, if any, of his associates. . . .

As already indicated, even if Watkins' associates were on the stand they could not decline to disclose their Communist connections on First Amendment grounds. While there may be no restraint by the Government of one's beliefs, the right of free belief has never been extended to include the withholding of knowledge of past events or transactions. There is no general privilege of silence. The First Amendment does not make speech or silence permissible to a person in such measure as he chooses. Watkins has here exercised his own choice as to when he talks, what questions he answers, and when he remains silent. A witness is not given such a choice by the Amendment. . . .

NOTES AND QUESTIONS

1. *Exposure for exposure's sake.* On what basis does the Court determine that the inquiries the defendant refused to answer were for the purpose of exposure only? If the defendant had refused to answer similar questions about his own background, would he have been similarly protected from contempt? Is exposure for exposure's sake a meaningful standard in the context of a legislative inquiry?

2. *The power to compel testimony.* The power to compel testimony or the production of documents, although infrequently exercised, is one of the most important powers of a legislative body. What is the source of this legislative power? What is its breadth? On what basis is a legislative committee able to exercise such power?

3. *Contempt of Congress.* On what authority can Congress punish for contempt? While Congress has enacted a statute that allows it to turn over contempt cases to the federal court system, each house of Congress retains the power to punish for contempt itself. This model also holds for many states.

4. *The rights of witnesses.* Assume you represent a witness compelled to appear before a legislative committee. You know from the *Watkins* decision that the inquiry must be rooted in some legitimate legislative purpose and that your client is protected against self-incrimination. What other rights does your client possess? In the House of Representatives, pursuant to Rule XI of the Rules of the House of Representatives, testimony cannot be taken without the presence of a committee quorum (two or more members), and the witness has a right to be accompanied by counsel, who can advise him or her on constitutional issues. The Senate has no similar rules, leaving decisions about such matters to the standing committees.

Many states have enacted statutes defining the rights of witnesses who appear before legislative committees. Typical rights are the receipt of notice of the time and place of the hearing and a statement of its subject; representation by counsel to advise the witness of his rights; the opportunity to enter a statement in the record and the right to review a transcript of the testimony; and some form of immunity from prosecution for those activities about which testimony is given.

5. *Immunity.* To compel testimony from witnesses who refuse to testify on the basis of their Fifth Amendment right against self-incrimination, Congress enacted a comprehensive immunity statute (18 U.S.C. §6002), part of which contained rules for granting immunity to witnesses before congressional committees. The immunity granted prohibits the government from using the immunized testimony or other compelled information

or evidence derived therefrom in any subsequent prosecution of the witness. Under 18 U.S.C. §6002, upon appropriate request from either house of Congress, a U.S. District Court must issue an order requiring the particular individual to testify or provide the requested information that he or she had previously refused to communicate on the basis of his or her privilege against self-incrimination. With respect to committees, an appropriate request for immunity is one that has been affirmatively supported by two-thirds of the members of the full committee. The statute also provides for notice to the Attorney General of a legislative request for immunity. This notice provides opportunity for the Attorney General to argue with the congressional committee over the appropriateness of granting immunity to a particular individual.

The granting of immunity for a legislative inquiry can sometimes lead to controversy. A prime example of this was the decision in United States v. North, 910 F.2d 843 (D.C. Cir. 1990). Oliver North, a U.S. Marine Corps officer who had served on the staff of the National Security Council, had appeared before a House and Senate committee under a grant of immunity. At these hearings, he gave extensive testimony about his role in the Iran-Contra scandal. This scandal involved the sale of arms to Iran to win the freedom of hostages in Lebanon and to "earn" money for the purchase of arms for the government-supported Contras in Nicaragua. It also included the cover-up of these activities. For his part in this scandal, North had been convicted of three counts of a 12-count indictment. The court of appeals determined that one of these convictions had been based on his testimony before Congress and that the other two may have been. The first count was struck down and the remaining two were remanded to the trial court to determine whether they had been based on immunized testimony. Ultimately, these remaining charges were dropped.

Executive Privilege and the Select Committee on Intelligence

As noted earlier, representatives of the executive branch of government are the most frequent witnesses before legislative committees, particularly when the committees are acting in their oversight capacity. Sometimes, notwithstanding the use of subpoenas, representatives of the executive branch may not want to provide the information requested. In these instances they may assert the protection of *executive privilege.* This extremely limited doctrine is explored in the following materials. These materials also provide an opportunity to witness the workings of a legislative committee performing its oversight function and the use and enforcement of subpoenas. The setting is a 1975 inquiry by a Select Committee on Intelligence of the House of Representatives. A select committee is a committee established by legislative resolution for a specific purpose. This committee was established in July of 1975 to investigate allegations concerning the lawfulness of U.S. intelligence agencies' activities and to make recommendations on how the House of Representatives could best exercise oversight of these agencies. Among the allegations that led to its creation was that the Central Intelligence Agency (CIA) had helped in efforts to topple the government of President Salvador Allende of Chile. The select committee consisted of 13 members, of whom 9 were Democrats and 4 were Republicans. Its chair was Otis Pike, a Democrat from New York.

U.S. Intelligence Agencies and Activities:
Committee Proceedings
Friday, November 14, 1975
House of Representatives
Select Committee on Intelligence
Washington, D.C.

The committee met, pursuant to notice, at 10:10 A.M. in room 2118, Rayburn House Office Building, Hon. Otis G. Pike [chairman], presiding.

Present: Representatives Pike (D), Dellums (D), Murphy (D), Aspin (D), Milford (D), Lehman (D), McClory (R), Treen (R), Johnson (R) and Kasten (R).

Also present: A. Searle Field, staff director; Aaron B. Donner, general counsel; Jack Boos, counsel; and Peter L. Hughes III, counsel.

Chairman PIKE.   The committee will come to order.

Yesterday we discussed the fact that it seemed rather clear there had been noncompliance with three separate subpoenas. The first subpoena addressed itself to recommendations by the State Department for covert actions — recommendations by the State Department to the National Security Council for covert actions. As to this particular subpoena, the issue was raised that executive privilege has — am I wrong, Mr. Donner; you are shaking your head? Why don't you tell us what the status of that particular subpoena is?

Mr. DONNER.   Executive privilege has not been raised, as of this date, with respect to any of them, sir.

Mr. FIELD.   There is a letter on its way from the State Department that should explain it.

Mr. McCLORY.   If the chairman will yield to me.

Chairman PIKE. Certainly, Mr. McClory. Your pipeline is much better than my pipeline.

Mr. McCLORY.   My pipeline, which was in operation shortly before I came to this meeting, included conversations by telephone with Mr. Philip Buchen, counsel to the President, as well as with Mr. Jack Marsh.

I will refer primarily to Mr. Phil Buchen. He stated that the doctrine of executive privilege would be raised with regard to the subpoena directed to the Secretary of State for covert operation recommendations by the State Department. I asked whether or not in each one of these instances, when a State Department recommendation for a covert operation was made, the President of the United States had personally made the decision to approve such a covert operation. He assured me that, in each instance, the President of the United States had personally made the decision.

Not this President, but a prior President — in all instances a prior President, and a prior administration.

I then stated that if the decision with respect to this was a personal communication with the President, it seemed to me that was an instance in which executive privilege might be raised.

I further pointed out that I felt the doctrine of executive privilege applied to the Office and not to the individual who happens to occupy the Office of President at a particular time; so it would be appropriate, under my interpretation of the law, for this President to have the right to invoke executive privilege on behalf of —

Chairman PIKE.   President Washington.

Mr. McCLORY.   President Washington, any deceased President or any prior President of the United States.

In other words — the chairman is being facetious — it applies to the Office and not to the individual who occupies the Office, in my interpretation; so I do think that this raises serious questions —

Chairman PIKE.   Mr. McClory, we have had testimony — and this was testimony from Mr. Kissinger — that the President, himself, has approved all of the covert operations since Mr. Kissinger has been in the Government and, according to his belief, prior to that time as well. Would not your doctrine, then, prohibit Congress from looking at any covert operation because of executive privilege?

Mr. McCLORY.   I am talking about communications with the President — recommendations made to the President, with decisions made by the President. It may be executive privilege could be expanded to include more than that which is being raised in this instance; but, calling your attention to the fact it is being raised, here, and the circumstances under which it is being raised, I think executive privilege has direct application where the President himself acts. . . .

Chairman PIKE.   Mr. Donner, can you enlighten us as to where, in your judgment, we are with regard to the legal precedents for denying information to Congress, and how those precedents apply to this situation?

Mr. DONNER.   There is only one Supreme Court case that we could uncover which directly considered the question of executive privilege, and that is United States v. Nixon. The line of cases leading up to it seem to be the only cases directly concerned with executive privilege.

The area of executive privilege is a gray and ambiguous one. There is no way of defining exactly where it begins or ends. Judicial interpretation of it has been sparse. However, United States v. Nixon was a case in which a President in office sought to assert the privilege as to communications received by him while he was in office. The extension of the doctrine in this instance, apparently, would cover communications to a deceased President — President Johnson — and also, apparently, a living ex-President — President Nixon.

That does create a rather anomalous situation. If President Ford can assert the privilege for President Nixon, it would seem that, by inference, if President Nixon then wanted — just hypothetically — to reveal information to this committee or give this committee documents in his possession, he would be precluded from doing so by a President in office. I personally find this a difficult doctrine to accept.

I could find no judicial interpretation which even seems to discuss this question, let alone support it or deny it.

From our research, the assertion of this doctrine seems to be a novel proposition in all of its parameters.

Mr. TREEN.   The *Nixon* case said the doctrine was not a universal doctrine; that it did not extend to all communications; that if there were evidence of criminal activity, that evidence would have to be examined, I think, in camera; and executive privilege could not be used to shield that sort of information. Is that the sum and substance of the Supreme Court decision?

Mr. DONNER.   Yes. The Court addressed itself only to the limited area of where there is evidence for a pending criminal action.

Mr. TREEN.   Did the Court in that decision, recognize that such a thing as executive privilege exists, in its dicta —

Mr. DONNER.   There is strong inference in the dicta in that case — and again, this was an area which the Court did not define — that there is an area where executive privilege could properly be asserted.

Again, they were addressing themselves — even if you extend the dictum to its broadest extension — to a President in office, and to communications to him while he was in office.

Mr. TREEN.   One other question then: In that case, did the Supreme Court reason, in suggesting that there is an area of executive privilege, that it was bottomed on the proposition that Presidents should be able to receive advice from their top aides in a perfectly confidential and candid manner? Isn't that the rationale for executive privilege?

Mr. DONNER.   That is an aspect of it, yes, sir; and that was the suggestion of the dictum in that case, sir.

Mr. TREEN.   I haven't decided how I am going to go on this issue. Most of these instances we are talking about today occurred in Democrat administrations, but it seems if the rationale of the Supreme Court decision is that we should preserve a channel of communication between a President and his top advisers, that channel could be destroyed if the exercise of the privilege is not extended to future Presidents; because the incentive of advisers to be candid would be destroyed to a certain extent if they felt that after the next election, or if the President died or something, all of their candor was going to be exposed completely.

The whole area troubles me.

[The decision referred to, United States v. Nixon 418 U.S. 683 (1974), is excerpted beginning on page 182.]

Mr. DONNER.   There are two points I would like to make in connection with that.

First, the material required by this subpoena would be received not for release or publication, but as classified information. In other words, the publicity aspect is somewhat diminished.

Mr. TREEN.   I hope you are right on your first point, sir.

Mr. DONNER.   The second point—and this again by interpretation rather than hard case law—is that it does not seem the Congress can decide the question of executive privilege on its own. It seems that is a judicial matter, and whether the privilege is validly exercised or not would be a question for the judiciary, not the legislative or executive branch.

Mr. McCLORY.   Will the gentleman yield for a further question? The doctrine of executive privilege has not been raised with regard to any of the other material that we have received. We have received a vast amount of material without having that doctrine raised before.

Mr. DONNER.   To be technical, sir, we do not have the assertion of executive privilege even at this moment.

Chairman PIKE.   It troubles me, Mr. McClory, that 3 days after the subpoena was returnable we have nothing. You have had phone calls; Mr. Donner and Mr. Field have had phone calls. The President has not asserted executive privilege. You have the assertion that he is going to assert executive privilege, but he hasn't done so.

Mr. McCLORY.   I am relying on a conversation with the President's counsel that the President is asserting executive privilege with regard to those matters, and I am communicating that to the committee here this morning. I have no reason not to believe that.

Let me say further that we are certainly in a position here to recognize what the law is. And if we recognize that the law does authorize the President to assert executive privilege in this instance, we have a right not to try to enforce a subpoena—if that is the decision we choose to make. We don't have to claim ignorance of what the law is and say we have to submit this to a tribunal. I would prefer not to present this particular instance to a tribunal. . . .

Mr. JOHNSON.   I thought we discussed the parameters of the claim of executive privilege—if in fact they do claim executive privilege, and to which materials it will apply—yesterday. It doesn't concern the matter of classification, but relates only to recommendations by prior Secretaries of State to the 40 Committee, to the National Security Council, or to the President.

In some instances it goes to the President. In some instances it goes to the National Security Council.

Chairman PIKE.   Mr. Johnson, I believe there are eight situations in which they said there were recommendations not only from prior Secretaries of State, but also from the present Secretary of State.

Mr. JOHNSON.   I didn't understand that. I thought they were all from prior Secretaries of State.

I further thought some of them went to the President directly, and others went to the National Security Council and/or the 40 Committee first.

Chairman PIKE.   Without having access to them, we really don't know where they went.

What we subpoenaed were State Department recommendations to the National Security Council. We did not subpoena any recommendations to the President.

Mr. JOHNSON.   The doctrine of executive privilege applies because the National Security Council is an arm of the President and the President is the Chairman of the National Security Council. We further established that the doctrine of executive privilege was not claimed by those Presidents to which the documents were directed, didn't we? President Johnson and President Kennedy — if they are the Presidents involved — did not observe the doctrine with regard to —

Chairman PIKE.   I think we may have President Kennedy, we may have President Johnson, we may have President Nixon; but the only person who allegedly is going to assert the privilege is President Ford. In fairness to the other Presidents, I don't think anybody ever tried to get these documents.

Mr. JOHNSON.   As a matter of fact, they were left in Government files and were not removed when these gentlemen left office.

Chairman PIKE.   That is correct.

Mr. JOHNSON.   They also were not private memoranda from the Secretaries involved or the President involved. They were State Department documents — not just little handwritten notes from one individual to another.

Chairman PIKE.   Once again, not having seen them, we can't really say.

Mr. FIELD.   It was our understanding — and perhaps the letter will clarify it — that three of them were direct communications to a President and five were not. I also believe the communications to President Nixon, which apparently are included among the documents, could not have been communications to him personally. All of his personal communications and records are now under court order, so we could not obtain them anyway. But in this case it has not been asserted that they are personal communications, and, in fact, they could not have culled the documents from those personal files because those files are under lock and key.

I think it is somewhat safe to say that at least the Nixon communications are not personal communications.

Mr. JOHNSON.   I stated yesterday—and I don't feel the need to fully reiterate my position—that I think that would be the worst possible extension of the doctrine of executive privilege. It should be very narrowly defined. I don't even recognize that the Executive has the right to waive it. I don't want to acknowledge that this is something they could assert, but choose not to. I don't think we ought to even acknowledge that there is a possibility that a President can control everything in Government files and Government documents and that the President has absolute control over this information dating from the inception of the Republic. . . .

Chairman PIKE.   Mr. Aspin.

Mr. ASPIN.   Mr. Chairman, we are talking now about the one issue of the subpoena directed to the Secretary of State. Perhaps you could tell us why we need this information, and what we are looking for in this document.

Chairman PIKE.   The question has come up throughout our hearings, and in the operations of the Central Intelligence Agency generally, whether the CIA was—to use a phrase frequently bandied about—a "rogue elephant," whether the CIA went off and did things on its own, or whether the CIA was in fact told to do things.

It has been our experience in those matters that we have gone into in some depth that in no instance did they go off and do things on their own. On the contrary, they were, from time to time, ordered to do things which they did not particularly want to do and, in fact, on occasion actively opposed.

The question then becomes—and Mr. Field stated this yesterday—whether those operations which are generated within the CIA, and in the normal course of business, are usually more responsible. Do they usually get our Nation into fewer difficulties than those which somebody outside of the intelligence operations department tells them to do?

So what we are trying to establish here is the nature of the operations that the CIA was told to do or that were generated in some other manner.

Most of the operations, I expect, are generated in the normal course of business, through normal CIA and DCI channels. Here we find a category of operations generated by the State Department. I think if the State Department is recommending operations to be carried out by the Central Intelligence Agency, it is part of our responsibility to see what kind of operations they are telling them to do or asking them to do.

Mr. ASPIN.   On this one, we have received absolutely zero; is that correct?

Mr. FIELD.   That is right.

Mr. ASPIN.   Nothing has happened since yesterday on this one?

Mr. FIELD.   That is correct.

Mr. ASPIN.   Could the chairman tell us what our alternatives are regarding this subpoena?

Chairman PIKE.   I won't give you all the alternatives, but I will tell you how I am going to vote. The alternatives range from doing nothing to seeking to cite the Secretary of State in this instance for contempt of Congress. I am going to vote in favor of citing the Secretary of State in contempt of Congress.

The one route we could take is to go back to the House for a resolution of necessity, but what has happened to that route is that time has kept running on us. I think by the time we went through that procedure, with two separate trips to the House of Representatives — let us assume the House had agreed to a resolution of necessity. We would then have to have some time frame within which the executive branch could comply with the House's assertion of the necessity for this information. If they then failed to comply, it would take some time to go the contempt route and I frankly think our charter would have expired before the issue were ever resolved. So I think at this point, that would be a meaningless exercise.

Mr. LEHMAN.   I recall the quotation that those who do not learn from history are bound to make the same mistakes. I think this is one way that this country can learn from history.

I do not find in these subpoenas the same possible question of invasion of a person's privacy that we had in a previous subpoena.

We have had not only Dr. Kissinger as a kind of imperious Secretary of State; we have also had others, such as Secretary of State Dulles and Secretary of State Acheson, who seemed to be larger than life and dominated the administration. I am very concerned that if we are to have a good professional organization — my information is the CIA is a good professional organization — we must give it some form of buffer from the kind of orders, the kind of compulsive direction, it can sometimes get from the administration that it serves under. This is the kind of knowledge that I think it is imperative this committee seek from the history of the actions of this administration or the previous administration, in order to prevent these kinds of things from happening in the future, and to construct the safeguards our intelligence community needs in order to perform the duty which it was originally committed to perform.

I would be willing to support enforcement of this subpoena at this time and let the chips fall where they may.

Chairman PIKE.   Mr. Dellums —

Mr. DELLUMS.   Mr. Chairman, I would like to move the following resolution:

Resolved, That the Speaker of the House of Representatives certify the report of the Select Committee on Intelligence of the House of Representatives as to the contumacious conduct of Henry A. Kissinger, as Secretary of State, in failing and refusing to produce certain pertinent materials in compliance with a subpoena duces tecum of said Select Committee served upon Henry A. Kissinger, as Secretary of State, and as ordered by the Select Committee, together with all the facts in connection therewith, under the seal of the House of Representatives, to the U.S. Attorney for the District of Columbia, to the end that Henry A. Kissinger, as Secretary of State, may be proceeded against in the manner and form provided by law.

Chairman PIKE.   Mr. Dellums, you are entitled to 5 minutes in support of your motion if you choose to use it.

Mr. DELLUMS.   Thank you, Mr. Chairman.

Mr. Chairman, we have been at this point once before. The majority of the committee by their vote several days ago decided not to challenge the Secretary of State with respect to certain information on the ground that the scope of the particular item before us then was very narrowly defined.

I think that the matter before us is obvious. I think it is important. I think it established the principle of the need for Congress to have access to information and I think if this committee is to go forward with its important work, we desperately need to take a stand. At this point I offer this resolution as an effort on the part of this committee to take a stand with regard to certain information which will allow it to go forward with its investigation.

Mr. McCLORY.   Mr. Chairman, I will oppose the resolution on the grounds previously mentioned, but I would also like to call the attention of the committee to the prior resolution they acted upon against the Director of the CIA, Mr. Colby.

It was based upon legal research of our counsel, and conformed to the requirement that we assert a necessity for the information. I think that our own counsel have advised us that this is a prerequisite to any kind of a proceeding to enforce a subpoena. If the committee wants to act in accordance with what I view as the procedure which is required to be followed for the purpose of truly enforcing a subpoena, I think the resolution of necessity is a prerequisite to any further action and, of course, it would have to be supported by action on the floor of the House.

I don't think it is a good idea for the committee to bypass any of the necessary preliminary steps in trying to get hastily at the business of going forward with a resolution to hold the Secretary of State in contempt of the Congress.

Chairman PIKE.   Mr. McClory, I would like to say first, I presume when you offered the subpoena, you deemed the documents to be necessary to this committee. I think that the committee members by voting for the subpoena, made the determination that they believed the documents to be necessary for this committee; I don't think there is any other requirement—any other procedural requirement—than that this committee feels the documents are necessary, in order to take a contempt resolution to the floor of the House. The House may not support us. We always recognize that; but I don't think it is necessary to go through any intermediate steps.

Mr. McCLORY.   Mr. Chairman, may I say that when the subpoena was offered originally, I was unaware of the fact that the President was going to assert executive privilege or that the documents covered by the subpoena involved personal action on the part of the President. In view of that assertion, I question our right to proceed. If there is a right to proceed, I think it does require this additional finding, at this time, on the part of the committee.

Mr. TREEN.   Who has possession of the documents we seek at this time?

Mr. FIELD.   The documents were sent from the State Department to the White House. They were then sent to the Justice Department, and I believe they are now back at the White House.

Mr. TREEN.   Wait a minute. They were sent from the State Department to the White House and then to Justice?

Mr. FIELD.   And then back to the White House.

Mr. TREEN.   The documents are in the possession of the White House, and not the Secretary of State, at this time?

Mr. FIELD.   I believe that is correct.

Mr. TREEN.   How does that affect our enforcement procedure?

Mr. FIELD.   The papers at the White House are copies of the documents.

Mr. TREEN.   Where are the originals?

Mr. FIELD.   The originals would be with the Secretary of State.

Mr. TREEN.   They are still there with him?

Mr. FIELD.   That is correct.

Mr. DONNER.   I would like to make an additional comment, Mr. Treen. I don't believe there is any way, under any basis of the law, that you can get rid of the papers and thereby avoid responsibility to respond to a subpoena.

Mr. KASTEN.   Mr. Chairman, I would like to offer an amendment in the nature of a substitute.

Chairman PIKE.   The gentleman will state his motion.

Mr. KASTEN.   The resolution be amended to read as follows:

Resolved, That the House of Representatives considers the work of the Select Committee on Intelligence to be necessary to the investigation which the House is resolved to make concerning intelligence operations and considers noncompliance with the subpoenas issued either before or after the adoption of this resolution by the Select Committee on Intelligence, to be a grave matter requiring appropriate enforcement.

That Henry A. Kissinger, Secretary of State, is directed to provide forthwith to the Select Committee on Intelligence of the House of Representatives the items specified in the schedule attached to and made part of the subpoena issued to Henry A. Kissinger, Secretary of State, under authority of the House of Representatives and dated November 6, 1975.

Chairman PIKE.   The gentleman is recognized for 5 minutes in support of his amendment.

Mr. KASTEN.   Thank you, Mr. Chairman.

I think it is important, especially in this particular case where we are dealing with — it is not hearsay, but at least insufficient information as to exactly what the position of the executive branch is going to be on this question. We have heard that a letter is on the way. None of us has it before us.

I think it is particularly important that we follow the correct procedure. The correct procedure is not contempt of Congress. The correct procedure is a resolution of necessity.

I think, also, Mr. Chairman and members of the committee, that in our effort to get the material, all of us agree we have a better chance of succeeding on the floor of the House and a better chance of eliciting the support of all of the Members — Republican and Democrat — in the House, through a resolution of necessity rather than through a contempt of Congress resolution.

I think that this is the proper procedure at this point. I think this is a resolution that we can win on. I think this is a resolution that addresses itself to the questions and the problems that we have. I would hope that we would adopt this resolution as a substitute for the contempt resolution, which I think is not the proper mechanism to deal with the problems with which the committee is faced at the present time. . . .

Chairman PIKE.   The Chair will recognize the Chair for 5 minutes in opposition to the substitute.

I think that I would have gone along with this procedure 3 months ago, because I would tend to agree with the gentleman that we would probably have a better chance of passing his substitute resolution on the floor of the House since it is a gentler route than the other one.

I will simply say that I could not support it at this time, because, while we could probably pass it on the floor of the House, to do so would, as I indicated earlier, be essentially a meaningless gesture. We would pass it on the floor of the House and still not get the documents because we would run out of time before anything was ever done.

I, for one, am weary of the whole business of waiting and delaying and waiting and delaying to get information to which this Congress is entitled.

As to the word "contumacious," it is a word of art which means "contempt," and that is what we are talking about. It happens to be the particular word which was in the last contempt citation which came to the floor of Congress and it is the word which is used if you are going to have a contempt of Congress citation.

I would agree that it is a strong and abrasive word. But I don't think that you can proceed with a powder puff when you are dealing with contempt. That is what we are dealing with and, in my judgment, time has simply run out on the route which the gentleman is prepared to go.

I will be happy to recognize anybody else. Mr. Johnson.

Mr. JOHNSON.   Mr. Chairman, I want to have the different alternatives clear. If either resolution is adopted, action will have to be taken by the full House of Representatives.

Chairman PIKE.   Action will have to be first taken by the Rules Committee, and in fairness to the members, I would like to make it very clear that this, itself, is not a foregone conclusion. The Rules Committee, as you know, is officially closed down for the year and it is going to take some action on my part and some support from the committee to get the Rules Committee to act. Then the full House will have to act on it.

Mr. JOHNSON.   If the Kasten substitute resolution, which states that the Secretary of State is directed to provide to the Select Committee the items specified in the schedule, were adopted on the floor of the House, and the documents were still not forthcoming, then we would have to go back through the contempt route.

Chairman PIKE.   We would have to go back through the contempt citation procedure — to the Rules Committee and then to the full House, and that is why we would just run out of time. . . .

Mr. JOHNSON.   Now, I would like to direct a question to counsel. I am concerned that in the event this matter does come up under the Dellums resolution and the House does take action on it, the U.S. attorney would enforce the contempt citation. What defenses might be available to the Secretary, other than the doctrine of executive privilege? In other words, is it clear that we have followed all of the legal requirements? Have we directed the subpoena to the proper person; is what we are after clearly identifiable? There won't be any means for the court to avoid the issue as a result of our not having done our legal homework on procedure, will there be?

Mr. DONNER.   I will always, Mr. Johnson, give credit to some clever lawyer someplace who might construct some argument. But as far as the preliminary procedural aspects for this committee go, they are to first of all authorize issuance of the subpoena. The subpoena itself demands production of fairly — in my opinion — identifiable documents and is specifically directed to a party who has not denied custody of these documents, and who has not indicated he did not have the documents to give to this committee.

To answer your question and develop it a little bit further, under the procedure, the contempt citation would then go to the U.S. attorney. There is a special statute — title 2, section 192 — which authorizes the U.S. attorney to bring proceedings for contempt of Congress, or failure to obey congressional subpoenas. At this point, the U.S. attorney would present it to a grand jury. Now, as to procedure, executive privilege could be raised at that time, either by motion or as a defense to an action. Presumptively, as I say, giving credit to imaginative attorneys, I am sure they would avail themselves of all the standard defenses to a subpoena.

Mr. JOHNSON.   Given a situation where the original documents were not in the hands of the Secretary but were someplace else, and only the Secretary had copies, would that be a defense to the subpoena?

Mr. DONNER.   No, sir. It may be urged by someone, but I would say that would be a rather fraudulent or facetious reply to a genuine request;

and if someone has possession of the documents, the subpoena charges them with the duty to deliver that material.

Mr. JOHNSON.   Mr. Chairman, under these circumstances, I intend to vote against the Kasten resolution and for the Dellums resolution. . . .

Chairman PIKE.   The question is on the substitute offered by Mr. Kasten and the clerk will call the roll. . . .

By a vote of two ayes, nine nays and one present, the substitute is not agreed to.

The question is on the resolution offered by Mr. Dellums and the clerk will call the roll. . . .

By a vote of 10 ayes and 2 nays, the resolution is agreed to.

U.S. Intelligence Agencies and Activities:
Committee Proceedings
Thursday, November 20, 1975
House of Representatives
Select Committee on Intelligence
Washington, D.C.

The committee met, pursuant to notice, at 10 A.M., in room 2118, Rayburn House Office Building, the Honorable Otis G. Pike [chairman], presiding.

Present: Representatives Pike, Giaimo, Stanton, Dellums, Murphy, Aspin, Milford, Hayes, Lehman, McClory, Treen, Johnson, and Kasten.

Also present: A. Searle Field, staff director; Aaron B. Donner, general counsel; and Jack Boos, counsel.

Chairman PIKE.   The committee will come to order.

Our first order of business will be to vote on a report, a draft of which has been prepared by our staff and copies of which have been made available to all of the members.

The chairman and all the members of the committee have received copies of a letter from the President of the United States. In view of the fact that it is four pages long and all the members have received it, I will not read it at this time. It will, however, be made available to the members of the press.

The essence of the letter — I shouldn't say the essence of the letter; I am not going to try to characterize the letter. The letter contains a request that members of the executive branch be permitted to argue in public before us this morning that which was argued in private with many of our members far into the night last night. I have no objection to their doing so.

[The letter from President Ford, dated November 19, 1975, is printed beginning on page 174.]

Mr. Leppert, it is my understanding that you are sort of managing your team. I have no idea who is supposed to appear for the executive branch, but the President has requested that witnesses be allowed to appear from the executive branch. Would whomever it is step forward and introduce themselves.

*Statement of Antonin Scalia, Assistant Attorney General, Office of
Legal Counsel, Accompanied by Monroe Leigh, Legal Adviser,
Department of State; Mrs. Jeanne Davis, Staff Secretary, NSC;
William Funk, Staff Attorney, Office of Legal Counsel; and
Daniel Christman, NSC Staff Member*

Mr. SCALIA. My name is Antonin Scalia. I am Assistant Attorney
General, Office of Legal Counsel. . . .

Mr. Chairman, I appreciate your permitting me to appear, at the President's request, to urge your reconsideration of the contempt resolutions
voted by this committee on November 14.

Chairman PIKE. That is your pitch — that we reconsider the contempt
citations; is that it?

Mr. SCALIA. Yes, sir; that is our request.

Chairman PIKE. Okay; all right.

Mr. SCALIA. We believe reconsideration is warranted because —

Chairman PIKE. Do you have a prepared statement, sir, and if so, could
we have a copy of it?

Mr. SCALIA. I do not have a prepared statement in a form that could be
copied, sir.

Chairman PIKE. I am sorry.

Mr. SCALIA. This meeting was set up rather quickly, as you know, and
I will be happy to have it typed in more presentable form and distribute it to
the committee afterward.

Chairman PIKE. I am sorry; I thought you were reading. Go ahead.

Mr. SCALIA. We believe, Mr. Chairman, that reconsideration is warranted because the action the committee took was based upon several misunderstandings which should not form the basis of action as serious as this.

Although I intend to make the only formal presentation, these other
ladies and gentlemen I have with me, who represent the various agencies
involved in this matter, may assist in responding to your questions. . . .

Chairman PIKE. Let's go ahead with the one on which executive
privilege by Presidents living and dead has been asserted.

Mr. SCALIA. Chairman, that subpoena as to which executive privilege
has been asserted was addressed to Henry A. Kissinger, Secretary of State,
and it was accepted on his behalf. If one were to attempt a description of
documents which would have the highest possible claim to an assertion of
executive privilege, one could only with difficulty surpass the description
contained in the subpoena. It asks for recommendations made to one of the
closest circles of Presidential advisers — namely, the National Security
Council and the 40 Committee, or its predecessors — on matters of the
most sensitive nature relating to foreign and military affairs — namely,
covert action. . . .

Not surprisingly, all of the documents originally identified as responsive
to this subpoena were found by the State Department to warrant

consideration for the assertion of executive privilege. On November 10 —
the day before the return date — the Department informed your staff director by telephone and later the same day by letter that, as they were being
identified, these materials were being brought to the attention of the appropriate office in the White House and that "the final decision on their release
to the committee will have to be taken in the White House."

On November 13, the day before your committee took its action on this
resolution, Mr. Buchen, Counsel to the President, wrote Chairman Pike
advising him that the documents were being reviewed "prior to a decision
by the President, concerning whether or not they should be made available
to the committee." . . .

Chairman PIKE.   We are familiar with all of these facts.

Mr. SCALIA.   I think the facts are important, Mr. Chairman.

Chairman PIKE.   We are familiar with the facts. All you are doing is
using up our time. We know the facts. Why don't you get to your legal
position? We have been trying to see what it is for months.

Mr. SCALIA.   I am saying categorically it won't include the entire minutes of every meeting that approved any single covert action project. That
was not my understanding of what the subpoena asked for. Nor was it
Mr. Field's. We cannot possibly deal with the committee if the understandings keep changing. I think the subpoena on its face is clear on this point,
and I think Mr. Field's description of it is clear.

Chairman PIKE.   I agree with you. We cannot deal with each other if the
understandings keep changing. You come in here this morning with a
brand new proposal and a brand new recommendation and we keep finding that the understandings do keep changing.

Mr. DELLUMS.   I think the Chair has a very good point. We know that
certain covert action programs are recommended by the CIA. We also
know that some projects are recommended by the State Department.
They come through different channels. All right. Then they come to the
40 Committee. The point that the Chair is making is, if we ask for all the
minutes approving covert operations by the 40 Committee, would that not
also then include the CIA-initiated projects as well as the State Department-
initiated projects? If that is correct, then it would seem to me that those
minutes would reflect "initiated by CIA," or "initiated by State."

Mr. Funk shakes his head no. Does that mean a project comes to the 40
Committee and the minutes don't indicate who initiated it? It is just a
project floated up from some place? That doesn't make sense to me and
you can't make me believe that.

If the project reflects that it was initiated by the CIA, or the project
indicates it was initiated by the State Department, would we not then
have access to that same information if you complied with the 40 Committee subpoena? On the one hand you are saying that on the subpoena
regarding the eight or more projects initiated by the State Department,
you invoke executive privilege; but you will give us access to the

40 Committee minutes, which any reasonable person would assume would also include the minutes approving projects initiated by the State Department.

Mr. SCALIA.   I understand your point, Mr. Dellums. What is wrong about it is we have already provided you, as I understand, the information about what projects were initiated by whom. What the subpoena to which executive privilege has been asserted would provide you is not just where it is initiated, but the particular individual who initiated it, his arguments pro and con, his advice to the President, his recommendations to the President, the alternatives he proposes — the very innermost portion of the consultative process within the executive branch.

Mr. DELLUMS.   Wouldn't that be discussed in the 40 Committee proceedings? Would not those matters be factors taken into consideration in making a determination as to whether there is efficacy in the approval or disapproval of a project?

Mr. SCALIA.   Yes, sir; but that discussion would not come within the portion of the minutes that could properly be described as committee "records of decisions taken since January 20, 1965, reflecting approvals."

Mr. DELLUMS.   Mr. Chairman, I have great difficulty following this. If these factors are included in the decision, but are excluded from the minutes, how do you justify that?

Chairman PIKE.   Mr. Dellums, you are supposed to have great difficulty in following it.

Mr. McCLORY.   Would the gentleman yield to me?

Chairman PIKE.   Mr. McClory.

Mr. McCLORY.   The point is, Mr. Chairman, what we are trying to find out is whether or not all covert activities are authorized and approved by the 40 Committee. The information with regard to State Department recommendations would disclose whether the State Department recommendations did go through the 40 Committee, or did not go through the 40 Committee. If they did, we would have a duplication of information; but if there is a discrepancy, then that would be of interest to us.

I think one of the important things for us to determine is whether covert activities — which may cost lots of money and may involve lots of risks — are carried out in a systematic, regular, orderly way, as contemplated by the legislation and by executive direction; or whether there is instead a kind of irregularity that is followed and, if there is, we ought to report on that and we ought to see to it that in the future there is no such irregularity.

Mr. SCALIA.   Mr. McClory, I think there is a real misunderstanding on this. The subpoena we are talking about now does not simply ask what covert action did the State Department initiate. It asks for all documents reflecting State Department initiations.

Mr. McCLORY.   Recommendations.

Mr. SCALIA.   Right. Recommendations. They are the lengthy documents containing discussions by Ambassadors and members of the

40 Committee concerning their thinking process, and their recommendations to the President. That goes much beyond whether it originated with the State Department. If you want to know that, we can provide that.

Chairman PIKE.   We keep referring to recommendations to the President, and I know that this is done intentionally; but the subpoena asked for recommendations to the National Security Council. It did not mention recommendations to the President.

The words "recommendation to the President" were nowhere in the subpoena. The language was "recommending covert action made to the National Security Council," which is what the statute requires. I know why you keep referring to recommendations to the President: You have to do that in order to bring it into the scope of executive privilege.

Mr. SCALIA.   I don't think that is right at all, Mr. Chairman.

Mr. McCLORY.   We want to determine whether or not covert operations do in all instances go through the 40 Committee or whether some are carried out on the recommendation of the State Department, without the 40 Committee actually meeting and providing its formal approval. That is the question, and we need a lot of information to come to a conclusion on it. . . .

Mr. SCALIA.   I would like to discuss some of the legal issues involved. I don't want to get into a full-blown discussion of the doctrine of executive privilege — the right to withhold certain documents from congressional inquiry that has been asserted by Presidents since George Washington and acknowledged in a recent case by the Supreme Court. It has most frequently been exercised with respect to military or foreign affairs secrets and with respect to confidential advice to the President or his closest advisers. Obviously, all of these elements are combined in the present case. In my view, there is no question that the subject matter is appropriate for an assertion of executive privilege, and this was the advice given to the President by the Attorney General. I understand that some members of the committee entertain doubts concerning the availability of a claim of executive privilege in the present case, because the documents in question were not addressed by the present President or his advisers, but rather to the President and advisers of earlier administrations. I confess, Mr. Chairman, that this is an entirely new asserted limitation upon the doctrine which I have never heard before, although I have done some considerable study in the field.

On its face, of course, it does not make much sense. Why does a fact which is a sensitive military or foreign affairs secret on January 19 suddenly become nonsecret on January 20, when a new President is sworn in? It makes no sense whatever to say that his predecessor could protect it from congressional inquiry but he cannot. Similarly, with that aspect of executive privilege which protects confidential advice giving. The purpose of this protection is to enable advice giving to be frank and forthright. It is hardly conducive to these values to maintain that advice can be protected only up to the date when a particular President leaves office, and that once he is gone the most unguarded statements of his advisers cannot be protected.

A look at the historic record discloses what one would expect: that no such limitation upon the privilege has been observed. The following instances should suffice. In 1846 President Polk refused a request of the House of Representatives to furnish it "an account of all payments made on the President's certificates ... from the 4th day of March 1841, until the retirement of Daniel Webster from the Department of State," a period which included the Presidency of President Harrison and a part of the Presidency of President Tyler. During the investigation of the attack on Pearl Harbor by a joint congressional committee in 1945, President Truman reserved the right to claim privilege in certain areas, and the committee's minority report indicates that there were some limitations on the access to information. Of course, President Truman was not President at the time of the attack on Pearl Harbor. During the investigation by the Senate Committee on Armed Services of the Military, Cold War Education and Speech Review Policies, which covered practices during the Eisenhower and Kennedy administrations, President Kennedy prohibited the disclosure of information not limited to acts which had occurred during his own tenure.

I understand that another reservation concerning the availability of executive privilege in this case, voiced by some members of the committee, pertains to a supposed requirement that the privilege must not only be asserted by the President, but must be communicated by him directly to the committee involved. This is again a limitation I confess I have never heard of. It would indeed seem strange that although the Congress may delegate not merely the communication of a demand, but even the assertion of a demand to one of its committees; and although that committee may serve the demand upon one of the President's subordinates, rather than upon the President himself, nevertheless the President must both personally decide upon the response of privilege and must personally convey it to the requesting committee.

There is again nothing in the historical record which would support such a requirement. The normal form of a claim of privilege is a letter from the President instructing a department head not to disclose certain information, with communication of the prohibition to the congressional committee involved, which is what happened here. For example, President Eisenhower's claim of privilege during the Army-McCarthy investigation took the form of a letter to the Secretary of Defense, not to the McCarthy committee. During the Senate investigation of Military Cold War Education and Speech Review Policies, President Kennedy's claim of privilege took the form of letters addressed to the Secretaries of Defense and State. There have been, of course, instances where Presidents have communicated directly with committees, especially where requests were directly addressed to the President. The examples set forth above, however, indicate that this procedure is not a requirement. Finally, I may note that the assertion of executive privilege against the judicial branch — which is another facet of the same doctrine — has been sanctioned by the Supreme Court when made by Cabinet secretaries without even evidence of specific Presidential consideration of the particular assertion, much less direct Presidential communication.

The simplicity of the executive privilege issue in the present case is marred by the fact that the final assertion was not made to the committee until the day of — probably after the hour of — the original contempt vote. In the present circumstances, however, I think this is inconsequential. Surely the Presidential power to assert the privilege carries with it the Presidential ability to take a reasonable period of time to consider its assertion. The 4 days — 2 business days — accorded to find the documents, identify the privileged material, obtain expert advice concerning the privilege and, as the President desired, to devote the President's own attention to the matter, was on its face insufficient. And the record shows the refusal of this committee to provide a reasonable period of grace.

In my view it is clear that the assertion in the present instance was both timely and proper. Even if it should be assumed, moreover, that the assertion of the privilege was improper, there still remains the issue of whether Secretary Kissinger could properly be held to be contumacious of the Congress for having obeyed the President's instruction on the matter. At least where the claim of privilege is colorable, I think that highly unlikely. The Secretary, after all, is a subordinate of the President, and must be permitted to follow apparently lawful instructions unless the executive branch is to become a house divided.

Indeed, it may be of questionable constitutionality to subject an executive branch officer in a manner such as this to the unavoidable risk of criminal liability for obeying an apparently lawful directive of the President.

I wish to make one final point, Mr. Chairman, which is in a sense quite technical and yet at bottom reflects basic considerations of fairness. I have been seeking this morning to induce this committee to reconsider an action it has already taken — a task which, as any lawyer knows, is an uphill struggle. It is to my knowledge the invariable practice of congressional committees, and indeed a practice that may be required by due process, to provide an opportunity to explain and to make a final categorical refusal before a citation of contempt is voted. This privilege was not accorded in the present case. I believe that if the executive branch had the opportunity before your action was initially taken to provide the explanation for apparent noncompliance, and the reasons for the areas of genuine noncompliance, which existed in the present case, you might have been disposed to reach a different result. Since we did not have that opportunity, I hope you will not merely reconsider the matter, but will consider it anew, without the inertia that a decision, once taken, normally provides.

In the one area covered by the State Department subpoena, I hope the committee will see that the spirit of mutual accommodation, which must enliven our system of Government, counsels this committee not to press for the production of material so close to the heart of the executive process—just as in many other areas during this inquiry (the SALT subpoena being one of them) the President has declined to make any assertion of executive privilege, though it might well have been available. As to the other areas covered by these three subpoenas, we have, I believe, made entire compliance with respect to the SALT documents and are willing to discuss reasonable alternatives with respect to the 40 Committee subpoena. I am confident these matters can be worked out. I believe that the actions which the executive branch officials have taken up until this time have not been meant to be contumacious of the role or the functions of this committee, and I am hopeful that you will see that it would harm rather than benefit the Nation to proceed with the present resolution.

Chairman PIKE.   Mr. Dellums.

Mr. DELLUMS.   I have two questions: Could we agree that where we are talking about abuse, wrongdoing or illegal acts, you should not exert executive privilege so as to hide any acts that would fall in the category of abuse of Government power, wrongdoing or illegal acts?

Mr. SCALIA.   I think President Ford has said he would not assert executive privilege to hide any wrongdoing, and that is one of the reasons we have not asserted it with respect to SALT. The committee expressed the view it was seeking to look into possible wrongdoing, so we have not chosen to assert it.

Mr. DELLUMS.   My follow-on questions are these: Suppose the committee has information in its possession, as a result of investigations and testimony, regarding certain covert operations initiated by the State Department which called into question their legality by virtue of the fact that they may not have been conducted within the prescribed manner laid down by certain laws. This committee would then be asserting either an abuse of power, wrongdoing, or outright illegal acts. How do you then assert executive privilege where we, on the one hand, are looking at the potential or the possibility of wrongdoing? Because, as Mr. McClory said, for example, we are looking at the question of whether certain covert operations were approved outside of the manner prescribed by law in the document that gave rise to the intelligence agencies. I haven't the document before me but it says "from time to time" certain projects shall be approved.

We feel some projects may very well have been approved outside of that legal mechanism. So if we are asserting wrongdoing, how can you, on the other hand, assert executive privilege when the President is saying; "I will not assert executive privilege to hide wrongdoing"?

Mr. SCALIA.   Mr. Congressman, I don't really see how this particular subpoena ties in with that. All this will get you is the State Department's recommendations. It won't show you what was approved and what wasn't approved.

Mr. DELLUMS.   We can check that when we get the information regarding the 40 Committee, so we do have a follow-up procedure.

Mr. SCALIA.   It is my understanding you already know what actions were proposed, and by what agency. If it is just a matter of knowing whether a particular action originated in one place or another, you don't need the full recommendation memorandum from an ambassador to the committee, or to the President in order to obtain that.

Mr. DELLUMS.   Let's use a hypothetical situation, where covert actions could possibly and conceivably have been approved outside the 40 Committee — with the involvement of an ambassador, of the Secretary of State, of the President, but not of the 40 Committee, as prescribed by law. Now, we would perceive that as wrongdoing or illegal acts or abuse of power. How can you then assert executive privilege to put a cloak over the necessary documentation we need to determine whether or not you have in fact engaged in wrongdoing, illegal acts, or abuse of Government powers? You know, we have documentation of information that certain projects have been approved outside of the 40 Committee process, and there we are alleging illegal action and impropriety.

Mr. SCALIA.   I don't see how this subpoena gets you anything like that. All this shows is what the Department — the State Department — recommended to the 40 Committee.

Mr. DELLUMS.   It will give us the thinking process; it will give us the information that led to a covert operation being approved and funded, using government moneys to carry out certain acts in certain places in the world —

Mr. SCALIA.   Through the 40 Committee. You have only requested those recommendations from the State Department to the 40 Committee or the NSC. I don't see how that can show you projects that didn't go through the 40 Committee or the NSC. That is why we don't see the connection with any seeking after wrongdoing in the case of this subpoena.

Mr. DELLUMS.   We would like to know how the projects got started and what the rationale for the process is. We have testimony on certain projects that at best are dubious and are at worst outright illegal, a sham, and a tragedy.

Mr. SCALIA.   Stupidity is still not unlawful.

Mr. DELLUMS.   We have a right to look at that blatant stupidity in the use of funds, in the involvement of activity in other countries —

Chairman PIKE.   Mr. Dellums, I am just going to caution you that this is an open session, and I think maybe you have gone as far as you ought to go on this particular point.

Mr. DELLUMS.   I appreciate that. I have been walking very delicately.

Chairman PIKE.   I know you have. Draw back.

Mr. DELLUMS.   My final question: Was executive privilege asserted after the fact? In other words, are you asserting executive privilege—in all candor—to cover the Secretary, or is the assertion of executive privilege being taken very seriously—in terms of this information being so sensitive that this committee cannot have access to it?

Mr. SCALIA.   No, sir, Mr. Dellums. I was asked earlier—I think Mr. Giaimo asked me—whether I was involved at all in these things, and I said there are only relatively narrow aspects of it I have been involved in. The assertion or nonassertion of executive privilege has been one area.

I can state of my own knowledge that by the time compliance with this subpoena was required, there was under active consideration the issue of whether it was proper to assert executive privilege. It isn't an afterthought; it is just as Mr. Buchen's letter to the committee reflected; it is that the executive branch wanted time to be able to make an intelligent decision—a decision that I am sure you gentlemen do not want the President to take lightly—about whether or not to assert executive privilege. It was in no way an afterthought, and the truth is that we needed more time to decide because the President was not about to jump to an unreasonable assertion of executive privilege.

I thought it was in the Congress' interest as well as the President's to have this time. He was not provided it. . . .

Mr. JOHNSON.   Mr. Scalia, you have raised the doctrine of executive privilege to a new and exalted level. I think you understand that. There is no legal basis, no court decision, on which to raise this kind of claim.

I find that totally unacceptable as an American citizen—not just as a Member of Congress, but as an American citizen. The idea that a President can, in effect, have censorship power over everything that occurred back to the time of George Washington is to be totally unacceptable.

If we as a committee accept that, and you continue to assert the privilege, you haven't offered us any means of resolving it or litigating it, outside of the contempt process. If you would make any kind of an offer as to a means of getting this settled in the courts—but I can't find this is an acceptable procedure, or acceptable claim—if you will offer us some means of doing this outside of the contempt process, I would personally be glad to consider it. But I am not willing to let it drop at this point and say, "OK, the doctrine of executive privilege, as you claim it, applies."

We are talking about the one directed to Dr. Kissinger as Secretary of State.

Mr. SCALIA.   Mr. Johnson, you know in 200 years—the reason I can't cite a decision is not because the doctrine hasn't been used, but because it has been used intelligently. There is good reason why the matter hasn't been decided by the courts. It hasn't gotten to the courts because the two other branches of Government have been farsighted enough to work it out between them.

There is another reason it hasn't come to the courts, and that is because the courts are not the place to decide it. It is not a rigid doctrine — so that you can exercise executive privilege as to this and you cannot as to the other. It depends on many variables, and variables not justiciable by a court. For example, some of the broadest assertions of executive privilege in history were made with respect to the McCarthy hearings, when the President just forbade any employee of the Department of Defense to appear. In ordinary circumstances, I would say that is not an appropriate manner of exercising executive privilege. In that circumstance, I think it was all right. But I don't know how a court could write an opinion to that effect and say, "Well, we think it is all right because we think this is a witch hunt and we don't like Joseph McCarthy."

Contrariwise, there were some assertions of executive privilege by President Nixon which were so narrow that one would normally say "that is a reasonable assertion of executive privilege." But in the context of those years, which we all recall, and the cloud of suspicion and distrust, it was not reasonable. Now, could a court have taken that case and said, "Well, normally this would be OK, but we don't trust President Nixon so we are not going to allow the assertion of the privilege?" Gentlemen, these issues are not issues for the courts. That is one of the reasons they have not gotten there. They should never get there. I do not apologize for not providing you an easy way to get them there.

Mr. JOHNSON.   You have raised the doctrine of executive privilege with respect to State Department documents sent to the National Security Council, which were not personal, which were not just little private memoranda, which do not take place in the context of a discussion at the Cabinet level. You are talking about American documents — American State papers over which a President says, "I can assert the doctrine of executive privilege all the way back."

That is an untenable claim as far as I personally am concerned. I don't know what the rest of the Members of Congress think. Your explanation to me is totally unacceptable as a legal, historical, constitutional principle. . . .

Mr. SCALIA.   Congressman, I think you have the argument inverted here. I am not asserting that executive privilege can properly be asserted all the way back. I find it very difficult to conceive of any —

Mr. JOHNSON.   How do you differentiate if the claim is allowed to stand?

Mr. SCALIA.   It is rather how you are asserting it cannot be exercised even one President back. So, even when you are dealing with an inquiry into — well, the one I mentioned in my testimony, about the censoring of military speeches: Although this was a process that had gone on, overlapping the administrations of Eisenhower and Kennedy, you would say that President Kennedy could assert the privilege with respect to documents dating from the time he took office and not before. That doesn't make any sense. If you are trying to protect the confidentiality of the process, he should be able to go back one President. I think sometimes you can go back two Presidents—but not to George Washington, sir.

Mr. JOHNSON.   We are not talking about a declassification system. We are not talking about making this public.

Mr. SCALIA.   I understand that.

Mr. JOHNSON.   We are talking about the right of the Congress to have access to documents.

Mr. SCALIA.   Yes, sir.

Mr. JOHNSON.   You say that the President is asserting that doctrine.

Mr. SCALIA.   And the right of the Congress to make it public if it chooses.

Mr. JOHNSON.   Oh, no. No, sir; that is not really a question. That has not been asserted before, and that isn't anything that is being considered by this committee, because those documents have a certain classification, I assume. That classification system will be honored by this committee. We are not talking about making them public. We are talking about our right to have them and your right to withhold them.

Mr. SCALIA.   I am not talking about your committee now and I am not talking about this context now. We were talking about executive privilege in general. I do not know that executive privilege in general only applies to providing documents to the Congress when there is no commitment by the Congress not to make them public. That is just not the doctrine we are talking about. In fact, the Congress usually asserts they don't have to make any commitments.

Mr. JOHNSON.   We are at an impasse with regard to that third subpoena so far as I am concerned.

Chairman PIKE.   Mr. Hayes.

Mr. HAYES.   Mr. Scalia, I think perhaps there are some other misunderstandings that you may have. You mentioned quite a bit earlier that we needed to have presented to us, in a fundamentally fair way, the counter-argument on what we were about to do. Your understanding was that we were about to cite the Secretary of State for contempt for the first time in history.

As the chairman has pointed out, we have already done that. We have before us draft reports. I want to compliment you because I think you have done an excellent job in presenting a good deal of new and fresh information. The chairman said, and I too believe, we have progressed quite a way. But we are rapidly running out of time, Mr. Chairman and members of the committee, and I believe we should act at this point on the draft reports before us. We would have sufficient time then to continue to consider not only Mr. Scalia's presentation today, but that further information which I am sure he will be able to furnish to us for our consideration, and that which Mr. Leigh undoubtedly has for us.

It is important, I believe, to move ahead with this process. We have a recess coming on. We have additional views both in agreement and in disagreement — and perhaps neutral — in regard to the action we are about to take.

Mr. Chairman, I would like to at this time move that we consider the —

Mr. Aspin, did you have a statement?

Chairman PIKE. Mr. Aspin is recognized.

Mr. ASPIN.   Just a couple of questions before we adjourn the meeting and finish.

You say, Mr. Scalia, that each executive privilege case must be decided on its merits. You cited several cases.

I agree with you; that is right. Given the facts about that, and given special consideration of the fact that this committee has agreed not to release information without the approval of the President, should that not have been a factor in deciding whether executive privilege was to be asserted in this case?

Mr. SCALIA.   Yes, sir. I think it should have been and it was. That is why long consideration was given and it is why, with respect to some information — to wit, the SALT information — we have agreed to provide it. But without meaning any disrespect of the committee, there is nonetheless some information which we believe should not be disclosed. With respect to the information in this subpoena, moreover, what is involved is not merely the fear that the information will become public. There is a point of principle at issue in the Congress — even if it does not distribute the information anywhere else — the Congress, itself, prying into the most internal deliberative processes of the executive branch. We like it no more than you would the executive being able to sit in on your staff meetings.

Mr. ASPIN.   Could you outline, in maybe a sentence or a paragraph or two, just exactly on what grounds you are asserting executive privilege in this case?

Mr. SCALIA.   Of course, it is the President's assertion and not mine. This case involves all three of the classic elements which underlie the majority of assertions of executive privilege. There are military secrets involved in some of these covert operations; there are foreign affairs secrets involved in virtually all of them; and there is the most confidential Presidential advice giving and consultation involved in all of the documents you have requested. You have specifically requested the recommendation of the Department of State to one of the closest advisory committees to the President. Those are the three.

Mr. ASPIN.   I just wanted to get on the record exactly what it was.

You see no way in which the executive can provide any kind of information on that document, or on that subpoena, at all — going back to what Mr. Johnson was saying — or to try to find some way to provide some information, without violating your concern about executive privilege.

Mr. SCALIA.   To the contrary, I think I said it was my belief that we have already told you what covert actions the State Department recommended — just which actions they were. I believe that is correct. If it is not correct, I will check on it.

Mr. ASPIN.   In what form were we told about it?

Mr. SCALIA.   It is on the list of the 40 Committee subpoena returns that you have. There is indicated in the margin the initiating agency with respect to each of those covert action approvals.

Chairman PIKE.   What we have, you are saying, is the State Department's recommending of a deleted action in a deleted country; and you are using this to say that you have told us what the State Department recommended?

Mr. SCALIA.   No sir, I have apologized for those deletions and told you we would remedy them.

Chairman PIKE.   I just wanted the record to be clear that we haven't got the slightest idea what the State Department recommended.

Mr. SCALIA.   I think in some of the cases you do by reason of other documents, but your point is substantially correct, I think, Mr. Chairman. But that is not our intent; we are willing to let you know that.

Mr. ASPIN.   It is your contention that once we have worked out the 40 Committee subpoena — the problems with compliance with the 40 Committee subpoena — at that point we will then have the essential information which would satisfy what we need to know under the subpoena to the Secretary of State?

Mr. SCALIA.   I have to make one reservation.

I didn't plan it this way, but it works this way: The 40 Committee subpoena only asks for approvals, and this present subpoena asks for State Department recommendations, whether they were approved or not approved by the 40 Committee. There would be a gap there. I am not sure we wouldn't be willing voluntarily to make up that gap. We might well. But you wouldn't get everything from the 40 Committee subpoena alone.

Mr. ASPIN.   To follow up, maybe there is something here.

It is hard to say in the abstract, without looking at — and I want to look at — what is being offered to comply with the 40 Committee subpoena; but if we have that information and supplement it with perhaps a similar kind of information about State Department recommendations which were disapproved, that would perhaps satisfy our needs and at the same time would not violate your concerns about executive privilege.

Mr. SCALIA.   I believe that is right, sir.

Mr. ASPIN.   Let me say I think it is important that we make some kind of an effort to comply with that; to get what information we were looking for in that particular subpoena.

Let me say secondly that I think that our chances of working out a substantive resolution of the other two issues — the SALT and the 40 Committee subpoenas — are probably better than our chances of working out the procedural questions of who is to be cited if that subpoena is not complied with.

That is just my observation from having listened to the discussion. It seems to me we have a better chance of reaching agreement on the substance than we have on the procedure, because I don't know whom we cite if we don't cite Mr. Kissinger.

I yield back the time.

Chairman PIKE.   The Chair recognizes Mr. Lehman.

Mr. LEHMAN.   Thank you, Mr. Chairman.

I just want to go back over this 40 Committee subpoena to be sure I understand what you are recommending for compliance. I understand your anxiety about the papers coming away from where you keep them, although I think you have no need to feel that kind of anxiety. But what you are saying now is that only Mr. Ratliff — Rob Roy Ratliff — has access to these documents. Only he of the staff of the 40 Committee?

Mr. SCALIA.   Yes, sir, that is my understanding.

Mr. LEHMAN.   Do you know whether he takes other appropriate staff in with him?

Mr. SCALIA.   My understanding is that he is the only one with access. That is one of the reasons we had trouble with compliance with the subpoena. He is the only one who can work on them.

Mr. LEHMAN.   If he can't come up here, but I can go down there, will I have the same privilege as a member of this committee, that Rob Roy Ratliff now has?

Mr. SCALIA.   Yes, sir, with respect to those portions of those documents the subpoena covers.

Mr. LEHMAN.   Will I have information available to me in those documents relating to the money involved, the countries involved, although not the particular person who may be endangered by that information?

Mr. SCALIA.   Yes, sir.

Mr. LEHMAN.   I will have access to all but the person's individual name.

Mr. SCALIA.   I didn't place that limitation on it, but if you offer it, I will take it.

Mr. LEHMAN.   I am trying to find out the difference between me as a member of the committee and Mr. Ratliff. I want to know what privilege he has that I won't have as a member of this committee.

Mr. SCALIA.   He will have the privilege to look at those portions of the documents that have nothing to do with decisions approving covert action.

Chairman PIKE.   We simply have to take your word for it as to what has been deleted from the documents.

Mr. SCALIA.   No, sir; I think we could work out a verification procedure somehow, too, in the spirit of SALT.

Chairman PIKE.   I will tell you, as a result of a private conversation I had out in the other room with one of the gentlemen at your table, I am not sure we are going to get all the documents on SALT either.

Mr. LEHMAN.   I am trying to find out what the hell "compliance" is.

Hegel said one thing we learn from history is that governments don't learn a damned thing from history. We are part of the Government and if we can't learn anything from history we are going to make the same mistakes. That is what I am trying to get to.

As a member of this committee, I want the members to have the same rights and privileges that Mr. Rob Roy Ratliff has. If they want to keep the name of the individual assigned secret, I am willing to accept that. Other than that, I think we are entitled to the information. We need this in order to have what I think is substantial compliance, and I will be willing to go down to your office to get it if you think you shouldn't send it to me.

I don't stand on that kind of ceremony. If you want something badly enough, you will go where it is. I yield back the balance of my time. . . .

Chairman PIKE.   Does anybody else seek recognition before Mr. Hayes makes his motion? Do you wish to make a motion, Mr. Hayes?

Mr. HAYES.   Mr. Chairman, I would like to move that the committee adopt the draft report of its action taken on November 14, 1975, in regard to the resolution on the contumacious behavior of Henry A. Kissinger as Secretary of State, certify the report to the Speaker of the House, and proceed in the manner and form prescribed by law.

Chairman PIKE.   Mr. Hayes, you are entitled to 5 minutes, if you want it, in support of your motion. Mr. Treen wants to speak in opposition, I presume, on the motion. Is that correct, Mr. Treen? I think we all understand the issues. Mr. Treen.

Mr. TREEN.   Thank you, Mr. Chairman. You are quite right. I think we do understand the issues. I didn't ask for this time to reargue all of the issues, but to state that I will vote against the report and I will vote Mr. McClory against the report by authority of the proxy he has left with me. The reason is that each of the reports contain the language recommending that the report be adopted by the full House — that is, the contempt citation be adopted by the full House.

Since we are opposed to that, we will vote against the reports and we will file our reasons in supplemental views to the report in accordance with the procedures of the committee.

Chairman PIKE.   Mr. Aspin.

Mr. ASPIN.   Mr. Chairman, just to clarify the record, what we are doing here is filing the report in connection with the citations that we voted last week.

Chairman PIKE.   That is correct.

Mr. ASPIN.   If we vote this report, it does not mean that if at some point, we work out something we cannot vote in favor of rescinding.

Chairman PIKE.   I would say more than that. The gentleman is absolutely correct. I would say that obviously, at any time we deem — and by "we" I mean the staff and our committee — there is substantial compliance with any of these three subpoenas, I want to assure the gentleman that I have no desire to take the issue to the floor on that basis.

By the same token, if we deem that there is not substantial compliance, I don't want to pretend to anybody that I don't have every intention of taking it to the floor.

Mr. ASPIN.   Thank you, Mr. Chairman, I just wanted to make sure that people understand.

The second point is, if we do vote for the report, that does not have any impact on whether we might want to file supplementary views or additional views.

Chairman PIKE.   I encourage all members to file dissenting, additional, supplemental, or any other views, and they will have until 1 week from tomorrow to get those views to the committee.

Mr. ASPIN.   Thank you, Mr. Chairman.

Mr. JOHNSON.   This motion, as I understand it, is just for the draft report with respect to the one subpoena to the Secretary of State.

Chairman PIKE.   That is correct. I think proper procedure would require that we have separate votes on each of these draft reports.

The clerk will call the roll. . . .

By a vote of 10 to 3, the draft report is agreed to. Do you wish to make another motion, Mr. Hayes?

Mr. HAYES.   Yes.

Mr. Chairman, I would make the same motion in regard to the draft report citing Henry A. Kissinger, which draft report is labeled "40 Committee."

Chairman PIKE.   We understand the motion, I think. Mr. Treen.

Mr. TREEN.   Mr. Chairman, I make the same remarks with regard to this motion. In the conclusion of the report there is a recommendation that the House of Representatives adopt the contempt resolution. Mr. McClory and I will vote against the report and file written reasons at a later time.

Chairman PIKE.   Mr. Kasten?

Mr. KASTEN.   Thank you, Mr. Chairman.

Mr. Chairman, on these two reports — the report of the 40 Committee and the report of the SALT compliance — I think that the committee this morning has received enough new evidence to make these reports no longer necessary or useful. We have been told by the President of the United States there is no basis — and I am quoting from his letter — "no basis for the resolutions addressed to Secretary Kissinger on these subpoenas." And through his answer to very detailed questions, I think the counsel before us has assured us that we simply have erred in the addressing of these subpoenas. I think the committee should not vote to adopt these reports. I think instead the committee should seek to amend the subpoenas so that they are addressed to the proper individual or individuals.

But, no matter what we do with the subpoenas, it seems to me the Secretary of State is no longer, or can be no longer, thought to be in contempt of Congress. That is the point that the President brought out in his letter. I think we should not adopt this report and that we should not adopt the report on the SALT agreement.

In no way do I believe the committee should not have the information; we ought to have the information. The subpoenas ought to be addressed properly. The staff and the people at the National Security Council and elsewhere ought to work to find the information that we need and make it available to the committee in the form that we want it. But I do not think that the Secretary of State is now in contempt of Congress or should be cited as being in contempt of Congress and that therefore these reports ought not to be adopted.

Mr. ASPIN. Briefly, in response to the point raised by the gentleman from Wisconsin, I think there is a lot to what he says. I think in part his remarks go to the citation rather than to the report. Second, I think we do have a question — if we have got the wrong man — about just exactly who the right man or woman is. I would think that the best procedure is to go ahead and vote for the report and see whether they comply with the subpoena. Then we don't have to worry about citing anyone.

Chairman PIKE. Mr. Johnson?

Mr. JOHNSON. Thank you, Mr. Chairman. The points raised by Mr. Kasten, I think are irrefutable. We are talking about a contempt citation. I have looked at this not as a matter of personalities of anybody involved, but as a legal matter. It is regrettable it wasn't pointed out to the committee at the time that Dr. Kissinger was not the assistant to the President; but as a matter of fact, that was not pointed out. Right now we are faced with a statement of the President of the United States saying Secretary Kissinger had no responsibility for responding to these subpoenas nor for supervising the response to them.

The only way it seems to me we can continue with the citation is to say that is an incorrect statement; that the President has in effect misled the committee. I will not accept that premise. I will accept the President's statement that Dr. Kissinger was not acting in that capacity at the time and therefore the contempt citation should not issue, and I intend to vote against the next two.

Chairman PIKE. The Chair would like to just express his own views on this subject. I would be inclined to accept the President's statement also, if he presented us with any alternative. We are told that Dr. Kissinger was not the proper person, he was not the Assistant to the President for National Security Affairs — there was no Assistant to the President for National Security Affairs. We are told that Mr. Ratliff is the only person who has access to all of these files, but no one has ever said that Mr. Ratliff is the person who has custody, in the sense of making the determination that these files will be made available to our committee.

We are told that General Scowcroft is not the Assistant to the President for National Security Affairs, and I believe that in the past there has been an opinion by the Justice Department to the effect that no person can serve in that capacity while he has a military commission.

I do not think that our acting on this resolution at this time is going to do anything but perhaps encourage that which has been held out to us this morning—that is, substantial compliance. I think we are being diverted from a procedure when the President said in his letter that the principal issue is that there will be substantial compliance, and I frankly would prefer to go the substantial compliance route. Mr. Milford.

Mr. MILFORD. Thank you, Mr. Chairman. I will be voting against the three reports before us today, and if it goes to the floor, against the resolution citing the Secretary of State for contempt. I do so not because I believe that the Congress does not have the right to this material. I feel clearly that the Congress does have a right to obtain this material. A no vote will be cast on the basis that while the Congress has a right to obtain it, it also has the responsibility for protecting this information and for preventing damage to the country that the release of the information would bring about. I contend that our present rules and mechanisms within the Congress are not such that we can responsibly protect this information whose release could be damaging to the country. For that reason, I will be voting against them and filing a dissenting view in the report.

Chairman PIKE. The clerk will call the roll. . . .

By a vote of eight ayes, five nays, the report is adopted. The draft report is adopted as the report of the committee.

Mr. HAYES. Mr. Chairman, I would like to move the committee adopt the draft report citing Henry A. Kissinger, which is labeled "SALT," in similar form to the previous motion. . . .

Chairman PIKE. The clerk will call the roll. . . .

By a vote of eight yeas and five nays, the draft report is adopted as the report of the committee. . . .

Mr. TREEN. A technical question, Mr. Chairman: Is it the intent to file three separate documents? Will we need to file separate dissenting views?

Chairman PIKE. That is a good question, and my opinion is that there will indeed be three separate reports; yes.

Mr. TREEN. Is it the intention to go to the Rules Committee for a rule?

Chairman PIKE. That is correct.

Mr. TREEN. If there is any change in the reports which have been adopted now, could we assume then that we would have additional time?

Chairman PIKE. There will be no changes in the reports which have been adopted now. I think it would be improper under our rules to change the reports which have been adopted.

Mr. TREEN. Thank you, Mr. Chairman.

Chairman PIKE. Let me say if there is a comma misplaced or a semicolon or something like that, it will be corrected.

The committee will stand in recess until after the recess, subject to the call of the Chair. . . .

Exchange of Letters between Chairman Pike and the Executive Branch

THE LEGAL ADVISER
Department of State
Washington, D.C.

November 14, 1975

The Honorable Otis G. Pike, Chairman
Select Committee on Intelligence
House of Representatives

Dear Mr. Chairman:

The Secretary of State has been instructed by the President respectfully to decline compliance with your subpoena to the Secretary of November 6, 1975, for the reason that it would be contrary to the public interest and incompatible with the sound functioning of the Executive branch to produce the documents requested.

The subpoena sought "all documents relating to State Department recommending covert action made to the National Security Council and the Forty Committee and its predecessor Committees from January 20, 1961, to present." The Committee staff has made clear that this is intended to cover recommendations originating with the State Department. An examination of our records has disclosed ten such documents, dating from the period 1962 through 1972. These consist of recommendations from officials in the State Department, sometimes the Secretary of State, to the Forty Committee or its predecessor, 303 Committee, or to the President himself in connection with consideration by one of those Committees.

The documents in question, in addition to disclosing highly sensitive military and foreign affairs assessments and evaluations, disclose the consultation process involving advice and recommendations of advisors to former Presidents, made to them directly or to Committees composed of their closest aides and counselors.

Therefore, I advise you that the Secretary of State is declining to comply with such subpoena on the basis of the President's assertion of Executive privilege.

Sincerely,

George H. Aldrich
Acting Legal Adviser
of the Department of State

THE WHITE HOUSE
Washington

November 19, 1975

Dear Mr. Chairman:

I want you to know of my deep concern because the Select Committee found it necessary on November 14 to vote in favor of three resolutions which could lead to a finding by the House of Representatives that Secretary of State Henry Kissinger is in contempt for failure to comply with three Committee subpoenas. This issue involves grave matters affecting our conduct of foreign policy and raises questions which go to the ability of our Republic to govern itself effectively. I know that you, Mr. Chairman, share my deep respect for the rights and powers of the House of Representatives — where our cumulative service spans nearly four decades — and for the obligations and responsibilities of the President. The two branches of government have an extremely serious responsibility to consider the issues raised in the ongoing foreign intelligence investigations dispassionately and with mutual respect.

Former Chief Justice Warren pointed out twenty years ago [in United States v. Watkins] that there can be no doubt as to the power of Congress and its committees to investigate fully matters relating to contemplated legislation. Without this power, which includes the authority to compel testimony and the production of documents, the Congress could not exercise its responsibilities under Article I of our Constitution. However, this power, as broad as it is, is subject to recognized limitations. Not only is it limited by powers given to the other two branches, but it also must respect requirements of procedural due process as they affect individuals.

The action of your Committee concerning the November 14th resolutions raises, in my mind, three principal issues: the extent to which the committee needs access to additional Executive Branch documents to carry out its legislative functions; the importance of maintaining the separation of powers between the branches and the ability of the Executive to function; and the individual rights of officials involved in this matter. I am not interested in recriminations and collateral issues which only serve to cloud the significant questions before us.

From the beginning of the investigations of the intelligence agencies, I have taken action to stop any possible abuses and to make certain that they do not recur as long as I am President. I have also endeavored to make available relevant information in a responsible manner to the appropriate committees of Congress. I have given great weight to my responsibility to maintain the integrity of our intelligence community and the ability of this Nation to develop and use foreign intelligence. This is one reason which I have insisted that much of the information I have made available to Congress be kept secret, so that current foreign intelligence operations, which are critical for the national security, can continue effectively. In accordance with those principles, your Committee and the Senate Select Committee have received unprecedented access to Executive Branch documents and information.

Your Committee's November 6th votes on seven subpoenas for additional Executive Branch documents came in the context of several months of working together on this very difficult subject and a record of cooperation on both sides. They were served on November 7. The documents were due on the morning of November 11, and the appropriate Administration officials immediately went to work completing the information. Four of the subpoenas were complied with fully. However, problems arose as to the remaining three issued to:

— "Henry A. Kissinger, Secretary of State, or any subordinate officer, official or employee with custody or control of . . . all documents relating to State Department recommending covert action made to the National Security Council and its predecessor committees from January 30, 1961 to present."

— "The Assistant to the President for National Security Affairs, or any subordinate officer, official or employee with custody or control of . . . all 40 Committee and predecessor Committee records of decisions taken since January 20, 1965 reflecting approvals of covert action projects. [Separate subpoena.] . . . All documents furnished by the Arms Control and Disarmament Agency's Standing Consultative Commission, and the Central Intelligence Agency, the National Security Agency, the Department of Defense, and the Intelligence Community staff, since May, 1972 relating to adherence to the provisions of the Strategic Arms Limitation Treaty of 1972 and the Vladivostok agreement of 1972."

These three subpoenas are the basis of the Committee resolutions of November 14.

The subpoena directed to the Secretary of State requests documents containing the recommendation of State Department officials to former Presidents concerning highly sensitive matters involving foreign intelligence activities of the United States. The appropriate State

Department officials identified and referred to the White House documents which apparently fall within the subpoena. None of these documents are from my Administration. These were carefully reviewed and, after I received the opinion of the Attorney General that these documents are of the type for which Executive privilege may appropriately be asserted, I directed Secretary Kissinger not to comply with the subpoena on the grounds of Executive privilege. I made a finding that, in addition to disclosing highly sensitive military and foreign affairs assessments and evaluations, the documents revealed to an unacceptable degree the consultation process involving advice and recommendations to Presidents Kennedy, Johnson and Nixon, made to them directly or to committees composed of their closest aides and counselors. Thus, in declining to comply with the subpoena, Secretary of State Kissinger was acting on my instructions as President of the United States.

With respect to the two subpoenas directed to ". . . the Assistant to the President for National Security Affairs, or any subordinate officer, official or employee with custody of control . . ." the really important point here is that the NSC staff has made a major effort to deliver the documents requested. As you know, additional documents were made available to the Committee after the deadline of the subpoenas and indeed after the Committee voted on the November 14th resolutions. There has been and continues to be an effort on the part of the NSC staff to provide the Committee with the information and documentation it needs. In fact, a very comprehensive volume of information has been made available which provides the Committee a substantial basis for its investigation.

This effort was undertaken, notwithstanding the fact that the subpoenas themselves were served on November 7, made returnable only four days later, and called for a broad class of documents, going back in one subpoena to 1965, and in the other to 1972. Substantial efforts were required to search files, identify items covered, and to review them for foreign policy and national security reasons in accordance with procedures which have been previously used with information requested by the Select Committee.

In addition to our efforts to substantially comply with these two subpoenas, I have been advised that there are serious and substantial legal and factual questions as to the basis on which the Committee seeks to find Secretary Kissinger to be in contempt. The subpoenas were directed to ". . . the Assistant to the President for National Security Affairs, or any subordinate officer . . ." and were in fact served on the Staff Secretary of the NSC. Secretary Kissinger had no responsibility for responding to these subpoenas nor for supervising the response to them. After November 3, he was no longer my Assistant for National Security Affairs, and he was neither named in the subpoenas nor were they served upon him. Thus there is no basis for the resolutions addressed to Secretary Kissinger on these subpoenas.

In summary, I believe that if the Committee were to reconsider the three resolutions of November 14, it would conclude that my claim of Executive privilege is a proper exercise of my Constitutional right and responsibility. As to the two subpoenas directed to the Assistant for National Security Affairs, they do not involve Secretary Kissinger, and there has been a substantial effort by the NSC staff to provide these documents. Furthermore, they will continue to work with you and your Committee to resolve any remaining problems.

It is my hope that the Select Committee will permit Executive Branch officials to appear at tomorrow's hearing to discuss the points I have raised in this letter.

It is my desire that we continue forward, working together on the foreign intelligence investigation. I believe that the national interest is best served through our cooperation and adoption of a spirit of mutual trust and respect.

Sincerely,

[Gerald R. Ford]

The Honorable Otis G. Pike
Chairman
House Select Committee on Intelligence
House of Representatives
Washington, D.C. 20515

Select Committee on Intelligence
U.S. House of Representatives
Washington, D.C. 20515

November 21, 1975

The President
White House
Washington, D.C.

Dear Mr. President:

I thank you for your letter of November 19 addressed to our Committee, and assure you that the issues as to which you voice concern are of equal concern to us.

As you are now aware, in compliance with your request, our Committee yesterday morning did allow representatives of the Executive branch to discuss the issues raised in your letter throughout our Committee meeting yesterday. While our Committee did thereafter act in such a manner as to keep our options practically viable I share with you the hope that the underlying issues may be resolved.

The additional material made available to the Committee night before last and today go a long way toward resolving our issues on two of the three subpoenas as to which there was concern. The NSC staff is now, as you state, making a real effort to provide the Committee with the information and documentation it needs.

As to the third subpoena on which executive privilege has been asserted, this is obviously the one on which you feel most strongly and it is also obviously the one on which the Committee feels most strongly, our report thereon having been approved yesterday by a bi-partisan 10-3 vote.

You have characterized that subpoena as requesting "documents containing the recommendation of State Department officials to former Presidents concerning highly sensitive matters involving foreign intelligence activities of the United States." The subpoena, in fact, does not request recommendations to Presidents, but requests recommendations to the National Security Council.

It is not addressed broadly to foreign intelligence activities, but specifically to covert actions.

It has appeared to our Committee that such operations generated outside of the normal channels have tended to be of higher risk and more questionable legality than those generated by the normal process, and it was largely for that reason that we felt such recommendations necessary for the successful conclusion of our investigation.

While we disagree on this issue, I wish you to understand our position on this matter as well as we understand your own.
With best personal regards,

Sincerely,

Otis G. Pike

OGP:o

THE WHITE HOUSE
Washington, D.C.

December 2, 1975

Dear Mr. Chairman:

On November 14, George H. Aldrich, Acting Legal Adviser of the Department of State, advised you by letter that the President had decided to invoke executive privilege with respect to documents sought in the Committee's subpoena of November 6, 1975, directed to the Secretary of State, and that Secretary Kissinger had accordingly been instructed respectfully to decline to comply with such subpoena. Mr. Aldrich stated in his letter that, as of that date, an examination of State Department records disclosed ten such documents covering the period 1961 through 1972.

This is to inform you that, since the date of Mr. Aldrich's letter, we have continued to search Executive Branch records for documents possibly subject to that subpoena and have, through information and documents not in the possession of the Department of State, identified an additional fifteen documents in which the Department of State proposed to the NSC, the 40 Committee or its predecessor, ten covert action projects. These documents cover the period from 1966 to 1971. Please be advised that the President has reviewed these additional documents and has decided to assert executive privilege with respect to them for the same reasons as compelled the assertion with respect to the documents previously identified.

Sincerely,

Philip W. Buchen
Counsel to the President

The Honorable Otis G. Pike
Chairman
Select Committee on Intelligence
House of Representatives
Washington, D.C. 20515

THE WHITE HOUSE
Washington
December 6, 1975

Dear Mr. Chairman:

The President has asked me to reply on his behalf to your thoughtful letter of November 21. He has further asked me to tell you that he appreciates the fact that you and your Committee permitted representatives of the Executive Branch to appear for testimony on November 20, and shares your hope that the remaining "underlying issues" may be removed.

As you know, in order to provide your Committee with the substance of the information it sought to obtain by the November 6 subpoenas, the Executive Branch identified the originating agency with respect to all covert actions conducted from 1965 to the present. The President authorized this step because of his desire to meet the legitimate needs of the Committee for information on covert operations although such detail was not required under any of the three subpoenas.

As a further demonstration of our desire for accommodation, the President has authorized me to inform you and your Committee that, since the 40 Committee subpoena covered only the period 1965 to the present, we will supplement the information already given to your Committee by providing similar information for the years 1961 through 1964 under the guidelines we have followed thus far. This additional step should, we believe, make it possible for the Committee to obtain the information that your letter indicated was necessary without affecting the President's claim of Executive privilege.

I sincerely hope, Mr. Chairman, that this further example of the President's desire to help the Committee carry out its important responsibilities will receive a favorable response by the Committee.

Sincerely,

Philip W. Buchen
Counsel to the President

The Honorable Otis G. Pike
Chairman
Select Committee on Intelligence
House of Representatives
Washington, D.C. 20515

NOTES AND QUESTIONS

1. *The exchange and its results.* The above exchanges at the committee hearings and through letters represent a dramatic confrontation between the legislature and the executive. At the heart of it is a fundamental reluctance on the part of the executive to accept Congress' power to oversee all executive actions. While there should be concern over compromising executive efforts in foreign policy and exposing government officials to unnecessary risk, in the end, the executive *is* accountable to the legislature for executive actions.

In this case, the executive ultimately relented and provided all of the materials requested by the committee. The select committee reported its findings and recommendations to the House of Representatives, and the House voted not to make the report public. It was, nevertheless, leaked in its entirety to the press. This leak immediately led to another investigation. This time it was of the thirteen members of the House subcommittee and their staff by the House Committee on Standards of Official Conduct. The leak was never revealed. For a detailed description of the work of this select committee, see Frank J. Smist, Jr., Congress Oversees the United States Intelligence Community, 1947-1989 (1990).

2. *Congressional oversight.* Congressman Pike's inquiry into CIA action is an example of the legislature performing one its most critical functions, oversight of the executive branch. This function was a power given to Congress by the Framers of the Constitution. The notion behind congressional oversight is that "policies formed through consultation and democratic process are better, and wiser, than those formed without it." Frederick A. O. Schwarz, Jr., and Aziz Z. Huq, Unchecked and Unbalanced 57-58 (2008). In recent years, however, particularly during the presidency of George W. Bush, Congress has been less attentive to this duty. UCLA political scientist Joel Aberbach reports that "the number of oversight hearings—excluding the appropriations committees—dropped from 782 during the first six months of 1983 to 287 during a comparable period in 1997. The falloff in the Senate between 1983 and 1997 . . . [was] from 429 to 175." Thomas E. Mann and Norman J. Ornstein, The Broken Branch 157 (2006).

As Mann and Ornstein have phrased it:

> The institutional rivalry designed by the framers gave way to a relationship in which Congress assumed a position subordinate to the executive. Party trumped institution. The president set the agenda of Congress and made clear he expected Republican leaders in Congress (his "lieutenants") to deliver.

Id. at 155. The result, according to them, has been "a series of governmental failures . . . that might have been prevented or mitigated if the Congress had exercised greater oversight and forced more debate." Id.

One such failure, it is argued, was in the realm of homeland security. The 9/11 Commission (created by the Bush administration to prepare a full and complete account of the circumstances surrounding the September 11, 2001, terrorist attacks — including any failures in preparation) came to the following conclusion:

> Of all our recommendations, strengthening congressional oversight may be among the most difficult and important. So long as oversight is governed by current congressional rules and resolutions, we believe the American people will not get the security they want and need. The United States needs a strong, stable and capable congressional structure to give America's national intelligence agencies oversight, support and leadership. . . .

Frederick A. O. Schwarz, Jr., and Aziz Z. Huq, Unchecked and Unbalanced 61 (2008). Along these lines, scholars argue that rather than acknowledging the calls by the Church Committee and 9/11 Commission for increased congressional oversight to reassert the proper balance between the executive and legislative branches, the Bush administration "instead resisted effective congressional inquiries into intelligence. . . . And it fought tooth and nail against any effort to ensure accountability beyond the opaque walls of the executive branch itself." Id.

Power without accountability risks unwise and abusive exercise. If the executive branch is not accountable to the legislative branch, as the Framers envisioned, then, due to congressional passivity and indifference toward executive power, the executive branch will remain uninhibited. The net effect will be a denial of transparency in executive decisionmaking to both the Congress and the public. While a degree of secrecy in presidential deliberation and decisionmaking is certainly necessary to serve certain aspects of national security, history reveals that too much secrecy often leads to an abuse of power. Consider the balance between the President's need for secrecy and Congress' need for information to further its oversight role as you read the following portions on executive privilege. Also consider the impact a further decline in congressional oversight could have on presidential claims of executive privilege.

3. *Executive privilege.* The letters above demonstrate how the claim of executive privilege can be asserted to avoid compliance with a congressional subpoena. What arguments were raised by the executive branch in both the testimony and the letters to support its claim for executive privilege? Consider these arguments in the context of the following case. Internal citations and footnotes have been omitted, except where particularly relevant.

United States v. Nixon
418 U.S. 683 (1974)

Chief Justice Burger delivered the opinion of the Court. . . .

On March 1, 1974, a grand jury of the United States District Court for the District of Columbia returned an indictment charging seven named individuals with various offenses, including conspiracy to defraud the United States and to obstruct justice. Although he was not designated as such in the indictment, the grand jury named the President, among others, as an unindicted co-conspirator. On April 18, 1974, upon motion of the Special Prosecutor, a subpoena duces tecum was issued pursuant to Rule 17(c) to the President by the United States District Court and made returnable on May 2, 1974. This subpoena required the production, in advance of the September 9th trial date, of certain tapes, memoranda, papers, transcripts, or other writings relating to certain precisely identified meetings between the President and others. The Special Prosecutor was able to fix the time, place, and persons present at these discussions because the White House daily logs and appointment records had been delivered to him. On April 30, the President publicly released edited transcripts of 43 conversations; portions of 20 conversations subject to subpoena in the present case were included. On May 1, 1974, the President's counsel filed a "special appearance" and a motion to quash the subpoena under Rule 17(c). This motion was accompanied by a formal claim of privilege. . . .

IV.   *The Claim of Privilege*

A

. . . [W]e turn to the claim that the subpoena should be quashed because it demands "confidential conversations between a President and his close advisors that it would be inconsistent with the public interest to produce." The first contention is a broad claim that the separation of powers doctrine precludes judicial review of a President's claim of privilege. The second contention is that if he does not prevail on the claim of absolute privilege, the court should hold as a matter of constitutional law that the privilege prevails over the subpoena duces tecum.

In the performance of assigned constitutional duties each branch of the Government must initially interpret the Constitution, and the interpretation of its powers by any branch is due great respect from the others. The President's counsel, as we have noted, reads the Constitution as providing an absolute privilege of confidentiality for all Presidential communications. Many decisions of this Court, however, have unequivocally reaffirmed the holding of Marbury v. Madison, 1 Cranch 137 (1803), that "[it] is emphatically the province and duty of the judicial department to say what the law is." Id. at 177.

No holding of the Court has defined the scope of judicial power specifically relating to the enforcement of a subpoena for confidential Presidential communications for use in a criminal prosecution, but other exercises of power by the Executive Branch and the Legislative Branch have been found invalid as in conflict with the Constitution. In a series of cases, the Court interpreted the explicit immunity conferred by express provisions of the Constitution on Members of the House and Senate by the Speech or Debate Clause, U.S. Const. Art. I, §6. Since this Court has consistently exercised the power to construe and delineate claims arising under express powers, it must follow that the Court has authority to interpret claims with respect to powers alleged to derive from enumerated powers.

Our system of government "requires that federal courts on occasion interpret the Constitution in a manner at variance with the construction given the document by another branch." Powell v. McCormack. . . .

B

In support of his claim of absolute privilege, the President's counsel urges two grounds, one of which is common to all governments and one of which is peculiar to our system of separation of powers. The first ground is the valid need for protection of communications between high Government officials and those who advise and assist them in the performance of their manifold duties; the importance of this confidentiality is too plain to require further discussion. Human experience teaches that those who expect public dissemination of their remarks may well temper candor with a concern for appearances and for their own interests to the detriment of the decisionmaking process. Whatever the nature of the privilege of confidentiality of Presidential communications in the exercise of Art. II powers, the privilege can be said to derive from the supremacy of each branch within its own assigned area of constitutional duties. Certain powers and privileges flow from the nature of enumerated powers; the protection of the confidentiality of Presidential communications has similar constitutional underpinnings.

The second ground asserted by the President's counsel in support of the claim of absolute privilege rests on the doctrine of separation of powers. Here it is argued that the independence of the Executive Branch within its own sphere insulates a President from a judicial subpoena in an ongoing criminal prosecution, and thereby protects confidential Presidential communications.

However, neither the doctrine of separation of powers, nor the need for confidentiality of high-level communications, without more, can sustain an absolute, unqualified Presidential privilege of immunity from judicial process under all circumstances. The President's need for complete candor and objectivity from advisers calls for great deference from the courts. However, when the privilege depends solely on the broad, undifferentiated claim of public interest in the confidentiality of such conversations, a confrontation with other values arises. Absent a claim of need to protect military, diplomatic, or sensitive national security secrets, we find it difficult to accept the argument that even the very important interest in confidentiality of Presidential communications is significantly diminished by production of such material for in camera inspection with all the protection that a district court will be obliged to provide.

The impediment that an absolute, unqualified privilege would place in the way of the primary constitutional duty of the Judicial Branch to do justice in criminal prosecutions would plainly conflict with the function of the courts under Art. III. In designing the structure of our Government and dividing and allocating the sovereign power among three co-equal branches, the Framers of the Constitution sought to provide a comprehensive system, but the separate powers were not intended to operate with absolute independence. . . .

C

Since we conclude that the legitimate needs of the judicial process may outweigh Presidential privilege, it is necessary to resolve those competing interests in a manner that preserves the essential functions of each branch. The right and indeed the duty to resolve that question does not free the Judiciary from according high respect to the representations made on behalf of the President.

The expectation of a President to the confidentiality of his conversations and correspondence, like the claim of confidentiality of judicial deliberations, for example, has all the values to which we accord deference for the privacy of all citizens and, added to those values, is the necessity for protection of the public interest in candid, objective, and even blunt or harsh opinions in Presidential decisionmaking. A President and those who assist him must be free to explore alternatives in the process of shaping policies and making decisions and to do so in a way many would be unwilling to express except privately. These are the considerations justifying a presumptive privilege for Presidential communications. The privilege is fundamental to the operation of Government and inextricably rooted in the separation of powers under the Constitution. . . .

But this presumptive privilege must be considered in light of our historic commitment to the rule of law. . . . We have elected to employ an adversary system of criminal justice in which the parties contest all issues before a court of law. The need to develop all relevant facts in the adversary system is both fundamental and comprehensive. The ends of criminal justice would be defeated if judgments were to be founded on a partial or speculative presentation of the facts. The very integrity of the judicial system and public confidence in the system depend on full disclosure of all the facts, within the framework of the rules of evidence. To ensure that justice is done, it is imperative to the function of courts that compulsory process be available for the production of evidence needed either by the prosecution or by the defense. . . .

In this case the President challenges a subpoena served on him as a third party requiring the production of materials for use in a criminal prosecution; he does so on the claim that he has a privilege against disclosure of confidential communications. He does not place his claim of privilege on the ground they are military or diplomatic secrets. As to these areas of Art. II duties the courts have traditionally shown the utmost deference to Presidential responsibilities. . . . No case of the Court, however, has extended this high degree of deference to a President's generalized interest in confidentiality. Nowhere in the Constitution, as we have noted earlier, is there any explicit reference to a privilege of confidentiality, yet to the extent this interest relates to the effective discharge of a President's powers, it is constitutionally based.

The right to the production of all evidence at a criminal trial similarly has constitutional dimensions. . . .

In this case we must weigh the importance of the general privilege of confidentiality of Presidential communications in performance of the President's responsibilities against the inroads of such a privilege on the fair administration of criminal justice. The interest in preserving confidentiality is weighty indeed and entitled to great respect. However, we cannot conclude that advisers will be moved to temper the candor of their remarks by the infrequent occasions of disclosure because of the possibility that such conversations will be called for in the context of a criminal prosecution.

On the other hand, the allowance of the privilege to withhold evidence that is demonstrably relevant in a criminal trial would cut deeply into the guarantee of due process of law and gravely impair the basic function of the courts. . . .

D

We have earlier determined that the District Court did not err in authorizing the issuance of the subpoena. If a President concludes that compliance with a subpoena would be injurious to the public interest he may properly, as was done here, invoke a claim of privilege on the return of the subpoena. Upon receiving a claim of privilege from the Chief Executive, it became the further duty of the District Court to treat the subpoenaed material as presumptively privileged. . . . Here the District Court treated the material as presumptively privileged, proceeded to find that the Special Prosecutor had made a sufficient showing to rebut the presumption, and ordered an in camera examination of the subpoenaed material. On the basis of our examination of the record we are unable to conclude that the District Court erred in ordering the inspection. . . .

NOTES AND QUESTIONS

1. *Applicability of the Nixon decision.* In your reading of the preceding case, we asked you to consider the arguments raised by the executive branch

under President Ford to support its claim of executive privilege regarding covert intelligence activities. How would the *Nixon* Court have evaluated these arguments? See Archibald Cox, Executive Privilege, 122 U. Pa. L. Rev. 1383 (1974); see also Presidential Records Act of 1978, 44 U.S.C. §§2201-2207 (1988) (restricting access to certain types of information for a specified number of years).

2. *Executive privilege and the Bush administration.* Claims of executive privilege have resurfaced under the administration of President George W. Bush. In contrast to a foreign affairs (as was the case in the letters above) or conspiracy (as in the *Nixon* case) context, the claims have been asserted in response to congressional investigations into the termination of public officials by former Attorney General Alberto Gonzales and other White House officials. Consider the arguments for and against the assertion of executive privilege in the discussion below. What does this tell us about the scope of executive privilege?

2.   *Executive Privilege: A Contemporary Problem*

In early 2007 the House Judiciary Committee and its Subcommittee on Commercial and Administrative Law commenced an inquiry into the propriety of the termination and replacement of nine United States Attorneys. Presidential Claims of Executive Privilege: History, Law, Practice and Recent Developments 24 (Cong. Research Serv., CRS Report for Congress Order Code RL 30319, Sept. 17, 2007). The dismissal of seven of the prosecutors en masse was preceded by the removal of two other attorneys, one of whom was a Mr. Cummins of Arkansas. Cummins' position was filled by J. Timothy Griffin, an ex-prosecutor and associate of Karl Rove—former chief political adviser to President Bush. The Griffin appointment was viewed as the most controversial: e-mail communications revealed that Justice Department and White House officials, including Rove and Harriet E. Miers (then White House counsel and aide to the President), "were preparing for President Bush's approval of the appointment as early as last summer [2005], five months before Griffin took the job." Dan Eggen and Amy Goldstein, E-Mails Show Machinations to Replace Prosecutor, Washington Post, Mar. 23, 2007 at A1. The substance of the e-mails tended to show that "D. Kyle Sampson, then the attorney general's chief of staff, and other Justice officials prepared to use a change in federal law [the Patriot Act] to bypass input from Arkansas' two Democratic senators, who had expressed doubts about placing a former Republican National Committee operative in charge of a U.S. attorney's office. The evidence runs contrary to assurances from Attorney General Alberto R. Gonzales that no such move had been planned." Id.

In another e-mail regarding Cummins' termination, Mr. Sampson wrote: " 'Getting him appointed was important to Harriet, Karl, etc.,' a reference to

Ms. Miers and Mr. Rove." David Johnston and Eric Lipton, "Loyalty" to Bush and Gonzales Was a Factor in Prosecutors' Firings, E-Mail Shows, N.Y. Times, Mar. 14, 2007. These communications and the secrecy involved in the decisionmaking sparked concern by Democrats and Republicans alike that the determination to remove the nine attorneys was politically motivated.

Extensive interviews ensued, and committees assembled thousands of pages of documents in an effort to determine who spearheaded the dismissals and how and why the individual attorneys removed were selected. In anticipation of a congressional committee using its subpoena power to fill in the gaps, the White House offered to allow committee members to privately interview Rove and Miers. In addition, they would have access to two other officials as well as e-mail messages regarding the dismissals (with the exception of those exchanged by White House officials). But the White House limited its offer in that "the officials would not testify under oath . . . there would be no transcript [and] Congress would not subsequently subpoena them." Sheryl Gay Stolberg, Bush Clashes with Congress on Prosecutors, N.Y. Times, Mar. 21, 2007. The Democratic leadership rejected this offer, and on March 21, 2007, the House Subcommittee authorized Chairman John Conyers, Jr., to issue subpoenas to a number of present and former White House officials. On June 13, 2007, Chairman Conyers issued subpoenas to White House Chief of Staff Joshua Bolten, as custodian of White House documents, and to former White House counsel Harriet Miers.

Former Attorney General Gonzales, in addition to Monica Goodling — who served as senior counsel to the attorney general and White House liaison until her resignation on April 7, 2007 — both testified before the committees. "On April 19, 2007, Gonzales repeatedly claimed not to recall important events surrounding the forced resignations — a performance roundly criticized in editorials from around the country and parodied mercilessly by the nation's comedians and late night talk show hosts." John McKay, Train Wreck at the Justice Department: An Eyewitness Account, 31 Seattle U. L. Rev. 265, 274 (2008). Monica Goodling informed the House Judiciary Committee that she would assert her Fifth Amendment right not to incriminate herself if she was called to testify. In response to this statement the committee approved, by a vote of 36-2, a limited immunity agreement for Monica Goodling in exchange for her subpoenaed testimony. She testified before the committee on May 23, and expressed regret that in reviewing candidates for lower-level prosecutorial jobs or positions at Justice headquarters she went "too far in asking political questions of applicants" and "may have taken inappropriate political considerations into account." Testimony of Monica Goodling before the S. Judiciary Comm., May 23, 2007, *available at* http://www.washingtonpost.com/wpsrv/politics/transcripts/goodling_testimony_052307.html.

On June 27, 2007, White House counsel Fred F. Fielding, at the direction of President Bush, advised the chairmen of the House and Senate Judiciary Committees that subpoenas issued to the White House custodian of documents and to two former White House officials were subject to executive privilege and subpoena recipients had been directed not to produce any documents. The Fielding letter noted that the "testimony sought from Ms. Miers and Ms. Taylor is also subject to a 'valid claim of Executive Privilege,' so as to protect the President's right to receive unfettered advice from his aides and the need for confidentiality in White House deliberations." Presidential Claims of Executive Privilege: History, Law, Practice and Recent Developments 24 (Cong. Research Serv., CRS Report for Congress Order Code RL 30319, Sept. 17, 2007); Sheryl Gay Stolberg, White House and Lawmakers Alike Face Risks in an Executive Privilege Fight, N.Y. Times, June 17, 2007 (also noting that "[t]he letter stated executive privilege will be asserted if the matter cannot be resolved before dates scheduled for their appearances"); David Johnston, Rove, Still under Subpoena, Remains Unlikely to Testify, N.Y. Times, Aug. 14, 2007.

Accompanying the Fielding letter was a legal memorandum prepared by interim Attorney General Paul D. Clement detailing the legal basis for a claim of executive privilege. The memo identified three categories of documents being sought: (1) internal White House communications; (2) communications by White House officials with individuals outside the executive branch, including individuals in the legislative branch; and (3) communications between White House and Justice Department officials. Presidential Claims of Executive Privilege: History, Law, Practice and Recent Developments 24 (2007). The substance of the memorandum is as follows:

> With respect to internal White House communications, which are said to consist of discussions of "the wisdom" of removal and replacement proposals, which U.S. Attorneys should be removed, and possible responses to Congressional and media inquiries, such discussions are claimed to be the "types of internal deliberations among White House officials [that] fall squarely within the scope of executive privilege" since their non-disclosure "promote[s] sound decisionmaking by ensuring that senior Government officials and their advisors may speak frankly and candidly during the decisionmaking process," citing U.S. v. Nixon. Since, it is argued, what is involved is the exercise of the presidential power to appoint and remove officers of the United States, a "quintessential and nondelegable Presidential power" (citing Espy), the President's protected confidentiality interests "are particularly" strong in this instance. As a consequence, an inquiring congressional committee would have to meet the standard established by the Senate Select Committee decision requiring a showing that the documents and information are "demonstrably critical to the responsible fulfillment of the Committee's function." Thus, it is claimed, there is doubt whether the Committees have oversight authority over deliberations essential to the exercise of this core

presidential power or that "their interests justify overriding a claim of executive privilege as to the matters at issue."

With respect to matters involving communications by White House officials with individuals outside the White House, the Clement memo asserts that confidentiality interests undergirding the privilege are not diminished if the President or his close advisors have to go outside the White House to obtain information to make an "informed decision," particularly about a core presidential power. Again, *Espy* and *Senate Select Committee* are referred as supporting authority. As to the final category, respecting communications between the Justice Department and the White House concerning proposals to dismiss and replace U.S. Attorneys, it is claimed that such communications "are deliberative and clearly fall within the scope of executive privilege. . . . [T]he President's need to protect deliberations about the selection of U.S. Attorneys is compelling, particularly given Congress' lack of legislative authority over the nomination or replacement of U.S. Attorneys," citing *Espy* and *Senate Select Committee*. The privilege is asserted to extend to White House–DOJ communications "that have been previously disclosed to the Committees by the Department." An argument that a waiver may have occurred is contrary to "relevant legal principles [that] should and do encourage, rather than punish, such accommodation[s] by recognizing that Congress' need for such documents is reduced to the extent similar materials have been provided voluntarily as part of the accommodation process." Since the Committees have these documents, seeking the relevant communications would be cumulative under *Senate Select Committee*. This rationale is argued to support the lack of any need for the testimony of the former White House officials subpoenaed.

Id. at 24-25.

On February 14, 2008, the House approved contempt citations against Bolten and Miers over their refusal to testify before the House Judiciary Committee by a 223-32 vote. The Senate Judiciary Committee has approved contempt citations for Bolten and Rove, who also refused to appear before that panel, but as of the date of this publication the full Senate has not acted on the matter. Paul Kane, West Wing Aides Cited for Contempt, Wash. Post, Feb. 15, 2008, at A4. The contempt citations are the first approved by Congress against the executive branch since the Reagan administration. Philip Shenon, House Votes to Issue Contempt Citations, N.Y. Times, Feb. 15, 2008. A congressional subpoena would normally be enforced by the Justice Department, but the White House and the Attorney General have said they would not pursue contempt charges because they believe that the testimony of the officials subpoenaed is protected by executive privilege. Id. As a result, the House brought an action through its Committee on the Judiciary seeking to compel Bolten and Miers to comply with the issued subpoenas. Bolten and Miers moved to dismiss contemporaneously with the Committee's motion for partial summary judgment. The Court denied the executives' claim of absolute immunity, but stopped short of requiring Miers and Bolten to produce a full privilege log — opting instead to compel the two to produce "a more detailed list and description of the nature and scope of the documents it seeks to withhold on the basis of executive privilege. . . ." See Comm. on the Judiciary v. Miers, 558 F. Supp. 2d 53 (D.D.C. 2008).

NOTES AND QUESTIONS

1. Presidential communications privilege and the deliberative process privilege. The legal memorandum discussed above detailed the legal basis for a claim of executive privilege and references the District of Columbia Circuit Court's decision in In re Sealed Case (*Espy*), 121 F.3d 729 (D.C. Cir. 1997). In *Espy*, the court bifurcated the over-generalized concept of executive privilege into the following categories: the presidential communications privilege and the deliberative process privilege. According to the court, the deliberative process privilege applies to "decisionmaking of executive officials generally" and is a common law privilege requiring a lower threshold of need to be overcome. Id. at 745. In fact, the deliberative process privilege "disappears altogether when there is any reason to believe government misconduct occurred." Id. at 746. On the other hand, the presidential communications privilege is rooted in "constitutional separation of powers principles and the President's unique constitutional role" and applies "specifically to decisionmaking of the President." Id. at 745. The privilege may be overcome only by a substantial showing that "the subpoenaed materials likely contain[] important evidence" and that "this evidence is not available with due diligence elsewhere." Id. at 754. As the court further distinguished, "The presidential communications privilege applies to documents in their entirety, and covers final and post-decisional materials as well as pre-deliberative ones." Id. at 745. See also Presidential Claims of Executive Privilege: History, Law, Practice and Recent Developments 18 (Cong. Research Serv., CRS Report For Congress Order Code RL 30319, Sept. 17, 2007).

With respect to the scope of the privilege (who was covered), the court held that the presidential communications privilege has to cover communications "made or received by presidential advisers in the course of preparing advice for the President even if those communications are not made directly to the President." Id. The familiar rationale for this position was the need for open and candid communication and the White House staff's "operational proximity" to direct presidential decisionmaking. Id. "Thus the privilege will 'apply both to communications which these advisers solicited and received from others as well as those they authored themselves.'" Id. at 19.

2. The Senate Select Committee case. The Clement memorandum also refers to the D.C. Circuit's decision in Senate Select Committee on Presidential Campaign Activities v. Nixon, 498 F.2d 725 (D.C. Cir. 1974). In this case the appellate court held that a committee must show that "subpoenaed evidence is demonstrably critical to the responsible fulfillment of the [c]ommittee's function" in order to overcome the presumption of privilege that presidential conversations enjoy. Id. at 730-31. Among the considerations the court took into account in deciding if evidence was "critical" was whether other committees had access to the subpoenaed information and if the information was critical to the performance of its legislative functions. See id. at 731-32.

3. *Executive privilege post-*Espy. In *Judicial Watch*, the D.C. Circuit Court examined executive privilege in the context of the pardon power of the President. The case involved a pair of Freedom of Information Act (FOIA) requests to the Office of the Pardon Attorney and the Office of the Deputy Attorney General for "pardon applications considered or granted by former President Clinton." Judicial Watch, Inc. v. U.S. Department of Justice, 2006 WL 2038513, at *1 (D.D.C. July 19, 2006).

> Over 4,300 pages were withheld on the grounds they were protected by the presidential communications and deliberative process privileges. The district court held that since the materials sought had been created solely for the purpose of advising the President on a "quintessential and nondelegable Presidential power"—the exercise of the President's constitutional pardon authority—the extension of the presidential communications privilege to internal Justice Department documents which had not been "solicited and received" by the President or the Office of the President was warranted. The appeals court reversed, concluding that "internal agency documents that are not solicited and received by the President or his Office are instead protected against disclosure, if at all, by the deliberative process privilege."

Presidential Claims of Executive Privilege: History, Law, Practice and Recent Developments 20 (Cong. Research Serv., CRS Report For Congress Order Code RL 30319, Sept. 17, 2007). Borrowing language from the *Espy* decision, the court emphasized the "solicited and received" limitation and clarified that the privilege may be invoked only by advisers in close proximity to the president who "have significant responsibility for advising him on non-delegable matters requiring direct presidential decisionmaking, have solicited and received such documents or communications or the President has received them himself." Id.

3.   Committee Deliberation: Markup, Amendment, and Voting

After a hearing on a bill has been completed, the committee (usually first a subcommittee) must next decide whether to act on the proposal. Whether a particular bill is part of the committee action agenda is, at least in the first instance, a decision for the committee chair. It is one of her most important powers. Once a committee decides to consider a bill, the bill enters into its markup phase.

It is during the markup period that a bill receives its most concentrated institutional study. The bill (or, if there are more than one on the same subject, the one chosen by the chair) becomes the "mark." It is read line by line to the members of the committee, usually in an open session of the committee. During this period, explanations for particular provisions are offered, discussions go on, and amendments are offered and considered. Sometimes this exacting process is repeated in the full committee after it has been finished in the subcommittee. The following description is illustrative:

> In the fullest form, markup may be lengthy and formal both at the subcommittee and at the full committee level. The Clean Air Act reauthorization in 1982 illustrates the extreme possibilities for formality. On the Senate side, markup was done only at the full committee, and it took the Environment and Public Works Committee nine months of markups before ordering S. 3041 reported on August 19. On the House side, the Health and Environment subcommittee . . . began markup on February 25. The subcommittee first voted on a proposed amendment on March 4, and continued subcommittee markups for several weeks, finally approving the bill on March 24.
>
> That sent the bill up to the full committee, Energy and Commerce, where the struggle began all over again. Full committee markup began on March 30, and then, after intense disputes, was broken off on April 29. It resumed in August, but without success, and the bill died. . . .

Id.

Voting in congressional committees, whether on amendment or on the question of reporting a bill to the floor, mimics voting on the floor of the legislatures. There can be voice votes and roll call votes. Which method is chosen depends on the committee rules. The only unique aspect of committee voting, at least in Congress, is the use of proxies, a practice not permitted in voting on the legislative floor. Under the rules of both houses, written proxies can be used if the committee authorizes their use. This practice has been criticized as strengthening the committee chair and allowing absenteeism. See Charles Tiefer, Congressional Practice and Procedure 172-73 (1989).

4. The Committee Report

In Congress (in particular) and state legislatures (to varying degrees from state to state), after a committee has voted to send (report) a bill to the floor of its parent chamber for action, the committee prepares a committee report that provides an explanation for the bill and its purpose, its committee procedural history, all votes of the committee, a section-by-section analysis, committee views, minority views and the supplemental views (in support or dissent) of committee members who choose to submit them, cost estimates, and regulatory impacts. In Congress this is an important step in the legislative process because both houses have standing rules that normally require that committee reports be available for members of Congress, for a time certain, before floor consideration of the bill that is the subject of the committee report.

The committee report is intended, in this context, as a source of information for legislators about pending legislation. The value of reports for this purpose is questionable. As one of the authors has written about his experience in Congress: "[t]he report . . . is relatively insignificant for purposes of floor action. At best, it serves to educate the legislative assistants of non-committee members." Abner J. Mikva and Patti B. Saris, The American Congress 216 (1983).

The committee report serves a far more important purpose in the interpretation of statutes than it does in their enactment. Private and public attorneys frequently use such reports as guides to the applicability of statutory provisions to either the proposed or accomplished behavior of their clients. Committee reports are also used with regularity by administrative agencies and the courts in determining the meaning of unclear statutes in the context of particular disputes.

The excerpts that follow are from the Report of the Senate Committee on the Judiciary on S. 1992 (the Voting Rights Act Amendments of 1982; these amendments are set forth in Chapter 10). It is illustrative of a typical congressional committee report. In reviewing it, consider the problem posed in Chapter 2, page 46.

Report of the Committee on the Judiciary on S. 1992

Calendar No. 598

97TH CONGRESS *2d Session* }	SENATE	{ REPORT No. 97-417

VOTING RIGHTS ACT EXTENSION

REPORT

OF THE

COMMITTEE ON THE JUDICIARY
UNITED STATES SENATE

ON

S. 1992

with

ADDITIONAL, MINORITY, AND SUPPLEMENTAL
VIEWS

MAY 25, 1982.- Ordered to be printed

U.S. GOVERNMENT PRINTING OFFICE

94-548 O   WASHINGTON : 1982

COMMITTEE ON THE JUDICIARY

(97th Congress)

STROM THURMOND, South Carolina, *Chairman*

CHARLES McC. MATHIAS, Jr., Maryland	JOSEPH R. BIDEN, Jr., Delaware
PAUL LAXALT, Nevada	EDWARD M. KENNEDY, Massachusetts
ORRIN G. HATCH, Utah	ROBERT C. BYRD, West Virginia
ROBERT DOLE, Kansas	HOWARD M. METZENBAUM, Ohio
ALAN K. SIMPSON, Wyoming	DENNIS DeCONCINI, Arizona
JOHN P. EAST, North Carolina	PATRICK J. LEAHY, Vermont
CHARLES E. GRASSLEY, Iowa	MAX BAUCUS, Montana
JEREMIAH DENTON, Alabama	HOWELL HEFLIN, Alabama
ARLEN SPECTER, Pennsylvania	

VINTON DeVANE LIDE, *Chief Counsel*
QUENTIN CROMMELIN, JR., *Staff Director*

SUBCOMMITTEE ON THE CONSTITUTION
ORRIN G. HATCH, Utah, *Chairman*

STROM THURMOND, South Carolina	DENNIS DeCONCINI, Arizona
CHARLES E. GRASSLEY, Iowa	PATRICK J. LEAHY, Vermont

STEPHEN MARKMAN, *Chief Counsel and Staff Director*
RANDALL RADER, *General Counsel*
PETER ORMSBY, *Professional Staff*
ROBERT FEIDLER, *Minority Counsel*

TABLE OF CONTENTS

PART I
Report of the Committee

VOTING RIGHTS ACT EXTENSION

MAY 25, 1982. — Ordered to be printed

Mr. THURMOND, from the Committee on the Judiciary,
submitted the following

R E P O R T

together with
ADDITIONAL, MINORITY, AND SUPPLEMENTAL VIEWS
[To accompany S. 1992]

The Committee on the Judiciary, to which was referred the bill (S. 1992) to amend the Voting Rights Act of 1965 to extend the effect of certain provisions and for other purposes, having considered the same, reports favorably thereon with an amendment (in the nature of a substitute) and recommends that the bill as amended do pass.

Senator Mathias filed the majority views of the Committee on the Judiciary.

I.   Introductory Summary

The Committee on the Judiciary, to which was referred the bill (S. 1992) to amend the Voting Rights Act of 1965, to extend the special coverage provisions, to adopt a new procedure by which jurisdictions can bail out of coverage under the special provisions, to amend section 2, to extend the language assistance provisions for an additional seven years, and to add a section governing assistance to voters who are blind, disabled or unable to read or write, having considered the same, reports favorably thereon with amendments and recommends that the bill as amended do pass.

The voting rights legislation which this Committee has considered is one of the most significant issues to come before this Congress. It has generated discussion not only in the Congress but throughout the Nation as well. This Committee has given the legislation detailed attention before coming to the conclusions reflected in this Report, which is the statement for the record of the intended meaning and operation of this bill.

Following the Committee Report on the bill are Additional Views and Minority Views of individual members.

II.   Purpose

The objectives of S. 1992, as amended, are as follows: (1) to extend the present coverage of the special provisions of the Voting Rights Act,

Sections 4, 5, 6, 7 and 8; (2) to amend Section 4(a) of the Act to permit individual jurisdictions to meet a new, broadened standard for termination of coverage by those special provisions; (3) to amend the language of Section 2 in order to clearly establish the standards intended by Congress for proving a violation of that section; (4) to extend the language-assistance provisions of the Act until 1992; and (5) to add a new section pertaining to voting assistance for voters who are blind, disabled, or illiterate.

Jurisdictions that meet the criteria set forth in Section 4(b) of the Act will continue to be subject to the special provisions of the Act until such time as they obtain a declaratory judgment granting termination of coverage as set forth in Section 4(a), as amended, but in any event not for a period exceeding 25 years.

The standard for bailout is also broadened by permitting political subdivisions in covered states, as defined in Section 14(c)(2), to bail out although the state itself remained covered. Under the new standard, which goes into effect on August 6, 1984, a jurisdiction must show, for itself and for all governmental units within its territory, that (1) for the 10 years preceding the filing of the bailout suit, it has a record of no voting discrimination and of compliance with the law; and (2) it has taken positive steps to increase the opportunity for full minority participation in the political process, including the removal of any discriminatory barriers.

S. 1992 amends Section 2 of the Voting Rights Act of 1965 to prohibit any voting practice or procedure resulting in discrimination. This amendment is designed to make clear that proof of discriminatory intent is not required to establish a violation of Section 2. It thereby restores the legal standards, based on the controlling Supreme Court precedents, which applied in voting discrimination claims prior to the litigation involved in Mobile v. Bolden. . . .

III.   History of Legislation and Committee Proceedings

The bulk of S. 1992 is virtually identical to legislation that was passed by an overwhelming margin by the House of Representatives in the fall of 1981. This Committee has reviewed the record of those proceedings, as well as the hearings of the Senate Subcommittee on the Constitution, in making its determinations on this legislation. . . .

On March 29, 1982, S. 1992 was briefly considered by the Committee, at which time a date certain was set for full Committee consideration. The Committee considered the measure on April 27, 28, 29, and May 4. Opening statements were given on April 27, 28, and 29. On May 4 the Committee voted on amendments, and ordered the bill, as amended, to be favorably reported.

The Committee first agreed to an amendment in the nature of a substitute for the Subcommittee bill. This amendment was offered by

Senator Dole for himself and the sponsors of the original S. 1992, Senators Mathias and Kennedy, as well as Senators DeConcini, Grassley, Metzenbaum, Biden, and Simpson. The substitute amendment reinstated most of the original text of S. 1992, but included three changes: (1) a further amendment to Section 2 of the Act; (2) a twenty-five year time limit on the special provisions of the Act; and (3) a new provision concerning the method by which voting assistance is provided to the blind, the disabled, and the illiterate. The substitute amendment was agreed to by a vote of 14–4.

A series of further amendments were then offered by Senator East. By a vote of 10–8, the Committee agreed to an East amendment relating to officials or agents of a voter's union assisting the blind, disabled, and illiterate in the polling booth under Section 5 of the substitute. . . .

The Committee then ordered the bill to be favorably reported to the full Senate by a vote of 17–1.

IV.   Background: Origin and Operation of the Voting Rights Act

The Committee bill will extend the essential protections of the historic Voting Rights Act. It will insure that the hard-won progress of the past is preserved and that the effort to achieve full participation for all Americans in our democracy will continue in the future.

Seventeen years ago, Americans of all races and creeds joined to persuade the Nation to confront its conscience and fulfill the guarantee of the Constitution.

From the effort came the Voting Rights Act of 1965. President Lyndon Johnson hailed its enactment as a "triumph for freedom as huge as any ever won on any battlefield." . . .

As a result of the Voting Rights Act of 1965, hundreds of thousands of Americans can now vote and, equally important, have their vote count as fully as do the votes of their fellow citizens. Men and women from racial and ethnic minorities now hold public office in places where that was once impossible.

Twice before, in 1970 and 1975, the crucial provisions of the Act have been extended. Each time the Act has come under attack. But each time, the Congress of the bipartisan basis has come to its rescue, with the support of Americans from every part of the country.

To appreciate the legacy of the Voting Rights Act and the need for its extension . . . an understanding of its history is essential. Traditionally, black Americans were denied the franchise throughout the South. After statutory bars to voting by blacks were lifted, the main device was denial of voter registration — by violence, by harassment, and by the use of literacy tests or other screening methods. Civil rights groups and the Justice Department challenged those barriers repeatedly in the courts. The Civil Rights Acts of 1957 and 1960 authorized the Attorney General to seek injunctions, and the bills also established a complex process to enroll black voters.

But case-by-case litigation proved wholly inadequate. . . .

VI.   *Amendment to Section 2 of the Voting Rights Act*

A.   Overview: Proposed Amendment to Section 2

The proposed amendment to Section 2 of the Voting Rights Act is designed to restore the legal standard that governed voting discrimination cases prior to the Supreme Court's decision in *Bolden.* In pre-*Bolden* cases plaintiffs could prevail by showing that a challenged election law or procedure, in the context of the total circumstances of the local electoral process, had the result of denying a racial or language minority an equal chance to participate in the electoral process. Under this results test, it was not necessary to demonstrate that the challenged election law or procedure was designed or maintained for a discriminatory purpose.

In *Bolden*, a plurality of the Supreme Court broke with precedent and substantially increased the burden on plaintiffs in voting discrimination cases by requiring proof of discriminatory purpose. The Committee has concluded that this intent test places an unacceptably difficult burden on plaintiffs. It diverts the judicial injury from the crucial question of whether minorities have equal access to the electoral process to a historical question of individual motives. . . .

B.   The Original Legislative Intent as to Section 2

The Committee amendment rejecting a requirement that discriminatory purpose be proved to establish a violation of Section 2 is fully consistent with the original legislative understanding of Section 2 when the Act was passed in 1965.

Advocates of an intent requirement for Section 2 cite statements in the legislative history of the 1965 Act to the effect that Section 2 was designed to track the Fifteenth Amendment, whose wording it follows. They suggest that the Fifteenth Amendment has always been understood to require proof of discriminatory purpose. They claim that, inasmuch as Congress chose to track the Fifteenth Amendment, Congress also must have sought to impose an intent standard in Section 2. Thus they argue that the Committee amendment is not consistent with the original understanding of Section 2.

Whether the Fifteenth or Fourteenth Amendment were understood by Congress in 1965 to embody an intent requirement is ultimately of limited relevance. However, the Committee has examined the legislative history of the 1965 enactment, relevant legislative history from the 1970 extension of the Act, and the general understanding in 1965 of what was required to establish a Fifteenth Amendment violation. We find no persuasive evidence to support the argument outlined above that Congress made proof of discriminatory purpose an essential requirement of Section 2 when it was first enacted. . . .

D.   The Operation of Amended Section 2

With the benefit of the record of explanation and analysis of Section 2 amendment by its Congressional sponsors and witnesses in the House of Representatives and the even more detailed, almost exhaustive, inquiry by our Subcommittee on the Constitution, the Committee has had an opportunity to examine all the aspects of the issues and implications raised by the new language. Based on this examination, the Committee believes that the amendment is sound, that it is necessary and appropriate to ensure full protection of the Fourteenth and Fifteenth Amendments rights, and that it will not present the dangers raised by those who have opposed it — a requirement of racial quotas, or an all-out assault on at-large election systems in general. . . .

If the plaintiff proceeds under the "results test," then the court would assess the impact of the challenged structure or practice on the basis of objective factors, rather than making a determination about the motivations which lay behind its adoption or maintenance. . . .

In adopting the "result standard" as articulated in White v. Regester, the Committee has codified the basic principle in that case as it was applied prior to the *Mobile* litigation. . . .

Section 2 protects the right of minority voters to be free from election practices, procedures or methods, that deny them the same opportunity to participate in the political process as other citizens enjoy.

If as a result of the challenged practice or structure plaintiffs do not have an equal opportunity to participate in the political processes and to elect candidates of their choice, there is a violation of this section. To establish a violation, plaintiffs could show a variety of factors, depending upon the kind of rule, practice, or procedure called into question.

Typical factors include:

1.   The extent of any history of official discrimination in the state or political subdivision that touched the right of the members of the minority group to register, to vote, or otherwise to participate in the democratic process;
2.   The extent to which voting in the elections of the state or political subdivision is racially polarized;
3.   The extent to which the state or political subdivision has used unusually large election districts, majority vote requirements, anti-single

shot provisions, or other voting practices or procedures that may enhance the opportunity for discrimination against the minority group;

4. If there is a candidate slating process, whether the members of the minority group have been denied access to that process;

5. The extent to which members of the minority group in the state or political subdivision bear the effects of discrimination in such areas as education, employment and health, which hinder their ability to participate effectively in the political process;

6. Whether political campaigns have been characterized by overt or subtle racial appeals;

7. The extent to which members of the minority group have been elected to public office in the jurisdiction.

Additional factors that in some cases have had probative value as part of plaintiffs' evidence to establish a violation are: whether there is a significant lack of responsiveness on the part of elected officials to the particularized needs of the members of the minority group; whether the policy underlying the state or political subdivision's use of such voting qualification, prerequisite to voting, or standard, practice or procedure is tenuous.

While these enumerated factors will often be the most relevant ones, in some cases other factors will be indicative of the alleged dilution.

The cases demonstrate, and the Committee intends that there is no requirement that any particular number of factors be proved, or that a majority of them point one way or the other.

Whitcomb, White, Zimmer, and their progeny dealt with electoral system features such as at-large elections, majority vote requirements and districting plans. However, Section 2 remains the major statutory prohibition of all voting rights discrimination. It also prohibits practices which, while episodic and not involving permanent structure barriers, result in the denial of equal access to any phase of the electoral process for minority group members.

If the challenged practice relates to such a series of events or episodes, the proof sufficient to establish a violation would not necessarily involve the same factors as the courts have utilized when dealing with permanent structural barriers. Of course, the ultimate test would be the *White* standard codified by this amendment of Section 2: whether, in the particular situation, the practice operated to deny the minority plaintiff an equal opportunity to participate and to elect candidates of their choice.

The requirement that the political processes leading to nomination and election be "equally open to participation by the group in question" extends beyond formal or official bars to registering and voting, or to maintaining a candidacy.

As the Court said in *White*, the question whether the political processes are "equally open" depends upon a searching practical evaluation of the "past and present reality."

Finally, the Committee reiterates the existence of the private right of action under Section 2, as has been clearly intended by Congress since 1965. See Allen v. Board of Elections, 393 U.S. 544 (1969).

Disclaimer

When a federal judge is called upon to determine the validity of a practice challenged under Section 2, as amended, he or she is required to act in full accordance with the disclaimer in Section 2 which reads as follows:

The extent to which members of a protected class have been elected to office in the State or political subdivision is one "circumstance" which may be considered, provided that nothing in this section establishes a right to have members of a protected class elected in numbers equal to their proportion in the population.

Contrary to assertions made during the full Committee markup of the legislation, this provision is both clear and straightforward.

This disclaimer is entirely consistent with the above mentioned Supreme Court and Court of Appeals precedents, which contain similar statements regarding the absence of any right to proportional representation. It puts to rest any concerns that have been voiced about racial quotas.

The basic principle of equity that the remedy fashioned must be commensurate with the right that has been violated provides adequate assurance, without disturbing the prior case law or prescribing in the statute mechanistic rules for formulating remedies in cases which necessarily depend upon widely varied proof and local circumstances. The court should exercise its traditional equitable powers to fashion the relief so that it completely remedies prior dilution of minority voting strength and fully provides equal opportunity for minority citizens to participate and to elect candidates of their choice.

The proposed results test was developed by the Supreme Court and followed in nearly two dozen cases by the lower federal courts. The results test is well-known to federal judges. It is not an easy test. As Arthur Flemming told the Subcommittee on the Constitution, "White v. Regester sets realistic standards for analyzing voting dilution cases." It was only after the adoption of the results test, and its application by the lower federal courts that minority voters in many jurisdictions finally began to emerge from virtual exclusion from the electoral process. We are acting to restore the opportunity for further progress. . . .

F.   The Limitations of the Intent Test

The intent test is inappropriate as the exclusive standard for establishing a violation of Section 2. This is so for several reasons. During the hearings, there was considerable discussion of the difficulty often encountered in meeting the intent test, but that is not the principal reason why we have rejected it.

The main reason is that, simply put, the test asks the wrong question. In the *Bolden* case on remand, the district court, after a tremendous expenditure of resources by the parties and the court, concluded that officials had acted more than 100 years ago for discriminatory motives. However, if an electoral system operates today to exclude blacks or Hispanics from a fair chance to participate, then the matter of what motives were in an official's mind 100 years ago is of the most limited relevance. The standard under the Committee amendment is whether minorities have equal access to the process of electing their representatives. If they are denied a fair opportunity to participate, the Committee believes that the system should be changed, regardless of what may or may not be provable about events which took place decades ago. . . .

XI.   *Recorded Votes in Committee*

1. Dole amendment offered in the nature of a substitute.

Yeas	Nays
Mathias	Hatch
Laxalt	East
Dole	Denton[*]
Simpson	Thurmond
Grassley[*]	
Specter	
Biden	
Kennedy	
Byrd[*]	
Metzenbaum[*]	
DeConcini[*]	
Leahy[*]	
Baucus	
Heflin	

*Voted by proxy

The Committee then ordered the bill to be favorably reported to the full Senate by a vote of 17-1.

XII.   *Estimated Costs*

In accordance with Section 252(a) of the Legislative Reorganization Act (2 U.S.C. §190(j)), the committee estimates that there will be the added cost due to the act and adopts the cost estimate prepared by the Congressional Budget Office (CBO) as follows:

Fiscal year:	Millions
1982	
1983	
1984	
1985	1.6
1986	1.7

On May 14, 1982, the following opinion was received from the Congressional Budget Office:

U.S. CONGRESS,
CONGRESSIONAL BUDGET OFFICE
Washington, D.C., May 14, 1982

Hon. Strom Thurmond,
Chairman, Committee on the Judiciary,
U.S. Senate, Washington, D.C.

Dear Mr. Chairman: Pursuant to Section 403 of the Congressional Budget Act of 1974, the Congressional Budget Office has prepared the attached cost estimate for S. 1992, the Voting Rights Act Amendments of 1982.

Should the Committee so desire, we would be pleased to provide further details on this estimate.

Sincerely,

Raymond C. Scheppach
(For Alice M. Rivlin, Director).

Congressional Budget Office — Cost Estimate

1. Bill number: S. 1992.
2. Bill title: Voting Rights Act Amendments of 1982.
3. Bill status: As ordered reported by the Senate Committee on the Judiciary, May 14, 1982.
4. Bill purpose: S. 1992 amends the requirements that states and other political subdivisions must meet to forgo review and approval by the Attorney General of proposed changes in their voting laws and procedures. These "preclearance" provisions affect nine states and parts of thirteen others.

Under the provisions of the bill, effective August 5, 1984, any state or political jurisdiction now subject to the preclearance provisions could be released from those requirements by a declaratory judgment if, over the preceding ten years, it met certain standards set forth in the bill. S. 1992 extends for five more years the time judicial jurisdiction over preclearance declaratory judgment matters is retained, allows any aggrieved person to move that the court reopen its action, and establishes certain conditions under which the court must vacate any previous declaratory judgment. The preclearance provisions are extended for 25 years after the effective date of the enactments, with interim Congressional review after 15 years.

The bill also establishes a new test of discrimination, whereby a judge could rule that discrimination occurred if state or local government actions had the effect or result of denying or abridging the right of any citizen to vote on account of race or color. Finally, the bill extends the 1975 requirement for bilingual ballots and other voting material to 1992, and provides that voters needing it may be given assistance, subject to certain restraints.

5.   Cost estimate:

Estimated authorization level:

Fiscal year:	*Millions*
1983	
1984	
1985	$1.6
1986	1.7
1987	1.8

Estimated outlays:

Fiscal year:	*Millions*
1983	
1984	
1985	1.5
1986	1.7
1987	1.8

The costs of this bill fall within budget function 750.

6.   Basis of estimate: Because no substantive change in law would occur until August 1984, no additional costs will be incurred until fiscal year 1985. CBO assumes that, beginning in fiscal year 1985, some political jurisdictions will ask the district court to release them from the preclearance requirement. For the purposes of this estimate, it was assumed that 400 jurisdictions would meet the requirements set forth in the bill by fiscal year 1985 and would request release. CBO estimates that the Department of

Justice would require an additional 40 positions beginning in fiscal year 1985 to handle the cases arising from the jurisdictions seeking release from preclearance. These are estimated to cost $1.6 million in 1985, with small increases thereafter.

The estimate of outlays is based on historical spending patterns for Justice Department activities.

7.   Estimate comparison: None.

8.   Previous CBO estimate: On September 14, 1981, CBO prepared an estimate on H.R. 3113, a bill to amend the Voting Rights Act of 1965 to extend the effects of certain provisions, and for other purposes, as ordered reported by the House Committee on the Judiciary, July 31, 1981. That bill was similar to S. 1992, and the estimated costs are identical.

9.   Estimate prepared by: Steven Martin.

10.   Estimate approved by: C. G. Nuckols (For James L. Blum, *Assistant Director for Budget Analysis*).

XIII.   Regulatory Impact Evaluation

In compliance with rule 29.5 of the Standing Rules of the Senate the Committee finds that no significant regulatory impact as defined by that subsection will result from the enactment of S. 1992.

XIV.   Changes in Existing Law Made by the Bill, as Reported

Changes in existing law made by the bill, as reported, are shown as follows (existing law proposed to be omitted is enclosed in black brackets, new matter is printed in italic, existing law in which no change is proposed is shown in roman). . . .

NOTES AND QUESTIONS

1. *Using the report to interpret a statute.* Does this report help you resolve the problem posed to you in Chapter 7, Section B? This report is drawn on heavily by the court to interpret the Voting Rights Act Amendments of 1982 in Thornburg v. Gingles, 478 U.S. 30 (1986). The *Thornburg* decision is excerpted and discussed in Chapters 6 and 12.

2. *Who drafts a report?* The reliance of courts on legislative reports for aiding the interpretation of unclear statutes has been the subject of substantial criticism over the years. The thrust of this criticism is that these reports are prepared by legislative staff, sometimes using language supplied by lobbyists, with an eye to future interpretation by administrative agencies and courts. In the extreme, Justice Scalia would forgo any

such use of committee reports. See, e.g., Blanchard v. Bergeron, 489 U.S. 87 (1989) (Scalia, J., concurring). While we leave to Part IV our analysis of the probative value of committee reports for purposes of statutory interpretation (we support it in some instances), it is important here to review the method by which committee reports are prepared. First, committee reports, as a general matter, are prepared by staff members. Second, the staff will sometimes use language provided by lobbyists. Third, committee reports are not voted on by the issuing committee. Fourth, the efforts of committee staff in these pursuits are, as a general matter, under the guidance of the legislator to whom the staff member is accountable. The insertion by a staff member of a view inconsistent with that of the member to whom he is responsible should never be expected or condoned.

CHAPTER 5
The Enactment of Legislation

A. INTRODUCTION

In Chapter 3 we focused on the organization and governing rules of legislatures, and in Chapter 4 we explored the workings of legislative committees. Together these form the framework for the consideration of legislation. In this chapter we will explore the enactment of legislation within this framework. We again turn to the Voting Rights Act of 1965 as our focal point for observing the formal steps of the enactment process.

B. THE STEPS OF ENACTMENT: FOLLOWING THE VOTING RIGHTS ACT OF 1965

The Voting Rights Act of 1965 was one of the most significant pieces of legislation ever adopted by Congress. Its passage, the result of an intense grassroots campaign by the civil rights movement, placed the federal government squarely behind efforts to create equal opportunities for African-Americans to participate in the political process. As the 89th Congress organized itself in January of 1965, passage of a broad voting rights reform was not a certainty. Although the newly elected president, Lyndon B.

Johnson, was committed to such reform and Congress was controlled by Democrats, many of the Democrats (along with many Republicans) opposed significant federal involvement in securing voting rights. Because of the then dominant seniority rules, many of these members held significant positions in Congress and could be counted on to take every opportunity to obstruct serious voting rights legislation.

In the presentation that follows we will watch the 89th Congress consider the voting rights bills that became the Voting Rights Act of 1965. Our window will be the Congressional Record, in which much of the formal work of Congress is recorded (while the style used for our excerpts is very close to that used in the Congressional Record, we are unable to present it in the news column format used in the Congressional Record). This presentation does not include every amendment proposed, nor does it set forth debate on the substance of the legislation. Rather, it is intended to introduce the formal mechanics and language of the legislative process and the methods for following it. The substance of the Voting Rights Act of 1965 will be explored in detail in Chapter 6.

1. Congressional and Other Records of Floor Activities

Congressional Record

United States of America   PROCEEDINGS AND DEBATES OF THE 89th CONGRESS, FIRST SESSION

Since 1873 the proceedings and debates of the United States Congress have been published daily in the Congressional Record. The Congressional Record is bound annually with an Index and Daily Digest. While the journal of each house (a constitutionally mandated document distinct from the Congressional Record) serves as the official record of legislative votes, the Congressional Record serves as an authoritative record of the proceedings of Congress. Users of the Congressional Record must be careful. Although a statute requires the Congressional Record to "be substantially a verbatim report of proceedings," 44 U.S.C. §901, congressional rules do allow some poststatement editing. A 1995 rules change in the House did limit this to grammatical errors of remarks by members of Congress and, under certain conditions, the insertion into the Congressional Record of remarks not made on the legislative floor, but critics of this process have argued that such remarks are misleading—particularly when such remarks may refer to an ambiguous provision in a statute. The inclusion of, at least, extended remarks—remarks explaining a member's stated position on a bill—does save floor time that might otherwise be used for their reading. Remarks not made on the floor are so designated in the Congressional Record by a different typeface or by placement in a section titled "Extensions of Remarks." For a more detailed discussion of Congressional Records, see Congressional Quarterly, Guide to Congress, 442 (4th ed. 1991); Richard A. Danner, Justice Jackson's Lament: Historical and Comparative Perspectives on the Availability of Legislative History, 13 Duke J. Comp. & Int'l L. 151 (2003).

State legislatures offer few comparable opportunities to follow their activities. While all state legislatures record or transcribe their sessions, the accessibility of these records varies from state to state.

2.   *Organization of the House of Representatives for the 89th Congress*

In the last chapter we explored the structures and rules that establish the framework under which Congress and state legislatures operate. In this section we will observe the organization of the House of Representatives of the 89th Congress, on January 4, 1965, in which it elected its leadership and adopted its rules. Prior to this organizational meeting, the representatives had been meeting in their respective party caucuses to choose their leaders and make their committee assignments.

HOUSE OF REPRESENTATIVES
Monday, January 4, 1965

This being the day fixed by the 20th amendment of the Constitution for the annual meeting of the Congress of the United States, the Members-elect of the House of Representatives of the 89th Congress met in their Hall, and at 12 o'clock noon were called to order by the Clerk of the House of Representatives, Hon. Ralph R. Roberts. . . .

The CLERK.   Representatives-elect to the 89th Congress: This is the day fixed by statute for the meeting of the 89th Congress.

As the law directs, the clerk of the House has prepared the official roll of the Representatives-elect.

Credentials covering the 435 seats in the 89th Congress have been received and are now on file with the Clerk of the 89th Congress.

The names of those persons whose credentials show they were regularly elected in accordance with the laws of the several States and of the United States will be called; and as the roll is called, following the alphabetical order of the States, beginning with the State of Alabama, Representatives-elect will answer to their names to determine whether or not a quorum is present.

The reading clerk will call the roll.

The Clerk called the roll by States and the following Representatives-elect answered to their names. . . .

Election of Speaker

The CLERK.   The next order of business is the election of a Speaker of the House of Representatives for the 89th Congress.

Nominations are now in order.

Mr. KEOGH.   Mr. Clerk, as chairman of the Democratic caucus, I am directed by the unanimous vote of that caucus to present for election to the office of the Speaker of the House of Representatives of the 89th Congress the name of the Honorable JOHN W. McCORMACK, a Representative-elect from the Commonwealth of Massachusetts.

Mr. LAIRD.   Mr. Clerk, by authority, by direction, and by unanimous vote of the Republican conference, I nominate for Speaker of the House of Representatives the Honorable GERALD R. FORD, a Representative-elect from the State of Michigan to the 89th Congress.

The CLERK.   The Honorable JOHN W. McCORMACK, a Representative-elect from the State of Massachusetts, and the Honorable GERALD R. FORD, Representative-elect from the State of Michigan, have been placed in nomination. Are there further nominations? [After a pause.] There being no further nominations, the Clerk will appoint the following to act as tellers: The gentleman from Texas, Mr. BURLESON, the gentleman from Pennsylvania, Mr. CORBETT, the gentlewoman from Missouri, Mrs. SULLIVAN, and the gentlewoman from Illinois, Mrs. REID.

Tellers will come forward and take their seats at the desk in front of the Speaker's rostrum.

The roll will now be called, and those responding to their name will indicate by surname the nominee of their choice.

The reading clerk will call the roll.

The tellers having taken their places, the House proceeded to vote for Speaker. . . .

The CLERK.   The tellers agree on their tallies. The total number of votes cast is 428, of which the Honorable JOHN W. McCORMACK, of Massachusetts, received 289, and the Honorable GERALD R. FORD received 139. Three voted "present."

Therefore, the Honorable JOHN W. McCORMACK, of Massachusetts, is the duly elected Speaker of the House of Representatives for the 89th Congress, having received a majority of the votes cast. . . .

Mr. McCORMACK. To my distinguished colleagues and valued associates, I appreciate very much the kind and generous remarks made about me by my friend, the minority leader, the gentleman from Michigan [Mr. GERALD R. FORD]. I can assure the gentleman that the deep, philosophical thoughts that he expressed are also entertained by me in relation to this great country of ours and in relation to the protection of the rights of all Members of the House under the rules of the House.

I am deeply grateful to my Democratic colleagues who on Saturday last selected me as their party's nominee for the office of Speaker.

I am grateful to the Members of the House for today officially electing me to the important position of Speaker of the U.S. House of Representatives for the 89th Congress. . . .

The 88th Congress just completed was one of the great Congresses of our history, and I have every confidence that the 89th Congress will make a most notable record.

Like you, I am looking forward to serving with the new Members who sincerely and in dedication to public service have already made a profound impression on me.

We meet, my colleagues, at the beginning of the 89th Congress under circumstances of monumental crises and of unlimited opportunities. Prospects are not totally but on the whole very bright and sound. Not only does our beloved country stand in the forefront of the nations as the most powerful force for peace and justice in the world, but for me the horizon seems bright, especially behind this philosophy of decency at home and our desire for understanding abroad.

We have, as a result of the politically historic election of last November, with his clear mandate, the leadership of LYNDON B. JOHNSON, as President, and of HUBERT H. HUMPHREY, as Vice President. They speak to the American people and to the world from the high quality of their individual gifts, their wide experience and great moral conviction and courage, and their dedication to our Nation and to our people.

On the legislative level, as a coordinate branch of the Government, I know the Congress will cooperate with President JOHNSON and Vice President HUMPHREY in the best interests of our country.

All of this contributes to an atmosphere of goodwill and unity. It fosters what I would like to call cooperation in depth. . . .

I am now ready to take the oath of office and will ask the dean of the House of Representatives, Hon. EMANUEL CELLER, of New York, to administer the oath.

Mr. CELLER then administered the oath of office to Mr. McCORMACK, of Massachusetts.

Swearing in of Members

The SPEAKER.   According to the precedent, the Chair is now ready to swear in all Members of the House.

The Members will rise.

Objection to Administration of Oath

Mr. RYAN.   Mr. Speaker.

The SPEAKER. For what purpose does the gentleman from New York rise?

Mr. RYAN.   Mr. Speaker, on my responsibility as a Member-elect of the 89th Congress, I object to the oath being administered to the gentlemen from Mississippi, Mr. ABERNETHY, Mr. WHITTEN, Mr. WILLIAMS, Mr. WALKER, and Mr. COLMER. I base this upon facts and statements which I consider to be reliable. I also make this objection on behalf of a significant number of colleagues who are now standing with me.

The SPEAKER.   Under the precedents, the Chair will ask the gentlemen who have been challenged not to rise to take the oath with the other Members, for the present at least.

The other Members will rise and I will now administer the oath of office to them.

The Members-elect and the Resident Commissioner-elect rose and the Speaker administered the oath of office to them.

Resolution Authorizing Oath of Office to Certain Members

Mr. ALBERT.   Mr. Speaker. I offer a resolution (H. Res. 1) which I send to the Clerk's desk.

The Clerk read the resolution, as follows:

H. Res. 1

Resolved, That the Speaker is hereby authorized and directed to administer the oath of office to the gentlemen from Mississippi, Mr. THOMAS G. ABERNETHY, Mr. JAMIE L. WHITTEN, Mr. JOHN BELL WILLIAMS, Mr. WILLIAM M. COLMER, and Mr. PRENTISS WALKER.

Mr. ALBERT.   Mr. Speaker, the Members-elect whose names are referred to in the resolution are here with certificates of election in due form on file with the Clerk of the House of Representatives just as all other members of the House.

Any question involving the validity of the regularity of the election of the Members in question is one which should be dealt with under the laws governing contested elections. I therefore urge the adoption of the resolution.

The SPEAKER.   The question is on the resolution.

Mr. ROOSEVELT.   Mr. Speaker, will the gentleman yield for a parliamentary inquiry?

Mr. ALBERT.   I yield for a parliamentary inquiry.

Mr. ROOSEVELT.   Mr. Speaker, will the first vote be on the resolution, or on the previous question?

The SPEAKER.   If the gentleman from Oklahoma moves the previous question, the vote will be on the previous question.

Mr. ROOSEVELT.   Mr. Speaker, if the motion for the previous question is voted down, would it then be in order to offer a substitute or an amendment providing that the five Representatives-elect from Mississippi not be sworn at this time and that the question of their rights to be seated be referred to the Committee on House Administration?

The SPEAKER.   The Chair will state that if the previous question is voted down, it would be in order to offer a proper amendment, which the Chair would not pass upon at this particular time, unless that situation arises.

Mr. ROOSEVELT.   I thank the Speaker.

Mrs. GREEN of Oregon.   Mr. Speaker, will the gentleman yield for a parliamentary inquiry?

Mr. ALBERT.   I yield for a parliamentary inquiry.

Mrs. GREEN of Oregon.   Since the rules of the House have not been adopted, am I correct in understanding that it would require 20 percent of the Members here to stand for a yea-and-nay vote?

The SPEAKER.   The Chair will state that under the Constitution, it would require one-fifth of the Members present to rise to order a yea-and-nay vote.

Mr. ALBERT.   Mr. Speaker, I move the previous question on the resolution.

Mrs. GREEN of Oregon.   Mr. Speaker, on that I demand the yeas and nays.

The yeas and nays were ordered.

The question was taken; and there were — yeas 276, nays 149, present 1, not sworn 8, as follows. . . .

The SPEAKER.   The question is on agreeing to the resolution.

The resolution was agreed to.

A motion to reconsider was laid on the table.

Swearing In of Members

The SPEAKER.   Will the Members-elect from Mississippi who have been challenged present themselves in the well of the House for the purpose of having the oath of office administered to them.

Messrs. ABERNETHY, WHITTEN, WILLIAMS, COLMER, and WALKER presented themselves at the bar of the House and the oath of office was administered to them. . . .

Majority Leader

Mr. KEOGH.   Mr. Speaker, as chairman of the Democratic caucus, I have been directed to report to the House that the Democratic Members have selected as majority leader the gentleman from Oklahoma, the Honorable CARL ALBERT.

Minority Leader

Mr. LAIRD.   Mr. Speaker, as chairman of the Republican conference, I am directed by that conference to notify the House officially that the gentleman from Michigan, the Honorable GERALD R. FORD, has been selected as the minority leader of the House.

Chairman of the Republican Policy Committee

Mr. LAIRD.   Mr. Speaker, further as chairman of the Republican conference, I am directed by that conference to notify the House that the gentleman from Wisconsin, Mr. BYRNES, has been elected chairman of the Republican policy committee of the House.

Election of Clerk, Sergeant at Arms, Doorkeeper, Postmaster, and Chaplain

Mr. KEOGH.   Mr. Speaker, I offer a resolution (H. Res. 3) and ask for its immediate consideration.

The Clerk read the resolution, as follows:

H. Res. 3

Resolved, That Ralph R. Roberts, of the State of Indiana, be, and he is hereby, chosen Clerk of the House of Representatives;

That Zeake W. Johnson, Jr., of the State of Tennessee, be, and he is hereby, chosen Sergeant at Arms of the House of Representatives;

That William M. Miller, of the State of Mississippi, be, and he is hereby, chosen Doorkeeper of the House of Representatives;

That H. H. Morris, of the State of Kentucky, be, and he is hereby, chosen Post-[master of the House of Representatives];

That Rev. Bernard Braskamp, D.D. of the master of the House of Representatives; District of Columbia, be, and he is hereby, chosen Chaplain of the House of Representatives.

The resolution was agreed to.
The SPEAKER. Will the officers elected present themselves at the bar of the House.
The officers-elect presented themselves at the bar of the House and took the oath of office.

Notification to Senate of Organization of House

Mr. MILLS. Mr. Speaker, I offer a resolution (H. Res. 4) and ask for its immediate consideration.
The Clerk read the resolution as follows:

H. RES. 4

Resolved, That a message be sent to the Senate to inform that body that a quorum of the House of Representatives has assembled; that JOHN W. McCORMACK, a Representative from the State of Massachusetts, has been elected Speaker; and Ralph R. Roberts, a citizen of the State of Indiana, Clerk of the House of Representatives of the Eighty-ninth Congress.
The resolution was agreed to.
A motion to reconsider was laid on the table.

Committee to Notify the President of the United States of the Assembly of the Congress

Mr. ALBERT. Mr. Speaker, I offer a resolution (H. Res. 5) and ask for its immediate consideration.
The Clerk read the resolution, as follows:

H. RES. 5

Resolved, That a committee of three Members be appointed by the Speaker on the part of the House of Representatives to join with a committee on the part of the Senate to notify the President of the United States that a quorum of each House has been assembled, and that Congress is ready to receive any communication that he may be pleased to make.

The resolution was agreed to.
A motion to reconsider was laid on the table.

The SPEAKER.   The Chair appoints as members of the committee to notify the President the gentleman from Oklahoma [Mr. ALBERT]; the gentleman from New York [Mr. CELLER]; and the gentleman from Michigan [Mr. FORD].

Authorizing the Clerk to Inform the President of the Election of the Speaker and the Clerk of the House of Representatives

Mr. MAHON,   Mr. Speaker, I offer a resolution (H. Res. 6) and ask for its immediate consideration.

The Clerk read the resolution, as follows:

H. Res. 6

Resolved, That the Clerk be instructed to inform the President of the United States that the House of Representatives has elected JOHN W. McCORMACK, a Representative from the State of Massachusetts, Speaker, and Ralph R. Roberts, a citizen of the State of Indiana, Clerk of the House of Representatives of the 89th Congress.

The resolution was agreed to.
A motion to reconsider was laid on the table. . . .

Rules of the House

Mr. ALBERT.   Mr. Speaker, I offer a resolution and ask for its immediate consideration.

The Clerk read as follows:

H. Res. 8

Resolved, That the Rules of the House of Representatives of the Eighty-eighth Congress, together with all applicable provisions of the Legislative Reorganization Act of 1946, as amended, be, and they are hereby adopted as the Rules of the House of Representatives of the Eighty-ninth Congress, with the following amendments therein as a part thereof, to wit:

In rule XI, strike out clause 23 and insert:

"23. . . . If the Committee on Rules shall adversely report or fail to report within twenty-one calendar days after reference, any resolution pending before the committee providing for an order of business for the consideration by the House of any public bill or joint resolution favorably reported by a committee of the House, on days when it is in order to call up motions to discharge committees, it may be in order as a matter of the highest privilege for the Speaker, in his discretion, to recognize the chairman or any member of the committee which reported such bill or joint resolution who has been so authorized by said committee to call up for consideration by the House the resolution which the Committee on Rules has so adversely reported, or failed to report, and it shall be in order to move the adoption by the House of said resolution adversely reported, or not reported, notwithstanding the adverse report, or the failure to report, of the Committee on Rules. Pending the consideration of said resolution the Speaker may entertain one motion that the House adjourn; but after the result is announced he shall not entertain any other dilatory motion until the said resolution shall have been fully disposed of." . . .

Mr. ALBERT.   Mr. Speaker, this resolution, if adopted, would restore the 21-day rule which was in effect during the 81st Congress, with some modifications.

Mr. Speaker, it would enable the Speaker, after a resolution had been before the Committee on Rules for 21 days or more, to recognize the chairman or other members of the legislative committee from which the bill emanated to discharge the Committee on Rules on a day set aside for discharging committees. . . .

The purpose of these . . . changes in the rules, of course, is to expedite the business of the House and to make available other methods of handling the legislative business of the House. They do not seek to change any of the rules governing the Committee on Rules or other procedures, all of which are left intact. . . .

Mr. Speaker, I urge the adoption of the resolution.

Mr. SMITH of Virginia.   Mr. Speaker, will the gentleman yield?

Mr. BROWN of Ohio.   Mr. Speaker, will the gentleman yield to me?

Mr. ALBERT.   I first yield to the distinguished gentleman from Virginia [Mr. SMITH] and then I shall yield to the gentleman from Ohio [Mr. BROWN].

Mr. SMITH of Virginia.   Mr. Speaker, I would like to propound a few questions. The first question on this resolution is this: Are copies of this resolution available so that the Members may know on what they are voting?

Mr. ALBERT.   In response to the gentleman from Virginia, I am not able to answer whether every Member has had copies of this resolution available. I do not know that many Members have had copies of the resolution.

Mr. SMITH of Virginia.   If the gentleman will yield further, I picked up a piece of paper here on the floor the other day which makes me think it is a copy of the typewritten copy of what is proposed. I do not know. But it seems to me that in a matter of this importance we should at least have the opportunity to have a copy available before us in order to see what we are doing.

Mr. ALBERT.   How many copies have been distributed to Members, I do not know.

Mr. SMITH of Virginia.   It was not distributed to me. I picked one up off the floor.

Mr. ALBERT.   The gentleman from Virginia has exercised his usual initiative in getting things.

Mr. SMITH of Virginia.   I assume the gentleman intends to move the previous question.

Mr. ALBERT.   I do, at the appropriate time.

Mr. SMITH of Virginia.   If the gentleman will yield further, what I want to know is whether or not there is going to be an opportunity for discussion and debate on this resolution?

Mr. ALBERT.   I say to the gentleman that I have yielded to the gentleman for the purpose of making a statement at this time.

Mr. SMITH of Virginia.   I thank the gentleman very much. I wonder if the gentleman will yield for the offering of an amendment?

Mr. ALBERT.   The gentleman is not in position to yield for the offering of an amendment. I may say to the gentleman from Virginia that many Members have spoken to me about the desirability of offering sundry amendments which have not been considered at all. The gentleman from Oklahoma is not in position to yield for the purpose of offering any amendments.

Mr. SMITH of Virginia.   I suspected that would be the answer I was going to get. . . .

Mr. ALBERT.   Mr. Speaker, I yield 5 minutes to the gentleman from Ohio [Mr. BROWN].

Mr. BROWN of Ohio.   Mr. Speaker, will the gentleman first yield for a question?

Mr. ALBERT.   I yield to the gentleman.

Mr. BROWN of Ohio.   May I say to the gentleman that I was not privileged to attend the conference, or the caucus, at which this rule was discussed, and it was not until late last night that I had an opportunity to study this new rule or resolution or, the effect thereof, or to read exactly the language of the resolution which the gentleman from Oklahoma has presented today.

As ranking minority member of the Rules Committee, I am, of course, vitally interested in what the rule may do. I should like to ask a question or two.

If I understand the language of the resolution, it would do more than restore the 21-day rule we had in the past, whereby if the Rules Committee did not take action on a bill within 21 days, it could automatically be brought up in the House. Apparently, this new rule goes beyond that so I should like to have the gentleman tell me if I have misinterpreted it, for I want to understand it. It goes beyond the old 21-day rule and gives authority to the Speaker greater than any which has been exercised by any Speaker for many, many years, to determine, in his own wisdom — and no one, questions the present Speaker's wisdom, patriotism, or good judgment — or to decide in his own judgment — whether he wants the bill to come up at all. No one else will have any authority except the Speaker, is that correct?

Mr. ALBERT. I would say to the distinguished gentleman that this would give the Speaker authority to recognize the chairman of the committee or a member designated by a legislative committee, but would not deprive the Committee on Rules of any authority it has to bring bills out under resolutions or rules and under the procedures governing the determination of legislation.

Mr. BROWN of Ohio. I understand that, yet I may not have made my question clear.

Mr. ALBERT. I believe the gentleman did.

Mr. BROWN of Ohio. If the Rules Committee does not act, and this new 21-day rule is applicable, it would be the Speaker, and the Speaker alone, who could decide whether the bill would be brought up, if it had been for 21 days before the Rules Committee.

Mr. ALBERT. The Speaker and the legislative committee having jurisdiction over the subject matter.

Mr. BROWN of Ohio. It does not say that.

Mr. ALBERT. The House will have the final determination in all instances. The House can decide whether the resolution should be adopted or whether it should be rejected, or even whether it should be referred to a committee. The House will have complete jurisdiction over the matter. . . .

Mr. BROWN of Ohio. One other question and then I am through. Will the gentleman yield for me to offer a perfecting amendment?

Mr. ALBERT. The gentleman will not yield for that purpose.

Mr. BROWN of Ohio. The gentleman refuses to yield for the purpose of offering an amendment at this time?

Mr. ALBERT. The gentleman cannot yield for that purpose.

Mr. BROWN of Ohio. I say to the gentleman I respect his position, but I want to make very clear what his position might be.

Mr. ALBERT. May I say to the gentleman that this resolution is being offered under instructions of the Democratic caucus. I am the agent of the caucus for that purpose. I have no authority to yield for amendment or to yield for any purpose in order to allow the bill to be divided.

Mr. BROWN of Ohio. May I say to my good friend, the distinguished gentleman from Oklahoma, I have the highest respect and regard for him. I know he is under instructions which he is attempting to carry out, and he always does carry out instructions to the best of his ability whether he likes them or not. I respect him for it.

Mr. ALBERT. In this case I like the instructions that I have had from the Democratic caucus. . . .

Mr. GERALD R. FORD. Mr. Speaker, I yield to the gentleman from Ohio [Mr. BROWN].

Mr. BROWN of Ohio. I would like to say to you that I, representing the minority in connection with these rules matters, have been under instructions from our party conference, as you have been from your caucus, to say to the House we have prepared certain amendments to the rules of the House that we would like to have considered, and that they may be offered as separate resolutions if they cannot be offered as amendments today. I think you are entitled to know this, and the House is entitled to know it, that those resolutions will be presented in due time.

Mr. ALBERT.   I thank the gentleman for giving me that information.

Mr. GERALD R. FORD.   Mr. Speaker, I appreciate the time given by the gentleman from Oklahoma, the majority leader. I intended to say much of what was said by the distinguished gentleman from Ohio [Mr. BROWN]. The House Republican conference has met twice within the last month. On December 16 we instructed a group, a task force, to undertake a study of the proposed changes in the rules that would be needed and desirable for the protection of the minority and for the orderly prosecution of parliamentary business. This committee, under the chairmanship of Mr. BROWN, has functioned and, as a consequence, we do have some proposals that, if we have an opportunity, will be offered if the previous question is defeated. They will be constructive, and I hope and trust that we can prevail in this next vote so that the House can work its will on these and other amendments.

Mr. CURTIS.   Mr. Speaker, will the gentleman yield?

Mr. ALBERT.   I yield for a brief question.

Mr. CURTIS.   The point I would like to make to the gentleman, having worked on these proposed rule changes, is that the procedure we are following right now demonstrates the difficulty that the minority finds itself in where we are considering one of the most serious matters we are going to face; namely, the rules we are going to operate under, and we are not able to debate the question or deliberate on it. I think the gentleman from Oklahoma sees the position that the minority is in, and I think the gentleman must recognize this is unfair. I hope he will, if these resolutions are brought out, take the matter to the Democratic caucus for reconsideration of these rules for fair play.

I thank the gentleman.

Mr. ALBERT.   I thank the gentleman and now I yield to our distinguished Speaker, the gentleman from Massachusetts [Mr. McCORMACK].

Mr. McCORMACK.   Mr. Speaker, as this resolution involves changes in the rules, I feel that my views should be made known to the Members of the House. I strongly favor the resolution offered by the gentleman from Oklahoma [Mr. ALBERT]. I think the 21-day rule is a rule that is for the benefit of the individual Members of the House without regard to party affiliation in giving them the opportunity of passing upon legislation that has been reported out of a standing committee. Some Members may construe it as an attack on the Committee on Rules, but it is not. It is a strengthening of the rules of the House in the direction of the individual Member having an opportunity to pass upon legislation that has been reported out of a standing committee and which has been pending before the Committee on Rules for 21 days or more. We had this rule some few Congresses ago for one Congress. The reason it was not continued is simply and frankly that we did not have the votes. When it was adopted, it was not adopted as a permanent part of the rules but for one Congress. In following Congresses we did not have the votes. So it is not a question whether the advocates of the 21-day rule felt that it was not workable. I have always felt throughout the years that it would be a strengthening influence not only on the rules of the House but on each Member of the House and on the House collectively in the matter of expressing the will of the House to have the 21-day rule incorporated as a part of the rules of the House. . . .

Mr. BROWN of Ohio.   Mr. Speaker, will the gentleman yield?

Mr. McCORMACK.   I yield to the gentleman from Ohio.

Mr. BROWN of Ohio.   Mr. Speaker, the gentleman has made a very able defense of the Committee on Rules for which I am grateful.

Mr. McCORMACK.   Mr. Speaker, I have profound respect for the Committee on Rules. May I say that as leader and as Speaker, knowing the power and the charm and the influence of the Committee on Rules, and when I meet individual members of that committee I bow to them.

Mr. BROWN of Ohio.   And we bow to the Speaker very humbly at times also; sometimes regretfully, but we do bow to him.

Mr. Speaker, may I ask the gentleman a question or two in connection with what is before us? I hate to correct the Speaker, but I believe we did adopt that rule not once, but twice.

Mr. McCORMACK.   I am always subject to correction.

Mr. BROWN of Ohio.   That was the 21-day rule, but that rule as it was adopted was different from the rule proposed.

Mr. McCORMACK.   Slightly different.

Mr. BROWN of Ohio.   Under this rule for the first time there is a provision that the Speaker may as a matter of the highest privilege and in his discretion call up a bill, or not call up a bill. It goes further than the 21-day rule that we had before. In other words, the Committee on Rules has had the power of life-and-death control over a bill — yes or no. Now you take it away from the Committee on Rules and put it in the hands of the Speaker, for whom, may I say, I have the greatest respect, love, and admiration.

Mr. McCORMACK.   I can conceive of no Speaker exercising his discretion but as a matter of high trust and as a matter of complete equity and fairness to all Members involved. I believe that the discretion of the Speaker is a reasonable provision to put in there in order to have it in connection with the 21-day rule. The original rule left it entirely in the hands of the chairman of the committee. This now, if adopted, would give the Speaker some authority to confer with the chairman of the committee.

Mr. BROWN of Ohio.   But not the chairman of the Committee on Rules?

Mr. McCORMACK.   Also, if the chairman of a committee should be recalcitrant or noncooperative then we could have the committee to direct some other member of the committee to call the bill up under the 21-day rule.

Mr. BROWN of Ohio. We have the highest respect and the highest regard for the character of the Speaker of this House, but we also realize that sometimes Speakers change. I mean by that we have had a change in the speakership and should this occur there might be someone on this side of the aisle who might abuse that privilege at the present time. There is a question as to whether or not we would want to do that by changing the rules of the House so as to permit any future Speaker — not you, because I am not worried about you, Mr. Speaker —

Mr. McCORMACK. That is very nice.

Mr. BROWN of Ohio. You are too nice a fellow. But I am thinking about some dirty dog that might come along some other time and say here is a nice little wrinkle in the rule which we can use to block this legislation.

In other words, should we give that power to every Speaker in the future?

We gave that power to "Uncle Joe" Cannon and Tom Reed as the gentleman recalls. We gave them too much power.

Mr. McCORMACK. This represents nothing comparable to what the gentleman is now referring. In those days the Speaker had the power to make all committee appointments. This is an entirely different situation. I can conceive of no Speaker doing anything other than exercising his discretion for the best interests of the membership of the House of Representatives. Frankly, I feel that is a minor if not insignificant argument to make against this proposed change.

Mr. BROWN of Ohio. Mr. Speaker, I salute you. You have again proven to the new membership of the House of Representatives why you have been selected as Speaker of this body. You are a very able man in the well of the House.

Mr. COOLEY. Mr. Speaker, will the gentleman yield?

Mr. McCORMACK. I yield to the gentleman from North Carolina.

Mr. COOLEY. I would like to propound a question, if I may:

Suppose the legislative committee passes a bill out and it goes to the Rules Committee and they have the ordinary usual hearing before the Rules Committee and the Rules Committee takes it under consideration and then denies the rule? Can you still bring that bill to the floor of the House?

Mr. McCORMACK. After 21 days.

Mr. COOLEY. If the gentleman will yield further, even though the Rules Committee has denied the rule?

Mr. McCORMACK. That is provided in the proposed change.

Mr. Speaker, I hope that the resolution which has been submitted by the gentleman from Oklahoma [Mr. ALBERT] will be agreed to.

Mr. ALBERT. Mr. Speaker, I move the previous question.

Mr. BROWN of Ohio. Mr. Speaker, on that I demand the yeas and nays. The yeas and nays were ordered.

The question was taken; and there were — yeas 224, nays 201, answered "present" 1, not voting 6. . . .

NOTES AND QUESTIONS

1. *Opening day.* The Twentieth Amendment to the Constitution provides that Congress shall meet at least once a year and that "such meeting shall begin at noon on the 3d day of January, unless they [Congress] shall decide otherwise." Before the adoption of this amendment in 1933, the Constitution established the first Monday in December as the commencement date. This particular amendment, along with the remaining provisions of the Twentieth Amendment, was intended to remedy several arcane congressional scheduling practices that resulted in one long session and one short lame-duck legislative session in each two-year term. This prior practice is described in Congressional Quarterly, Guide to Congress 54 (4th ed. 1991).

2. *The receipt of credentials.* The Constitution (Art. I, §4) grants each state the power to regulate its own elections for members of Congress, but reserves for Congress the power to preempt such regulation. Each house of Congress is also granted the power to be the judge of the elections of its own members. The practice is for each state through its own processes to certify the winner of its congressional races and to forward those certifications to each respective house. Generally, these certifications are accepted, but sometimes objections may be raised. One such objection that proved successful — the refusal to seat member-elect Richard McIntyre — is discussed in Chapter 7 on pages 440-443.

3. *Choosing the Speaker.* The most important organizational decision of the House of Representatives is the choice of its Speaker, who then becomes the second most powerful political officer in the country. In 1995, the House of Representatives, to weaken the power of individual Speakers, amended its rules to provide that no member could hold that office for longer than eight consecutive years. Although the Speaker is elected by the House as a whole, the choice is really that of the majority caucus, whose nominee is inevitably elected. Once the Speaker is elected, his first task, after taking his oath, is to administer the oath to the other representatives-elect.

4. *Administering the oath of office.* Normally the administration of the oath of office to representatives-elect is perfunctory, but for the 89th Congress, it was disturbed by the motion of Representative-elect Ryan to exclude the representatives from Mississippi. Although Ryan's objection was quickly overcome, it is a window on the political environment in which the voting rights legislation will be considered. During the prior summer's Democratic Convention, delegates from the Mississippi Freedom Democratic Party (MFDP), an integrated pro–civil rights party, had tried to replace the all-white delegation of the Mississippi Democrats, which had adopted a platform opposing civil rights and rejecting the civil rights planks of the national party. The MFDP's efforts were defeated, although they were supported by a number of delegates, including the delegations from

Michigan and New York. At the start of the 89th Congress, the MFDP went to Washington to object to the seating of the five-member, all-white Mississippi delegation. While this effort was unsuccessful, it was supported by close to 150 representatives, of which Representative Ryan was one.

On what basis do you think Congress could have voted to refuse to seat the Mississippi delegation? The Constitution, Article 1, §5, provides: "Each House shall be the Judge of the Elections, Returns and Qualifications of its own Members. . . ." In Chapter 7 we will discuss the authority to judge elections and returns and the authority to judge qualifications.

5. *The amendment to the rules.* We discussed the importance of legislative rules in Chapter 3. At the commencement of each new Congress, the House must adopt new rules. The traditional procedure is to adopt the rules of the prior Congress with, if necessary, amendments. The determination of what rules will remain in effect and which will be amended is generally made by the majority party and the rules are almost always sent to the floor without opportunity for amendment. The politics surrounding rules changes can be intense because such changes can have substantial impacts on political power and public policy. In this case several amendments were offered. The amendment to establish a 21-day rule illustrates the impact a rule can have on legislative politics and policy. The rule reduces the power of the Chair of the Rules Committee. The Speaker and Democratic caucus were concerned that the Rules Committee, which controls the scheduling and terms of legislative debate, had become too independent and might thwart the caucus' legislative goals, even though the committee has a Democratic majority. This was of particular concern for voting rights legislation, which was opposed by the committee's chair. The 21-day rule was introduced to circumvent any logjam. A different procedural change to effect the same end was adopted in the Senate. In later years, the 21-day rule was again repealed, and, at present, has been replaced by a discharge procedure, which is discussed in Chapter 4. See Note 4 on page 266 of this chapter for an example of another rule (three-fifths voting for any federal tax rate increase) adopted by the House in the 104th Congress (1995-1996) that could have a profound effect on policy.

3.   Introduction of Bills

In Chapter 1, we presented a statute. A bill is a proposal for a change in the law that becomes a statute after it has been enacted. The bills that ultimately led to the adoption of Public Law 89-110, the Voting Rights Act of 1965, were recorded as introduced into the 89th Congress, 1st Session, on March 17, 1965, in the House of Representatives (H.R. 6400) and on March 18, 1965, in the Senate (S. 1564).

HOUSE OF REPRESENTATIVES
Wednesday, March 17, 1965

The House met at 12 o'clock noon.

Public Bills and Resolutions

Under clause 4 of rule XXII, public bills and resolutions were introduced and severally referred as follows:
By Mr. CELLER:
H.R. 6400. A bill to enforce the 15th amendment to the Constitution of the United States; to the Committee on the Judiciary.

SENATE
Thursday, March 18, 1965

The Senate met at 12 o'clock meridian, and was called to order by the Vice President.

Bills Introduced

Bills were introduced, read the first time, and, by unanimous consent, the second time, and referred as follows:
By Mr. MANSFIELD (for himself and Senators DIRKSEN, KUCHEL, AIKEN, ALLOTT, ANDERSON, BARTLETT, BASS, [plus many others]:
S. 1564. A bill to enforce the 15th amendment to the Constitution of the United States.

In Congress, as in most legislative bodies, ideas for legislation are introduced in the form of a bill. While such ideas can emanate from a variety of sources, e.g., the executive branch, lobbyists, constituents, legislative staffs (see Chapter 2), only members of a legislature can introduce bills. However, the budget processes in some states require the governor of that state to submit budget bills to the legislature. See, e.g., Art. IV, §12 of the California State Constitution; Art. VII, §2 of the New York State Constitution; and Art. VIII, §2 of the Illinois State Constitution. In the U.S. House of Representatives, bills are introduced by depositing a bill in the "hopper," provided for that purpose in the chamber. In the Senate, bills are usually introduced in a similar manner. On occasion, if a senator seeks some particular procedural treatment for a bill, the Senator will rise and introduce the bill from the floor. The latter path was followed for the introduction of S. 1564. In state legislative bodies, bills are usually introduced by depositing them with the legislative clerk of the house of which the introducer is a member. After introduction, bills are assigned numbers by clerks of the legislative bodies and referred to the appropriate committees by the presiding officer of each house. The numbers usually run sequentially, based on time of introduction, but sometimes certain numbers will be held for particular legislation. After a bill is introduced, in most legislative bodies, it is printed.

Only a small percentage of bills become law. The system, politically and administratively, winnows the number of bills enacted to a minimal percentage of those introduced. Bills are divisible into a number of cubbyholes that roughly bespeak their possibilities for passage: bills with little support; noncontroversial bills; controversial bills; major bills; and "must" bills. Bills with little support, the most frequently introduced bill, are not introduced with an enactment expectation, at least, on the part of the legislator. They are intended generally to publicize an issue, initiate debate on such issue, or curry political favor with a constituent or interest group. The introduction of a bill can shift political "heat" from the legislator to a legislative committee. Noncontroversial bills, by definition, are bills that can be expedited through the process without opposition, generally by the use of special calendars. They include bills to exchange real property, to rename parks or streets, or to name a building after a former legislator. Controversial bills, of course, are those surrounded by political controversy. Mostly they are major bills, those pieces of legislation that have broad redistributive or regulatory impact. The likelihood of their enactment is unpredictable. It is on these bills that legislative bodies focus most of their attention. "Must" bills are, generally, controversial bills about which there is general legislative agreement that there must be a solution before the end of a legislative session. These bills generally garner the most attention as members struggle to find compromises to build majorities. The Voting Rights Act is an example of major, controversial, "must" legislation. For a fuller discussion of the division of bills into similar categories, see Walter Oleszek, Congressional Procedures and the Policy Process 81-84 (1989).

Excerpts from H.R. 6400 and S. 1564 follow. Their form is similar to the form of bills used in the nation's state legislatures (though the style and typeface do not exactly duplicate that used by Congress).

89TH CONGRESS
1ST SESSION

H.R. 6400

IN THE HOUSE OF REPRESENTATIVES

MARCH 17, 1965

Mr. CELLER introduced the following bill; which was
referred to the Committee on the Judiciary

A BILL

To enforce the fifteenth amendment to the Constitution of the
United States.

*Be it enacted by the Senate and House of Representatives of the United
States of America in Congress assembled,* That this Act shall be known as
the "Voting Rights Act of 1965."

Sec. 2. No voting qualification or procedure shall be imposed or applied to deny or abridge the right to vote on account of race or color. . . .

89th CONGRESS
1st Session

S. 1564

IN THE SENATE OF THE UNITED STATES

March 18, 1965

Mr. Mansfield (for himself, Mr. Dirksen, Mr. Kuchel, Mr. Aikin,
Mr. Allott, Mr. Anderson, Mr. Bartlett, Mr. Bass, Mr. Bath, Mr. Ben-
nett, Mr. Boggs, Mr. Brewster, Mr. Burdick, Mr. Case, Mr. Church,
Mr. Clark, Mr. Cooper, Mr. Cotton, Mr. Dodd, Mr. Dominick,
Mr. Douglas, Mr. Fong, Mr. Gruening, Mr. Harris, Mr. Hart, Mr.
Hartke, Mr. Inouye, Mr. Jackson, Mr. Javits, Mr. Jordan of Idaho,
Mr. Kennedy of Massachusetts, Mr. Kennedy of New York, Mr.
Lausche, Mr. Long of Missouri, Mr. Magnuson, Mr. McCarthy, Mr.
McGee, Mr. McGovern, Mr. McIntyre, Mr. McNamara, Mr. Metcalf,
Mr. Mondale, Mr. Monroney, Mr. Montoya, Mr. Morse, Mr. Morton,
Mr. Moss, Mr. Mundt, Mr. Murphy, Mr. Muskie, Mr. Nelson, Mrs.
Neuberger, Mr. Pastore, Mr. Pearson, Mr. Pell, Mr. Prouty, Mr. Prox-
mire, Mr. Randolph, Mr. Ribicoff, Mr. Saltonstall, Mr. Scott, Mr.
Symington, Mr. Tydings, Mr. Williams of New Jersey, Mr. Yarbor-
ough, and Mr. Young of Ohio) introduced the following bill, which
was read twice and referred to the Committee on the Judiciary.

A BILL

To enforce the fifteenth amendment to the Constitution of the
United States.

*Be it enacted by the Senate and House of Representatives of the United
States of America in Congress assembled,* That this Act shall be known as
the "Voting Rights Act of 1965."

Sec. 2. No voting qualification or procedure shall be imposed or applied to deny or abridge the right to vote on account of race or color. . . .

4.   *Assignment of Bills to Committees*

One of the most important decisions about a bill is the choice of committee to which it is assigned. Committee decisions to kill bills are rarely overturned, and committee amendments usually frame the ensuing legislative debate. References to committees are usually routine acts by legislative staff under the formal authority of the legislative leadership of the particular house in which the bill has been introduced. For example, in the Congress, it is the parliamentarians who usually make the referrals. Most referrals are simple, based on the subject of the bill and the jurisdiction of the particular committee. But, while each legislative committee has its own jurisdiction (either codified or set forth in the legislative rules of the particular house), there are many jurisdictional ambiguities. As one observer has written about the House of Representatives:

> The House . . . suffers from a chronic case of jurisdictional ambiguities. In 1973, the Bolling Committee examination of the House jurisdictional lines found "disarray" and "endemic" jurisdictional conflict, of which "hundreds of such cases, involving virtually every committee, were detailed in the staff-prepared monographs." A classic 1980s example was nuclear waste disposal, an area that was claimed by Energy and Commerce (with jurisdiction over nuclear energy), Science and Technology (technology), and Interior (public lands, where the disposal sites would be), among others. When the issue came to a head in 1982, the bill referrals reflected the overlap. The Chair referred one bill . . . to Interior; another bill . . . to Energy and Commerce; and a third . . . to Science and Technology.

Charles Tiefer, Congressional Practice and Procedure 111-12 (1989). The present rules of the House of Representatives provide for multiple referrals of bills whose subject matter comes within the jurisdiction of more than one committee. Rule XII, cl. 2 of the Rules of the House of Representatives.

The decision about which committee to refer a bill to can be of life or death significance, and the selection of a committee may be part of the overall strategy for the passage of a bill. For example, the Civil Rights Act of 1964 was drafted to permit its referral to a friendly Senate Commerce Committee rather than to a hostile Senate Judiciary Committee. But in all referrals there must be some relationship between the bill's subject matter and the committee's jurisdiction. New York provides another example. For years, a "bottle" bill (providing for refunds for the return of bottles) had been sent to the State Assembly's commerce committee because of its impact on industry. After years of having the bill killed in this committee, it was finally sent by a new Speaker to the committee charged with responsibility for environmental issues, where it was quickly reported to the floor and passed. The functions and procedures of committees are the subject of Chapter 4.

When the Voting Rights Act of 1965 was introduced in the Senate, it was accompanied by a motion that the Senate Judiciary Committee report the bill within a specific number of days. The motion triggered a procedural dispute that signaled the rugged debate the passage of this bill would entail.

Mr. MANSFIELD.   Mr. President, on behalf of the distinguished minority leader and myself, I move that the bill be referred to the Committee on the Judiciary, with instructions to report back not later than April 9, 1965.

The VICE PRESIDENT.   The question is on agreeing to the motion of the Senator from Montana.

Mr. EASTLAND.   Mr. President —.

The VICE PRESIDENT.   The motion is debatable.

The Senator from Mississippi [Mr. EASTLAND] is recognized.

Mr. EASTLAND.   Mr. President, as I understand, the motion is to refer the bill to the Judiciary Committee, the bill to be reported back not later than the 9th day of April.

The VICE PRESIDENT.   That is the understanding of the Chair.

Mr. EASTLAND.   Mr. President, this is a bill which flies directly in the face of the Constitution of the United States. What is being proposed is an unheard of thing. It is proposed to give the Judiciary Committee only 15 days to study a bill as far reaching as this. Of course, there cannot be the attention paid to it which it should have. I assure the Senate that the Committee on the Judiciary will hold hearings expeditiously and will go into all phases of the bill.

Let me make myself clear: I am opposed to every word and every line in the bill. I believe that it is an unheard of thing. I believe that it is bad procedure to refer a bill of this character to a committee with instructions to report after only 15 days.

Consider the poll tax amendment. We passed an amendment to the Constitution to prohibit the poll tax as a qualification for voting in Federal elections. Some of those who signed the bill took the position that it would require a constitutional amendment. Now, they are backing up and attempting to do by statute what they said would require an amendment to the Constitution.

This bill would apply to only five States. It is sectional legislation. It is regional legislation. I tell the Senate now that when it considers a regional bill, such a bill is suspect, not only in this instance, but also in every other instance. Certainly, there should be study and deliberation. If the committee is dragging its feet, all the Senate has to do is to adopt a motion to discharge the committee and bring the bill back to the floor.

The Attorney General of the United States — if I read the press reports correctly — and all his staff of lawyers have been working for a number of weeks on the bill. The majority leader and his staff have been working for a number of weeks on the bill. The minority leader and his staff have been working for a number of weeks on the bill.

My information is that they were able to come together only yesterday morning. Then the bill was dropped in the hopper, and it is proposed to refer it to the Judiciary Committee, with only 15 days' time to consider it.

(At this point, Mr. Tydings took the chair as Presiding Officer.)

Mr. EASTLAND.   I do not see that is an orderly, legislative process. It seems to me that when a Senator believes he has the votes to pass a bill, regardless of its merits, the roll should be called.

This bill would lodge vast discretionary power in the Attorney General without any guidelines. I believe there is a very grave question involved.

Are we delegating legislative responsibility? Are we delegating legislative power which the Constitution of the United States prohibits?

Should not the Judiciary Committee have the opportunity to study that phase?

The Constitution of the United States provides that the Congress shall have power to regulate the time and place of holding Federal elections. That is as far as it goes.

There is one basic fact: The Federal Government cannot go into voter qualifications in the States. I do not believe that there is any room for argument on that point. That is basic to our system of government. This bill would do violence to that provision in the Constitution.

Is the Senate willing to undertake a study which would show whether it should proceed by constitutional amendment or by statute?

Is that not the legal way to do it? Is that not the proper way to consider legislation?

The asserted basis of the bill is the 15th amendment to the Constitution. The 15th amendment does not provide that the Congress may assert a single standard for voter qualifications for alleged discrimination on account of race.

I call the attention of the Senate to section 2 of the Constitution, which clearly lodges the authority within the States themselves.

Mr. President, 15 days is wholly inadequate. The Judiciary Committee will expeditiously proceed to consider the bill. I remember that in 1960, the committee made a number of amendments to one bill, which greatly improved it, and reported it back to the Senate, and the Senate agreed to the committee amendments.

I do not see how we are gaining anything, but we are certainly destroying the legislative process by this procedure.

I tell Senators now that there will not be adequate or full consideration of the bill in 15 days.

The PRESIDING OFFICER.   The question is on agreeing to the motion to refer the bill to the Committee on the Judiciary with instructions.

On this question, the yeas and nays have been ordered; and the clerk will call the roll.

The legislative clerk proceeded to call the roll.

Mr. MANSFIELD   (when his name was called). On this vote I have a pair with the junior Senator from Alabama [Mr. SPARKMAN]. If he were present and voting he would vote "nay." If I were at liberty to vote, I would vote "yes." I therefore withhold my vote.

Mr. METCALF   (when his name was called). On this vote I have a pair with the senior Senator from Louisiana [Mr. ELLENDER]. If he were present and voting he would vote "nay." If I were at liberty to vote, I would vote "yea." I therefore withhold my vote.

The roll call was concluded.

Mr. LONG of Louisiana.   I announce that the Senator from Idaho [Mr. CHURCH], the Senator from Louisiana [Mr. ELLENDER], the Senator from Alaska [Mr. GRUENING], the Senator from Missouri [Mr. LONG], the Senator from Minnesota [Mr. McCARTHY], the Senator from Oklahoma [Mr. MONRONEY], and the Senator from Florida [Mr. SMATHERS] are absent on official business.

I also announce that the Senator from North Carolina [Mr. ERVIN], the Senator from New York [Mr. KENNEDY], the Senator from Wyoming [Mr. McGEE], the Senator from Utah [Mr. MOSS], the Senator from Georgia [Mr. RUSSELL], and the Senator from Alabama [Mr. SPARKMAN] are necessarily absent.

On this vote, the Senator from New York [Mr. KENNEDY] is paired with the Senator from North Carolina [Mr. ERVIN]. If present and voting, the Senator from New York would vote "yea," and the Senator from North Carolina would vote "nay."

I further announce that, if present and voting, the Senator from Idaho [Mr. CHURCH], the Senator from Missouri [Mr. LONG], the Senator from Utah [Mr. MOSS], the Senator from Oklahoma [Mr. MONRONEY], and the Senator from Alaska [Mr. GRUENING] would each vote "yea."

Mr. KUCHEL.   I announce that the Senator from Utah [Mr. BENNETT], the Senator from Arizona [Mr. FANNIN], the Senator from California [Mr. MURPHY], and the Senator from Texas [Mr. TOWER] are necessarily absent.

The Senator from Massachusetts [Mr. SALTONSTALL] is absent on official business.

If present and voting, the Senator from Utah [Mr. BENNETT], the Senator from Massachusetts [Mr. SALTONSTALL], the Senator from Texas [Mr. TOWER], and the Senator from California [Mr. MURPHY] would each vote "yea."

So the motion of Mr. Mansfield and other Senators to refer the bill (S. 1564) to the Committee on the Judiciary with instructions was agreed to.

The result was announced — yeas 67, nays 13, as follows:

[No. 40. Leg.]
Yeas — 67

Aiken	Fulbright	Morton
Allott	Gore	Mundt
Anderson	Harris	Muskie
Bartlett	Hart	Nelson
Bass	Hartke	Neuberger
Bayh	Hayden	Pastore
Bible	Hickenlooper	Pearson
Boggs	Hruska	Pell
Brewster	Inouye	Prouty
Burdick	Jackson	Proxmire
Byrd, WV	Javits	Randolph
Cannon	Jordan, ID	Ribicoff
Carlson	Kennedy, MA	Scott
Case	Kuchel	Simpson
Clark	Lausche	Symington
Cooper	Magnuson	Tydings
Cotton	McGovern	Williams, NJ
Curtis	McIntyre	Williams, DE
Dirksen	McNamara	Yarborough
Dodd	Miller	Young, ND
Dominick	Mondale	Young, OH
Douglas	Montoya	
Fong	Morse	

Nays — 13

Byrd, VA	Jordan, NC	Stennis
Eastland	Long, LA	Talmadge
Hill	McClellan	Thurmond
Holland	Robertson	
Johnston	Smith	

Not Voting — 20

Bennett	Long, MO	Murphy
Church	Mansfield	Russell
Ellender	McCarthy	Saltonstall
Ervin	McGee	Smathers
Fannin	Metcalf	Sparkman
Gruening	Monroney	Tower
Kennedy, NY	Moss	

Mr. JAVITS.   Mr. President, I move that the Senate reconsider the vote by which the motion was agreed to.

Mr. KUCHEL.   I move to lay that motion on the table.

The VICE PRESIDENT.   The question is on agreeing to the motion of the Senator from California to lay on the table the motion of the Senator from New York to reconsider.

The motion to lay on the table was agreed to.

Typically, no formal limits circumscribe a committee's consideration of a bill. Senator Mansfield's motion, which led to the debate, was atypical and intended to ensure that the committee process could not tie up the legislation. This concern was particularly justified by proponents of the bill because the Chair of the Judiciary Committee, Senator Eastland, was opposed to the legislation, and it was feared that he would exercise whatever prerogatives available to delay its movement.

5.   *Legislative Voting*

For an initial observer of the legislative process, legislative voting often seems confusing and sometimes unsettling. In addition to archaic terminology ("ayes and nays"), depending on the legislative jurisdiction one is viewing, bills can pass with few legislators on the floor, and absent legislators can be counted as voting in favor of the legislation.

On this later point, recall the facts in Heimbach v. State of New York (Chapter 3, page 109). The New York State Senate voted in succession on five separate tax bills intended to provide revenues for transportation-related subjects. A review of the journal for that particular day reflects that one particular minority party senator voted yes on three of the taxes and was marked absent for the other two. Witnesses to the votes would note that this particular senator was not on the Senate floor for any of the votes. In fact, he was in the hospital. To make matters worse on several of these taxes, the missing senator was the deciding vote in favor of the taxes, taxes he later testified he opposed. What happened? From the legislative perspective, nothing unusual. The senator had checked in early on the morning of the day in question. That meant, under New York rules, that on a fast roll call vote (the three on which he was noted in support) he was considered voting yes unless he personally signified his opposition, which he could not do because he was out of the chamber. The other two votes on which he was recorded absent, were slow roll calls during which he had to cast his own vote. As he was not on the floor at the time the vote was taken, he was considered absent. If he had not checked in, he would have been considered absent for all of the votes.

The particulars of the above example make voting somewhat unsettling. But the types of voting rules that resulted in this peculiar fact pattern are intended as efficiencies that usually reduce unnecessary legislative delay.

Basically there are two general voting methods: nonrecorded votes, in which individual votes are not recorded (mostly limited to Congress), and recorded votes in which individual votes are noted. Nonrecorded votes are divided into three forms: voice votes, division votes, and teller votes.

On a *voice vote*, votes are cast in chorus by answering "aye" or "no" to a particular question with the presiding officer determining the outcome of the vote, based on the volume of the response. A *division vote*, which may be demanded by any member, is a more accurate form of voice vote because it requires members to stand to be counted rather than to just express their view by voice. Even more accurate is the *teller vote*, in which members are assigned responsibility of making an actual count. This vote must be required by one-fifth of a quorum. In none of these forms are individual votes recorded. The rules of the House of Representatives provide as follows:

> The Speaker shall rise to put a question but may state it sitting. The Speaker shall put a question in this form: "Those in favor (of the question), say 'Aye.'"; and after the affirmative voice is expressed, "Those opposed, say 'No.'" After a vote by voice under this clause, the Speaker may use such voting procedures as may be invoked under rule XX.

Rule I, cl. 6 of the Rules of the House of Representatives. On a nonrecorded vote the count of the presiding officer is not appealable and the outcome is recorded in the journal and in the Congressional Record. The voice vote will, on occasion, result in legislation passing with no member on the floor of the legislature except for the presiding officer. Such a result can be avoided by a call for a quorum by any member. While nonrecorded votes, particularly voice votes, may afford some legislative efficiency in consideration of noncontroversial legislation, it can also be used to deny the public the opportunity to know how members voted on controversial legislation, like pay-raise bills.

Recorded votes compel the notation of individual votes on the legislative record. As is illustrated by the New York example above, there can be several types of recorded votes. Under the New York Senate rules, all votes are recorded. The normal vote is the fast roll call during which the first and last names on the roll call list (an alphabetically arranged list) are called and everyone who is checked in is recorded "yes" unless they personally indicate "no" by raising their hand or standing. A slow roll call, triggered by five members standing, forces members to come to the floor to vote.

The Mansfield motion, noted earlier, required a recorded vote (yeas and nays). Article I, §5 of the U.S. Constitution requires such a vote on any question, in either house of Congress, whenever demanded by one-fifth of the members present. In the Senate, after a member requests a recorded vote, the presiding officer asks the body whether such a vote is "the desire of one-fifth of those present," and those in support raise their hands. Although the Constitution only requires one-fifth of those present, under Senate practice this has been interpreted to mean at least 11 members — one-fifth of a quorum (51 members). If more than a quorum is present, then more than 11 members are necessary to "second" a call for a roll call vote. The need for "seconders" has allowed the Senate leadership over the years some discretion in whether roll call votes would occur. See Charles Tiefer, Congressional Practice and Procedure 532-34 (1989) (generally an extraordinary compendium on congressional practice). In the House, a recorded vote can be obtained in one of two ways: through the constitutionally mandated desire of one-fifth of those present (not necessarily a quorum); and through Rule XX, which compels a roll call when desired by one-fifth of a quorum (44 members). What are the advantages of each method?

A recorded vote is also required in the House if there has been a successful objection to the absence of a quorum for any formal action. This is known as an *automatic roll call.*

6. (a) When a quorum fails to vote on a question, a quorum is not present, and objection is made for that cause (unless the House shall adjourn) —

(1) there shall be a call of the House;

(2) the Sergeant-at-Arms shall proceed forthwith to bring in absent Members; and

(3) the yeas and nays on the pending question shall at the same time be considered as ordered.

(b) The Clerk shall record Members by the yeas and nays on the pending question, using such procedure as the Speaker may invoke under clause 2, 3, or 4. Each Member arrested under this clause shall be brought by the Sergeant-at-Arms before the House, whereupon he shall be noted as present, discharged from arrest, and given an opportunity to vote; and his vote shall be recorded. If those voting on the question and those who are present and decline to vote together make a majority of the House, the Speaker shall declare that a quorum is constituted, and the pending question shall be decided as the requisite majority of those voting shall have determined. Thereupon further proceedings under the call shall be considered as dispensed with.

Rule XX, cl. 6 of the Rules of the House of Representatives.

In the Senate, a recorded vote is accomplished by each member answering the clerk's call of his or her name. In the House, most recorded votes are taken by use of electronic voting machines into which each member inserts a personal voting card.

In a roll call vote, members of the Congress who are not in attendance can have their view on a particular bill expressed through pairing with members holding opposite views, either present in the chamber (live pair) or absent (dead pair). As can be seen from the roll call on the Mansfield motion to instruct the Judiciary Committee, pairs are not recorded as votes. If a live pair is made, the present legislator cannot cast his or her vote. (See Senator Mansfield above: "If I were at liberty to vote, I would vote 'yea.' ") In the Senate, absent members can also have their view of a bill expressed by a present member, while in the House, nonpaired (absent) members can only be listed without reference to their preference on a bill.

6. *Reporting a Bill from Committee*

Pursuant to the Mansfield motion referring S. 1564 to the Senate Judiciary Committee with instructions, the committee reported the voting rights bill on April 9, 1965, with amendments.

Reports of Committees

The following reports of committees were submitted:

By Mr. EASTLAND, from the Committee on the Judiciary, with amendments, without recommendation. . . .

S. 1564. A bill to enforce the 15th amendment to the Constitution of the United States (Rept. No. 162).

Usually a committee will make a recommendation to its legislative body with respect to a bill as amended. In this case, the committee made no recommendation. A consensus could not be reached on a number of issues, and the committee was required to report a bill by April 9. Recall, also, that Senator Eastland, chair of the committee, was opposed to *every* line of the legislation. Note also the form in which the bill is reported. The original bill is reported with amendments. This means that both the bill and the amendments will be before the parent chamber. The committee could have reported a "clean" bill, one with a new number, in which all adopted amendments had been incorporated. There is no rule that determines which method a committee will follow on this point. But, as you will see, the form chosen can make a difference in the way a bill may be considered, particularly for purposes of subsequent amendment.

The Congressional Record does not record much about committee proceedings, only a notice that a committee has reported a bill and the committee's recommendation, if any. To find out what happened at the committee, including the votes of its members, one must turn to the committee report, in this case S. Rep. No. 162 (of the Judiciary Committee), or other committee records, such as transcripts of committee meetings (if made) or voting sheets. Committee reports are printed by the U.S.

Government Printing Office and can be found, at least in part, in the U.S. Code Congressional and Administrative News. Excerpts from a committee report are found in Chapter 4.

On April 13, 1965, Senator Mansfield moved that the Senate consider the bill, which motion was agreed to by voice vote.

Voting Rights Act of 1965

Mr. MANSFIELD.   Mr. President, I move that the Senate proceed to the consideration of Calendar No. 149, Senate bill 1564.

The ACTING PRESIDENT pro tempore.   The bill will be stated by title.

The LEGISLATIVE CLERK.   A bill (S. 1564) to enforce the 15th amendment of the Constitution of the United States.

The ACTING PRESIDENT pro tempore.   The question is on agreeing to the motion of the Senator from Montana.

Mr. ELLENDER.   Mr. President, before the question is put, I should like to ask what the intention of the leadership is.

Mr. MANSFIELD.   The intention is not to debate the bill until the Senate convenes on April 21.

Mr. ELLENDER.   At 12 o'clock noon on that day.

Mr. MANSFIELD.   At 12 o'clock noon.

Mr. ELLENDER.   No action will be taken in respect to the bill in the mean-time.

Mr. MANSFIELD.   Nothing before that time. There will be a morning hour when we return. Then we shall lay down the bill and again make it the pending business.

The ACTING PRESIDENT pro tempore.   The question is on agreeing to the motion of the Senator from Montana.

The motion was agreed to, and the Senate proceeded to consider the bill, which had been reported from the Committee on the Judiciary with an amendment, to strike out all after the enacting clause and insert. . . .

This motion did not require any immediate action on the bill but only signaled the commencement of its consideration. In fact, later that day, consideration of the bill was resumed and Senator Williams offered an amendment to add certain prohibitions to the bill.

Voting Rights Act of 1965

The Senate resumed the consideration of the bill (S. 1564) to enforce the 15th amendment of the Constitution of the United States.

Mr. WILLIAMS of Delaware.   Mr. President, I understand from the able majority leader that no action will be taken on the pending measure until April 21. However, on behalf of the Senator from Iowa [Mr. MILLER] and myself, I send to the desk an amendment and ask that it be stated. I shall discuss the amendment when the Senate reconvenes and I ask that the amendment be made the pending business.

The Presiding Officer (Mr. KENNEDY of New York in the chair).   The amendment will be stated.

The legislative clerk read as follows:

On page 29, line 20, strike all down to and including line 4 on page 30 and insert in lieu the following:

"Whoever knowingly or wilfully gives false information as to his name, address, or period of residence in the voting district for the purpose of establishing his eligibility to register or vote, or conspires with another individual for the purpose of encouraging his false registration or illegal voting, or pays or offers to pay or accepts payment either for registration or for voting shall be fined not more than $10,000 or imprisoned not more than five years, or both."

Mr. WILLIAMS of Delaware.   Mr. President, I ask that the amendment just read be made the pending business. I shall discuss it next week.

---

7.   Floor Amendments

As noted above, the Judiciary Committee reported S. 1564 to the floor with amendments. In Congress, as in many states, floor amendments are a very important part of the process and are often adopted. In some states, however, floor amendments, although frequently offered, are almost *never* adopted due to strict party discipline. (New York State is one such example.)

In the Senate, a decision to consider a bill opens the floor amendment process. In the House, where size requires floor actions to be far more controlled, the amendatory process is circumscribed by "rules" from the Rules Committee that must be adopted by the House. In either case, the offering of a floor amendment requires a response from a bill's sponsor or manager.

> The moment of truth ... comes when a ... [legislator] has offered a floor amendment and the bill manager must decide how to respond. Floor managers work in two dimensions. They work strategically, to obtain passage of the bill in some form, which motivates them to oppose amendments that would kill or reshape the bill, but to accept amendments that

move the bill towards passage in acceptable shape. Also they work tactically. . . .

Charles Tiefer, Congressional Practice and Procedure 640 (1989).

Amendments are frequently characterized as either "friendly" or "hostile." A friendly amendment, such as the Williams amendment, is one that is acceptable to a bill's sponsor, either because it resolves a substantive problem or furthers its chances for passage. A hostile amendment is one that is intended to make it impossible to achieve the goals of the bill's sponsor.

Under the rules of the Senate, an amendment can be offered at any time on any subject, without regard to the germaneness of the amendment to the bill. This procedure creates opportunities for confusing or obstructing the process. It also creates opportunities for forcing unpopular votes on Senators. For example, in 1993, members of the Senate who were opposed to President Clinton's decision to permit gays in the military offered an amendment, prohibiting such action, to the Home Leave Act of 1992 in order to create a possible election issue against those who voted against the amendment. This procedure would have been considered out of order in the House of Representatives.

> Senate rules permitting members to offer non-germane amendments to most legislation allow senators to bypass committee consideration and force a floor vote on pet proposals. Just last month, for example, Howard M. Metzenbaum, D-Ohio, won Senate approval of stiffer infant-formula standards as an amendment to another bill (H.R. 1848), although he had been unable to get even a hearing on his proposal in the Labor and Human Resources Committee.

Hook, Senate Rules, Closeness of GOP Margin . . . Keeps Democrats Influential in Minority, 44 Cong. Q. Week. Prep. 1394 (1986) (quoted in Charles Tiefer, Congressional Practice and Procedure 585 (1989)).

To amend a bill in the House the "rule" that governs floor consideration will set forth the conditions, if any, for amendment. In addition, the House has a standing rule prohibiting nongermane amendments, which is in effect unless there is a contrary rule. Whether a particular amendment is germane is, of course, another question that is sometimes quite difficult to resolve.

By introducing his amendment well before commencement of the bill's consideration, Senator Williams chose a tactical path that maximizes notice of his intention and his opportunities to garner support for his view. Contrast this tactic with a surprise amendment — one called up for debate on the same day as it is introduced — which is frequently intended to slow consideration of a bill or embarrass a member by forcing a vote on a particular issue.

The debate on the proposed amendment of Senator Williams started on April 22, 1965.

Voting Rights Act of 1965

Mr. MANSFIELD.   Mr. President, I ask unanimous consent that the Chair lay before the Senate the unfinished business.

The PRESIDING OFFICER.   The Chair lays before the Senate the unfinished business, which is S. 1564.

The Senate resumed the consideration of the bill (S. 1564) to enforce the 15th amendment of the Constitution of the United States.

The PRESIDING OFFICER.   The question is on agreeing to the amendment of the Senator from Delaware [Mr. WILLIAMS] numbered 82, to the committee substitute.

Under the precedents of the Senate, in such a case, the substitute, for the purpose of amendment, is regarded as original text. Any amendment proposed thereto is therefore in the first degree, and any amendment to such amendment is in the second degree, and not open to amendment.

Any amendment to the original text of the bill, or any amendment to such an amendment, would have precedence over the committee substitute or any amendment thereto.

In the event the committee amendment is agreed to, no further amendment is in order.

Senator Williams had moved to amend the committee's substitute (amendment in the nature of a substitute) for the original bill S. 1564. The substitute was an amendment that replaced everything following the bill's enactment clause. Both S. 1564 and the committee substitute were before the Senate, and, at some point, the Senate had to adopt the substitute as an amendment to S. 1564 before it then adopted S. 1564 as amended. The procedural point under discussion above related to certain limits on the amendment process. According to Senate practice, an amendment in the first degree is subject to further amendment, but an amendment to amend such an amendment (an amendment in the second degree) is not subject to further amendment. This serves the obvious purpose of avoiding the confusion and delay that would accompany the freedom of unlimited amendments.

This point is illustrated by Senator Ervin, who on April 29 offered an amendment to the amendment of Senator Williams. The Williams amendment was in the first degree, so the Ervin amendment was appropriate. If the Williams amendment had been an amendment in the second degree, the Ervin amendment would not have been in order. Procedurally, this amendment was accepted by Senator Williams, which normally would have ended the matter. But because the Senate had ordered a recorded vote on the Williams amendment, unanimous consent was required to permit this amendment. Unanimous consent is a procedure generally used to temporarily amend the normal legislative rules for a particular purpose.

Voting Rights Act of 1965

The Senate resumed the consideration of the bill (S. 1564) to enforce the 15th amendment of the Constitution of the United States.

Amendment No. 117

Mr. ERVIN.   Mr. President, I send to the desk an amendment to amendment No. 82 of the Senator from Delaware [Mr. WILLIAMS], and ask that it be stated.

The PRESIDING OFFICER.   The amendment to the amendment will be stated for the information of the Senate.

The LEGISLATIVE CLERK.   On page 1, line 10, of the amendment numbered 82, change the period to a colon and add this additional sentence:

"*Provided, however,* That this provision shall be applicable only to elections held for the selection of presidential electors, Members of the United States Senate, and Members of the United States House of Representatives."

Mr. ERVIN.   Mr. President, let me state briefly the reason why I offer my amendment to the pending amendment of the Senator from Delaware. I am in favor of amendment No. 82. However, in my opinion amendment No. 82 in its present form is unconstitutional because it is not restricted to Federal elections. By the term "Federal elections," I mean elections in which presidential electors and Members of the U.S. Senate and Members of the U.S. House of Representatives are chosen. The only effect of my amendment would be to confine the application of amendment No. 82 to Federal elections and thereby make it constitutional under the interpretation placed on the 15th amendment by the Supreme Court of the United States in a number of cases.

Mr. WILLIAMS of Delaware.   Mr. President, I concur in the statement just made by the Senator from North Carolina [Mr. ERVIN]. I find his amendment to my amendment to be perfectly acceptable. In fact, I believe that it would make my amendment stronger, which is the objective we are trying to achieve.

Since the yeas and nays have been ordered on the amendment I ask unanimous consent that I be allowed to modify my amendment to accept the provision of the amendment offered by the Senator from North Carolina.

The PRESIDING OFFICER.   Is there objection? The Chair hears none, and it is so ordered.

On April 30, the day after the Williams proposal (as amended by the Ervin amendment) passed on a roll call vote, the majority and minority leaders, Senators Mansfield and Dirksen, offered an amendment in the form of a substitute for the voting rights legislation.

Voting Rights Act of 1965

The Senate resumed the consideration of the bill (S. 1564) to enforce the 15th amendment of the Constitution of the United States.

Amendment No. 124

Mr. MANSFIELD.   Mr. President, on behalf of the distinguished minority leader and myself, I send to the desk a substitute for the voting rights bill which was reported by the Judiciary Committee about 2 weeks ago. The substitute does not differ greatly from the committee bill. On the contrary it recognizes and adopts most of the legal contributions which were made by the distinguished lawyers of the Judiciary Committee. The brilliant work in committee of the able Senator from Michigan [Mr. HART], the Senator from Missouri [Mr. LONG], the Senator from Massachusetts [Mr. KENNEDY], the Senator from Indiana [Mr. BAYH], the Senator from North Dakota [Mr. BURDICK], the Senator from Maryland [Mr. TYDINGS], the Senator from Nebraska [Mr. HRUSKA], the Senator from Hawaii [Mr. FONG], the Senator from Pennsylvania [Mr. SCOTT], the Senator from New York [Mr. JAVITS], as well, of course, as that of the distinguished minority leader [Mr. DIRKSEN]—the great contributions of these Senators to more effective insurance of the right to vote for all, have been, for the most part, retained in the substitute.

The actual changes from the committee version of the bill originally introduced by the joint leadership are not great. I now list them in summary form.

The first appears in the so-called cleansing portion of the bill, section 4(a). Our amendment strikes the escape clauses of the present bill, including the controversial 60 percent escape hatch. In brief, it provides that a State or subdivision may get out from under the act only when the effects of the denial and abridgement of the right to vote have been effectively corrected and there is no reasonable cause to believe that a test or device will be used for the purpose or will have the effect of discrimination in voting. As in the present bill, the court maintains jurisdiction of the matter for 5 years to insure against backsliding.

In section 7 the substitute simplifies the procedure for listing voters by Federal examiners. An applicant to an examiner need only allege that he is not registered and that he has been denied the opportunity to do so. The Attorney General may waive the latter requirement.

The amended bill contains a new poll tax provision — section 9 — which is clearly constitutional, which places the Congress clearly on record against discriminatory poll taxes, and which assures a speedy determination on the matter by the Supreme Court. It is true that this provision does not automatically abolish all poll taxes as some would have the Congress attempt by legislation. But we are convinced, largely by the arguments of the Attorney General, that there would be a significant constitutional question involved in such an attempt. Indeed, it might, in the end, result in no action at all being taken on poll taxes. We are persuaded, too, that the language of the substitute not only insures against the use of poll taxes where there is even the slightest suggestion of discriminatory purpose or use but also provides for the most rapid and direct court test of the constitutionality of this question.

Finally, a new section 10 assures that persons listed by Federal examiners will actually have the ballot placed in their hands.

The amendment proposed by the senior Senator from Delaware [Mr. WILLIAMS], as modified by the senior Senator from North Carolina [Mr. ERVIN] and adopted by the Senate yesterday, is included.

The distinguished minority leader and I are in agreement in our belief that these changes will strengthen the effectiveness of the legislation. We believe they will be helpful in bringing about at the earliest possible moment the equal treatment of all citizens in their right to vote in all elections — Federal, State, and local.

I realize that other Members may not feel the same way. Each lawyer in the Senate as well as all those outside has his own ideas about how to achieve the same legal purpose. There are many roads which lead to the same end and they are followed by Senators who are at least as able as the lawyers who worked with us to perfect this substitute. But, in the end, Senators who are generally trying to go in the same direction must also try to get together on the same road, if there is to be any legislation in the Senate at all. The joint leadership is hopeful that this substitute provides such a road. We are hopeful that, with the key questions now placed in focus, the Senate will proceed steadily until the matter is resolved. For the information of the Senate, it is our intention to consider the substitute at the earliest possible moment consistent with respect for the rights of all other Members. Once it is before the Senate we will stay with it until a decision is made one way or the other. In view of the amount of time already spent on the voting rights legislation, moreover, the Senate is on notice that beginning Monday, sessions will be lengthened. The intention is to come in at noon as heretofore in order to permit committees to meet on other essential business. But Members should anticipate that the Senate will be in session until about 7 p.m. or later every day. Beginning on Monday the possibility of quorums and votes at any time will exist. Senators should make their plans accordingly.

The PRESIDING OFFICER.   The amendment will be stated.

Note that this amendment was offered by the leadership of both parties of the legislative body. This meant that the bipartisan leadership of the Senate had been spending time negotiating differences with Senators in order to build a majority around compromises reflected in this legislation. This is evident in the comments on the amendment by one of its sponsors, Senator Dirksen.

Mr. DIRKSEN.   I believe the distinguished majority leader has very clearly stated the case. Insofar as possible, we have sought to preserve the text in all sections of the bill that was first offered as it came to the Senate from the committee before the deadline on April 9. We were careful to preserve that language so that it could not be said that we were coming here with an entirely new bill.

However, there were provisions concerning which deep conviction reposed on both sides of the aisle. I come within that orbit of conviction. That concern related, first, to the poll tax; second, with respect to making clear the real objective of the bill; third, with respect to the cleansing provision. Those are the major items as to which modifications have been made.

As the majority leader has indicated, we hope that the subject of the poll tax, without actually being resolved in the Senate, and leaving it in the status which it presently enjoys, will finally go to the Supreme Court with as much dispatch as possible for the purpose of obtaining a declaratory judgment. Then we shall know, notwithstanding the recent decision — in fact, this week — in the Virginia case, and notwithstanding the dicta in that case, where we stand on the subject of the poll tax.

I was afraid an impression might go abroad that there was something punitive about the bill and that we were missing the objective of trying to secure the voting rights of people. That was the reason for section 10, verifying and simplifying it, and going to the heart of the subject.

Finally, there was the so called cleansing provision in section 4.

Those items constitute the real improvements in the bill. I earnestly hope that when we resume explanation and discussion, not merely today, but in the next week, we can move apace and finally get the bill out of the Senate and on the way to the House of Representatives.

---

8. A Legislative Quorum

The debate on the Williams amendment (which occurred before the Mansfield-Dirksen amendment was offered) was interrupted for a quorum call.

Mr. ELLENDER.   Mr. President, I suggest the absence of a quorum.
The PRESIDING OFFICER.   The clerk will call the roll.
The legislative clerk called the roll, and the following Senators answered to their names:

[No. 59 Leg.]

Aiken	Hart	Miller
Bennett	Holland	Mondale
Boggs	Inouye	Monroney
Brewster	Jackson	Mundt
Clark	Javits	Murphy
Cooper	Jordan, ID	Nelson
Cotton	Kuchel	Pastore
Dirksen	Long, MO	Pell
Ellender	Long, LA	Sparkman
Fannin	Mansfield	Tydings
Gruening	McCarthy	Williams, DE
Harris	McNamara	Young, OH

Mr. LONG of Louisiana.   I announce that the Senator from New Mexico [Mr. ANDERSON], the Senator from Alaska [Mr. BARTLETT], the Senator from. Tennessee [Mr. BASS], the Senator from Nevada [Mr. BIBLE], the Senator from Virginia [Mr. BYRD], the Senator from Nevada [Mr. CANNON], the Senator from Connecticut [Mr. DODD], the Senator from Arkansas [Mr. FULBRIGHT], the Senator from Massachusetts [Mr. KENNEDY], the Senator from Washington [Mr. MAGNUSON], the Senator from Wyoming [Mr. McGEE], the Senator from Oregon [Mr. MORSE], the Senator from Utah [Mr. MOSS], the Senator from Oregon [Mr. NEUBERGER], the Senator from Mississippi [Mr. STENNIS], the Senator from Texas [Mr. YARBOROUGH], and the Senator from Tennessee [Mr. GORE] are absent on official business.

I also announce that the Senator from North Dakota [Mr. BURDICK], the Senator from West Virginia [Mr. BYRD], the Senator from Illinois [Mr. DOUGLAS], the Senator from North Carolina [Mr. JORDAN], the Senator from Ohio [Mr. LAUSCHE], the Senator from South Dakota [Mr. McGOVERN], the Senator from New Hampshire [Mr. McINTYRE], the Senator from Montana [Mr. METCALF], the Senator from Maine [Mr. MUSKIE], the Senator from West Virginia [Mr. RANDOLPH], the

Senator from Connecticut [Mr. RIBICOFF], the Senator from Georgia [Mr. RUSSELL], the Senator from Florida [Mr. SMATHERS], the Senator from Missouri [Mr. SYMINGTON], and the Senator from Georgia. [Mr. TALMADGE] are necessarily absent.

Mr. KUCHEL.   I announce that the Senator from Colorado [Mr. ALLOTT], the Senator from Vermont [Mr. PROUTY] and the Senator from Massachusetts [Mr. SALTONSTALL] are necessarily absent.

The Senator from Hawaii [Mr. FONG], the Senator from Iowa [Mr. HICKENLOOPER], the Senator from Pennsylvania [Mr. SCOTT] and the Senator from Wyoming [Mr. SIMPSON] are absent on official business.

The Senator from Kansas [Mr. CARLSON], the Senator from New Jersey [Mr. CASE], the Senator from Nebraska [Mr. CURTIS], the Senator from Texas [Mr. TOWER], and the Senator from North Dakota [Mr. YOUNG] are detained on official business.

The PRESIDING OFFICER.   A quorum is not present.

Mr. HART.   Mr. President, I move that the Sergeant at Arms be directed to request the attendance of absent Senators.

The PRESIDING OFFICER (Mr. MONDALE in the chair).   The question is on agreeing to the motion of the Senator from Michigan.

The motion was agreed to.

The PRESIDING OFFICER.   The Sergeant at Arms will execute the order of the Senate.

After a little delay, Mr. BAYH, Mr. CHURCH, Mr. DOMINICK, Mr. EASTLAND, Mr. ERVIN, Mr. HARTKE, Mr. HAYDEN, Mr. HRUSKA, Mr. KENNEDY of New York, Mr. McCLELLAN, Mr. MONTOYA, Mr. MORTON, Mr. PROXMIRE, Mr. ROBERTSON, Mrs. SMITH, Mr. THURMOND, and Mr. WILLIAMS of New Jersey entered the Chamber and answered to their names.

The PRESIDING OFFICER.   A quorum is present. The Senator from Michigan is recognized.

A quorum is the number of members of a legislative body necessary to be present for the conduct of legislative business. The Constitution (Art. 1, §5) requires a quorum of a majority of members to be present to conduct business in either house of Congress.

Both houses of Congress operate under the presumption of a quorum's presence, which means that the absence of a quorum must be suggested, through a point of order, by a member. Generally, a member must be recognized to make this point. The consequence of denying such recognition, at least on more than the most infrequent occasions, would almost certainly be chaos. Calling for a quorum has a variety of purposes. First, for purposes of a recorded vote, a quorum call can serve to bring needed seconders to the floor and to maximize the number of members whose vote is recorded. Second, all quorum calls take time. Such time can be used to temporarily delay proceedings in order to negotiate a procedural point or to convince a member to support the legislation. Sometimes the intent of the delay is to actually bring members to the floor; to second a request for a recorded vote; to make as many members as possible cast a recorded vote; to locate and bring to the floor supporters or opponents of legislation; to harass the majority party by generally slowing down the process. Third, a quorum call can be used to tarnish the attendance record of a member who is not present in the capitol. On occasion, the request for a quorum can result in an adjournment if an insufficient number are available to answer the call. In this case, a quorum was not present and the Sergeant-at-Arms was instructed to find the absent members.

9.   Unanimous Consent Agreements

On May 4, after debates on numerous amendments, Senate Majority Leader Mansfield offered a "unanimous consent agreement" for the purpose of regulating the continuing debate. As noted earlier, a request for unanimous consent is a request to amend the normal legislative rules for a particular purpose. In the Senate, unanimous consent requests are frequently requests for agreements on the management of the debate on a particular piece of legislation. In this sense they are, if adopted, agreements (called unanimous consent agreements) to limit debate and the freedom of amendment. In the House, this function is served by "rules" from the Committee on Rules (see page 253) and the germaneness rule. In most state legislatures, the function is served by legislative rules limiting debate and requiring germaneness.

In this case the proposed agreement was objected to by Senator Ellender and was, thus, defeated.

Proposed Unanimous-Consent Agreement

Mr. MANSFIELD.   Mr. President, I send to the desk a proposed unanimous-consent agreement and ask that it be read by the clerk.

The PRESIDING OFFICER.   The clerk will read the proposal.

The legislative clerk read as follows:

Ordered, that at the conclusion of routine morning business on Thursday, May 6, 1965, during the further consideration of S. 1564, debate on the amendment of the senior Senator from North Carolina [Mr. ERVIN] shall be limited to 4 hours, to be equally divided and controlled by Senator ERVIN and the junior Senator from Michigan [Mr. HART]: that debate on the amendment to be offered by the junior Senator from Massachusetts [Mr. KENNEDY] and others dealing with the poll tax shall be limited to 4 hours, to be equally divided and controlled by the mover of said amendment and the majority leader, and that debate on any other amendment, motion, or appeal, except a motion to lay on the table, shall be limited to 2 hours, to be equally divided and controlled by the mover of any such amendment or motion and the junior Senator from Michigan [Mr. HART]:

Provided, That in the event the junior Senator from Michigan [Mr. HART] is in favor of any such amendment or motion, the time in opposition thereto shall be controlled by the majority leader or some Senator designated by him: *Ordered further,* that on the question of the final passage of the said bill, debate shall be limited to 6 hours, to be equally divided and controlled, respectively, by the junior Senator from Michigan [Mr. HART] and the senior Senator from Louisiana [Mr. ELLENDER]: *Provided,* That the said leaders, or either of them, may, from the time under their control, on the passage of the said bill, allot additional time to any Senator during the consideration of any amendment, motion, or appeal.

The PRESIDING OFFICER.   Is there objection?

Mr. ELLENDER.   I object.

In response to the objection to the proposed unanimous consent agreement, the majority leader warned the members that the leadership was considering filing a motion for cloture.

Voting Rights Act of 1965

The Senate resumed the consideration of the bill (S. 1564) to enforce the 15th amendment of the Constitution of the United States.

Notice of Possibility of Cloture Motion

Mr. MANSFIELD.   Mr. President, in view of the fact that it seems impossible to arrive at a unanimous consent agreement on the amendments and the bill, I think it is only fair that the leadership should announce at this time, so that all Senators may be informed, that because of the objection raised, we shall have to give very serious consideration to filing a motion for cloture at an appropriate time.

---

10.   Filibuster and Cloture

A filibuster is a delay tactic that takes advantage of the Senate's unlimited debate rule. Cloture is the process for ending a filibuster in the Senate. A motion for cloture, under Senate Rule XXII, §2, requires the signature of

16 senators to be introduced and must be approved by three-fifths of the membership. The need for 60 votes to close debate creates extraordinary power for a large minority of senators to oppose a particular bill through a filibuster and makes particularly powerful a minority party that has greater than 30 members in the Senate. In 1965, at the time of the debate on the Voting Rights Act, the cloture rule required two-thirds of the members, or 66 votes of the 100.

After some additional weeks of debate on the bill and various other amendments, on May 21 Senator Hart filed a motion to bring debate on S. 1564 to a close.

Voting Rights Act of 1965

Mr. HART.   Mr. President, I ask unanimous consent that the Chair lay before the Senate the unfinished business.

The ACTING PRESIDENT pro tempore.   The bill will be stated by title.

The LEGISLATIVE CLERK.   A bill (S. 1564) to enforce the 15th amendment to the Constitution of the United States.

The ACTING PRESIDENT pro tempore.   Is there objection?

There being no objection, the Senate resumed the consideration of the bill (S. 1564) to enforce the 15th amendment to the Constitution of the United States.

Cloture Motion

Mr. HART.   Mr. President, I send to the desk a cloture motion filed under rule XXII and ask that it be read.

The ACTING PRESIDENT pro tempore.   The cloture motion will be stated.

The LEGISLATIVE CLERK read the motion, as follows:

Cloture Motion

We, the undersigned Senators, in accordance with the provisions of rule XXII of the Standing Rules of the Senate, hereby move to bring to a close the debate upon the bill (S. 1564) to enforce the 15th amendment to the Constitution of the United States.

(1) MIKE MANSFIELD; (2) EVERETT M. DIRKSEN; (3) PHILIP A. HART; (4) THOMAS H. KUCHEL; (5) LEVERETT SALTON-STALL; (6) PAT McNAMARA; (7) JOHN O. PASTORE; (8) FRANK E. MOSS; (9) JACOB K. JAVITS; (10) HUGH SCOTT; (11) HIRAM L. FONG; (12) CLAIBORNE PELL; (13) EDMUND S. MUSKIE; (14) WAYNE

MORSE; (15) JOHN SHERMAN COOPER; (16) STEPHEN M. YOUNG; (17) CLIFFORD P. CASE; (18) EUGENE J. McCARTHY; (19) WALTER F. MONDALE; (20) DANIEL BREWSTER; (21) FRED R. HARRIS; (22) DANIEL K. INOUYE; (23) PAUL H. DOUGLAS; (24) JOSEPH S. CLARK; (25) GAYLORD NELSON; (26) JENNINGS RANDOLPH; (27) ABRAHAM RIBICOFF; (28) FRANK J. LAUSCHE; (29) THOMAS J. DODD; (30) VANCE HARTKE; (31) JOSEPH D. TYDINGS; (32) EDWARD V. LONG; (33) BIRCH BAYH; (34) EDWARD KENNEDY; (35) LEE METCALF; (36) GORDON ALLOTT; (37) HARRISON WILLIAMS; (38) QUENTIN BURDICK.

Mr. HART subsequently said: Mr. President, on behalf of the junior Senator from New Jersey [Mr. WILLIAMS] and the junior Senator from North Dakota [Mr. BURDICK], I ask unanimous consent that their signatures may be permitted to be added to the cloture motion filed today under rule XXII with respect to the voting rights bill.

The ACTING PRESIDENT pro tempore.   Without objection, it is so ordered.

Mr. ALLOTT subsequently said: Mr. President, I ask unanimous consent that my signature may be added to the cloture motion notwithstanding the fact that it has already been filed.

The ACTING PRESIDENT pro tempore.   Without objection, it is so ordered.

This motion was adopted on May 25. It was only the second time, after a long history of defeating civil rights legislation through filibustering, that debate had been forcibly closed. A successful cloture motion dramatically changes the procedure on the Senate floor:

> And if that question shall be decided in the affirmative . . . then said measure, motion or other matter pending before the Senate . . . shall be the unfinished business to the exclusion of all other business until disposed of.
>
> Thereafter no Senator shall be entitled to speak in all more than one hour on the measure. . . . Except by unanimous consent, no amendment shall be proposed after the vote to bring the debate to a close [with certain limited exceptions]. . . . No dilatory motion or dilatory amendment, or amendment not germane shall be in order. . . . After no more than thirty hours of consideration of the . . . matter on which cloture has been invoked, the Senate shall proceed, without any further debate on any question, to vote on the final disposition thereof . . . [which time may be extended, only once, by a three-fifths vote of the members].

Senate Rule XXII, §2. For a full and excellent exploration of the filibuster and cloture procedures, see Charles Tiefer, Congressional Practice and Procedure, ch. 10 (1989).

The successful motion for cloture brought an end to the Senate debate, and on May 26, 1965, the Senate adopted, by roll call vote, the Mansfield-Dirksen substitute, as amended, for the committee substitute for the bill. The Senate then adopted, by voice vote, the committee amendment in the nature of a substitute as amended by the Mansfield-Dirksen substitute. Finally, it adopted, by roll call vote, S. 1564 as so amended.

11. Governing the House Debate: Rules Committee and Its Rules

Floor action on the voting rights issue resumed in the House of Representatives on June 1, 1965, when H.R. 6400, as amended and having passed the Committee on the Judiciary, was referred to the Committee of the Whole House on the State of the Union (Committee of the Whole) under a "rule" from the House Committee on Rules. This Committee of the Whole is the subject of the next section. The scheduling of legislation for the Committee of the Whole (and, usually, in the House itself) is up to the House Rules Committee, which is responsible for scheduling consideration of legislation and the terms for such consideration. Because of this committee's relationship to the procedure on the floor, it will be considered here and not in Chapter 4, in which committee functions are addressed. There is a rules committee in the Senate and in almost all houses of state legislatures, but, for the most part, they serve other functions that need not be addressed here.

> The [House] Rules Committee is "specifically designed to function as the responsible agent of the majority party, using its great discretionary authority over pending legislation to facilitate the consideration and adoption of the majority party's programs." . . . [T]he Rules committee performs the critical task of assuring the orderly consideration of legislation. Although it generally works in harmony with the majority leadership today, the committee can and sometimes does act contrary to the leadership's wishes and to the will of the House.

Walter J. Oleszek, Congressional Procedures and the Policy Process 131-33 (1989) (quoting former chairman of the committee Representative Bolling).

The committee's instrument for communicating its determination is a "rule." Such a rule is distinct from the standing rules of the House and functions as the procedural guide under which a particular piece of legislation will be considered. The authority to control scheduling and procedure makes this committee extremely powerful.

The process for obtaining a rule is begun by a sponsor of the bill or the chair of the substantive committee that reported the bill (in this case, the Committee on the Judiciary) requesting a rule from the chair of the Rules Committee. If the Rules Committee, mostly through its chairperson, agrees to proceed with this request, hearings will generally be held. If it does not, the bill is most frequently killed. It is to this problem that the 21-day procedure (page 155) is addressed.

Hearings before the Rules Committee usually include discussion of the substance of the bill as well as discussion of the terms of debate. The Rules Committee cannot amend a bill but can express its view of the bill by the rule it fashions, including authorizing the consideration of particular amendments, or by not granting a rule, or by recommending that the bill be recommitted to the substantive committee. The committee can also trade a rule for changes in the bill.

A rule from the Rules Committee, in the form of a House Resolution (H.R.), must be approved by the House prior to the commencement of the consideration of the bill that the rule addresses. In effect, it is treated as a separate piece of legislation.

Voting Rights Act of 1965

Mr. BOLLING. Mr. Speaker, by direction of the Committee on Rules, I call up a resolution (H. Res. 440) and ask for its immediate consideration. The Clerk read as follows:

H. RES. 440

Resolved, That upon the adoption of this resolution it shall be in order to move that the House resolve itself into the Committee of the Whole House on the State of the Union for the consideration of the bill (H.R. 6400) to enforce the fifteenth amendment to the Constitution of the United States. After general debate, which shall be confined to the bill and shall continue not to exceed ten hours, to be equally divided and controlled by the chairman and ranking minority member of the Committee on the Judiciary, the bill shall be read for amendment under the five-minute rule. It shall be in order to consider the amendment in the nature of a substitute recommended by the Committee on the Judiciary now in the bill and such amendment shall be considered under the five-minute rule as an original bill for the purpose of amendment. It shall also be in order to consider the text of the bill H.R. 7896 as a substitute for the committee amendment in the nature of a substitute printed in the bill. At the conclusion of such consideration the Committee shall rise and report the bill to the House with such amendments as may have been adopted, and any Member may demand a separate vote in the House on any of the amendments adopted in the Committee of the Whole to the bill or the committee amendment in the nature of a substitute. The previous question shall be considered as ordered on the bill and amendments thereto to final passage without intervening motion except one motion to recommit with or without instructions. After the passage of the bill H.R. 6400, it shall be in order in the House to take from the Speaker's table the bill S. 1564 and to move to strike out all after the enacting clause of said Senate bill and to insert in lieu thereof the provisions contained in H.R. 6400 as passed by the House.

There are basically three types of rules: open, closed, and modified closed. All of the rules fix the time for general debate on the bill. Under an open rule, the most typical and the type granted for H.R. 6400, any germane amendment, simple or complex, may be offered after the general debate has occurred. Such amendments in the Committee of the Whole are subject to the five-minutes rule. A member may speak in favor of his or her amendment for five minutes, and an opponent has five minutes to reply. In practice, debate over an amendment can last significantly longer by a successful request for unanimous consent to continue or by a motion to "strike out the last word" of the amendment under debate: This latter motion is a ploy that permits continued debate on the same amendment (minus its last word). Under H.R. 440 an amendment cannot be discussed beyond the five-minute exchange. The motion to "strike the last word" puts a new amendment for debate before the body, although it is effectively the same amendment for which time to debate has expired.

Closed rules prohibit floor amendments. They are controversial because they contradict the democratic values of the House. Historically, tax bills and other products of the Ways and Means Committee were debated under closed rules, ostensibly because their highly technical nature was inconsistent with the limited consideration available in the floor amendment process. This custom has been considerably weakened over the years with no apparent increased tendencies toward irrationality.

Modified closed rules are a cross between open and closed rules, with some parts of the bill open to amendment and other parts closed. Within these broad contours, the Rules Committee can be quite creative in fashioning particular rules to effect various goals. In addition to authorizing an open amendment period, H.R. 440 contained additional instructions, relating to the treatment of certain proposed amendments. As noted earlier, the Judiciary Committee had proposed an amendment in the nature of a substitute. H.R. 440 allowed the committee substitute to be treated as the original bill which meant that it, and not the original bill, was the bill that would be the subject of debate and proposed amendments. Also, Representatives Ford and McCulloch planned to offer H.R. 7896 as an amendment to the committee's bill. The rule allowed this bill to be treated as a substitute amendment, which meant that it could be the subject of further amendment under the five-minute rule (normally amendments to amendments cannot be further amended). Most likely this special treatment was part of an agreement with supporters in the minority party (Republicans) that gave them an opportunity to present a somewhat different bill for consideration in return for support of the committee substitute, if their amendment did not pass. (As noted later, this amendment failed and both of its sponsors supported the committee substitute.)

H.R. 440 was approved by the House on July 6, 1965, by a voice vote, which was converted into an automatic recorded vote by a successful quorum call by Representative Williams, an opponent of the bill.

Mr. BOLLING.   Mr. Speaker, I move the previous question.

The previous question was ordered.

The SPEAKER.   The question is on agreeing to the resolution.

The question was taken; and the Speaker announced that the ayes appeared to have it.

Mr. WILLIAMS.   Mr. Speaker, I object to the vote on the ground that a quorum is not present and make the point of order that the quorum is not present.

The SPEAKER.   Evidently a quorum is not present.

The Doorkeeper will close the doors, the Sergeant at Arms will notify absent Members, and the Clerk will call the roll.

The question was taken; and there were — yeas 308, nays 58, not voting 68, as follows: [Roll No. 167]

While the adoption of a rule by the House, particularly an open rule, is usually perfunctory, sometimes the consideration of a rule precipitates a major fight, either on the terms of the rule or on the substance of the legislation to which the rule is addressed. If the motion to cut off such debate is defeated, sponsors of the underlying legislation will frequently withdraw the bill for further coalition-building. An example of a major fight over a rule was the battle that surrounded the 1994 federal crime legislation. The rule was defeated and the bill replaced by one much more palatable to its opponents. For an in-depth study of the Rules Committee, its processes, and its products, see S. Bach and S. S. Smith, Managing Uncertainty in the House of Representatives (1988); Walter Oleszek, Congressional Procedures and the Policy Process (2007); Charles Tiefer, Congressional Practice and Procedure (1989).

12.   The Committee of the Whole House on the State of the Union

All bills that involve a tax, an appropriation, or the authorization of an appropriation (almost all bills) are by House rules referred to the Committee of the Whole House on the State of the Union (the Committee of the Whole). The Committee of the Whole is, in effect, the House of Representatives, operating under some different procedures designed, in some part, to make the consideration of bills more efficient. All representatives are members, but a quorum consists of only 100 members instead of the 218 required for the House. A recorded vote needs 25 members. There are no automatic roll call votes. It is in the Committee of the Whole where the House debate occurs and where amendments are offered.

When the House constitutes itself as the Committee of the Whole, the Speaker steps down as presiding officer and is replaced by the chair of the Committee of the Whole, a member so designated by the Speaker. This action is accompanied by the removal of the Speaker's mace (a traditional symbol of the Speaker's authority consisting of a bundle of 13 ebony rods bound in silver, topped with a silver globe and a silver eagle). Both of these acts are rooted in the historically close relationship between the English kings and parliamentary speakers and the determination of the House of Commons during the rule of King John to create a forum in which debate could occur outside of the King's "ears."

Pursuant to the rule, general debate commenced in the Committee of the Whole on July 6, 1965.

Mr. CELLER.   Mr. Speaker, I move that the House resolve itself into the Committee of the Whole House on the State of the Union for the consideration of the bill (H.R. 6400) to enforce the 15th amendment to the Constitution of the United States.

The SPEAKER.   The question is on the motion offered by the gentleman from New York.

The motion was agreed to.

In the Committee of the Whole

Accordingly, the House resolved itself into the Committee of the Whole House on the State of the Union for the consideration of the bill H.R. 6400, with Mr. Bolling in the chair.

The Clerk read the title of the bill.

By unanimous consent, the first reading of the bill was dispensed with.

The CHAIRMAN.   Under the rule, the gentleman from New York [Mr. CELLER], will be recognized for 5 hours, and the gentleman from Ohio [Mr. McCULLOCH], will be recognized for 5 hours. The Chair recognizes the gentleman from New York.

Mr. CELLER. Mr. Chairman, I yield myself such time as I may consume.

Debate in legislative bodies serves various purposes, only one of which is occasionally affecting the vote of members who remain undecided at that time. Professor Oleszek sums it up nicely:

> General debate is both symbolic and practical. It assures both legislators and the public that the House makes its decision in a democratic fashion,

with due respect for majority and minority opinions. "Debate appropriately tests the conclusions of the majority." General debate forces members to come to grips with the issues at hand; difficult and controversial sections of the bill are explained; constituents and interest groups are alerted to a measure's purpose through press coverage of the debate; member sentiment can be assessed by the floor leaders; a public record, or legislative history, for administrative agencies and the courts is built, revealing the intentions of the proponents and opponents alike; legislators may take positions for reelection purposes; and, occasionally, fence-sitters may be influenced.

Not all legislators agree on the last point. Some doubt that debate can really change views or affect the outcome of a vote. But debate, especially by party leaders just before a key vote, can change opinion. . . .

In sum, reasoned deliberation is important in decision making. Lawmaking consists of more than log rolling, compromises, or power plays. General debate enables members to gain a better understanding of complex issues, and it may influence the collective decision of the House.

Walter Oleszek, Congressional Procedures and the Policy Process 149 (1989). In recent years, several scholars have become concerned about the decline of general debate in the House of Representatives, a phenomenon more noticeable in many state legislatures. Such decline to them represents increasingly lost opportunities to educate and inform a public hungry for such information. General debate on a bill is defined as "a time of pure discussion about a bill, without amendments or votes." The purpose would be to explore the bill as a whole and hopefully the larger policy context into which it fits. Indeed, to emphasize the significance of this latter purpose, these scholars have proposed that each house of the Congress set aside time each week for debates on issues such as America in the post-Cold War world and the need for a national industrial policy. See The American Enterprise Institute and the Brookings Institution, Renewing Congress, a First Report (1992).

The ten-hour debate on H.R. 6400 was held over a three-day period. On July 8, after general debate had ended, the amendment process began. In the House, this is normally done on a section-by-section basis starting with the enactment clause. In this manner, amendments are offered after the section to which they relate has been read. Under the rule, it was in order for the House to consider H.R. 7896 (Ford-McCulloch) as a substitute for the committee amendment in the nature of a substitute. No time for such consideration was explicit in the rule, but two hours were agreed to by unanimous consent of the Committee of the Whole.

The CHAIRMAN.   All time has expired. The Clerk will read.

The Clerk read as follows:

Be it enacted by the Senate and House of Representatives of the United States of America in Congress assembled, That this Act shall be known as the "Voting Rights Act of 1965."

Amendment Offered by Mr. McCulloch

Mr. McCULLOCH.   Mr. Chairman, I offer an amendment.

The Clerk read as follows:

Amendment offered by Mr. McCULLOCH as a substitute for the committee amendment:

Mr. McCULLOCH (interrupting the reading).   Mr. Chairman, I ask unanimous consent that further reading of the amendment be dispensed with, and that the amendment be printed in the RECORD and be open for amendment at any point.

The CHAIRMAN.   Is there objection to the request of the gentleman from Ohio?

There was no objection.

Mr. CELLER.   Mr. Chairman, I ask unanimous consent that all debate on the so-called McCulloch substitute and all amendments thereto be limited to 2 hours, and that such time be equally divided and controlled by myself and the gentleman from Ohio [Mr. McCULLOCH].

The CHAIRMAN.   Is there objection to the request of the gentleman from New York?

There was no objection.

On July 9, 1965, H.R. 7896, which had been amended, was defeated on a teller vote.

The CHAIRMAN.   All time has expired.

The question is on the amendment offered by the gentleman from Ohio, as amended.

Mr. McCULLOCH.   Mr. Chairman, I demand tellers.

Tellers were ordered, and the Chairman appointed as tellers Mr. McCULLOCH and Mr. CELLER.

The Committee divided, and the tellers reported that there were — ayes 166, noes 215.

The amendment process continued throughout the day, with some amendments adopted and some rejected. One amendment, offered by Congressman Cramer, illustrates the value of different forms of nonrecorded voting, as a ruling of the chair was overturned by a teller vote.

The CHAIRMAN.   The time of the gentleman has expired. All time has expired. The question is on the amendment offered by the gentleman from Florida.

The question was taken; and the Chairman announced that the noes appeared to have it.

Mr. CRAMER.   Mr. Chairman, I demand tellers.

Tellers were ordered and the Chairman appointed as tellers Mr. CRA-
MER and Mr. RODINO. The Committee divided and the tellers reported
that there were—ayes 136, noes 132.

The amendment was agreed to.

At 7:20 P.M. on July 9, 1965, with debate concluded in the Committee of
the Whole, a voice vote on H.R. 6400 (as amended by the Judiciary Committee and by the Committee of the Whole) was taken, the amended bill
was adopted, the Committee of the Whole rose, the Speaker took the rostrum, and the bill was ready for consideration by the House.

The CHAIRMAN.   All debate is concluded even with a preferential
motion. The agreement was that all debate would conclude at 7:20 P.M.
The hour is now 7:20 P.M. There is no further time.

The question is on the committee amendment, as amended.

The committee amendment, as amended, was agreed to.

Mr. GERALD R. FORD.   Mr. Chairman, a parliamentary inquiry.

The CHAIRMAN.   The gentleman will state his parliamentary inquiry.

Mr. GERALD R. FORD.   At what point in this process will we have an
opportunity to ask for separate votes on the Cramer vote-fraud amendment
and on the Boggs amendment?

The CHAIRMAN.   In the House, after the previous question has been
announced by the Speaker.

Under the rule, the Committee rises.

Accordingly, the Committee rose; and the Speaker having resumed the
chair, Mr. BOLLING, Chairman of the Committee of the Whole House on
the State of the Union, reported that Committee having had under consideration the bill (H.R. 6400) to enforce the 15th amendment to the Constitution of the United States, pursuant to House Resolution 440, he reported the
bill back to the House with an amendment adopted in the Committee of the
Whole.

The SPEAKER.   Under the rule, the previous question is ordered.

Is a separate vote demanded on any amendment to the committee
amendment?

---

13.   A Bill on the Floor of the House

After the Committee of the Whole has completed its work, including the
amendment process, the bill moves to the House for final action. In
the House, members must first consider any amendments approved by

the Committee of the Whole and then consider the bill in its reported or amended form. New amendments may not be offered nor may amendments defeated in the Committee of the Whole be offered. A motion to recommit the bill with or without instruction on what is to be reconsidered, if the bill is recommitted, is in order. This recommittal motion gives the opposition one last chance to reshape or to kill the bill.

On the floor of the House, each of the amendments that had been adopted in the Committee of the Whole was considered. One, the Cramer amendment, was adopted; two remaining ones were rejected. After the amendments adopted by the Committee of the Whole were disposed of, pursuant to the rule, the House turned to the amendment of the Judiciary Committee, which had been considered in the Committee of the Whole along with the original version of H.R. 6400. This amendment was adopted, and now the House was ready for action on H.R. 6400 as amended.

The SPEAKER.   The question is on the committee amendment as amended.

The committee amendment as amended was agreed to.

The SPEAKER.   The question is on engrossment and third reading of the bill.

The bill was ordered to be engrossed and read a third time and was read the third time.

Motion to Recommit by Mr. Collier

Mr. COLLIER.   Mr. Speaker, I offer a motion to recommit.

The SPEAKER.   Is the gentleman opposed to the bill?

Mr. COLLIER.   In its present form I am, Mr. Speaker.

The SPEAKER.   The gentleman qualifies.

The Clerk will report the motion to recommit.

Notice in the Speaker's call of the question the reference to the engrossed bill. An engrossed bill is the final copy of the bill passed by either house (with all of the adopted amendments) certified by that house's clerk. Each bill in Congress and in state legislatures is supposed to be read three times before passage. This procedure reflects an earlier history when many members of legislatures could not read. In modern practice, bills are not read aloud three times, although in the House, they may be read once in the Committee of the Whole.

After the motion to recommit was defeated on a recorded vote, H.R. 6400 (as amended) was adopted on a recorded vote by the House. Immediately thereafter, in accordance with the terms of the rule, the House amended the

Senate bill (S. 1564) by replacing everything following its enacting clause with the text of the House bill.

Mr. CELLER.   Mr. Speaker, pursuant to House Resolution 440, I call up from the Speaker's table for immediate consideration the bill S. 1564, an act to enforce the 15th amendment to the Constitution of the United States, and for other purposes.

The Clerk read the title of the bill.

Amendment Offered by Mr. Celler

Mr. CELLER.   Mr. Speaker, I offer an amendment.

The Clerk read as follows:

Amendment offered by Mr. CELLER: Strike out all after the enacting clause of S. 1564 and insert in lieu thereof the text of H.R. 6400, as passed.

The amendment was agreed to.

The bill was ordered to be read a third time, was read the third time, and passed.

The title was amended so as to read:

"A bill to enforce the 15th amendment to the Constitution of the United States, and for other purposes."

This process of amendment in effect created a single bill, S. 1564, which had been acted upon by both houses, but it did not resolve the substantive disagreements between the version adopted by the Senate and the one adopted by the House; rather it set the stage for the next step in the legislative process. On July 12, 1965, the Senate requested a conference, after it rejected the House amended version of S. 1564.

Enforcement of the 15th Amendment to the Constitution

Mr. MANSFIELD.   Mr. President, I ask the Chair to lay before the Senate the amendments of the House of Representatives to the bill (S. 1564).

The PRESIDING OFFICER laid before the Senate the amendments of the House of Representatives to the bill (S. 1564) to enforce the 15th amendment to the Constitution of the United States, and for other purposes, which were, to strike out all after the enacting clause and insert: . . .

Mr. MANSFIELD.   Mr. President, I move that the Senate disagree to the amendments of the House to the bill (S. 1564) and request a conference on the disagreeing votes of the two Houses, and that conferees on the part of the Senate be appointed by the Chair.

The motion was agreed to; and the PRESIDING OFFICER appointed Mr. EASTLAND, Mr. DODD, Mr. HART, Mr. LONG of Missouri, Mr. DIRKSEN, and Mr. HRUSKA conferees on the part of the Senate.

14. *The Conference*

The conference is the means by which the two houses of Congress resolve the differences between them on a bill that both houses have considered and adopted. Such agreement is necessary if a bill is to become law, because each house must pass an identical version of the same bill. The Speaker and the presiding officer of the Senate name conferees to the conference committee. Conferees are usually members of the substantive committee that reported the legislation and are recommended by the committee chair and ranking minority member. A conference report must be approved by a majority of the conferees from each house (it does not matter how many members are appointed from each house), although it may change the dynamics of arriving at an intrahouse compromise.

In many instances, although not in this case, conferees are instructed on the position they are to take at a conference committee, although these instructions do not strictly bind them. Conferees are not authorized to address provisions of the bill that are not in dispute in the bill. However, during the bargaining process that goes on in the conference, other issues can be put on the table, even if not in dispute in the bill or germane to the bill. An extreme example of using the conference to bring an unrelated issue to the table is recalled by one of the authors, Judge Mikva. In the mid-1970s, each house of Congress had passed a different bill amending the Social Security law. A conference committee was established, chaired by Representative Al Ullman, chair of the House Ways and Means Committee. A meeting was scheduled during the Christmas vacation because of the urgency of the Social Security issue. Senator Russell Long, a member of the conference committee and chair of the Senate Finance Committee, opened the conference by informing the members from the House that he was concerned about a piece of legislation, sponsored by a Senate colleague, dealing with tuition tax credits for parochial schools. This bill had been bottled up by Representative Ullman in the House Ways and Means Committee. Simply stated, Senator Long insisted that the bill be moved as a cost of reaching an agreement on Social Security. After this request was rejected, the conference was adjourned. A number of days later, as time started to run out, Long agreed to proceed with the conference and drop his intransigence if Ullman could win approval for such action from the Senate colleague whose bill was being held. After such approval was granted, a conference report was negotiated and adopted. Sometime later, it was reported to Representative Mikva, who had been a member of the

conference committee, that the object of Long's ploy had not been his colleague's bill but rather another bill, on oil taxes, which he was trying to
have moved in the Ways and Means Committee. For a detailed description
of the working of conference committees, see L. D. Longley and W. J. Oleszek, Bicameral Politics and the Conference Committees (1989).

When a conference committee reaches an agreement, it issues a conference report that details the agreement. This report then becomes the vehicle
for further legislative action. It may contain exact bill language, but it may
only contain references to prior legislative action, such as an amendment of
one house or the other. The report is then considered by the house that
accepted the request for a conference (in this case the House, which agreed
to the conference on July 14). The report is not subject to amendment, and, if
not adopted by both houses, it must go back to another conference. When
both houses agree to a conference report, that report becomes the mandate
for the bill's enrollment.

The conference report on S. 1564, as amended, was called up in the
House of Representatives on August 3, 1965.

Voting Rights

Mr. CELLER.   Mr. Speaker, I call up the conference report on the bill
(S. 1564) to enforce the 15th amendment to the Constitution of the United
States, and for other purposes, and ask unanimous consent that the state-
ment of the managers on the part of the House be read in lieu of the report.

The Clerk read the title of the bill.

The SPEAKER.   Is there objection to the request of the gentleman from
New York?

There was no objection.

The Clerk read the statement.

The conference report and statement are as follows:

Conference Report (Rept. No. 711)

The committee of conference on the disagreeing votes of the two Houses
on the amendment of the House to the bill (S. 1564) to enforce the fifteenth
amendment of the Constitution of the United States, and for other purposes, having met, after full and free conference, have agreed to recommend and do recommend to their respective Houses as follows:

That the Senate recede from its disagreement to the amendment of the
House to the substantive provisions of the bill and agree to the same with
an amendment as follows: In lieu of the matter proposed to be inserted by
the House amendment insert the following:

"That this Act shall be known as the 'Voting Rights Act of 1965.' . . ."

The House adopted the Conference Report on August 3, and the Senate followed on August 4. The bill, now passed by both houses, was ready for presidential action. Before a bill can be sent to the President, it has to be enrolled (produced as a final copy), printed on parchment and certified by the clerk of the house of origin (the Senate, in this case) and signed by both the Speaker of the House and the Senate president pro tempore. In the House, the Committee on House Administration is charged with responsibility for verifying the bill prior to the Speaker's signing it. The enrollment process is extremely important because the bill that is sent to the President must reflect *exactly* the text mandated by the conference report. On August 6, 1965, the President signed the enrolled S. 1564, and the Voting Rights Act of 1965 became law.

NOTES AND QUESTIONS

1. *The nature of the legislation.* While no legislation is typical, the legislation above is somewhat atypical because of its bipartisan support in both houses of Congress. Also, while the American legislative process is marked by the multitude of opportunities for derailing or compromising legislation, the description above is of a bill that encompasses far-reaching regulatory changes and that passes without major substantive amendments. This success is reflective of a clear legislative understanding that the bill addressed a problem that needed to be solved and solved through federal legislation with substantial federal administrative involvement. This legislation was "must" legislation for a newly elected President (Lyndon B. Johnson) and for most members of Congress. A description of the events surrounding the enactment of this legislation is found in Chapter 6.

2. *Legislative voting — recorded votes.* Notice the number of unrecorded votes that occur. Every legislative body develops some method for quickly voting on issues over which there is little or no dispute and the unrecorded vote is Congress'. About the unrecorded vote Justice Story wrote: "an unlimited power to call the yeas and nays on every question, at the mere will of a single member, would interrupt and retard, and, in many cases, wholly defeat, the public business." Joseph Story, The Constitution of the United States 117-18 (Regnery Gateway Bicentennial ed. 1986). How does this method of voting compare with New York's fast roll call? What are the advantages or disadvantages of each from an efficiency and accountability perspective? Do you think that any of the unrecorded votes taken on the Voting Rights Act of 1965 (as excerpted in the materials) should have been recorded? In 1995, as part of the proposed constitutional amendment to require a balanced budget, the sponsors included mandatory roll call voting on tax and debt ceiling increases. As one sponsor, Senator Larry E. Craig, argued: "We want people to stand up and be counted if they

want to raise taxes." David E. Rosenbaum, I'll Sleep on the Idea, But Must I Vote on It?, N.Y. Times, Feb. 2, 1995, at B8.

3. *Legislative voting — majority vote.* Historically, in Congress (and all American legislatures), the standard for legislative enactment has been one of majority rule. In 1995, at the impetus of a newly elected Republican majority, the House of Representatives adopted a rule that requires a three-fifths vote for an increase in the federal income tax rate. The Constitution contains no express requirement that calls for a majority vote, but does specifically call for a supermajority (two-thirds) in five instances: the Senate's advice and consent to a treaty (Art. II, §2); the Senate's vote for guilt on impeachment (Art. 1, §3); the vote to expel a member in either house (Art. I, §5); the override of a veto by either house (Art. I, §7); and the vote in either house to approve a constitutional amendment (Art. V). What do you think of the constitutionality of the three-fifths standard? Who and under what circumstances might a party have standing to challenge such a rule?

4. *Legislative voting — majority vote redux.* As discussed in Note 3, the traditional standard for congressional legislative enactment has been majority rule, changed in the House in 1995 for certain tax bills. Does this rule require a majority of the membership of the legislative body (at least 218 in the House of Representatives and at least 51 in the Senate) or of the members present on the floor? As noted earlier, the Constitution requires an absolute majority for a quorum. Do you think that it requires an absolute majority for enactment? Compare the language of Article I, §5 ("a majority of each shall constitute a Quorum to do Business, but a smaller number may adjourn from day to day. . . . The Yeas and Nays of the members of either House on any question shall at the Desire of one fifth of those Present, be entered on the journal") with that of Article III, §14 of the New York State Constitution ("nor shall any bill be passed or become law except by the assent of a majority of the members elected to each branch of the legislature"). See United States v. Ballon, 144 U.S. 1 (1891). What policy reasons might be offered to support the enactment of a statute by fewer than a majority of the whole number of members? Consider the comments of James Madison on this point (applicable also to consideration of the questions in Note 3):

> It has been said that more than a majority ought be required for a quorum and more than a majority of a quorum for a decision. That some advantages might have resulted from such a precaution cannot be denied. It might have been an additional shield to some particular interests, and another obstacle generally to hasty and partial measures. But these considerations are outweighed by the inconveniences in the opposite scale. In all cases where justice or the general good might require new laws to be passed, or active measures to be pursued, the fundamental principle of free government would be reversed. It would no longer be the majority that would rule: the power would be transferred to the minority.

The Federalist No. 58, at 396-97 (J. Madison) (Jacob Cooke ed. 1961). Interestingly, as part of the effort to achieve a balanced budget amendment in 1995, see Note 2 above, one proposal required a three-fifths vote to pass all tax increases, but a three-fifths vote of an absolute majority.

5. *The filibuster.* Historically, the filibuster was used on a limited basis, on issues about which Senators felt great passion. Its use brought business in the Senate to a halt. To avoid the latter interference with legislative work, the Senate installed a two-track system that allows the consideration of other legislation, if cloture cannot be achieved. This has made the filibuster almost painless and encouraged its use. So commonplace did it become that in 1994 an editorial in USA Today aptly opined: "Instead of providing a dramatic final forum for individuals against a stampeding majority, it has become a pedestrian tool of partisans and gridlock-meisters." Nov. 25, 1994, at 8A, col. 1. In 1995 several senators proposed a scheme by which cloture could, after a time, be effected by a majority vote. This proposal was easily defeated. If the three-fifths vote is unconstitutional, do you think that the filibuster is also unconstitutional?

PART *III*

The Legitimizing Characteristics of American Legislatures

Axiomatic to the formation and structure of this nation's governments is the Americans' fear of centralized and removed governmental power. This fear engendered the great federalist-antifederalist debates that followed the adoption of the Constitution by the convention in Philadelphia and required the addition of a Bill of Rights to assure its ratification. (And it has continued as a significant factor in American political debate.) Such fear was not directed only against powers concentrated in the hands of an executive or against a federal government, but also against the domination of a representative legislative body by a majority "who are united and actuated by some common impulse of passion, or of interest, adverse to the rights of other citizens, or to the permanent and aggregate interests of the community." The Federalist No. 10, at 57 (James Madison) (Jacob E. Cooke ed. 1961).

To protect against such domination, Americans constructed legislative bodies whose salient characteristics are representativeness, accessibility, and deliberativeness. These characteristics grant legitimacy to acts of legislative bodies. Like the country's growth and changing demographics, the details of these features have not been frozen in time. They have followed the many changes in attitudes and policies of the nation and have been crafted in the nation's political ovens. The purpose of this part is to examine these characteristics of American legislative bodies and to explore their effectiveness in legitimizing the actions of American legislatures.

CHAPTER **6**

Representativeness — The Electorate

The political legitimacy of laws depends upon their public acceptance. As Alexander Hamilton admonished, "no laws have any validity or binding force without the consent and approbation of the people." Quoted in G. Wood, The Creation of the American Republic, 1776-1787, 162 (1969). In the United States, consent and approbation are achieved through delegating lawmaking power to legislatures that consist of popularly elected representatives. "The real importance of the legislatures came from their being the constitutional repository of the democratic element of the society or, in other words, the people themselves." G. Wood, The Creation of the American Republic, 1776-1787, 163 (1969). But who can elect a legislator and who that legislator serves are the defining tests for the representativeness of a legislature. This chapter focuses on how these questions have been answered.

A. A BRIEF HISTORY OF SUFFRAGE

The real measure of a government's representativeness is the breadth of its suffrage. Since the formation of this country, the ability of excluded groups to gain and exercise the right to vote has presented an ongoing test of the legitimacy of the government. The success of these efforts has allowed this government to become a model of democratic stability.

The concept of universal suffrage was a radical one at the time of the writing of the Constitution. None of the Framers of the Constitution advocated it with any intensity. Only a small percentage of the population was eligible to elect ratifiers of the Constitution itself.

The first effort to expand the franchise revolved around the removal of property (freehold) qualifications. At the Constitutional Convention, efforts were made to limit the federal franchise to freeholders. Some consider the constitutional provisions for suffrage in Article I, §2 — "Electors in each State shall have the Qualifications requisite for Electors of the most numerous Branch of the State Legislature" — as a victory over such attempts. C. Williamson, American Suffrage from Property to Democracy 1760-1860, 124-25 (1960). James Madison even argued that this provision meant that the electorate would "[n]ot [be] the rich more than the poor; not the learned more than the ignorant; not the haughty heirs of distinguished names, more than the humble sons of obscure and unpropitious fortune." The Federalist No. 57, at 385 (James Madison) (Jacob E. Cooke ed. 1961). Contrary to this sentiment, it took considerable additional efforts to approach the realization of this goal.

1.   An End to Freehold Qualifications

At the time the Constitution was adopted and into the early decades of the 1800s, state constitutions generally contained freehold qualifications in order to "exclude such persons as are in so mean a situation as to be esteemed to have no will of their own." 1 W. Blackstone, Commentaries on the Laws of England 171 (5th ed. 1773). A typical example of such a provision is found in New York's 1777 Constitution: "[E]very male inhabitant of full age . . . shall . . . be entitled to vote for representative of the said county in assembly; if . . . he shall have been a freeholder, possessing a freehold of the value of twenty pounds . . . or have rented a tenement . . . of the yearly value of forty shillings, and been rated and actually paid taxes to this State." 7 Sources and Documents of U.S. Constitutions 174 (W. Swindler ed. 1976).

By the mid-1800s such qualifications had all but disappeared from state constitutions. This was largely a result of the demands for more democratic institutions pressed by the nation's increasing and changing white population and its changing economic base. The press for this democratization was aided by the representative philosophy and rhetoric that were part of the nation's constitutional heritage and was charged by the competition for support between the emerging political parties.

While the freehold qualifications were discarded with relative ease, the demands of other groups to participate in the political process met with considerable resistance. New York, for example, while removing freehold qualifications in its 1821 Constitution, added qualifications making it almost impossible for nonwhite men to vote. New Jersey, in its 1844 Constitution, deleted a gender and race neutral suffrage provision of its 1776 Constitution and replaced it with a "white male only" provision.

2. The Nineteenth Amendment

The struggle for female suffrage lasted until the ratification of Article XIX of the Constitution in 1920, following World War I. It was both violent and arduous. An enormous political and legal effort, commencing with the Seneca Falls Convention in 1848, preceded this amendment. One of its most noteworthy legal moments was the decision in Minor v. Happersett, 88 U.S. 162 (1874), in which the Supreme Court told Virginia Minor that her citizenship did not include the right to vote by stating that "[f]or nearly ninety years the people have acted upon the idea that the Constitution, when it conferred citizenship, did not necessarily confer the right of suffrage. . . . Our province is to decide what the law is, not to declare what it should be." Id. at 177-78. Another was the political prosecution and conviction of Susan B. Anthony on the charge of having voted without the lawful right to vote.

Finally, in 1919 Congress, in a very close vote, approved and submitted to the states the Nineteenth Amendment. The battle then raged state by state. In 1920, Tennessee became the thirty-sixth and last state necessary for ratification. The amendment was approved by one vote in the Tennessee legislature, when its youngest member, Harry Burns, switched sides after receiving a pro-amendment telegram from his mother. Burns was then reportedly chased from the capitol by an angry mob.

So on the vote of the swift-footed Burns, the country officially completed a task set in motion 131 years earlier. The farmers had argued in 1787 that broader representation would make a stronger, freer country and produce better decisions. But only in 1920 did the country finally complete the essence of this challenge. In one act, the nation enfranchised more voters than at any other time in its history. Struggles over the vote would continue, of course. The enfranchisement of African Americans was official but not yet real, and would not be for another forty years. Younger people, who were dying for the country in its wars, would eventually be allowed to vote too as a result of the pain of Vietnam.

But at this moment when women were admitted to the vote was the moment the last philosophical divide was crossed. The country had recognized constitutionally that a country built on the participation of its citizens needed to allow all its citizens to participate.

Did the enfranchisement of women change the nature of government? That is a subject of endless and continuing debate. At first, women were more likely than men to vote Republican, the party more favorable to their enfranchisement. In 1928, political analysts said Herbert Hoover, a defender of Prohibition, was helped into office by women voters. What is clear is that less than a generation after women were given the vote, the nature of the federal government would be radically altered. Perhaps that participation of women played a role. Clearly, the crises of the Great Depression and World War II did.

The 1920 presidential election was the first in which women voted. Warren G. Harding and Calvin Coolidge, the Republicans, defeated James Cox and

Franklin D. Roosevelt by a landslide. . . . But Roosevelt would be back. In 1932, he would defeat Herbert Hoover, whose scruples against big government restrained his actions against the Depression. The stage was being set for both the nation's greatest success and for its current challenge.

Eric Lane and Michael Oreskes, The Genius of America 142-43 (2007).

3.   The Post–Civil War Amendments and the Voting Rights Act of 1965

African-Americans faced an even more harrowing battle. As a consequence of the Civil War, the Fourteenth Amendment (1868), which made all people born in the United States citizens, and the Fifteenth Amendment (1870), which barred race as a basis for denying citizens the opportunity to vote, were ratified. Despite the struggle for and the promise of these amendments, resistance to their implementation long delayed their realization. Through use of "white only" primaries (declared unconstitutional in Nixon v. Herndon, 273 U.S. 536 (1927); Terry v. Adams, 345 U.S. 461 (1953); Smith v. Allwright, 321 U.S. 649 (1944); see also Nixon v. Condon, 286 U.S. 73 (1932)), literacy tests (subsequently prohibited by the 1972 amendments to the Voting Rights Act), poll taxes (prohibited by the Twenty-fourth Amendment and Harper v. Virginia Board of Elections, 383 U.S. 663 (1966), prohibiting poll taxes in state elections under the equal protection provision of the Fourteenth Amendment), and physical intimidation, the promise of these amendments, and of a variety of statutes enforcing them, was continually frustrated. On the eve of the famous 1965 march on Selma, Alabama, Dallas County (where Selma is located) listed only 383 black registrants out of an eligible 15,000, despite years of federal litigation and court decisions finding violations of the Fifteenth Amendment.

This march, part of a well-organized and widely reported voter registration campaign, riveted congressional attention on voting rights. Senator Mondale's response to the television and print pictures and descriptions of the violent attack by Alabama state police on peaceful marchers crossing the Edmund Pettus Bridge on March 7, 1965, is illustrative. "Sunday's outrage in Selma, Alabama, makes passage of legislation to guarantee Southern Negroes the right to vote an absolute imperative for Congress this year." 111 Cong. Rec. 4350 (1965). And these images were continuously reinforced by the registration campaign and the march from Selma to Montgomery. Prior to the march, the new Johnson administration had been working on various ideas for voting rights legislation, and numerous legislators and civil rights lobbyists had been pushing for stronger federal legislation. On March 15, 1965, President Johnson, with the support of congressional leaders, presented his voting rights legislation to a joint session of Congress to provide federal registration officials. In August of that year, Congress acknowledged the past failure to secure equal opportunities for African-Americans to participate in the political process by enacting the Voting Rights Act of 1965. As set forth in the Committee Report of the House Judiciary Committee:

> A salient obligation and responsibility of the Congress is to provide appropriate implementation of the guarantees of the 15th amendment to the Constitution. . . . The historic struggle for the realization of this constitutional guarantee indicates clearly that our national achievements in this area have fallen far short of our aspirations. The history of the 15th amendment litigation in the Supreme Court reveals both the variety of means used to bar Negro voting and the durability of such discriminatory practices. . . .
>
> [A]lthough these laws [federal civil rights statutes passed in 1957, 1960, and 1964] were intended to supply strong and effective remedies, their enforcement has encountered serious obstacles in various regions of the country. Progress has been painfully slow in part because of the intransigence of the State and local officials and repeated delays in the judicial process.

Committee on the Judiciary, H.R. Rep. No. 439, 89th Cong., 1st Sess. 8-11 (1965). For accounts of events leading up to the passage of the Civil Rights Act of 1965, see Juan Williams, Eyes on the Prize (Blackside ed. 1987); David J. Garrow, Protest at Selma (1978).

The Voting Rights Act of 1965 contained a radically different approach to the protection of voting rights than had been previously attempted. It contemplated complete federal involvement in the enforcement of voting rights. While the general prohibition of §2 — "no voting qualification . . . or procedure shall be imposed or applied by any State . . . to deny or abridge the right of any Citizen of the United States to vote on account of race or color" — was not dissimilar from earlier approaches, other sections triggered substantial involvement of the federal government in the implementation and enforcement of the act. For example, various sections provided authority for the use of federal examiners to enforce voting rights. Section 4 created an irrebuttable presumption of discrimination against any state or political subdivision in which the Attorney General determined that a test or device was in use on November 1, 1964, and with respect to which the Director of the Census determined that less than 50 percent of the persons of voting age residing therein were registered on November 1, 1964, or that less than 50 percent of such persons voted in the presidential election of November 1964. If a state or political subdivision became "covered" under §4 of the Act, it could not use any test or device (e.g., literacy test, standard of educational achievement, evidence of good moral character) as a qualification for voting, and it would be subject to §5 of the Act, which requires "preclearance" by the United States Department of Justice before any such jurisdiction "shall enact or seek to administer any voting qualification or prerequisite to voting, or standard, practice or procedure with respect to voting [e.g., reapportioning legislative districts, moving a polling place, changing times for voting] different from that in force or effect on November 1, 1964." Finally, additional sections provided jurisdiction to the federal courts to hear cases arising under the act's provisions. This scheme of intense federal involvement in state elections processes was upheld by the Supreme Court in South Carolina v. Katzenbach, 383 U.S. 301 (1966).

4.   Amendments to the Voting Rights Act of 1965 and the Twenty-sixth Amendment

The Voting Rights Act of 1965 has been amended substantially three times since 1965: in 1970, 1975, and 1982. In each instance the amendments broadened the scope of the Act beyond its original focus on Southern discrimination against African-Americans. Each of the amendments is an important part of the evolution of suffrage, and each was aided by the successes of the preceding amendment.

The 1970 amendments. The 1970 amendments extended the provisions of §§4 and 5 for an additional five years and used the results of the 1968 presidential election to determine the applicability of those sections to a political jurisdiction. It also created a five-year national ban on literacy tests. Additionally, the amendments lowered the voting age from 21 to 18 for national and state elections. The applicability of this provision to state elections was declared unconstitutional in Oregon v. Mitchell, 400 U.S. 112 (1970). As a consequence of this case, the Twenty-sixth Amendment to the Constitution, making 18-year-olds eligible to vote in all elections, was adopted and ratified July 1, 1971.

One consequence of this Amendment was a substantial expansion of the Act's coverage to non-Southern jurisdictions. (Alaska and several subdivisions of non-Southern states were covered in 1965.) The application of the 50 percent test to the 1968 presidential election registration and vote resulted in a number of non-Southern states and subdivisions being covered by §§4 and 5 of the Act. Included among these were three New York counties: Kings, New York, and Bronx. At the time of the 1968 presidential election, New York had a literacy test.

The inclusion of non-Southern jurisdictions under the Act's coverage precipitated a line of criticism against the Act that continues today. The thrust of this criticism is that the purpose of the Act was being distorted by its amendments, as one of the Act's (as amended) most ardent critics argues:

> In 1965 those who wrote the Voting Rights Act knew which states they wanted to cover and designed a test to single them out. Few jurisdictions outside the South were caught in the federal net, and few offenders in the South eluded it. True, some southern counties that were in fact registering blacks were caught, while those in eastern Texas with poor records of black

enfranchisement were not. But if the fit was not perfect, it was extraordinarily close.

Applying the benchmark of 50-percent turnout to the 1968 figures, however, had a very different result: an assorted collection of counties with no history of black disfranchisement were brought under coverage. None of these counties were in the South, and no other evidence suggested that these were jurisdictions in which minority voters were at a distinctive disadvantage. The evidence, in fact, pointed in quite another direction. For example, under the revised act, three counties in New York City were covered. But turnout for the 1968 presidential election had been low across the nation, and participation in New York, reflecting the national trend, had dropped slightly to just under the determining 50-percent mark. . . .

If, indeed, there were northern counties in which the extraordinary requirement of preclearance was required, some new test was needed to identify them. The discovery that a jurisdiction used a literacy test and that voter participation had dropped a few points in the last presidential election was not revealing.

Abigail Thernstrom, Whose Votes Count? 39 (1987). Criticisms of the Voting Rights Act are discussed in this chapter on pages 302-307. Set forth below is a typical literacy test used in New York in 1968. What do you think its purpose was?

New York State Regents Literacy Test: The First Railroads

England was the first country to have railroads. These railroads were used at the iron mines. At first, the cars were pulled by mules. Then, in 1814, an English miner named George Stephenson made a steam engine. This engine could pull a train of 8 cars loaded with iron ore. In 1830, an American named Peter Cooper built a small engine. It was called the *Tom Thumb*. In 1831, an engine called the *De Witt Clinton* was tried on a railroad track in New York State. The railroad track started in Albany and went to Schenectady. The engineer and fireman stood on a platform behind the engine. The passengers rode in old stagecoaches which were fitted with special wheels. At first the railroad tracks were made of wood. Later iron rails were used. By 1860, a person could travel by railroad from the Atlantic coast as far west as the Mississippi River.

The answers to the following questions are to be taken from the above paragraph.

Sample: Which country was the first to have railroads? England

1. At first, what animals pulled the cars? _____
2. What was the name of the English miner who made a steam engine in 1814?

   _____

3. How many cars loaded with iron ore could this steam engine pull?

   _____

4. What was the name of the American who built a small engine in 1830?
    _____

5. What was this small engine called? _____
6. In what city did the railroad track in New York State start?
    _____

7. In what did the passengers ride? _____
8. Of what were the first railroad tracks made? _____

The 1975 amendments. In 1975, Congress again amended the Voting Rights Act. It extended the provisions of §§4 and 5 for 17 years and made permanent the national ban on literacy tests. It also made the Act applicable to the 1972 presidential election. More significantly, from the perspective of representativeness, Congress added "language minorities" to the list of protected classes under §§2, 4, and 5 of the Act. Henceforth "no voting qualification or prerequisite to voting, or standard, practice, or procedure shall be imposed or applied . . . to deny or abridge the right of any citizen of the United States to vote because he is a member of a language minority group." Language minorities are defined by the amendment as "persons who are American Indian, Asian Americans, Alaskan Natives or of Spanish heritage." For coverage under §4, which effectively prohibits the use of tests or devices in covered jurisdictions and which triggers preclearance under §5 for various election-related changes, the 1975 amendments add to the definition of tests or devices the use of English-only voting-related materials, including ballots. Such a standard is only applicable in states or jurisdictions in which voting-age members of single language minorities make up 5 percent or more of the voting age population. The need for the term "language minorities," at least in part, reflected a concern that the term "race" might not be broad enough to cover Spanish-speaking Mexican-Americans. The addition of language minorities to the Act reflected growing acceptability of its processes, the increased voting power of protected minorities during the Act's ten-year history, and the growing strength of the large Mexican-American population of the Southwest. Indeed, one result of these amendments was to add to the list of covered jurisdictions the states of Texas, Arizona, and Alaska and counties of various additional states.

B. THE 1982 AMENDMENTS TO §2: AN END TO DISCRIMINATION OR PROPORTIONAL REPRESENTATION?

In 1982, Congress again amended the Voting Rights Act. This time the goal was to revamp §2. The stimulus for these amendments was provided by a forceful lobbying campaign, the consequence of two events that generated great concern within the civil rights community. The first was the 1980 Supreme Court decision in City of Mobile v. Bolden, 446 U.S. 55 (1980), and the second was the election of Ronald Reagan as President (along with a Republican Senate majority) on a platform perceived to be hostile to civil rights. In the *Mobile* decision, a plurality of the Court characterized §2 as a restatement of the Fifteenth Amendment, which "prohibits only purposefully discriminatory denial or abridgment by government of the freedom to vote on account of race, color, or previous condition of servitude." Id. at 65. For civil rights advocates, this rendering of the scope of §2 called into question a basic assumption that they had held about the meaning of representativeness in the context of voting rights legislation. From their perspective, the purpose of the Voting Rights Act had been to expand the opportunities of protected minorities to participate in the electoral processes, without regard to whether the obstacles to participation were intentional. The *Mobile* plurality suggested that the Voting Rights Act had a far more limited purpose: preventing intentional discrimination. The lobbying campaign that surrounded the amendments to §2 is described later in this chapter.

The Voting Rights Act, as fully amended, is found in Chapter 2. Section 2, as amended and in its amendatory form, reads as follows (omitted language is struck out; new language is underlined):

SEC. 2. (a) No voting qualification or prerequisite to voting or standard, practice, or procedure shall be imposed or applied by any State or political subdivision to deny or abridge in a manner which results in a denial or abridgement of the right of any citizen of the United States to vote on account of race or color, or in contravention of the guarantees set forth in section 4(f)(2), as provided in subsection (b).

(b) A violation of subsection (a) is established if, based on the totality of circumstances, it is shown that the political processes leading to nomination or election in the State or political subdivision are not equally open to participation by members of a class of citizens protected by subsection (a) in that its members have less opportunity than other members of the electorate to participate in the political process and to elect representatives of their choice. The extent to which members of a protected class have been elected to office in the State or political subdivision is one circumstance which may be considered: *Provided*, that nothing in this section establishes a right to have members of a protected class elected in numbers equal to their proportion in the population.

NOTES AND QUESTIONS

1. *Compare and contrast.* Consider the differences between the original and amended §2. The amendment to §2 of the act did more than simply remedy the problem raised by Mobile v. Bolden. This problem could have

been remedied by the changes found in §2(a) alone. Indeed, the bill that was adopted by the House of Representatives included only that amendment, plus a provision against proportional representation (new language is underscored; omitted language is struck out):

> SEC. 2. (a) No voting qualification or prerequisite to voting or standard, practice, or procedure shall be imposed or applied by any State or political subdivision ~~to deny or abridge~~ in a manner which results in a denial or abridgement of the right of any citizen of the United States to vote on account of race or color, or in contravention of the guarantees set forth in section 4(f)(2), as provided in subsection (b). The fact that members of a minority group have not been elected in numbers equal to the group's proportion of the population shall not, in and of itself, constitute a violation of this section.

On what basis do you think that the bill was further amended to its present language? This is the subject of the following material.

Senators Hatch and Dole — The Making of §2

In the Senate, the House bill was referred to the Subcommittee on the Constitution of the Committee of the Judiciary, of which Senator Hatch was chairperson. This subcommittee amended the House version of the bill by striking the results test and restoring the existing language of the act. In that form, the bill was reported to the Senate Committee of the Judiciary. There, Senator Dole, noting the impasse between the House version of the bill and the bill reported by the subcommittee, offered a compromise amendment, which ultimately became §2. At the heart of the impasse between the two versions of the bill is one of the thorniest issues of representativeness, one that continues to provoke controversy today — proportional representation.

Voting Rights Act, Hearings before the Subcommittee on the Constitution of the Committee on the Judiciary
97th Cong., 2d Sess. 16-19 (1982)

Senator Hatch

Thank you, Mr. Chairman. Once in a great while this body considers legislation that must be looked upon as a watershed with respect to the direction in which this Nation is going to go. One of these occurred in 1965 in which this Nation committed itself to the goal of insuring that no citizen, whatever his or her race or color, would be denied the opportunity to participate in the electoral process. As there are to all great objectives, there was a cost involved, a cost relating to the transformation of traditional values of federalism itself. Under the 1965 act, sovereign States would be required to secure the approval of the Federal Government prior to enacting changes in their voting laws and procedures, an obligation that many at the time viewed as inconsistent with the respective roles of the State and National Governments.

Despite these costs, the Voting Rights Act of 1965 was necessary and is necessary legislation. It was necessary in order to overcome a clear and indisputable history of discrimination in various parts of the country that had worked to deny individuals their constitutional rights not to be denied suffrage on the basis of race or color. It was an extraordinary piece of legislation, but it was necessary to secure the most basic, fundamental right of all rights in a free and democratic society, the right to vote for the candidate of one's choice.

Mr. Chairman, today the Judiciary Committee again considers legislation that, in my view, is a watershed and is likely to define in an important manner what this Nation is all about. Again, the legislation to be considered is described as voting rights legislation. This time, however, the objectives are different, vastly different. Instead of leading ultimately to the nonconsideration of race in the electoral process as was the objective of the original Voting Rights Act, the present legislation would make the consideration of race the overriding consideration in decisions in this area. Instead of directing its protections toward the individual as did the original act, and as does the Constitution, the present legislation would make racial groups the focus of protection. Instead of reinforcing in the law the great constitutional principle of equal protection, the present legislation would substitute a totally alien principle of equal results and equal outcome.

Mr. Chairman, in short, the debate on the new version of the Voting Rights Act will focus upon one of the most important public policy issues ever to be considered by this body. . . . This is legislation with both profound constitutional implications and profound practical consequences. In summary, the issue is how this Nation is going to define "civil rights" and "discrimination."

Both in popular parlance and within judicial forums, the concept of racial discrimination has always implied the maltreatment or disparate treatment of individuals because of race or skin color. . . .

Proof of discriminatory intent or purpose is the essence of any civil rights violation for the simple reason that there has never been an obligation upon either public or private entities to conduct their affairs in a manner designed to insure racial balance or proportional representation by minorities in employment, housing, education, voting, and the like. Rather, the traditional and entirely proper obligation under civil rights law has been to conduct such affairs in a manner that does not involve disparate treatment of individuals because of race or skin color. And the important words are because of race or skin color.

What is being proposed in the present Voting Rights Act or the House Voting Rights Act debate is that Congress amend the Voting Rights Act and alter this traditional intent standard. In its place would be substituted a new results standard. Rather than focusing upon the process of discrimination, the new standard would focus upon electoral results or outcome. . . .

To speak of "discriminatory results" is to speak purely and simply of racial balance and racial quotas. The premise of the results test is that any disparity between minority population and minority representation evidences discrimination. . . .

Senator Dole

Mr. Chairman. Again, I want to express my thanks to the Chairman for his patience and for his willingness to meet with us a number of times, a couple of times on Friday, in helping us take, as the Senator said, a step in the right direction. Maybe it does not go as far as some would like. Maybe it goes a bit further than others would like. But it is an honest effort to try to compromise differences in a very controversial and emotional subject, and that is voting rights for Americans. . . .

In the course of discussing this bill — and I know that the Senator from Utah [Senator Hatch] spent countless hours in hearings, as did other members of this committee, and I commend them for that; and I know of the strong views they hold with reference to intent and results. I do not, say, quarrel with that, but I will try to explain in a minute why I believe that we should move quickly on what I will offer as a compromise for myself, the Senator from Arizona, Senator DeConcini; the Senator from Iowa, Senator Grassley. And then the original sponsors of the major provision have joined in the compromises, Senators Kennedy and Mathias, along with, I think, Senator Metzenbaum, who has an important provision in that bill. . . .

I would say at the outset that supporting the compromise does not indicate that everybody is totally satisfied with the final product. There are some who have reservations that we do not do enough, as I said earlier, and some will probably — and I certainly respect that right — attempt to amend the compromise in the committee and on the Senate floor.

As the members of the committee are aware, late yesterday afternoon I along with Senators DeConcini, Grassley, Kennedy, and Metzenbaum and Senator Mathias, who could not be there, announced that we had worked out a compromise on the matter now under consideration. The compromise is the result of extensive negotiation and discussion with our colleagues on the committee as well as with leaders in the civil rights community. I believe that, as I try to count the present support for the compromise, there are about 13 members of this committee who will support the compromise. Hopefully, that number will grow before a vote is taken. . . .

With regard to the compromise itself, we are all aware that the most controversial aspect of the committee's consideration of S. 1992 relates to section 2 of the Voting Rights Act. Section 2 lies at the heart of the act insofar as it contains the basic guarantee that the voting rights of our citizens should not be denied or abridged on account of race, color, or membership in a language minority. In the 1980 case of Mobile v. Bolden, the Supreme Court interpreted section 2 as prohibiting only intentional discrimination. The Mathias/Kennedy bill would amend section 2 to prohibit any voting practice discriminatory in result. The bill recommended by the Constitution Subcommittee, however, would not amend section 2, thus leaving the intent requirement of the *Mobile* decision intact.

Proponents of the results standard in the Mathias/Kennedy bill [the House version of the bill] persuasively argue that intentional discrimination is too difficult to prove to make enforcement of the law effective. Perhaps more importantly, they have asked, if the right to exercise a franchise has been denied or abridged, why should plaintiffs have to prove that the deprivation of this fundamental right was intentional. On the other hand, many on the committee have expressed legitimate concerns that a results standard could be interpreted by the courts to mandate proportional representation. . . .

The supporters of this compromise believe that a voting practice or procedure which is discriminatory in result should not be allowed to stand, regardless of whether there exists a discriminatory purpose or intent. For this reason, the compromise retains the results standards of the Mathias/Kennedy bill. However, we also feel that the legislation should be strengthened with additional language delineating what legal standard should apply under the results tests and clarifying that it is not a mandate for proportional representation. Thus, our compromise adds a new subsection to section 2, which codified language from the 1973 Supreme Court decision of White v. Regester. *White* was a controlling precedent for voting rights cases prior to the controversial *Mobile* decision.

The new subsection clarifies, as did *White* and previous cases, that the issue to be decided is whether members of a protected class enjoy equal access. I think that is the thrust of our compromise: equal access, whether it is open; equal access to the political process; not whether they have achieved proportional election results.

The new subsection also provides . . . that the extent to which minorities have been elected to office is one circumstance which may be considered. But it explicitly states—let me make that very clear—in the compromise that nothing in this section establishes a right to proportional representation. . . .

I would just say in summary that, so everybody clearly understands, the compromise maintains the results standard of the House bill but adds language—and this is the key part that I think Senator Thurmond and others are concerned about—to address the proportional representation issue. Specifically, the compromise provides that the issue to be decided is whether political processes are equally open, thus placing focus on access to the process, not election results. To the extent which minorities have been elected is one circumstance to be considered. We talk about the totality of circumstances, the White v. Regester criteria. But it also expressly states that there is no right, there is no right to proportional representation.

NOTES AND QUESTIONS

1. *A typical challenge.* Under §2 of the Voting Rights Act, every challenge to a legislative districting plan is motivated by an opinion that the existing plan does not result in the election of a sufficient number of representatives from a minority group protected by the Voting Rights Act, based on that group's percentage of total population. The goal of all of these suits is to increase minority representation in the belief that such representation will help improve the condition of the protected minority. As Professor Lani Guinier has written: "For almost two decades, the conventional civil rights political empowerment agenda of black activists, lawyers and scholars has focused on the election of black representatives." Lani Guinier, The Triumph of Tokenism: The Voting Rights Act and the Theory of Black Electoral Success, 89 Mich. L. Rev. 1077, 1078 (1991). To focus on the debate between Senator Hatch and the bill's proponents, consider the impact of each of their views on such a litigation. Does the Dole compromise resolve the disagreement?

2. *The "electoral success" circumstance and the proviso against proportional representation.* As a result of the Dole compromise, §2 sets forth electoral success as one circumstance that may be probative of discrimination, and then adds to that a proviso against proportional representation. What is the significance of these provisions? Is the failure to achieve proportional representation in a particular jurisdiction evidence of discrimination? Assuming the answer to that question is yes, is there a right to proportional representation? The issues set forth in this note and in Note 1 are among the many points discussed in the following section.

C. APPLYING THE VOTING RIGHTS ACT OF 1965, AS AMENDED

Thornburg v. Gingles
478 U.S. 30 (1986)

Brennan, J., announced the judgment of the Court and delivered the opinion of the Court with respect to Parts I, II, III-A, III-B, IV-A, and V, in which White, Marshall, Blackmun, and Stevens, JJ., joined, an opinion with respect to Part III-C, in which MARSHALL, BLACKMUN, and STEVENS, JJ., joined, and an opinion with respect to Part IV-B, in which WHITE, J., joined. [Internal citations and footnotes have been omitted, except where particularly relevant.]

This case requires that we construe for the first time §2 of the Voting Rights Act of 1965, as amended June 29, 1982. . . .

I. Background

In April 1982, the North Carolina General Assembly enacted a legislative redistricting plan for the State's Senate and House of Representatives. Appellees, black citizens of North Carolina who are registered to vote, challenged seven districts, one single-member and six multimember districts, alleging that the redistricting scheme impaired black citizens' ability to elect representatives of their choice in violation of the Fourteenth and Fifteenth Amendments to the United States Constitution and of §2 of the Voting Rights Act.

After appellees brought suit, but before trial, Congress amended §2. The amendment was largely a response to this Court's plurality opinion in Mobile v. Bolden, 446 U.S. 55 (1980). . . . Congress substantially revised §2 to make clear that a violation could be proved by showing discriminatory effect alone and to establish as the relevant legal standard the "results test," applied by this Court in White v. Regester. . . .

The Senate Judiciary Committee majority Report accompanying the bill that amended §2 elaborates on the circumstances that might be probative of a §2 violation, noting the following "typical factors":

> 1. the extent of any history of official discrimination in the state or political subdivision that touched the right of the members of the minority group to register, to vote, or otherwise to participate in the democratic process;
> 2. the extent to which voting in the elections of the state or political subdivision is racially polarized;
> 3. the extent to which the state or political subdivision has used unusually large election districts, majority vote requirements, antisingle shot provisions, or other voting practices or procedures that may enhance the opportunity for discrimination against the minority group;
> 4. if there is a candidate slating process, whether the members of the minority group have been denied access to that process;
> 5. the extent to which members of the minority group in the state or political subdivision bear the effects of discrimination in such areas as education, employment and health, which hinder their ability to participate effectively in the political process;
> 6. whether political campaigns have been characterized by overt or subtle racial appeals;
> 7. the extent to which members of the minority group have been elected to public office in the jurisdiction.

Additional factors that in some cases have had probative value as part of plaintiffs' evidence to establish a violation are:

whether there is a significant lack of responsiveness on the part of elected officials to the particularized needs of the members of the minority group.

whether the policy underlying the state or political subdivision's use of such voting qualification, prerequisite to voting, or standard, practice or procedure is tenuous.

S. Rep., at 28-29.

The District Court applied the "totality of the circumstances" test set forth in §2(b) to appellees' statutory claim, and, relying principally on the factors outlined in the Senate Report, held that the redistricting scheme violated §2 because it resulted in the dilution of black citizens' votes in all seven disputed districts.

II.   Section 2 and Vote Dilution Through Use of Multimember Districts . . .

A.   Section 2 and Its Legislative History . . .

The Senate Report which accompanied the 1982 amendments elaborates on the nature of §2 violations and on the proof required to establish these violations. . . . The "right" question, as the report emphasizes repeatedly, is whether "as a result of the challenged practice or structure plaintiffs do not have an equal opportunity to participate in the political processes and to elect candidates of their choice."

In order to answer this question, a court must assess the impact of the contested structure or practice on minority electoral opportunities "on the basis of objective factors." The Senate Report specifies factors which typically may be relevant to a §2 claim. . . . The Report stresses, however, that this list of typical factors is neither comprehensive nor exclusive. While the enumerated factors will often be pertinent to certain types of §2 violations, particularly to vote dilution claims, other factors may also be relevant and may be considered. Furthermore, the Senate Committee observed that "there is no requirement that any particular number of factors be proved, or that a majority of them point one way or the other." Rather, the Committee determined that "the question whether the political processes are 'equally open' depends upon a searching practical evaluation of the 'past and present reality,'" and on a "functional" view of the political process.

Although the Senate Report espouses a flexible, fact-intensive test for §2 violations, it limits the circumstances under which §2 violations may be proved in three ways. First, electoral devices, such as at-large elections, may not be considered per se violative of §2. Plaintiffs must demonstrate that, under the totality of the circumstances, the devices result in unequal access to the electoral process. Second, the conjunction of an allegedly dilutive electoral mechanism and the lack of proportional representation alone does not establish a violation. Third, the results test does not assume the existence of racial bloc voting; plaintiffs must prove it.

B. Vote Dilution Through the Use of Multimember Districts

Appellees contend that the legislative decision to employ multimember, rather than single-member, districts in the contested jurisdictions dilutes their votes by submerging them in a white majority, thus impairing their ability to elect representatives of their choice.

The essence of a §2 claim is that a certain electoral law, practice, or structure interacts with social and historical conditions to cause an inequality in the opportunities enjoyed by black and white voters to elect their preferred representatives. This Court has long recognized that multimember districts and at-large voting schemes may "operate to minimize or cancel out the voting strength of racial [minorities in] the voting population." The theoretical basis for this type of impairment is that where minority and majority voters consistently prefer different candidates, the majority, by virtue of its numerical superiority, will regularly defeat the choices of minority voters. Minority voters who contend that the multi-member form of districting violates §2 must prove that the use of a multi-member electoral structure operates to minimize or cancel out their ability to elect their preferred candidates.

While many or all of the factors listed in the Senate Report may be relevant to a claim of vote dilution through submergence in multimember districts, unless there is a conjunction of the following circumstances, the use of multimember districts generally will not impede the ability of minority voters to elect representatives of their choice. Stated succinctly, a bloc voting majority must usually be able to defeat candidates supported by a politically cohesive, geographically insular minority group. These circumstances are necessary preconditions for multimember districts to operate to impair minority voters' ability to elect representatives of their choice for the following reasons. First, the minority group must be able to demonstrate that it is sufficiently large and geographically compact to constitute a majority in a single-member district. If it is not, as would be the case in a substantially integrated district, the multimember form of the district cannot be responsible for minority voters' inability to elect its candidates. Second, the minority group must be able to show that it is politically cohesive. If the minority group is not politically cohesive, it cannot be said that the selection of a multimember electoral structure thwarts distinctive minority group interests. Third, the minority must be able to demonstrate that the white majority votes sufficiently as a bloc to enable it — in the absence of special circumstances, such as the minority candidate running unopposed — usually to defeat the minority's preferred candidate.

In establishing this last circumstance, the minority group demonstrates that submergence in a white multimember district impedes its ability to elect its chosen representatives.

Finally, we observe that the usual predictability of the majority's success distinguishes structural dilution from the mere loss of an occasional election.

III.   Racially Polarized Voting . . .

A.   The District Court's Treatment of Racially Polarized Voting

The investigation conducted by the District Court into the question of racial bloc voting credited some testimony of lay witnesses, but relied principally on statistical evidence presented by appellees' expert witnesses, in particular that offered by Dr. Bernard Grofman. Dr. Grofman collected and evaluated data from 53 General Assembly primary and general elections involving black candidacies. These elections were held over a period of three different election years in the six originally challenged multimember districts. . . .

The court's initial consideration of these data took the form of a three-part inquiry: did the data reveal any correlation between the race of the voter and the selection of certain candidates; was the revealed correlation statistically significant; and was the difference in black and white voting patterns "substantively significant"? The District Court found that blacks and whites generally preferred different candidates and, on that basis, found voting in the districts to be racially correlated. The court accepted Dr. Grofman's expert opinion that the correlation between the race of the voter and the voter's choice of certain candidates was statistically significant. Finally, adopting Dr. Grofman's terminology, the court found that in all but 2 of the 53 elections the degree of racial bloc voting was "so marked as to be substantively significant, in the sense that the results of the individual election would have been different depending upon whether it had been held among only the white voters or only the black voters."

. . . The court then considered the relevance to the existence of legally significant white bloc voting of the fact that black candidates have won some elections. It determined that in most instances, special circumstances, such as incumbency and lack of opposition, rather than a diminution in usually severe white bloc voting, accounted for these candidates' success. The court also suggested that black voters' reliance on bullet voting was a significant factor in their successful efforts to elect candidates of their choice. Based on all of the evidence before it, the trial court concluded that each of the districts experienced racially polarized voting "in a persistent and severe degree."

B. The Degree of Bloc Voting That Is Legally Significant under §2 . . .

2. *The Standard for Legally Significant Racial Bloc Voting . . .*

The purpose of inquiring into the existence of racially polarized voting is twofold: to ascertain whether minority group members constitute a politically cohesive unit and to determine whether whites vote sufficiently as a bloc usually to defeat the minority's preferred candidates. Thus, the question whether a given district experiences legally significant racially polarized voting requires discrete inquiries into minority and white voting practices. A showing that a significant number of minority group members usually vote for the same candidates is one way of proving the political cohesiveness necessary to a vote dilution claim, and, consequently, establishes minority bloc voting within the context of §2. And, in general, a white bloc vote that normally will defeat the combined strength of minority support plus white "crossover" votes rises to the level of legally significant white bloc voting. The amount of white bloc voting that can generally "minimize or cancel" black voters' ability to elect representatives of their choice, however, will vary from district to district according to a number of factors, including the nature of the allegedly dilutive electoral mechanism; the presence or absence of other potentially dilutive electoral devices, such as majority vote requirement, designated posts, and prohibitions against bullet voting; the percentage of registered voters in the district who are members of the minority group; the size of the district; and, in multimember districts, the number of seats open and the number of candidates in the field. . . .

Because loss of political power through vote dilution is distinct from the mere inability to win a particular election, a pattern of racial bloc voting that extends over a period of time is more probative of a claim that a district experiences legally significant polarization than are the results of a single election. . . . Also for this reason, in a district where elections are shown usually to be polarized, the fact that racially polarized voting is not present in one or a few individual elections does not necessarily negate the conclusion that the district experiences legally significant bloc voting. Furthermore, the success of a minority candidate in a particular election does not necessarily prove that the district did not experience polarized voting in that election; special circumstances, such as the absence of an opponent, incumbency, or the utilization of bullet voting, may explain minority electoral success in a polarized contest.

As must be apparent, the degree of racial bloc voting that is cognizable as an element of a §2 vote dilution claim will vary according to a variety of factual circumstances. Consequently, there is no simple doctrinal test for the existence of legally significant racial bloc voting. However, the foregoing general principles should provide courts with substantial guidance in determining whether evidence that black and white voters generally prefer different candidates rises to the level of legal significance under §2.

3.   Standard Utilized by the District Court . . .

The District Court's findings concerning black support for black candidates in the five multimember districts at issue here clearly establish the political cohesiveness of black voters. . . . In all but 5 of 16 primary elections, black support for black candidates ranged between 71% and 92%; and in the general elections, black support for black Democratic candidates ranged between 87% and 96%.

In sharp contrast to its findings of strong black support for black candidates, the District Court found that a substantial majority of white voters would rarely, if ever, vote for a black candidate. In the primary elections, white support for black candidates ranged between 8% and 50%, and in the general elections it ranged between 28% and 49%. The court also determined that, on average, 81.7% of white voters did not vote for any black candidate in the primary elections. In the general elections, white voters almost always ranked black candidates either last or next to last in the multicandidate field, except in heavily Democratic areas where white voters consistently ranked black candidates last among the Democrats, if not last or next to last among all candidates. The court further observed that approximately two-thirds of white voters did not vote for black candidates in general elections, even after the candidate had won the Democratic primary and the choice was to vote for a Republican or for no one. . . .

We conclude that the District Court's approach, which tested data derived from three election years in each district, and which revealed that blacks strongly supported black candidates, while, to the black candidates' usual detriment, whites rarely did, satisfactorily addresses each facet of the proper legal standard.

C.   Evidence of Racially Polarized Voting

1.   Appellants' Argument

North Carolina and the United States . . . argue that the term "racially polarized voting" must, as a matter of law, refer to voting patterns for which the principal cause is race. They contend that the District Court utilized a legally incorrect definition of racially polarized voting by relying on . . . analyses which merely demonstrated a correlation between the race of the voter and the level of voter support for certain candidates, but which did not prove that race was the primary determinant of voters' choices. . . .

Whether appellants and the United States believe that it is the voter's race or the candidate's race that must be the primary determinant of the voter's choice is unclear. . . . In either case, we disagree: For purposes of §2, the legal concept of racially polarized voting incorporates neither causation nor intent. It means simply that the race of voters correlates with the selection of a certain candidate or candidates; that is, it refers to the situation where different races (or minority language groups) vote in blocs for different candidates. . . .

3. Race of Voter as Primary Determinant of Voter Behavior

Appellants and the United States contend that the legal concept of "racially polarized voting" refers not to voting patterns that are merely correlated with the voter's race, but to voting patterns that are determined primarily by the voter's race, rather than by the voter's other socioeconomic characteristics.

The first problem with this argument is that it ignores the fact that members of geographically insular racial and ethnic groups frequently share socioeconomic characteristics, such as income level, employment status, amount of education, housing and other living conditions, religion, language, and so forth. . . . Where such characteristics are shared, race or ethnic group not only denotes color or place of origin, it also functions as a shorthand notation for common social and economic characteristics. Appellants' definition of racially polarized voting is even more pernicious where shared characteristics are causally related to race or ethnicity. The opportunity to achieve high employment status and income, for example, is often influenced by the presence or absence of racial or ethnic discrimination. A definition of racially polarized voting which holds that black bloc voting does not exist when black voters' choice of certain candidates is most strongly influenced by the fact that the voters have low incomes and menial jobs — when the reason most of those voters have menial jobs and low incomes is attributable to past or present racial discrimination — runs counter to the Senate Report's instruction to conduct a searching and practical evaluation of past and present reality, and interferes with the purpose of the Voting Rights Act to eliminate the negative effects of past discrimination on the electoral opportunities of minorities. . . .

Congress could not have intended that courts employ this definition of racial bloc voting. First, this definition leads to results that are inconsistent with the effects test adopted by Congress when it amended §2 and with the Senate Report's admonition that courts take a "functional" view of the political process, [and] conduct a searching and practical evaluation of reality. A test for racially polarized voting that denies the fact that race and socioeconomic characteristics are often closely correlated permits neither a practical evaluation of reality nor a functional analysis of vote dilution. And, contrary to Congress' intent in adopting the "results test," appellants' proposed definition could result in the inability of minority voters to establish a critical element of a vote dilution claim, even though both races engage in "monolithic" bloc voting, and generations of black voters have been unable to elect a representative of their choice. . . .

IV.   The Legal Significance of Some Black Candidates' Success

A

North Carolina and the United States maintain that the District Court failed to accord the proper weight to the success of some black candidates in the challenged districts. Black residents of these districts, they point out, achieved improved representation in the 1982 General Assembly election. They also note that blacks in House District 23 have enjoyed proportional representation consistently since 1973 and that blacks in the other districts have occasionally enjoyed nearly proportional representation. This electoral success demonstrates conclusively, appellants and the United States argue, that blacks in those districts do not have "less opportunity than other members of the electorate to participate in the political process and to elect representatives of their choice." 42 U.S.C. §1973(b). . . .

Nothing in the statute or its legislative history prohibited the court from viewing with some caution black candidates' success in the 1982 election, and from deciding on the basis of all the relevant circumstances to accord greater weight to blacks' relative lack of success over the course of several recent elections. Consequently, we hold that the District Court did not err, as a matter of law, in refusing to treat the fact that some black candidates have succeeded as dispositive of appellees' §2 claim. Where multimember districting generally works to dilute the minority vote, it cannot be defended on the ground that it sporadically and serendipitously benefits minority voters.

B

The District Court did err, however, in ignoring the significance of the sustained success black voters have experienced in House District 23. In that district, the last six elections have resulted in proportional representation for black residents. This persistent proportional representation is inconsistent with appellees' allegation that the ability of black voters in District 23 to elect representatives of their choice is not equal to that enjoyed by the white majority. . . .

JUSTICE WHITE, concurring.

I join Parts I, II, III-A, III-B, IV-A, and V of the Court's opinion and agree with Justice Brennan's opinion as to Part IV-B. I disagree with Part III-C of Justice Brennan's opinion.

Justice Brennan states in Part III-C that the crucial factor in identifying polarized voting is the race of the voter and that the race of the candidate is irrelevant. Under this test, there is polarized voting if the majority of white voters vote for different candidates than the majority of the blacks, regardless of the race of the candidates. I do not agree. Suppose an eight-member multimember district that is 60% white and 40% black, the blacks being geographically located so that two safe black single-member districts could be drawn. Suppose further that there are six white and two black Democrats running against six white and two black Republicans. Under Justice Brennan's test, there would be polarized voting and a likely §2 violation if all the Republicans, including the two blacks, are elected, and 80% of the blacks in the predominantly black areas vote Democratic. I take it that there would also be a violation in a single-member district that is 60% black, but enough of the blacks vote with the whites to elect a black candidate who is not the choice of the majority of black voters. This is interest-group politics rather than a rule hedging against racial discrimination. I doubt that this is what Congress had in mind in amending §2 as it did. . . . Furthermore, on the facts of this case, there is no need to draw the voter/candidate distinction. The District Court did not and reached the correct result except, in my view, with respect to District 23.

JUSTICE O'CONNOR, with whom THE CHIEF JUSTICE, JUSTICE POWELL, and JUSTICE REHNQUIST join, concurring in the judgment. . . .

In construing this compromise legislation, we must make every effort to be faithful to the balance Congress struck. This is not an easy task. We know that Congress intended to allow vote dilution claims to be brought under §2, but we also know that Congress did not intend to create a right to proportional representation for minority voters. There is an inherent tension between what Congress wished to do and what it wished to avoid, because any theory of vote dilution must necessarily rely to some extent on a measure of minority voting strength that makes some reference to the proportion between the minority group and the electorate at large. In addition, several important aspects of the "results" test had received little attention in this Court's cases or in the decisions of the Courts of Appeals employing that test on which Congress also relied. Specifically, the legal meaning to be given to the concepts of "racial bloc voting" and "minority voting strength" had been left largely unaddressed by the courts when §2 was amended.

The Court attempts to resolve all these difficulties today. First, the Court supplies definitions of racial bloc voting and minority voting strength that will apparently be applicable in all cases and that will dictate the structure of vote dilution litigation. Second, the Court adopts a test, based on the level of minority electoral success, for determining when an electoral scheme has sufficiently diminished minority voting strength to constitute vote dilution. Third, although the Court does not acknowledge it expressly, the combination of the Court's definition of minority voting strength and its test for vote dilution results in the creation of a right to a form of proportional representation in favor of all geographically and politically cohesive minority groups that are large enough to constitute majorities if concentrated within one or more single-member districts. In so doing, the Court has disregarded the balance struck by Congress in amending §2. . . .

I

In order to explain my disagreement with the Court's interpretation of §2, it is useful to illustrate the impact that alternative districting plans or types of districts typically have on the likelihood that a minority group will be able to elect candidates it prefers, and then to set out the critical elements of a vote dilution claim as they emerge in the Court's opinion.

Consider a town of 1,000 voters that is governed by a council of four representatives, in which 30% of the voters are black, and in which the black voters are concentrated in one section of the city and tend to vote as a bloc. It would be possible to draw four single-member districts, in one of which blacks would constitute an overwhelming majority. The black voters in this district would be assured of electing a representative of their choice, while any remaining black voters in the other districts would be submerged in large white majorities. This option would give the minority group roughly proportional representation.

Alternatively, it would usually be possible to draw four single-member districts in two of which black voters constituted much narrower majorities of about 60%. The black voters in these districts would often be able to elect the representative of their choice in each of these two districts, but if even 20% of the black voters supported the candidate favored by the white minority in those districts the candidates preferred by the majority of black voters might lose. This option would, depending on the circumstances of a particular election, sometimes give the minority group more than proportional representation, but would increase the risk that the group would not achieve even roughly proportional representation.

It would also usually be possible to draw four single-member districts in each of which black voters constituted a minority. In the extreme case, black voters would constitute 30% of the voters in each district. Unless approximately 30% of the white voters in this extreme case backed the minority candidate, black voters in such a district would be unable to elect the candidate of their choice in an election between only two candidates even if they unanimously supported him. This option would make it difficult for black voters to elect candidates of their choice even with significant white support, and all but impossible without such support.

Finally, it would be possible to elect all four representatives in a single at-large election in which each voter could vote for four candidates. Under this scheme, white voters could elect all the representatives even if black voters turned out in large numbers and voted for one and only one candidate. . . . [T]he at-large or multimember district has an inherent tendency to submerge the votes of the minority. The minority group's prospects for electoral success under such a district heavily depend on a variety of factors such as voter turnout, how many candidates run, how evenly white support is spread, how much white support is given to a candidate or candidates preferred by the minority group, and the extent to which minority voters engage in "bullet voting." . . .

There is no difference in principle between the varying effects of the alternatives outlined above and the varying effects of alternative single-district plans and multimember districts. The type of districting selected and the way in which district lines are drawn can have a powerful effect on the likelihood that members of a geographically and politically cohesive minority group will be able to elect candidates of their choice.

Although §2 does not speak in terms of "vote dilution," I agree with the Court that proof of vote dilution can establish a violation of §2 as amended. The phrase "vote dilution," in the legal sense, simply refers to the impermissible discriminatory effect that a multimember or other districting plan has when it operates "to cancel out or minimize the voting strength of racial groups." This definition, however, conceals some very formidable difficulties. Is the "voting strength" of a racial group to be assessed solely with reference to its prospects for electoral success, or should courts look at other avenues of political influence open to the racial group? Insofar as minority voting strength is assessed with reference to electoral success, how should undiluted minority voting strength be measured? How much of an impairment of minority voting strength is necessary to prove a violation of §2? What constitutes racial bloc voting and how is it proved? What weight is to be given to evidence of actual electoral success by minority candidates in the face of evidence of racial bloc voting?

The Court resolves the first question summarily: minority voting strength is to be assessed solely in terms of the minority group's ability to elect candidates it prefers. Under this approach, the essence of a vote dilution claim is that the State has created single-member or multimember districts that unacceptably impair the minority group's ability to elect the candidates its members prefer.

In order to evaluate a claim that a particular multimember district or single-member district has diluted the minority group's voting strength to a degree that violates §2, however, it is also necessary to construct a measure of "undiluted" minority voting strength. . . . Put simply, in order to decide whether an electoral system has made it harder for minority voters to elect the candidates they prefer, a court must have an idea in mind of how hard it "should" be for minority voters to elect their preferred candidates under an acceptable system.

Several possible measures of "undiluted" minority voting strength suggest themselves. First, a court could simply use proportionality as its guide:

if the minority group constituted 30% of the voters in a given area, the court would regard the minority group as having the potential to elect 30% of the representatives in that area. Second, a court could posit some alternative districting plan as a "normal" or "fair" electoral scheme and attempt to calculate how many candidates preferred by the minority group would probably be elected under that scheme. There are, as we have seen, a variety of ways in which even single-member districts could be drawn, and each will present the minority group with its own array of electoral risks and benefits; the court might, therefore, consider a range of acceptable plans in attempting to estimate "undiluted" minority voting strength by this method. Third, the court could attempt to arrive at a plan that would maximize feasible minority electoral success, and use this degree of predicted success as its measure of "undiluted" minority voting strength. If a court were to employ this third alternative, it would often face hard choices about what would truly "maximize" minority electoral success. An example is the scenario described above, in which a minority group could be concentrated in one completely safe district or divided among two districts in each of which its members would constitute a somewhat precarious majority.

The Court today has adopted a variant of the third approach, to wit, undiluted minority voting strength means the maximum feasible minority voting strength. In explaining the elements of a vote dilution claim, the Court first states that "the minority group must be able to demonstrate that it is sufficiently large and geographically compact to constitute a majority in a single-member district." If not, apparently the minority group has no cognizable claim that its ability to elect the representatives of its choice has been impaired. Second, "the minority group must be able to show that it is politically cohesive," that is, that a significant proportion of the minority group supports the same candidates. Third, the Court requires the minority group to "demonstrate that the white majority votes sufficiently as a bloc to enable it — in the absence of special circumstances . . . — usually to defeat the minority's preferred candidate." If these three requirements are met, "the minority group demonstrates that submergence in a white multimember district impedes its ability to elect its chosen representatives." That is to say, the minority group has proved vote dilution in violation of §2.

The Court's definition of the elements of a vote dilution claim is simple and invariable: a court should calculate minority voting strength by assuming that the minority group is concentrated in a single-member district in which it constitutes a voting majority. Where the minority group is not large enough, geographically concentrated enough, or politically cohesive enough for this to be possible, the minority group's claim fails. Where the minority group meets these requirements, the representatives that it could elect in the hypothetical district or districts in which it constitutes a majority will serve as the measure of its undiluted voting strength. Whatever plan the State actually adopts must be assessed in terms of the effect it has on this undiluted voting strength. If this is indeed the single, universal standard for evaluating undiluted minority voting strength for vote dilution purposes, the standard is applicable whether what is challenged is a multimember district or a particular single-member districting scheme.

The Court's statement of the elements of a vote dilution claim also supplies an answer to another question posed above: how much of an impairment of undiluted minority voting strength is necessary to prove vote dilution. The Court requires the minority group that satisfies the threshold requirements of size and cohesiveness to prove that it will usually be unable to elect as many representatives of its choice under the challenged districting scheme as its undiluted voting strength would permit. This requirement, then, constitutes the true test of vote dilution. Again, no reason appears why this test would not be applicable to a vote dilution claim challenging single-member as well as multimember districts.

This measure of vote dilution, taken in conjunction with the Court's standard for measuring undiluted minority voting strength, creates what amounts to a right to usual, roughly proportional representation on the part of sizable, compact, cohesive minority groups. If, under a particular multimember or single-member district plan, qualified minority groups usually cannot elect the representatives they would be likely to elect under the most favorable single-member districting plan, then §2 is violated. Unless minority success under the challenged electoral system regularly approximates this rough version of proportional representation, that system dilutes minority voting strength and violates §2.

To appreciate the implications of this approach, it is useful to return to the illustration of a town with four council representatives given above. Under the Court's approach, if the black voters who constitute 30% of the town's voting population do not usually succeed in electing one representative of their choice, then regardless of whether the town employs at-large elections or is divided into four single-member districts, its electoral system violates §2. Moreover, if the town had a black voting population of 40%, on the Court's reasoning the black minority, so long as it was geographically and politically cohesive, would be entitled usually to elect two of the four representatives, since it would normally be possible to create two districts in which black voters constituted safe majorities of approximately 80%.

To be sure, the Court also requires that plaintiffs prove that racial bloc voting by the white majority interacts with the challenged districting plan so as usually to defeat the minority's preferred candidate. In fact, however, this requirement adds little that is not already contained in the Court's requirements that the minority group be politically cohesive and that its preferred candidates usually lose. . . .

II

In my view, the Court's test for measuring minority voting strength and its test for vote dilution, operating in tandem, come closer to an absolute requirement of proportional representation than Congress intended when it codified the results test in §2. It is not necessary or appropriate to decide in this case whether §2 requires a uniform measure of undiluted minority voting strength in every case, nor have appellants challenged the standard employed by the District Court for assessing undiluted minority voting strength. . . .

In my view, we should refrain from deciding in this case whether a court must invariably posit as its measure of "undiluted" minority voting strength single-member districts in which minority group members constitute a majority. There is substantial doubt that Congress intended "undiluted minority voting strength" to mean "maximum feasible minority voting strength." Even if that is the appropriate definition in some circumstances, there is no indication that Congress intended to mandate a single, universally applicable standard for measuring undiluted minority voting strength, regardless of local conditions and regardless of the extent of past discrimination against minority voters in a particular State or political subdivision. . . .

On the same reasoning, I would reject the Court's test for vote dilution. The Court measures undiluted minority voting strength by reference to the possibility of creating single-member districts in which the minority group would constitute a majority, rather than by looking to raw proportionality alone. The Court's standard for vote dilution, when combined with its test for undiluted minority voting strength, makes actionable every deviation from usual, rough proportionality in representation for any cohesive minority group as to which this degree of proportionality is feasible within the framework of single-member districts. Requiring that every minority group that could possibly constitute a majority in a single-member district be assigned to such a district would approach a requirement of proportional representation as nearly as is possible within the framework of single-member districts. Since the Court's analysis entitles every such minority group usually to elect as many representatives under a multi-member district as it could elect under the most favorable single-member district scheme, it follows that the Court is requiring a form of proportional representation. This approach is inconsistent with the results test and with §2's disclaimer of a right to proportional representation. . . .

I would adhere to the approach outlined in *Whitcomb* and *White*. . . . Under that approach, a court should consider all relevant factors bearing on whether the minority group has "less opportunity than other members of the electorate to participate in the political process and to elect representatives of their choice." 42 U.S.C. §1973 (emphasis omitted). The court should not focus solely on the minority group's ability to elect representatives of its choice. Whatever measure of undiluted minority voting strength the court employs in connection with evaluating the presence or absence of minority electoral success, it should also bear in mind that "the power to influence the political process is not limited to winning elections." Davis v. Bandemer. Of course, the relative lack of minority electoral success under a challenged plan, when compared with the success that would be predicted under the measure of undiluted minority voting strength the court is employing, can constitute powerful evidence of vote dilution. Moreover, the minority group may in fact lack access to or influence upon representatives it did not support as candidates. . . . Nonetheless, a reviewing court should be required to find more than simply that the minority group does not usually attain an undiluted measure of electoral success. The court must find that even substantial minority success will be highly infrequent under the challenged plan before it may conclude, on this basis alone, that the plan operates "to cancel out or, minimize the voting strength of [the] racial [group]." *White.*

III

Only three Justices of the Court join Part III-C of Justice Brennan's opinion, which addresses the validity of the statistical evidence on which the District Court relied in finding racially polarized voting in each of the challenged districts. Insofar as statistical evidence of divergent racial voting patterns is admitted solely to establish that the minority group is politically cohesive and to assess its prospects for electoral success, I agree that defendants cannot rebut this showing by offering evidence that the divergent racial voting patterns may be explained in part by causes other than race, such as an underlying divergence in the interests of minority and white voters. I do not agree, however, that such evidence can never affect the overall vote dilution inquiry. Evidence that a candidate preferred by the minority group in a particular election was rejected by white voters for reasons other than those which made that candidate the preferred choice of the minority group would seem clearly relevant in answering the question whether bloc voting by white voters will consistently defeat minority candidates. Such evidence would suggest that another candidate, equally preferred by the minority group, might be able to attract greater white support in future elections.

I believe Congress also intended that explanations of the reasons why white voters rejected minority candidates would be probative of the likelihood that candidates elected without decisive minority support would be willing to take the minority's interests into account. In a community that is polarized along racial lines, racial hostility may bar these and other indirect avenues of political influence to a much greater extent than in a community where racial animosity is absent although the interests of racial groups diverge. Indeed, the Senate Report clearly stated that one factor that could have probative value in §2 cases was "whether there is a significant lack of responsiveness on the part of elected officials to the particularized needs of the members of the minority group." The overall vote dilution inquiry neither requires nor permits an arbitrary rule against consideration of all evidence concerning voting preferences other than statistical evidence of racial voting patterns. Such a rule would give no effect whatever to the Senate Report's repeated emphasis on "intensive racial politics," on "racial political considerations," and on whether "racial politics ... dominate the electoral process" as one aspect of the "racial bloc voting" that Congress deemed relevant to showing a §2 violation. ...

V

When members of a racial minority challenge a multimember district on the grounds that it dilutes their voting strength, I agree with the Court that they must show that they possess such strength and that the multimember district impairs it. A court must therefore appraise the minority group's undiluted voting strength in order to assess the effects of the multimember district. I would reserve the question of the proper method or methods for making this assessment. But once such an assessment is made, in my view the evaluation of an alleged impairment of voting strength requires consideration of the minority group's access to the political processes generally, not solely consideration of the chances that its preferred candidates will actually be elected. Proof that white voters withhold their support from minority-preferred candidates to an extent that consistently ensures their defeat is entitled to significant weight in plaintiffs' favor. However, if plaintiffs direct their proof solely towards the minority group's prospects for electoral success, they must show that substantial minority success will be highly infrequent under the challenged plan in order to establish that the plan operates to "cancel out or minimize" their voting strength. *White.*

Compromise is essential to much if not most major federal legislation, and confidence that the federal courts will enforce such compromises is indispensable to their creation. I believe that the Court today strikes a different balance than Congress intended to when it codified the results test and disclaimed any right to proportional representation under §2. For that reason, I join the Court's judgment but not its opinion.

Justice Stevens, with whom Justice Marshall and Justice Blackmun join, concurring in part and dissenting in part.

In my opinion, the findings of the District Court ... adequately support the District Court's judgment concerning House District 23 as well as the balance of that judgment. ...

White, J., filed a concurring opinion [omitted]. O'Connor, J., filed an opinion concurring in the judgment, in which Burger, C.J., Powell and Rehnquist, JJ., joined [omitted]. Stevens, J., filed an opinion concurring in part and dissenting in part, in which Marshall and Blackmun, JJ., joined [omitted]. ...

NOTES AND QUESTIONS

1. *Gingles and the Dole compromise.* On pages 280-284 of this chapter, we describe the compromise offered by Senator Dole that resolved the impasse between the House and the Senate Subcommittee on the Constitution. In her concurrence, Justice O'Connor claims that the decision of the Court fails to honor that compromise, thereby undermining the legislative process. What aspect of the Court's opinion occasions such criticism? What approach would Justice O'Connor take to avoid this problem?

2. *Totality of the circumstances.* In applying the statute, the Court makes reference to the Senate report that accompanied the bill from the Senate Judiciary Committee to the Senate floor. This report sets forth a list of circumstances that should be considered in determining whether the terms of §2 have been violated. As your answer to the previous question should make clear, the Court, despite its reference to the report, narrows the list to the single circumstance of electoral success, the one circumstance set forth in the statute. As Professor Guinier has written:

> In search of a statutory core value and judicially manageable standards, the courts have cobbled from the statute a right to minority electoral success. The courts have ignored statutory language providing for the "opportunity . . . to participate [equally] in the political process" and instead have focused exclusively on language securing the "opportunity . . . *to elect* the representatives of [the protected group's] choice." . . . The submergence of black electoral potential and the subsequent emergence of black voting majorities capable of electing black candidates have become the preferred indicia of a statutory violation. Issues of voter participation, effective representation, and policy responsiveness are omitted from the calculus.

Lani Guinier, The Triumph of Tokenism: The Voting Rights Act and the Theory of Black Electoral Success, 89 Mich. L. Rev. 1077, 1093 (1991). Of course, this brings us full circle to Senator Hatch's concern. While a plaintiff is not entitled to proportional representation and cannot complain if an approved plan does not result in proportional representation, each decision striking a districting plan results from a court's view that roughly proportional representation has not been reached.

3. *Judicially manageable standards.* Consider Professor Guinier's reference to judicially manageable standards. The statutory definition of representativeness is not very clear. The definition of representativeness that emerges from *Gingles* is quite clear. How do you square the two? What is lost by *Gingles'* exclusive focus on polarized voting?

4. *The Gingles test.* The use of electoral success as the circumstance to determine whether a districting plan discriminates against protected minorities requires a determination of what an appropriate plan would be. In other words, to determine whether one plan is insufficient one must be able to determine that another plan produces the possibility of

greater electoral success. In *Gingles*, the Court establishes a test to make such a determination. What is this test, and what is the significance of each of its elements?

5. *Polarized voting.* One of the key elements of the *Gingles* test is polarized voting. Does the Court offer a standard to determine when polarized voting has occurred? For example, is there polarized voting under the *Gingles* test in a district that is 20 percent minority by registration and in which minority candidates have never won but have lost by margins of only 2 or 3 percent, meaning that they have consistently received at least 27 or 28 percent of the white vote?

1.   The Circumstance of Electoral Success — Three Views

What is the purpose of the Voting Rights Act, and how does it effect representativeness? Below are excerpts from three scholars with different answers. Each looks at the Voting Rights Act and assesses its ability to achieve its goals as each scholar defines the goals of the Voting Rights Act. As you read each excerpt, ascertain what goal each scholar thinks the Voting Rights Act is designed to meet.

Abigail M. Thernstrom, Whose Vote Counts? 240-43 (1987): I have argued that the Senate report . . . properly focused the section 2 inquiry. Nevertheless, an implied trust in the political process left substantially to its own devices is not shared by most spokesmen for the civil rights organizations. They see America as too racially divided to sustain a political life that transcends color. They believe that minority representation means minority office-holding, that whites cannot represent blacks, and that blacks elected with white support have questionable credentials. In "Hands That Picked Cotton," a defeated black candidate says of his victorious black opponent: "He got all the white votes. . . . Doc is not classified as black to me. You black when black folks elect you. White folks don't vote for black folks."

This is too bleak a picture, too hard a line, and it confuses the issues. The "two societies" argument rests on the fact of severe and continuing economic and other problems in the black community to which whites appear largely indifferent. But the appalling level of black teenage pregnancy is not an argument for creating a maximum number of 65 percent black districts. Racially mixed dinner parties may still be rare, but a mix of blacks, browns, and whites in politics is not. "To start and stop analyses on the assumption that race is all that matters," Harold Stanley has written, "distorts rather than delivers an understanding of southern politics." The same can be said about northern politics. Not all whites are racists (whether in Boston or in Selma, Alabama), and whites vote for whites for reasons other than skin color. Personalities and issues divide the black community as well as the white. Most blacks who vote for whites are neither intimidated nor mis-guided. Furthermore, when blacks and Hispanics fail to vote, factors other than racist electoral obstacles are often at work. And when blacks and Hispanics do vote, they do not necessarily vote together; a black candidate cannot count on Hispanic support, or vice versa. Nonwhite groups, that is, are not interchangeable; categorizing citizens as either white or nonwhite distorts reality.

Charles Hamilton has argued that affirmative action goals and timeta-bles resulted from experience showing the inadequacy of good intentions. But reliance on good intentions in the political sphere is by and large unnecessary. As a black scholar in Mississippi has remarked, "Racists . . . know how to count. No matter what you think of their past, many white politicians count the black vote." Political necessity drove Dixiecrat politi-cians such as Strom Thurmond and George Wallace to seek black support, and the same pressures operate at every level of government in most jur-isdictions with significant black populations. "I vote the same way a black would," a three-term white Democrat from a largely black New York district told a reporter. These votes were political, not charitable. In Ernest J. Gaines's novel A Gathering of Old Men, a lynch mob forms to take care of a black who has murdered a white. But the expected leader backs out, persuaded by two sons whose futures have come to rest with blacks as well as whites. "Those days are gone. . . . The world has changed, Papa," one son says. Especially in the South, "the world has changed"; in politics the conditions of success have permanently altered. There remain places, I have made clear, where only federal intervention will break the firm hold of whites on elected office. But black and Hispanic political exclusion in a "frozen" setting is now the exception, not the rule.

If a community of citizens is an unattainable ideal, and if blacks and Hispanics are represented only by one of their own, then aggressive federal action to restructure methods of voting to promote minority officeholding is appropriate. But if the logic of politics works for inclusion (once basic enfranchisement has been assured), then a lighter touch, a more hesitant intervention, is possible.

Why not err on the side of safety, though? Why risk the underprotection of historically oppressed groups? Because there is a dark side to affirmative action in the electoral sphere, as in others. I do not have in mind, needless to say, the defeat of whites who could win at-large, or in a differently consti-tuted district, or with the benefit of a majority-vote requirement. Whites denied medical school admission as a consequence of minority preference have been arguably denied a right; those disadvantaged by a change in the electoral rules cannot make that claim. There are no "objective" criteria for elected office — no equivalent of the Medical College Aptitude Test. A white denied a seat on a city council cannot claim entitlement on the ground of "merit." In addition, safe black and Hispanic districts carry no stigma with respect to minority self-esteem. If it is true, as often contended, that whites and blacks alike suspect the ability of blacks promoted by affirmative action on a job, no comparable stigma attaches to election from a safe black district. Qualification for office is not measured by meritocratic standards in the customary sense.

At various points in this book I have touched upon the potential costs attached to maximizing minority officeholding. Perhaps most important is the danger that categorizing individuals for political purposes along lines of race and sanctioning group membership as a qualification for office may inhibit political integration. As James Blumstein argued at the 1982 Senate hearings, such categorization amounts to a racial "piece-of-the-action approach," perhaps freezing rather than thawing the previous system of racial politics. The heightened sense of group membership works against that of a common citizenship. And as Donald Horowitz pointed out at those same hearings, ethnic boundaries, by diminishing the sense of common citizenship, may "ultimately smother democratic choice and threaten democratic institutions." . . .

The pressure for such interracial, interethnic coalitions lessens with the existence of single-member districts drawn to maximize the minority officeholding. Political necessity brings groups together.

What underlying values lead Thernstrom to her conclusion? Is Professor Thernstrom ignoring the purpose of the Act when she writes, "Perhaps most important [of those potential costs attached to maximizing minority officeholding] is the danger that categorizing individuals for political purposes along lines of race and sanctioning group membership as qualification for office may inhibit political integration. . . . [T]he heightened sense of group membership works against that of a common citizenship"? Is attaining a common citizenship the end goal of §2? If so, from where does she draw that? Is there a connection between common citizenship and representativeness?

Samuel Issacharoff, Polarized Voting and the Political Process: The Transformation of Voting Rights Jurisprudence, 90 Mich. L. Rev. 1833, 1860-61 (1992): Behind each judicial determination that a particular voting system frustrates the electoral aspiration of minority voters stands an indictment of majoritarian processes. The racially polarized voting inquiry gives the Court a healthy basis for skepticism concerning the majoritarian premise implicit in respect for the outcomes of elections. In the context of persistent racially polarized voting, the problem is not simply that some win and some lose. Rather, there is a predictability to who wins and loses, and that predictability falls along racial lines. . . . Simple electoral defeat does not trigger the Voting Rights Act. . . .

The existence of this racially defined majority voting faction raises concerns as old as the republic. Madison in The Federalist cautioned of the venomous role of factions in political life. But his particular concern was with majority factions that would be unrestrainable through the operation of the franchise.... Political institutions must provide safeguards to "guard one part of the society against the injustice of the other part." Madison affirmatively assigned to government the role of protecting against the tyranny bred of the ruling passions of interests and to the judiciary the independent power to effectuate that protection.

Persistent polarized voting is the courtroom proof of the existence of not only a permanent faction, but a majority faction. There are innumerable majority factions in American life.... Majority factionalism does not in itself provide a legitimating trigger for judicial intervention. Rather, courts must look to the defining features of the majority and minority factions to justify countermajoritarian review. The polarized voting inquiry provides this justification by identifying a particular form of majority factionalism, one based on a repudiation [by the majority] of the political choices of historically disadvantaged minorities.

———————

Although Issacharoff uses The Federalist Papers as support for legislative and judicial intervention in the event of polarized voting, the emphasis on polarized voting may go one step beyond the concerns raised in The Federalist Papers. There the goal was to protect the minority from an overreaching majority. Is that the goal of §2? Or is §2's goal to give legislative voice to protected minorities? Professor Lani Guinier takes the latter goal. She elaborates on how a polarized voting test, which rests on assumptions following from black electoral success, fails to assure that the goal of giving legislative voice to protected minorities is met.

Lani Guinier, The Triumph of Tokenism: The Voting Rights Act and the Theory of Black Electoral Success, 89 Mich. L. Rev. 1077, 1115-20 (1991):
According to the polarization assumption, racial bloc voting within the electorate eliminates pluralistic bargaining among shifting intergroup coalitions. Where members of the majority consistently refuse to vote for minority-sponsored candidates, blacks are unable to attract enough dissatisfied majority group members to create an effective race neutral majority....

While pluralist theories of democracy do contemplate minority losses, they do not necessarily envision a minority that never wins. In other words, Madison's reliance on checks and balances to control "factions" was both a way to monitor the "special interest" problem *as well* as a hedge against the tyranny of a hostile majority. To fight permanent majority tyranny based on prejudice, voting rights litigation focused on promoting electoral opportunities for black candidates.

The polarization assumption posits that black incumbency tends to diminish prejudice and weaken stereotypes of black incompetence. Black elected officials will assuage white fears by engaging more intimately in legislative deliberations after the election. Black representation is a "crucial lever for obtaining the benefits — patronage contracts, public services — that must be bargained for in the political arena." Regarding black interests, black representatives will "exert special influence on their colleagues," providing "internal leadership" to which people defer.

Black electoral success advocates assume that prejudice results from ignorance and unfamiliar difference. Once knowledge of similarities is present, or familiarity with difference is facilitated, these advocates contend that black and white elected officials will rationally overcome prejudice and engage freely and equally in pluralistic bargaining or dialogic debate. . . .

Black activists have long recognized that blacks cannot become an *effective political majority* without legislative allies. Yet, electing black representatives may simply relocate to the legislature polarization experienced at the polls. Indeed, some political scientists studying "the new black politics" in Cleveland, Chicago, and Atlanta have challenged the working assumption that black electoral success will ultimately reduce polarization. . . . Because the individual black elected official may not be able to overcome polarization to "infiltrate the decisionmaking process" at the legislative level, the election of black representatives does not, by itself, translate into intergroup cooperation. . . .

To consider effectively all viewpoints, deliberation requires sustained communication and participation among equals. Effective deliberation also demands that group members be receptive to relevant information and willing to compromise. Members of a deliberating body should share information, exchange views, and debate the issues. In addition, the deliberation ideal contemplates consensus and cooperation derived from honest, good-faith interaction, and not heavy-handed normative pressure.

Is Professor Guinier discussing the Voting Rights Act or the larger topic of representativeness? Her challenge to the assumptions of black electoral success advocates rests on her vision of what will happen as a result of black electoral success — continued discrimination against minorities but, this time, in the legislature rather than in the electorate. From her perspective, the Voting Rights Act does not go far enough to ensure representativeness.

How does Professor Guinier's view compare to that of Professor Thernstrom? How do Professors Guinier and Thernstrom differ from Professor Issacharoff?

2. A Note on §5 of the Voting Rights Act

Jurisdictions covered under §5 of the Voting Rights Act of 1965, as amended, have a special burden in redistricting. Before they can implement a redistricting plan, they must have it "precleared" by the Attorney General of the United States or the Federal District Court of the District of Columbia. Such preclearance is required of the redistricting plans of non-covered states if those plans apply to covered counties or other subdivisions within that state. Lopez v. Monterey County, 525 U.S. 266 (1999). In either of these processes, the submitting jurisdiction has the burden of proving that the plan "does not have the purpose and will not have the effect of denying or abridging the right to vote on account of race or color." If the submitting jurisdiction does not satisfy this burden, the plan will be objected to and will be void. The Supreme Court, in Beer v. United States, 528 U.S. 320 (2000), held that an *effect* of denying or abridging the right to vote on account of race or color equates to a retrogressive effect, one that reduces minority representation. And in Reno v. Bossier Parish School Board, 120 S. Ct. 866 (2000), the Court (5-4), building on the *Beer* decision, held that the *purpose* of denying or abridging the right to vote on account of race or color similarly equates to a retrogressive purpose. While from a narrow interpretive perspective the decision has a certain logic, contextually the decision seems more a product of a five-Justice majority intent on cabining the reach of the Voting Rights Act.

3. The Voting Rights Act and Equal Protection

Section 5 of the Voting Rights Act of 1965 has had a powerful (and, editorially speaking, beneficial) impact on the redistricting process. In short, those people redistricting covered areas have had to have a constant eye on the practices of the Justice Department. An objection to a redistricting plan for failing to satisfy the §5 standard could result in political eruptions within the submitting state. As a result, most redistricting in covered areas tended to draw lines to maximize minority districts either initially or immediately after receiving a Justice Department objection. Few attempted to circumvent the Justice Department through the courts.

In 1993, this focus on satisfying Justice Department concerns ran into a judicial backwash, similar to the narrowing of congressional authority discussed in Chapter 1, pages 32-34, that has unsettled all subsequent redistricting efforts, including, importantly, those going on at this time in the post-2000 census period. In Shaw v. Reno, 509 U.S. 630 (1993), the Supreme Court recognized the claim of white plaintiffs that North Carolina's District 12, a barbell-shaped district running 160 miles along highway I-85 that evidently was intended to connect within one district a number of distant African-American neighborhoods, deprived them of their rights under the equal protection clause of the U.S. Constitution. According to the Court:

> [A] plaintiff challenging a reapportionment statute under the Equal Protection Clause may state a claim by alleging that the legislation, though race-neutral on its face, rationally cannot be understood as anything other than an effort to separate voters into different districts on the basis of race, and that the separation lacks sufficient justification.

In effect, the majority found that District 12 was presumptively discriminatory, apparently because of its quite odd appearance.

The dissenters questioned mostly the standing of the plaintiffs, by challenging the idea that members of a racial majority could be injured by drawing lines that favor a minority, particularly when such efforts were the result of a §5 objection to an earlier districting plan. In short, the minority suggested that at issue was the constitutionality of the Voting Rights Act itself, or at least its application to districting plans. (Both Justices Thomas and Scalia had argued, in dissent, in Holder v. Hall (excerpted in Chapter 12, page 844), that redistricting was not within the reach of the Voting Rights Act.) If line-drawers were not allowed to act on race alone, what mix of considerations would be necessary to satisfy the Voting Rights Act and the new equal protection doctrine? See United Jewish Organizations v. Carey, 430 U.S. 144 (1977), for a decision supporting race consciousness in districting. This question is the subject of the case and notes that follow. [Internal citations and footnotes have been omitted, except where particularly relevant.]

Miller v. Johnson
515 U.S. 900 (1995)

KENNEDY, J., delivered the opinion of the Court, in which REHNQUIST, C.J., and O'CONNOR, SCALIA, and THOMAS, JJ., joined. . . .

The question we now decide is whether Georgia's new Eleventh District gives rise to a valid equal protection claim under the principles announced in *Shaw*, and, if so, whether it can be sustained nonetheless as narrowly, tailored to serve a compelling governmental interest. . . .

In 1965, the Attorney General designated Georgia a covered jurisdiction under §4(b) of the Voting Rights Act. In consequence, §5 of the Act requires Georgia to obtain either administrative preclearance by the Attorney General or approval by the United States District Court for the District of Columbia of any change in a "standard, practice, or procedure with respect to voting" made after November 1, 1964. The preclearance mechanism applies to congressional redistricting plans, and requires that the proposed change "not have the purpose and will not have the effect of denying or abridging the right to vote on account of race or color." "The purpose of §5 has always been to insure that no voting-procedure changes would be made that would lead to a retrogression in the position of racial minorities with respect to their effective exercise of the electoral franchise." . . .

Twice spurned [two redistricting acts had been rejected by the Justice Department under §5], Georgia's General Assembly set out to create three majority-minority districts to gain preclearance. Using the ACLU's "max-black" plan [a plan intended to maximize the number of African-American seats] as its benchmark, the General Assembly enacted a plan that "bore all the signs of [the Justice Department's] involvement. . . . The dense population centers of the approved Eleventh District were all majority-black, all at the periphery of the district, and in the case of Atlanta, Augusta and Savannah, all tied to a sparsely populated rural core by even less populated land bridges. Extending from Atlanta to the Atlantic, the Eleventh covered 6,784.2 square miles, splitting eight counties and five municipalities along the way."

The Almanac of American Politics has this to say about the Eleventh District: "Geographically, it is a monstrosity, stretching from Atlanta to Savannah. Its core is the plantation country in the center of the state, lightly populated, but heavily black. It links by narrow corridors the black neighborhoods in Augusta, Savannah and southern DeKalb County." M. Barone & G. Ujifusa, Almanac of American Politics 356 (1994). Georgia's plan included three majority-black districts, though, and received Justice Department preclearance on April 2, 1992. . . .

Finding that the "evidence of the General Assembly's intent to racially gerrymander the Eleventh District is overwhelming, and practically stipulated by the parties involved," the District Court held that race was the predominant, overriding factor in drawing the Eleventh District. Appellants do not take issue with the court's factual finding of this racial motivation. Rather, they contend that evidence of a legislature's deliberate classification of voters on the basis of race cannot alone suffice to state a claim under *Shaw*. They argue that, regardless of the legislature's purposes, a plaintiff must demonstrate that a district's shape is so bizarre that it is unexplainable other than on the basis of race, and that appellees failed to make that showing here. Appellants' conception of the constitutional violation misapprehends our holding in *Shaw* and the Equal Protection precedent upon which *Shaw* relied. . . .

Our observation in *Shaw* of the consequences of racial stereotyping was not meant to suggest that a district must be bizarre on its face before there is a constitutional violation. . . . Our circumspect approach and narrow holding in *Shaw* did not erect an artificial rule barring accepted equal protection analysis in other redistricting cases. Shape is relevant not because bizarreness is a necessary element of the constitutional wrong or a threshold requirement of proof, but because it may be persuasive circumstantial evidence that race for its own sake, and not other districting principles, was the legislature's dominant and controlling rationale in drawing its district lines. The logical implication, as courts applying *Shaw* have recognized, is that parties may rely on evidence other than bizarreness to establish race-based districting. . . .

Federal court review of districting legislation represents a serious intrusion on the most vital of local functions. It is well settled that "reapportionment is primarily the duty and responsibility of the State." Electoral districting is a most difficult subject for legislatures, and so the States must have discretion to exercise the political judgment necessary to balance competing interests. . . . The courts, in assessing the sufficiency of a challenge to a districting plan, must be sensitive to the complex interplay of forces that enter a legislature's redistricting calculus. Redistricting legislatures will, for example, almost always be aware of racial demographics; but it does not follow that race predominates in the redistricting process. The distinction between being aware of racial considerations and being motivated by them may be difficult to make. This evidentiary difficulty, together with the sensitive nature of redistricting and presumption of good faith that must be accorded legislative enactments, requires courts to exercise extraordinary caution in adjudicating claims that a state has drawn district lines on the basis of race. The plaintiff's burden is to show, either through circumstantial evidence of a district's shape and demographics or more direct evidence going to legislative purpose, that race was the predominant factor, motivating the legislature's decision to place a significant number of voters within or without a particular district. To make this showing, a plaintiff must prove that the legislature subordinated traditional race-neutral districting principles, including but not limited to compactness, contiguity, respect for political subdivisions or communities defined by actual shared interests, to racial considerations. Where these or other race-neutral considerations are the basis for redistricting legislation, and are not subordinated to race, a state can "defeat a claim that a district has been gerrymandered on racial lines." . . .

In our view, the District Court applied the correct analysis, and its finding that race was the predominant factor motivating the drawing of the Eleventh District was not clearly erroneous. The court found it was "exceedingly obvious" from the shape of the Eleventh District, together with the relevant racial demographics, that the drawing of narrow land bridges to incorporate within the District outlying appendages containing nearly 80% of the district's total black population was a deliberate attempt to bring black populations into the district. Although by comparison with other districts the geometric shape of the Eleventh District may not seem bizarre on its face, when its shape is considered in conjunction with its racial and population densities, the story of racial gerrymandering seen by the District Court becomes much clearer. Although this evidence is quite compelling, we need not determine whether it was, standing alone, sufficient to establish a *Shaw* claim that the Eleventh District is unexplainable other than by race. The District Court had before it considerable additional evidence showing that the General Assembly was motivated by a predominant, overriding desire to assign black populations to the Eleventh District and thereby permit the creation of a third majority-black district in the Second.

The court found that "it became obvious," both from the Justice Department's objection letters and the three preclearance rounds in general, "that [the Justice Department] would accept nothing less than abject surrender to its maximization agenda." It further found that the General Assembly acquiesced and as a consequence was driven by its overriding desire to comply with the Department's maximization demands. . . .

In light of its well-supported finding, the District Court was justified in rejecting the various alternative explanations offered for the District. Although a legislature's compliance with "traditional districting principles such as compactness, contiguity, and respect for political subdivisions" may well suffice to refute a claim of racial gerrymandering, appellants cannot make such a refutation where, as here, those factors were subordinated to racial objectives. Georgia's Attorney General objected to the Justice Department's demand for three majority-black districts on the ground that to do so the State would have to "violate all reasonable standards of compactness and contiguity." This statement from a state official is powerful evidence that the legislature subordinated traditional districting principles to race when it ultimately enacted a plan creating three majority-black districts, and justified the District Court's finding that "every [objective districting] factor that could realistically be subordinated to racial tinkering in fact suffered that fate." . . .

Nor can the State's districting legislation be rescued by mere recitation of purported communities of interest. The evidence was compelling "that there are no tangible 'communities of interest' spanning the hundreds of miles of the Eleventh District." . . . A State is free to recognize communities that have a particular racial makeup, provided its action is directed toward some common thread of relevant interests. . . . But where the State assumes from a group of voters' race that they "think alike, share the same political interests, and will prefer the same candidates at the polls," it engages in racial stereotyping at odds with equal protection mandates. . . .

To satisfy strict scrutiny, the State must demonstrate that its districting legislation is narrowly tailored to achieve a compelling interest. There is a "significant state interest in eradicating the effects of past racial discrimination." The State does not argue, however, that it created the Eleventh District to remedy past discrimination, and with good reason: there is little doubt that the State's true interest in designing the Eleventh District was creating a third majority-black district to satisfy the Justice Department's preclearance demands. Whether or not in some cases compliance with the Voting Rights Act, standing alone, can provide a compelling interest independent of any interest in remedying past discrimination, it cannot do so here. . . .

We do not accept the contention that the State has a compelling interest in complying with whatever preclearance mandates the Justice Department issues. When a state governmental entity seeks to justify race-based remedies to cure the effects of past discrimination, we do not accept the government's mere assertion that the remedial action is required. Rather, we insist on a strong basis in evidence of the harm being remedied. . . .

Georgia's drawing of the Eleventh District was not required under the Act because there was no reasonable basis to believe that Georgia's earlier enacted plans violated §5. Wherever a plan is "ameliorative," a term we have used to describe plans increasing the number of majority-minority districts, it "cannot violate §5 unless the new apportionment itself so discriminates on the basis of race or color as to violate the Constitution." Georgia's first and second proposed plans increased the number of majority-black districts from 1 out of 10 (10%) to 2 out of 11 (18.18%). These plans were "ameliorative" and could not have violated §5's non-retrogression principle. . . . The Government justifies its preclearance objections on the ground that the submitted plans violated §5's purpose element. The key to the Government's position, which is plain from its objection letters if not from its briefs to this Court is and always has been that Georgia failed to proffer a nondiscriminatory purpose for its refusal in the first two submissions to take the steps necessary to create a third majority-minority district. . . .

Based on this historical understanding, we recognized in *Beer* [v. United States, 425 U.S. 130 (1976),] that "the purpose of §5 has always been to insure that no voting-procedure changes would be made that would lead to a retrogression in the position of racial minorities with respect to their effective exercise of the electoral franchise." The Justice Department's maximization policy seems quite far removed from this purpose. We are especially reluctant to conclude that §5 justifies that policy given the serious constitutional concerns it raises. . . .

JUSTICE O'CONNOR, concurring.

I understand the threshold standard the Court adopts — "that the legislature subordinated traditional race-neutral districting principles . . . to racial considerations" — to be a demanding one. To invoke strict scrutiny, a plaintiff must show that the State has relied on race in substantial disregard of customary and traditional districting practices. Those practices provide a crucial frame of reference and therefore constitute a significant governing principle in cases of this kind. The standard would be no different if a legislature had drawn the boundaries to favor some other ethnic group; certainly the standard does not treat efforts to create majority-minority districts less favorably than similar efforts on behalf of other groups. Indeed, the driving force behind the adoption of the Fourteenth Amendment was the desire to end legal discrimination against blacks.

Application of the Court's standard does not throw into doubt the vast majority of the Nation's 435 congressional districts, where presumably the States have drawn the boundaries in accordance with their customary districting principles. That is so even though race may well have been considered in the redistricting process. But application of the Court's standard helps achieve *Shaw's* basic objective of making extreme instances of gerrymandering subject to meaningful judicial review. I therefore join the Court's opinion.

JUSTICE STEVENS dissenting. [Justice Stevens does not believe that plaintiffs have suffered any "legally cognizable wrong."]

JUSTICE GINSBURG, with whom JUSTICES STEVENS and BREYER, and with whom JUSTICE SOUTER joins except as to Part III-B, dissenting.

Two Terms ago, in Shaw v. Reno, this Court . . . authorized judicial intervention in "extremely irregular" apportionments, in which the legislature cast aside traditional districting practices to consider race alone — in the *Shaw* case, to create a district in North Carolina in which African-Americans would compose a majority of the voters.

Today the Court expands the judicial role, announcing that federal courts are to undertake searching review of any district with contours "predominantly motivated" by race: "strict scrutiny" will be triggered not only when traditional districting practices are abandoned, but also when those practices are "subordinated to" — given less weight than — race. . . .

Before Shaw v. Reno, this Court invoked the Equal Protection Clause to justify intervention in the quintessentially political task of legislative districting in two circumstances: to enforce the one-person-one-vote requirement, see Reynolds v. Sims [page 325 of this text]; and to prevent dilution of a minority group's voting strength.

In *Shaw*, the Court recognized a third basis for an equal protection challenge to a State's apportionment plan. The Court wrote cautiously, emphasizing that judicial intervention is exceptional: "[S]trict [judicial] scrutiny" is in order, the Court declared, if a district is "so extremely irregular on its face that it rationally can be viewed only as an effort to segregate the races for purposes of voting." . . .

The problem in *Shaw* was not the plan architects' consideration of race as relevant in redistricting. Rather, in the Court's estimation, it was the virtual exclusion of other factors from the calculus. Traditional districting practices were cast aside, the Court concluded, with race alone steering placement of district lines.

The record before us does not show that race similarly overwhelmed traditional districting practices in Georgia. Although the Georgia General Assembly prominently considered race in shaping the Eleventh District, race did not crowd out all other factors, as the Court found it did in North Carolina's delineation of the *Shaw* district.

In contrast to the snake-like North Carolina district inspected in *Shaw*, Georgia's Eleventh District is hardly "bizarre," "extremely irregular," or "irrational on its face." Instead, the Eleventh District's design reflects significant consideration of "traditional districting factors (such as keeping political subdivisions intact) and the usual political process of compromise and trades for a variety of nonracial reasons." The District covers a core area in central and eastern Georgia, and its total land area of 6,780 square miles is about average for the State. The border of the Eleventh District runs 1,184 miles, in line with Georgia's Second District, which has a 1,243-mile border, and the State's Eighth District, with a border running 1,155 miles.

Nor does the Eleventh District disrespect the boundaries of political subdivisions. . . . Eighty-three percent of the Eleventh District's geographic area is composed of intact counties, above average for the State's congressional districts. And notably, the Eleventh District's boundaries largely follow precinct lines.

Evidence at trial similarly shows that considerations other than race went into determining the Eleventh District's boundaries. For a "political reason" — to accommodate the request of an incumbent State Senator regarding the placement of the precinct in which his son lived — the DeKalb County portion of the Eleventh District was drawn to include a particular (largely white) precinct. The corridor through Effingham County was substantially narrowed at the request of a (white) State Representative. . . .

The Court suggests that it was not Georgia's legislature, but the U.S. Department of Justice, that effectively drew the lines, and that Department officers did so with nothing but race in mind. . . .

And although the Attorney General refused preclearance to the first two plans approved by Georgia's legislature, the State was not thereby disarmed; Georgia could have demanded relief from the Department's objections by instituting a civil action in the United States District Court for the District of Columbia, with ultimate review in this Court. Instead of pursuing that avenue, the State chose to adopt the plan here in controversy — a plan the State forcefully defends before us. We should respect Georgia's choice by taking its position on brief as genuine.

Along with attention to size, shape, and political subdivisions, the Court recognizes as an appropriate districting principle, "respect for . . . communities defined by actual shared interests." The Court finds no community here, however, because a report in the record showed "fractured political, social, and economic interests within the Eleventh District's black population."

But ethnicity itself can tie people together, as volumes of social science literature have documented — even people with divergent economic interests. For this reason, ethnicity is a significant force in political life. . . .

To accommodate the reality of ethnic bonds, legislatures have long drawn voting districts along ethnic lines. Our Nation's cities are full of districts identified by their ethnic character — Chinese, Irish, Italian, Jewish, Polish, Russian, for example. The creation of ethnic districts reflecting felt identity is not ordinarily viewed as offensive or demeaning to those included in the delineation. . . .

The Court derives its test from diverse opinions on the relevance of race in contexts distinctly unlike apportionment. The controlling idea, the Court says, is "the simple command [at the heart of the Constitution's guarantee of equal protection] that the Government must treat citizens as individuals, not as simply components of a racial, religious, sexual or national class."

In adopting districting plans, however, States do not treat people as individuals. Apportionment schemes, by their very nature, assemble people in groups. States do not assign voters to districts based on merit or achievement, standards States might use in hiring employees or engaging contractors. Rather, legislators classify voters in groups — by economic, geographical, political, or social characteristics — and then "reconcile the competing claims of [these] groups." Davis v. Bandemer.

That ethnicity defines some of these groups is a political reality. Until now, no constitutional infirmity has been seen in districting Irish or Italian voters together. . . . If Chinese-Americans and Russian-Americans may seek and secure group recognition in the delineation of voting districts, then African-Americans should not be dissimilarly treated. Otherwise, in the name of equal protection, we would shut out "the very minority group whose history in the United States gave birth to the Equal Protection Clause." . . .

Special circumstances justify vigilant judicial inspection to protect minority voters — circumstances that do not apply to majority voters. A history of exclusion from state politics left racial minorities without clout to extract provisions for fair representation in the lawmaking forum. . . . The majority, by definition, encounters no such blockage. White voters in Georgia do not lack means to exert strong pressure on their state legislators. The force of their numbers is itself a powerful determiner of what the legislature will do that does not coincide with perceived majority interests.

State legislatures like Georgia's today operate under federal constraints imposed by the Voting Rights Act — constraints justified by history and designed by Congress to make once-subordinated people free and equal citizens. But these federal constraints do not leave majority voters in need of extraordinary judicial solicitude. The Attorney General, who administers the Voting Rights Act's preclearance requirements, is herself a political actor. She has a duty to enforce the law Congress passed, and she is no doubt aware of the political cost of venturing too far to the detriment of majority voters. Majority voters, furthermore, can press the State to seek judicial review if the Attorney General refuses to preclear a plan that the voters favor. Finally, the Act is itself a political measure, subject to modification in the political process.

The Court's disposition renders redistricting perilous work for state legislatures. Statutory mandates and political realities may require States to consider race when drawing district lines. But today's decision is a counterforce; it opens the way for federal litigation if "traditional . . . districting principles" arguably were accorded less weight than race. Genuine attention to traditional districting practices and avoidance of bizarre configurations seemed, under *Shaw*, to provide a safe harbor. In view of today's decision, that is no longer the case.

Only after litigation — under either the Voting Rights Act, the Court's new *Miller* standard, or both — will States now be assured that plans conscious of race are safe. Federal judges in large numbers may be drawn into the fray. This enlargement of the judicial role is unwarranted. The reapportionment plan that resulted from Georgia's political process merited this Court's approbation, not its condemnation. Accordingly, I dissent.

NOTES AND QUESTIONS

1. *The equal protection test.* What test has the Court established to determine a violation of equal protection for racial majorities in redistricting? How does the test in *Miller* differ from that in *Shaw?*

2. *The view of Justice O'Connor.* How, if at all, does Justice O'Connor's view differ from that of the plurality? This is a very important practical question because of the slimness of the majority in this case. This slimness is particularly accentuated in Bush v. Vera, 517 U.S. 952 (1996), in which a three-member plurality (Justice O'Connor writing the plurality opinion and also a separate concurrence) is added to by a concurrence by Justice Thomas, joined by Justice Scalia, to find that particular Texas congressional districts violate the equal protection clause. But this majority seems irreconcilably separated over the question of whether any racial considerations can be a motivation for the drawing of majority-minority districts. The plurality answers yes (but not to the extent found in this particular case), while Justices Thomas and Scalia answer no. The view of the dissent, as in *Miller*, is that plaintiffs have suffered no injury and that the insistence on the applicability of equal protection in these cases undermines the national commitment to voting rights as expressed through the Voting Rights Act of 1965 and its amendments.

3. *An awareness of race.* According to the majority in *Miller*, race need not be ignored in redistricting, but should not subordinate traditional

districting criteria. This is, as the majority acknowledges, a hard line to draw: "The distinction between being aware of racial considerations and being motivated by them may be difficult to make." Assume, for example, that the first Georgia plan increased the number of majority black districts from 0 out of 10 to 1 out of 11 (there was an increase in population) and that this plan was disapproved by the Justice Department. Assume then that the second plan increased the number of majority black districts to 2 out of 11 and that it was approved. Assume also that a third majority African-American district (a so-called max black plan) was possible. Do you think this fact pattern would have resulted in a different decision?

In Bush v. Vera, 517 U.S. 952 (1996), there is no extensive record of exchanges between Texas and the Justice Department or state reactions to Justice Department actions because the congressional plan was approved in the first instance. According to the plurality, this case was a "mixed motive" case, meaning that both racial and non-racial considerations motivated the crafting of the three districts under challenge. The plurality determined that strict scrutiny applied because the shapes of the districts (although not "bizarre"), along with some additional although not particularly strong evidence, was sufficient to establish that racial motivations predominated.

4. *Plaintiffs' injuries.* What are the injuries plaintiffs suffered in *Miller*? How would you evaluate them? What role do you think such an evaluation plays in the case?

5. *The Voting Rights Act.* One of the most important questions in the post-*Shaw* era is the health of the Voting Rights Act of 1965, as amended, in the face of equal protection clause challenges. How does *Miller* deal with the state's claims that it had a compelling interest to follow the Voting Rights Act of 1965, as amended?

As with *Miller*, in Shaw v. Hunt, 517 U.S. 899 (1996) (*Shaw II*), and in *Bush*, the state claims compliance with the Voting Rights Act as a compelling interest to overcome strict scrutiny. In *Shaw II*, this defense, as it relates to §5, is treated as it is in *Miller*. Regarding §2, the state argued that their action was intended to avoid voting rights liability. On this point the *Shaw* Court stated:

> Where, as here, we assume avoidance of §2 liability to be a compelling state interest, we think that the racial classification would have realized that goal; the legislative action must, at a minimum, remedy the anticipated violation or achieve compliance to be narrowly tailored. District 12 could not remedy any potential §2 violation. . . . [A] plaintiff must show that the minority group is "geographically compact" to establish §2 liability.

Id. at 915-16. (See Thornburg v. Gingles, page 284.) To add emphasis to the theoretical point made by the majority in *Bush*, Justice O'Connor in her concurrence added: "I write separately to express my view on two points.

First, compliance with the results test of §2 of the Voting Rights Act is a compelling state interest. Second, that test can co-exist in principle and in practice with Shaw v. Reno, and its progeny." Bush v. Vera, 517 U.S. 952, 990 (1996). Time, of course, will measure the wisdom of these words, but, from a practitioner's view, the balance will be hard to measure without more definition, despite an attempt at such by Justice O'Connor following her above declaration in *Bush:*

> [I]f a state has a strong basis in evidence for concluding the *Gingles* factors are present, it may create a majority-minority district without awaiting judicial findings. Its "strong basis in evidence" need not take any particular form, although it cannot simply rely on generalized assumptions about the pre-valence of racial bloc voting. [I]f a state pursues that compelling interest by creating a district that "substantially addresses the potential liability . . . and does not deviate substantially from a hypothetical court-drawn §2 district for predominantly racial reasons (citations omitted), its districting plan will be deemed narrowly tailored."

Id. at 994.

6. *Abrams v. Johnson — Georgia revisited.* In *Miller* the Court rejected a plan with three majority-minority districts. This plan was Georgia's second attempt at redistricting. Its original plan, objected to by the Justice Depart-ment, had contained two majority-minority districts. Following the *Miller* decision, the state legislature was unable to agree on a new plan and finally a districting plan was effected by a federal district court. This plan contained one majority-minority district. This time the plan was challenged by plaintiffs who argued that the court-drawn plan provided insufficient majority-minority districts. Plaintiffs' view was that at least two such dis-tricts were required by prior Court doctrine, covering court-drawn plans, and under §§2 and 5 of the Voting Rights Act. The basis for this claim was the 1992 plan involving two majority-minority districts enacted by the state legislature, but rejected by the Justice Department. The Supreme Court (5-4) upheld the court-drawn plan in Abrams v. Johnson, 521 U.S. 74 (1997). While this case is somewhat unusual because its subject was not a legisla-tively enacted plan, Justice Breyer, writing for the dissenters, argues force-fully that the majority view effectively deprives legislatures of any way of reasonably regarding race as a basis for drawing legislative lines.

7. *Hunt v. Cromartie* (Shaw III), *Hunt v. Cromartie* (Shaw IV). In Hunt v. Cromartie, 526 U.S. 541 (1999), the Court was again confronted with a challenge to North Carolina's Twelfth Congressional District. Again the question, this time on an appeal from a lower court's summary judgment order, was whether a newly drawn, bizarrely (less bizarrely) shaped district with concentrations of black voters violated the Fourteenth Amend-ment. In reversing the lower court's decision, the Court held that the leg-islature's motivation is itself a factual question and, on the basis of post facto statements by legislators and the report of an expert, that the shape of

the district and its minority concentration could also have been motivated by party preferences. According to the expert there was "a strong correlation between racial composition and party preference." Id. at 550. As discussed earlier with respect to Davis v. Bandemer, the Court has created an almost impossible test for striking down a redistricting plan based on party preferences. While it is hard to assign any larger significance to this case, at this point, several points are interesting. First, a district's shape no longer seems to be determinative of racial preferences, as it may have been in *Shaw I*, although the majority was careful to note "we doubt that a bizarre shape equally supports a political inference and a racial one." Id. at 548. Second, the use of post facto testimony of bill sponsors as to legislative motivation would seem to be extremely problematic given the tendency of legislators to shape every contemporary comment with an eye on the contemporary political context. It is also ironic given the makeup of the majority, some of whom would in other contexts be less likely to allow even the pre-passage declarations of a bill's sponsors to speak for legislative meaning or intent. See Chapter 10, pages 702-703. Finally, the important question that remains unanswered is what will be the impact of this group of decisions on the national redistricting that commences in the next several years?

A clue to the answer to that question may come from *Shaw IV*, 121 S. Ct. 1452 (2001). A three-day retrial, following the remand ordered by *Shaw III*, resulted in a determination by a three-judge court that, although the legislature had used a number of criteria to draw its new lines, it had also "used criteria . . . that are facially race driven without any compelling justification for doing so." To the Supreme Court, the three-judge court's evidence for this conclusion was:

> [T]he district's snakelike shape, the way in which it split cities and towns, and its heavily African-American (47%) voting population, — all matters that this Court had considered when it found summary judgment inappropriate (citation omitted). The court also based this conclusion upon a specific finding — absent when we previously considered this litigation — that the legislature had drawn the boundaries in order "to collect precincts with *high racial identification rather than political identification.*"

(Citation omitted, emphasis in original.) Relying on the uniquely legislative nature of redistricting, the Court, in reversing the lower court (5-4, with Justice O'Connor in the majority), first restated the premise that courts must "exercise *extraordinary caution* in adjudicating claims that a State has drawn district lines on the basis of race" (emphasis in the original) and then determined:

> In a case such as this one where majority-minority districts (or the approximate equivalent) are at issue and where racial identification correlates highly with political affiliation, the party attacking the legislatively drawn boundaries must show at the least that the legislature could have achieved its

legitimate political objectives in alternative ways that are comparably consistent with traditional districting principles. That party must also show that those districting alternatives would have brought about significantly greater racial balance. Appellees failed to make any such showing here.

What this predicts for this round of redistricting is uncertain. In the Court's above summary of its view, it makes clear that, for a majority of the Court, the phenomenon of minority districts or of minority voters and the creation of majority-minority or minority impact districts for political or other traditional districting purposes does not constitute racially motivated districting — that is, districting in which race rather than politics predominantly explains the challenged district. But to what extent can the racial considerations of the Voting Rights Act play an open role? The rhetorical answer is that race may not play the predominant role, but it may play some role (Justice O'Connor's ongoing view) in redistricting. How would you describe that role? What does the majority mean when it states that a plaintiff "must also show that those districting alternatives [the ones suggested by the challenger] would have brought about significantly greater racial balance"? Assume the legislature enacts a plan that has one more majority-minority district than previously existed. They do so, in their words, to both conform to the Voting Rights Act and to establish another Democratic district. Plaintiff, a white resident of this new district, claims that it is predominantly racially motivated. He shows that you can create an additional Democratic district without establishing an additional majority-minority district. Does this satisfy the Court's standard for a challenger? If not, on what basis do you think the Court can require otherwise?

Of course, as the Voting Rights Act is still in effect, none of these cases would support a plan that reduces minority voting strength on the basis of furthering a party's political goals.

D.   ONE PERSON, ONE VOTE

The movement by Congress to broaden the franchise to all the nation's adults and to reduce obstacles to the exercise of that franchise was not paralleled by congressional and state legislative action to ensure that the vote of each of the enfranchised counted equally. Despite the apparent directive of Article I, §2 of the Constitution and similar provisions in various state constitutions, legislative redistricting did not reflect the growth and shifts of population throughout most of the century. For example, in 1946 the Seventh Congressional District in Illinois had a population of 914,053, while the Fifth Congressional District had a population of only 112,116; the Third District in California had 409,404, while the

Twenty-first had 194,199; the Twenty-fifth District in New York had 365,918, while the Forty-fifth had 235,913; and the Eighth District in Texas had 528,961, while the Seventeenth had 230,010. Colegrove v. Green, 328 U.S. 549, 557-59 (1946). This unequal distribution of the population among legislative districts arose not only from racially or regionally discriminatory motives, but also from an unwillingness on the part of incumbent legislators to make even the slightest unfavorable change in their districts. The motivation usually fueling any legislatively drawn district plan is the protection of incumbents. Other goals are a gain in party advantage and the reward or punishment of particular members.

The reluctance of legislative bodies to remedy malapportionment resulted in attempts to use the courts to accomplish the change. Through 1949, these attempts were frustrated by refusals by the judiciary to view population equality as an issue that could be judicially resolved. The exemplar of this view is Colegrove v. Green, in which petitioners challenged the large population deviations among Illinois congressional districts. Writing for the Court, Justice Frankfurter held: "[w]e are of the opinion that the petitioners ask of this Court what is beyond its competence, to grant. This is one of those demands on judicial power which cannot be met by verbal fencing about 'jurisdiction.' It must be resolved by considerations on the basis of which this Court, from time to time, has refused to intervene in controversies. It has refused to do so because due regard for the effective workings of our Government revealed this issue to be of a peculiarly political nature and therefore not meat for judicial determination." Id. at 552. And later in the opinion he wrote, "It is hostile to a democratic system to involve the judiciary in the politics of the people. . . . [T]he short of it is that the Constitution has conferred upon Congress exclusive authority to secure fair representation by the States in the popular House and left to that House determination whether States have fulfilled their responsibility. . . . [W]hether Congress faithfully discharges its duty or not, the subject has been committed to the exclusive control of Congress." Id. at 553-54.

Judicial resistance to entering what Frankfurter referred to as the "political thicket," id. at 556, of legislative redistricting was overcome by the Court in its landmark 1962 decision Baker v. Carr, 369 U.S. 186 (1962). This case, in effect, overruled *Colegrove* and other earlier cases by allowing challenges to districting plans based on claims under the equal protection clause of the Constitution. *Baker* represents the type of consequence that may result from legislative failure, over a long period of time, to recognize and respond to significant and meaningful political demands. (One result of this case is further and questionable involvement of the federal courts in legislative affairs.) In *Baker*, the Court was asked to review a districting plan of the state of Tennessee that had not been changed since 1901, despite dramatic demographic changes. In declaring this matter "justiciable" and not subject to the political question doctrine (the doctrine that protects the constitutional separation of powers), the Court created a fact-sensitive (case-by-case) test for making such determinations:

> Prominent on the surface of any case held to involve a political question is found a textually demonstrable constitutional commitment of the issue to a coordinate political department; or a lack of judicially discoverable and manageable standards for resolving it; or the impossibility of deciding without an initial policy determination of a kind clearly for nonjudicial discretion; or the impossibility of a court's undertaking independent resolution without expressing lack of the respect due coordinate branches of government; or an unusual need for unquestioning adherence to a political decision already made; or the potentiality of embarrassment from multifarious pronouncements by various departments on one question.

Id. at 217.

Two landmark redistricting cases immediately followed *Baker*, Wesberry v. Sanders (congressional districts) and Reynolds v. Sims (state legislative districts). Excerpts from these cases follow. Internal citations and footnotes have been omitted except where particularly relevant.

Wesberry v. Sanders
376 U.S. 1 (1964)

JUSTICE BLACK delivered the opinion of the Court.

Appellants are citizens and qualified voters of Fulton County, Georgia, and as such are entitled to vote in congressional elections in Georgia's Fifth Congressional District. That district, one of ten created by a 1931 Georgia statute, includes Fulton, DeKalb, and Rockdale Counties and has a population according to the 1960 census of 823,680. The average population of the ten districts is 394,312, less than half that of the Fifth. One district, the Ninth, has only 272,154 people, less than one-third as many as the Fifth. Since there is only one Congressman for each district, this inequality of population means that the Fifth District's Congressman has to represent from two to three times as many people as do Congressmen from some of the other Georgia districts. . . .

II

This brings us to the merits. We agree with the District Court that the 1931 Georgia apportionment grossly discriminates against voters in the Fifth Congressional District. A single Congressman represents from two to three times as many Fifth District voters as are represented by each of the Congressmen from the other Georgia congressional districts. The apportionment statute thus contracts the value of some votes and expands that of others. If the Federal Constitution intends that when qualified voters elect members of Congress each vote be given as much weight as any other vote, then this statute cannot stand.

We hold that, construed in its historical context, the command of Art. I, §2, that Representatives be chosen "by the People of the several States" means that as nearly as is practicable one man's vote in a congressional election is to be worth as much as another's. This rule is followed automatically, of course, when Representatives are chosen as a group on a statewide basis, as was a widespread practice in the first 50 years of our Nation's history. It would be extraordinary to suggest that in such statewide elections the votes of inhabitants of some parts of a State, for example, Georgia's thinly populated Ninth District, could be weighted at two or three times the value of the votes of people living in more populous parts of the State, for example, the Fifth District around Atlanta. We do not believe that the Framers of the Constitution intended to permit the same vote-diluting discrimination to be accomplished through the device of districts containing widely varied numbers of inhabitants. To say that a vote is worth more in one district than in another would not only run counter to our fundamental ideas of democratic government, it would cast aside the principle of a House of Representatives elected "by the People," a principle tenaciously fought for and established at the Constitutional Convention. The history of the Constitution, particularly that part of it relating to the adoption of Art. I, §2, reveals that those who framed the Constitution meant that, no matter what the mechanics of an election, whether statewide or by districts, it was population which was to be the basis of the House of Representatives. . . .

The question of how the legislature should be constituted precipitated the most bitter controversy of the Convention. One principle was uppermost in the minds of many delegates: that, no matter where he lived, each voter should have a voice equal to that of every other in electing members of Congress.

Some delegates opposed election by the people. The sharpest objection arose out of the fear on the part of small States like Delaware that if population were to be the only basis of representation the populous States like Virginia would elect a large enough number of representatives to wield overwhelming power in the National Government. . . .

The dispute came near ending the Convention without a Constitution. Both sides seemed for a time to be hopelessly obstinate. Some delegations threatened to withdraw from the Convention if they did not get their way. Seeing the controversy growing sharper and emotions rising, the wise and highly respected Benjamin Franklin arose and pleaded with the delegates on both sides to "part with some of their demands, in order that they may join in some accommodating proposition." At last those who supported representation of the people in both houses and those who supported it in neither were brought together, some expressing the fear that if they did not reconcile their differences, "some foreign sword will probably do the work for us." The deadlock was finally broken when a majority of the States agreed to what has been called the Great Compromise, based on a proposal which had been repeatedly advanced by Roger Sherman and other delegates from Connecticut. It provided on the one hand that each State, including little Delaware and Rhode Island, was to have two Senators. As a further guarantee that these Senators would be considered state emissaries, they were to be elected by the state legislatures, Art. I, §3, and it was specially provided in Article V that no State should ever be deprived of its equal representation in the Senate. The other side of the compromise was that, as provided in Art. I, §2, members of the House of Representatives should be chosen "by the People of the several States" and should be "apportioned among the several States . . . according to their respective Numbers." While those who wanted both houses to represent the people had yielded on the Senate, they had not yielded on the House of Representatives. William Samuel Johnson of Connecticut had summed it up well: "in one branch the people ought to be represented; in the other, the States."

The debates at the Convention make at least one fact abundantly clear: that when the delegates agreed that the House should represent "people" they intended that in allocating Congressmen the number assigned to each State should be determined solely by the number of the State's inhabitants. The Constitution embodied Edmund Randolph's proposal for a periodic census to ensure "fair representation of the people," an idea endorsed by Mason as assuring that "numbers of inhabitants" should always be the measure of representation in the House of Representatives. The Convention also overwhelmingly agreed to a resolution offered by Randolph to base future apportionment squarely on numbers and to delete any reference to wealth. . . .

It would defeat the principle solemnly embodied in the Great Compromise — equal representation in the House for equal numbers of people — for us to hold that, within the States, legislatures may draw the lines of congressional districts in such a way as to give some voters a greater voice in choosing a Congressman than others. . . .

It is in the light of such history that we must construe Art. I, §2, of the Constitution, which, carrying out the ideas of Madison and those of like views, provides that Representatives shall be chosen "by the People of the several States" and shall be "apportioned among the several States . . . according to their respective Numbers." . . .

While it may not be possible to draw congressional districts with mathematical precision, that is no excuse for ignoring our Constitution's plain objective of making equal representation for equal numbers of people the fundamental goal for the House of Representatives. That is the high standard of justice and common sense which the Founders set for us.

Reynolds v. Sims
377 U.S. 533 (1964)

CHIEF JUSTICE WARREN delivered the opinion of the Court.

I

On August 26, 1961, the original plaintiffs (appellees in No. 23), residents, taxpayers and voters of Jefferson County, Alabama, filed a complaint in the United States District Court for the Middle District of Alabama, in their own behalf and on behalf of all similarly situated Alabama voters, challenging the apportionment of the Alabama Legislature. Defendants below (appellants in No. 23), sued in their representative capacities, were various state and political party officials charged with the performance of certain duties in connection with state elections.... Plaintiffs below alleged that the last apportionment of the Alabama Legislature was based on the 1900 federal census, despite the requirement of the State Constitution that the legislature be reapportioned decennially. They asserted that, since the population growth in the State from 1900 to 1960 had been uneven, Jefferson and other counties were now victims of serious discrimination with respect to the allocation of legislative representation. As a result of the failure of the legislature to reapportion itself, plaintiffs asserted, they were denied "equal suffrage in free and equal elections . . . and the equal protection of the laws" in violation of the Alabama Constitution and the Fourteenth Amendment. . . .

On July 12, 1962, an extraordinary session of the Alabama Legislature adopted two reapportionment plans to take effect for the 1966 elections. One was a proposed constitutional amendment, referred to as the "67-Senator Amendment." It provided for a House of Representatives consisting of 106 members, apportioned by giving one seat to each of Alabama's 67 counties and distributing the others according to population by the "equal proportions" method. Using this formula, the constitutional amendment specified the number of representatives allotted to each county until a new apportionment could be made on the basis of the 1970 census. The Senate was to be composed of 67 members, one from each county. The legislation provided that the proposed amendment should be submitted to the voters for ratification at the November 1962 general election.

The other reapportionment plan was embodied in a statutory measure adopted by the legislature and signed into law by the Alabama Governor, and was referred to as the "Crawford-Webb Act." It was enacted as standby legislation to take effect in 1966 if the proposed constitutional amendment should fail of passage by a majority of the State's voters, or should the federal courts refuse to accept the proposed amendment (though not rejected by the voters) as effective action in compliance with the requirements of the Fourteenth Amendment. The act provided for a Senate consisting of 35 members, representing 35 senatorial districts established along county lines, and altered only a few of the former districts. In apportioning the 106 seats in the Alabama House of Representatives, the statutory measure gave each county one seat, and apportioned the remaining 39 on a rough population basis, under a formula requiring increasingly more population for a county to be accorded additional seats. . . .

II

Undeniably the Constitution of the United States protects the right of all qualified citizens to vote, in state as well as in federal elections. . . . The right to vote freely for the candidate of one's choice is of the essence of a democratic society, and any restrictions on that right strikes at the heart of representative government. And the right of suffrage can be denied by a debasement or dilution of the weight of a citizen's vote just as effectively as by wholly prohibiting the free exercise of the franchise. . . .

III

A predominant consideration in determining whether a State's legislative apportionment scheme constitutes an invidious discrimination violative of rights asserted under the Equal Protection Clause is that the rights allegedly impaired are individual and personal in nature. . . .

Legislators represent people, not trees or acres. Legislators are elected by voters, not farms or cities or economic interests. As long as ours is a representative form of government, and our legislatures are those instruments of government elected directly by and directly representative of the people, the right to elect legislators in a free and unimpaired fashion is a bedrock of our political system. It could hardly be gainsaid that a constitutional claim had been asserted by an allegation that certain otherwise qualified voters had been entirely prohibited from voting for members of their state legislature. And, if a State should provide that the votes of citizens in one part of the State should be given two times, or five times, or 10 times the weight of votes of citizens in another part of the State, it could hardly be contended that the right to vote of those residing in the disfavored areas had not been effectively diluted. It would appear extraordinary to suggest that a State could be constitutionally permitted to enact a law providing that certain of the State's voters could vote two, five, or 10 times for their legislative representatives, while voters living elsewhere could vote only once. And it is inconceivable that a state law to the effect that, in counting votes for legislators, the votes of citizens in one part of the State would be multiplied by two, five, or 10, while the votes of persons in another area would be counted only at face value, could be constitutionally sustainable. Of course, the effect of state legislative districting schemes which give the same number of representatives to unequal numbers of constituents is identical. Overweighting and overvaluation of the votes of those living here has the certain effect of dilution and undervaluation of the votes of those living there. The resulting discrimination against those individual voters living in disfavored areas is easily demonstrable mathematically. Their right to vote is simply not the same right to vote as that of those living in a favored part of the State. Two, five, or 10 of them must vote before the effect of their voting is equivalent to that of their favored neighbor. Weighting the votes of citizens differently, by any method or means, merely because of where they happen to reside, hardly seems justifiable. . . .

Logically, in a society ostensibly grounded on representative government, it would seem reasonable that a majority of the people of a State could elect a majority of that State's legislators. To conclude differently, and to sanction minority control of state legislative bodies, would appear to deny majority rights in a way that far surpasses any possible denial of minority rights that might otherwise be thought to result. Since legislatures are responsible for enacting laws by which all citizens are to be governed, they should be bodies which are collectively responsive to the popular will. And the concept of equal protection has been traditionally viewed as requiring the uniform treatment of persons standing in the same relation to the governmental action questioned or challenged. . . .

VI

By holding that as a federal constitutional requisite both houses of a state legislature must be apportioned on a population basis, we mean that the Equal Protection Clause requires that a State make an honest and good faith effort to construct districts, in both houses of its legislature, as nearly of equal population as is practicable. We realize that it is a practical impossibility to arrange legislative districts so that each one has an identical number of residents, or citizens, or voters. Mathematical exactness or precision is hardly a workable constitutional requirement.

In Wesberry v. Sanders, the Court stated that congressional representation must be based on population as nearly as is practicable. In implementing the basic constitutional principle of representative government as enunciated by the Court in *Wesberry* — equality of population among districts — some distinctions may well be made between congressional and state legislative representation. Since, almost invariably, there is a significantly larger number of seats in state legislative bodies to be distributed within a State than congressional seats, it may be feasible to use political subdivision lines to a greater extent in establishing state legislative districts than in congressional districting while still affording adequate representation to all parts of the State. To do so would be constitutionally valid, so long as the resulting apportionment was one based substantially on population and the equal-population principle was not diluted in any significant way. Somewhat more flexibility may therefore be constitutionally permissible with respect to state legislative apportionment than in congressional districting. . . .

History indicates, however, that many States have deviated, to a greater or lesser degree, from the equal-population principle in the apportionment of seats in at least one house of their legislatures. So long as the divergences from a strict population standard are based on legitimate considerations incident to the effectuation of a rational state policy, some deviations from the equal-population principle are constitutionally permissible with respect to the apportionment of seats in either or both of the two houses of a bicameral state legislature. But neither history alone, nor economic or other sorts of group interests, are permissible factors in attempting to justify disparities from population-based representation. Citizens, not history or economic interests, cast votes. Considerations of area alone provide an insufficient justification for deviations from the equal-population principle. Again, people, not land or trees or pastures, vote. . . .

A consideration that appears to be of more substance in justifying some deviations from population-based representation in state legislatures is that of insuring some voice to political subdivisions, as political subdivisions. Several factors make more than insubstantial claims that a State can rationally consider according political subdivisions some independent representation in at least one body of the state legislature, as long as the basic standard of equality of population among districts is maintained. Local governmental entities are frequently charged with various responsibilities incident to the operation of state government. In many States much of the legislature's activity involves the enactment of so-called local legislation, directed only to the concerns of particular political subdivisions. And a State may legitimately desire to construct districts along political subdivision lines to deter the possibilities of gerrymandering. However, permitting deviations from population-based representation does not mean that each local governmental unit or political subdivision can be given separate representation, regardless of population. Carried too far, a scheme of giving at least one seat in one house to each political subdivision (for example, to each county) could easily result, in many States, in a total subversion of the equal-population principle in that legislative body. This would be especially true in a State where the number of counties is large and many of them are sparsely populated, and the number of seats in the legislative body being apportioned does not significantly exceed the number of counties. Such a result, we conclude, would be constitutionally impermissible.

NOTES AND QUESTIONS

1. *"People, not trees."* The doctrine of "one person, one vote," found in both *Wesberry* and *Reynolds*, is based on the view that "legislators represent people, not trees or acres," *Reynolds*, 377 U.S. at 562, and that inequality in numerical representation debases the value of a vote in more populated districts. Under this doctrine the Court has struck down a New Jersey congressional plan in which the maximum deviations between districts was .6984 percent, Karcher v. Daggett, 462 U.S. 725 (1983), and approved a Virginia state legislative plan in which the maximum deviation between districts was 16.4 percent. Mahan v. Howell, 410 U.S. 315 (1973).

What constitutional doctrines from *Wesberry* and *Reynolds* explain the Court's rejection of the almost immeasurable deviation in *Karcher* and its protection of the large deviation in *Mahan?*

Although the Court has permitted greater population deviation in state and local legislative districting plans than in congressional plans, population remains the predominant factor. "[A] State's policy urged in justification of disparity in district population, however rational, cannot constitutionally be permitted to emasculate the goal of substantial equality." *Mahan*, 410 U.S. at 326. What state policies may justify population deviations in state and local legislative districts?

2. *"People, not trees" revisited.* During the same term in which *Wesberry* and *Reynolds* were decided, the Court also decided another "one person, one vote" case, Lucas v. Forty-fourth General Assembly of Colorado, 377 U.S. 713 (1964). Dissenter Justice Stewart took issue with this doctrine, writing, "legislators do not represent faceless numbers. They represent people, or more accurately, a majority of the voters in their districts . . . with identifiable needs and interests . . . which can often be related to the geographical areas in which these people live." Id. at 750. He also argued that the logic of the Court's equal representation argument required "the abolition of districts and the holding of elections at large." Id. At-large elections are ones in which more than one legislator is elected from a particular district by giving each voter as many votes as there are representatives from such district. An example would be a state congressional delegation of five members, all of whom ran statewide.

What would be the effect of such elections on a legislative body? What would be the effect on various minority groups throughout the state?

3. *Single-member districts.* Several years after *Wesberry* and *Reynolds*, Congress adopted a law that prohibits at-large elections for Congress by requiring single-member districts for the House of Representatives. Pub. L. No. 90-196, 81 Stat. 581 (1967). In debate on this law, Senator Baker urged that the proposal would "effectuate the principles of one man, one vote, and . . . give life to and vitality to the concept that the Constitution contemplates," 113 Cong. Rec. 34, 364-65 (1967). He characterized this concept as immediate and direct access of the people to their representative. Id.

Because many political interests are geographically identifiable (i.e., urban or rural poor, suburban middle class, rural agricultural), does the requirement of districts serve to accommodate both the concerns of the Court for equality and the concerns of Justice Stewart for interest representation?

4. *The U.S. Senate: a special case.* One argument rejected in *Reynolds* was that the Alabama senate plan replicated the federal model by assigning one senator and only one senator to each of the state's counties, regardless of population. The decision triggered a change in the legislative structure of a number of state legislatures that had population-based lower houses and geography-based upper houses. How do you justify the continued allocation of U.S. Senate seats under the "one person, one vote" equation?

As discussed earlier, the test set forth in Baker v. Carr for evaluating the applicability of the "political question" doctrine to districting plans has also brought to the Court's attention the politically sensitive claim of gerrymandering. In Vieth v. Jubelirer, 541 U.S. 267 (2004), and Davis v. Bandemer, 478 U.S. 109 (1986), the Court determined that such claims were justiciable, but struggled over standards by which to judge such claims. An excerpt of the *Vieth* decision follows. Internal citations and footnotes have been omitted except where particularly relevant.

Vieth v. Jubelirer
541 U.S. 267 (2004)

SCALIA, J., announced the judgment of the Court and delivered an opinion, in which REHNQUIST, C.J., and O'CONNOR and THOMAS, JJ., joined.

Plaintiffs-appellants Richard Vieth, Norma Jean Vieth, and Susan Furey challenge a map drawn by the Pennsylvania General Assembly establishing districts for the election of congressional Representatives, on the ground that the districting constitutes an unconstitutional political gerrymander. In *Davis v. Bandemer*, 478 U.S. 109, 106 S. Ct. 2797, 92 L. Ed. 2d 85 (1986), this Court held that political gerrymandering claims are justiciable, but could not agree upon a standard to adjudicate them. The present appeal presents the questions whether our decision in *Bandemer* was in error, and, if not, what the standard should be.

The facts, as alleged by the plaintiffs, are as follows. The population figures derived from the 2000 census showed that Pennsylvania was entitled to only 19 Representatives in Congress, a decrease in 2 from the Commonwealth's previous delegation. Pennsylvania's General Assembly took up the task of drawing a new districting map. At the time, the Republican Party controlled a majority of both state Houses and held the Governor's office. Prominent national figures in the Republican Party pressured the

General Assembly to adopt a partisan redistricting plan as a punitive measure against Democrats for having enacted pro-Democrat redistricting plans elsewhere. The Republican members of Pennsylvania's House and Senate worked together on such a plan. On January 3, 2002, the General Assembly passed its plan, which was signed into law by Governor Schweiker as Act 1.

Plaintiffs, registered Democrats who vote in Pennsylvania, brought suit in the United States District Court for the Middle District of Pennsylvania, seeking to enjoin implementation of Act 1 under Rev. Stat. §1979, 42 U.S.C. §1983. Defendants-appellees were the Commonwealth of Pennsylvania and various executive and legislative officers responsible for enacting or implementing Act 1. The complaint alleged, among other things, that the legislation created malapportioned districts, in violation of the one-person, one-vote requirement of Article I, §2, of the United States Constitution, and that it constituted a political gerrymander, in violation of Article I and the Equal Protection Clause of the Fourteenth Amendment. With regard to the latter contention, the complaint alleged that the districts created by Act 1 were "meandering and irregular," and "ignor[ed] all traditional redistricting criteria, including the preservation of local government boundaries, solely for the sake of partisan advantage." . . .

II

Political gerrymanders are not new to the American scene. One scholar traces them back to the Colony of Pennsylvania at the beginning of the 18th century, where several counties conspired to minimize the political power of the city of Philadelphia by refusing to allow it to merge or expand into surrounding jurisdictions, and denying it additional representatives. . . . There were allegations that Patrick Henry attempted (unsuccessfully) to gerrymander James Madison out of the First Congress. And in 1812, of course, there occurred the notoriously outrageous political districting in Massachusetts that gave the gerrymander its name—an amalgam of the names of Massachusetts Governor Elbridge Gerry and the creature ("salamander") which the outline of an election district he was credited with forming was thought to resemble. "By 1840 the gerrymander was a recognized force in party politics and was generally attempted in all legislation enacted for the formation of election districts. It was generally conceded that each party would attempt to gain power which was not proportionate to its numerical strength."

It is significant that the Framers provided a remedy for such practices in the Constitution. Article I, §4, while leaving in state legislatures the initial power to draw districts for federal elections, permitted Congress to "make or alter" those districts if it wished. . . .

The power bestowed on Congress to regulate elections, and in particular to restrain the practice of political gerrymandering, has not lain dormant.

In the Apportionment Act of 1842, 5 Stat. 491, Congress provided that Representatives must be elected from single-member districts "composed of contiguous territory." Congress again imposed these requirements in the Apportionment Act of 1862, 12 Stat. 572, and in 1872 further required that districts "contai[n] as nearly as practicable an equal number of inhabitants." In the Apportionment Act of 1901, Congress imposed a compactness requirement. The requirements of contiguity, compactness, and equality of population were repeated in the 1911 apportionment legislation, 37 Stat. 13, but were not thereafter continued. Today, only the single-member-district requirement remains. Recent history, however, attests to Congress's awareness of the sort of districting practices appellants protest, and of its power under Article I, §4, to control them. Since 1980, no fewer than five bills have been introduced to regulate gerrymandering in congressional districting.

Eighteen years ago, we held that the Equal Protection Clause grants judges the power — and duty — to control political gerrymandering, see *Davis v. Bandemer*, 478 U.S. 109, 106 S. Ct. 2797, 92 L. Ed. 2d 85 (1986). It is to consideration of this precedent that we now turn.

III

As Chief Justice Marshall proclaimed two centuries ago, "[i]t is emphatically the province and duty of the judicial department to say what the law is." *Marbury v. Madison*, 1 Cranch 137, 177, 2 L. Ed. 60 (1803). Sometimes, however, the law is that the judicial department has no business entertaining the claim of unlawfulness — because the question is entrusted to one of the political branches or involves no judicially enforceable rights. Such questions are said to be "nonjusticiable," or "political questions."

In *Baker v. Carr*, 369 U.S. 186 (1962), we set forth six independent tests for the existence of a political question: . . . [2] a lack of judicially discoverable and manageable standards for resolving it. . . .

The second is at issue here, and there is no doubt of its validity. "The judicial Power" created by Article III, §1, of the Constitution is not *whatever* judges choose to do or even *whatever* Congress chooses to assign them. It is the power to act in the manner traditional for English and American courts. One of the most obvious limitations imposed by that requirement is that judicial action must be governed by *standard*, by *rule*. Laws promulgated by the Legislative Branch can be inconsistent, illogical, and ad hoc; law pronounced by the courts must be principled, rational, and based upon reasoned distinctions.

Over the dissent of three Justices, the Court held in *Davis v. Bandemer* that, since it was "not persuaded that there are no judicially discernible and manageable standards by which political gerrymander cases are to be decided," such cases *were* justiciable. The clumsy shifting of the burden of proof for the premise (the Court was "not persuaded" that standards do not exist, rather than "persuaded" that they do) was necessitated by the uncomfortable fact that the six-Justice majority could not discern what the judicially discernible standards might be. There was no majority on that point. Four of the Justices finding justiciability believed that the standard was one thing, two believed it was something else. The lower courts have lived with that assurance of a standard (or more precisely, lack of assurance that there is no standard), coupled with that inability to specify a standard, for the past 18 years. In that time, they have considered numerous political gerrymandering claims; this Court has never revisited the unanswered question of what standard governs. . . .

Eighteen years of judicial effort with virtually nothing to show for it justify us in revisiting the question whether the standard promised by *Bandemer* exists. As the following discussion reveals, no judicially discernible and manageable standards for adjudicating political gerrymandering claims have emerged. Lacking them, we must conclude that political gerrymandering claims are nonjusticiable and that *Bandemer* was wrongly decided.

A

We begin our review of possible standards with that proposed by Justice White's plurality opinion in *Bandemer* because, as the narrowest ground for our decision in that case, it has been the standard employed by the lower courts. The plurality concluded that a political gerrymandering claim could succeed only where plaintiffs showed "both intentional discrimination against an identifiable political group and an actual discriminatory effect on that group." As to the intent element, the plurality acknowledged that "[a]s long as redistricting is done by a legislature, it should not be very difficult to prove that the likely political consequences of the reapportionment were intended." However, the effects prong was significantly harder to satisfy. Relief could not be based merely upon the fact that a group of persons banded together for political purposes had failed to achieve representation commensurate with its numbers, or that the apportionment scheme made its winning of elections more difficult. Rather, it would have to be shown that, taking into account a variety of historic factors and projected election results, the group had been "denied its chance to effectively influence the political process" as a whole, which could be achieved even without electing a candidate. It would not be enough to establish, for example, that Democrats had been "placed in a district with a supermajority of other Democratic voters" or that the district "departs from pre-existing political boundaries." Rather, in a challenge to an individual district the inquiry would focus "on the opportunity of members of the group to participate in party deliberations in the slating and nomination of candidates, their opportunity to register and vote, and hence their chance to directly influence the election returns and to secure the attention of the winning candidate." A statewide challenge, by contrast, would involve an analysis of "the voters' direct *or indirect* influence on the elections of the state legislature as a whole." With what has proved to be a gross understatement, the plurality acknowledged this was "of necessity a difficult inquiry." . . .

In the lower courts, the legacy of the plurality's test is one long record of puzzlement and consternation. . . . The test has been criticized for its indeterminacy by a host of academic commentators. . . . Because this standard was misguided when proposed, has not been improved in subsequent application, and is not even defended before us today by the appellants, we decline to affirm it as a constitutional requirement.

B

Appellants take a run at enunciating their own workable standard based on Article I, §2, and the Equal Protection Clause. We consider it at length not only because it reflects the litigant's view as to the best that can be derived from 18 years of experience, but also because it shares many features with other proposed standards, so that what is said of it may be said of them as well. Appellants' proposed standard retains the two-pronged framework of the *Bandemer* plurality — intent plus effect — but modifies the type of showing sufficient to satisfy each.

To satisfy appellants' intent standard, a plaintiff must "show that the mapmakers acted with a *predominant intent* to achieve partisan advantage," which can be shown "by direct evidence or by circumstantial evidence that other neutral and legitimate redistricting criteria were subordinated to the goal of achieving partisan advantage." As compared with the *Bandemer* plurality's test of mere intent to disadvantage the plaintiff's group, this proposal seemingly makes the standard more difficult to meet — but only at the expense of making the standard more indeterminate.

"Predominant intent" to disadvantage the plaintiff's political group refers to the relative importance of that goal as compared with all the other goals that the map seeks to pursue — contiguity of districts, compactness of districts, observance of the lines of political subdivision, protection of incumbents of all parties, cohesion of natural racial and ethnic neighborhoods, compliance with requirements of the Voting Rights Act of 1965 regarding racial distribution, etc. Appellants contend that their intent test *must* be discernible and manageable because it has been borrowed from our racial gerrymandering cases. To begin with, in a very important respect that is not so. In the racial gerrymandering context, the predominant intent test has been applied to the challenged district in which the plaintiffs voted. Here, however, appellants do not assert that an apportionment fails their intent test if any single district does so. Since "it would be quixotic to attempt to bar state legislatures from considering politics as they redraw district lines," appellants propose a test that is satisfied only when "partisan advantage was the predominant motivation *behind the entire statewide plan*." Vague as the "predominant motivation" test might be when used to evaluate single districts, it all but evaporates when applied statewide. Does it mean, for instance, that partisan intent must outweigh all other goals — contiguity, compactness, preservation of neighborhoods, etc. — *statewide*? And how is the statewide "outweighing" to be determined? If three-fifths of the map's districts forgo the pursuit of partisan ends in favor of strictly observing political-subdivision lines, and only two-fifths ignore those lines to disadvantage the plaintiffs, is the observance of political subdivisions the "predominant" goal between those two? We are sure appellants do not think so.

Even within the narrower compass of challenges to a single district, applying a "predominant intent" test to *racial* gerrymandering is easier and less disruptive. The Constitution clearly contemplates districting by political entities, see Article I, §4, and unsurprisingly that turns out to be root-and-branch a matter of politics. By contrast, the purpose of segregating voters on the basis of race is not a lawful one, and is much more rarely encountered. Determining whether the shape of a particular district is so substantially affected by the presence of a rare and constitutionally suspect motive as to invalidate it is quite different from determining whether it is so substantially affected by the excess of an ordinary and lawful motive as to invalidate it. Moreover, the fact that partisan districting is a lawful and common practice means that there is almost *always* room for an election-impeding lawsuit contending that partisan advantage was the predominant motivation; not so for claims of racial gerrymandering. Finally, courts might be justified in accepting a modest degree of unmanageability to enforce a constitutional command which (like the Fourteenth Amendment obligation to refrain from racial discrimination) is clear; whereas they are not justified in inferring a judicially enforceable constitutional obligation (the obligation not to apply *too much* partisanship in districting) which is both dubious and severely unmanageable. For these reasons, to the extent that our racial gerrymandering cases represent a model of discernible and manageable standards, they provide no comfort here.

The effects prong of appellants' proposal replaces the *Bandemer* plurality's vague test of "denied its chance to effectively influence the political process," with criteria that are seemingly more specific. The requisite effect is established when "(1) the plaintiffs show that the districts systematically 'pack' and 'crack' the rival party's voters, *and* (2) the court's examination of the 'totality of circumstances' confirms that the map can thwart the plaintiffs' ability to translate a majority of votes into a majority of seats." This test is loosely based on our cases applying §2 of the Voting Rights Act of 1965, 42 U.S.C. §1973, to discrimination by race. But a person's politics is rarely as readily discernible — and *never* as permanently discernible — as a person's race. Political affiliation is not an immutable characteristic, but may shift from one election to the next; and even within a given election, not all voters follow the party line. We dare say (and hope) that the political party which puts forward an utterly incompetent candidate will lose even in its registration stronghold. These facts make it impossible to assess the effects of partisan gerrymandering, to fashion a standard for evaluating a violation, and finally to craft a remedy.

Assuming, however, that the effects of partisan gerrymandering can be determined, appellants' test would invalidate the districting only when it prevents a majority of the electorate from electing a majority of representatives. Before considering whether this particular standard is judicially manageable we question whether it is judicially discernible in the sense of being relevant to some constitutional violation. Deny it as appellants may (and do), this standard rests upon the principle that groups (or at least political-action groups) have a right to proportional representation. But the Constitution contains no such principle. It guarantees equal protection of the law to persons, not equal representation in government to equivalently sized groups. It nowhere says that farmers or urban dwellers, Christian fundamentalists or Jews, Republicans or Democrats, must be accorded political strength proportionate to their numbers.

Even if the standard were relevant, however, it is not judicially manageable. To begin with, how is a party's majority status to be established? Appellants propose using the results of statewide races as the benchmark of party support. But as their own complaint describes, in the 2000 Pennsylvania statewide elections some Republicans won and some Democrats won. Moreover, to think that majority status in statewide races establishes majority status for district contests, one would have to believe that the only factor determining voting behavior at all levels is political affiliation. That is assuredly not true.

But if we could identify a majority party, we would find it impossible to ensure that that party wins a majority of seats-unless we radically revise the States' traditional structure for elections. In any winner-take-all district system, there can be no guarantee, no matter how the district lines are drawn, that a majority of party votes statewide will produce a majority of seats for that party. The point is proved by the 2000 congressional elections in Pennsylvania, which, according to appellants' own pleadings, were conducted under a judicially drawn district map "free from partisan gerrymandering." On this "neutral playing fiel[d]," the Democrats' statewide majority of the major-party vote (50.6%) translated into a minority of seats (10, versus 11 for the Republicans). Whether by reason of partisan districting or not, party constituents may always wind up "packed" in some districts and "cracked" throughout others. Consider, for example, a legislature that draws district lines with no objectives in mind except compactness and respect for the lines of political subdivisions. Under that system, political groups that tend to cluster (as is the case with

Democratic voters in cities) would be systematically affected by what might be called a "natural" packing effect.

Our one-person, one-vote cases have no bearing upon this question, neither in principle nor in practicality. Not in principle, because to say that each individual must have an equal say in the selection of representatives, and hence that a majority of individuals must have a majority say, is not at all to say that each discernible group, whether farmers or urban dwellers or political parties, must have representation equivalent to its numbers. And not in practicality, because the easily administrable standard of population equality adopted by *Wesberry* and *Reynolds* enables judges to decide whether a violation has occurred (and to remedy it) essentially on the basis of three readily determined factors — where the plaintiff lives, how many voters are in his district, and how many voters are in other districts; whereas requiring judges to decide whether a districting system will produce a statewide majority for a majority party casts them forth upon a sea of imponderables, and asks them to make determinations that not even election experts can agree upon.

For these reasons, we find appellants' proposed standards neither discernible nor manageable. . . .

The judgment of the District Court is affirmed.

It is so ordered.

Justice STEVENS, dissenting.

The central question presented by this case is whether political gerrymandering claims are justiciable. Although our reasons for coming to this conclusion differ, five Members of the Court are convinced that the plurality's answer to that question is erroneous. Moreover, as is apparent from our separate writings today, we share the view that, even if these appellants are not entitled to prevail, it would be contrary to precedent and profoundly unwise to foreclose all judicial review of similar claims that might be advanced in the future. That we presently have somewhat differing views — concerning both the precedential value of some of our recent cases and the standard that should be applied in future cases — should not obscure the fact that the areas of agreement set forth in the separate opinions are of far greater significance.

The concept of equal justice under law requires the State to govern impartially. Today's plurality opinion would exempt governing officials from that duty in the context of legislative redistricting and would give license, for the first time, to partisan gerrymanders that are devoid of any rational justification. In my view, when partisanship is the legislature's sole motivation — when any pretense of neutrality is forsaken unabashedly and all traditional districting criteria are subverted for partisan advantage — the governing body cannot be said to have acted impartially.

Although we reaffirm the central holding of the Court in *Davis v. Bandemer*, 478 U.S. 109 (1986), we have not reached agreement on the standard that should govern partisan gerrymandering claims. I would decide this case on a narrow ground. Plaintiffs-appellants urge us to craft new rules that in effect would authorize judicial review of statewide election results to protect the democratic process from a transient majority's abuse of its power to define voting districts. I agree with the plurality's refusal to undertake that ambitious project. I am persuaded, however, that the District Court failed to apply well-settled propositions of law when it granted the defendants' motion to dismiss plaintiff-appellant Susan Furey's gerrymandering claim.

According to the complaint, Furey is a registered Democrat who resides at an address in Montgomery County, Pennsylvania, that was located under the 1992 districting plan in Congressional District 13. Under the new plan adopted by the General Assembly in 2002, Furey's address now places her in the "non-compact" District 6. Furey alleges that the new districting plan was created "solely" to effectuate the interests of Republicans, and that the General Assembly relied "exclusively" on a principle of "maximum partisan advantage" when drawing the plan. In my judgment, Furey's allegations are plainly sufficient to establish: (1) that she has standing to challenge the constitutionality of District 6; (2) that her district-specific claim is not foreclosed by the *Bandemer* plurality's rejection of a statewide claim of political gerrymandering; and (3) that she has stated a claim that, at least with respect to District 6, Pennsylvania's redistricting plan violates the equal protection principles enunciated in our voting rights cases both before and after *Bandemer*. The District Court therefore erred when it granted the defendants' motion to dismiss Furey's claim.

I

Prior to our seminal decision in *Baker v. Carr*, 369 U.S. 186 (1962), a majority of this Court had heeded Justice Frankfurter's repeated warnings about the dire consequences of entering the "political thicket" of legislative districting. As a result, even the most egregious gerrymanders were sheltered from judicial review. It was after *Baker* that we first decided that the Constitution prohibits legislators from drawing district lines that diminish the value of individual votes in overpopulated districts. In reaching that conclusion, we explained that "legislatures . . . should be bodies which are collectively responsive to the popular will," and we accordingly described "the basic aim of legislative apportionment" as "achieving . . . fair and effective representation for all citizens." Consistent with that goal, we also reviewed claims that the majority had discriminated against particular groups of voters by drawing multimember districts that threatened "to minimize or cancel out the voting strength of racial or political elements of the voting population." Such districts were "vulnerable" to constitutional challenge "if racial or political groups ha[d] been fenced out of the political process and their voting strength invidiously minimized." Our holding in *Bandemer*, that partisan gerrymandering claims are justiciable followed ineluctably from the central reasoning in *Baker*. . . .

At issue in this case, as the plurality states, is *Baker*'s second test — the presence or absence of judicially manageable standards. . . .

With purpose as the ultimate inquiry, other considerations have supplied ready standards for testing the lawfulness of a gerrymander. In his dissent in *Bandemer*, Justice Powell explained that "the merits of a gerrymandering claim must be determined by reference to the configurations of the districts, the observance of political subdivision lines, and other criteria that have independent relevance to the fairness of redistricting." . . .

The Court has made use of all three parts of Justice Powell's standard in its recent racial gerrymandering jurisprudence. In those cases, the Court has examined claims that redistricting schemes violate the equal protection guarantee where they are "so highly irregular" on their face that they "rationally cannot be understood as anything other than an effort" to segregate voters by race, *Shaw v. Reno*, 509 U.S. 630 (1993) (*Shaw I*), or where "race for its own sake, and not other districting principles, was the legislature's dominant and controlling rationale in drawing its district lines." The *Shaw* line of cases has emphasized that "reapportionment is one area in which appearances do matter," and has focused both on the shape of the challenged districts and the purpose behind the line-drawing in assessing the constitutionality of majority-minority districts under the Equal Protection Clause. These decisions, like Justice Powell's opinion in *Bandemer*, have also considered the process by which the districting schemes were enacted, looked to other evidence demonstrating that purely improper considerations motivated the decision, and included maps illustrating outlandish district shapes.

Given this clear line of precedents, I should have thought the question of justiciability in cases such as this — where a set of plaintiffs argues that a single motivation resulted in a districting scheme with discriminatory effects — to be well settled. The plurality's contrary conclusion cannot be squared with our long history of voting rights decisions. . . .

To begin with, the plurality errs in assuming that politics is "an ordinary and lawful motive." We have squarely rejected the notion that a "purpose to discriminate on the basis of politics" is never subject to strict scrutiny. On the contrary, "political belief and association constitute the core of those activities protected by the First Amendment," and discriminatory governmental decisions that burden fundamental First Amendment interests are subject to strict scrutiny. Thus, unless party affiliation is an appropriate requirement for the position in question, government officials may not base a decision to hire, promote, transfer, recall, discharge, or retaliate against an employee, or to terminate a contract, on the individual's partisan affiliation or speech. It follows that political affiliation is not an appropriate standard for excluding voters from a congressional district. . . .

State action that discriminates against a political minority for the sole and unadorned purpose of maximizing the power of the majority plainly violates the decisionmaker's duty to remain impartial. Gerrymanders necessarily rest on legislators' predictions that "members of certain identifiable groups . . . will vote in the same way." "In the line-drawing process, racial, religious, ethnic, and economic gerrymanders are all species of political gerrymanders." Thus, the critical issue in both racial and political gerrymandering cases is the same: whether a single nonneutral criterion controlled the districting process to such an extent that the Constitution was offended. This Court has treated that precise question as justiciable in *Gomillion* and in the *Shaw* line of cases, and today's plurality has supplied no persuasive reason for distinguishing the justiciability of partisan gerrymanders. . . .

III

Elected officials in some sense serve two masters: the constituents who elected them and the political sponsors who support them. Their primary obligations are, of course, to the public in general, but it is neither realistic nor fair to expect them wholly to ignore the political consequences of their decisions. "It would be idle . . . to contend that any political consideration taken into account in fashioning a reapportionment plan is sufficient to invalidate it." Political factors are common and permissible elements of the art of governing a democratic society.

But while political considerations may properly influence the decisions of our elected officials, when such decisions disadvantage members of a minority group — whether the minority is defined by its members' race, religion, or political affiliation — they must rest on a neutral predicate. The Constitution enforces "a commitment to the law's neutrality where the rights of persons are at stake." Thus, the Equal Protection Clause implements a duty to govern impartially that requires, at the very least, that every decision by the sovereign serve some nonpartisan public purpose.

In evaluating a claim that a governmental decision violates the Equal Protection Clause, we have long required a showing of discriminatory purpose. That requirement applies with full force to districting decisions. The line that divides a racial or ethnic minority unevenly between school districts can be entirely legitimate if chosen on the basis of neutral factors — county lines, for example, or a natural boundary such as a river or major thoroughfare. But if the district lines were chosen for the purpose of limiting the number of minority students in the school, or the number of families holding unpopular religious or political views, that invidious purpose surely would invalidate the district.

Consistent with that principle, our recent racial gerrymandering cases have examined the shape of the district and the purpose of the districting body to determine whether race, above all other criteria, predominated in the line-drawing process. We began by holding in *Shaw I* that a districting scheme could be "so irrational on its face that it [could] be understood only as an effort to segregate voters into separate voting districts because of their race." Then, in *Miller*, we explained that *Shaw I*'s irrational-shape test did not treat the bizarreness of a district's lines itself as a constitutional violation; rather, the irregularity of the district's contours in *Shaw I* was "persuasive circumstantial evidence that race for its own sake, and not other districting principles, was the legislature's dominant and controlling rationale in drawing its district lines." Under the *Shaw* cases, then, the use of race as a criterion in redistricting is not *per se* impermissible, but when race is elevated to paramount status — when it is the be-all and end-all of the redistricting process — the legislature has gone too far. "Race must not simply have been *a* motivation . . . but the *predominant* factor motivating the legislature's districting decision."

Just as irrational shape can serve as an objective indicator of an impermissible legislative purpose, other objective features of a districting map can save the plan from invalidation. We have explained that "traditional districting principles," which include "compactness, contiguity, and respect for political subdivisions," are "important not because they are constitutionally required . . . but because they are objective factors that may serve to defeat a claim that a district has been gerrymandered on racial lines." "Where these or other race-neutral considerations are the basis for redistricting legislation, and are not subordinated to race, a State can 'defeat a claim that a district has been gerrymandered on racial lines.'"

In my view, the same standards should apply to claims of political gerrymandering, for the essence of a gerrymander is the same regardless of whether the group is identified as political or racial. Gerrymandering always involves the drawing of district boundaries to maximize the voting strength of the dominant political faction and to minimize the strength of one or more groups of opponents. In seeking the desired result, legislators necessarily make judgments about the probability that the members of identifiable groups — whether economic, religious, ethnic, or racial — will vote in a certain way. The overriding purpose of those predictions is political. It follows that the standards that enable courts to identify and redress a racial gerrymander could also perform the same function for other species of gerrymanders.

The racial gerrymandering cases therefore supply a judicially manageable standard for determining when partisanship, like race, has played too great of a role in the districting process. Just as race can be a factor in, but cannot dictate the outcome of, the districting process, so too can partisanship be a permissible consideration in drawing district lines, so long as it does not predominate. If, as plaintiff-appellant Furey has alleged, the predominant motive of the legislators who designed District 6, and the sole justification for its bizarre shape, was a purpose to discriminate against a political minority, that invidious purpose should invalidate the district.

The plurality reasons that the standards for evaluating racial gerrymanders are not workable in cases such as this because partisan considerations, unlike racial ones, are perfectly legitimate. Until today, however, there has not been the slightest intimation in any opinion written by any Member of this Court that a naked purpose to disadvantage a political minority would provide a rational basis for drawing a district line. On the contrary, our opinions referring to political gerrymanders have consistently assumed that they were at least undesirable, and we always have indicated that political considerations are among those factors that may not dominate districting decisions. Purely partisan motives are "rational" in a literal sense, but there must be a limiting principle. "[T]he word 'rational' — for me at least — includes elements of legitimacy and neutrality that must always characterize the performance of the sovereign's duty to govern impartially." A legislature controlled by one party could not, for instance, impose special taxes on members of the minority party, or use tax revenues to pay the majority party's campaign expenses. The rational basis for government decisions must satisfy a standard of legitimacy and neutrality; an acceptable rational basis can be neither purely personal nor purely partisan. . . .

Accordingly, I respectfully dissent.

KENNEDY, J., filed an opinion concurring in the judgment [omitted].

SOUTER, J., filed a dissenting opinion, in which GINSBURG, J., joined [omitted].

BREYER, J., filed a dissenting opinion [omitted].

NOTES AND QUESTIONS

1. *Finding a manageable standard.* Baker v. Carr made inevitable equal protection challenges to political gerrymandering. In *Davis* and *Vieth*, the Court struggled with both the justiciability of such claims and the standards that must be applied, if they are in fact justiciable. In *Davis*, the three dissenters argued that there were no discernible standards, and in *Vieth* that number increased to four. In *Davis* the majority, as its standard, required a plaintiff to show that "the electoral system is arranged in a manner that will consistently degrade a voter's or a group of voters' influence on the political [not electoral] process as a whole." *Davis v. Bandemer*, 478 U.S. 109, 132 (1986). In *Vieth*, this standard was abandoned by the four dissenting Justices, who offered three new and differing tests for establishing the discriminatory effects of political gerrymandering. The majority this time consisted of the four Justices for whom there was no manageable standard, and one concurring Justice. The result of all of this seems to be

that the *Davis* standard remains intact — although no Justice seems willing to apply it. And how can you? What is the actual injury that you would need to prove, and what evidence would you need to prove it to satisfy the *Davis* test? In League of United Latin American Citizens v. Perry, 548 U.S. 399 (2006), the Supreme Court determined that a mid-decade redistricting by the Texas legislature of its own and its congressional districts, solely motivated by partisan politics, did not establish per se a burden on the plaintiffs' representational rights.

2. *Adequate representation?* Part of the Court's determination in *Davis* was based on its view that individuals who cast votes for losing candidates are usually adequately represented by winning candidates. Consequently, they are not disadvantaged in the political process. What does this view reflect in the American political system — the absence of substantial ideological differences between parties, a particularly open process of relating to legislators regardless of party, or the absence of party loyalty as a determining factor in legislative voting? Isn't the Voting Rights Act based on a legislative finding that certain minorities have not been able to adequately participate in the political process?

A Problem for the Governor's Counsel

Assume you are the counsel to your state governor. The state legislature has just passed a bill for the reapportionment of the state's congressional and state legislative districts. Your state has 100,000 of its citizens (1 percent of its population) enrolled in the Socialist party. They live in close proximity to each other, and this number is sufficient to elect at least one representative to the state assembly if most of these citizens were placed in the same district. But rather than placing these Socialists into one district, the state legislature has quartered the area in which the Socialists live to maximize the number of seats for the majority party of each house. The governor is concerned about the application of *Vieth* and *Davis* to this legislation. What is your view?

Would it make a difference if the area were quartered for the *purpose of preventing* a Socialist from being elected? If so, is the remedy in this particular example proportional representation?

Can a distinction be made based on the small-minority status of Socialist party members statewide? Isn't the "quartering" of the potential Socialist district just another way to politically defeat the Socialist platform?

"One Person, One Vote" and the Census

Underlying the regulation of legislative redistricting is the constitutionally mandated decennial census. U.S. Const., Art. I, §2. The census controls the number of representatives apportioned to each state. Representatives are apportioned pursuant to a formula found in 2 U.S.C. §2a. The total number of representatives, presently 435, was established in 1912. See 2 U.S.C. §2 (presently omitted). The census also forms the statistical basis for drawing district lines for the House of Representatives and most state and local legislative bodies under the doctrine of one person, one vote. (The census additionally controls the amount of federal aid that states and localities receive under certain population-determined programs.) After the 1980 census, a number of states and municipalities complained that there had been a substantial undercounting of minorities and the poor in cities. It is generally agreed that New York City, among other cities, suffered a substantial undercount. This undercount meant that New York State may have had apportioned to it one fewer member of Congress than its entitlement and that it was underrepresented in its congressional and state legislative delegations. Numerous lawsuits were brought to challenge the 1980 census on the basis of the undercount and its impact on minorities and the poor. While these suits failed, the courts affirmed the view that there was no constitutional bar to statistical adjustments. See, e.g., Cuomo v. Baldridge, 674 F. Supp. 1089 (S.D.N.Y. 1987). In 1988, the City of New York and other cities brought an action against the Department of Commerce to enjoin the taking of the 1990 census unless a method for adjusting the undercount was established. City of New York v. Department of Commerce, No. 88 Civ. 3474 (E.D.N.Y). A settlement of the case was reached in July 1989. This settlement required the promulgation of guidelines for determining whether adjustments to the 1990 census should be made.

In anticipation of the 2000 census, a heated battle ensued among an array of parties over the census undercount issue. Basically, Democrats advocated the use of sampling while Republicans argued for a continuation of individual enumeration. Under President Clinton, the Department of Commerce pushed for sampling and became engaged in constant budget and legislative battles with the Republican Congress over the issue. In response, for example, to the Bureau of the Census' announcement that it planned to use statistical sampling for the 2000 census, Congress amended the Census Act to prohibit such action and President Clinton vetoed the amendment. As a substitute for that bill, Congress passed and the President signed a bill calling essentially for the Bureau to set forth a clear and detailed plan on how it intended to conduct the 2000 census. After the Bureau's publication of the plan, suits were brought against it, challenging the constitutionality and statutory legality of the sampling techniques. The Supreme Court responded to this challenge in Department of Commerce v. House of Representatives, 525 U.S. 316 (1999), holding on the basis of the text of the Census Act and its legislative history that statistical sampling for purposes of apportioning congressional districts among states was prohibited.

Although sampling is banned, the Court has held that statistical tools can be used to avoid the undercounting issue. The following case illustrates how the use of such tools is not subject to heightened scrutiny. Internal citations and footnotes have been omitted except where particularly relevant.

Wisconsin v. City of New York et al.
517 U.S. 1 (1996)

CHIEF JUSTICE REHNQUIST delivered the opinion of the Court.

In conducting the 1990 United States Census, the Secretary of Commerce decided not to use a particular statistical adjustment that had been designed to correct an undercount in the initial enumeration. The Court of Appeals for the Second Circuit held that the Secretary's decision was subject to heightened scrutiny because of its effect on the right of individual respondents to have their vote counted equally. We hold that the Secretary's decision was not subject to heightened scrutiny, and that it conformed to applicable constitutional and statutory provisions.

I

The Constitution requires an "actual Enumeration" of the population every 10 years and vests Congress with the authority to conduct that census "in such Manner as they shall by Law direct." Art. I, §2. Through the Census Act, 13 U.S.C. §1 et seq., Congress has delegated to the Secretary of the Department of Commerce the responsibility to take "a decennial census of [the] population . . . in such form and content as he may determine. . . ." §141(a). . . .

The Constitution provides that the results of the census shall be used to apportion the Members of the House of Representatives among the States. See Art. I, §2, cl. 3 ("Representatives . . . shall be apportioned among the several States . . . according to their respective Numbers . . ."); Amdt. 14, §2 ("Representatives shall be apportioned among the several States according to their respective numbers, counting the whole number of persons in each State . . ."). Because the Constitution provides that the number of Representatives apportioned to each State determines in part the allocation to each State of votes for the election of the President, the decennial census also affects the allocation of members of the electoral college. Today, census data also have important consequences not delineated in the Constitution: The Federal Government considers census data in dispensing funds through federal programs to the States, and the States use the results in drawing intrastate political districts.

There have been 20 decennial censuses in the history of the United States. Although each was designed with the goal of accomplishing an "actual Enumeration" of the population, no census is recognized as having been wholly successful in achieving that goal. Despite consistent efforts to improve the quality of the count, errors persist. Persons who should have been counted are not counted at all or are counted at the wrong location; persons who should not have been counted (whether because they died before or were born after the decennial census date, because they were not a resident of the country, or because they did not exist) are counted; and persons who should have been counted only once are counted twice. It is thought that these errors have resulted in a net "undercount" of the actual American population in every decennial census. In 1970, for instance, the Census Bureau concluded that the census results were 2.7% lower than the actual population. . . .

The Census Bureau has recognized the undercount and the differential undercount as significant problems, and in the past has devoted substantial effort toward achieving their reduction. Most recently, in its preparations for the 1990 census, the Bureau initiated an extensive inquiry into various means of overcoming the impact of the undercount and the differential undercount. As part of this effort, the Bureau created two task forces: the Undercount Steering Committee, responsible for planning undercount research and policy development; and the Undercount Research Staff (URS), which conducted research into various methods of improving the accuracy of the census. In addition, the Bureau consulted with state and local governments and various outside experts and organizations.

In preparing for the 1990 census, the Bureau and the task forces also looked into the possibility of using large-scale statistical adjustment to compensate for the undercount and differential undercount. Although the Bureau had previously considered that possibility (most recently in 1980), it always had decided instead to rely upon more traditional methodology and the results of the enumeration. In 1985, preliminary investigations by the URS suggested that the most promising method of statistical adjustment was the "capture-recapture" or "dual system estimation" (DSE) approach. . . .

In the context of the census, the initial enumeration of the entire population (the "capture") would be followed by the post-enumeration survey (PES) (the "recapture") of certain representative geographical areas. The Bureau would then compare the results of the PES to the results of the initial enumeration for those areas targeted by the PES, in order to determine a rate of error in those areas for the initial enumeration (i.e., the rate at which the initial enumeration undercounted people in those areas). That rate of error would be extrapolated to the entire population, and thus would be used to statistically adjust the results of the initial enumeration. . . .

In July 1991, the Secretary issued his decision not to use the PES to adjust the 1990 census. The Secretary began by noting that large-scale statistical adjustment of the census through the PES would "abandon a two hundred year tradition of how we actually count people." Before taking a "step of that magnitude," he held, it was necessary to be "certain that it would make the census better and the distribution of the population more accurate." Emphasizing that the primary purpose of the census was to apportion political representation among the States, the Secretary concluded that "the primary criterion for accuracy should be distributive accuracy — that is, getting most nearly correct the proportions of people in different areas."

After reviewing the recommendations of his advisers and the voluminous statistical research that had been compiled, the Secretary concluded that although numerical accuracy (at the national level) might be improved through statistical adjustment, he could not be confident that the distributive accuracy of the census — particularly at the state and local level — would be improved by a PES-based adjustment. In particular, the Secretary noted, the adjusted figures became increasingly unreliable as one focused upon smaller and smaller political subdivisions.

The Secretary stated that his decision not to adjust was buttressed by a concern that adjustment of the 1990 census might present significant problems in the future. Because small changes in adjustment methodology would have a large impact upon apportionment — an impact that could be determined before a particular methodology was chosen — the Secretary found that statistical adjustment of the 1990 census might open the door to political tampering in the future. The Secretary also noted that statistical adjustment might diminish the incentive for state and local political leaders to assist in the conduct of the initial enumeration. In conclusion, the Secretary stated that the Bureau would continue its research into the possibility of statistical adjustment of future censuses, and would maintain its efforts to improve the accuracy and inclusiveness of the initial enumeration. . . .

II

We think that the Court of Appeals erred in holding the "one person–one vote" standard of *Wesberry* and its progeny applicable to the action at hand. For several reasons, the "good-faith effort to achieve population equality" required of a State conducting intrastate redistricting does not translate into a requirement that the Federal Government conduct a census that is as accurate as possible. First, we think that the Court of Appeals understated the significance of the two differences that it recognized between state redistricting cases and the instant action. The court failed to recognize that the Secretary's decision was made pursuant to Congress' direct delegation of its broad authority over the census. See Art. I, §2, cl. 3 (Congress may conduct the census "in such Manner as they shall by Law direct"). The court also undervalued the significance of the fact that the Constitution makes it impossible to achieve population equality among interstate districts. As we have noted before, the Constitution provides that "[t]he number of Representatives shall not exceed one for every 30,000 persons; each State shall have at least one Representative; and district boundaries may not cross state lines."

While a court can easily determine whether a State has made the requisite "good-faith effort" toward population equality through the application of a simple mathematical formula, we see no way in which a court can apply the *Wesberry* standard to the Federal Government's decisions regarding the conduct of the census. The Court of Appeals found that *Wesberry* required the Secretary to conduct a census that would "achieve voting-power," which it understood to mean a census that was as accurate as possible. But in so doing, the court implicitly found that the Constitution prohibited the Secretary from preferring distributive accuracy to numerical accuracy, and that numerical accuracy — which the court found to be improved by a PES-based adjustment — was constitutionally preferable to distributive accuracy.... As in [previous cases], where we could see no constitutional basis upon which to choose between absolute equality and relative equality, so here can we see no ground for preferring numerical accuracy to distributive accuracy, or for preferring gross accuracy to some particular measure of accuracy. The Constitution itself provides no real instruction on this point, and extrapolation from our intrastate districting cases is equally unhelpful. Quite simply, "[t]he polestar of equal representation does not provide sufficient guidance to allow us to discern a single constitutionally permissible course." ...

[W]e [have] held that Congress' "apparently good-faith choice of a method of apportionment of Representatives among the several States 'according to their respective Numbers'" was not subject to strict scrutiny under *Wesberry*. With that conclusion in mind, it is difficult to see why or how *Wesberry* would apply to the Federal Government's conduct of the census — a context even further removed from intrastate districting than is congressional apportionment. Congress' conduct of the census, even more than its decision concerning apportionment, "commands far more deference than a state districting decision that is capable of being reviewed under a relatively rigid mathematical standard."

Rather than the standard adopted by the Court of Appeals, we think that it is the standard established by this Court in *Montana* [Department of Commerce v. Montana, 503 U.S. 442 (1992)] and *Franklin* [Franklin v. Massachusetts, 505 U.S. 788 (1992)] that applies to the Secretary's decision not to adjust. The text of the Constitution vests Congress with virtually unlimited discretion in conducting the decennial "actual Enumeration," and notwithstanding the plethora of lawsuits that inevitably accompany each decennial census, there is no basis for thinking that Congress' discretion is more limited than the text of the Constitution provides. Through the Census Act, Congress has delegated its broad authority over the census to the Secretary. Hence, so long as the Secretary's conduct of the census is "consistent with the constitutional language and the constitutional goal of equal representation," it is within the limits of the Constitution. In light of the Constitution's broad grant of authority to Congress, the Secretary's decision not to adjust need bear only a reasonable relationship to the accomplishment of an actual enumeration of the population, keeping in mind the constitutional purpose of the census. . . .

III

The Constitution confers upon Congress the responsibility to conduct an "actual Enumeration" of the American public every 10 years, with the primary purpose of providing a basis for apportioning political representation among the States. Here, the Secretary of Commerce, to whom Congress has delegated its constitutional authority over the census, determined that in light of the constitutional purpose of the census, an "actual Enumeration" would best be achieved without the PES-based statistical adjustment of the results of the initial enumeration. We find that conclusion entirely reasonable. Therefore we hold that the Secretary's decision was well within the constitutional bounds of discretion over the conduct of the census provided to the Federal Government. The judgment of the Court of Appeals is Reversed.

CHAPTER 7

Representativeness — Elections, Qualifications, Representative Duties

In Chapter 6, we explored representativeness from the perspective of the electorate. The subject was the right of citizens to vote for legislative candidates and to have their votes count equally. Underlying this attention was the basic premise that, in a representative democracy, "[e]llections provide the chief means through which most voters influence the formation of government policy and exercise the right responsibilities of citizenship." A. James Reichley, The Electoral System, in Elections American Style 1, 1 (1987).

In this chapter we continue our focus on representativeness, but shift our view to the candidate and representative. In this effort, three topics are examined: qualifications for legislative office, the election to legislative office, and representative obligations of legislators.

A. THE REPRESENTATIVE: QUALIFICATIONS FOR OFFICE

Age, Citizenship, Residence

The U.S. Constitution and many state constitutions contain qualifications for legislative office. Article I, §2 of the Constitution requires a member of the House of Representatives to be 25 years of age, a citizen for 7 years, and an inhabitant of the state in which the member's district is located. A senator, according to Art. I, §3 of the Constitution, must be 30, 9 years a citizen, and an inhabitant of the state to be represented. For examples of similar state constitutional provisions, see Ala. Const. Art. IV, §47; Md. Const. Art. II, §9; and Penn. Const. Art. II, §5. The U.S. Constitution (Art. I, §5) also charges each house of the Congress with being the judge of the qualifications of its members and authorizes each house to punish a member and, on the basis of a two-thirds vote, expel a member. Similar provisions are contained in most state constitutions. Among these are Cal. Const. Art. IV, §5; Iowa Const. Art. III, §7; La. Const. Art. III, §7.

Prior to 1969, Congress had broadly interpreted its power to judge the qualifications of prospective members. On eight occasions the House of Representatives had excluded prospective members from taking their seats on grounds other than those explicitly set forth in the Constitution. These grounds included loyalty in the Civil War cases (Brown and Young, Wimpy and Simpson, 1867), malfeasance (Whittemore, 1870); polygamy (Roberts, 1900), and sedition (Berger, 1919, 1920). In opposition to the seating of Whittemore in 1870, Congressman John A. Logan presented the prototypical argument for exclusion: that, notwithstanding representative government, the people did not have the right to "destroy their own liberties, by filling Congress with men who, from their conduct, show themselves capable of the destruction of the Government." Cong. Globe, 41st Cong., 2d Sess. 4670-73 (1870), *quoted in* Richard A. Baker, The History of Congressional Ethics, in Representation and Responsibility 3, 13 (1985). (Whittemore had been charged with selling admissions to the military academies.) See Cong. Q., Guide to Congress 825 (3d ed. 1982).

The Supreme Court established limits on this interpretation of congressional power in the following case. Internal citations have been omitted except where particularly relevant.

Powell v. McCormack
395 U.S. 486 (1969)

CHIEF JUSTICE WARREN delivered the opinion of the Court. . . .

Facts

During the 89th Congress, a Special Subcommittee on Contracts of the Committee on House Administration conducted an investigation into the expenditures of the Committee on Education and Labor, of which petitioner Adam Clayton Powell, Jr., was chairman. The Special Subcommittee issued a report concluding that Powell and certain staff employees had deceived the House authorities as to travel expenses. The report also indicated there was strong evidence that certain illegal salary payments had been made to Powell's wife at his direction. See H.R. Rep. No. 2349, 89th

Cong., 2d Sess. 6-7 (1966). No formal action was taken during the 89th Congress. However, prior to the organization of the 90th Congress, the Democratic members-elect met in caucus and voted to remove Powell as chairman of the Committee on Education and Labor. See H.R. Rep. No. 27, 90th Cong., 1st Sess. 1-2 (1967).

When the 90th Congress met to organize in January 1967, Powell was asked to step aside while the oath was administered to the other members-elect. Following the administration of the oath to the remaining members, the House discussed the procedure to be followed in determining whether Powell was eligible to take his seat. After some debate, by a vote of 363 to 65 the House adopted House Resolution No. 1, which provided that the Speaker appoint a Select Committee to determine Powell's eligibility. 113 Cong. Rec. 26-27. Although the resolution prohibited Powell from taking his seat until the House acted on the Select Committee's report, it did provide that he should receive all the pay and allowances due a member during the period.

The Select Committee, composed of nine lawyer-members, issued an invitation to Powell to testify before the Committee. The invitation letter stated that the scope of the testimony and investigation would include Powell's qualifications as to age, citizenship, and residency; his involvement in a civil suit (in which he had been held in contempt); and "[m]atters of . . . alleged official misconduct since January 3, 1961." See Hearings on H.R. Res. No. 1 before Select Committee Pursuant to H.R. Res. No. 1, 90th Cong., 1st Sess. 5 (1967) (hereinafter Hearings). Powell appeared at the Committee hearing held on February 8, 1967. After the Committee denied in part Powell's request that certain adversary-type procedures be followed, Powell testified. He would, however, give information in relation only to his age, citizenship, and residency; upon the advice of counsel, he refused to answer other questions. . . .

Then, on February 23, 1967, the Committee issued its report, finding that Powell met the standing qualifications of Art. I, §2. H.R. Rep. No. 27, 90th Cong., 1st Sess. 31 (1967). However, the Committee further reported that Powell had asserted an unwarranted privilege and immunity from the processes of the courts of New York; that he had wrongfully diverted House funds for the use of others and himself; and that he had made false reports on expenditures of foreign currency to the Committee on House Administration. Id., at 31-32. The Committee recommended that Powell be sworn and seated as a member of the 90th Congress but that he be censured by the House, fined $40,000 and be deprived of his seniority. Id., at 33.

The report was presented to the House on March 1, 1967, and the House debated the Select Committee's proposed resolution. At the conclusion of the debate, by a vote of 222 to 202 the House rejected a motion to bring the resolution to a vote. An amendment to the resolution was then offered; it called for the exclusion of Powell and a declaration that his seat was vacant.

The Speaker ruled that a majority vote of the House would be sufficient to pass the resolution if it were so amended. 113 Cong. Rec. 5020. After further debate, the amendment was adopted by a vote of 248 to 176. Then the House adopted by a vote of 307 to 116 House Resolution No. 278 in its amended form, thereby excluding Powell and directing that the Speaker notify the Governor of New York that the seat was vacant.

Powell and 13 voters of the 18th Congressional District of New York subsequently instituted this suit in the United States District Court for the District of Columbia. Five members of the House of Representatives were named as defendants individually and "as representatives of a class of citizens who are presently serving ... as members of the House of Representatives." John W. McCormack was named in his official capacity as Speaker, and the Clerk of the House of Representatives, the Sergeant at Arms and the Doorkeeper were named individually and in their official capacities. . . .

We granted certiorari. 393 U.S. 949 (1968). While the case was pending on our docket, the 90th Congress officially terminated and the 91st Congress was seated. In November 1968, Powell was again elected as the representative of the 18th Congressional District of New York and he was seated by the 91st Congress. The resolution seating Powell also fined him $25,000. See H.R. Res. No. 2, 91st Cong., 1st Sess., 115 Cong. Rec. H21 (daily ed., January 3, 1969). . . .

Respondents press upon us a variety of arguments to support the court below; they will be considered in the following order. (1) Events occurring subsequent to the grant of certiorari have rendered this litigation moot. (2) The Speech or Debate Clause of the Constitution, Art. I, §6, insulates respondents' action from judicial review. (3) The decision to exclude petitioner Powell is supported by the power granted to the House of Representatives to expel a member. (4) This Court lacks subject matter jurisdiction over petitioners' action. (5) Even if subject matter jurisdiction is present, this litigation is not justiciable either under the general criteria established by this Court or because a political question is involved. . . .

IV.   Exclusion or Expulsion

The resolution excluding petitioner Powell was adopted by a vote in excess of two-thirds of the 434 Members of Congress — 307 to 116. 113 Cong. Rec. 5037-38. Article I, §5, grants the House authority to expel a member "with the Concurrence of two thirds." Respondents assert that the House may expel a member for any reason whatsoever and that, since a two-thirds vote was obtained, the procedure by which Powell was denied his seat in the 90th Congress should be regarded as an expulsion, not an exclusion. . . .

Although respondents repeatedly urge this Court not to speculate as to the reasons for Powell's exclusion, their attempt to equate exclusion with expulsion would require a similar speculation that the House would have voted to expel Powell had it been faced with that question. Powell had not been seated at the time House Resolution No. 278 was debated and passed. After a motion to bring the Select Committee's proposed resolution to an immediate vote had been defeated, an amendment was offered which mandated Powell's exclusion. Mr. Celler, chairman of the Select Committee, then posed a parliamentary inquiry to determine whether a two-thirds vote was necessary to pass the resolution if so amended "in the sense that it might amount to an expulsion." 113 Cong. Rec. 5020. The Speaker replied that "action by a majority vote would be in accordance with the rules." Ibid. Had the amendment been regarded as an attempt to expel Powell, a two-thirds vote would have been constitutionally required. The Speaker ruled that the House was voting to exclude Powell, and we will not speculate what the result might have been if Powell had been seated and expulsion proceedings subsequently instituted.

Nor is the distinction between exclusion and expulsion merely one of form. The misconduct for which Powell was charged occurred prior to the convening of the 90th Congress. On several occasions the House has debated whether a member can be expelled for actions taken during a prior Congress and the House's own manual of procedure applicable in the 90th Congress states that "both Houses have distrusted their power to punish in such cases." Rules of the House of Representatives, H.R. Doc. No. 529, 89th Cong., 2d Sess., 25 (1967). . . .

Finally, the proceedings which culminated in Powell's exclusion cast considerable doubt upon respondents' assumption that the two-thirds vote necessary to expel would have been mustered. These proceedings have been succinctly described by Congressman Eckhardt:

> The House voted 202 votes for the previous question leading toward the adoption of the [Select] Committee report. It voted 222 votes against the previous question, opening the floor for the Curtis Amendment which ultimately excluded Powell. "Upon adoption of the Curtis Amendment, the vote again fell short of two-thirds, being 248 yeas to 176 nays. Only on the final vote, adopting the Resolution as amended, was more than a two-thirds vote obtained, the vote being 307 yeas to 116 nays. On this last vote, as a practical matter, members who would not have denied Powell a seat if they were given the choice to punish him had to cast an aye vote or else record themselves as opposed to the only punishment that was likely to come before the House. Had the matter come up through the processes of expulsion, it appears that the two-thirds vote would have failed, and then members would have been able to apply a lesser penalty.

We need express no opinion as to the accuracy of Congressman Eckhardt's prediction that expulsion proceedings would have produced a different result. However, the House's own views of the extent of its power to expel combined with the Congressman's analysis counsel that exclusion and expulsion are not fungible proceedings. The Speaker ruled that House Resolution No. 278 contemplated an exclusion proceeding. We must reject respondents' suggestion that we overrule the Speaker and hold that, although the House manifested an intent to exclude Powell, its action should be tested by whatever standards may govern an expulsion. . . .

VI.   *Justiciability*

. . . Respondents maintain that even if this case is otherwise justiciable, it presents only a political question. It is well established that the federal courts will not adjudicate political questions. . . .

Respondents' first contention is that this case presents a political question because under Art. I, §5, there has been a "textually demonstrable constitutional commitment" to the House of the "adjudicatory power" to determine Powell's qualifications. Thus it is argued that the House, and the House alone, has power to determine who is qualified to be a member.

In order to determine whether there has been a textual commitment to a co-ordinate department of the Government, we must interpret the Constitution. In other words, we must first determine what power the Constitution confers upon the House through Art. 1, §5, before we can determine to what extent, if any, the exercise of that power is subject to judicial review. Respondents maintain that the House has broad power under §5, and, they argue, the House may determine which are the qualifications necessary for membership. On the other hand, petitioners allege that the Constitution provides that an elected representative may be denied his seat only if the House finds he does not meet one of the standing qualifications expressly prescribed by the Constitution.

If examination of §5 disclosed that the Constitution gives the House judicially unreviewable power to set qualifications for membership and to judge whether prospective members meet those qualifications, further review of the House determination might well be barred by the political question doctrine. On the other hand, if the Constitution gives the House power to judge only whether elected members possess the three standing qualifications set forth in the Constitution, further consideration would be necessary to determine whether any of the other formulations of the political question doctrine are "inextricable from the case at bar." . . .

In order to determine the scope of any "textual commitment" under Art. I, §5, we necessarily must determine the meaning of the phrase to "be the Judge of the Qualifications of its own Members." Petitioners argue that the records of the debates during the Constitutional Convention; available commentary from the post-Convention, pre-ratification period; and early congressional applications of Art. I, §5, support their construction of the section. Respondents insist, however, that a careful examination of the pre-Convention practices of the English Parliament and American colonial assemblies demonstrates that by 1787, a legislature's power to judge the qualifications of its members was generally understood to encompass exclusion or expulsion on the ground that an individual's character or past conduct rendered him unfit to serve. When the Constitution and the debates over its adoption are thus viewed in historical perspective, argue respondents, it becomes clear that the "qualifications" expressly set forth in the Constitution were not meant to limit the long-recognized legislative power to exclude or expel at will, but merely to establish "standing incapacities," which could be altered only by a constitutional amendment. Our examination of the relevant historical materials leads us to the conclusion that petitioners are correct and that the Constitution leaves the House without authority to *exclude* any person, duly elected by his constituents, who meets all the requirements for membership expressly prescribed in the Constitution. . . .

NOTES AND QUESTIONS

1. *The final judge.* The Court in *Powell* seems to be ruling that the House of Representatives, in judging the qualifications of prospective members, may not impose more qualifications than those set forth in the Constitution. See also Bond v. Floyd, 385 U.S. 116 (1966) (prohibiting the Georgia state senate from excluding Julian Bond from membership on the grounds that his views on the Vietnam War were inconsistent with a constitutionally required oath of office). But is the House (or Senate) the final judge of whether an elected representative satisfies the qualifications required by the Constitution? Assume, for example, that a 20-year-old was elected representative and was seated by the House. Is the House the final judge of this action?

2. *Exclusion versus expulsion.* In defense of its vote to exclude Representative Powell, the House argued that, while Powell fulfilled all of the constitutional qualifications for office, its action was, in effect, an expulsion authorized by Article I, §5 in order to give the House of Representatives the power to protect its institutional integrity. Considering that the vote for exclusion was greater than two-thirds of the House, why did the Court reject this argument?

3. *The effect of an election.* Assume that Powell had been seated and then expelled for acts committed prior to his last election. What role should that election have played in the deliberations of the House of Representatives? How would the *Powell* Court have analyzed this issue?

4. *The grounds for expulsion.* In *Powell*, the House also argued that it could expel a member for any reason. Assume that Powell had espoused disfavored political views during a session of Congress, for which he was then expelled. Are there any limits on the substantive grounds Congress may use to expel a member? Should there be?

5. *Protecting the electorate?* In 1989 a member of the Louisiana state legislature, Representative Odon Bacque, attempted to exclude David Duke from membership. Duke was a self-acknowledged former member (and

reputed current member) of the Ku Klux Klan and head of the suspect National Association for the Advancement of Whites. His campaign had received notoriety throughout the country because of his views on race relations. In the legislature, Bacque unsuccessfully moved to exclude Duke on the basis of Louisiana's constitutional rule requiring one-year residency in the district from which he was elected. While there were some questions about Duke's residency, the issue unavoidably became Duke's "politics" and the right of his constituents to have his representation. Duke was seated. Should Bacque have next moved for expulsion, using the argument of Congressman Logan in the *Whittemore* case that, notwithstanding representative government, a legislative body had the right to protect citizens from their own bad choices?

6. *Drug-free candidates.* Assume that a state required drug testing for its legislative candidates and barred the candidacy of a candidate who tested positive. If the constitution of that state set forth only age and citizenship qualifications, do you think such a bar would be a constitutionally impermissible qualification? See Chandler v. Miller, 520 U.S. 305 (1997) (holding that the test itself was an unconstitutional search). See discussion in U.S. Term Limits v. Thornton to determine whether testing positive for drugs (assuming the search was permissible) could be a state-imposed disqualification for Congress.

B.   TERM LIMITS

In earlier chapters, we discussed some of the historical criticisms of legislative bodies and the impact such criticisms have had on the legislative process. Reflective of such criticism are efforts, successful in a number of states, to impose term limits on state and federal legislators. Term limits prohibit incumbents from seeking reelection to the same office, after they have served a fixed number of terms in that office. The goal of term limits, according to its advocates, is to weaken the grip of career legislators, break the hold of "special interests," and return policy making power to the people. See, e.g., The California Ballot Pamphlet: The Pros and Cons of Proposition 140, *reprinted in* Limiting Legislative Terms 477 (Gerald Benjamin and Michael J. Malbin eds., 1992). (This document was prepared by the California Secretary of State for use in the referendum and contains, among other things, competing arguments.) There is an ironic aspect to these efforts. This is pointed out by the political scientist David Everson in the following passage:

> Fewer than thirty years ago excessive membership turnover in state legislature was considered to be a significant problem, the source of far too

much amateurism in the legislative process. The remedy prescribed by political scientists? Make the job of state legislator a more attractive career through legislative modernization and professionalization. The reformers of that era sought to do this by altering the incentives for service to recruit lawmakers who would stay around long enough to become seasoned professionals.

To a significant degree, the reformers achieved their objectives. Beginning in the 1960s, a great wave of legislative reform swept the states. By the 1980s it had clearly produced its intended effects: more professionalized state legislators and greater state legislative membership stability.

David H. Everson, The Impact of Term Limitations on the States: Cutting the Underbrush or Chopping Down the Tall Timber, in Limiting Legislative Terms 189, 189 (Gerald Benjamin and Michael J. Malbin eds., 1992).

The idea of term limits is not new. Indeed, it was a significant part of the debate over ratification of the Constitution.

Mark P. Petracca, Rotation in Office: The History of an Idea, in Limiting Legislative Terms
19, 31-34 (Gerald Benjamin and Michael J. Malbin eds., 1992)

The absence of a rotation requirement in the finished Constitution was denounced by the Antifederalists, who viewed the principle as a "truly republican institution." Most of the Antifederalist criticism reflected fear that the Senate would become "a fixed and unchangeable body of men" and the president "a king for life, like the king of Poland." Delegates at the ratification conventions in New York, Virginia, and North Carolina proposed amending the new Constitution to include rotation for the presidency.

The process of ratifying the Constitution was punctuated by great debates over the wisdom of rotation in office, debates every bit as passionate and far more informed than any of the contemporary quarrels over term limitations.

New York's "Brutus" advocated rotation for the Senate on the grounds that it would give more people the opportunity to serve in government: "It would give opportunity to bring forward a greater number of men to serve their country, and would return those, who had served, to their state, and afford them the advantage of becoming better acquainted with the condition and politics of their constituents." This view was shared by Elbridge Gerry of Massachusetts, who criticized the new Constitution at the Massachusetts ratification convention in 1788:

> There is not provision for a rotation, nor anything to prevent the perpetuity of office in the same hands for life; which by a little well timed bribery, will probably be done, to the exclusion of men of the best abilities from their share in the offices of government.

New York's Melancton Smith was the Antifederalist's most articulate and thoughtful advocate of rotation in office. In June of 1788, Smith reaffirmed the potential of rotation to check tyranny and the abuse of power. Calling for a constitutional amendment to remedy the "evil" of the proposed Senate, Smith proposed:

> [R]otation . . . as the best possible mode of affecting a remedy. The amendment will not only have a tendency to defeat any plots, which may be formed against the liberty and authority of the state governments, but will be the best means to extinguish the factions which often prevail, and which are sometimes so fatal in legislative bodies. . . . We have generally found, that perpetual bodies have either combined in some scheme of usurpation, or have been torn and distracted with cabals — Both have been the source of misfortune to the state. Our Congress would have been a fine field for party spirit to act in — That body would undoubtedly have suffered all the evils of faction, had it not been secured by the rotation established by the articles of the confederation.

Smith and Brutus understood that it would be very difficult to get rid of individuals once they were elected to office. . . .

The argument that rotation in office helps to secure fidelity between the representative and the represented, to paraphrase [Thomas] Paine, was made rather simply by James Monroe of Virginia, who argued that "the rotative principle is preserved" for the sake of legislative responsibility "which will I hope never be given up." "Even good men in office," said Virginia's Richard Henry Lee, "in time, imperceptibly lose sight of the people, and gradually fall into measures prejudicial to them." The need for rotation as a means to assure quality representation was also emphasized by John Lansing in New York, who urged passage of an amendment to require rotation for senators so as to "oblige them to return, at certain periods, to their fellow-citizens, that, by mingling with the people, they may recover that knowledge of their interests, and revive that sympathy with their feelings, which power and an exalted station are too apt to efface from the minds of rulers." . . .

The Federalists Strike Back

The Antifederalist critique of the Constitution did not go unchallenged. In New York, Robert R. Livingston provided a scathing response to the rotation proposal of John Lansing and Gilbert Livingston:

> The people are the best judges of who ought to represent them. To dictate and control them, to tell them whom they shall not elect, is to abridge their natural rights. This rotation is an absurd species of ostracism — a mode of proscribing eminent merit, and banishing from stations of trust those who have filled them with the greatest faithfulness. Besides, it takes away the strongest stimulus to public virtue — the hopes of honors and rewards.

Similarly, Roger Sherman lashed out against rotation for the president and senate in "A Citizen of New Haven," printed in 1788:

> It is proposed to make the president and senators ineligible after certain periods. But this would abridge the privilege of the people and remove one great motive to fidelity in office, and render persons incapable of serving in offices, on account of their experience, which would best qualify them for usefulness in office — but if their services are not acceptable they may be left out at any new election.

But the strongest argument against rotation was once again Hamilton's delivered at the New York ratification convention. Hamilton's final response to Melancton Smith merits attention here as a balance to the case made by the Antifederalists:

> Sir, in contending for a rotation, the gentlemen carry their zeal beyond all reasonable bounds. I am convinced that no government, founded on their feeble principal, can operate well. . . . [R]otation would be productive of many disadvantages: under particular circumstances, it might be extremely inconvenient, *if not fatal to the prosperity of our country.* [Emphasis added.]

Livingston, Sherman and Hamilton made three arguments, which reappear frequently in contemporary clashes about term limitation:

1. The people have a right to judge who they will and will not elect to public office.
2. Rotation reduces the incentives for political accountability.
3. Rotation deprives the polity of experienced public servants.

1. The Impact of Term Limits on the Legislative Process

In the excerpts below we turn our attention to the impact of term limits on the legislative procedure. Professor Rosenthal is among the nation's leading scholars on state legislatures. Although he warns that his analysis is applicable only to state legislatures, the authors believe that it is also relevant to Congress. Professors Malbin and Benjamin are also specialists in legislative process. Professor Benjamin once served as a member of the Ulster County (New York) legislature and as its majority leader.

Alan Rosenthal, The Effect of Term Limits
on Legislatures: A Comment, in Limiting Legislative Terms
205, 205-08 (Gerald Benjamin and Michael J. Malbin eds., 1992)

Term limitations might have several effects on the legislature as an institution. The observations that follow are limited to state legislatures and are not meant to refer to Congress. Although my remarks will be general, it must be remembered that there are real differences among the states.

Parenthetically, I do not think there is any relationship between present conditions in the individual state legislatures and the desire to have term limits. That desire stems from a variety of motives, including anger at Congress. It would not be surprising if a term-limit movement began in New Hampshire, where the citizen legislature model is the strongest, not because such a movement was called for by legislative conditions but because it reflected the public's anger.

The first point to examine concerns what difference there will be in the kinds of people who serve in the legislature. There is good reason to doubt that the people will be very different from the members of today. People who go into politics do not think in terms of ten or fifteen years; they think in terms of what they want now, and do not worry about tomorrow. Their time perspective has to be short, because they are subject to so many uncertainties.

Second, will there be a difference in the way people adjust to legislative life? I doubt there will be much difference in that either. Legislatures today are fairly malleable institutions. Of course, in New York, New Jersey, or Pennsylvania, it is better to be in the majority than the minority. Aside from that, nobody serves an apprenticeship anywhere. If you come in with an education program or a feminist agenda, you can accomplish a lot in a very short span of time. Legislators do not come in thinking "I have twenty years to do it." They want it now. They want instant gratification of their programmatic needs. It will be the same with term limits. The limits will not change the members' time perspectives significantly because the perspectives already are short.

A third subject would be in the members' information networks and the sources of their behavioral cues. There, the effects of term limits might be subtle, especially if a reduction in staff accompanies the limitation on terms, as is happening in California. If there are no senior members with more than six or seven years of service to serve as a repository of knowledge, then members may have to rely more on somebody like the old-time director of the office of legislative counsel, the nonpartisan staff agency in many states. The director, who typically had years of service, was powerful in the period before there were many staff or senior legislators specializing in policy domains. . . . Maybe lobbyists will play that role; I do not know. What develops will vary from state to state and the differences will be extraordinarily subtle.

Fourth, will term limits bring about any differences in the level of specialization or expertise? I doubt it. If there are any differences, they would also be subtle. Members already jump from committee to committee in order to get a chairmanship or vice-chairmanship, or to get from a minor committee to judiciary, or from judiciary to appropriations. We political scientists have a congressional picture in our heads in which the committee is a repository of expertise. That is not the way it is in state legislatures, nor should it be. There are a few expert legislators in each area, but only a few.

Even though we may not be cutting down on expertise and specialized knowledge with term limits, we will be reducing the level of general knowledge. In my opinion, the longer members are in, the more they learn. This is not true of everyone, but it is probably true of those who are skillful and like what they are doing. They get more savvy and more knowledgeable over time. Their judgment improves, too. But a lot of what they learn is political knowledge, not substantive knowledge about policy. That kind of knowledge is going to dissipate with term limits, and I do not know what will substitute for it. In addition, members today have time to build up their reputations and the respect they are accorded for their political knowledge and skills. Other members, therefore, will turn to them for cues. Term limits afford legislators less time to develop such reputations. That is bound to affect the way members pick up their cues within the legislature. Consequently, it is also bound to affect the legislature's informal networks of leadership.

The fifth area is one where I do foresee significant change in a relatively short time: the internal distribution of power within a legislative body. Term limitations will accelerate the ongoing dispersion of power. For ten or twenty years, members have been becoming more individualistic as a result of the weakening of parties and the development of candidate-centered campaigns. Legislative reform and modernization have facilitated this by spreading the resources around. In the good old days, only a few people got to read the bills. They just were not available. Everybody can read bills now. Leaders had more control then. Today, resources are much more widely distributed, members put in more time, and the knowledge gap between the leaders and members is shrinking. . . .

With term limits, members are not going to tolerate anyone serving six, eight, ten, or twelve years as leader. The rest of the members will have very little time to wait for their own chances. No leader will be able to serve very long, and certainly not long enough to become even vaguely familiar with the job. Leadership will have to rotate — maybe even annually if the members have six-year term limits. Chairmanships will also rotate until committees mean very little. From some point of view this may be a dream to hope for; from another it is a horror story. But it is a real possibility.

So, term limits will mean that leaders' powers will be weakened still further. They will not have control over committee appointments; committees will generate on a rotational system. They will not control bills; members will manage their own bills. Calendaring will become automatic. The term-limited legislature will resemble the Indiana legislature when it was tied, with a Republican speaker one day and a Democratic speaker the next day. Everything passed in the House, although a lot of it was stopped in the Senate. The little bills, the special-interest bills, probably will go through a kind of a logrolling process, but the tough ones may well be stalemated.

My final point concerns the power of the legislature vis-à-vis the executive. A legislature needs some sort of responsible leadership to deal with the executive. Without effective legislative leaders, a governor can knock off the members one by one, buying them cheaply and easily. What you are going to see with term limits is a shift, generally speaking, back to executive dominance.

Maybe that is good. Maybe that is what we need, but I doubt it. If that is what you want, term limits will get you there.

Gubernatorial dominance will be accompanied by bureaucratic dominance as well. The government will be ruled by bureaucrats building up their programs and their budgets without having to contend with strong legislatures. That will be a splendid irony for those advocates of term limits who prefer a small government.

Michael J. Malbin and Gerald Benjamin,
Legislatures after Term Limits, in Limiting Legislative Terms
209, 210-17 (Gerald Benjamin and Michael J. Malbin eds., 1992)

Inside the Legislature

If term limits are to affect the distribution of power inside the legislature, they must first alter the incentives, norms and expectations of individual legislators. Therefore, we shall consider norms and incentives before turning to leadership and structure.

Incentives and Norms

Advocates of term limits believe that under a new system members will be more motivated than current members by a desire to "do the right thing" for its own sake, and less by a constant seeking after reelection. Perhaps amateur politicians would be willing to ignore reelection concerns. If so, term limits that produce amateurs *might* also produce legislatures filled with members who act out of their pure commitment to the merits of a proposal, unsullied by any concerns about how their support or opposition might affect their careers. Before anyone begins dancing with joy at this prospect, however, it should be noted that a desire to do the right thing does not guarantee success. For example, although many commentators have argued that stalemate results when politicians are too cowardly to make tough decisions, stalemate occurs at least as often among members who are quite willing to do the right thing but disagree sharply over just what the right thing *is.*

But however one thinks amateur legislators would behave under term limits, it is clear that a completely different kind of analysis is necessary for those term-limit proposals that would encourage musical chairs by professional politicians. For one thing, such limits would mean that politicians could never rest content with maintaining a safe constituency. Perhaps they would, in fact, *be* safe in their current office. But they could never be content with that. If they wanted to remain active in politics, they would have to plan ahead for a future run for another office. As a result, far from seeing term limits decrease the members' feeling of dependence, the limits might well make some members feel even less free to take policy risks than they do now. The difference is that the members' focus might shift from their current to their potential constituencies. If so, the members would simply replace reelection behavior with preelection behavior. . . .

Many scholars have noted that the declining importance of the party in the electorate has been associated with a more individualistic style of behavior inside the legislature. More members play to the press galleries today than a few decades ago. But that is not all they do.

The U.S. House and Senate, and most state legislatures, still have many mechanisms for rewarding members who do the unpublicized but crucial kind of work that goes under the heading of "institutional maintenance." Members get nothing politically out of serving on an ethics committee, but they do gain credit and prestige with their colleagues. A job well done today can mean more internal power later. Similarly, the role of the chairman of the budget committee can be a political negative during a time of fiscal constraint, but it is important for the institution and therefore important for the chairman's long-term power inside the institution.

Clearly, term limits would reduce the incentives for individual members to engage in long-term strategies for increasing their power inside the institution. Similarly, they would make members less likely to put any of their personal emphasis on maintaining the power or prestige of their current institution as a whole. When combined with the incentives for media attention, the net effect of term limits therefore probably would intensify the individualism that has marked Congress and many state legislatures in recent decades.

Leadership and Internal Organization

The effect of term limits on incentives and norms in turn would spill over to affect every other aspect of institutional life. For example, it almost goes without saying that term limits would make seniority all but untenable as a basis for allocating power within the legislature. The shorter the limit, the more untenable seniority would be.

It is possible, as some have argued, that this could strengthen the hand of party leaders by weakening the independence of committee and subcommittee chairmen. In the late nineteenth through early twentieth centuries, party leaders lost power in Congress as legislative careerism took hold and members with long-term stakes in the institution revolted against putting their internal power in arbitrary hands. That, in part, was what the 1910 uprising against Speaker Joseph Cannon was about. After the 1910 revolt, seniority became all but inviolate, reducing leaders to the role of brokers and facilitators.

There can be no question that eliminating seniority, perhaps even eliminating the presumption of reappointment, would weaken the independent power of committees and subcommittees. And there is some historical plausibility to the assumption that weakening committees would increase the power of party leaders. The problem with the assumption, however, is that it presupposes that the same members who refuse to tolerate seniority would be willing to grant their party leaders an independent power base. The shorter the term limit, the less likely this would be. Remember that these would be the very same members just described as having every reason to behave as media-oriented individualists. There is no reason for them to turn the reins of power over to anyone else.

On the contrary, we expect that members with defined term limits will be unlikely to let strong party leadership develop. In fact, we would not be surprised to see a more fluid party leadership, with leaders changing every few years. Members would trade their votes for favorable committee positions, as the potential leaders seek to put together majority coalitions for their leadership races. In addition, because the leaders would have no ability to impose sanctions that pinch over the long term, there is every possibility that the resulting factionalism would encourage leadership fights in an increasing number of states to become cross-party factional contests.

Thus, even if term limits do away with seniority, it should not simply be assumed that the average member of Congress, or of a state legislature, would follow somebody else. If the term limits produce amateur legislators, amateurs might be more inclined than contemporary careerists to follow his personal convictions.

On the other hand, if the limits merely encourage professionals to run for new offices periodically, the professionals would become more entrepreneurial. In neither case would most members be likely to feel a long-term, institutionally based incentive for following a collective institutional leadership.

Legislatures and Executives

. . . [B]oth the advocates and opponents of term limits agree that limiting legislative terms will bring about a major shift in the balance between the legislative and executive branches of government. The two sides differ over what is desirable, but both seem to assume that term limits will produce a legislature that is more inclined to vote yes to whatever the governor or president might want. In our view, there is no reason to make this assumption. . . .

Historically, governors — and, to a lesser extent, presidents — have been at their strongest when they sat at the top of electorally important party organizations. The executive's party before the 1960's was generally the majority party in the legislature. Party members would support the executive's program not only out of conviction, but because they felt a sense of common political fate before the electorate, linked as they were to the executive through the political party. This is the situation we look to, therefore, for examples in which legislators feel a positive political incentive to cooperate.

For the typical contemporary member, by comparison, the political party has become less important in elections. Most incumbents more or less control their own fates. To the extent the members think about making common cause with their president or governor for electoral reasons, they are thinking about building up their party in the legislature, or retaining control over the government more than about their personal reelection. As a result, the incentives for cooperation are more mixed for today's members than was true for their counterparts of decades ago. Cooperation is not important for the member's personal reelection, but it can be important for the effective power the members exercise inside the legislature. . . .

To the extent that a legislature tends toward the purely amateur, then — almost by definition — the members will have no personal electoral motivation for supporting or resisting the chief executive. . . .

The amateur will have no personal, career-based reason to help make the chief executive look good, and there is little an executive or legislative leader can do to hurt the amateur's career. Therefore, the amateur legislator is our best example of the middle of our three logical possibilities. The members' personal political incentives leave them more or less neutral between cooperating with or resisting the executive because, by definition, the true amateur will not have a long-term political career inside or outside the legislature.

The situation will be different for professionals facing term limits. Professionals cannot afford to let their futures depend solely upon a governor's or president's popularity. If they want to remain in politics, they will have to try to stand out from the crowd. Their career interests will lead them to promote legislation in their own names, conduct oversight, or, perhaps, become gadflies to the governor and legislative party leaders. No professional faced with a term limit could afford to accept a governor's or a president's lead passively. If anything, the incentives run in the opposite direction. (For example, contrary to those who predict term limits will produce an unchecked bureaucracy, we believe the political incentives for high-visibility oversight would increase under term limits.) The term-limited legislature of itinerant professionals thus is the kind most likely to fit our third logical possibility; neither cooperative nor neutral, this will be a legislature whose members have a personal stake in opposing the executive.

So far, we have concentrated on incentives. However, term limit supporters and opponents seem to base their predictions about a shift in legislative-executive relations more upon capacity than incentives. If legislatures lose their most experienced members, the reasoning goes, then the institution will be less able to withstand the executive. . . .

If a legislature does suffer a significant loss in technical skill or experience, that in turn would compromise its ability to substitute its considered judgment for the executive's. That is, it would probably be less able to pass a fully developed legislative package on its own initiative. But a lack of capacity does not automatically imply a lack of incentive. If legislators are less able to develop intricate packages on their own, it does not mean they will stop trying. If the incentives are strong, they can draw upon lobbyists or simply ignore some of the technical details. Of course, a legislature that ignores details would also lose some of its control over how policy is implemented. In other words, it would be a weakened legislature in some respects, and the content of policy would be affected. But the crucial point for legislative-executive relations is this: governors and presidents are *not* automatically made stronger when the legislatures they face are made weaker. Legislators will let their political interests and goals dictate whether to resist the executive, whatever their technical capacities. In that respect, as in so many others, interbranch politics are not a zero-sum game.

This point is seen even more graphically if we move away from the subject of technical competence to one we believe will be more important for legislative-executive relations: legislative leadership. We have already mentioned that leaders in term-limited legislatures are likely to change rapidly and to have a relatively weak set of resources at their disposal. That means, among other things, that the leaders will have less ability to set agendas and mobilize majorities. This could be interpreted as a sign of a weakened institutional capacity. At the same time, however, it would probably cause problems for chief executives.

Many opponents of term limits have argued that the loss of experienced, long-serving leaders would weaken the legislature in its negotiations with the executive over policy. Our point in some ways is just the opposite: the governor has a stake in strong legislative leadership. It is easier for the chief executive to develop a relationship with a few leaders in each house who can deliver majorities on a range of tough issues — even including leaders of the opposite party — than it is to assemble separate majorities on each issue. Insofar as term limitations weaken the capacity of legislative leaders to provide disciplined majorities, they are likely to make it harder, not easier, for governors to achieve their objectives.

Governors could, in theory, try to turn themselves into legislative leaders. With term-limited legislatures, they may have to try. . . .

NOTES AND QUESTIONS

1. *The impact of term limits.* Professor Rosenthal opposes term limits, while Professors Malbin and Benjamin are supportive. On what points do they agree and disagree regarding the impact of term limits on the legislative process? How does this debate affect your view?

2. *The effect of term limits.* For an article arguing that Congress would become less effective if term limits were in place, see Professor Elizabeth Garrett, Term Limitations and the Myth of the Citizen-Legislator, 81 Cornell L. Rev. 623 (1996). For a critical journalistic look at the impact of term limits, see B. Drummond Ayres, Jr., State Term Limits Are Transforming the Legislatures, N.Y. Times, Apr. 28, 1997, at A1.

3. *A voting rights problem.* Viewing the impact of term limits on the legislative process, one observer has raised the question of whether term limits on members of Congress would violate Section 2 of the Voting Rights Act. "In the estimation of some, term limits would herald both legislative responsiveness and civic empowerment. In actuality . . . term limits would cause a detrimental shift in power from the legislative to the executive branch of government, reducing the influence of minorities in national politics. . . .

[T]his would occur because while minorities have more influence over Congress than over the president, their influence is dependent on having a Congress with the seniority and expertise necessary to counterbalance the president's substantial powers." Anthony E. Gay, Congressional Term Limits: Good Government or Minority Vote Dilution, 141 U. Pa. L. Rev. 2311 (1983). How would you evaluate this argument? The Voting Rights Act is discussed in Chapter 6. See Lowe v. Kansas City Board of Election Commissioners, 752 F. Supp. 897 (W.D. Mo. 1990) (holding that city charter amendment limiting council members' terms to eight years did not violate the Voting Rights Act).

2.   The Legal Restraints on Term Limits

State efforts to impose term limits on state legislators have raised a number of legal issues. For example, in Legislature v. March Fong Eu, 816 P.2d 1309 (Cal. 1991), petitioners argued that California's state legislative term limits violated their First and Fourteenth Amendment rights to vote and stand for office. The court found to the contrary, holding that even under a compelling state interest standard (which they did not apply), California's stated interest in turning out long-term incumbents trumped petitioners' First Amendment rights.

State attempts to limit legislative terms have not been restricted to the terms of their own legislators, but, in a number of states, have reached the terms of members of Congress. These laws have raised a separate legal question concerning the power of the state to regulate congressional terms.

The Supreme Court answered this question in U.S. Term Limits v. Thornton. Internal citations and footnotes have been omitted except where particularly relevant.

U.S. Term Limits v. Thornton
514 U.S. 779 (1995)

JUSTICE STEVENS delivered the opinion of the Court.

The Constitution sets forth qualifications for membership in the Congress of the United States. Article I, §2, cl. 2, which applies to the House of Representatives, provides:

> No Person shall be a Representative who shall not have attained to the Age of twenty five Years, and been seven Years a Citizen of the United States, and who shall not, when elected, be an Inhabitant of that State in which he shall be chosen.

Article 1, §3, cl. 3, which applies to the Senate, similarly provides:

> No Person shall be a Senator who shall not have attained to the Age of thirty Years, and been nine Years a Citizen of the United States, and who shall not, when elected, be an Inhabitant of that State for which he shall be chosen. . . .

Twenty-six years ago, in Powell v. McCormack, we reviewed the history and text of the Qualifications Clauses in a case involving an attempted exclusion of a duly elected Member of Congress. The principal issue was whether the power granted to each House, in Art. I, §5, to judge the "Qualifications of its own Members" includes the power to impose qualifications other than those set forth in the text of the Constitution. In an opinion by Chief Justice Warren for eight Members of the Court, we held that it does not. . . .

Our reaffirmation of *Powell* does not necessarily resolve the specific questions presented in these cases. For petitioners argue that . . . the historical and textual materials discussed in *Powell* do not support the conclusion that the Constitution prohibits additional qualifications imposed by States. In the absence of such a constitutional prohibition, petitioners argue, the Tenth Amendment and the principle of reserved powers require that States be allowed to add such qualifications. . . .

Petitioners argue that the Constitution contains no express prohibition against state-added qualifications, and that Amendment 73 is therefore an appropriate exercise of a State's reserved power to place additional restrictions on the choices that its own voters may make. We disagree for two independent reasons. First, we conclude that the power to add qualifications is not within the "original powers" of the States, and thus is not reserved to the States by the Tenth Amendment. Second, even if States possessed some original power in this area, we conclude that the Framers intended the Constitution to be the exclusive source of qualifications for members of Congress, and that the Framers thereby "divested" States of any power to add qualifications. . . .

Contrary to petitioners' assertions, the power to add qualifications is not part of the original powers of sovereignty that the Tenth Amendment reserved to the States. Petitioners' Tenth Amendment argument misconceives the nature of the right at issue because that Amendment could only "reserve" that which existed before. As Justice Story recognized, "the states can exercise no powers whatsoever, which exclusively spring out of the existence of the national government, which the constitution does not delegate to them. . . . No state can say, that it has reserved, what it never possessed." . . .

With respect to setting qualifications for service in Congress, no such right existed before the Constitution was ratified. The contrary argument overlooks the revolutionary character of the government that the Framers conceived. Prior to the adoption of the Constitution, the States had joined together under the Articles of Confederation. . . . After the Constitutional Convention convened, the Framers were presented with, and eventually adopted a variation of, "a plan not merely to amend the Articles of Confederation but to create an entirely new National Government with a National Executive, National Judiciary, and a National Legislature." In adopting that plan, the Framers envisioned a uniform national system, rejecting the notion that the Nation was a collection of States, and instead creating a direct link between the National Government and the people of the United States. . . .

We believe that the Constitution reflects the Framers' general agreement with the approach later articulated by Justice Story. For example, Art. I, §5, cl. 1 provides: "Each House shall be the Judge of the Elections, Returns and Qualifications of its own Members." The text of the Constitution thus gives the representatives of all the people the final say in judging the qualifications of the representatives of any one State. For this reason, the dissent falters when it states that "the people of Georgia have no say over whom the people of Massachusetts select to represent them in Congress."

Two other sections of the Constitution further support our view of the Framers' vision. First . . . the Constitution provides that the salaries of representatives should "be ascertained by Law, and paid out of the Treasury of the United States," Art. I, §6, rather than by individual States. The salary provisions reflect the view that representatives owe their allegiance to the people, and not to States. Second, the provisions governing elections reveal the Framers' understanding that powers over the election of federal officers had to be delegated to, rather than reserved by, the States. It is surely no coincidence that the context of federal elections provides one of the few areas in which the Constitution expressly requires action by the States, namely that "[t]he Times, Places and Manner of holding Elections for Senators and Representatives, shall be prescribed in each State by the Legislature thereof." Art. I, §4, cl. 1. This duty parallels the duty under Article II that "Each State shall appoint, in such Manner as the Legislature thereof may direct, a Number of Electors." Art. II, §1, cl. 2. These Clauses are express delegations of power to the States to act with respect to federal elections. . . .

In short, as the Framers recognized, electing representatives to the National Legislature was a new right, arising from the Constitution itself. The Tenth Amendment thus provides no basis for concluding that the States possess reserved power to add qualifications to those that are fixed in the Constitution. Instead, any state power to set the qualifications for membership in Congress must derive not from the reserved powers of state sovereignty, but rather from the delegated powers of national sovereignty. In the absence of any constitutional delegation to the States of power to add qualifications to those enumerated in the Constitution, such a power does not exist. . . .

Even if we believed that States possessed as part of their original powers some control over congressional qualifications, the text and structure of the Constitution, the relevant historical materials, and, most importantly, the "basic principles of our democratic system" all demonstrate that the Qualifications Clauses were intended to preclude the States from exercising any such power and to fix as exclusive the qualifications in the Constitution.

Much of the historical analysis was undertaken by the Court in *Powell*. There is, however, additional historical evidence that pertains directly to the power of States. That evidence, though perhaps not as extensive as that reviewed in *Powell*, leads unavoidably to the conclusion that the States lack the power to add qualifications. . . .

The available affirmative evidence indicates the Framers' intent that States have no role in the setting of qualifications. In Federalist Paper No. 52, dealing with the House of Representatives, Madison addressed the "qualifications of the electors and the elected." Madison first noted the difficulty in achieving uniformity in the qualifications for electors, which resulted in the Framers' decision to require only that the qualifications for federal electors be the same as those for state electors. Madison argued that such a decision "must be satisfactory to every State, because it is comfortable to the standard already established, or which may be established, by the State itself." Madison then explicitly contrasted the state control over the qualifications of electors with the lack of state control over the qualifications of the elected:

> The qualifications of the elected, being less carefully and properly defined by the State constitutions, and being at the same time more susceptible of uniformity, have been very properly considered and regulated by the convention. A representative of the United States must be of the age of twenty-five years; must have been seven years a citizen of the United States; must, at the time of his election be an inhabitant of the State he is to represent;

and, during the time of his service must be in no office under the United States. Under these reasonable limitations, the door of this part of the federal government is open to merit of every description, whether native or adoptive, whether young or old, and without regard to poverty or wealth, or to any particular profession of religious faith. . . .

The provisions in the Constitution governing federal elections confirm the Framers' intent that States lack power to add qualifications. The Framers feared that the diverse interests of the States would undermine the National Legislature, and thus they adopted provisions intended to minimize the possibility of state interference with federal elections. For example, to prevent discrimination against federal electors, the Framers required in Art. I, §2, cl. 1, that the qualifications for federal electors be the same as those for state electors. . . . Similarly, in Art. I, §4, cl. 1, though giving the States the freedom to regulate the "Times, Places and Manner of holding Elections," the Framers created a safeguard against state abuse by giving Congress the power to "by Law make or alter such Regulations." The Convention debates make clear that the Framers' overriding concern was the potential for States' abuse of the power to set the "Times, Places and Manner" of elections. . . .

The dissent nevertheless contends that the Framers' distrust of the States with respect to elections does not preclude the people of the States from adopting eligibility requirements to help narrow their own choices. As the dissent concedes, however, the Framers were unquestionably concerned that the States would simply not hold elections for federal officers, and therefore the Framers gave Congress the power to "make or alter" state election regulations. Yet under the dissent's approach, the States could achieve exactly the same result by simply setting qualifications for federal office sufficiently high that no one could meet those qualifications. In our view, it is inconceivable that the Framers would provide a specific constitutional provision to ensure that federal elections would be held while at the same time allowing States to render those elections meaningless by simply ensuring that no candidate could be qualified for office. Given the Framers' wariness over the potential for state abuse, we must conclude that the specification of fixed qualifications in the constitutional text was intended to prescribe uniform rules that would preclude modification by either Congress or the States.

We find further evidence of the Framers' intent in Art. I, §5, cl. 1, which provides: "Each House shall be the Judge of the Elections, Returns and Qualifications of its own Members." That Art. I, §5, vests a federal tribunal with ultimate authority to judge a Member's qualifications is fully consistent with the understanding that those qualifications are fixed in the Federal Constitution, but not with the understanding that they can be altered by the States. If the States had the right to prescribe additional qualifications — such as property, educational, or professional qualifications — for their own representatives, state law would provide the standard for judging a Member's eligibility. . . .

Our conclusion that States lack the power to impose qualifications vindicates the same "fundamental principle of our representative democracy" that we recognized in *Powell*, namely, that "the people should choose whom they please to govern them." . . .

Finally, state-imposed restrictions, unlike the congressionally imposed restrictions at issue in *Powell*, violate a third idea central to this basic principle: that the right to choose representatives belongs not to the States, but to the people. . . . [T]he Framers, in perhaps their most important contribution, conceived of a Federal Government directly responsible to the people, possessed of direct power over the people, and chosen directly, not by States, but by the people. The Framers implemented this ideal most clearly in the provision, extant from the beginning of the Republic, that calls for the Members of the House of Representatives to be "chosen every second Year by the People of the several States." Art. I, §2, cl. 1. Following the adoption of the Seventeenth Amendment in 1913, this ideal was extended to elections for the Senate. The Congress of the United States, therefore, is not a confederation of nations in which separate sovereigns are represented by appointed delegates, but is instead a body composed of representatives of the people. . . .

Permitting individual States to formulate diverse qualifications for their representatives would result in a patchwork of state qualifications, undermining the uniformity and the national character that the Framers envisioned and sought to ensure. . . . Such a patchwork would also sever the direct link that the Framers found so critical between the National Government and the people of the United States. . . .

Petitioners argue that, even if States may not add qualifications, Amendment 73 is constitutional because it is not such a qualification, and because Amendment 73 is a permissible exercise of state power to regulate the "Times, Places and Manner of Holding Elections." We reject these contentions.

Unlike §§1 and 2 of Amendment 73, which create absolute bars to service for long-term incumbents running for state office, §3 merely provides that certain Senators and Representatives shall not be certified as candidates and shall not have their names appear on the ballot. They may run as write-in candidates and, if elected, they may serve. Petitioners contend that only a legal bar to service creates an impermissible qualification, and that Amendment 73 is therefore consistent with the Constitution. . . .

In our view, Amendment 73 is an indirect attempt to accomplish what the Constitution prohibits Arkansas from accomplishing directly. . . . Indeed, it cannot be seriously contended that the intent behind Amendment 73 is other than to prevent the election of incumbents. The preamble of Amendment 73 states explicitly: "[T]he people of Arkansas . . . herein limit the terms of elected officials." Sections 1 and 2 create absolute limits on the number of terms that may be served. There is no hint that §3 was intended to have any other purpose.

Petitioners do, however, contest the Arkansas Supreme Court's conclusion that the Amendment has the same practical effect as an absolute bar. They argue that the possibility of a write-in campaign creates a real possibility for victory, especially for an entrenched incumbent. One may reasonably question the merits of that contention. Indeed, we are advised by the state court that there is nothing more than a faint glimmer of possibility that the excluded candidate will win. Our prior cases, too, have suggested that write-in candidates have only a slight chance of victory. But even if petitioners are correct that incumbents may occasionally win reelection as write-in candidates, there is no denying that the ballot restrictions will make it significantly more difficult for the barred candidate to win the election. In our view, an amendment with the avowed purpose and obvious effect of evading the requirements of the Qualifications Clauses by handicapping a class of candidates cannot stand. To argue otherwise is to suggest that the Framers spent significant time and energy in debating and crafting Clauses that could be easily evaded. More importantly, allowing States to evade the Qualifications Clauses by "dress[ing] eligibility to stand for Congress in ballot access clothing" trivializes the basic principles of our democracy that underlie those Clauses. Petitioners' argument treats the Qualifications Clauses not as the embodiment of a grand principle, but rather as empty formalism. . . .

Petitioners make the related argument that Amendment 73 merely regulates the "Manner" of elections, and that the Amendment is therefore a permissible exercise of state power under Article I, §4, cl. 1 (the Elections Clause), to regulate the "Times, Places and Manner" of elections. We cannot agree. . . .

A necessary consequence of petitioners' argument is that Congress itself would have the power to "make or alter" a measure such as Amendment 73. Art. I, §4, cl. 1. That the Framers would have approved of such a result is unfathomable. As our decision in *Powell* and our discussion above make clear, the Framers were particularly concerned that a grant to Congress of the authority to set its own qualifications would lead inevitably to congressional self-aggrandizement and the upsetting of the delicate constitutional balance. Petitioners would have us believe, however, that even as the Framers carefully circumscribed congressional power to set qualifications, they intended to allow Congress to achieve the same result by simply formulating the regulation as a ballot access restriction under the Elections Clause. We refuse to adopt an interpretation of the Elections Clause that would so cavalierly disregard what the Framers intended to be a fundamental constitutional safeguard.

Moreover, petitioners' broad construction of the Elections Clause is fundamentally inconsistent with the Framers' view of that Clause. The Framers intended the Elections Clause to grant States authority to create procedural regulations, not to provide States with license to exclude classes of candidates from federal office. . . .

The merits of term limits, or "rotation," have been the subject of debate since the formation of our Constitution, when the Framers unanimously rejected a proposal to add such limits to the Constitution. The cogent arguments on both sides of the question that were articulated during the process of ratification largely retain their force today. Over half the States have adopted measures that impose such limits on some offices either directly or indirectly, and the Nation as a whole, notably by constitutional amendment, has imposed a limit on the number of terms that the President may serve. Term limits, like any other qualification for office, unquestionably restrict the ability of voters to vote for whom they wish. On the other hand, such limits may provide for the infusion of fresh ideas and new perspectives, and may decrease the likelihood that representatives will lose touch with their constituents. It is not our province to resolve this longstanding debate.

We are, however, firmly convinced that allowing the several States to adopt term limits for congressional service would effect a fundamental change in the constitutional framework. Any such change must come not by legislation adopted either by Congress or by an individual State, but rather — as have other important changes in the electoral process — through the Amendment procedures set forth in Article V. . . .

The judgment is affirmed.

It is so ordered.

JUSTICE THOMAS, with whom THE CHIEF JUSTICE, JUSTICE O'CONNOR, and JUSTICE SCALIA join, dissenting. . . .

Our system of government rests on one overriding principle: All power stems from the consent of the people. To phrase the principle in this way, however, is to be imprecise about something important to the notion of "reserved" powers. The ultimate source of the Constitution's authority is the consent of the people of each individual State, not the consent of the undifferentiated people of the Nation as a whole.

The ratification procedure erected by Article VII makes this point clear. The Constitution took effect once it had been ratified by the people gathered in convention in nine different States. But the Constitution went into effect only "between the States so ratifying the same," Art. VII; it did not bind the people of North Carolina until they had accepted it. . . .

When they adopted the Federal Constitution, of course, the people of each State surrendered some of their authority to the United States (and hence to entities accountable to the people of other States as well as to themselves). They affirmatively deprived their States of certain powers, see, *e.g.,* Art. I, §10, and they affirmatively conferred certain powers upon the Federal Government, see, *e.g.,* Art. I, §8. Because the people of the several States are the only true source of power, however, the Federal Government enjoys no authority beyond what the Constitution confers: The Federal Government's powers are limited and enumerated. . . .

In each State, the remainder of the people's powers . . . are either dele-gated to the state government or retained by the people. The Federal Con-stitution does not specify which of these two possibilities obtains; it is up to the various state constitutions to declare which powers the people of each State have delegated to their state government. As far as the Federal Con-stitution is concerned, then, the States can exercise all powers that the Constitution does not withhold from them. The Federal Government and the States thus face different default rules: where the Constitution is silent about the exercise of a particular power — that is, where the Consti-tution does not speak either expressly or by necessary implication — the Federal Government lacks that power and the States enjoy it.

These basic principles are enshrined in the Tenth Amendment, which declares that all powers neither delegated to the Federal Government nor prohibited to the States "are reserved to the States respectively, or to the people." With this careful last phrase, the Amendment avoids taking any position on the division of power between the state governments and the people of the States: It is up to the people of each State to determine which "reserved" powers their state government may exercise. But the Amend-ment does make clear that powers reside at the state level except where the Constitution removes them from that level. All powers that the Constitu-tion neither delegates to the Federal Government nor prohibits to the States are controlled by the people of each State.

To be sure, when the Tenth Amendment uses the phrase "the people," it does not specify whether it is referring to the people of each State or the people of the Nation as a whole. But the latter interpretation would make the Amendment pointless: There would have been no reason to provide that where the Constitution is silent about whether a particular power resides at the state level, it might or might not do so. In addition, it would make no sense to speak of powers as being reserved to the undiffer-entiated people of the Nation as a whole, because the Constitution does not contemplate that those people will either exercise power or delegate it. The Constitution simply does not recognize any mechanism for action by the undifferentiated people of the Nation. . . .

In short, the notion of popular sovereignty that undergirds the Consti-tution does not erase state boundaries, but rather tracks them. The people of each State obviously did trust their fate to the people of the several States when they consented to the Constitution; not only did they empower the governmental institutions of the United States, but they also agreed to be bound by constitutional amendments that they themselves refused to rat-ify. See Art. V (providing that proposed amendments shall take effect upon ratification by three-quarters of the States). At the same time, however, the people of each State retained their separate political identities. . . .

I take it to be established, then, that the people of Arkansas do enjoy "reserved" powers over the selection of their representatives in Congress. Purporting to exercise those reserved powers, they have agreed among themselves that the candidates covered by §3 of Amendment 73—those whom they have already elected to three or more terms in the House of Representatives or to two or more terms in the Senate—should not be eligible to appear on the ballot for reelection, but should nonetheless be returned to Congress if enough voters are sufficiently enthusiastic about their candidacy to write in their names. . . .

The majority settles on "the Qualifications Clauses" as the constitutional provisions that Amendment 73 violates. . . .

Although the Qualifications Clauses neither state nor imply the prohibition that it finds in them, the majority infers from the Framers' "democratic principles" that the Clauses must have been generally understood to preclude the people of the States and their state legislatures from prescribing any additional qualifications for their representatives in Congress. But the majority's evidence on this point establishes only two more modest propositions: (1) the Framers did not want the Federal Constitution itself to impose a broad set of disqualifications for congressional office, and (2) the Framers did not want the Federal Congress to be able to supplement the few disqualifications that the Constitution does set forth. The logical conclusion is simply that the Framers did not want the people of the States and their state legislatures to be constrained by too many qualifications imposed at the national level. The evidence does not support the majority's more sweeping conclusion that the Framers intended to bar the people of the States and their state legislatures from adopting additional eligibility requirements to help narrow their own choices. . . .

The fact that the Framers did not grant a qualification-setting power to Congress does not imply that they wanted to bar its exercise at the state level. One reason why the Framers decided not to let Congress prescribe the qualifications of its own members was that incumbents could have used this power to perpetuate themselves or their ilk in office. . . .

As the majority argues, democratic principles also contributed to the Framers' decision to withhold the qualification-setting power from Congress. But the majority is wrong to suggest that the same principles must also have led the Framers to deny this power to the people of the States and the state legislatures. . . .

Indeed, the invocation of democratic principles to invalidate Amendment 73 seems particularly difficult in the present case, because Amendment 73 remains fully within the control of the people of Arkansas. If they wanted to repeal it (despite the 20-point margin by which they enacted it less than three years ago), they could do so by a simple majority vote.

The majority appears to believe that restrictions on eligibility for office are inherently undemocratic. But the Qualifications Clauses themselves prove that the Framers did not share this view; eligibility requirements to which the people of the States consent are perfectly consistent with the Framers' scheme. . . .

It is radical enough for the majority to hold that the Constitution implicitly precludes the people of the States from prescribing any eligibility requirements for the congressional candidates who seek their votes. This holding, after all, does not stop with negating the term limits that many States have seen fit to impose on their Senators and Representatives. Today's decision also means that no State may disqualify congressional candidates whom a court has found to be mentally incompetent, who are currently in prison, or who have past vote-fraud convictions. Likewise, after today's decision, the people of each State must leave open the possibility that they will trust someone with their vote in Congress even though they do not trust him with a vote in the election for Congress. See, *e.g.*, R.I. Gen. Laws 17-14-1.2 (1988) (restricting candidacy to people "qualified to vote"). . . .

The majority nonetheless thinks it clear that the goal of §3 is "to prevent the election of incumbents." . . . One of petitioners' central arguments is that congressionally conferred advantages have artificially inflated the pre-existing electoral chances of the covered candidates, and that Amendment 73 is merely designed to level the playing field on which challengers compete with them.

To understand this argument requires some background. Current federal law (enacted, of course, by congressional incumbents) confers numerous advantages on incumbents, and these advantages are widely thought to make it "significantly more difficult" for challengers to defeat them. For instance, federal law gives incumbents enormous advantages in building name recognition and good will in their home districts. See, *e.g.*, 39 U.S.C. §3210 (permitting Members of Congress to send "franked" mail free of charge); 2 U.S.C. §§61-1, 72a, 332 (permitting Members to have sizable taxpayer-funded staffs); 2 U.S.C. §123b (establishing the House Recording Studio and the Senate Recording and Photographic Studios). At the same time that incumbent Members of Congress enjoy these in-kind benefits, Congress imposes spending and contribution limits in congressional campaigns that "can prevent challengers from spending more . . . to overcome their disadvantage in name recognition." Many observers believe that the campaign-finance laws also give incumbents an "enormous fund-raising edge" over their challengers by giving a large financing role to entities with incentives to curry favor with incumbents. In addition, the internal rules of Congress put a substantial premium on seniority, with the result that each Member's already plentiful opportunities to distribute benefits to his constituents increase with the length of his tenure. In this manner, Congress effectively "fines" the electorate for voting against incumbents. . . .

The voters of Arkansas evidently believe that incumbents would not enjoy such overwhelming success if electoral contests were truly fair — that is, if the government did not put its thumb on either side of the scale. The majority offers no reason to question the accuracy of this belief. Given this context, petitioners portray §3 of Amendment 73 as an effort at the state level to offset the electoral advantages that congressional incumbents have conferred upon themselves at the federal level. . . .

I do not mean to suggest that States have unbridled power to handicap particular classes of candidates, even when those candidates enjoy federally conferred advantages that may threaten to skew the electoral process. But laws that allegedly have the purpose and effect of handicapping a particular class of candidates traditionally are reviewed under the First and Fourteenth Amendments rather than the Qualifications Clauses. . . . Term-limit measures have tended to survive such review without difficulty. . . .

NOTES AND QUESTIONS

1. *Powell v. McCormack revisited.* Both the majority and dissent must address the *Powell* decision in arriving at their own opinion concerning term limits. Both affirm its doctrine. For the majority that affirmation is basically determinative. For the dissent it seems almost insignificant. What are the different analytical views of *Powell* that lead to such different evaluations of *Powell's* importance?

2. *Of states and people.* Another key difference between the majority and dissent is their views of the Tenth Amendment. What are their different views and how do they affect each opinion?

3. *Term limits as the regulation of elections.* Respondents argue that term limits are not qualifications for office, but a ballot-access issue, the regulation of which is permitted under Article I, §4 of the Constitution. The argument characterizing term limits as regulatory is premised on the existence of the write-in alternative available to the incumbent. Why is this a pivotal point to the advocates?

The Scarlet Letter Alternative

U.S. Term Limits v. Thornton did not halt the efforts of congressional term limit proponents. Attention shifted to efforts to amend the Constitution to include a term limit provision. In March of 1995, a vote in the House of Representatives fell short of the two-thirds majority required for adoption of the proposed amendment to limit congressional service to no more than 12 years. A bill establishing an advisory referendum on term limits was introduced in the House of Representatives in June of 1997, but no action has yet been taken. Proponents of term limits attempted a somewhat unusual approach on the state level. In about a dozen states (as of 1998) initiative laws required the placement of ballot designations, such as "violated voter instruction on term limits" next to the names of candidates who did not support the term limit amendment in specific ways set forth in the initiative law. These "scarlet letter" laws were successfully challenged in various courts on a number of theories before finally ending up before the Supreme Court in Cook v. Gralike. Internal citations and footnotes have been omitted except where particularly relevant.

Cook v. Gralike
531 U.S. 510 (2001)

JUSTICE STEVENS delivered the opinion of the Court.

In U.S. Term Limits, Inc. v. Thornton, we reviewed a challenge to an Arkansas law that prohibited the name of an otherwise eligible candidate for the United States Congress from appearing on the general election ballot if he or she had already served three terms in the House of Representatives or two terms in the Senate. We held that the ballot restriction was an indirect attempt to impose term limits on congressional incumbents that violated the Qualifications Clauses in Article I of the Constitution rather than a permissible exercise of the State's power to regulate the "Times, Places and Manner of holding Elections for Senators and Representatives" within the meaning of Article I, §4, cl. 1.

In response to that decision, the voters of Missouri adopted in 1996 an amendment to Article VIII of their State Constitution designed to lead to the adoption of a specified "Congressional Term Limits Amendment" to the Federal Constitution. At issue in this case is the constitutionality of Article VIII.

I

Article VIII "instruct[s]" each Member of Missouri's congressional delegation "to use all of his or her delegated powers to pass the Congressional Term Limits Amendment" set forth in §16 of the Article. Mo. Const., Art. VIII, §17(1). That proposed amendment would limit service in the United States Congress to three terms in the House of Representatives and two terms in the Senate. . . .

Three provisions in Article VIII combine to advance its purpose. Section 17 prescribes that the statement "DISREGARDED VOTERS' INSTRUCTION ON TERM LIMITS" be printed on all primary and general ballots adjacent to the name of a Senator or Representative who fails to take any one of eight legislative acts in support of the proposed amendment. Section 18 provides that the statement "DECLINED TO PLEDGE TO SUPPORT TERM LIMITS" be printed on all primary and general election ballots next to the name of every nonincumbent congressional candidate who refuses to take a "Term Limit" pledge that commits the candidate, if elected, to performing the legislative acts enumerated in §17. And §19 directs the Missouri Secretary of State to determine and declare, pursuant to §§17 and 18, whether either statement should be printed alongside the name of each candidate for Congress. . . .

Respondent Don Gralike was a nonincumbent candidate for election in 1998 to the United States House of Representatives from Missouri's Third Congressional District. . . .

II

Article VIII furthers the State's interest in adding a term limits amendment to the Federal Constitution in two ways. It encourages Missouri's congressional delegation to support such an amendment in order to avoid an unfavorable ballot designation when running for reelection. And it encourages the election of representatives who favor such an amendment. Petitioner argues that Article VIII is an exercise of the "right of the people to instruct" their representatives reserved by the Tenth Amendment, and that it is a permissible regulation of the "manner" of electing federal legislators within the authority delegated to the States by the Elections Clause, Art. I, §4, cl. 1. Because these two arguments rely on different sources of state power, it is appropriate at the outset to review the distinction in kind between powers reserved to the States and those delegated to the States by the Constitution.

As we discussed at length in *U.S. Term Limits*, the Constitution "draws a basic distinction between the powers of the newly created Federal Government and the powers retained by the preexisting sovereign States." On the one hand, in the words of Chief Justice Marshall, "it was neither necessary nor proper to define the powers retained by the States. These powers proceed, not from the people of America, but from the people of the several States; and remain, after the adoption of the constitution, what they were before, except so far as they may be abridged by that instrument." The text of the Tenth Amendment delineates this principle:

> The powers not delegated to the United States by the Constitution, nor prohibited by it to the States, are reserved to the States respectively, or to the people.

On the other hand, as Justice Story observed, "the states can exercise no powers whatsoever, which exclusively spring out of the existence of the national government, which the constitution did not delegate to them." Simply put, "[n]o state can say, that it has reserved, what it never possessed."

III

To be persuasive, petitioner's argument that Article VIII is a valid exercise of the State's reserved power to give binding instructions to its representatives would have to overcome three hurdles. First, the historical precedents on which she relies for the proposition that the States have such a reserved power are distinguishable. Second, there is countervailing historical evidence. Third, and of decisive significance, the means employed to issue the instructions, ballots for congressional elections, are unacceptable unless Article VIII is a permissible exercise of the State's power to regulate the manner of holding elections for Senators and Representatives. Only a brief comment on the first two points is necessary.

Petitioner relies heavily on the part instructions played in the Second Continental Congress, the Constitutional Convention, the early Congress, the selection of United States Senators before the passage of the Seventeenth Amendment, and the ratification of certain federal constitutional amendments. However, unlike Article VIII, none of petitioner's examples was coupled with an express legal sanction for disobedience. At best, as an *amicus curiae* for petitioner points out, and as petitioner herself acknowledges, such historical instructions at one point in the early Republic may have had "de facto binding force" because it might have been "political suicide" not to follow them. This evidence falls short of demonstrating that either the people or the States had a right to give legally binding, *i.e.*, nonadvisory, instructions to their representatives that the Tenth Amendment reserved, much less that such a right would apply to federal representatives. . . .

Indeed, contrary evidence is provided by the fact that the First Congress rejected a proposal to insert a right of the people "to instruct their representatives" into what would become the First Amendment. The fact that the proposal was made suggests that its proponents thought it necessary, and the fact that it was rejected by a vote of 41 to 10, suggests that we should give weight to the views of those who opposed the proposal. It was their view that binding instructions would undermine an essential attribute of Congress by eviscerating the deliberative nature of that National Assembly. ("[W]hen the people have chosen a representative, it is his duty to meet others from the different parts of the Union, and consult, and agree with them to such acts as are for the general benefit of the whole community. If they were to be guided by instructions, there would be no use in deliberation; all that a man would have to do, would be to produce his instructions, and lay them on the table, and let them speak for him"). . . .

In any event, even assuming the existence of the reserved right that petitioner asserts (and that Article VIII falls within its ambit), the question remains whether the State may use ballots for congressional elections as a means of giving its instructions binding force.

IV

The federal offices at stake "aris[e] from the Constitution itself." U.S. Term Limits, Inc. v. Thornton, 514 U.S., at 805. Because any state authority to regulate election to those offices could not precede their very creation by the Constitution, such power "had to be delegated to, rather than reserved by, the States." ... Through the Elections Clause, the Constitution delegated to the States the power to regulate the "Times, Places and Manner of holding Elections for Senators and Representatives," subject to a grant of authority to Congress to "make or alter such Regulations." No other constitutional provision gives the States authority over congressional elections, and no such authority could be reserved under the Tenth Amendment. By process of elimination, the States may regulate the incidents of such elections, including balloting, only within the exclusive delegation of power under the Elections Clause.

With respect to the Elections Clause, petitioner argues that Article VIII "merely regulates the manner in which elections are held by disclosing information about congressional candidates." As such, petitioner concludes, Article VIII is a valid exercise of Missouri's delegated power.

We disagree. To be sure, the Elections Clause grants to the States "broad power" to prescribe the procedural mechanisms for holding congressional elections. Nevertheless, Article VIII falls outside of that grant of authority. As we made clear in *U.S. Term Limits*, "the Framers understood the Elections Clause as a grant of authority to issue procedural regulations, and not as a source of power to dictate electoral outcomes, to favor or disfavor a class of candidates, or to evade important constitutional restraints." Article VIII is not a procedural regulation. It does not regulate the time of elections; it does not regulate the place of elections; nor, we believe, does it regulate the manner of elections. As to the last point, Article VIII bears no relation to the "manner" of elections as we understand it, for in our commonsense view that term encompasses matters like "notices, registration, supervision of voting, protection of voters, prevention of fraud and corrupt practices, counting of votes, duties of inspectors and canvassers, and making and publication of election returns." In short, Article VIII is not among "the numerous requirements as to procedure and safe-guards which experience shows are necessary in order to enforce the fundamental right involved."

Rather, Article VIII is plainly designed to favor candidates who are willing to support the particular form of a term limits amendment set forth in its text and to disfavor those who either oppose term limits entirely or would prefer a different proposal. As noted, the state provision does not just "instruct" each member of Missouri's congressional delegation to promote in certain ways the passage of the specified term limits amendment. It also attaches a concrete consequence to noncompliance — the printing of the statement "DISREGARDED VOTERS' INSTRUCTIONS ON TERM LIMITS" by the candidate's name on all primary and general election ballots. Likewise, a nonincumbent candidate who does not pledge to follow the instruction receives the ballot designation "DECLINED TO PLEDGE TO SUPPORT TERM LIMITS."

In describing the two labels, the courts below have employed terms such as "pejorative," "negative," "derogatory," "intentionally intimidating," "particularly harmful," "politically damaging," "a serious sanction," "a penalty," and "official denunciation." The general counsel to petitioner's office, no less, has denominated the labels as "the Scarlet Letter." We agree with the sense of these descriptions. They convey the substantial political risk the ballot labels impose on current and prospective congressional members who, for one reason or another, fail to comply with the conditions set forth in Article VIII for passing its term limits amendment. . . .

Indeed, it seems clear that the adverse labels handicap candidates "at the most crucial stage in the election process — the instant before the vote is cast." At the same time, "by directing the citizen's attention to the single consideration" of the candidates' fidelity to term limits, the labels imply that the issue "is an important — perhaps paramount — consideration in the citizen's choice, which may decisively influence the citizen to cast his ballot" against candidates branded as unfaithful. While the precise damage the labels may exact on candidates is disputed between the parties, the labels surely place their targets at a political disadvantage to unmarked candidates for congressional office. Thus, far from regulating the procedural mechanisms of elections, Article VIII attempts to "dictate electoral outcomes." Such "regulation" of congressional elections simply is not authorized by the Elections Clause. . . .

Accordingly, the judgment of the Court of Appeals is affirmed.

It is so ordered.

Justice Kennedy, concurring.

I join the opinion of the Court, holding §15 et seq. of Article VIII of the Missouri Constitution violative of the Constitution of the United States. It seems appropriate, however, to add these brief observations with respect to Part III of the opinion. The Court does not say the States are disabled from requesting specific action from Congress or from expressing their concerns to it. As the Court holds, however, the mechanism the State seeks to employ here goes well beyond this prerogative.

A State is not permitted to interpose itself between the people and their National Government as it seeks to do here. Whether a State's concern is with the proposed enactment of a constitutional amendment or an ordinary federal statute it simply lacks the power to impose any conditions on the election of Senators and Representatives, save neutral provisions as to the time, place, and manner of elections pursuant to Article I, §4. . . .

The dispositive principle in this case is fundamental to the Constitution, to the idea of federalism, and to the theory of representative government. The principle is that Senators and Representatives in the National Government are responsible to the people who elect them, not to the States in which they reside. The Constitution was ratified by Conventions in the several States, not by the States themselves, U.S. Const., Art. VII, a historical fact and a constitutional imperative which underscore the proposition that the Constitution was ordained and established by the people of the United States. U.S. Const., preamble. The idea of federalism is that a National Legislature enacts laws which bind the people as individuals, not as citizens of a State; and, it follows, freedom is most secure if the people themselves, not the States as intermediaries, hold their federal legislators to account for the conduct of their office. . . .

This said, it must be noted that when the Constitution was enacted, respectful petitions to legislators were an accepted mode of urging legislative action. This right is preserved to individuals (the people) in the First Amendment. Even if a State, as an entity, is not itself protected by the Petition Clause, there is no principle prohibiting a state legislature from following a parallel course and by a memorial resolution requesting the Congress of the United States to pay heed to certain state concerns. From the earliest days of our Republic to the present time, States have done so in the context of federal legislation. Indeed, the situation was even more complex in the early days of our Nation, when Senators were appointed by state legislatures rather than directly elected. At that time, it appears that some state legislatures followed a practice of instructing the Senators whom they had appointed to pass legislation, while only requesting that the Representatives, who had been elected by the people, do so. I do not believe that the situation should be any different with respect to a proposed constitutional amendment, and indeed history bears this out. . . .

CHIEF JUSTICE REHNQUIST, with whom JUSTICE O'CONNOR joins, concurring in the judgment.

I would affirm the judgment of the Court of Appeals, but on the ground that Missouri's Article VIII violates the First Amendment to the United States Constitution. Specifically, I believe that Article VIII violates the First Amendment right of a political candidate, once lawfully on the ballot, to have his name appear unaccompanied by pejorative language required by the State. . . .

. . . Article VIII is not only not content neutral, but it actually discriminates on the basis of viewpoint because only those candidates who fail to conform to the State's position receive derogatory labels. The result is that the State injects itself into the election process at an absolutely critical point — the composition of the ballot, which is the last thing the voter sees before he makes his choice — and does so in a way that is not neutral as to issues or candidates. The candidates who are thus singled out have no means of replying to their designation which would be equally effective with the voter. . . .

NOTES AND QUESTIONS

1. *The meaning of representation.* On pages 444-447 we discuss the representative relationship. What view of that relationship does this case

favor? Does the case depend on a trustee theory, or could you rule the same way even if you were a fan of the delegate theory? Would it have made a difference to the court if the designation was simply a symbol indicating support or opposition to the term limit amendment?

2. *Constitutional amendment versus statute?* Assume that a state wanted to make sure that its congressional representatives always voted against Medicaid funding for abortion. Through a referendum that state adopted a "law" that required candidates to take an oath to always vote against Medicaid funding of abortions, and required the secretary of state of that state to place the phrase "OATH REFUSER" next to the name of any candidate who refused to take such an oath and the phrase "OATH BREAKER" next to the name of any incumbent who had voted contrary to the oath. How would the *Gralike* Court rule on such a law?

C.   THE ELECTION FOR LEGISLATIVE OFFICE

Elections, as noted earlier, are the most significant legitimizing steps of the legislative process. It is through elections, primarily, that the public exercises power over the legislative process and the behavior of its elected representatives. It is also through elections that the public's views begin their path to becoming public policy. On this James Madison wrote:

> As it is essential to liberty that the government in general, should have a common interest with the people; so it is particularly essential that the branch of it under consideration [legislative branch] should have an immediate dependence on, & an intimate sympathy with the people. Frequent elections are unquestionably the only policy by which this dependency and policy can be effectually secured.

The Federalist No. 52, at 355 (James Madison) (Jacob E. Cooke ed., 1961).

For candidates, of course, elections are the way they become and remain legislators. As the political scientist David Mayhew has observed about members of Congress "[r]e-election underlies everything else, as indeed it should, if we are to expect that the relation between politicians and public will be one of accountability." David R. Mayhew, The Electoral Connection and the Congress, *reprinted in* Congress: Structure and Policy 19 (Matthew D. McCubbins and Terry Sullivan eds., 1987). The connection between election and the behavior of legislators, as might be expected, has been the subject of considerable study by political scientists, and it is one we touch on a number of times in this book. The general view (one that the authors share based on their experience) is that while reelection is extremely important to legislators, it is not their sole goal nor their sole consideration, but a means for them to accomplish their other goals:

> Its [Congress'] members — most of them, anyway — have other goals besides reelection. Holding office may be essential to the achievement of these other ends, but it is only worth the effort because it allows their pursuit. Richard Fenno has identified making good public policy and earning influence and respect in Washington as the most important of these goals.

Gary C. Jacobson, The Politics of Congressional Elections 182 (2d ed. 1987). See generally id.; John W. Kingdon, Congressmen's Voting Decisions (3d ed. 1989); Congress: Structure and Policy (Matthew D. McCubbins and Terry Sullivan eds., 1987). The election-legislative behavior relationship raises some thorny questions. Philosophically, there is the question of how much duty is owed by the legislator to the wishes of his or her constituents. Politically, there is the almost unresolvable question of how a legislator is to account for the conflicting demands of the public that a legislator simultaneously be above the political fray and yet remain the advocate of local interests. These problems will be explored later in Section D of this chapter.

In this section, attention is on the electoral process and its regulation. Four topics are covered: access to the ballot for prospective legislative candidates; financing of legislative campaigns; use of legislative resources by incumbents in campaigns; and the power of legislative bodies to judge legislative elections.

The regulation of the election process has historically been a matter of state jurisdiction. For state legislative elections, this is a matter of federalism, although, as is evident from the cases in the preceding section, state discretion is circumscribed by the Constitution. But for Congress, this is a tradition that flows from Article I, §4 of the Constitution: "The Time, Places and Manner of holding Elections for Senators and Representatives, shall be prescribed in each State by the Legislature thereof; but the Congress may at any time by Law make or alter such Regulations, except as to the Places of Chusing Senators." Over the years, Congress has acted to impose some regulation on federal legislative elections: requiring a national election day; establishing single member districts for the House of Representatives; regulating the financing of congressional campaigns; and lowering the voting age for federal elections to 18. Numerous subjects, such as those that relate to ballot access, remain under state control.

1. Ballot Access

The decision to run for legislative office does not assure a candidacy. Since the advent of ballots printed and provided by state government (known as

"Australian" ballots) in the latter part of the nineteenth century, states have increasingly regulated ballot access to reduce corruption and the confusion from multiple candidacies for the same office. See Eldon C. Evans, A History of the Australian Ballot in the United States (1917). Every state has some regulatory channels that must be navigated to gain a ballot berth, whether as the candidate of a political party or as an independent candidate. Requirements of petition signatures or fees or both are typical.

Such regulation has also had the effect, in some cases, to reduce opportunities for political participation. Simply put, the higher the barriers to ballot access, the fewer the candidates. It is this point that is explored in all of the ballot access cases, as exemplified by the following case. Internal citations and footnotes have been omitted except where particularly relevant.

Lubin v. Panish
415 U.S. 709 (1974)

CHIEF JUSTICE BURGER delivered the opinion of the Court.

We granted certiorari to consider petitioner's claim that the California statute requiring payment of a filing fee of $701.60 in order to be placed on the ballot in the primary election for nomination to the position of County Supervisor, while providing no alternative means of access to the ballot, deprived him, as an indigent person unable to pay the fee, and others similarly situated, of the equal protection guaranteed by the Fourteenth Amendment and rights of expression and association guaranteed by the First Amendment.

The California Elections Code provides that forms required for nomination and election to congressional, state, and county offices are to be issued to candidates only upon prepayment of a nonrefundable filing fee. Cal. Elections Code §6551. Generally, the required fees are fixed at a percentage of the salary for the office sought. The fee for candidates for United States Senator . . . is 2% of the annual salary. Candidates for Representative to Congress, State Senator or Assemblyman . . . must pay 1% . . .

Under the California statutes in effect at the time this suit was commenced, the required candidate filing fees ranged from $192 for State Assembly, $425 for Congress, . . . [to] $850 for United States Senator. . . .

The California statute provides for the counting of write-in votes subject to certain conditions. §18600 et seq. (Supp. 1974). Write-in votes are not counted, however, unless the person desiring to be a write-in candidate files a statement to that effect with the Registrar-Recorder at least eight days prior to the election, §18602, and pays the requisite filing fee, §18603. . . .

In his complaint, petitioner maintained that he was a citizen and a voter and that he had sought nomination as a candidate . . . [and that he] was denied the requested nomination papers orally and in writing solely because he was unable to pay the $701.60 filing fee required of all would-be candidates for the office of Board of Supervisors. . . .

Historically, since the Progressive movement of the early 20th century, there has been a steady trend toward limiting the size of the ballot in order to "concentrate the attention of the electorate on the selection of a much smaller number of officials and so afford to the voters the opportunity of exercising more discrimination in their use of the franchise." This desire to limit the size of the ballot has been variously phrased as a desire to minimize voter confusion, to limit the number of runoff elections, to curb "ballot flooding," and to prevent the overwhelming of voting machines— the modern counterpart of ballot flooding. A majority of States have long required the payment of some form of filing fee, in part to limit the ballot and in part to have candidates pay some of the administrative costs.

In sharp contrast to this fear of an unduly lengthy ballot is an increasing pressure for broader access to the ballot. Thus, while progressive thought in the first half of the century was concerned with restricting the ballot to achieve voting rationality, recent decades brought an enlarged demand for an expansion of political opportunity. The Twenty-fifth Amendment, the Twenty-sixth Amendment, and the Voting Rights Act of 1965, 79 Stat. 437, 42 U.S.C. §1973 et seq., reflect this shift in emphasis. There has also been a gradual enlargement of the Fourteenth Amendment's equal protection provision in the area of voting rights. . . . This principle flows naturally from our recognition that

> legislators are elected by voters, not farms or cities or economic interests. As long as ours is a representative form of government, and our legislatures are those instruments of government elected directly by and directly representative of the people, the right to elect legislators in a free and unimpaired fashion is a bedrock of our political system.

Reynolds v. Sims, 377 U.S. 533, 562 (1964) (Warren, C.J.).

The present case draws these two means of achieving an effective, representative political system into apparent conflict and presents the question of how to accommodate the desire for increased ballot access with the imperative of protecting the integrity of the electoral system from the recognized dangers of ballots listing so many candidates as to undermine the process of giving expression to the will of the majority. The petitioner stated on oath that he is without assets or income and cannot pay the $701.60 filing fee although he is otherwise legally eligible to be a candidate on the primary ballot. Since his affidavit of indigency states that he has no resources and earned no income whatever in 1972, it would appear that he would make the same claim whether the filing fee had been fixed at $1, $100, or $700. The State accepts this as true but defends the statutory fee as necessary to keep the ballot from being overwhelmed with frivolous or otherwise nonserious candidates, arguing that as to indigents the filing fee is not intended as a test of his pocketbook but the extent of his political support and hence the seriousness of his candidacy.

In Bullock v. Carter, 405 U.S. 134 (1972), we recognized that the State's interest in keeping its ballots within manageable, understandable limits is of the highest order. The role of the primary election process in California is underscored by its importance as a component of the total electoral process and its special function to assure that fragmentation of voter choice is minimized. That function is served, not frustrated, by a procedure that tends to regulate the filing of frivolous candidates. A procedure inviting or permitting every citizen to present himself to the voters on the ballot without some means of measuring the seriousness of the candidate's desire and motivation would make rational voter choices more difficult because of the size of the ballot and hence would tend to impede the electoral process. That no device can be conjured to eliminate every frivolous candidacy does not undermine the State's effort to eliminate as many such as possible.

That "laundry list" ballots discourage voter participation and confuse and frustrate those who do participate is too obvious to call for extended discussion. The means of testing the seriousness of a given candidacy may be open to debate; the fundamental importance of ballots of reasonable size limited to serious candidates with some prospects of public support is not. Rational results within the framework of our system are not likely to be reached if the ballot for a single office must list a dozen or more aspirants who are relatively unknown or have no prospects of success.

This legitimate state interest, however, must be achieved by a means that does not unfairly or unnecessarily burden either a minority party's or an individual candidate's equally important interest in the continued availability of political opportunity. The interests involved are not merely those of parties or individual candidates; the voters can assert their preferences only through candidates or parties or both and it is this broad interest that must be weighed in the balance. The right of a party or an individual to a place on a ballot is entitled to protection and is intertwined with the rights of voters.

> The right to vote is heavily burdened if that vote may be cast only for one of two parties at a time when other parties are clamoring for a place on the ballot.

Williams v. Rhodes, 393 U.S. 23, 31 (1968). This must also mean that the right to vote is "heavily burdened" if that vote may be cast only for one of two candidates in a primary election at a time when other candidates are clamoring for a place on the ballot. It is to be expected that a voter hopes to find on the ballot a candidate who comes near to reflecting his policy preferences on contemporary issues. This does not mean every voter can be assured that a candidate to his liking will be on the ballot, but the process of qualifying candidates for a place on the ballot may not constitutionally be measured solely in dollars. . . .

Filing fees, however large, do not, in and of themselves, test the genuineness of a candidacy or the extent of the voter support of an aspirant for public office. A large filing fee may serve the legitimate function of keeping ballots manageable but, standing alone, it is not a certain test of whether the candidacy is serious or spurious. A wealthy candidate with not the remotest chance of election may secure a place on the ballot by writing a check. Merchants and other entrepreneurs have been known to run for public office simply to make their names known to the public. We have also noted that prohibitive filing fees, such as those in *Bullock*, can effectively exclude serious candidates. Conversely, if the filing fee is more moderate, as here, impecunious but serious candidates may be prevented from running. Even in this day of high-budget political campaigns some candidates have demonstrated that direct contact with thousands of voters by "walking tours" is a route to success. Whatever may be the political mood at any given time, our tradition has been one of hospitality toward all candidates without regard to their economic status.

The absence of any alternative means of gaining access to the ballot inevitably renders the California system exclusionary as to some aspirants. As we have noted, the payment of a fee is an absolute, not an alternative, condition, and failure to meet it is a disqualification from running for office. Thus, California has chosen to achieve the important and legitimate interest of maintaining the integrity of elections by means which can operate to exclude some potentially serious candidates from the ballot without providing them with any alternative means of coming before the voters. Selection of candidates solely on the basis of ability to pay a fixed fee without providing any alternative means is not reasonably necessary to the accomplishment of the State's legitimate election interests. Accordingly, we hold that in the absence of reasonable alternative means of ballot access, a State may not, consistent with constitutional standards, require from an indigent candidate filing fees he cannot pay.

In so holding, we note that there are obvious and well-known means of testing the "seriousness" of a candidacy which do not measure the probability of attracting significant voter support solely by the neutral fact of payment of a filing fee. States may, for example, impose on minor political parties the precondition of demonstrating the existence of some reasonable quantum of voter support by requiring such parties to file petitions for a place on the ballot signed by a percentage of those who voted in a prior election. . . .

JUSTICE BLACKMUN, with whom JUSTICE REHNQUIST joins, concurring in part.

For me, the difficulty with the California election system is the absence of a realistic alternative access to the ballot for the candidate whose indigency renders it impossible for him to pay the prescribed filing fee.

In addition to a proper petitioning process suggested by the Court in its opinion, I would regard a write-in procedure, free of fee, as an acceptable alternative. Prior to 1968, California allowed this, and write-in votes were counted, although no prior fee had been paid. But the prior fee requirement for the write-in candidate was incorporated into the State's Elections Code in that year, Laws 1968, c. 79, §3, and is now §18603(b) of the Code. It is that addition, by amendment, that serves to deny the petitioner the equal protection guaranteed to him by the Fourteenth Amendment. . . .

I would hold that the California election statutes are unconstitutional insofar as they presently deny access to the ballot. If §18603(b) were to be stricken, the Code, as before, would permit write-in access with no prior fee. The presence of that alternative, although not perfect, surely provides the indigent would-be candidate with as much ease of access to the ballot as the alternative of obtaining a large number of petition signatures in a relatively short time. The Court seemingly would reject a write-in alternative while accepting many petition alternatives. In my view, a write-in procedure, such as California's before 1968, satisfies the demands of the Equal Protection Clause as well as most petitioning procedures. I, therefore, join the Court in reversing the order of the Supreme Court of California denying petitioner's petition for writ of mandate and in remanding the case for further proceedings.

NOTES AND QUESTIONS

1. *The rights protected and balanced.* What are the rights of the petitioner the Court seeks to protect, and where are they found in the Constitution? What is the right of the state? How does the Court evaluate the competing interests?

2. *The California response.* California responded to the *Lubin* decision by amending its election law to provide a petition alternative. What do you think of this as a solution?

3. *The write-in alternative.* Justices Rehnquist and Blackmun concurred in the decision but stated that if California had a write-in alternative without a fee, they would have dissented. How do you think the majority would have ruled? A write-in candidacy takes a special organizing effort. Voters must make a unique effort to ignore the familiar party candidates, whose names are printed on the ballots, and the ease of using levers or electronic buttons to vote. They must affirmatively write the name of the candidates in the spaces provided. Is this a real alternative? Can you think of any race in which a write-in candidate ran, did well, or won?

4. *Lee v. Keith — signature, filing date, and primary election restrictions.* In 1975 and 1979 the state of Illinois made two major changes to its ballot access laws with regard to independent candidates. The deadline for

independents to file nominating petitions was pushed back from 92 days before the November general election to 323 days, and the signature requirement for independent candidates was increased from 5 percent to 10 percent of the vote in the last general election for the office sought. Additionally, the legislature imposed a restriction whereby any voter who signed an independent candidate's nominating petition was disqualified from voting in the primary election. "These changes had a dramatic impact. Before 1975, independent candidates for the state legislature qualified for the ballot occasionally, though not frequently. Since 1980, however — the year following the second of these changes — not a single independent candidate for state legislative office has qualified for ballot access." Lee v. Keith, 463 F.3d 763, 764 (7th Cir. 2006).

David Lee, who wished to run as an independent candidate for the Illinois State Senate in the 2004 general election, was unable to acquire the necessary signatures by the filing deadline. After failing in his campaign bid, Lee filed suit against the members of the Illinois State Board of Elections to challenge the ballot access restrictions. He claimed that "the restrictions violated his First and Fourteenth Amendment rights as a candidate and voter by erecting an unconstitutionally high barrier to ballot access for independent candidates running for the state legislature." Id. at 765. The Court of Appeals for the 7th Circuit held that "the ballot access restrictions Illinois places on independent . . . candidates — the early filing deadline and the 10% signature requirement, together with the corresponding restriction disqualifying an independent candidate's petition signers from voting in the primary — combine to severely burden Lee's . . . rights as a candidate and voter." Id. at 772.

In finding the statutes unconstitutional, the court concluded that "[b]allot access barriers this high — they are the most restrictive in the nation and have effectively eliminated independent legislative candidacies from the Illinois political scene for a quarter of a century — are not sustainable on the state's asserted interest in deterring party splintering, factionalism, and frivolous candidacies." Id. at 765. Are there other state interests involved that may have justified the use of Illinois' ballot access devices? What are they? Would the court have come to a different conclusion if Illinois' ballot access restrictions were less restrictive than those in other states?

5. *A question of mootness.* In *Lee*, the Court of Appeals assumed jurisdiction on the theory that, despite the fact the general election was long over, this was a "case where the controversy is capable of repetition, yet evading review." Id. at 767 (quoting Nader v. Keith, 385 F.3d 729, 735 (7th Cir. 2004)). On the issue of standing, does it matter that Lee withdrew his bid for the Illinois State Senate prior to the 2004 November election? What if Lee were seeking an injunction placing his name on the ballot? What if he sought an injunction before the submission or even the collection of any petitions? See, e.g., Tobin for Governor v. Ill. State Bd. of Elections, 268 F.3d 517, 528-29 (7th Cir. 2001).

A Problem on Ballot Access

New York is among the most difficult states for non-party-backed candidates to gain ballot access. Almost 50 percent of the nation's election litigation flows from the New York system. Its complexity is described in the critical findings of the New York State Commission on Government Integrity in its 1991 report:

> [In New York] a candidate seeking to run in a party's primary election is required to file petitions containing the signatures of a substantial number of voters enrolled in the party. The petition process has been justly criticized by one appellate court as "a maze, whose corridors are compounded by hurdles, to be negotiated by only the wariest of candidates." The procedural vagaries of the law are indeed overwhelming both in their complexity and their rigidity.
>
> The genuine signature of an eligible voter may be invalidated for any one of a number of technical reasons. For example, as in only a handful of other states, a voter's signature must be accompanied by the voter's assembly and election districts as well as the voter's address; if that information is not correctly provided, the voter's signature will not be counted. Likewise, a voter's signature will not be counted if it is not dated or if the voter makes an alteration which the subscribing witness neglects to initial.
>
> Other technical defects may result in the invalidation of entire petitions. For example, the law requires a subscribing witness to reside within the political district in which the witness gathers signatures. A petition may be invalidated simply because the subscribing witness is registered to vote in a district in New York State other than the one in which the signatures must be obtained. Similarly, if the subscribing witness fails to date a petition, or misstates or omits various information, such as the witness' address or assembly and election districts, the entire petition will be invalidated.
>
> Moreover, New York is the only state that requires cover sheets to be filed along with petitions. Cover sheets must state the total number of pages in the petition as well as the total number of signatures. If the petition designates more than one candidate for public office, the cover sheet must also include additional information, such as the total number of signatures in support of each individual candidate and the page numbers of the sheets on which those signatures are located. A petition containing the required number of valid signatures may be totally discounted if the cover sheet contains an innocent misstatement or omission.
>
> There are additional requirements when the petitions contain more than one volume. The pages in each volume must be numbered consecutively, and each volume must include a cover sheet listing such information as the number of the volume, the total number of pages in the volume, and the total number of signatures in the volume. When some of the volumes of a petition fail to comply with these procedural requirements, the entire petition may be ruled invalid, even if the other volumes are free of error and contain more than enough genuine signatures.
>
> Finally, the law strictly regulates how and when petitions are filed. For example, a petition may be invalidated if its pages are not correctly bound

together and consecutively numbered. Likewise, if a petition is not filed during the precise period of time specified by the law, the candidate may be denied a place on the ballot.

Government Ethics Reform for the 1990s, 304-07 (Bruce A. Green ed., 1991). Assume you are a district court judge weighing a challenge to this ballot access system. What is your judgment and its basis? The courts in New York have traditionally interpreted the state election law narrowly, claiming that changes have to come from the legislature. In 1993, the New York system was slightly amended to permit the courts more discretion in enforcing cover page requirements.

2.   *The Financing of Campaigns*

Campaigns for legislative office cost money. Money enables the candidates to wage their campaigns and it is through this money that they inform the public of their candidacy. As Professor Herbert Alexander, one of the nation's leading campaign finance scholars, has remarked, "Money — lots of it — is essential to the smooth conduct of our system of free elections." Herbert E. Alexander, Financing Politics 2 (3d ed. 1984).

To conduct campaigns in the 2004 election cycle, congressional candidates spent $1.3 billion, an increase of about $560 million over 1998. This increase may partly be attributable to the ban on soft money instituted with the passage of the Bipartisan Campaign Reform Act of 2002 (BCRA) (Pub. L. No. 107-155), which we discuss in depth on pages 401-403.

Soft money, or the unregulated money contributed to and spent by political parties on behalf of their legislative candidates, was once a major component of every political campaign at the national level. Regardless, campaign expenditures have been seen by some scholars as relatively small for the task they are intended to accomplish. For example, Professor Alexander has written:

> Relatively speaking, the dollar price of U.S. elections is not high. The $2.7 billion spent for campaigns in 1988 was a fraction of 1 percent of the amounts spent by federal, state, county, and municipal governments — and that is what politics is all about, gaining control of governments to decide policies on, among other things, how tax money will be spent. The $500 million spent to elect a president in 1988, including prenomination campaigns and minor party candidates, was only a little more than what Americans spend in one year on cosmetic surgery. And compared with what is spent in other nations on elections, the U.S. total is not excessive — the average costs fall somewhere near the middle, clustered with costs in India and Japan. The cost per voter in Israel is far higher than in the United States.

Herbert E. Alexander, Financing Politics 91 (4th ed. 1992).

Campaign finance has been a subject of considerable public and political concern since the beginning of the twentieth century. In recent decades, at least, campaigns seem expensive. The costs are, except for the presidential campaigns after 1972 and some state and municipal campaigns, funded privately. This has meant that those with substantial wealth can fund their own campaigns, but most candidates must raise their campaign funds from others. In this latter process, efficiency dictates that those with more wealth or access to wealth will receive more attention than those with less. Both situations impact public attitudes toward campaign financing. The more candidates search for money, the more the public believes that candidates' policy views are influenced by wealth. This skepticism undermines the legitimacy of legislative policy making.

> The American system is rooted in the assumption of political equality — "one person, one vote." But money, which candidates need to harvest votes, is not distributed equally. The substantial inequities of political financing have hindered the quest for political equality and have worried concerned Americans since the beginning of the twentieth century.

Herbert E. Alexander, Financing Politics 2 (4th ed. 1992).

The nature of political campaigns has also changed since the 1960s. Increased dependency on electronic media and the decline of the political party have dramatically increased the cost of campaigns and required candidates to pay more and more attention to the fund-raising task, increasing public skepticism.

Frank J. Sorauf, Inside Campaign Finance 2-5 (1992): For most of the twentieth century American campaign finance was ruled by the political parties and their sleekly affluent "fat cats." The parties dominated finance because they dominated the campaigns themselves. . . . Much of the party-centered campaigning needed no cash; it rested heavily on services volunteered or bartered for some party-controlled favor. But when the campaign needed cash, the party raised it — often from the candidates themselves, since providing money for the campaign, either from acquaintances or from one's own resources, was frequently a condition of receiving the party's nomination.

When cash in large sums was needed, the parties went to men of wealth. . . .

The reign of the parties and the big contributors continued well into the 1950s and 1960s, but important changes were afoot both in the campaigns themselves and in their financing. Whereas in 1952 only 34 percent of American households had a television set, 92 percent did by 1964. Campaigning was never the same again.

. . . Not surprisingly, it was in the first full flush of television expenditures for campaigning, during the 1960s, that the costs of campaigning first rose at a rate sharply greater than that of inflation. . . .

In the race to provide the fuel for the new electronic engines of campaigning, the big contributors remained essential. . . .

At the same time, an even more fundamental, if less visible, change was under way. The political parties . . . began to lose their vaunted role. . . . Just as important, voters reduced their emotional commitments to the parties; fewer and fewer thought of themselves as loyal "members" of a party, and more and more split their tickets at the polling place. . . .

Whereas the people and events of the old campaigning had pivoted around the political party, the new configuration centered on the candidate. . . . They could in fact rent most of the old party service from the new specialists. . . . To rent media time and the new campaign technocrats one needed cash — lots of it. And so the burden of raising campaign money passed from party to candidate, and the fat cats became as important to the candidates as they had been for the parties. Moreover, because it was so candidate-centered, American campaign finance became much more . . . expensive.

Public skepticism over campaign financing, along with some actual examples of political corruption surrounding presidential campaigns (for example, the Teapot Dome scandal, the Watergate scandal, and the Whitewater scandal), have led to a number of campaign finance reforms on all levels of government. These efforts culminated on the federal level, after the exposure of extensive fund-raising improprieties by the 1974 presidential campaign of President Richard M. Nixon, with the enactment of the Federal Election Campaign Act (FECA) Amendments of 1974 (Pub. L. No. 99-443). (Although this statute was a series of amendments to the Federal Election Campaign Act of 1971, it effectively rewrote the major provisions of that law.) This statute established the bipartisan Federal Election Commission, which was granted extensive authority to give advisory opinions, conduct audits and investigations, conduct hearings, and seek injunctions. The statute created limits on congressional candidates' campaign contributions and expenditures and set up requirements for broad disclosure. For presidential campaigns, the statute established a voluntary public financing program.

These provisions did not go unchallenged. In *Buckley*, the Court was asked to resolve the question of how to balance the rights secured by the First Amendment against Congress' determination to protect the electoral system from corruption and to temper the influence of money in the electoral system. Plaintiffs' primary argument was that the Act's contribution and expenditure limitations violated the First Amendment's guarantees of political association and political expression. In upholding the constitutionality of the Act's limitations on contributions and striking down the limitations on expenditures, the Court drew a stark distinction between the two:

> A restriction on the amount of money a person or group can spend on political communication during a campaign necessarily reduces the quantity of expression by restricting the number of issues discussed, the depth of their exploration, and the size of the audience reached. . . . The expenditure limitations contained in the Act represent substantial rather than merely theoretical restraints on the quantity and diversity of political speech. The $1,000 ceiling on spending "relative to a clearly identified candidate" would appear to exclude all citizens and groups except candidates, political parties, and the institutional press from any significant use of the most effective modes of communication. . . . By contrast . . . a limitation upon the amount that any one person or group may contribute to a candidate or political committee entails only a marginal restriction upon the contributor's ability to engage in free communication. . . . In sum, although the Act's contribution and expenditure limitations both implicate fundamental First Amendment interests, its expenditure ceilings impose significantly more severe restrictions on protected freedoms of political expression and association than do its limitations on financial contributions.

Buckley v. Valeo, 424 U.S. 1 (1976) (internal citations omitted).

What would become known as the *Buckley* doctrine did not settle the debate over campaign finance reform. The Court's compelled breakage of the statutory link between expenditure and contribution limits created new and greater pressures on candidates to raise, or have and use their own, money. And these pressures grew as the costs of campaigns inflated and the value of the $1,000 contribution limit deflated.

One place to which candidates looked for help was political parties. Under FECA's Party Expenditure Provision, 2 U.S.C. §441a(d)(3), each national and state party committee's expenditures on each candidate were limited to the greater of $20,000, or two cents multiplied by the voting-age population of the state where the election is held. If expenditure limitations on candidates violated the First Amendment, would the same be true for expenditure limitations on political parties? And, if so, could application of the *Buckley* doctrine open the way for, in effect, greater campaign expenditures? The Supreme Court answered these questions in two decisions. Colorado Republican Federal Campaign Committee v. FEC, 518 U.S. 604 (1996) (*Colorado I*) and FEC v. Colorado Republican Federal Campaign Committee, 531 U.S. 923 (2001) (*Colorado II*) revisited *Buckley's* contribution/expenditure distinction, as applied to political party spending on federal candidates.

In *Colorado I*, the Court determined that the independent expenditures of a political party could not be limited by the Party Expenditure Provision, but remanded for consideration the question of whether limitations on coordinated party expenditures similarly violated the First Amendment under the *Buckley* doctrine. In *Colorado II*, the Court decided that expenditures by parties in coordination with a political campaign were contributions subject to FECA's $20,000 limitation.

Political action committees (PACs), and their use of soft money, also became a vehicle by which money could be raised and spent without the limitations imposed on political campaigns. PACs are organizations formed to raise and contribute money to the campaigns of legislative candidates who support their views, although many PACs, mostly those representing business interests, contribute to incumbents to ensure access. From 1974 to 2000 the number of PACs grew from 608 to 4,499, and from the 1977-1978 election cycle to the 1999-2000 cycle PAC contributions grew from $35.2 million to $259.8 million.

The growth of PACs is a direct result of the limitation on campaign expenditures. Originally many PACs were used as a means to boost voter registration. But as the limited reach of campaign finance laws became more and more apparent, PACs became conduits for channeling money — "soft money" — in support of one candidate or another.

Soft money is generally thought of as money spent on a candidate that is not subject to FECA's contribution and expenditure limitations. This money was increasingly funneled into issue advertising (or issue advocacy), which spurred most of its criticism. Senator Russell D. Feingold (D, Wis.) has described issue advertising as "broadcast advertisements that may bitterly attack an opponent but avoid certain magic words like 'vote for' or 'vote against.'" Special Interest and Soft Money, 10 Stan. L. & Pol'y Rev. 59, 60 (1998).

This reference to "magic words" in ads is a direct result of the *Buckley* Court's reading of §608 of FECA. In *Buckley*, the Court held that FECA §608's limitation on expenditures "relative to a clearly identified candidate" must be construed to apply only to those expenditures for communication that in express terms advocate the election or defeat of a clearly identified candidate for federal office. Buckley v. Valeo, 424 U.S. 1, 44 n.52 (1976). The Court noted that application of the provision should be restricted to "communications containing express advocacy of election or defeat, such as 'vote for,' 'elect,' 'support,' 'cast your ballot for,' 'Smith for Congress,' 'vote against,' 'defeat,' [and] 'reject.'" Id. Thus, advertisements not invoking these "magic words" (issue advertisements) were excluded from FECA §608's scope, creating an outlet for the expenditure of millions in soft money. By contrast, express advocacy uses the "magic words" to directly advocate on behalf of a particular candidate or group of candidates and are therefore subject to the FECA expenditure limitations. To gain a sense of the impact that soft money has had on campaigns, compare the $21.6 million raised by campaigns in the

1984 presidential election cycle with the $498 million raised by campaigns in 2000.

The extraordinary amounts of soft money spent in the 2000 federal elections led to new initiatives to reform the campaign finance laws. What emerged was the Bipartisan Campaign Reform Act of 2002, jointly sponsored by Senators John McCain (R, Ariz.) and Russell Feingold. This Act's most important provisions regulated, and in some instances banned, the use of soft money; restricted television and radio communications that referred to a "clearly identifiable candidate" and imposed new disclaimer requirements; increased the contribution limits for individuals and political committees; modified recordkeeping and reporting requirements; prohibited certain contributions by minors; strengthened the regulation of a candidate's personal use of funds; and increased civil penalties for the Act's violation.

The Bipartisan Campaign Reform Act (BCRA) of 2002

The following are highlights from the 2002 statute that amended FECA. Most of these provisions were declared constitutional by the Supreme Court's decision in McConnell v. Federal Election Commission (excerpted below). Some were held unconstitutional in either *McConnell* or its progeny (discussed in the Notes and Questions following McConnell v. FEC).

Soft Money Regulation

- Soft money of political parties (2 U.S.C. §441i):
  - —Bans a national committee of a political party from soliciting, receiving, or directing to another person a contribution, donation, or transfer of funds not subject to the limitations, prohibitions, and reporting requirements of the Act
  - —Requires amounts disbursed for Federal election activity by a State, district, or local committee of a political party to be made from funds subject to the limitations, prohibitions, and reporting requirements of the Act
  - —Restricts the solicitation of funds from or the donation to tax-exempt organizations described in 26 U.S.C. §501(c) or an organization described in 26 U.S.C. §527
  - —Prohibits Federal candidates from soliciting, receiving, directing, transferring, or spending funds in connection with an election for Federal office unless the funds are subject to the limitations, prohibitions, and reporting requirements of the Act

Increased Contribution Limits

- Limitations on contributions and expenditures (2 U.S.C. §441a):

  — Increases the limitation on contributions by an individual to any single candidate and his authorized political committees from $1,000 to $2,000 in the aggregate, per election for Federal office

  — Increases the limitation on contributions by an individual to any political committee established and maintained by a national political party from $20,000 to $25,000 in the aggregate, per calendar year

  — Increases the limitation on contributions by an individual to any political committee established and maintained by a State committee of a political party to $10,000, per calendar year

  — Increases the limitation on all contributions by an individual to all Federal candidates and their authorized committees from $25,000 to $37,500 in the aggregate during a two-year period beginning on January 1 of an odd-numbered year; or $57,500 in the case of any other contributions, of which not more than $37,500 may be attributable to contributions to political committees which are not of national political parties, during the same period

  — Increases limits on contributions to a candidate for nomination for election, or for election to the U.S. Senate from $17,500 to $35,000, made by any Senatorial Campaign Committee or national committee of a political party, for the year in which an election is held in which he is such a candidate

  — Provides for an increase in the ceiling on individual contributions to a candidate under circumstances where the personal funds of that candidate's opposition exceed a threshold value

  — Provides for the indexing of limitations on contributions to inflation on an annual basis

Disclosure Requirements

- Reports (2 U.S.C. §434):

  — Requires the treasurer of a political committee to report all receipts and disbursements

  — Requires the itemization of receipts or disbursements from or to any person in excess of $200 in the aggregate

  — Institutes additional reporting requirements that are dependent upon the substantiality and timing of the expenditure

Party-Specific Prohibitions

- Disclosure of electioneering communications (2 U.S.C. §434(f)):

  — Requires every person who makes a disbursement for the direct costs of producing and airing electioneering communications in an amount in excess of $10,000 in the aggregate to file a disclosure statement

- Contributions or expenditures by national banks, corporations, or labor organizations (2 U.S.C. §441b):

  —Makes it unlawful for any national bank, corporation or labor organization to make a contribution or expenditure in connection with any election to a political office—does not apply to certain Section 501 organizations or Section 527 political organizations

- Prohibition of contributions by minors (2 U.S.C. §441k):

  —Prohibits individuals seventeen years old or younger from making contributions to a candidate or donations to a political party committee

Penalties

- Penalties; defenses; mitigation of offenses (2 U.S.C. §437g(d)):

  —Provides for a fine or up to five years imprisonment, or both, for a knowing and willful violation of the Act, where the individual makes contributions of $25,000 or more in the aggregate; or a fine or one year imprisonment, or both, for violations dealing with less than $25,000 and more than $2,000 in the aggregate

NOTES AND QUESTIONS

1. *Translating public concerns into public policy.* The BCRA was motivated by a number of public concerns described earlier in this section. How does the statute address these various concerns?

2. *The BCRA and the Constitution.* Do you see any constitutional problems with the above provisions? Senator Mitch McConnell, the former Senate Majority Whip from Kentucky, along with the California Democratic Party, the National Rifle Association, and the American Civil Liberties Union, among others, perceived many and challenged the statute in several cases that culminated in the following decision. Internal citations and footnotes have been omitted except where particularly relevant.

McConnell v. FEC
540 U.S. 93 (2003)

JUSTICE STEVENS and JUSTICE O'CONNOR delivered the opinion of the Court with respect to BCRA Titles I and II. JUSTICE SOUTER, JUSTICE GINSBURG, and JUSTICE BREYER join this opinion in its entirety.

The Bipartisan Campaign Reform Act of 2002 (BCRA) contains a series of amendments to the Federal Election Campaign Act of 1971 (FECA or Act), the Communications Act of 1934, and other portions of the United States Code, that are challenged in these cases. . . .

I

BCRA is the most recent federal enactment designed "to purge national politics of what was conceived to be the pernicious influence of 'big money' campaign contributions." . . .

Congress' historical concern with the "political potentialities of wealth" and their "untoward consequences for the democratic process" has long reached beyond corporate money. . . . As we noted in a unanimous opinion recalling this history, Congress' "careful legislative adjustment of the federal electoral laws, in a 'cautious advance, step by step,' to account for the particular legal and economic attributes of corporations and labor organizations warrants considerable deference." . . .

In early 1972 Congress continued its steady improvement of the national election laws by enacting FECA. As first enacted, that statute required disclosure of all contributions exceeding $100 and of expenditures by candidates and political committees that spent more than $1,000 per year. It also prohibited contributions made in the name of another person, and by Government contractors. The law ratified the earlier prohibition on the use of corporate and union general treasury funds for political contributions and expenditures, but it expressly permitted corporations and unions to establish and administer separate segregated funds (commonly known as political action committees, or PACs) for election-related contributions and expenditures.

As the 1972 Presidential elections made clear, however, FECA's passage did not deter unseemly fundraising and campaign practices. Evidence of those practices persuaded Congress to enact the Federal Election Campaign Act Amendments of 1974. Reviewing a constitutional challenge to the amendments, the Court of Appeals for the District of Columbia Circuit described them as "by far the most comprehensive . . . reform legislation [ever] passed by Congress concerning the election of the President, Vice-President and members of Congress."

The 1974 amendments closed the loophole that had allowed candidates to use an unlimited number of political committees for fundraising purposes and thereby to circumvent the limits on individual committees' receipts and disbursements. They also limited individual political contributions to any single candidate to $1,000 per election, with an overall annual limitation of $25,000 by any contributor; imposed ceilings on spending by candidates and political parties for national conventions; required reporting and public disclosure of contributions and expenditures exceeding certain limits; and established the Federal Election Commission (FEC) to administer and enforce the legislation.

This Court . . . concluded that each set of limitations raised serious — though different — concerns under the First Amendment. We treated the limitations on candidate and individual expenditures as direct restraints on speech, but we observed that the contribution limitations, in contrast, imposed only "a marginal restriction upon the contributor's ability to engage in free communication." Considering the "deeply disturbing examples" of corruption related to candidate contributions . . . we determined that limiting contributions served an interest in protecting "the integrity of our system of representative democracy." In the end, the Act's primary purpose — "to limit the actuality and appearance of corruption resulting from large individual financial contributions" — provided "a constitutionally sufficient justification for the $1,000 contribution limitation." . . .

We upheld all of the disclosure and reporting requirements in the Act that were challenged on appeal to this Court after finding that they vindicated three important interests: providing the electorate with relevant information about the candidates and their supporters; deterring actual corruption and discouraging the use of money for improper purposes; and facilitating enforcement of the prohibitions in the Act. . . .

Three important developments in the years after our decision in *Buckley* persuaded Congress that further legislation was necessary to regulate the role that corporations, unions, and wealthy contributors play in the electoral process. As a preface to our discussion of the specific provisions of BCRA, we comment briefly on the increased importance of "soft money," the proliferation of "issue ads," and the disturbing findings of a Senate investigation into campaign practices related to the 1996 federal elections.

Soft Money

Under FECA, "contributions" must be made with funds that are subject to the Act's disclosure requirements and source and amount limitations. Such funds are known as "federal" or "hard" money. FECA defines the term "contribution," however, to include only the gift or advance of anything of value "made by any person for the purpose of influencing any election for Federal office." 2 U.S.C. §431(8)(A)(i). Donations made solely for the purpose of influencing state or local elections are therefore unaffected by FECA's requirements and prohibitions. As a result, prior to the enactment of BCRA, federal law permitted corporations and unions, as well as individuals who had already made the maximum permissible contributions to federal candidates, to contribute "nonfederal money" — also known as "soft money" — to political parties for activities intended to influence state or local elections.

Shortly after *Buckley* was decided, questions arose concerning the treatment of contributions intended to influence both federal and state elections. Although a literal reading of FECA's definition of "contribution" would have required such activities to be funded with hard money, the FEC ruled that political parties could fund mixed-purpose activities — including get-out-the-vote drives and generic party advertising — in part with soft money. In 1995 the FEC concluded that the parties could also use soft money to defray the cost of "legislative advocacy media advertisements," even if the ads mentioned the name of a federal candidate, so long as they did not expressly advocate the candidate's election or defeat.

As the permissible uses of soft money expanded, the amount of soft money raised and spent by the national political parties increased exponentially. Of the two major parties' total spending, soft money accounted for 5% ($21.6 million) in 1984, 11% ($45 million) in 1988, 16% ($80 million) in 1992, 30% ($272 million) in 1996, and 42% ($498 million) in 2000. The national parties transferred large amounts of their soft money to the state parties, which were allowed to use a larger percentage of soft money to finance mixed-purpose activities under FEC rules. In the year 2000, for example, the national parties diverted $280 million — more than half of their soft money — to state parties.

Many contributions of soft money were dramatically larger than the contributions of hard money permitted by FECA. For example, in 1996 the top five corporate soft-money donors gave, in total, more than $9 million in nonfederal funds to the two national party committees. In the most recent election cycle the political parties raised almost $300 million — 60% of their total soft-money fundraising — from just 800 donors, each of which contributed a minimum of $120,000. Moreover, the largest corporate donors often made substantial contributions to both parties. Such practices corroborate evidence indicating that many corporate contributions were motivated by a desire for access to candidates and a fear of being placed at a disadvantage in the legislative process relative to other contributors, rather than by ideological support for the candidates and parties. . . .

The solicitation, transfer, and use of soft money thus enabled parties and candidates to circumvent FECA's limitations on the source and amount of contributions in connection with federal elections.

Issue Advertising

In *Buckley* we construed FECA's disclosure and reporting requirements, as well as its expenditure limitations, "to reach only funds used for communications that expressly advocate the election or defeat of a clearly identified candidate." As a result of that strict reading of the statute, the use or omission of "magic words" such as "Elect John Smith" or "Vote Against Jane Doe" marked a bright statutory line separating "express advocacy" from "issue advocacy." Express advocacy was subject to FECA's limitations and could be financed only using hard money. The political parties, in other words, could not use soft money to sponsor ads that used any magic words, and corporations and unions could not fund such ads out of their general treasuries. So-called issue ads, on the other hand, not only could be financed with soft money, but could be aired without disclosing the identity of, or any other information about, their sponsors.

While the distinction between "issue" and express advocacy seemed neat in theory, the two categories of advertisements proved functionally identical in important respects. Both were used to advocate the election or defeat of clearly identified federal candidates, even though the so-called issue ads eschewed the use of magic words. . . . Indeed, the ads were attractive to organizations and candidates precisely because they were beyond FECA's reach, enabling candidates and their parties to work closely with friendly interest groups to sponsor so-called issue ads when the candidates themselves were running out of money.

Because FECA's disclosure requirements did not apply to so-called issue ads, sponsors of such ads often used misleading names to conceal their identity. "Citizens for Better Medicare," for instance, was not a grassroots organization of citizens, as its name might suggest, but was instead a platform for an association of drug manufacturers. And "Republicans for Clean Air," which ran ads in the 2000 Republican Presidential primary, was actually an organization consisting of just two individuals — brothers who together spent $25 million on ads supporting their favored candidate. . . .

II

. . . BCRA's central provisions are designed to address Congress' concerns about the increasing use of soft money and issue advertising to influence federal elections. Title I regulates the use of soft money by political parties, officeholders, and candidates. Title II primarily prohibits corporations and labor unions from using general treasury funds for communications that are intended to, or have the effect of, influencing the outcome of federal elections. . . .

III

Title I is Congress' effort to plug the soft-money loophole. The cornerstone of Title I is new FECA §323(a), which prohibits national party committees and their agents from soliciting, receiving, directing, or spending any soft money. 2 U.S.C. §441i(a) (Supp. II). In short, §323(a) takes national parties out of the soft-money business. The remaining provisions of new FECA §323 largely reinforce the restrictions in §323(a). . . .

Plaintiffs mount a facial First Amendment challenge to new FECA §323, as well as challenges based on the Elections Clause, U.S. Const., Art. I, §4, principles of federalism, and the equal protection component of the Due Process Clause. . . .

A

In *Buckley* and subsequent cases, we have subjected restrictions on campaign expenditures to closer scrutiny than limits on campaign contributions. In these cases we have recognized that contribution limits, unlike limits on expenditures, "entai[l] only a marginal restriction upon the contributor's ability to engage in free communication." . . .

Because the communicative value of large contributions inheres mainly in their ability to facilitate the speech of their recipients, we have said that contribution limits impose serious burdens on free speech only if they are so low as to "preven[t] candidates and political committees from amassing the resources necessary for effective advocacy."

. . . The less rigorous standard of review we have applied to contribution limits (*Buckley*'s "closely drawn" scrutiny) shows proper deference to Congress' ability to weigh competing constitutional interests in an area in which it enjoys particular expertise. It also provides Congress with sufficient room to anticipate and respond to concerns about circumvention of regulations designed to protect the integrity of the political process. . . .

Like the contribution limits we upheld in *Buckley*, §323's restrictions have only a marginal impact on the ability of contributors, candidates, officeholders, and parties to engage in effective political speech. Complex as its provisions may be, §323, in the main, does little more than regulate the ability of wealthy individuals, corporations, and unions to contribute large sums of money to influence federal elections, federal candidates, and federal officeholders. . . .

For example, while §323(a) prohibits national parties from receiving or spending nonfederal money, and §323(b) prohibits state party committees from spending nonfederal money on federal election activities, neither provision in any way limits the total amount of money parties can spend. 2 U.S.C. §§441i(a), (b) (Supp. II). Rather, they simply limit the source and individual amount of donations. That they do so by prohibiting the spending of soft money does not render them expenditure limitations. . . .

Section 323 thus shows "due regard for the reality that solicitation is characteristically intertwined with informative and perhaps persuasive speech seeking support for particular causes or for particular views." The fact that party committees and federal candidates and officeholders must now ask only for limited dollar amounts or request that a corporation or union contribute money through its PAC in no way alters or impairs the political message "intertwined" with the solicitation. And rather than chill such solicitations, as was the case in *Schaumburg*, the restriction here tends to increase the dissemination of information by forcing parties, candidates, and officeholders to solicit from a wider array of potential donors. As with direct limits on contributions, therefore, §323's spending and solicitation restrictions have only a marginal impact on political speech. . . .

With these principles in mind, we apply the less rigorous scrutiny applicable to contribution limits to evaluate the constitutionality of new FECA §323.

New FECA §323(a)'s Restrictions on National Party Committees

The core of Title I is new FECA §323(a), which provides that "national committee[s] of a political party . . . may not solicit, receive, or direct to another person a contribution, donation, or transfer of funds or any other thing of value, or spend any funds, that are not subject to the limitations, prohibitions, and reporting requirements of this Act." 2 U.S.C. §441i(a)(1) (Supp. II). The prohibition extends to "any officer or agent acting on behalf of such a national committee, and any entity that is directly or indirectly established, financed, maintained, or controlled by such a national committee." §441i(a)(2).

The main goal of §323(a) is modest. In large part, it simply effects a return to the scheme that was approved in *Buckley* and that was subverted by the creation of the FEC's allocation regime, which permitted the political parties to fund federal electioneering efforts with a combination of hard and soft money. Under that allocation regime, national parties were able to use vast amounts of soft money in their efforts to elect federal candidates. Consequently, as long as they directed the money to the political parties, donors could contribute large amounts of soft money for use in activities designed to influence federal elections. New §323(a) is designed to put a stop to that practice.

1. Governmental Interests Underlying New FECA §323(a)

The Government defends §323(a)'s ban on national parties' involvement with soft money as necessary to prevent the actual and apparent corruption of federal candidates and officeholders. Our cases have made clear that the prevention of corruption or its appearance constitutes a sufficiently important interest to justify political contribution limits. . . . Of "almost equal" importance has been the Government's interest in combating the appearance or perception of corruption engendered by large campaign contributions. Take away Congress' authority to regulate the appearance of undue influence and "the cynical assumption that large donors call the tune could jeopardize the willingness of voters to take part in democratic governance."

. . . The idea that large contributions to a national party can corrupt or, at the very least, create the appearance of corruption of federal candidates and officeholders is neither novel nor implausible. For nearly 30 years,

FECA has placed strict dollar limits and source restrictions on contributions that individuals and other entities can give to national, state, and local party committees for the purpose of influencing a federal election. The premise behind these restrictions has been, and continues to be, that contributions to a federal candidate's party in aid of that candidate's campaign threaten to create — no less than would a direct contribution to the candidate — a sense of obligation. . . .

The question for present purposes is whether large soft-money contributions to national party committees have a corrupting influence or give rise to the appearance of corruption. Both common sense and the ample record in these cases confirm Congress' belief that they do. . . . [T]he FEC's allocation regime has invited widespread circumvention of FECA's limits on contributions to parties for the purpose of influencing federal elections. Under this system, corporate, union, and wealthy individual donors have been free to contribute substantial sums of soft money to the national parties, which the parties can spend for the specific purpose of influencing a particular candidate's federal election. It is not only plausible, but likely, that candidates would feel grateful for such donations and that donors would seek to exploit that gratitude. . . .

Particularly telling is the fact that, in 1996 and 2000, more than half of the top 50 soft-money donors gave substantial sums to both major national parties, leaving room for no other conclusion but that these donors were seeking influence, or avoiding retaliation, rather than promoting any particular ideology. . . .

Plaintiffs argue that without concrete evidence of an instance in which a federal officeholder has actually switched a vote (or, presumably, evidence of a specific instance where the public believes a vote was switched), Congress has not shown that there exists real or apparent corruption. But the record is to the contrary. The evidence connects soft money to manipulations of the legislative calendar, leading to Congress' failure to enact, among other things, generic drug legislation, tort reform, and tobacco legislation. . . .

The record in the present cases is replete with similar examples of national party committees peddling access to federal candidates and officeholders in exchange for large soft-money donations. . . .

Despite this evidence and the close ties that candidates and officeholders have with their parties, Justice Kennedy would limit Congress' regulatory interest only to the prevention of the actual or apparent quid pro quo corruption "inherent in" contributions made directly to, contributions made at the express behest of, and expenditures made in coordination with, a federal officeholder or candidate. . . . This crabbed view of corruption, and particularly of the appearance of corruption, ignores precedent, common sense, and the realities of political fundraising exposed by the record in this litigation. . . .

In sum, there is substantial evidence to support Congress' determination that large soft-money contributions to national political parties give rise to corruption and the appearance of corruption.

2.   New FECA §323(a)'s Restriction on Spending and Receiving Soft Money

Plaintiffs and The Chief Justice contend that §323(a) is impermissibly overbroad because it subjects all funds raised and spent by national parties to FECA's hard-money source and amount limits, including, for example, funds spent on purely state and local elections in which no federal office is at stake. Such activities, The Chief Justice asserts, pose "little or no potential to corrupt . . . federal candidates and officeholders." This observation is beside the point. Section 323(a), like the remainder of §323, regulates contributions, not activities. As the record demonstrates, it is the close relationship between federal officeholders and the national parties, as well as the means by which parties have traded on that relationship, that have made all large soft-money contributions to national parties suspect. . . .

The nexus between national parties and federal officeholders prompted one of Title I's framers to conclude:

> Because the national parties operate at the national level, and are inextricably intertwined with federal officeholders and candidates, who raise the money for the national party committees, there is a close connection between the funding of the national parties and the corrupting dangers of soft money on the federal political process. The only effective way to address this [soft-money] problem of corruption is to ban entirely all raising and spending of soft money by the national parties. 148 Cong. Rec. H409 (Feb. 13, 2002) (statement of Rep. Shays). . . .

3.   New FECA §323(a)'s Restriction on Soliciting or Directing Soft Money

Plaintiffs also contend that §323(a)'s prohibition on national parties' soliciting or directing soft-money contributions is substantially overbroad. The reach of the solicitation prohibition, however, is limited. It bars only solicitations of soft money by national party committees and by party officers in their official capacities. The committees remain free to solicit hard money on their own behalf, as well as to solicit hard money on behalf of state committees and state and local candidates. They also can contribute hard money to state committees and to candidates. In accordance with FEC regulations, furthermore, officers of national parties are free to solicit soft money in their individual capacities, or, if they are also officials of state parties, in that capacity. . . .

4. New FECA §323(a)'s Application to Minor Parties

The McConnell and political party plaintiffs contend that §323(a) is substantially overbroad and must be stricken on its face because it impermissibly infringes the speech and associational rights of minor parties such as the Libertarian National Committee, which, owing to their slim prospects for electoral success and the fact that they receive few large soft-money contributions from corporate sources, pose no threat of corruption comparable to that posed by the RNC and DNC. In *Buckley*, we rejected a similar argument concerning limits on contributions to minor-party candidates, noting that "any attempt to exclude minor parties and independents en masse from the Act's contribution limitations overlooks the fact that minor-party candidates may win elective office or have a substantial impact on the outcome of an election." We have thus recognized that the relevance of the interest in avoiding actual or apparent corruption is not a function of the number of legislators a given party manages to elect. It applies as much to a minor party that manages to elect only one of its members to federal office as it does to a major party whose members make up a majority of Congress. It is therefore reasonable to require that all parties and all candidates follow the same set of rules designed to protect the integrity of the electoral process. . . .

5. New FECA §323(a)'s Associational Burdens

Finally, plaintiffs assert that §323(a) is unconstitutional because it impermissibly interferes with the ability of national committees to associate with state and local committees. By way of example, plaintiffs point to the Republican Victory Plans, whereby the RNC acts in concert with the state and local committees of a given State to plan and implement joint, full-ticket fundraising and electioneering programs. The political parties assert that §323(a) outlaws any participation in Victory Plans by RNC officers, including merely sitting down at a table and engaging in collective decisionmaking about how soft money will be solicited, received, and spent. Such associational burdens, they argue, are too great for the First Amendment to bear.

We are not persuaded by this argument because it hinges on an unnaturally broad reading of the terms "spend," "receive," "direct," and "solicit." 2 U.S.C. §441i(a) (Supp. II). Nothing on the face of §323(a) prohibits national party officers, whether acting in their official or individual capacities, from sitting down with state and local party committees or candidates to plan and advise how to raise and spend soft money. As long as the national party officer does not personally spend, receive, direct, or solicit soft money, §323(a) permits a wide range of joint planning and electioneering activity. . . .

Moreover, §323(a) leaves national party committee officers entirely free to participate, in their official capacities, with state and local parties and candidates in soliciting and spending hard money; party officials may also solicit soft money in their unofficial capacities.

Accordingly, we reject the plaintiffs' First Amendment challenge to new FECA §323(a).

[The plaintiffs made substantially similar arguments as those set forth above, only with regard to: FECA §323(b)'s restrictions on state and local party committees; FECA §323(d)'s restrictions on parties' solicitation for, and donations to, tax-exempt organizations; FECA §323(e)'s restrictions on federal candidates and officeholders; and FECA §323(f)'s restrictions on state candidates and officeholders. As the Court approached each issue utilizing substantially the same analysis, and came to the same conclusion, discussions of FECA §§323(b), (d), (e), and (f) have been omitted.]

B

Several plaintiffs contend that Title I exceeds Congress' Election Clause authority to "make or alter" rules governing federal elections, U.S. Const., Art. I, §4, and, by impairing the authority of the States to regulate their own elections, violates constitutional principles of federalism. In examining congressional enactments for infirmity under the Tenth Amendment, this Court has focused its attention on laws that commandeer the States and state officials in carrying out federal regulatory schemes. By contrast, Title I of BCRA only regulates the conduct of private parties. It imposes no requirements whatsoever upon States or state officials, and, because it does not expressly pre-empt state legislation, it leaves the States free to enforce their own restrictions on the financing of state electoral campaigns. It is true that Title I, as amended, prohibits some fundraising tactics that would otherwise be permitted under the laws of various States, and that it may therefore have an indirect effect on the financing of state electoral campaigns. But these indirect effects do not render BCRA unconstitutional. It is not uncommon for federal law to prohibit private conduct that is legal in some States. . . .

C

Finally, plaintiffs argue that Title I violates the equal protection component of the Due Process Clause of the Fifth Amendment because it discriminates against political parties in favor of special interest groups such as the National Rifle Association, American Civil Liberties Union, and Sierra Club. As explained earlier, BCRA imposes numerous restrictions on the fundraising abilities of political parties, of which the soft-money ban is only the most prominent. Interest groups, however, remain free to raise soft money to fund voter registration, GOTV activities, mailings, and broadcast advertising (other than electioneering communications). We conclude that this disparate treatment does not offend the Constitution.

As an initial matter, we note that BCRA actually favors political parties in many ways. Most obviously, party committees are entitled to receive individual contributions that substantially exceed FECA's limits on contributions to nonparty political committees; individuals can give $25,000 to political party committees whereas they can give a maximum of $5,000 to nonparty political committees. In addition, party committees are entitled in effect to contribute to candidates by making coordinated expenditures, and those expenditures may greatly exceed the contribution limits that apply to other donors. See 2 U.S.C. §441a(d) (Supp. II).

More importantly, however, Congress is fully entitled to consider the real-world differences between political parties and interest groups when crafting a system of campaign finance regulation. Interest groups do not select slates of candidates for elections. Interest groups do not determine who will serve on legislative committees, elect congressional leadership, or organize legislative caucuses. Political parties have influence and power in the Legislature that vastly exceeds that of any interest group. As a result, it is hardly surprising that party affiliation is the primary way by which voters identify candidates, or that parties in turn have special access to and relationships with federal officeholders. . . .

Accordingly, we affirm the judgment of the District Court insofar as it upheld §§323(e) and 323(f). We reverse the judgment of the District Court insofar as it invalidated §§323(a), 323(b), and 323(d).

IV

Title II of BCRA, entitled "Noncandidate Campaign Expenditures," is divided into two subtitles: "Electioneering Communications" and "Independent and Coordinated Expenditures." We consider each challenged section of these subtitles in turn.

BCRA §201's Definition of "Electioneering Communications"

The first section of Title II, §201, comprehensively amends FECA §304, which requires political committees to file detailed periodic financial reports with the FEC. The amendment coins a new term, "electioneering communications," to replace the narrowing construction of FECA's disclosure provisions adopted by this Court in *Buckley*. As discussed further below, that construction limited the coverage of FECA's disclosure requirement to communications expressly advocating the election or defeat of particular candidates. By contrast, the term "electioneering communication" is not so limited, but is defined to encompass any "broadcast, cable, or satellite communication" that

> (I)   refers to a clearly identified candidate for Federal office;
> (II) is made within—
>> (aa) 60 days before a general, special, or runoff election for the office sought by the candidate; or
>> (bb) 30 days before a primary or preference election, or a convention or caucus of a political party that has authority to nominate a candidate, for the office sought by the candidate; and
> (III) in the case of a communication which refers to a candidate for an office other than President or Vice President, is targeted to the relevant electorate. 2 U.S.C. §434(f)(3)(A)(i) (Supp. II).

New FECA §304(f)(3)(C) further provides that a communication is " 'targeted to the relevant electorate' " if it "can be received by 50,000 or more persons" in the district or State the candidate seeks to represent. 2 U.S.C. §434(f)(3)(C).

In addition to setting forth this definition, BCRA's amendments to FECA §304 specify significant disclosure requirements for persons who fund electioneering communications. BCRA's use of this new term is not, however, limited to the disclosure context: A later section of the Act (BCRA §203, which amends FECA §316(b)(2)) restricts corporations' and labor unions' funding of electioneering communications. Plaintiffs challenge the constitutionality of the new term as it applies in both the disclosure and the expenditure contexts.

The major premise of plaintiffs' challenge to BCRA's use of the term "electioneering communication" is that *Buckley* drew a constitutionally mandated line between express advocacy and so-called issue advocacy, and that speakers possess an inviolable First Amendment right to engage in the latter category of speech. Thus, plaintiffs maintain, Congress cannot constitutionally require disclosure of, or regulate expenditures for, "electioneering communications" without making an exception for those "communications" that do not meet *Buckley*'s definition of express advocacy.

That position misapprehends our prior decisions, for the express advocacy restriction was an endpoint of statutory interpretation, not a first principle of constitutional law. . . . [A] plain reading of *Buckley* makes clear that the express advocacy limitation, in both the expenditure and the disclosure contexts, was the product of statutory interpretation rather than a constitutional command. In narrowly reading the FECA provisions in *Buckley* to avoid problems of vagueness and overbreadth, we nowhere suggested that a statute that was neither vague nor overbroad would be required to toe the same express advocacy line. Nor did we suggest as much in *MCFL*, in which we addressed the scope of another FECA expenditure limitation and confirmed the understanding that *Buckley*'s express advocacy category was a product of statutory construction.

In short, the concept of express advocacy and the concomitant class of magic words were born of an effort to avoid constitutional infirmities. We have long " 'rigidly adhered' " to the tenet " 'never to formulate a rule of constitutional law broader than is required by the precise facts to which it is to be applied,' " for "[t]he nature of judicial review constrains us to consider the case that is actually before us." Consistent with that principle, our decisions in *Buckley* and *MCFL* were specific to the statutory language before us; they in no way drew a constitutional boundary that forever fixed the permissible scope of provisions regulating campaign-related speech.

Nor are we persuaded, independent of our precedents, that the First Amendment erects a rigid barrier between express advocacy and so-called issue advocacy. That notion cannot be squared with our longstanding recognition that the presence or absence of magic words cannot meaningfully distinguish electioneering speech from a true issue ad. Indeed, the unmistakable lesson from the record in this litigation, as all three judges on the District Court agreed, is that *Buckley*'s magic-words requirement is functionally meaningless. Not only can advertisers easily evade the line by eschewing the use of magic words, but they would seldom choose to use such words even if permitted. And although the resulting advertisements do not urge the viewer to vote for or against a candidate in so many words, they are no less clearly intended to influence the election. *Buckley*'s express advocacy line, in short, has not aided the legislative effort to combat real or apparent corruption, and Congress enacted BCRA to correct the flaws it found in the existing system.

Finally we observe that new FECA §304(f)(3)'s definition of "electioneering communication" raises none of the vagueness concerns that drove our analysis in *Buckley*. The term "electioneering communication" applies only (1) to a broadcast (2) clearly identifying a candidate for federal office, (3) aired within a specific time period, and (4) targeted to an identified audience of at least 50,000 viewers or listeners. These components are both easily understood and objectively determinable. Thus, the constitutional objection that persuaded the Court in *Buckley* to limit FECA's reach to express advocacy is simply inapposite here. . . .

[Discussions of BCRA §§201 and 202 omitted.]

BCRA §203's Prohibition of Corporate and Labor Disbursements for Electioneering Communications

Since our decision in *Buckley*, Congress' power to prohibit corporations and unions from using funds in their treasuries to finance advertisements expressly advocating the election or defeat of candidates in federal elections has been firmly embedded in our law. The ability to form and administer separate segregated funds authorized by FECA §316, 2 U.S.C. §441b (2000 ed. and Supp. II), has provided corporations and unions with a constitutionally sufficient opportunity to engage in express advocacy. That has been this Court's unanimous view, and it is not challenged in this litigation.

Section 203 of BCRA amends FECA §316(b)(2) to extend this rule, which previously applied only to express advocacy, to all "electioneering communications." . . . Thus, under BCRA, corporations and unions may not use their general treasury funds to finance electioneering communications, but they remain free to organize and administer segregated funds, or PACs, for that purpose. Because corporations can still fund electioneering communications with PAC money, it is "simply wrong" to view the provision as a "complete ban" on expression rather than a regulation. As we explained in *Beaumont*:

> The PAC option allows corporate political participation without the temptation to use corporate funds for political influence, quite possibly at odds with the sentiments of some shareholders or members, and it lets the government regulate campaign activity through registration and disclosure . . . without jeopardizing the associational rights of advocacy organizations' members.

Rather than arguing that the prohibition on the use of general treasury funds is a complete ban that operates as a prior restraint, plaintiffs instead challenge the expanded regulation on the grounds that it is both overbroad and underinclusive. Our consideration of plaintiffs' challenge is informed by our earlier conclusion that the distinction between express advocacy and so-called issue advocacy is not constitutionally compelled. In that light, we must examine the degree to which BCRA burdens First Amendment expression and evaluate whether a compelling governmental interest justifies that burden. The latter question — whether the state interest is compelling — is easily answered by our prior decisions regarding campaign finance regulation, which "represent respect for the 'legislative judgment that the special characteristics of the corporate structure require particularly careful regulation.'" We have repeatedly sustained legislation aimed at "the corrosive and distorting effects of immense aggregations of wealth that are accumulated with the help of the corporate form and that have little or no correlation to the public's support for the corporation's political ideas."

In light of our precedents, plaintiffs do not contest that the Government has a compelling interest in regulating advertisements that expressly advocate the election or defeat of a candidate for federal office. Nor do they contend that the speech involved in so-called issue advocacy is any more core political speech than are words of express advocacy. . . . Rather, plaintiffs argue that the justifications that adequately support the regulation of express advocacy do not apply to significant quantities of speech encompassed by the definition of electioneering communications.

This argument fails to the extent that the issue ads broadcast during the 30- and 60-day periods preceding federal primary and general elections are the functional equivalent of express advocacy. The justifications for the regulation of express advocacy apply equally to ads aired during those periods if the ads are intended to influence the voters' decisions and have that effect. The precise percentage of issue ads that clearly identified a candidate and were aired during those relatively brief preelection time spans but had no electioneering purpose is a matter of dispute between the parties and among the judges on the District Court. Nevertheless, the vast majority of ads clearly had such a purpose. Moreover, whatever the precise percentage may have been in the past, in the future corporations and unions may finance genuine issue ads during those time frames by simply avoiding any specific reference to federal candidates, or doubtful cases by paying for the ad from a segregated fund.

We are therefore not persuaded that plaintiffs have carried their heavy burden of proving that amended FECA §316(b)(2) is overbroad. Even if we assumed that BCRA will inhibit some constitutionally protected corporate and union speech, that assumption would not "justify prohibiting all enforcement" of the law unless its application to protected speech is substantial, "not only in an absolute sense, but also relative to the scope of the law's plainly legitimate applications." Far from establishing that BCRA's application to pure issue ads is substantial, either in an absolute sense or relative to its application to election-related advertising, the record strongly supports the contrary conclusion. . . .

In addition to arguing that §316(b)(2)'s segregated-fund requirement is underinclusive, some plaintiffs contend that it unconstitutionally discriminates in favor of media companies. FECA §304(f)(3)(B)(i) excludes from the definition of electioneering communications any "communication appearing in a news story, commentary, or editorial distributed through the facilities of any broadcasting station, unless such facilities are owned or controlled by any political party, political committee, or candidate." 2 U.S.C. §434(f)(3)(B)(i) (Supp. II). Plaintiffs argue this provision gives free rein to media companies to engage in speech without resort to PAC money. Section 304(f)(3)(B)(i)'s effect, however, is much narrower than plaintiffs suggest. The provision excepts news items and commentary only; it does not afford carte blanche to media companies generally to ignore FECA's provisions. The statute's narrow exception is wholly consistent with First Amendment principles. "A valid distinction . . . exists between corporations that are part of the media industry and other corporations that are not involved in the regular business of imparting news to the public." Numerous federal statutes have drawn this distinction to ensure that the law "does not hinder or prevent the institutional press from reporting on, and publishing editorials about, newsworthy events."

We affirm the District Court's judgment to the extent that it upheld the constitutionality of FECA §316(b)(2); to the extent that it invalidated any part of §316(b)(2), we reverse the judgment.

[Discussions of BCRA §§204, 212, 213, and 214 omitted.]

Accordingly, we affirm in part and reverse in part the District Court's judgment with respect to Titles I and II.

It is so ordered.

[The following constitutes the Court's opinion as to BCRA Titles III and IV.]

CHIEF JUSTICE REHNQUIST delivered the opinion of the Court with respect to BCRA Titles III and IV. JUSTICE O'CONNOR, JUSTICE SCALIA, JUSTICE KENNEDY, and JUSTICE SOUTER join this opinion in its entirety. JUSTICE STEVENS, JUSTICE GINSBURG, and JUSTICE BREYER join this opinion, except with respect to BCRA §305. JUSTICE THOMAS joins this opinion with respect to BCRA §§304, 305, 307, 316, 319, and 403(b).

This opinion addresses issues involving miscellaneous Title III and IV provisions of the Bipartisan Campaign Reform Act of 2002 (BCRA), 116 Stat. 81. For the reasons discussed below, we affirm the judgment of the District Court with respect to these provisions. . . .

[Discussions of BCRA §§305, 307, 304, 316, and 319 omitted.]

BCRA §311

FECA §318 requires that certain communications "authorized" by a candidate or his political committee clearly identify the candidate or committee or, if not so authorized, identify the payor and announce the lack of authorization. 2 U.S.C. §441d (2000 ed. and Supp. II). BCRA §311 makes several amendments to FECA §318, among them the expansion of this identification regime to include disbursements for "electioneering communications" as defined in BCRA §201.

The McConnell and Chamber of Commerce plaintiffs challenge BCRA §311 by simply noting that §311, along with all of the "electioneering communications" provisions of BCRA, is unconstitutional. We disagree. We think BCRA §311's inclusion of electioneering communications in the FECA §318 disclosure regime bears a sufficient relationship to the important governmental interest of "shed[ding] the light of publicity" on campaign financing. Assuming as we must that FECA §318 is valid to begin with, and that FECA §318 is valid as amended by BCRA §311's amendments other than the inclusion of electioneering communications, the challenged inclusion of electioneering communications is not itself unconstitutional. We affirm the District Court's decision upholding §311's expansion of FECA §318(a) to include disclosure of disbursements for electioneering communications.

BCRA §318

BCRA §318, which adds FECA §324, prohibits individuals "17 years old or younger" from making contributions to candidates and contributions or donations to political parties. 2 U.S.C. §441k (Supp. II). The McConnell and Echols plaintiffs challenge the provision; they argue that §318 violates the First Amendment rights of minors. We agree.

Minors enjoy the protection of the First Amendment. Limitations on the amount that an individual may contribute to a candidate or political committee impinge on the protected freedoms of expression and association. When the Government burdens the right to contribute, we apply heightened scrutiny. . . . We ask whether there is a "sufficiently important interest" and whether the statute is "closely drawn" to avoid unnecessary abridgment of First Amendment freedoms. The Government asserts that the provision protects against corruption by conduit; that is, donations by parents through their minor children to circumvent contribution limits applicable to the parents. But the Government offers scant evidence of this form of evasion. Perhaps the Government's slim evidence results from sufficient deterrence of such activities by §320 of FECA, which prohibits any person from "mak[ing] a contribution in the name of another person" or "knowingly accept[ing] a contribution made by one person in the name of another," 2 U.S.C. §441f. Absent a more convincing case of the claimed evil, this interest is simply too attenuated for §318 to withstand heightened scrutiny.

Even assuming, arguendo, the Government advances an important interest, the provision is over-inclusive. The States have adopted a variety of more tailored approaches — e.g., counting contributions by minors against the total permitted for a parent or family unit, imposing a lower cap on contributions by minors, and prohibiting contributions by very young children. Without deciding whether any of these alternatives is sufficiently tailored, we hold that the provision here sweeps too broadly. We therefore affirm the District Court's decision striking down §318 as unconstitutional. . . .

[Discussions of BRCA §403(b) and Title V omitted.]

It is so ordered.

NOTES AND QUESTIONS

1. *The First Amendment protections.* In *McConnell,* the Court was asked once again to resolve the question of how to balance the rights secured by the First Amendment against Congress' determination to enhance the system of protections it has employed in the American electoral system. What are the First Amendment rights impacted by the Act's provisions and how does the Act impact them? For an argument that FECA violates the

First Amendment, see Stephen E. Gottlieb, The Dilemma of Election Campaign Finance Reform, 18 Hofstra L. Rev. 213 (1989). Despite the criticisms made by Professor Gottlieb and others of the Act, the Court has reaffirmed its First Amendment standards. In Nixon v. Shrink Missouri, 528 U.S. 377 (2000), the Court held that *Buckley* was authority for state contribution limits on state campaigns. The Court also addressed another interesting question that flowed from *Buckley*. The question was whether a contribution limit of $1,000, adjusted for inflation to $1,075, was constitutionally too low because of the erosion of the dollar's value over the preceding 30 years. In other words, had inflation driven the $1,000 *Buckley* contribution limit so low that it now, in its *Missouri* formulation, had become violative of the First Amendment? On this point the Court wrote:

> In *Buckley*, we specifically rejected the contention that $1,000, or any other amount, was a constitutional minimum below which legislatures could not regulate. As indicated above, we referred instead to the outer limits of contribution regulation by asking whether there was any showing that the limits were so low as to impede the ability of candidates to "amas[s] the resources necessary for effective advocacy," 424 U.S., at 21. We asked, in other words, whether the contribution limitation was so radical in effect as to render political association ineffective, drive the sound of a candidate's voice below the level of notice, and render contributions pointless. Such being the test, the issue in later cases likely cannot be truncated to a narrow question about the power of the dollar, but must go to the power to mount a campaign with all the dollars likely to be forthcoming.

Id. at 909. What if the value of the dollar dramatically dropped in the span of a few months; would the Court's view likely change? Does it matter that Congress has subsequently implemented a system that indexes limitations on contributions to inflation under the BCRA?

2. *Contributions versus expenditures*. In arriving at its conclusions in both *Buckley* and *McConnell*, the Court made a distinction between contribution and expenditure limitations. What is the distinction, on what is it based, and what is its consequence for the decisions? Do you find satisfactory the Court's rendering of the free speech harms associated with each of the limitations? Assume, for example, that you are very much in favor of a particular candidate because of her ideological bearings and you want to offer your financial support to that candidate, to the extent you deem possible. You decide to spend $15,000. You consider the independent steps of taking out an ad or undertaking a mailing, but in the end you determine that the money will be more efficiently used if contributed to the candidate. Is this a protected interest? Is it less important an interest than that of spending the $15,000 independently? On what basis is it barred? Is it a greater danger to the integrity of the political process or is it a tempering of the advantages of money? If the latter, is it an appropriate interest to balance against First Amendment concerns?

On this point, Justice Thomas, in dissent, has written:

> But the practical judgment by a citizen that another person or organization
> can more effectively deploy funds for the good of a common cause than
> he can ought not deprive that citizen of his First Amendment rights. . . .
> A contribution is simply an indirect expenditure; though contributions
> and expenditures may thus differ in form, they do not differ in substance.

Colorado Republican Federal Campaign Committee v. Federal Election
Commission, 518 U.S. 604, 638 (1996). What do you think of this view?

3. *FEC v. Wisconsin Right to Life — McConnell unwinding?* In *McConnell*
the Court upheld BCRA §203 against a facial challenge under the First
Amendment. Even though the provision banned both "express advocacy"
and "issue advocacy" within 30 days of a primary election and 60 days of a
general election paid for by a corporation out of its general treasury, the
Court determined that there was no overbreadth concern to the extent that
the speech was the "functional equivalent of express campaign speech." In
Wisconsin Right to Life, plaintiff ideological advocacy corporation (WRTL), a
nonprofit organization formed under §501(c)(4) of the Internal Revenue
Code, began broadcasting a radio advertisement as a part of a "grassroots
lobbying campaign." FEC v. Wisconsin Right to Life, Inc., 127 S. Ct. 2652,
2660 (2007). WRTL had planned on paying for the radio spots out of its
general treasury throughout August 2004. However, as of August 15, 30
days prior to the Wisconsin primary, the ads would have become illegal
"electioneering communication[s]" under BCRA §203. Id. at 2661. WRTL
sued the FEC, seeking declaratory and injunctive relief, alleging that
BCRA's prohibition under §203 was unconstitutional as applied.

The Court held that "[b]ecause WRTL's ads may reasonably be interpreted as something other than an appeal to vote for or against a specific
candidate, they are not the functional equivalent of express advocacy, and
therefore fall outside of *McConnell*'s scope." Id. at 2670.

> *McConnell* held that express advocacy of a candidate or his opponent by a
> corporation shortly before an election may be prohibited, along with the
> functional equivalent of such advocacy. . . . But when it comes to defining
> which speech qualifies as the functional equivalent of express advocacy
> subject to such a ban . . . we give the benefit of the doubt to speech, not
> censorship.

Id. at 2674. Thus, since the government failed to identify an interest sufficiently compelling to burden WRTL's speech, the Court felt compelled to
invalidate the provision.

Chief Justice Roberts, joined by Justice Alito, as well as Justices Kennedy,
Scalia, and Thomas in separate concurring opinions, held BCRA §203
unconstitutional as applied to the particular ads at issue. Does this case
represent a shift in the Supreme Court's view of the validity of the issue

advocacy versus express advocacy distinction, or is it merely the result of a shift in the makeup of the Court itself?

4. *Post-BCRA problems emerge.* In 2007 the New York Times reported on a "new channel" for soft money emerging on the political scene. Groups registered as 501(c)(4) nonprofit corporations are allowed to raise and spend unlimited amounts from individuals without any disclosure, as long as they can argue they are more concerned with the promotion of an issue than with the election of a candidate, in accordance with the *Buckley* and *McConnell* decisions. "The lack of disclosure makes it hard to tell how the group spends its money, and impossible to say where it gets its money, and whether its donors have already donated directly to candidates." Jim Rutenburg and David D. Kirkpatrick, A New Channel for Soft Money Appears in Race, N.Y. Times, Nov. 12, 2007, at A1. Should Congress be working to enact new legislation to close this "loophole" as well? On what basis might such a statute be challenged, and what is the likelihood of success?

5. *The millionaire's amendment.* Section 319(a) of the BCRA also provided a scheme which, when in force, augmented the normal limits imposed on campaign contributions. Often referred to as the "Millionaire's Amendment," this provision was meant to level the playing field when one candidate for office possessed such vast personal wealth that the campaign finance contribution limits effectively foreclosed the ability of a "non-self-financed" candidate to contend with him (at least with regard to expenditures). Under §319(a), when a candidate's "opposition personal funds amount" (OFPA — a statistic based on campaign assets and anticipated personal expenditures) exceeded $350,000, the "self-financed" candidate remained subject to the normal contribution limits, while the non-self-financed candidate was allowed to receive three times the normal limits. Once the non-self-financed candidate's receipts exceeded the OFPA, the standard limits once again took effect. Any contributions received under the augmented scheme that were not spent during that election had to be returned. See Davis v. FEC, 128 S. Ct. 2759 (2008). Since certain information was necessary in order to determine a candidate's OFPA, §319(b) required candidates to file certain disclosures with the FEC.

In 2004 and 2006 Jack Davis was the Democratic candidate for the House of Representatives from New York's 26th Congressional District. During the 2006 campaign, Davis was informed by the FEC that he had violated the OFPA disclosure requirements during the 2004 election. Consequently, Davis sued the FEC, seeking a declaration of §319's unconstitutionality and an injunction against its enforcement during the 2006 election. Id. Davis claimed that §319 amounted to a violation of the First Amendment, since it:

> burden[ed] his exercise of his First Amendment right to make unlimited expenditures of his personal funds because making expenditures that create

the imbalance has the effect of enabling his opponent to raise more money and to use that money to finance speech that counteracts and thus diminish[ed] the effectiveness of [his] own speech.

Id.

In agreeing with Davis' position, the majority turned to "*Buckley's* emphasis on the fundamental nature of the right to spend personal funds for campaign speech." They viewed §319 as imposing "an unprecedented penalty on any candidate who robustly exercises that First Amendment right." Id. The dissenters to this opinion saw no injury to the First Amendment whatsoever, claiming §319 "does no more than assist the opponent of a self-funding candidate in his attempts to make his voice heard; this amplification in no way mutes the voice of the millionaire." Id.

What is your view of §319's effect on the First Amendment? Are you more inclined to side with the majority or minority view here? Can you think of another way to view this situation? Davis also challenged §319 under the Fifth Amendment, but due to the Court's conclusion on the First Amendment claim, this point was never reached on the merits. If §319 had passed muster under the First Amendment, would the Court have nonetheless found it unconstitutional under the equal protection component of the Fifth Amendment's due process clause?

Despite spending a combined $3.5 million — almost entirely out of his own pocket — Davis failed to unseat the incumbent in both elections.

3.   *The Incumbency Factor*

Incumbent legislators are reelected with great frequency (over 90 percent of the time) in the United States. It is the frequency of reelection that fuels the efforts for term limits and for restricting or prohibiting the contributions of PACs. While many such reelection efforts are successful because of the esteem in which most districts hold their own representatives, there can be no doubt that this esteem is enhanced by the many resources available to the incumbent legislator. Legislators have a responsibility to communicate with their constituents on the issues of the day and to help their constituents with problems created by the regulatory state. To accomplish these goals, legislators have access to public funds for staff, mailing, travel, and for maintaining district offices. And, because legislators never believe their seats are safe, they tend to maximize the use of these resources under the theory that the more visible the legislator, the more reelectable. Congressional scholar Professor Gary Jacobson provides an apt description:

> Meanwhile members of Congress continue to act as if they felt anything but safe; indeed, the pursuit of reelection seemed to absorb even more of

their time and energy. Anyone observing the incessant scramble for attention and credit, the constant shuttling between Washington and the district, the vast outpouring of newsletters, pamphlets, questionnaires, booklets, letters, and other messages from the member to his constituents, the increasingly hectic and undignified hustling of campaign contributions, could hardly come away with the sense that incumbent security is a major fact of political life. Yet, from the perspective of raw statistics, it is.

Gary C. Jacobson, Running Scared: Elections and Congressional Politics in the 1980s, in Congress: Structure and Policy 39, 39 (Matthew D. McCubbins and Terry Sullivan eds., 1987).

The use of public resources for the above-described purposes raises important and difficult questions about the use of public funds to advantage the reelection campaigns of legislators. Congress and a number of states have attempted to address these questions by statute or legislative rule regulating the use of public resources.

HOUSE OF REPRESENTATIVES

House employees are compensated from funds of the Treasury for regular performance of official duties. They are not paid to do campaign work. In the words of the United States District Court for the District of Columbia: It is clear from the record that Congress has recognized the basic principle that government funds should not be spent to help incumbents gain reelection.

Common Cause v. Bolger, 574 F. Supp. 672, 683 (D.C. Cir. 1983).

As noted in Chapter 4, however, the "Hatch Act" does not apply to congressional employees. "Once House employees have completed their official duties, they are free to engage in campaign activities on their own time, as volunteers or for pay, as long as they do not do so in congressional offices or facilities, or otherwise use official resources." Additionally, employees may engage in campaign activities while on annual leave, on a leave of absence, or in part-time employment status, provided the time spent on both official and campaign activities is carefully documented. Staff may not be required to do political work as a condition of House employment. Committee on Standards of Official Conduct, 110th Congress, House Ethics Manual 135-37 (2008).

UNITED STATES SENATE

A Senator or an individual who is a candidate for nomination for election, or election, to the Senate may not use the frank for any mass mailing . . . if such mass mailing is mailed at or delivered to any postal facility less than sixty days immediately before the date of any primary or general election . . . in which the Senator is a candidate for public office or the individual is a candidate for Senator. . . . Senate Rule XL, Standing Rules of the Senate (2008); see also 39 U.S.C. §3210(a)(6)(A)(i) (2006).

FLORIDA

. . . [N]o employee in the career service shall . . . take any active part in a political campaign while on duty or within any period of time during which the employee is expected to perform services for which he or she receives compensation from the state. Fla. Stat. Ann. §110.233(4)(a) (2001).

NEW JERSEY

. . . If any candidate is a holder of public office to whom there is attached or assigned, by virtue of said office, any aide or aides whose service are of a personal or confidential nature in assisting him to carry out the duties of said office, and whose salary or other compensation is paid in whole or part out of public funds, the services of such aide or aides which are paid out of public funds shall be for public purposes only. . . . N.J. Rev. Stat. §19:44A-3(f) (2008).

WASHINGTON

No elective official nor any employee of his [or her] office . . . may use or authorize the use of any of the facilities of a public office or agency, directly or indirectly, for the purpose of assisting a campaign for election of any person. . . . Facilities of public office . . . include, but are not limited to, use of stationery, postage, machines and equipment, use of employees of the office . . . during working hours, vehicles, office space, publications of the office. . . . Wash. Rev. Code §42.17.130 (2008).

For the most part, the regulations governing the use of public resources are either very narrow (for example, Senate Rule XL) or leave unanswered the central questions of what representative tasks and election tasks really are. In some instances, definition is left to state commissions, which can promulgate rules, issue advisory opinions, and render decisions. An example of this type of commission is the California Fair Political Practices Commission. In other instances, courts have had to struggle with these issues, as exemplified by the cases below. Internal citations and footnotes have been omitted except where particularly relevant.

United States ex rel. Joseph v. Cannon
642 F.2d 1373 (D.C. Cir. 1981)

Opinion for the Court filed by Circuit Judge SPOTTSWOOD W. ROBINSON, III. . . .

I.   Background

Howard W. Cannon is a United States Senator from the State of Nevada. At all times relevant to this case, Chester B. Sobsey was a Senate employee serving as his administrative assistant. In 1969, Senator Cannon, compliably with then Senate Rule 43, filed a written designation with the Secretary of the Senate authorizing Sobsey to solicit, receive, distribute, and act as custodian of the Senator's campaign funds.

According to appellant, however, Sobsey did far more for the 1976 Cannon campaign than administer contributions. From March, 1975, through November, 1976, Sobsey allegedly worked "extensively and exclusively" for the Senator's reelection. Throughout this period, the complaint avers, "Sobsey accepted his regular pay for services ostensibly performed as Senator Cannon's administrative assistant even though such services were not performed or (were) performed in a perfunctory or nominal manner." Appellant maintains that Senator Cannon was aware of the nature of his assistant's activities, yet authorized these salary payments. . . .

Invoking the False Claims Act, appellant brought suit against Senator Cannon and Sobsey. . . .

II.   The Count One Claim

Appellant theorizes that Senator Cannon's authorization of salary payments to Sobsey while the aide was not performing "official legislative and representational duties" made out an actionable false claim. . . .

A.   The Requirements of Section 232(C)

The False Claims Act was adopted during the Civil War, a time when massive frauds were being committed against the Government. To encourage action against defrauders, Congress authorized private citizens to bring civil actions against wrongdoers on the Government's behalf, and to retain half of any recovery. . . .

B.   Liability under the Act

. . . [W]e are . . . constrained to hold that dismissal of appellant's first count was appropriate. . . .

1.   Limits on Judicial Power

We approach our interpretation of the False Claims Act mindful of long-established principles governing the scope of judicial power in our constitutional scheme. We maintain, too, a candid recognition of functional limitations on the ability of the judiciary to deal with certain types of problems. Constitutionally speaking, federal courts may decide only "cases" and "controversies," and while neither of these terms has proven susceptible to precise definition, the courts traditionally have refused to undertake decisions on questions that are ill-suited to judicial resolution. This concept of justiciability appears in many guises, and traces its origins both to inherent limitations on the capabilities of judicial tribunals as well as to the separation-of-powers concerns central in our system of government.

. . . A challenge to the interworkings of a Senator and his staff member raises at the outset the specter that such a question lurks, and it is to an investigation of that possibility that we first turn.

2. *Lack of Judicially Discernible Rules or Standards*

Although the precise boundaries of the political-question doctrine are obscure, " '[i]n determining whether a question falls within (that) category, the appropriateness under our system of government of attributing finality to the action of the political departments and also the lack of satisfactory criteria for a judicial determination are dominant considerations.' " Prominent characteristics of political questions are a textually demonstrable constitutional commitment of the issue to a coordinate political department; or a lack of judicially discoverable and manageable standards for resolving it; or the impossibility of deciding without an initial policy determination of a kind clearly for nonjudicial discretion; or the impossibility of a court's undertaking independent resolution without expressing lack of the respect due coordinate branches of government. . . .

We perceive no "textually demonstrable commitment" of the issue before us to any other branch of the Federal Government. Nor do we believe that judicial review of congressional employment decisions necessarily involves a "lack of the respect due coordinate branches of government." We do find, however, a complete absence "of judicially discoverable and manageable standards for resolving" the question whether Senators may use paid staff members in their campaign activities.

a. Lack of Statutory, Administrative and Case Law

Appellant cites no judicial decision or administrative ruling, nor has our own research revealed any, establishing a standard to guide a court in determination of the issue generated by the first count of the complaint. Nor have we encountered any statute affording that kind of assistance. It is true that "sums appropriated for the various branches of expenditure in the public service" are statutorily confined "to the objects for which they are respectively made," and consequently are available "for no others." But we are unable to agree with the American Law Division of the Library of Congress in its conclusion that this statutory directive perforce bars public compensation of congressional staff members for the performance of campaign activities. The unambiguous meaning of this relatively straightforward provision is simply that appropriated funds are to be applied solely to statutorily-enumerated purposes, and the appropriations bills covering the era of Senator Cannon's reelection campaign tells us no more than that their purpose was "compensation of officers, employees, clerks to Senators." Even assuming, as fairly we may, that the funds appropriated were intended solely to compensate staffers for performance of their "official" duties, we are left with the perplexing question whether campaign work is official activity. Not even the Senate itself has been able to reach a consensus on the propriety of using staff members in reelection campaigns; rather, the history of its attempts to develop a suitable rule reveals the lack of a firm standard during the period relevant to this case, and vividly portrays the keen difficulties with which courts would be faced were they to attempt to design guidelines on their own.

b. Senatorial Treatment

When, in 1976, Senator Cannon launched his reelection drive, the Senate restricted campaign activity by staff members only in the area of fund-handling. Senate Resolution 266, adopted in 1966, had established standards of conduct for Members, officers and employees, and the sole provision dealing with staffers' participation in campaigns was Rule 43, which allowed only designated employees to receive, solicit, hold, or distribute campaign funds.

Quite significantly the Senate Select Committee on Standards, in recommending Rule 43, noted the high degree of personal allegiance owed a Member of Congress by his immediate staff, and the undesirability of interference with a Member's discretion in assigning duties to staff personnel. Resultantly, the Committee disavowed any intention to deter campaign activity by Senate employees beyond involvement with campaign monies. The floor debate on Resolution 266 similarly was a reaffirmation that a Senator's staff was generally free to assist in his reelection efforts. Both Senator Stennis, the chairman of the Select Committee, and Senator Cooper, a member of the Committee, emphasized that, except for fundraising, the Committee had imposed no limits on staffers' campaign activities.

It was not until after Senator Cannon's 1976 reelection that the Senate began to reconsider the role of staff in senatorial campaigns. In early 1977, a Special Committee on Official Conduct was instructed to formulate standards of behavior for Members, officers and employees. On March 10 of that year, the Committee reported favorably on Senate Resolution 110, which recommended major changes in the standing rules of the Senate.

One suggested revision was a new Rule 49, designed to refine the provisions of the older Rule 43 respecting the handling of campaign funds by forbidding staff members from soliciting such funds. Paragraph 3 of Rule 49 also "attempted . . . to deal with some of the complicated and delicate issues relating to the political activity of officers and employees whose salaries are paid by the Senate." The Committee readily acknowledged difficulties in distinguishing between a staffer's official duties and his campaign assistance, but nevertheless proposed removal from the Senate payroll of officers and employees "engag(ing) substantially in campaign activities." The Committee said:

> While the prohibition applies equally to activities on behalf of any candidate for Federal office, the particular concern of the Committee was that Senate staff not stay on the payroll if they are engaging in substantial campaign activities on behalf of the reelection effort of the Senator for whom they work.
>
> The Committee considered writing this rule in terms of the number of hours spent on campaigning for the percentage of time spent on campaign activities, but concluded that this approach would be futile. However, the Committee believes that the intention of the rule is clear enough: If a Senate employee is substantially engaged in campaign activities on behalf of a candidate, that the employee should not be receiving his salary from the Government. The Committee understands that this is the approach currently taken by most Members of the Senate.

Because of the complexity of the issue, however, the rule's injunction was to be qualified by exceptions for an individual's "political activity directly related to his official duties," for "campaign activity of a de minimis nature," and for "voluntary campaign activity on the officer's or employee's own time."

Paragraph 3 of Rule 49 represents the most serious effort a Senate unit has yet made to regulate the use of Members' personal staffs in reelection campaigns. It met a very early demise, however, a fate reflective of the still-continuing inability of the Senate to prescribe binding standards of behavior in that regard, as well as of the perceived need for further study of the problem. Before Resolution 110 was introduced on the floor of the Senate, Paragraph 3 was withdrawn. . . . [and] was replaced with a provision requiring the Committee on Rules and Administration to report, within 180 days, "proposals to prohibit the misuse of official staff by holders of public office in campaigns for . . . election, to Federal office." Resolution 110, as thus altered, was adopted by the Senate.

The report summoned by Resolution 110 did not issue early. While it was awaited, there were developments in the Senate, but these too mirrored the body's usual ambivalence on the problem. On May 11, 1977, the Senate Select Committee on Ethics rendered an interpretive ruling on the use of staff in campaigns pending availability of the report of the Committee on Rules and Administration. The Committee advised:

> In the iterim [sic], Members must use their best judgment in taking staff off the Senate payroll to devote substantial portions of their time or to participate for any extended period in such activities. The Committeee [sic] on Ethics recognizes staff frequently will be reinstated after campaign activities.

Additionally, on June 13, 1977, the Senate agreed to Resolution 188, which effectuated a recommendation by the Committee on Rules and Administration that Rule 49 be amended to allow designated employees to solicit as well as handle campaign funds. It is of no little moment for this case that the Committee's report called attention to Rule 49's proposed ban on fund-solicitation by staffers, and declared that aside from fund-raising rules

> [t]he committee is not aware of any laws which prohibit individuals who are part of a Senator's staff from participating in a Senator's reelection campaign as long as they do not neglect their Senate duties, and the committee does not feel there should be such proscriptions.

Meanwhile, the Committee on Rules and Administration pressed forward in the mission directed by Senate Resolution 110. . . .

The Committee issued its first report on October 17, 1977. With respect to staff use in election campaigns, the report recounted the salient events discussed earlier in this opinion. On the basis of this review, the Committee concluded that "[o]ther than the actual handling of campaign funds, the Senate has not imposed any restrictions on the participation of a member of a Senator's staff in that Senator's reelection campaign." The Committee therefore supported the general rule . . . that members of a Senator's staff are permitted to engage in the reelection campaign of a Senator, as long as that staff member does not neglect his or her Senate duties. The nature and scope of a staff member's Senate duties are determined by each Member of the Senate. Such duties necessarily encompass political and representational responsibilities, as well as legislative, administrative, or clerical ones, and are often performed during irregular and unconventional work hours. A similar rule of practice has been followed in the House of Representatives, and would be generally applicable to other Federal employees not covered by the Hatch Act.

The Committee announced its intention to study, as the second stage of its work, the role of staff members in political campaigns, a project in which the Committee presumably is still engaged.

3. Manageability and Need for Initial Policy Determinations

As this historical resume makes abundantly clear, there were in 1976 and there are now no "manageable standards" for a court to apply when viewing staff participation in a Senate reelection campaign. Moreover, the inability of the Senate, a body constitutionally authorized and institutionally equipped to formulate national policies and internal rules of conduct, to solve the problem demonstrates "the impossibility of deciding" the issue appellant poses "without an initial policy determination of a kind clearly for nonjudicial discretion." Indeed, the interpretation of the False Claims Act suggested by appellant would license the courts to monitor every action taken by a Senator and his aide in an effort to determine whether it is sufficiently "official" or too "political." . . .

In the absence of any discernible legal standard or even of a congressional policy determination that would aid consideration and decision of the question raised by appellant's first count, we are loathe to give the False Claims Act an interpretation that would require the judiciary to develop rules of behavior for the Legislative Branch. We are unwilling to conclude that Congress gave the courts a free hand to deal with so sensitive and controversial a problem, or invited them to assume the role of political overseer of the other branches of Government. . . .

NOTES AND QUESTIONS

1. *Political question.* At issue in *Cannon* was an allegation of exclusive use of staff services for campaign work. Why did the court determine that such an allegation did not make out a claim under the False Claims Act? Would you have ruled this way? The Supreme Court denied certiorari in *Cannon*, 454 U.S. 810 (1982). This decision and its underlying policy were sharply criticized in Ivan Kline, Note, Use of Congressional Staff in Election Campaigning, 82 Colum. L. Rev. 998 (1982).

2. *Applying another statute.* Assume that the Washington statute excerpted on page 426 governed in this case. Would the result have been different? What about applying the Florida statute? California makes it illegal to use public funds for purposes not authorized by law. Cal. Penal Code §424 (2008). Would this law, if applicable, have affected the *Cannon* court? Consider its applicability in California in the following case. Internal citations and footnotes have been omitted except where particularly relevant.

Fair Political Practices Commission v. Suitt
90 Cal. App. 3d 125 (1979)

Paras, Judge.
This is a consolidated appeal from a portion of the judgment entered in Friends of Tom Suitt v. The Fair Political Practices Commission (FPPC) . . . and from the judgment entered in Fair Political Practices Commission v. Suitt et al. . . .

The legal dispute arises out of the activities of Michael O'Key, an employee of the State of California and more specifically of the Caucus, an association of the Democratic members of the California Assembly. The Caucus is authorized by statute and by Assembly resolution to hire and direct employees, whose salaries are paid by the state.

The FPPC v. Suitt complaint alleges that in May and June of 1976, O'Key was relieved of some of his normal working responsibilities to enable him to perform campaign work for the Suitt Committee (Committee), a political committee working for the reelection of Assemblyman Tom Suitt. O'Key spent at least three of the twenty working days of May and at least three of the twenty-two working days of June on campaign activities. On these days he solicited campaign contributions and engaged in and was substantially responsible for campaign strategy and planning, coordination of the activities of volunteer workers, and preparation of the campaign budget. Such work was done at the behest of Suitt.

While allegedly performing campaign work, O'Key continued to receive his full state salary. He received no compensation from Suitt or the Committee; and neither the Committee nor anyone else reimbursed the state for his salary accumulation while doing the campaign work.

Pursuant to sections 84200 and 84210, the Committee was required to file periodic campaign disclosure statements, revealing contributions received and disbursements made. The FPPC contends that as a consequence of O'Key's campaign work the Committee received a nonmonetary contribution in the form of personal services, which it was required to disclose on the campaign disclosure statements covering the two months. The Committee made no such disclosure. . . .

The Political Reform Act was adopted as an initiative measure in June 1974, effective January 7, 1975. It covers a wide range of matters involving public officials, including lobbying, conflict of interest, and campaign disclosure. Section 81002 recites the public policy applicable to campaign disclosures and declares "Receipts and expenditures in election campaigns should be fully and truthfully disclosed in order that the voters may be fully informed and improper practices may be inhibited." To accomplish this purpose, section 84200 et seq. require all candidates and committees supporting or opposing candidates and ballot measures to file periodic campaign disclosure statements. The act also requires records to be kept, prohibits anonymous and cash contributions, and regulates payments by agents and intermediaries.

Campaign statements must disclose, inter alia, the "full name of each *person* from whom a contribution or contributions totaling fifty dollars ($50) or more has been received. . . ." (Italics added.) The term "contribution" includes not only cash and cash-equivalent contributions but also nonmonetary or "in-kind" contributions of goods and services. Specifically, "contribution" is defined to include "the payment of compensation *by any person* for the personal services or expenses of any other person if such services are rendered or expenses incurred on behalf of a candidate or committee without payment of full and adequate consideration." (Italics added.) This provision is intended to prevent a potential subterfuge; it assures that when an employer allows an employee to spend compensated time in campaign work for a campaign committee, the committee must report that benefit, just as it would if the employer made a direct cash contribution to the committee which in turn used it to pay a campaign worker.

The term "person" is broadly defined in section 82047 to mean ". . . an individual, proprietorship, firm, partnership, joint venture, syndicate, business trust, company, corporation, association, committee, and *any other organization or group of persons acting in concert.*" (Italics added.) The emphasized segment of the definition, broad as it is, appears at first blush to include the Caucus and other governmental entities like it, but because governmental entities are not actually specified respondents offer several reasons for the supposition that they were intentionally omitted.

Respondents assert first that "much of what is done by the Legislature, and consequently by legislative aides, is done for a political purpose," therefore application of the act to the Legislature would result in ". . . an interference with the normal functioning of the sovereign powers of the Legislature." Just how this comes about is not clear to us; presumably the claim is that the effort of legislators would be hampered by their inability to distinguish work on a political campaign from work on legislation in deciding what is or is not a contribution under section 82015. As the FPPC points out in response, this argument is not convincing; for even if the definition of "contribution" might be unclear as applied to certain legislative activities not here involved, the Act obviously does not infringe on the performance of Suitt's official duties insofar as the activities alleged in this case are concerned. The use of state employees by a legislator's campaign committee to solicit contributions, plan campaign strategy, coordinate volunteers, and prepare the campaign budget, all at state expense, is in no way a proper part of a legislator's official functions; that is not to be questioned. If it is to be done at all, the public has a serious interest in its disclosure.

The Legislature's asserted difficulty here, if indeed it exists, is no different from that faced by government officials in distinguishing between the improper expenditure of public funds for "campaign" purposes and the proper expenditure thereof for "informational" activities. In Stanson v. Mott (1976) 17 Cal. 3d 206, 223, the Supreme Court resolved that problem by holding governmental officials liable only if they fail to use due care in authorizing the expenditure. Analogously the Legislature need not be absolutely perfect in distinguishing between the performance by its employees of proper legislative functions as distinguished from election campaigning; it should nonetheless exercise due care in separating the two activities.

Respondents emphasize however that the Legislature is so political that it is impossible to distinguish campaigning from legislating. In particular, they state:

> . . . Government Code Section 82015 defines "contribution" as "a payment . . . except to the extent that full and adequate consideration is received unless it is

clear from the surrounding circumstances that it is not made for a political purpose."

This definition makes a payment a "contribution" unless it is not made for a political purpose. The use of the double negative means that if there is a single political purpose, then a payment made with such purpose is a contribution. That is, if there are multiple purposes, one of which is a political purpose, a payment made for the multiple purposes is a contribution notwithstanding the existence of non-political purposes.

Since the definition of "payment" in Government Code Section 82044 includes *in-kind* services, any rendering of service, one of the purposes of which is a political purpose, is a contribution within the meaning of Section 82015. The Administrative Code further defines political purposes . . . as meaning, "made for the purpose of influencing or attempting to influence the action of the voters for or against the nomination or election of a candidate. . . ."

As we have previously indicated, however, the alleged activities in the present case were unambiguously political. Of course, there may be certain marginal activities which are neither specifically included by the act's campaign disclosure provisions nor excluded from them. Thus, there may be some ambiguity as to whether certain activities by legislators are "contributions." However, any ambiguity can be cured through regulations or judicial constructions which draw clear lines for the marginal cases. . . .

With respect to campaign activities by publicly paid staff, the FPPC acknowledges that a situation may arise in which lines are difficult to draw, although no such difficulty is presented by the instant case. Therefore, the FPPC advises us in its reply brief that pursuant to its rule making authority, it is now preparing to take public testimony and to develop guidelines which will eliminate any possible ambiguity with respect to campaign activities involving public employees, office facilities and supplies. The solution to any ambiguity that may exist in the statute is to develop clear, enforceable standards for the marginal cases, not, as respondents suggest, to eliminate the reporting requirement entirely. . . .

The judgments in both cases are reversed, except only for the portion of the *Suitt v. FPPC* judgment which awards attorney fees (no appeal having been taken therefrom). Appellant shall recover costs on appeal.

REGAN, ACTING P.J., and REYNOSO, J., concurred.

NOTES AND QUESTIONS

1. *Compare and contrast.* Compare and contrast the facts and statutes in *Suitt* and *Cannon*. Can the decision in *Suitt* be rationalized on the basis of different behavior or different regulatory schemes? Or is the difference reflective of a difference in judicial approaches to questions of separation of power?

2. *A New York example.* New York has historically left it up to individual legislators to set staff functions. In 1987, legislators and legislative staff were indicted by the New York County District Attorney for theft under various generic sections of the state penal statutes. The charge was that legislative staff had worked in campaigns, some exclusively, and that this work represented a theft of state resources. Excerpts from an opinion of New York's highest court, dismissing the charges, follow. In reading them, consider how they compare to the reasoning in *Cannon* and *Suitt*:

> Under the State Constitution, the Legislature alone has the power to authorize expenditures from the State treasury, and to "regulate and fix the wages or salaries and the hours of work or labor . . . of persons employed by the state" (N.Y. Const., art. XIII, §14). The Legislative Law delegates to the Minority Leader the power to "appoint such employees to assist him in the performance of his duties as may be authorized and provided for in the legislative appropriation bill" (§6[2]) and to determine their tenure (§8) and salaries (§10). Similar powers are delegated with respect to committees (§9). However, there is no statute fixing the hours of work for such employees or defining the duties of legislative aides or the duties of the Minority Leader they are hired to assist. And at the times relevant here, there was no rule or regulation concerning these matters. The Legislature is not always in session, and when it is in session, legislators and their staffs often work late into the night and through holidays and weekends until the Legislature's work is done. They were not required to account for their time and received no additional compensation or formal compensatory time allowances for overtime. Legislative staff members worked when they were needed and were often given free time when they were not needed, at the discretion of the particular legislator.
>
> The appropriation bill that authorized the salaries in this case limited the amount of money available but did not otherwise limit the legislator's powers with respect to the allocation of staff time or function. It provided simply that the funds were to be used for "personal service of employees and for temporary and expert services of legislative and program operations . . . [and] of standing committees."
>
> Thus the statutes permitted the individual legislator to appoint staff members, to determine the terms and conditions of their employment and to assign duties and the hours of work as the legislator deemed necessary to fulfill the broad range of legislative duties. Despite this extensive grant of authority, the prosecutor urges that a Senator's power to assign duties to legislative assistants should be limited to governmental activities and should not include purely political ones. Although this distinction may be relevant to other State employees, the line between political and governmental activities is not so easily drawn in cases dealing with legislators and their assistants.
>
> The Legislature is the "political" branch of government. All of its members are elected every two years and all legislation is the product of political activity both inside and outside the Legislature. Indeed, by statute the State Legislature itself is structured along party lines with the majority

and minority parties in both houses organized behind elected party leaders. As noted, the Minority Leader is expressly authorized to appoint persons to assist him with his duties, and annual appropriations specifically authorize the expenditure of State funds to compensate these employees and enable the party leaders to carry out that party's "program operations." In addition to political activities formally recognized at law, there are additional functions which a legislator performs to gain support in the community, such as distributing newsletters and meeting constituents. Although these activities may be fairly characterized as political, as opposed to governmental, they are considered an inherent part of the job of an elected representative and thus perfectly legitimate acts for a legislator or legislative assistant to perform (Hutchinson v. Proxmire, 443 U.S. 111). Indeed, the prosecutor does not suggest that every legislator who uses State facilities or personnel for any type of political activity should be indicted for misuse of government funds. As the People make clear in their reply brief, for example: "The People recognize that some 'political' activities of legislators and their aides do fall into an uncertain or 'gray' area." Conduct is not illegal "merely because legislative employees worked on election campaigns." It has "never been [the People's] position that legislative employees are prohibited from engaging in political campaign activity." Thus the prosecutor's objection to the defendants' use of Senate staff for the campaigns is not based on the fact that it is a political activity but on the belief that it is too political.

People v. Ohrenstein, 77 N.Y.2d 38, 46-47 (N.Y. 1990).

3. *Defining representative and campaign activities.* Both *Cannon* and *Ohrenstein* resulted in dismissals because of the absence of clear rules under which to evaluate legislative activity. As the *Cannon* decision indicates, legislators are reluctant line drawers. This reluctance is based on the difficulty of the task and on an unwillingness to limit themselves in their reelection efforts. What rules would you impose on a legislative body regarding the use of staff or resources? Consider the following findings from a report issued by a blue ribbon commission established by the New York State Legislature in response to the indictments in the *Ohrenstein* case. The commission was composed of a former governor, Malcolm Wilson; a former dean of the New York University Law School, Robert McCabe; and a former state senator, Carol Bellamy. Among its staff members was the noted legal ethicist Professor Stephen Gillers.

*Report of the New York State Blue Ribbon Commission
to Review Legislative Practices in Relation to Political
Campaign Activities of Legislative Employees*
5, 9-11 (1988)

Perhaps the heart of our assignment is to define the conduct in which a legislative employee may not engage when he or she is being paid to do legislative work. . . .

Much of what legislative employees *legitimately* do is "political" in the conventional sense of that word: Keeping constituents informed on issues, for example, or helping a member develop support for a bill. Many of these political activities will properly help a member in future campaigns. The Legislature is a political body and a member is the political representative of his or her constituents. If a member does his or her political job well, the member's campaign chances are enhanced.

On the other hand, some work that can also be labeled "political" would clearly be off-limits to legislative employees when acting in their official capacities.

We have been instructed to recommend guidelines regulating "political campaign activity," which for convenience we shall refer to as "campaign work." One is generic; the other is with examples. We do both. . . .

Guideline One: Campaign Work

I. In these guidelines, a legislative employee is any person compensated by the state of New York in any manner for the performance of official duties on behalf of a member or officer of the legislature or a legislative commission, committee or office. . . .

II. Except in accordance with guideline two [voluntary campaign work], a legislative employee may not assign or engage in campaign work. Campaign work is work that does not reasonably fulfill the employee's official duties while materially contributing to (A) a person's chance of election or reelection to public or party office, or (B) the financial prospects or the electoral advantage of a political party.

III. Work that would otherwise be campaign work within the meaning of paragraph II is not prohibited if it occurs on rare and isolated occasions and its performance imposes little or no cost on the state.

Commentary

1. Examples of work that would be considered campaign work within the definition of paragraph II are the following, taken in part from the California Administrative Code. This list is illustrative:

   a. acting in the capacity of campaign manager or coordinator;
   b. arranging or coordinating a campaign related event;
   c. soliciting, receiving or acknowledging campaign contributions or arranging for the raising of contributions;
   d. developing, writing or distributing campaign literature or making arrangements for campaign literature;
   e. arranging for the development, production or distribution of campaign literature;

> f.   preparing television, radio or newspaper campaign advertisements;
> g.   establishing liaison with or coordinating activities of campaign volunteers;
> h.   preparing campaign budgets;
> i.   preparing campaign statements;
> j.   participating in partisan get-out-the-vote drives;
> k.   posting campaign placards;
> l.   analyzing polling data that deal with voter profiles or preferences;
> m. transporting voters to the polls.

2. By contrast, some work is not within the definition of campaign work although it may materially contribute to a person's electoral chances. This is because the work reasonably fulfills the employee's official duties. Examples include helping a legislator prepare speeches to constituents and assisting a legislator's effort to transmit his or her views to the public and press, except when these activities may be prohibited because of the proximity of an election. See Guideline Five.

3. Situations will arise when it will be difficult to determine whether work is campaign work. In deciding whether work is campaign work it is proper to consider the factual context, including the nature of the work in question; its proximity to, and likely influence on, an election; and the official duties of the employee who engages in the work. The Guidelines Oversight Commission will be available to give advice on these questions. Over time, its opinions will provide further guidance on the dividing line between campaign work and legislative work. . . .

5. It is impossible to catalogue an employee's "official duties" as that term is used in Paragraph II. There are many kinds of employees and many kinds of official duties. Generally, the term refers to the work assignments of an employee that advance the representational and lawmaking tasks of the Legislature and its constituents. Our purpose in using the term "official duties" is to make it clear that if work reasonably fulfills such duties, then its effect on a future campaign or on a party's finances is unimportant. Representational tasks include constituent casework, preparation of newsletters to constituents, and public appearances. . . .

7. The definition of campaign work refers to work that substantially increases the "financial prospects or electoral advantage of a political party." This includes, but is not limited to, fundraising for a party and efforts to get out the vote for a party.

4. *Legislatures as Judges of Elections*

The constitutions of the United States and of the states delegate to their legislative bodies the power to be the judge of their own elections. An example is Article I, §5, cl. 1 of the federal Constitution that provides that "each House shall be the Judge of the Elections, Returns and Qualifications of its own Members."

For the most part, election returns are certified by administrative officials, with challenges directed to the courts. But, on occasion, the challenge to election returns is decided by the legislative body for which the race is run. This infrequent phenomenon is explored in the following materials. Internal citations and footnotes have been omitted except where particularly relevant.

Morgan v. United States
801 F.2d 445 (D.C. Cir. 1986)

SCALIA, Circuit Judge:
This case presents the question whether we have jurisdiction to review the substance or procedure of a determination by the House of Representatives that one of two contestants was lawfully elected to that body. . . .

I

This litigation grows out of one of the closest congressional elections in history. Initial returns in November 1984 showed that Democrat Frank McCloskey had won the House seat in the Eighth Congressional District of Indiana by 72 votes. After corrections to the returns, the count showed that his opponent, Republican Richard McIntyre, had won by 34 votes. On December 13, 1984 the Secretary of State of Indiana certified that McIntyre had won. A subsequent recount supervised by the state courts and completed January 22, 1985 showed that McIntyre had won by 418 votes. Before this recount could be completed, however, the House of Representatives assembled. On January 3, by a party-line vote, the House declined to seat McIntyre and appointed a Task Force of the House Administration Committee to investigate the election. The Task Force decided to conduct its own recount and to employ its own rules rather than those of Indiana state election law. Its report, issued April 29, concluded that McCloskey had won by four votes out of the more than 230,000 votes cast. H.R. Rep. No. 58, 99th Cong., 1st Sess. 2 (1985). On May 1, again by a party-line vote, the House seated McCloskey.

In this suit . . . a group of registered Republicans residing in Indiana, Maryland, and Virginia named the United States, the House of Representatives, three Democratic House leaders, and three House employees as defendants. The plaintiffs, proceeding *pro se*, alleged that the refusal to seat McIntyre violated their rights of free speech and association, their first amendment right to petition the government for redress of grievances, their rights under the due process clause and the tenth amendment, along with several other constitutional provisions and the Federal Contested Election Act, Pub. L. No. 91-138, 83 Stat. 284 (1969). They requested an injunction seating McIntyre with full seniority rights retroactive to January 3, 1985, a declaration that the House proceedings pursuant to the election investigation and the seating of McCloskey are void, and monetary damages.

The District Court dismissed the suit with prejudice. . . . On the subsequent appeal to this court, we denied the appellants' motions for summary reversal and expedition and directed the appellants to show cause why the decision of the District Court should not be summarily affirmed. The appellants have now responded to that order, and the appellees have submitted a reply.

II

Summary affirmance is appropriate where the merits of an appeal "are so clear as to justify expedited action." Because the Constitution so unambiguously proscribes judicial review of the proceedings in the House of Representatives that led to the seating of McCloskey, we believe that further briefing and oral argument in this case would be pointless, and that the decision of the District Court should be summarily affirmed.

It is difficult to imagine a clearer case of "textually demonstrable constitutional commitment" of an issue to another branch of government to the exclusion of the courts, see Baker v. Carr, 369 U.S. 186, 217 (1962), than the language of Article I, section 5, clause 1 that "each House shall be the Judge of the Elections, Returns and Qualifications of its own Members." The provision states not merely that each House "may judge" these matters, but that each House "shall be *the* Judge." The exclusion of others — and in particular of others who are judges — could not be more evident. Hence, without need to rely upon the amorphous and partly prudential doctrine of "political questions," we simply lack jurisdiction to proceed.

The history of the Elections Clause is entirely consistent with its plain exclusion of judicial jurisdiction. In the formative years of the American republic, it was "the uniform practice of England and America" for legislatures to be the final judges of the elections and qualifications of their members. There was no opposition to the Elections Clause in the Federal Constitutional Convention, and the minor opposition in the ratification debates focused upon the clause's removal of final authority not from the courts, but from the state legislatures, where the Articles of Confederation had vested an analogous power. It is noteworthy that none of the responses to the opposition mentions the safeguard of judicial review. Such a safeguard was evidently unthinkable, since the determination of the legislative House was *itself* deemed to be a *judicial* one. . . . As far as we are aware, in none of the discussions of the clause did there appear a trace of suggestion that the power it conferred was not exclusive and final. . . .

In almost two centuries of numerous election contests resolved by the House and Senate, beginning in the very first Congress, no court, as far as we are aware, has ever undertaken to review the legislative judgment or (until the present litigation) even been asked to do so. . . .

It is true, as the appellants point out, that this court has found no absolute prohibition of judicial review in the clause, adjacent the Elections Clause, which states that "each House may determine the Rules of its Proceedings." Art. I, §5, cl. 2. But the language of that clause is not comparable. Authorization to determine rules of proceedings does not inevitably exclude, review of the lawfulness of those rules; the command to "be the judge of . . . Elections" excludes other judges. The other constitutional text in which the appellants seek to find a helpful analogy, which provides that state legislatures may prescribe "the Times, Places and Manner of holding Elections for Senators and Representatives," Art. I, §4, cl. 1, is even less comparable. Moreover, even while undertaking judicial review of such state prescriptions, the Supreme Court held in no uncertain terms that the authority of the states must not preclude the exclusive authority of each House to decide whether to seat its members.

While it is not our role to examine the wisdom of a disposition that appears so clearly in the text and history of the Constitution, we may observe that it makes eminent practical sense. The pressing legislative demands of contemporary government have if anything increased the need for quick, decisive resolution of election controversies. Adding a layer of judicial review, which would undoubtedly be resorted to on a regular basis, would frustrate this end. What is involved, it should be borne in mind, is not judicial resolution of a narrow issue of law, but review of an election recount, with all the fact-finding that that entails. If it be said that the relevant House is not the appropriate body to make the determination because of the possibility of improper political motivation, the response is that "all power may be abused if placed in unworthy hands. But it would be difficult . . . to point out any other hands in which this power would be more safe, and at the same time equally effectual." . . .

The major evil of interference by other branches of government is entirely avoided, while a substantial degree of responsibility is still provided by regular elections, the interim demands of public opinion, and the desire of each House to preserve its standing in relation to the other institutions of government. . . .

Our holding today does not, of course, preclude all judicial challenges bearing any relationship to legislative resolution of disputed elections. It is conceivable, for example, that in investigating such a dispute a House might go beyond its constitutional power to compel witnesses. In that event, "a clear showing of such arbitrary and improvident use of the power as will constitute a denial of due process of law" would justify limited "judicial interference." Such a due process violation, however, must rest on violation of some individual interest beyond the failure to seat an individual or to recognize that person as the winner of an election. That substantive determination, which is the issue in the present case, resides entirely with the House.

On this court's own motion, the decision of the District Court is summarily affirmed.

NOTES AND QUESTIONS

1. *The history of House judgments.* From 1933 to the date of the McCloskey-McIntyre dispute, 82 challenges had been brought to the House, and the House has seated the certified winner pending completion of its inquiry 81 times. The only exception was in 1961, when one candidate was certified by the secretary of state, who later wrote to the House stating he was mistaken and that the other contestant should be certified.

2. *The Committee on House Administration.* After receiving the matter described in *Morgan*, the Committee on House Administration appointed a three-member task force to investigate the election. The Task Force met 23 times over several months and conducted a number of public hearings at which hours of testimony was received. It found considerable inconsistencies in standards applied by each of the 15 counties that were conducting the recount. Among these inconsistencies were the treatment of absentee ballots and the application of various technicalities of Indiana law. The consequence of this finding was the ordering of an additional recount.

Government auditors and outside experts were appointed to the task. Under rules established by the task force for, among other things, determining the validity of absentee ballots, they determined that McCloskey had won by four votes. The Committee then certified McCloskey the winner by a count of 116,645 to 116,641.

3. *Federal Contested Election Act* (2 U.S.C. §§381-396). The Federal Contested Election Act provides a procedural framework for the prosecution of election challenges in the House of Representatives. It does not set forth substantive standards. See McIntyre v. Fallahay, 766 F.2d 1078 (7th Cir. 1985).

4. *The case of Senator Packwood.* In 1993, a group of Oregonians petitioned the United States Senate to exclude Senator Bob Packwood from the Senate and to declare his seat vacant. Petitioners claimed that Senator Packwood, in his reelection campaign of 1992, had defrauded the voters by making deliberate misstatements about material facts regarding his sexual behavior toward women. Particularly, the petitioners claimed that Senator Packwood lied to reporters about his history of sexual aggression toward female employees and other women and that he threatened to harm women who made his actions public. Further, according to the petitioners, but for the lies, Packwood would have lost the election. The Senate referred the petition to the Senate Committee on Rules and Administration, which

undertook its deliberation. At issue was whether, assuming the truth of these allegations, such behavior (lying about material facts) was grounds for declaring a Senate seat vacant or whether the issue was a question of legislative ethics (the misconduct toward female staff members) that should be dealt with by the Senate Ethics Committee. Both sides argued ethics, policy, and precedent. The latter argument focused on whether authority to be the judge of elections is limited to judging voting procedures and vote counting. If you were a member of the Rules Committee, how would you vote? For an interesting discussion of false campaign promises, see Stephen D. Sencer, Note, Read My Lips: Examining the Legal Implications of Knowingly False Campaign Promises, 90 Mich. L. Rev. 428 (1991).

D.   THE REPRESENTATIVE RELATIONSHIP

Central to the debates over qualifications for legislative office, the electoral process, and the question of legislative ethics (discussed in the next section) is the concept of the representative relationship—the relationship between the representative and her constituents—in the legislative process. The nature of this relationship was the subject of considerable attention and controversy during the debate over the ratification of the Constitution and has continued to be debated among political scientists and ethicists. It is confusion about this relationship that also underlies much of the criticism of legislators, as the public either wants legislators to ignore district interests, for the public interest, or pay attention to district interests, as the district's representative.

The debate has revolved around the question of what is and what ought to be the duty of an elected representative. Answers range from acting pursuant to the wishes of a majority of constituents (the delegate theory) to acting pursuant to his or her best judgment or conscience (the trustee theory). See generally J. Roland Pennock, Democratic Political Theory (1979); Hannah F. Pitkin, The Concept of Representation (1967); Gordon Wood, The Creation of the American Republic, 1776-1787 (1969). This debate can only provide some guideposts for an understanding of representation. The legislative process is too complex and the rational need for compromise too great to permit neat categories. Nor are most issues susceptible to such categorization. A legislator may also have a variety of allegiances, concerns, and sensibilities on any given issue that he factors into the making of a particular decision. What can be observed is that legislators reflect the dominant attitudes and status of their constituents and believe they are responsible for expressing the same in the legislative arena. In the experience of both of the authors, legislators first respond to proposed legislation on the basis of their own policy views and then, when appropriate, refract them through other relevant prisms such as constituent and party demands. On what basis a decision is made depends on the intensity of each factor. The notion, propounded by some commentators, that the voting choices of individual legislators are generally determined by materialistic (what's-in-it-for-me) views is simply wrong. As one observer, who spent a year following then Speaker Wright, has written:

> Legislators . . . wanted solutions. That was far different from being [individuals] . . . who exploited an issue for political gain rather than trying to solve it. Legislators were problem solvers, solution seekers. They did not deal in rhetoric or theory; they had to write real laws which had real effects on real people. If an issue was too large or complex to resolve, legislators . . . "often times will deal with a minute part of a problem." If an issue had to be compromised to pass and if principle was not involved, so be it. Half a loaf was better than none — it was a solution.

John M. Barry, The Ambition and the Power 98 (1989). For a detailed study of the influences on voting decisions of members of the House of Representatives, see John W. Kingdon, Congressmen's Voting Decisions (1989). See also Hannah F. Pitkin, The Concept of Representation (1967):

> Thus in legislative behavior a great complexity and plurality of determinants are at work, any number of which may enter into a legislative decision. The legislator represents neither by a simple response to constituency desires nor by detached, Olympian judgment on the merits of a proposal. None of the analogies of acting for others on the individual level seems satisfactory for explaining the relationship between a political representative and his constituents. He is neither agent nor trustee nor deputy nor commissioner; he acts for a group of people without a single interest, most of whom seem incapable of forming an explicit will on political questions.

Hannah F. Pitkin, The Concept of Representation 220-21 (1967).

Sometimes legislators actually do join issue at the extremes of this debate. This arises when an issue becomes so poignant that it touches a legislator's personal sense of morality. Examples of this type of issue are abortion and the death penalty. Consider the exchange below from a 1978 New York State Senate debate on the death penalty:

> The PRESIDENT: Senator Solomon.
> SENATOR SOLOMON: Thank you. Madam President, this is the first time I have addressed this Chamber. As one of the newer members of the House, along with Mr. Connor and Mr. Gallagher, I also have the opportunity to be out in the streets. In fact, I continue to be out in my district. As late as Sunday night I was out in my district on a forum on crime and the overwhelming majority of constituents in my area are in favor of the death penalty. They realize it is not the sole solution. I realize that also, but it is one of the solutions

which has to be put into effect. We have to go back to it if only for the reason that the psychology of the constituents that I represent demands it. It is the issue which is constantly brought up time and time again.

Now, I feel that as an elected representative, on an issue where such an overwhelming majority of the constituents are in favor of the Volker bill, and particularly in restoring capital punishment, it is my moral obligation to vote to restore capital punishment in this state. . . .

SENATOR BURSTEIN: Madam President.

The PRESIDENT: Senator Burstein.

SENATOR BURSTEIN: I just want to say to my colleagues, Senator Solomon and Senator Tauriello, that somebody once addressed himself to the particular problem that they are confronting. It was Edmund Burke upon his election as a member of Parliament. We will excuse the fact that at that time there were no women elected. He said, "[c]ertainly, gentlemen, it ought to be the happiness and glory of a representative to live in the strictest union, the closest correspondence, and the most unreserved communication with his constituents. Their wishes ought to have great weight with him; their opinion, high respect; their business, unremitted attention. It is his duty to sacrifice his repose, his pleasures, his satisfaction to theirs; and above all, ever, and in all cases, to prefer their interests to his own. But his unbiased opinion, his mature judgment, his enlightened conscience, he ought not to be sacrificed to you, to any man, or to any set of men living," or women. "These he does not derive from your pleasure; no, nor from the law and the constitution. They are a trust from Providence, for the abuse of which he is deeply answerable. Your representative owes you, not his industry only, but his judgment; and he betrays, instead of serving you, if he sacrifices it to your opinion."

I vote no.

NOTES AND QUESTIONS

1. *The right choice?* Which view of representation do you share with respect to this issue? At the time of this vote, both senators' districts were overwhelmingly in favor of the death penalty. What significance do you attach to the fact that such an unpopular vote might cause the senator to be defeated at the next election? What significance do you attach to the fact that Senator Burstein's opponent in her last election, prior to the above debate, had used her position on the death penalty as a campaign issue against her?

2. *Local versus national.* A more frequent example of a voting dilemma is the choice between an obvious local interest and an obvious national interest. Extreme examples of this are votes on the closing of military bases or votes adversely affecting the tobacco industry by representatives from tobacco-producing states. In each case, successful legislation may cause substantial economic disruption to the legislator's district and raise serious campaign issues. Consider the comments of Senator Robert C. Byrd of West Virginia explaining his opposition to an otherwise broadly supported clean air bill, which passed the Senate by a vote of 89-11: "I cannot

vote for legislation that can bring economic ruin to communities throughout the Appalachian region and the Midwest." N.Y. Times, Apr. 4, 1990, at A20. Senator Byrd had unsuccessfully advocated an appropriation for support of mine workers who would lose their jobs as a result of the limitations on the production of high-sulfur coal. Is Senator Byrd correct? Does it make a difference that the coal mining regions of West Virginia are considered to be among the nation's poorest areas?

3. *National versus local.* During this same period of time, Representative Byron Dorgan of North Dakota was winning praise for opposing construction in his district of part of the MX missile system. Despite the fact that the installation represented a multimillion-dollar investment in his district, Dorgan argued "[t]o those in my district who yearn for the economic activity generated by the MX program . . . I must say that that's not the economic activity that builds a better future for us and our children." N.Y. Times, Mar. 31, 1990, at A24.

4. *The American tradition.* The concept of an "instructed" representative is consistent with founding American experience, however impractical or philosophically unsavory this idea may have become. See Gordon Wood, The Creation of the American Republic, 1776-1787, 162-75 (1969). The American concept of representation was forged in an environment hostile to the English concept of "virtual" representation. Under this English concept, Parliament was not, in the words of Edmund Burke, "a *congress* of ambassadors from different and hostile interests, which interest each must maintain, as an agent and advocate, against other agents and advocates; but Parliament is a *deliberative* assembly of *one* nation, with *one* interest, that of the whole, where not local purposes, not local prejudices ought to guide, but the general good, resulting from the general reason of the whole." Quoted in Wood, id. at 163.

5. *A practical view.* Judge Mikva recalls that, as part of an orientation program upon his first entering Congress in 1969, he was told by Congressman Morris Udall of Arizona that every elected representative came to Congress with a certain number of "chits" to use in expressing views unpopular with large groups of constituents. According to Udall, the representative who used all of his chits in the first term would be a failure as a public servant because he would be an ex-public servant. But, Udall continued, if these chits were not used at all, the representative would have wasted the opportunity to be a leader. "One should not leave this blessed place with unused 'chits,'" Udall concluded. Consider the wisdom of Udall's admonition in relation to the following statement of Carter Esqew, media consultant to Joseph Lieberman, the successful challenger in 1988 to incumbent Senator Lowell Weicker from Connecticut: "We beat him by showing what he was good at. . . . Lieberman made the case that Weicker cares deeply about issues, that he is a man of principle. But they are not often principles shared by the majority of people." Michael Specter, N.Y. Times, Sunday Magazine, Dec. 15, 1991, at 41.

E. CONFLICTS OF INTEREST

1. Norms for Legislative Behavior

American legislative bodies, historically, have had little success fashioning either norms of ethical behavior for their members or effective enforcement mechanisms. Despite the extraordinary self-regulating power granted by constitutions to legislative bodies, legislatures have basically chosen to rely on the election process for both defining ethical behavior and punishing members, except for the adoption of antibribery statutes (see, e.g., 18 U.S.C. §201) and the occasional and inconsistent punishment of "errant" members. See, e.g., Richard A. Baker, The History of Congressional Ethics, in Representation and Responsibility 3 (1985); Congressional Quarterly, Guide to Congress 828-61 (3d ed. 1982). This reliance has been the product of a number of factors: the collegial environment that permeates legislative bodies and dictates against judging colleagues in other than political terms; the belief by legislators that representative government places the primary responsibility for the regulation of a legislator's behavior with the electorate and the resultant difficulty in defining ethical standards; the institutional influence of legislators who have benefited from the absence of formal constraints; and the absence of public pressure for change.

This legislative reluctance to prescribe and judge the behavior of members was jarred during the 1960s and 1970s by a number of highly visible scandals involving legislators and legislative staff, all heightened by the resignation of President Nixon and the conviction of many of his aides as a result of the Watergate investigation. Throughout the nation, legislative bodies began to enact financial disclosure laws (see, e.g., 2 U.S.C. §701 et seq.), adopt codes of conduct, and consider meaningful mechanisms for enforcement.

The present rules of the House of Representatives exemplify these efforts to regulate the behavior of legislators. Adopted first in 1968, and strengthened in 1977, these rules were further tightened as part of the Ethics Reform Act of 1989, Pub. L. No. 101-194, 103 Stat. 1716 (1989). Excerpts from House Rule XXIII (Code of Official Conduct) and House Rule XXV (Limitations on Outside Earned Income and Acceptance of Gifts) follow:

HOUSE RULE XXIII

CODE OF OFFICIAL CONDUCT

There is hereby established by and for the House the following code of conduct, to be known as the "Code of Official Conduct":

1. A Member, Delegate, Resident Commissioner, officer, or employee of the House of Representatives shall conduct himself at all times in a manner which shall reflect creditably on the House.

2. A Member, Delegate, Resident Commissioner, officer, or employee of the House shall adhere to the spirit and the letter of the Rules of the House and to the rules of duly constituted committees thereof.

3. A Member, Delegate, Resident Commissioner, officer, or employee of the House may not receive compensation and may not permit compensation to accrue to his beneficial interest from any source, the receipt of which would occur by virtue of influence improperly exerted from his position in Congress.

4. A Member, Delegate, Resident Commissioner, officer, or employee of the House may not accept gifts except as provided by clause 5 of rule XXV.

5. A Member, Delegate, Resident Commissioner, officer, or employee of the House may not accept an honorarium for a speech, a writing for publication, or other similar activity, except as otherwise provided under rule XXV.

HOUSE RULE XXV

LIMITATIONS ON OUTSIDE EARNED INCOME AND ACCEPTANCE OF GIFTS

1. (a) Except as provided by subparagraph (b), a Member, Delegate, Resident Commissioner, officer, or employee of the House may not —

(1) have outside earned income attributable to such calendar year which exceeds 15 percent of the annual rate of basic pay for level II of the Executive Schedule under section 5313 of title 5, United States Code, as of January 1 of such calendar year; or

(2) receive any honorarium, except that an officer or employee of the House who is paid . . . less than 120 percent of the minimum rate of basic pay for GS-15 of the General Schedule may receive an honorarium unless the subject matter is directly related to the official duties of the individual, the payment is made because of the status of the individual with the House, or the person offering the honorarium has interests that may be substantially affected by the performance or nonperformance of the official duties of the individual. . . .

4. . . . (b) In this rule the term "honorarium" means a payment of money or any thing of value for an appearance, speech, or article (including a series of appearances, speeches, or articles) by a Member, Delegate, Resident Commissioner, officer, or employee of the House, excluding any actual and necessary travel [includes lodging and meals] expenses incurred by that Member . . . to the extent that such expenses are paid or reimbursed by any other person. . . .

(d) (1) In this rule the term "outside earned income" means, with respect to a Member . . . wages, salaries, fees, and other amounts received or to be received as compensation for personal services actually rendered, but does not include — . . .

(E) copyright royalties received from established publishers under usual and customary contractual terms. . . .

5. (a) (1) (A) (i) A Member, Delegate, Resident Commissioner, officer, or employee of the House may not knowingly accept a gift except as provided in this clause.

> (ii) A Member . . . may not knowingly accept a gift from a
> registered lobbyist or agent of a foreign principal or from a private
> entity that retains or employs registered lobbyists of agents of a
> foreign principal. . . .
>   (B) (i) A Member . . . may accept a gift (other than cash or cash
> equivalent) . . . that the Member . . . reasonably and in good faith
> believes to have a value of less than $50 and a cumulative value
> from one source during a calendar year of less than $100. A gift
> having a value of less than $10 does not count toward the $100
> annual limit. . . .
>   (2) (A) In this clause the term "gift" means a gratuity, favor, dis-
> count, entertainment, hospitality, loan, forbearance, or other item hav-
> ing monetary value. The term includes gifts of services, training,
> transportation, lodging, and meals, whether provided in kind, by
> purchase of a ticket, payment in advance, or reimbursement after the
> expense has been incurred. . . .

NOTES AND QUESTIONS

1. *A minimalist effort.* The efforts of Congress to regulate the behavior of
its members, matched by those of many state legislatures and local legislative
bodies, follows the historical focus of legislatures on individual pecuniary
gain or the public perception of such gain as the root of legislative evil. See
generally Council on Governmental Ethics Law, The Blue Book: A Compilation of Campaign, Ethics, and Lobbying Reform Laws (1988); Robert M. Stein,
Ethics in the States: The Laboratories of Reform, in Representation and
Responsibility 243 (Bruce Jennings and Daniel Callahan eds., 1985); Cal.
Govt. Code §§8920-8926 (2008); Fla. Stat. §§112.311-112.321 (2008); Mass.
Gen. Laws ch. 268A, §§1-25 (2008); N.Y. Exec. Law §94 (2008). The political
philosopher Dennis Thompson, in his book Political Ethics and Public
Office 97 (1987), has characterized this approach as "minimalist" and has
attributed its attraction to the following factors:

> It proscribes only a small area of conduct, and it prescribes relatively
> objective rules, which can be accepted by legislators who disagree on
> fundamental moral and political values. It does not dictate any particular
> role or any substantive political theory on which representatives must act. By
> circumscribing the scope of ethics in this way, it gives greater play to the
> give-and-take of pluralist politics. The conflict between the generic require-
> ments of ethics and its representational requirements is thus reduced.

As noted earlier, critics of this approach consider that its silence on
representative values and legislative goals (advocating for the "national
interest" or "common good" or "justice") empties it of meaning. See generally id. at 96-116; The Hastings Center, The Ethics of Legislative Life
(1984); The Hastings Center, Revising the United States Senate Code of

Ethics (1981) (containing an inclusive model code); and John Rawls, A Theory of Justice (1971). This criticism challenges the concept that the legislative process itself creates the "national interest" or "common good" through the accommodation, moderation, and compromising of interests.

Thompson and other critics accept the proposition that legislative ethics must be considered in the context of the existing legislative process but still argue for ethical considerations broader than the avoidance of financial conflicts of interest. See generally Representation and Responsibility (Bruce Jennings and Daniel Callahan eds., 1985). Thompson, for example, offers a number of suggestions concerning legislative diligence and openness that he believes would enhance the existing political strengths of the legislative process. Dennis Thompson, Political Ethics and Public Office 96-112 (1989). See also Amy Gutmann and Dennis Thompson, The Theory of Legislative Ethics, in Representation and Responsibility 167 (Bruce Jennings and Daniel Callahan eds., 1985). These critics do acknowledge that the political and representational needs of the legislative process make neat ethical formulations problematic.

2. *Honoraria.* Criticism of the legislative codes of ethics has not been limited to the failure of these codes to expand their scope beyond financial conflicts of interest or the appearance of such conflicts. Critics contend that these codes do not fulfill their intended purposes. One example has been the collection of fees (honoraria) by legislators (particularly members of Congress) from interest groups whose trade conventions or dinners they attend as speakers. Prior to the 1989 amendments to the ethics code of the House of Representatives (effective 1991), members of the House were permitted to receive up to $2,000 for a speech. Such fees and other outside income could not exceed 30 percent of the legislative salary (then $89,500). Exempted from these limits were contributions to charity.

In 1989, Dan Rostenkowski, chair of the tax writing House Ways and Means Committee, received $285,000 (by far more than any other member) in speaking fees. Representative Rostenkowski kept $26,850 (10 percent of his salary) and donated the remainder to charities. Among the sources of these fees were many entities that had substantial interests in the work of his committee. Critics, including some members of Congress, claimed that "[e]lected officials should be beholden to people that elect them for their compensation, not to vested interest groups" (N.Y. Times, May 30, 1990, at D24, col. 1, *quoting* Rep. Jolene Unsoeld) and that such fees "fuel a growing perception that favoritism and self-interest are more important in the legislative process than merit and the public interest." J. Hedlund, Lobbying and Legislative Ethics, in Representation and Responsibility 89, 100 (Bruce Jennings and Daniel Callahan eds., 1985).

3. *Legislative fact-finding.* Legislators have also been criticized for attending interest group conventions or presentations, at the expense of the sponsoring group, for the purpose of "fact-finding." While fact-finding is an

important part of the legislator's job, and travel is sometimes necessary to fulfill this obligation, the sites of these conventions and presentations are frequently resorts, and much time is used by legislators for vacationing. At these events, legislators are constantly surrounded by representatives of the particular sponsor. These events are intended to advance the interests of their sponsors, and they often succeed. Whether they succeed or not, the public believes they do, and the events create cynicism about the integrity of the legislative process. But critics claim that restrictions on accepting free travel for the purpose of fact-finding only hinder the representative's ability to become better informed about subject matters related to his or her official duties. What solutions might remedy the problem? Can you design different alternatives — some that protect useful fact-finding by a representative?

4. *A context for ethics reform.* Despite these criticisms, the major impetus behind the adoption of the Ethics Reform Act of 1989 was a salary increase for members of the House of Representatives. Historically, salary increases have presented intractable problems for legislators. Early in 1989, a salary increase proposal resulted in an extraordinary political battle, no increase in salary, and perhaps, as discussed below, the forced resignation of the Speaker of the House. The ethics provisions of the Ethics Reform Act of 1989 were tied to a salary increase that was contained in the bill. The relationship between the salary increase and the ethics provisions is demonstrated by §603 of the Act, under which the prior existing rules relating to outside income would be reinstated if the pay increase provisions of the act were subsequently repealed. The Senate refused the salary increase and exempted itself from the ethics provisions of the Act.

5. *A statute or rules?* The provisions of the Ethics Reform Act of 1989 recast the standards on outside earned income for members of the House of Representatives. These provisions, while adopted as part of a statute, are only rules of the House of Representatives. "The provisions of this Act that are applicable to Members . . . of the legislative branch are enacted by the Congress . . . as an exercise of the rulemaking power of the House of Representatives . . . with full recognition of the constitutional right of the [House of Representatives] to change such rules . . . at any time, in the same manner, and to the same extent as any other rule of such House." Ethics Reform Act of 1989, §1001. What is the significance of using rules to accomplish these purposes?

6. *Appearing before regulated agencies.* One issue that has been addressed in varying ways by many of the recently adopted state codes is the practice of legislators of appearing for compensation before various state agencies. See generally Council on Governmental Ethics Law, The Blue Book: A Compilation of Campaign, Ethics, and Lobbying Reform Laws (1988). See, e.g., Cal. Govt. Code §8920 (2008); Fla. Const. art. II, §8(e); Mass. Gen. Laws Ann. ch. 268A, §5 (2008); N.Y. Pub. Off. Law §73(7)(a) (2008). Historically, this has been a common legislative practice, although it has been prohibited for

members of Congress for a considerable time (18 U.S.C. §203). Daniel Webster was a member of Congress and lawyer for the Bank of the United States during periods of intense legislative activity on bank issues (in a now infamous letter to bank president Nicholas Biddle dated December 21, 1833, he warned that "[i]f it be wished that my relation to the bank be continued, it may be well to send me the usual retainers"). Letter from Daniel Webster to Nicholas Biddle (Dec. 21, 1833), in 2 The Papers of Daniel Webster, Legal Papers 320 (1983). State and local legislative bodies have been slower to regulate such activity because many of their members continue to be part-time and pursue other vocations, often the practice of law. In recognition of this fact, many states do not prohibit legislator-lawyers from litigating in most of their courts, although legislatures control the salaries and other expenses of the judiciary. Is this exception justified? On the other hand, litigation against the state is generally prohibited. Why?

7. *The appearance of conflict.* Assume that when a legislator appears before a state agency, as described in Note 6, she does not receive any special treatment. Is there anything wrong with this appearance? This question was raised, in a different context, in the Senate's 1990 investigation of the ties of several of its members to savings and loan executive Charles H. Keating, Jr. The investigation was governed by Senate Resolution 338, which prohibited "improper conduct which may reflect upon the Senate." The allegations were that Keating had made substantial contributions to several senators in order to have them influence a federal regulatory agency's treatment of Keating's bank, the Lincoln Savings and Loan Association. To hear the case, the Senate Ethics Committee appointed Robert S. Bennett as its special counsel. In publicly televised hearings of the Committee in 1990, Bennett suggested, among other things, that there was a link between senators' solicitation and receipt of contributions and their meetings with regulators. In response to these charges, some of the named senators argued that the purpose of these meetings was to question federal investigators about why they were treating unfairly certain important economic concerns in their states. Bennett answered this justification by arguing that, even assuming there was nothing substantively wrong with these meetings, the senators violated an appearance standard. "Legislators who appear to reasonable persons to do wrong actually do wrong by eroding the trust between citizens and their representatives." Congressional Quarterly Inc., Congressional Ethics 128 (1992). One senator replied, "We must do what we think is right, not just what appears to be right." Id. at 128. Ultimately, the Senate based its decisions to reprimand (formally and publicly criticize before the Senate) one of the members and to rebuke others on actual improprieties, but did not deal with the appearance standard. What do you think of Bennett's argument? In answering this question, consider the comments of Professor Ronald M. Levin below.

8. *Gifts galore.* Lobbyists are always buying legislators dinner, giving them tickets to events, and otherwise providing what they would

characterize as small gifts. Criticism of the practice is typically met with outraged comments such as "no one could think that my vote could be bought for such a small amount." And most codes of legislative ethics permit some level of gift taking. Looming in the background of this long practice of gift giving on the federal level has been 18 U.S.C. §201(c)(1)(A), which provides, in relevant part, that anyone who:

> otherwise than as provided by law for the proper discharge of official duty ... directly or indirectly gives, offers, or promises anything of value to any public official, former public official, or person selected to be a public official, for or because of any official act performed or to be performed by such public official, former public official, or person selected to be a public official ... shall be fined under this title or imprisoned for not more than two years, or both.

The Supreme Court, in United States v. Sun-Diamond Growers of California, 526 U.S. 398 (1999), has narrowly read this provision to apply only if there is a proven nexus between the gift made and an official act previously performed or to be performed by the public recipient. See also Damon Chappie and Paul Kane, Gift Cases Often Favor Members, Roll Call, April 30, 2001, at 1.

Ronald M. Levin, *Congressional Ethics and Constituent Advocacy in an Age of Distrust*
95 Mich. L. Rev. 1 (1996)

In the specific context of congressional ethics, use of an appearance standard as a disciplinary standard poses special hazards. The charges are likely to be highly visible and subject to intense public controversy before the ethics committee even begins its inquiry. Moreover, the adjudicators are not Article III judges but elected officials who are themselves highly accountable to the public. Under these circumstances, an appearance standard, if taken seriously, would virtually guarantee a finding of liability. How can a member of the ethics committee say to his or her own constituents that the conduct does *not* appear improper, if *they* think it does? Indeed, such a standard could give rise to an insidious circularity: hostile editorials might not only trigger an ethics investigation of a member, but also become conclusive evidence that a sanction should be imposed. The distinction between ethics regulation and public disapproval would be totally erased.

Special Counsel Bennett apparently tried to avoid this problem by suggesting that appearances be assessed from the perspective of a "reasonable nonpartisan, fully informed person." Aside from the fact that these qualifications tend to sever the link between the appearance standard and its theoretical justification of respecting public opinion, the additional criteria are not a realistic solution to the dilemma. They would put the ethics committee member in the hopeless position of saying to constituents, "Well, if you disagree with me, you must either be unreasonable, uninformed, or have a political ax to grind."

Finally, some might argue that the appearance standard is attractive precisely because of its stringency: even if it is overbroad, the argument might run, congressional ethics is in such a deplorable state that members should be encouraged to err, if at all, on the side of self-restraint. An *in terrorem* standard may be appealing where the conduct to be deterred involves only the member's self-interest, as is arguably true of limitations on outside income, gift restrictions, and the like. Constituent service, however, has affirmative value to the political system, and the realities of campaign finance make fundraising at least a necessary evil. Overdeterrence of casework or of normal solicitation of political support should not be shrugged off as cost-free.

2.   *The Enforcement of Legislative Ethics*

The mechanisms for enforcing legislative codes of conduct have been the subject of considerable debate. This debate has usually centered on enforcement structures rather than procedures. The procedures generally conform to basic due process requirements with the right to notification of particularized charges, to a hearing, and to counsel. The pervasive legislative structure that provokes the debate is the legislative committee. Legislators argue that this model protects legislative independence in highly charged political environments and assures that the "judges" of a legislator's acts will be familiar with the legislative process. Critics argue that legislative committees are reluctant to punish their colleagues; such critics favor "independent" commissions, meaning entities not dominated by legislators. See, e.g., Robert M. Stern, Ethics in the States, in Representation and Responsibility 243 (Bruce Jennings and Daniel Callahan eds., 1985).

The rules of the House of Representatives are enforced by the bipartisan House Standards on Official Conduct Committee, consisting of an equal number of Democratic and Republican members of the House. The Senate rules are enforced by the bipartisan Senate Select Ethics Committee, also consisting of an equal number of senators from each party. The rules of both committees afford members under investigation adequate notice and the opportunity to be heard, as demonstrated in the discussion of Representative James Wright, Jr. below. Most state legislatures employ similar models. Some states have commissions. Among these, Florida and California have established commissions by referendum. See Fla. Const. art. 2, §8; Cal. Govt. Code §8940 (2008). Massachusetts has created a commission by statute. Mass. Gen. Laws Ann. ch. 286A (2008). The California commission is appointed by the state senate and assembly;

the Florida commission is appointed by the Governor (five appointments) and the legislative leaders (a total of four appointments); and the Massachusetts commission is appointed by the Governor (three appointments), the State Secretary (one appointment) and the Attorney General (one appointment).

Despite the criticism that legislative ethics committees are lax in the performance of their tasks, these committees, on occasion, produce extraordinary results, as a brief detailing of the resignation of Speaker James Wright in 1989 demonstrates.

The Fall of a Speaker

On May 26, 1988, a Republican member of Congress from Georgia, Representative Newt Gingrich, set the federal political world afire by taking the extraordinary act of filing a complaint with the Committee on Standards of Official Conduct against the Speaker of the House of Representatives, James C. Wright, Jr. Gingrich charged that Wright had violated various sections of the United States Code and the House Code of Official Conduct by scheming to evade limits on outside income and by accepting improper gifts. In response to these charges, the Committee decided to conduct a preliminary inquiry into Gingrich's assertions and, because of Representative Wright's position, retained special outside counsel to perform the task.

In February 1989, after examining more than 70 witnesses and thousands of documents, the outside counsel reported to the Committee that "[t]he facts discovered during the Preliminary Inquiry demonstrate that Wright has violated, at times repeatedly, House Rule XLIII, clauses 1 (conduct reflecting discreditably on the House) and 4 (accepting improper gifts); House Rule XLIV (failing to disclose income and gifts); House Rule XLVII, clause 1 (exceeding the limit on outside earned income); Code of Ethics of Government Service, consideration 5 (receiving favors that may influence performance of government duties); and 2 U.S.C. §441i (retaining excessive honoraria)." House Comm. on Standards of Official Conduct, Report of the Special Outside Counsel 3 (Feb. 21, 1989) (the Code of Ethics for Government Service provides conduct standards for government employees; it was adopted in 1958 by Congress as a concurrent resolution, expressing the sense of Congress, and is without legally binding effect (72 Stat., pt. II, B 12)). Particularly, the special counsel found that: (1) Wright had, through a number of schemes (including one dealing with the publication and sale of a book he wrote, Reflections of a Public Man, for which he received royalties of 55 percent of retail sales), circumvented various restrictions on outside income for representatives; (2) Wright had failed to report this additional income; and (3) Wright had used his position in the House leadership to "exercise undue influence on the actions taken by the

Federal Home Loan Bank Board to control the burgeoning savings and loan crisis in Texas and elsewhere." House Comm. on Standards of Official Conduct, Report of the Special Outside Counsel 3 (Feb. 21, 1989).

In April 1989, the Committee, after having heard initially from Representative Wright in September 1988 and having received the special counsel's report, issued its Statement of the Committee on Standards of Official Conduct in the Matter of Representative James C. Wright, Jr. (Committee Statement), which contained a five-count Statement of Alleged Violations. The first count related to the marketing and sale of the book, which the Committee believed was "intended to avoid the limitations of law and House Rules on the reporting and receipt of outside earned income, honoraria, and gifts." Id. at 36. This was clearly the most significant of the charges. The abnormally large royalty percentage and the sale of quantities of books to groups before whom Representative Wright was speaking strongly suggested a scheme for honoraria in excess of the then-$2,000 limit. The remaining four counts also dealt with various alleged gifts received by Wright, but were considered weaker than the first charge. A number of charges of the special counsel were dropped on a determination of the Committee that there was no reason to believe that the alleged violations had occurred.

Under the Rules of the Committee, a representative charged is entitled to a disciplinary hearing at which the Committee's staff must establish the facts alleged in the Statement of Alleged Violations by clear and convincing evidence. Such a hearing may be preceded by various motions to the Committee to force review of the Statement of Alleged Violations. Speaker Wright challenged the Statement in a televised hearing before the Committee in May 1989, his counsel arguing that, while the Speaker may have come close to the line of permitted behavior, he had not crossed it.

While the legal process of the House affords due process protection to a member charged with violations of House rules, the political process, particularly in the case of a Speaker, can be far less restrained. In the case of Speaker Wright, it became unforgiving. The public business in the House was coming to a standstill. Substantial political anger was being directed against Wright by a number of representatives, both Republicans and Democrats, who considered him arrogant in his handling of a number of matters, including a bungled attempt to secure a pay raise for members. The pending charges became a vent for this political steam. The press, which had already spent considerable time and resources in the examination of Wright, became further invigorated in their review of his affairs after release of the Committee report. This situation is presented in detail by John M. Barry in his book The Ambition and the Power (1989) and by the considerable news coverage generated by the investigation. On May 31, 1989, on the floor of the House, Representative Wright resigned as a member of the House of Representatives (he would not consider the option of resigning as Speaker and remaining as a member).

NOTES AND QUESTIONS

1. *The press for enforcement.* The case of Speaker Wright illustrates the workings of an active legislative ethics committee. Despite the historical reluctance of legislators to judge their colleagues, the political environment that spurred the widespread adoption of ethics codes has also encouraged more activity by legislative ethics committees. One of this book's authors, Professor Lane, recalls that the major campaign issue raised by a challenger in a 1984 state senate election in New York was that the incumbent, as chair of the New York State Senate Ethics Committee, had called only a few meetings of the committee in two years. The challenger's upset victory in a district with a registration and voting history that favored the incumbent resulted in the next chair of the committee holding regular and frequent meetings. Knowledge of this campaign also became part of the atmosphere in the New York state legislature as it restructured its ethics code.

2. *A fair hearing.* The Wright case raises a question about such activity. Can an individual subject to the committee's jurisdiction receive a fair hearing from a committee operating in such a politicized environment? Must political accountability come at the cost of individual rights? Do the commission models discussed earlier provide better alternatives?

CHAPTER *8*
Accessibility

Representative government requires public accessibility to ensure its accountability and integrity. Accessibility includes the right of the people to petition their legislators for the redress of problems. As Justice Black has said, "the whole concept of representation depends upon the ability of the people to make their wishes known to their representatives." Eastern Railroad Presidents Conference v. Noerr Motors, Inc., 365 U.S. 127, 137 (1961). This right to petition enjoys protection against formal limitation under the United States (the First Amendment) and state constitutions. But the right to petition does not require a petition to be heard. That obligation of legislators is established by the election process and the ethos of the legislative environment.

Accessibility also includes the right of people to know what their legislators are doing (and not doing) in the conduct of public business. This was underscored early in our history by James Madison when he wrote, "A popular government, without popular information, or the means of acquiring it, is but a prologue to a farce or a tragedy, or perhaps both." (Letter to W. T. Barby, August 4, 1822, 9 Writings of James Madison 103 (Hunt ed. 1910).) This "right to know" is formalized in constitutions and statutes that require, for example, public notice of prospective legislative meetings and legislation, the maintenance of public journals of legislative votes, and open legislative meetings. Many of these requisites have been hard won against the opposition of legislators. Legislators have been reluctant to open their processes to public view, believing in part that too much openness impedes the necessary process of compromise, militates against legislative effectiveness, and may injure their reelection opportunities.

These requirements, which vary from jurisdiction to jurisdiction, focus on the formal steps of lawmaking: the introduction of legislation, consideration of legislation by both committees (at hearings or in meetings) and the legislative body, and any final outcome of any such consideration. But advocacy and the exchange of information in the legislative process, unlike the judicial process, are not restricted to formal, recorded settings at which all interested parties are present. Many communications occur at informal forums and at meetings (including phone conversations) with constituents, lobbyists, and other legislators, none of which are covered by the rules defining the right to know. Nor do these rules open to public view the informal forums at which compromises on legislation or trades for support of legislation are made. Often exchanges of information, advocacy by legislators, compromises, trades, and debates occur at party caucuses. These caucuses are used to shape party positions on particular legislation. This is of particular significance in a two-party political system in which members of the party may share widely varying views. These meetings, when they are of the majority party of a legislative body, take on added importance and almost formal status, in the event that a caucus decision is determinative of legislative action. Most jurisdictions do not require that caucus meetings be open to public view or records be kept of their proceedings, but in a number of jurisdictions considerable debate has surrounded this practice. The structure and operation of party caucuses are discussed in Chapter 3.

This chapter examines accessibility. It focuses first on lobbying as the political expression of the constitutional right to petition government, and then on notice requirements and open meetings as a means to study the right to know. A case study on legislative party caucuses is included to explore a more informal arena for communication in the legislative process and the debate over whether such communication should be private or public.

A.   LOBBYING THE LEGISLATURE

Each year, legislators in all of the nation's legislative bodies receive countless communications (written and oral) from their constituents and various interest groups, urging them to advance or defeat some particular idea in the legislative arena. It is this activity that is broadly characterized as *lobbying*. These communications vary greatly in detail, from simple expressions of desire or support for new or pending legislation to detailed, factually intensive argumentation. Many of these are spontaneous and personalized communications from individual constituents. Others are the direct or indirect products of efforts by organized interests. This section will focus on these organized efforts (which, for purposes of this section, are characterized as lobbying).

Lobbying is a constitutionally protected activity. See Buckley v. Valeo, 424 U.S. 1, 45 (1976). The First Amendment guarantees that no law shall abridge "the right of the people . . . to petition the Government for a redress of grievances." This is consistent with a theory of representative government. As characterized in an American Bar Association–sponsored study of lobbying:

> . . . [W]e have traditionally believed that our elected representatives should be responsive to the desires of their constituents; thus our system of politics assumes a vigorous contest among competing interests for the attention, and votes, of legislators. This model of government suggests that individuals and groups should be permitted, in fact encouraged, to make their views known to their representatives. This is reflected in the First Amendment's guarantee that no law shall abridge the people's right to petition the government for redress of grievances. One of the goals of the right to petition is to encourage and foster a pressure system of politics, in which interest groups are expected to influence representatives through a wide array of techniques, with very few out of bounds in a continuing game of struggle and domination.

William N. Eskridge, Jr., and the ABA Section of Administrative Law and Regulatory Practice, The Lobbying Manual: A Compliance Guide for Lawyers and Lobbyists, ch. 1, at 5 (William V. Luneburg and Thomas M. Susman eds., 3d ed. 2005).

Lobbying is also vital to the legislative process. The movement of almost all bills through legislatures is accompanied by a lobbying effort. Bills would not move without such efforts, as it is most frequently the lobbying efforts alone that create the pressure for action. Without the efforts of lobbyists, many significant problems would remain unaddressed and many resolutions to problems would be inadequate:

> Every Member of Congress is faced with a continuous problem of securing reliable information on a myriad of problems. There are by far too many issues coming before the Congress each session for every Member to be fully informed on the relative merits and demerits of all of them. As a result, he must rely on information and advice from other sources. Among the sources . . . are the deliberations of congressional committees and their recommendations, the executive departments of the Government, . . . the position of the President . . . and other Members who have chosen to specialize in particular policy areas. Each of these sources will provide him with some information, but interest representatives will view legislation from a different perspective — that of one of the parties most directly affected.

Abner J. Mikva, Interest Representation in Congress: The Social Responsibilities of the Washington Lawyer, 38 Geo. Wash. L. Rev. 651, 661 (1970).

Lobbying is also perceived with great skepticism by the public. They often see organized lobbying as the rapacious efforts of "special" interests to get their way at the cost of democracy. Sometimes this is true.

Both lobbyists and legislators have been guilty of excesses in the enactment process. But to a large extent, this view is grounded in a rhetoric of politics that casts opposition views as corrupt rather than different. Almost all nonincumbents, for example, run on a platform of "ending the grip of special interests on" whatever legislative body they are running for. Of course, if they win, this same issue is used against them by their challenger. Unfortunately, little public effort is made to consider lobbying from a more accurate perspective.

> The fact is that many people belong to or are represented directly or indirectly by special-interest groups that are trying to get a fair shake, an advantage, or a program from government or are trying to stop something from being done that would adversely affect them. It is understandable, therefore, that when people are asked about particular interest groups, they are more favorably inclined than when they are asked about "special interests" as such. A Gallup poll (April 1989) shows favorable views, particularly with regard to groups that might not appear to have a special interest. Of those responding, 93 percent felt positively about the American Cancer Society, 82 percent about Planned Parenthood, 71 percent about the National Organization for Women, 58 percent about the National Rifle Association, 55 percent the National Right to Life Commission, 55 percent Handgun Control, and 54 percent the American Civil Liberties Union.

Alan Rosenthal, The Third House 6 (1993).

1.   A Story of Lobbying

In the excerpts that follow, we view the legislative process from a lobbyist's perspective, as their author describes the lobbying strategy and implementation behind the successful efforts to adopt the Voting Rights Act Amendments of 1981. These amendments were intended to assure that the applicability of Section 2 of the Voting Rights Act would be governed by an effects test, rather than an intent test. This latter standard had been advocated by a plurality of the Court in Mobile v. Bolden, a view that had caused grave concern in the civil rights advocacy community. These points are detailed in Chapter 6.

The breadth of access to the legislative process and the number of participants make each lobbying effort unique. And the effort described below is particularly unique because, unlike most, this one ends with the enactment of legislation, without significant alteration to the original bill. The hallmark of the American legislative process is the difficulty of legislative enactment, not its ease. It is, as intended by the Framers, far easier to kill legislation than to enact it. See Chapter 9.

All organized lobbying efforts; on the other hand, have some similarities. They require a recognition of the problems that the lobbyist will face in either advocating or opposing a particular bill and a strategy for resolving these problems. Lobbying efforts also require a familiarity with the legislative players, particularly those on the committees with jurisdiction over the subject matter at issue. Such familiarity includes an awareness of each player's policy and political views of the bill and of how these views might be impacted by potential compromises.

Michael Pertschuk, Giant Killers
151-78 (1986)

In January 1981, the civil rights community confronted the political ravages of the 1980 elections. They had lost a president, Jimmy Carter, with a commitment to civil rights, while the country elected Ronald Reagan who had opposed every civil rights act. And the new president, within a month of his election, signaled his doubts about those voting rights provisions which subjected the states of the old Confederacy to special supervision.

In the Senate, the Leadership Conference [on Civil Rights, made up of representatives from some 165 civil rights, labor, education, minority, women, disabled, senior citizen, and religious organizations] had been able to count on the unwavering leadership of Democrats Ted Kennedy of Massachusetts as chairman of the Senate Judiciary Committee, and Birch Bayh of Indiana as chairman of the Constitutional Rights Subcommittee. Now Bayh was gone, defeated. Kennedy had lost his chairmanship, as the Republicans gained a majority and took charge of the Senate. In Kennedy's place as committee chairman now sat Republican Strom Thurmond of South Carolina, leader in 1948 of the Dixiecrat rebellion against the civil rights policies of the Democratic party. From his new eminence, Thurmond vowed that either the preclearance procedures or the entire Voting Rights Act must go.

And that very same Orrin Hatch, who had employed such mastery of parliamentary mischief to lead the sidetracking of the Fair Housing Bill, was now chairman of the Constitutional Rights Sub-committee.

In the spring of 1980, the Supreme Court delivered a heavy blow to civil rights litigators. In the *Mobile* case, the Court held that a Voting Rights Act violation could be established only by evidence of an actual "intent" to discriminate, not simply by a pattern of discriminatory "effects."

Hatch and his fellow conservatives would draw strength and legitimacy from the Court's decision in their single-minded crusade to eliminate *effects* tests in all civil rights laws — and to prevent an *effects* test from being applied to voting rights.

In gaining the extension of the Voting Rights Act unimpaired and in persuading Congress to instruct the Supreme Court to apply the *effects*, not the *intent* test, the Leadership Conference faced one of the most formidable tasks in its 30-year history. . . .

The conference also bore the scars of recent conflicts. In the Voting Rights Act extension debates of 1975, some members of the conference, fearing that the whole act would be jeopardized, had balked at backing the extension of the act to mandate bilingual ballots and otherwise extend coverage of the act to areas of the Southwest where Hispanic voters had been systemically disenfranchised. Though these provisions survived, there lingered distrust of the conference among Hispanic leaders, a residue of the internal conflicts.

Because the conference harbored within the folds of its umbrella moderate groups such as the AFL-CIO, as well as black and Hispanic activists, and new feminist and handicapped advocacy groups, each with divergent priorities, it had experienced increasing inner stress.

In the voting rights campaign, there was another source of tension . . . between litigators and lobbyists. So crucial were the expiring *preclearance* procedures to the success of voter discrimination cases, that a group of lawyers who had been fighting these cases, often in remote rural areas of the South and Southwest, had come to Washington to work for the extension — and would stay there until it was ensured. These litigators had often been forced to try their cases before skeptical, sometimes hostile judges, often coming from the very communities whose practices were being challenged. So they pressed for explicit legislative language that would make it impossible for a reluctant judge to twist ambiguities in the law to thwart voter discrimination cases.

The lobbyists, while sympathetic, had learned over time that the broad congressional consensus on civil rights principles could break down when embodied in harsh detail — and that ambiguity was often the key to legislative movement.

The litigators, however, remained convinced that, coming (as most did) from the communities they served, they were closer to the people than the Washington-acculturated lobbyists. They suspected they would have to bear the burdens of the lobbyists' chronic urge to compromise. . . .

The first decision made by the conference was to seek not only extension of the act, but affirmative action to reverse a Supreme Court decision — an action Congress ordinarily shies from.

The conference was a strong lobby. There was no doubt that they could line up majorities of the Democratic House and, probably, even the Republican Senate in support of a strong bill.

But Neas [the newly appointed executive director of the conference] also knew that majorities would not be enough. A bill which passed the House with a bare majority against conservative opposition would be stopped dead in the Senate. Hatch and Thurmond, as the designated committee "generals" responsible for marshalling the bill through the Senate, would be afflicted with what Lincoln diagnosed in his generals as "the slows." They would make certain that no bill reached the Senate floor until late in 1982, whereupon it would fall easy victim to the filibuster.

And, even if the conference could overcome the filibuster, the bill would get the veto of any bill which troubled President Reagan, a veto which could be overridden only by a two-thirds vote of both houses.

What Neas needed was timely passage in the House by an overwhelming majority—a majority so large as to convey a sense of inevitability to wavering senators, incipient filibusterers, and a reluctant White House.

But to achieve that goal, Neas had to reach out not just to Republican moderates, but to hard-core conservatives. And that meant not only talking to members whom the activists neither liked nor trusted, but remaining open to compromises which might allay the reasonable concerns of conservatives.

The litigators, however, knew that a majority of the House would support a strong bill without compromise. Why explore compromise before it was clear that compromise was necessary? If the bill ran into trouble in the Senate, then compromise could be explored. For the litigators, even early exploration of compromise presaged sell-out. . . .

On one of the first issues to occupy the coalition, Neas sided with the risk takers. Several of the more cautious congressional leaders feared that the reactionary climate in Congress and the administration barred any chance of overturning the *Mobile* decision's *intent* test—so much so that even the attempt to include an *effects* amendment in the bill would jeopardize the extension of the act. They had pleaded for seeking only a simple extension of the act.

But Neas and others on the steering committee were convinced that Hatch and his allies were prepared to seek the substitution of an *intent* test in all civil rights legislation. They knew that of all civil rights, voting rights enjoyed the broadest popular—and congressional—support. If they were ever to beat Hatch, they argued, it would be on voting rights. And they believed they could win.

The first task for the steering committee was the shaping of the House hearings. They had the good fortune to be working with House Judiciary Committee chairman, Democrat Peter Rodino of New Jersey, and the chairman of its Subcommittee on Civil and Constitutional Rights, Don Edwards of California. Both Rodino and Edwards were strong civil rights champions, and both had worked closely with the Leadership Conference for decades. The Rodino-Edwards bill, on which the hearings would be held, embodied the conference's legislative objectives. . . .

The depth and quality of the hearings provided compelling evidence that systematic, though disguised, voter discrimination persisted where it had historically been acute, in the old South and parts of the Southwest.

Almost 120 witnesses testifying in support were orchestrated by the steering committee. And the hearings were completed by the second week of June, within the timetable set out by Neas and the steering committee.

At that moment, the conference experienced a breakthrough, an opportunity, and a risk—all simultaneously, and all in the person of Henry Hyde, an unlikely benefactor.

The Republican Hyde represented the conservative, mostly white citizens of Cicero, Illinois, and some black and Hispanic voters on the west side of Chicago. His national fame, or notoriety, rests almost entirely on his zealous and canny leadership of congressional efforts to stamp out abortion.

On the Judiciary Committee, he served as the senior, or "ranking," Republican on the Civil Rights Subcommittee. Hence, his vote for the Voting Rights Act would send an important signal to conservative Republicans in the House and Senate, and to the White House. His opposition meant trouble.

And trouble he appeared to be, as the Edwards hearings got underway in early May. In his opening statement, Hyde deplored the mandatory preclearance provisions imposed upon the southern states. . . .

Hyde, who had attended every hearing, had grown increasingly restive as the testimony unfolded. That morning, he had erupted:

> I want to say that I have listened with great interest and concern, and I will tell you, registration hours from 9 to 4 [are] outrageous. It is absolutely designed to keep people who are working and who have difficulty traveling from voting.
>
> If that persists and exists, it is more than wrong.
>
> The lack of deputy registrars — only 12 counties have them — demonstrates a clear lack of enthusiasm for getting people registered, obviously.
>
> The location of voting places is a subtle intimidation of black people and is also wrong.
>
> The lack of blacks working as polling officials is also wrong.
>
> [Now] we have all heard where it is all done on the table; there is no privacy.
>
> That is outrageous, absolutely outrageous. . . .

That was the breakthrough.

Neas and Taylor also believed that they could persuade Hyde to cosponsor the Rodino-Edwards bill. That was the opportunity.

The risk materialized in the form of a concept called "bailout." The act provided that jurisdictions covered by the preclearance procedures because of past discriminatory practices could escape supervision, or "bailout," if they could convince a federal court in Washington that their hands had been clean since 1965. The burden of proof on the covered jurisdictions was so heavy, however, and the incentive to escape from the status quo so slight, that few jurisdictions had invoked the bailout provisions.

Hyde was convinced, both as a matter of fairness and as a positive inducement, that the bailout provisions should be substantially revised. Specifically, he proposed that jurisdictions should be allowed to escape supervision if they could demonstrate that they had not discriminated for at least 10 years, and that they had made affirmative efforts "to enhance minority participation in the electoral process."

Hyde's proposal threatened to sunder the Leadership Conference. The moderate members believed it was not inherently troublesome, but could be shaped, through good faith negotiation, to achieve a positive result. . . .

So what if Hyde had reasons other than sabotaging the Voting Rights Act, asked the skeptics. Why should we meet him halfway, when we've got the votes to pass an undiluted bill out of the committee and the full House? Why compromise now? Later, in the Senate, then was the time to talk compromise! . . .

Central to Neas's strategy was "building public perception that the reasonable position was pro-voting rights extension, and that only isolated extremists were against extension." If they could win over the likes of Henry Hyde, they could withstand any future challenge by the administration.

Lurking in the shadows was the specter of the Reagan administration, still preoccupied with such pressing national priorities as relieving the tax and regulatory burdens of oppressed corporate citizens, but beginning to formulate an administrative position on the Voting Rights Act extension. The Leadership Conference had made some effort to gain the support of the attorney general, but discovered, in their brief live encounters, a near-total vacuum of knowledge or understanding in Reagan's attorney general, William French Smith.

Pulled in several directions, the president did what presidents often do: he ducked for a while. The White House announced that the president had asked his attorney general to study the history of the Voting Rights Act's enforcement and come back in a few months with a recommendation.

Some members of the Leadership Conference, recalling the benign leadership of past administrations, expressed disappointment, even outrage at this buck passing. But others, including Neas and Taylor, were delighted. They knew that nothing good could be forthcoming from this administration on civil rights. "Some people regarded the delay as a major setback," recalled Taylor, "but I think most of us regarded it as the opportunity to capture and continue the initiative, without the administration coming in."

By the first week of July, Neas had hammered out a brittle consensus within the steering committee: They had agreed on a firm memorandum of understanding, listing eight critical requirements that had to be met in any bailout compromise. Though it was contemplated that the lowest priority points might be yielded in order to secure the rest, neither Neas nor Taylor nor anyone else was to be authorized to yield on any point without the express approval of the steering committee. . . .

Next, Neas had to persuade Edwards of the wisdom of pursuing compromise with Hyde. Having done so, he then had to let his congressional leaders know that they would have to do so without public support from the steering committee, which wanted to maintain its public opposition to all compromise to avoid weakening its bargaining position.

Third, the negotiations should remain secret (in a town where intended secrecy makes even a bad joke newsworthy), and, finally, that it was the considered wisdom of the steering committee that no negotiations should be initiated with Hyde until the subcommittee had made a show of its civil rights strength by reporting the unamended bill to the full committee. . . .

The presentation went well. Indeed, it went almost too well. Rodino was so persuaded of the virtues of negotiating with Hyde that he rushed off to open negotiations with Hyde, ignoring Neas's counsel that he wait until the subcommittee had voted out an uncompromised bill in a show of civil rights strength.

Then Joe Rauh decided on his own that the Leadership Conference should not only act reasonably, but be publicly perceived reasonable. So he leaked to columnist Bill Raspberry of the *Washington Post* the news that the conference looked with favor upon a fair bailout provision — thereby shattering the fragile consensus that the conference's willingness to compromise was to remain secret. Throats tightened; Neas recalls phlegmatically, "People were now a little bit nervous." . . .

Meanwhile, Hyde was proving an unaccommodating negotiating partner. Believing that he held a strong bargaining hand, he refused to accept safeguards, such as the requirement that "saintly jurisdictions" show that no fewer than 60 percent of its minority citizens register and vote, and that judges in the District of Columbia, not in the petitioning jurisdiction, make the decision. On the critical importance of these provisions, there was no division within the steering committee. . . .

Ralph Neas, with unbounded irony, marks Wednesday, July 29, 1981, as "the brightest day of my professional life." The Judiciary Committee was within a few days of "mark-up" (deliberating and voting), and negotiations between Parker [Counsel to the Judiciary Committee] and Hyde's staff had intensified.

At midnight on the 28th, Neas received a call summoning him, Althea Simmons, and Laura Murphy (of the American Civil Liberties Union) — all perceived as among the least contentious steering committee members — to a meeting with Parker at 11:00 the next morning. Neas had a number of queasy sensations, among them that they ought not to meet with Parker without at least one of the litigators present. But it seemed more important to find out what Parker was up to than to fight over the make-up of the delegation, a decision Neas was later to regret. . . .

Parker greeted them with the news that he had forged the best compromise that could be worked out and that it ought to be satisfactory to all reasonable parties. He was, Parker noted, not asking, but telling. He had cleared his compromise with key black congressmen and the subcommittee and committee chairmen, Edwards and Rodino, had signed off. It was a fait accompli.

The three quickly caucused with Taylor, who had been waiting outside Parker's office, and hurriedly reviewed the Parker compromise.

It was patently unacceptable — again, not just to the litigators but to the others, the "moderates," as well.

At this moment, Neas faced a difficult choice. The members of the steering committee were waiting, restlessly he knew, for a briefing on the Parker meeting.

On the other hand, there was at least a chance that they could convince Edwards, before it was too late, to withdraw support from the compromise. Yet to do so, they had to persuade Edwards to repudiate the committee's own staff, a rare event. . . .

But Edwards agreed. He informed Parker that he had only tentatively agreed to the compromise, contingent upon its being acceptable to the Leadership Conference. Since it plainly wasn't, he would not support it. Then he turned to Taylor, with whom he had worked closely for almost 20 years, saying, "You now have to stay here and try to put this thing back together again." And he set Taylor to work, along with Simmons and Murphy, drafting an acceptable counteroffer to Hyde. . . .

Throughout the late afternoon, Edwards shuttled back and forth to Hyde's office, armed with Taylor's nonstop drafting and redrafting. Hyde began to give ground, and the gap between them began to close, and a compromise acceptable to most of the Leadership Conference was within reach. . . .

Neas decided that the compromise was worth supporting, though it was not perfect. The calendar hung heavy on his mind. It was July 29; Congress would recess for a month on August 1. Without the compromise, there was a substantial risk that Hyde and his supporters on the committee could prevent any bill from being reported out before the recess, and that meant that the conference's grass-roots efforts during the recess could not be focused on a consensus bill: reported out of committee and gathering momentum. And if they turned Hyde down, he would have gained the moral advantage as the rejected reasonable man.

Neas had consulted with the representatives of the major membership organizations within the conference. They had agreed to support the new compromise. . . .

It came. At 1:45 A.M. Neas received a call from one of the litigators. She wanted him to know that the compromise was unacceptable and that her group would oppose it. The dissident group had spent the evening calling civil rights leaders throughout the country, sounding the alarm that a rape of the Voting Rights Act was about to take place, with the Leadership Conference as an accomplice. And they sought to blow the compromise up the next morning. . . .

At that moment, Henry Hyde stepped forward to save the Voting Rights Act, and the Leadership Conference, and Ralph Neas's day.

Not intentionally; Hyde simply overreached. He refused to remove a provision, obnoxious to the steering committee, which would allow state legislatures to "bail out" of the preclearance procedures even though there remained cities or counties within that state which were still covered. Hyde evidently considered his bargaining position so strong, the desire of the civil rights lobby for compromise so compelling, that he had decided to hang tough and resist Edwards' and Rodino's last, best offer. . . .

The committee met, locked in impasse, and adjourned. In the ensuing uproar and confusion, the press were distracted and even failed to report the damaging appearance of confusion and divisiveness within the Leadership Conference, a divisiveness which, with the heroic exception of Althea Simmons and the NAACP, broke painfully along racial lines, the most disaffected representing black and Hispanic groups.

For the next several hours, Edwards sought to reopen negotiations with Hyde, but to no avail. Then, at about 4:00 in the afternoon, Hyde issued a press release denouncing Edwards, Rodino, and the Leadership Conference as unrealistic and unreasonable, and declared his effort to reach a compromise at an end.

Edwards, normally the calmest of legislators, was furious. And Neas was ready with a plan. A week to ten days before marking-up, Neas had asked a group of the litigators, just in case the compromise negotiations were to fail, "to draft up what they considered to be the perfect bailout provision — what we would like in the best of all possible situations." That draft had been prepared, and Neas proposed that the committee be reconvened the next morning, and that this ideal bailout provision be the basis for a new, substitute bill, to be offered to the full Judiciary Committee at 10:00 the next morning. They had to take on Hyde in an open fight. . . .

Alan Parker and the other committee staffers were dead set in opposition. "If you do this," they argued, "we will not have a Voting Rights Act extended. You will doom this entire effort to defeat, if not in the House, for sure in the Senate. Negotiations with Hyde are essential, and you should give us the time, during the August recess, to reach an accommodation with Hyde. If you don't, it's the end." . . .

The revamped bill was very similar to the draft spurned by Hyde the day before. It contained a bailout provision that was significantly tighter than that proposed by Hyde, but which would still permit "angelic" jurisdictions to become exempt if they could demonstrate a record of compliance and good behavior.

By 10:00 the next morning, the group had produced a bill so carefully drafted and technically sound that it would remain essentially intact in its future passage through House and Senate. They had also prepared a technical section-by-section analysis of the bill and summaries for the press, a work product which, under normal time pressures, would take three to four intensive weeks to produce.

Between 7:30 and 10:00, Edwards had convinced two senior and respected House Republicans to cosponsor the new bill: Hamilton Fish, Jr. of New York, a long-time supporter of the act, and James Sensenbrenner of Wisconsin, who ranked just behind Hyde on the subcommittee.

Edwards and Neas had calculated correctly that these members would not want to see the Republicans now portrayed as the stumbling block to reasonable civil rights legislation. They also banked upon Republican disaffection with Hyde, whose arrogance and lack of deference to colleagues who had led on civil rights issues in the past had become a growing irritant. Besides, the Republican congressmen were being handed, on a silver platter, the opportunity to become two main sponsors of an historic civil rights law — no mean incentive. . . .

Hyde, of course, was not happy when he realized what was happening. But Edwards began by explaining what it was he proposed to do, paying elaborate credit to Hyde: "Henry, we've taken 95 percent of your bill and we give you great credit and we thank you."

There followed a vigorous one hour debate. Despite the brevity of their briefings, Fish and Sensenbrenner proved eloquent advocates, as did Edwards and Rodino.

At first, Hyde was simply furious that he had not received advance notice of the substitute bill. But when he realized he had been out-maneuvered and did not have the votes, he chose not to make the fight. He thundered that a drastic mistake had been made, and that the proponents of the bill would rue the day that they had forced it through the Judiciary Committee:

"You might get it through the House of Representatives, but let me assure you, you will fail in the United States Senate!"

But he would not vote against it.

The vote was 25-1 in favor of the bill.

In less than 36 hours, Neas and the conference had gone from looming disaster to a 25-1 victory, on a bill which compromised not a single Leadership Conference objective!

The painful effort to seek a middle ground by accepting a modified bailout provision had been worth it: the combination of co-sponsorship by Republicans Fish and Sensenbrenner and the lack of hard opposition from Hyde set in motion a bipartisan steamroller effect.

On October 5, 1981, the full House passed the bill by a vote of 389-24.

Wavering senators could not help but be influenced by the size of that vote. By December, 61 senators had cosponsored the House-passed bill — precisely the number needed to close off a filibuster. By the following spring, the number of cosponsors had risen to 65, almost enough to override a presidential veto.

And, yet, one more compromise was still forthcoming.

By late April, the Reagan administration had joined Hatch and other conservatives in full-throated opposition to the *effects* test. Hatch's subcommittee had voted favorably on a bill maintaining the *intent* standard, and the full Senate Judiciary Committee was deadlocked, with Chairman Thurmond controlling the timetable. The August 6 deadline — the date the Voting Rights Act was due to expire was close on the horizon. A filibuster or a presidential veto was still a serious threat.

Again, the Leadership Conference's strategy was to cleave a wedge between moderate, mainstream Republicans and the radical right. . . .

The embodiment of mainstream Republicanism was Kansas Senator Robert Dole, now Senate Republican leader. Dole had remained "uncommitted" within the Judiciary Committee, holding the balance.

Once again, there was resistance to compromise. The New York Times quoted an anonymous member of the steering committee, plausibly, "We've got 65 votes. That's two-thirds of the Senate. What do we want to compromise for?"

But, with Neas, Taylor, Simmons, and Elaine Jones (of the NAACP Legal Defense Fund) in the lead, the Dole compromise emerged — a compromise that gained the support of 14 of the 18 Judiciary Committee members and, at the final hour, the reluctant acquiescence of the president.

What was compromised away? The Dole-Kennedy-Mathias amendment spelled out more clearly than the House version the intention of Congress that voting rights for minorities does not mandate proportional representation. (The Leadership Conference had never taken the position that voting rights require proportional representation.) Also, using language from earlier Supreme Court decisions which had been referenced in the House committee's report on the bill, the compromise spelled out in the bill the components of the *effects* test — and it provided that the supervisory provisions of the act would expire, unless again extended, in 25 years — three and a half times longer, than any previous Voting Rights Act extension! The Dole compromise gave reassurance to legislators who had genuine reservations but believed in voting rights. . . .

In return, Dole acted as the Senate general in maneuvering the bill around the procedural shoals of the Senate. On June 18, the Senate voted 85-5 to pass the bill, and on June 29, 1982, President Reagan, in a signing ceremony at the White House pronounced the right to vote "the crown jewel of American liberties" adding, "this legislation proves our, unbending commitment to voting rights. It also proves that differences can be settled in the spirit of good will and good faith."

And good lobbying. . . .

NOTES AND QUESTIONS

1. *Problems and strategies.* Lobbying requires the identification of enactment problems and strategies for their resolution. What problems were identified, and what strategies were employed? What problems were misperceived, and what strategies failed?

2. *Why did the amendments pass?* The political environment in which the amendments were enacted would, at first glance, have seemed hostile to the passage of such a substantial amendment to the Voting Rights Act.

Why did the bill pass? Do you think that it was exclusively the consequence of the efforts described by Michael Pertschuk?

3. *The legislative process and the applicability of statutes.* In Chapters 11 and 12 we discuss statutory ambiguities and their judicial resolution. In those chapters, we point out that legislatures often use ambiguities to resolve particular problems, leaving the courts with the problem of establishing their meaning in the context of a particular case. This point is illustrated in the above materials by the differing views between the civil rights lobbyists and litigators on bill language. These views were dictated by the different institutions in which they worked. For the lobbyists, ambiguities were part of their strategy for gaining support among otherwise hostile legislators. For the litigators, they were seen as an opportunity for hostile judges to impose their policy preferences. For the lobbyists, ambiguities were a path to victory. For the litigators, ambiguities were a path to defeat. For the lobbyists, ambiguities could result in moving their legislative agenda forward, if not as far as they would like. For the litigators, ambiguities could result in their agenda being frustrated. For cases dealing with ambiguities in the Voting Rights Act, planned or otherwise, see Thornburg v. Gingles, Shaw v. Reno (Chapter 6), Chisom v. Roemer, and Holder v. Hall (Chapter 12).

4. *Compromise as the heart of the process.* In Chapter 1, we noted the significance of the compromise to the legislative process. The above description illustrates the compromise as part of a lobbying strategy. For each compromise, something is intended to be gained and something can be lost. This applies to both policy and support. What are the various compromises considered in the above materials, and what is each of their impacts on the legislation and its support?

5. *Legislators and lobbyists.* How would you characterize the relationship between lobbyists, legislators, and legislative staff, as described in these materials? Later in this chapter, we make the point that while the relationships between lobbyists, legislators, and legislative staff are often close, they are not symbiotic; the goal of a lobbyist is to prevail for his client, not to vindicate the representative or institutional responsibilities of legislators. How is this point illustrated in the Pertschuk description?

6. *The legislative hearing.* In Chapter 4, we described the committee hearing. The hearing described in the above material is one at which concentrated oral testimony made a difference. What was that difference? Observe how, because of the relationship between the lobbyists and committee leadership, the hearing is structured to accomplish strategic goals.

7. *Grass-roots efforts.* Notice the reference to grass-roots efforts to put pressure on legislators. While grass-roots lobbying has been a long staple of the civil rights community, it has in recent years gained greater use among a far broader range of lobbying interests. The growing use of grass-roots lobbying is discussed in Section A.3 of this chapter.

2. The Efforts of Organized Interests

De Tocqueville, Democracy in America
106-07 (Vol. II 1980)

Americans of all ages, all conditions, and all dispositions constantly form associations. They, have not only commercial and manufacturing companies, in which all take part, but associations of a thousand other kinds, religious, moral, serious, futile, general or restricted, enormous or diminutive. The Americans make associations to give entertainments, to found seminaries, to build inns, to construct churches, to diffuse books, to send missionaries to the antipodes; in this manner they found hospitals, prisons, and schools. If it is proposed to inculcate some truth or to foster some feeling by the encouragement of a great example, they form a society. . . .

Among democratic nations, all the citizens are independent and feeble; they can do hardly anything by themselves, and none of them can oblige his fellow men to lend him their assistance. They all, therefore, become powerless if they do not learn voluntarily to help one another. If men living in democratic countries had no right and no inclination to associate for political purposes, their independence would be in great jeopardy, but they might long preserve their wealth and their cultivation: whereas if they never acquired the habit of forming associations in ordinary life, civilization itself would be endangered. A people among whom individuals lost the power of achieving great things single-handed, without acquiring the means of producing them by united exertions, would soon relapse into barbarism.

We noted earlier in Chapter 1 the historical significance of interest groups in spurring legislative activity. As national resources dwindled and society became more diverse, more societal cleavages appeared from which grew more interest groups. And these groups turned more and more to the legislative arena to accommodate their concerns.

Such efforts have not been limited to traditional economic or business interests. De Tocqueville's observations remain accurate, as groups, representing every issue imaginable, form to advocate or resist the adoption of some legislation or changes to the legislative process. The Congressional Quarterly's Guide to Congress (1982) lists numerous categories of lobbying groups, which include those representing business, labor, the environment, farmers, civil rights, state and local interests, foreign interests, senior citizens, education, and various single interests (for example, the pro-choice and pro-life movements, the National Rifle Association). Consumer groups and groups interested primarily in reforming legislative process (the so-called good government groups) can also be added to this list. Groups, in a sense, breed new groups. "Groups formed from an imbalance of interests in one area induce a subsequent disequilibrium, which acts as a catalyst for individuals to form groups as counterweights to the new perceptions of inequity. Group politics thus is characterized by successive waves of mobilization and countermobilization." Cigler and Loomis, Introduction, Interest Group Politics 7 (3d ed. 1991).

The involvement of organized interests in the legislative process is not exceptional. To be effective in the legislative process people must band together and apply pressure. This is at the heart of electorally enforced representation. "Practical politicians and scholars alike generally have concurred that interest groups (also known as factions, pressure groups, and special interests) are natural phenomena in a democratic regime — that is, individuals will band together to protect their interests." Cigler and Loomis, Introduction, Interest Group Politics 2 (3d ed. 1991). But their impact on the legislative process has been a matter of considerable concern.

For the Constitution's Framers, such concern provided the rationale for designing our elaborate system of checks and balances. Both the representative (Chapters 6 and 7) and deliberative (Chapter 9) characteristics of the nation's legislative process partly address this concern by promoting competition and frustrating the easy passage of legislation.

James Madison, The Federalist No. 10
58-59 (J. Cooke ed., 1961)

As long as the reason of man continues fallible, and he is at liberty to exercise it, different opinions will be formed. As long as the connection subsists between his reason and his self-love, his opinions and his passions will have a reciprocal influence on each other; and the former will be objects to which the latter will attach themselves. This diversity in the faculties of men from which the rights of property originate, is not less an insuperable obstacle to a uniformity of interests. The protection of these faculties is the first object of Government. From the protection of different and unequal faculties of acquiring property, the possession of different degrees and kinds of property immediately results: and from the influence of these on the sentiments and views of the respective proprietors, ensues a division of the society into different interests and parties.

The latent causes of faction are thus sown in the nature of man; and we see them everywhere brought into different degrees of activity, according to the different circumstances of civil society. A zeal for different opinions concerning religion, concerning Government and many other points, as well of speculation as of practice; an attachment to different leaders ambitiously contending for pre-eminence and power; or to persons of other descriptions whose fortunes have been interesting to the human passions, have in turn divided mankind into parties, inflamed them with mutual animosity, and rendered them much more disposed to vex and oppress each other, than to cooperate for their common good. So strong is this propensity of mankind to fall into mutual animosities, that where no substantial occasion presents itself, the most frivolous and fanciful distinctions have been sufficient to kindle their unfriendly passions, and excite their most violent conflicts. But the most common and durable source of factions, has been the various and unequal distribution of property. Those who hold, and those who are without property, have ever formed distinct interests in society. Those who are creditors, and those who are debtors, fall under a like discrimination. A landed interest, a manufacturing interest, a mercantile interest, a monied interest, with many lesser interests, grow up of necessity in civilized nations, and divide them into different classes, actuated by different sentiments and views. The regulation of these various and interfering interests forms the principal task of modern legislation, and involves the spirit of party and faction in the necessary and ordinary operations of Government.

The proliferation of interest groups since the early years of the twentieth century has engendered a debate on their impact. Fundamentally, this continuous debate recapitulates the concern expressed by Madison. The contours of the debate are well illuminated in the following excerpts.

Allan J. Cigler and Burdett A. Loomis, Introduction, *Interest Group Politics*
3-5 (3d ed. 1991)

Hostility toward interest groups became more virulent in an industrialized America, where the great concentrations of power that developed far outstripped anything Madison might have imagined. After the turn of the century many Progressives railed at various monopolistic "trusts" and intimate connections between interests and corrupt politicians. Later, in 1935, Hugo Black, then a senator (and later a Supreme Court justice), painted a grim picture of group malevolence: "Contrary to tradition, against the public morals, and hostile to good government, the lobby has reached such a position of power that it threatens government itself. Its size, its power, its capacity for evil, its greed, trickery, deception and fraud condemn it to the death it deserves."

Similar suspicions are expressed today, especially in light of the substantial growth of PACs [Political Action Committees] since 1974. PAC contributions to congressional candidates rose from almost $23 million in 1976 to $148 million in 1988, which amounted to almost a third of all their funds. Still, the number of PACs has leveled off at just over 4,000, and only a fraction of these are major players in electoral politics. Reformers in and out of Congress have sought to limit purported PAC influence, but as of 1990 legislators could not agree on major changes in laws regulating campaign spending or group activity. PACs continue to be an attractive target for reformers. One typical expression of dismay came from Common Cause, the self-styled public interest lobby: "The Special Interest State is a system in which interest groups dominate the making of government policy. These interests legitimately concentrate on pursuing their own immediate — usually economic — agendas, but in so doing they pay little attention to the impact of their agendas on the nation as a whole."

Despite the considerable popular distrust of interest group politics, political scientists and other observers often have viewed groups in a much more positive light. This perspective also draws upon Madison's Federalist writings, but it is tied more closely to the growth of the modern state. Political science scholars such as Arthur Bentley, circa 1910, and David Truman, forty years later, placed groups at the heart of politics and policy making in a complex, large, and increasingly specialized governmental system. The interest group becomes an element of continuity in a changing political world. Truman noted the "multiplicity of co-ordinate or nearly co-ordinate points of access to governmental decisions," and concluded that "the significance of these many points of access and of the complicated texture of relationships among them is great. This diversity assures various ways for interest groups to participate in the formation of policy, and this variety is a flexible, stabilizing element."

Derived from Truman's work, and that of other group-oriented scholars, is the notion of the pluralist state in which competition among interests, in and out of government, will produce policies roughly responsive to public desires, and no single set of interests will dominate. As one student of group politics summarized:

> Pluralist theory assumes that within the public arena there will be counter-vailing centers of power within governmental institutions and among outsiders. Competition is implicit in the notion that groups, as surrogates for individuals, will produce products representing the diversity of opinions that might have been possible in the individual decision days of democratic Athens.

In many ways the pluralist vision of American politics corresponds to the basic realities of policy making and the distribution of policy outcomes, but a host of scholars, politicians, and other observers have roundly criticized this perspective. Two broad (although sometimes contradictory) critiques have special merit.

The first critique argues that some interests systematically lose in the policy process; others habitually win. Without making any elite theory contentions that a small number of interests and individuals conspire together to dominate societal policies, one can make a strong case that those interests with more resources (money, access, information, and so forth) usually will obtain better results than those who possess fewer assets and employ them less effectively. The numerically small, cohesive, well-heeled tobacco industry, for example, does well year in and year out in the policy-making process; marginal farmers and the urban poor produce a much less successful track record. Based on the continuing unequal results, critics of the pluralist model argue that interests are still represented unevenly and unfairly.

A second important line of criticism generally agrees that inequality of results remains an important aspect of group politics. But this perspective, most forcefully set out by Theodore Lowi, sees interests as generally succeeding in their goals of influencing government — to the point that the government itself, in one form or another, provides a measure of protection to almost all societal interests. Everyone thus retains some vested interest in the ongoing structure of government and array of public policies. This does not mean that all interests obtain just what they desire from governmental policies; rather, all interests get at least some rewards. From this point of view the tobacco industry surely wishes to see its crop subsidies maintained, but the small farmer and the urban poor also have pet programs, such as guaranteed loans and food stamps, which they seek to protect.

Lowi labels the proliferation of groups and their growing access to government "interest-group liberalism," and he sees this phenomenon as pathological for a democratic government: "Interest-group liberal solutions to the problem of power [who will exercise it] provide the system with stability by spreading a *sense* of representation at the expense of genuine flexibility, at the expense of democratic forms, and ultimately at the expense of legitimacy." Interest group liberalism is pluralism, but it is *sponsored* pluralism; and the government is the chief sponsor.

NOTES AND QUESTIONS

1. *Two definitions of interest, groups.* One important aspect of the debate between Professors Truman and Lowi can be illustrated by two definitions of interest groups:

> A. By faction I understand a number of citizens, whether amounting to a majority or minority of the whole, who are united and actuated by some common impulse of passion, or of interest adverse to rights of other citizens, or to the permanent and aggregate interests of the community.

The Federalist No. 10, at 57 (J. Madison) (J. Cooke ed., 1961).

> B. [A]ny group that, on the basis of one or more shared attitudes, makes certain claims upon other groups in the society for the establishment, maintenance or enhancement of forms of behavior that are implied by the shared attitudes.

D. Truman, The Governmental Process 33 (1951).

What is the difference between these two definitions? Professor Lowi views this difference as central to his criticism of the pluralist vision. "To the Madisonians, and also to the early twentieth century progressives, groups were necessary evils much in need of regulation. To the modern pluralist, groups are good; they require accommodation." T. Lowi, The End of Liberalism 296 (1969).

2. *Determining the public good.* To the Madisonians, groups were evil when they pursued interests adverse to the interests of the community or what now is deemed the public interest. What is the community or public interest? Earlier we discussed this issue in terms of representativeness. See Chapter 7. In the next chapter, we will discuss the issue in terms of deliberativeness. How can we determine the public interest? How can we determine if a statute is adverse to the public interest? The pluralists' response to this question is, basically, that the public interest can only be determined by the outcome of the legislative process. If this is so, might an appropriate legislative reform be one that provided resources for lobbying to groups without adequate resources to petition a legislature?

3. *Private bargains.* Another criticism presented by Lowi, stated in the extreme, is what he sees as a willingness on the part of government to accept as governmental policy bargains between competing interest groups that are arrived at outside of the legislative process and without consideration of the overall significance of the "solution." This picture cannot be attractive. The idea that policy is made without its consideration by representatives within the legislative process raises grave concern.

But how accurate is the Lowi vision? The experience of both authors would suggest a contrary view. While without doubt interest groups, alone or in concert, occasionally get their way—that is, have their view adopted without legislative attention—this is exceptional and generally confined to very narrowly focused legislation. Even then such "private lawmaking" may not end with the adoption of the private agreement. One of the authors, Professor Lane, recalls such a situation. Sometime in the early eighties, a debate ensued in the New York State Capitol over the appropriate level of workers' compensation. After a series of meetings between groups representing management and labor, a deal was struck between them. The terms of this deal were reduced to legislation and presented to the legislature, with the admonition that "if we can live with this, you can also." Essentially what was being asked was that the bill be introduced and adopted as delivered, without regard to its broader implications, if any, and without regard to the normal processes through which debate might occur. The deal failed when the then Speaker of the New York State Assembly, Stanley Fink, informed everyone that there would be at least an Assembly view of this proposal.

3.   The Function of the Lobbyist

Both of the authors entered their legislative service with a negative and narrow view of lobbying. This view was defined by a somewhat Madisonian attitude (the republic must be saved from the private interests pursued by lobbyists) and the powerful, historical (and not inaccurate) nineteenth-century image of lobbyists as cigar-chomping, backslapping, frequent practitioners of questionable activities on behalf of grasping economic interests. For both authors this view was short-lived. Lobbyists enriched the legislative debate rather than corrupting it. Through the efforts of lobbyists, different views could be heard and a legislator's own political and policy views could be tested. From this perspective, the function of lobbyist was to broaden the market for ideas, not to co-opt the legislator.

Modern lobbying is a far different enterprise from its "backslapping" antecedents. Although personal relationships remain important, other factors have become more so. Lobbying as practiced today is described in the following passage.

Hedrick Smith, Old-Breed Lobbying, New-Breed Lobbying,
American Politics, Classic and Contemporary Readings
370 (Cigler and Loomis eds., 1989)

The essence of the old-breed game is *retail* lobbying: the one-on-one pitch. It is Bob Strauss's note to Treasury Secretary Jim Baker to help a friend seek appointment to the World Bank. It is Howard Baker's contact with an old Senate colleague to see that some client gets a break on the "transition rules" of a tax bill. It is Bob Gray's phone call to the White House to ask the president to address some convention or to wangle an invitation to a state dinner for an industrial big shot. It is breakfast with a committee staff director who is drafting intricate legislation. It is little favors such as tickets to a Washington Redskins football game or helping Ed Meese's wife get a job. It is knowing which buttons to push.

"The best lobbyists' work is basically just socializing," former Speaker O'Neill's spokesman, Chris Matthews, advised me. "They know members of Congress are here three nights a week, alone, without their families. So they say, 'Let's have dinner. Let's go see a ballgame.' Shmooze with them. Make friends. And they don't lean on it all the time. Every once in a while, they call up — maybe once or twice a year — ask a few questions. Call you up and say, 'Say, what's Danny going to do on this tax-reform bill?' Anne Wexler [a former Carter White House official, now a lobbyist] will call up and spend half an hour talking about leftwing politics, and suddenly she'll pop a question, pick up something. They want that little bit of access. That's what does it. You can hear it. It clicks home. They'll call their chief executive officer, and they've delivered. That's how it works. It's not illegal. They work on a personal basis." . . .

Old-breed lobbying also thrives on an aura of influence, a promise of the inside track, the hint of priceless contacts. A certain amount of this promise of influence is hokum. There is no year-in, year-out box-score, but even the big-name lobbyist "rainmakers" lose major battles or settle for much less than they had hoped for. "One of the great myths around is that wheelers and dealers can come in there and write policy and have their way in whatever they want — it's simply not the case," asserts Norm Ornstein, one of the best-known scholars on Congress, who is at the American Enterprise Institute for Public Policy Research. "You pick any big shot, and you're dealing with *some* wins and losses. Any sophisticated person is going to know that you hire a Tommy Boggs, and that doesn't mean you buy victory. What you buy with a Tommy Boggs is access. Very few people are gonna say they won't see him. You buy acumen. This is somebody who understands how the process works."

Ornstein's skepticism is well taken, for lobbyists are prone to oversell their influence; but his assertion that lobbyists do not write policy is too sweeping. Their effectiveness, suggested David Cohen, codirector of the Advocacy Institute, depends largely on the public visibility of issues. Large issues like the MX missile, environmental legislation, the Voting Rights Act, or broad provisions of tax law are "less susceptible to the superlobbyists because they are highly visible," Cohen argues — correctly, I think. "But, when you're dealing with invisible issues and the narrower details of legislation, you can still use the superlawyers and the super-lobbyists."

Access is the first arrow in any lobbyist's quiver, especially lobbyists of the old breed. Scores of times I have been told that votes are won simply by gaining an audience with a time-harassed congressman, so he could hear your case. In this access game, the lobbyist's first rule is to make his own services so reliable and indispensable that officeholders become dependent on him — for his information, his contacts, his policy advice, not to mention his money. "A good lobbyist is simply an extension of a congressional member's staff," I was told by Terry Lierman, an energetic health lobbyist and former staff aide for the Senate Appropriations Committee. "If you're a good lobbyist and you're working something, all the members know where you're coming from," Lierman said. "So if they want information and they trust you, they'll call *you* for that information." . . .

The new-breed game reflects the organic changes in American politics and the institutional changes in Congress. Its medium is mass marketing; its style is packaging issues; its hallmark is wholesale lobbying. New-breed lobbying borrows heavily from the techniques of political campaigns, with their slick P.R., television advertising, orchestrated coalitions, targeted mass mailings, and their crowds of activists. It is the National Rifle Association generating three million telegrams in seventy-two hours and blanketing Capitol Hill with so many phone calls that members cannot make outgoing calls. It is the "gray lobby" dumping up to fifteen million postcards and letters on Jim Wright in one day to warn Congress not to tamper with Social Security cost-of-living adjustments. It is legions of insurance or real estate lobby agents swarming Capitol Hill as a tax markup nears a climax. It is political consultants and campaign strategists elbowing superlawyers aside, to generate grass-roots support for their lobbying clients or to do public-relations campaigns. . . .

The essence of the new-breed game is grass-roots lobbying. It developed in the 1960s with the advent of citizen protest. The civil rights movement, mass marches against the Vietnam War, and then Ralph Nader and public-interest groups such as Common Cause opened up mass lobbying. Those movements spawned a new generation, a new cadre of players trained in grass-roots activism, many of whom settled into the Washington power game. Business was initially slow to react, but it arrived with a vengeance to play on the new terrain in the late 1970s and gained the upper hand in the 1980s. Now old-breed and new-breed lobbyists jostle, borrowing techniques from each other.

The new game has made lobbying a boom industry. It takes a lot more money and manpower than it did in the old days to touch all the power bases in Congress, and the campaign techniques of working the grass roots shoot costs up exponentially. The swarm of lobbyists in Washington seems to reach new highs every year: from 5,662 registered with the secretary of the Senate in 1981 to 23,011 in mid-1987 (registration is required to work the halls of Congress legally), plus another fifty or sixty thousand more lobbyists and workers in law firms and trade association offices. In the new Washington, practically no big client will settle these days for a single lobbying firm. The style now is "team lobbying" to make all the necessary contacts and to handle all aspects of the influence game: a law firm, a public-relations outfit, a lobbying firm, plus grass-roots political specialists. . . .

The swarm of lobbyists is so great that members of Congress have grown jaded—quick to challenge Washington lobbyists for evidence that their case has real pull among the voters. Danny Rostenkowski, chairman of the House Ways and Means Committee, told me that while his committee was drafting the 1986 tax bill, he refused to see Washington lobbyists— though he would grant time to constituents from home. And Tom Korologos, an old-breed lobbyist who learned the power game in the 1960s under Utah Senator Wallace Bennett and as congressional liaison in the Nixon White House concedes: "We have a different breed of congressman who is more active, more publicity prone, more responsive to his district." . . .

"On the Senate side in the old days you could go talk to two or three committee chairmen," Korologos recalled, "you could talk to John Stennis and Russell Long and Allen Ellender and Warren Magnuson, and you had a policy. You had a defense bill. You had an oil policy. Now, you've got to talk to fifty-one guys. So you fly in the Utah plant manager to see Orrin Hatch and Jake Garn [Utah's two senators], and the Utah plant manager gets in to see 'em. If he doesn't get in, he goes back home and goes to church on Sunday and bowling on Monday and to coffee on Tuesday and says, 'I was in Washington, and the son of a bitch wouldn't see me.' And let that spread around for a while. Political graveyards are filled with statesmen who forgot the folks back home."

"The logistics of trying to persuade Congress have changed enormously," agreed Jim Mooney, for years a top House Democratic staff aide and now chief lobbyist for the cable-television industry. "What's changed is there are so many more groups now and simultaneously a diminution of power in the power centers of Congress. You've got to persuade members one by one."

In the new game, another maxim is that lobbyists must demonstrate that the home folks are with them to prove their political legitimacy. "There's a suspicion on the part of elected officials toward paid lobbyists," acknowledged David Cohen, the public-interest lobbyist. "They often sense a gap between leaders and the rank and file, whether labor unions or other organizations like church groups. I don't think you're a player unless you have a constituency to mobilize."

In an earlier era, labor unions had a near monopoly on lobbying with a mass base. Disgruntled farmers also rolled their tractors onto the capitol Mall to demonstrate mass anger. Business has now entered that game. Mass-marketing techniques are being used even by people like Charles Walker, a traditional Washington insider whose normal style is lobbying at intimate dinners for selected members of Congress. After serving as an inside tax adviser to the 1980 Reagan campaign, Walker got important tax write-offs for business written into the 1981 tax bill. But more recently he has enlisted help from new-breed lobbyists.

"When a member says to you, 'Go convince my constituents,' then you are thrown into those arenas," Walker explained to me. "You get into targeted mail and all that sort of stuff. The lobbying business is moving toward a full service which will include not just your legislative experts and administration experts, but your public-relations experts, experts in grass-roots communications, targeted communications, cluster-group approaches, grass-roots coalition building." Charles Walker was talking the lingo of the modern political campaign, and in fact, the old-breed lobbyists are turning increasingly to campaign consultants.

The evolution of lobbying from its early rendition to its modern form has followed the extraordinary expansion of legislative law-making at all levels of government from its late nineteenth century focus on private petitions, grants, charters, and franchises to its broad modern focus on the regulation of most major aspects of life in society and the enormous growth in government spending. This expansion of legislative attention to increasingly complex problems has required far more sophisticated efforts by legislators and their staffs. These efforts have been paralleled by the efforts of an ever increasing number of interest groups and their lobbyists. As described by the legal historian Professor Willard Hurst:

> The staple work of the representatives of major interests concerned with legislation began to center around detailed, technical craftsmanship in the drafting of bills, the gathering of statistics and descriptive material, collection and analysis of legislation and legislative documents from all over the country, the careful, bill-by-bill scrutiny of all that was fed into the legislative hopper session by session, the assembling of briefs on pending proposals and the formal appearance before legislative committees, the preparation and dissemination of large quantities of printed material presenting a point of view for the education of the members of an interest group itself or of the general public.

J. Willard Hurst, The Growth of American Law, The Law Makers 63-64 (1950).

The growth of lobbying is described in a 1976 report of the United State Senate:

> Efforts to influence Congress have, in fact, become big business. While it is impossible to estimate accurately the true extent of the effort because of the inadequacies of the present lobbying law, the committee received testimony suggesting that as many as 10,000 people may be paid at any one time to engage in efforts to influence legislation. In 1950, a select House committee on lobbying activities concluded on the basis of its own research that, "If the full truth were ever known, this committee has little doubt that lobbying, and all its ramifications, would prove to be a billion dollar industry." The total amount of money actually expended on lobbying must have significantly increased since this estimate was made in 1950. (General Interim Report of the House Select Committee on Lobbying Activities. Rept. No. 3138, 81st Cong., 2d sess., p. 8.)

S. Rep. No. 763, 94th Cong., 2d Sess. 2 (1976). One lobbyist has even claimed, perhaps cynically, that "[e]ssentially, we operate as an extension of congressmen's staffs. Occasionally we come up with the legislation, or speeches — and questions [for legislative hearings] all the time. We look at it as providing staff work for allies." Wall St. J., Oct. 5, 1987, at 54. Despite this lobbyist's view, the relationship between lobbyist and legislator, no matter how useful, is not symbiotic. The goal of a lobbyist is to prevail for his interest, not to vindicate the representative or institutional responsibilities of legislators.

Gaining Access to Legislative Decisionmaking

To influence legislative decisionmaking, a lobbyist must first gain access to the legislative process. In the legislative arena, access means securing a legislator's attention on a particular position, or on the need for specific legislation, or on the need to defeat specific legislation. Of particular importance is getting the attention of legislators who have a significant role in the process affecting the issue, for example, the speaker or majority leader of the legislative body or relevant committee or subcommittee chairpersons or members. Access is an extremely important currency in the legislative process. While it does not in any way assure a favorable outcome for the lobbyist, given the great demand for and limited supply of a legislator's time, access can provide an advantage for those who have it. This is especially true in efforts to delay, weaken, or defeat legislation, which require far less energy than does its passage.

To gain access, a lobbyist will play on a number of factors: the legislator's political interest in the issue, the legislator's personal interest in the issue, and the legislator's sense of obligation to the particular lobbyist or the interest represented.

The first and foremost factor, political interest, generally relates to the relationship of the subject matter to the legislator's constituency. Senator Byrd's explanation for his vote against the Clean Air Act of 1990, described in Chapter 7, Note 2, pages 446-447, is illustrative of this point. A legislator's political interest also may relate to the legislator's ambition for higher office. The second factor, personal interest, relates to a legislator's own substantive interests, her own sense of "public interest." Judge Mikva's interest in repealing the Emergency Detention Act of 1950, described in Chapter 2, page 61, is an example of a personal interest. A legislator's self-image as, for example, an "environmentalist" or "foreign policy expert" comes within this classification of interest. The final factor, sense of obligation, is a miscellaneous category relating to obligations owing from campaign contributions, requests of friends and colleagues, and similar relationships.

Access to the process includes both direct and indirect contact between the lobbyist and the legislators. Direct contact includes written communications by the lobbyist to members of the legislature, testimony before legislative committees, and meetings with legislators. An appearance before a legislative committee is the most formal method of organized lobbying. It is also the one instance of lobbying that becomes part of the "official" legislative history of a particular bill. Notwithstanding this, the significance of such testimony to the legislator depends upon the evaluation of factors noted earlier.

Meetings with relevant legislators (those that make a difference on a particular issue) are the most favored form of direct communications, but the hardest to accomplish. Most legislators do not have enough time (or interest) to meet with everyone who wishes to meet with them. Nor can legislative staff accommodate all of the demands for meetings. A prime reason why lobbyists are frequently found in public spaces (chamber lobbies or near elevators) is to create an opportunity for even casual communication with a legislator — "to grab his or her ear." Whether a meeting is scheduled depends on a lobbyist's ability to appeal to a legislator's varied political, personal, or other interests.

Indirect contacts are communications to a legislator by his or her constituents inspired by a lobbyist or lobbying interest, but usually intended to seem as independent from the lobbyist as possible — the so-called grass-roots campaigns. These campaigns potentially have significant effects on legislators, as they may appear (and are intended to appear) to the legislator as involving large numbers of constituents operating with intensity. Usually these communications take the form of letters or phone calls from constituents but can include other forms of contacts, such as visits by constituents with the legislator.

> The objective of a grass-roots campaign is to prove to legislators that their constituents are concerned about a particular issue. . . . In the words of a Maryland lobbyist, "the old politics don't work anymore, you have to get back home where it really hurts." According to this line of reasoning, the legislator's district is where political power resides, and grass-roots lobbying puts legislators into contact with constituents who hold that power. . . . In a grass-roots campaign, constituents tell legislators how the measure will affect them instead of the lobbyist doing it; "don't believe me," the lobbyist can say to the legislator, "just ask Charlie," a "key contact" from back home.

Alan Rosenthal, The Third House 155 (1993).

One of the authors, Judge Mikva, recalls that when he was a state legislator in Illinois he had proposed legislation to move state gasoline tax revenues from an earmarked fund, available only for highway repairs, to a general fund, available for general state purposes. Suddenly Representative Mikva started receiving a considerable amount (over 15 messages would probably qualify on an issue of this sort) of unfavorable constituent mail on his proposal. Each letter was written and addressed by hand and contained the same message in slightly different form. Mikva discovered that they had one similarity: All had his middle initial incorrect, an error found on the mailing list of the Illinois Automobile Association, an organization that opposed the legislation. What difference would this make to you if you were a state legislator?

On this point consider the following material from a handbook on lobbying published by a New York State lobbying group, New York Public Interest Research Group [emphasis added]:

What Makes an Effective Letter to a Legislator?

1. Use personal stationery rather than a post card or form letter.
2. Type it if you can. If you can't, make sure your handwriting is legible.
3. Keep the letter short; it should fit on one page. If you have more information than will fit on one page, summarize it; include the surplus as background material.
4. Write it in your own words, and include your own thoughts.
5. Discuss just one issue. Make it clear which issue you are discussing by writing at the top of the page (below the date) "Re_____," filling in the blank with the issue or the bill number.
6. Refer to the bill in question by name and number, if possible.
7. Demonstrate your familiarity with the issue and/or the bill, and with its current status.
8. Clearly state your position, and give reasons for it. Cite personal experience and personal observation, if possible. Mention the local impact or implications of the bill or issue; remember, the first concern of legislators is the welfare and well-being of their constituents.
9. *Don't mention your membership in NYPIRG or any other organization. The individual's letter counts more than one obviously inspired by an organization.*
10. Be specific about what you want your legislator to do.
11. Ask your legislator to indicate his position on the bill or issue.
12. If you can, mention your legislator's vote on a recent (and preferably related) issue to show your awareness of his/her record.
13. In general, be helpful, not threatening. Be courteous, not angry or sarcastic. Even if you disagree with your legislator's position, be polite.
14. When the legislature is in session, address your letter to your representative's office in Washington or Albany. At other times, use your representative's home address, if available.
15. Write a follow-up letter praising an action or expressing disappointment after the issue has been resolved. This shows you are following your legislator's actions and are truly concerned.
16. Finally, remember: any letter is better than no letter.

In recent years, grass-roots lobbying efforts have multiplied. This has been a product of their success, aided by loopholes in lobbying *legislation* that permits such activity without disclosure. These modern practices are summed up by one observer as follows:

> Rarely now does a well-connected Washington lobbyist work alone. Instead, the lobbyist has become just one of many players running national campaigns designed to create a "grass-roots" ground swell in support, or more often in opposition, to legislation before Congress.
>
> In their million-dollar costs and in their reliance on television, polling and grass-roots constituency building, these efforts most resemble Presidential campaigns. And they are now so pervasive and sophisticated that it has become difficult to distinguish between a lobbying effort, an issue advocacy campaign and a citizens movement.

Alison Mitchell, A New Form of Lobbying Puts a Public Face on Private Interest, N.Y. Times, Sept. 30, 1998, at A1.

Indirect contacts include the use of the media. Media attention on an issue, particularly sustained media attention, is a galvanizing method for capturing a legislator's attention. Consider the following material from a training manual prepared by the Advocacy Institute, an organization established for teaching lobbying techniques and strategies.

Advocacy Institute, The Elements of a Successful Public Interest Advocacy Campaign
11-12 (1990)

Effective use of the media is essential to the success of any advocacy campaign. The media focuses public concern and spurs public action; it is also an important tool for legislators to assess public sentiment. But in order to use media correctly, the campaign must catch and hold the media's attention, despite its notoriously short attention span.

For better or worse, in the mass media, labels and symbols frame the issue. The media are the battleground in which each side seeks to secure to its cause the most powerful affirmative symbols, and to attribute to its adversaries the most negative symbols. How issues are framed in the media — and how they can be strategically reframed — can determine the outcome of an issue campaign. Media advocacy promotes broad-based media coverage that frames and captures the symbols of public debate, thereby building public support for policy initiatives. "Framing the issue" is the process by which advocates convey their message to maximize the affirmative, and minimize the negative, values associated with it.

Most issue campaigns begin with a core group of supporters within the general population, who quickly resonate to the themes naturally evoked by the initiative. The critical framing task for the campaign, then, is to broaden that core base of supporters by finding and using themes that engage the intellect and emotions of those who are not ready supporters of the initiative.

- Though we are a notoriously heterogeneous nation, Americans resonate with surprising unanimity to a set of core public values: freedom, security, family, health, fairness, opportunity, caring. The more an issue initiative positively evokes one or more of these values, the more likely it is that public attitudes toward that initiative will be favorable.
- Mirroring these affirmative public values are a set of negative values which evoke negative responses: unfairness, government or corporate oppression, harm, deceit, greed, favoritism, dependency. When an issue campaign succeeds in associating one or more affirmative values with its initiative — and associating its opposition with one or more negative values, its chances of generating broad public support are greatly enhanced.
- There are certain sub-values which tend to be more powerful for some groups than others. Thus, peace, public health, corporate accountability, freedom from government regulation of dissent or artistic expression, family security, all tend to be salient values with political liberals; while military security, freedom from government economic restraint, and maintenance of civic order, tend to be more salient values with conservatives.
- The most successful issue campaigns succeed in appropriating those values which have almost equal appeal to liberals and conservatives, such as privacy and freedom of choice, and they frame their appeals in ways which allow both liberals and conservatives to associate their own values and sub-values with the initiative.

NOTES AND QUESTIONS

1. *The public interest.* The growth of lobbying has created a continuing, intense debate among political scientists and other observers of the legislative process on how to define the public interest. On one side are those who essentially argue that in this country's pluralistic society all groups are special pleaders and that the public interest can only be forged by the advocacy of the interests of these groups in the legislative arena. On the other side are those who argue for a more abstract notion of the public interest against which to measure legislative activity.

Consider these two views. Surely many of you have viewed certain legislative decisions as contrary to the public interest. On what basis have you made that decision? Would your view change if you were certain that all groups had adequate access to the legislative process? If you think that the legislative process is not well served by the lobbying efforts of organized interests, what changes would you adopt?

2. *Legislative access and judicial access.* In light of the discussion in this section, consider the differences between "accessing" the legislative

process and "accessing" the judicial process. What do the differences tell you about the underlying goals and purposes of legislatures and courts? What similarities do you see?

4. The Regulation of Lobbying

The scope and complexity of modern legislative endeavors have turned lobbying into a big business with high stakes and breathtaking competition for success. While lobbyists have, in the words of the congressional scholar Walter Oleszek, helped "to inform both Congress and the public about problems and issues" and to stimulate "public debate" on such issues (Walter J. Oleszek, Congressional Procedures and the Policy Process (1989)), not everything that lobbyists do may be considered helpful to the legislative process. The negative impacts of various lobbying efforts to influence the legislative process are discussed throughout this chapter. Activities of the sort covered by these pages are a distasteful, but foreseeable, by-product of the intensity and competitiveness within the legislative arena and can be subject to reasonable regulation.

A problem more intrinsic to the growth of organized lobbying efforts is the potential these efforts have for drowning out the voices of a legislator's constituents, skewing the representative relationship between representatives and their electorate. Recall Judge Mikva's experience (page 486) with the letters from "disguised" members of the Illinois Automobile Association. How could he evaluate the communications? Did this sudden outpouring represent the spontaneous views of his constituents, which might deliver one message about the bill, or did it represent the view of more limited interests, which might result in another? This worry is enforced by the report from the New York Times found on page 502. Consider this excerpt from the 1976 Senate Report cited on page 484:

> The power of the modern lobbying organization may be vast. A lobbying organization can generate hundreds of thousands of telegrams in a few days opposing or favoring a particular piece of legislation. With the help of sophisticated computers, it can target within a matter of hours thousands of key individuals or organizations and solicit them to communicate with particularly influential or undecided Senators or Congressmen. At the request of this committee the Library of Congress surveyed 115 large organizations which issue publications readily available to the Library of Congress, and which have a staff of 25 or more in Washington. The survey found that 38, or approximately one-third of the organizations, used their publications for purposes of soliciting their members to communicate with Congress. These 38 organizations had a combined membership of just under 18 million individuals.

Concerned about the consequences of such large-scale lobbying efforts, Congress enacted the Regulation of Lobbying Act of 1946. Its purpose was well stated by the Supreme Court in United States v. Harriss, 347 U.S. 612, 625 (1954):

> Present-day legislative complexities are such that individual members of Congress cannot be expected to explore the myriad pressures to which they are regularly subjected. Yet full realization of the American ideal of government by elected representatives depends to no small extent on their ability to properly evaluate such pressures. Otherwise the voice of the people may all too easily be drowned out by the voices of special interest groups seeking favored treatment while masquerading as proponents of the public weal. This is the evil which the Lobbying Act was designed to help prevent.

This statute, in effect until its repeal in 1995, was a poorly drafted, extremely confusing statute that created considerable confusion over who was covered and the nature of their obligations. To one observer, the statute was an example of the need for legislative speed outweighing the need for legislative thought.

After decades of occasionally intense but frustrating effort, Congress enacted comprehensive federal lobbying regulation almost by accident in 1946. The Federal Regulation of Lobbying Act succeeded where so many other lobbying bills had failed in the past, partly because it was a component (Title III) of the much larger Legislative Reorganization Act. The Lobbying Act provisions had been placed in this larger bill because the Joint Committee on the Organization of Congress had "heard many complaints during its hearings of the attempts of organized pressure groups to influence the decisions of the Congress on legislation pending before the two Houses or their committees."

The mere fact that the Joint Committee was interested in the lobbying provisions did not mean that lobbying was the focus of its activities, however. Apparently, the Joint Committee had held no hearings on lobbying, and its report devoted little more than a page to the contours of lobbying regulation. Based upon this report, the Office of Legislative Counsel drafted the Lobbying Act provisions of the Reorganization Act. Given the scant legislative guidance and great time pressure (only a few months to draft comprehensive lobbying rules and the remainder of the Reorganization Act), the Legislative Counsel simply adopted the 1936 compromise, with a few modifications.

The reports of the standing committees that considered the Reorganization Act are not much more illuminating than the Joint Committee's report on the proposed requirements of the lobbying title. Thus, the Senate Judiciary Committee reported that lobbying regulation should not apply to newspaper publishers, witnesses in committee hearings, those seeking to influence Congress without compensation, and organizations whose lobbying activities were only "incidental." On the other hand, the Committee believed that the regulation should embrace those who inspire letter campaigns, those who come to Washington "under the false impression that they exert some mysterious influences over Members of Congress," and "honest and respectable representatives of business" who seek openly and frankly to influence legislation. Floor discussion of the lobbying provisions reflected confusion over their effect and some concern that the provisions would "intimidate" citizens desiring to petition Congress. But, as Senator John Kennedy later wrote, "Congress was in no mood to hold up the Legislative Reorganization Act and Title III was in effect carried through on the coattails of the other Congressional reforms regarded as most important by Congress."

William v. Luneburg and the ABA Section of Administrative Law and Regulatory Practice, The Lobbying Manual, ch. 1, 9-10 (2005).

Claims about the vagueness of the Regulation of Lobbying Act of 1946 surfaced in the courts in National Association of Manufacturers v. McGrath, 103 F. Supp. 510 (1952). This case was instituted by the National Association of Manufacturers (NAM) against the Attorney General of the United States to enjoin him from initiating a prosecution against NAM for violations of the act. NAM claimed that the act violated its right to notice under the Fifth Amendment (the vagueness argument) and its right to petition the government under the First Amendment. NAM also claimed that the act was not applicable to it. Without reaching NAM's last claim, the three-judge district court concluded that basic provisions of the act "are invalid as contravening the due process clause of the Fifth Amendment in failing to define the offense with sufficient precision. . . ." Id. at 514. The court also declared the penalty in Section 310(b) (prohibiting violators of the act from lobbying for a period of three years) to be in violation of the First Amendment. The decision in this case was vacated as moot by the Supreme Court in McGrath v. National Association of Manufacturers, 344 U.S. 804 (1952).

The Supreme Court revisited this issue the following year in United States v. Harriss, 347 U.S. 612 (1954), after the United States District Court for the District of Columbia had again declared the statute unconstitutional. *Harriss* reversed the lower court's judgment of the act's unconstitutionality and, "to avoid a danger of unconstitutionality," provided an extremely narrow reading of the statute. Under the Court's view, characterized by Justice Jackson, in dissent, as leaving "the country under an Act which is not much like any Act passed by Congress," the Act's coverage was limited to persons who solicit, collect, or receive contributions and situations in which the principal purpose of either the persons or the contributions is to influence the passage or defeat of legislation through direct communications with members of Congress. In the Court's view such a narrow reading of the statute was consistent with legislative intent:

> The legislative history of the Act makes clear that, at the very least, Congress sought disclosure of such direct pressures, exerted by the lobbyists themselves or through their hirelings or through an artificially stimulated letter campaign. . . . It is likewise clear that Congress would have intended the Act to operate on this narrower basis, even if a broader application to organizations seeking to propagandize the general public were not permissible.

Id. at 620-21.

The *Harriss* decision was the subject of substantial criticism. This criticism is captured by a Senate Report that declared that the Court had destroyed the law. (To make it clear that the law being discussed is the now repealed Lobbying Regulation Act of 1946 and not the Lobbying Disclosure Act of 1995, we have changed the tense of the Report's verbs from present to past and removed the adjective "present" from before the term "law." For example, in the original text paragraph (2) started: "The current law does not apply. . . ." It now reads: "The law did not apply. . . .")

(1) Groups which utilized their own funds in an attempt to influence legislation were not required to register their efforts unless they solicited, collected, or received funds from others for that purpose.

(2) The law did not apply to organizations or individuals unless lobbying was their principal purpose. There was a wide disparity in the way the "principal purpose" definition was interpreted. Due to the vagueness of the definition, many organizations did not register at all, concluding that lobbying was not their "principal purpose."

(3) The law did not clearly cover efforts by a lobbyist which did not involve direct contact with Congress. Thus, lobbyists who attempted to influence Congress by soliciting others to communicate with Congress were not required to report these grass roots lobbying efforts.

(4) The law did not clearly include lobbying communications with staff employees of Senators or Congressmen. Thus, a large portion of the lobbying process was outside the scope of the act's coverage.

(5) In general, the law's reporting requirements were so vague and ambiguous that the lobbyists who did report often filed incomplete information or interpreted the requirements differently. Some groups considered far more types of expenses to be related to lobbying than others. As a result, it was difficult to make a meaningful comparison between the reports filed by any two lobbyists, or to reach any overall conclusion about the true nature or extent of the activities of those who did register. The act also imposed very detailed and unworkable financial disclosure requirements. In many cases, each expenditure over $50 had to be itemized. This further discouraged full and accurate financial reporting.

(6) No agency of the Federal Government was given clear responsibility and adequate investigatory powers to ensure compliance with the act.

After *Harriss*, Congress attempted several times to remedy the above-noted problems. In each instance, the efforts were vigorously opposed by groups intended to be covered, and in each case, the efforts failed. For a detailed presentation of these efforts, see William v. Luneburg and the ABA Section of Administrative Law and Regulatory Practice, The Lobbying Manual, ch. 2 (2005). One cause for such failure may have been the *Harriss* decision itself. By saving part of the act and jettisoning some of its most controversial provisions, the Court may have undermined the compromises that led to its enactment. In effect, the decision created a political situation that made reform more difficult by splitting from the regulated lobbyists those who lobby "indirectly" (grassroots lobbyists). On this point, consider the proposed 1993 amendments to the act that would have broadened the disclosure requirements to cover some forms of grass-roots lobbying. The bill, supported by President Clinton, was on the verge of being passed (there was a conference report) but was defeated by a Senate filibuster on that report after "opposition grew exponentially among Republicans in the days before the cloture vote as outside groups, many of which would have been forced to disclose their lobbying activities for the first time, began to voice objections about the bill's scope. In particular, they said it could require grassroots lobbying organizations to disclose information about their contributors that would chill citizen involvement in politics." David S. Cloud, 52 Cong. Q. Wkly. Rep. 2854 (1993).

Finally, in 1995, Congress repealed the 1946 act and replaced it with the Lobbying Disclosure Act of 1995. The 1995 Act focused largely on the role of lobbyists in the political arena and targets regulation thereof. It attempted to address many of the problems noted above, but in 2007, following well-publicized lobbying and ethics scandals that rocked the national political scene, the Lobbying Disclosure Act was amended by the Honest Leadership and Open Government Act of 2007 (2007 Act). The 2007 Act, while overlapping with the 1995 Act in many respects, significantly shifted the focus onto the lawmakers themselves and sought to regulate their relationships with lobbyists as well as other legislators. As such, the combination of the 1995 Act and 2007 Act is integral in understanding the national landscape of lobbying and ethical legislation.

Relevant portions of the 1995 Act, as modified by the 2007 Act, are included below. The events preceding the 2007 Act are discussed following the Notes and Questions.

The Lobbying Disclosure Act of 1995
Pub. L. No. 104-65, 2 U.S.C. §§1601 et seq.

Sec. 1.   Short Title

This Act may be cited as the "Lobbying Disclosure Act of 1995."

Sec. 2.   Findings

The Congress finds that—
(1) responsible representative Government requires public awareness of the efforts of paid lobbyists to influence the public decision making process in both the legislative and executive branches of the Federal Government;

(2) existing lobbying disclosure statutes have been ineffective because of unclear statutory language, weak administrative and enforcement provisions, and an absence of clear guidance as to who is required to register and what they are required to disclose; and

(3) the effective public disclosure of the identity and extent of the efforts of paid lobbyists to influence Federal officials in the conduct of Government actions will increase public confidence in the integrity of Government.

Sec. 3. Definitions

As used in this Act: . . .

(2) Client. — The term "client" means any person or entity that employs or retains another person for financial or other compensation to conduct lobbying activities on behalf of that person or entity. A person or entity whose employees act as lobbyists on its own behalf is both a client and an employer of such employees. In the case of a coalition or association that employs or retains other persons to conduct lobbying activities, the client is the coalition or association and not its individual members. . . .

(4) Covered legislative branch official. — The term "covered legislative branch official" means —

(A) a Member of Congress;

(B) an elected officer of either House of Congress;

(C) any employee of, or any other individual functioning in the capacity of an employee of —

(i) a Member of Congress;

(ii) a committee of either House of Congress;

(iii) the leadership staff of the House of Representatives or the leadership staff of the Senate;

(iv) a joint committee of Congress; and

(v) a working group or caucus organized to provide legislative services or other assistance to Members of Congress; . . .

(7) Lobbying activities. — The term "lobbying activities" means lobbying contacts and efforts in support of such contacts, including preparation and planning activities, research and other background work that is intended, at the time it is performed, for use in contacts, and coordination with the lobbying activities of others.

(8) Lobbying contact. —

(A) Definition. — The term "lobbying contact" means any oral or written communication (including an electronic communication) to a covered executive branch official or a covered legislative branch official that is made on behalf of a client with regard to —

(i) the formulation, modification, or adoption of Federal legislation (including legislative proposals);

(ii) the formulation, modification, or adoption of a Federal rule, regulation, Executive order . . . ;

(iii) the administration or execution of a Federal program or policy ... ; or

(iv) the nomination or confirmation of a person for a position subject to confirmation by the Senate.

(B) Exceptions — The term "lobbying contact" does not include a communication that is — ...

(ii) made by a representative of a media organization if the purpose of the communication is gathering and disseminating news and information to the public;

(iii) made in a speech, article, publication or other material that is distributed and made available to the public, or through radio, television, cable television, or other medium of mass communication; ...

(v) a request for a meeting, a request for the status of an action, or any other similar administrative request, if the request does not include an attempt to influence a covered executive branch official or a covered legislative branch official;

(vii) testimony given before a committee, subcommittee, or task force of the Congress, or submitted for inclusion in the public record of a hearing conducted by such committee, subcommittee, or task force;

(viii) information provided in writing in response to an oral or written request by a covered executive branch official or a covered legislative branch official for specific information;

(ix) required by subpoena, civil investigative demand, or otherwise compelled by statute, regulation, or other action of the Congress or an agency; ...

(xiv) a written comment filed in the course of a public proceeding or any other communication that is made on the record in a public proceeding;

(xvii) a disclosure by an individual that is protected under the amendments made by the Whistleblower Protection Act of 1989, under the Inspector General Act of 1978, or under another provision of law;

(xviii) made by —

(I) a church, its integrated auxiliary, or a convention or association of churches that is exempt from filing a Federal income tax return under paragraph 2(A)(i) of section 6033(a) of the Internal Revenue Code of 1986, or

(II) a religious order that is exempt from filing a Federal income tax return under paragraph (2)(A)(iii) of such section 6033(a); ...

(9) Lobbying Firm. — The term "lobbying firm" means a person or entity that has 1 or more employees who are lobbyists on behalf of a client other than that person or entity. The term also includes a self-employed individual who is a lobbyist.

(10) Lobbyist. — The term "lobbyist" means any individual who is employed or retained by a client for financial or other compensation for services that include more than one lobbying contact, other than an

individual whose lobbying activities constitute less than 20 percent of the time engaged in the services provided by such individual to that client over a 3-month period. . . .

Sec. 4.   Registration of Lobbyists

(a) Registration. —
    (1) General Rule. — No later than 45 days after a lobbyist first makes a lobbying contact or is employed or retained to make a lobbying contact, whichever is earlier, such lobbyist . . . shall register with the Secretary of the Senate and the Clerk of the House of Representatives.
    (2) Employer Filing. — Any organization that has 1 or more employees who are lobbyists shall file a single registration under this section on behalf of such employees for each client on whose behalf the employees act as lobbyists.
    (3) Exemption. —
        (A) General Rule. — Notwithstanding paragraphs (1) and (2), a person or entity whose —
            (i) total income for matters related to lobbying activities on behalf of a particular client (in the case of a lobbying firm) does not exceed and is not expected to exceed $2,500; or
            (ii) total expenses in connection with lobbying activities (in the case of an organization whose employees engage in lobbying activities on its own behalf) do not exceed or are not expected to exceed $10,000 (as estimated under section 5) in the quarterly period described in section 5 (a) during which the registration would be made is not required to register under subsection (a) with respect to such client. . . .
(b) Contents of Registration. — Each registration under this section shall contain —
    (1) the name, address, business telephone number, and principal place of business of the registrant, and a general description of its business or activities;
    (2) the name, address, and principal place of business of the registrant's client, and a general description of its business or activities (if different from paragraph (1));
    (3) the name, address, and principal place of business of any organization, other than the client, that —
        (A) contributes more than $5,000 to the registrant or the client in the quarterly period to fund the lobbying activities of the registrant; and
        (B) actively participates in the planning, supervision or control of such lobbying activities;
    (4) the name, address, principal place of business, amount of any contribution of more than $5,000 to the lobbying activities of the

registrant, and approximate percentage of equitable ownership in the client (if any) of any foreign entity . . . ;

   (5) a statement of—

      (A) the general issue areas in which the registrant expects to engage in lobbying activities on behalf of the client; and

      (B) to the extent practicable, specific issues that have (as of the date of the registration) already been addressed or are likely to be addressed in lobbying activities; and

   (6) the name of each employee of the registrant who has acted or whom the registrant expects to act as a lobbyist on behalf of the client. . . . No disclosure is required under paragraph (3)(B) if the organization that would be identified as affiliated with the client is listed on the client's publicly accessible Internet website as being a member of or contributor to the client, unless the organization in whole or in major part, plans, supervises, or controls such lobbying activities. If a registrant relies upon the preceding sentence, the registrant must disclose the specific Internet address of the web page containing the information relied upon. Nothing in paragraph (3)(B) shall be construed to require the disclosure of any information about individuals who are members of, or donors to, an entity treated as a client by this chapter or an organization identified under that paragraph. . . .

Sec. 5.   *Reports by Registered Lobbyists*

(a) Quarterly Report—No later than 20 days after the end of the quarterly period beginning on the first day of January, April, July and October of each year in which a registrant is registered under section 4 of this title, or on the first business day after the 20th day if the 20th is not a business day, each registrant shall file a report with the Secretary of the Senate and the Clerk of the House of Representatives on its lobbying activities during such quarterly period. A separate report shall be filed for each client of the registrant.

(b) Contents of Report—Each quarterly report filed under subsection (a) shall contain—

   (1) the name of the registrant, the name of the client, and any changes or updates to the information provided in the initial registration . . . ;

   (2) for each general issue area in which the registrant engaged in lobbying activities on behalf of the client during the quarterly period —

      (A) a list of the specific issues upon which a lobbyist employed by the registrant engaged in lobbying activities. . . .

      (B) a statement of the Houses of Congress and the Federal agencies contacted by lobbyists employed by the registrant on behalf of the client . . . ;

Sec. 6. Disclosure and Enforcement

(a) In general-The Secretary of the Senate and the Clerk of the House of Representatives shall—

(1) provide guidance and assistance on the registration and reporting requirements of this Act and develop common standards, rules, and procedures for compliance with this Act;

(2) review, and, where necessary, verify and inquire to ensure the accuracy, completeness, and timeliness of registration and reports; . . .

(4) make available for public inspection and copying at reasonable times the registrations and reports filed under this Act; . . .

Sec. 7. Penalties

(a) Civil Penalty. — Whoever knowingly fails to—

(1) remedy a defective, filing within 60 days after notice of such a defect by the Secretary of the Senate or the Clerk of the House of Representatives; or

(2) comply with any other provision of this Act; shall, upon proof of such knowing violation by a preponderance of the evidence, be subject to a civil fine of not more than $200,000 depending on the extent and gravity of the violation.

(b) Criminal Penalty. — Whoever knowingly and corruptly fails to comply with any provision of this Act shall be imprisoned for not more than 5 years or fined under Title 18, United States Code, or both.

Sec. 8. Rules of Construction

(a) Constitutional Rights. — Nothing in this Act shall be construed to prohibit or interfere with—

(1) the right to petition the Government for the redress of grievances;

(2) the right to express a personal opinion; or

(3) the right of association, protected by the first amendment to the Constitution.

(b) Prohibition of Activities. — Nothing in this Act shall be construed to prohibit, or to authorize any court to prohibit, lobbying activities or lobbying contacts by any person or entity, regardless of whether such person or entity is in compliance with the requirements of this Act.

(c) Audit and Investigations. — Nothing in this Act shall be construed to grant general audit or investigative authority to the Secretary of the Senate or the Clerk of the House of Representatives. . . .

Sec. 14.   Identification of Clients and Covered Officials

(a) Oral Lobbying Contacts. — Any person or entity that makes an oral lobbying contact with a covered legislative branch official or a covered, executive branch official shall, on the request of the official at the time of the lobbying contact —

(1) state whether the person or entity is registered under this Act and identify the client on whose behalf the lobbying contact is made. . . .

Sec. 18.   Exempt Organizations

An organization described in section 501(c)(4) of the Internal Revenue Code of 1986 which engages in lobbying activities shall not be eligible for the receipt of federal funds constituting an award, grant, contract, loan or any other form. . . .

Sec. 23.   Sense of the Senate that Lobbying Expenses Should Remain Nondeductible . . .

(a) Findings. — The Senate finds that ordinary Americans generally are not allowed to deduct the costs of communicating with their elected representatives.

(b) Sense of the Senate. — It is the sense of the Senate that lobbying expenses should not be tax deductible. . . .

Sec. 25.   Prohibition on Provision of Gifts or Travel by Registered Lobbyists to Members of Congress and to Congressional Employees

(a) Prohibition. — Any person described in subsection (b) may not make a gift or provide travel to a covered legislative branch official if the person has knowledge that the gift or travel may not be accepted by that covered legislative branch official under the Rules of the House of Representatives or the Standing Rules of the Senate (as the case may be).

(b) Persons Subject to Prohibition. — The persons subject to the prohibition under subsection (a) are any lobbyist that is registered or is required to register under section 4(a)(1), any organization that employs 1 or more lobbyists and is registered or is required to register under section 4(a)(2) and any employee listed or required to be listed as a lobbyist by a registrant under section 4(b)(6) or 5(b)(2)(C).

NOTES AND QUESTIONS

1. *Disclosure and prohibition.* The regulatory approach followed in the Regulation of Lobbying Act of 1946 and Lobbying Disclosure Act of 1995 was one of disclosure. Another approach might be to prohibit certain activities. Consider the following provisions from the 1877 Constitution of the State of Georgia: "Lobbying is declared to be a crime, and the General Assembly shall enforce this provision by suitable penalties." Ga. Const. of 1877, art. I, §2. What is its defect?

2. *Responding to criticisms.* Consider the criticisms of the earlier bill by the Senate Report. Does the bill address and resolve each of these criticisms? One clear result of the act in its first year (1995) was that registrations almost doubled (from approximately 6,000 to 12,000). See Mary Jacoby, The Newly Registered Lobbyists: "Coalitions" Roll Call at 1 (Apr. 18, 1996).

3. *Goals and results.* Senator Carl Levine, one of the co-sponsors of the 1995 Act, summarized the broad impact of the legislation in the foreword to the third edition of the ABA Section of Administrative Law and Regulatory Practice, The Lobbying Manual:

> Under the LDA, lobbying of congressional staff is no longer exempt; lobbying of executive branch officials is no longer ignored; lobbying on non-legislative issues is no longer left out; and the much-abused "primary purpose" test has been eliminated. For the first time, all paid professional lobbyists are required to disclose who is paying them how much to lobby Congress and the executive branch — and on what issues.

4. *Grass-roots lobbying revisited.* Earlier in this chapter (Gaining Access to Legislative Decisionmaking on page 485), we explored the prevalence of organized grass-roots lobbying, labeled "astro-turf" mobilization by one observer because of its manufactured nature. Theda Skocpol, Boomerang 139 (1996). Recall Judge Mikva's experience, as a congressman, with the Illinois Automobile Association. This certainly would be considered "astro-turf" mobilization. Would any registration or reporting be required under the 1995 Act, assuming that the IAA had no other communication on any issue with Mikva or other parties covered by the Act? If not, what else would be necessary? Of course, it is unlikely that a lobbying effort would be so limited without any attempt at additional contact with other legislators. Assume that the IAA, while running its mail campaign, also contacted the chair of the committee with jurisdiction over the bill. Or assume that the IAA had registered as a lobbyist on some other issue. Would this affect your registration or reporting decision? During the debate on the Lobbying Disclosure Act of 1995, Senators McConnell (R, Kentucky) and Levin (D, Michigan) successfully proposed an amendment to the bill that removed all reference to grass-roots lobbying. According to Senator McConnell, the goal of this amendment was to clarify that the Act "will not require any reporting or disclosure whatsoever of grassroots activity." What importance do you place on this statement in answering the question concerning Congressman Mikva?

5. *Creating a special exception?* The Lobbying Disclosure Act of 1995 met a small snag in the enactment process at the door of the Senate enrollment clerk. (For a description of the enrollment process see Chapter 2, pages 75-79.) According to a report in the New York Times (Adam Clymer, One Bill's Detour on the Way to the White House, N.Y. Times, Dec. 14, 1995, at A1, A14), the bill was held up in the office of the Senate's enrolling clerk for more than two weeks while the clerk waited for orders from Senate Majority Leader Bob Dole, because Senator Alan K. Simpson (R, Wyoming) and Senator Larry E. Craig (R, Idaho) were trying to rewrite part of the bill that would force nonprofit organizations to choose between lobbying and taking federal dollars. Clymer reported that Senator Simpson's target had been the American Association of Retired Persons. Blue Cross and Blue Shield complained because they had contracts to handle Medicare claims and insure federal workers, and they did not want to lose their ability to lobby. The Blues had been lobbying in favor of some parts of the Republican Medicare program that would result in more business for them, and against parts they felt would offer unfair competition. As a result of these complaints, the two senators had been trying to eliminate the word "contracts" from the bill's description of federal funding (Section 18) so that the Blues would be unaffected. As a vehicle for their effort they seized on a resolution of the Senate intended to instruct the enrollment clerk to fix some typographical errors in the bill. In Congress, if errors are found during the enrolling process, they can be corrected if both houses adopt an identical resolution directing the enrollment clerk to make the correction. Ultimately, the Senate passed two versions of a typographical error resolution, one with a change to accommodate the Blues, and one without it, leaving the final decision to the House. The House passed the resolution without the substantive change.

5.   The K Street Scandal and the Honest Leadership and Open Government Act of 2007

Technically speaking, K Street is nothing more than just that: a major street that runs through a powerful Georgetown neighborhood in the nation's capital. However, the street is much more infamous than its simple name suggests. K Street is home to the nation's most powerful lobbying groups, think tanks, advocacy groups, and media bureaus — in short, those offices on K Street wield a lot of influence.

Following the 1994 congressional elections, which gave Republicans control of the House of Representatives after a 40-year Democratic stronghold, Republican strategist Grover Norquist launched the K Street Project, which was portrayed simply as a nonpartisan employment service. The areas of employment the project focused on were lobbying firms, law firms, and trade associations. Yet in 2004, with the unfolding of the Jack Abramoff lobbying scandal, the entrenched purpose of the project also came to light. In a January 14, 2007, New York Times Book Review discussion of *Heist*, a book by Peter H. Stone, Norman J. Ornstein explained that in fact "the goal [of the project] was to get trusted people into jobs where they could use campaign cash to help Republicans stay in power while enabling them to live comfortably by sharing in the munificence of the moneyed interests." Certainly, the idea of placing individuals in positions of power that support certain ideological positions was not conceived by the K Street project; this practice, in a sense, is at the very heart of the lobbying profession. Instead, it was the depth of the Project's power and the scope of its leadership that seems to have caught Washington off guard.

In February 2004 the Department of Justice and the FBI began investigating Jack Abramoff, one of the nation's most prominent Republican lobbyists, for corrupt lobbying practices. That investigation opened a Pandora's box of lobbying and ethical transgressions, which implicated various members of the Congress, powerful lobbyists, and noted strategists. Fittingly, the scandal has been dubbed the "Enron of Lobbying." Susan Schmidt and James V. Grimaldi, The Fast Rise and Steep Fall of Jack Abramoff, Wash. Post, Dec. 29, 2005, at A1.

The Abramoff scandal centered on payments by multiple Indian gaming tribes to Abramoff and his associates, which totaled upwards of $60 million over a three-year period. This amount was remarkable both because of the total absence of any gaming tribe issues in the legislative arena during the period of these mammoth payouts, and the fact that those payments eclipsed what most large corporations — such as pharmaceutical companies — were paying Washington lobbyists in the same three-year period. What was even more remarkable was where the money was going. Over the course of the two-year investigation, it was revealed that various members of the House, including then House Majority Leader Tom DeLay and Representative Bob Ney, had benefited in various ways from that money — for example, in the form of lavish trips overseas, meals, and sporting event tickets — all in exchange for their support of Abramoff's Indian gaming clients.

Abramoff had very close ties with Grover Norquist, the founder of the K Street project, and ultimately it was revealed that so too did Majority Leader DeLay and numerous congressional aides. On January 3, 2006, Abramoff pleaded guilty to charges of conspiracy, fraud, and tax evasion. Following Abramoff's plea, on January 7, 2006, DeLay permanently resigned from his position amidst pressures stemming from the Abramoff scandal as well as an unrelated Texas state criminal indictment for conspiracy to violate campaign finance laws (which was ultimately dropped). The fallout continued when, on October 13, 2006, Representative Bob Ney pleaded guilty for conspiracy and making false statements in connection with the Abramoff investigation. For further readings on the Abramoff lobbying scandal, see the sequence of articles by Washington Post writer Susan Schmidt detailing the investigation and its culmination over the entire two-year period. See also Peter H. Stone, Heist: Superlobbyist Jack Abramoff, His Republican Allies, and the Buying of Washington (2006).

While this scandal raged, the 109th Congress, and subsequently the 110th, recognized that an overhaul of both the federal lobbying laws and its own internal ethics rules were necessary. Not only had Congress taken note; the American voting public were equally concerned. A January 10, 2006, CNN/ USA Today/Gallup poll indicated that 43 percent of those polled cited government corruption as an "extremely important" issue in the 2006 congressional elections. A flurry of House and Senate bills quickly proliferated, making lobbying and ethics reform the hot topic. To name but a few, there were S. 2349, S. 2118, H.R. 4975, H.R. 4920, and H.R. 5677, all of which concerned the topic of ethics and lobbying reform. Ultimately, the 110th Congress streamlined the various reform proposals and passed the Honest Leadership and Open Government Act of 2007, on January 4 of that year.

The Honest Leadership and Open Government Act of 2007

The Honest Leadership and Open Government Act of 2007 is divided into seven titles, all of which are aimed at closing the loopholes that the K Street scandal exposed. The following chart, which was compiled by the American Society of Association Executives and is available at http:// www.asaecenter.org/, compares *relevant* changes in the law due to the passage of the 2007 Act. It should be noted that the comparison outlines the differences not only between the 1995 Act and the 2007 Act, but also between the 2007 Act and some of the relevant House and Senate ethics rules (discussed in Note 3 below).

2007 Act Section	Area of Focus	Law Pre–2007 Act	Law as Amended by the Honest Leadership and Open Government Act of 2007
Title I: Closing the Revolving Door			
101	Former members' lobbying restrictions/ "cooling off" period	A member of Congress must wait one year before he or she can lobby Congress	A senator must now wait two years before being allowed to lobby Congress. A representative still must wait one year before lobbying Congress. Senate staff are also required to wait one year before lobbying any Senate office.
102	Ending the K Street Project	No specific mention of "influencing" the hiring practices of outside companies	No member of Congress can influence the hiring of a person on a partisan basis by any private entity without being subject to a fine or imprisonment.

2007 Act Section	Area of Focus	Law Pre–2007 Act	Law as Amended by the Honest Leadership and Open Government Act of 2007
103	Notifying members of post-congressional restrictions	N/A	The Secretary of the Senate/Clerk of the House is responsible for notifying members leaving Congress of their post-congressional job restrictions, and may post these on the Internet.
104	Tribal work exception	N/A	Members or executive branch officials representing a tribal organization or intertribal consortium are exempt from certain lobbying provisions.

Title II: Full Public Disclosure of Lobbying

201	Quarterly filing of lobbying reports	Lobbying reports are filed semi-annually within 45 days after the end of 6 months.	Lobbying reports must now be filed quarterly, and the reports must be filed within 20 days of the end of the quarter.
202	Disclosure of state government lobbying	N/A	The lobbying report now must include whether a client is a state or local government, or any entity controlled by a state or local government.
203	Reporting of lobbyists' campaign contributions	N/A	Twice a year lobbyists are required to disclose any contribution over $200 to any federal candidate, PAC, or party organization; and money spent on an event honoring a member or given to a presidential library. The disclosure would also include a certification that the lobbyist has

2007 Act Section	Area of Focus	Law Pre–2007 Act	Law as Amended by the Honest Leadership and Open Government Act of 2007
			read the Rules of the Senate and House and has not violated those rules.
204	Bundling disclosure	N/A	This section amends the Federal Election Campaign Act of 1971 to require a candidate's PAC to disclose the name of a person who has bundled two or more contributions over $15,000 (not including those contributions made by the bundler). The FEC should disclose all reported bundled contributions on their website.
205	Electronic filing of lobbying disclosure report	There is no requirement that the semiannual lobbying report be filed online.	This section requires the House and Senate to use the same software to allow the Lobbying Disclosure Act to be filed over the Internet.
206	Gift and travel prohibitions	Members and staff are not allowed to accept any one gift valued over $50 or any combination over $100 in a year.	Members and staff are prohibited from accepting gifts or privately financed travel from lobbyists except as specified by each chamber's rules. The rules currently abolish the $50 gift rule and place restrictions on who can finance congressional travel and for how long (see ASAE summary of House Rules regarding gifts and travel).

2007 Act Section	Area of Focus	Law Pre–2007 Act	Law as Amended by the Honest Leadership and Open Government Act of 2007
207	Disclosure of funds from coalitions and associations	N/A	Associations or coalitions that receive over $5,000 in a quarter from other associations or coalitions for lobbying purposes must disclose these donations on their lobbying disclosure report or post them on their website.
208	Lobbyists' disclosing executive branch employment	The LDA of 1995 required a lobbyist to disclose employment in the executive branch over the past two years.	This section requires a lobbyist to disclose any employment within the executive branch within the past 20 years.
209	Public's ability to view lobbying disclosure	Lobbying disclosure reports were available to the public through each chamber's respective administrative offices.	This section allows for the Secretary of the Senate and the Clerk of the House to post lobbying disclosure reports on the Internet.
210	Reporting of violations	The respective chambers' administrative offices notify a lobbyist of noncompliance with this act.	The section requires making public periodically the number of violations of this act, and the Attorney General for D.C. must report to Congress semiannually the number of enforcement actions taken regarding this bill.
211	Penalties for violations of the law	A fine of no more than $50,000 will be charged to a lobbyist violating the law.	The fine for violation increases to $200,000 and the section adds jail time of up to five years.

2007 Act Section	Area of Focus	Law Pre–2007 Act	Law as Amended by the Honest Leadership and Open Government Act of 2007
212	Electronic access to foreign government lobbying registration	N/A	All lobbying disclosures for foreign governments are to be available online for free under the Attorney General's office.
213	Comptroller General's annual audit of lobbying records	N/A	The Comptroller General's office is to randomly sample registered lobbyists to determine if they are compliant with lobbying disclosure requirements. These results will be reported to Congress annually. This section also allows the Comptroller General's office to request information directly from the registered lobbyists used in the study.
214	Sense of Congress resolutions	N/A	Congress disparages using family to circumvent lobbying requirements and feels the lobbying community should create a standard of conduct for the industry.

Title III: Matters Relating to the House of Representatives

2007 Act Section	Area of Focus	Law Pre–2007 Act	Law as Amended by the Honest Leadership and Open Government Act of 2007
301	Members and staff disclosing employment negotiations	The House Rules do not address this.	This section creates House Rule XXVII, which states that any House member may not be hired or negotiate employment with an outside entity until their successor is elected or they file a statement with the Ethics Committee. They are prohibited from

2007 Act Section	Area of Focus	Law Pre–2007 Act	Law as Amended by the Honest Leadership and Open Government Act of 2007
			voting on anything that is or can be perceived to be a conflict of interest. Highly paid staff (75% of the member's salary) also fall under these rules.
302	Prohibiting lobbying by a spouse	The House Rules do not address this.	All staff within a member's office are prohibited from making a "lobbying contact" with a member's spouse if that spouse is a lobbyist.
303	Prohibiting lobbying firms from serving as legal counsel for House offices	Lawyers who are consultants for House members may not lobby the offices that employ them but may lobby Congress on matters not related to their contracted cause.	This section amends the House Rules, extending the prohibition on the individual to the entire firm.
304	Travel disclosure reports on the Internet	The House Rules do not address this.	The Clerk of the House must post all travel disclosure forms filed in the office, with certain personal information redacted.

Title IV: Congressional Pension Accountability

2007 Act Section	Area of Focus	Law Pre–2007 Act	Law as Amended by the Honest Leadership and Open Government Act of 2007
401	Removing right to pension for Convicted members	N/A	Members who commit crimes listed in this section (bribery, perjury, etc.) lose their right to a congressional pension.

2007 Act Section	Area of Focus	Law Pre–2007 Act	Law as Amended by the Honest Leadership and Open Government Act of 2007

Subtitle C: Revolving-Door Reform

2007 Act Section	Area of Focus	Law Pre–2007 Act	Law as Amended by the Honest Leadership and Open Government Act of 2007
531	Former senators' lobbying restrictions	Former senators may not lobby the Senate for one year, according to Senate Rule XXXVII.	The prohibition in Senate Rule XXXVII is extended to two years. The prohibition is also extended to highly paid staff (those who make 75% of a member's salary).
532	Members and staff disclosing employment negotiations	The Senate Rules do not address this.	This section amends Senate Rule XXXVII, preventing senators from being hired by or negotiating employment with an outside entity until a successor is elected or a statement is filed with the Ethics Committee. They are prohibited from voting on anything that is or could be perceived to be a conflict of interest. Highly paid staff (making 75% of the member's salary) also fall under this rule.
533	Banishing former senators, now lobbyists, from the Senate floor	Senate Rule XXIII lists all persons allowed on the Senate floor.	Senate Rule XXIII is amended to prohibit former senators, Senate officers, and Speakers of the House who are registered lobbyists from receiving Senate floor privileges, and from using the Senate gym and Senate parking spaces.
534	Ending the K Street Project	The Senate Rules do not address this.	No senator can influence the hiring of a person on a partisan basis by any private entity.

2007 Act Section	Area of Focus	Law Pre–2007 Act	Law as Amended by the Honest Leadership and Open Government Act of 2007
		Subtitle D: Gift and Travel Reform	
541	Gift ban	A senator or staff is prohibited from receiving a gift of more than $50 in value or gifts totaling $100 over a year. This excludes gifts from family, participation in events as an official duty, awards, etc.	Senate Rule XXXV is modified to prohibit a gift of any cost from a lobbyist, except as permitted in the existing Senate Rules.
544	Privately funded travel restrictions	Prior approval is required for senators wishing to travel when the travel is sponsored by an outside group.	Included in the prohibition is funding of private travel by an organization that employs lobbyists. Funding of travel for a member is allowed if the trip is for one day or is paid for by a 501(c)(3) organization. Before the trip, the member and sponsoring organization must file paperwork with the Ethics Committee. The Ethics Committee sets the guidelines for how the travel is to be conducted and what constitutes reasonable expenses for reimbursement. Members must reimburse corporate flights at the charter rate.

2007 Act Section	Area of Focus	Law Pre–2007 Act	Law as Amended by the Honest Leadership and Open Government Act of 2007
545	Constituent events	Events in the district fall under the gift requirements.	A senator may attend an event in his or her home state if the meal cost is less than $50, the event is sponsored by constituents, at least five constituents will be present, none of the attendees shall be lobbyists, the senator participates in the event in some way, and the event is within the senator's official duties.
546	Creating a website to track privately funded travel	The Senate Rules do not address this.	The Secretary of the Senate will create a website containing information on senators' privately funded travel.
Subtitle E: Other Reforms			
552	Prohibiting lobbying by a spouse	The Senate Rules do not address this.	Senate Rule XXXVII is amended to prohibit a senator or senator's staffer to make a lobbying contact with the senator's spouse or any other senator's spouse if that spouse became a lobbyist after that senator was elected or the two were married.
554	Ethics Committee's annual report on violations	The Senate Rules do not address this.	The Ethics Committee is required to annually present a report to Congress on the number of LDA violations by members and the outcome of investigations.

2007 Act Section	Area of Focus	Law Pre–2007 Act	Law as Amended by the Honest Leadership and Open Government Act of 2007
Title VI: Prohibited Use of Private Aircraft			
601	Restrictions on using campaign funds for air travel	N/A	All candidates (including current lawmakers) for federal office may not take reduced-rate flights on corporate aircraft. House members are prohibited from flying on any private aircraft. Flights on privately owned aircraft and aircraft owned by family members are permitted.

NOTES AND QUESTIONS

1. *The revolving door.* The term "revolving door" generally refers to the practice of hiring former legislators, or their aides, as lobbyists. The concern is over the ties such individuals have with their former colleagues. As noted in the chart above, the 2007 Act increased the so-called cooling-off period before former senators or senior Senate staff members may lobby in the Senate from one to two years. In contrast, the House rules remain unchanged by the legislation; former House members cannot lobby either house of Congress for a one-year period following the end of their terms, and senior House staff may not lobby the member's office or committee at which they were employed for one year following the end of their employment. Do you think the two-year increase results in an adequate time period in light of the concerns noted above? It should be mentioned that former campaign consultants are wholly exempt from this provision, which means that a senior consultant from a winning (or losing, for that matter) campaign may immediately be hired as a lobbyist once his or her duties have ended. What are your thoughts on this?

2. *Disclosure requirements.* Under the original 1995 Act lobbyists were required to register with the Secretary of the Senate and the Clerk of the House of Representatives on a semi-annual basis. In addition, pursuant to Section 7, a lobbyist who knowingly failed to remedy a defective filing with the Secretary of the Senate or the Clerk of the House of Representatives was subject to civil penalties. It was the job of the Secretary and the Clerk to report any alleged violations of the 1995 Act to the Department of Justice;

incidents in those reports, however, were unavailable to the public. This lack of any transparency made the regulation seem somewhat self-defeating. As Senator Chris Dodd noted at a February 8, 2006, hearing of the Senate Committee on Rules and Administration, "since 2003, the Office of Public Records has referred over 2,000 cases to the Department of Justice, and nothing's been heard from them again." Eric Peterson, Lobbying Reform: Background and Legislative Proposals, 109th Congress, Congressional Research Service (CRS) Report for Congress, at CRS-6, 7 (updated March 23, 2006).

The 2007 Act sought to rectify this problem in two ways. First, the Act not only increased the civil penalty from $50,000 to $200,000, but it also added stiff criminal penalties for any registrant who knowingly fails to comply with the provisions. In addition, instead of investing the oversight responsibility solely in the Secretary of the Senate and the Clerk of the House, the 2007 Act requires the Comptroller General to audit lobbyist reports and convey the findings to the Congress on an annual basis. Finally, the Senate Secretary and the House Clerk now must electronically post all reports on a publicly available website.

3. *Congressional ethics rules and federal lobbying regulations.* The federal regulations that pertain to lobbying are not the only set of laws a lobbyist must be aware of when navigating the complicated path of compliance. Indeed, each house of the Congress has its own set of ethical rules. While the rules are generally binding only on members of Congress, their staff, and other congressional officers, the implications for any lobbyist found to be involved in an ethics violation are quite profound. Reputation is the most important commodity a lobbyist has to offer a client, and involvement in a congressional ethics scandal clearly puts that commodity in jeopardy. For more on congressional ethics and their relationship to lobbying, see ABA Section of Administrative Law and Regulatory Practice, The Lobbying Manual: A Compliance Guide for Lawyers and Lobbyists, ch. 22 (William V. Luneburg and Thomas M. Susman eds., 3d ed. 2005).

6. Applying the Lobbying Act — A Problem

Consider the applicability of the registration requirements of the act to the following activities. Who, if anybody, must register and for which activities?

1. A letter to a legislator or testimony before a legislative committee, by an environmentalist in favor of a particular piece of environmental legislation.

2. A letter to a legislator or testimony before a legislative committee, by the same environmentalist in favor of the same legislation as above, but prepared by an attorney for a fee paid by the environmentalist.

3. A letter to a legislator or testimony before a legislative committee, by a staff member of a national environmental organization in favor of the same

Clerk of the House of Representatives	Secretary of the Senate
Legislative Resource Center	Office of Public Records
B-106 Cannon Building	232 Hart Building
Washington, DC 20515	Washington, DC 20510
http://lobbyingdisclosure.house.gov	http://senate.gov/lobby

LOBBYING REPORT

Lobbying Disclosure Act of 1995 (Section 5) - **All Filers Are Required to Complete This Page**

1. Registrant name ☒ Organization/Lobbying Firm   ☐ Self Employed Individual

    Organization

2. Address   ☐ Check if different than previously reported

    Address1   Address 2

    City   State   Zip Code   Country USA

3. Principal place of business (if different than line 2)

    City   State   Zip Code   Country

City   State/Zip or Country

4a. Contact Name	b. Telephone number	c. E-mail	5. Senate ID #
Prefix Full Name			
Ms.			

7. Client Name ☐ Self ☐ *Click if the client is a state or local government or instrumentality*   6. House ID #

TYPE OF REPORT   8. Year   Q1 (1/1 - 3/31) ☐   Q2 (4/1 - 6/30) ☐   Q3 (7/1 - 9/30) ☐   Q4 (10/1 - 12/31) ☐

9. Check if this filing amends a previously filed version of this report ☐

10. Check if this is a Termination Report ☐ ⇨ Termination Date _____   11. No Lobbying Issue Activity ☐

INCOME OR EXPENSES - You MUST Complete Either Line 12 OR Line 13

12. Lobbying Firms	13. Organizations
INCOME relating to lobbying activities for this reporting period was:	**EXPENSES** relating to lobbying activities for this reporting period were:
Less than $5,000 ☐	Less than $5,000 ☐
$5,000 or more ☐ ⇨ $ _____	$5,000 or more ☐ ⇨ $ _____

Provide a good faith estimate, rounded to the nearest $10,000, of all lobbying related income from the client (including all payments to the registrant by any other entity for lobbying activities on behalf of the client).

14. REPORTING METHOD. Check box to indicate expense accounting method. See instructions for description of options.

☐ **Method A.**   Reporting amounts using LDA definitions only
☐ **Method B.**   Reporting amounts under section 6033(b)(8) of the Internal Revenue Code
☐ **Method C.**   Reporting amounts under section 162(e) of the Internal Revenue Code

Printed Name and Title _____

LD-2DS (Rev. 6.0.0 Mac)

Registrant Name _____   Client Name _____

LOBBYING ACTIVITY. Select as many codes as necessary to reflect the general issue areas in which the registrant engaged in lobbying on behalf of the client during the reporting period. **Using a separate page for each code,** provide information as requested. Attach additional page(s) as needed.

15. General issue area code _____ (one per page)

16. Specific lobbying issues

17. House(s) of Congress and Federal agencies contacted ☐ Check if None

House of Representatives		
Senate	[Add >]	
Administration for Children & Families (ACF)		
Administration on Aging	[< Remove]	
Advisory Council on Historic Preservation (ACHP)		

18. Name of each individual who acted as a lobbyist in this issue area

First Name	Name Last Name	Suffix	Covered Official Position (if applicable)	New
				☐
				☐
				☐
				☐
				☐
				☐
				☐
				☐
				☐

19. Interest of each foreign entity in the specific issues listed on line 16 above ☐ Check if None

Printed Name and Title _____

LD-2DS (Rev. 6.0.0 Mac)

Registrant Name _____ Client Name _____

Information Update Page - Complete ONLY where registration information has changed.

20. Client new address

Address			
City	State	Zip Code	Country

21. Client new principal place of business (if different than line 20)

City	State	Zip Code	Country

22. New general description of client's business or activities

LOBBYIST UPDATE

23. Name of each previously reported individual who is no longer expected to act as a lobbyist for the client

	First Name	Last Name	Suffix		First Name	Last Name	Suffix
1				3			
2				4			

ISSUE UPDATE

Find the code to select below.

24. General lobbying issues that no longer pertain

AFFILIATED ORGANIZATIONS 25. Add the following affiliated organization(s)

Internet Address:

Name	Address	Principal place of Business (city and state or country)
	Address	City
	C/S/Z	State Country
	Address	City
	C/S/Z	State Country

26. Name of each previously reported organization that is no longer affiliated with the registrant or client

1	2	3

FOREIGN ENTITIES

27. Add the following foreign entities

Name	Address Street Address City State/Province Country	Principal place of business (city and state or country)	Amount of contribution for lobbying activities	Ownership percentage in client
		City		
		State Country		%

28. Name of each previously reported foreign entity that no longer owns, or controls, or is affiliated with the registrant, client or affiliated organization

1	3	5
2	4	6

LD-2DS (Rev. 6.0.0 Mac)

legislation as before. This organization was established to perform educational functions relating to the environment; included among these functions is the provision of information to legislative bodies. The staff member who presented the organization's view on the legislation is a member of the professional staff of the organization. Funds to support the organization are raised through membership dues and special activities such as concerts.

4. A national letter writing campaign organized by this same organization in favor of the same legislation. The campaign includes direct requests to members of the organization to write to their legislators and the placement of advertisements in newspapers requesting people who agree with the group's position on the legislation to write to their legislators. All of the advertisements are paid out of the general funds of the organization, except for an ad in the New York Times, which is paid for by a special grant from a wealthy donor.

5. An educational campaign by this environmental group intended to be conducted through all of the nation's various media outlets: radio, television, and print. The campaign includes the staging of events throughout the country to highlight certain dangers to the environment, the visiting of editorial boards to gain editorial support for the organization's views, the placing of guest editorials in newspapers, and appearances on local television and radio shows throughout the country.

6. The preparation and distribution to members of Congress of books and pamphlets by this environmental group on the general condition of the environment.

7. A meeting among members of the group, staff of the group, and favorable legislators to discuss strategies for passage of the legislation. This meeting is held at the organization's headquarters in Washington, D.C. Lunch is served and paid for by the organization.

Being subject to the Lobbying Act requires submission of a quarterly report to the Clerk of the House of Representatives and the Clerk of the Senate. A copy of a form for such report follows.

7. State Statutes Governing Lobbying

Laws requiring the registration of lobbyists are common among the states. For the most part, they follow the federal model, focusing on the registration of those who are compensated for attempting to directly influence the enactment of legislation. In 1993, the Illinois legislature amended its Lobbyist Registration Act to include the following definition:

> "Lobbying" means any direct or indirect communication or contact with an official of the . . . legislative branch of state government . . . for the ultimate purpose of influencing . . . legislative . . . action.

How does this provision differ from the federal Act? How would substituting it in the questions posed in Section A.6 above change your answers?

8. The Lawyer as Lobbyist: Unique Problems

Lawyers make effective lobbyists. By training they are well suited to influencing legislative action. They are familiar with statutory law and its constitutional framework. They are skilled in legal research, drafting, and interpretation. They are also trained to marshal facts and argue positions. Additionally because many legislators are lawyers, the lawyer-lobbyist may have an advantage in understanding the thinking of the lawyer-legislator.

Although the lawyer-lobbyist may have some advantages, she also faces dilemmas not confronted by non-lawyer-lobbyists. A lawyer-lobbyist must comply with the ethics code of the jurisdiction in which she is admitted. As a comment to the code of the District of Columbia states:

> Lawyers have no exclusive right to appear before nonadjudicative bodies, as they do before a court. The requirements of this Rule therefore may subject lawyers to regulations inapplicable to advocates, such as nonlawyer lobbyists, who are not lawyers. However, legislatures and administrative agencies have a right to expect lawyers to deal with them as they deal with courts.

1 D.C. Court Rules, App. A, Rule 3.9, comment 2.

In this section, we will review some of the unique issues that can arise for lawyer-lobbyists as a result of the applicability of codes of ethics to lobbying. Of particular concern will be the conflict of interest provisions. A question to consider is whether such provisions are realistic as applied to lobbying. The code explored in this section is the Rules of Professional Conduct of the District of Columbia (1 D.C. Court Rules, App. A) (D.C. Rules). Not only do these rules regulate the behavior of a large concentration of lawyer-lobbyists, but the manner of their implementation will also naturally influence the regulation of lobbying activity by other states. We do not provide a fully detailed exposition of these rules. For more detail and analysis, see generally ABA Section of Administrative Law and Regulatory Practice, The Lobbying Manual: A Compliance Guide for Lawyers and Lobbyists, (William V. Luneburg and Thomas M. Susman eds., 3d ed. 2005).

Each state and the District of Columbia has its own code of ethics, promulgated by its legislature or highest court. Two major models exist. The first is the ABA's Model Code, which is in effect in some form or other in one-third of the states. The second is the ABA's Model Rules (adopted by the ABA in 1983 as a reform of the Model Code), which has been adopted by more than one-half of the states. The D.C. code is a variant of the Model Rules. What this means is that lawyers lobbying state or municipal legislatures must become familiar with the rules of ethics of those particular states. Also, lawyers who are subject to the D.C. Rules and to those of some other jurisdiction must be aware of potential conflicts. See ABA Model Rule 8.5 for a recent proposal on how such conflicts should be resolved.

Selected D.C. Rules of Professional Conduct

Rule 1.6.   Confidentiality of Information

(a) Except when permitted under paragraph (c) or (d), a lawyer shall not knowingly:

(1) Reveal a confidence or secret of the lawyer's client;

(2) Use a confidence or secret of the lawyer's client to the disadvantage of the client;

(3) Use a confidence or secret of the lawyer's client for the advantage of the lawyer or of a third person.

(b) "Confidence" refers to information protected by the attorney-client privilege under applicable law; and "secret" refers to other information gained in the professional relationship that the client has requested be held inviolate, or the disclosure of which would be embarrassing, or would be likely to be detrimental, to the client. . . .

Rule 1.7.   Conflict of Interest: General Rule

(a) A lawyer shall not represent a client with respect to a position to be taken in a matter if that position is adverse to a position taken or to be taken in the same matter by another client represented with respect to that position by the same lawyer.

(b) Except as permitted by paragraph (c) below, a lawyer shall not represent a client with respect to a matter if:

(1) A position to be taken by that client in that matter is adverse to a position taken or to be taken by another client in the same matter;

(2) Such representation will be or is likely to be adversely affected by representation of another client;

(3) Representation of another client will be or is likely to be adversely affected by such representation; or

(4) The lawyer's professional judgment on behalf of the client will be or reasonably may be adversely affected by the lawyer's responsibilities to or interests in a third party or the lawyer's own financial, business, property, or personal interests.

(c) A lawyer may represent a client with respect to a matter in the circumstances described in paragraph (b) above if:

(1) Each potentially affected client provides consent to such representation after full disclosure of the existence and nature of the possible

conflict and the possible adverse consequences of such representation; and

     (2) The lawyer is able to comply with all other applicable rules with respect to such representation.

Rule 1.10. Imputed Disqualification: General Rule

(a) While lawyers are associated in a firm, none of them shall knowingly represent a client when any one of them practicing alone would be prohibited from doing so by Rules 1.7, 1.8(b), 1.9, or 2.2. . . .

Rule 3.9. Advocate in Nonadjudicative Proceedings

    A lawyer representing a client before a legislative or administrative body in a nonadjudicative proceeding shall disclose that the appearance is in a representative capacity and shall conform to the provisions of Rules 3.3, 3.4(a) through (c), and 3.5.

Problems for the Lawyer-Lobbyist

    Assume you have been retained by a U.S. car manufacturer (A-Auto) on an annual retainer, first, to draft and lobby for an amendment reducing the number of foreign car imports permitted under an existing statute and, second, to protect it against pending or potential adverse legislation, particularly tax legislation. At the time you accept the retainer, your law firm represents, on annual retainer, the "general legislative" interests of a number of other corporate interests, including a U.S. corporation that makes parts for foreign car producers (P-Parts). You do not represent this client, but you do represent a number of clients of the firms who are concerned about being adversely affected by changes to the tax code. None of this latter group is in auto-related businesses. Set forth below are a series of questions addressing the applicability of the D.C. Rules to a number of situations that might confront the lawyer-lobbyist. The following Comments to Rule 1-7, promulgated, along with the Rules, by the District of Columbia Court of Appeals, may prove helpful:

> [3] The concept of a "matter" is typically apparent in on-the-record adversary proceedings or other proceedings in which a written record of the position of parties exists. In other situations, it may not be clear to a lawyer whether the representation of one client is adverse to the interests of another client. For example, a lawyer may represent a client only with respect to one or a few of the client's areas of interest. Other lawyers, or

nonlawyers (such as lobbyists), or employees of the client (such as government relations personnel) may be representing that client on many issues whose scope and content are unknown to the lawyer. A lawyer may not undertake a representation known to be adverse to the interests of another client, whether that representation is in a court proceeding, an on-the-record administrative hearing, a notice-and-comment rulemaking, or in an effort to influence policy or achieve a legislative result. . . .

[4] the absolute prohibition of paragraph (a) applies only to situations in which a lawyer would be called upon to espouse adverse positions in the same matter. . . .

[11] A number of types of situations frequently arise in which disclosure and informed consent are usually required. These include joint representation of parties to criminal and civil litigation, joint representation of incorporators of a business, joint representation of a business or government agency and its employees, representation of family members seeking estate planning or the drafting of wills, joint representation of an insurer and an insured, representation in circumstances in which the personal or financial interests of the lawyer, or the lawyer's family, might be affected by the representation and other similar situations in which experience indicates that conflicts are likely to exist or arise. For example, a lawyer might not be able to represent a client vigorously if the client's adversary is a person with whom the lawyer has longstanding personal or social ties. The client is entitled to be informed of such circumstances so that an informed decision can be made concerning the advisability of retaining the lawyer who has such ties to the adversary. The principles of disclosure and consent are equally applicable to all such circumstances, except that if the positions to be taken by two clients in a matter as to which the lawyer represents both are actually adverse, then, as provided in paragraph (a), the lawyer may not undertake or continue the representation with respect to those issues even if disclosure has been made and consent obtained. . . .

[17] All of the references in Rule 1.7 and its accompanying Comment to the limitation upon a "lawyer" must be read in light of the imputed disqualification provisions of Rule 1.10, which affect lawyers practicing in a firm.

In formulating your answer to these questions, consider also whether the rules make sense in the lobbying arena.

1. *At the start of the session.* Does the act of being retained by A-Auto violate the D.C. Rules? If so, is there a remedy short of ending the lawyer-client relationship? Do you think one remedy would be to lobby only legislative staff and not elected representatives? (Recall that under the Regulation of Lobbying Act of 1946, pages 490-491 of this chapter, it is questionable whether lobbying legislative staff is a regulated activity.)

2. *A grass-roots approach?* Assume that the problem set forth in Question 1 is not remedial with respect to the particular amendment. A-Auto asks you to draft the protective amendment and then to organize a grass-roots campaign for its enactment, leaving the direct lobbying of this amendment to its in-house lobbyists. Would such lobbying be permitted under the D.C. Rules, all other facts remaining the same?

·

3. *A bill forthcoming?* Assume that during the course of the year, Congress decides, on short notice, that it must raise taxes to reduce the deficit. As Congress has been attempting to reduce personal taxes, it focuses on corporate tax increases to produce the necessary revenues. A number of your clients and those of your firm believe that they should be exempted from any tax increase either as a class of business or individually. There is no bill yet, but you have the above information from good legislative sources. One thing that is certain is that if there is a bill, you and your firm's clients will be competing against each other for exemptions, if there are any. Do the D.C. Rules require any action at this point in the legislative process? Should they?

4. *A legislative hearing.* As session days pass, a bill is noticed for hearing before the House Ways and Means Committee. It would raise the taxes on several of your clients but exempt entirely one category of your clients. In the exempted class are start-up research and development companies. Both your covered and exempted clients want you to testify on the bill. Both want you to oppose the legislation, but, of course, if a statute is forthcoming, your exempt clients want you to support their exemption. What, if any, is your obligation under the Rules at this point? Would it make a difference if your clients, whose taxes were to be increased, instructed you, as an alternative to opposing the bill, to oppose the exemption in order to reduce the rate of tax increase? Assume you only represented the firm clients who were exempted from the increase, and other members of your firm represented the non-exempted clients. How would the Rules apply?

5. *A meeting with the Chair.* The Chair of the Ways and Means Committee has given you an opportunity to meet with him to discuss the tax bill. You have been scheduled for a 15-minute meeting. No one else in your firm is to have such a meeting. Should you attend the meeting? If so, what position should you take on the bill?

Public Service and the Lawyer-Lobbyist

Judge Mikva has written that, while the Washington lawyer is a skillful representative of his client's interests, the lawyer-lobbyist's services are not equally available to individuals and groups who might need them. Their services are primarily available to those who can pay for them. Thus, "only the groups or interests who already possess the resources for effective representation can afford the services of Washington lawyers." Abner J. Mikva, Interest Representation in Congress: The Social Responsibilities of the Washington Lawyer, 38 Geo. Wash. L. Rev. 651, 667 (1970). It is the social responsibility of the Washington lawyer to see that "minority and diffused majority interests" are represented in lobbying Congress and administrative agencies so that their policy preferences are not completely ignored. Id. at 669-70.

The D.C. Rules contain the following provision:

RULE 6.1. PRO BONO PUBLICO SERVICE

A lawyer should participate in serving those persons, or groups of persons, who are unable to pay all or a portion of reasonable attorneys' fees or who are otherwise unable to obtain counsel. A lawyer may discharge this responsibility by providing professional services at no fee, or at a substantially reduced fee, to persons and groups who are unable to afford or obtain counsel, or by active participation in the work of organizations that provide legal services to them. When personal representation is not feasible, a lawyer may discharge this responsibility by providing financial support for organizations that provide legal representation to those unable to obtain counsel.

Do you think that it would be appropriate fulfillment of this responsibility for lawyer-lobbyists to lobby for groups that have legislative needs but cannot afford the fees of lobbyists?

B. NOTICE OF LEGISLATIVE ACTIVITY

Meaningful participation in the legislative process requires information about its activities. Such notice includes information about the timing of various legislative meetings; matters to be considered at such meetings; the outcome of such consideration; and the votes of individual members.

The most important vehicle for noticing legislative activity is the committee and floor calendar, on which is set forth, usually by bill title, the matters to be considered on the stated date. The use of bill titles as notice of the substance of legislation is discussed in Chapter 2.

Journals

The federal Constitution and state constitutions require Congress and state legislatures to keep journals of their proceedings. Journals are intended to provide public notice of the official activities of legislative bodies and their votes. Justice Story makes this point in writing about the federal provision:

[T]he object of the whole clause is to insure publicity to the proceedings of the legislature, and a correspondent responsibility of the members to their respective constituents. And it is founded in sound policy and deep political foresight. Intrigue and cabal are thus deprived of some of their main resources, by plotting and devising measures in secrecy. The public mind is enlightened by an attentive examination of the public measures; patriotism, and integrity, and wisdom obtain their due reward; and votes are ascertained, not by vague conjecture, but by positive facts. . . . So long as known and open responsibility is valuable as a check or an incentive among the representatives of a free people, so long a journal of their proceedings and their votes, published in the face of the world, will continue to enjoy public favor and be demanded by public opinion.

Joseph Story, Constitution §§840, 841.

Article 1, §5 of the Constitution requires that "[e]ach house shall keep a journal of its proceedings, and from time to time publish the same, excepting such parts as may, in their judgment, require secrecy; and the yeas and nays of the members of either house on any question, shall at the desire of one-fifth of those present, be entered on the journal." The term "proceedings" refers to the business before the houses — for example, consideration of motions, resolutions, or bills — but does not include the debate or comments on such business. Debate and comments of members of Congress are part of the Congressional Record, which is discussed in Chapter 5. The proceedings include votes on a particular piece of business. Because, in most instances, individual votes of legislators are not recorded, the journal will only indicate whether the particular piece of legislative business has been adopted or rejected. When a roll call vote is required (yeas and nays), then individual votes will be recorded. The various methods of voting in Congress are discussed in Chapter 5. Votes to reconsider legislation vetoed by the President are always roll call votes, and individual votes are recorded in the journal. U.S. Const. Art. I, §7.

State constitutional provisions contain similar requirements, although differing sometimes on the issues of publication (e.g., Alabama requires its journal to be published immediately after the adjournment of each legislative session (Ala. Const, art. IV, §55)) and on the number of members necessary to have individual votes recorded (e.g., Pennsylvania requires a roll call vote if two members of any house call for it (Pa. Const, art. 2, §12)). Also, some states permit comments in their journals in the form of dissents or protests against specific acts or resolutions to be recorded (e.g., Ala. Const, art. IV, §55; Kan. Const, art. 2, §10).

The everyday use of journals is far more limited than that envisioned by Justice Story. Publicity about the adoption of statutes and the votes of legislators is the task of the media and interest groups, which have, as their ongoing purpose, the need to publicly disseminate such information. One reason the continuing use of journals remains significant is demonstrated in the following excerpts from a 1983 decision of the Illinois Supreme Court. Citations have been omitted except where particularly relevant.

Yarger v. The Board of Regents
456 N.E.2d 39 (Ill. 1983)

WARD, JUDGE.

On April 7, 1982, the plaintiffs, William C. and Orval J. Yarger, filed a complaint in the circuit court of Sangamon County. The first count asked that the defendant Board of Regents of Regency Universities (the Board), which operates Illinois State University in Normal, be enjoined from permitting the leasing of space on that campus for use as a bookstore. . . . The plaintiffs are members of a partnership which owns and operates a retail store selling books and school supplies in Normal. . . .

The Board filed a motion to dismiss on October 18, 1982, alleging the unconstitutionality of the legislative procedure under which the statute was enacted. The Board's motion . . . was granted by the trial court. The court determined that the Act, which became effective in 1967, had not been enacted in accordance with section 12 of article IV and section 16 of article V of the Constitution of Illinois of 1870. (Ill. Const. 1870, art. IV, sec. 12; Ill. Const. 1870, art. V, sec. 16.) The former section required, inter alia, that a bill had to be passed by a majority of the members elected to each house before becoming law. The latter section provided for the submission for the Governor's approval of every bill passed by the General Assembly. The court found that "[t]he enrolled bill reflecting the legislation signed by the President of the Senate and the Speaker of the House and approved by the Governor failed to include material and substantive amendments enacted by the General Assembly and in the form submitted to the Governor for signature was not in the form enacted by the General Assembly." . . .

The legislative history of the Act as set out in the House Journal shows the following sequence of events: the bill was taken up, read by title, and ordered printed; the bill was referred to the Committee on Higher Education; when printed, the bill was read a second time with an amendment offered by the Committee on Higher Education. . . . The amendment was adopted; the bill was transcribed and typed with the adopted amendment, read a third time, and passed by a vote of 157 yeas to 5 nays. The 1967 Senate Journal shows that the bill was read at large a first time and referred to the Committee on Assignment of Bills; the bill was assigned to the Committee on Education, which recommended that the bill "do pass"; the bill was read a second time; the bill was read at large a third time and passed by a vote of 47 yeas and no nays. On April 3, 1967, a printed copy of the bill which was in its original form and did not include the amendment was approved by the Governor and signed by the Speaker of the House and the President of the Senate. In our State, courts have allowed resort to the journals of the two branches of the legislature to show compliance or noncompliance with constitutionally mandated procedures for enacting statutes. . . . This is commonly referred to as the "journal entry" rule.

On July 1, 1971, our constitution of 1970 became effective. Section 8 of article IV provides, inter alia, that each bill that passes both houses shall be signed by the Speaker of the House and the President of the Senate "to certify that the procedural requirements for passage have been met." (Ill. Const. 1970, art. IV, sec. 8.) The quoted language, the plaintiffs say, changed

our State from one following the journal-entry rule to a jurisdiction applying the "enrolled bill" rule in cases of challenged statutes. Under one version of the enrolled-bill rule, the plaintiff argues here, the signatures on the
enrolled bill evidence conclusively that the statute's procedural enactment
has been proper. The enactment's propriety may not be attacked by resort
to the journals or any other evidence. 1 Sutherland, Statutory Construction
sec. 15.03, at 410 (4th ed. 1972).

Even if it were to be assumed for sake of the plaintiffs' argument that our
present constitution calls for application of the enrolled-bill rule, the statute
here was considered and purportedly adopted by the General Assembly in
1967. Thus it must be examined under the journal-entry rule, which was
applicable under the Constitution of 1870. . . .

Under the journal-entry rule there is a presumption that a statute signed
by the presiding officers of each branch of the General Assembly and
approved by the Governor was enacted in accordance with constitutional
requirements. . . . This presumption may be overcome by clear and convincing proof that the constitutional procedure was not followed. . . . Too,
the journals may be employed to show noncompliance with constitutionally prescribed procedures. . . . As we noted, the journals do not show compliance with the constitutionally mandated procedure for enactment. To
the contrary, they present clear and convincing evidence that the bill which
passed both houses was not the bill which the Governor approved. The
amendment by the House of Representatives was omitted. The journals do
not affirmatively show that the bill was amended again so it cannot be said
that the original version of the bill may have been restored. . . . It is undeniable that the Act signed by the Governor did not contain the amendatory
language. It cannot be presumed that the Governor would have approved
the Act if the amendment had been included. . . . Further, the House of
Representatives' amendment of the original bill demonstrates that the
bill was unacceptable to it as originally proposed. . . .

For the reasons given, the judgment of the circuit court of Sangamon
County is affirmed.

NOTES AND QUESTIONS

1. *Journal entry and enrolled bill rule.* This case not only demonstrates the
use of a journal but discusses the difference between a journal entry
rule and enrolled bill rule. In both cases, the issue is whether a particular
piece of legislation has been adopted in accordance with appropriate
legislative procedure. The enrolled bill rule creates less opportunity for
judicial review of legislative proceedings.

2. *The federal rule.* In Field v. Clark, 143 U.S. 649 (1891), the Court applied
the enrolled bill rule to Congress. Importers of various cloth materials pro-
tested assessments under a tariff act. They claimed that the statute was a

nullity because, per the journal and other evidence, "a section of the bill, as it finally passed, was not in the bill authenticated by the signatures of the presiding officers of the respective houses of Congress, and approved by the President." Id. at 669. In rendering its decision, the Court wrote:

In regard to certain matters, the Constitution expressly requires that they shall be entered on the journal. To what extent the validity of legislative action may be affected by the failure to have those matters entered on the journal, we need not inquire. No such question is presented for determination. But it is clear that, in respect to the particular mode in which, or with what fullness, shall be kept the proceedings of either house relating to matters not expressly required to be entered on the journals; whether bills, orders, resolutions, reports and amendments shall be entered at large on the journal, or only referred to and designated by their titles or by numbers; these and like matters were left to the discretion of the respective houses of Congress. Nor does any clause of that instrument, either expressly or by necessary implication, prescribe the mode in which the fact of the original passage of a bill by the House of Representatives and the Senate shall be authenticated, or preclude Congress from adopting any mode to that end which its wisdom suggests. . . .

The signing by the Speaker of the House of Representatives, and by the President of the Senate, in open session, of an enrolled bill, is an official attestation by the two houses of such bill as one that has passed Congress. It is a declaration by the two houses, through their presiding officers, to the President, that a bill, thus attested, has received, in due form, the sanction of the legislative branch of the government, and that it is delivered to him in obedience to the constitutional requirement that all bills which pass Congress shall be presented to him. And when a bill, thus attested, receives his approval, and is deposited in the public archives, its authentication as a bill that has passed Congress should be deemed complete and unimpeachable. . . .

It is admitted that an enrolled act; thus authenticated, is sufficient evidence of itself—nothing to the contrary appearing upon its face—that it passed Congress. But the contention is, that it cannot be regarded as a law of the United States if the journal of either house fails to show that it passed in the precise form in which it was signed by the presiding officers of the two houses, and approved by the President. It is said that, under any other view, it becomes possible for the Speaker of the House of Representatives and the President of the Senate to impose upon the people as a law a bill that was never passed by Congress. But this possibility is too remote to be seriously considered in the present inquiry. It suggests a deliberate conspiracy. . . . Judicial action based upon such a suggestion is forbidden by the respect due to a coordinate branch of the government. The evils that may result from the recognition of the principle that an enrolled act, in the custody of the Secretary of State, attested by the signatures of the presiding officers of the two houses of Congress, and the approval of the President, is conclusive evidence that it was passed by Congress, according to the forms of the Constitution, would be far less than those that would certainly result from a rule making the validity of Congressional enactments depend upon the manner in which the journals of the respective houses are kept by the subordinate officers charged with the duty of keeping them.

Id. at 671-73. What does it mean to enroll a bill?

3. *The accuracy of journals.* The use of journals to test conformity with legislative procedures assumes their accuracy. Some state constitutions expressly require that "[t]he journal shall accurately reflect the proceedings." La. Const, art. 3, §10; cf. Ohrenstein v. Thompson, 444 N.Y.S.2d 196 (App. Div. 1981) (the accuracy of the journal is nonjusticiable).

C.   THE OPENNESS OF THE LAWMAKING PROCESS

We noted earlier that accessibility not only includes the right to petition the legislature, but also the opportunity to observe its processes and know how legislators vote. Such opportunity is fundamental to the legitimacy of elected, representative government. Observation provides a check against legislative temptation to stray from the mores of representativeness and provides knowledge that electors can use to evaluate the performance of their representatives. "The people must be able to remain informed if they are to retain control over those who are their public servants. It is the only climate under which the commonweal will prosper and enable the governmental process to operate for the benefit of those who created it." N.Y. Pub. Off. Law §100 (McKinney 1988).

Open Meetings

Formal legislative action occurs in legislative sessions and at committee meetings. All of the nation's legislative bodies afford the public the opportunity to observe legislative sessions, either by custom (as in the case of Congress) or by constitutional instruction, statute, or legislative rule. While provision is generally made for secret sessions (see, e.g., Rule XXI of the Rules of the United States Senate (Session with Closed Doors); Rule XXVII of the Rules of the House of Representatives (Secret Sessions); N.Y. Const., art. III, §10 ("[t]he door of each house shall be kept open, except when the public welfare shall require secrecy")), such secrecy is rarely invoked. What subject matter would justify the closing of legislative sessions?

The bulk of lawmaking work is performed by legislative committees. See Chapter 5. Committee meetings have, historically, been closed to public view. Concern over this veil was minimal when legislative debate and decisionmaking occurred in the legislative session. The importance of the legislative committee to modern lawmaking makes the openness of committee meetings as significant as the openness of legislative sessions.

This reasoning resulted in Congress amending its rules in 1975 to require open meetings.

Rule XXVI, §5, Rules of the United States Senate

(b) Each meeting of a committee, or any subcommittee thereof, including meetings to conduct hearings, shall be open to the public, except that a meeting or series of meetings by a committee or a subcommittee thereof on the same subject for a period of no more than fourteen calendar days may be closed to the public on a motion made and seconded to go into closed session to discuss only whether the matters enumerated in clauses (1) through (6) would require the meeting to be closed, followed immediately by a record vote in open session by a majority of the members of the committee or subcommittee when it is determined that the matters to be discussed or the testimony to be taken at such meeting or meetings —

(1) will disclose matters necessary to be kept secret in the interests of national defense or the confidential conduct of the foreign relations of the United States;

(2) will relate solely to matters of committee staff personnel or internal staff management or procedure;

(3) will tend to charge an individual with crime or misconduct, to disgrace or injure the professional standing of an individual, or otherwise to expose an individual to public contempt or obloquy, or will represent a clearly unwarranted invasion of the privacy of an individual;

(4) will disclose the identity of any informer or law enforcement agent or will disclose any information relating to the investigation or prosecution of a criminal offense that is required to be kept secret in the interests of effective law enforcement;

(5) will disclose information relating to the trade secrets of financial or commercial information pertaining specifically to a given person if —

(A) an Act of Congress requires the information to be kept confidential by Government officers and employees; or

(B) the information has been obtained by the Government on a confidential basis, other than through an application by such person for a specific Government financial or other benefit, and is required to be kept secret in order to prevent undue injury to the competitive position of such person; or

(6) may divulge matters required to be kept confidential under other provisions of law or Government regulations.

(c) Whenever any hearing conducted by any such committee or subcommittee is open to the public, that hearing may be broadcast by radio or television, or both under such rules as the committee or subcommittee may adopt.

Rule XI, Rules of the United States House of Representatives

Open Meetings and Hearings

(g) (1) Each meeting for the transaction of business, including the markup of legislation, by a standing committee or subcommittee thereof (other than the Committee on Standards of Official Conduct or its subcommittees) shall be open to the public, including to radio, television, and still photography coverage, except when the committee or subcommittee, in open session and with a majority present, determines by record vote that all or part of the remainder of the meeting on that day shall be in executive session because disclosure of matters to be considered would endanger national security, would compromise sensitive law enforcement information, would tend to defame, degrade, or incriminate any person, or otherwise would violate a law or rule of the House. Persons, other than members of the committee and such noncommittee Members, Delegates, Resident Commissioner, congressional staff, or departmental representatives as the committee may authorize, may not be present at a business or markup session that is held in executive session. This subparagraph does not apply to open committee hearings, which are governed by clause 4(a)(1) of rule X or by subparagraph (2).

(2) (A) Each hearing conducted by a committee or subcommittee (other than the Committee on Standards of Official Conduct or its subcommittees) shall be open to the public, including to radio, television, and still photography coverage, except when the committee or subcommittee, in open session and with a majority present, determines by record vote that all or part of the remainder of that hearing on that day shall be closed to the public because disclosure of testimony, evidence, or other matters to be considered would endanger national security, would compromise sensitive law enforcement information, or would violate a law or rule of the House.

(B) Notwithstanding the requirements of subdivision (A), in the presence of the number of members required under the rules of the committee for the purpose of taking testimony, a majority of those present may—

(i) agree to close the hearing for the sole purpose of discussing whether testimony or evidence to be received would endanger national security, would compromise sensitive law enforcement information, or would violate clause 2(k)(5); or

(ii) agree to close the hearing as provided in clause 2(k)(5).

(C) A Member, Delegate, or Resident Commissioner may not be excluded from non-participatory attendance at a hearing of a committee or subcommittee (other than the Committee on Standards of Official Conduct or its subcommittees) unless the House by majority vote authorizes a particular committee or subcommittee, for purposes of a particular series of hearings on a particular article of legislation or on a particular subject of investigation, to close its hearings to Members, Delegates, and the Resident Commissioner by the same procedures specified in this subparagraph for closing hearings to the public.

(D) The committee or subcommittee may vote by the same procedure described in this subparagraph to close one subsequent day of hearing, except that the Committee on Appropriations, the Committee on Armed Services, and the Permanent Select Committee on Intelligence and the subcommittees therein may, by the same procedure, vote to close up to five additional consecutive days of hearings.

NOTES AND QUESTIONS

1. *House versus Senate.* Consider the differences between the Senate and House rules. While both houses establish a presumption in favor of openness, both permit closed meetings and hearings. Which set of rules requires more openness? Consider the reasons set forth in the Senate Rules for closing committee meetings. Do you think they justify public preclusion? State legislatures have also been slow to open their committee doors for public observation, but by statute and rule have generally followed the congressional model.

2. *Openness versus efficiency.* The opening of the committee meeting has raised a concern about the efficiency of the legislative process in promoting representativeness and forging compromise. One close observer of the legislative process has written:

> With the movement in the 1970's to open to the public more committee meetings, most markups today are conducted in open session. However, important measures (tax, defense, and appropriations, for example) are still, marked up in private without much protest from the press, media, or others. Even proponents of openness admit that members can reach compromises and make tough decisions more easily when they are away from the glare of lobbyists sitting in the audience.

Walter J. Oleszek, Congressional Procedures and the Policy Process 102 (1989). What do you think about this rationale for closing committee meetings?

3. *Harriss revisited.* Consider again the Lobbying Registration Act and United States v. Harriss, both found in Section A.4. Assume that the compromises that permitted the act's passage had occurred at an open committee meeting or conference. Would a record of such compromises have made a difference in the Court's approach to the case?

The Political Caucus Exception to
the Open Meetings Law

Notwithstanding the open meeting requirements adopted by legislatures, legislators continue to look for ways to meet outside of public view. In New York, as in most states, a forum frequently used for this purpose is the legislative caucus or conference. See Chapter 3 for a discussion of these caucuses. In New York, "majority building generally occurs in private non-recorded conferences, where legislative leaders express their view on bills, staff are given an opportunity to fully brief the legislators on the provisions of each controversial bill, members most openly discuss the policies and politics of each bill, and conference negotiators are given their instructions." Lane, Legislative Process and Its Judicial Renderings: A Study in Contrast, 48 U. Pitt. L. Rev. 639, 648-49 (1987). Party conferences in New York were considered protected from the state's open meeting law by §108 of the Public Officers Law, which exempted from coverage "deliberations of political committees, conferences and caucuses." In 1981 the privacy of these conferences was challenged by an appellate court decision. Citations have been omitted except where particularly relevant.

Sciolino v. Ryan
440 N.Y.S.2d 795 (1981)

MOULE, JUDGE.

The question presented on this appeal is whether certain gatherings of members of the Rochester City Council, and other public officers, are required to be open to the public under the Open Meetings Law. . . .

The Rochester City Council (Council), the legislative governing body of the City of Rochester, holds regular public meetings twice a month on Tuesdays. On most Thursday afternoons respondents, the eight Democratic members of the nine member Council, meet in the office of the Mayor of Rochester at his invitation. Members of the city's administrative staff, including the City Manager and City Clerk, are frequently invited and attend these sessions, with occasional invitations extended to members of advisory boards and commissions, and consultants under contract with the City of Rochester. The sole Republican member of the Council, representatives of the news media and the general public are excluded from these meetings. These closed sessions held prior to the public meeting are apparently a custom, having also been conducted by the Republican members of the Council when they were in the majority.

At these sessions the majority receives information relating to city government matters likely to come before the entire Council, and discusses such matters. The frequent result of these discussions is decisions to include or not to include an item on the agenda of the regular public

Council meeting, to communicate with the leader of another legislative body or to support a bill in the State Legislature.

On May 8, 1980 petitioner in the first proceeding, Anthony J. Sciolino, the Republican member of the Council, attempted to attend one of these closed sessions but was denied admission. On May 22, 1980 and June 5, 1980 newspaper reporters for petitioner in the second proceeding, Gannett Co., Inc., also requested admission to these sessions but were denied. On these three occasions, petitioners observed at least six members of the Council's Democratic majority.

On June 4, 1980 petitioner Sciolino commenced a CPLR article 78 proceeding seeking a judgment that the term "meeting" within the meaning of the Open Meetings Law includes a majority gathering of the Council, regardless of political affiliation, where topics of discussion and decision are such as would arise at a regular meeting; that the closed sessions held by the Democratic majority are public meetings within the Open Meetings Law, and not a "political caucus"; and that further closed sessions be prohibited unless petitioner and the public are notified and allowed to attend. Petitioner Gannett Co., Inc., commenced a . . . proceeding on July 17, 1980 seeking a judgment that respondents closed sessions were public meetings and an order that respondents admit petitioner to the sessions. . . .

The intent behind the enactment of the Open Meetings Law was the performance of public business in an open and public manner, with the public able to attend and listen to the deliberations and decisions that go into the making of public policy (Public Officers Law, §95). Every meeting of a public body is required to be open to the general public (Public Officers Law, §98). A "meeting" is the official convening of a public body to conduct public business; a "public body" is any entity for which a quorum consisting of two or more members is required to conduct public business (Public Officers Law, §97, subds. 1, 2).

By enactment of the Open Meetings Law, the Legislature intended to affect the entire decision-making process, not just the formal act of voting or the formal execution of an official document. The statute encompasses private meetings, attended by only a quorum of the members of a public entity, at which the matters for discussion and eventual decision are such as would otherwise arise at a public meeting. It is not necessary that an entity have binding authority for it to be considered a public body; it is within the meaning of the Open Meetings Law if its determinations affect the public and eventually obtain substance in official form.

The closed sessions of the Council's Democratic majority constitute meetings within the scope of the Open Meetings Law. A majority of the nine member Council constitutes a quorum (Rochester City Charter, §5-7), and it is undisputed that a quorum was present at the three closed sessions to which petitioners sought admission. The decisions of these sessions, the legislative future of items before the Council, although not binding, affect, the public and directly relate to the possibility of a municipal matter becoming an official enactment. To keep the decision-making process of all but one of the members of the Council secret, simply because they term themselves a "majority" instead of a "quorum," allows the public to be aware of only legislative results, not deliberations, violating the spirit of the Open Meetings Law and exalting form over substance.

Respondents' second contention on appeal is that the closed sessions are within the exemption from the Open Meetings Law extended to the "deliberations of political . . . caucuses" (Public Officers Law, §103, subd. 2). The term "political caucuses" is not defined by the statute.

Respondents contend that the phrase "political caucus" should be interpreted to apply to a political majority of a legislative body regardless of what it discusses.

An expansive definition of a political caucus, as urged by respondents, would defeat the purpose of the Open Meetings Law that public business be performed in an open and public manner (Public Officers Law, §95), for such a definition could apply to exempt regular meetings of the Council from the statute. To assure that the purpose of the statute is realized, the exemption for political caucuses should be narrowly, not expansively, construed. The entire exemption is for the "deliberations of political committees, conferences and caucuses" (Public Officers Law, §103, subd. 2), indicating that it was meant to prevent the statute from extending to the private matters of a political party, as opposed to matters which are public business yet discussed by political party members. To allow the majority party members of a public body to exclude minority members, and thereafter conduct public business in closed sessions under the guise of a political caucus, would be violative of the statute.

Accordingly, the judgments appealed from should be affirmed.

Legislative Response to the *Ryan* Decision

In response to this decision, the New York State legislature, in 1985, amended §108 of the Public Officers Law by adding the following provision:

> 2. b. For purposes of this section, the deliberations of political committees, conferences and caucuses means a private meeting of members of the senate or assembly of the state of New York, or of the legislative body of a county, city, town or village, who are members or adherents of the same political party, without regard to (i) the subject matter under discussion, including discussion of public business, (ii) the majority or minority status of such political committees, conferences and caucuses or (iii) whether such political committees, conferences and caucuses invite staff or guests to participate in their deliberations. . . .

In support of this amendment the legislature made the following declaration:

The legislature hereby reaffirms that the public business of public bodies of the state of New York should generally be conducted at open and public meetings. Nonetheless, as recognized by the court of appeals of the state of New York in Matter of Orange County Publications v. Council of the City of Newburgh, 45 N.Y.2d 947, 949, "neither public nor private meetings of governmental bodies are inherently desirable or undesirable. Whichever kind of meeting is permitted or required there are . . . offsetting losses or gains." When enacting the open meetings law, the legislature intended and provided that the "deliberations of political committees, conferences and caucuses" should be exempt from the coverage of such law. Such exemption was enacted in furtherance of the legislature's recognition that the public interest is well served by the political party system in legislative bodies because such parties serve as mediating institutions between disparate interest groups and government and promote continuity, stability and orderliness in government. The performance of this function requires the private, candid exchange of ideas and points of view among members of each political party concerning the public business to come before legislative bodies. Recent judicial decisions have, however, eroded this exemption by holding that it applied only to discussions of political business. Accordingly, the legislature hereby declares its adherence to the original intent of the legislature, that the provisions of the open meetings law are not applicable to the deliberations of political committees, conferences and caucuses of legislative bodies regardless of (i) the subject matter under discussion, including discussions of public business, (ii) the majority or minority status of such political committees, conferences and caucuses or (iii) whether such political committees, conferences and caucuses invite staff or guests to participate in their deliberations.

What do you think of this reasoning? It was challenged by the New York Commission on Government Integrity, a temporary state commission established to review a number of governmental practices throughout the state. In the excerpts from its report that follow, the Commission is directly addressing the legislative decision to overrule *Sciolino*.

Government Ethics Reform for the 1990s
328-32 (Bruce A. Green ed., 1991)

a. Impact on Deliberations.   The primary justification advanced for closed caucuses is that members of public bodies need to discuss in private their views on public issues in order to reach a consensus. As one political scientist and local legislator has written, "a degree of confidentiality is needed to facilitate a free exchange of ideas *before* a decision is reached." . . .

In our judgment, the public is entitled to make an informed decision about the quality of its representatives, and cannot do so if the significant deliberations of those representatives are held behind closed doors. In Anthony Sciolino's words, "The public has a right to know who's contributing, who's not; who's being petty, who's being statesmanlike. Unfortunately, when the door is closed nobody knows who is doing the job." In fact, discussions of the most difficult and controversial issues are precisely those that legislators might most want to hold in private—such as the location of low-income housing or a major waterfront development, removal of asbestos from schools, solid waste disposal, or increases in their salaries. These are discussions in which the public has great interest and which should clearly be held in public. These are issues which have, on occasion, been discussed behind closed doors. Yet, because the provisions exempting caucuses do not contain any requirements for giving notice or taking minutes, it is difficult if not impossible to know for sure when such caucuses have occurred.

The deliberations of public officials also show why, not merely how, a particular legislator voted on a particular issue. Closed caucuses prevent the public from knowing what considerations led to the decisions of the majority of a legislative body, what alternatives the members of that body examined, and what consequences they weighed.[1]

b. *Effect on the Two-Party System.*   Secondly, proponents in favor of the political caucus exemption have argued that open caucuses weaken parties and thereby the two-party system. One commentator has explained that the majority political party in a legislative body "needs a confidential forum in which its members can frankly discuss alternatives and hammer out compromises. Applying the open meeting law to political caucuses inhibits intraparty compromise" on issues and thereby inhibits the ability of the majority to forge a policy position for which the majority, as majority, is responsible.

This argument, in our view, does not withstand close scrutiny. First, no one who made this claim could provide the Commission with a concrete example of party structures having suffered these adverse consequences as a result of open caucuses.

Furthermore, any arguably positive effects that closed caucuses might have upon intraparty strength are outweighed by their palpable negative effects upon intraparty vitality, at least in those numerous localities in New York where the minority party is vastly outnumbered by the majority. In those communities, to the extent that information relevant to the public's

---

1. Proponents of closed caucuses respond that a legislator will normally consider it necessary to explain and justify a vote on a crucial issue, typically in open debate at the meeting of the full body or in statements to the media before or after the vote, and that, if legislators do not adequately account for their performance, then their constituents, who have the greatest stake in the matter, can vote them out of office. In the Commission's view, such after-the-fact statements may not reflect the true motives of the legislator as fully as does the actual deliberative discussion.

business is conveyed in private meetings of the majority, excluded minority members are deprived of information vital to their informed participation in the public debate which is essential to the proper functioning of the two-party system. In these circumstances, closed caucuses may in fact weaken the system. . . .

The proponents of closed caucuses respond that this handicap might actually increase if the 1985 amendment were repealed. Discussions would lawfully take place in smaller groups, in telephone conversations, and in informal communications among key leaders. To the extent that discussions of public issues were displaced from the caucus to other channels of communication, some legislators would receive less information and would have less opportunity to participate in crucial decisions, and collective party responsibility would be blurred.

We do not agree. In our view, a series of private discussions of even critical issues of substance is qualitatively different than a single gathering of a majority of a public body, where the majority discusses and even decides the public business. The majority can make decisions; smaller groups of lawmakers cannot.

Some witnesses testifying before the Commission also suggested that the pre-1985 Open Meetings Law unfairly discriminated against the majority party, since only the majority was prohibited from discussing public business in closed session. One Rochester City Council member is quoted as having said: "It's like telling the winning team at half time that it can't go into the locker room to discuss strategy for the second half while the losing team can."

The differing impact open caucus requirements may have on the majority than on the minority party is, in the Commission's view, justifiable. As the Democratic minority leader of the Monroe County Legislature pointed out, the majority party has an obligation different from that of the minority. What the majority decides in caucus is, effectively, the decision of the legislative body itself. Particularly in politically lopsided bodies, closed caucuses effectively preclude any meaningful debate between opposing parties; the real business may be conducted behind closed doors, and the public meeting may become a pro-forma exercise.

c. Impact on Integrity in Government.   Some perceive the need for private conferences among lawmakers and elected officials to be so great that secret meetings will be held no matter what the law provides. In this vein, it has been argued that prohibiting closed caucuses which discuss public business would encourage disrespect for the law, since the majority party would seek a way to disobey or evade it. A former Rochester City Council member testified, "[A]bolition of closed caucuses is sheer hypocrisy. You'll never abolish them. . . . [I]f abolished in one form, [they] would only be held in another, even if at midnight in my basement behind the furnace."

Again, the Commission does not agree. Perhaps the most compelling reason for abandoning the political caucus exemption lies precisely in its impact upon the appearance of integrity in government. The public almost invariably perceives closed door meetings of public bodies as evidence that the members of that body have something to hide. That perception alone lends an appearance of impropriety to such a meeting and detracts from public confidence in the integrity of public officials. When such closed door meetings involve a number of lawmakers sufficient to decide a public issue, and take place without notice, minutes, or a clear delineation of the issues considered, that appearance of impropriety is heightened. Until 1985, the circumstances in which closed meetings of legislative bodies could be held were circumscribed by law to reflect fairly narrow areas, with clear procedural safeguards. Since the 1985 amendment, the boundaries are far less clear, and the public's confidence in its lawmakers suffers.

The remedy to the temptation to try to meet behind closed doors to debate and decide public issues, the Commission believes, is a clearer statement in the law that such attempts are prohibited, together with improved enforcement mechanisms. With those changes, the Commission is confident that lawmakers will strive to obey, not flout, the law.

NOTES AND QUESTIONS

1. *The concern over compromising.* Can compromise occur as easily in open forums as in forums that are closed? Should compromise be facilitated?

2. *The presence of the opposition.* In our two-party legislative system, it takes considerable debate and compromise to arrive at a party position on most legislation. Can such a position be achieved at a public meeting, a meeting at which members of the opposition party can be in attendance?

3. *The Democratic caucus of the House of Representatives.* In the 1970s, the Democratic caucus (the majority party) of the House of Representatives adopted a rule making their caucus open to the public unless members voted to close it. This decision was the result of the initiative of a number of conservative southern members. These members, who opposed busing and similar remedies to discrimination, had been warned in the caucus that, if they failed to support the party position in favor of such legislation, they would be stripped of committee positions and other party-bestowed status. To counter these efforts, they successfully pushed to open the caucus, in which they were joined by a number of liberal legislators who were concerned about voting against openness in government.

CHAPTER *9*
Deliberativeness

A. INTRODUCTION

In republican government the legislative authority, necessarily, predominates. The remedy for this inconveniency is, to divide the legislature into different branches; and to render them by different modes of election, and different principles of action, as little connected with each other, as the nature of their common functions, and their common dependence on the society, will admit. It may even be necessary to guard against dangerous encroachments by still further precautions. As the weight of the legislative authority requires that it should be thus divided, the weakness of the executive may require, on the other hand, that it should be fortified.

The Federalist No. 51, at 350 (J. Madison) (J. Cooke ed., 1961).

The most distinctive characteristic of American legislatures is their deliberativeness. "Deliberativeness" is not a synonym for "debate," although debate may be one of its elements. Rather, the term defines those steps of the legislative process that slow legislative decisionmaking and distance it from the passions and immediacy of the prevailing desires of individual legislators and of various constituencies. Deliberativeness is intended as an anchor against change, protecting the status quo from precipitous upset. It reflects a skepticism about centralized power and, to a lesser extent today, a natural fear of sacrificing local control to centralized and distant legislatures. Affirmatively, deliberativeness works toward assuring that enacted legislation is based on a public consensus on the need for, as well as the type of, change.

Each phase of the enactment process creates a point at which a bill's progress can be delayed or halted. Advancement requires support from varying numbers or coalitions of colleagues, almost none of whom share each others' exact ideas, concerns, or constituencies. As discussed throughout the book, winning such support can be the product of numerous factors, including persuasive debate, compromises, favors, trades, and political force.

> Political life is not merely the making of arbitrary choices, nor merely the resultant of bargaining between separate, private wants. It is always a combination of bargaining and compromise where there are irresolute and conflicting commitments, and common deliberation about public policy, to which facts and rational arguments are relevant.

Hannah F. Pitkin, The Concept of Representation 212 (1967).

Set forth below is the legislative chronology for the Cable Television Consumer Protection and Competition Act of 1992. Consider this chronology in a political context. Review the number of points in this enactment process at which support is necessary for the advancement of the legislation. Not all legislation is subject to such extensive process. The more complex and the more controversial the proposed legislation, the more extensive the process will be. This legislation was extremely complex and controversial, pitting various high-powered interest groups, both commercial and consumer, against one another.

Legislative Chronology — Cable Television Consumer Protection and Competition Act of 1992

1st Session Activity

01/14/91	137 Cong. Rec. S434	Referred to the Senate Commerce, Science, and Transportation Committee
01/14/91	137 Cong. Rec. S582	Remarks by Sens. Danforth, Gore, Hollings, Lieberman
01/15/91	137 Cong. Rec. S576	Cosponsors added
02/05/91	137 Cong. Rec. S1606	Cosponsors added
03/14/91	137 Cong. Rec. D305	Senate Subcommittee on Communications held hearings
03/14/91	137 Cong. Rec. S3434	Cosponsors added

1st Session Activity

05/14/91	137 Cong. Rec. D580	Senate Commerce, Science, and Transportation Committee ordered favorably reported, with an amendment in the nature of a substitute
06/04/91	137 Cong. Rec. S7047	Gorton Amendment No. 281, submitted and ordered to lie on the table
06/28/91	137 Cong. Rec. S9115	Reported in the Senate (S. Rept. No. 102-92)
08/02/91	137 Cong. Rec. S12313	Cosponsors added

2d Session Activity

01/21/92	138 Cong. Rec. S18	Senate reached a unanimous-consent agreement providing for the consideration of the bill
01/23/92	138 Cong. Rec. S309	Senate reached a unanimous-consent agreement providing for the consideration of the bill, on Monday, January 27
01/27/92	138 Cong. Rec. S400	Senate began consideration of the bill, with a committee amendment in the nature of a substitute
01/28/92	138 Cong. Rec. S542	Senate reached a unanimous-consent agreement providing for further consideration of the bill, with a committee amendment in the nature of a substitute, on Wednesday, January 29
01/29/92	138 Cong. Rec. S561	Senate resumed consideration of the bill, with a committee amendment in the nature of a substitute, taking action on amendments proposed thereto
01/29/92	138 Cong. Rec. S564	Senate adopted Inouye Amendment No. 1498, of a perfecting nature, by voice vote
01/29/92	138 Cong. Rec. S567	Senate adopted Gorton-Metzenbaum Amendment No. 1499, to prohibit cable operators from charging subscribers for services and equipment not affirmatively requested by name, by voice vote
01/29/92	138 Cong. Rec. S568	Senate adopted Gorton Amendment No. 1500, to protect the privacy of cable television subscribers, by voice vote
01/29/92	138 Cong. Rec. S569	Senate adopted Lott Amendment No. 1497, to permit cable operators to itemize on subscribers' bills not only franchise fees, but also other taxes and regulatory costs, by voice vote
01/29/92	138 Cong. Rec. S570	Senate adopted Inouye Amendment No. 1501, to provide for designation of channel capacity for commercial programming from a qualified minority programming source, by voice vote
01/29/92	138 Cong. Rec. S570	Senate adopted Breaux Amendment No. 1502, regarding a programming service that is predominantly utilized for the transmission of sales presentations or program-length commercials, by voice vote
01/29/92	138 Cong. Rec. S580	Senate failed to table Graham Modified Amendment No. 1503 (to Amendment No. 1502), to require an inquiry by the Federal Communications Commission concerning broadcast television stations whose programming consists predominantly of sales presentations, by a recorded vote of 33 yeas and 64 nays with 1 voting present (D 20-35, R 13-29) Vote No. 10

2d Session Activity

01/29/92	138 Cong. Rec. S582	Senate adopted Leahy Amendment No. 1504, to require cable television operators to provide notice and options to consumers regarding the use of converter boxes and remote control devices, and to assure compatibility between cable systems and consumer electronics, by voice vote
01/29/92	138 Cong. Rec. S589	Senate adopted Helms Amendment No. 1505 (to Amendment No. 1502), to provide notice to cable subscribers before they receive unsolicited sexually explicit programs, by voice vote
01/29/92	138 Cong. Rec. S592	Senate adopted Inouye (for Dole) Amendment No. 1506, to provide for carriage of closed caption transmission, by voice vote

01/29/92	138 Cong. Rec. S604	Senate adopted Pressler Amendment No. 1508, to require a report to Congress on direct broadcast satellite services, by voice vote
01/29/92	138 Cong. Rec. S605	Senate adopted Pressler Amendment No. 1509, relating to costs necessary for C-band distribution, by voice vote
01/29/92	138 Cong. Rec. S605	Senate will continue consideration of the bill and amendments to be proposed thereto, on Thursday, January 30
01/29/92	138 Cong. Rec. S608	Lott (and Burns) Amendment No. 1497, submitted and ordered to lie on the table
01/29/92	138 Cong. Rec. S609	Inouye Amendment No. 1498, submitted
01/29/92	138 Cong. Rec. S610	Gorton (and Metzenbaum) Amendment No. 1499, submitted
01/29/92	138 Cong. Rec. S610	Gorton Amendment No. 1500, submitted
01/29/92	138 Cong. Rec. S610	Inouye Amendment No. 1501, submitted
01/29/92	138 Cong. Rec. S610	Breaux Amendment No. 1502, submitted
01/29/92	138 Cong. Rec. S610	Graham (and Bryan) Amendment No. 1503, submitted
01/29/92	138 Cong. Rec. S610	Leahy (and Gore) Amendment No. 1504, submitted
01/29/92	138 Cong. Rec. S611	Helms (and Thurmond) Amendment No. 1505, submitted
01/29/92	138 Cong. Rec. S611	Dole Amendment No. 1506, submitted
01/29/92	138 Cong. Rec. S611	Pressler Amendment No. 1508, submitted
01/29/92	138 Cong. Rec. S611	Pressler (and McCain) Amendment No. 1509, submitted
01/30/92	138 Cong. Rec. S635	Senate resumed consideration of the bill, with a committee amendment in the nature of a substitute, taking action on amendments proposed thereto
01/30/92	138 Cong. Rec. S636	Bingaman Amendment No. 1511, to require cable operators to have at least one channel designated for instructional use, withdrawn in the Senate
01/30/92	138 Cong. Rec. S644	Senate rejected Brown Amendment No. 1512, to modify provisions relating to the requirement to carry local broadcast signals, by voice vote
01/30/92	138 Cong. Rec. S645	Senate adopted Helms Amendment No. 1514, to limit the access of children to indecent programming by a cable operator, by a recorded vote of 95 yeas and 0 nays with 1 voting present (D 54-0, R 41-0) Vote No. 12

2d Session Activity

01/30/92	138 Cong. Rec. S645	Helms Amendment No. 1513, to limit the access of children to indecent programming by a cable operator, withdrawn in the Senate
01/30/92	138 Cong. Rec. S649	Senate adopted Fowler Amendment No. 1515, to empower cable operators to prohibit programming of sexually explicit or unlawful conduct, by voice vote
01/30/92	138 Cong. Rec. S652	Senate adopted Helms Amendment No. 1516, to make cable companies liable for carrying obscene programs on leased access channels, by voice vote
01/30/92	138 Cong. Rec. S652	Senate adopted Thurmond-DeConcini Amendment No. 1517, to express the sense of the Congress that the television networks and producers should increase their activity to monitor and remove offensive sexual material from their television broadcast programming, by voice vote
01/30/92	138 Cong. Rec. S661	Senate adopted Metzenbaum Amendment No. 1518, relating to the applicability of anti-trust laws, by voice vote
01/30/92	138 Cong. Rec. S663	Senate adopted Wallop Amendment No. 1519, to provide for an analysis of the regulations on employment and economic competitiveness, by voice vote

01/30/92	138 Cong. Rec. S666	Senate adopted Gorton Amendment No. 1520, to provide for the expansion of the rural exemption to the cable telephone cross-ownership prohibition, and to clarify franchising authority, by voice vote
01/30/92	138 Cong. Rec. S667	Senate adopted Inouye (for Levin) Amendment No. 1521, to express the sense of the Senate that cable and television network and local television stations should establish and follow voluntary guidelines to keep commercials depicting acts or threats of violence out of family programming hours, by voice vote
01/30/92	138 Cong. Rec. S668	Garn (for Packwood) Amendment No. 1522, in the nature of a substitute, pending in the Senate
01/30/92	138 Cong. Rec. S671	Senate reached a unanimous-consent time-agreement providing for further consideration of the bill and the pending amendment proposed thereto, on Friday, January 31
01/30/92	138 Cong. Rec. S686	Cosponsors added
01/30/92	138 Cong. Rec. S687	Bingaman (and Byrd) Amendment No. 1511, submitted
01/30/92	138 Cong. Rec. S687	Brown Amendment No. 1512, submitted
01/30/92	138 Cong. Rec. S688	Helms Amendment No. 1513, submitted
01/30/92	138 Cong. Rec. S688	Helms (and others) Amendment No. 1514, submitted
01/30/92	138 Cong. Rec. S688	Fowler (and Wirth) Amendment No. 1515, submitted
01/30/92	138 Cong. Rec. S688	Helms Amendment No. 1516, submitted
01/30/92	138 Cong. Rec. S688	Thurmond (and others) Amendment No. 1517, submitted
01/30/92	138 Cong. Rec. S688	Metzenbaum Amendment No. 1518, submitted
01/30/92	138 Cong. Rec. S688	Wallop Amendment No. 1519, submitted
01/30/92	138 Cong. Rec. S689	Gorton Amendment No. 1520, submitted

2d Session Activity

01/30/92	138 Cong. Rec. S689	Levin (and Simon) Amendment No. 1521, submitted
01/30/92	138 Cong. Rec. S689	Packwood (and others) Amendment No. 1522, submitted
01/31/92	138 Cong. Rec. S711	Passed in the Senate, after agreeing to a committee amendment in the nature of a substitute, and taking action on an amendment proposed thereto, by a recorded vote of 73 yeas and 18 nays (D 46-4, R 27-14) Vote No. 14
01/31/92	138 Cong. Rec. S711	Senate rejected Garn (for Packwood) Amendment No. 1522, in the nature of a substitute, by a recorded vote of 35 yeas and 54 nays with 1 voting present (D 7-42, R 28-12) Vote No. 13
02/04/92	138 Cong. Rec. H217	Senate requested the concurrence of the House
07/23/92	138 Cong. Rec. H6571	Passed in the House, after striking all after the enacting clause and inserting in lieu thereof the text of H.R. 4850, as amended, by voice vote
07/23/92	138 Cong. Rec. H6571	House Clerk was authorized to make technical and conforming changes including section numbers, punctuation, spelling, and cross references, and any other necessary technical and conforming changes in the engrossment of the bill
07/31/92	138 Cong. Rec. H7115	The Speaker appointed the following members as conferees in the conference on the disagreeing vote of the two Houses on the House Amendments to the bill: Reps. Dingell, Markey, Tauzin, Eckart, Manton, Hall (TX), Harris, Lent, Rinaldo, Bilirakis, and Fields: Provided, that Mr. Ritter is appointed in place of Mr. Fields for consideration of so much of section 16 of the Senate bill

08/06/92	138 Cong. Rec. D1014	Senate reached a unanimous-consent agreement providing that just prior to the adjournment or recess of the Senate for the August recess, the Majority Leader may make a motion to disagree to the amendments of the House to the bill and that the Senate agree to the request for a conference thereon and the Chair be authorized to appoint conferees
08/12/92	138 Cong. Rec. S12557	Pursuant to the order of Thursday, August 6, 1992, Senate disagreed to the amendments of the House to the bill
08/12/92	138 Cong. Rec. S12557	Senate agreed to the request for a conference thereon, and the Chair appointed the following conferees: Senators Hollings, Inouye, Ford, Danforth, and Packwood
09/09/92	138 Cong. Rec. D1084	Conferees agreed to file a conference report on the differences between the Senate- and House-passed versions of the bill
09/14/92	138 Cong. Rec. H8357	Conference report on S. 12, reported in the House (H. Rept. 102-862)
09/15/92	138 Cong. Rec. D1114	House Rules Committee heard testimony from Chairman Dingell, and Representatives Markey, Brooks, Hughes, Lent, Moorhead, and Oxley, but no action was taken on the conference report to accompany S. 12
09/16/92	138 Cong. Rec. D1123	House Rules Committee granted a rule waiving all points of order against the conference report to accompany the bill, and against its consideration
09/16/92	138 Cong. Rec. H8646	H. Res. 571, the rule waiving all points of order against the conference report on S. 12, reported in the House (H. Rept. 102-869)
09/17/92	138 Cong. Rec. H8649	House agreed to H. Res. 571, the rule waiving all points of order against the conference report, by a recorded vote of 263 yeas and 134 nays (D 230-8; R 33-126) (Roll No. 397)
09/17/92	138 Cong. Rec. H8671	House agreed to the conference report by a recorded vote of 280 yeas and 128 nays and 1 voting present (D 209-38; R 71-90) (Roll No. 398)—clearing the measure for Senate action
09/18/92	138 Cong. Rec. S14027	A motion was entered in the Senate to close further debate on the conference report on S. 12
09/18/92	138 Cong. Rec. S14198	Subsequently, the cloture motion was withdrawn in the Senate, and a unanimous-consent time-agreement was reached providing for consideration of the conference report on Monday, September 21, with a vote to occur on adoption of the conference report at 2:15 P.M., on Tuesday, September 22
09/21/92	138 Cong. Rec. S14222	Senate resumed consideration of the conference report on the bill
09/21/92	138 Cong. Rec. S14222	By prior unanimous-consent agreement, Senate will vote on adoption of the conference report at 2:15 P.M., on Tuesday, September 22
09/22/92	138 Cong. Rec. H8964	Enrolled in the House
09/22/92	138 Cong. Rec. S14600	Senate agreed to the conference report on the bill, by a recorded vote of 74 yeas and 25 nays and 1 voting present (D 50-7; R 24-18) (Vote No. 225)—clearing the measure for the President
10/03/92	138 Cong. Rec. S16460	Senate reached a unanimous-consent time-agreement providing that upon the receipt of the veto message on the bill, the reading be dispensed with, and that the Senate proceed to consideration of the veto message on Monday, October 5, with a vote on reconsideration, the objections of the President notwithstanding, to occur at 6 P.M.

10/05/92	138 Cong. Rec. H11477	House read a message from the President wherein he announces his veto of the bill
10/05/92	138 Cong. Rec. H11477	Subsequently, the House voted to override the President's veto of the bill, by a recorded vote of 308 yeas and 114 nays, with 1 voting "present" (D 231-29; R 77-85) (Roll No. 477) — clearing the measure
10/05/92	138 Cong. Rec. S16652	Senate voted to override the President's veto of the bill by a recorded vote of 74 yeas and 25 nays (D 50-7; R 24-18) (Vote No. 264) — two-thirds of those Senators duly chosen and sworn having voted in the affirmative
10/07/92	138 Cong. Rec. D1316	Signed by the President on October 5, 1992 (P.L. 102-385)

This chapter examines the deliberative characteristic of American legislatures. It focuses first on bicameralism, the most important construct for restraining legislative lawmaking, and then on the veto power, which inserts the executive into the legislative process. Within this latter section, considerable attention is paid to the various forms of item vetoes found in state constitutions, with some discussion added on the various proposals to incorporate item vetoes into the federal process. A third section deals with legislative rules as restraints on precipitous action, with particular reference to certain typical rules found in state constitutions. A study of the speech and debate clauses of American constitutions, which are intended to protect legislators from executive interference, constitutes the chapter's fourth section. Finally, the last section explores the initiative and referendum as a public expression of dissatisfaction with the deliberative characteristic of the legislative process.

Deliberativeness weighs heavily against hasty action. It is intended to do so. In the age of statutes, the delay caused by the deliberative process can be seen as painfully insensitive to the public needs. It was on this string that President Bush played in his unsuccessful 1992 election attempt to blame the Democrat-controlled Congress for failing to solve the economic problems that permeated the last two years of his tenure (this, despite the fact that he had vetoed a number of bills in which Congress had addressed these economic issues). Governmental inaction frequently does not represent a failure to recognize a public problem but a failure to develop a consensus on how to resolve it. The development of such consensus is at the heart of deliberativeness. The political scientist Morris P. Fiorina has written:

> Though The Founding Fathers believed in the necessity of establishing a genuinely national government, they took great pains to design one that could not lightly do things *to* its citizens; what government might do *for* its citizens was to be limited to the functions of what we know now as the "watchman state." Thus the Founders . . . distributed and blended powers

within and across the federal levels, and they encouraged the occupants of the various positions to check and balance each other by structuring incentives so that one officeholder's ambitions would be likely to conflict with others'. The resulting system of institutional arrangements predictably hampers efforts to undertake major initiative and favors maintenance of the status quo.

Given the historical record faced by the Founders, their emphasis on constraining government is understandable. But we face a later historical record, one that shows two hundred years of increasing demands for government to act positively. Moreover, developments unforeseen by the Founders increasingly raise the likelihood that the uncoordinated actions of individuals and groups will inflict serious damage on the nation as a whole. The by-products of the industrial and technological revolutions impose physical risks not only on us, but on future generations as well. . . . None of this is to suggest that we should forget about what government can do *to* us. . . . But the modern age demands as well that we worry about our ability to make government work *for* us.

Morris P. Fiorina, The Decline of Collective Responsibility in American Politics 1, 2 (1980). For Professor Fiorina, the principal problem with the deliberative process is that, in an effort to prevent evil, it prevents good. Such an observation, if accurate, must cause concern. The legitimacy of American government depends on its ability to recognize and respond to serious problems. But, while it may be argued that modern expectations of the role of government and unceasing demands for governmental solutions to problems require more efficient models of government than offered by our present system, it can be similarly argued that, in the face of such expectations and demands, the need for deliberativeness and consensus is all the more acute. These points and possible alternatives should be considered in studying the sections below. By way of example, the following excerpts are from an article written by Lloyd Cutler, who held the position of Counsel to President Carter. (Cutler also served on a temporary basis as Counsel to President Clinton.) They are spurred by his frustration over the inability of the Carter administration to effect its domestic and foreign policy initiatives.

Lloyd N. Cutler, To Form a Government
59 Foreign Aff. 126 (1980)

We are all children of this faith in a rational written arrangement for governing. Our faith should encourage us to consider changes in our Constitution—for which the framers explicitly allowed—that would assist us in adjusting to the changes in the world in which the Constitution must function. Yet we tend to resist suggestions that amendments to our existing constitutional framework are needed to govern our portion of the interdependent world society we have become, and to cope with the resulting problems that all contemporary governments must resolve.

A particular shortcoming in need of a remedy is the structural inability of our government to propose, legislate and administer a balanced program for governing. In parliamentary terms, one might say that under the U.S. Constitution it is not now feasible to "form a Government." The separation of powers between the legislative and executive branches, whatever its merits in 1793, has become a structure that almost guarantees stalemate today. As we wonder why we are having such a difficult time making decisions we all know must be made, and projecting our power and leadership, we should reflect on whether this is one big reason.

We elect one presidential candidate over another on the basis of our judgment of the overall program he presents, his ability to carry it out, and his capacity to adapt his program to new developments as they arise. . . .

But because we do not "form a Government," it has not been possible for [the] President . . . to carry out this major part of his program. . . .

The Constitution does not require or even permit in such a case the holding of a new election, in which those who oppose the President can seek office to carry out their own overall program. Indeed, the opponents of each element of the President's overall program usually have a different makeup from one element to another. They would probably be unable to get together on any overall program of their own, or to obtain the congressional votes to carry it out. As a result the stalemate continues, and because we do not form a Government, we have no overall program at all. We cannot fairly hold the President accountable for the success or failure of his overall program, because he lacks the constitutional power to put that program into effect.

Compare this with the structure of parliamentary governments. A parliamentary government may have no written constitution, as in the United Kingdom. Or it may have a written constitution, as in West Germany, Japan and Ireland, that in other respects — such as an independent judiciary and an entrenched Bill of Rights — closely resembles our own. But while there may be a ceremonial President or, as in Japan, an Emperor, the executive consists of those members of the legislature chosen by the elected legislative majority. The majority elects a Premier or Prime Minister from among its number, and he selects other leading members of the majority as the members of his Cabinet. The majority as a whole is responsible for forming and conducting the "government." If any key part of its overall program is rejected by the legislature, or if a vote of "no confidence" is carried, the "Government" must resign and either a new "Government" must be formed out of the existing legislature or a new legislative election must be held. If the program is legislated, the public can judge the results, and can decide at the next regular election whether to reelect the majority or turn it out. At all times the voting public knows who is in charge, and whom to hold accountable for success or failure. . . .

President Carter's party has a much larger majority percentage in both Houses of Congress than Chancellor Schmidt or Mrs. Thatcher. But this comfortable majority does not even begin to assure that President Carter or any other President can rely on that majority to vote for each element of his program. No member of that majority has the constitutional duty or the practical political need to vote for each element of the President's program. Neither the President nor the leaders of the legislative majority have the means to punish him if he does not. In the famous phrase of Joe Jacobs, the fight manager, "it's every man for theirself."

Let me cite an example. In the British House of Commons, just as in our own House, some of the majority leaders are called the Whips. In the Commons, the Whips do just what their title implies. If the Government cares about the pending vote, they "whip" the fellow members of the majority into compliance, under pain of party discipline if a member disobeys. On the most important votes, the leaders invoke what is called a three-line whip, which must be obeyed on pain of resignation or expulsion from the party.

In our House, the Majority Whip, who happens to be one of our very best Democratic legislators, can himself feel free to leave his Democratic President and the rest of the House Democratic leadership on a crucial vote, if he believes it important to his constituency and his conscience to vote the other way. When he does so, he is not expected or required to resign his leadership post; indeed he is back a few hours later "whipping" his fellow members of the majority to vote with the President and the leadership on some other issue. But all other members are equally free to vote against the President and the leadership when they feel it important to do so. The President and the leaders have a few sticks and carrots they can use to punish or reward, but nothing even approaching the power that Mrs. Thatcher's Government or Chancellor Schmidt's Government can wield against any errant member of the majority. . . .

In the drawing this comparison, I am not blind to the proven weaknesses of parliamentary government, or to the virtues which our forefathers saw in separating the executive from the legislature. In particular, the parliamentary system lacks the ability of a separate and vigilant legislature to investigate and curb the abuse of power by an arbitrary or corrupt executive. Our own recent history has underscored this virtue of separating these two branches.

Moreover, our division of executive from legislative responsibility also means that a great many more voters are represented in positions of power, rather than as mere members of a "loyal opposition." If I am a Democrat in a Republican district, my vote in the presidential election may still give me a proportional impact. And if my party elects a President, I do not feel — as almost half the voters in a parliamentary constituency like Oxford must feel — wholly unrepresented. One result of this division is a sort of a permanent centrism. While this means that no extreme or Thatcher-like program can be legislated, it means also that there are fewer wild swings in statutory policy.

This is also a virtue of the constitutional division of responsibility. It is perhaps what John Adams had in mind when, at the end of his life, he wrote to his old friend and adversary, Thomas Jefferson, that "checks and balances, Jefferson . . . are our only Security, for the progress of Mind, as well as the Security of Body."

But these virtues of separation are not without their costs. I believe these costs have been mounting in the last half-century, and that it is time to examine whether we can reduce the costs of separation without losing its virtues. . . .

We are not about to revise our own Constitution so as to incorporate a true parliamentary system. But we do need to find a way of coming closer to the parliamentary concept of "forming a Government," under which the elected majority is able to carry out an overall program, and is held accountable for its success or failure.

There are several reasons why it is far more important in 1980 than it was in 1940, 1900 or 1800 for our government to have the capability to formulate and carry out an overall program.

1) The first reason is that government is now constantly required to make a different kind of choice than usually in the past, a kind for which it is difficult to obtain a broad consensus. That kind of choice, which one may call "allocative," has become the fundamental challenge to government today. . . .

During the second half of this century, our government has adopted a wide variety of national goals. Many of these goals — checking inflation, spurring economic growth, reducing unemployment, protecting our national security, assuring equal opportunity, increasing social security, cleaning up the environment, improving energy efficiency — conflict with one another, and all of them compete for the same resources. There may have been a time when we could simultaneously pursue all of these goals to the utmost. But even in a country as rich as this one, that time is now past. One of the central tasks of modern government is to make wise balancing choices among courses of action that pursue one or more of our many conflicting and competing objectives. . . .

If we decide we want the capability of forming a Government, the only way to do so is to amend the Constitution. . . .

The most one can hope for is a set of modest changes that would make our structure work somewhat more in the manner of a parliamentary system, with somewhat less separation between the executive and the legislature than now exists.

There are several candidate proposals. Here are some of the more interesting ideas:

1) We now vote for a presidential candidate and a vice-presidential candidate as an inseparable team. We could provide that in presidential election years, voters in each congressional district would be required to vote for a trio of candidates, as a team, for President, Vice President and the House of Representatives. This would tie the political fortunes of the party's presidential and congressional candidates to one another, and provide some incentive for sticking together after they are elected. Such a proposal could be combined with a four-year term for members of the House of Representatives. This would tie the presidential and congressional candidates even more closely, and has the added virtue of providing members with greater protection against the pressures of single-issue political groups. . . .

2) Another idea is to permit or require the President to select 50 percent of his Cabinet from among the members of his party in the Senate and House, who would retain their seats while serving in the Cabinet. . . .

3) A third intriguing suggestion is to provide the President with the power, to be exercised not more than once in his term, to dissolve Congress and call for new congressional elections. This is the power now vested in the President under the French Constitution. . . .

4) Another variant on the same idea is that in addition to empowering the President to call for new congressional elections, we might empower a majority or two-thirds of both Houses to call for new presidential elections. . . .

7) One final proposal may be mentioned. It would be possible, through constitutional amendment, to revise the legislative process in the following way. Congress would enact broad mandates first, declaring general policies and directions, leaving the precise allocative choices, within a congressionally approved budget, to the President. All agencies would be responsible to the President. By dividing up tasks among them, and making the difficult choices of fulfilling some congressional directions at the expense of others, the President would fill in the exact choices, the allocative decisions. Then any presidential action would be returned to Congress where it would await a two-house legislative veto. If not so vetoed within a specified period, the action would become law.

If the legislative veto could be overturned by a presidential veto — subject in turn to a two-thirds override — then this proposal would go a long way to enhance the President's ability to "form a Government." In any event, it would enable the elected President to carry out the program he ran on, subject to congressional oversight, and end the stalemate over whether to legislate the President's program in the first instance. It would let Congress and the President each do what they have shown they now do best.

NOTES AND QUESTIONS

1. *The Cutler perspective.* Cutler speaks from an enormous frustration with the failures of the Carter administration to effect many of its policy goals. His argument is that President Carter was elected because of his programmatic goals and his ability to effect them, but that his efforts were thwarted by an unaccommodating governmental structure. What do you think of this argument?

2. *Reforming government.* To effect what he characterizes as a "wide variety of national goals," Cutler argues that we must reduce the costs of deliberativeness by amending our governmental structure-procedure. How would his suggested constitutional amendments serve to accomplish these goals? What costs would they impose on the goals of deliberativeness? How does he address these costs? Consider the following perspective on Cutler's philosophies.

Eric Lane and Michael Oreskes, The Genius of America
186-88 (2007)

The supporters of the initiative movement were so determined to win that they ignored the lessons of half a century earlier. No one could accuse Lloyd Cutler of forgetting American political history. By 1980, he felt the Constitution had outlived its usefulness. Cutler was the consummate Washington insider. "A commanding presence among the capital's power elite for decades and at home in the highest levels of industry, government and politics," wrote one reporter. A graduate of Yale and Yale Law School, Cutler had apprenticed for a major New York law firm, moved to Washington, D.C., served the government in a number of roles, including in army intelligence, and started one of the nation's largest law firms. In 1980, he was just ending his services as counsel to President Jimmy Carter.

The Carter administration had experienced great frustration over the refusal of a Democratic Congress to submit to the president's views on how to resolve the energy crisis and economic stagnation. No matter the efforts he exerted, Carter could not persuade his fellow Democrats of the wisdom of his proposals. In truth he was not a good politician. As he observed, Congress was "twisted and pulled in every direction by hundreds of well-financed and powerful interests." But it was his job to forge a consensus from these competing interests.

Cutler saw Carter's inability to build a consensus for his programs as a failure of the system, not a failure of his president. A president elected by all the people should have the support of Congress, Cutler reasoned. So in 1980 he wrote in the influential magazine *Foreign Affairs*: "The separation of powers between the legislative and executives branches, whatever its merits in 1793, has become a structure that almost guarantees stalemates today. As we wonder why we are having such a difficult time making decisions we all know must be made, and projecting our power and leadership we should reflect on whether this is one big reason."

And for this reason Cutler went on to call for a form of government in which the president would have far more control over Congress.

Lloyd Cutler's profound criticism of the American form of government seems startling at first. If a man so steeped in the American constitutional tradition and so advantaged by it was now so willing to overthrow it, there must have been something truly wrong with the system. But here was a man committed to the vision of his leader and clear in his own mind of that vision's public virtue. Hence its rejection by Congress had to be wrong, the work of "special interests." Just the kind of narrow motivation the framers built the system to guard against.

One analyst of the Reagan era, John Ehrman, identifies Cutler's proposal as an example of a frustration among liberal intellectuals, who for forty years had been at the heart of the American consensus. With the end of that consensus, they felt isolated. So "they began by deciding that America's ruling institutions needed a complete overhaul, one borrowing from foreign models." Cutler proposed an English-style Parliament. Ezra Vogel, a Harvard sociologist, urged the country to adopt a Japanese approach to solving problems "through study and consensus rather than American Style competition."

These proposals ignored the intrinsically homegrown nature of American democracy, as if something else could be grafted on our roots. But there was more: "a desire to avoid politics, either by placing authority in the hands of technocrats or by reducing the power of the president's opponents." This spared liberals "from having to explain how their ideas would work, gain popular support, and be put into action." Ehrman's critique of the liberals is a mirror image of the critique others offered of the conservatives who were pushing the initiative movement at the same time.

Thus on the right, through initiative and referendum, and on the left, through proposals for institutional overhaul, efforts were under way to escape the complicated demands and constraints of the democratic process the framers had developed.

NOTES AND QUESTIONS

1. Professor Lane categorizes Cutler's efforts as an attempt "to escape the complicated demands and constraints of the democratic process the framers had developed." Do you agree with this view of our system of government? Are there ways to escape the constraints built into the system?

2. Have the problems in our system identified by Lloyd Cutler increased or decreased in the years since Cutler's letter to *Foreign Affairs* magazine? For a discussion concerning the growth of presidential powers under George W. Bush, see Eric Lane and Michael Oreskes, The Genius of America (2007); Frederick A. O. Schwarz, Jr. and Aziz Z. Huq, Unchecked and Unbalanced: Presidential Power in a Time of Terror (2007); Thomas E. Mann and Norman J. Ornstein, The Broken Branch: How Congress Is Failing America and How to Get It Back on Track (2006).

B. BICAMERALISM

1. In General

Charles Warren, The Making of the Constitution
158-59 (reprinted 1967)

Thursday, May 31, 1787

In Convention

A Legislature of Two Branches

On this day, the arrival of Major William Pierce and William Houstoun of Georgia gave that State a representation — the eleventh State to Appear.

The Committee took up and agreed to Randolph's second Resolution, without debate (Pennsylvania alone dissenting), viz.: "That the National Legislature ought to consist of two branches." While this provision was in accord with the Constitutions of eleven of the States, nevertheless, a Legislature of only one branch existed in Georgia and Pennsylvania, and in the Congress under the Articles of Confederation. Moreover, the existence of a second branch of the Legislature — the Senate — had been, in Massachusetts, one of the chief grievances of those who sympathized with the movement which took outward shape in the Shays Rebellion, only six months prior; for it was regarded as the representative of property. In many of the other States also, since the property qualification for members of the Senate was greater than for members of the lower House, and the property qualification required of the electors of the Senate was greater than those of the electors of the other branch, the State Senates were regarded as representative of the property interests. Under these conditions, it would not have been unnatural if there should have been considerable discussion over the adoption of a two-branch Legislature. On this date, however, there was no difference of opinion on the subject. Later in the Convention (on

June 16), John Lansing of New York raised the point that the only object of having two branches was that one should serve as a check, but, said he, in a Congress, "the delegations of the different States are checks on each other." To this James Wilson replied that "in a single House, there is no check but the inadequate one of the virtue and good sense of those who compose it." Roger Sherman of Connecticut (on June 20) also stated that he saw no necessity for two branches, and that the complaints of the Congress of the Confederation had not been of the unwisdom of its acts, but the insufficiency of its powers. To these statements, George Mason of Virginia replied with finality, that while "the mind of the people of America . . . was unsettled as to some points . . . in two points he was sure it was settled, in an attachment to republican government — in an attachment to more than one branch in the Legislature." Undoubtedly, also, many of the delegates had been strongly impressed by the forceful argument against a one-house Legislature, which had been made by John Adams in his book, then recently published. When this Resolution adopted by the Committee of the Whole came up for vote in the Convention, on June 21, seven States voted aye (after striking out the word "National"), with New York, New Jersey, and Delaware voting no, and Maryland divided.

Congress and the legislatures of every state, except Nebraska, are divided into two houses. Under this arrangement, each house must pass identical bills to enact law, but neither house must consider bills adopted by the other nor defer to the other house in any way. One exception to this proposition is that revenue bills must be initiated in the House of Representatives in Congress and in the lower houses of legislatures.

The intent and consequence of this division of American legislatures into separate but equal chambers is to make the adoption of legislation very difficult. For the Framers, the wisdom of such arrangement was so indisputable as to be self-evident. Bicameralism "is a precaution founded on such clear principles, and now so well understood in the United States, that it would be more than superfluous to enlarge on it." The Federalist No. 62, 418 (J. Madison) (Jacob E. Cooke ed., 1961). A unicameral legislature would "entail upon our posterity one of the most execrable forms of government that human infatuation ever contrived." The Federalist No. 22, 145 (A. Hamilton) (Jacob E. Cooke ed., 1961).

In contrast, the advantages of bicameralism were seen as multitudinous:

> The Constitution . . . adopts, as a fundamental rule, the exercise of the legislative power by two distinct and independent branches. The advantages of this division are, in the first place, that it interposes a great check upon undue, hasty, and oppressive legislation. In the next place, it interposes a barrier against the strong propensity of all public bodies to accumulate all

power, patronage, and influence in their own hands. In the next place, it operates, indirectly, to retard, if not wholly to prevent, the success of the efforts of a few popular leaders, by their combinations and intrigues in a single body, to carry their own personal, private, or party objects into effect, unconnected with the public good. In the next place, it secures a deliberate review of the same measures, by independent minds, in different branches of government, engaged in the same habits of legislation, but organized upon a different system of elections. And, in the last place, it affords great securities to public liberty, by requiring the cooperation of different bodies, which can scarcely ever, if properly organized, embrace the same sectional or local interests, or influences, in exactly the same proportion, as a single body. The value of such a separate organization will, of course, be greatly enhanced, the more the elements, of which each body is composed, differ from each other, in the mode of choice, in the qualifications, and in the duration of office of the members, provided due intelligence and virtue are secured in each body.

Joseph Story, A Familiar Exposition of the Constitution of the United States 70-71 (1986).

Today the chambers of the nation's legislative bodies are less distinguishable from each other than they were at the time of Judge Story's comments — Senators are now popularly elected (XVII Amendment, 1913) and state legislators are all chosen on the basis of population — but the vitality of bicameralism remains. Over this time, Congress and most of the chambers of state legislative bodies have:

> evolved their own rules, precedents, traditions, and customs. These distinctions are enduring. "Institutional differences between the House and Senate," wrote one scholar, "are real and important in and of themselves, whether or not exacerbated by differences in policy approaches or partisan control."
>
> Over the decades these bicameral devices have spawned rivalry, conflict, and competition between House and Senate.

Lawrence D. Longley and Walter J. Oleszek, Bicameral Politics and the Conference Committees 21-21 (1989). So strong is bicameralism that one of the authors, after retiring from Congress, wrote:

> It is difficult to believe that the country's founders envisioned the full impact of bicameralism. The interplay between the House and the Senate, which are totally separate and, for all practical purposes, equal in power — but are completely dependent on each other to pass any legislation or otherwise perform their functions — defies description by even the most avid Hill-watchers. Jealousy, suspicion, condescension, distrust, petulance, are only some of the angry emotions expressed by the members of one body toward the members of the other, especially when their committees share a legislative jurisdiction, or when they come from the same state. Yet they cannot succeed in any endeavor unless they cooperate.

Perhaps the most astonishing aspect of the two-chamber Congress is the lack of communication between the two bodies; indeed, it is practically a miracle that any legislation passes, given the differences in the perspectives, the constituencies, and the procedures. Previous reference was made to the variety of groups within each chamber that work on various projects and exchange information. However, no such groups operate bicamerally, with the possible exception of the Members of Congress for Peace Through Law, which was most active during the Vietnam War. Although state delegations in each chamber meet occasionally on a bipartisan basis, they seldom meet on a bicameral basis. (The House members never refer to the Senate by name; it is always called "the other body.")

Instead, lobby groups (including the administration) act as lines of communication between the two bodies. Staff find out more from lobbyists about activities on "the other side" than they do from picking up the phone and calling counterparts on the other committee.

Abner J. Mikva and Patti B. Saris, The American Congress 201 (1983).

This has not meant that Congress or bicameral bodies have not been effective. That we live in an age of statutes attests to the energy and activity of the legislative process. But overcoming the centrifugal forces of bicameralism takes considerable focus, energy, and ingenuity. On this point consider the following passage.

Lawrence D. Longley and Walter J. Oleszek,
Bicameral Politics and the Conference Committees
22-24 (1989)

Despite such institutional disagreements and rivalry, cooperation rather than conflict typically characterizes intercameral spirit. Without bicameral compromise, no legislative proposal could be forwarded to the president. There are many ties that bind the two chambers together, partisan, individual, strategic, and structural-procedural, to name a few.

At the partisan level, House and Senate party leaders frequently consult about legislative priorities. This pattern of cooperative relations occurs even when both houses are controlled by different parties. "The inescapable necessity of bicameral cooperation" necessitates such interchamber cooperation: "The President and the public may attempt to set policy directions and goals for the Congress, but the institutional problems of bicameralism remain for the House and Senate themselves to resolve." During the early 1980s, for instance, there was arguably more bipartisanship between Democratic Speaker Thomas P. O'Neill of Massachusetts and Republican Senate Majority Leader Howard H. Baker of Tennessee than between Congress and the White House. "Congress may still save the [budget] process over the President's objections," declared Speaker O'Neill at one point in 1983. "If we do it, it will be because of bipartisan cooperation." When the Democrats took control of both chambers after the 1986 election, new House Speaker Jim Wright (D, Tex.) and Senate Majority Leader Robert C. Byrd (D, W. Va.) worked together to facilitate bicameral cooperation, a task now further made easier by their partisan common bond.

Individually, senators and representatives work together to pass or defeat legislation. During the Ninety-seventh and Ninety-eighth congresses, for instance, Senator Alan Simpson (R, Wy.) and Representative Romano Mazzoli (D, Ky.) sponsored legislation to revise the nation's immigration laws. As chairmen of Judiciary subcommittees with jurisdiction over this issue, Simpson and Mazzoli were well positioned to advance immigration reform legislation. The two members in effect worked as a bipartisan and bicameral team to mobilize support for their measure, which eventually became law during the Ninety-ninth Congress.

Strategically, members of each chamber are mindful that the success or failure of their policy proposals can hinge on how well they involve the other body in their lawmaking plans. Representatives who find their bill stymied in the House may turn to sympathetic senators to promote it in that chamber. Or members of one chamber might maneuver to avoid having their proposal sent to an unfavorable panel in the other body.

On one occasion, Senator Robert C. Byrd (D, W. Va.) persuaded the Senate to support a strip mining measure. When the bill was sent to the House, it was referred to the House Interior Committee; Morris Udall (D, Ariz.), chairman of that panel, opposed Senator Byrd's bill and successfully prevented any action on it. The next year, however, Senator Byrd managed to bypass Udall's House committee. He attached the strip mining proposal in the Senate as an amendment to a noncontroversial House-passed bill initially reported by the House Merchant Marine Committee. When the measure was returned to the House, the Merchant Marine Committee, not the less friendly Interior panel, assumed jurisdiction over the Byrd proposal.

Legislative strategists must, therefore, be mindful of the personalities, structures, and biases of the other body as they bear on a particular bill. Sometimes compromises can be made in one chamber with confidence that the other legislative body will restore the lost provisions. On the other hand, if the other chamber is thought to be hostile to a policy initiative, a broader bill might be pressed to provide a stronger position for subsequent conference negotiations. Sometimes a bill of questionable merit is pushed in anticipation (unrealized at times) that the other chamber will kill it. In sum, the expected stance of the other body is anticipated by members and their actions planned accordingly.

Finally, before any measure can become law, it must pass both chambers in absolutely identical form. "What the Constitution has divided, it also demands be united," writes Charles O. Jones. Two parliamentary methods are employed to achieve bicameral reconciliation: motions and conference committees. Under the first, the House and Senate can motion, or "ping-pong," measures back and forth between them until their disagreements are resolved. Congressional rules, however, limit each chamber to "two shots" at perfecting the legislation in observance of the parliamentary principle that forbids amendments in the third degree. One chamber, to be sure, can simply adopt the other's bill verbatim and obviate the motion or conference route.

Members and staff aides from each chamber often consult in advance to facilitate the compromise-making process. These consultations sometimes result in one chamber accepting the other's legislative version. In 1981, for example, the House passed a measure involving agencies' internal accounting and administrative control systems. It was sent to the Senate, where the legislation was amended and then returned to the House. Representative Jack Brooks (D, Tex.), chairman of the House committee that reported the measure, asked unanimous consent that the House concur in the Senate amendment to H.R. 1526. He explained, "Mr. Speaker, we have worked with the Senate on the language of their amendment and I can assure my colleagues that the Senate amendment is consistent with the original intent of the bill as passed by the House." The House granted the unanimous consent request. This action completed Congress's lawmaking steps, and the measure was transmitted to the president for his consideration.

The other major device for resolving interchamber differences on legislation is the conference committee — "a device well-suited to the purpose [of interchamber reconciliation] because it permits free discussion and negotiation in a relatively informal setting, in comparison with formal floor action by one chamber on the amendments of the other." Composed of members from each chamber, typically from the committees that originally reported the legislation, conference committees are ad hoc bargaining units whose fundamental task is twofold: first, to negotiate an agreement that a majority of the conferees from each chamber can support, and, second, to report an agreement acceptable to a majority of both the House and Senate. This task gives rise to an "inherent tension central to the conference process, [for] producing an acceptable compromise bill necessarily means each house must to some extent yield on their chamber's position." The process of reaching such an agreement involves a complex mix of many forces, including institutional, committee, and individual. Their interactions shape significantly the character and content of the national policies that emerge from conference and define interchamber and conference committee politics.

Recall Professor Fiorina's comments on pages 547-548. His concern is that the structure of American government may work against effective governance in the modern world. How would you evaluate bicameralism in this context? One way of exploring this question is to consider alternative structures. For example, what would be the effect of establishing unicameral legislatures? This was the course followed by municipalities with bicameral bodies during the Progressive Era and by Nebraska in 1934.

Of course, to adopt such a model, one would have to considerably devalue or discount the concerns about factions, oppression, irrationality, concentrations of power, and the desire for competition that underlie the original commitment to the bicameral structure. What has been the impact of such change? Do factions dominate? Is legislation poorly drawn? Is the Founders' view of human nature wrong or no longer applicable?

There has been little evaluation of the Nebraska experience. But some brief observations about municipalities are in order. First, the functions of municipalities are historically administrative, and their powers to effect substantial regulatory and distributive changes relative to Congress and state legislatures are minor. Secondly, in the shaping of municipal legislation, concerns about the mobility of the governed are more relevant than at other levels of government. See Saul Levmore, Bicameralism: When Are Two Decisions Better Than One?, 12 Int'l Rev. L. & Econ. 143, 161 (1992). Additionally, in recent years there has been some renewed interest in bicameral legislatures for municipalities. In 1989, for example, a proposal to create a bicameral city council was considered by a New York City Charter Revision Commission because of fears that a proposed newly empowered council would not be adequately checked. It was only dropped from the agenda after concern was expressed that the proposal might run afoul of the Voting Rights Act of 1965. See Chapter 5.

Another proposal might be for a unicameral body that requires a supermajority for the enactment of legislation. Would such a structure be more or less democratic than a bicameral body? Would it be easier or harder to adopt legislation? On this point, see Saul Levmore, Bicameralism: When Are Two Decisions Better Than One?, 12 Int'l Rev. L. & Econ. 143 (1992). (Supermajoritarianism defeats opportunities to enact strongly favored legislation.)

What other change can you think of that might make the legislative process more efficient but still protect the public against an overzealous government?

2.   The Legislative Veto

Bicameralism has also proved an obstacle, at least on the federal level, to legislative attempts to oversee administrative activities. The legislative veto, depending on its type, permits either both houses of a legislature, acting concurrently, or one house of the legislature, acting alone (and, in some rare cases, legislative committees) to veto the rule of a federal department or independent agency. During the 1970s, the legislative veto had become a major method of legislative control over agency actions. Broadly written legislation, which granted agencies enormous policymaking discretion, was countered by the requirement that these policies be reviewed through the legislative veto process. From a legislative perspective, this was a far more powerful tool for control than the normal oversight process or the amendment of these broad statutes to narrow their scope. On the federal level, all this came to an end with the adoption by the House of the following resolution.

H.R. RES. 926 (1975)
Disapproving Granting of Permanent Residence in the United
States to Certain Aliens

Mr. EILBERG.   Mr. Speaker, I ask unanimous consent that the Committee on the Judiciary be discharged from the further consideration of the resolution (H. Res. 926) disapproving the granting of permanent residence in the United States to the aliens hereinafter named, in which cases the Attorney General has submitted reports to the Congress pursuant to section 244(a)(1) of the Immigration and Nationality Act, as amended, and ask for its immediate consideration.

The Clerk read the title of the resolution.

The SPEAKER.   Is there objection to the request of the gentleman from Pennsylvania?

Mr. WYLIE.   Mr. Speaker, I reserve the right to object.

Mr. Speaker, I reserve the right to object—and I will not object. This resolution has not been available to the Members of the House for review because it was not printed. The Private Calendar objectors met this morning, and we decided that there are extenuating circumstances and will make this resolution an exception so it can be considered by the Members of this body.

The Private Calendar objectors think this resolution does deserve immediate consideration. We would like the Record to show, however, that we do not regard this "expediting" procedure as a precedent as far as the minority Members of the Private Calendar objectors are concerned.

Mr. Speaker, I would yield to the gentleman from Pennsylvania for an explanation of the resolution.

Mr. EILBERG.   Mr. Speaker, this resolution has been brought to the floor under the provision of section 244 of the Immigration and Nationality Act which establishes procedures for suspending the deportation of aliens who have had long periods of residence in the United States.

Under that section of law, the Congress is required to review administrative decisions which have recommended the suspension of deportation of aliens who have satisfied the following statutory requirements: First, 7 years of continuous physical presence in the United States; second, good moral character during that time; and third, unusual hardship in the event of their deportation.

It was the feeling of the committee, after reviewing 340 cases, that the aliens contained in the resolution did not meet these statutory requirements, particularly as it relates to hardship; and it is the opinion of the committee that their deportation should not be suspended.

I should emphasize that this is a disapproval resolution and unless it is adopted in this session of Congress permanent residence will be granted to those aliens named in the resolution.

Mr. WYLIE.   Mr. Speaker, I withdraw my reservation of objection.

The SPEAKER.   Is there objection to the request of the gentleman from Pennsylvania?

There was no objection.

The Clerk read the resolution as follows:

H. Res. 926

Resolved, That the House of Representatives does not approve the granting of permanent residence in the United States to the aliens herein-after named, in which cases the Attorney General has submitted reports to the Congress pursuant to section 244(a)(1) of the Immigration and Nationality Act, as amended:

A17 926 460, Cantu-Trinidad.

A17 385 958, Jagdish Rai Chadha.

A14 862 226, Jeffrey H. K. Dowa.

A14 007 721, Lucia Paulino.

A13 601 720, Adib Sami Salem.

A13 950 009, Jose Jesus Villalobos-Calderon.

The resolution was agreed to.

A motion to reconsider was laid on the table.

Immigration & Naturalization Service v. Chadha
462 U.S. 919 (1983)

CHIEF JUSTICE BURGER delivered the opinion of the Court. . . .

I

Chadha is an East Indian who was born in Kenya and holds a British passport. He was lawfully admitted to the United States in 1966 on a non-immigrant student visa. His visa expired on June 30, 1972. . . . Section 244(a)(1), at the time in question, provided:

> As hereinafter prescribed in this section, the Attorney General may, in his discretion, suspend deportation and adjust the status to that of an alien lawfully admitted for permanent residence, in the case of an alien who applies to the Attorney General for suspension of deportation. . . .

After Chadha submitted his application for suspension of deportation, the deportation hearing was resumed. . . .

Pursuant to §244(c)(1) of the Act, 8 U.S.C. §1254(c)(1), the Immigration Judge suspended Chadha's deportation and a report of the suspension was transmitted to Congress. Section 244(c)(1) provides:

> Upon application by any alien who is found by the Attorney General to meet the requirements of subsection (a) of this section the Attorney General may in his discretion suspend deportation of such alien. If the deportation of any alien is suspended under the provisions of this subsection, a complete and detailed statement of the facts and pertinent provisions of law in the case shall be reported to the Congress with the reasons for such suspension. Such reports shall be submitted on the first day of each calendar month in which Congress is in session.

Once the Attorney General's recommendation for suspension of Chadha's deportation was conveyed to Congress, Congress had the power under §244(c)(2) of the Act, 8 U.S.C. §1254(c)(2), to veto the Attorney General's determination that Chadha should not be deported. Section 244(c)(2) provides:

> (2) In the case of an alien specified in paragraph (1) of subsection (a) of this subsection —
>
> if during the session of the Congress at which a case is reported, or prior to the close of the session of the Congress next following the session at which a case is reported, either the Senate or the House of Representatives passes a resolution stating in substance that it does not favor the suspension of such deportation, the Attorney General shall thereupon deport such alien or authorize the alien's voluntary departure at his own expense under the order of deportation in the manner provided by law. If, within the time above specified, neither the Senate nor the House of Representatives shall pass such a resolution, the Attorney General shall cancel deportation proceedings.

The June 25, 1974, order of the Immigration Judge suspending Chadha's deportation remained outstanding as a valid order for a year and a half. For reasons not disclosed by the record, Congress did not exercise the veto authority reserved to it under §244(c)(2) until the first session of the 94th Congress. This was the final session in which Congress, pursuant to §244(c)(2), could act to veto the Attorney General's determination that Chadha should not be deported. The session ended on December 19, 1975. 121 Cong. Rec. 42014, 42277 (1975). Absent congressional action, Chadha's deportation proceedings would have been canceled after this date and his status adjusted to that of a permanent resident alien.

On December 12, 1975, Representative Eilberg, Chairman of the Judiciary Subcommittee on Immigration, Citizenship, and International Law, introduced a resolution opposing "the granting of permanent residence in the

United States to [six] aliens," including Chadha. The resolution was referred to the House Committee on the Judiciary. On December 16, 1975, the resolution was discharged from further consideration by the House Committee on the Judiciary and submitted to the House of Representatives for a vote. The resolution had not been printed and was not made available to other Members of the House prior to or at the time it was voted on. So far as the record before us shows, the House consideration of the resolution was based on Representative Eilberg's statement from the floor that:

> It was the feeling of the committee, after reviewing 340 cases, that the aliens contained in the resolution [Chadha and five others] did not meet these statutory requirements, particularly as it relates to hardship; and it is the opinion of the committee that their deportation should not be suspended.

The resolution was passed without debate or recorded vote. Since the House action was pursuant to §244(c)(2), the resolution was not treated as an Art. I legislative act; it was not submitted to the Senate or presented to the President for his action. . . .

III

A

We turn now to the question whether action of one House of Congress under §244(c)(2) violates strictures of the Constitution. We begin, of course, with the presumption that the challenged statute is valid. Its wisdom is not the concern of the courts; if a challenged action does not violate the Constitution, it must be sustained. . . .

By the same token, the fact that a given law or procedure is efficient, convenient, and useful in facilitating functions of government, standing alone, will not save it if it is contrary to the Constitution. Convenience and efficiency are not the primary objectives — or the hallmarks — of democratic government and our inquiry is sharpened rather than blunted by the fact that congressional veto provisions are appearing with increasing frequency in statutes which delegate authority to executive and independent agencies:

> Since 1932, when the first veto provision was enacted into law, 295 congressional veto-type procedures have been inserted in 196 different statutes. . . .

Justice White undertakes to make a case for the proposition that the one-House veto is a useful "political invention," and we need not challenge that assertion. We can even concede this utilitarian argument although the long-range political wisdom of this "invention" is arguable. . . . But policy arguments supporting even useful "political inventions" are subject to the demands of the Constitution which defines powers and, with respect to this subject, sets out just how those powers are to be exercised.

Explicit and unambiguous provisions of the Constitution prescribe and define the respective functions of the Congress and of the Executive in the legislative process. Since the precise terms of those familiar provisions are critical to the resolution of this case, we set them out verbatim. Article I provides:

> All legislative Powers herein granted shall be vested in a Congress of the United States, which shall consist of a Senate *and* House of Representatives. [Art. I, §1 (emphasis added).]
>
> Every Bill which shall have passed the House of Representatives *and* the Senate, *shall*, before it becomes a law, be presented to the President of the United States. . . . [Art. I, §7, cl. 2 (emphasis added).]
>
> *Every* Order, Resolution, or Vote to which the Concurrence of the Senate and House of Representatives may be necessary (except on a question of Adjournment) *shall* be presented to the President of the United States; and before the Same shall take Effect, *shall* be approved by him, or being disapproved by him, *shall* be repassed by two thirds of the Senate and House of Representatives, according to the Rules and Limitations prescribed in the Case of a Bill. [Art. I, §7, cl. 3 (emphasis added).]

These provisions of Art. I are integral parts of the constitutional design for the separation of powers. We have recently noted that "[t]he principle of separation of powers was not simply an abstract generalization in the minds of the Framers: it was woven into the document that they drafted in Philadelphia in the summer of 1787." Buckley v. Valeo, 424 U.S., at 124. Just as we relied on the textual provision of Art. II, §2, cl. 2, to vindicate the principle of separation of powers in *Buckley*, we see that the purposes underlying the Presentment Clauses, Art. I, §7, cls. 2, 3, and the bicameral requirement of Art. I, §1, and §7, cl. 2, guide our resolution of the important question presented in these cases. The very structure of the Articles delegating and separating powers under Arts, I, II, and III exemplifies the concept of separation of powers, and we now turn to Art. I.

B.   The Presentment Clauses

The records of the Constitutional Convention reveal that the requirement that all legislation be presented to the President before becoming law was uniformly accepted by the Framers. Presentment to the President and the Presidential veto were considered so imperative that the draftsmen took special pains to assure that these requirements could not be circumvented. During the final debate on Art. I, §7, cl. 2, James Madison expressed concern that it might easily be evaded by the simple expedient of calling a proposed law a "resolution" or "vote" rather than a "bill." As a consequence, Art. I, §7, cl. 3 was added. . . .

C. Bicameralism

The bicameral requirement of Art. I, §§1, 7, was of scarcely less concern to the Framers than was the Presidential veto and indeed the two concepts are interdependent. By providing that no law could take effect without the concurrence of the prescribed majority of the Members of both Houses, the Framers reemphasized their belief, already remarked upon in connection with the Presentment Clauses, that legislation should not be enacted unless it has been carefully and fully considered by the Nation's elected officials. . . .

However familiar, it is useful to recall that apart from their fear that special interests could be favored at the expense of public needs, the Framers were also concerned, although not of one mind, over the apprehensions of the smaller states. Those states feared a commonality of interest among the larger states would work to their disadvantage; representatives of the larger states, on the other hand, were skeptical of a legislature that could pass laws favoring a minority of the people. It need hardly be repeated here that the Great Compromise, under which one House was viewed as representing the people and the other the states, allayed the fears of both the large and small states.

We see therefore that the Framers were acutely conscious that the bicameral requirement and the Presentment Clauses would serve essential constitutional functions. The President's participation in the legislative process was to protect the Executive Branch from Congress and to protect the whole people from improvident laws. The division of the Congress into two distinctive bodies assures that the legislative power would be exercised only after opportunity for full study and debate in separate settings. The President's unilateral veto power, in turn, was limited by the power of two-thirds of both Houses of Congress to overrule a veto thereby precluding final arbitrary action of one person. It emerges clearly that the prescription for legislative action in Art. I, §§1, 7, represents the Framers' decision that the legislative power of the Federal Government be exercised in accord with a single, finely wrought and exhaustively considered, procedure.

IV

Not every action taken by either House is subject to the bicameralism and presentment requirements of Art. I. Whether actions taken by either House are, in law and fact, an exercise of legislative power depends not on their form but upon "whether they contain matter which is properly to be regarded as legislative in its character and effect." S. Rep. No. 1335, 54th Cong., 2d Sess., 8 (1897).

Examination of the action taken here by one House pursuant to §244(c)(2) reveals that it was essentially legislative in purpose and effect. In purporting to exercise power defined in Art. I, §8, cl. 4, to "establish an uniform Rule of Naturalization," the House took action that had the purpose and effect of altering the legal rights, duties, and relations of persons, including the Attorney General, Executive Branch officials and Chadha, all outside the Legislative Branch. Section 244(c)(2) purports to authorize one House of Congress to require the Attorney General to deport an individual alien whose deportation otherwise would be canceled under §244. The one-House veto operated in these cases to overrule the Attorney General and mandate Chadha's deportation; absent the House action, Chadha would remain in the United States. Congress has acted and its action has altered Chadha's status. . . .

Since it is clear that the action by the House under §244(c)(2) was not within any of the express constitutional exceptions authorizing one House to act alone, and equally clear that it was an exercise of legislative power, that action was subject to the standards prescribed in Art. I. The bicameral requirement, the Presentment Clauses, the President's veto, and Congress' power to override a veto were intended to erect enduring checks on each Branch and to protect the people from the improvident exercise of power by mandating certain prescribed steps. . . .

The veto authorized by §244(c)(2) doubtless has been in many respects a convenient shortcut; the "sharing" with the Executive by Congress of its authority over aliens in this manner is, on its face, an appealing compromise. In purely practical terms, it is obviously easier for action to be taken by one House without submission to the President; but it is crystal clear from the records of the Convention, contemporaneous writings and debates, that the Framers ranked other values higher than efficiency. The records of the Convention and debates in the States preceding ratification underscore the common desire to define and limit the exercise of the newly created federal powers affecting the states and the people. There is unmistakable expression of a determination that legislation by the national Congress be a step-by-step, deliberate and deliberative process.

The choices we discern as having been made in the Constitutional Convention impose burdens on governmental processes that often seem clumsy, inefficient, even unworkable, but those hard choices were consciously made by men who had lived under a form of government that permitted arbitrary governmental acts to go unchecked. There is no support in the Constitution or decisions of this Court for the proposition that the cumbersomeness and delays often encountered in complying with explicit constitutional standards may be avoided, either by the Congress or by the President. See Youngstown Sheet & Tube Co. v. Sawyer, 343 U.S. 579

(1952). With all the obvious flaws of delay, untidiness, and potential for abuse, we have not yet found a better way to preserve freedom than by making the exercise of power subject to the carefully crafted restraints spelled out in the Constitution.

V

We hold that the congressional veto provision in §244(c)(2) is severable from the Act and that is unconstitutional. . . .

JUSTICE POWELL, concurring in the judgment.

The Court's decision, based on the Presentment Clauses, Art. I, §7, cls. 2 and 3, apparently will invalidate every use of the legislative veto. The breadth of this holding gives one pause. Congress has included the veto in literally hundreds of statutes, dating back to the 1930's. Congress clearly views this procedure as essential to controlling the delegation of power to administrative agencies. One reasonably may disagree with Congress' assessment of the veto's utility, but the respect due its judgment as a coordinate branch of Government cautions that our holding should be no more extensive than necessary to decide these cases. In my view, the cases may be decided on a narrower ground. When Congress finds that a particular person does not satisfy the statutory criteria for permanent residence in this country it has assumed a judicial function in violation of the principle of separation of powers. Accordingly, I concur only in the judgment. . . .

On its face, the House's action appears clearly adjudicatory. The House did not enact a general rule; rather it made its own determination that six specific persons did not comply with certain statutory criteria. It thus undertook the type of decision that traditionally has been left to other branches. Even if the House did not make a de novo determination, but simply reviewed the Immigration and Naturalization Service's findings, it still assumed a function ordinarily entrusted to the federal courts. . . .

The impropriety of the House's assumption of this function is confirmed by the fact that its action raises the very danger the Framers sought to avoid — the exercise of unchecked power. In deciding whether Chadha deserves to be deported, Congress is not subject to any internal constraints that prevent it from arbitrarily depriving him of the right to remain in this country. Unlike the judiciary or an administrative agency, Congress is not bound by established substantive rules. Nor is it subject to the procedural safeguards, such as the right to counsel and a hearing before an impartial tribunal, that are present when a court or an agency adjudicates individual rights. The only effective constraint on Congress' power is political, but Congress is most accountable politically when it prescribes rules of general applicability. When it decides rights of specific persons, those rights are subject to "the tyranny of a shifting majority."

Chief Justice Marshall observed: "It is the peculiar province of the legislature to prescribe general rules for the government of society; the application of those rules to individuals in society would seem to be the duty of other departments." Fletcher v. Peck, 6 Cranch 87, 136 (1810). In my view, when Congress undertook to apply its rules to Chadha, it exceeded the scope of its constitutionally prescribed authority. I would not reach the broader question whether legislative vetoes are invalid under the Presentment Clauses.

JUSTICE WHITE, dissenting.

Today the Court not only invalidates §244(c)(2) of the Immigration and Nationality Act, but also sounds the death knell for nearly 200 other statutory provisions in which Congress has reserved a "legislative veto." For this reason, the Court's decision is of surpassing importance. . . .

The prominence of the legislative veto mechanism in our contemporary political system and its importance to Congress can hardly be overstated. It has become a central means by which Congress secures the accountability of executive and independent agencies. Without the legislative veto, Congress is faced with a Hobson's choice: either to refrain from delegating the necessary authority, leaving itself with a hopeless task of writing laws with the requisite specificity to cover endless special circumstances across the entire policy landscape, or in the alternative, to abdicate its lawmaking function to the Executive Branch and independent agencies. . . .

The Court holds that the disapproval of a suspension of deportation by the resolution of one House of Congress is an exercise of legislative power without compliance with the prerequisites for lawmaking set forth in Art. I of the Constitution. Specifically, the Court maintains that the provisions of §244(c)(2) are inconsistent with the requirement of bicameral approval, implicit in Art. I, §1, and the requirement that all bills and resolutions that require the concurrence of both Houses be presented to the President, Art. I, §7, cls. 2 and 3.

I do not dispute the Court's truismatic exposition of these Clauses. There is no question that a bill does not become a law until it is approved by both the House and the Senate, and presented to the President. . . .

If Congress may delegate lawmaking power to independent and Executive agencies, it is most difficult to understand Art. I as prohibiting Congress from also reserving a check on legislative power for itself. Absent the veto, the agencies receiving delegations of legislative or quasi-legislative power may issue regulations having the force of law without bicameral approval and without the President's signature. It is thus not apparent why the reservation of a veto over the exercise of that legislative power must be subject to a more exacting test. In both cases, it is enough that the initial statutory authorizations comply with the Art. I requirements.

JUSTICE REHNQUIST filed a dissenting opinion [omitted].

NOTES AND QUESTIONS

1. *A sweeping decision. Chadha* is one of the most sweeping decisions in Supreme Court history. By this single decision, the Court ended a frequently employed congressional method of overseeing administrative agencies and put into jeopardy a multitude of statutes. Either clauses providing for legislative vetoes would be struck or statutes would be struck. What would determine the choice?

2. *An alternative solution.* Could the Court have done less and still protected Chadha? How does Justice Powell respond to that question? How would you evaluate his response?

3. *The dangers of particular legislation.* The facts of *Chadha* make clear the dangers inherent in legislatures enacting bills of particular applicability or private bills. Such bills are of minimal concern to a large majority of legislators because they do not have palpable policy implications or impact on the constituents of most members. For most members, their only value is to gain credit for support for similar legislation of interest to them. About his vote in favor of deporting Chadha, Representative Mikva has written:

> [T]he Court remarked in a footnote that it was "not at all clear whether the House . . . correctly understood what it was doing." Notwithstanding the loyalty I retain toward the first branch, I must agree with that observation. I was a member of the House when that body passed on Chadha's suspension of deportation. I voted to exercise the legislative veto, and to override the decision of the immigration judge. After *Chadha* was decided, I reexamined the Congressional Record for that day. I cannot, for the life of me, remember why I voted to deport the gentleman.

Abner J. Mikva, The Changing Role of Judicial Review, 38 Admin. L. Rev. 115, 117 (1986).

A State Perspective on the Legislative Veto

A number of state legislatures have adopted some form of the legislative veto for overseeing administrative agencies. These legislative vetoes have also been the subject of challenges, under an analysis similar to one found in the *Chadha* decision. All, except one, have proven successful. In Idaho, on a challenge to the legislative veto, the Idaho Supreme Court decided:

> Rule making that comes from a legislative delegation of power is neither the legal nor functional equivalent of constitutional power.
>
> It is not constitutionally mandated; rather it comes to the executive department through delegation from the legislature. This Court, as noted, has consistently found the executive rule making authority to be rooted in a legislative delegation, not a power constitutionally granted to the executive.

Mead v. Arnell, 791 P.2d 410, 417 (Idaho 1990).

Some states have remedied judicial decisions striking legislative vetoes. Connecticut requires all rules to be reviewed by a joint legislative committee, which has the power to disapprove them. Conn. Gen. Stat. §4-170. West Virginia, on the other hand, prohibited agency rulemaking, requiring every proposed rule to be the subject of a statute. W. Va. Code §29A-3-11. For a detailed study of this subject, see National Conference of State Legislatures, Legislative Review of Administrative Rules and Regulations (1990); Arthur E. Bonfield, State Administrative Rule Making (1986).

C. THE VETO

1. In General

The United States Constitution and the constitutions of all states, except for North Carolina, grant to the executive the power to veto legislation. The power is not absolute; its exercise may be over-ridden by a supermajority of legislators in each legislative chamber. Article I, §7, cl. 2 of the United States Constitution is typical:

> Every Bill which shall have passed the House of Representatives and the Senate, shall, before it becomes a Law, be presented to the President of the United States; if he approve he shall sign it, but if not he shall return it, with his Objections to that House in which it shall have originated, who shall enter the Objections at large on their Journal, and proceed to reconsider it. If after such Reconsideration two thirds of that House shall agree to pass the Bill, it shall be sent, together with the Objections, to the other House, by which it shall likewise be reconsidered, and if approved by two thirds of that House, it shall become a Law. But in all such Cases the Votes of both Houses shall be determined by Yeas and Nays, and the Names of the Persons voting for and against the Bill shall be entered on the Journal of each House respectively. If any Bill shall not be returned by the President within ten Days (Sundays excepted) after it shall have been presented to him, the Same shall be a Law, in the like Manner as if he had signed it, unless the Congress by their Adjournment prevent its Return, in which Case it shall not be a Law.

The executive veto is the most important external check on legislative activity. "It establishes a salutary check upon the legislative body, calculated to guard the community against the effects of faction, precipitancy, or of any impulse unfriendly to the public good, which may happen to influence a majority of that body." The Federalist No. 73, at 495 (A. Hamilton) (Jacob E. Cooke ed., 1961). While Hamilton thought its use would be infrequent—"[i]t is evident that there would be greater danger of his not using his power when necessary, than of his using it too often, or too much," id. at 497 — recent Presidents have used or threatened to use the power with some frequency.

In modern practice, the exercise of the veto power has not signaled executive displeasure with the legislative process but rather with the legislative product. No executive objects to the "precipitous" passage of legislation he or she favors. In the age of statutes, Presidents have increasingly participated vigorously in the legislative process, drafting legislation and lobbying for its adoption, and it has been the veto power that has added special weight to their participation. Through the veto power the President becomes a "third branch of the legislature." Woodrow Wilson, Congressional Government 53 (Johns Hopkins ed., 1981). For example, consider the following veto of the proposed Cable Television Consumer Protection and Competition Act of 1992. Recall its enactment process from pages 542-547. On what basis is the President objecting to the legislation?

Veto of Cable Television Consumer Protection and Competition Act of 1992

To the Senate of the United States:

I am returning herewith without my approval S. 12, the "Cable Television Consumer Protection and Competition Act of 1992." This bill illustrates good intentions gone wrong, fallen prey to special interests.

Contrary to the claims made by its proponents, this legislation will not reduce the price Americans pay for cable television service. Rather, the simple truth is that under this legislation cable television rates will go up, not down. Competition will not increase, it will stagnate. In addition, this legislation will cost American jobs and discourage investment in telecommunications, one of our fastest growing industries.

S. 12 is clearly long on promises. Unfortunately, it is just as clearly short on relief to the American families who are quite rightly concerned about significant increases in their cable rates and poor cable service. Although the proponents of S. 12 describe the bill as procompetitive, it simply is not. Indeed, the only truly competitive provision, one that would have expanded the ability of telephone companies to compete with cable companies in rural areas, was dropped from the bill at the last minute.

S. 12 tries to address legitimate consumer concerns, but it does so by requiring cable companies to bear the costs of meeting major new federally imposed regulatory requirements and by adopting costly special interest provisions. For example, the bill requires cable companies for the first time to pay broadcasting companies, who have free access to the airwaves, to carry the broadcasters' programs. The undeniable result: higher rates for cable viewers.

Beyond increasing consumer costs, the bill takes certain key business decisions away from cable operators and puts them in the hands of the Federal Government. One provision, which is unconstitutional, requires cable companies to carry certain television stations regardless of whether the viewing public wants to see these stations. Another special interest provision would put the Federal Government in the position of dictating to cable companies to whom and at what price they could sell their programs. These types of federally mandated outcomes will discourage continued investment in new programs to the detriment of cable subscribers who have come to expect a wide variety of programming and new services.

I believe that the American people deserve cable television legislation that, unlike S. 12, will deliver what it promises: fair rates, good programming, and sound service.

/s/ George Bush

The White House
October 3, 1992

Overriding an executive veto is an immensely difficult task. First, there is the obvious problem of gaining a supermajority in any chamber in which the bill had passed by only a simple majority. Second, even if a particular bill has passed by a veto-proof margin in both houses, maintaining such margins can prove problematic. The executive veto puts enormous pressure on members of the president's party who previously supported the bill. And even for members of the opposition party, the prospect of voting against the will of an executive causes concern. These problems are explored below in the excerpts from the Senate debate on overriding the executive veto on the Cable Television Consumer Protection and Competition Act of 1992. Prior to this successful override attempt, Congress had failed to override 35 previous vetoes by President Bush.

Overriding the Veto of Cable Television Regulation

CONGRESSIONAL RECORD—SENATE
Monday, October 5, 1992

The PRESIDING OFFICER.   Under the previous order, the Senate will now proceed to the consideration of the President's veto message on S.12, which the clerk will report. . . .

The PRESIDING OFFICER.   Under the previous order, there will now be 1 hour of debate with the time to be equally divided and controlled by the two leaders or their designees.

Mr. MITCHELL.   Mr. President, I ask unanimous consent that the time on the bill be controlled by Senator Danforth and Senator Burns.

The PRESIDING OFFICER.   Without objection, it is so ordered.

Who yields time? . . .

The PRESIDING OFFICER.   The Senator from Montana is recognized.

Mr. BURNS.   Mr. President, I will just have an opening statement here, as we start down this road. This whole debate today regarding cable reregulation has been set up by some speeches made previously here on this floor this afternoon. One of them has to do with jobs. We beat up on our President because the economy has not grown and job creation has not really happened like we would all like to see it. Yet, we are starting right down another pathway here that is going to cost jobs here in America — reregulation. I find it ironic that this is the President's fault, and it is not the Congress' fault. No other industry has enjoyed the growth through slow economic times like that of the cable industry. It did not do that until it was unregulated. There are a lot of things that this Government does and a lot of things this Congress does and about 2 years later we come back and look at it and say, "Woops, we made a mistake there, maybe we should undo that." We find out that is very, very hard to do.

Mr. President, we are in another one of those situations where we might have to say woops again. So as we look at this situation — and we will have some statements later on down the line — the underlying fact in this country is that jobs are a result of the creation of goods and services which are sold to consumers and users. This bill restrains cable's ability to create new jobs, clear and simple. There is no other argument that could even come up to that.

Senator Gore, with this bill, wants to stop this new job creation, and President Bush wants new jobs to continue to be created. If that is not a defining point, I do not know what is. President Bush has been doing everything in his power to create jobs this last 4 years, and the Congress has stood in his way every step of the way.

Then we stand back and say, "Aren't we in bad shape?" This country is not nearly as bad as everybody thinks it is. We are still the largest economy in the world, largest exporter in the world. In fact, our economy is bigger than the next three put together, and I do not see anybody making a big exodus out of this country to live somewhere else. I do not get one letter from people wanting out. But we will, if this continues, because we are heading right down that old track.

This bill is just another example of a regulatory Congress that is trying to ram a bad piece of legislation down the President's throat.

Mr. President, I do not see my colleague on the floor, and I reserve the remainder of my time.

The PRESIDING OFFICER.   Who seeks recognition?

Mr. Danforth addressed the Chair.

The PRESIDING OFFICER.   The Senator from Missouri is recognized.

Mr. DANFORTH.   Mr. President, I yield 6 minutes to the Senator from Hawaii.

Mr. INOUYE.   Mr. President, I rise today to urge my colleagues to support S. 12, the Cable Television Consumer Protection and Competition Act of 1992 and override the President's veto.

The purpose of this legislation is very simple and straightforward: To promote competition in the video industry and to protect consumers from excessive rates and poor customer service where no competition exists. At the same time, it continues to permit the cable industry to grow and bring to the American public a new array of programming and other services. This bill represents a balanced and bipartisan package.

There is an effort underfoot to make this a partisan issue. It is not. This bill passed the Senate by a vote of 74 to 25, with a majority of both Democrats and Republicans voting for the bill.

If this measure does not become law the only losers will be America's consumers. This bill would not be here before us today were it not for the consumer outrage over the way they have been treated by the cable industry. I hope that my colleagues will not let this measure fall over partisan politics. Our first responsibility is to the American people who want us to put in place protections against cable's monopoly power.

To promote competition, the bill ensures that competitors receive access to cable programming, not for free, but for the same price that the programming is sold to cable operators.

Contrary to the President's assertion, this bill does not require the government to set prices for programming nor dictate to whom it is sold. It simply provides that programmers owned by cable operators cannot discriminate. This bill also permits municipalities to construct their own cable systems in competition with the existing operator, and it prohibits a franchising authority from unreasonably refusing to award a second franchise.

The President says that competition will not increase under this bill. He is wrong. If we do not pass this bill, there will never be competition to cable. . . . The President's contention that the conference report drops the provision that would have permitted the telephone companies to provide cable service in communities with up to 10,000 residents, ignores the fact that the FCC is presently conducting a proceeding to do just that. Moreover, if the conferees had retained that provision then the FCC would have been precluded from raising the limit should it find that telephone companies should provide cable service in communities with more than 10,000 residents.

This measure also addresses the exorbitant rate increases many consumers have suffered since deregulation. Rates for cable service have risen three times faster than inflation, and complaints about poor customer service have been numerous. To protect consumers, S. 12 gives the FCC, and in some cases, local authorities, the ability to ensure that rates are reasonable where no competition exists. It also directs the FCC to establish customer service standards.

Regarding retransmission consent and must carry, I want to note that when the Senate considered this legislation in January, the cable industry and the President supported the Packwood substitute which contained both retransmission consent and must carry. Thus, every Member that voted for the substitute of S. 12 voted for both of these provisions. . . .

S. 12 passed the Senate earlier this year by a vote of 73 to 18.

Because of its wide support and logic, a majority of both Republicans and Democrats voted in support of this bill. Supporters of S. 12 include: cities, consumer groups, unions, public and commercial broadcast stations, the religious broadcasters, and senior citizens.

S. 12 will promote competition and impose regulation until that competition develops. I urge all of my colleagues to look beyond the rhetoric being employed by the cable industry and the President to the solid foundation that supports S. 12. I urge all of my colleagues to support S. 12 and override the President's veto.

In closing, Mr. President, may I just say that, as much as I admire my friend from Montana, I am certain he will agree with me that history has demonstrated that monopolies never create jobs. It is the system that we all admire and love, the free enterprise system, the competitive system, that provides jobs. Everyone agrees, Mr. President, that the cable industry is a monopoly. It is anticompetitive. If we put into practice the free enterprise system, that is when jobs will be created. Mr. President, I yield the floor. . . .

The PRESIDING OFFICER.   Who yields time? The Senator from Missouri.

Mr. DANFORTH.   How much time is left on my side?

The PRESIDING OFFICER.   A little over 9 minutes.

Mr. DANFORTH.   Mr. President, I yield myself 6 minutes. I speak as a Republican politician and as a strong supporter of President Bush. And I speak as the Senator whose name happens to be first on S. 12. Along with Senator Hollings and Inouye, I introduced this bill almost 2 years ago.

I want to say first of all that there are good arguments on both sides of this legislation. The President, in vetoing the bill, is true to what he takes to be basic Republican philosophy, which is that Government regulation is a problem for this country and we have to try to reduce that problem and reduce the amount of regulation.

Mr. President, I generally agree with that position. I certainly do not agree with some of the more partisan things that have been said attacking the President of the United States for his position on this bill. I do not agree, for example, with the statement of Mr. George Stephanopoulos, the communications director of the Clinton campaign, who made a statement October 3 saying that "George Bush slapped the American consumers across the face."

And I do not agree with Senator Gore's speech of September 29, when he said that the President was "owned lock, stock and barrel by the cable TV industry."

I do not agree with those statements. I do not think they are right. I do not think they are fair.

The President is doing what he thinks is correct and he believes he is opposing overregulation. The difference of opinion here has to do with when regulation is appropriate and when it is not. The President is against overregulation, against reregulation. The philosophy that is espoused by those of us who support this bill is that without regulation, cable companies in each particular community amount to unregulated monopolies, monopolies which have allowed consumer rates to go up three times the rate of inflation since 1986.

That is the difference of opinion. It is an opinion that can be fairly held by people on both sides. I would hope whoever ends up winning this argument does not gloat about it and does not try to rub it in.

I want to say a word about the role of Republicans particularly in the Senate with respect to this legislation, because Republicans have had a big hand in this legislation. Those of us who support it believe that we are very much in the tradition of a great Republican President, Theodore Roosevelt. In 1989, when the predecessor of this bill, S. 1880, was introduced, there were 7 Republican cosponsors for the bill and 8 out of 9 Republicans on the Commerce Committee voted to report the bill out of the committee. Then when S. 12 was introduced and reported out of the Commerce Committee, 6 of the Republicans on that committee voted to report S. 12 out, and 27 Republicans voted for final passage in the Senate and 24 Republicans voted for the conference report. And in the House, 98 Republican House Members voted for the bill and 71 voted for the conference report. Since passage of the bill, when the bill was in conference, an effort was made to move in the direction of the President and during conference the President won some victories. For example, with respect to the definition of the basic tier of cable television that could be regulated by the communities, that was a victory for the administration. And there was another victory for the administration during the Senate debate in the prohibition of cities from granting exclusive franchises, moving in the administration's direction with respect to the importance of competition.

I would also like to say that I am sure that many of my friends on my side of the aisle are concerned about voting against the President, particularly this close to an election, and are concerned about what is the effect of overriding a Presidential veto. I know that a lot of weight has gone on the President's perfect record on vetoes so far. But I would simply like to point out that a lot of Presidents have had vetoes overridden and a lot of them have been very strong Presidents.

Franklin Roosevelt, for example, had 9 vetoes overridden; Harry Truman had 12 vetoes overridden by Congress; Dwight Eisenhower was overridden twice; Richard Nixon 7 times; Gerald Ford 12 times; Jimmy Carter twice; Ronald Reagan was overridden 9 times.

So it is no weakness on the part of the President of the United States if he happens to have a veto overridden. It is no point of disrespect at all. It is a matter simply of disagreement. . . .

Mr. BURNS.   The Republican leader wants about 5 minutes, and he will take that out of his leader time, if that is possible.

So I ask unanimous consent that the Republican leader be able to take 5 minutes of his leader time to speak.

Mr. MITCHELL.   What is the request, Mr. President?

Mr. BURNS.   The Republican leader wants 5 minutes, but he wants to take it out of his leader time.

Mr. MITCHELL.   I have no objection to that.

The PRESIDING OFFICER.   Without objection, it is so ordered. . . .

Mr. DOLE.   Mr. President, when it comes to protecting cable consumers, the sponsors of this bill have tuned into the wrong channel.

As I see it, Congress has two responsibilities in addressing consumer problems with the cable industry. First and foremost we must ensure that consumers are not gouged and that they are protected both today and tomorrow. And second, we should establish a strong communications policy that ensures our Nation's edge in the communications industry. Unfortunately the bill the President vetoed fails on both counts.

Consumers have asked us to address the very real problems of cable rates and service shortcomings. I cannot recall a town meeting or chamber of commerce breakfast back in Kansas that did not hear at least one complaint about this industry.

So the urge to do something is understandable and justifiable. But that something should not be a measure that will cut off the development of the programming and information that consumers really want, should not be a reregulatory scheme which will entrench and perpetuate the existing cable monopolies, and above all, should not be something that in the end will leave consumers paying more for less, still captive to a government sanctioned monopoly.

Mr. President, from the perspective of genuine consumer protection and common sense communications policy, this bill flunks the test.

S. 13 dictates cable system architecture for the 10 years and thereby ignores more cost effective delivery systems that may come with innovation. This mandate is an expensive gambit, raising costs of cable operators up to an estimated 5.8 billion.

S. 12 was stripped of any true competitive provisions. I supported a provision to promote competition in rural areas by permitting telephone companies to offer cable services to communities with populations smaller than 10,000. This provision would have gone a long way toward reasonable cable rates for rural America. Unfortunately, it was completely eliminated in conference.

While S. 12 does not understand competition, the FCC does. Earlier this year, the FCC authorized telephone companies to deliver video programming to consumers through video dialtone services, which I encouraged. If we were really serious about promoting free-market competition, we would have provided in this bill for telephone company entry — the only entity strong enough to go head to head with the cable companies. True competition spurs better services, innovation, and jobs. And let us face it, S. 12 is not the consumer's Robin Hood. It does not take from the rich and give back to the poor. Cable companies are not going to get stuck with this bill. The consumer is. That means that under this bill, cable customers will pay even more to watch the proceedings of Congress on C-SPAN, or whatever their favorite programming may be.

Mr. President, as we approach the 21st century, we must also have a coherent communications policy. America has a rich history in the communications field — from the pony express to the telegraph, telephones, radios, and televisions, we have always been innovators and world leaders.

With recent and rapid developments in the communications field, including computers, fiber optics, fax machines, cellular phones, and satellites, America needs a flexible, forward-looking communications policy more than ever before. Restrictive regulatory policies will be counterproductive and will mean that the United States will lose its global competitive edge. Competition, not Federal regulations, is the only regulator that can accommodate the opportunities that will accompany advances in technology.

Mr. President, this bill is not the answer to the justifiable frustrations of cable consumers. This cable bill is neither good for the consumer nor good communications policy. We all want to address the concerns of cable consumers, so let us change the channel, tune in next year, and do it in a responsible way.

I urge my colleagues to sustain the President's veto. Mr. President, for all the reasons I set forth in my statement, I think the veto should be sustained. I am not certain the veto will be sustained. But I would just add one additional thing. Like any other bill near the election, there has been a lot of politics and a lot of talk about politics and a lot of comments about the President's position and others' positions with reference to this bill.

My junior colleague from Tennessee was quoted as saying in the Chicago Tribune, September 29, 1992: "George Bush knows that on this issue this cable monopoly owns him lock, stock, and barrel. If you veto the cable bill, you will have sided with the monopolies and against the American people."

Another quote in the Associated Press just a couple days ago: "President Bush has vetoed important consumer legislation to protect his rich friends in the cable monopolies."

Another in Reuters, the same date: "So he can protect the ability of big cable companies to keep soaking their consumers."

In my view, this is partisanship to the nth degree, and it makes it rather difficult, I hope, for some of my colleagues on this side of the aisle to understand that this has become a political game. This is politics. The merits of this legislation went out the window 2 weeks ago, 3 weeks ago, 30 days ago. And now we have one candidate for Vice President, my distinguished junior colleague from Tennessee, out saying the President is owned lock, stock, and barrel by the cable industry. Where is the proof? Where is the proof? And how can we continue to make reckless charges just because it may be campaign season?

So I say to my colleagues on this side of the aisle, this is politics. This is an effort to embarrass President Bush 30 days before the election, 1 week before the first debate. That is what it is all about. The merits of this legislation have been forgotten. We have a fight between big money interests on both sides; the networks, the cable companies, the movie industry, the big newspapers, and the consumer has been forgotten.

So I urge my colleagues to sustain the President's veto. He has not asked for much. We have sustained 10 vetoes in the Senate. They have sustained 10 vetoes in the House. Some have been pocket vetoed, some have been referred to committees. This is an important piece of legislation. It should not have been politicized, but it has been politicized. So I ask my colleagues on this side and the others who have voted with us before to sustain the President's veto. We will get good legislation next year based on competition and not reregulation, based on policy and not based on politics. . . .

Mr. DANFORTH.   I ask unanimous consent to proceed for 1 minute.

The PRESIDING OFFICER.   The Senator indeed has 1 minute. He will be recognized.

Mr. DANFORTH.   Mr. President, this is not a partisan bill. This bill was reported out of the Senate Commerce Committee with a majority of Republicans voting for it. The fact that a Presidential veto is overridden is not a slap in the face to the President. President Reagan had 9 vetoes overridden. President Nixon had 7. President Eisenhower had 2. President Truman, whom everybody is citing this year, had 12 vetoes overridden. It is not an insult to the President. It is merely a disagreement on an issue.

The PRESIDING OFFICER.   The question is, Shall the bill pass, the objections of the President of the United States to the contrary notwithstanding? The yeas and nays are mandatory under the Constitution. The clerk will now call the roll. . . .

Mr. MACK (*when his name was called*).   Present.

The yeas and nays resulted — yeas 74, nays 25. . . .

The PRESIDING OFFICER.   If there is no other Senator wishing to vote, on this vote the yeas are 74, the nays are 25. One Senator responded "present." Two-thirds of the Senators voting, a quorum being present, having voted in the affirmative, the bill, on reconsideration, is passed, the objections of the President of the United States to the contrary notwithstanding. . . .

Sometimes a legislature will pass a bill knowing that it will be vetoed and that the veto cannot be overridden. The purpose of this exercise is to create a political issue. A good illustration of this is Congress' adoption of H.R. 11. This bill contained the urban aid package promised by the President and legislative leaders after the Los Angeles riots in April 1992. The bill also contained numerous revenue raisers, which it was politically impossible for the President to support because of his attacks on then-Governor Clinton's alleged 128 percent tax increase and President Bush's pledge to raise no new taxes. Prior to its passage, the White House warned that the President would veto such a bill, a promise he honored. During the presidential campaign debates of that year, Governor Clinton and legislative leaders used the promise of such veto as evidence of the President's insensitivity to the urban problems, notwithstanding his call for action after the riots.

2. The Pocket Veto

In most instances, the executive veto process occurs within the confines of the executive and legislative chambers, under the dictates of the policies and politics of the time. Occasionally these processes break down or are perceived to break down, and the courts are asked to intercede.

Kennedy v. Sampson
511 F.2d 430 (D.C. Cir. 1974)

TAMM, Circuit Judge:

Appellee, a United States Senator, filed suit against the Administrator of the General Services Administration and the Chief of White House Records seeking a declaration that the Family Practice of Medicine Act (hereinafter, S. 3418) became law on December 25, 1970, and an order requiring the appellants to publish the Act was a validly enacted law. S. 3418 was passed by overwhelming majorities in both the House and Senate in the Fall of 1970. Appellee was among those Senators who voted in favor of the bill which was presented to the President on December 14, 1970. On December 22 both Houses of Congress adjourned for the Christmas holidays, the Senate until December 28 and the House until December 29. Before adjourning, the Senate authorized the Secretary of the Senate to receive messages from the President during the adjournment. On December 24, the President issued a memorandum of disapproval announcing that he would withhold his signature from S. 3418. The President took no further action with respect to the bill. Appellants maintain that this series of events resulted in a pocket veto under article I, section 7 of the United States Constitution. Appellee, relying upon the same provision, contends that the bill became law without the President's signature at the expiration of the ten-day period following its presentation to him. . . .

Two questions are presented for review: (1) does appellee have standing to maintain this suit; and (2) did S. 3418 become a law? We conclude that both questions must be answered in the affirmative. . . .

I

The requirement of standing derives from the limitation upon judicial power expressed in the "case" or "controversy" formula of article III of the Constitution. . . .

One approach to the question is to inquire whether a "logical nexus" exists between the status asserted by a litigant and the claim sought to be adjudicated. Examination of appellee's complaint reveals that such a nexus is present in this case. While the complaint is literally addressed to the ministerial duties of certain officials, the legal issue turns on the validity of executive action which purports to have disapproved an Act of Congress by means of a constitutional procedure which does not permit Congress to override the disapproval. If appellants' arguments are accepted, then appellee's vote in favor of the bill in question has been nullified and appellee has no right to demand or participate in a vote to override the President's veto. Conversely, if appellee's interpretation of the veto clause is correct, then the bill became law without the President's signature. In short, disposition of the substantive issue will determine the effectiveness *vel non* of appellee's actions as a legislator with respect to the legislation in question. This demonstrates a relationship between appellee and his claim which is not only logical but real, a relationship which assures that the issues have been litigated with the vigor and thoroughness necessary to assist the court in rendering an informed judgment.

A somewhat different analysis of standing has been employed with respect to parties who challenge administrative action. In Association of Data Processing Service Organizations, Inc. v. Camp, 397 U.S. 150 (1970), the Supreme Court framed the standing issue as follows: (1) does the plaintiff allege that the challenged action has caused him "injury in fact, economic or otherwise"; (2) is the interest sought to be protected "arguably within the zone of interests to be protected or regulated by the statute or constitutional guarantee in question." Appellee's pleading satisfies both inquiries. The complaint alleges an injury to him in his capacity as a United States Senator. . . . Appellee's asserted interest plainly falls among those contemplated by the constitutional provision upon which he relies. That provision, article I, section 7, is one of several in the Constitution which implement the "separation of powers" doctrine. Taken together, these provisions define the prerogatives of each governmental branch in a manner which prevents overreaching by any one of them. The provision under discussion allocates to the executive and legislative branches their respective roles in the lawmaking process. When either branch perceives an intrusion upon its legislative power by the other, this clause is appropriately invoked. The gist of appellee's complaint is that such an intrusion has occurred as a result of the President's misinterpretation of this clause and that a consequence of this intrusion is the nullification of appellee's vote in favor of the bill in question; hence, the complaint alleges injury to an

interest of appellee as a member of the legislative branch of the government, and interest among those protected by article I, section 7. Appellants
insist that only the interests of the Congress or one of its Houses as a body
are protected by this provision. . . .

Appellants' argument to the contrary is based upon a distinction which
is more formal than substantive. While conceding that Congress as a whole
(or even one of its Houses) has standing to challenge the President's purported use of the pocket veto, appellants insist that an individual member
of Congress does not, even if he voted for the bill in controversy. The
interest of the Congress in preserving its role in the law-making process
is said to be "direct" while that of appellee is labelled "indirect or
derivative." Appellants base this distinction upon the self-evident
proposition that appellee is not the Congress. . . . The prerequisite to
standing is that a party be "among the injured," in the words of *Sierra
Club*, not that he be the most grievously or most directly injured. We
think that appellee is "among the injured" in this case. . . .

II

Article I, section 7, paragraph 2 of the United States Constitution
prescribes the manner in which laws of the United States are enacted:

> Every Bill which shall have passed the House of Representatives and the
> Senate, shall, before it becomes a Law, be presented to the President of the
> United States; if he approve he shall sign it, but if not he shall return it, with
> his Objections to that House in which it shall have originated, who shall enter
> the Objections at large on their Journal, and proceed to reconsider it. . . . If
> any Bill shall not be returned by the President within ten Days (Sundays
> excepted) after it shall have been presented to him, the Same shall be a
> Law, in the like Manner as if he had signed it, *unless the Congress by their
> Adjournment prevent its Return, in which Case it shall not be a Law.* (Emphasis
> added.)

At issue in this case is whether the Christmas adjournment of 1970 was
one which "prevented" the return of S. 3418 by the President. If so, then the
President's failure to approve the bill within ten days of its presentation to
him constituted a pocket veto. If the adjournment did not prevent
the return of S. 3418, then the bill became law without the President's
signature. . . . [W]e affirm the district court's declaration that S. 3418
became law on December 25, 1970.

Our analysis begins with the premise that the pocket veto power is an
exception to the general rule that Congress may override presidential disapproval of proposed legislation. Rejection of an absolute presidential veto
is explicit both in the proceedings of the Constitutional Convention and
in contemporaneous commentary. . . . Since it operates as an "absolute

negative," the pocket veto power is a departure from the central scheme of the Constitution. As such, it must be limited by the specific purpose it is intended to serve, a purpose explained in the following passage from Story's Commentaries:

> But the President might effectually defeat the wholesome restraint [i.e., congressional override], thus intended, upon his qualified negative, if he might silently decline to act after a bill was presented to him for approval or rejection. The Constitution, therefore, has wisely provided, that, if any bill shall not be returned by the President within ten days (Sundays excepted) after it shall have been presented to him, it shall be a law, in like manner as if he had signed it. But if this clause stood alone, Congress might, in like manner, defeat the due exercise of his qualified negative by a termination of the session, which would render it impossible for the President to return the bill. It is therefore added, unless the Congress, by their adjournment, prevent its return, in which case it shall not be a law.

The pocket veto power is one component of a constitutional mechanism designed to enforce respect on the part of each of the lawmaking branches of the government for the legislative authority of the other. This understanding of the purpose of the clause has led the Supreme Court to adopt a rule of construction which governs in this case:

> The constitutional provisions [i.e., article I, section 7, paragraph 2] have two fundamental purposes: (1) that the President shall have suitable opportunity to consider the bills presented to him, and (2) that the Congress shall have suitable opportunity to consider his objections to bills and on such consideration to pass them over his veto provided there are the requisite votes. Edwards v. United States, 286 U.S. 482, 486. We should not adopt a construction which would frustrate either of these purposes.

Wright v. United States, 302 U.S. 583, 596 (1938). Where possible, then, the pocket veto clause should be construed in a manner which preserves both purposes. Since a pocket veto always has the effect of frustrating Congress' right to reconsider a vetoed bill, the preferred construction of the clause is that return of a bill was not prevented by an adjournment. Only two decisions of the Supreme Court have addressed the question of whether an adjournment prevented the return of a bill. Appellant relies upon the first of these and seeks to distinguish the later decision from the present case.

The decision relied upon by appellant is The Pocket Veto Case, 279 U.S. 655 (1929), which held that the intersession adjournment of the 69th Congress prevented the return of a bill which had been presented to the President eight days (excluding Sunday) before the adjournment of the first session. The opinion states two reasons for the holding: (1) the word "House" in the return veto clause means house in session and does not permit return of a bill to an officer or agent of the originating House during an adjournment; (2) return of a bill during an intersession adjournment would result in a long delay in the final disposition of the bill attended by public uncertainty as to its status. Id. at 682-684. A significant exception to this holding was established in the Supreme Court's only other pocket veto decision, Wright v. United States. Addressing the first part of the Pocket Veto Case rationale, the Court held that the return of a bill may, in certain instances, be accomplished by delivery to an appropriate agent of the originating House:

> Nor was there any practical difficulty in making the return of the bill during the recess. The organization of the Senate continued and was intact. The Secretary of the Senate was functioning and was able to receive, and did receive, the bill. Under the constitutional act with reasonable promptitude upon the President's objections Provision [article I, section 5, paragraph 4] the Senate was required to reconvene in not more than three days and thus would be able to act with reasonable promptitude upon the President's objections. There is no greater difficulty in returning a bill to one of the two Houses when it is in recess during the session of Congress than in presenting a bill to the President by sending it to the White House in his temporary absence. Such a presentation is familiar practice. The bill is sent by a messenger and is received by the President. It is returned by a messenger, and why may it not be received by the accredited agent as the legislative body? To say that the President cannot return a bill when the House in which it originated is in recess during the session of Congress, and thus afford an opportunity for the passing of the bill over the President's objections, is to ignore the plainest practical considerations and by implying a requirement of an artificial formality to erect a barrier to the exercise of a constitutional right.

Id. at 589-90.

The five-day recess in this case was only two days longer than that considered in *Wright*. Moreover, the most significant portion of the recess, that which extended beyond the ten-day period for return of a bill, was only one day longer than that which occurred in *Wright*, and was actually within the maximum delay explicitly approved in *Wright*. As in the former case, the Senate continued in existence during the Christmas recess of 1970 and the Secretary of the Senate was available to receive messages from the President during the adjournment. There was no danger that the bill could not be reconsidered "with reasonable promptitude" should it be returned by the President during the adjournment. For these reasons, the mere fact that the Senate was not in session to physically receive the President's objections does not require the conclusion that the Congress had, by its adjournment, prevented the return of S. 3418.

The fact that the House of Representatives had not adjourned in the *Wright* case is also a distinction without a difference. Assuming that the conclusion of the foregoing paragraph is correct, it is difficult to see how the presence or absence of the nonoriginating House at the time of the return could affect our decision. To hold that a return veto is possible while the originating House alone is in brief recess but not when both Houses are in recess would embrace ritual at the expense of logic. As the foregoing discussion demonstrates, the present case falls within the exception — or, at least, within a logical extension of the exception — to the Pocket Veto Case established in *Wright*. Even if *Wright* were not applicable, however, appellants' reliance upon the Pocket Veto Case would be misplaced. The modern practice of Congress with respect to intrasession adjournments creates neither of the hazards — long delay and public uncertainty — perceived in the Pocket Veto Case. First of all, intrasession adjournments are much shorter than the intersession adjournment considered in the Pocket Veto Case. At the time of that decision, intersession adjournments of five or six months were still common. By contrast, only four intrasession adjournments in the history of the Congress have exceeded sixty days in duration. Of these, only two occurred in this century. . . .

More importantly, return of a bill during an intrasession adjournment, whatever its length, can no longer cause the public uncertainty envisioned in the Pocket Veto Case. Modern methods of communication make it possible for the return of a disapproved bill to an appropriate officer of the originating House to be accomplished as a matter of public record accessible to every citizen. The status of such a bill would be clear; it has failed to receive presidential approval but may yet become law if Congress, upon resumption of its deliberations, passes the bill again by a two-thirds majority. This state of affairs generates no more public uncertainty than does the return of a disapproved bill while Congress is in actual session. The only possible uncertainty about this situation arises from the absence of a definitive ruling as to whether an intrasession adjournment "prevents" the return of a vetoed bill. Hopefully, our present opinion eliminates that ambiguity.

NOTES AND QUESTIONS

1. *Standing.* One of the most important questions presented in Kennedy v. Sampson is the standing of a legislator or legislative body to bring such a challenge. How do the courts resolve this question? Consider the following comments from Judge Bork in dissent in a subsequent case raising almost the identical issues:

> The issue of standing is jurisdictional. If a court concludes that a party lacks standing, the court may not proceed to decide the merits of the suit. . . .
> It is thus an aspect of democratic theory. Questions of jurisdiction are questions of power, power not merely over the case at hand but power over issues and over other branches of government. Article III of the Constitution confers the "judicial Power of the United States" and limits that

power in several ways. Among the most important limitations is that expressed in section 2 of article III, confining our jurisdiction to "Cases" and "Controversies." The meaning of those terms, however, is decided by federal courts. It follows that judges can determine the extent of their own power within American government by how they define cases and controversies. It is for this reason that the proper definition of those terms is crucial to the maintenance of the separation of powers that is central to our constitutional structure.

"Standing" is one of the concepts courts have evolved to limit their jurisdiction and hence to preserve the separation of powers. A critical aspect of the idea of standing is the definition of the interests that courts are willing to protect through adjudication. A person may have an interest in receiving money supposedly due him under law. Courts routinely regard an injury to that interest as conferring upon that person standing to litigate. Another person may have an equally intensely felt interest in the proper constitutional performance of the United States government. Courts have routinely regarded injury to that interest as not conferring standing to litigate. The difference between the two situations is not the reality or intensity of the injuries felt but a perception that according standing in the latter case would so enhance the power of the courts as to make them the dominant branch of government. There would be no issue of governance that could not at once be brought into the federal courts for conclusive disposition. Every time a court expands the definition of standing, the definition of the interests it is willing to protect through adjudication, the area of judicial dominance grows and the area of democratic rule contracts. That is what is happening in this case. My disagreement with the majority, therefore, is about first principles of constitutionalism. . . .

The first problem with this court's doctrine of congressional standing is that, on the terms of its own rationale, the concept is uncontrollable. Congress is not alone in having governmental powers created or contemplated by the Constitution. This means that the vindication-of-constitutional-powers rationale must confer standing upon the President and the judiciary to sue other branches just as much as it does upon Congress. "Congressional standing" is merely a subset of "governmental standing." . . .

No avoidance of these implications is possible unless courts lay down fiats, resting upon no discernible principle, that arbitrarily limit those institutions whose members may vindicate constitutional and legal interests.

Barnes v. Kline, 759 F.2d 21, 44 (1985). The standing issue is also raised in Chapter 5.

2. *An absolute veto.* In effect, the pocket veto provides the executive with an absolute veto. Given our historical aversion to granting the executive such power, why is it granted within constitutional limits?

3. *The schedule of the modern Congress.* This decision recognizes the substantial technological changes that have occurred since the founding of the Republic and the fact that Congress now is a year-round operation. The practice of Congress is now to take a number of short intrasession

recesses. This practice, if not for the *Kennedy* decision, would result in more opportunities for pocket vetoes than offered in the past when Congress would work through a period of time and then recess or adjourn for a number of months. See generally Comment, The Veto Power and Kennedy v. Sampson; Burning a Hole in the President's Pocket, 69 Nw. U. L. Rev. 587 (1974). This logic was also followed in Barnes v. Kline, 759 F.2d 21 (D.C. Cir. 1985), which declared an intersession pocket veto unconstitutional. What would be the consequence of a pocket veto following the last session of a congressional term (between the adjournment of the session and the sitting of the new Congress)?

3. The Item Veto: A Special Power for Many State Executives

The governors of many of the nation's states possess the power to exercise vetoes on parts of a bill rather than the bill as a whole. This is known as the *item veto.* The term is inclusive, intended to cover the power to veto amounts of appropriations (the most typical), the language of appropriations, bills, or the language of non-appropriations bills (for example, in the state of Washington). The term also covers what is known as the *amendatory veto,* the power of the governor to condition the approval of a bill on the enactment by the legislature of recommended amendments. Each of these powers makes the executive a more significant player in the legislative process than the general veto power. Each of these powers also creates additional opportunities for court involvement in the legislative process. In this section, we explore each type of item veto. In recent years, insecurities about the federal budgeting process have renewed national interest in granting item veto power to the President. In the last subsection, we address a proposal for item veto power on the federal level.

a. Items of Appropriation

Most common of the item vetoes are those that permit the executive to veto an item of appropriation in an appropriation bill. This power is included in the constitutions of 43 states. Typical language allows a governor to approve an appropriation bill "in whole or in part," with the part approved becoming law and the part disapproved sent back to the legislature for override consideration.

Some state constitutions also authorize the executive to reduce an item of appropriation rather than to simply veto it. For example, the California Constitution authorizes the governor to "reduce or eliminate one or more items of appropriation while approving other portions of a bill." Art. 4, §10(e).

The granting to governors of item veto power over appropriation bills is a "reform" of the late 1800s. As two commentators have written about the advent of this grant of executive power:

> Three factors contributed to the proliferation of the gubernatorial item veto: the state's antilegislative bias; balanced budget requirements in forty-nine states; and state budget cycles.
>
> The most significant consideration is the fear of legislative excesses, manifested in the belief that state budgetary decisions ultimately should be made by an executive officer. Fear of irresponsible legislative actions fueled the initial push for the item veto in the late nineteenth century. According to one observer, state legislatures during this period were perceived . . . as being "corrupt, open to bribes for introducing private and special legislation," while governors were considered "less venal than legislators. Thus being the lesser of evils, trust ought to be given to governors to act as guardians of the purse against avaricious legislators."
>
> In general, the governor's power over the budget grew from 1900 to 1970 due to the popular perception that the executive branch was a more capable manager than the legislature. This view was rooted in the belief that the government should operate as a business with the governor as chief administrator. Gubernatorial power was further enhanced during the Depression era, in an effort to eliminate nonessential spending. Until Vietnam and Watergate shook the nation's confidence in the President, trust in executive responsibility remained strong. By the time legislatures reasserted themselves at the state and national levels, the item veto was an established gubernatorial power.
>
> Constitutional constraints on legislative action were closely tied to, and in part responsible for, the growth of the item veto. Limitations were placed on state borrowing. Prohibitions also barred a host of private, special, and local laws. State constitutions included detailed prohibitions on the enactment of private or local laws that attempted to fix the rate of interest, remit fines, penalties, or forfeitures, exempt property from taxation . . . and impose other restrictions that would be totally inappropriate for the federal Constitution. These constraints, by impeding the legislature's authority to pass laws and appropriate funds, further enhanced the governor's power over the budget.

Louis Fisher and Neal Devins, How Successfully Can the States' Item Veto Be Transferred to the President?, 75 Geo. L.J. 159, 178 (1986). Most of the passage above refers to the antilegislative bias in the states that motivated many changes in state constitutions during the late nineteenth and early twentieth centuries. The item veto, as noted, is also intended to effect balanced budget requirements by allowing the executive to bring appropriations in line with anticipated revenues. Also, in states with a biennial budget, this power, along with the power to impound funds, provides some flexibility to the executive in managing the state budget.

The possession of line item veto power over appropriation bills clearly provides the executive with additional power at the expense of the legislature. But whether such power results in fiscal restraint is open to debate.

State experience with item veto has been unquestionably mixed. Although some evidence supports the notion that the item veto can be a significant deficit reduction measure several studies call into question the item veto's effectiveness for reducing expenditures. Moreover, available evidence suggests that the item veto often functions as a partisan political tool and causes strife between the executive and legislative branches in state government.

The item veto has a reputation for saving money. A recent legislative analysis prepared by the American Enterprise Institute concluded that "governors have vetoed or reduced appropriations to achieve substantial savings." . . .

Opponents of the item veto, however, cite contrary examples and question the methodology utilized by proponents. . . .

Gubernatorial reductions may merely cancel spending that the legislature added because the governor possessed item veto authority. A study in Pennsylvania suggested, "When a legislator, even though opposed in principle to an appropriation, is reasonably certain that the governor will slice it down to more moderate size, he is tempted to bolster himself politically by voting large sums of money to a popular cause." Another author claimed that the item veto at the state level "encouraged legislators to please their constituents by voting for appropriations far in excess of anticipated revenues thus forcing the governor to make inevitable reductions and incur the wrath of interests adversely affected." In other words, the availability of an item veto allows legislators to shift more of the responsibility for the fiscal process to the executive.

Louis Fisher and Neal Devins, How Successfully Can the States' Item Veto Be Transferred to the President?, 75 Geo. L.J. 159, 182-84 (1986).

Another consequence of the item veto not referred to in the above passage is the threat to use the item veto to force policy changes in non-appropriation legislation. For example, a legislator may have a particular project in which he or she is interested. This interest is reflected in the budget as an item of appropriation. The threat of an item veto to such appropriation can make the legislator more pliant on other legislation desired by the executive. This, of course, enhances executive power over policy initiatives but not over the budget. For an analytical take of this proposition, see Maxwell L. Stearns, The Public Choice Case Against the Item Veto, 49 Wash. & Lee L. Rev. 385 (1992).

While, as noted above, 43 state constitutions grant executives the power to line item veto appropriation bills and, with some variations, the language is similar, there is considerable variation among states on the scope of the executive veto. As Professor Richard Briffault has written:

> These variations . . . seem to relate to differences among state supreme courts over questions of constitutional interpretation, and to differences in state institutional traditions.

Thus states have disagreed over how to define an appropriation and what constitutes an appropriations bill; whether a governor may veto items within an appropriation or must veto the entire lump sum; whether the governor may reduce as well as disallow an item; whether the governor may veto non-monetary items; whether the governor may veto conditions, provisos or restrictions on appropriations without vetoing the appropriation itself; and whether the governor may exercise the veto power in a manner which changes the policy the legislature intended to enact.

All these disputes have a common theme — how to assure the governor authority broad enough to consider and determine each item of appropriation separately without giving the governor unwarranted legislative power. In other words, how is the item veto and the power it gives to the governor to be integrated into the traditional concepts of the appropriate role of the executive and the legislature?

Richard Briffault, The Item Veto, 2 Emerging Issues in State Constitutional Law 85, 90-91 (1989).

The following two cases are illustrative of Professor Briffault's observations. Internal citations have been omitted except where particularly relevant.

State ex rel. Kleczka v. Conta
82 Wis. 2d 679, 264 N.W.2d 539 (1978)

The petitioners in this original action are Gerald D. Kleczka, a member of the Wisconsin Senate, and John C. Shabaz, a member of the Assembly. . . .

The principal respondent named in the petition is Martin J. Schreiber, Acting Governor (hereafter Governor) of the State of Wisconsin. . . .

Assembly Bill 664, as subsequently amended, was concurred in by the Senate on September 28, 1977. The enrolled bill was presented to the Governor on October 11, 1977. On that same day the Governor purported to exercise the partial-veto authority conferred upon him by art. V, sec. 10, of the Wisconsin Constitution. A message and a letter from the Governor was sent to the Assembly Chief Clerk on that same date. He stated that he had exercised his partial veto "to restore the check-off provision that existed in the original bill" (sec. 51) and exercised his partial veto "in Section 53 of the bill because the September 30, 1977, effective date is unnecessary to implement the law for the 1978 elections." . . .

Subsequent to the commencement of this action and following the date of oral arguments in this court, the legislature on January 24, 1978, acted on the Governor's partial veto, but failed to secure the necessary two-thirds vote to override the veto.

The petitioners' contentions are directed principally to the partial vetoes of the Governor of secs. 51 and 53 of the enrolled bill. Sec. 51 of the enrolled bill created sec. 71.095 of the Wisconsin Statutes to provide in part as follows:

(1) Every individual filing an income tax statement may designate that their income tax liability be increased by $1 for deposit into the Wisconsin Election Campaign Fund for the use of eligible candidates under s. 11.50.

Acting Governor Schreiber exercised his partial veto by lining out the words, "that their income tax liability be increased by," and the words, "deposit into." The section as changed by the partial veto reads:

> (1) Every individual filing an income tax statement may designate $1 for the Wisconsin Election Campaign Fund for the use of eligible candidates under s. 11.50.

It is conceded that the bill as enrolled would require taxpayers to "add on" to their tax liabilities the sum of $1 if they wished that sum to go to the campaign fund. As changed by the Governor's partial veto, a taxpayer instead elects to designate that the sum of $1 be "checked off" or expended from the state general funds for the purposes of the Election Campaign Fund.

The parties have stipulated that the change made in sec. 51 will result in approximately $600,000 in tax funds being expended directly for political purposes per annum. Under the bill as passed by the Legislature, only the sum which taxpayers agreed to have added to their tax liability would have been used for political purposes. Under the provisions of sec. 51 as partially vetoed, the sums used for political purposes will come out of general tax revenues.

The change in sec. 53 was made by the veto of the portion which provided:

> (1) Section 71.095 of the statutes, as created by this act, shall apply to all individual income tax returns for any calendar year or corresponding fiscal year which commences not more than 9 months preceding the effective date of this act and to each calendar year or corresponding fiscal year thereafter.

It is alleged by the Attorney General that the partial veto of sec. 53 accelerated the effective date of the bill by one year. . . .

The petitioners . . . contend that Bill 664 was not an appropriation bill and, therefore, not subject to the partial-veto provisions of art. V, sec. 10. The Attorney General, although he contends that the partial veto was unauthorized, acknowledges that Bill 664 was an appropriation bill within the meaning of the Constitution.

The petitioners also contend that, even were the bill held to be "returned" in accordance with the Constitution and even were it an appropriation bill, the vetoes attempted here were unauthorized by the Constitution, because the Governor may not, in the exercise of a partial veto, strike language from a bill unless it is severable and cannot strike from the bill provisos or conditions on an appropriation that were placed thereon by the Legislature. . . .

It is our conclusion that Enrolled Bill 664 was an appropriation bill. . . . We conclude that the portions stricken were severable from the enrolled bill; and corollary to the latter conclusion, we conclude that the bill as partially vetoed by the Governor and published by the Secretary of State was a complete, workable bill, which meets the requirements here-tofore stated by this court to be mandated by the Constitution. The portion approved by the Governor became effective upon publication by the Secretary of State.

We give attention to each contention in turn, considering first whether the bill was an appropriation bill in the terms of the Constitution.

The constitutional provision applicable is art. V, sec. 10. The Constitution as amended by the referendum of November 30, 1930, provides:

GOVERNOR TO APPROVE OR VETO BILLS; PROCEEDINGS ON VETO

SECTION 10 [as amended Nov. 1908 and Nov. 1930]. Every bill which shall have passed the legislature shall, before it becomes a law, be presented to the governor; if he approve, he shall sign it, but if not, he shall return it, with his objections, to that house in which it shall have originated, who shall enter the objections at large upon the journal and proceed to reconsider it. Appropri-ation bills may be approved in whole or in part by the governor, and the part approved shall become law, and the part objected to shall be returned in the same manner as provided for other bills. If, after such reconsideration, two-thirds of the members present shall agree to pass the bill, or the part of the bill objected to, it shall be sent, together with the objections, to the other house, by which it shall likewise be reconsidered, and if approved by two-thirds of the members present it shall become a law. But in all such cases the votes of both houses shall be determined by yeas and nays, and the names of the members voting for or against the bill or the part of the bill objected to, shall be entered on the journal of each house respectively. If any bill shall not be returned by the governor within six days (Sundays excepted) after it shall have been presented to him, the same shall be a law unless the legislature shall, by their adjournment, prevent its return, in which case it shall not be a law.

Under the Constitution only appropriation bills are susceptible to a partial veto. In the event Bill 664 was not an appropriation bill and not subject to a partial veto, the petitioners are correct and the Governor was not authorized to disapprove less than the whole of the bill. . . .

The petitioners concede that the bill as it left the Governor's hands was an appropriation bill, but they contend, properly, that it is not in that posture that the nature of a bill should be determined. The question is whether it was an appropriation bill when it was delivered to the Governor. They argue that the bill in its enrolled form as submitted to the Governor was not an appropriation bill.

Under the provisions of the enrolled bill, the sums added on to the taxpayers' liability and paid into the treasury are to be deposited to the general funds. The Secretary of Revenue is designated to certify the amount of money deposited in the general fund as the result of the add-on to tax liability. The amount determined under sec. 71.095, Stats., by the Secretary is then to be paid into the Wisconsin Election Campaign Fund annually, on

August 15, by the State Treasurer. From that fund, there is made a continuing appropriation of money as certified under sec. 71.095 to provide for payments to the candidates who qualify under sec. 11.50.

It is clear, from these provisions, that the bill as it went to the Governor authorized the expenditure of public moneys. The bill set apart a portion of the public funds for a public purpose — the financing of election campaigns. This meets the definitions of an appropriation bill. . . .

The words removed had the effect of replacing taxpayers' voluntary add-on to their personal tax liabilities the sum of $1 for political purposes, with an election by the taxpayer to direct that $1 be paid out of general funds and general tax revenues.

The additional charge to the general fund is estimated to be $600,000 per annum. This the petitioners claim created an appropriation where none existed before. Implicit in the petitioners' argument and explicit in the argument of the Attorney General is the additional argument that voluntary contributions were a proviso or condition upon which the appropriation depended and that such proviso or condition was ipso facto inseverable from the appropriation itself.

The petitioners acknowledge that the Legislature cannot, by a statement incorporated in the legislation, frustrate the Governor's partial-veto power by declaring that certain portions of a bill are inseverable. In that respect, the petitioners are correct. Severability, petitioners acknowledge, is the test of the partial-veto power. Petitioners concede that what is severable may be excised from the legislation by the Governor's partial veto.

The petitioners correctly assert that severability must be determined, not as a matter of form, but as a matter of substance. The brief of the petitioners argues that a partial veto which would make an appropriation where none existed before is not a severable change.

As stated above, we conclude that, for a Governor to exercise a partial veto, the bill must, as it comes to the Governor, contain an appropriation. The principal thrust of the petitioners is based on the assumption that this bill contained no appropriation when it reached the Governor. We have concluded that assumption is incorrect. The bill clearly provided for an appropriation of funds obtained by a voluntary add-on option afforded a taxpayer. Those funds were then appropriated for election purposes by the bill.

Hence, it is incorrect, under the facts, for the petitioners to assert that the bill as altered by the Governor created an appropriation where none existed before. The Governor's veto left the appropriation untouched. Rather, it affected the source from which the appropriated funds were to be derived. Accordingly, to conclude, as the petitioners would have us do, that this bill is inseverable because it created an appropriation where none existed before is patently incorrect.

Severability is indeed the test of the Governor's constitutional authority to partially veto a bill. . . . but the test of severability is that established by the Wisconsin court and not by courts which operate under a different constitution. . . .

Three major Wisconsin cases have discussed the power of the Governor to partially veto a bill under the authority of art. V, sec. 10. . . .

Each of these cases emphasizes that the power of the Governor to approve or disapprove a bill "in part" is a far broader power than that conferred upon Governors under the partial-veto provisions of most state constitutions. In most instances, the power of the Governor is confined to the excision of appropriations or items in an appropriation bill. . . .

We conclude that the test of severability has clearly and repeatedly been stated by this court to be simply that what remains be a complete and workable law. The power of the Governor to disassemble the law is coextensive with the power of the Legislature to assemble its provisions initially.

This conclusion in respect to severability is consistent with the Legislature's own declaration. In sec. 990.001(11), Stats., the Legislature stated, "The provisions of the statutes are severable. The provisions of any session law are severable. . . ."

While that legislative declaration is concerned primarily with the construction and effect of legislation which may be in part defective, it evinces a general legislative purpose to give force to portions of legislation which survive a constitutionally authorized nullification, whether that nullification be by the courts or by the Governor.

In the present case it is undisputed that what remained after the Governor's partial veto is a complete, entire, and workable law. As such, it is severable and reflects the proper exercise of the partial-veto power conferred on the Governor by the Constitution of the state.

In addition, the cases decided by this court have repeatedly pointed out that, because the Governor's power to veto is coextensive with the legislature's power to enact laws initially, a governor's partial veto may, and usually will, change the policy of the law. . . .

It should be borne in mind, of course, that the very section of the Constitution which gives to the Governor the authority to change policy by the exercise of a partial veto also gives the final disposition and resolution of policy matters to the Legislature. The Governor's changed policy can ultimately remain in effect only if the Legislature acquiesces in a partial veto by its refusal or failure to override the Governor's objections. . . .

There remains yet another facet of the authority of the Governor to exercise a partial-veto power that should be explored. It is urged by the petitioners and by the Attorney General that provisos and conditions of an appropriation may not be severed from the appropriation itself. It is argued that, even when a workable bill remains after the exercise of the partial veto, the fulfillment of that test alone does not make what remains a properly severable and independent bill. The position of the antagonists to the Governor's partial veto in this case is that, whenever an appropriation is made on the basis of a legislatively established proviso or condition, the provisos themselves may not be separately vetoed, but the entire appropriation, including the provisos, must be excised by the Governor.

In the instant case it is argued that the appropriation of moneys for political purposes was conditioned by the Legislature upon the voluntary contribution to be made by taxpayers and that proviso or condition is inseverable from the appropriation itself.

The conclusion urged by the petitioners and the Attorney General reasonably could be reached from the dicta of Wisconsin cases. We are satisfied, however, that those pronouncements are dicta only and, more importantly, have no relevance to interpretation of the partial-veto provisions of the Wisconsin Constitution. . . .

No provision of art. V, sec. 10, of the Constitution limits the Governor's authority to veto appropriations because of any legislatively imposed conditions. . . .

[T]he Acting Governor vetoed what is arguably a condition which the Legislature had placed on the appropriation. By so doing, he changed the policy of the law as envisaged by the Legislature. He caused the general fund to be charged with an obligation which the Legislature did not anticipate; and also, it is contended, he accelerated the effective date of the bill. These are policy changes, legislative in nature, which the Constitution authorized him to make.

The bill was an appropriation bill. What remained after the Governor's partial veto was a complete, entire, and workable bill. As such it was severable from the legislative package of the enrolled bill. The Acting Governor complied with the constitutional mandates by timely and appropriately messaging his objections to the house of the Legislature in which the bill originated. He made an appropriate return of the vetoed legislation as the Constitution contemplates it. We accordingly hold that Acting Governor Schreiber constitutionally exercised the power of partial veto as conferred upon governors of Wisconsin by art. V, sec. 10, of the Constitution. . . .

CONNOR T. HANSEN, J. (concurring in part, dissenting in part). . . .

I respectfully dissent from the holding of the majority that the power of partial veto, as exercised in this case, is a valid exercise of that authority.

In the Wisconsin Constitution, as in the federal constitution, the principle of separation of powers is nowhere expressly stated, but it is recognized as implicit in the provisions vesting the legislative, executive and judicial powers of the state in the respective branches of government. Our constitution provides for three branches of government, separate and coordinate, each supreme in its sphere and independent of the others. None may perform the functions or exercise the powers of another. This court has jealously guarded this concept, in the belief that an invasion of the province of one branch by another is an attack upon the constitutional foundation of the government itself, and in a sense, upon the liberty of our citizens. . . .

Article IV, section 1, of our constitution provides that "The legislative power shall be vested in a senate and an assembly." The constitutional role of the governor in the legislative process includes the power to convene special sessions of the legislature; to communicate with, and make recommendations to, the legislature; to direct the preparation of the financial budget; and to veto bills which have been passed by the legislature, Art. V, secs. 4 and 10, Wisconsin Constitution. . . . Nevertheless, the fundamental concept of Art. IV, sec. 1, is that the legislative power of this state is confined exclusively to the legislature. Unless we are prepared to abandon that concept—and I am not prepared to do so—then there must be some palpable limit to the power of the governor to rewrite, by the device of the partial veto, bills which have passed the legislature.

In recent years, partial vetoes have not only increased greatly in number; they have been applied to ever smaller portions of bills. Several years ago, an attempt was made to exercise the power so as to strike the digit "2" from a $25 million bonding authorization. Even this may not mark the limits of the use of the power. Advisors to a recent governor were reported to have considered striking the letter "t" from the word "thereafter" in order to alter the effective date of a liquor tax increase. Only the limitations on one's imagination fix the outer limits of the exercise of the partial veto power by incision or deletion by a creative person. At some point this creative negative constitutes the enacting of legislation by one person, and at precisely that point the governor invades the exclusive power of the legislature to make laws.

Long before the advent of the partial veto, the father of the doctrine of separation of powers, Baron de Montesquieu, warned that liberty would be endangered if the executive were to have the power of ordaining laws by his own authority or of amending what had been ordained by others, and he urged that the executive should have no part in legislating other than the privilege of rejecting what had been enacted by the legislature. I believe Montesquieu was correct. In the scheme of our constitution, the governor is to review the laws and not to write them. He is not, by careful and ingenious deletions, to effectively "write with his eraser" and to devise new bills which will become law unless disapproved by two-thirds of the legislators who are elected by the people of the state.

In principle, this is clear enough. What gives pause to the majority, I suspect, is the difficulty of applying these principles to concrete cases. . . . This is so because the exercise of the partial veto power by the executive shades into the powers of the legislature. As the *Sundby Case* recognized, every veto has both an affirmative and a negative ring about it. Every veto necessarily works some change of policy, and in a sense partakes of legislating. Here lies the difficulty the majority confronts in saying precisely where the proper sphere of the executive ends and that of the legislature begins.

The majority is rightfully wary of the elusive tests enunciated in some other jurisdictions. To hold that the exercise of the partial veto power may not have an "affirmative," "positive" or "creative" effect on legislation, or that the veto may not change the "meaning" or "policy" of a bill, as some courts elsewhere have done, would be to involve this court in disingenuous semantic games. While these tests may be appealing in the abstract, they are unworkable in practice. Every veto may be perceived in affirmative or negative terms, and as either conforming to or defying the general legislative intent, depending upon the observer's perspective. These tests are inescapably subjective. Without an objective point of reference, this court would be reduced to deciding cases upon its subjective assessment of the respective policies espoused by the legislature and the executive, an unseemly result which would foster uncertainty in the legislative process. More importantly, such a result would defeat its own purpose; the judicial department may no more assume the proper functions of the legislature, or interfere with their discharge, than may the governor.

Perhaps for this reason, the decisions of this court have steadily fashioned a standard which affords the governor virtually unlimited power to rework legislation by means of the partial veto. . . .

However, this writer is unable to find language in art. V, sec. 10, to support such a sweeping construction of the partial veto power, nor has attention been directed to authorities in this state or any other state which would suggest that such was the intent of the 1930 constitutional amendment which created that power. . . .

The standard approved today gives the governor wide, and for all practical purposes, unlimited, authority to exercise power reserved by the constitution to the legislature. In reality, the purported limitation that the remainder of any bill, after the exercise of a partial veto, must be a workable law, imposes little constraint upon such a usurpation of legislative power. It is difficult to envisage a governor deliberately exercising the partial veto power so as to produce a fragmentary or unworkable law. . . .

[T]he test stated by the majority affords no discernible basis for objection to such a veto, if the remainder of the bill is workable. Further, in the case before us, the legislature provided for the collection and disbursement of a voluntary payment by the taxpayer. By exercise of the partial veto power, the governor has effectively increased an appropriation by producing a charge on the general fund of an estimated $600,000 per annum. Under the test pronounced by the majority it therefore becomes unobjectionable to increase an appropriation by the exercise of the partial veto power.

Even more disturbingly, the standard adopted by the court poses no discernible obstacle to the use of deletions to produce a complete, entire and workable bill concerning a subject utterly unrelated to that of the bill as passed by the legislature. Might an appropriation for a gubernatorial commission be transformed to provide the governor with a second salary? In all probability we will not soon face such a question, but the clear lesson of experience is that we ought not discount such ingenuity. I am unable to identify, in the majority opinion, even an implicit obstacle to such an abuse of the veto power. I fear that the court may now have painted itself into a corner, and that a time may come when we regret having done so.

The original purposes of the partial veto power, and the language of this court's early decisions defining that power, suggest an alternative solution, a solution that, in my opinion, would be consistent with the purposes of the partial veto power, provide a neutral benchmark from which the actions of the governor might be measured, and also preserve the prerogatives of the legislature. . . .

The partial veto power was . . . directed toward the legislative practice of uniting in a single bill various proposals, each of which would have constituted a complete and workable bill in itself.

Prior to the constitutional amendment, the improper joinder of such proposals prevented the governor from dealing separately with each "part" which would otherwise have constituted a separate proposal. The partial veto provisions gave the governor power to unpack omnibus appropriation bills, and to pass separately upon each of the constituent parts which, if not for the practice of jumbling bills together, would have been enacted individually, and would have constituted a complete, entire and workable bill.

The governor's power to dismantle an appropriations bill was made as extensive as the legislative's power to construct such a bill from independent proposals capable of separate enactment. . . .

The power thus conferred is not a power to reduce a bill to its single phrases, words, letters, digits and punctuation marks. Rather the partial veto power should be exercised only as to the individual components, capable of separate enactment, which have been joined together by the legislature in an appropriation bill. That is, the portions stricken must be able to stand as a complete and workable bill.

Also, as stated by the majority, the portions of a bill approved by the governor must constitute a complete, entire, and workable law. However, I do not consider this "limitation" to say anything which is not implicitly true of every legislative enactment. Any enactment, whether passed by the legislature and approved by the governor, or created by use of the partial veto power, will fail if it is fragmentary, patently incomplete, or incapable of execution.

The approach here set forth would effectively define the limits of the constitutional role of the governor. He would be able to veto independent elements of multisubject appropriation bills, and would in most cases be unable to effectively add elements to the bills enacted by the legislature. His veto would be directed to portions of an appropriation bill which were grammatically and structurally distinct, and he would not be able to deal individually with numbers or words, or single digits or letters.

Equally important, this standard would be capable of evenhanded and predictable application, and this court would not be required to mediate policy disagreements between the two other coordinate branches of our government. Most important, this approach would protect the prerogatives reserved to the legislature by the constitution and would fulfill the responsibility of this court to determine when the exclusive territory of one of our independent branches has been invaded by another. . . .

There can be no question that the partial vetoes presently before the court do not meet the standard herein set forth. The governor partially vetoed section 51 of the bill as passed by the legislature by striking the words "that their income tax liability be increased by," and the words "deposit into." There is no method by which these portions can be said to constitute an independent legislative proposal capable of separate enactment, and I would therefore hold that the governor has exceeded the limits of the power conferred upon him by the partial veto provision, and has improperly assumed power reserved to the legislature.

State of New Mexico ex rel. Sego v. Kirkpatrick
86 N.M. 359, 524 P.2d 975 (1974)

We are here concerned with vetoes and attempted vetoes of certain language contained in the General Appropriations Act of 1974, commonly and hereinafter referred to as House Bill 300. In accomplishing these vetoes and attempted vetoes, the Governor was acting under the authority vested and claimed to be vested in him by Art. IV, §22, Constitution of New Mexico which provides:

> Every bill passed by the legislature shall, before it becomes a law, be presented to the governor for approval. If he approves, he shall sign it, and deposit it with the secretary of state; otherwise, he shall return it to the house in which it originated, with his objections, which shall be entered at large upon the journal; and such bill shall not become a law unless thereafter approved by two-thirds of the members present and voting in each house by yea and nay vote entered upon its journal. Any bill not returned by the governor within three days, Sundays excepted, after being presented to him, shall become a law, whether signed by him or not, unless the legislature by adjournment prevent such return. Every bill presented to the governor during the last three days of the session shall be approved by him within twenty days after the adjournment and shall be by him immediately deposited with the secretary of state. Unless so approved and signed by him such bill shall not become a law. *The governor may in like manner approve or disapprove any part or parts, item or items, of any bill appropriating money,* and such parts or items approved shall become a law, and such as are disapproved shall be void unless passed over his veto, as herein provided. (As amended September 15, 1953.)

[Emphasis added.] The disapproval by the Governor of an item or part of a bill under this authority is commonly referred to as a "line item veto."

However, the word "line" does not appear in the constitutional language conferring this authority, and the use thereof in relation to a veto under this authority is misleading and has caused some confusion. . . .

Petitioner is a citizen, an elector, a taxpayer, a State Senator, a member of the Senate Finance and Rules Committee, and a member of the Legislative Finance Committee. By failing to predicate our holding as to standing on one or more of these facts, we in no way suggest that one or more thereof would not be sufficient to give petitioner standing in these proceedings. We simply elect to confer standing on the basis of the importance of the public issues involved. . . .

We shall next consider the remaining seven challenged vetoes. However, before undertaking an individual consideration of these challenged vetoes, a resolution, insofar as necessary, as to what is meant by the following quoted language from Art. IV, §22 . . . would be helpful, since all of these vetoes and attempted vetoes were accomplished pursuant to the authority vested in the Governor by this language:

> . . . The governor may . . . disapprove any part or parts, item or items, or any bill appropriating money, and such parts or items . . . as are disapproved shall be void unless passed over his veto. . . .

The legislative power of the State of New Mexico is vested in the Legislature. Article IV, §1, Constitution of New Mexico. Except for interest or other payments on the public debt, money shall be paid out of the treasury of the State only upon appropriations made by the Legislature, and every law making an appropriation shall distinctly specify the sum appropriated and the object to which it is to be applied. Article IV, §30, Constitution of New Mexico. The supreme executive power of the State is vested in the Governor, whose principal function, insofar as legislatively enacted law is concerned, is to faithfully execute these laws. Article V, §4, Constitution of New Mexico. He does, however, have the power to exercise veto control over the enactments of the Legislature to the extent that this power or authority is vested in him by Art. IV, §22, supra. As to bills appropriating money, he clearly has the power to veto a "part or parts" or "item or items" thereof. The Legislature may not properly abridge that power by subtle drafting of conditions, limitations or restrictions upon appropriations, and the Governor may not properly distort legislative appropriations or arrogate unto himself the power of making appropriations by carefully striking words, phrases or sentences from an item or part of an appropriation.

What is meant by "part or parts" and "item or items" in the context and manner in which these terms appear in the above quoted language from Art. IV, §22 . . . and what is the nature and purpose of the veto power conferred upon the Governor by this section of our constitution? . . .

[T]he purpose or purposes for the inclusion of the terms "part or parts," "item or items" and "parts or items" in our Constitution were to extend or enlarge the partial veto power thereby conferred beyond the partial veto power conferred by the constitutions of other states wherein that power is limited to (1) items of appropriation, and (2) to general appropriation bills. However, the extension or enlargement of the partial veto power to cover (1) bills of general legislation, which contain incidental items of appropriation, as well as general appropriation bills, and (2) to "items or parts" thereof in addition to "items of appropriation," does not mean there are no limitations on the partial veto of bills appropriating money.

The power of partial veto is the power to disapprove. This is a negative power, or a power to delete or destroy a part or item, and is not a positive power, or a power to alter, enlarge or increase the effect of the remaining parts or items. It is not the power to enact or create new legislation by selective deletions. Thus, a partial veto must be so exercised that it eliminates or destroys the whole of an item or part and does not distort the legislative intent, and in effect create legislation inconsistent with that enacted by the Legislature, by the careful striking of words, phrases, clauses or sentences.

We now turn our attention to the challenged vetoes. We shall consider them in the order in which they were presented and argued by the parties in their respective briefs.

The Legislature unconditionally appropriated for the State Planning Office the sum of $324,800 from the State's general fund and $712,800 from Federal funds. This appropriation of both State and Federal funds in the total amount of $1,037,600 has not been questioned. It was followed by a contingent appropriation to this office of $150,000, which was stated as follows:

> In addition to the above appropriation, there is appropriated the sum of $150,000 from the general fund for the purpose of saving harmless the state planning office from loss of federal funds available for continuing the present operations of the office. ~~This contingent appropriation shall be disbursed only upon certification in writing by the state planning officer, approved by the director of the department of finance and administration, that federal funds to continue the agency's operation are not available; provided, however, that no funds shall be disbursed from this appropriation which would allow an operating budget greater than 1,037,600.~~

The language shown as stricken or lined out in this and in the hereinafter quoted portions of House Bill 300 are the portions purportedly vetoed by the Governor. He gave as his reasons for this particular veto:

> . . . This language would have had the effect of negating the contingent appropriation made [in the first quoted sentence] in that no part of the contingent appropriation could be utilized if any federal funds continued to be available to the Planning Office. I do not believe that it was the intent of the legislature to so restrict this contingent appropriation.

It is plain to us that the Legislature placed a very explicitly worded contingency upon the disbursement of this appropriation and a very explicitly worded limiting or restrictive proviso, provision or condition upon the amount of funds from this appropriation which could be disbursed. We do not question the sincerity of the Governor's effort to evaluate the intent of the Legislature, and we do not purport to know upon what he based this evaluation. However, as already stated, we find the language to be very clear, and we have no reason to believe the Legislature meant something other than what is plainly expressed in its language. . . .

We have heretofore held that the Legislature has the power to affix reasonable provisions, conditions or limitations upon appropriations and upon the expenditure of the funds appropriated. The Governor may not distort, frustrate or defeat the legislative purpose by a veto of proper legislative conditions, restrictions, limitations or contingencies placed upon an appropriation and permit the appropriation to stand. He would thereby create new law, and this power is vested in the Legislature and not in the Governor. Therefore, the attempted veto was invalid. . . .

The next challenged veto consisted of striking language from a conditional or contingent appropriation to the State Racing Commission. This contingent appropriation and the portions thereof purportedly vetoed, follow:

> ~~In the event the state scientific laboratory cannot provide~~ necessary chemical tests requiring specialized equipment, an additional 58,000 is hereby appropriated to the commission ~~to contract for such services.~~

The Governor gave the following reasons for his attempt to veto the stricken language:

> . . . The legislature was evidently concerned with the over-all ability of our Racing Commission to detect small quantities of drugs which may affect the stamina or speed of a race horse. The appropriation of an additional 58,000 was made to up-grade the type of chemical tests to be conducted. More advanced methods of testing will of course cost additional money. House Memorial 10 requests the Racing Commission to consider the State Police laboratory as the laboratory for such tests. House Bill 300 indicates consideration should be given to the use of the new state scientific laboratory. The veto of this language will give the Racing Commission the flexibility of choosing the laboratory which will best serve the need of the people of this State.

Obviously the Governor was endeavoring to substitute his judgment for that of the Legislature as to how to best spend the 58,000 appropriated for chemical tests. Regardless of whether or not his judgment in this regard is better than that of the Legislature, the fact remains it was for the Legislature to determine the condition or contingency under which the Racing Commission could spend this appropriation for contract services. . . .

We also observe that this effort to distort and frustrate the legislative purpose, by striking portions of a complete and readily understandable sentence, is an attempt to appropriate funds for an uncertain purpose by grammatically incorrect language.

The next challenged veto relates to the appropriation for the State Personnel Board. This appropriation was in the amount of 688,800, but was subject to the following limitation which the Governor undertook to veto:

> ~~None of the above appropriation shall be spent for promulgating or filing rules, policies or plans which have significant financial impact or would require significant future appropriations to maintain without prior specific legislative approval.~~

The reasons assigned by the Governor in his executive message for this attempted veto were:

> . . . This is an attempt to place substantive law in House Bill 300. In addition it would severely limit the discretionary powers of the State Personnel Board. Opinions of the Attorney General indicate that requiring legislative approval of the promulgation of rules for executive agencies violates the separation of powers provision of our State Constitution. I have the assurance of the State Personnel Board that they will not take any action which will have a significant effect upon State expenditures without placing a delayed date on such action in order to give the legislature ample time to consider such action. . . .

. . . The Legislature, which has the power and is charged with the responsibility of appropriating State money, is certainly concerned with matters which would have a significant financial impact upon or require significant future appropriations of State funds, and may properly limit the expenditure of appropriated funds for uses which will have such impact or require such future appropriations.

This veto must fail for the same reasons recited for the failure of the previously discussed attempted vetoes.

The next veto which has been challenged is concerned with an appropriation of 4,000 to the Construction Industries Commission for the purpose of establishing a revolving fund for the purchase and resale of literature. The Governor in no way disturbed the appropriation or the fact that "it shall be used only for the purpose of establishing a revolving fund to be used for the purchase and resale of literature." His veto went only to the following language:

> ~~There shall be an amount of 4,000 to the credit of the fund at the end of each fiscal year.~~

The Governor gave as his reason for his veto:

> The language vetoed . . . would have prohibited the Construction Indus-
> tries Commission from having an inventory of literature at the end of the
> fiscal year. I do not believe that the legislature desired such a rigid restriction.
> Rather I believe that the purpose of this provision was for the Commission to
> maintain a revolving fund whose balance at the end of the fiscal year would
> be 4,000. This would include cash, receivables and inventory on hand. I will
> instruct this Commission to accomplish this purpose.

Respondents now contend, and we believe correctly, that the Governor's
action did not change the purpose for which the revolving fund was established. We are unable to agree with the position of petitioner that the language deleted by the Governor "thereby purportedly authorized the
expenditure of 4,000 for other than the creation of a revolving fund."
This appears to us to be a futile attempt to create an issue or find a
difference between the positions of the Legislature and the Governor,
when in fact there is no such issue or difference. This being so, the veto
should stand.

The two challenged vetoes we now consider relate to each other and
represent perhaps the greatest divergence in views of the parties as to
the constitutional powers vested in the Governor by Art. IV, §22. . . .

The Governor sought to veto the qualifying prepositional phrase, consisting of five words, to Subsection G, Section 3 — General Provisions — of
House Bill 300:

> ~~In categories wherein specifically authorized,~~ the department of finance
> and administration may approve increases in budgets of state agencies
> whose actual revenue from sources other than the general fund and unre-
> verted and unencumbered balances exceed appropriations made in the
> General Appropriation Act of 1974. Such actual revenues exclusive of shared
> revenue are hereby appropriated. In approving such budget increases, the
> department shall advise the legislature through its officers and appropriate
> committees in writing of the conditions under which the increased budget is
> approved and the expenditures authorized together with justification for the
> adjustments.

The Governor also struck the following language from the appropriations made under nine separately designated categories:

> ~~The department of finance and administration may approve budget
> increases in agencies in this category pursuant to Section 3, subsection G
> of this act.~~

Comparable language was also included in that portion of the vetoed
language from the "Higher Education" category, which language shall
hereinafter be quoted and discussed.

Since these ten categories, including that of Higher Education, do not constitute all the categories contained in House Bill 300 and do not include all the State agencies to which appropriations were made, the effect of these attempted vetoes was to conditionally appropriate additional funds, or at least authorize their appropriation, to the agencies not included in the ten stated categories. Respondents deny this was the effect of these attempted vetoes, and assert that, even if the effect thereof be so construed, the Governor was acting within his authority in so doing. We disagree. As above stated, the power of partial veto is a power to disapprove and to thereby delete or destroy a part or item, and it is not the positive power to alter, enlarge or increase appropriations by enacting legislation through the device of selective deletions. These attempted vetoes were constitutionally invalid. . . .

The final veto which has been challenged and with which we are here concerned was the striking by the Governor of the following language from the category of Higher Education:

~~In the event that actual revenues to state agencies in this category exceed the amounts appropriated from:~~
~~1. federal finds; or~~
~~2. other state funds in the form of revenues received in the sixty third fiscal year; or~~
~~3. other state funds in the form of receipts, earnings or balances from bond issue proceeds; or~~
~~4. other state funds in the form of receipts, or balances resulting from acts of the 1974 legislative session; or~~
~~5. other state funds in the form of scholarships, gifts, donations, private endowments or other gratuities received from an outside source; or~~
~~6. other state funds in the form of increased income from auxiliary activities;~~
~~the department of finance and administration may approve the expenditure of such excess funds received pursuant to Section 3, subsection G of this act. Provided, that the department of finance and administration may approve the temporary use of balances which shall be restored to the original amount prior to the close of the 63rd fiscal year.~~

The Governor gave as his reason for striking this language:

Article XI, Section 13 of the New Mexico Constitution provides that the legislature shall provide for the control and management of each of the State's educational institutions by a board of regents. The effect of [the vetoed language] would be to cause confusion and to severely limit the flexibility of the boards of regents in the control and management of the institutions. . . .

As to the authority of the Governor to veto this language under his partial veto power, we are of the opinion that this was a proper exercise of his power. This item or part of House Bill 300 related solely to Higher Education and to an attempt on the part of the Legislature to authorize additional appropriations to or expenditures by the agencies in this category of actual revenues, in the event these revenues should exceed the amounts appropriated from the six numbered and named funds and the Department of Finance and Administration should approve. However, these additional appropriations or expenditures were conditioned upon or limited by the provisions that "the department of finance and administration may approve the temporary use of balances which shall be restored to the original amount prior to the close of the 63rd fiscal year."

This item or part of House Bill 300 stands as a separate and distinct conditional and provisional appropriation or authorization to expend funds, and the veto thereof operated to delete or destroy it. The deletion or destruction of this item or part does not alter the effect of the remaining parts or items, except to the extent that striking or removing a part always effects a change in the whole. . . .

The final matter to be considered in these proceedings is respondent's contention that "a finding that the governor's veto authority has been unconstitutionally applied nullifies the Appropriation Bill [House Bill 300] as a whole." Respondents cite no authority for this contention, and we are not impressed with their arguments in support thereof. An unconstitutional veto must be disregarded and the bill given the effect intended by the Legislature. . . .

NOTES AND QUESTIONS

1. *The decision's impact.* What is the impact of each of these decisions on their state's legislative process? How can a legislature protect itself against a decision such as *Kleczka*?

2. *Think of a judicial standard.* Can you think of a standard by which a court can evaluate the validity or invalidity of an item veto?

b.   Sections of Bills: The State of Washington

Article 3, §12 of the Constitution of the State of Washington provides its governors with one of the most unique item veto powers: that of applying the item veto to nonappropriation bills.

> If any bill presented to the governor contains several sections or appropriation items, he may object to one or more sections or appropriation items while approving other portions of the bill: *Provided* that he may not object to less than an entire section except that if the section contain one or more items he may object to any such appropriation item or items. In case of

objection . . . the section or sections, appropriation item or items, so objected to, shall not take effect unless passed over the governor's objection. . . .

Such provision broadly expands the legislative power of the governor. How broad do you think this power is? Review the 1982 amendments to the Voting Rights Act of 1965 set forth in Chapter 2. Assume that this is a state bill before the Governor of Washington. What could he do to this bill? The scope of such power is the subject of the following case. Internal citations have been omitted except where particularly relevant.

State Motorcycle Dealers Association v. The State of Washington
111 Wash. 2d 667, 763 P.2d 442 (1988)

Facts of Case

The 62nd amendment to the Constitution of the State of Washington sets forth the veto power of the Governor. It provides that a governor "may not object to less than an entire section" of a non-appropriation bill. Const. art. 3, §12 (amend. 62). We hold that the 62nd Amendment means what it says, and that the Governor's vetoes of less than entire sections of the Motorcycle Dealers' Franchise Act (a nonappropriation bill), enacted at the 1985 regular session, are void.

In 1985 the Legislature passed . . . the Motorcycle Dealers' Franchise Act. The act as passed by the Legislature contained 15 numbered sections and many more numbered and lettered subsections. The purpose of the act is to regulate relations between motorcycle dealers and motorcycle manufacturers.

On May 21, 1985, Governor Booth Gardner vetoed certain of the language in sections 3(2), 3(8), 3(16), 4(1)(a), 4(1)(b), 4(1)(c), 4(1)(g), 4(7), 4(11), 4(17), 4(18), 4(20), 4(21), 4(22), 4(24), 5(4), 5(5), 8(1), 8(2), and 10, and vetoed all of sections 6, 7, 11 and 12. As partially vetoed, the bill became law (RCW 46.94) on July 28, 1985. The Legislature took no action to override the vetoes. . . .

A single issue is dispositive. . . .

Under Const. art. 3, §12 (amend. 62), were the Governor's vetoes of parts of numbered sections of the Motorcycle Dealers' Franchise Act valid? . . .

Conclusion

We answer the question posed by this issue in the negative. Under the veto powers clause of the constitution in its present form (Const. art. 3, §12

(amend. 62)), gubernatorial vetoes of less than entire sections of nonappropriation bills are void.

Before the 62nd Amendment was adopted, the veto powers clause of the
constitution, Const. art. 3, §12, provided that the Governor "may object to
one or more sections or items." . . .

In the 1950's a new trend in the use of gubernatorial partial vetoes
emerged, and then in the 1960's and thereafter that trend escalated. This
resulted in part from the decisions of this court in Cascade Tel. Co. v. State
Tax Comm'n, 176 Wash. 616, 30 P.2d 976 (1934) (holding that a "section" in
the original Const. art. 3, §12 would be construed to mean any portion of a
bill with separate, distinct and independent subject matter), and State ex
rel. Ruoff v. Rosellini, 55 Wash. 2d 554, 348 P.2d 971 (1960) (holding that an
"item" under original Const. art. 3, §12 was not limited to matters in an
appropriation bill). This trend peaked in about 1971-72 when the then
Governor exercised 149 partial vetoes on bills passed by the 42nd Legislature, 123 of which removed less than an entire section from nonappropriation bills, and 26 of which removed less than an entire item from
appropriation bills.

In response to the greatly expanded use of the partial veto, the voters
were asked to approve the placement of curbs on this power in the state
constitution. The proposed changes were submitted to them in 1974 as
Senate Joint Resolution 140. The "Statement for" the constitutional amendment in the Official Voters Pamphlet made clear what was intended:

Washington is the only state in the nation in which the Governor exercises practically unlimited power to remove portions from laws passed by
the Legislature. This "item veto" power has been interpreted by recent
Governors to apply to any element of a bill down to a single word.

It empowers our Governors to act in effect as an unseparated third house
of the Legislature to alter measures substantially prior to signing them into
law. This is contrary to the grant of authority allowed our nation's Presidents under the Federal Constitution — which is to reject entire pieces of
legislation by veto, not to change them.

*SJR 140 is a moderate compromise proposal passed with bipartisan support. It
will not completely eliminate this unparalleled power, but limit it to the veto of
sections of bills as well as entire bills, and even provides that budget bills would still
be subject to the item veto.* (Italics ours.) SJR 140 was adopted by the voters
with some 498,745 votes being cast in favor of what is now Amendment 62
to the Constitution of the State of Washington. . . .

The amendment wrought three things. First, it limited use of the item
veto to appropriation bills. Second, it added a new express prohibition
against partially vetoing anything less than "an entire section" of a nonappropriation bill. And third, it provided the Legislature with authority to
reconvene itself into extraordinary session within 45 days after adjournment to override vetoes. The case now before us concerns the second of
these three changes, the Governor's veto power over entire sections of nonappropriation bills.

All of the arguments supporting the Governor's vetoes of less than full sections of the bill in question in this case boil down to a single conclusion—that when the people wrote into the constitution the limitation that the Governor "may not object to less than an entire section" of a nonappropriation bill, what they really meant was that the Governor may object to less than an entire section of such a bill! To adopt this reasoning would skew the state constitution off the course set by the people and violate the basic constitutional precepts that the constitution means what it says, and when it is not ambiguous there is nothing for the courts to construe.

Even were we to consider the 62nd Amendment ambiguous, which it is not, it was directly enacted by the voters and must therefore be read "' . . . as the average informed lay voter would read it.'" There is no reasonable way that "entire section" in the 62nd Amendment could have been read by an informed lay voter as meaning "part of a section."

The importance of the case before us is that it deals directly with one of the cardinal and fundamental principles of the American constitutional system, both state and federal: the separation of powers doctrine. "It has been declared that the division of governmental powers into executive, legislative, and judicial represents probably the most important principle of government declaring and guaranteeing the liberties of the people, and preventing the exercise of autocratic power, and that it is a matter of fundamental necessity, and is essential to the maintenance of a republican form of government." In this same connection, it is also the law that "American courts are constantly wary not to trench upon the prerogatives of other departments of government or to arrogate to themselves any undue powers, lest they disturb the balance of power; and this principle has contributed greatly to the success of the American system of government and to the strength of the judiciary itself."

In the opinion of the people of the State of Washington, the balance of power between the executive and legislative branches of government had gotten out of kilter, and they reacted directly and forcefully to restore that balance when they adopted the 62nd Amendment. By our opinion herein, we honor the balance of power between the executive and legislative branches that the people struck by adopting the 62nd Amendment, and we will not trench upon that balance under the guise of "interpretation" or "construction." . . .

It must be conceded that in the past this court has been less than entirely clear or consistent in favoring our governors with guidelines as to what governors constitutionally can and cannot veto. Originally, this court ruled that the *affirmative-negative* test was to be used. Under that test, the Governor could only exercise the partial veto power in a negative or destructive way, i.e., the veto could only be used to prevent some provision from becoming law, but could not be used to add a new or different result from that which the Legislature intended. That test was formulated about 1910 and last applied in 1980 when it was used to uphold the veto of an election provision in a bill creating judgeships. Then in 1984, the court entirely abandoned the test, declaring that it had "outlived its usefulness," was subjective, unworkable and that no one could safely predict whether any given partial veto would be upheld or struck down. As the court also explained when it abandoned the affirmative-negative test, it "is an intrusion into the legislative branch, contrary to the separation of powers doctrine, and substitutes judicial judgment for the judgment of the legislative branch."

Another test used by this court in the past to determine the validity of partial vetoes to nonappropriation bills is *the separate subject test*, also mentioned above. Under that test, the focus of the veto is on the subject matter vetoed, with the veto being upheld if the portion vetoed contained separate, distinct and independent subject matter. This test is every bit as vague and uncertain as the affirmative-negative test. As one commentator who recently analyzed this issue recommends:

> Just as it abandoned the affirmative-negative test, the court should abandon the separate subject matter test for a section. Both tests have been relied on when the court has apparently not been comfortable with the constitutional allocation of powers, and the application of either test shifts the constitutional balance of legislative power. Moreover, the separate subject matter test is just as flawed in practical terms as the affirmative-negative test. It is equally difficult to apply and is no more predictable. . . .

It is this "separate subject" test which the trial court applied to uphold some of the vetoes of less than full sections of the bill in this case. . . .

We conclude that there is no longer valid reason to perpetuate an outmoded subjective test like this that renders predictability virtually impossible. When this court recently discarded the "affirmative-negative" test after many years of frustration on the part of all concerned, it leveled a number of criticisms at the test. Each of those criticisms is equally applicable to the "separate subject" test. The "separate subject" test too has outlived its usefulness because it too is "unworkable and subjective," with "no standards to predict" whether any given partial veto will be upheld or struck down; and it "is an intrusion into the legislative branch, contrary to the separation of powers doctrine, and substitutes judicial judgment for the judgment of the legislative branch." . . .

We now decline to continue to use either of the subjective semantic tests this court has seen fit to resort to in the past. They are no longer necessary or justified. The 62nd Amendment obviates the need for either of those artificial tests where, as here, vetoes of parts of nonappropriation bills are concerned. Henceforth, should a governor in such situations wish to veto anything in any section, the governor should veto the "entire section" containing the material considered to be objectionable; then the Legislature may or may not attempt to override the gubernatorial veto as it deems fit. . . .

For the foregoing reasons, it is necessary to void all of the Governor's vetoes of less than an entire section of the bill before us.

c. Amendatory Veto

The constitutions of a number of states grant to their executives the power to formally condition the approval of bills on the adoption by the legislature of executive recommended amendments. Typical of this power is Article 4, §9(e) of the Constitution of the State of Illinois:

> The Governor may return a bill together with specific recommendations for change to the house in which it originated. The bill shall be considered in the same manner as a vetoed bill but the specific recommendations may be accepted by a record vote of a majority of the members elected to each house. Such bills shall be presented again to the Governor and if he certifies that such acceptance conforms to his specific recommendation, the bill shall become law. If he does not so certify, he shall return it as a vetoed bill to the house in which it originated.

A governor always has the power to tell a legislature, either before or after the passage of a bill, that he will not approve the bill without certain amendments. What does the above provision from the Illinois Constitution add to this power? Is it just a question of shifting the formal burden for killing legislation from the executive to the legislature? Consider the following ruling by the Speaker of the Illinois House of Representatives in response to a motion by a bill's sponsor that certain recommendations of the governor be accepted.

> ... The Governor's specific recommendations for change with respect to House Bill 1867 change the fundamental purpose of this Bill and made substantial and expansive changes contrary to the Illinois Supreme Court decisions. ... After careful consideration of the issue, the Chair rules that with respect to his veto of House Bill 1867, the Governor has exceeded the scope of his authority, granted to him under Article IV, section 9e of the Illinois Constitution of 1970, to return a bill with specific recommendations for change. Therefore, Mr. Kulas's motion which incorporates the Governor's specific recommendations for change is out of order.

Quoted in Kirk W. Dillard, The Amendatory Veto Revisited: How Far Can the Governor's Magic Constitutional Pen Reach?, July 1988 Ill. Bar J. 598, 602.

In most instances the scope of the amendatory veto power will be determined through the political processes, as illustrated above. Sometimes, if the legislature likes the proposed amendments, it may not be so protective of its prerogatives. In such instances the courts may be requested to rule on the propriety of particular amendatory vetoes.

People ex rel. Klinger v. Howlett
50 Ill. 2d 242, 278 N.E.2d 84 (1972)

JUSTICE SCHAEFER delivered the opinion of the court. . . . [Internal citations have been omitted except where particularly relevant.]

On October 29, 1971, this court granted leave to file an original petition for mandamus to compel the respondent Auditor of Public Accounts to process vouchers and issue warrants in connection with Senate Bills 1195, 1196, and 1197, passed by both houses in the 77th General Assembly. These bills are also identified as "Public Acts 77—1656, 77—1657 and 77—1658." They relate to financial assistance for nonpublic school education. The respondent answered, denying the constitutionality of the bills. . . .

The briefs of the parties have discussed the validity of the bills under the first amendment to the constitution of the United States and under the article I, section 3, and article X, section 3 of the 1970 constitution of Illinois. Issues were also discussed as to the proper interpretation of authority given to the Governor, under section 9(e) of article IV of the constitution of 1970, to return a bill passed by the General Assembly with his "specific recommendations for change." . . .

The three bills were passed by the Senate on June 2, 1971, and by the House on June 22, 1971. By messages dated September 10, 1971, the Governor, stating that he was acting pursuant to the authority vested in him under article IV, section 9(e) of the constitution of 1970, returned each bill with the recommendation that the title of each bill be amended and that everything in each bill after the enacting clause be stricken and entirely new textual material be substituted therefore. On October 14, 1971, a motion to accept the Governor's recommendations was adopted by the Senate and a similar motion was adopted by the House of Representatives on October 28, 1971. On that date the Governor certified that the acceptance of the General Assembly conformed to his specific recommendations for change. . . .

Senate bills 1195, 1196 and 1197 were passed on October 28, 1971, and they became law when the Governor certified them pursuant to article IV, section 9(e) on October 28, 1971. But under section 10 of article IV they are not effective until July 1, 1972, because they were passed after June 30 and the legislature did not fix an earlier effective date.

What has been said is sufficient to dispose of the issues that are before us in this case, and ordinarily we would say no more. It has been pointed out, however, that there are several other bills adopted by the 77th General Assembly with respect to which the Governor has made specific recommendations for changes under section 9(e) of article IV. This fact prompts us to observe that the scope of the Governor's authority under that section has not been clearly stated either in the constitution itself or in the committee reports or debates in the constitutional convention. . . .

Our examination of the records of the Convention shows that the following terms were used to describe the kinds of "specific recommendations for change" that were contemplated: "corrections"; "precise corrections"; "technical flaws"; "simple deletions"; "to clean up the language." In response to the following question put by Delegate Netsch, however, "Then was it the Committee's thought that the conditional veto would be available only to correct technical errors?" a committee member answered, "No, Ma'am."

Upon the basis of the imprecise text of the constitutional provision and the materials before us in this case, we cannot now attempt to delineate the exact kinds of changes that fall within the power of the Governor to make specific recommendations for change. It can be said with certainty, however, that the substitution of complete new bills, as attempted in the present case, is not authorized by the constitution. . . .

JUSTICE GOLDENHERSH, specially concurring [omitted].

NOTES AND QUESTIONS

1. *Why aren't they law?* Klinger v. Howlett instructs that the amendatory vetoes cannot be used to substitute new bills for the ones passed by the legislature. Why not? Weren't they passed by both houses of the legislature and signed by the governor?

2. *The scope of the power.* The court in *Klinger* finds an evident limit on the use of this power. For a more subtle case, consider the following: In 1985 the Illinois legislature created a system of collective bargaining for a broad group of public employees and employers. Upon receipt of the bills, the governor returned the bills to legislature with recommended amendments: that educational employees be deleted from the act; that a provision concerning a bistate development agency, which was intended to transfer to the State Board jurisdiction over labor matters involving that agency while adhering to federal labor requirements applicable to its employees, be added to the act; that the state's anti-injunction act be made applicable to the provisions here; and that two departmental directors be added to the membership of the state's governing body, the special group that reviews impasse arbitration decisions involving the state. The legislature concurred in the governor's recommendations. Do you think this comes within the ambit of amendatory veto provisions? See Kane County v. Carlson, 507 N.E.2d 482 (Ill. 1987).

d. A Federal Line Item Veto

Following nearly a century of steadfastly rejecting proposals to constitutionally provide line item veto authority to the President, Congress in

1996 enacted the Line Item Veto Act (effective January 1, 1997), under which Presidents were granted line item veto authority over appropriations, new direct spending, and certain tax benefits. The statute was first attacked by several members of Congress, who were ruled not to have standing to bring the action. Raines v. Byrd, 521 U.S. 81 (1997). The merits of the statute are the subject of the following case. Internal citations have been omitted except where particularly relevant.

Clinton v. The City of New York
524 U.S. 417 (1998)

STEVENS, J., delivered the opinion of the Court.

The Line Item Veto Act (Act) was enacted in April 1996 and became effective on January 1, 1997. The following day, six Members of Congress who had voted against the Act brought suit in the District Court for the District of Columbia challenging its constitutionality. . . . We determined, however, that the Members of Congress did not have standing to sue because they had not "alleged a sufficiently concrete injury to have established Article III standing."

Less than two months after our decision in that case, the President exercised his authority to cancel one provision in the Balanced Budget Act of 1997 and two provisions in the Taxpayer Relief Act of 1997. . . .

I

We begin by reviewing the canceled items that are at issue in these cases.

Section 4722(c) of the Balanced Budget Act

Title XIX of the Social Security Act, 79 Stat. 343, as amended, authorizes the Federal Government to transfer huge sums of money to the States to help finance medical care for the indigent. In 1991, Congress directed that those federal subsidies be reduced by the amount of certain taxes levied by the States on health care providers. In 1994, the Department of Health and Human Services (HHS) notified the State of New York that 15 of its taxes were covered by the 1991 Act, and that as of June 30, 1994, the statute therefore required New York to return $955 million to the United States. The notice advised the State that it could apply for a waiver on certain statutory grounds. New York did request a waiver for those tax programs, as well as for a number of others, but HHS has not formally acted on any of those waiver requests. New York has estimated that the amount at issue for the period from October 1992 through March 1997 is as high as $2.6 billion.

Because HHS had not taken any action on the waiver requests, New York turned to Congress for relief. On August 5, 1997, Congress enacted a law that resolved the issue in New York's favor. Section 4722(c) of the Balanced Budget Act of 1997 identifies the disputed taxes and provides that they "are deemed to be permissible health care related taxes and in compliance with the requirements" of the relevant provisions of the 1991 statute.

On August 11, 1997, the President sent identical notices to the Senate and to the House of Representatives canceling "one item of new direct spending," specifying §4722(c) as that item, and stating that he had determined that "this cancellation will reduce the Federal budget deficit." He explained that §4722(c) would have permitted New York "to continue relying upon impermissible provider taxes to finance its Medicaid program" and that "[t]his preferential treatment would have increased Medicaid costs, would have treated New York differently from all other States, and would have established a costly precedent for other States to request comparable treatment."

Section 968 of the Taxpayer Relief Act

A person who realizes a profit from the sale of securities is generally subject to a capital gains tax. Under existing law, however, an ordinary business corporation can acquire a corporation, including a food processing or refining company, in a merger or stock-for-stock transaction in which no gain is recognized to the seller; the seller's tax payment, therefore, is deferred. If, however, the purchaser is a farmers' cooperative, the parties cannot structure such a transaction because the stock of the cooperative may be held only by its members, see 26 U.S.C. §521(b)(2); thus, a seller dealing with a farmers' cooperative cannot obtain the benefits of tax deferral.

In §968 of the Taxpayer Relief Act of 1997, Congress amended §1042 of the Internal Revenue Code to permit owners of certain food refiners and processors to defer the recognition of gain if they sell their stock to eligible farmers' cooperatives. The purpose of the amendment, as repeatedly explained by its sponsors, was "to facilitate the transfer of refiners and processors to farmers' cooperatives." The amendment to §1042 was one of the 79 "limited tax benefits" authorized by the Taxpayer Relief Act of 1997 and specifically identified in Title XVII of that Act as "subject to [the] line item veto."

On the same date that he canceled the "item of new direct spending" involving New York's health care programs, the President also canceled this limited tax benefit. In his explanation of that action, the President endorsed the objective of encouraging "value-added farming through the purchase by farmers' cooperatives of refiners or processors of agricultural goods," but concluded that the provision lacked safeguards and also "failed to target its benefits to small- and medium-size cooperatives." ...

IV

The Line Item Veto Act gives the President the power to "cancel in whole" three types of provisions that have been signed into law: "(1) any dollar amount of discretionary budget authority; (2) any item of new direct spending; or (3) any limited tax benefit." It is undisputed that the New York case involves an "item of new direct spending" and that the Snake River case involves a "limited tax benefit" as those terms are defined in the Act. It is also undisputed that each of those provisions had been signed into law pursuant to Article I, §7, of the Constitution before it was canceled.

The Act requires the President to adhere to precise procedures whenever he exercises his cancellation authority. In identifying items for cancellation he must consider the legislative history, the purposes, and other relevant information about the items. He must determine, with respect to each cancellation, that it will "(i) reduce the Federal budget deficit; (ii) not impair any essential Government functions; and (iii) not harm the national interest." Moreover, he must transmit a special message to Congress notifying it of each cancellation within five calendar days (excluding Sundays) after the enactment of the canceled provision. It is undisputed that the President meticulously followed these procedures in these cases.

A cancellation takes effect upon receipt by Congress of the special message from the President. If, however, a "disapproval bill" pertaining to a special message is enacted into law, the cancellations set forth in that message become "null and void." The Act sets forth a detailed expedited procedure for the consideration of a "disapproval bill," but no such bill was passed for either of the cancellations involved in these cases. A majority vote of both Houses is sufficient to enact a disapproval bill. The Act does not grant the President the authority to cancel a disapproval bill, but he does, of course, retain his constitutional authority to veto such a bill.

The effect of a cancellation is plainly stated in §691e, which defines the principal terms used in the Act. With respect to both an item of new direct spending and a limited tax benefit, the cancellation prevents the item "from having legal force or effect." . . .

In both legal and practical effect, the President has amended two Acts of Congress by repealing a portion of each. . . . There is no provision in the Constitution that authorizes the President to enact, to amend, or to repeal statutes. Both Article I and Article II assign responsibilities to the President that directly relate to the lawmaking process, but neither addresses the issue presented by these cases. The President "shall from time to time give to the Congress Information on the State of the Union, and recommend to their Consideration such Measures as he shall judge necessary and expedient. . . ." Art. II, §3. Thus, he may initiate and influence legislative proposals. Moreover, after a bill has passed both Houses of Congress, but "before it become[s] a Law," it must be presented to the President. If he approves it, "he shall sign it, but if not he shall return it, with his Objections to that House in which it shall have originated, who shall enter the Objections at large on their Journal, and proceed to reconsider it." Art. I, §7, cl. 2. His "return" of a bill, which is usually described as a "veto," is subject to being overridden by a two-thirds vote in each House.

There are important differences between the President's "return" of a bill pursuant to Article I, §7, and the exercise of the President's cancellation authority pursuant to the Line Item Veto Act. The constitutional return takes place before the bill becomes law; the statutory cancellation occurs after the bill becomes law. The constitutional return is of the entire bill; the statutory cancellation is of only a part. Although the Constitution expressly authorizes the President to play a role in the process of enacting statutes, it is silent on the subject of unilateral Presidential action that either repeals or amends parts of duly enacted statutes.

There are powerful reasons for construing constitutional silence on this profoundly important issue as equivalent to an express prohibition. The procedures governing the enactment of statutes set forth in the text of Article I were the product of the great debates and compromises that produced the Constitution itself. Familiar historical materials provide abundant support for the conclusion that the power to enact statutes may only "be exercised in accord with a single, finely wrought and exhaustively considered, procedure." Our first President understood the text of the Presentment Clause as requiring that he either "approve all the parts of a Bill, or reject it in toto." What has emerged in these cases from the President's exercise of his statutory cancellation powers, however, are truncated versions of two bills that passed both Houses of Congress. They are not the product of the "finely wrought" procedure that the Framers designed.

At oral argument, the Government suggested that the cancellations at issue in these cases do not effect a "repeal" of the canceled items because under the special "lockbox" provisions of the Act, a canceled item "retain[s] real, legal budgetary effect" insofar as it prevents Congress and the President from spending the savings that result from the cancellation. The text of the Act expressly provides, however, that a cancellation prevents a direct spending or tax benefit provision "from having legal force or effect." That a canceled item may have "real, legal budgetary effect" as a result of the lockbox procedure does not change the fact that by canceling the items at issue in these cases, the President made them entirely inoperative as to appellees. Section 968 of the Taxpayer Relief Act no longer provides a tax benefit, and §4722(c) of the Balanced Budget Act of 1997 no longer relieves New York of its contingent liability. Such significant changes do not lose their character simply because the canceled provisions may have some continuing financial effect on the Government. . . .

V

The Government advances two related arguments to support its position that despite the unambiguous provisions of the Act, cancellations do not amend or repeal properly enacted statutes in violation of the Presentment Clause. First, relying primarily on Field v. Clark the Government contends that the cancellations were merely exercises of discretionary authority granted to the President by the Balanced Budget Act and the Taxpayer Relief Act read in light of the previously enacted Line Item Veto Act. Second, the Government submits that the substance of the authority to cancel tax and spending items "is, in practical effect, no more and no less than the power to 'decline to spend' specified sums of money, or to 'decline to implement' specified tax measures." Neither argument is persuasive.

In Field v. Clark, the Court upheld the constitutionality of the Tariff Act of 1890. That statute contained a "free list" of almost 300 specific articles that were exempted from import duties "unless otherwise specially provided for in this act." Section 3 was a special provision that directed the President to suspend that exemption for sugar, molasses, coffee, tea, and hides "whenever, and so often" as he should be satisfied that any country producing and exporting those products imposed duties on the agricultural products of the United States that he deemed to be "reciprocally unequal and unreasonable. . . ."

[There are] three critical differences between the power to suspend the exemption from import duties and the power to cancel portions of a duly enacted statute. First, the exercise of the suspension power was contingent upon a condition that did not exist when the Tariff Act was passed: the imposition of "reciprocally unequal and unreasonable" import duties by other countries. In contrast, the exercise of the cancellation power within five days after the enactment of the Balanced Budget and Tax Reform Acts necessarily was based on the same conditions that Congress evaluated when it passed those statutes. Second, under the Tariff Act, when the President determined that the contingency had arisen, he had a duty to suspend; in contrast, while it is true that the President was required by the Act to make three determinations before he canceled a provision those determinations did not qualify his discretion to cancel or not to cancel. Finally, whenever the President suspended an exemption under the Tariff Act, he was executing the policy that Congress had embodied in the statute. In contrast, whenever the President cancels an item of new direct spending or a limited tax benefit he is rejecting the policy judgment made by Congress and relying on his own policy judgment. . . .

Neither are we persuaded by the Government's contention that the President's authority to cancel new direct spending and tax benefit items is no greater than his traditional authority to decline to spend appropriated funds. The Government has reviewed in some detail the series of statutes in which Congress has given the Executive broad discretion over the expenditure of appropriated funds. For example, the First Congress appropriated "sum[s] not exceeding" specified amounts to be spent on various Government operations. In those statutes, as in later years, the President was given wide discretion with respect to both the amounts to be spent and how the money would be allocated among different functions.

It is argued that the Line Item Veto Act merely confers comparable discretionary authority over the expenditure of appropriated funds. The critical difference between this statute and all of its predecessors, however, is that unlike any of them, this Act gives the President the unilateral power to change the text of duly enacted statutes. None of the Act's predecessors could even arguably have been construed to authorize such a change.

VI

... [O]ur decision rests on the narrow ground that the procedures authorized by the Line Item Veto Act are not authorized by the Constitution. The Balanced Budget Act of 1997 is a 500-page document that became "Public Law 105-33" after three procedural steps were taken: (1) a bill containing its exact text was approved by a majority of the Members of the House of Representatives; (2) the Senate approved precisely the same text; and (3) that text was signed into law by the President. The Constitution explicitly requires that each of those three steps be taken before a bill may "become a law." Art. I, §7. If one paragraph of that text had been omitted at any one of those three stages, Public Law 105-33 would not have been validly enacted. If the Line Item Veto Act were valid, it would authorize the President to create a different law — one whose text was not voted on by either House of Congress or presented to the President for signature. Something that might be known as "Public Law 105-33 as modified by the President" may or may not be desirable, but it is surely not a document that may "become a law" pursuant to the procedures designed by the Framers of Article I, §7, of the Constitution.

If there is to be a new procedure in which the President will play a different role in determining the final text of what may "become a law," such change must come not by legislation but through the amendment procedures set forth in Article V of the Constitution.

JUSTICE KENNEDY, concurring.

I write to respond to my colleague JUSTICE BREYER, who observes that the statute does not threaten the liberties of individual citizens, a point on which I disagree. The argument is related to his earlier suggestion that our role is lessened here because the two political branches are adjusting their own powers between themselves. To say the political branches have a somewhat free hand to reallocate their own authority would seem to require acceptance of two premises: first, that the public good demands it, and second, that liberty is not at risk. The former premise is inadmissible.

The Constitution's structure requires a stability which transcends the convenience of the moment. The latter premise, too, is flawed. Liberty is always at stake when one or more of the branches seek to transgress the separation of powers.

Separation of powers was designed to implement a fundamental insight: concentration of power in the hands of a single branch is a threat to liberty. The Federalist states the axiom in these explicit terms: "The accumulation of all powers, legislative, executive, and judiciary, in the same hands ... may justly be pronounced the very definition of tyranny." The Federalist No. 47. So convinced were the Framers that liberty of the person inheres in structure that at first they did not consider a Bill of Rights necessary. The Federalist No. 84. It was at Madison's insistence that the First Congress enacted the Bill of Rights. It would be a grave mistake, however, to think a Bill of Rights in Madison's scheme then or in sound constitutional theory now renders separation of powers of lesser importance.

In recent years, perhaps, we have come to think of liberty as defined by that word in the Fifth and Fourteenth Amendments and as illuminated by the other provisions of the Bill of Rights. The conception of liberty embraced by the Framers was not so confined. They used the principles of separation of powers and federalism to secure liberty in the fundamental political sense of the term, quite in addition to the idea of freedom from intrusive governmental acts. The idea and the promise were that when the people delegate some degree of control to a remote central authority, one branch of government ought not possess the power to shape their destiny without a sufficient check from the other two. In this vision, liberty demands limits on the ability of any one branch to influence basic political decisions. . . .

The principal object of the statute, it is true, was not to enhance the President's power to reward one group and punish another, to help one set of taxpayers and hurt another, to favor one State and ignore another. Yet these are its undeniable effects. The law establishes a new mechanism which gives the President the sole ability to hurt a group that is a visible target, in order to disfavor the group or to extract further concessions from Congress. The law is the functional equivalent of a line item veto and enhances the President's powers beyond what the Framers would have endorsed. . . .

JUSTICE SCALIA, with whom JUSTICE O'CONNOR joins, and with whom JUSTICE BREYER joins as to Part III, concurring in part and dissenting in part. . . .

III . . .

Article I, §7 of the Constitution obviously prevents the President from canceling a law that Congress has not authorized him to cancel. Such action cannot possibly be considered part of his execution of the law, and if it is legislative action, as the Court observes, "'repeal of statutes, no less than enactment, must conform with Art. I.'" But that is not this case. It was certainly arguable, as an original matter, that Art. I, §7 also prevents the President from canceling a law which itself authorizes the President to cancel it. But as the Court acknowledges, that argument has long since been made and rejected. . . . This Court upheld the constitutionality of [such an] . . . Act in Field v. Clark. . . .

As much as the Court goes on about Art. I, §7, therefore, that provision does not demand the result the Court reaches. It no more categorically prohibits the Executive reduction of congressional dispositions in the course of implementing statutes that authorize such reduction, than it categorically prohibits the Executive augmentation of congressional dispositions in the course of implementing statutes that authorize such augmentation—generally known as substantive rulemaking. There are, to be sure, limits upon the former just as there are limits upon the latter—and I am prepared to acknowledge that the limits upon the former may be much more severe. Those limits are established, however, not by some categorical prohibition of Art. I, §7, which our cases conclusively disprove, but by what has come to be known as the doctrine of unconstitutional delegation of legislative authority: When authorized Executive reduction or augmentation is allowed to go too far, it usurps the nondelegable function of Congress and violates the separation of powers. . . .

Insofar as the degree of political, "law-making" power conferred upon the Executive is concerned, there is not a dime's worth of difference between Congress's authorizing the President to cancel a spending item, and Congress's authorizing money to be spent on a particular item at the President's discretion. And the latter has been done since the Founding of the Nation. . . . From a very early date Congress also made permissive individual appropriations, leaving the decision whether to spend the money to the President's unfettered discretion. In 1803, it appropriated $50,000 for the President to build "not exceeding fifteen gun boats, to be armed, manned and fitted out, and employed for such purposes as in his opinion the public service may require." President Jefferson reported that "[t]he sum of fifty thousand dollars appropriated by Congress for providing gun boats remains unexpended. The favorable and peaceable turn of affairs on the Mississippi rendered an immediate execution of that law unnecessary." . . . During the Great Depression, Congress appropriated $950 million "for such projects and/or purposes and under such rules and regulations as the President in his discretion may prescribe." . . .

The short of the matter is this: Had the Line Item Veto Act authorized the President to "decline to spend" any item of spending contained in the Balanced Budget Act of 1997, there is not the slightest doubt that authorization would have been constitutional. What the Line Item Veto Act does instead—authorizing the President to "cancel" an item of spending—is technically different. But the technical difference does not relate to the technicalities of the Presentment Clause, which have been fully complied with; and the doctrine of unconstitutional delegation, which is at issue here, is preeminently not a doctrine of technicalities. The title of the Line Item Veto Act, which was perhaps designed to simplify for public comprehension, or perhaps merely to comply with the terms of a campaign pledge, has succeeded in faking out the Supreme Court. The President's action it authorizes in fact is not a line-item veto and thus does not offend Art. I, §7; and insofar as the substance of that action is concerned, it is no different from what Congress has permitted the President to do since the formation of the Union. . . .

JUSTICE BREYER, with whom JUSTICE O'CONNOR and JUSTICE SCALIA join as to Part III, dissenting. . . .

II

I approach the constitutional question before us with three general considerations in mind. First, the Act represents a legislative effort to provide the President with the power to give effect to some, but not to all, of the expenditure and revenue-diminishing provisions contained in a single massive appropriations bill. And this objective is constitutionally proper.

When our Nation was founded, Congress could easily have provided the President with this kind of power. In that time period, our population was less than four million, see U.S. Dept. of Commerce, Census Bureau, Historical Statistics of the United States: Colonial Times to 1970, federal employees numbered fewer than 5,000, annual federal budget outlays totaled approximately $4 million. . . .

At that time, a Congress, wishing to give a President the power to select among appropriations, could simply have embodied each appropriation in a separate bill, each bill subject to a separate Presidential veto.

Today, however, our population is about 250 million, the Federal Government employs more than four million people, the annual federal budget is $1.5 trillion, and a typical budget appropriations bill may have a dozen titles, hundreds of sections, and spread across more than 500 pages of the Statutes at Large. Congress cannot divide such a bill into thousands, or tens of thousands, of separate appropriations bills, each one of which the President would have to sign, or to veto, separately. Thus, the question is whether the Constitution permits Congress to choose a particular novel means to achieve this same, constitutionally legitimate, end.

Second, the case in part requires us to focus upon the Constitution's generally phrased structural provisions, provisions that delegate all "legislative" power to Congress and vest all "executive" power in the President. The Court, when applying these provisions, has interpreted them generously in terms of the institutional arrangements that they permit. . . .

Third, we need not here referee a dispute among the other two branches. . . .

These three background circumstances mean that, when one measures the literal words of the Act against the Constitution's literal commands, the fact that the Act may closely resemble a different, literally unconstitutional, arrangement is beside the point. To drive exactly 65 miles per hour on an interstate highway closely resembles an act that violates the speed limit. But it does not violate that limit, for small differences matter when the question is one of literal violation of law. No more does this Act literally violate the Constitution's words. . . .

III

The Court believes that the Act violates the literal text of the Constitution. A simple syllogism captures its basic reasoning:

Major Premise: The Constitution sets forth an exclusive method for enacting, repealing, or amending laws.

Minor Premise: The Act authorizes the President to "repea[l] or amen[d]" laws in a different way, namely by announcing a cancellation of a portion of a previously enacted law.

Conclusion: The Act is inconsistent with the Constitution.

I find this syllogism unconvincing, however, because its Minor Premise is faulty. When the President "canceled" the two appropriation measures now before us, he did not repeal any law nor did he amend any law. He simply followed the law, leaving the statutes, as they are literally written, intact.

To understand why one cannot say, literally speaking, that the President has repealed or amended any law, imagine how the provisions of law before us might have been, but were not, written. Imagine that the canceled New York health care tax provision at issue here, had instead said the following:

> Section One. Taxes . . . that were collected by the State of New York from a health care provider before June 1, 1997 and for which a waiver of provisions [requiring payment] have been sought . . . are deemed to be permissible health care related taxes . . . *provided however that the President may prevent the just-mentioned provision from having legal force or effect if he determines x, y and z.* (Assume x, y and z to be the same determinations required by the Line Item Veto Act).

Whatever a person might say, or think, about the constitutionality of this imaginary law, there is one thing the English language would prevent one from saying. One could not say that a President who "prevent[s]" the deeming language from "having legal force or effect," has either repealed or amended this particular hypothetical statute. Rather, the President has followed that law to the letter. He has exercised the power it explicitly delegates to him. He has executed the law, not repealed it.

It could make no significant difference to this linguistic point were the italicized proviso to appear, not as part of what I have called Section One, but, instead, at the bottom of the statute page, say referenced by an asterisk, with a statement that it applies to every spending provision in the act next to which a similar asterisk appears. And that being so, it could make no difference if that proviso appeared, instead, in a different, earlier-enacted law, along with legal language that makes it applicable to every future spending provision picked out according to a specified formula.

But, of course, this last-mentioned possibility is this very case. The earlier law, namely, the Line Item Veto Act, says that "the President may . . . prevent such [future] budget authority from having legal force or effect." Its definitional sections make clear that it applies to the 1997 New York health care provision, just as they give a special legal meaning to the word "cancel." For that reason, one cannot dispose of this case through a purely literal analysis as the majority does. Literally speaking, the President has not "repealed" or "amended" anything. . . .

This is not the first time that Congress has delegated to the President or to others this kind of power — a contingent power to deny effect to certain statutory language.

All of these examples, like the Act, delegate a power to take action that will render statutory provisions "without force or effect." Every one of these examples, like the present Act, delegates the power to choose between alternatives, each of which the statute spells out in some detail. None of these examples delegates a power to "repeal" or "amend" a statute, or to "make" a new law. Nor does the Act. Rather, the delegated power to nullify statutory language was itself created and defined by Congress, and included in the statute books on an equal footing with (indeed, as a component part of) the sections that are potentially subject to nullification. . . .

Because one cannot say that the President's exercise of the power the Act grants is, literally speaking, a "repeal" or "amendment," the fact that the Act's procedures differ from the Constitution's exclusive procedures for enacting (or repealing) legislation is beside the point. The Act itself was enacted in accordance with these procedures, and its failure to require the President to satisfy those procedures does not make the Act unconstitutional.

IV

Because I disagree with the Court's holding of literal violation, I must consider whether the Act nonetheless violates Separation of Powers principles — principles that arise out of the Constitution's vesting of the "executive Power" in "a President," U.S. Const., Art. II, §1, and "[a]ll legislative Powers" in "a Congress," Art. I, §1. There are three relevant Separation of Powers questions here: (1) Has Congress given the President the wrong kind of power, i.e., "non-Executive" power? (2) Has Congress given the President the power to "encroach" upon Congress' own constitutionally reserved territory? (3) Has Congress given the President too much power, violating the doctrine of "nondelegation"? These three limitations help assure "adequate control by the citizen's representatives in Congress," upon which JUSTICE KENNEDY properly insists. And with respect to this Act, the answer to all these questions is "no."

A

Viewed conceptually, the power the Act conveys is the right kind of power. It is "executive." As explained above, an exercise of that power "executes" the Act. Conceptually speaking, it closely resembles the kind of delegated authority—to spend or not to spend appropriations, to change or not to change tariff rates — that Congress has frequently granted the President, any differences being differences in degree, not kind.

The fact that one could also characterize this kind of power as "legislative," say, if Congress itself (by amending the appropriations bill) prevented a provision from taking effect, is beside the point. This Court has frequently found that the exercise of a particular power, such as the power to make rules of broad applicability . . . can fall within the constitutional purview of more than one branch of Government. The Court does not "carry out the distinction between legislative and executive action with mathematical precision" or "divide the branches into watertight compartments," for, as others have said, the Constitution "blend[s]" as well as "separat[es]" powers in order to create a workable government.

The Court has upheld congressional delegation of rulemaking power and adjudicatory power to federal agencies. . . . If there is a Separation of Powers violation, then, it must rest, not upon purely conceptual grounds, but upon some important conflict between the Act and a significant Separation of Powers objective.

B

The Act does not undermine what this Court has often described as the principal function of the Separation of Powers, which is to maintain the tripartite structure of the Federal Government—and thereby protect individual liberty. . . .

[O]ne cannot say that the Act "encroaches" upon Congress' power, when Congress retained the power to insert, by simple majority, into any future appropriations bill, into any section of any such bill, or into any phrase of any section, a provision that says the Act will not apply. Congress also retained the power to "disapprov[e]," and thereby reinstate, any of the President's cancellations. And it is Congress that drafts and enacts the appropriations statutes that are subject to the Act in the first place—and thereby defines the outer limits of the President's cancellation authority. . . .

And, if an individual Member of Congress, who say, favors aid to Country A but not to Country B, objects to the Act on the ground that the President may "rewrite" an appropriations law to do the opposite, one can respond, "But a majority of Congress voted that he have that power; you may vote to exempt the relevant appropriations provision from the Act; and if you command a majority, your appropriation is safe." Where the burden of overcoming legislative inertia lies is within the power of Congress to determine by rule. Where is the encroachment?

Nor can one say the Act's, grant of power "aggrandizes" the Presidential office. The grant is limited to the context of the budget. It is limited to the power to spend, or not to spend, particular appropriated items, and the power to permit, or not to permit, specific limited exemptions from generally applicable tax law from taking effect. These powers, as I will explain in detail, resemble those the President has exercised in the past on other occasions. The delegation of those powers to the President may strengthen the Presidency, but any such change in Executive Branch authority seems minute when compared with the changes worked by delegations of other kinds of authority that the Court in the past has upheld. . . .

The Act before us seeks to create such a principle in three ways. The first is procedural. The Act tells the President that, in "identifying dollar amounts [or] . . . items . . . for cancellation" (which I take to refer to his selection of the amounts or items he will "prevent from having legal force or effect"), he is to "consider," among other things, "the legislative history, construction, and purposes of the law which contains [those amounts or items, and] . . . any specific sources of information referenced in such law or . . . the best available information. . . ."

The second is purposive. The clear purpose behind the Act, confirmed by its legislative history, is to promote "greater fiscal accountability" and to "eliminate wasteful federal spending and . . . special tax breaks."

The third is substantive. The President must determine that, to "prevent" the item or amount "from having legal force or effect" will "reduce the Federal budget deficit; . . . not impair any essential Government functions; and . . . not harm the national interest."

The resulting standards are broad. But this Court has upheld standards that are equally broad, or broader. See, e.g., National Broadcasting Co. v. United States (upholding delegation to Federal Communications Commission to regulate broadcast licensing as "public interest, convenience, or necessity" require).

Indeed, the Court has only twice in its history found that a congressional delegation of power violated the "nondelegation" doctrine. . . .

The case before us does not involve any such "roving commission," nor does it involve delegation to private parties, nor does it bring all of American industry within its scope. It is limited to one area of government, the budget, and it seeks to give the President the power, in one portion of that budget, to tailor spending and special tax relief to what he concludes are the demands of fiscal responsibility. Nor is the standard that governs his judgment, though broad, any broader than the standard that currently governs the award of television licenses, namely "public convenience, interest, or necessity." To the contrary, (a) the broadly phrased limitations in the Act, together with (b) its evident deficit reduction purpose, and (c) a procedure that guarantees Presidential awareness of the reasons for including a particular provision in a budget bill, taken together, guide the President's exercise of his discretionary powers. . . .

NOTES AND QUESTIONS

1. *Not a dime's worth of difference.* Both Justices Scalia and Breyer in dissent argue that the issue in the case is really whether the Line Item Veto Act is an appropriate delegation of power to the President rather than whether that Act allows the President to repeal or amend part of a statute. According to Justice Scalia, "there is not a dime's worth of difference between Congress authorizing the President to cancel a spending item, and Congress authorizing money to be spent on a particular item at the President's discretion." And Justice Breyer makes this same point through the use of his "rewritten" version of the New York–related provisions in question. (They apparently make the same argument about tax provisions, although there is some difference.) Do you agree with this analysis or do you think that there is something actually protected by requiring a literal reading of Article I, §7? Do you think that this distinction is the foundation to the majority's decision?

2. *The delegation issue.* If Justices Scalia and Breyer are correct, then the remaining issue would seem to be whether the Line Item Veto Act contains a constitutionally proper delegation of power to the President. Justice Scalia, for example, states that if the Act authorized the President to decline to spend an item of appropriation, that undoubtedly would have been constitutional. And Justice Breyer argues similarly that a number of laws grant the President equal amounts of power, for example, a delegation to the Federal Communications Commission to regulate broadcast licensing as "public interest, convenience, or necessity" requires. Also included in his list are:

("Section 620(x) of the Foreign Assistance Act of 1961 shall be of no further force and effect upon the President's determination and certification to the Congress that the resumption of full military cooperation with Turkey is in the national interest of the United States and [other criteria]"); 28 U.S.C. §2072

(Supreme Court is authorized to promulgate rules of practice and procedure in federal courts, and "[a]ll laws in conflict with such rules shall be of no further force and effect"); 41 U.S.C. §405b (subsection (a) requires the Office of Federal Procurement Policy to issue "[g]overnment-wide regulations" setting forth a variety of conflict of interest standards, but subsection (e) says that "if the President determine[s]" that the regulations "would have a significantly adverse effect on the accomplishment of the mission" of government agencies, "the requirement [to promulgate] the regulations . . . shall be null and void"); Gramm-Rudman-Hollings Act (authorizing the President to issue a "final order" that has the effect of "permanently cancell[ing]" sequestered amounts in spending statutes in order to achieve budget compliance); "Pub. L. 89-732 [dealing with immigration from Cuba] is repealed . . . upon a determination by the President . . . that a democratically elected government in Cuba is in power"); Pub. L. 99-498 (amending §758 of the Higher Education Act of 1965) (Secretary of Education "may" sell common stock in an educational loan corporation; if the Secretary decides to sell stock, and "if the Student Loan Marketing Association acquires from the Secretary" over 50 percent of the voting stock, "section 754 [governing composition of the Board of Directors] shall be of no further force or effect"); Pub. L. 104-134 (President is "authorized to suspend the provisions of the [preceding] proviso" which suspension may last for entire effective period of proviso, if he determines suspension is "appropriate based upon the public interest in sound environmental management . . . [or] the protection of national or locally-affected interests, or protection of any cultural, biological or historic resources").

What do you think of this analysis? Are the delegations offered for comparison the same as the delegation granted to the President in the Act? How do you think the dissenters would rule on the item veto exercise by the governor of Wisconsin in Kleczka v. Conta (affirming governor's vetoes of appropriation bill language even though veto changed the meaning of the bill), on page 592 of this book?

3. *The question of liberty.* In his concurrence, Justice Kennedy states the following: "In recent years, perhaps, we have come to think of liberty as defined by that word in the Fifth and Fourteenth Amendments and as illuminated by the other provisions of the Bill of Rights. The conception of liberty embraced by the Framers was not so confined." What does he mean by his last sentence and how does it apply to this use?

D.   RULES OF PROCEDURE AND DELIBERATIVENESS

In Chapter 3, we focused on rules of legislative procedure that order the enactment of legislation. One of the functions of legislative rules that we noted was the protection they offered to legislative minorities against the rashness of majorities. Almost all legislative procedural rules can assist a minority of members in obstructing the legislative process. A clear example is the Senate filibuster that allows a minority of Senators to block any legislation. In this manner the legislative process becomes more deliberative, forcing more consideration of a bill. A somewhat different spin is placed on this deliberative method by the following comments.

Using the Rules to Obstruct the House
Congressional Quarterly, Guide to Congress 422 (3d ed. 1982)

Obstructionist tactics in Congress change with the years. When an abused loophole in the rules is plugged up, ingenious members are able to devise new ones that serve the same purpose.

House members bent on blocking legislation have had to be more imaginative than their colleagues in the Senate, where the filibuster always has been available to those wishing to delay congressional action. Stringent House curbs on debate preclude a filibuster in the Senate mold, and in recent years the House has closed other avenues of delay, for example, by giving the Speaker additional authority aimed at speeding up legislative business and severely curbing the use of quorum calls.

Until the late 1970s the quorum call was one of the most useful delaying devices. A dramatic example, which became the equivalent of a Senate filibuster, occurred on the eve of adjournment of the 1968 session. At issue were bills on legislative reorganization, campaign spending reform and televising the presidential candidates' debates. All three bills failed to win approval before Congress went home.

The stalling began in earnest on Oct. 8 when House Republicans, saying they sought action on the first two reform bills, forced the House to stay in session for more than 32 hours before it passed the television debate bill. When Senate Republicans, also using dilatory tactics, succeeded in killing that measure, a group of House Democrats then employed stalling tactics of their own to hold up adjournment from Oct. 10 to 14 in an effort to force the Senate to accept the television bill.

On Oct. 8 the House Republicans combined a demand for the full reading of the Journal, 33 quorum calls, three roll-call votes and other procedures to delay the day's proceedings for 20 hours before the House was able to consider the television bill. Democrats charged that Republican presidential candidate Richard Nixon did not want to debate his Democratic opponent, Vice President Hubert H. Humphrey, while the Republicans responded that they were concerned about the two reform measures.

During the Oct. 8-9 House session — lasting 32 hours and 17 minutes — there were 37 quorum calls and eight roll-call votes. And in those days, before the advent of electronic voting, a single roll-call vote took between 30 and 45 minutes to complete. According to the Congressional Research Service of the Library of Congress, that session was surpassed in length only twice: by a 48-hour, 25-minute session in 1875 on a civil rights bill, and by a 35-hour, 30-minute session in 1854 on the Kansas-Nebraska bill repealing the Missouri Compromise of 1820.

As seen by the 1968 example, it is much easier for obstruction to succeed near the end of a session when usually there is not enough time to counter repeated delaying tactics. Another example occurred 10 years later, at adjournment time of the 95th Congress. This time, obstructionists employed the "disappearing quorum" to defeat a water projects development bill. Opposed by environmentalists, the bill was hurriedly brought to the floor by its sponsors under a shortcut procedure, known as suspension of the rules, that required a two-thirds vote for passage.

It was the last day of the session, and members already had started to leave for home. The previous roll call had drawn only 11 more votes than were necessary for a quorum (218). Opponents knew the popular water projects bill had overwhelming support in the House. Because their only hope was to prevent a quorum from voting, they mobilized like-minded colleagues to stay away from the chamber. On the final tally, the bill was backed by a 129-31 vote, but this was more than 50 short of a quorum. The House then was forced to adjourn, ending any chance of reviving the water bill.

At other times, dilatory tactics merely delay legislation, presenting scheduling irritations for the leadership. For example, on April 23, 1975, House members opposed to quick action on a Ford administration aid bill for Vietnamese refugees used the one-minute-speeches period at the opening of the day's session, along with demands for roll calls on normally routine motions, to delay the bill's consideration.

These one-minute speeches also gave members an opportunity to vent their frustrations with other aspects of America's Vietnam policy, including the administration's belated evacuation of U.S. and high Vietnamese government personnel from South Vietnam. In all, 26 members used the period to attack the bill and U.S. Southeast Asia policies.

In 1980, on the eve of a July recess, approval of a crucial emergency appropriations bill was in jeopardy because of differences over budget priorities and the eagerness of members to leave town. Conservatives were critical of providing aid to Nicaragua, and there was much opposition to Senate cuts in revenue sharing. It appeared that a delicate compromise could unravel.

At one point Rep. Robert E. Bauman, R-Md. (1973-81), a leading foreign aid opponent, refused to relinquish the floor despite entreaties from Speaker Thomas P. O'Neill Jr., D-Mass. When the presiding officer permitted O'Neill to proceed anyway, Bauman charged the chair's action was based on partisan politics.

In a rare move, Bauman appealed the ruling to the full House. Though the rules appeared to support Bauman, the House supported O'Neill, 199-163. Eventually, the pending recess worked to the congressional leaders' advantage. They hinted members would be called back to Washington if the measure was not passed. This convinced lawmakers to stop stalling and clear the bill.

NOTES AND QUESTIONS

1. *Deliberativeness or obstructionism?* How would you evaluate the example set forth above? Does it reflect deliberativeness or obstructionism? What is the difference between the two?

2. *An anecdote.* A personal experience of one of the authors, Professor Lane, illustrates the point. In 1983, the New York State Senate Majority wanted to punish the Senate Minority for its election successes in the 1982 elections. They decided to deny all marginal members (those whom the majority believed that they could beat in the next elections) all "member items" in the budget. Member items (sometimes referred to as "pork") are items of appropriation directed to particular projects within a member's district. They can range from enhancement money for some particular social service program to purchasing a new ambulance for a volunteer ambulance group or a shell for a high school rowing team.

The traditional practice had been to divide a sum of money between the majority and minority that would then be allocated by each caucus's leadership. In these allocations marginal members would be paid special attention because it was believed that these appropriations were significant for reelection efforts. In this context, the Republican decision to deny certain members their item caused a great storm. In response to this decision, the Senate Democrats decided to take advantage of a number of Senate Rules to slow the process almost to a halt. First, every bill was debated for the maximum permissible time (two hours). Second, amendments were offered to almost every bill, and these amendments were debated. Third, every vote was made a roll call vote, and every Democrat rose for several minutes to explain their vote. What generally took an hour began to take a week. So severe was the paralysis that the Republican's Conference publicly considered changing the rules to severely limit the time for debate. Ultimately the time pressures placed on these part-time legislators became so severe that they capitulated by reinstating the appropriations and assuring the passage of a number of Democratic caucus bills.

Do you consider this action by the minority caucus in furtherance of the deliberative process or an obstruction to the legislative process?

3. *State approaches.* Some states have laws that are uniquely addressed to issues of deliberativeness. Among the most frequent of these provisions is one which directs that a bill must be read on three separate days in each house before it is passed. Florida's instruction is illustrative. "It [a bill] shall be read in each house on three separate days, unless this rule is waived by two-thirds vote." New York has a special spin on the three-day rule,

requiring that the executive play a role in avoiding its consequences. Article III, §14 of the Constitution of the State of New York provides:

> No bill shall be passed or become a law unless it shall first have been printed and upon the desks of the members, in its final form, at least three calendar legislative days prior to its final passage, unless the governor, or the acting governor, shall have certified, under his hand and the seal of the state, that facts which in his opinion necessitate an immediate vote thereon, in which case it must nevertheless be upon the desks of the members in final form not necessarily printed, before its final passage . . .

The purpose of all such waiting periods is "to prevent hasty and careless legislation, to prohibit amendments at the last moment, and to insure that the proposed legislation receives adequate publicity and consideration." Schneider v. Rockefeller, 340 N.Y.S.2d 889, 900 (1972). Three days is usually more than enough time for interest groups to organize opposition to legislation. Indeed, aside from the end of the session rush discussed below, the main reason that the three-day rules are shortened by legislative or executive action is to avoid opposition from forming. For part-time legislatures, the three-day rules can prove a major obstacle to the passage of end of session legislation. For example, in New York the legislative session usually ends at the end of June. The last days of these sessions are a whirl of activity with legislators, staff members, and lobbyists all running around trying to either improve, pass, or stop legislation. The three-day rule is intended to temper some of this activity by allowing, in theory, only the most essential newly introduced legislation or amendments to pass. The practice is sometimes considerably different. While the requirement for a message of necessity from the governor kills much legislation, it can sometimes become a currency for winning the support of legislators for executive initiatives or for rewarding or punishing legislators.

E.   SPEECH AND DEBATE CLAUSES

The United States Constitution and those of all of the states have provisions that provide that "for any speech or debate in either house, [senators and representatives] shall not be questioned in any place." U.S. Constitution, Article I, §6. From the deliberativeness perspective, the provision is intended to protect the legislative branch from executive intrusion and "to secure independence, firmness, and fearlessness on the part of the members, so that, in discharging their high trusts, they may not be overawed by wealth, or power, or dread of prosecution." Joseph Story, A Familiar Exposition of the Constitution of the United States, §144, 135 (Gateway ed. 1986). Today the discharge of such trust is carried not only by legislators but by large staffs and in various arenas beyond the floors of legislative chambers. Can the speech and debate clause accommodate such changes?

Gravel v. United States
408 U.S. 606 (1972)

JUSTICE WHITE wrote the opinion of the Court. . . . [Internal citations have been omitted except where particularly relevant.]

These cases arise out of the investigation by a federal grand jury into possible criminal conduct with respect to the release and publication of a classified Defense Department study entitled History of the United States Decision-Making Process on Viet Nam Policy. This document, popularly known as the Pentagon Papers, bore a Defense security classification of Top Secret-Sensitive. The crimes being investigated included the retention of public property or records with intent to convert (18 U.S.C. §641), the gathering and transmitting of national defense information (18 U.S.C. §793), the concealment or removal of public records or documents (18 U.S.C. §2071), and conspiracy to commit such offenses and to defraud the United States (18 U.S.C. §371).

Among the witnesses subpoenaed were Leonard S. Rodberg, an assistant to Senator Mike Gravel of Alaska and a resident fellow at the Institute of Policy Studies, and Howard Webber, Director of M.I.T. Press. Senator Gravel, as intervenor, filed motions to quash the subpoenas. . . . He asserted that requiring these witnesses to appear and testify would violate his privilege under the Speech or Debate Clause of the United States Constitution, Art. I, §6, cl. 1.

It appeared that on the night of June 29, 1971, Senator Gravel, as Chairman of the Subcommittee on Buildings and Grounds of the Senate Public Works Committee, convened a meeting of the subcommittee and there read extensively from a copy of the Pentagon Papers. He then placed the entire 47 volumes of the study in the public record. Rodberg had been added to the Senator's staff earlier in the day and assisted Gravel in preparing for and conducting the hearing. Some weeks later there were press reports that Gravel had arranged for the papers to be published by Beacon Press and that members of Gravel's staff had talked with Webber as editor of M.I.T. Press. . . .

I

Because the claim is that a Member's aide shares the Member's constitutional privilege, we consider first whether and to what extent Senator Gravel himself is exempt from process or inquiry by a grand jury investigating the commission of a crime. Our frame of reference is Art. I, §6, cl. 1, of the Constitution:

The Senators and Representatives shall receive a Compensation for their Services, to be ascertained by Law, and paid out of the Treasury of the United States. They shall in all Cases, except Treason, Felony and Breach of the Peace, be privileged from Arrest during their Attendance at the Session of their respective Houses, and in going to and returning from the same; and for any Speech or Debate in either House, they shall not be questioned in any other Place. . . .

Senator Gravel disavows any assertion of general immunity from the criminal law. But he points out that the last portion of §6 affords Members of Congress another vital privilege — they may not be questioned in any other place for any speech or debate in either House. The claim is not that while one part of §6 generally permits prosecutions for treason, felony, and breach of the peace, another part nevertheless broadly forbids them. Rather, his insistence is that the Speech or Debate Clause at the very least protects him from criminal or civil liability and from questioning elsewhere than in the Senate, with respect to the events occurring at the subcommittee hearing at which the Pentagon Papers were introduced into the public record. To us this claim is incontrovertible. The Speech or Debate Clause was designed to assure a co-equal branch of the government wide freedom of speech, debate, and deliberation without intimidation or threats from the Executive Branch. It thus protects Members against prosecutions that directly impinge upon or threaten the legislative process. We have no doubt that Senator Gravel may not be made to answer — either in terms of questions or in terms of defending himself from prosecution — for the events that occurred at the subcommittee meeting. Our decision is made easier by the fact that the United States appears to have abandoned whatever position it took to the contrary in the lower courts.

Even so, the United States strongly urges that because the Speech or Debate Clause confers a privilege only upon "Senators and Representatives," Rodberg himself has no valid claim to constitutional immunity from grand jury inquiry. In our view, both courts below correctly rejected this position. . . .

It is true that the Clause itself mentions only "Senators and Representatives," but prior cases have plainly not taken a literalistic approach in applying the privilege. The Clause also speaks only of "Speech or Debate," but the Court's consistent approach has been that to confine the protection of the Speech or Debate Clause to words spoken in debate would be an unacceptably narrow view. Committee reports, resolutions, and the act of voting are equally covered; "in short . . . things generally done in a session of the House by one of its members in relation to the business before it." Kilbourn v. Thompson, 103 U.S. 168, 204 (1881). . . . Rather than giving the Clause a cramped construction, the Court has sought to implement its fundamental purpose of freeing the legislator from executive and judicial oversight that realistically threatens to control his conduct as a legislator.

We have little doubt that we are neither exceeding our judicial powers nor mistakenly construing the Constitution by holding that the Speech or Debate Clause applies not only to a Member but also to his aides insofar as the conduct of the latter would be a protected legislative act if performed by the Member himself. . . .

The United States fears the abuses that history reveals have occurred when legislators are invested with the power to relieve others from the operation of otherwise valid civil and criminal laws. But these abuses, it seems to us, are for the most part obviated if the privilege applicable to the aide is viewed, as it must be, as the privilege of the Senator, and invocable only by the Senator or by the aide on the Senator's behalf, and if in all events the privilege available to the aide is confined to those services that would be immune legislative conduct if performed by the Senator himself. This view places beyond the Speech or Debate Clause a variety of services characteristically performed by aides for Members of Congress, even though within the scope of their employment. It likewise provides no protection for criminal conduct threatening the security of the person or property of others, whether performed at the direction of the Senator in preparation for or in execution of a legislative act or done without his knowledge or direction. Neither does it immunize Senator or aide from testifying at trials or grand jury proceedings involving third-party crimes where the questions do not require testimony about or impugn a legislative act. Thus our refusal to distinguish between Senator and aide in applying the Speech or Debate Clause does not mean that Rodberg is for all purposes exempt from grand jury questioning.

II

We are convinced also that the Court of Appeals correctly determined that Senator Gravel's alleged arrangement with Beacon Press to publish the Pentagon Papers was not protected speech or debate within the meaning of Art. I, §6, cl. 1, of the Constitution.

Historically, the English legislative privilege was not viewed as protecting republication of an otherwise immune libel on the floor of the House. . . .

Prior cases have read the Speech or Debate Clause "broadly to effectuate its purposes," United States v. Johnson, 383 U.S., at 180, and have included within its reach anything "generally done in a session of the House by one of its members in relation to the business before it." Kilbourn v. Thompson, 103 U.S., at 204; United States v. Johnson, 383 U.S., at 179. Thus, voting by Members and committee reports are protected; and we recognize today . . . that a Member's conduct at legislative committee hearings, although subject to judicial review in various circumstances, as is legislation itself, may not be made the basis for a civil or criminal judgment against a Member because that conduct is within the "sphere of legitimate legislative activity."

But the Clause has not been extended beyond the legislative sphere. That Senators generally perform certain acts in their official capacity as Senators does not necessarily make all such acts legislative in nature. Members of Congress are constantly in touch with the Executive Branch of the Government and with administrative agencies—they may cajole, and exhort with respect to the administration of a federal statute—but such conduct, though generally done, is not protected legislative activity. United States v. Johnson decided at least this much. "No argument is made, nor do we think that it could be successfully contended, that the Speech or Debate Clause reaches conduct, such as was involved in the attempt to influence the Department of Justice, that is in no way related to the due functioning of the legislative process." 383 U.S., at 172.

Legislative acts are not all-encompassing. The heart of the Clause is speech or debate in either House. Insofar as the Clause is construed to reach other matters, they must be an integral part of the deliberative and communicative processes by which Members participate in committee and House proceedings with respect to the consideration and passage or rejection of proposed legislation or with respect to other matters which the Constitution places within the jurisdiction of either House. . . .

Here, private publication by Senator Gravel through the cooperation of Beacon Press was in no way essential to the deliberations of the Senate; nor does questioning as to private publication threaten the integrity or independence of the Senate by impermissibly exposing its deliberations to executive influence. The Senator had conducted his hearings; the record and any report that was forthcoming were available both to his committee and the Senate. Insofar as we are advised, neither Congress nor the full committee ordered or authorized the publication. We cannot but conclude that the Senator's arrangements with Beacon Press were not part and parcel of the legislative process. . . .

There are additional considerations. Article I, §6, cl. 1, as we have emphasized, does not purport to confer a general exemption upon Members of Congress from liability or process in criminal cases. Quite the contrary is true. While the Speech or Debate Clause recognizes speech, voting, and other legislative acts as exempt from liability that might otherwise attach, it does not privilege either Senator or aide to violate an otherwise valid criminal law in preparing for or implementing legislative acts. If republication of these classified papers would be a crime under an Act of Congress, it would not be entitled to immunity under the Speech or Debate Clause. It also appears that the grand jury was pursuing this very subject in the normal course of a valid investigation. The Speech or Debate Clause does not in our view extend immunity to Rodberg, as a Senator's aide, from testifying before the grand jury about the arrangement between Senator Gravel and Beacon Press or about his own participation, if any, in the alleged transaction, so long as legislative acts of the Senator are not impugned. . . .

JUSTICE BRENNAN, with whom JUSTICE DOUGLAS, and JUSTICE MARSHALL, join, dissenting.

. . . My concern is with the narrow scope accorded the Speech or Debate Clause by today's decision. I fully agree with the Court that a Congressman's immunity under the Clause must also be extended to his aides if it is to be at all effective. The complexities and press of congressional business make it impossible for a Member to function without the close cooperation of his legislative assistants. Their role as his agents in the performance of official duties requires that they share his immunity for those acts. The scope of that immunity, however, is as important as the persons to whom it extends. In my view, today's decision so restricts the privilege of speech or debate as to endanger the continued performance of legislative tasks that are vital to the workings of our democratic system.

I

In holding that Senator Gravel's alleged arrangement with Beacon Press to publish the Pentagon Papers is not shielded from extra-senatorial inquiry by the Speech or Debate Clause, the Court adopts what for me is a far too narrow view of the legislative function. The Court seems to assume that words spoken in debate or written in congressional reports are protected by the Clause, so that if Senator Gravel had recited part of the Pentagon Papers on the Senate floor or copied them into a Senate report, those acts could not be questioned "in any other Place." Yet because he sought a wider audience, to publicize information deemed relevant to matters pending before his own committee, the Senator suddenly loses his immunity and is exposed to grand jury investigation and possible prosecution for the republication. The explanation for this anomalous result is the Court's belief that "Speech or Debate" encompasses only acts necessary to the internal deliberations of Congress concerning proposed legislation. "Here," according to the Court, "private publication by Senator Gravel through the cooperation of Beacon Press was in no way essential to the deliberations of the Senate." . . .

Thus, the Court excludes from the sphere of protected legislative activity a function that I had supposed lay at the heart of our democratic system. I speak, of course, of the legislator's duty to inform the public about matters affecting the administration of government. That this "informing function" falls into the class of things "generally done in a session of the House by one of its members in relation to the business before it," Kilbourn v. Thompson, was explicitly acknowledged by the Court in Watkins v. United States, 354 U.S. 178 (1957). In speaking of the "power of the Congress to inquire into and publicize corruption, maladministration or inefficiency in agencies of the Government," the Court noted that "from the earliest times in its history, the Congress has assiduously performed an 'informing function' of this nature." Id., at 200 n.33.

We need look no further than Congress itself to find evidence supporting the Court's observation in *Watkins*. Congress has provided financial support for communications between its Members and the public, including the franking privilege for letters, telephone and telegraph allowances, stationery allotments, and favorable prices on reprints from the Congressional Record. Congressional hearings, moreover, are not confined to gathering information for internal distribution, but are often widely publicized, sometimes televised, as a means of alerting the electorate to matters of public import and concern. . . .

The informing function has been cited by numerous students of American politics, both within and without the Government, as among the most important responsibilities of legislative office. Woodrow Wilson, for example, emphasized its role in preserving the separation of powers by ensuring that the administration of public policy by the Executive is understood by the legislature and electorate:

> It is the proper duty of a representative body to look diligently into every affair of government and to talk much about what it sees. It is meant to be the eyes and the voice, and to embody the wisdom and will of its constituents. Unless Congress have and use every means of acquainting itself with the acts and the disposition of the administrative agents of the government, the country must be helpless to learn how it is being served; and unless Congress both scrutinize these things and sift them by every form of discussion, the country must remain in embarrassing, crippling ignorance of the very affairs which it is most important that it should understand and direct.

Congressional Government 303 (1885). . . . Though I fully share these and related views on the educational values served by the informing function, there is yet another, and perhaps more fundamental, interest at stake. It requires no citation of authority to state that public concern over current issues — the war, race relations, governmental invasions of privacy — has transformed itself in recent years into what many believe is a crisis of confidence, in our system of government and its capacity to meet the needs and reflect the wants of the American people. Communication between Congress and the electorate tends to alleviate that doubt by exposing and clarifying the workings of the political system, the policies underlying new laws and the role of the Executive in their administration. To the extent that the informing function succeeds in fostering public faith in the responsiveness of Government, it is not only an "ordinary" task of the legislator but one that is essential to the continued vitality of our democratic institutions.

Unlike the Court, therefore, I think that the activities of Congressmen in communicating with the public are legislative acts protected by the Speech or Debate Clause. I agree with the Court that not every task performed by a legislator is privileged; intervention before Executive departments is one that is not. But the informing function carries a far more persuasive claim to the protections of the Clause. It has been recognized by this Court as something "generally done" by Congressmen, the Congress itself has established special concessions designed to lower the cost of such communication, and, most important, the function furthers several well-recognized goals of representative government. To say in the face of these facts that the informing function is not privileged merely because it is not necessary to the internal deliberations of Congress is to give the Speech or Debate Clause an artificial and narrow reading unsupported by reason. . . .

Similarly, the Government cannot strip Senator Gravel of the immunity by asserting that his conduct "did not relate to any pending Congressional business." The Senator has stated that his hearing on the Pentagon Papers had a direct bearing on the work of his Subcommittee on Buildings and Grounds, because of the effect of the Vietnam war on the domestic economy and the lack of sufficient federal funds to provide adequate public facilities. If in fact the Senator is wrong in this contention, and his conduct at the hearing exceeded the subcommittee's jurisdiction, then again it is the Senate that must call him to task. This Court has permitted congressional witnesses to defend their refusal to answer questions on the ground of nongermaneness. Watkins v. United States, 354 U.S. 178 (1957). Here, however, it is the Executive that seeks the aid of the judiciary, not to protect individual rights, but to extend its power of inquiry and interrogation into the privileged domain of the legislature. In my view the Court should refuse to turn the freedom of speech or debate on the Government's notions of legislative propriety and relevance. We would weaken the very structure of our constitutional system by becoming a partner in this assault on the separation of powers.

Whether the Speech or Debate Clause extends to the informing function is an issue whose importance goes beyond the fate of a single Senator or Congressman. What is at stake is the right of an elected representative to inform, and the public to be informed, about matters relating directly to the workings of our Government. The dialogue between Congress and people has been recognized, from the days of our founding, as one of the necessary elements of a representative system. We should not retreat from that view merely because, in the course of that dialogue, information may be revealed that is embarrassing to the other branches of government or violates their notions of necessary secrecy. A Member of Congress who exceeds the bounds of propriety in performing this official task may be called to answer by the other Members of his chamber. We do violence to the fundamental concepts of privilege, however, when we subject that same conduct to judicial scrutiny at the instance of the Executive. The threat of "prosecution by an unfriendly executive and conviction by a hostile judiciary," United States v. Johnson, 383 U.S., at 179, that the Clause was designed to avoid, can only lead to timidity in the performance of this vital function. The Nation as a whole benefits from the congressional investigation and exposure of official corruption and deceit. It likewise suffers when that exposure is replaced by muted criticism, carefully hushed behind congressional walls.

II

Equally troubling in today's decision is the Court's refusal to bar grand jury inquiry into the source of documents received by the Senator and placed by him in the hearing record. The receipt of materials for use in a congressional hearing is an integral part of the preparation for that legislative act. . . . It would accomplish little toward the goal of legislative freedom to exempt an official act from intimidating scrutiny, if other conduct leading up to the act and intimately related to it could be deterred by a similar threat. The reasoning that guided that Court in *Johnson* is no less persuasive today, and I see no basis, nor does the Court offer any, for departing from it here. I would hold that Senator Gravel's receipt of the Pentagon Papers, including the name of the person from whom he received them, may not be the subject of inquiry by the grand jury.

I would go further, however, and also exclude from grand jury inquiry any knowledge that the Senator or his aides might have concerning how the source himself first came to possess the Papers. This immunity, it seems to me, is essential to the performance of the informing function. Corrupt and deceitful officers of government do not often post for public examination the evidence of their own misdeeds. That evidence must be ferreted out, and often is, by fellow employees and subordinates. Their willingness to reveal that information and spark congressional inquiry may well depend on assurances from their contact in Congress that their identities and means of obtaining the evidence will be held in strictest confidence. To permit the grand jury to frustrate that expectation through an inquiry of the Congressman and his aides can only dampen the flow of information to the Congress and thus to the American people. There is a similar risk, of course, when the Member's own House requires him to break the confidence. But the danger, it seems to me, is far less if the Member's colleagues, and not an "unfriendly executive" or "hostile judiciary," are charged with evaluating the propriety of his conduct. In any event, assuming that a Congressman can be required to reveal the sources of his information and the methods used to obtain that information, that power of inquiry, as required by the Clause, is that of the Congressman's House, and of that House only.

JUSTICE STEWART filed an opinion dissenting in part [omitted].

JUSTICE DOUGLAS filed a dissenting opinion [omitted].

NOTES AND QUESTIONS

1. *A more typical case.* In *Gravel* the speech and debate clause was used to shelter the legislative process from the executive in the battle between these two branches. More often the issue comes up in far less poignant circumstances—for example, the challenge is not intended as a direct challenge to the separation of power doctrine. Professor Lane recalls that during his tenure as counsel to the New York State Senate Minority, he was requested by an assistant district attorney from a particular county to provide information regarding why a particular item was appropriated in one particular budget. The prosecutor believed that the entity to which the appropriation was made was a shell, established to enable a particular legislator to hire his family from whom he then received kickbacks. He wanted to review any documents that might refer to this appropriation and to interview relevant legislators and staff members, for example, members and staff of the finance committee. The relevant legislators determined that such inquiry would be too intrusive and instructed Lane to raise the speech and debate privilege. Why? Like many states, New York interprets its speech and debate clause, identical to the federal provision, in much the same way as the Court did in *Gravel*. Does the reasoning of *Gravel* cover this situation?

2. *Federal inquiry into state legislative activities.* Assume that the inquiry referred to above had come from federal prosecutors. Would the instructions to Lane have been sound? Consider the following case.

United States v. Gillock
445 U.S. 360 (1980)

BURGER, C.J., delivered the opinion of the Court. . . . [Internal citations have been omitted except where particularly relevant.]

I

Respondent Edgar H. Gillock was indicted on August 12, 1976, in the Western District of Tennessee on five counts of obtaining money under color of official right in violation of 18 U.S.C. §1951, one count of using an interstate facility to distribute a bribe in violation of 18 U.S.C. §1952, and one count of participating in an enterprise through a pattern of racketeering activity in violation of 18 U.S.C. §1962. The indictment charged Gillock, then a Tennessee state senator and practicing attorney, with accepting money as a fee for using his public office to block the extradition of a defendant from Tennessee to Illinois, and for agreeing to introduce in the State General Assembly legislation which would enable four persons to obtain master electricians' licenses they had been unable to obtain by way of existing examination processes.

Before trial, Gillock moved to suppress all evidence relating to his legislative activities. The District Court granted his motion, holding that as a state senator, Gillock had an evidentiary privilege cognizable under Rule 501 of the Federal Rules of Evidence. This privilege, deemed by the District Court to be equivalent to that granted Members of both Houses of Congress under the Speech or Debate Clause, Art. I, §6, cl. 1, was limited to prohibiting the introduction of evidence of Gillock's legislative acts and his underlying motivations. The court stated that the privilege is necessary "to protect the integrity of the [state's] legislative process by insuring the independence of individual legislators" and "to preserve the constitutional relation between our federal and state governments in our federal system." . . .

On remand, the Government submitted a formal offer of proof and requested a ruling on the applicability of the legislative privilege to 15 specifically described items of evidence. . . .

Based on this offer of proof, the District Court granted Gillock's renewed motion to exclude evidence of his legislative acts under Rule 501. It ruled inadmissible Gillock's official request for an opinion from the Attorney General regarding extradition and the answer to that request, and Gillock's statements to Howard that he could exert pressure on the extradition hearing officer to block the extradition because the hearing officer had appeared before Gillock's legislative committee. Similarly, the court ruled that all evidence regarding Gillock's introduction and support of the electricians' reciprocal licensing bill, his conversation with the private individuals who opposed the legislation, and the Governor's veto letter would be inadmissible. . . .

II

Gillock urges that we construct an evidentiary privilege barring the introduction of evidence of legislative acts in federal criminal prosecutions against state legislators. He argues first that a speech or debate type privilege for state legislators in federal criminal cases is an established part of the federal common law and is therefore applicable through Rule 501. Second, he contends that even apart from Rule 501, a legislative speech or debate privilege is compelled by principles of federalism rooted in our constitutional structure.

It is clear that were we to recognize an evidentiary privilege similar in scope to the Federal Speech or Debate Clause, much of the evidence at issue here would be inadmissible. . . . Under that standard, evidence of Gillock's participation in the state senate committee hearings and his votes and speeches on the floor would be privileged and hence inadmissible.

The language and legislative history of Rule 501 give no aid to Gillock. The Rule provides in relevant part that "the privilege of a witness . . . shall be governed by the principles of the common law as they may be interpreted by the courts of the United States in the light of reason and experience." Congress substituted the present language of Rule 501 for the draft proposed by the Advisory Committee of the Judicial Conference of the United States to provide the courts with greater flexibility in developing rules of privilege on a case-by-case basis. Under the Judicial Conference proposed rules submitted to Congress, federal courts would have been permitted to apply only nine specifically enumerated privileges, except as otherwise required by the Constitution or provided by Acts of Congress. Neither the Advisory Committee, the Judicial Conference, nor this Court saw fit, however, to provide the privilege sought by Gillock. Although that fact standing alone would not compel the federal courts to refuse to recognize a privilege omitted from the proposal, it does suggest that the claimed privilege was not thought to be either indelibly ensconced in our common law or an imperative of federalism. . . .

III

Gillock argues that the historical antecedents and policy considerations which inspired the Speech or Debate Clause of the Federal Constitution should lead this Court to recognize a comparable evidentiary privilege for state legislators in federal prosecutions. The important history of the Speech or Debate Clause has been related abundantly in opinions of this Court and need not be repeated. . . .

Two interrelated rationales underlie the Speech or Debate Clause: first, the need to avoid intrusion by the Executive or Judiciary into the affairs of a coequal branch, and second, the desire to protect legislative independence. . . .

The first rationale, resting solely on the separation of powers doctrine, gives no support to the grant of a privilege to state legislators in federal criminal prosecutions. It requires no citation of authorities for the proposition that the Federal Government has limited powers with respect to the states, unlike the unfettered authority which English monarchs exercised over the Parliament. By the same token, however, in those areas where the Constitution grants the Federal Government the power to act, the Supremacy Clause dictates that federal enactments will prevail over competing state exercises of power. Thus, under our federal structure, we do not have the struggles for power between the federal and state systems such as inspired the need for the Speech or Debate Clause as a restraint on the Federal Executive to protect federal legislators.

Apart from the separation of powers doctrine, it is also suggested that principles of comity require the extension of a speech or debate type privilege to state legislators in federal criminal prosecutions. However, as we have noted, federal interference in the state legislative process is not on the same constitutional footing with the interference of one branch of the Federal Government in the affairs of a coequal branch. . . .

The second rationale underlying the Speech or Debate Clause is the need to insure legislative independence. Gillock relies heavily on Tenney v. Brandhove, 341 U.S. 367 (1951), where this Court was cognizant of the potential for disruption of the state legislative process. The issue there, however, was whether state legislators were immune from civil suits for alleged violations of civil rights under 42 U.S.C. §1983. The claim was made by a private individual who alleged that a state legislative committee hearing was conducted to prevent him from exercising his First Amendment rights. . . .

Although *Tenney* reflects this Court's sensitivity to interference with the functioning of state legislators, we do not read that opinion as broadly as Gillock would have us. First, *Tenney* was a civil action brought by a private plaintiff to vindicate private rights. . . . Thus, in protecting the independence of state legislators, *Tenney* and subsequent cases on official immunity have drawn the line at civil actions.

We conclude, therefore, that although principles of comity command careful consideration, our cases disclose that where important federal interests are at stake, as in the enforcement of federal criminal statutes, comity yields. We recognize that denial of a privilege to a state legislator may have some minimal impact on the exercise of his legislative function; however, similar arguments made to support a claim of Executive privilege were found wanting in United States v. Nixon, 418 U.S. 683 (1974), when balanced against the need of enforcing federal criminal statutes. There, the genuine risk of inhibiting candor in the internal exchanges at the highest levels of the Executive Branch was held insufficient to justify denying judicial power to secure all relevant evidence in a criminal proceeding. . . .

IV

The Federal Speech or Debate Clause, of course, is a limitation on the Federal Executive, but by its terms is confined to federal legislators. The Tennessee Speech or Debate Clause is in terms a limit only on the prosecutorial powers of that State. Congress might have provided that a state legislator prosecuted under federal law should be accorded the same evidentiary privileges as a Member of Congress. Alternatively, Congress could have . . . directed federal courts to apply to a state legislator the same evidentiary privileges available in a prosecution of a similar charge in the courts of the state. But Congress has chosen neither of these courses. . . .

JUSTICE REHNQUIST filed a dissenting statement, in which JUSTICE POWELL joined [omitted].

F.   INITIATIVE AND REFERENDUM—CHALLENGE TO LEGISLATIVE LEGITIMACY

We introduced Part III of this book by reference to Federalist No. 10 and its particular concern about majorities "who are united and actuated by some common impulse of passion, or of interest, adverse to the permanent and aggregate interests of the community." The Federalist No. 10, at 57 (James Madison) (Jacob E. Cooke ed., 1961). As an antidote to this concern, the Framers proposed a model of representative democracy that through its structures and procedures was intended to temper passions, provide a framework for rational policy making and protect minority interests. History demonstrates how well this system of government has worked in making the enactment of legislation extremely difficult. As has been pointed out in earlier sections of this chapter, this enactment difficulty has proved extremely frustrating for proponents of various policies. Such frustration is exemplified by the views of Lloyd Cutler found on pages 548-552.

One avenue for the expression of this disenchantment has been the use of the initiative and referendum to circumvent the need for legislative enactment of statutes or consideration of constitutional amendments. Initiative, the main focus of this section, refers to the process of having legislation (or constitutional amendments) placed directly on the ballot, usually through a petitioning process, and then voted on by the public. There is a modified form of this process (sometimes referred to as an indirect initiative) that uses the petition process to trigger legislative consideration of a particular proposal. Such a proposal is only subject to referendum in the event that the legislature does not adopt it. Referendum refers to the process by which legislative enactments are required to be approved by the electorate before they can become effective. In some states particular types of legislation (for example, creating debt) must be subject to referendum. Another form of referendum is to allow the public, through a petition process, to require an enacted bill to be submitted to the voters. One example of a state constitutional provision authorizing initiatives and referendums is set forth below:

ARTICLE IV, CONSTITUTION OF OREGON

SECTION 1. LEGISLATIVE POWER; INITIATIVE AND REFERENDUM

(1) The legislative power of the state, except for the initiative and referendum powers reserved to the people, is vested in a Legislative Assembly, consisting of a Senate and a House of Representatives.

(2) (a) The people reserve to themselves the initiative power, which is to propose laws and amendments to the Constitution and enact or reject them at an election independently of the Legislative Assembly.

(b) An initiative law may be proposed only by a petition signed by a number of qualified voters equal to six percent of the total number of votes cast for all candidates for Governor at the election at which a Governor was elected for a term of four years next preceding the filing of the petition.

(c) An initiative amendment to the Constitution may be proposed only by a petition signed by a number of qualified voters equal to eight percent of the total number of votes cast for all candidates for Governor at the election at which a Governor was elected for a term of four years next preceding the filing of the petition.

(d) An initiative petition shall include the full text of the proposed law or amendment to the Constitution. A proposed law or amendment to the Constitution shall embrace one subject only and matters properly connected therewith.

(e) An initiative petition shall be filed not less than four months before the election at which the proposed law or amendment to the Constitution is to be voted upon.

(3) (a) The people reserve to themselves the referendum power, which is to approve or reject at an election any Act, or part thereof, of the Legislative Assembly that does not become effective earlier than 90 days after the end of the session at which the Act is passed.

(b) A referendum on an Act or part thereof may be ordered by a petition signed by a number of qualified voters equal to four percent of the total number of votes cast for all candidates for Governor at the election at which a Governor was elected for a term of four years next preceding the filing of the petition. A referendum petition shall be filed not more than 90 days after the end of the session at which the Act is passed.

Initiatives are not new to American government. They were introduced to state constitutions as part of the Progressive movement's attempt to bring government "back to the people." But despite their early introduction, they were little used until the 1970s. Today more than one-third of the states have provisions authorizing initiatives. Since the 1970s, initiatives have addressed subjects as diverse as public morality, governmental processes, taxation, labor regulation, business regulation, utility rates, zoning and land use, health, welfare reform, housing, homelessness, education, civil rights, environmental protection, and nuclear power. During the early 1990s, the most noted initiatives were a California effort to limit the rights of illegal aliens and their children, a California effort to prohibit affirmative actions, the efforts of several states to restrict the rights of homosexuals, and Oregon's doctor-assisted suicide law.

1.   Initiatives — The Democratic Context

The frequent use of the initiatives since the 1970s has led to considerable debate about their efficacy. This debate has basically addressed two issues:

(1) how successful initiatives have been as measured against their goals; and (2) how they compare, as a law-making process, with representative democracy. The following excerpts from two of the major students of initiatives exemplify this debate.

David B. Magleby, Direct Legislation
181-88 (1984)

Not only do direct and indirect forms of democracy differ in the institutional arrangements they advocate but they pursue quite different ends and values as well. Direct democracy values participation, open access, and political equality. It tends to deemphasize compromise, continuity, and consensus. In short, direct democracy encourages conflict and competition and attempts to expand the base of participants. Indirect democracy values stability, consensus, and compromise and seeks institutional arrangements that insulate fundamental principles from momentary passions or fluctuations in opinion. While direct and indirect forms of democracy maximize different ends, there are several important dimensions of democratic governance upon which the two can be compared: participation, representation, accountability, accommodation, authority and deliberation.

Participation and Representation

The case for establishing and enlarging direct legislation has one fundamental premise: all citizens should be able to initiate and decide upon legislation themselves. . . .

Just as direct democracy is central to the argument for the initiative and referendum, the idea of a republic and representation is the central premise of direct legislation's opponents. The "representationists" not only criticize the operation of direct legislation in practice but assert that the people can best rule themselves through regular election of public officials. Opponents of direct legislation challenge the claims that direct legislation is necessary for free and open government and that it fosters better government. . . .

Both the participationists and the representationists would agree with the popular sentiment that the people should rule, but they would have very different views on how the people can effectively rule. . . .

Which people rule in direct legislation? Those who set the legislative agenda and those who actually vote on that agenda. Neither the issues put before the voters nor those voters who actually decide them are representative. The people who rule under direct legislation tend to be those who can understand and use the process. Less educated, poorer, and nonwhite citizens are organizationally and financially excluded from setting the direct legislation agenda because their own issue agendas are less articulated and because they lack the resources and personal efficacy to attempt a petition circulation and direct legislation campaign. These same people are less likely to vote on ballot propositions because they cannot comprehend the wording of the proposition and need the assistance of such ballot-organizing devices as political parties.

Despite the high hopes of reformers that direct legislation would increase turnout and reduce alienation, neither has occurred. In fact, direct legislation has not activated uninterested or alienated voters. . . .

Accommodation, Accountability, and Authority

Difference of opinion about public policy will exist in any society. An important characteristic of a democratic system is the presence of institutional structures that reflect public opinion in the determination of public policy and can also resolve conflicts over policy by peaceful accommodation. For instance, in the legislative arena rarely will any one side have its way completely. Rather, the legislative product typically will be the result of compromise, allowing consensus to emerge around a policy choice.

In direct legislation the voter is only partially a legislator. The voter is not party to the drafting and compromising process and can play no part in the determination of the policy choice he will confront. Thus, voters are faced with statutes that they did not help to write and that they must affirm or reject in toto. Direct legislation does not face the procedural constraints of the legislative process: hearings, amendments, markup, scheduling, floor debate, and conference. In contrast, rarely do the sponsors of an initiative circulate their bill prior to the petition phase — and once this phase begins, the language cannot be changed. The process of direct legislation is not built upon the principle of compromise and accommodation but instead forces an all-or-nothing policy decision on the question as formulated by the sponsors alone.

Another important distinction between the two forms of legislation is that the direct means does not permit an assessment of the participants' intensity of opinion. In direct legislation all votes are counted equally, but not all voters feel equally positive or negative about the proposition. Some voters may be only slightly opposed or slightly in favor of the proposition, but their votes have the same weight as the votes cast by those who are sure of their opinions and feel strongly about them. In the legislative process, elected representatives can calculate the varying degrees of intensity and include them in their legislative decisions. . . . This advantage of the legislative process works to facilitate accommodation. The strength of feeling among all partisans to an issue is weighted as legislators arrive at compromises acceptable to a majority of legislators. This is not the case in direct legislation, which helps to explain why direct legislation measures are often more extreme than measures produced by legislatures. . . .

One of the frequently cited positive consequences of the initiative is that it often stimulates the legislature to take action or, at the least, provides a means to determine in part the agenda of legislative action. Whether the initiative serves as a "gun behind the door" or a legislative "bit and bridle," most students of the process have concluded that on balance, it fosters legislative responsibility. On at least some issues, however, the initiative serves as an easy way for the legislature to avoid deciding an issue, passing it along instead to the voters. In this respect direct legislation discourages legislative accountability. An additional problem for legislative accountability is the fact that voters can hold only themselves accountable for an unsuccessful initiative. Precisely because of the nature of initiative politics, legislators are legally prohibited from tampering with a successful initiative measure or are politically unlikely to do so.

Deliberation

The legislative process is frequently criticized for being slow, cumbersome, and biased against action. These factors, however, have benefits as well as costs, including the open and deliberative nature of the process. In the legislature, proposed statutes and constitutional amendments are reviewed and modified several times before they are submitted to a final vote. As a measure obtains sponsors, survives hearings, and then is opened for amendment in markup, the expertise and experience of legislators, staff, and interested groups and individuals is brought to bear. These same procedures are repeated in the second house of the legislature in every state except Nebraska, which has a unicameral legislature. The process of drafting and modifying initiatives is not subject to the same open and deliberative review. This frequently puts the voters in the position of deciding a measure with flaws that emerge in the campaign but cannot be changed even if the sponsors desire to make the change.

When comparing the more open and public nature of legislative drafting conducted in state legislature with the more closed and private drafting of initiatives, it is important to consider not only the final product of the process but also the decision-making process of the participants: the voters, in the context of direct legislation, and the legislators, in the legislatures.

Unfortunately, I do not have comparable data on the levels of knowledge and information most legislators have for their voting decisions; but the data I have reviewed on voter decision making on direct legislation raise serious questions about the operation of that process. Voters rarely use more than one source of information, typically television; they rarely consult with others about the proposed legislation; and they often decide their vote late in the campaign or in the polling booth. There is voter confusion on ballot propositions generally because of the legal and technical language that is so much a part of direct legislation. In short, voters appear to reach their voting decision on most propositions with very little deliberation, discussion, or study.

Legislators face some of the same problems as voters, but they have some resources at their disposal that voters do not have. In addition, legislators have structured the decision-making process on the basis of specialization. The committee system, the seniority principle, and professional staff mean that expertise is brought to bear on legislation in the formative states. In the final voting phase, legislators call upon the knowledge and experience of their colleagues to inform their vote. For any issue there are legislative specialists on both sides of the question. In addition, there are lobbyists, again on both sides of virtually all issues, who seek the ear of any potentially interested legislator. Legislators have not only these resources but also the time and political interest to study proposed laws. They also know that they may be held accountable for their vote and therefore have a stake in understanding the issue. Modern legislatures with trained professional staffs possess a tremendous advantage over individual voters in the knowledge and information aspects of decision making.

There are, in sum, important differences between direct and representative legislation. The electorate as a whole cannot function as a deliberative assembly in the same way that a legislature can. Voters do not develop expertise in the same way or to the same extent that legislators do. The elected legislator will weight in his voting calculus his personal views on the issue, his perception of his constituents' views on the issue, and his view of the long-range interest of the polity. In direct legislation, voting is more individualistic. Theoretically, the outcome of direct legislation should reflect the majority will; however, given dropoff and voter confusion, this may not be true in practice. What is true of direct legislation is that the outcome, which may or may not reflect the majority will, is subject to fewer institutional checks and safeguards than the legislative process.

A concern with the relative absence of checks and balances is recurrent in the debate over the initiative process. Opponents of the process often cite this as one of their chief procedural concerns, along with oversimplification and overdramatization. Under direct legislation, the task of safeguarding minority rights from majority tyranny is effectively left to the courts. Elected legislatures guard against majority tyranny by the use of indirect rather than direct popular input, by bicameral checks, and by the executive veto. James Madison argued in number 10 of The Federalist Papers that the function of a representative assembly is "to refine and enlarge the public views, by passing them through the medium of a chosen body of citizens." The translation of public views into public policy is more likely to be refined and enlarged under representative systems than under direct democratic systems.

The initiative and referendum permit an authoritarian (publicly accepted) resolution of a difficult policy choice and serve as a safety valve for issues that slip between the legislative cracks. In several other respects, however, direct legislation does not compare as favorably. Under direct legislation the decision is limited to a yes or no response to a typically complex issue. The legislative process provides more room for adjustment and accommodation of competing viewpoints. Direct legislation is a closed and private process until the matter goes out for signature. The legislative process, especially in the formulative phase, is open and public, particularly since the passage of sunshine laws. Direct legislation presents an agenda of issues that does not represent the issue concerns of the general citizenry, and the process is inflexible, providing little opportunity to correct error. Voter decision making in direct legislation is typically the result of snap judgments based upon superficial emotional appeals broadcast on television. The legislative process is more deliberative, substantive, and rational.

The legislative process is not without problems. Last-minute consideration of bills often lacks deliberation, and the closing rush may mean that legislators will cast votes without understanding the substance of measures. The sometimes dominant role played by interest groups makes the process less democratic. Complexity prompts creation of specialized committees and subcommittees, which in turn may exclude some legislators from influence until the bill is brought to the floor. In short, both direct legislation and the legislative process have shortcomings. Much of what has been written about direct legislation in the past, however, has only focused on the weaknesses of the legislative process, ignoring its strengths.

Eric Lane, Men Are Not Angels: The Realpolitik of Direct Democracy and What We Can Do About It
34 Willamette L. Rev. 579 (1998)

The direct democracy movement was not, at least in its advocacy, simply a nihilistic attack on the reigning institutions of power. It was not posited merely as an alternative to representative democracy, but as means for capturing the civic spirit of American citizens. Premised on a view of human conduct unlike that of representative democracy, "[i]t was not," according to Professor Morone, "merely a negative vision, restricted to razing the party state. Along with popular participation came the restoration of the classic republican constituency. Reformers would put Madison aside." Understanding what it means to "put Madison aside" is fundamental to comparing representative democracy and direct democracy. It references the idea that government is the greatest reflection on human nature. To "put Madison aside," then, means to put Madison's view of human nature aside and substitute a view of human nature justifying direct democracy.

What is Madison's need-to-be-disposed-of view? Simply put, it is that individuals within society organize themselves into factions to advance their individual interests and passions. The term "passion" refers to non-economic interests such as religion or ideology. Factions are groups "who are united and actuated by some common impulse of passion, or of interest, adverse to the permanent and aggregate interests of the community." In The Federalist No. 10, Madison expressed the view of human conduct on which our system of representative democracy is based:

> The latent causes of faction are thus sown in the nature of man; and we see them everywhere brought into different degrees of activity, according to the different circumstances of civil society. A zeal for different opinions concerning religion, concerning Government and many other points, as well of speculation as of practice; an attachment to different leaders ambitiously contending for preeminence and power; or to persons of other descriptions whose fortunes have been interesting to the human passions, have in turn divided mankind into parties, inflamed them with mutual animosity, and rendered them much more disposed to vex and oppress each other, than to co-operate for their common good. So strong is this propensity of mankind to fall into mutual animosities, that where no substantial occasion presents itself, the most frivolous and fanciful distinctions have been sufficient to kindle their unfriendly passions, and excite their most violent conflicts. But the most common and durable source of factions, has been the various and unequal distribution of property.

It is this view of human conduct that had to be "put aside" by the advocates of direct democracy in order to justify the very form of government Madison and the other Framers believed would result in the triumph of passions and interests. To acknowledge the Madisonian view of human conduct would have meant that the Progressives were advocating a system in which people's narrow interests and passions would triumph. To avoid this consequence, they returned to the same romantic image of man popularized by the radical Whig republicans to contest British rule at the time of Independence and rejected by the Framers as untrue. This was the rustic, sturdy yeoman — frugal, industrious, temperate, and simple. And its Progressive Period progeny was John Q. Public, the Average Man, the Man of Good Will, the Forgotten Man possessing all of the virtues of the sturdy yeoman plus more. As Professor Hofstadter described him:

> His approach to politics was, in a sense, individualistic: He would study the issues and think them through, rather than learn them through pursuing his needs. Furthermore, it was assumed that somehow he would be really capable of informing himself in ample detail about the many issues that he would come to pass on, and that he could master their intricacies sufficiently to pass intelligent judgment.

Therein lies the premise for direct democracy. A man, John Q. Public, possesses the inclination and time to participate continuously in the lawmaking of his nation, state, or locality and is able to discern and pursue the common good without regard to self-interest.

This view of human nature was the wave upon which the ship Progressive predictably foundered. John Q. Public, as used by the Progressives, was a necessary construct to rationalize a government that conflicted with representative democracy. As Hofstadter wrote: "Without such assumptions the entire movement for such reforms as the initiative and referendum ... is unintelligible." As its supporters soon recognized, the movement quickly became unintelligible. Walter Lippmann, an early advocate of the selfless man, best described this phenomenon in stating:

> In ordinary circumstances voters cannot be expected to transcend their particular, localized and self-regarding opinions. [We might as] well expect men laboring in the valley to see the land as from a mountain top. In their circumstances, which as private persons they cannot readily surmount, the voters are most likely to suppose that whatever seems obviously good to them must be good for the country, and good in the sight of God.

Likewise, Hofstadter wrote:

> Confronted by an array of technical questions, often phrased in legal language, the voters shrank from the responsibilities the new system attempted to put upon them. Small and highly organized groups with plenty of funds and skillful publicity could make use of these devices, but such were not the results the proponents of initiative and referendum sought; nor was the additional derationalization of politics that came with the propaganda campaigns demanded by referendums. ...

In addition to John Q. Public's demasking, the corrupt railroad and robber baron legislatures of the last century have been virtually eliminated. This does not mean that today's legislatures are free from direct corruption, or that campaign costs and regulations have not had a corrupting effect on some legislators. However, as legislative activity in every government level has grown exponentially throughout this century because of the public's demand for regulatory and redistributive changes, legislative corruption has diminished.

Thomas E. Cronin, Direct Democracy
224-32 (1989)

Has direct democracy enhanced government responsiveness and accountability? The answer is at best a maybe. States that have adopted direct democracy devices are more accountable than they once were. Yet other factors, not limited to states that have the initiative and referendum, also help to account for this change, including better education, vastly increased revenues, professional staffs, and more experience with rule by law. ...

Do direct democracy devices provide an effective safety valve when legislators prove timid, corrupt, or dominated by narrow special interests? Generally, yes. Indeed, the mere circulation of petitions for an initiative, referendum, or recall sometimes "encourages" officials to reconsider what they are doing and how they are doing it. . . .

Direct democracy processes have *not* brought about rule by the common people. Government by the people has been a dream for many, but most Americans want their legislators and other elected officials to represent them as best they can and to make the vast bulk of public policy decisions. Direct democracy devices occasionally permit those who are motivated and interested in public policy issues to have a direct personal input by recording their vote, but this is a long way from claiming that direct democracy gives a significant voice to ordinary citizens on a regular basis. That early claim was considerably overstated.

A related claim was that direct democracy devices would lessen the undesirable influences of special interests. These devices may have done this in some respects, but special interests are still present and can still afford highly paid, high-caliber lobbyists at every state legislature. And there are many more lobbyists now than there were in 1900.

On the other hand, direct democracy devices have sometimes allowed less well-represented interests to bring their messages before the public. Environmentalists, for example, have used the initiative process to force legislatures to give greater consideration to conservation and environmental protection issues. Other groups, such as those favoring the death penalty and mandatory sentences, have been able to get their ideas heard and often enacted into law. Ultimately, however, single individuals unwilling to join groups and form coalitions are unable to use direct democracy processes. In the larger states the initiative process has come to be dominated by large organizations, displacing the citizen groups it was once intended to serve. Only in groups and in concert with several groups can a few individuals make these devices work for them. The much-talked-about "common man" is required to become an uncommon joiner and organizer in order to realize the aspirations of the proponents of direct democracy. And it helps to be wealthy and to have access to professional campaign management technologies, especially in California.

Direct democracy was also supposed to stimulate educational debate about important policy issues. It does, yet the debates usually last only five or six weeks. Direct democracy processes do allow debate in public forums well beyond the legislative hearing chambers, and as a result, public officials, newspapers, radio and television stations, and various interest groups often take a stand and trigger at least limited public discussion debate. . . .

The most unfortunate deficiency of this claim, one not adequately anticipated by the early advocates of initiative, referendum, and recall, is that the side with more money too often gets to define the issue and structure the debate in an unbalanced way. Whereas a town meeting gives all sides an equal chance to speak, money and court rulings permitting unlimited spending promote a system in which the better-financed side can, and often does, outspend the other by a dramatic margin.

Direct democracy was also intended to stimulate voter interest in issues and encourage higher election-day turnouts. It often does stir interest and sometimes even polarizes factions. Certainly it heightens interest at election time, although interest in candidate races . . . ordinarily is greater. . . .

Finally, proponents of direct democracy claimed that their innovations would increase civic pride and trust in government and thereby diminish apathy and alienation. This was a proud boast and a noble aspiration. Trust in or alienation from government is difficult to measure. Americans tend to love their country and to dislike their government. Government reminds them of taxes, regulations, and restrictions. Pride in government is cyclical and is related in part to war or its absence, prosperity or its absence, Olympic successes, bicentennials, and similar events. It would be difficult to prove that Minnesotans or Virginians are less proud or less trusting of their state governments than Coloradans or Californians. Many states without direct democracy devices appear to enjoy as much citizen respect and acceptance as states that have them. In one area civic pride did increase. In states in the West that once were dominated by a few large special interests and often by party bosses — including the Dakotas, Oregon, and California — direct democracy devices doubtless did play a role in encouraging state governments to become more responsive to ordinary citizens. But better education, better and more media, increased competition between the political parties, and other factors also contributed to this same end. Clearly, direct democracy's advocates overstated their claim.

Have the initiative, referendum, and recall undermined representative democracy? Have the devices weakened our legislatures? Although experts still argue about the consequences, most would say that direct democracy has not weakened our regular legislative processes. Even in areas where these devices are used, 98 or 99 percent of the laws remain the responsibility of legislators. Legislatures are more important today than ever, as growing population and growing demands on government force them to assume greater responsibilities. Americans overwhelmingly endorse leaving the job of making laws to their elected representatives and view direct democracy devices almost entirely as a last alternative to the legislative process. . . .

A second major objection to direct democracy held that it would produce unsound legislation and unwise or bad policy. Unwise legislation does get onto ballots, but the record indicates that voters reject most really unsound ideas. When defective legislation has been approved by direct democracy procedures, it has often been contested later in the courts, resulting in modification or outright invalidation.

Critics say, with some justification, that direct legislation is less well prepared than institutional legislation. Legislators have access to veteran legislative draftsmen, researchers, and counsel — resources that can seldom be matched by interest groups or concerned activists trying to get a measure on the ballot. This problem could be remedied, and safeguards have been adopted in some states, but the number of judicial reversals of initiatives attests to the reality that direct democracy efforts sometimes produce poorly drafted legislation.

A related fear was that minority rights might be sacrificed on the altar of majority rule. However, remarkably few ballot issues of this type have prevailed. When compared with the work of the nation's legislatures, the outcomes of initiative and referendum campaigns can be characterized as equally tolerant of minority rights. In some regions of the country state legislatures, even in the twentieth century, have been notably intolerant of women, minorities, and members of a minority party or even the major opposition political party. Most of these same states do not permit their voters the initiative, referendum, and recall.

Opponents also have long objected to direct democracy on the grounds that the typical voter would not be informed enough to cast an intelligent vote. According to this view, few voters consider all the possible alternatives to and consequences of a single vote; they are asked to render a verdict on a specific point but not on its context. American voters themselves would agree that their votes are often not as informed as they should be. Even people who feel strongly that citizens ought to be able to vote directly on issues admit that many citizens, including themselves, are often not able to cast a well-informed vote. Survey data confirm that as many as one-third to a majority of those voting acknowledge that they felt uncomfortable about voting because they needed more information or more time to discuss the issue or to read the voter pamphlet more carefully, or found that the statement was too hard to read and comprehend. . . . So, too, members of the state and national legislatures — especially in those frantic days near the end of a session — yearn for more information about consequences, and more discussion and compromise than time will permit. Despite the misgivings of critics, voters judge reasonably well when faced with initiative, referendum, or recall choices. It is partly a matter of the gap between the ideal and real worlds. In the ideal context, voters would prepare for their votes in a judicious, scholarly, and textbook-citizen fashion. But seldom is the time available. This is also true, but obviously to a lesser extent, for local, state, and national legislators. There too, a gap exists between the textbook legislator and the legislator with a family to raise, campaign funds to collect, a second job to maintain, and party loyalties to sustain. . . .

Critics of direct democracy predicted that special interests would turn these devices to their own advantage. Has this in fact been the case? To get things accomplished, individuals have to join a group with which they share common interest. America has become a nation of interest groups — and this is likely to be even more the case in the future than in the past. . . .

Legislatures, to be sure, are usually the best place to reconcile the divergent interests of a state or nation, but they need not be the only place.

Parties, the media, and the processes provided for in direct democracy can sometimes perform the reconciliation and compromising functions we usually assign, and should assign, to our institutionalized legislatures.

The final objection to direct democracy was that it would weaken the political accountability of elected officials. Voters in ballot issue elections seldom have to live with the consequence of their decisions; they seldom understand the longer-term needs and interests of the region; they are likely to think only of the short term and usually of their own self-interest.

These are serious objections. The sharing and checking of powers among elected officials in the three branches of government do provide for greater continuity and consideration of long-range consequences than do the initiative, referendum, and recall. Indeed, one criterion voters use in deciding whom to elect to office is the candidate's ability to comprehend the overall needs of a state or nation. Yet the record suggests that the public can also act responsibly . . . on environmental matters the public appears to be more responsible than most state legislatures. . . . The fear that populist democracy via initiative, referendum, and recall would lead to irresponsible, mercurial, or even bizarre decision making has not been borne out. The outcomes of direct democracy are similar to the outcomes of indirect democratic processes. One reason is that several safeguards regulate the existing forms of direct democracy. Another is that most Americans take their civic responsibilities seriously and have worked hard to make the initiative, referendum, and recall reasonable safe supplements to the traditional Madisonian checks and balances system.

NOTES AND QUESTIONS

1. *The differences between indirect and direct democracy.* Professors Magleby, Lane, and Cronin posit a number of goals and characteristics of representative and direct democracy. What are they, and how do they compare with each other? What is the view of each regarding the impact of initiatives on the legislative process? Do you think initiatives create incentives for legislators to allow tough political issues to be dealt with by the public? If so, does this matter? In 1994, voters of California overwhelmingly adopted an initiative (Proposition 187) limiting their government's ability to provide services to illegal aliens and their children. Efforts to have the California legislature, a relatively diverse bicameral body, enact similar methods had failed. Consider how the enactment of Proposition 187 reflects the various points made by each of the commentators.

2. *An idealized legislative model.* In a review of Professor Magleby's book, Professor Richard Briffault suggests that a weakness of Magleby's work is that it measures initiatives against idealized legislative process. See Richard Briffault, Distrust of Democracy, 63 Tex. L. Rev. 1347 (1985). What does this mean? If it means that outcome of legislative deliberation

is not always the product of rational debate, this is of course true. As discussed in Chapter 7, legislative voting decisions are the products of numerous factors. But does this deny the validity of the proposition that the process tempers majority rashness? In fact, isn't it the very deliberative characteristic of representative democracy that results in a growing frequency in the use of initiatives? And in the 1990s, many of these initiatives have been aimed at limiting minority rights and benefits. Professor Julian Eule, a leading student of initiatives, makes this point well:

> No one would be so naive as to deny that the deliberative ideal breaks down with disturbing frequency. The legislature often has trouble hearing voices from the margin. The Framers' vision, however, combined a deliberative idealism — which inspired representative government — with a pluralistic realism — which prompted cautionary checks. In other words, the process anticipates its own frailties by subdividing lawmaking authority. . . .
>
> The problem with substitutive democracy is different. When naked preferences emerge from a plebiscite, it is not a consequence of system breakdown. Naked preferences are precisely what the system seeks to measure. Aggregation is all that it cares about. The threat to minority rights and interests here is structural. This is how the system is supposed to work.

Julian N. Eule, Judicial Review of Direct Democracy, 99 Yale L.J. 1503, 1550-51 (1990).

3. *Initiative as escape valve.* One of the popular arguments in favor of initiatives is that they serve as an escape valve for representative democracy. What does this mean? Isn't this escape valve for majoritarian views the very phenomenon that the Framers were attempting to curb?

4. *Initiatives, minority groups, and the Voting Rights Act.* One of the arguments raised against the use of initiatives is that they disfavor the nation's minority groups. This point is sharply raised by Derrick A. Bell, Jr. See The Referendum: Democracy's Barrier to Racial Equality, 54 Wash. L. Rev. 1 (1978). This raises an interesting question about the relationship between the Voting Rights Act of 1965 and its amendments (discussed in Chapter 6) and initiatives. Does the success of minorities in the electoral process trigger more initiatives to circumvent their influence? Consider, for example, tax reduction initiatives. Aren't they, effectively, ways of reducing expenditures for social programs, which to a large extent benefit minority communities? Wouldn't it be much more difficult to reduce these programs in the give and take of the legislative process? Do you think that, on this basis, initiatives could be subject to the Voting Rights Act? Consider the comments of Professor Bell:

> Throughout this country's history, politicians have succumbed to the temptation to wage a campaign appealing to the desire of whites to dominate blacks. More recently, however, the growing black vote has begun to have an impact and even effected "Road to Damascus" conversions on more than a

few political Pauls, some of whom even claim "born again" experiences during mid-term. This impact may be subverted if voting majorities may enact controversial legislation directly.

Id. at 13.

2. Initiatives — The Legal Context

Legislative plebiscites also raise some fundamental legal questions. First, does the use of legislative plebiscites by states violate the guarantee clause of the United States Constitution? And second, should laws enacted through the initiative process be subject to different standards of judicial review than those enacted through the legislative process?

Article IV, §4 of the Constitution provides that "the United States shall guarantee to every State in this Union a Republican Form of Government." What form of government did the Framers contemplate here? Most scholars argue that a republican form of government, as contrasted to "pure democracy," was one in which representatives were chosen by the electorate. See, for example, The Federalist Nos. 10, 14, and 39. As Judge Hans Linde has written: "[t]hat a republican form of government meant representative, not direct, democracy could not be stated more emphatically." Hans A. Linde, When Initiative Lawmaking Is Not "Republican Government": The Campaign Against Homosexuality, 72 Or. L. Rev. 19, 24 (1993). But does this guarantee require judicial invalidation of initiatives? Early decisions in state courts answered the question arguing that initiatives did not interfere with representative government, but complemented it. Legislatures, it was argued, were free to repeal or amend (either through statute or through their powers to amend their constitutions) laws adopted through initiatives. See, for example, State v. Pacific States Tel. & Tel. Co., 53 Or. 162, 99 P. 427 (1909); Kiernan v. City of Portland, 57 Or. 454, 111 P. 379 (1910). For a provocative challenge to the logic of these cases, see Hans A. Linde, When Initiative Lawmaking Is Not "Republican Government": The Campaign Against Homosexuality, 72 Or. L. Rev. 19 (1993).

Federal jurisprudence has treated the question differently, as evidenced by the decision below. Internal citations have been omitted except where particularly relevant.

Pacific States Tel. & Tel. Co. v. Oregon
223 U.S. 1184 (1912)

CHIEF JUSTICE WHITE delivered the opinion of the Court.

In 1902 Oregon amended its constitution (Art. IV, §1). This amendment while retaining an existing clause vesting the exclusive legislative power in a General Assembly consisting of a senate and house of representatives added to that provision the following: "But the people reserve to themselves power to propose laws and amendments to the constitution and to enact or reject the same at the polls, independent of the legislative assembly, and also reserve power at their own option to approve or reject at the polls any act of the legislative assembly." . . .

By resort to the initiative in 1906 a law taxing certain classes of corporations was submitted, voted on and promulgated by the Governor in 1906 . . . as having been duly adopted. . . .

The Pacific States Telephone and Telegraph Company, an Oregon corporation engaged in business in that State, made a return of its gross receipts as required by the statute and was accordingly assessed two per cent upon the amount of such return. The suit which is now before us was commenced by the State to enforce payment of this assessment and the statutory penalties for delinquency. . . .

[The company defended the suit by making several different arguments, among others, that the initiative and referendum violated the guarantee clause of the United States Constitution.]

Thus dispelling any mere confusion resulting from forms of expression and considering the substance of things, it is apparent that the second proposition, which rests upon the affirmative assertion that by the adoption of the initiative and referendum the State "violates the right to a republican form of government which is guaranteed by section 4 of Article IV of the Federal Constitution," and the two subdivisions made of that proposition, the first that "the guarantee in question is to the people of the States and to each citizen, as well as to the States as political entities," and the second asserting "section 4 of Article IV therefore prohibits the majority in any State from adopting an unrepublican constitution," are the basic propositions upon which all the others rest. That is to say, all the others and their subdivisions are but inducements tending to show the correctness of the second and fundamental one. This conclusion is certain, as they all but point out the various modes by which the adoption of the initiative and referendum incapacitated the State from performing the duties incumbent upon it as a member of the Union or its obligations towards its citizens, thus causing the State to cease to be a government republican in form within the intendment of the constitutional provision relied upon. In other words, the propositions each and all proceed alone upon the theory that the adoption of the initiative and referendum destroyed all government republican in form in Oregon. This being so, the contention, if held to be sound, would necessarily affect the validity, not only of the particular statute which is before us, but of every other statute passed in Oregon since the adoption of the initiative and referendum. And indeed the propositions go further than this, since in their essence they assert that there is no governmental function, legislative or judicial, in Oregon, because it cannot be assumed, if the proposition be well founded, that there is at one and the same time one and the same government which is republican in form and not of that character.

Before immediately considering the text of §4 of Art. IV, in order to uncover and give emphasis to the anomalous and destructive effects upon both the state and national governments which the adoption of the proposition implies, as illustrated by what we have just said, let us briefly fix the inconceivable expansion of the judicial power and the ruinous destruction of legislative authority in matters purely political which would necessarily be occasioned by giving sanction to the doctrine which underlies and would be necessarily involved in sustaining the propositions contended for. First. That however perfect and absolute may be the establishment and dominion in fact of a state government, however complete may be its participation in and enjoyment of all its powers and rights as a member of the national Government, and however all the departments of that Government may recognize such state government, nevertheless every citizen of such State or person subject to taxation therein, or owing any duty to the established government, may be heard, for the purpose of defeating the payment of such taxes or avoiding the discharge of such duty, to assail in a court of justice the rightful existence of the State. Second. As a result, it becomes the duty of the courts of the United States, where such a claim is made, to examine as a justiciable issue the contention as to the illegal existence of a State and if such contention be thought well founded to disregard the existence in fact of the State, of its recognition by all of the departments of the Federal Government, and practically award a decree absolving from all obligation to contribute to the support of or obey the laws of such established state government. And as a consequence of the existence of such judicial authority a power in the judiciary must be implied, unless it be that anarchy is to ensue, to build by judicial action upon the ruins of the previously established government a new one, a right which by its very terms also implies the power to control the legislative department of the Government of the United States in the recognition of such new government and the admission of representatives therefrom, as well as to strip the executive department of that government of its otherwise lawful and discretionary authority.

Do the provisions of §4, Art. IV, bring about these strange, farreaching and injurious results? That is to say, do the provisions of that Article obliterate the division between judicial authority and legislative power upon which the Constitution rests? In other words, do they authorize the judiciary to substitute its judgment as to a matter purely political for the judgment of Congress on a subject committed to it and thus overthrow the Constitution upon the ground that thereby the guarantee to the States of a government republican in form may be secured, a conception which after all rests upon the assumption that the States are to be guaranteed a government republican in form by destroying the very existence of a government republican in form in the Nation. . . .

It is indeed a singular misconception of the nature and character of our constitutional system of government to suggest that the settled distinction which the doctrine just stated points out between judicial authority over justiciable controversies and legislative power as to purely political questions tends to destroy the duty of the judiciary in proper cases to enforce the Constitution. The suggestion but results from failing to distinguish between things which are widely different, that is, the legislative duty to determine the political questions involved in deciding whether a state government republican in form exists, and the judicial power and ever-present duty whenever it becomes necessary in a controversy properly submitted to enforce and uphold the applicable provisions of the Constitution as to each and every exercise of governmental power.

How better can the broad lines which distinguish these two subjects be pointed out than by considering the character of the defense in this very case? The defendant company does not contend here that it could not have been required to pay a license tax. It does not assert that it was denied an opportunity to be heard as to the amount for which it was taxed, or that there was anything inhering in the tax or involved intrinsically in the law which violated any of its constitutional rights. If such questions had been raised they would have been justiciable, and therefore would have required the calling into operation of judicial power. Instead, however, of doing any of these things, the attack on the statute here made is of a wholly different character. Its essentially political nature is at once made manifest by understanding that the assault which the contention here advanced makes is not on the tax as a tax, but on the State as a State. It is addressed to the framework and political character of the government by which the statute levying the tax was passed. It is the government, the political entity, which (reducing the case to its essence) is called to the bar of this court, not for the purpose of testing judicially some exercise of power assailed, on the ground that its exertion has injuriously affected the rights of an individual because of repugnancy to some constitutional limitation, but to demand of the State that it establish its right to exist as a State, republican in form.

As the issues presented, in their very essence, are, and have long since by this court been, definitely determined to be political and governmental, and embraced within the scope of the powers conferred upon Congress, and not therefore within the reach of judicial power, it follows that the case presented is not within our jurisdiction, and the writ of error must therefore be, and it is, dismissed for want of jurisdiction.

NOTES AND QUESTIONS

1. *The Court's dubious argument?* What do you think of the Court's logic? Do you agree with the following observation?

The Court overstated the effects of declaring this issue justiciable, however. While citizens would be able to turn to the federal courts to enforce their right to a republican form of government, the resulting suits need not be characterized as attacks on the very existence of the state. Rather, these suits could be characterized as challenges to an allegedly unconstitutional practice by an existing state government. The citizen would not be seeking to have the state's existence nullified, but merely to enforce a constitutional right to have a state govern in the constitutionally prescribed way.

Cynthia L. Fountaine, Note, Lousy Lawmaking: Questioning the Desirability and Constitutionality of Legislating by Initiative, 61 S. Cal. L. Rev. 733, 760 (1988). See Laurence H. Tribe, American Constitutional Law 99 (2d ed. 1988) (arguing that Chief Justice White's argument was "dubious"). But see Baker v. Carr, 369 U.S. 186, 218 (1962) (the "Guaranty clause claims involve those elements which define a 'political question' and for that reason and no other, they are nonjusticiable").

2. *A question of degree?* Assume that, by initiative, a state removed the taxing power or the appropriation power from its legislature. Do you think that the Court would maintain that this action was not justiciable? The Court has changed its views on the justiciability of particular issues. For example, the Supreme Court in Baker v. Carr, 369 U.S. 186 (1962), made legislative districting justiciable, after the Court had earlier determined this to be a political question. See Colegrove v. Green, 328 U.S. 549 (1946). Both of these cases are discussed in Chapter 6. On this point, Professor Robin Charlow has written:

> The Supreme Court has decided that the constitutionality of plebiscites under the Guarantee Clause is a nonjusticiable political question. . . . The Court did not always adhere, however, to the view that all Guarantee Clause cases are nonjusticiable. The Court may not find nonjusticiability in every future instance in which such claims are raised. See Reynolds v. Sims, 377 U.S. 533, 582 (1964) ("*some* questions raised under the Guaranty Clause are nonjusticiable") (emphasis added). Cf. New York v. United States, 112 S. Ct. 2408, 2433 (1992) (discussing that the view that the Guarantee Clause implicates only nonjusticiable political questions may not hold true according to recent cases).

Robin Charlow, Judicial Review, Equal Protection and the Problem with Plebiscites, 79 Cornell L. Rev. 527, 543 n.54 (1994). One such case in which a court considered an issue under the guarantee clause is VanSickle v. Shanahan, 511 P.2d 223 (Kan. 1973). In this case, the Kansas Supreme Court, after reviewing *Pacific* and *Baker*, concluded that the guarantee clause might provide a basis for a challenge to state actions depending on "the facts and circumstances surrounding the litigation, as well as the theory upon which the constitutional challenge is premised." Id. at 234. For an alternative approach to guarantee clause litigation, see Hans A. Linde, When Initiative Lawmaking Is Not "Republican Government": The Campaign Against

Homosexuality, 72 Or. L. Rev. 19 (1993) (asserting that the clause invalidates only those initiatives based on motives most feared by the Framers, including economic self-interest and majority passion).

Initiatives are frequently challenged on the basis of other constitutional provisions. These range from suits based on conformity to particular state requirements (for example, single subject rules to broader constitutional challenges. The focus of many initiatives on limiting the rights of and services to particular societal groupings has grounded many of these suits in equal protection jurisprudence. For a recent decision declaring an initiative denying homosexuals the right to any protected status a violation of the equal protection clause, see Evans v. Roemer, 854 P.2d 1270 (Colo. 1994). In reviewing the validity of an initiative, courts have treated them as they have treated legislation.

> The rare recognition that the law under attack originated with the electorate is most often followed by a boilerplate statement like Chief Justice Burger's in Citizens Against Rent Control/Coalition for Fair Housing v. City of Berkeley: "It is irrelevant that the voters rather than a legislative body enacted [this law] because the voters may no more violate the Constitution by enacting a ballot measure than a legislative body may do so by enacting legislation."

Julian N. Eule, Judicial Review of Direct Democracy, 99 Yale L.J. 1503, 1505-06 (1990).

In recent years, several scholars, including Professor Eule, have argued that laws adopted by initiatives receive a "harder look" by the courts than those legislatively enacted. Professor Eule's view and a criticism of it by Professor Robin Charlow follow. How would you evaluate each?

Julian N. Eule, Judicial Review of Direct Democracy
99 Yale L.J. 1503, 1548-49, 1559-61, 1572-73 (1990)

The thesis to this point may be roughly summarized as follows: The Constitution seeks to balance majority rule and minority rights. It enforces the government's obligation to the majority by requiring frequent elections. Legislative agents periodically return to the people for a renewal of their transitory mandates. They are held accountable for past actions and are exposed to shifting waves of public sentiment. Yet, government has an obligation to all of its citizens; the rights of individuals and minority groups must be protected against the actions of the majority. The Constitution seeks to enforce this obligation by (i) investing primary lawmaking authority in representatives rather than the people themselves; (ii) dividing the power of the lawmakers so that each unit may check the others; and (iii) placing certain principles beyond the reach of ordinary majorities. These protections are enforced by the mechanism of judicial review. Much sentiment exists for the proposition that the judiciary should exercise substantial self-restraint in performing its role. The argument for judicial deference, however, rests on the assumption that the structure itself — (i) and (ii) — guards against neglect of minority interests. In its substitutive form direct democracy bypasses internal safeguards designed to filter out or negate factionalism, prejudice, tyranny, and self-interest. The judiciary must compensate for these process defects. It must serve as the first line of defense for minority interests; a back-up role is no longer adequate. The absence of structural safeguards demands that the judge take a harder look. . . .

2. The Outlines of a Hard Judicial Look

. . . On occasions when the people eschew representation, courts need to protect the Constitution's representational values. . . . Where the structure itself is unable to guarantee a hearing for a variety of voices or to prevent factional domination, courts must pick up the slack and ensure that the majority governs in the interests of the whole people.

I shall not attempt here to provide a detailed primer for judicial application of such an intensified review. Substitutive plebiscites cover a dazzling array of subject matters and are challenged under a variety of specific constitutional provisions, including equal protection, impairment of contract, First Amendment, taking without just compensation, cruel and unusual punishment, and procedural due process. With all signs advising caution, I nonetheless cannot resist a number of general suggestions.

Because the harder look is prompted by a concern for individual rights and equal application of laws, it is principally in these areas that the courts should treat substitutive plebiscites with particular suspicion. Where, on the other hand, the electorate acts to improve the processes of legislative representation, the justification for judicial vigilance is absent. Measures to enforce ethics in government, regulate lobbyists, or reform campaign finance practices pose no distinctive threat of majoritarian tyranny. These measures install new filters rather than seeking to bypass the existing ones. Interestingly enough, only one of the nearly three dozen plebiscites reviewed by the Supreme Court has involved such a measure.

I am unwilling, however, to group alterations of government structure and reapportionment efforts in the category of governmental reform. Too often these "reforms" are a facade for disfranchising minorities; courts should be watchful of such chicanery. Neither do I ignore the threat of majority tyranny in fiscal measures like taxation and spending limitations. The beneficiaries of these so-called taxpayer revolts are principally upper and upper-middle class white citizens. The brunt of the burdens, in contrast, is borne by the underrepresented poor and by racial minorities.

This raises the problematic question of how to measure discrimination against minorities. The traditional approach holds that "the invidious quality of a law claimed to be racially discriminatory must ultimately be traced to a racially discriminatory purpose." Disparate impact on acknowledged minorities without more does not suffice to invite close judicial scrutiny. The search for a bigoted decision-maker seems particularly elusive in the context of substitutive plebiscites. Public debate is minimal and voting is private. Furthermore, lower courts have barred inquiry into motivations of individual voters. . . .

Altering the manner in which discrimination is measured is just a portion of what I mean to convey by the concept of a hard judicial look. There are scores of other situations in which courts might take account of the ways in which the substitutive plebiscite operates differently from the legislative process. In the hope that it will leave the reader with some small sense of the breadth of possibilities, a few brief examples follow.

Rationality review under the equal protection clause entails enormous deference to the lawmakers' classification scheme. Courts have generally been willing to uphold any classification based upon facts that reasonably can be conceived to constitute a distinction. It has made little difference whether the conceivable facts actually exist, justify the classification, or were ever presented to the lawmakers. In part, this deferential approach is premised on a presumption that legislatures conduct hearings, that it is impossible for courts to review all that the legislature considered, and that legislatures are more competent factfinders than the courts. Courts sporadically move away from this deferential stance to a heightened scrutiny in response to factors they regard as suspect in some sense but are unwilling to label as such. The absence of structured factfinding in the substitutive plebiscite and the dangers of classification inherent in a process of naked aggregation suggest that the substitutive plebiscite may be one of those situations that warrants heightened ends-means review.

I do not perceive the concept of a hard judicial look to be a rigid one. Unlike "strict scrutiny"—a standard which on paper at least can be reduced to precise formulation—it is not intended to take on a unitary form. What I have in mind is more a general notion that courts should be willing to examine the realities of substitutive plebiscites — that the unspoken assumptions about the legislative process that so often induce judicial restraint deserve less play in a setting where they are more fanciful.

Robin Charlow, Judicial Review, Equal Protection
and the Problem with Plebiscites
79 Cornell L. Rev. 527, 607-09 (1994)

Putting aside for a moment the problem of different constitutional restrictions on federal and state lawmaking, what might remain constitutionally problematic is that, as the special review thesis argues, plebiscitary law is made directly by the public, and not that the public's numerical support behind it is improper. In the most fundamental sense, why should it matter whether law is made directly or indirectly by the public, when in either case law need not reflect the desires of any specific number of the populace? It appears that proponents of the special review thesis attack this prospect principally because they worry that certain groups will be less successful in promoting their interests when policy is determined by the populace directly. They fear that this will occur because they assume that direct citizen voting will more often reflect the will of the popular majority than legislation does (a point that has not been empirically established) and will reflect majoritarianism at its worst.

But, if this were really the problem, then every plebiscite would have to occasion special judicial review. Some minority, that is, some group comprised of less than fifty percent of the public, loses virtually every time a plebiscite is enacted. Therefore, every plebiscite potentially poses a special danger of majoritarian tyranny and should require special judicial attention. Not surprisingly, proponents of special review do not advocate special treatment of every plebiscite, and do not even advocate the same treatment of every supposedly suspicious plebiscite. Their agenda does not appear to be the elimination of the dreaded plebiscite, but rather a selective, differential oversight of plebiscitary results. The questions that naturally follow are: precisely which plebiscites deserve special scrutiny; why those; what oversight; and, why that particular oversight? Interestingly, these questions do not get answered except in the most vague and anecdotal fashion.

Many, if not all, of the proposals appear to attack plebiscites affecting certain identified groups, such as African-Americans, Latinos, aliens, the poor, and the powerless. The crucial issue thus becomes whether there is something especially hostile about the plebiscitary process to these or other groups, such that they should be singled out from the innumerable "minorities" that lose in plebiscitary votes. One cannot answer this question on a wholesale level. Each group must be examined separately to see whether there is something about it and about its role in the functioning of the plebiscitary process that results in a special disadvantage to the group. This disadvantage must distinguish this minority from other minorities that routinely lose plebiscitary votes. More importantly, to justify different judicial treatment of plebiscites than of legislation, the characteristics must render the group generally more ineffective in the plebiscitary process than in the legislative process. In other words, what is really called for is nothing more than traditional equal protection analysis to determine whether the groups or individuals in question receive their fair shake in the plebiscitary, rather than in the legislative, process. If they do not, then the situation would call for judicial review analogous to that accorded to groups that do not receive proper consideration in the legislative process. The problem thus becomes one of applying standard equal protection analysis to certain groups within the plebiscitary process, and it is unclear how this analysis would differ from the traditional equal protection analysis of legislative laws that run afoul of the equal protection principle.

---

3. *The initiative process.* Over the years a number of reforms to the initiative process have been adopted by states. Most have centered on the petitioning process to curb misrepresentations by petitioners. Colorado is among the states that had adopted such reforms. In Buckley v. American Constitutional Law Foundation, 525 U.S. 182 (1999), the Court determined that Colorado provisions that required petitioners to be registered voters, to wear name tags, and that required proponents of initiatives to make certain filings were violative of the First Amendment.

PART *IV*

Establishing the Meaning of a Statute

Parts II and III mainly addressed the dynamic processes by which bills become law, the values that inform these processes, and the legal framework within which these processes occur. The focus up to this point has been the enactment of legislation. We have stressed the extreme difficulties encountered in converting an idea into a statute, the buffeting from many sides to which all serious bills are subjected, and the inevitable compromises that take place before a bill becomes law. Although the process of enactment is shaped by federal and state constitutions, statutes, and legislative rules, its direction and energy stem from what one commentator has characterized as "the essential techniques of politics in real life persuasion, exchange of services, rewards and benefits, alliances and deals." Michael Finley, Politics in the Ancient World 51 (1983). The enactment of a bill into a statute shifts the focus from the rawness of legislative politics to the seemingly calmer arenas in which law is applied. Now we have a law, but determination of its precise meaning with respect to particular conduct awaits the action of the parties it is intended to cover and the institution to which its implementation has been charged.

Chapter 10 is an introduction to statutory interpretation. It is a primer on both judicial and scholarly approaches. Chapters 11 and 12 divide statutes into those that are clear and those that are unclear. Chapter 11 explores cases in which a statute is clear, but a court or a minority of a court does not agree with the outcome from the application of the clear meaning. Chapter 12 examines cases in which the meaning of the statute is unclear regarding the question before the court.

CHAPTER *10*

The Interpretation
of Statutes

Once a statute has been enacted and published, it must be applied. In other words, parties must determine whether particular conduct comes within the statute's regulatory reach. In the age of statutes, advising a client on the applicability of statutes to particular conduct is one of an attorney's most important functions. For reasons discussed in this chapter, this is sometimes a difficult task. In short, the text of a statute does not always provide a certain answer to whether particular conduct comes under its regulation.

In this chapter we offer a primer on statutory interpretation. Mostly our focus is on how judges interpret statutes, which should guide the interpretive efforts of attorneys. We start with a problem through which students can begin to understand the interpretive process. We then follow with a critical and historical discussion of various judicial approaches to statutory interpretation and the tools judges use in these efforts. We end with a discussion of the current theoretical debate over the "proper" approach to reading a statute.

A. APPLYING A STATUTE: AN INTRODUCTORY PROBLEM

Assume you are a judge in the highest appellate court of your state. In the case before you, petitioners are the sheriffs of all of the counties in your state. Sheriffs in your state are responsible for the supervision of the county jails. Jails are county or locally financed facilities in which defendants are held for trial or sentenced to terms of imprisonment of less than one year. Jails are also used to hold prisoners sentenced to terms of one year or more, until such prisoners are transferred to the state prisons (state-financed facilities for prisoners sentenced to one or more years of imprisonment). The respondent is the state commissioner of corrections, who is in charge of the state prison system. The sheriffs are complaining that the correction commissioner is violating the state's criminal procedure law by refusing to accept "state-ready" prisoners. State-ready prisoners are those who are ready for transfer from jails to prisons.

Under the state Criminal Procedure Law:

> when a sentence of imprisonment is pronounced . . . the defendant must *forthwith* be committed to the custody of the appropriate public servant and detained until the sentence is complied with (emphasis added).

The respondent argues that the statute provides some discretion for the state to refuse to accept state-ready prisoners. In this case, respondent points out, the record indicates that the state prisons are at 100 percent capacity (on the basis of various standards that govern imprisonment); if the prisons exceed this capacity by, for example, double bunking or reducing recreational areas, they might be compelled by a court to release prisoners. Assume also that the record indicates that, on average, the state's jails are only at 95 percent of their capacity.

At this point, how would you rule on the case, and on what basis would you make your ruling?

Now assume that the record is amended to reflect that the state's jails are at 100 percent of capacity. Would this change your ruling, and, if so, on what basis?

Would your rulings change if the statute was amended in any of the following ways?

> *Amendment 1:* When a sentence of imprisonment is pronounced . . . the defendant must <u>immediately</u> ~~forthwith~~ be committed to the custody of the appropriate public servant and detained until the sentence is complied with.

> *Amendment 2:* When a sentence of imprisonment is pronounced . . . <u>within three days of such pronouncement</u>, the defendant must ~~forthwith~~ be committed to the custody of the appropriate public servant and detained until the sentence is complied with.

> *Amendment 3:* When a sentence of imprisonment is pronounced . . . the defendant must, ~~forthwith~~ <u>as soon as is practical</u>, be committed to the custody of the appropriate public servant and detained until the sentence is complied with.

Amendment 4: When a sentence of imprisonment is pronounced . . . the defendant must ~~forthwith~~ be committed to the custody of the appropriate public servant and detained until the sentence is complied with.

Assume that the statute in its unamended form was enacted 50 years ago. In its bill form, when it was reported to the floor of your state senate by the committee to which it was referred, it was accompanied by a committee report that contained the following passage:

One of the purposes of this statute is to resolve the confusion surrounding the relationship between the state and localities regarding their respective responsibilities for state prisoners. With the present-day crowding of the state's jails, and the relative underutilization of the state's prisons, state reluctance to immediately accept state-ready prisoners places an unfair burden on the resources of the state's counties.

This passage was not found in the report that accompanied the bill to the floor of the state assembly.

Would this passage from the senate report make any difference in any of your rulings? Why or why not?

Assume that in 1985, at the beginning of a prison building boom in your state, your state legislature enacted as part of the prison building budget a law that set forth, among other things, the capacity for each prison in the state and stated that no new prison could be built until it was projected by the Commissioner of Corrections that in the following year the prison system population would be more than 15 percent above its then-existing capacity. Assume also that at the time of the dispute between the sheriffs and the state, there were no further appropriations for prison building, and that the prisons were on average 20 percent above their legislatively enacted capacities. Would this make any difference in any of your rulings? Why or why not?

For the record, the facts on which this problem is built are drawn from a real decision of the New York State Court of Appeals, in which the state sheriffs prevailed. The statute, in its unamended form, is §430.20(1) of New York State Criminal Procedure Law. The decision is set forth below; internal citations have been omitted except where particularly relevant.

Ayers v. Coughlin
530 N.E.2d 373 (N.Y. 1988)

KAYE, JUDGE.

Under New York's bipartite corrections system, individuals ultimately subject to State custody may initially be confined in county jails, to be transferred to State correctional facilities after conviction and sentencing.

This appeal focuses on the point when the State must accept State prisoners from county jails. In a situation where State and county correction officials each claim dangerous overcrowding at their facilities, the point when inmates must be accepted into State custody — already the subject of extensive litigation — obviously has great practical importance.

The legal issue centers on CPL 430.20(1), which directs — with apparent simplicity — that "[when] a sentence of imprisonment is pronounced ... the defendant must forthwith be committed to the custody of the appropriate public servant and detained until the sentence is complied with." What is the meaning of the statutory term "forthwith"? We conclude that the State's responsibility under the statute is to accept without delay inmates in local facilities who have been committed to the custody of the State Department of Correctional Services. ... While there may be some limited flexibility in CPL 430.20(1), the statute does not vest discretion in the State to delay accepting State-ready inmates on the basis of relative overcrowding at State and local facilities. ...

Petitioners contend that, owing to State prison overcrowding, DOCS as a matter of policy has delayed accepting inmates from county jails, sometimes for six months or more, unless otherwise judicially ordered. The Sheriffs urge that failure to accept defendants and parole violators promptly, as directed by statute, has resulted in overcrowding of county jails, threatening the health, welfare and safety of petitioners, their staffs, the inmates and the community. ...

[R]espondent DOCS Commissioner does not dispute the underlying proposition that relative conditions at detention facilities are considered in determining when to accept inmates into State custody. Indeed, he contends that it is entirely appropriate under CPL 430.20(1) ... to weigh crowding in the respective facilities as well as the options available to the county officials to increase the capacity of local jails; he maintains that these are necessary components of the statutory term "forthwith." ...

I

The modern-day prison overcrowding crisis has suddenly focused attention on the statutory term "forthwith," a word which has been in the English language for centuries and in CPL 430.20(1) and its predecessor since at least 1881, without significant controversy. ...

We reiterate that the statutory mandate to commit individuals to the officials responsible for their custody "forthwith" means that it is to be done without delay, at once, promptly. "Forthwith" signals immediacy. ... Thus, we conclude that State-ready inmates (including adjudicated parole violators) committed to State custody must be accepted by respondent Commissioner without delay, it being the statutory responsibility of the State to provide for their detention until their sentence is carried out.

While the Legislature made clear its intention that commitment to the custody of the appropriate public servant should take place without delay, its choice of "forthwith" rather than the specification of a hard-and-fast number of days left certain limited flexibility in implementing, its mandate. But any such flexibility in "forthwith" simply cannot accommodate the Commissioner's view that the statute vests discretion in DOCS to accept defendants from county jails when it deems it prudent or appropriate to do so.

Respondent Commissioner urges that the issue can be resolved only after a court analyzes the circumstances in each locality, determines which facilities are overcrowded and what steps are being taken to alleviate overcrowding, and "prioritizes" the allocation of space in State correctional facilities, dependent in part on a locality's effort to alleviate overcrowding. Such a construction, however, ignores the fact that it is the State's statutory responsibility to house these inmates and it ignores the plain direction of CPL 430.20(1) that they are to be committed to appropriate custody without delay. The Legislature did not provide for transfer to State custody in the Commissioner's discretion, upon his conclusion that State facilities were safe, healthy and humane; and inmates classified according to their needs; it said "forthwith." Any limited flexibility in "forthwith" obviously must be reserved for exigent circumstances in particular cases, not for evaluation of relative capacity of State and local detention facilities that would in effect reallocate a portion of the State's responsibility to the localities. The Commissioner's construction robs the legislative direction "forthwith" of any force. . . .

The Commissioner's argument, in the end, is a plea to the courts to redistribute responsibility for housing the State's vastly expanded prison population, placing a greater burden on the localities, who (he alleges) have — relative to the State — failed to meet increased needs by enlarging their facilities. Such a plea for change in the law is appropriately directed to the legislative and executive branches of government, not to the courts. . . .

NOTES AND QUESTIONS

1. *The role of the court.* On what basis does the court reach its decision in *Ayers,* and how does it define its role in the legislative process?

2. *The legislative command.* Judge Richard Posner has characterized a statute as "a command issued by a superior body (the legislature) to a subordinate body (the judiciary). . . ." Richard A. Posner, The Problems of Jurisprudence 265 (1990). If the command is clear, it is to be followed, but what if the command is unclear? For example, what if the statute being applied is Amendment 3 on page 674? How will the court know the meaning of the command? Should and can the answer be drawn from the legislative history, in this instance the portion of the committee report

that follows the amendments on page 675? What if there is no relevant legislative history?

Leaving the statute in its unamended form, assume that a second case is brought. In this case, the localities argue that the term "forthwith," interpreted by the *Ayers* court to mean "immediately," requires the state to take the prisoners the very minute they are sentenced to state time. This would require the state to have appropriate representatives and transportation at every sentencing for which state prison time is a possible sanction. Is that the meaning of "immediate"? If not, how is the court to determine the meaning of the term? It is these and similar questions that are the subject of the remainder of this chapter and of Chapters 11 and 12.

B. THE CONTEXT FOR JUDICIAL INTERPRETATION

In Chapter 2, we defined a statute simply as a law enacted by a legislature. A statute is also a command of a particular legislature (Congress, state, municipal) that must be obeyed, under threat of governmental sanction, by those whose behavior it regulates. For a member of the public, the question then is whether the statute regulates particular behavior. Answering this question usually is not difficult because the meaning of the statute in the context of the particular behavior is clear. Statutes are written in English and generally use terms that carry common enough meanings or contain definitions of terms. For example, some state penal codes provide that: "A person is guilty of theft if he unlawfully takes, or exercises unlawful control over, movable property of another with purpose to deprive him thereof." While the language of this provision is perhaps technical, its application would be clear to most people in most instances. Even terms that are somewhat less than common to laypeople are frequently understood by the parties under the statute's ambit. All of this is to mark the obvious, but sometimes overlooked, point that statutes are overwhelmingly interpreted and implemented informally, that is, without invoking the formal processes of administrative agencies or the courts.

This, of course, is not always the case. In the age of statutes, their interpretation constitutes a major part of the judicial function. This is evidenced by court dockets filled with cases emanating from disputes over the meaning of statutory language, in the context of a particular fact pattern. It is also evidenced by the attention of law school curricula to the interpretation of statutes. These disputes arise, for the most part, because statutory provisions do not provide clear answers to questions concerning particular behavior. As Justice, then Judge, Antonin Scalia observed during the hearing for his nomination to the Supreme Court, "we do not normally have a lawsuit in front of us if the language of a statute is clear." Hearings before the Senate Committee on the Judiciary, 99th Cong., 2d Sess. 65 (Aug. 5-6, 1986). Sometimes, though, cases are initiated in order to gain a delay in the implementation of a statute or because a party is simply unwilling to comply with the law.

Once such a case is before the court, lawyers, regardless of their client's motivation, must argue why the statute covers or does not cover the behavior in question and judges must "find the meaning" of the statute to decide whether it regulates the particular conduct at issue. It is this search for "meaning" that constitutes judicial interpretation. Sometimes, even when the language of a statute is clear with respect to a particular fact pattern, judges will still conduct a "search for its meaning," because they do not believe that the application of clear language results in the outcome the legislature intended or because of some preference they have for an outcome different from that imposed by the statute's language. The willingness of courts to ignore a particular statute's plain meaning in certain instances is an important part of any study of statutory interpretation and is integral to an understanding of the history of statutory interpretation and the theoretical debates that continue to swirl around this important judicial function. An awareness of such potential judicial action is also important to the lawyer who must advise his or her client on the applicability of a particular statute to particular behavior. Such awareness should not lead to a conclusion that statutory interpretation is a random judicial function, but only to a more contextual and historical look at statutory interpretation and a more careful study of the approaches of individual judges to statutory interpretation. In the following sections of this chapter, we will discuss the judicial approaches to statutory interpretation, provide some historical and theoretical context for their exercise, and explore some of the modern theoretical debates that surround the exercise of this judicial function.

C. HOW JUDGES INTERPRET A STATUTE

All approaches to statutory interpretation are framed by the constitutional truism that the judicial will must bend to the legislative command. It is through the subordination of the judiciary to the legislature that our laws are assured their "democratic pedigree." Cass R. Sunstein, After the Rights Revolution 113 (1990). What this has traditionally meant is that, in cases of statutory interpretation, judges are not free to simply substitute their policy views for those of the legislature that enacted the statute. They must at least in construing a statute make reference to statutory language or legislative intent found through the use of a canon of interpretation or evidence by some piece of legislative history. As Judge Patricia Wald has written:

> Personal experience has revealed that the nearly universal view among federal judges is that when we are called upon to interpret statutes, it is our primary responsibility, within constitutional limits, to subordinate our wishes to the will of Congress because the legislators' collective intention, however discerned, trumps the will of the court.

Patricia M. Wald, The Sizzling Sleeper: The Use of Legislative History in Construing Statutes in the 1988-89 Term of the United States Supreme Court, 39 Am. U. L. Rev. 277, 281 (1990). Or as Judge Judith Kaye, Chief Judge of the New York State Court of Appeals, has written, "[u]nless a statute in some way contravenes the state or federal constitution, we are obliged to follow it—and of course we do." Judith S. Kaye, State Courts at the Dawn of a New Century: Common Law Courts Reading Statutes and Constitutions, 70 N.Y.U. L. Rev. 1, 19-20 (1995).

Judge Wald's rendition of legislative supremacy may catch an uninitiated reader off guard, because of the normal assumption that the "will" of a legislative body would be found in a statute's text. As noted earlier, often it is, but, as we also noted, often the text is unclear in the context of a particular fact pattern and a statute's meaning must be drawn from other sources. But the existence of unclear statutes does not alone explain her reference to a "legislators' collective intention *however discerned."* (Emphasis added.) Rather, her observation also frames a historical and continuing debate over what Judge Richard Posner has characterized as "the important question concerning statutory interpretation, which is political rather than epistemic: how free *should* judges feel themselves to be from the fetters of text and legislative intent in applying statutes." Richard A. Posner, The Problems of Jurisprudence 271 (1990). The question is not only what the legislature meant by a certain statutory provision in the context of a particular fact pattern, but also how to square such legislative meaning with a judicial preference for what a decision should be. This is what one observer has characterized as the "tension between literal and non-literal interpretations" of statutes. William S. Blatt, The History of Statutory Interpretation: A Study in Form and Substance, 6 Cardozo L. Rev. 799, 811 (1985).

On reflection, the existence of judicial outcome preferences should come as no surprise. Judges are not automatons. They have, to varying degrees, ideological and policy preferences and, in a particular case, empathy for a particular party, all of which combine to form outcome preferences in particular cases. As Federal District Court Judge Nicolas Politan has stated: "Query, whether or not having gone through all of that you don't bring to it your own view of what you think it should be, which is a problem that we try to guard against. I suspect in any judicial decision, you bring to that decision your own background, your own thought about the matter, and in essence perhaps you do put yourselves in the position of being the super legislators. Somebody had to do it. The buck stops with the judiciary." Twenty-first Annual United States Judicial Conference for the District of New Jersey, 35 (March 13, 1997). Contrary to the advocacy views of Alexander Hamilton, who wrote that the courts would not, "on the pretence of repugnancy . . . substitute their own pleasure to the constitutional intentions of the legislature . . . [or] be disposed to exercise WILL instead of JUDGEMENT," The Federalist No. 78 (Cooke ed. 1987), these preferences are sometimes so compelling that a judge may want to impose them as the law in a particular case despite statutory language to the contrary or evidence of statutory meaning to the contrary. As Justice Holmes wrote:

> The language of judicial decision is mainly the language of logic. And the logical method and form flatter that longing for certainty and for repose which is in every human mind. But certainty generally is illusion, and repose is not the destiny of man. Behind the logical form lies a judgment as to the relative worth and importance of competing legislative rounds, often an inarticulate and unconscious judgment, it is true, and yet the very root and nerve of the whole proceeding.

Oliver W. Holmes, The Path of the Law, 10 Harv. L. Rev. 457, 468-69 (1897).

Whether a judge follows such a course and imposes his or her own preference in a particular case depends on a number of factors, including the intensity of the preference, the clarity of the contrary statute's meaning, and his or her view of the obligation to obey statutory commands. A judge may have a strong preference that is not imposed because the statute, either through its language or its legislative history, commands otherwise. In a case in which a judge wants to impose his or her outcome preference, notwithstanding a legislative command to the contrary, the judge will not simply state that he or she is trumping the statute, but will argue that this view is consistent with legislative meaning, intent, or purpose. This is the larger point Judge Wald is making and that we will be demonstrating in the cases excerpted in Chapters 11 and 12.

1. Legislative Meaning, Intent, and Purpose

Statutory interpretation is a search for legislative meaning in the context of the particular question before the court. If the statutory language is clearly determinative of the question before the court, the inquiry ends, in most instances, because courts view statutory language as the best evidence of legislative meaning. But sometimes even when the language is clear, interpreters ask the question. Did the legislature intend the particular result achieved by applying the statute's plain meaning to a particular fact pattern? For example, in Tennessee Valley Authority v. Hill, 437 U.S. 153 (1978), the court was asked whether a statute that required governmental agencies to take "such actions necessary to insure that actions authorized, funded, or carried out by them do not jeopardize the continued existence of such endangered species" applied to an almost completed dam and reservoir project for which many millions of tax dollars had been spent and for which there were great economic expectations. While the majority answered the question affirmatively, based on the clear meaning of the statutory text, the dissenters argued that such an application of the statute was absurd and inconsistent with legislative intent. This case is excerpted and discussed in Chapter 12, page 726.

When a statute is unclear with respect to a particular question, lawyers and courts generally commence their search for statutory meaning by asking the question: Did the legislature intend this particular statutory provision to cover this particular fact pattern? An example of such an inquiry is found in Chisom v. Roemer, 501 U.S. 380 (1991), a case in which the Court was asked to determine whether the method of electing judges in Louisiana was covered by the Voting Rights Act of 1965, as amended. This case is excerpted in Chapter 12, page 834.

Historically, reference by the courts to legislative intent has been the subject of intense critical analysis in which it was argued that judges frequently used legislative intent to trump statutory language the judges disfavored. In other words, if they did not like the outcome effected by the statutory language, they would declare that a favored outcome was required by legislative intent. For example, to the legal realist Max Radin this was a

> transparent and absurd fiction. . . . That the intention of the legislature is undiscoverable in any real sense is almost an immediate inference from the statement of the proposition. The chances that of several hundred men each will have exactly the same determinate situation in mind as possible reductions of a given determinable, are infinitesimally small. The chance is still smaller that a given determinate, the litigated issue, will not only be within the minds of all these men but will be certain to be selected by all of them as the present limit to which the determinable should be narrowed.

Max Radin, Statutory Interpretation, 43 Harv. L. Rev. 863, 870 (1929-1930). The denial of legislative intent as a reference point for statutory interpretation left its critics with somewhat of a problem. If reference could not be made to legislative intent, on what basis would a court be able to find the meaning of an unclear statute, or, for some proponents of broader judicial discretion, on what basis would a court be able to exercise discretion beyond the language of a statute? After all, courts still needed to find some legislative peg on which to hang their decision. The response was to refer to a statute's "purpose," which was seen by its proponents as a more objective standard that is "evident from the thing [statute] itself." Id.

This emphasis on purpose is sometimes referred to as *purposivism*. Purpose, to its proponents, is found by "comparing the new law with the old" and asking "[w]hy would reasonable men, confronted with the law as it was, have enacted this new law to replace it?" Henry Hart and Albert Sacks, The Legal Process: Basic Problems in the Making and Application of Law 1415 (10th ed. 1958). For an example of a case in which the Supreme Court focuses on purpose to the exclusion of clear statutory language, see United Steelworkers v. Weber, 443 U.S. 193 (1979), excerpted in Chapter 11, page 749. Not every scholar abandoned intent as a result of the assault of the legal realists. Professor Reed Dickerson, for example, characterized intent as "indispensable. . . . [L]egislative intent underlies the very idea of a legislative process." Reed Dickerson, The Interpretation and Application of Statutes 78 (1975).

Whether or not there is a real distinction between legislative *intent or purpose*, other than that made in historical context, courts have basically ignored this debate in their search for statutory meaning. Courts often use *intent* unanalytically and interchangeably with *purpose* to refer to a source of statutory meaning (the intent of the legislature, the purpose of the legislation) outside of the language of the statute at issue in the litigation. The Supreme Court, for example, in Liporata v. United States, 471 U.S. 419 (1985), a case included or referred to in most criminal law casebooks, stated that "the interpretations proffered by both . . . accord with congressional intent. . . . The legislative history . . . contains nothing that would clarify the Congressional purpose on this point." Id. at 424-25. For a full exploration of the debate on legislative intent, see U.S. Department of Justice, Office of Legal Policy, Using and Misusing Legislative History: A Re-evaluation of the Status of Legislative History in Statutory Interpretation, 6-20 (1989).

One cautionary note: Sometimes a statement of legislative purpose is actually enacted into law as a provision of a statute. On such occasion, reference to legislative "purpose" and "intent" should not be used interchangeably. The term "purpose" should be used to designate the purpose provision, while intent should maintain its traditional role as a reference point outside the statute. The following example of an enacted purpose clause is taken from the Americans with Disability Act of 1990, 42 U.S.C. §§21101 et seq.

(b) Purpose. —

It is the purpose of this Act—

(1) to provide a clear and comprehensive national mandate for the elimination of discrimination against individuals with disabilities;

(2) to provide clear, strong, consistent, enforceable standards addressing discrimination against individuals with disabilities;

(3) to ensure that the Federal Government plays a central role in enforcing the standards established in this Act on behalf of individuals with disabilities; and

(4) to invoke the sweep of congressional authority, including the power to enforce the fourteenth amendment and to regulate commerce, in order to address the major areas of discrimination faced day-to-day by people with disabilities.

An example of this purpose clause being used in the interpretation of a statute is found in Sutton v. United Airlines, discussed in Chapter 2, page 65.

2.   Clear and Unclear Statutory Language

In our exploration of statutory interpretation, we divide statutes into two categories: those for which the text provides a clear answer to the issue in question and those for which the textual answer is unclear. It is not our determination of what is clear that governs the categorizations, but the particular courts. We make this division because we think that judicial avoidance of a clear legislative command, whether based on a judicial view of legislative intent or on a judicial policy preference, is a unique exercise of judicial power even though the approaches used to "find the legislative meaning" outside the text are the same as those used when the statute is unclear. Consistent with this division, Chapter 11 contains examples of courts applying plain or clear statutes and Chapter 12 contains examples of courts applying unclear statutes.

3.   Applying a Clear Statute

The starting place for any search for statutory meaning must obviously be its language, for the language of a statute is that which is enacted by the legislature. "It is elementary that the meaning of a statute must, in the first instance, be sought in the language in which the act is framed. . . ." Caminetti v. United States, 242 U.S. 470, 485 (1917). And if a reading of the statute provides a clear answer to the case (a determination often subject to debate), most judges and commentators would agree, at least in theory, that the inquiry should be ended because "if that is plain, and if the law is within the constitutional authority of the law-making body which passed it, the sole function of the courts is to enforce it according to its terms." Id. This is known as the plain meaning rule. This is the rule the New York State Court of Appeals applied to the problem set forth in Section A of this chapter.

Cases in which the statutory text provides a plain or clear answer to a dispute generally do not reach the appellate courts, though there are several exceptions to this rule. Sometimes the rigid application of the plain meaning of a statute can lead to absurd results because "[m]eaning depends on context as well as on the semantic and other formal properties of sentences." Richard A. Posner, The Problems of Jurisprudence 269 (1990). As Professor Daniel Farber has written: "For example, virtually no one doubts the correctness of the ancient decision that a statute prohibiting 'letting blood in the streets' did not ban emergency surgery." Daniel A. Farber, Statutory Interpretation and Legislative Supremacy, 78 Geo. L.J. 281, 289 (1989). Think again of the problem set forth in Section A. Assume that the sheriffs were arguing that the term "immediate" required the state to accept every defendant sentenced to state time immediately upon that defendant's sentencing, without regard to the administrative concerns of the locality or state, or the near impossibility of having state officials and transportation available at every sentencing at which state prison time is a possible sanction. The application of the literal language in such situations would lead to absurd consequences, ones that, constructively, could not have been within the purpose of the enacting legislature.

This exception to the plain meaning rule is largely theoretical. Rarely is a court faced with clear statutory language, which, if applied in a particular case, would be so illogical or contrary to reason that the application constructively could not reflect the will of the enacting legislature. An example of such an application of a statute that almost reached the New York courts is drawn from the New York City Charter. A provision of the charter provides that no elected official may serve more than "two full terms" in office. After the disastrous attacks on New York's World Trade Center, Mayor Giuliani, nearing the end of his second term in office, suggested he might resign a day or two before the end of his term so that he could serve another four years. He had been offered the Conservative Party line for the general election and it was suggested by some of his aides that there would be no procedural obstacles to his running and, if he won, serving again in spite of his resignation. According to his aides, he would not have served two full terms (but would fall one or two days short). What do you think of this reading of the statute?

More typically, a court will choose not to apply a statute's plain meaning because it judges that such application of a statue's plain meaning in a particular case is inconsistent with the enacting legislature's intent or purpose or because it does not agree with the policy outcome dictated by the statute's language. In either case, the court will declare the plain meaning inapplicable as inconsistent with legislative intent or purpose as determined through the application of some canon of interpretation or as evidenced by some piece of legislative history. We underscore, in reference to this traditional exception, the need for relating the decision to legislative intent or purpose. Even if the decision is one based on judicial willfulness, reference to legislative intent is necessary to preserve the concept of legislative supremacy. (A rare exception to this latter point is Judge Posner's dissent in United States v. Marshall, 908 F.2d 1312, presented in Chapter 11, page 774.)

Again revisit the problem set forth in Section A of this chapter. Don your judicial mantle and assume that your sympathies rest with the position of the state in the situation of overcrowded state prisons and underutilized jails. Would you argue that sending the state-ready prisoners to the state facilities immediately is absurd? If not, you might say that the legislature could not have intended to send more prisoners to overcrowded prisons. Assuming that you believed this, would you be willing to support the state on the basis of the statute alone? If not, would you decide in favor of the state's position on the basis of the senate committee report, arguing that it showed a different legislative intent or purpose from the statute? Why?

Exceptions to the plain meaning rule have been, off and on, the subject of considerable debate. At the heart of this debate have been competing visions of the role of courts and legislatures in society. In essence the questions asked and argued are: How far can the courts move away from the plain meaning of statutory language in applying that statute to a particular case; on what basis can a court argue that, despite the plain language of a statute, the statute really means something else; isn't the arguable consequence of such a decision that "either (a) the statute consists of the string of words actually on the rolls [books], in which case that statute (i.e., that string of words) is not binding, or (b) the statute is binding but consists of a different string of words from that on the rolls [books]"? Gerald C. MacCallum, Jr., Legislative Intent, 75 Yale L.J. 754, 763 (1966).

The issues raised in this section will be explored in the cases in Chapter 11 and the notes and questions that follow those cases.

4. *Applying an Unclear Statute*

Most cases of statutory interpretation, especially at the appellate level, involve language that does not provide courts with clear answers to the question of whether particular conduct is within the statute's reach. As the Supreme Court noted in its *Liporata* opinion (page 683), "the words themselves provide little guidance. Either interpretation would accord with ordinary usage." *Liporata*, 471 U.S. at 424.

Several factors account for this. First, words are not perfect symbols for the communication of ideas and may be understood differently by different audiences. The meaning of words may also change over time. For example, in the problem in Section A of this chapter, the word "forthwith" (made part of the statute in 1891) is no longer generally used, having been replaced by "immediately." A modern reader familiar with the term "immediately" might suppose that "forthwith" had some other meaning, creating some room for argument that the word could support discretion on the part of the state.

Second, and most important, while particular events may stimulate the enactment of a statute, statutes are, for the most part, drafted in general terms, addressing *categories* of conduct. No matter how carefully any statute might be drafted, a dispute over its applicability to a particular fact pattern is the natural consequence of its generality. Illustrative of this point is a 1991 decision of the Supreme Court, Chisom v. Roemer, 501 U.S. 380 (1991) (Chapter 12, page 834), in which the Court was asked to decide whether "elected judges" came within the definition of the statutory term "representatives," thereby subjecting the election of judges to §2 of the Voting Rights Act of 1965, as amended. As Charles Breitel, former Chief Judge of the New York Court of Appeals, has written: "The words men use are never absolutely certain in meaning; the limitations of finite man and the even greater limitations of his language see to that." Bankers Ass'n v. Albright, 343 N.E.2d 735, 738 (N.Y. 1975).

Third, legislatures sometimes use general language, contemplating that it will be defined by administrative agencies. The constitutional propriety of such provisions is the province of administrative law. This is the topic characterized as the delegation doctrine. But within an appropriate delegation much is often left to administrative discretion through the use of general or nonspecific language. In cases of such statutory ambiguity, the Supreme Court, in Chevron v. Natural Resources Defense Council, 467 U.S. 837 (1984) (Chapter 10, page 715), determined that the judicial role is to defer to the agency's interpretation of its guiding statute. Also revisit the problem in Section A of this chapter and consider Amendment 3, which provides that the transfer between jails and prisons take place "as soon as is practical."

Fourth, sometimes statutes are unclear because legislative compromises are struck to secure votes for the enactment of a statute. Compromises can be struck by an agreement to leave undefined a general word or phrase in order to protect a particular political position. Compromises can also be struck by an agreement to remain silent on a particular point. On these points, consider the discussion in Chapter 2, pages 67-69, on the effective date of the Civil Rights Act of 1991. Consider also Landgraf v. USI Film Products, 511 U.S. 24 (1994) (Chapter 12, page 869).

Fifth, sometimes ambiguities are created by insufficient legislative thought to the meaning of the language employed or because the legislature has simply not considered the question that has become the subject of litigation. A probable and interesting example of the latter is the absence of any reference to "burden of proof or persuasion" in Title VII of the Civil Rights Act of 1965. This silence resulted in two contrary decisions of the Supreme Court, Griggs v. Duke Power Co., 401 U.S. 424 (1971) (holding, among other things, that Congress placed the burden of persuasion to establish a business justification on the employer), and Wards Cove Packing Co. v. Antonio, 490 U.S. 642 (1989) (holding, among other things, that the statute required the employee to disprove a business justification raised by the employer). The issue was finally resolved in the Civil Rights Act of 1991, in which Congress placed the burden of proving business justifications on the employer.

Finally, in the rush of the legislative process, sometimes provisions are added or subtracted without sufficient thought given to their effect on the rest of the statute.

When the language of a statute is unclear, courts are confronted with the problem of giving meaning to a provision of a statute without clear direction from its language. In essence, they are asked to make policy choices. As courts are not simply "free" to "enact" their policy views into law, they have relied on: (1) general presumptions about legislative intent, known as canons of construction; and (2) specific presumptions about legislative intent, usually discernible through legislative history, but sometimes gleaned through examining other provisions of a particular statute or the statute as a whole. These tools of construction are, as noted earlier, the same ones used to establish legislative intent outside of the language of a statute. Again turning to *Liporata* for an example, the Court in searching for the meaning of the ambiguous statute found that "the legislative history of the statute contains nothing that would clarify the congressional purpose on this point," but based its decision to require mens rea in this case on several interpretive canons, including the often cited one that "ambiguity concerning the ambit of criminal statutes should be resolved in favor of lenity." Supra at *Liporata*, 471 U.S. at 427.

Note the term "presumptions" in the above paragraph. Legislative bodies speak through statutes, and the use of any source but the statute itself to determine its meaning is problematic. Canons of construction pose a particularly difficult case because they are judicial visions of what legislatures, in general, mean when they enact a statute. Legislative history avoids this problem because it addresses the particular procedural history of the statute in question, but it is troublesome for a different reason. Although it is grounded in the legislative process and particular to the statute in question, it is not the product of the entire legislature. Rather, it is the work of some lesser number of members, such as a committee.

5.   Two Tools for Statutory Interpretation: Canons of Construction and Legislative History

We noted above the court's use of canons of construction and legislative history as tools for interpreting a statute. Both will be explored in the cases and notes and questions set forth in Chapters 11 and 12. The use of canons and legislative history as tools for statutory interpretation has been the subject of considerable debate. Its focus, like the focus on almost all writing about statutory interpretation, is the relationship between legislatures and courts and the relative prowess of each institution. We explore in brief the issues raised in this debate to provide some context for approaching the judicial use of these devices.

Canons of Construction

Canons of construction are judicially crafted maxims or aphorisms for determining the meaning of statutes. Canons are expressly intended to limit judicial discretion by rooting interpretive decisions in a system of aged and shared principles from which a judge may draw a "'correct,' unchallengeable rule[ ] of 'how to read.'" Karl N. Llewellyn, Remarks on the Theory of Appellate Decision and the Rules or Canons about How Statutes Are to Be Construed, 3 Vand. L. Rev. 395, 399 (1950). A typical expression of this view is set forth below:

> Among all civilized nations, we have always seen, formed by the side of the sanctuary of the laws, and under the controlling guidance of judicial and legislative wisdom, a fund of maxims, rules, and decisions and doctrine, which have been sifted by the constant practice, and the collision, consequent upon judicial debates. These rules and maxims have been incessantly increasing the store of wisdom and knowledge thus acquired, until they have become the supplement of legislation in the establishment of law, and are regarded as the highest attainment towards the perfection of human reason, in the exposition of law.
>
> The judicial power, established to declare and apply the laws, needs, and is greatly aided, by such a fund of rules and maxims. These maxims apply equally to all men. They regard men in the aggregate, never as individuals. They are rules as proper to be known to the legislator, as to the magistrate, though their duties are variant. The science of the legislator, and his consequent duty, consists in searching in each case for principles most favorable to the common welfare; that of the judge, is to put these principles in action; to extend them by a wise and thoughtful application to private assumptions; and to study the spirit of the law, when perhaps, the letter destroys.

Sir Fortunatus Dwarris, A General Treatise on Statutes 121 (J. Platter Potter ed., 1885).

There are a multitude of canons; some traditional examples are listed below (commonly used Latin phrases are noted in parentheses). The authors do not, as some others do, define the plain meaning rule as a canon of construction. This is based on our view that the plain meaning rule is the constitutionally compelled starting place for any statutory construction and that tools of interpretation are only applicable when, for whatever reason, the plain meaning rule fails to provide the answer.

- A thing may be within the letter of the statute and yet not within the statute because it is not within the spirit or within the intention of the statute's makers.
- Statutes in derogation of the common law are to be read narrowly.
- Remedial statutes are to be read broadly.

- Criminal statutes are to be read narrowly.
- Statutes should be read to avoid constitutional questions.
- Statutes that relate to the same subject matter (*in pari materia*) are to be construed together.
- The general language of a statute is limited by specific phrases that have preceded the general language (*ejusdem generis*).
- Explicit exceptions are deemed exclusive (*expressio unius est exclusio alterius*).
- Repeals by implication are not favored.
- Words and phrases that have received judicial construction before enactment are to be understood according to that construction.
- A statute should be construed such that none of its terms is redundant.
- A statute should be read to avoid internal inconsistencies.
- Words are to be given their common meaning, unless they are technical terms or words of art.
- Titles do not control meaning.
- Punctuation will govern when the statute is open to two constructions.

The use of canons of construction for the interpretation of statutes has been held in scholarly ill repute for over a century. At the end of the nineteenth century, Sir Frederick Pollock observed that the only explanation for the use of canons was "the theory that Parliament generally changes the law for the worse, and that the business of the judges is to keep the mischief of its interference within the narrowest possible bounds." Frederick Pollock, Essays in Jurisprudence and Ethics 85 (1882). The one-time popular canon that the courts should narrowly construe statutes in derogation of the common law illustrates this point. See Jefferson B. Fordham and J. Russell Leach, Interpretation of Statutes in Derogation of the Common Law, 3 Vand. L. Rev. 438 (1950). The criticism of the use of canons over this period of time has been so consistently unfavorable that two recent scholars of statutory interpretation have matter-of-factly written that "almost everybody thinks that canons are bunk." William N. Eskridge, Jr., and Philip P. Frickey, Cases and Materials on Legislation 630 (1988).

Two basic observations underlie this criticism of the use of canons: first, canons are not a coherent, shared body of law from which correct answers can be drawn; and second, viewed individually, many canons are wrong.

It has become commonplace to recognize that the canons are not a system or body of principles that provide the "correct reading," but are a grab bag of individual rules, from which a judge can choose to support his view of the case. This was Karl Llewellyn's point when he observed that "there are two opposing canons on almost every point." Karl N. Llewellyn, Remarks on the Theory of Appellate Decision and the Rules or Canons about How Statutes Are to Be Construed, 3 Vand. L. Rev. 395, 401 (1950). Few have taken issue with Llewellyn's observation. Indeed, it has been almost universally adopted as the starting place for all criticism of canons. "The usual criticism of the canons . . . is that for every canon one might bring to bear on a point there is an equal and opposite canon so that the outcome of the interpretive process depends on the choice between paired opposites — a choice the canons themselves do not illuminate. (You need a canon for choosing between competing canons, and there isn't any.)" Richard A. Posner, Statutory Interpretation — in the Classroom and in the Courtroom, 50 U. Chi. L. Rev. 800, 806 (1983).

Several of Llewellyn's examples illustrate the point:

- "[a] statute cannot go beyond its text," **except** "[t]o effect its purpose a statute may be implemented beyond its text";
- "[s]tatutes in derogation of the common law will not be extended by construction," **except** "[s]uch acts will be liberally construed if their nature is remedial";
- "statutes *in pari materia* must be construed together," **except** "[a] statute is not *in pari materia* . . . where a legislative design to depart from the general purpose or policy of previous enactments may be apparent";
- "[e]very word and clause must be given effect," **except** "[i]f inadvertently inserted or if repugnant to the rest of the statute they may be rejected as surplusage."

Karl N. Llewellyn, Remarks on the Theory of Appellate Decision and the Rules or Canons about How Statutes Are to Be Construed, 3 Vand. L. Rev. 395, 401-06 (1950).

Canons, as individual rules, are considered equally flawed. Canons are considered presumptions about legislative intent. To see this clearly, reread the listed canons, adding the word "why" to each. For example: Why should remedial statutes be read broadly? The answer to this question must be that this is what the enacting legislature intended, unless there is constitutional authority for another answer. But how do we know as a general proposition that when a legislature passes a remedial statute that it intends for it to be broadly applied? It is just as probable that the enacting legislature intends the statute to be moderately or narrowly applied. The point is that, as a rule, the canon bars the inquiry and is at odds with legislative supremacy (and the supremacy of legislative values of weighing, sifting, and balancing interests) by forcing the burden on the legislature to overcome a judicial presumption, rather than requiring the court to dig for the meaning. Also, assuming that a legislative body could or would undertake this burden, how would it know which canon to follow given the menu of contradictory canons?

As presumptions about the legislative process, a number of the canons are also more wrong than right and reflect little, if any, knowledge about

the legislative process. Take, for example, the canon that remedial legislation should be construed broadly:

> Since the building of majorities necessarily requires compromise, a broad
> reading of a controversial statute is far more likely to undermine legislative
> intent than to support it. Moreover, a bill drafter's awareness of this rule of
> interpretation would not influence the legislative process except to guarantee
> the defeat of the bill if he or she were to take the position that no compromise
> is possible because the courts will ignore it. If a canon of interpretation is
> necessary, a more accurate one would be "all statutes should be construed
> moderately."

Eric Lane, Legislative Process and Its Judicial Renderings: A Study in Contrast, 48 U. Pitt. L. Rev. 639, 657 (1987).

This tide of scholarly criticism has not eroded the judicial employment of
canons as tools of interpretation. Faced with unclear statutes or statutes
with which they disagree, judges continue to turn to canons either to find
meaning beyond their own views or to justify the imposition of their own
views. For an interesting discussion of the continued use of canons by the
courts, see Jonathan R. Macey and Geoffrey P. Miller, The Canons of
Statutory Construction and Judicial Preferences, 45 Vand. L. Rev. 647
(1992) (the continued use of canons reflects an "era of moral and intellectual
uncertainty," id. at 667); Lawrence C. Marshall, The Canons of Statutory
Construction and Judicial Constraints: A Response to Macey and Miller, 45
Vand. L. Rev. 673 (1992) (the use of canons helps fulfill judicial obligation to
legislative supremacy). But see Eric Lane, How to Read a Statute in New
York: A Response to Judge Kaye and More, 25 Hofstra L. Rev. 85 (1999).

Recognizing the continued force of canons, a number of scholars have
been urging the adoption of "new" canons. Judge (then Professor) Easterbrook, for example, would re-create a form of nineteenth-century judicial
conservatism by limiting the redistributive or regulatory effects of statutes
through a "meta" canon, which constrains the applicability of statutes "to
cases anticipated by the framers and expressly resolved in the legislative
process." Frank H. Easterbrook, Statutes' Domain, 50 U. Chi. L. Rev. 533,
544 (1983). Professor Sunstein, on the other hand, advocates a far more
creative role for courts confronting unclear statutes. He argues for a series
of canons "that improve[s] the performance of modern government, and
that [is] not based on pre–New Deal understandings, which seem to have
overstayed their welcome." Cass R. Sunstein, Interpreting Statutes in the
Regulatory State, 103 Harv. L. Rev. 405, 412 (1989). Under this series of
canons, courts would be authorized "to promote accountability and deliberation in government, to furnish surrogates when both [accountability and
deliberation] are absent, to limit factionalism and self-interested representation, and to further political equality." Id. at 477. Finally, Professor
Eskridge argues that courts should (and do) look to "current policies

and societal conditions" to resolve unclear statutes. William N. Eskridge, Jr., Dynamic Statutory Interpretation, 135 U. Pa. L. Rev. 1479, 1484 (1987).

On what basis can the court adopt such "new" canons? As Justice Breyer has asked:

> [C]an the Court legally adopt new up-to-date canons, such as those Professor Sunstein has suggested? . . . [C]an the Court simply adopt them? Where would it find the legal authority for doing so? Unlike the older canons, these new canons lack the legitimacy provided by continuous judicial use over many years. The traditional canons may seem out-of-date, but they possess a time-honored acceptance that newer, up-to-date canons lack.

Stephen Breyer, On the Uses of Legislative History in Interpreting Statutes, 65 S. Cal. L. Rev. 845, 870 (1992). Indeed, as Professor Ross points out, these canons are not intended to "describe accurately what Congress actually intended or what the words of a statute mean, but rather to direct courts to construe any ambiguity in a particular way in order to further some policy objective." Stephen Ross, Where Have You Gone, Karl Llewellyn? Should Congress Turn Its Lonely Eyes to You?, 45 Vand. L. Rev. 561, 563 (1992).

Legislative History

The formal steps of the legislative process are officially documented. In Congress, ideas for legislation are introduced as bills or as amendments to bills; committee hearings and debates and markups are transcribed; committee actions are set forth and explained in committee reports; legislative debate is transcribed; and votes are recorded. For all legislatures, the documentation of these steps is part of the process of building majorities and providing the public with access to the work of the legislature. For the courts, this documentation is legislative history. Significant steps in the legislative process are not recorded. The discussion of a bill in a political party caucus or in the offices of the legislative leadership, for example, might, if documented, reveal very probative evidence of legislative intent, but to serve various legislative purposes they are not documented.

A legislative history of a statute might contain all or some of the following documents or documentation. (The parenthetical references are to chapters and sections of the book in which the particular step of the enactment process is discussed.)

Introduction (Chapter 5, Sections B.1 and B.2): the bill or bills through which the statute was introduced; the transcript of introductory remarks; memoranda that accompany such introduction (New York, for example, requires introductory memoranda); and the record of a bill's assignment to committee.

> *Committee proceedings* (Chapter 4): transcripts of committee hearings, debates, and markup sessions; amendments; committee votes; and, finally, committee reports, which in Congress contain a statement of a bill's purpose and scope, a statement of the reasons for which a bill should be enacted, a section-by-section analysis, a statement of changes the bill would make in existing law, committee amendments to the bill, votes taken in committee, and a minority report setting forth reasons for opposition to the bill.
> *Floor proceedings* (Chapter 5, Sections B.7-B.13): transcripts of debates; floor amendments; and votes.
> *Conference committee proceedings* (Chapter 5, Section B.14): conference committee reports.
> *Executive proceedings:* (Chapter 9, Section C): signing or veto statements and memoranda submitted in favor of or opposition to the bill.

All of these pieces of legislative history, except for the executive proceedings, are what we characterize as, borrowing a term from Professor Charles Tiefer, institutional legislative history, meaning legislative history on which Congress relies to establish meaning. Charles Tiefer, The Reconceptualization of Legislative History in the Supreme Court, 2000 Wis. L. Rev. 205 (2000).

Not every statute will have as complete a legislative history as set forth above. Not every statute goes through every possible step of the legislative process. For example, not every statute has a hearing or is debated. Not every state legislature transcribes committee debates or includes conference committees as part of its legislative process. In beginning a search for legislative history, two initial inquiries are important: First, what legislative steps has the statute been through and, second, which of these steps is documented?

Judges use legislative history as a tool for statutory interpretation. As Justice Breyer has written, "[u]sing legislative history to help interpret unclear statutory language seems natural. Legislative history helps a court understand the context and purpose of a statute." Stephen Breyer, On the Uses of Legislative History in Interpreting Statutes, 65 S. Cal. L. Rev. 845, 848 (1992). It seems natural because, if the judicial goal is to discover whether the legislature intended to cover the particular conduct under litigation, reference to relevant legislative history logically advances that goal.

The value of legislative history as a tool of statutory construction is not universally perceived. Much of the criticism has been stoked by an apparent overuse of legislative history in the last several decades.

> Two preliminary observations may be made. First, although the Court still refers to the "plain meaning" rule, the rule has effectively been laid to rest. No occasion for statutory construction now exists when the Court will *not*

look at the legislative history. When the plain meaning rhetoric is invoked, it becomes a device not for ignoring legislative history but for shifting onto legislative history the burden of proving that the words do mean what they appear to say. Second, the Court has greatly expanded the types of materials and events that it will recognize in the search for Congressional intent.

Patricia M. Wald, Some Observations on the Use of Legislative History in the 1981 Supreme Court Term, 68 Iowa L. Rev. 195 (1982).

The criticism of the use of legislative history for statutory construction is two-pronged. First, it is argued that the use of it is inconsistent with the democratic theory encapsulated in the Constitution. "Committee reports, floor speeches, and even colloquies between Congressmen . . . are frail substitutes for bicameral vote upon the text of a law and its presentment to the President." Thompson v. Thompson, 484 U.S. 174, 191 (1987) (Scalia, J., concurring). In this same vein, it is said that if the goal is to find the intent of the legislature, "[l]egislative material . . . at best can shed light only on the 'intent' of that small portion of Congress in which such records originate; [the legislative materials] therefore lack the holistic 'intent' found in the statute itself." Kenneth W. Starr, Observations about the Use of Legislative History, 1987 Duke L.J. 371, 375.

Second, serious questions have been raised about the reliability of legislative history. The most extreme example of this criticism comes from Justice Scalia:

> That the Court should refer to the citation of three District Court cases in a document issued by a single committee of a single house as the action *of Congress* displays the level of unreality that our unrestrained use of legislative history has attained. . . . As anyone who is familiar with modern-day drafting of a congressional committee report is well aware, the references to the cases were inserted, at best by a committee staff member on his or her own initiative, and at worst by a committee staff member at the suggestion of a lawyer-lobbyist; and the purpose of those references was not primarily to inform the Members of Congress what the bill meant . . . but rather to influence judicial construction. What a heady feeling it must be for a young staffer, to know that his or her citation of obscure district court cases can transform them into law of the land, thereafter dutifully to be observed by the Supreme Court itself.

Blanchard v. Bergeron, 489 U.S. 87, 98 (1989) (Scalia, J., concurring) (emphasis in original). While Justice Scalia's general skepticism about the creation of legislative history far overstates the problem (in the view of the authors), some corruption of the legislative record does take place. This corruption is described, in legislative terms, as the "planting of legislative history." This refers to adding to the legislative record (e.g., committee reports, the Congressional Record) language that is not intended to influence the legislative enactment process but rather to influence the judicial interpretive process.

As one of the authors has previously written about his experience in Congress:

> Two members will rise and engage in a colloquy for the purpose of making "legislative history." Frequently, however, the colloquy is written by just one of the members, not both. It is handed to the other actor and the two of them read it like a grade B radio script. And that is the material that judges later will solemnly pore over, under the guise of "studying the legislative history." This, of course, is ridiculous.

Abner J. Mikva, A Reply to Judge Starr's Observations, 1987 Duke L.J. 380, 384.

The more the courts rely on legislative history, the greater the incentive for such corruption of the legislative record. Judicial ignorance of the legislative process also adds to the problem because, without knowledge of the process, courts are unable to properly assess the relative value of different pieces of legislative history.

Consider the remarks of Senator Danforth with respect to the enactment of the Civil Rights Act of 1991. The legislative debate over its enactment clause is discussed in Chapter 2. Cases interpreting this statute are set forth in Chapter 12.

> Mr. DANFORTH: Mr. President. I would like to say a word this morning on the difficult, contentious subject of legislative history, what its limitations are, and how the issue of legislative history is now before the Senate.
>
> Justice Scalia has taken the position that the Supreme Court should not get into the business of interpreting legislative history but that instead the Court should attempt to construe legislative language as it appears in statutes themselves.
>
> I think that the odyssey of the present legislation is a strong argument for Justice Scalia's position. One of the interesting things about this particular bill is that whereas with much controversial legislation when a compromise is reached, *all kinds of people say we really do not like this bill but we are not going to be able to do any better, therefore, we will support it.*
>
> This bill is different in that a whole variety of people have come forward and have expressed support and even enthusiasm for the bill. People as diverse as the administration, on one hand, Senator Dole, Senator Hatch and, on the other hand, for example, Senator Kennedy, Senator Mitchell all have expressed support. They have all said there is a lot to be said for this legislation.
>
> *One of the reasons that this is possible is that there are slightly different interpretations among Members of the Senate and between the Senate and the administration on the precise meaning of some of the provisions in the law.* That is not unusual. What the courts are for is to interpret what is meant by the Congress in passing laws.
>
> It is very common for Members of the Senate to try to affect the way in which a court will interpret a statute by putting things into the Congressional Record. Sometimes statements are made on the floor of the Senate.

Sometimes the Senator will say, but for such and such a provision, which I interpret in such and such a way, I never could support this bill. That is one method of trying to doctor the legislative history and influence the future course of litigation.

Another way is to put an interpretive memorandum in the Congressional Record. These memoranda typically are not read on the floor of the Senate. They are just stuck into the Record.

Another way to do it is for agreed colloquies to be signed by various Senators and for those to be stuck into the Record. This is what is happening with respect to this bill. Last Friday, Senator Kennedy made a speech on the floor of the Senate. He stated his views of what the bill does. Senator Hatch has just made a very extensive speech on the floor. He stated his views of what the bill does.

My guess, Mr. President, is that if Senator Kennedy would give us his analysis of Senator Hatch's position he would disagree with it. If Senator Hatch would give us his analysis of Senator Kennedy's position, Senator Hatch would disagree with Senator Kennedy. I might disagree with both of them. I anticipate that I am going to have an interpretive memorandum which will be put into the Record signed by the other original six Republican cosponsors for the legislation. That will be our interpretation of various provisions, but it may not be the interpretation of Senator Hatch or Senator Kennedy or anybody else.

So what I am saying is that Justice Scalia, I think, has a good point in stating that it is risky business to try to piece together from floor statements or from agreed memoranda legislative history which is informative to the court in interpreting the meaning of a statute. . . .

I believe, Mr. President, we should go ahead and pass the bill. I believe that it will be passed. But I simply want to state that a court would be well advised to take with a large grain of salt floor debate and statements placed into the Congressional Record which purport to create an interpretation for the legislation that is before us.

Congressional Record, Senate, Oct. 29, 1991, S.15324-25 (emphasis added). The passages emphasized in the above quote from the debate over the Civil Rights Act of 1991 are intended to demonstrate why the language of a statute may sometimes be unclear. The need to pass a statute brings with it the need to compromise. Sometimes such compromises can be in the form of obscuring the particular meaning of a statute, allowing different legislators to read the obscured provisions the way they wish. Again this demonstrates the very practical side of the legislative process.

A third criticism of the use of legislative history comes from a legislative perspective. This criticism was well stated by M. Douglass Bellis, Assistant Legislative Counsel, U.S. House of Representatives, at the 1996 American Association of Law Professors annual conference: "If we decide that the legislative history . . . is more important than the legislation, legislators will never really know what they have to do, what levers they need to pull in order to get their ideas firmly cemented in place."

The debate over the use of legislative history has another focus beyond the reliability of particular pieces of such history and its democratic legitimacy. As we noted earlier, approaches to statutory interpretation also reflect choices concerning the exercise of political power. From this perspective, the failure to use appropriate legislative history as a basis for resolving a dispute over the meaning of an ambiguous statute can be seen as opting for judicial dominance of the interpretive arena. If legislative history is ignored, what is effectively left as a basis for decision are canons of construction, which effectively permit unfettered discretion.

This point is well evidenced by the decisions of Justice Scalia who, in our view, has developed a "new" canon of interpretation, namely that ambiguous statutes should be read narrowly. As we have attempted to demonstrate elsewhere, through an analysis primarily of his 1999 judicial writings, "Justice Scalia's most probable reason for ignoring legislative history may be the freedom it provides him for limiting statutory scope. A choice in almost every statutory dispute is whether a broad or narrow reading of a statute is to be applied. Justice Scalia's most consistent view of how to read a statute seems to be to read it narrowly. Hence, fealty to a regimen that might compel a broader reading in any given case must be eschewed in all cases." Abner J. Mikva and Eric Lane, The Muzak of Justice Scalia's Revolutionary Call to Read Unclear Statutes Narrowly, 53 SMU L. Rev. 121 (2000).

What seems in order is not the avoidance of legislative history, but its careful use. Legislative history is, after all, part of the legislative process, and the outright refusal to acknowledge it as a vehicle for expressing legislative intent raises constitutional questions. Consider the following view of Judge Wald:

> If we are serious about respecting the will of Congress, how can we ignore Congress' chosen methods for expressing that will? For all its imperfections, legislative history, in the form of committee reports, hearings, and floor remarks, is available to courts because Congress has made those documents available to us. . . . As Justice Scalia has recognized, there does indeed exist a congressional practice of including information in legislative history for the purpose, among others, of informing later judicial construction of the statute. But, to the extent that Congress performs its responsibilities through committees and delegates to staff the writing of its reports it is Congress' evident intention that an explanation of what it has done be obtained from these extrinsic materials. If only a few of the "sneakier" members of Congress were slipping information past the congressional membership at large, I might share Justice Scalia's skepticism of giving any weight to legislative history. That, however, is not the case; legislative history is the authoritative product of the institutional work of the Congress. It records the manner in which Congress enacts its legislation, and it represents the way Congress communicates with the country at large.
>
> To disregard committee reports as indicators of congressional understanding because we are suspicious that nefarious staffers have

planted certain information for some undisclosed reason, is to second-guess Congress' chosen form of organization and delegation of authority, and to doubt its ability to oversee its own constitutional functions effectively. It comes perilously close, in my view, to impugning the way a coordinate branch conducts its operations and, in that sense, runs the risk of violating the spirit if not the letter of the separation of powers principle.

Patricia Wald, The Sizzling Sleeper: The Use of Legislative History in Construing Statutes in the 1988-89 Term of the United States Supreme Court, 39 Am. U. L. Rev. 277, 306-07 (1990).

Careful usage would prevent the use of legislative history to contradict clear language, unless its application was clearly absurd. Too frequently a court will refer to legislative history, notwithstanding its own recognition of the clarity of the language. For example, the New York Court of Appeals, where possible, supports its clear meaning findings with references to legislative history as if to support the clarity of their initial application. What it would do if it found a conflict remains a question, although some of its opinions suggest it would still favor the clear text. See Eric Lane, How to Read a Statute in New York: A Response to Judge Kaye and More, 25 Hofstra L. Rev. 85 (1999). After all, legislatures vote on bill language; no bill can become law unless identical text is agreed on by a majority of each house of the legislature; the President must have an opportunity to approve or veto this language; if vetoed, the legislature is given the opportunity to override the veto of that language; and it is the statute that informs the public of the regulation. An example of a Supreme Court decision in which legislative history trumps clear text is Train v. Colorado Public Interest Research Group, Inc., 426 U.S. 1 (1976) (Chapter 11, page 820).

Restricting the use of legislative history to statutes in which the language is unclear should calm constitutional anxiety. As Justice Breyer has written:

> The "statute-is-the-only-law" argument misses the point. No one claims that legislative history is a statute, or even that, in any strong sense, it is "law." Rather, legislative history is helpful in trying to understand the meaning of the words that do make up the statute or the "law." A judge cannot interpret the words of an *ambiguous* statute without looking beyond its words for the words have simply ceased to provide univocal guidance to decide the case at hand. Can the judge, for example, ignore a dictionary or the historical interpretive practice of the agency that customarily applies some words? Is a dictionary or an historic agency interpretive practice "law"? It is "law" only in a weak sense that does not claim the status of a statute, and in a sense that violates neither the letter nor the spirit of the Constitution.

Stephen Breyer, On the Uses of Legislative History in Interpreting Statutes 65 S. Cal. L. Rev. 845, 863 (1992) (emphasis added).

Careful use would also entail a judicial understanding of the legislative process and a good-faith attempt on the part of the courts to choose legislative history that is most probative of legislative intent and not legislative history that supports their views. For, as Justice Jackson stated, "[i]t is a poor cause that cannot find some plausible support in legislative history. . . ." Robert H. Jackson, Problems of Statutory Interpretation, 8 F.R.D. 121, 125 (1948).

For a piece of legislative history to be probative of legislative intent, it must bear a significant relationship to the enactment process. Within this broad category, legislative history can then be prioritized by levels of significance. For Congress, the following rough pecking order for choosing legislative history makes sense: committee reports (including conference reports); markup transcripts; committee debate and hearing transcripts; transcripts of "hot" (actual) floor debate. The significance of committee reports needs reemphasis. Congress acts through committees (see Chapter 4), and "in the ordinary course of legislation, committee reports should be looked to for the most coherent, thorough, and authoritative explanation of a bill's purpose and intended meaning." George A. Costello, Average Voting Members and Other "Benign Fictions": The Relative Reliability of Committee Reports, Floor Debates, and Other Sources of Legislative History, 1990 Duke L.J. 39, 72.

Statements made on the floor, which are not part of an actual debate, or statements inserted in the Congressional Record should mostly be ignored. So, too, should statements by the opponents of legislation, except in the hot debate context. Consider the following experience of Judge Mikva during his tenure in Congress:

> When the provisions of the Organized Crime Act of 1970 [RICO] came up for floor debate, I expressed my opposition in hyperbolic terms, parading one horrible example after another before the House. Since the managers had the number of votes needed for passage, and I was speaking mostly to an empty House, they did not even bother to answer me. My remarks have been used ever since as legislative history to prove the broad scope of RICO.

Abner J. Mikva, Reading and Writing Statutes, 48 U. Pitt. L. Rev. 627, 632 (1987). Statements made on the floor as part of the debate must be weighted according to their significance to the debate. For example, Professor Ross suggests two categories of statement that he considers most reliable:

> (1) statements by the sponsor of the legislation or the particular provision at issue when it appears that members who might otherwise desire to amend the bill have relied on those statements; and (2) colloquies between the "major players" concerning a legislative provision when it appears that the majority of members are prepared to follow any consensus reached by these individuals.

Stephen Ross, Where Have You Gone, Karl Llewellyn? Should Congress Turn Its Lonely Eyes to You?, 45 Vand. L. Rev. 561, 576 (1992).

On occasion, courts will refer to the rejection of amendments during the enactment process as evidence of one of the meanings being urged in litigation. This is a dangerous exercise, for "[t]here are many reasons for saying no." Reed Dickerson, The Interpretation and Application of Statutes 160 (1975). For example, the rejection of an amendment could reflect the view that the amendment is superfluous. Another problematic interpretive exercise is the use of legislative silence to confirm prior judicial statutory constructions. "It is at best treacherous to find in legislative silence alone the adoption of a controlling rule of law." Girouard v. United States, 328 U.S. 61, 69 (1946). The typical case unfolds as follows: Confronted with an unclear statute, a court finds an earlier decision that interprets the language in a particular way. The court then justifies its use of this earlier interpretation by stating that the earlier interpretation has been legislatively adopted because the legislature has failed to overturn it. Assuming that legislators are generally aware of judicial decisions (which, in most instances, is a false assumption) there are numerous reasons why a legislature might not overturn the decision. Professors Hart and Sacks, in their landmark book, offer many:

> Complete disinterest; Belief that other measures have a stronger claim on the limited time and energy of the body; Belief that the bill is sound in principle but politically inexpedient to be connected with; Unwillingness to have the bill's sponsors get credit for its enactment; Belief that the bill is sound in principle but defective in material particulars; Tentative approval, but belief that action should be withheld until the problem can be attacked on a broader front; Indecision, with or without one or another of the foregoing attitudes also; Belief that the matter should be left to be handled by the normal processes of judicial development of decisional law, including the overruling of outstanding decisions to the extent that the sound growth of the law requires; Positive approval of existing law as expressed in outstanding decisions of the Supreme Court; Ditto of the court of appeals' decisions also; Ditto also of district court decisions; Ditto also of one or more varieties of outstanding administrative determinations; Etc., etc., etc., etc., etc.

Henry M. Hart, Jr., and Albert M. Sacks, The Legal Process: Basic Problems in the Making and Application of Law 1395-96 (1958).

A variation on the "use" of legislative silence is found in *Girouard*. At issue was whether Girouard's stated unwillingness to take up arms on behalf of the United States (he was willing to serve in the armed forces) disqualified him for citizenship. The question was the meaning of the statutorily prescribed oath of allegiance for becoming a citizen. Neither the oath nor other provisions of the statute answered the question, but, prior to 1942, several Supreme Court decisions had interpreted the language of the oath as requiring an applicant to be willing to take up arms in defense of the country. Many attempts to reverse these decisions had died in legislative committees.

Standing alone, these efforts should have no impact on the statute's interpretation for the reasons discussed earlier. What makes this case particularly interesting is that in 1942, Congress reenacted the oath without change, raising the question for the court of whether this reenactment without change incorporated the interpretation of the oath stated in the Court's several earlier decisions. In other words, the question after the reenactment became whether Congress had adopted the Court's earlier view that the oath of allegiance included implicitly an obligation to bear arms for the United States. The Court, as noted by the earlier quoted passage, refused to infuse legislative silence with such meaning, but it was clear from the decision that the Court thought its earlier decisions incorrect. Despite our wariness over the use of legislative silence, and without consideration of the policies in dispute in *Girouard*, it would seem that such a procedural record could reasonably be read to support the view that in 1942 Congress had adopted the interpretation of the oath declared by the earlier Court decisions. This is the rule that most courts apply.

Post-enactment explanations of legislative meaning would seem absolutely taboo. For example, a post-enactment letter from a senator to an administrative agency head informing him what the senator believed a piece of legislation meant because that senator was involved in its enactment should have no probative value. First, such post-enactment statements are not part of the enactment process. Second, they are absolutely unreliable. All post-enactment statements by legislators are influenced by post-enactment political considerations. An experience of one of the authors, Professor Lane, illustrates this point. The New York state legislature wanted to block an attempt by a county legislature to take over a nuclear power plant. To accomplish its purpose, the state legislature enacted preemptive legislation. In a subsequent litigation over whether the state statute preempted the local law, several members of the state legislature, who had voted in favor of the state legislation, attempted to submit affidavits declaring that the legislation was not intended to be preemptive. All of these members had participated in negotiating the bill and were well aware of its purpose. But subsequent to the adoption of the state legislation, they had become the target of intense protests by local legislators and community groups, who claimed that the state legislation denied them home rule and was inadequate for protecting local interests. The affidavits were reflective of these later pressures, rather than of the legislative history.

In recent years some commentators have argued for judicial use of executive signing statements in statutory interpretation. The argument in favor of this position rests on the role of the executive in the legislative process. (See Chapter 1, Section B.3.) The signing message is not a part of the enactment process. While the President has the power to veto a bill and the legislature has the power to override the veto, the legislature has no power to veto or override the executive's signing message, which can contain any statement the executive chooses to include. For example, at issue in a 1995 Supreme Court decision, Chisom v. Roemer, 501 U.S. 380 (1995) (Chapter 12, page 834), was whether the word "representative" in §2 of the Voting Rights Act of 1965, as amended by the Voting Rights Amendments of 1982, included elected judges. The majority decided that it did. Assume that in signing the Voting Rights Amendments of 1982, President Reagan had specifically stated that he was signing the bill based on his understanding that the term "representative" did not include elected judges. In our view, this signing statement should not be used in interpreting the statute because it has not been the subject of legislative consideration, but is simply executive gloss about which the legislature can do nothing. By this we mean that Congress cannot debate or override, as part of the enactment process, a signing statement accompanying an approved bill. We would make one exception to this view. Assume that in the signing statement the executive made reference to some communication or negotiation between the executive and the legislative leadership in which agreement had been reached over the meaning declared in the signing statement. In such a case, a signing statement might have some probative value. Despite our view on signing statements, they should not be ignored in the practice of law, particularly on the state level. State courts often make reference to them, probably because of the absence of legislatively generated materials and the need of courts to hang their decisions on some peg of the enactment process. The New York Court of Appeals, for example, constantly refers to executive documents as legislative history. See Eric Lane, How to Read a Statute in New York: A Response to Judge Kaye and Some More, 25 Hofstra L. Rev. 85 (1999).

A cautionary lesson should be evident from the above discussion. Generalizations about the probative value of legislative history are only useful as guidelines for statutory interpretation. Knowing, for example, that the committee reports are an extremely important part of congressional practice alerts one to the importance of committee reports, but does not answer the question of whether a particular committee report is important for determining legislative intent with respect to a particular provision of a statute. Every statute has its own legislative history that must be explored in the search for the meaning of the particular statutory language.

State legislatures offer little comparable opportunities to follow their activities. While all state legislatures record or transcribe their sessions, the accessibility of these records varies from state to state. Less available are the transcripts of committee meetings and hearings. Some state legislatures produce committee reports, others do not. For example, New York does not, but does require a sponsor's explanatory memorandum with the introduction of legislation.

6.   *"Showdown" Questions*

Sometimes the meaning of an unclear statute cannot be clarified by reference to other provisions of the statute, traditional canons, or legislative history. In other words, sometimes the meaning of a statute cannot be found through an exploration of the legislative process. This is particularly true on the state level, where legislative history is sparsely documented and access to those documents is not easy. "[I]n New York and likely other states as well, legislative history is relatively sparse with legislative intent evidenced primarily by the language of the statute itself." Judith S. Kaye, State Courts at the Dawn of a New Century: Common Law Courts Reading Statutes and Constitutions, 70 N.Y.U. L. Rev. 1, 30 (1995).

It is such a situation that Professor Harry W. Jones characterized as a "'serious business' situation" or "showdown question," one for which statutory sources or legislative procedures cannot provide an answer and yet the court must answer. Harry W. Jones, An Invitation to Jurisprudence, 74 Colum. L. Rev. 1023, 1041 (1974). According to Jones:

> In "serious business" situations, the positive law is not a command to the judge but, at most, an authorization of alternative decisions. Judges, by and large are reluctant lawmakers, but the role is thrust upon even the most modest of them by the realities of their function. The case must be decided, one way or the other. Unlike the pure social scientist, the judge cannot withhold his action until all the returns are in. There is no hiding place from the political and moral obligation to decide.

Harry W. Jones, id. at 1041. The phrase "serious business" is drawn from Justice Cardozo: "It is when the colors do not match, when the references in the index fail, when there is no decisive precedent, that the serious business of the judge begins." Benjamin N. Cardozo, The Nature of the Judicial Process 21 (1921). One point of Professor Jones' observation needs particular emphasis. Faced with a showdown question, even the most deferential judges must become "activists" in the sense that they must resolve the question before them without legislative guidance. This point is illustrated by federal District Court Judge Nicolas Politan in answer to a question concerning showdown cases: "You have litigators in front of you, you have people who want answers to their problems. What do you have to do? It seems to me in a situation where there is nothing to look to you have to search out the legislative intent in any method that you deem proper." Proceedings of the Twenty-first Annual United States Judicial Conference for the District of New Jersey (March 13, 1997).

Assume that in the problem in Section A of this chapter the statute read:

> When a sentence of imprisonment is pronounced . . . the defendant must, as soon as practical, be committed to the custody of the appropriate public servant and detained until the sentence is complied with.

Assume also that there is no discoverable legislative history to explain this provision. Finally, assume that the jail system is 95 percent filled and the prison system is at 100 percent capacity. On what basis is a court to make a decision in this case? For example, what would you think about a judge simply flipping a coin? Or what would you think about a judge deciding, based on his or her judgment, that the best policy would be to keep the prisoners in the jails until there was more room in the prisons or, to the contrary, ordering the state to accept the prisoners? How do you think the judge should write the opinion, with reference to the coin flip or to her own policy preference?

In practice, judges do not clearly signal that a particular question of interpretation is a showdown question. Such expression offends concepts of separation of power and could lead to questions about the judge's willingness to obey his or her obligation to effect legislative purpose. Instead, judges frame these decisions along traditional lines, with strained references to legislative purpose or intent. As Professor Jones observed:

> Why is it so hard to tell, on a first reading of the court's opinion in a "serious business" case, that the controversy was originally a stand-off, as concerns formal legal doctrine, and was decided as it was chiefly in accordance with the court's views — informed judgment, intuitive impression, or largely unconscious predilection, depending on judge or judges involved — of what is sound public policy? The source of the analytical difficulty is in the syllogistic form characteristic of judicial opinions, which operates, as often as not to obscure policy decision in a wrapping of essentially secondary doctrinal explanations. For courts must not only reach decisions, they also have to justify them, and, as John Dewey wrote a long time ago, there is always danger that the logic of justification will overpower and conceal the logic of search inquiry by which a decision was actually arrived at.

Harry W. Jones, An Invitation to Jurisprudence, 74 Colum. L. Rev. 1023, 1041 (1974). An example of a decision in which a court signals that it is faced with a showdown question and basically confronts it head on is Braschi v. Stahl Associates, 74 N.Y.2d 201 (1989). This case is excerpted and discussed in Chapter 12, page 896.

It is also difficult to determine whether a court is facing a showdown for a second reason. The judges deciding the case may simply disagree on the question. As easy as it is to define a showdown question in general, such definition can be very elusive in the context of a particular case. Judges, on a panel, may disagree over whether a particular case presents such a question, based on each one's reading of a statute or the importance each places on legislative history or particular items thereof. For example, is the question of whether "a voluntary affirmative action plan that discriminates against whites prohibited by the Civil Rights Act of 1964" (presented in United Steelworkers of America v. Weber, 443 U.S. 193 (1979)), a showdown question? To the dissenters and to many commentators, including the authors, it is not. To the majority, or to some of its members (certainly Justice Blackmun), it might have been. To Judge Posner and Ronald Dworkin it is. The *Weber* decision is excerpted and discussed in Chapter 11, page 749.

7. Theories of Statutory Interpretation

The Traditional Theory

In Section B of this chapter, we explored the methods by which courts, with rare exception, establish (or claim to establish) the meaning of statutes, providing some critiques along the path. From a theoretical perspective, this constitutes a statement of the traditional theory of statutory interpretation with some criticisms of its implementation. Stated simply, statutes are commands of the legislature that must be followed by the courts. The starting point is the language of the statute. Sometimes, and for different reasons, a court will not or cannot apply the language of a statute and will look elsewhere, to other provisions of the statute or to the legislative history or to canons of interpretation, to find the statute's meaning in the context of the particular case. But the search for the legislative meaning, even in the hardest of cases, is the defining characteristic of the traditional approach. This is true even in the show-down cases in which, by definition, legislative meaning is elusive and in which judicial reference to legislative meaning is almost fictional. The notion is to avoid opening the door to at least blatant judicial lawmaking. This explains Judge Posner's "imaginative reconstruction" direction, which instructs judges, confronted with an unclear statute for which no legislative guidance is apparent, to "place themselves in the position of the legislators who enacted the statute that they [judges] are being asked to interpret." Richard A. Posner, The Problems of Jurisprudence 273 (1990). In other words, it is not the bald policy preference of the judge that is to determine the litigation, but the policy preference of the enacting legislature, no matter how difficult the reach for such preference might be.

This traditional theory is merited both from a constitutional perspective and from a political theory perspective. Both separation of powers doctrine and representative democratic theory require this approach. The theoretical underpinnings for this theory of statutory interpretation are set forth and discussed in Chapter 1.

Since the early 1980s, some scholars and judges have expressed significant disagreement with the traditional theory or with various aspects of it. For the most part, they have not argued directly against legislative supremacy, but for a far more limited definition of such supremacy in the application of unclear statutes. An example of this is the normative canons proposed by Professor Sunstein. These are discussed in this chapter, on page 692. Another example is the refusal of Justice Scalia to refer to legislative history. See pages 695-696. Below are set forth four additional views. In reading them, consider how each compares and contrasts with the traditional theory and with each other.

Ronald Dworkin, *A Matter of Principle*
328-29 (1985)

How is a court to choose between two justifications for a statute, each of which fits the statute and finds a basis in political opinion? If one of these justifications has been attached to the statute as an institutionalized intention, through some legislative convention of the sort described earlier, then the court must apply that justification even though it prefers another. If the legislative history shows that while one justification had great support among a number of legislators, the other went unnoticed or was rejected by all who noticed it, then that might well be some evidence that the second does not, after all, reflect any widespread political opinion. But in most hard cases testing whether a statute applies in controversial circumstances, when there are two justifications available that point in opposite directions, both justifications will fit well enough both the text of the statute and the political climate of the day, and neither will be attached to the statute by convention. . . .

In these cases I see no procedure for decision — no theory of legislation — other than this: one justification for a statute is better than another, and provides the direction of coherent development of the statute, if it provides a more accurate or sounder analysis of the underlying moral principles. So judges must decide which of the two competing justifications is superior as a matter of political morality, and apply the statute so as to further that justification. Different judges, who disagree about morality, will therefore disagree about the statute. But this is inevitable, and if each judge faces the moral decision openly, an informed public will be in a better position to understand and criticize them than if the moral ground of decision lies hidden under confused arguments about nonexistent legislative intents.

It is no use protesting that this procedure allows judges to substitute their own political judgment for the judgment of elected representatives of the people. That protest is doubly misleading. It suggests, first, that the legislators have in fact made a judgment so that it is wrong for the judges to displace that judgment. But if there is not institutionalized intention, no pertinent collective understanding, and two competing justifications, there is no such judgment. Second, the protest suggests that judges have some way to decide such a case that does *not* require them to make a political judgment. But there is no such procedure, except a method that leaves the decision to chance, like flipping a coin.

Frank H. Easterbrook, Statute's Domain
50 U. Chi. L. Rev. 533, 544-52 (1983)

My suggestion is that unless the statute plainly hands courts the power
to create and revise a form of common law [e.g., federal antitrust legisla-
tion], the domain of the statutes should be restricted to cases anticipated by
its framers and expressly resolved in the legislative process. Unless the
party relying on the statute could establish either express resolution or
creation of the common law power of revision, the court would hold the
matter in question outside the statute's domain. The statute would become
irrelevant, the parties (and court) remitted to whatever other sources of law
might be applicable. . . .

This approach is faithful to the nature of compromise in private interest
legislation. . . . This approach also is supported by a number of other considerations. First, it recognizes that courts cannot reconstruct an original
meaning because there is none to find. Second, it prevents legislatures from
extending their lives beyond the terms of their members. Third, it takes a
liberal view of the relation between the public and private spheres. Fourth,
it takes a realistic view of judges' powers. . . .

1. Original Meaning. Because legislatures comprise many members, they
do not have "intents" or "designs," hidden yet discoverable. Each member
may or may not have a design. The body as a whole, however, has only
outcomes. It is not only impossible to reason from one statute to another but
also impossible to reason from one or more sections of a statute to a
problem not resolved. . . .

2. Legislatures Expire. Judicial interpolation of legislative gaps would be
questionable even if judges could ascertain with certainty how the legislature would have acted. Every legislative body's power is limited by a
number of checks, from the demands of its internal procedures to bicameralism to the need to obtain the executive's assent. The foremost of these
checks is time. Each session of Congress . . . lasts but two years. . . . What
each Congress does binds the future until another Congress acts, but what a
Congress might have done, had it the time, is simply left unresolved. The
unaddressed problem is handled by a new legislature with new instructions from the voters.

If time is classified with the veto as a limit on the power of legislatures,
then one customary argument for judicial gap-filling — that legislatures
lack the time and foresight to resolve every problem — is a reason why
judges should not attempt to fill statutory gaps. . . .

In a sense, gap-filling construction has the same effects as extending the
term of the legislature and allowing that legislature to avoid submitting its
plan to the executive for veto. Obviously no court would do this directly. If
the members of the Ninety-third Congress reassembled next month and
declared their legislative meaning, the declaration would have absolutely
no force. . . .

The meta-rule I have suggested reduces the number of times judges must summon up the ghouls of legislative past. In order to authorize judges (or agencies) to fill statutory gaps, the legislature must deny itself life after death and permit judges or agencies to supply their own conception of the public interest.

3. *Liberal Principles.* A principle that statutes are inapplicable unless they either plainly supply a rule of decision or delegate the power to create such a rule is consistent with the liberal principles underlying our political order. Those who wrote and approved the Constitution thought that most social relations would be governed by private agreements, customs, and understanding, not resolved in the halls of government. There is still at least a presumption that people's arrangements prevail unless expressly displaced by legal doctrine. All things are permitted unless there is some contrary rule. . . .

4. *Judicial Abilities.* Statutory construction is an art. Good statutory construction requires the rarest of skills. The judge must find clues in the structure of the statute, hints in the legislative history, and combine these with mastery of history, command of psychology, and sensitivity to nuance to divine how deceased legislators would have answered unasked questions.

It is all very well to say that a judge able to understand the temper of 1871 (and 1921), and able to learn the extent of a compromise in 1936, may do well when construing statutes. How many judges meet this description? . . . The number of judges living at any time who can, with plausible claim to accuracy, "think [themselves] . . . into the minds of the enacting legislators and imagine how they would have wanted the statute applied to the case at bar" [referring to Judge Posner's notion of imaginative reconstruction] may be counted on one hand.

To deny that judges have the skills necessary to construe statutes well — at least when construction involves filling gaps in the statutes rather than settling the rare case that arises from conflicts in the rules actually laid down — is not to say that stupid and irresponsible judges can twist any rule. Doubtless the "judge's role should be limited, to protect against willful judges who lack humility and self-restraint." Yet there is a more general reason for limiting the scope of judicial discretion. Few of the best intentioned, most humble, and most restrained among us have the skills necessary to learn the temper of time before our births, to assume the identity of people we have never met, and to know how 535 disparate characters from regions of great political and economic diversity would have answered questions that never occurred to them. Anyone of reasonable skill could tell that some answers would have been beyond belief in 1866. After putting the impossible to one side, though, a judge must choose from among the possible solutions, and here human ingenuity is bound to fail, often. When it fails, even the best intentioned will find that the imagined dialogues of departed legislators have much in common with their own conceptions of the good.

William N. Eskridge, Jr., Dynamic Statutory Interpretation
135 U. Pa. L. Rev. 1479, 1482-84 (1987)

The static vision of statutory interpretation prescribed by traditional doctrine is strikingly outdated. In practice, it imposes unrealistic burdens on judges, asking them to extract textual meaning that makes sense in the present from historical materials whose sense is often impossible to recreate faithfully. As doctrine, it is intellectually antediluvian, in light of recent developments in the philosophy of interpretation. Interpretation is not static, but dynamic. Interpretation is not an archaeological discovery, but a dialectical creation. Interpretation is not mere exegesis to pinpoint historical meaning, but hermeneutics to apply that meaning to current problems and circumstances.

The dialectic of statutory interpretation is the process of understanding a text created in the past and applying it to a present problem. This process cannot be described simply as the recreation of past events and past expectations, for the "best" interpretation of a statute is typically the one that is most consonant with our current "web of beliefs" and policies surrounding the statute. That is, statutory interpretation involves the present-day interpreter's understanding and reconciliation of three different perspectives, no one of which will always control. These three perspectives relate to (1) the statutory text, which is the formal focus of interpretation and a constraint on the range of interpretive options available (textual perspective); (2) the original legislative expectations surrounding the statute's creation, including compromises reached (historical perspective); and (3) the subsequent evolution of the statute and its present context, especially the ways in which the societal and legal environment of the statute has materially changed over time (evolutive perspective).

Under dynamic statutory interpretation, the textual perspective is critical in many cases. The traditional understanding of the "rule of law" requires that statutes enacted by the majoritarian legislature be given effect, and that citizens have reasonable notice of the legal rules that govern their behavior. When the statutory text clearly answers the interpretive question, therefore, it normally will be the most important consideration. Exceptions, however, do exist because an apparently clear text can be rendered ambiguous by a demonstration of contrary legislative expectations or highly unreasonable consequences. The historical perspective is the next most important interpretive consideration; given the traditional assumptions that the legislature is the supreme lawmaking body in a democracy, the historical expectations of the enacting legislature are entitled to deference. Hence, when a clear text and supportive legislative history suggest the same answer, they typically will control.

The dynamic model, however, views the evolutive perspective as most important when the statutory text is not clear and the original legislative expectations have been overtaken by subsequent changes in society and

law. In such cases, the pull of text and history will be slight, and the interpreter will find current policies and societal conditions most important.
The hardest cases, obviously, are those in which a clear text or strong historical evidence or both, are inconsistent with compelling current values
and policies.

Guido Calabresi, A Common Law for the Age of Statutes
2 (1982)

... [B]ecause a statute is hard to revise once it is passed, laws are governing us that would not and could not be enacted today, and that *some* of
these laws not only could not be reenacted but also do not fit, are in some
sense inconsistent with, our whole legal landscape.

The combination of lack of fit and lack of current legislative support I will
call the problem of legal obsolescence. ...

There is an alternative way of dealing with the problem of legal obsolescence: granting to courts the authority to determine whether a statute is
obsolete, whether in one way or another it should be consciously reviewed.
At times this doctrine would approach granting to courts the authority to
treat statutes as if they were no more and no less than part of the common
law. At other times it would be used to enable courts to encourage, or even
to induce, legislative reconsideration of the statute. Employing a variety of
techniques, the court might begin a "common law" process of renovation in
the obsolete law, update the statute directly by replacing it with new rules
(derived either from the common law or from statutory sources), or do no
more than create a situation in which conscious legislative reconsideration
of the law was made likely. The object in all cases would be to permit courts
to keep anachronistic laws from governing us without thereby requiring
them to do tasks for which they are not suited, or denying to the legislatures
the decisive word in the making of constitutionally valid laws.

NOTES AND QUESTIONS

1. *Compare and contrast.* How do each of the above approaches compare to
each other and to the traditional theory? How would each resolve the differing issues presented in the problem set forth in Section A of this chapter?

2. *Theories about interpretation or the legislative process.* Consider the
following passage:

> The point is general. The interpretation of statutes is highly sensitive to
> theories of the legislative process, and these are controversial political theo-
> ries and hence do not provide sure footing for judicial decisions. Those who
> believe that legislatures embody the popular will and who venerate popular

democracy are likely to attach great weight to any indications of how a majority of the legislature might have answered the interpretive question that has arisen. Those who regard the impediments to the legislative process as salutary checks on the excesses of democracy are likely to be distrustful of any expressions of legislative preference that have not run the gauntlet. There is no basis in law — maybe no basis period, in current political theory — for choosing between these positions. Interpretation is not foundational; it sits uneasily on shifting political foundations.

Richard A. Posner, The Problems of Jurisprudence 292 (1990). What are the political foundations that underlie each of the above passages and those views of Justice Scalia and Professor Sunstein discussed on pages 692 and 695?

3. *The role of judges.* What role does the traditional theory of statutory interpretation assign to judges? How does this differ from the role assigned by the theories of Scalia, Sunstein, Dworkin, Easterbrook, Eskridge, and Calabresi? How is each of these views grounded in democratic theory? In this regard, consider the views of one of the authors about Professor Calabresi's theory:

> I question whether common law rulemaking itself has been democratic: it has worked more as a tool for those with sufficient resources to influence the legal system than it has as a compact among all citizens. . . . For all of its virtues, the common law has never been a beacon of democracy for the average consumer-citizen. Indeed, the failure of the common law to meet the needs of the common many may itself have given rise to the age of statutes. . . .
>
> A more troublesome aspect of Calabresi's thesis is the crucial role that lack of fit with the legal landscape plays in his definition of statutory obsolescence, in his assumption of the legitimacy of judicial updating power, and in his effort to limit the exercise of the power. Is the concept of a "legal landscape" firm enough to bear the weight Calabresi places upon it? I doubt it. . . .
>
> Moreover, an unrestrained updating power could actually undermine the independence of the judiciary. Not only might judges occasionally gauge incorrectly whether use of the updating power is justified, and thus come under fire from the statute's supporters, but they also might come to think of themselves as, and increasingly try to act like, legislators. When judges act like legislators, they lose some of their traditional authority. The power of judicial updating cannot be justified in the same manner as can the power of judicial review. When a court decides a question on the basis of the Constitution, the document itself justifies and delimits the decision. . . . When a judge engages in updating without legislative authorization, however, neither the statute itself nor the electoral process constrains or legitimizes his action.
>
> Finally, and perhaps most disturbingly, judicial updating may generate perceptions of judges as legislators and buttress the argument that judges should be selected — and retired — as are legislators. Like Alexander

Hamilton, I think that the election of judges would be the most serious threat to the independence of the judiciary.

Abner J. Mikva, The Shifting Sands of Legal Topography, 96 Harv. L. Rev. 534, 540-43 (1982). How would Judge Mikva's analysis apply to Judge Easterbrook's approach to statutory interpretation?

8. A View from the States

The discussion of the interpretation of statutes to this point has made no distinction between federal and state statutes, except for the section on legislative history, which focused on Congress. Such an approach has received some criticism by Judge Judith Kaye, the Chief Judge of the New York State Court of Appeals. According to Judge Kaye:

> Despite the outpouring of scholarly ink, analysis has focused almost entirely on how *federal* courts read *federal* statutes. Few, if any, of the recent commentators have considered whether the subject of statutory interpretation presents a different set of issues for state judges reading state statutes.
>
> I submit that it does. And of the many reasons that come to mind, perhaps most important, as is evident in the area of state constitutional law, is the fact that state courts regularly, openly, and legitimately speak the language of the common law whereas federal courts do not.

Judith S. Kaye, State Courts at the Dawn of a New Century: Common Law Courts Reading Statutes and Constitutions, 70 N.Y.U. L. Rev. 1, 19-20 (1995).

Our own observations are that federal and state judges apply the same approaches to statutory interpretation. Differences in interpretive approaches are the product of individual judicial sensibilities and not, for the most part, of particular jurisdictions. As one of the authors has written:

> The use of a common law approach as defined by Judge Kaye is what judges must do and do to make a decision. "Must do" because the judicial role is to decide cases and "do" because, in the words of Judge Abner J. Mikva, cited by Judge Kaye, this "is really judicial naturalism — judges doing what comes naturally. . . ."
>
> From this perspective federal judges are not different from state judges. They must decide the case before them. They are required to follow legislative dictates. They have views about the legislative process. They have general policy preferences and form outcome preferences in particular cases. Whether a judge will impose his or her own conscious preference in a particular case depends upon a number of factors, including, the clarity of the statute's command in the particular case, the intensity of the preference

and his or her sense of obligation to obey statutory commands. And when a statute is unclear and the road to its meaning unmapped, federal judges also will apply common law techniques of the common law. Judge Robert Cowen (then of the Third Circuit) on his federal judicial experience in searching for the meaning of unmapped statutes makes this point clearly: "I think I have to be brutally honest with you and say the unspeakable, that I would decide the case based on what I perceive the most just manner of resolving the matter before me."

Eric Lane, How to Read a Statute in New York, 28 Hofstra L. Rev. 85, 87 (1999) (citations omitted).

The major difference between federal and state interpretive approaches results from the scarcity and inaccessibility of the legislative history in many states. This results in either the redefinition of legislative history, as in New York with its frequent reliance on executive records, or in an increase of show-down cases. While the maturation of state legislatures has resulted in better and more accessible documentation in many states, no state legislature matches this aspect of the congressional process. While all state legislative bodies maintain and make public some form of journal (see Chapter 8, Section B), no state has anything like the Congressional Record. In fact, records of floor debates in almost all states are only available through the office of the clerk of the house of the state legislature in which the debate occurred and then usually with some difficulty. Also, most are indexed only by date. Access to committee debates is even more difficult and in some states no record of such debates is made. For a detailed listing of many state practices, see National Conference of State Legislatures, Inside the Legislative Process (1992). For examples of the documentation practices of particular states, see Malinda Allison, Research in Texas Legislative History, Tex. B.J. March 1984, at 314; Robert M. Rhodes and Susan Seereiter, The Search for Intent: Aids to Statutory Construction in Florida — An Update, 13 Fla. St. U. L. Rev. 485 (1985); Arthur C. Wang, Note, Legislative History in Washington, 7 U. Puget Sound L. Rev. 751 (1984); Note, Researching Illinois Legislative Histories: A Practical Guide, 1982 S. Ill. U. L.J. 601.

D.   A NOTE ON ADMINISTRATIVE AGENCIES

In the age of statutes administrative agencies have been the vehicle for implementing many of the statutory schemes. Each major regulatory effort, from efforts to regulate trusts and the air waves to the social legislation of the 1930s, civil rights legislation of the 1960s, and environmental legislation of the 1970s, to name only a few, has birthed a new agency or enhanced the regulatory power of an old one: for example, following the above examples, the Federal Trade Commission, the Federal Communications Commission, the Social Security Administration, the Equal Employment Opportunity Commission, and the Environmental Protection Agency. Central to the agency function is the interpretation of its enabling legislation, which establishes its mission. This means that, in many lawsuits, courts are reviewing decisions by agencies about the meaning of their enabling statutes. Agencies, like the courts, are required to defer to the plain meaning rule and the failure of an agency to do so is reversible by a court. But in a case in which the statute is unclear, the Supreme Court has held that federal courts must defer to the interpretation given to the statute by that agency to which Congress has delegated the power to apply the statute. Internal citations and footnotes have been omitted except where particularly relevant.

Chevron v. Natural Resources Defense Council
467 U.S. 837 (1984)

Statute: 42 U.S.C. §7502(b)(6) (Clean Air Act Amendments of 1977, §172(b)(6))
The plan required by subsection (a) shall . . .
"(6) require permits for the construction and operation of new or modified major stationary sources in accordance with section 173 (relating to permit requirements)." 91 Stat. 747.

JUSTICE STEVENS delivered the opinion of the Court.

In the Clean Air Act Amendments of 1977, Pub. L. 95-95, 91 Stat. 685, Congress enacted certain requirements applicable to States that had not achieved the national air quality standards established by the Environmental Protection Agency (EPA) pursuant to earlier legislation. The amended Clean Air Act required these "nonattainment" States to establish a permit program regulating "new or modified major stationary sources" of air pollution. Generally, a permit may not be issued for a new or modified major stationary source unless several stringent conditions are met. The EPA regulation promulgated to implement this permit requirement allows a State to adopt a plantwide definition of the term "stationary source." Under this definition, an existing plant that contains several pollution-emitting devices may install or modify one piece of equipment without meeting the permit conditions if the alteration will not increase the total emissions from the plant. The question presented by these cases is whether EPA's decision to allow States to treat all of the pollution-emitting devices within the same industrial grouping as though they were encased within a single "bubble" is based on a reasonable construction of the statutory term "stationary source." . . .

II

When a court reviews an agency's construction of the statute which it administers, it is confronted with two questions. First, always, is the question whether Congress has directly spoken to the precise question at issue. If the intent of Congress is clear, that is the end of the matter; for the court, as well as the agency, must give effect to the unambiguously expressed intent of Congress. If, however, the court determines Congress has not directly addressed the precise question at issue, the court does not simply impose its own construction on the statute, as would be necessary in the absence of an administrative interpretation. Rather, if the statute is silent or ambiguous with respect to the specific issue, the question for the court is whether the agency's answer is based on a permissible construction of the statute. . . .

If Congress has explicitly left a gap for the agency to fill, there is an express delegation of authority to the agency to elucidate a specific provision of the statute by regulation. Such legislative regulations are given controlling weight unless they are arbitrary, capricious, or manifestly contrary to the statute. Sometimes the legislative delegation to an agency on a particular question is implicit rather than explicit. In such a case, a court may not substitute its own construction of a statutory provision for a reasonable interpretation made by the administrator of an agency. . . .

Based on the examination of the legislation and its history . . . we agree with the Court of Appeals that Congress did not have a specific intention on the applicability of the bubble concept in these cases, and conclude that the EPA's use of that concept here is a reasonable policy choice for the agency to make. . . .

As previously noted, prior to the 1977 Amendments, the EPA had adhered to a plantwide definition of the term "source." . . .

After adoption of the 1977 Amendments . . . the EPA rejected the plantwide definition [in certain circumstances]; on the other hand, it expressly concluded that the plantwide approach would be permissible in certain [other] circumstances. . . .

In August 1980, however, the EPA adopted a regulation that, in essence, applied the basic reasoning of the Court of Appeals in these cases. The EPA took particular note of the two then-recent Court of Appeals decisions, which had created the bright-line rule that the "bubble concept" should be employed in a program designed to maintain air quality but not in one designed to enhance air quality. . . .

In 1981 a new administration took office and initiated a "Government-wide reexamination of regulatory burdens and complexities." . . . In the context of that review, the EPA reevaluated the various arguments that had been advanced in connection with the proper definition of the term "source" and concluded that the term should be given the same definition in both nonattainment areas and PSD areas. . . .

Our review of the EPA's varying interpretations of the word "source" — both before and after the 1977 Amendments — convinces us that the agency primarily responsible for administering this important legislation has consistently interpreted it flexibly — not in a sterile textual vacuum, but in the context of implementing policy decisions in a technical and complex arena. The fact that the agency has from time to time changed its interpretation of the term "source" does not, as respondents argue, lead us to conclude that no deference should be accorded the agency's interpretation of the statute. An initial agency interpretation is not instantly carved in stone. On the contrary, the agency, to engage in informed rulemaking, must consider varying interpretations and the wisdom of its policy on a continuing basis. Moreover, the fact that the agency has adopted different definitions in different contexts adds force to the argument that the definition itself is flexible, particularly since Congress has never indicated any disapproval of a flexible reading of the statute. . . .

Policy

The arguments over policy that are advanced in the parties' briefs create the impression that respondents are now waging in a judicial forum a specific policy battle which they ultimately lost in the agency and in the 32 jurisdictions opting for the "bubble concept," but one which was never waged in the Congress. Such policy arguments are more properly addressed to legislators or administrators, not to judges.

In these cases the Administrator's interpretation represents a reasonable accommodation of manifestly competing interests and is entitled to deference: the regulatory scheme is technical and complex, the agency considered the matter in a detailed and reasoned fashion, and the decision involves reconciling conflicting policies. Congress intended to accommodate both interests, but did not do so itself on the level of specificity presented by these cases. Perhaps that body consciously desired the Administrator to strike the balance at this level, thinking that those with great expertise and charged with responsibility for administering the provision would be in a better position to do so; perhaps it simply did not consider the question at this level; and perhaps Congress was unable to forge a coalition on either side of the question, and those on each side decided to take their chances with the scheme devised by the agency. For judicial purposes, it matters not which of these things occurred.

Judges are not experts in the field, and are not part of either political branch of the Government. Courts must, in some cases, reconcile competing political interests, but not on the basis of the judges' personal policy preferences. In contrast, an agency to which Congress has delegated policymaking responsibilities may, within the limits of that delegation, properly rely upon the incumbent administration's views of wise policy to inform its judgments. While agencies are not directly accountable to the people, the Chief Executive is, and it is entirely appropriate for this political branch of the Government to make such policy choices—resolving the competing interests which Congress itself either inadvertently did not resolve, or intentionally left to be resolved by the agency charged with the administration of the statute in light of everyday realities.

When a challenge to an agency construction of a statutory provision, fairly conceptualized, really centers on the wisdom of the agency's policy, rather than whether it is a reasonable choice within a gap left open by Congress, the challenge must fail. In such a case, federal judges—who have no constituency—have a duty to respect legitimate policy choices made by those who do. The responsibilities for assessing the wisdom of such policy choices and resolving the struggle between competing views of the public interest are not judicial ones: "Our Constitution vests such responsibilities in the political branches." TVA v. Hill. . . .

NOTES AND QUESTIONS

1. *The continuing debate over Chevron. Chevron* is an extremely significant case and has been the subject of extensive scholarly comment and debate. For example, see Stephen Breyer, Judicial Review of Questions of Law and Policy, 38 Admin. L. Rev. 363 (1986); Thomas W. Merrill, Judicial Deference to Executive Precedent, 101 Yale L.J. 969 (1992); Richard J. Pierce, *Chevron* and Its Aftermath: Judicial Review of Agency Interpretations of Statutory Provisions, 41 Vand. L. Rev. 301 (1988); Kenneth W. Starr, Cass R. Sunstein, Richard K. Willard, Alan B. Morrison, and Ronald M. Levin, Judicial Review of Administrative Action in a Conservative Era, 39 Admin. L. Rev. 353 (1987); Cass R. Sunstein, Law and Administration after *Chevron,* 90 Colum. L. Rev. 2071 (1990). Much of this comment is beyond the scope of this book. The several notes that follow address the impact of the decision on Congress. These notes assume the strongest reading of *Chevron*— deference to agency interpretations of all unclear regulatory statutes. For some interesting views on the meaning of *Chevron,* see the two *Sweet Home* decisions in Chapter 12.

2. *A new canon. Chevron* sets forth a general principle of statutory inter-pretation to be followed after a court determines that an agency enabling statute is unclear. As discussed earlier in this chapter, such principles are based on presumptions of legislative intent. To again test this proposition, answer the following question: Why should courts give deference to agency interpretations of unclear statutes? As a presumption of legislative

intent, this one, like many of the others discussed earlier, is sometimes correct and sometimes not. Congress frequently delegates policy making to administrative agencies either through broad grants of power or through general language. But not every provision of a regulatory statute is a delegation of power to an agency:

> Such a rule is quite appealing, especially when Congress has delegated law-interpreting power to the agency or when the question involves the agency's specialized fact finding and policy making competence. . . .
>
> For several reasons, however, a general rule of judicial deference to all agency interpretations of law would be unsound. The case for deference depends in the first instance on congressional instructions. If Congress has told courts to defer to agency interpretations, courts must do so. But many regulatory statutes were born out of legislative distrust for agency discretion; they represent an effort to limit administrative authority through clear legislative specifications. A rule of deference in the face of ambiguity would be inconsistent with understandings, endorsed by Congress, of the considerable risks posed by administrative discretion. An ambiguity is simply not a delegation of law-interpreting power. *Chevron* confuses the two.

Cass R. Sunstein, Interpreting Statutes in the Regulatory State, 103 Harv. L. Rev. 405, 445 (1989). How would you classify the language in question in *Chevron?*

3. *Narrowing Chevron's applicability.* In Gonzales v. Oregon, the Court refused to apply the canon propounded in *Chevron* and favored instead a more expansive review of the rule at issue. Justice Kennedy explains, in writing the opinion for the majority:

> In 1994, Oregon became the first State to legalize assisted suicide when voters approved a ballot measure enacting the Oregon Death With Dignity Act (ODWDA). ODWDA . . . exempts from civil or criminal liability state-licensed physicians who, in compliance with the specific safeguards in ODWDA, dispense or prescribe a lethal dose of drugs upon the request of a terminally ill patient.
>
> The drugs Oregon physicians prescribe under ODWDA are regulated under a federal statute, the Controlled Substances Act (CSA or Act). The CSA allows these particular drugs to be available only by a written prescription from a registered physician. . . .
>
> A November 9, 2001, Interpretive Rule issued by the Attorney General addresses the implementation and enforcement of the CSA with respect to ODWDA. It determines that using controlled substances to assist suicide is not a legitimate medical practice and . . . is unlawful under the CSA. The Interpretive Rule's validity under the CSA is the issue before us. . . .
>
> [T]he Interpretive Rule receives no . . . deference under *Chevron*. If a statute is ambiguous, judicial review of administrative rulemaking often demands *Chevron* deference; and the rule is judged accordingly. All would agree . . . that the statutory phrase "legitimate medical purpose"

is a generality, susceptible to more precise definition and open to varying constructions. . . . *Chevron* deference, however, is not accorded merely because the statute is ambiguous and an administrative official is involved. To begin with, the rule must be promulgated pursuant to authority Congress has delegated to the official. . . .

Since the Interpretive Rule was not promulgated pursuant to the Attorney General's authority, its interpretation of "legitimate medical purpose" does not receive *Chevron* deference. Instead, it receives deference only in accordance with *Skidmore*. "The weight of such a judgment in a particular case will depend upon the thoroughness evident in its consideration, the validity of its reasoning, its consistency with earlier and later pronouncements, and all those factors which give it power to persuade, if lacking power to control." Skidmore v. Swift & Co., 323 U.S. 134, 140 (1944).

Gonzales v. Oregon, 546 U.S. 243, 249, 255, 269 (2006) (citations omitted).

In invalidating the Attorney General's rule, the Court noted that while he did hold rulemaking power under the CSA, such power simply did not extend to the ability to "define the substantive standards of medical practice." Id. at 264. Under the Court's reading of the CSA, Congress placed this authority solely "in the hands of the Secretary. . . . The Attorney General cannot control a substance if the Secretary disagrees." Id.

4. *A new role for the President in the interpretive process. Chevron* makes the President a direct player in the process of statutory interpretation. Prior to *Chevron,* the President's affirmative role (not including the veto power) was essentially one of lobbyist, as the legislative intent of the Congress that enacted the legislation would, at least in theory, control any interpretive decision. Since *Chevron,* the President, through the control of administrative agencies, has a far more important role. Consider the following provision from President Bush's signing statement for the Civil Rights Act of 1991:

> This change in the burden of proof . . . means it is especially important to ensure that all the legislation's other safeguards against unfair application of disparate impact law are carefully observed. These highly technical matters are addressed in detail in the analyses of S. 1745 placed in the legislative record by Senator Dole on behalf of himself and several other Senators and of the Administration. I direct that these documents be treated as authoritative interpretive guidance by all officials in the Executive branch with respect to the law of disparate impact as well as other matters covered in the documents.

Senator Dole, along with the administration, had argued for a narrow statute, which view is reflected in the materials referred to in the signing statement. In the end, although the statute was not as narrow as the bill Senator Dole had advocated, he supported the enacted legislation, offering his narrow reading (the analysis referred to in the signing statement) as justification for his vote. Assume that the relevant agencies followed the command of the President set forth in his signing statement. Compare how the courts would have treated the agencies' use of the Dole analysis before and after *Chevron*. Assume that the particular language under challenge is unclear. See generally Cynthia Farina, Statutory Interpretation and the Balance of Power in the Administrative State, 89 Colum. L. Rev. 452 (1989).

5. *Old Congress versus new Congress.* By removing references to legislative intent as a tool for interpreting unclear regulatory statutes, *Chevron* reduces the power of the Congress that enacted the statute. While much of the power goes to the President and the relevant agencies, the decision also enhances the authority of the current Congress and especially its oversight committees. Why? See generally Peter Strauss, When the Judge Is Not the Primary Official with Responsibility to Read: Agency Interpretation and the Problem of Legislative History, 66 Chi.-Kent L. Rev. 321, 335 (1990). Of course, in enacting a statute, Congress can avoid subsequent shifts of power by drafting its statutes to avoid step two of the *Chevron* analysis. See Michael Herz, Judicial Textualism Meets Congressional Micromanagement: A Potential Collision in Clean Air Interpretation, 16 Harv. Envtl. L. Rev. 175 (1992). Congress could also amend §706 of the Administrative Procedure Act to prohibit the courts from giving deference to administrative interpretations of unclear statutes.

6. *The politics of administrative policy making.* Among the traditional justifications for the legislative delegation of rulemaking power to agencies is that agencies can provide technical expertise that is not otherwise available to the delegating legislature. What weight does the Court give to agency expertise in *Chevron?* For example, how does the EPA justify its continuous redefinition of "stationary source"? At the heart of *Chevron* and of its criticism is the level of protection the decision gives to the politics of agency policy making. As Peter Strauss has written, "part of what distinguishes agencies from courts in the business of statute-reading is that we accept a legitimate role for current politics in the work of agencies; the question then becomes . . . how much law there is in the mixture." Peter Strauss, When the Judge Is Not the Primary Official with Responsibility to Read: Agency Interpretation and the Problem of Legislative History, 66 Chi.-Kent L. Rev. 321, 335 (1990).

7. *Chevron in the states.* State courts have generally not adopted the *Chevron* canon. While state courts will give weight in various circumstances to agency interpretations of their enabling statutes, they tend to reserve to themselves, in some form or another, the authority to impose their interpretations of statutes that do not call for the application of an agency's particular expertise. For example, in *Seittelman v. Sabol*, 697 N.E.2d 154 (N.Y. 1998), New York's highest court, in overruling an agency's narrow interpretation of a statute, held:

> "It is settled law that an agency's interpretation of the statutes it administers must be upheld absent demonstrated irrationality or unreasonableness"

(citation omitted). However, where "the question is one of pure statutory reading and analysis, dependent only on accurate apprehension of legislative intent, there is little basis to rely on any special competence or expertise of the administrative agency" (citations omitted). In such a case, courts are "free to ascertain the proper interpretation from the statutory language and legislative intent" (citation omitted).

Id. at 158. See generally Arthur E. Bonfield and Michael Asimow, State and Federal Administrative Law (1989).

E.   THE INTERPRETATION OF LAW ENACTED THROUGH INITIATIVE AND REFERENDUM

In the sections above, we have discussed the interpretation of statutes enacted through the legislative process. Not all statutes are enacted in that fashion. For example, law students and lawyers in California quite regularly are required to interpret statutes enacted through an initiative process. Today some 20 states have direct initiative processes that allow citizens to initiate and enact legislation, totally bypassing their state legislatures. Some additional states have a form of initiative that gives the legislature an opportunity to enact the initiated legislation. If the legislation is not enacted within a specific time period, it then goes to referendum.

Since the 1970s initiatives have addressed subjects as diverse as public morality, governmental processes, taxation, labor regulation, business regulation, utility rates, zoning and land use, health, welfare reform, housing, homelessness, education, civil rights, environmental protection, and nuclear power. During the early 1990s, the most noted initiatives were a California effort to limit the rights of illegal aliens and their children, a California effort to prohibit affirmative action, the efforts of several states to restrict the rights of homosexuals, and Oregon's doctor-assisted suicide law.

Initiative refers to the process of having legislation (or constitutional amendments) placed directly on the ballot, usually through a petitioning process, and then voted on by the public. A modified form of this process (sometimes referred to as an indirect initiative) uses the petition process to trigger legislative consideration of a particular proposal. Such a proposal is only subject to referendum in the event that the legislature does not adopt it. *Referendum* refers to the process by which legislative enactments are required to be approved by the electorate before they can become effective. In some states, particular types of legislation (for example, creating debt) must be subject to referendum. Another form of referendum is to allow the public, through a petition process, to require an enacted bill to be submitted to the voters.

The frequent use of initiatives since the 1970s has led to considerable debate about their efficacy. This debate has basically addressed two issues: (1) How successful initiatives have been as measured against their goals; and (2) how they compare, as a lawmaking process, with representative democracy. There is also debate over their constitutional validity. For a discussion of this debate, see Chapter 9, Section F.

The increasingly frequent use of initiatives raises another important question about their statutory product: How are they to be interpreted? The application of such statutes produces the same problems of "meaning" as legislative enacted statutes, but are these problems susceptible to the same interpretive approaches used in the interpretation of legislative law? More particularly, if the language of the statute does not provide an answer to the question under litigation, what sources of meaning are available to provide an answer? As Professor Jane S. Schacter, in an article about the interpretation of initiatives, has written:

> Consider, for example, the mass size of the electorate; the absence of legislative hearings, committee reports, or other recorded legislative history; and the inability of citizen lawmakers to deliberate about, or to amend proposed ballot measures. In addition, voters are not professional lawmakers so it is problematic to impute to the electorate the same knowledge about law, legal terminology, and legislative context that courts routinely ascribe — if sometimes only as aspiration — to legislators.

Jane S. Schacter, The Pursuit of "Popular Intent": Interpretive Dilemmas in Direct Democracy, 105 Yale L.J. 107, 110 (1995).

Aside from the work of Professor Schacter, little scholarly attention has been focused on this problem and we rely heavily on her work to describe the approaches most courts have adopted. According to Schacter, "courts widely subject citizen-lawmakers to the same standards as legislators and generally confine their search to sources commonly used in construing legislative law," despite the fact that the interpretive sources for initiative laws might "differ from those used in construing legislative law because of, for example, the absence of a legislative record and the fact that voters are not professional." Id. at 119-20. For example, in their search for the meaning of a provision in an initiative law, courts have relied on "popular intent" (as an analogy to legislative intent), drawn from sources used for legislative law: the statute's language, the body of existing law and its legislative history, legal text, judicial and administrative decisions, and canons of construction.

This reliance on a traditional methodology is to be expected. The language of the initiative, read or not read, understood or not understood, is that which is enacted. If it is ambiguous, the court's search for the law's meaning in traditional sources, along with ballot material, would seem natural. But such approaches require careful analysis. Professor Schacter, for example, is very critical, arguing that interpretive rules consistent with characteristics of the initiative process need to be judicially framed.

CHAPTER *11*

The Applicability of Plain Meaning

In Section B of Chapter 10, we discussed the plain meaning rule and its exceptions. In this chapter, we provide some cases illustrating the points of that discussion. The questions raised by these cases remain a continuing focus of scholars, legislators, and judges. They relate, importantly, to the legislative and judicial powers and functions and to the strengths and weaknesses of each. They relate, also, very pragmatically to the practice of law. For as long as judges are willing to depart from the plain meaning of a statute to look elsewhere for legislative meaning, lawyers must know about and remain alert for other sources of meaning than the applicable statutory language itself.

The overarching question in each of the following cases is whether to apply the plain meaning of the statute in a particular case. In some cases, the plain meaning is applied; in others, it is not. Where it is not applied or where there is a dissent against its application, the court or dissenting judges argue, on some basis, that the application of the plain meaning is inconsistent with some definition of legislative intent or purpose. While all of the cases fit this pattern, we divide them into several sections to emphasize different points. There is overlapping among these sections. Section A provides a general look at the applicability of plain meaning through a series of well-known and frequently discussed cases. Section B contains two cases in which courts agree that there has been a drafting error in a statute, but seemingly address these errors differently. In Section C, we explore private rights of action. The question in each of these cases is whether the Court may grant private rights of action when the statute is silent on this point. Finally, in Section D, we take a more detailed look at the uses of legislative history in cases in which the statutory meaning is plain.

725

A.   LANGUAGE AND PURPOSE

Tennessee Valley Authority v. Hill
437 U.S. 153 (1978)

Statute: 16 U.S.C. §1536 (Endangered Species Act of 1973)

The Secretary [of the Interior] shall review other programs administered by him and utilize such programs in furtherance of the purposes of this chapter. All other Federal departments and agencies shall, in consultation with and with the assistance of the Secretary, utilize their authorities in furtherance of the purposes of this chapter by carrying out programs for the conservation of endangered species and threatened species listed pursuant to section 1533 of this title and by taking such action necessary to insure that actions authorized, funded, or carried out by them do not jeopardize the continued existence of such endangered species and threatened species or result in the destruction or modification of habitat of such species which is determined by the Secretary, after consultation as appropriate with the affected States, to be critical.

CHIEF JUSTICE BURGER delivered the opinion of the Court. [Internal citations have been omitted except where particularly relevant.]

The questions presented in this case are (a) whether the Endangered Species Act of 1973 requires a court to enjoin the operation of a virtually completed federal dam — which had been authorized prior to 1973 — when, pursuant to authority vested in him by Congress, the Secretary of the Interior has determined that operation of the dam would eradicate an endangered species; and (b) whether continued congressional appropriations for the dam after 1973 constituted an implied repeal of the Endangered Species Act, at least as to the particular dam.

I

The Little Tennessee River originates in the mountains of northern Georgia and flows through the national forest lands of North Carolina into Tennessee, where it converges with the Big Tennessee River near Knoxville. The lower 33 miles of the Little Tennessee takes the river's clear, free-flowing waters through an area of great natural beauty. Among other environmental amenities, this stretch of river is said to contain abundant trout. Considerable historical importance attaches to the areas immediately adjacent to this portion of the Little Tennessee's banks. To the south of the river's edge lies Fort Loudon, established in 1756 as England's southwestern outpost in the French and Indian War. Nearby are also the ancient sites of several native American villages, the archeological stores of which are to a large extent unexplored. These include the Cherokee towns of Echota and Tennase, the former being the sacred capital of the Cherokee Nation as early as the 16th century and the latter providing the linguistic basis from which the State of Tennessee derives its name.

In this area of the Little Tennessee River the Tennessee Valley Authority, a wholly owned public corporation of the United States, began constructing the Tellico Dam and Reservoir Project in 1967, shortly after Congress appropriated initial funds for its development. Tellico is a multipurposed regional development project designed principally to stimulate shoreline development, generate sufficient electric current to heat 20,000 homes, and provide flatwater recreation and flood control, as well as improve economic conditions in "an area characterized by underutilization of human resources and outmigration of young people." . . .

The Tellico Dam has never opened, however, despite the fact that construction has been virtually completed and the dam is essentially ready for operation. Although Congress has appropriated monies for Tellico every year since 1967, progress was delayed, and ultimately stopped, by a tangle of lawsuits and administrative proceedings. . . .

[In 1973] a discovery was made in the waters of the Little Tennessee which would profoundly affect the Tellico Project. . . . [A] University of Tennessee ichthyologist, Dr. David A. Etnier, found a previously unknown species of perch, the snail darter. . . .

Until recently the finding of a new species of animal life would hardly generate a cause célèbre. . . . The moving force behind the snail darter's sudden fame came some four months after its discovery, when the Congress passed the Endangered Species Act of 1973 (Act), 87 Stat. 884, 16 U.S.C. §1531 et seq. (1976 ed.). This legislation, among other things, authorizes the Secretary of the Interior to declare species of animal life "endangered" and to identify the "critical habitat" of these creatures. When a species or its habitat is so listed, the following portion of the Act — relevant here — becomes effective:

> The Secretary [of the Interior] shall review other programs administered by him and utilize such programs in furtherance of the purposes of this chapter. All other Federal departments and agencies shall, in consultation with and with the assistance of the Secretary, utilize their authorities in furtherance of the purposes of this chapter by carrying out programs for the conservation of endangered species and threatened species listed pursuant to section 1533 of this title and *by taking such action necessary to insure that actions authorized, funded, or carried out by them do not jeopardize the continued existence of such endangered species and threatened species* or result in the destruction or modification of habitat of such species which is determined by the Secretary, after consultation as appropriate with the affected States, to be critical.

16 U.S.C. §1536 (1976 ed.) (emphasis added).

In January 1975, the respondents in this case and others petitioned the Secretary of the Interior to list the snail darter as an endangered species. After receiving comments from various interested parties, including TVA and the State of Tennessee, the Secretary formally listed the snail darter as an endangered species on October 8, 1975. In so acting, it was noted that "the snail darter is a living entity which is genetically distinct and reproductively isolated from other fishes." More important for the purposes of this case, the Secretary determined that the snail darter apparently lives only in that portion of the Little Tennessee River which would be completely inundated by the reservoir created as a consequence of the Tellico Dam's completion. . . .

Subsequent to this determination, the Secretary declared the area of the Little Tennessee which would be affected by the Tellico Dam to be the "critical habitat" of the snail darter. Using these determinations as a predicate, and notwithstanding the near completion of the dam, the Secretary declared that pursuant to §7 of the Act, "all Federal agencies must take such action as is necessary to insure that actions authorized, funded, or carried out by them do not result in the destruction or modification of this critical habitat area." This notice, of course, was pointedly directed at TVA and clearly aimed at halting completion or operation of the dam. . . .

Meanwhile, Congress had . . . become involved in the fate of the snail darter. Appearing before a Subcommittee of the House Committee on Appropriations in April 1975 — some seven months before the snail darter was listed as endangered — TVA representatives described the discovery of the fish and the relevance of the Endangered Species Act to the Tellico Project. At that time TVA presented a position which it would advance in successive forums thereafter, namely, that the Act did not prohibit the completion of a project authorized, funded, and substantially constructed before the Act was passed. . . . Thereafter, the House Committee on Appropriations, in its June 20, 1975, Report, stated the following in the course of recommending that an additional $29 million be appropriated for Tellico:

> The *Committee* directs that the project, for which an environmental impact statement has been completed and provided the Committee, should be completed as promptly as possible. . . .

(Emphasis added.) Congress then approved the TVA general budget, which contained funds for continued construction of the Tellico Project. In December 1975, one month after the snail darter was declared an endangered species, the President signed the bill into law.

In February 1976 . . . respondent filed the case now under review. . . . Shortly thereafter the House and Senate held appropriations hearings which would include discussions of the Tellico budget.

At these hearings, TVA Chairman Wagner reiterated the agency's position that the Act did not apply to a project which was over 50% finished by the time the Act became effective and some 70% to 80% complete when the snail darter was officially listed as endangered. . . .

[O]n May 25, 1976, the court entered its memorandum opinion and order denying respondents their requested relief and dismissing the complaint. . . .

In reaching this result, the District Court stressed that the entire project was then about 80% complete. . . . To accept the plaintiffs' position, the District Court argued, would inexorably lead to what it characterized as the absurd result of requiring "a court to halt impoundment of water behind a fully completed dam if an endangered species were discovered in the river on the day before such impoundment was scheduled to take place. We cannot conceive that Congress intended such a result."

Less than a month after the District Court decision, the Senate and House Appropriations Committees recommended the full budget request of $9 million for continued work on Tellico. In its Report accompanying the appropriations bill, the Senate Committee stated:

> During subcommittee hearings . . . TVA informed the Committee that it was continuing its efforts to preserve the darter, while working towards the scheduled 1977 completion date. TVA repeated its view that the Endangered Species Act did not prevent the completion of the Tellico project, which has been under construction for nearly a decade. The subcommittee brought this matter, as well as the recent U.S. District Court's decision upholding TVA's decision to complete the project, to the attention of the full Committee. *The Committee does not view* the Endangered Species Act as prohibiting the completion of the Tellico project at its advanced stage and directs that this project be completed as promptly as possible in the public interest.

(Emphasis added.) On June 29, 1976, both Houses of Congress passed TVA's general budget, which included funds for Tellico; the President signed the bill on July 12, 1976.

Thereafter . . . [t]he Court of Appeals . . . reversed, remanding "with instructions that a permanent injunction issue halting all activities incident to the Tellico Project which may destroy or modify the critical habitat of the snail darter." . . .

Following the issuance of the permanent injunction, members of TVA's Board of Directors appeared before Subcommittees of the House and Senate Appropriations Committees to testify in support of continued appropriations for Tellico. The Subcommittees were apprised of all aspects of Tellico's status, including the Court of Appeals' decision. TVA reported that the dam stood "ready for the gates to be closed and the reservoir filled," and requested funds for completion of certain ancillary parts of the project, such as public use areas, roads, and bridges. As to the snail darter itself; TVA commented optimistically on its transplantation efforts, expressing the opinion that the relocated fish were "doing well and [had] reproduced."

Both Appropriations Committees subsequently recommended the full amount requested for completion of the Tellico Project. In its June 2, 1977, Report, the House Appropriations Committee stated:

> *It is the Committee's view* that the Endangered Species Act was not intended to halt projects such as these in their advanced stage of completion, and [the Committee] strongly recommends that these projects not be stopped because of misuse of the Act.

(Emphasis added.) As a solution to the problem, the House Committee advised that TVA should cooperate with the Department of the Interior "to relocate the endangered species to another suitable habitat so as to permit the project to proceed as rapidly as possible." . . . Toward this end, the Committee recommended a special appropriation of $2 million to facilitate relocation of the snail darter and other endangered species which threatened to delay or stop TVA projects. Much the same occurred on the Senate side, with its Appropriations Committee recommending both the amount requested to complete Tellico and the special appropriation for transplantation of endangered species. Reporting to the Senate on these measures, the Appropriations Committee took a particularly strong stand on the snail darter issue:

> *This committee has not viewed* the Endangered Species Act as preventing the completion and use of these projects which were well under way at the time the affected species were listed as endangered. If the act has such an effect, which is contrary to *the Committee's understanding* of the intent of Congress in enacting the Endangered Species Act, funds should be appropriated to allow these projects to be completed and their benefits realized in the public interest, the Endangered Species Act notwithstanding.

(Emphasis added.)

TVA's budget, including funds for completion of Tellico and relocation of the snail darter, passed both Houses of Congress and was signed into law on August 7, 1977.

II

We begin with the premise that operation of the Tellico Dam will either eradicate the known population of snail darters or destroy their critical habitat. . . .

Starting from the above premise, two questions are presented: (a) Would TVA be in violation of the Act if it completed and operated the Tellico Dam as planned? (b) If TVA's actions would offend the Act, is an injunction the appropriate remedy for the violation? For the reasons stated hereinafter, we hold that both questions must be answered in the affirmative.

A

It may seem curious to some that the survival of a relatively small number of three-inch fish among all the countless millions of species extant would require the permanent halting of a virtually completed dam for which Congress has expended more than $100 million. The paradox is not minimized by the fact that Congress continued to appropriate large sums of public money for the project, even after congressional Appropriations Committees were apprised of its apparent impact upon the survival of the snail darter. We conclude, however, that the explicit provisions of the Endangered Species Act require precisely that result.

One would be hard pressed to find a statutory provision whose terms were any plainer than those in §7 of the Endangered Species Act. Its very words affirmatively command all federal agencies *"to insure that actions authorized, funded, or carried out* by them do not *jeopardize* the continued existence"* of an endangered species or *"result* in the destruction or modification of habitat of such species. . . ."* 16 U.S.C. §1536 (1976 ed.). (Emphasis added.) This language admits of no exception. . . .

Concededly, this view of the Act will produce results requiring the sacrifice of the anticipated benefits of the project and of many millions of dollars in public funds. But examination of the language, history, and structure of the legislation under review here indicates beyond doubt that Congress intended endangered species to be afforded the highest of priorities. . . .

When Congress passed the Act in 1973, it was not legislating on a clean slate. The first major congressional concern for the preservation of the endangered species had come with passage of the Endangered Species Act of 1966. . . .

Section 7 of the Act, which of course is relied upon by respondents in this case, provides a particularly good gauge of congressional intent. As we have seen, this provision had its genesis in the Endangered Species Act of 1966, but that legislation qualified the obligation of federal agencies by stating that they should seek to preserve endangered species only *"insofar as is practicable and consistent with the[ir] primary purposes. . . ."* Likewise, every bill introduced in 1973 contained a qualification similar to that found in the earlier statutes. . . . This type of language did not go unnoticed by those advocating strong endangered species legislation. A representative of the Sierra Club, for example, attacked the use of the phrase "consistent with the primary purpose" in proposed H.R. 4758, cautioning that the qualification "could be construed to be a declaration of congressional policy that other agency purposes are necessarily more important than protection of endangered species and would always prevail if conflict were to occur."

What is very significant in this sequence is that the final version of the 1973 Act carefully omitted all of the reservations described above. . . .

It is against this legislative background that we must measure TVA's claim that the Act was not intended to stop operation of a project which, like Tellico Dam, was near completion when an endangered species was discovered in its path. While there is no discussion in the legislative history of precisely this problem, the totality of congressional action makes it abundantly clear that the result we reach today is wholly in accord with both the words of the statute and the intent of Congress. The plain intent of Congress in enacting this statute was to halt and reverse the trend toward species extinction, whatever the cost. . . .

It is not for us to speculate, much less act, on whether Congress would have altered its stance had the specific events of this case been anticipated. In any event, we discern no hint in the deliberations of Congress relating to the 1973 Act that would compel a different result than we reach here. Indeed, the repeated expressions of congressional concern over what it saw as the potentially enormous danger presented by the eradication of any endangered species suggest how the balance would have been struck had the issue been presented to Congress in 1973. . . .

In passing the Endangered Species Act of 1973, Congress was also aware of certain instances in which exceptions to the statute's broad sweep would be necessary. Thus, §10 creates a number of limited "hardship exemptions," none of which would even remotely apply to the Tellico project. In fact, there are no exemptions in the Endangered Species Act for federal agencies, meaning that under the maxim *expressio unius est exclusio alterius*, we must presume that these were the only "hardship cases" Congress intended to exempt.

Notwithstanding Congress' expression of intent in 1973, we are urged to find that the continuing appropriations for Tellico Dam constitute an implied repeal of the 1973 Act, at least insofar as it applies to the Tellico Project. . . .

There is nothing in the appropriations measures, as passed, which states that the Tellico Project was to be completed irrespective of the requirements of the Endangered Species Act. These appropriations, in fact, represented relatively minor components of the lump-sum amounts for the *entire* TVA budget. To find a repeal of the Endangered Species Act under these circumstances would surely do violence to the "'cardinal rule . . . that repeals by implication are not favored.'" . . .

The doctrine disfavoring repeals by implication "applies with full vigor when . . . the subsequent legislation is an *appropriations* measure." (Emphasis added.) This is perhaps an understatement since it would be more accurate to say that the policy applies with even greater force when the claimed repeal rests solely on an Appropriations Act. We recognize that both substantive enactments and appropriations measures are "Acts of Congress," but the latter have the limited and specific purpose of providing funds for authorized programs. When voting on appropriations measures, legislators are entitled to operate under the assumption that the funds will be devoted to purposes which are lawful and not for any purpose forbidden. Without such an assurance, every appropriations measure would be pregnant with prospects of altering substantive legislation, repealing by implication any prior statute which might prohibit the expenditure. Not only would this lead to the absurd result of requiring Members to review exhaustively the background of every authorization before voting on an appropriation, but it would flout the very rules the Congress carefully adopted to avoid this need. House Rule XXI(2), for instance, specifically provides:

> No appropriation shall be reported in any general appropriation bill, or be in order as an amendment thereto, for any expenditure not previously authorized by law, unless in continuation of appropriations for such public works as are already in progress. *Nor shall any provision in any such bill or amendment thereto changing existing law be in order.*

(Emphasis added.)

JUSTICE POWELL, with whom JUSTICE BLACKMUN joins, dissenting.

In my view §7 cannot reasonably be interpreted as applying to a project that is completed or substantially completed when its threat to an endangered species is discovered. Nor can I believe that Congress could have intended this Act to produce the "absurd result" . . . of this case. If it were clear from the language of the Act and its legislative history that Congress intended to authorize this result, this Court would be compelled to enforce it. It is not our province to rectify policy or political judgments by the Legislative Branch, however egregiously they may disserve the public interest. But where the statutory language and legislative history, as in this case, need not be construed to reach such a result, I view it as the duty of this Court to adopt a permissible construction that accords with some modicum of common sense and the public weal. . . .

A

The starting point in statutory construction is, of course, the language of §7 itself. I agree that it can be viewed as a textbook example of fuzzy language, which can be read according to the "eye of the beholder." The critical words direct all federal agencies to take "such action [as may be] necessary to insure that actions authorized, funded, or carried out by them do not jeopardize the continued existence of . . . endangered species . . . or result in the destruction or modification of [a critical] habitat of such species. . . ."

Under the Court's reasoning, the Act covers every existing federal installation, including great hydroelectric projects and reservoirs, every river and harbor project, and every national defense installation — however essential to the Nation's economic health and safety. The "actions" that an agency would be prohibited from "carrying out" would include the continued operation of such projects or any change necessary to preserve their continued usefulness. The only precondition, according to respondents, to thus destroying the usefulness of even the most important federal project in our country would be a finding by the Secretary of the Interior that a continuation of the project would threaten the survival or critical habitat of a newly discovered species of water spider or amoeba.

"[Frequently] words of general meaning are used in a statute, words broad enough to include an act in question, and yet a consideration of the whole legislation, or of the circumstances surrounding its enactment, or of the absurd results which follow from giving such broad meaning to the words, makes it unreasonable to believe that the legislator intended to include the particular act." Church of the Holy Trinity v. United States (citation omitted). The result that will follow in this case by virtue of the Court's reading of §7 makes it unreasonable to believe that Congress intended that reading. Moreover, §7 may be construed in a way that avoids an "absurd result" without doing violence to its language.

The critical word in §7 is "actions" and its meaning is far from "plain." It is part of the phrase: "actions authorized, funded or carried out." In terms of planning and executing various activities, it seems evident that the "actions" referred to are not all actions that an agency can ever take, but rather actions that the agency is deciding whether to authorize, to fund, or to carry out. In short, these words reasonably may be read as applying only to prospective actions, i.e., actions with respect to which the agency has reasonable decisionmaking alternatives still available, actions not yet carried out. At the time respondents brought this lawsuit, the Tellico Project was 80% complete at a cost of more than $78 million. . . .

B

The Court recognizes that the first purpose of statutory construction is to ascertain the intent of the legislature. . . .

If the relevant Committees that considered the Act, and the Members of Congress who voted on it, had been aware that the Act could be used to terminate major federal projects authorized years earlier and nearly completed, or to require the abandonment of essential and long-completed federal installations and edifices, we can be certain that there would have been hearings, testimony, and debate concerning consequences so wasteful, so inimical to purposes previously deemed important, and so likely to arouse public outrage. The absence of any such consideration by the Committees or in the floor debates indicates quite clearly that no one participating in the legislative process considered these consequences as within the intendment of the Act. . . .

[T]his view of legislative intent at the time of enactment is abundantly confirmed by the subsequent congressional actions and expressions.

We have held, properly, that post-enactment statements by individual Members of Congress as to the meaning of a statute are entitled to little or no weight. The Court also has recognized that subsequent Appropriations Acts themselves are not necessarily entitled to significant weight in determining whether a prior statute has been superseded. But these precedents are inapposite. There was no effort here to "bootstrap" a post-enactment view of prior legislation by isolated statements of individual Congressmen. Nor is this a case where Congress, without explanation or comment upon the statute in question, merely has voted apparently inconsistent financial support in subsequent Appropriations Acts. Testimony on this precise issue was presented before congressional committees, and the Committee Reports for three consecutive years addressed the problem and affirmed their understanding of the original congressional intent. We cannot assume — as the Court suggests — that Congress, when it continued each year to approve the recommended appropriations, was unaware of the contents of the supporting Committee Reports. All this amounts to strong corroborative evidence that the interpretation of §7 as not applying to completed or substantially completed projects reflects the initial legislative intent.

III

I have little doubt that Congress will amend the Endangered Species Act to prevent the grave consequences made possible by today's decision. Few, if any, Members of that body will wish to defend an interpretation of the Act that requires the waste of at least $53 million and denies the people of the Tennessee Valley area the benefits of the reservoir that Congress intended to confer. There will be little sentiment to leave this dam standing before an empty reservoir, serving no purpose other than a conversation piece for incredulous tourists.

But more far reaching than the adverse effect on the people of this economically depressed area is the continuing threat to the operation of every federal project, no matter how important to the Nation. If Congress acts expeditiously, as may be anticipated, the Court's decision probably will have no lasting adverse consequences. But I had not thought it to be the province of this Court to force Congress into otherwise unnecessary action by interpreting a statute to produce a result no one intended.

Justice Rehnquist filed a dissenting opinion.

NOTES AND QUESTIONS

1. *Is the meaning plain?* This decision provides a good illustration of many of the points discussed in Chapter 10. The question being addressed by the

decision is whether the words "taking such actions necessary to insure that actions . . . do not jeopardize the continued existence of such endangered species . . . or result in the destruction . . . of habitat of such species . . ." apply to projects that are substantially completed. The majority finds the statute clear and applies the language. The dissent argues, as its first point, that the statute is unclear; indeed, that it is a "textbook example of fuzzy language."

What is your view?

One of the decision's critics has written:

Our doubts whether that statute gave the secretary power to halt projects well begun cannot be located in the ambiguity or vagueness or abstraction of some phrase or word. No one would claim that it is unclear whether the act applies to dams at all, although dams are not explicitly mentioned. Once again we think the statute unclear about projects already begun because it strikes many people as silly that so much money should be wasted to save an unappealing and scientifically unimportant species.

Ronald Dworkin, Law's Empire 352 (1986).

2. *An absurd result?* The main argument urged by the dissent is that the application of the statute in this case would be absurd. You will see this argument used in other cases. On what basis does the dissent reach this conclusion? After reading the dissent, how would you define the term "absurd"? Is the dissent arguing that applying the statute in this case would be constructively absurd or that there is actual evidence on which to base the claim of absurdity? If the latter, what evidence supports their view? Recall Professor Dworkin's characterization of the snail darter in Note 1. Do you think that the dissent would have reached the same decision if the species were one of the bear family, or wolf family, or eagle family?

3. *Legislative process—legislative history.* Note the references to the legislative process in the decision. They are divided into two categories: first, the legislative history of the statute and, second, postenactment meetings of the congressional appropriations committees and their reports. (These postenactment proceedings are not part of the statute's legislative history.) Identify each part of the legislative process referred to and evaluate its value for establishing the point for which it is being offered.

4. *Legislative process—the appropriations bills.* Appropriations bills enacted by Congress are law. Since the appropriation for the TVA included sufficient funds to complete the dam, on what basis did the majority ignore the legislative command? What relevance did the Court attach to the testimony before, and committee reports of, the appropriations committees?

5. *A canon of construction.* In rejecting the TVA's argument that the appropriations bill mandated completion of a dam, the Court used a canon of construction:

To find a repeal of the Endangered Species Act under these circumstances would surely do violence to the "cardinal rule . . . that repeals by implication are not favored." ... The doctrine disfavoring repeals by implication "applies with full vigor when ... the subsequent legislation is an *appropriations* measure."

Do you think this is a reasonable presumption of legislative intent? What would be the consequence of a contrary canon?

6. *And what happened to the dam?* As a partial justification for their decision, the dissent in *Tennessee Valley Authority* declares with certainty the inevitability of remedial action by Congress. And Congress did act immediately, but not to assure the completion of the dam. In the summer of 1978, Congress enacted an extension to the Endangered Species Act that established a cabinet-level committee for the purpose of resolving conflicts between the protection of endangered species and the effectuation of federal public projects. Early in 1979, this committee voted unanimously in favor of the snail darter, barring the completion of the dam. Finally, in July of 1979, Congress's cabinet-level committee did *expressly* mandate the completion of the program in an appropriations bill:

> For the purpose of carrying out the provisions of the Tennessee Valley Authority Act of 1933, as amended ... $148,677,000 ... *Provided,* That notwithstanding the provisions of 16 U.S.C., chapter 35 or any other law, the Corporation is authorized and directed to complete construction, operate and maintain the Tellico Dam and Reservoir project for navigation, flood control, electric power generation and other purposes, including the maintenance of a normal summer reservoir pool of 813 feet above sea level.

Pub. L. No. 96-69 (Sept. 25, 1979). In September 1979, President Carter signed the bill, after his opposition to it was softened by fears of congressional retaliation against two of the administration's major legislative efforts: ratification of the Panama Canal Treaties and creation of a separate department of education.

7. *And what happened to the snail darter?* Apparently it is alive and well in other tributaries of the Tennessee River.

Griffin v. Oceanic Contractors, Inc.
458 U.S. 564 (1982)

Statute: 46 U.S.C. §596
The master or owner of any vessel making coasting voyages shall pay to every seaman his wages within two days after the termination of the agreement under which he was shipped, or at the time such seaman is discharged, whichever first happens; and in case of vessels making foreign voyages, or from a port on the Atlantic to a port on the Pacific, or vice versa, within twenty-four hours after the cargo has been discharged, or within four days after the seaman has been discharged, whichever first happens;

and in all cases the seaman shall be entitled to be paid at the time of his discharge on account of wages a sum equal to one-third part of the balance due him. Every master or owner who refuses or neglects to make payment in the manner hereinbefore mentioned without sufficient cause shall pay to the seaman a sum equal to two days' pay for each and every day during which payment is delayed beyond the respective periods, which sum shall be recoverable as wages in any claim made before the court. . . .

JUSTICE REHNQUIST delivered the opinion of the Court. Internal citations have been omitted except where particularly relevant.

I

On February 18, 1976, petitioner signed an employment contract with respondent in New Orleans, agreeing to work as a senior pipeline welder on board vessels operated by respondent in the North Sea. The contract specified that petitioner's employment would extend "until December 15, 1976 or until Oceanic's 1976 pipeline committal in the North Sea is fulfilled, whichever shall occur first." The contract also provided that respondent would pay for transportation to and from the worksite, but that if petitioner quit the job prior to its termination date, or if his services were terminated for cause, he would be charged with the cost of transportation back to the United States. Respondent reserved the right to withhold $137.50 from each of petitioner's first four paychecks "as a cash deposit for the payment of your return transportation in the event you should become obligated for its payment." On March 6, 1976, petitioner flew from the United States to Antwerp, Belgium, where he reported to work at respondent's vessel, the "Lay Barge 27," berthed in the Antwerp harbor for repairs.

On April 1, 1976, petitioner suffered an injury while working on the deck of the vessel readying it for sea. Two days later he underwent emergency surgery in Antwerp. On April 5, petitioner was discharged from the hospital and went to respondent's Antwerp office, where he spoke with Jesse Williams, the welding superintendent, and provided a physician's statement that he was not fit for duty. Williams refused to acknowledge that petitioner's injury was work-related and denied that respondent was liable for medical and hospital expenses, maintenance, or unearned wages. Williams also refused to furnish transportation back to the United States, and continued to retain $412.50 in earned wages that had been deducted from petitioner's first three paychecks for that purpose. Petitioner returned to his home in Houston, Tex., the next day at his own expense. He was examined there by a physician who determined that he would be able to resume work on May 3, 1976. On May 5, petitioner began working as a welder for another company operating in the North Sea.

In 1978 he brought suit against respondent. . . . Petitioner also sought penalty wages under Rev. Stat. §4529, as amended, 46 U.S.C. §596, for respondent's failure to pay over the $412.50 in earned wages allegedly due upon discharge. The District Court found for petitioner and awarded damages totalling $23,670.40.

Several findings made by that court are particularly relevant to this appeal. First, the court found that petitioner's injury was proximately caused by an unseaworthy condition of respondent's vessel. Second, the court found that petitioner was discharged from respondent's employ on the day of the injury, and that the termination of his employment was caused solely by that injury. Third, it found that respondent's failure to pay petitioner the $412.50 in earned wages was "without sufficient cause." Finally, the court found that petitioner had exercised due diligence in attempting to collect those wages.

In assessing penalty wages under 46 U.S.C. §596, the court held that "[the] period during which the penalty runs is to be determined by the sound discretion of the district court and depends on the equities of the case." It determined that the appropriate period for imposition of the penalty was from the date of discharge, April 1, 1976, through the date of petitioner's reemployment, May 5, 1976, a period of 34 days. Applying the statute, it computed a penalty of $6,881.60. Petitioner appealed the award of damages as inadequate. . . .

II

A

The language of the statute first obligates the master or owner of any vessel making coasting or foreign voyages to pay every seaman the balance of his unpaid wages within specified periods after his discharge. It then provides:

> Every master or owner who refuses or neglects to make payment in the manner hereinbefore mentioned without sufficient cause shall pay to the seaman a sum equal to two days' pay for each and every day during which payment is delayed beyond the respective periods. . . .

The statute in straightforward terms provides for the payment of double wages, depending upon the satisfaction of two conditions. First, the master or owner must have refused or failed to pay the seaman his wages within the periods specified. Second, this failure or refusal must be "without sufficient cause." Once these conditions are satisfied, however, the unadorned language of the statute dictates that the master or owner "shall pay to the seaman" the sums specified "for each and every day during which payment is delayed." The words chosen by Congress, given their plain meaning, leave no room for the exercise of discretion either in deciding whether to exact payment or in choosing the period of days by which the payment is to be calculated. . . . Our task is to give effect to the will of Congress, and where its will has been expressed in reasonably plain terms, "that language must ordinarily be regarded as conclusive." Consumer Product Safety Comm'n v. GTE Sylvania, Inc. . . .

B

Nevertheless, respondent urges that the legislative purpose of the statute is best served by construing it to permit some choice in determining the length of the penalty period. In respondent's view, the purpose of the statute is essentially remedial and compensatory, and thus it should not be interpreted literally to produce a monetary award that is so far in excess of any equitable remedy as to be punitive.

Respondent, however, is unable to support this view of legislative purpose by reference to the terms of the statute. "There is, of course, no more persuasive evidence of the purpose of a statute than the words by which the legislature undertook to give expression to its wishes." United States v. American Trucking Assns. Nevertheless, in rare cases the literal application of a statute will produce a result demonstrably at odds with the intentions of its drafters, and those intentions must be controlling. We have reserved "some 'scope for adopting a restricted rather than a literal or usual meaning of its words where acceptance of that meaning . . . would thwart the obvious purpose of the statute.' " This, however, is not the exceptional case.

As the Court recognized in Collie v. Fergusson, the "evident purpose" of the statute is "to secure prompt payment of seamen's wages . . . and thus to protect them from the harsh consequences of arbitrary and unscrupulous action of their employers, to which, as a class, they are peculiarly exposed." This was to be accomplished "by the imposition of a liability which is not exclusively compensatory, but designed to prevent, by its coercive effect, arbitrary refusals to pay wages, and to induce prompt payment when payment is possible." Thus, although the sure purpose of the statute is remedial, Congress has chosen to secure that purpose through the use of potentially punitive sanctions designed to deter negligent or arbitrary delays in payment.

The legislative history of the statute leaves little if any doubt that this understanding is correct. . . .

III

Respondent argues, however, that a literal construction of the statute in this case would produce an absurd and unjust result which Congress could not have intended. The District Court found that the daily wage to be used in computing the penalty was $101.20. If the statute is applied literally, petitioner would receive twice this amount for each day after his discharge until September 17, 1980, when respondent satisfied the District Court's judgment. Petitioner would receive over $300,000 simply because respondent improperly withheld $412.50 in wages. In respondent's view, Congress could not have intended seamen to receive windfalls of this nature without regard to the equities of the case.

It is true that interpretations of a statute which would produce absurd results are to be avoided if alternative interpretations consistent with the legislative purpose are available. . . .

It is highly probable that respondent is correct in its contention that a recovery in excess of $300,000 in this case greatly exceeds any actual injury suffered by petitioner as a result of respondent's delay in paying his wages. But this Court has previously recognized that awards made under this statute were not intended to be merely compensatory. . . .

It is in the nature of punitive remedies to authorize awards that may be out of proportion to actual injury; such remedies typically are established to deter particular conduct, and the legislature not infrequently finds that harsh consequences must be visited upon those whose conduct it would deter. It is probably true that Congress did not precisely envision the grossness of the difference in this case between the actual wages withheld and the amount of the award required by the statute. But it might equally well be said that Congress did not precisely envision the trebled amount of some damages awards in private antitrust actions or that, because it enacted the Endangered Species Act, "the survival of a relatively small number of three-inch fish . . . would require the permanent halting of a virtually completed dam for which Congress [had] expended more than $1 million," TVA v. Hill [citation omitted]. It is enough that Congress intended that the language it enacted would be applied as we have applied it. The remedy for any dissatisfaction with the results in particular cases lies with Congress and not with this Court. Congress may amend the statute; we may not. . . .

JUSTICE STEVENS, with whom JUSTICE BLACKMUN joins, dissenting.

In final analysis, any question of statutory construction requires the judge to decide how the legislature intended its enactment to apply to the case at hand. The language of the statute is usually sufficient to answer that question, but "the reports are full of cases" in which the will of the legislature is not reflected in a literal reading of the words it has chosen.

Qualifying language in 46 U.S.C. §596 supports a much narrower construction than the Court adopts. For over 50 years after the statute's most recent amendment in 1915, federal judges consistently construed it to avoid the absurd result the Court sanctions today. Their reading of the statute was consistent with the specific purposes achieved by the amendments in 1898 and 1915, as well as with the meaning of the statute when an award for unearned wages was first authorized.

I ...

The question of statutory construction that is before us is what "sum shall be recoverable as wages" to compensate petitioner for respondent's refusal to pay him $412.50 on April 5, 1976. The District Court computed that sum by doubling his daily wage of $101.20 and multiplying that amount by 34—the number of days between the injury on April 1 and petitioner's reemployment on May 5, 1976. The District Court's award thus amounted to $6,881.60. This Court holds that the sum recoverable as wages amounts to at least $302,790.40.

II ...

The text of the statute admittedly supports the construction given it by the Court—if there was not sufficient cause for the refusal to make payment within four days of the discharge, then the seaman is entitled to double wages for the entire period between the fourth day and the date the payment is finally made. The statute, however, is susceptible of another interpretation. Indeed, for a half century following its latest amendment the federal courts, including this Court, consistently exercised some discretion in determining the sum recoverable as wages under this section.

A

In fixing the amount of the award of double wages, the District Court in this case may have reasoned that respondent had sufficient cause for its delay in paying the earned wages after petitioner obtained employment with another shipmaster, but that there was not sufficient cause for its failure to make payment before that time. Although this reasoning conflicts with a literal reading of §596, it is perfectly consistent with this Court's contemporary construction of the statute in Pacific Mail S.S. Co. v. Schmidt, 241 U.S. 245 (1916). The teaching of Justice Holmes' opinion for the Court in that case is that the wrongful character of the initial refusal to pay does not mean that all subsequent delay in payment is also "without sufficient cause" within the meaning of the statute. . . .

C

Flexibility also has characterized the applications of the statute rendered by the lower federal courts. For decades those courts consistently concluded that Congress intended to allow judicial discretion to play a part in determining the amount of the double-wage recovery. Whether those decisions were entirely consistent with the meaning a grammarian might have placed on the statute is less significant than the fact that they were entirely consistent with this Court's decisions and with one another, and the fact that their holdings must have come to the attention of Congress.

It was not until 1966 that a contrary reading of the statute was adopted by the Third Circuit in Swain v. Isthmian Lines, Inc., and another eight years before that case was followed in another Circuit. I cannot deny that there is wisdom in the rule of construction that mandates close adherence to literal statutory text, but it is also true that a consistent course of judicial construction can become as much a part of a statute as words inserted by the legislature itself. The construction consistently followed by the federal judiciary between 1898 and 1966 was presumably acceptable to Congress, and I find this more persuasive than the literal reading on which the Court places its entire reliance. Moreover, since the result that construction produces in this case is both absurd and palpably unjust, this is one of the cases in which the exercise of judgment dictates a departure from the literal text in order to be faithful to the legislative will.

III

The construction permitting the district court to exercise some discretion in tailoring the double-wage award to the particular equities of the case is just as consistent with the legislative history of §596 as the Court's new literal approach to this statute. . . .

NOTES AND QUESTIONS

1. *Plain meaning.* In this case, the Justices agree that the statutory language is plain with respect to the case before them. How do the dissenters justify their positions?

2. *An unfair award?* As in Tennessee Valley Authority v. Hill, it is not the language of the statute that is creating the dispute, it is the facts — in this case, the seeming unfairness of the award. But even if you think the award is unfair, does it reach a level in which you could say that the statute's application would be absurd? Do you think that the enacting Congress, if it knew these facts, would not have enacted the statute in its existing form? Should this make a difference?

3. *A problem for a legislative counsel.* Assume you are a legislative drafter for a legislator sympathetic to the dissent in *Griffin*. Prepare an amendment to the statute excepting from its coverage fact patterns or situations similar to one before the Court in *Griffin*.

Church of the Holy Trinity v. United States
143 U.S. 457 (1892)

Statute: 23 Stat. 332, ch. 164

An act to prohibit the importation and migration of foreigners and aliens under contract or agreement to perform labor in the United States, its Territories and the District of Columbia.

Be it enacted . . . That from and after the passage of this act it shall be unlawful for any person, company, partnership, or corporation, in any manner whatsoever, to repay the transportation, or in any way assist or encourage the importation or migration of any alien or aliens, any foreigner or foreigners, into the United States, its Territories, or the District of Columbia, under contract or agreement, parol or special, express or implied, made previous to the importation or migration of such alien or aliens, foreigner or foreigners, to perform labor or service of any kind in the United States, its Territories, or the District of Columbia. . . .

Sec. 5. That nothing in this act shall be so construed as to prevent any citizen . . . from engaging under contract or otherwise, persons not residents or citizens of the United States to act as private secretaries, servants . . . nor shall this act be so construed as to prevent any person or persons, partnership, or corporation from engaging . . . skilled workmen in foreign countries to perform labor in the United States in or upon any new industry not at present established in the United States: *Provided* that skilled labor for that purpose cannot be otherwise obtained; nor shall the provisions of this act apply to professional actors, artists, lecturers, or singers, nor to persons employed strictly as personal or domestic servants. . . .

JUSTICE Brewer delivered the opinion of the Court. Internal citations have been omitted except where particularly relevant.

Plaintiff in error is a corporation, duly organized and incorporated as a religious society under the laws of the State of New York. E. Walpole Warren was, prior to September, 1887, an alien residing in England. In that month the plaintiff in error made a contract with him, by which he was to remove to the city of New York and enter into its service as rector and pastor; and in pursuance of such contract, Warren did so remove and enter upon such service. It is claimed by the United States that this contract on the part of the plaintiff in error was forbidden by the act of February 26, 1885. . . . The Circuit Court held that the contract was within the prohibition of the statute. . . .

It must be conceded that the act of the corporation is within the letter of this section, for the relation of rector to his church is one of service, and implies labor on the one side with compensation on the other. Not only are the general words labor and service both used, but also, as it were to guard against any narrow interpretation and emphasize a breadth of meaning, to them is added "of any kind"; and, further, as noticed by the Circuit Judge in his opinion, the fifth section, which makes specific exceptions, among them professional actors, artists, lecturers, singers and domestic servants, strengthens the idea that every other kind of labor and service was intended to be reached by the first section. While there is great force to this reasoning, we cannot think Congress intended to denounce with penalties a transaction like that in the present case. It is a familiar rule, that a thing may be within the letter of the statute and yet not within the statute, because not within its spirit, nor within the intention of its makers. . . . This is not the substitution of the will of the judge for that of the legislator, for frequently words of general meaning are used in a statute, words broad enough to include an act in question, and yet a consideration of the whole legislation, or of the circumstances surrounding its enactment, or of the absurd results which follow from giving such broad meaning to the words, makes it unreasonable to believe that the legislator intended to include the particular act. . . .

Among other things which may be considered in determining the intent of the legislature is the title of the act. We do not mean that it may be used to add to or take from the body of the statute, but it may help to interpret its meaning. . . .

It will be seen that words as general as those used in the first section of this act were by that decision limited, and the intent of Congress with respect to the act was gathered partially, at least, from its title. Now, the title of this act is, "An act to prohibit the importation and migration of foreigners and aliens under contract or agreement to perform labor in the United States, its Territories and the District of Columbia." Obviously the thought expressed in this reaches only to the work of the manual laborer, as distinguished from that of the professional man. No one reading such a title would suppose that Congress had in its mind any purpose of staying the coming into this country of ministers of the gospel, or, indeed, of any class whose toil is that of the brain. The common understanding of the terms labor and laborers does not include preaching and preachers; and it is to be assumed that words and phrases are used in their ordinary meaning. So whatever of light is thrown upon the statute by the language of the title indicates an exclusion from its penal provisions of all contracts for the employment of ministers, rectors and pastors.

Again, another guide to the meaning of a statute is found in the evil which it is designed to remedy; and for this the court properly looks at contemporaneous events, the situation as it existed, and as it was pressed upon the attention of the legislative body. The situation which called for this statute was briefly but fully stated by Mr. Justice Brown when, as District Judge, he decided the case of United States v. Craig:

> The motives and history of the act are matters of common knowledge. It had become the practice for large capitalists in this country to contract with their

agents abroad for the shipment of great numbers of an ignorant and servile class of foreign laborers, under contracts, by which the employer agreed, upon the one hand, to prepay their passage, while, upon the other hand, the laborers agreed to work after their arrival for a certain time at a low rate of wages. The effect of this was to break down the labor market, and to reduce other laborers engaged in like occupations to the level of the assisted immigrant. The evil finally became so flagrant that an appeal was made to Congress for relief by the passage of the act in question, the design of which was to raise the standard of foreign immigrants, and to discountenance the migration of those who had not sufficient means in their own hands, or those of their friends, to pay their passage.

It appears, also, from the petitions, and in the testimony presented before the committees of Congress, that it was this cheap unskilled labor which was making the trouble, and the influx of which Congress sought to prevent. It was never suggested that we had in this country a surplus of brain toilers, and, least of all, that the market for the services of Christian ministers was depressed by foreign competition. Those were matters to which the attention of Congress, or of the people, was not directed. So far, then, as the evil which was sought to be remedied interprets the statute, it also guides to an exclusion of this contract from the penalties of the act.

A singular circumstance, throwing light upon the intent of Congress, is found in this extract from the report of the Senate Committee on Education and Labor, recommending the passage of the bill:

> The general facts and considerations which induce the committee to recommend the passage of this bill are set forth in the Report of the Committee of the House. The committee reported the bill back without amendment, although there are certain features thereof which might well be changed or modified, in the hope that the bill may not fail of passage during the present session. Especially would the committee have otherwise recommended amendments, substituting for the expression "labor and service," whenever it occurs in the body of the bill, the words "manual labor" or "manual service," as sufficiently broad to accomplish the purposes of the bill, and that such amendments would remove objections which a sharp and perhaps unfriendly criticism may urge to the proposed legislation. The committee, however, believing that the bill in its present form will be construed as including only those whose labor or service is manual in character, and being very desirous that the bill become a law before the adjournment, have reported the bill without change.

Page 6059, Congressional Record, 48th Congress. And, referring back to the report of the Committee of the House, there appears this language:

> It seeks to restrain and prohibit the immigration or importation of laborers who would have never seen our shores but for the inducements and allurements of men whose only object is to obtain labor at the lowest possible rate,

regardless of the social and material well-being of our own citizens and regardless of the evil consequences which result to American laborers from such immigration. This class of immigrants care nothing about our institutions, and in many instances never even heard of them; they are men whose passage is paid by the importers; they come here under contract to labor for a certain number of years; they are ignorant of our social condition, and that they may remain so they are isolated and prevented from coming into contact with Americans. They are generally from the lowest social stratum, and live upon the coarsest food and in hovels of a character before unknown to American workmen. They, as a rule, do not become citizens, and are certainly not a desirable acquisition to the body politic. The inevitable tendency of their presence among us is to degrade American labor, and to reduce it to the level of the imported pauper labor.

Page 5359, Congressional Record, 48th Congress.

We find, therefore, that the title of the act, the evil which was intended to be remedied, the circumstances surrounding the appeal to Congress, the reports of the committee of each house, all concur in affirming that the intent of Congress was simply to stay the influx of this cheap unskilled labor.

But beyond all these matters no purpose of action against religion can be imputed to any legislation, state or national, because this is a religious people. This is historically true. From the discovery of this continent to the present hour, there is a single voice making this affirmation. . . .

As the happiness of a people and the good order and preservation of civil government essentially depend upon piety, religion and morality, and as these cannot be generally diffused through a community but by the institution of the public worship of God and of public instructions in piety, religion and morality: Therefore, to promote their happiness and to secure the good order and preservation of their government, the people of this commonwealth have a right to invest their legislature with power to authorize and require, and the legislature shall, from time to time, authorize and require, the several towns, parishes, precincts and other bodies-politic or religious societies to make suitable provision, at their own expense, for the institution of the public worship of God and for the support and maintenance of public Protestant teachers of piety, religion and morality in all cases where such provision shall not be made voluntarily. . . .

Even the Constitution of the United States, which is supposed to have little touch upon the private life of the individual, contains in the First Amendment a declaration common to the constitutions of all the States, as follows: "Congress shall make no law respecting an establishment of religion, or prohibiting the free exercise thereof," etc. And also provides in Article 1, section 7 (a provision common to many constitutions), that the Executive shall have ten days (Sundays excepted) within which to determine whether he will approve or veto a bill.

There is no dissonance in these declarations. There is a universal language pervading them all, having one meaning; they affirm and reaffirm that this is a religious nation. . . .

The judgment will be reversed, and the case remanded for further proceedings in accordance with this opinion.

NOTES AND QUESTIONS

1. *The plain meaning.* In this case, as in *Griffin*, there is no argument over the clarity of the statute. What rationale does the Court offer for departing from the statute's plain meaning?

2. *A canon on the spirit of the law.* *Holy Trinity* is famous for its "creation" of one of the best-known canons of statutory construction: "A thing may be within the language of the law but not within its spirit." It is frequently cited as a starting place for departing from a statute's plain meaning. What does this canon mean? On what basis does the Court determine, in this case, that the canon is applicable?

3. *Absurdity.* In the decision, the Court characterizes the prohibition of contracting with the Reverend Warren as an absurd application of the statute. What is the definition of "absurd" applied by the Court? Was it evident at the time the statute was passed or at the time the decision was rendered? Does the answer to the last question make a difference? Would such a statute be presently absurd?

4. *The exception to the general prohibition — an ignored canon.* The statute contains an explicit provision (§5) that excepts certain professions from the general prohibition. Is a reverend or pastor included? For purposes of interpretation, what is the significance of this exception? How does the Court deal with it? After reading the decision, how would you draft this statute to include reverends within the general prohibition?

In reaching its conclusion, the Court ignored one of the most frequently employed canons of construction: Explicit exceptions are deemed exclusive (*expressio unius est exclusio alterius*). What would be the consequence of applying this canon to this case?

5. *Purpose and purpose.* The Court makes considerable hay out of its view that the enacting legislature did not consider the applicability of the statute to the clergy. Must an enacting legislature have considered a particular application of a statute for the application to be intended by the statute?

6. *The dictionary.* In Question 4, we asked whether reverends or pastors were included within the exception. These terms are clearly not there. Could any of the excepted forms of service cover these terms? How would you make such a determination? If your reference is to a dictionary, is it a recent one or one that comes from the period in which the statute was adopted? What difference does it make? Do you think that a dictionary is an appropriate source for determining the meaning of statutory language?

7. *Legislative history.* What use does the Court make of the House committee reports? How would you evaluate this use?

8. *A "hail Mary" pass.* Professor Philip Frickey has made the following (appropriate) comment about *Holy Trinity Church:*

> In my legislation course, I tell my students that *Holy Trinity Church* is the case you always cite when the statutory text is hopelessly against you, and the case title lends some additional mirth to this observation. The tactic of relying upon the case does sometimes resemble the "hail Mary" pass in football. As a matter of attorney advocacy, that may be all well and good, but as a matter of judicial resolution of a critical social issue, it may seem like something altogether different.

Philip P. Frickey, From the Big Sleep to the Big Heat: The Revival of Theory in Statutory Interpretation, 77 Minn. L. Rev. 241, 247 (1992). Bear this criticism in mind as you read the next case. (Internal citations have been omitted except where particularly relevant.)

United Steelworkers of America, AFL-CIO-CLC v. Weber
443 U.S. 193 (1979)

Statute: 42 U.S.C. §2000e-2(a) (Civil Rights Act of 1964, tit. VII, §703(a))

(a) . . . It shall be an unlawful employment practice for an employer —

(1) to fail or refuse to hire or to discharge any individual, or otherwise to discriminate against any individual with respect to his compensation, terms, conditions, or privileges of employment, because of such individual's race, color, religion, sex, or national origin; or

(2) to limit, segregate, or classify his employees or applicants for employment in any way which would deprive or tend to deprive any individual of employment opportunities or otherwise adversely affect his status as an employee, because of such individual's race, color, religion, sex, or national origin.

Statute: 42 U.S.C. §2000e-2(d) (Civil Rights Act of 1964, tit. VII, §703(d))

It shall be an unlawful employment practice for any employer, labor organization, or joint labor-management committee controlling apprenticeship or other training or retraining, including on-the-job training programs to discriminate against any individual because of his race, color, religion, sex, or national origin in admission to, or employment in, any program established to provide apprenticeship or other training.

JUSTICE BRENNAN delivered the opinion of the Court. JUSTICE POWELL and JUSTICE STEVENS took no part in the consideration or decision of the cases.

Challenged here is the legality of an affirmative action plan—collectively bargained by an employer and a union—that reserves for black employees 50% of the openings in an in-plant craft-training program until the percentage of black craftworkers in the plant is commensurate with the percentage of blacks in the local labor force. The question for decision is whether Congress, in Title VII of the Civil Rights Act of 1964, left employers and unions in the private sector free to take such race-conscious steps to eliminate manifest racial imbalances in traditionally segregated job categories. We hold that Title VII does not prohibit such race-conscious affirmative action plans.

I

In 1974, petitioner United Steelworkers of America (USWA) and petitioner Kaiser Aluminum & Chemical Corp. (Kaiser) entered into a master collective-bargaining agreement covering terms and conditions of employment at 15 Kaiser plants. The agreement contained, inter alia, an affirmative action plan designed to eliminate conspicuous racial imbalances in Kaiser's then almost exclusively white craftwork forces. . . .

This case arose from the operation of the plan at Kaiser's plant in Gramercy, La. Until 1974, Kaiser hired as craft workers for that plant only persons who had had prior craft experience. Because blacks had long been excluded from craft unions, few were able to present such credentials. . . .

Pursuant to the national agreement Kaiser altered its craft-hiring practice in the Gramercy plant. Rather than hiring already trained outsiders, Kaiser established a training program to train its production workers to fill craft openings. Selection of craft trainees was made on the basis of seniority, with the proviso that at least 50% of the new trainees were to be black until the percentage of black skilled craftworkers in the Gramercy plant approximated the percentage of blacks in the local labor force.

During 1974, the first year of the operation of the Kaiser-USWA affirmative action plan, 13 craft trainees were selected from Gramercy's production work force. Of these, seven were black and six white. The most senior black selected into the program had less seniority than seven white production workers whose bids for admission were rejected. Thereafter one of those white production workers, respondent Brian Weber (hereafter respondent), instituted this class action in the United States District Court for the Eastern District of Louisiana. . . .

The District Court held that the plan violated Title VII. . . . A divided panel of the Court of Appeals for the Fifth Circuit affirmed, holding that all employment preferences based upon race, including those preferences incidental to bona fide affirmative action plans, violated Title VII's prohibition against racial discrimination in employment. . . . We reverse.

II

We emphasize at the outset the narrowness of our inquiry. . . . The only question before us is the narrow statutory issue of whether Title VII forbids private employers and unions from voluntarily agreeing upon bona fide affirmative action plans that accord racial preferences in the manner and for the purpose provided in the Kaiser-USWA plan. That question was expressly left open in McDonald v. Santa Fe Trial Transp. Co. [citation omitted], which held, in a case not involving affirmative action, that Title VII protects whites as well as blacks from certain forms of racial discrimination. . . .

Respondent's argument rests upon a literal interpretation of §§703(a) and (d) of the Act. Those sections make it unlawful to "discriminate . . . because of . . . race" in hiring and in the selection of apprentices for training programs. Since, the argument runs, McDonald v. Santa Fe Trail Transp. Co. settled that Title VII forbids discrimination against whites as well as blacks, and since the Kaiser-USWA affirmative action plan operates to discriminate against white employees solely because they are white, it follows that the Kaiser-USWA plan violates Title VII.

Respondent's argument is not without force. But it overlooks the significance of the fact that the Kaiser-USWA plan is an affirmative action plan voluntarily adopted by private parties to eliminate traditional patterns of racial segregation. In this context respondent's reliance upon a literal construction of §§703(a) and (d) and upon *McDonald* is misplaced. It is a "familiar rule, that a thing may be within the letter of the statute and yet not within the statute, because not within its spirit, nor within the intention of its makers." Holy Trinity Church v. United States [citation omitted]. The prohibition against racial discrimination in §§703(a) and (d) of Title VII must therefore be read against the background of the legislative history of Title VII and the historical context from which the Act arose. Examination of those sources makes clear that an interpretation of the sections that forbade all race-conscious affirmative action would "bring about an end completely at variance with the purpose of the statute" and must be rejected.

Congress' primary concern in enacting the prohibition against racial discrimination in Title VII of the Civil Rights Act of 1964 was with "the plight of the Negro in our economy" [remarks of Sen. Humphrey]. Before 1964, blacks were largely relegated to "unskilled and semi-skilled, jobs" [remarks of Sen. Humphrey, Sen. Clark, Sen. Kennedy]. Because of automation the number of such jobs was rapidly decreasing [remarks of Sen. Humphrey, Sen. Clark]. As a consequence, "the relative position of the Negro worker [was] steadily worsening. In 1947 the nonwhite unemployment rate was only 64 percent higher than the white rate; in 1962 it was 124 percent higher" [remarks of Sen. Humphrey]. Congress considered this a serious social problem. As Senator Clark told the Senate:

The rate of Negro unemployment has gone up consistently as compared with white unemployment for the past 15 years. This is a social malaise and a social situation which we should not tolerate. That is one of the principal reasons why the bill should pass.

Congress feared that the goals of the Civil Rights Act — the integration of blacks into the mainstream of American society — could not be achieved unless this trend were reversed. And Congress recognized that that would not be possible unless blacks were able to secure jobs "which have a future" [remarks of Sen. Clark]. . . . As Senator Humphrey explained to the Senate:

What good does it do a Negro to be able to eat in a fine restaurant if he cannot afford to pay the bill? What good does it do him to be accepted in a hotel that is too expensive for his modest income? How can a Negro child be motivated to take full advantage of integrated educational facilities if he has no hope of getting a job where he can use that education? . . .

Without a job, one cannot afford public convenience and accommodations. Income from employment may be necessary to further a man's education, or that of his children. If his children have no hope of getting a good job, what will motivate them to take advantage of educational opportunities?

These remarks echoed President Kennedy's original message to Congress upon the introduction of the Civil Rights Act in 1963.

There is little value in a Negro's obtaining the right to be admitted to hotels and restaurants if he has no cash in his pocket and no job.

Accordingly, it was clear to Congress that "[t]he crux of the problem [was] to open employment opportunities for Negroes in occupations which have been traditionally closed to them" [remarks of Sen. Humphrey], and it was to this problem that Title VII's prohibition against racial discrimination in employment was primarily addressed.

It plainly appears from the House Report accompanying the Civil Rights Act that Congress did not intend wholly to prohibit private and voluntary affirmative action efforts as one method of solving this problem. The Report provides:

No bill can or should lay claim to eliminating all of the causes and consequences of racial and other types of discrimination against minorities. There is reason to believe, however, that national leadership provided by the enactment of Federal legislation dealing with the most troublesome problems will create an atmosphere conducive to voluntary or local resolution of other forms of discrimination.

Given this legislative history, we cannot agree with respondent that Congress intended to prohibit the private sector from taking effective steps to accomplish the goal that Congress designed Title VII to achieve. . . . It would be ironic indeed if a law triggered by a Nation's concern over centuries of racial injustice and intended to improve the lot of those who had "been excluded from the American dream for so long" [remarks of Sen. Humphrey], constituted the first legislative prohibition of all voluntary, private, race-conscious efforts to abolish traditional patterns of racial segregation and hierarchy.

Our conclusion is further reinforced by examination of the language and legislative history of §703(j) of Title VII. Opponents of Title VII raised two related arguments against the bill. First, they argued that the Act would be interpreted to require employers with racially imbalanced work forces to grant preferential treatment to racial minorities in order to integrate. Second, they argued that employers with racially imbalanced work forces would grant preferential treatment to racial minorities, even if not required to do so by the Act. Had Congress meant to prohibit all race-conscious affirmative action, as respondent urges, it easily could have answered both objections by providing that Title VII would not require or *permit* racially preferential integration efforts. But Congress did not choose such a course. Rather, Congress added §703(j) which addresses only the first objection. The section provides that nothing contained in Title VII "shall be interpreted to *require* any employer . . . to grant preferential treatment . . . to any group because of the race . . . of such . . . group on account of" a de facto racial imbalance in the employer's work force. The section does *not* state that "nothing in Title VII shall be interpreted to *permit*" voluntary affirmative efforts to correct racial imbalances. The natural inference is that Congress chose not to forbid all voluntary race-conscious affirmative action.

The reasons for this choice are evident from the legislative record. Title VII could not have been enacted into law without substantial support from legislators in both Houses who traditionally resisted federal regulation of private business. Those legislators demanded as a price for their support that "management prerogatives, and union freedoms . . . be left undisturbed to the greatest extent possible." Section 703(j) was proposed by Senator Dirksen to allay any fears that the Act might be interpreted in such a way as to upset this compromise. The section was designed to prevent §703 of Title VII from being interpreted in such a way as to lead to undue "Federal Government interference with private businesses because of some Federal employee's ideas about racial balance or racial imbalance" [remarks of Sen. Miller]. . . . Clearly, a prohibition against all voluntary, race-conscious, affirmative action efforts would disserve these ends. Such a prohibition would augment the powers of the Federal Government and diminish traditional management prerogatives while at the same time impeding attainment of the ultimate statutory goals. In view of this legislative history and in view of Congress's desire to avoid undue federal regulation of private businesses, use of the word "require" rather than the phrase "require or permit" in §703(j) fortifies the conclusion that Congress did not intend to limit traditional business freedom to such a degree as to prohibit all voluntary, race-conscious affirmative action.

We therefore hold that Title VII's prohibition in §§703(a) and (d) against racial discrimination does not condemn all private, voluntary, race-conscious affirmative action plans.

JUSTICE BLACKMUN filed a concurring opinion [omitted].

CHIEF JUSTICE BURGER, dissenting.

The Court reaches a result I would be inclined to vote for were I a Member of Congress considering a proposed amendment of Title VII. I cannot join the Court's judgment, however, because it is contrary to the explicit language of the statute and arrived at by means wholly incompatible with long-established principles of separation of powers. Under the guise of statutory "construction," the Court effectively rewrites Title VII to achieve what it regards as a desirable result. It "amends" the statute to do precisely what both its sponsors and its opponents agreed the statute was not intended to do. . . .

When Congress enacted Title VII after long study and searching debate, it produced a statute of extraordinary clarity, which speaks directly to the issue we consider in this case. In §703(d) Congress provided:

> It shall be an unlawful employment practice for any employer, labor organization, or joint labor-management committee controlling apprenticeship or other training or retraining, including on-the-job training programs to discriminate against any individual because of his race, color, religion, sex, or national origin in admission to, or employment in, any program established to provide apprenticeship or other training.

42 U.S.C. §2000e-2(d).

Often we have difficulty interpreting statutes either because of imprecise drafting or because legislative compromises have produced genuine ambiguities. But here there is no lack of clarity, no ambiguity. The quota embodied in the collective-bargaining agreement between Kaiser and the Steelworkers unquestionably discriminates on the basis of race against individual employees seeking admission to on-the-job training programs. And, under the plain language of §703(d), that is "an unlawful employment practice."

Oddly, the Court seizes upon the very clarity of the statute almost as a justification for evading the unavoidable impact of its language. The Court blandly tells us that Congress could not really have meant what it said, for a "literal construction" would defeat the "purpose" of the statute — at least the congressional "purpose" as five Justices divine it today. But how are judges supposed to ascertain the *purpose* of a statute except through the words Congress used and the legislative history of the statute's evolution? One need not even resort to the legislative history to recognize what is apparent from the face of Title VII—that it is specious to suggest that §703(j) contains a negative pregnant that permits employers to do what §§703(a) and (d) unambiguously and unequivocally *forbid* employers from doing. Moreover, as Justice Rehnquist's opinion—which I join—conclusively demonstrates, the legislative history makes equally clear that the supporters and opponents of Title VII reached an agreement about the statute's intended effect. That agreement, expressed so clearly in the language of the statute that no one should doubt its meaning, forecloses the reading which the Court gives the statute today. . . .

JUSTICE REHNQUIST, with whom THE CHIEF JUSTICE joins, dissenting.

The operative sections of Title VII prohibit racial discrimination in employment *simpliciter*. Taken in its normal meaning, and as understood by all Members of Congress who spoke to the issue during the legislative debates . . . this language prohibits a covered employer from considering race when making an employment decision, whether the race be black or white. Several years ago, however, a United States District Court held that "the dismissal of white employees charged with misappropriating company property while not dismissing a similarly charged Negro employee does not raise a claim upon which Title VII relief may be granted." McDonald v. Santa Fe Trail Transp. Co. [citation omitted]. This Court unanimously reversed, concluding from the "uncontradicted legislative history" that "Title VII prohibits racial discrimination against the white petitioners in this case upon the same standards as would be applicable were they Negroes. . . ."

We have never wavered in our understanding that Title VII "prohibits *all* racial discrimination in employment, without exception for any group of particular employees" (emphasis in original). . . .

Today, however . . . without even a break in syntax, the Court rejects "a literal construction of §703(a)" in favor of newly discovered "legislative history," which leads it to a conclusion directly contrary to that compelled by the "uncontradicted legislative history" unearthed in *McDonald* and our other prior decisions. Now we are told that the legislative history of Title VII shows that employers are free to discriminate on the basis of race: an employer may, in the Court's words, "trammel the interests of the white employees" in favor of black employees in order to eliminate "racial imbalance." . . .

As if this were not enough to make a reasonable observer question this Court's adherence to the oft-stated principle that our duty is to construe rather than rewrite legislation, United States v. Rutherford [citation omitted], the Court also seizes upon §703(j) of Title VII as an independent, or at least partially independent, basis for its holding. Totally ignoring the wording of that section, which is obviously addressed to those charged with the responsibility of interpreting the law rather than those who are subject to its proscriptions, and totally ignoring the months of legislative debates preceding the section's introduction and passage, which demonstrate clearly that it was enacted to prevent precisely what occurred in this case, the Court infers from §703(j) that "Congress chose not to forbid all voluntary race-conscious affirmative action."

Thus, by a tour de force reminiscent not of jurists such as Hale, Holmes, and Hughes, but of escape artists such as Houdini, the Court eludes clear statutory language, "uncontradicted" legislative history, and uniform precedent in concluding that employers are, after all, permitted to consider race in making employment decisions. It may be that one or more of the principal sponsors of Title VII would have preferred to see a provision allowing preferential treatment of minorities written into the bill. Such a provision, however, would have to have been expressly or impliedly excepted from Title VII's explicit prohibition on all racial discrimination in employment. There is no such exception in the Act. And a reading of the legislative debates concerning Title VII, in which proponents and opponents alike uniformly denounced discrimination in favor of, as well as discrimination against, Negroes, demonstrates clearly that any legislator harboring an unspoken desire for such a provision could not possibly have succeeded in enacting it into law. . . .

II

Were Congress to act today specifically to prohibit the type of racial discrimination suffered by Weber, it would be hard pressed to draft language better tailored to the task than that found in §703(d) of Title VII. . . . Equally suited to the task would be §703(a)(2), which makes it unlawful for an employer to classify his employees "in any way which would deprive or tend to deprive any individual of employment opportunities or otherwise adversely affect his status as an employee, because of such individual's race, color, religion, sex, or national origin."

Entirely consistent with these two express prohibitions is the language of §703(j) of Title VII, which provides that the Act is not to be interpreted "to require any employer . . . to grant preferential treatment to any individual or to any group because of the race . . . of such individual or group" to correct a racial imbalance in the employer's work force. Seizing on the word "require," the Court infers that Congress must have intended to "permit" this type of racial discrimination. Not only is this reading of §703(j) outlandish in the light of the flat prohibitions of §§703(a) and (d), but also, as explained in Part III, it is totally belied by the Act's legislative history.

Quite simply, Kaiser's racially discriminatory admission quota is flatly prohibited by the plain language of Title VII. This normally dispositive fact, however, gives the Court only momentary pause. An "interpretation" of the statute upholding Weber's claim would, according to the Court, "'bring about an end completely at variance with the purpose of the statute.'"

To support this conclusion, the Court calls upon the "spirit" of the Act, which it divines from passages in Title VII's legislative history indicating that enactment of the statute was prompted by Congress' desire "'to open employment opportunities for Negroes in occupations which [had] been traditionally closed to them.'" But the legislative history invoked by the Court to avoid the plain language of §§703(a) and (d) simply misses the point. To be sure, the reality of employment discrimination against Negroes provided the primary impetus for passage of Title VII. But this fact by no means supports the proposition that Congress intended to leave employers free to discriminate against white persons. . . . [T]he legislative history of Title VII is as clear as the language of §§703(a) and (d), and it irrefutably demonstrates that Congress meant precisely what it said in §§703(a) and (d) — that no racial discrimination in employment is permissible under Title VII, not even preferential treatment of minorities to correct racial imbalance.

III

In undertaking to review the legislative history of Title VII, I am mindful that the topic hardly makes for light reading, but I am also fearful that nothing short of a thorough examination of the congressional debates will fully expose the magnitude of the Court's misinterpretation of Congress' intent.

A

Introduced on the floor of the House of Representatives on June 20, 1963, the bill — H.R. 7152 — that ultimately became the Civil Rights Act of 1964 contained no compulsory provisions directed at private discrimination in employment. The bill was promptly referred to the Committee on the Judiciary, where it was amended to include Title VII. With two exceptions, the bill reported by the House Judiciary Committee contained §§703(a) and (b) as they were ultimately enacted. Amendments subsequently adopted on the House floor added §703(d)'s prohibition against sex discrimination and §703(d)'s coverage of "on-the-job training."

After noting that "[t]he purpose of [Title VII] is to eliminate . . . discrimination in employment based on race, color, religion, or national origin," the Judiciary Committee's Report simply paraphrased the provisions of Title VII without elaboration. In a separate Minority Report, however, opponents of the measure on the Committee advanced a line of attack which was reiterated throughout the debates in both the House and Senate and which ultimately led to passage of §703(j). Noting that the word "discrimination" was nowhere defined in H.R. 7152, the Minority Report charged that the absence from Title VII of any reference to "racial imbalance" was a "public relations ruse" and that "the administration intends to rely upon its own construction of 'discrimination' as including the lack of racial balance. . . ." To demonstrate how the bill would operate in practice, the Minority Report posited a number of hypothetical employment situations, concluding in each example that the employer "*may be forced to hire according to race*, to 'racially balance' those who work for him in every job classification or be in violation of Federal law" (emphasis in original).

When H.R. 7152 reached the House floor, the opening speech in support of its passage was delivered by Representative Celler, Chairman of the House Judiciary Committee and the Congressman responsible for introducing the legislation. A portion of that speech responded to criticism "seriously misrepresen[ting] what the bill would do and grossly distort [ing] its effects":

> [T]he charge has been made that the Equal Employment Opportunity Commission to be established by title VII of the bill would have the power to prevent a business from employing and promoting the people it wished, and that a "Federal inspector" could then order the hiring and promotion only of employees of certain races or religious groups. This description of the bill is entirely wrong. . . .
>
> Even [a] court could not order that any preference be given to any particular race, religion or other group, but would be limited to ordering an end of discrimination. The statement that a Federal inspector could order the employment and promotion only of members of a specific racial or religious group is therefore patently erroneous. . . .
>
> The Bill would do no more than prevent . . . employers from discriminating against or in favor of workers because of their race, religion, or national origin.
>
> It is likewise not true that the Equal Employment Opportunity Commission would have power to rectify existing "racial or religious imbalance" in employment by requiring the hiring of certain people without regard to their qualifications simply because they are of a given race or religion. Only actual discrimination could be stopped.
>
> 110 Cong. Rec. 1518 (1964). Representative Celler's construction of Title VII was repeated by several other supporters during the House debate.

Thus, the battle lines were drawn early in the legislative struggle over Title VII, with opponents of the measure charging that agencies of the Federal Government such as the Equal Employment Opportunity Commission (EEOC), by interpreting the word "discrimination" to mean the existence of "racial imbalance," would "require" employers to grant preferential treatment to minorities, and supporters responding that the EEOC would be granted no such power and that, indeed, Title VII prohibits discrimination "in favor of workers because of their race." Supporters of H.R. 7152 in the House ultimately prevailed by a vote of 290 to 130, and the measure was sent to the Senate to begin what became the longest debate in that body's history.

B

The Senate debate was broken into three phases: the debate on sending the bill to Committee, the general debate on the bill prior to invocation of cloture, and the debate following cloture.

1

When debate on the motion to refer the bill to Committee opened, opponents of Title VII in the Senate immediately echoed the fears expressed by their counterparts in the House, as is demonstrated by the following colloquy between Senators Hill and Ervin:

> Mr. ERVIN. I invite attention to . . . Section [703(a)]. . . .
>
> I ask the Senator from Alabama if the Commission could not tell an employer that he had too few employees, that he had limited his employment, and enter an order, under [Section 703(a)], requiring him to hire more persons, not because the employer thought he needed more persons, but because the Commission wanted to compel him to employ persons of a particular race.
>
> Mr. HILL. The Senator is correct. That power is written into the bill. The employer could be forced to hire additional persons. . . .

110 Cong. Rec. 4764 (1964). Senator Humphrey, perhaps the primary moving force behind H.R. 7152 in the Senate, was the first to state the proponents' understanding of Title VII. Responding to a political advertisement charging that federal agencies were at liberty to interpret the word "discrimination" in Title VII to require racial balance, Senator Humphrey stated: "[T]he meaning of racial or religious discrimination is perfectly clear. . . . [I]t means a distinction in treatment given to different individuals because of their different race, religion, or national origin." Stressing that Title VII "does not limit the employer's freedom to hire, fire, promote or demote for any reasons — or no reasons — so long as his action is not based on race," Senator Humphrey further stated that "nothing in the bill would permit any official or court to require any employer or labor union to give preferential treatment to any minority group."

After 17 days of debate, the Senate voted to take up the bill directly, without referring it to a committee. Consequently, there is no Committee Report in the Senate.

2

Formal debate on the merits of H.R. 7152 began on March 30, 1964. Supporters of the bill in the Senate had made elaborate preparations for this second round. Senator Humphrey, the majority whip, and Senator Kuchel, the minority whip, were selected as the bipartisan floor managers on the entire civil rights bill. Responsibility for explaining and defending each important title of the bill was placed on bipartisan "captains." Senators Clark and Case were selected as the bipartisan captains responsible for Title VII.

In the opening speech of the formal Senate debate on the bill, Senator Humphrey addressed the main concern of Title VII's opponents, advising that not only does Title VII not require use of racial quotas, it does not permit their use. "The truth," stated the floor leader of the bill, "is that this title forbids discriminating against anyone on account of race. This is the simple and complete truth about title VII." Senator Humphrey continued:

> Contrary to the allegations of some opponents of this title, there is nothing in it that will give any power to the Commission or to any court to require hiring, firing, or promotion of employees in order to meet a racial "quota" or to achieve a certain racial balance.
>
> That bugaboo has been brought up a dozen times; but it is nonexistent. In fact, the very opposite is true. Title VII prohibits discrimination. In effect, it says that race, religion and national origin are not to be used as the basis for hiring and firing. Title VII is designed to encourage hiring on the basis of ability and qualifications, not race or religion.

At the close of his speech, Senator Humphrey returned briefly to the subject of employment quotas: "It is claimed that the bill would require racial quotas for all hiring, when in fact it provides that race shall not be a basis for making personnel decisions."

Senator Kuchel delivered the second major speech in support of H.R. 7152. In addressing the concerns of the opposition, he observed that "[n]othing could be further from the truth" than the charge that "Federal inspectors" would be empowered under Title VII to dictate racial balance and preferential advancement of minorities. Senator Kuchel emphasized that seniority rights would in no way be affected by Title VII: "Employers and labor organizations could not discriminate *in favor of or against* a person because of his race, his religion, or his national origin. In such matters . . . the bill now before us . . . is color-blind." (Emphasis added.)

A few days later the Senate's attention focused exclusively on Title VII, as Senators Clark and Case rose to discuss the title of H.R. 7152 on which they shared floor "captain" responsibilities. In an interpretative memorandum submitted jointly to the Senate, Senators Clark and Case took pains to refute the opposition's charge that Title VII would result in preferential treatment of minorities. Their words were clear and unequivocal:

> There is no requirement in title VII that an employer maintain a racial balance in his work force. On the contrary, any deliberate attempt to maintain a racial balance, whatever such a balance may be, would involve a violation

of title VII because maintaining such a balance would require an employer to hire or to refuse to hire on the basis of race. It must be emphasized that discrimination is prohibited as to any individual.

Of particular relevance to the instant litigation were their observations regarding seniority rights. As if directing their comments at Brian Weber, the Senators said:

> Title VII would have no effect on established seniority rights. Its effect is prospective and not retrospective. Thus, for example, if a business has been discriminating in the past and as a result has an all-white working force, when the title comes into effect the employer's obligation would be simply to fill future vacancies on a nondiscriminatory basis. He would not be obliged — or *indeed permitted* — to fire whites in order to hire Negroes, *or to prefer Negroes for future vacancies, or, once Negroes are hired, to give them special seniority rights at the expense of the white workers hired earlier.*

(Emphasis added.)

Thus, with virtual clairvoyance the Senate's leading supporters of Title VII anticipated precisely the circumstances of this case and advised their colleagues that the type of minority preference employed by Kaiser would violate Title VII's ban on racial discrimination. To further accentuate the point, Senator Clark introduced another memorandum dealing with common criticisms of the bill, including the charge that racial quotas would be imposed under Title VII. The answer was simple and to the point: "Quotas are themselves discriminatory."

Despite these clear statements from the bill's leading and most knowledgeable proponents, the fears of the opponents were not put to rest. Senator Robertson reiterated the view that "discrimination" could be interpreted by a federal "bureaucrat" to require hiring quotas. Senators Smathers and Sparkman, while conceding that Title VII does not in so many words require the use of hiring quotas, repeated the opposition's view that employers would be coerced to grant preferential hiring treatment to minorities by agencies of the Federal Government. Senator Williams was quick to respond:

> Those opposed to H.R. 7152 should realize that to hire a Negro solely because he is a Negro is racial discrimination, just as much as a "white only" employment policy. Both forms of discrimination are prohibited by Title VII of this bill. The language of that title simply states that race is not a qualification for employment. . . . Some people charge that H.R. 7152 favors the Negro, at the expense of the white majority. But how can the language of equality favor one race or one religion over another? Equality can have only one meaning, and that meaning is self-evident to reasonable men. Those who say that equality means favoritism do violence to common sense.

Senator Williams concluded his remarks by noting that Title VII's only purpose is "the elimination of racial and religious discrimination in employment." . . .

While the debate in the Senate raged, a bipartisan coalition under the leadership of Senators Dirksen, Mansfield, Humphrey, and Kuchel was working with House leaders and representatives of the Johnson administration on a number of amendments to H.R. 7152 designed to enhance its prospects of passage. The so-called "Dirksen-Mansfield" amendment was introduced on May 26 by Senator Dirksen as a substitute for the entire House-passed bill. The substitute bill, which ultimately became law, left unchanged the basic prohibitory language of §§703(a) and (d), as well as the remedial provisions in §706(g). It added, however, several provisions defining and clarifying the scope of Title VII's substantive prohibitions. One of those clarifying amendments, §703(j), was specifically directed at the opposition's concerns regarding racial balancing and preferential treatment of minorities, providing in pertinent part: "Nothing contained in [Title VII] shall be interpreted to require any employer . . . to grant preferential treatment to any individual or to any group because of the race . . . of such individual or group on account of" a racial imbalance in the employer's work force.

The Court draws from the language of §703(j) primary support for its conclusion that Title VII's blanket prohibition on racial discrimination in employment does not prohibit preferential treatment of blacks to correct racial imbalance. Alleging that opponents of Title VII had argued (1) that the Act would be interpreted to require employers with racially imbalanced work forces to grant preferential treatment to minorities and (2) that "employers with racially imbalanced work forces would grant preferential treatment to racial minorities, even if not required to do so by the Act," the Court concludes that §703(j) is responsive only to the opponents' first objection and that Congress therefore must have intended to permit voluntary, private discrimination against whites in order to correct racial imbalance.

Contrary to the Court's analysis, the language of §703(j) is precisely tailored to the objection voiced time and again by Title VII's opponents. . . .

In light of the background and purpose of §703(j), the irony of invoking the section to justify the result in this case is obvious. The Court's frequent references to the "voluntary" nature of Kaiser's racially discriminatory admission quota bear no relationship to the facts of this case. Kaiser and the Steelworkers acted under pressure from an agency of the Federal Government, the Office of Federal Contract Compliance, which found that minorities were being "under utilized" at Kaiser's plants. . . . That is, Kaiser's work force was racially imbalanced. Bowing to that pressure, Kaiser instituted an admissions quota preferring blacks over whites, thus confirming that the fears of Title VII's opponents were well founded. Today, §703(j), adopted to allay those fears, is invoked by the Court to uphold imposition of a racial quota under the very circumstances that the section was intended to prevent. . . .

On June 9, Senator Ervin offered an amendment that would entirely delete Title VII from the bill. In answer to Senator Ervin's contention that Title VII "would make the members of a particular race special favorites of the laws," Senator Clark retorted:

> The bill does not make anyone higher than anyone else. It establishes no quotas. It leaves an employer free to select whomever he wishes to employ. . . .
> All this is subject to one qualification, and that qualification, is to state: "In your activity as an employer . . . you must not discriminate because of the color of a man's skin. . . ."
> That is all this provision does. . . .
> It merely says, "When you deal in interstate commerce, you must not discriminate on the basis of race. . . ."

The Ervin amendment was defeated. . . .

3

On June 10, the Senate, for the second time in its history, imposed cloture on its Members. . . .

As the civil rights bill approached its final vote, several supporters rose to urge its passage. Senator Muskie adverted briefly to the issue of preferential treatment: "It has been said that the bill discriminates in favor of the Negro at the expense of the rest of us. It seeks to do nothing more than to lift the Negro from the status of inequality to one of equality of treatment." Senator Moss, in a speech delivered on the day that the civil rights bill was finally passed, had this to say about quotas:

> The bill does not accord to any citizen advantage or preference — it does not fix quotas of employment or school population — it does not force personal association. What it does is to prohibit public officials and those who invite the public generally to patronize their businesses or to apply for employment, to utilize the offensive, humiliating, and cruel practice of discrimination on the basis of race. In short, the bill does not accord special consideration; it establishes equality.

Later that day, June 19, the issue was put to a vote, and the Dirksen-Mansfield substitute bill was passed.

C

The Act's return engagement in the House was brief. The House Committee on Rules reported the Senate version without amendments on

June 30, 1964. By a vote of 289 to 126, the House adopted H. Res. 789, thus agreeing to the Senate's amendments of H.R. 7152. Later that same day, July 2, the President signed the bill and the Civil Rights Act of 1964 became law.

IV

Reading the language of Title VII, as the Court purports to do, "against the background of [its] legislative history . . . and the historical context from which the Act arose," . . . one is led inescapably to the conclusion that Congress fully understood what it was saying and meant precisely what it said. Opponents of the civil rights bill did not argue that employers would be permitted under Title VII voluntarily to grant preferential treatment to minorities to correct racial imbalance. The plain language of the statute too clearly prohibited such racial discrimination to admit of any doubt. They argued, tirelessly, that Title VII would be interpreted by federal agencies and their agents to require unwilling employers to racially balance their work forces by granting preferential treatment to minorities. Supporters of H.R. 7152 responded, equally tirelessly, that the Act would not be so interpreted because not only does it not require preferential treatment of minorities, it also does not permit preferential treatment of any race for any reason. It cannot be doubted that the proponents of Title VII understood the meaning of their words, for "[s]eldom has similar legislation been debated with greater consciousness of the need for 'legislative history,' or with greater care in the making thereof, to guide the courts in interpreting and applying the law."

To put an end to the dispute, supporters of the civil rights bill drafted and introduced §703(j). Specifically addressed to the opposition's charge, §703(j) simply enjoins federal agencies and courts from interpreting Title VII to require an employer to prefer certain racial groups to correct imbalances in his work force. The section says nothing about voluntary preferential treatment of minorities because such racial discrimination is plainly proscribed by §§703(a) and (d). . . .

V

Our task in this case, like any other case involving the construction of a statute, is to give effect to the intent of Congress. To divine that intent, we traditionally look first to the words of the statute and, if they are unclear, then to the statute's legislative history. Finding the desired result hopelessly foreclosed by these conventional sources, the Court turns to a third source — the "spirit" of the Act. But close examination of what the Court proffers as the spirit of the Act reveals it as the spirit animating the present majority, not the 88th Congress. For if the spirit of the Act eludes the cold words of the statute itself, it rings out with unmistakable clarity in the words of the elected representatives who made the Act law. It is *equality.* . . .

NOTES AND QUESTIONS

1. *A "hail Mary" pass?* On what basis does Justice Brennan make his decision? How do you evaluate his reasoning? (For the reference to the term " 'hail Mary' pass," see Note 8 on page 749.)

2. *The statute's purpose.* Would the statute, as applied by Justice Rehnquist, be in conflict with Justice Brennan's statement that the statute's purpose was to further employment opportunities for African-Americans? Can't the purpose have been to effect what Justice Brennan says without authorizing everything imaginable to further that purpose? Do you think that the Congress that enacted Title VII in 1964 would have voted for a bill that included a provision authorizing racial quotas in private employment? Are these questions relevant and, if so, why?

3. *Legislative history.* Note the pieces of legislative history cited by Justices Brennan and Rehnquist. Putting aside the question of whether it should be referred to at all, how probative of the statute's meaning is each piece cited?

The *Weber* Controversy

Weber is one of the most controversial statutory interpretation decisions of modern times. It has led to probing debates about the powers and functions of legislative and judicial branches of government. The debate has been framed not by the opinion of Justice Brennan, which many considered not well reasoned, but by the positions of two other Justices: Justice Burger (and Justice Rehnquist), in dissent, and Justice Blackmun, in concurrence.

JUSTICE BURGER: The Court reaches a result I would be inclined to vote for were I a Member of Congress considering a proposed amendment of Title VII. I cannot join the Court's judgment, however, because it is contrary to the explicit language of the statute and arrived at by means wholly incompatible with long-established principles of separation of powers. Under the guise of statutory "construction," the Court effectively rewrites Title VII to achieve what it regards as a desirable result. It "amends" the statute to do precisely what both its sponsors and its opponents agreed the statute was not intended to do. It is controversial because of the difficulty in justifying it without solely referring to its outcome.

JUSTICE BLACKMUN: While I share some of the misgivings expressed in Mr. Justice Rehnquist's dissent concerning the extent to which the legislative history of Title VII clearly supports the result the Court reaches today, I believe that additional considerations, practical and equitable, only partially perceived, if perceived at all, by the 88th Congress, support the conclusion reached by the Court today. . . .

United Steelworkers of America v. Weber, 443 U.S. 193, 209 (1979). What is the role of the Court in statutory interpretation envisioned by each of these Justices? What does Justice Blackmun mean by the last sentence in the above passage? Is this a recognizable basis for a court's application of a statute? How does this fit in with our concepts of representative democracy and legislative supremacy? As one scholar has written about the decision: "It is difficult to escape the conclusion that the Court went 'not merely *beyond,* but directly *against* title VII's language and legislative history.' In displacing congressional policy to allow preferential hiring, the Court appears to have violated the supremacy principles." Daniel A. Farber, Statutory Interpretation and Legislative Supremacy, 78 Geo. L.J. 281, 305 (1989).

Consider the following comments, which exemplify some of the scholarship on the subject.

William N. Eskridge, Spinning Legislative Supremacy, 78 Geo. L.J. 319, 334-37 (1989): Looking first at the text, the crucial statutory term, "discriminate" is not defined in title VII. Although "discriminates" denotes "differentiating" in many ways, it also has strong connotations of "invidious" differentiation. For example, it would be correct denotative usage of the term "discriminate" to say that one "discriminates" against pears because one prefers apples to pears; however, under the term's connotative meaning, use of the term would be inappropriate because the preference for apples probably is not borne out of an "invidious" prejudice against pears. Similarly, under the connotative meaning of the statutory term, passing over Brian Weber and other white workers because of an affirmative desire to redress past injustice to black workers is not the same as passing over him because the company or union is prejudiced against whites. . . .

Although there are other textual arguments, which cut both ways, on the whole I consider the text of title VII to be ambiguous on the issue of voluntary affirmative action in training programs. A better case can be made that the legislative history is unambiguous, because the leading congressional supporters of the statute repeatedly reassured their colleagues that title VII would not impose quotas upon employers. . . .

One wonders why there is no "smoking gun" in the legislative history — why there is no senator who said: "We don't care if racial disparities persist over time — there can be no preferences for minorities, ever." . . .

Indeed even if there were smoking guns galore in the debates, backed by a clearer statutory text, the changed circumstances — the unbundling of two originally consistent statutory purposes — would lend some support to *Weber's* reading of the statute. . . . When an assumption behind legislative passage is revealed as flawed, blind adherence to the textual language and legislative history premised on that assumption does not serve the values of legislative supremacy. Rather, when there have been changed circumstances, those values are best served by a dynamic interpretation of the statute based on the purposes behind the assumption.

For an extraordinarily elaborate attempt to provide theory for the *Weber* decision, see Ronald Dworkin, How to Read the Civil Rights Act, N.Y. Rev., Dec. 20, 1979.

Bernard D. Meltzer, The *Weber* Case: The Judicial Abrogation of the Antidiscrimination Standard in Employment, 47 U. Chi. L. Rev. 423, 456-58 (1980): The Court's approach cannot be justified on the ground that the change made by *Weber* is only a response to a minor hitch, unforeseen by "Congress, that often emerges as a statute is administered." That change goes to the roots of the bargain struck by the 88th Congress, and to the roots of our colorblind aspiration. *Weber* is, in fact, an important step in the transformation of the classic and widely supported liberal ideal of equal opportunity for individuals into a new program of equal outcomes for groups that is both more divisive than the older ideal and fundamentally inconsistent with it. . . .

The meanings of "equality" and of "equal opportunity" and their relationship to equity and efficiency have been the subjects of a vast literature that cannot and need not be reviewed here. But what merits emphasis is that choosing between competing values underlying those concepts — under the guise of statutory construction — appears to have strained the Court's institutional competence. The Court's opinion does not even notice some basic and troubling questions relevant to a disinterested and informed choice. One need not romanticize the process of legislative investigation or legislative decision to recognize that litigation is as ill-suited for informing the Court about the pertinent questions as the Court is for resolving them. In any event, in illustrating questions neglected by the court, I will point to those pivotal to the Court's stated objective — helping blacks, and especially unemployed blacks, into the mainstream of our economy.

Is official pressure for affirmative action a substantial factor in the flight of business from the centers of black population, as employers attempt to avoid pressure for quota hiring? As a consequence, are the most disadvantaged blacks being hurt by regulation designed to help them? Will those hoping to cultivate the grievances of whites in order to promote bigotry now be able to march under an honorable banner — equal opportunity for all? Will the fallout from *Weber* intensify racial politics and further polarize our work forces and our communities? Will it obstruct important job training across racial lines — the spontaneous on-the-job instruction of one worker by another? Will *Weber* and the centrifugal tendencies that it promotes create further obstacles to legislative action necessary for programs designed to help all disadvantaged, black and white? Will quota hiring result in significant inefficiencies — thereby retarding economic growth, to the particular disadvantage of minorities? . . .

These illustrative questions are not only legislative and political but also critical . . . to the achievement of the purpose the Court imputed to Congress. There is no indication that the Court considered them.

Richard A. Posner, The Problems of Jurisprudence, 284-85 (1990): The problem with all this evidence in favor of *Weber* is that it can be sidestepped by observing that Congress in 1964 never considered the possible application of the statute to voluntary private efforts by white employers (or employers controlled by white people, as Kaiser surely was and is) to promote employment of blacks. The problem at that time was discrimination against blacks, not in favor of them. The legislature did foresee the possibility that impatient courts or enforcement agencies would use racial quotas to advance the goals of the statute, and made clear that it did not want them to do this merely on grounds of race imbalance, as distinct from doing so as a remedy for violations of the statute. But apparently it did not foresee the possibility that an employer would adopt such quotas voluntarily.

Since textual arguments can be traps, the fact that the affirmative action practiced by Kaiser and the union is embraced by the semantics of Title VII does not compel a conclusion that the statute prohibits the practice. Anyway, the textual arguments in *Weber* are not as one-sided as I have implied. The statutory proviso against a court's compelling affirmative action except as a remedy for discrimination would be unnecessary if, but for the proviso, the statute prohibited nonremedial affirmative action. "Otherwise to discriminate" could refer to the form (that is, other than to fire or fail to hire) rather than to the purpose (that is, whether invidious or benign) of the discrimination. And the exception for the use of sex, religion, or national origin when it is a bona-fide occupational qualification could be thought to support a distinction between deliberate and incidental discrimination: between wanting to exclude blacks — or whites — or women, or whomever, and excluding them as the incidental consequence of favoring another group on non-invidious grounds. It could be argued that only the first type of discrimination requires the discriminator to establish a bona-fide occupational qualification, and that the second is not even a prima facie violation of the statute.

In the absence of Title VII, an employer could discriminate in favor of blacks all he wanted. It seems odd to use a statute whose primary purpose was to benefit blacks as a weapon against them, although it can be argued that they must take the bitter with the sweet, and the argument is supported by the generality of the statutory definition of discrimination. A further point, however, is that the imbalance between the percentage of black craftworkers at Kaiser's plant and the percentage of black workers in the area's skilled work force, coupled with the long history of discrimination against blacks by craft unions, made Kaiser and the union likely targets for investigation and complaint on grounds of discriminating against blacks. In this light the affirmative action plan becomes a prudent measure of anticipatory compliance. Did Congress mean to forbid *this* back in 1964, and thereby place employers on a razor's edge?

United States v. Marshall
908 F.2d 1312 (7th Cir. 1990)

Statute: 21 U.S.C. §§841(b)(1)(A)(v) and (B)(v)

(b) (1) (A) In the case of a violation of subsection (a) of this section involving—

(v) 10 grams or more of a mixture or substance containing a detectable amount of lysergic acid diethylamide (LSD) . . . such person shall be sentenced to a term of imprisonment which may not be less than 10 years or more than life and if death or serious bodily injury results from the use of such substance shall be not less than 20 years or more than life, a fine not to exceed the greater of that authorized in accordance with the provisions of Title 18, or $4,000,000 if the defendant is an individual or $10,000,000 if the defendant is other than an individual, or both. . . .

(B) In the case of a violation of subsection (a) of this section involving—

(v) 1 gram or more of a mixture or substance containing a detectable amount of lysergic acid diethylamide (LSD) . . . such person shall be sentenced to a term of imprisonment which may not be less than 5 years and not more than 40 years and if death or serious bodily injury results from the use of such substance shall be not less than 20 years or more than life, a fine not to exceed the greater of that authorized in accordance with the provisions of Title 18, $2,000,000 if the defendant is an individual or $5,000,000 if the defendant is other than an individual, or both.

EASTERBROOK, CIRCUIT JUDGE. [Internal citations have been omitted except where particularly relevant.]

. . . Stanley J. Marshall was . . . sentenced to 20 years' imprisonment for conspiring to distribute, and distributing, more than ten grams of LSD, enough for 11,751 doses. Patrick Brumm, Richard L. Chapman, and John M. Schoenecker were convicted of . . . selling ten sheets (1,000 doses) of paper containing LSD. Because the total weight of the paper and LSD was 5.7 grams, a five-year mandatory minimum applied. The district court sentenced Brumm to 60 months' (the minimum), Schoenecker to 63 months', and Chapman to 96 months' imprisonment. . . .

I

According to the Sentencing Commission, the LSD in an average dose weighs 0.05 milligrams. Twenty thousand pure doses are a gram. But 0.05 mg is almost invisible, so LSD is distributed to retail customers in a carrier. Pure LSD is dissolved in a solvent such as alcohol and sprayed on paper or gelatin; alternatively the paper may be dipped in the solution. After the solvent evaporates, the paper or gel is cut into one-dose squares and sold by the square. Users swallow the squares or may drop them into a beverage, releasing the drug. Although the gelatin and paper are light, they weigh much more than the drug. Marshall's 11,751 doses weighed 113.32 grams; the LSD accounted for only 670.72 mg of this, not enough to activate the five-year mandatory minimum sentence, let alone the ten-year minimum. The ten sheets of blotter paper carrying the 1,000 doses Chapman and confederates sold weighed 5.7 grams; the LSD in the paper did not approach the one-gram threshold for a mandatory minimum sentence. This disparity between the weight of the pure LSD and the weight of LSD-plus-carrier underlies the defendants' arguments.

A

If the carrier counts in the weight of the "mixture or substance containing a detectable amount" of LSD, some odd things may happen. Weight in the hands of distributors may exceed that of manufacturers and wholesalers. Big fish then could receive paltry sentences or small fish draconian ones. Someone who sold 19,999 doses of pure LSD (at 0.05 mg per dose) would escape the five-year mandatory minimum of §841(b)(1)(B)(v) and be covered by §841(b)(1)(C), which lacks a minimum term and has a maximum of "only" 20 years. Someone who sold a single hit of LSD dissolved in a tumbler of orange juice could be exposed to a ten-year mandatory minimum. Retailers could fall in or out of the mandatory terms depending not on the number of doses but on the medium: sugar cubes weigh more than paper, which weighs more than gelatin. One way to eliminate the possibility of such consequences is to say that the carrier is not a "mixture or substance containing a detectable amount" of the drug. Defendants ask us to do this.

Defendants' submission starts from the premise that the interaction of the statutory phrase "mixture or substance" with the distribution of LSD by the dose in a carrier creates a unique probability of surprise results. The premise may be unwarranted. The paper used to distribute LSD is light stuff, not the kind used to absorb ink. Chapman's 1,000 doses weighed about 0.16 ounces. More than 6,000 doses, even in blotter paper, weigh less than an ounce. Because the LSD in one dose weighs about 0.05

milligrams, the combination of LSD-plus paper is about 110 times the weight of the LSD. The impregnated paper could be described as "0.9% LSD." . . .

This is by no means an unusual dilution rate for illegal drugs. Heroin sold on the street is 2% to 3% opiate and the rest filler. . . .

So there may be nothing extraordinary about LSD, no reason to think that the statute operates differently for LSD than for heroin. Heroin comes into this country pure; it is sold diluted on the street, creating the possibility that §841 will require higher sentences for retailers than for smugglers or refiners. The dilution factor for retail heroin is not significantly different from the factor for LSD on blotter paper. LSD in solution weighs more than LSD on blotter paper; pure heroin weighs (much) less per dose than the dilute heroin sold on the street. Heroin is sold in different cities at different dilution rates; that implies that the weight of a packet of heroin for a single administration weighs more in some cities than in others. . . .

B

It is not possible to construe the words of §841 to make the penalty turn on the net weight of the drug rather than the gross weight of carrier and drug. The statute speaks of a "mixture or substance containing a detectable amount" of a drug. "Detectable amount" is the opposite of "pure"; the point of the statute is that the "mixture" is not to be converted to an equivalent amount of pure drug.

The structure of the statute reinforces this conclusion. The 10-year minimum applies to any person who possesses, with intent to distribute, "100 grams or more of phencyclidine (PCP) or 1 kilogram or more of a mixture or substance containing a detectable amount of phencyclidine (PCP)," §841(b)(1)(A)(iv). Congress distinguished the pure drug from a "mixture or substance containing a detectable amount of" it. All drugs other than PCP are governed exclusively by the "mixture or substance" language. Even brute force cannot turn that language into a reference to pure LSD. Congress used the same "mixture or substance" language to describe heroin, cocaine, amphetamines, and many other drugs that are sold after being cut — sometimes as much as LSD. There is no sound basis on which to treat the words "substance or mixture containing a detectable amount of," repeated verbatim for every drug mentioned in §841 except PCP, as different things for LSD and cocaine although the language is identical, while treating the "mixture or substance" language as meaning the same as the reference to pure PCP in 21 U.S.C. §841(b)(1)(A)(iv) and (B)(iv).

Although the "mixture or substance" language shows that the statute cannot be limited to pure LSD, it does not necessarily follow that blotter paper is a "mixture or substance containing" LSD. That phrase cannot include all "carriers." One gram of crystalline LSD in a heavy glass bottle is still only one gram of "statutory LSD." So is a gram of LSD being "carried" in a Boeing 747. How much mingling of the drug with something else is essential to form a "mixture or substance"? The legislative history is silent, but ordinary usage is indicative.

"Substance" may well refer to a chemical compound, or perhaps to a drug in a solvent. LSD does not react chemically with sugar, blotter paper, or gelatin, and none of these is a solvent. "Mixture" is more inclusive. Cocaine often is mixed with mannitol, quinine, or lactose. These white powders do not react, but it is common ground that a cocaine-mannitol mixture is a statutory "mixture."

LSD and blotter paper are not commingled in the same way as cocaine and lactose. What is the nature of their association? The possibility most favorable to defendants is that LSD sits on blotter paper as oil floats on water. Immiscible substances may fall outside the statutory definition of "mixture." The possibility does not assist defendants — not on this record, anyway. LSD is applied to paper in a solvent; after the solvent evaporates, a tiny quantity of LSD remains. Because the fibers absorb the alcohol, the LSD solidifies inside the paper rather than on it. You cannot pick a grain of LSD off the surface of the paper. Ordinary parlance calls the paper containing tiny crystals of LSD a mixture.

United States v. Rose [authored by Judge Posner, who dissents in this case; citation omitted], like every other appellate decision that has addressed the question, concludes that the carrier medium for LSD, like the "cut" for heroin and cocaine, is a "mixture or substance containing a detectable amount" of the drug. . . . Without knowing more of the chemistry than this record reveals, we adhere to the unanimous conclusion of the other courts of appeals that blotter paper treated with LSD is a "mixture or substance containing a detectable quantity of" LSD.

C

Two reasons have been advanced to support a contrary conclusion: that statutes should be construed to avoid constitutional problems, and that some members of the sitting Congress are dissatisfied with basing penalties on the combined weight of LSD and carrier. Neither is persuasive.

A preference for giving statutes a constitutional meaning is a reason to construe, not to rewrite or "improve." Canons are doubt-resolvers, useful when the language is ambiguous. . . . "Substance or mixture containing a detectable quantity" is not ambiguous. . . . Neither the rule of lenity nor the preference for avoiding constitutional adjudication justifies disregarding unambiguous language.

The canon about avoiding constitutional decisions, in particular, must be used with care, for it is a closer cousin to invalidation than to interpretation.

It is a way to enforce the constitutional penumbra, and therefore an aspect of constitutional law proper. Constitutional decisions breed penumbras, which multiply questions. Treating each as justification to construe laws out of existence too greatly enlarges the judicial power. And heroic "construction" is unnecessary, given our conclusion in Part III that Congress possesses the constitutional power to set penalties on the basis of gross weight.

As for the pending legislation: subsequent debates are not a ground for avoiding the import of enactments. Although the views of a subsequent Congress are entitled to respect, ongoing debates do not represent the views of Congress. Judge Wilkins, Chairman of the Sentencing Commission, wrote a letter to Senator Biden, Chairman of the Judiciary Committee, remarking that "it is unclear whether Congress intended the carrier to be considered as a packaging material, or since it is commonly consumed along with the illicit drug, as a diluent ingredient in the drug mixture." The Chairman of the Commission invited the Chairman of the Committee to introduce legislation choosing one or the other explicitly.

Senator Biden introduced an amendment to S. 1711, the Administration's omnibus drug bill, stating in materials read into the Congressional Record that the amendment changes the statute to omit the weight of the carrier. So far as we can determine, the language he actually introduced did not contain the text to which his prepared statement referred. No language of this kind appears in the version the Senate passed (text of bill that Senate sent to House). The House is yet to act. Senator Kennedy has introduced an amendment to other legislation affecting the criminal code, which, like Senator Biden's, would exclude the carrier. But this proposal, too, awaits enactment. Both Senator Kennedy's proposal and Senator Biden's statement are more naturally understood as suggestions for change than as evidence of today's meaning. At all events, the Senators were speaking for themselves, not for Congress as an institution.

Statements supporting proposals that have not been adopted do not inform our reading of the text an earlier Congress passed and the President signed. We may not, in the name of faithful interpretation of what the political branches enacted, treat as authoritative the statements of legislators supporting change. Opinion polls of Senators are not law.

CUMMINGS, Circuit Judge, with whom BAUER, Chief Judge, and WOOD, JR., CUDAHY, and POSNER, Circuit Judges, join, dissenting:

Two assumptions lie at the heart of the majority opinion. The first is that the words "mixture or substance" are not ambiguous and are not therefore susceptible of interpretation by the courts. The second is that the due process clause of the Fifth Amendment guarantees process but not substance. Both of these assumptions are unwarranted.

Six courts, including the district court in *Marshall,* have explicitly considered whether the carrier in an LSD case is a mixture or substance within the meaning of 21 U.S.C. §841. Five of these courts have concluded that the blotter paper is a "mixture or substance" within the meaning of the statute. These courts rely primarily on the 1986 amendments to Section 841, which altered the references to various drugs, including LSD, by adding the words "mixture or substance containing a detectable amount of [the drug in question]." The earlier version of the statute referred merely to the drugs themselves.

The sixth court, the United States District Court for the District of Columbia, held that blotter paper was not a mixture or substance within the meaning of the statute. United States v. Healy, [citation omitted]. The court relied not only on ordinary dictionary definitions of the words mixture and substance but also on a November 30, 1988, Sentencing Commission publication, entitled "Questions Most Frequently Asked About the Sentencing Guide-lines," which states that the Commission has not taken a position on whether the blotter paper should be weighed. The conclusion that the Commission has not yet resolved this question is further supported by a Sentencing Commission Notice issued on March 3, 1989, which requested public comments on whether the Commission should exclude the weight of the carrier for sentencing purposes in LSD cases.

The *Healy* court also stated that Congress could have intended the words "mixture or substance" to refer to the liquid in which the pure LSD is dissolved. . . .

The court in *Healy* did not refer to the legislative history of the statute to support the proposition that Congress did not intend the weight of the carrier to be included in LSD cases. This is not surprising since the only reference to LSD in the debates preceding the passage of the 1986 amendments to Section 841 was a passing reference that does not address quantities or weights of drugs.

Two subsequent pieces of legislative history, however, do shed some light on this question. [Here the dissent refers to the letter from Judge Wilkins, the statement by Senator Biden, and an amendatory bill introduced by Senator Kennedy, all of which are described in the court's opinion.] . . .

To be sure there are difficulties inherent in relying heavily on this subsequent legislative history. The first is that these initiatives to clarify the manner in which 21 U.S.C. §841 and the sentencing guidelines treat LSD offenders may never be enacted. The second is that a given amendment may be viewed not as a clarification of Congress' original intent, but as the expression of an entirely new intent. At the very least, however, this subsequent legislative history, coupled with the fact that the Sentencing Commission has yet to resolve its position on the matter, refutes the proposition that the language of the statute and the Guidelines "couldn't be clearer."

POSNER, Circuit Judge, joined by BAUER, Chief Judge, and CUMMINGS, WOOD, JR., and CUDAHY, Circuit Judges, dissenting.

Based as it is on weight, the system . . . works well for drugs that are sold by weight; and ordinarily the weight quoted to the buyer is the weight of the dilute form, although of course price will vary with purity. The dilute form is the product, and it is as natural to punish its purveyors according to the weight of the product. . . .

LSD, however, is sold to the consumer by the dose; it is not cut, diluted, or mixed with something else. Moreover, it is incredibly light. An average dose of LSD weighs .05 milligrams, which is less than two millionths of an ounce. To ingest something that small requires swallowing something much larger. Pure LSD in granular form is first diluted by being dissolved, usually in alcohol, and then a quantity of the solution containing one dose of LSD is sprayed or eyedropped on a sugar cube, or on a cube of gelatin, or, as in the cases before us, on an inch-square section of "blotter" paper. (LSD blotter paper, which is sold typically in sheets ten inches square containing a hundred sections each with one dose of LSD on it, is considerably thinner than the paper used to blot ink but much heavier than the LSD itself.) After the solution is applied to the carrier medium, the alcohol or other solvent evaporates, leaving an invisible (and undiluted) spot of pure LSD on the cube or blotter paper. The consumer drops the cube or the piece of paper into a glass of water, or orange juice, or some other beverage, causing the LSD to dissolve in the beverage, which is then drunk. This is not dilution. It is still one dose that is being imbibed. . . . It would be like basing the punishment for selling cocaine on the combined weight of the cocaine and of the vehicle (plane, boat, automobile, or whatever) used to transport it or the syringe used to inject it or the pipe used to smoke it. . . .

The weight of the carrier is vastly greater than that of the LSD, as well as irrelevant to its potency. There is no comparable disparity between the pure and the mixed form (if that is how we should regard LSD on blotter paper or other carrier medium) with respect to the other drugs in section 841, with the illuminating exception of PCP. There Congress specified alternative weights, for the drug itself and for the substance or mixture containing the drug. For example, the five-year minimum sentence for a seller of PCP requires the sale of either ten grams of the drug itself or one hundred grams of a substance or mixture containing the drug. 21 U.S.C. §841(b)(1)(B)(iv).

Ten sheets of blotter paper, containing a thousand doses of LSD, weigh almost six grams. The LSD itself weighs less than a hundredth as much. If the thousand doses are on gelatin cubes instead of sheets of blotter paper, the total weight is less, but it is still more than two grams, which is forty times the weight of the LSD. In both cases, if the carrier plus the LSD constitutes the relevant "substance or mixture" (the crucial "if" in this case), the dealer is subject to the minimum mandatory sentence of five years. One of the defendants before us (Marshall) sold almost 12,000 doses of LSD on blotter paper. This subjected him to the ten-year minimum, and the Guidelines then took over and pushed him up to twenty years.

Since it takes 20,000 doses of LSD to equal a gram, Marshall would not have been subject to even the five-year mandatory minimum had he sold the LSD in its pure form. And a dealer who sold fifteen times the number of doses as Marshall — 180,000 — would not be subject to the ten-year mandatory minimum sentence if he sold the drug in its pure form, because 180,000 doses is only nine grams.

At the other extreme, if Marshall were not a dealer at all but dropped a square of blotter paper containing a single dose of LSD into a glass of orange juice and sold it to a friend at cost (perhaps 35 cents), he would be subject to the ten-year minimum. The juice with LSD dissolved in it would be the statutory mixture or substance containing a detectable amount of the illegal drug and it would weigh more than ten grams (one ounce is about 35 grams, and the orange juice in a glass of orange juice weighs several ounces). So a person who sold one dose of LSD might be subject to the ten-year mandatory minimum sentence while a dealer who sold 199,999 doses in pure form would be subject only to the five-year minimum. Defendant Dean sold 198 doses, crowded onto one sheet of blotter paper: this subjected him to the five-year mandatory minimum, too, since the ensemble weighed slightly more than a gram. . . .

All this seems crazy but we must consider whether Congress might have had a reason for wanting to key the severity of punishment for selling LSD to the weight of the carrier rather than to the number of doses or to some reasonable proxy for dosage (as weight is, for many drugs). The only one suggested is that it might be costly to determine the weight of the LSD in the blotter paper, sugar cube, etc., because it is so light! That merely underscores the irrationality of basing the punishment for selling this drug on weight rather than on dosage. But in fact the weight is reported in every case I have seen, so apparently it can be determined readily enough; it has to be determined in any event, to permit a purity adjustment under the Guidelines. If the weight of the LSD is difficult to determine, the difficulty is easily overcome by basing punishment on the number of doses, which makes much more sense in any event. To base punishment on the weight of the carrier medium makes about as much sense as basing punishment on the weight of the defendant. . . .

This is a quilt the pattern whereof no one has been able to discern. The legislative history is silent, and since even the Justice Department cannot explain the why of the punishment scheme that it is defending, the most plausible inference is that Congress simply did not realize how LSD is sold. . . .

That irrationality is magnified when we compare the sentences for people who sell other drugs prohibited by 21 U.S.C. §841. Marshall, remember, sold fewer than 12,000 doses and was sentenced to twenty years. Twelve thousand doses sounds like a lot, but to receive a comparable sentence for selling heroin Marshall would have had to sell ten kilograms, which would yield between one and two million doses. To receive a comparable sentence for selling cocaine he would have had to sell fifty kilograms, which would yield anywhere from 325,000 to five million doses. While the corresponding weight is lower for crack — half a kilogram — this still translates into 50,000 doses. . . .

Well, what if anything can we judges do about this mess? The answer lies in the shadow of a jurisprudential disagreement that is not less important by virtue of being unavowed by most judges. It is the disagreement between the severely positivistic view that the content of law is exhausted in clear, explicit, and definite enactments by or under express delegation from legislatures, and the natural lawyer's or legal pragmatist's view that the practice of interpretation and the general terms of the Constitution (such as "equal protection of the laws") authorize judges to enrich positive law with the moral values and practical concerns of civilized society. Judges who in other respects have seemed quite similar, such as Holmes and Cardozo, have taken opposite sides of this issue. Neither approach is entirely satisfactory. The first buys political neutrality and a type of objectivity at the price of substantive injustice, while the second buys justice in the individual case at the price of considerable uncertainty and, not infrequently, judicial willfulness. It is no wonder that our legal system oscillates between the approaches. The positivist view, applied unflinchingly to this case, commands the affirmance of prison sentences that are exceptionally harsh by the standards of the modern Western world, dictated by an accidental, unintended scheme of punishment nevertheless implied by the words (taken one by one) of the relevant enactments. The natural law or pragmatist view leads to a freer interpretation, one influenced by norms of equal treatment; and let us explore the interpretive possibilities here. One is to interpret "mixture or substance containing a detectable amount of [LSD]" to exclude the carrier medium — the blotter paper, sugar or gelatin cubes, and orange juice or other beverage. That is the course we rejected in United States v. Rose, as have the other circuits. I wrote *Rose*, but I am no longer confident that its literal interpretation of the statute, under which the blotter paper, cubes, etc. are "substances" that "contain" LSD, is inevitable. The blotter paper, etc. are better viewed, I now think, as carriers, like the package in which a kilo of cocaine comes wrapped or the bottle in which a fifth of liquor is sold.

Interpreted to exclude the carrier, the punishment schedule for LSD would make perfectly good sense; it would not warp the statutory design. The comparison with heroin and cocaine is again illuminating. The statute imposes the five-year mandatory minimum sentence on anyone who sells a substance or mixture containing a hundred grams of heroin, equal to 10,000 to 20,000 doses. One gram of pure LSD, which also would trigger the five-year minimum, yields 20,000 doses. The comparable figures for cocaine are 3250 to 50,000 doses, placing LSD in about the middle. So Congress may have wanted to base punishment for the sale of LSD on the weight of the pure drug after all, using one and ten grams of the pure drug to trigger the five-year and ten-year minima (and corresponding maxima — twenty years and forty years). This interpretation leaves "substance or mixture containing" without a referent, so far as LSD is concerned. But we must remember that Congress used the identical term in each subsection that specifies the quantity of a drug that subjects the seller to the designated minimum and maximum punishments. In thus automatically including the same term in each subsection, Congress did not necessarily affirm that, for each and every drug covered by the statute, a substance or mixture containing the drug must be found.

The flexible interpretation that I am proposing is decisively strengthened by the constitutional objection to basing punishment of LSD offenders on the weight of the carrier medium rather than on the weight of the LSD. Courts often do interpretive handsprings to avoid having even to decide a constitutional question. In doing so they expand, very questionably in my view, the effective scope of the Constitution, creating a constitutional penumbra in which statutes wither, shrink, are deformed. A better case for flexible interpretation is presented when the alternative is to nullify Congress's action: when in other words there is not merely a constitutional question about, but a constitutional barrier to, the statute when interpreted literally. This is such a case. . . .

The point is not that the judicial imagination can conjure up anomalous applications of the statute. A statute is not irrational because its draftsmen lacked omniscience. The point is that graduating punishment to the weight of the carrier medium produces, in the case of LSD, a systematically, unavoidably bizarre schedule of punishments that no one is able to justify. I would give respectful consideration to any rationale for the schedule advanced by the legislators, the framers of the Guidelines, or the Department of Justice. None has been advanced. And such given as there is in the Guidelines (the purity adjustment) is unavailing when defendants are subject to the mandatory minimum sentences in section 841, as all the defendants before us (plus Dean) are. . . .

Our choice is between ruling that the provisions of section 841 regarding LSD are irrational, hence unconstitutional, and therefore there is no punishment for dealing in LSD — Congress must go back to the drawing boards, and all LSD cases in the pipeline must be dismissed — and ruling that, to preserve so much of the statute as can constitutionally be preserved, the statutory expression "substance or mixture containing a detectable amount of [LSD]" excludes the carrier medium. Given this choice, we can be reasonably certain that Congress would have preferred the second course; and this consideration carries the argument for a flexible interpretation over the top. . . .

The literal interpretation adopted by the majority is not inevitable. All interpretation is contextual. The words of the statute — interpreted against a background that includes a constitutional norm of equal treatment, a (closely related) constitutional commitment to rationality, an evident failure by both Congress and the Sentencing Commission to consider how LSD is actually produced, distributed, and sold, and an equally evident failure by the same two bodies to consider the interaction between heavy mandatory minimum sentences and the Sentencing Guidelines — will bear an interpretation that distinguishes between the carrier vehicle of the illegal drug and the substance or mixture containing a detectable amount of the drug. The punishment of the crack dealer is not determined by the weight of the glass tube in which he sells the crack; we should not lightly attribute to Congress a purpose of punishing the dealer in LSD according to the weight of the LSD carrier. We should not make Congress's handiwork an embarrassment to the members of Congress and to us.

NOTES AND QUESTIONS

1. *What's going on here?* Defendants are convicted and sentenced for distributing and selling LSD. One receives 20 years, the others between 5 and 8 years. The statute's language plainly dictates these sentences. Yet the court, en banc, splits, with the majority arguing that "even brute force cannot turn that language into pure LSD." This language is occasioned by the dissent's almost incredible unwillingness to accept the statute's consequence — incredible, in a positive law sense, because none of the traditional justifications for departing from the plain meaning of the statute seem to exist. Do you agree with this latter statement? If not, what do the dissenters point to that evidences a meaning of the enacting legislature different from the language of the statute? On what basis do the various dissenters justify their dissents?

2. *Judge Posner's flexible interpretation.* Judge Posner's dissent is most provocative. In an earlier decision, United States v. Rose, 881 F.2d 386 (7th Cir. 1989), he had affirmed a decision under the statute and now, changing course, he attempts to rewrite the statute, to replace "dose" with "weight." He would undertake such effort based on what he boldly characterizes as "natural law" judicial authority "to enrich positive law with the moral values and practical concerns of civilized society." This approach is, as Judge Posner himself warns, fraught with danger, inviting judicial willfulness. This approach is not new (see Chapter 1, Section A), but is one of the approaches taken, historically, by judges who do not like the constraints of statutes. As Judge Posner himself has written, "the important question concerning statutory interpretation . . . is political rather than epistemic: how free *should* judges feel themselves to be from the fetters of text and legislative intent in applying statutes? . . ." Richard A. Posner, The Problems of Jurisprudence 271 (1990). How free does Judge Posner feel himself to be from the "fetters of text and legislative intent"? When is it appropriate to exercise such judicial freedom? What are the moral values and practical concerns that lead him to dissent in this case, notwithstanding the statutory language? Does the punishment of the defendants in this case reach such level of concern?

3. *Is the statute irrational?* To Judge Posner, the statute is irrational because the LSD provision is not tied to drug weight. What makes the statute irrational to Judge Posner: his substantive view that the penalties are unfair or his procedural view that the legislative history is silent on this provision? Assume Judge Posner, in his search for meaning, had found within a relevant committee report the following passage:

> The fact that sentencing provisions contained in this statute may result, in certain instances, in stiffer penalties being imposed on sellers of certain types of drugs than on their importers is noted. A number of members of this committee believe that sellers even of the smallest amounts of drugs ought to receive the stiffest penalties to stem the sale of drugs. To these members, it is appropriate that the highest societal costs (long-term imprisonment) might be imposed on the lowest end of the drug trade organization chart market. Their view is that this is an effective way of stopping the sale of drugs.

Do you think this would have changed Judge Posner's view of the case?

Consider the view of Justice Rehnquist, writing for the majority in affirming the sentencing of Chapman, one of the defendants in *Marshall:*

> The current penalties reflect a "market-oriented" approach to punishing drug trafficking. . . . To implement that principle, Congress . . . intended the penalties for drug trafficking to be graduated according to the weight of the drugs in whatever form they were found — cut or uncut, pure or impure, ready for wholesale or ready for distribution at the retail level. Congress did not want to punish retail traffickers less severely, even though they deal in smaller quantities of the pure drug, because such traffickers keep the street markets going. . . .

United States v. Chapman, 500 U.S. 453 (1991). The Court denied Marshall's certiorari application. United States v. Marshall, 500 U.S. 453 (1991).

4. *Legislative versus judicial perspectives.* Judge Posner makes much of his view that Congress was not aware of the particular problems of LSD marketing when enacting the statute. Does this really matter? Consider the record on which Judge Posner is making his decision: What is its focus? On the other hand, what do you suppose the record before Congress was like? What difference does this point out between legislative and judicial decisionmaking? In answering this question, revisit the discussion in Chapter 1.

B. MISTAKES

The following case, National Bank of Oregon v. Insurance Agents, should be familiar. We referred to it in Chapter 2 to demonstrate the relationship between statutes and unenacted codes. *National Bank of Oregon* is somewhat difficult to follow. Think of it as a puzzle. The question is how to make the boldface provisions in the statutory text below part of §13 of that same statute notwithstanding the punctuation.

National Bank of Oregon v. Insurance Agents
508 U.S. 439 (1993)

Statute: 39 Stat. 752, ch. 461 (1916)

An Act To amend certain sections of the Act entitled "Federal Reserve Act," approved December twenty-third, nineteen hundred and thirteen. . . . *Be it enacted* . . . That the Act entitled the "Federal Reserve Act," approved December twenty-third, nineteen hundred and thirteen, be, and is hereby, amended as follows:

At the end of section eleven insert a new clause as follows: ". . ."

That section thirteen be, and is hereby, amended to read as follows: ". . ."

Section fifty-two hundred and two of the Revised Statutes of the United States is hereby amended so as to read as follows: "No national banking association shall at any time be indebted, or in any way liable, to an amount exceeding the amount of its capital stock at such time actually paid in and remaining undiminished by losses or otherwise, except on account of demands of the nature following:

"First. Notes of circulation.

"Second. Moneys deposited with or collected by the association.

"Third. Bills of exchange or drafts drawn against money actually on deposit to the credit of the association, or due thereto.

"Fourth. Liabilities to the stockholders of the association for dividends and reserve profits.

"Fifth. Liabilities incurred under the provisions of the Federal Reserve Act.

"The discount and rediscount and the purchase and sale by any Federal reserve bank of any bills receivable and of domestic and foreign bills of exchange, and of acceptances authorized by this Act, shall be subject to such restrictions, limitations, and regulations as may be imposed by the Federal Reserve Board.

"That in addition to the powers now vested by law in national banking associations organized under the laws of the United States any such association located and doing business in any place the population of which does not exceed five thousand inhabitants, as shown by the last preceding decennial census, may, under such rules and regulations as may be prescribed by the Comptroller of the Currency, act as the agent

**for any fire, life, or other insurance company authorized by the author-
ities of the State in which said bank is located to do business in said
State. . . .**

"Any member bank may accept drafts or bills of exchange drawn
upon it having not more than three months' sight to run, exclusive of
days of grace, drawn under regulations to be prescribed by the Federal
Reserve Board by banks or bankers in foreign countries or dependencies
or insular possessions of the United States for the purpose of furnishing
dollar exchange as required by the usages of trade in the respective
countries, dependencies, or insular possessions. Such drafts or bills
may be acquired by Federal reserve banks in such amounts and subject
to such regulations, restrictions, and limitations as may be prescribed by
the Federal Reserve Board. . . ."

That subsection (e) of section fourteen be, and is hereby, amended to
read as follows:

" . . . "

That the second paragraph of section sixteen be, and is hereby, amended
to read as follows:

" . . . "

That section twenty-four be, and is hereby, amended to read as follows:

" . . . "

That section twenty-five be, and is hereby, amended to read as follows:

" . . . "

Statute: 40 Stat. 506, ch. 45 (1918) (War Finance Corporation Act of 1918)

Sec. 20. Section fifty-two hundred and two of the Revised Statutes of the
United States is hereby amended so as to read as follows:

"Sec. 5202. No national banking association shall at any time be
indebted, or in any way liable, to an amount exceeding the amount of its
capital stock at such time actually paid in and remaining undiminished by
losses or otherwise, except on account of demands of the nature following:
[provisions "First" through "Fifth" from Rev. Stat. §5202, excluding any
reference to the paragraphs in bold print following the paragraph labeled
"Fifth in the 1916 Act"]. . . .

"Sixth. Liabilities incurred under the provisions of the War Finance
Corporation Act."

Justice Souter delivered the opinion for a unanimous Court. [Internal
citations have been omitted except where particularly relevant.]

The Comptroller of the Currency recently relied on a statutory provision
enacted in 1916 to permit national banks located in small communities to
sell insurance to customers outside those communities. These cases present
the unlikely question whether Congress repealed that provision in 1918.
We hold that no repeal occurred.

I

Almost 80 years ago, Congress authorized any national bank "doing business in any place the population of which does not exceed five thousand inhabitants . . . [to] act as the agent for any fire, life, or other insurance company." Act of Sept. 7, 1916. In the first compilation of the United States Code, this provision appeared as section 92 of title 12. See 12 U.S.C. §92 (1926 ed.); see also United States Code editions of 1934, 1940, and 1946. The 1952 edition of the Code, however, omitted the insurance provision, with a note indicating that Congress had repealed it in 1918. See 12 U.S.C. §92 (1952 ed.) (note). Though the provision has also been left out of the subsequent editions of the United States Code, including the current one . . . the parties refer to it as "section 92," and so will we.

Despite the absence of section 92 from the Code, Congress has assumed that it remains in force, on one occasion actually amending it. . . . The regulators concerned with the provision's subject, the Comptroller of the Currency and the Federal Reserve Board, have likewise acted on the understanding that section 92 remains the law, and indeed it was a ruling by the Comptroller relying on section 92 that precipitated these cases.

The ruling came on a request by United States National Bank of Oregon, a national bank with its principal place of business in Portland, Oregon, to sell insurance through its branch in Banks, Oregon (population: 489), to customers nationwide. The Comptroller approved the request in 1986, interpreting section 92 to permit national bank branches located in communities with populations not exceeding 5,000 to sell insurance to customers not only inside but also outside those communities. . . .

III

A

Though the appearance of a provision in the current edition of the United States Code is "prima facie" evidence that the provision has the force of law, 1 U.S.C. §204(a), it is the Statutes at Large that provides the "legal evidence of laws," §112, and despite its omission from the Code section 92 remains on the books if the Statutes at Large so dictates. The analysis that underlies our conclusion that section 92 is valid law calls for familiarity with several provisions appearing in the Statutes at Large. . . .

The background begins in 1863 and 1864, when the Civil War Congress enacted and then reenacted the National Bank Act. . . . In a section important for [this case] . . . the National Bank Act set limits on the indebtedness of national banks, subject to certain exceptions. Ten years later, Congress adopted the indebtedness provisions again as part of the Revised Statutes of the United States, a massive revision, reorganization, and reenactment of all statutes in effect at the time, accompanied by a simultaneous repeal of all prior ones. Title 62 of the Revised Statutes, containing §§5133 through 5243, included the Nation's banking laws, and, with a few stylistic alterations the National Bank Act's indebtedness provision became §5202 of the Revised Statutes. . . .

In 1913 Congress amended Rev. Stat. §5202 by adding a fifth exception to the indebtedness limit. The amendment was a detail of the Federal Reserve Act of 1913 (Federal Reserve Act or 1913 Act), which created Federal Reserve banks and the Federal Reserve Board and required the national banks formed pursuant to the National Bank Act to become members of the new Federal Reserve System. The amendment came in §13 of the 1913 Act, the first five paragraphs of which set forth the powers of the new Federal Reserve banks. . . .

> [SEC. 13] . . . Section fifty-two hundred and two of the Revised Statutes of the United States is hereby amended so as to read as follows: . . .
>   Fifth . . .

In 1916, Congress enacted what became section 92. It did so as part of a statute that amended various sections of the Federal Reserve Act and that, in the view of respondents and the Court of Appeals, also amended Rev. Stat. §5202. Unlike the 1913 Act, the 1916 Act employed quotation marks, and those quotation marks proved critical to the Court of Appeals's finding that the 1916 Act placed section 92 in Rev. Stat. §5202. . . .

The final relevant statute is the War Finance Corporation Act, ch. 45, 40 Stat. 506 (1918 Act), which in §20 amended Rev. Stat. §5202 by, at least, adding a sixth exception to the indebtedness limit. . . .

B

The argument that section 92 is no longer in force . . . is simply stated: the 1916 Act placed section 92 in Rev. Stat. §5202, and the 1918 Act eliminated all of Rev. Stat. §5202 except the indebtedness provision (to which it added a sixth exception), thus repealing section 92. Our discussion begins with the first premise of that argument, and there it ends, for we conclude with petitioners that the 1916 Act placed section 92 not in Rev. Stat. §5202 but in §13 of the Federal Reserve Act; since the 1918 Act did not touch §13, it did not affect, much less repeal, section 92.

A reader following the path of punctuation of the 1916 Act would no doubt arrive at the opposite conclusion, that the statute added section 92 to Rev. Stat. §5202. The 1916 Act reads, without quotation marks, *Section fifty-two hundred and two of the Revised Statutes of the United States is hereby amended so as to read as follows.* 39 Stat. 753. That phrase is followed by a colon and then opening quotation marks; closing quotation marks do not appear until several paragraphs later, and the paragraph that was later codified as 12 U.S.C. §92 is one of those within the opening and closing quotation marks. The unavoidable inference from familiar rules of punctuation is that the 1916 Act placed section 92 in Rev. Stat. §5202.

A statute's plain meaning must be enforced, of course, and the meaning of a statute will typically heed the commands of its punctuation. But a purported plain-meaning analysis based only on punctuation is necessarily incomplete and runs the risk of distorting a statute's true meaning. Along with punctuation, text consists of words living "a communal existence," in Judge Learned Hand's phrase, the meaning of each word informing the others and "all in their aggregate taking their purport from the setting in which they are used." . . . No more than isolated words or sentences is punctuation alone a reliable guide for discovery of a statute's meaning. . . .

Here, though the deployment of quotation marks in the 1916 Act points in one direction, all of the other evidence from the statute points the other way. It points so certainly, in our view, as to allow only the conclusion that the punctuation marks were misplaced and that the 1916 Act put section 92 not in Rev. Stat. §5202 but in §13 of the Federal Reserve Act.

The first thing to notice, we think, is the 1916 Act's structure. The Act begins by stating *[t]hat the Act entitled the "Federal Reserve Act," approved [1913], be, and is hereby, amended as follows.* 39 Stat. 752. It then contains what appear to be seven directory phrases not surrounded by quotation marks, each of which is followed by one or more paragraphs within opening and closing quotation marks. These are the seven phrases (the numbers and citation are ours):

[1] At the end of section eleven insert a new clause as follows: "..." [39 Stat. 752]

[2] That section thirteen be ... amended to read as follows: "..." [39 Stat. 752]

[3] Section fifty-two hundred and two of the Revised Statutes of the United States is hereby amended so as to read as follows: "..." [39 Stat. 753] [It is within the preceding quotation marks that §92 is found — EDS.]

[4] That subsection (e) of section fourteen, be, and is hereby, amended to read as follows: "..." [39 Stat. 754]

[5] That the second paragraph of section sixteen be, and is hereby, amended to read as follows: "..." [39 Stat. 754]

[6] That section twenty-four be, and is hereby, amended to read as follows: "..." [39 Stat. 754]

[7] That section twenty-five be, and is hereby, amended to read as follows: "..." [39 Stat. 755]

The paragraph eventually codified as 12 U.S.C. §92 is one of several inside the quotation marks that open after the third phrase, which "hereby amended" Rev. Stat. §5202, and that close before the fourth, and the argument that the 1916 Act placed section 92 in Rev. Stat. §5202 hinges on the assumption that the third phrase is a directory phrase like each of the others. But the structure of the Act supports another possibility, that the third phrase does not introduce a new amendment at all. Of the seven phrases, only the third does not in terms refer to a section of the Federal Reserve Act. Congress, to be sure, was free to take a detour from its work on the Federal Reserve Act to revise the Revised Statutes. But if Congress had taken that turn, one would expect some textual indication of the point where once its work on Rev. Stat. §5202 was done it returned to revision of the Federal Reserve Act. None of the directory phrases that follow the phrase mentioning Rev. Stat. §5202, however, refers back to the Federal Reserve Act. The failure of the fourth phrase, for example, to say something like "subsection (e) of section fourteen *of the Federal Reserve Act of 1913* is hereby amended" suggests that the Congress never veered from its original course, that the object of the 1916 Act was singlemindedly to revise sections of the Federal Reserve Act, and that amending the Revised Statutes was beyond the 1916 law's scope.

Further evidence that the 1916 Act amended only the Federal Reserve Act comes from the 1916 Act's title: *An Act To amend certain sections of the Act entitled "Federal reserve Act," approved December twenty-third, nineteen hundred and thirteen.* During this era the titles of statutes that revised pre-existing laws appear to have typically mentioned each of the laws they revised. . . . Absent a comprehensive review it is impossible to know the extent of exceptions to this general rule, if any, and we would not cast aside the 1916 Act's punctuation based solely on the Act's title. Nevertheless, the omission of the Revised Statutes from the 1916 Act's title does provide supporting evidence for the inference from the Act's structure, that the Act did not amend Rev. Stat. §5202.

One must ask, however, why the 1916 Act stated that *Section fifty-two hundred and two of the Revised Statutes of the United States is hereby amended so as to read as follows,* 39 Stat. 753, if it did not amend Rev. Stat. §5202. The answer emerges from comparing the 1916 Act with the statute that all agree it did amend, the Federal Reserve Act of 1913, and noticing that the identical directory phrase appeared in §13 of the 1913 Act, which did amend Rev. Stat. §5202. As enacted in 1913, §13 contained several paragraphs granting powers to Federal Reserve banks; it then included a paragraph amending Rev. Stat. §5202 (by adding a fifth exception to the indebtedness limit for "liabilities incurred under the provisions of the Federal Reserve Act"), a paragraph that began *Section fifty-two hundred and two of the Revised Statutes of the United States is hereby amended so as to read as follows.* 38 Stat. 264. The 1916 Act, in the portion following the phrase introducing a revision of §13 of the 1913 Act, proceeded in the same manner. It contained several paragraphs granting powers to Federal Reserve banks, paragraphs that are somewhat revised versions of the ones that appeared in the 1913 Act, followed by the phrase introducing an amendment to Rev. Stat. §5202 and then the language of Rev. Stat. §5202 as it appeared in the 1913 Act.

The similarity of the language of the 1916 and 1913 Acts suggests that, in order to amend §13 in 1916, Congress restated the 1913 version of §13 in its entirety, revising the portion it intended to change and leaving the rest unaltered, including the portion that had amended Rev. Stat. §5202.

In defending the Court of Appeals's contrary conclusion that the 1916 Act amended Rev. Stat. §5202, respondents argue that any other reading would render meaningless the language in the 1916 Act that purports to amend that section of the Revised Statutes. But the 1916 Congress would have had good reason to carry forward that portion of the 1913 Act containing Rev. Stat. §5202, even though in 1916 it did not intend to amend it any further. The 1916 Act revised §13 of the 1913 Act by completely restating it with a mixture of old and new language (providing that §13 is amended "to read as follows," 39 Stat. 752), and a failure to restate Rev. Stat. §5202 with its 1913 amendment could have been taken to indicate its repeal.

The final and decisive evidence that the 1916 Act placed section 92 in §13 of the Federal Reserve Act rather than Rev. Stat. §5202 is provided by the language and subject matter of section 92 and the paragraphs surrounding it, paragraphs within the same opening and closing quotation marks. In the paragraph preceding section 92, the 1916 Act granted the Federal Reserve Board authority to regulate the discount and rediscount and the purchase and sale by any Federal reserve bank of any bills receivable and of domestic and foreign bills of exchange, and of acceptances authorized by this Act. . . . 39 Stat. 753. "This Act" must mean the Federal Reserve Act, since it was §13 of the Federal Reserve Act that granted banks the authority to discount and rediscount. Use of "this Act" in the discount-and-rediscount paragraph is powerful proof that the 1916 Act placed that paragraph in the Act to which it necessarily refers, the Federal Reserve Act. That is crucial because section 92 travels together with the paragraphs that surround it; neither the language nor, certainly, the punctuation of the 1916 Act justifies separating them. Because the 1916 Act placed the paragraph preceding section 92 in §13 of the Federal Reserve Act, it follows that the 1916 Act placed section 92 there too.

We are not persuaded by respondents' argument that the term "this Act" in the discount-and-rediscount paragraph is an antecedent reference to "the Federal reserve Act," which is mentioned in the prior paragraph (in the fifth exception clause of Rev. Stat. §5202). If respondents are right, then the 1916 Act may be read as placing the discount-and-rediscount paragraph (and section 92, which necessarily accompanies it) in Rev. Stat. §5202. But while the antecedent interpretation is arguable as construing "this Act" in the discount-and-rediscount paragraph, that reading cannot attach to the other uses of "this Act" in the 1916 Act . . . since none is within the vicinity of a reference to the Federal Reserve Act. Presumptively, "'identical words used in different parts of the same act are intended to have the same meaning,'" and since nothing rebuts that presumption here, we are of the view that each use of "this Act" in the 1916 Act refers to the Act in which the language is contained. Rather than aiding respondents, then, the single full reference to "the Federal reserve Act" in the portion of the 1916 Act that amended Rev. Stat. §5202 cuts against them. The fact that it was not repeated in the next paragraph confirms that the statute's quotation of Rev. Stat. §5202 had ended.

Finally, the subject matter of the discount-and-rediscount paragraph (located, again, within the same opening and closing quotation marks as section 92) confirms that the 1916 Act placed section 92 in the Federal Reserve Act. The discount-and-rediscount paragraph subjects certain powers of Federal Reserve banks to regulation by the Federal Reserve Board. The logic of locating this provision in the Federal Reserve Act is obvious, whereas there would have been no reason for Congress to place it in Rev. Stat. §5202, which narrowly addressed the indebtedness of national banks, or even in the National Bank Act (from which Rev. Stat. §5202 derived), which concerned not public Federal Reserve banks or the Federal Reserve Board, but private national banks. Similarly, the paragraph following section 92, which authorizes Federal Reserve banks to acquire foreign drafts or bills of exchange from member banks and subjects transactions involving foreign acceptances to Federal Reserve Board regulations, fits far more comfortably with §13 of the Federal Reserve Act than with Rev. Stat. §5202. While we do not disagree with respondents insofar as they assert that Congress could have placed section 92, granting powers of insurance agency to some national banks (and without mentioning Federal Reserve banks or the Federal Reserve Board), in Rev. Stat. §5202, Congress could also reasonably have dealt with the insurance provision as part of the Federal Reserve Act, which Congress had before it for amendment in 1916. There is no need to break that tie, however, because there is no way around the conclusion that the 1916 Act placed section 92 in the same statutory location as it must have placed its neighbors, in §13 of the Federal Reserve Act.

Against the overwhelming evidence from the structure, language, and subject matter of the 1916 Act there stands only the evidence from the Act's punctuation, too weak to trump the rest. In this unusual case, we are convinced that the placement of the quotation marks in the 1916 Act was a simple scrivener's error, a mistake made by someone unfamiliar with the law's object and design. Courts, we have said, should "disregard the punctuation, or repunctuate, if need be, to render the true meaning of the statute." The true meaning of the 1916 Act is clear beyond question, and so we repunctuate. The 1916 Act should be read as if closing quotation marks do not appear at the end of the paragraph before the phrase *Section fifty-two hundred and two of the Revised Statutes of the United States is hereby amended so as to read as follows,* 39 Stat. 753, and as if the opening quotation marks that immediately follow that phrase instead precede it. Accordingly, the 1916 Act placed within §13 of the Federal Reserve Act each of the paragraphs between the phrases that introduce the amendments to §§13 and 14 of the Federal Reserve Act, including the paragraph that was later codified as 12 U.S.C. §92. Because the 1918 Act did not amend the Federal Reserve Act, it did not repeal section 92, despite the Court of Appeals' conclusion to the contrary.

NOTES AND QUESTIONS

1. *The answer to the puzzle.*

39 STAT. 752 (1916) CH. 461

An Act To amend certain sections of the Act entitled "Federal reserve Act," approved December twenty-third, nineteen hundred and thirteen. . . . *Be it enacted* . . . That the Act entitled the "Federal Reserve Act," approved December twenty-third, nineteen hundred and thirteen, be, and is hereby, amended as follows:

At the end of section eleven insert a new clause as follows:
"..."

That section thirteen be, and is hereby, amended to read as follows:
"..."

"Section fifty-two hundred and two of the Revised Statutes of the United States is hereby amended so as to read as follows: No national banking association shall at any time be indebted, or in any way liable, to an amount exceeding the amount of its capital stock at such time actually paid in and remaining undiminished by losses or otherwise, except on account of demands of the nature following:

"First. Notes of circulation. . . .

"That in addition to the powers now vested by law in national banking associations organized under the laws of the United States any such association located and doing business in any place the population of which does not exceed five thousand inhabitants, as shown by the last preceding decennial census, may, under such rules and regulations as may be prescribed by the Comptroller of the Currency, act as the agent for any fire, life, or other insurance company authorized by the authorities of the State in which said bank is located to do business in said State. . . .

"Any member bank may accept drafts or bills of exchange drawn upon it having not more than three months' sight to run, exclusive of days of grace, drawn under regulations to be prescribed by the Federal Reserve Board by banks or bankers in foreign countries or dependencies or insular possessions of the United States for the purpose of furnishing dollar exchange as required by the usages of trade in the respective countries, dependencies, or insular possessions. Such drafts or bills may be acquired by Federal reserve banks in such amounts and subject to such regulations, restrictions, and limitations as may be prescribed by the Federal Reserve Board."

On what basis does the Court arrive at this conclusion?

2. *The importance of punctuation.* How importantly should the Court treat punctuation? Should it be treated the same as statutory language or a misused word or a misspelling?

3. *Should the court correct an error?* Do you think the Court is right in its finding that there was an error? If so, do you think the Court ought to correct it? This is the issue in the case that follows.

Harris v. Shanahan
192 Kan. 183, 387 P.2d 771 (1963)

FATZAR, JUDGE.

This action attacks the apportionment of the senate and house of representatives of the Kansas legislature. . . .

Both houses of the 1963 legislature introduced bills to apportion their respective legislative districts. . . . Senate bill 440 repealed the 1947 apportionment of the senate and reapportioned the 40 seats of that body. Based upon the 1962 census of state population of 2,165,009, an average-sized senatorial district should contain approximately 54,125 people. As introduced and passed by the legislature, senate bill 440 apportioned the state into 40 districts of approximately equal population, none of which varied more than approximately 10 percent from the average population figure of 54,125. The bill represented diligent and good-faith effort by the legislature to achieve the standard of equality of representation demanded by Article 10, Section 2, as hereafter noted, and we believe the minds of reasonable men could not doubt that a range of variance above and below the average district of not more than approximately 10 percent constituted as close an approximation to exactness as possible.

Subsequent to the adjournment of the 1963 legislature this court held hearings with respect to the validity of the 1961 apportionment of the multidistrict seats in the house of representatives. At the first hearing counsel for both parties orally stated that the 1963 apportionment of the senate met all the requirements of equal representation imposed by Article 10, Section 2, of the Kansas Constitution and that senate bill 440 should be judicially approved. Since that time, however, it has come to the court's attention that all of the city of Leawood in Johnson County, consisting of approximately 8,800 people, was omitted from senatorial district No. 15 and was not included in any senatorial district. . . .

The existing apportionment of the house of representatives was enacted in 1961 and that of the senate in 1963. Thus, both being current in terms of time within the meaning of Article 10, Section 2, those acts are not subject to change by the legislature until the next constitutional apportionment period unless held to be invalid. Since there is a presumption that laws passed by the legislature are valid and constitutional until judicially determined to be otherwise, the legislature will be powerless to lawfully reapportion until the next apportionment period, unless this court adjudges the present senate apportionment act to be invalid. Accordingly, the effect of the omission of the city of Leawood from any senatorial district must be carefully considered at this time and touched upon in the court's opinion if opportunity for the correction of the senate apportionment is to be afforded prior to the primary and general elections in 1964. . . .

[W]e turn to the contention of the parties as to the validity of senate bill 440. In deciding the question it will be helpful to set out in chronological order the legislative history of the bill. On March 27, 1963, the Senate Committee on Legislative and Congressional Apportionment introduced the bill to apportion the state into 40 senatorial districts. . . . The bill was read the second time on March 28, and referred to the Committee of the Whole Senate. On March 29, the Committee of the Whole recommended that it be passed. On the same day and on an emergency motion, the bill was advanced to third reading and roll call and passed by a vote of 24 yeas and 6 nays. As introduced and passed by the senate, the designation of senatorial district No. 15 commenced on line 48 of the bill and ended on line 54. That part of the bill, including the line numbers, reads:

"48 15. *All* of Aubry and Oxford townships in Johnson county,
"49 *the city of Leawood in Johnson county, all of the territory in*
"50 precincts 3, 4, 5 and 6 of ward 2 and all of the territory in
"51 wards 3, 4, and 5 of the city of Overland Park in Johnson county
"52 and all of the territory in wards 4, 5 and 6 of the city of Prairie
"53 Village in Johnson county shall constitute the fifteenth senatorial
"54 district."

(Emphasis added.)

The bill was messaged to the house on April 1, 1963, and read the first time. The following day the bill was read the second time and referred to the House Committee on Legislative Apportionment. On April 10, and with respect to senatorial district No. 15, the House committee recommended the bill be amended . . .

in line 48, by striking out all of the line after the word "of"; by striking out all of lines 50 to 54, inclusive, and inserting in lieu thereof the following: "all of precincts 4, 5 and 6 of ward 2 and precincts 3, 4, 5, 6 and 7 of ward 3, and all of wards 4 and 5 in the city of Overland Park in Johnson county and precinct 4 in ward 2 and all of wards 4, 5 and 6 in Prairie Village in Johnson county, shall constitute the fifteenth senatorial district." . . .

Thus, it is noted that after the house committee amendments, the only portion remaining in the bill establishing senatorial district 15 was the emphasized portion quoted above. When that language is added to the language inserted by the house committee amendments, senatorial district No. 15 was established to include the following:

> All of the city of Leawood in Johnson county, all of the territory in all of precincts 4, 5 and 6 of ward 2 and precincts 3, 4, 5, 6 and 7 of ward 3, and all of wards 4 and 5 in the city of Overland Park in Johnson county and precinct 4 in ward 2 and all of wards 4, 5 and 6 in Prairie Village in Johnson county, shall constitute the fifteenth senatorial district.

On the same day, April 10, the committee recommended that the bill be passed as amended and the committee report was adopted by the house. On the same day, and on an emergency motion, the bill was advanced to third reading subject to amendment and debate. Thereupon the bill passed the house upon roll call by a vote of 90 yeas and 11 nays. On that same day, April 10, the senate received the bill from the house as amended, and concurred in the house amendments by a vote of 28 yeas and 8 nays. On April 13, under the heading of "Report on Engrossed Bills," senate bill 440 was reported as correctly engrossed. On April 16, under the heading of "Report on Enrolled Bills," the journal of the senate shows that senate bill 440 was correctly enrolled, properly signed, and presented to the governor on that date for his signature. On April 16, under the heading of "Messages from the Governor" the journal of the senate shows that the bill was signed by the governor on April 17, 1963.

Enrolled senate bill 440 appears in the 1963 Session Laws as Chapter 13, pages 29 through 37. Beginning on page 30 of the fourth line from the top, the paragraph pertaining to senatorial district No. 15 reads as follows:

> 15. All of precincts 4, 5 and 6 of ward 2 and precincts 3, 4, 5, 6 and 7 of ward 3, and all of wards 4 and 5 in the city of Overland Park in Johnson county and precinct 4 in ward 2 and all of wards 4, 5 and 6 in Prairie Village in Johnson county, shall constitute the fifteenth senatorial district.

From the foregoing it is obvious that the minds of the house and senate met in common agreement that senate bill 440, as amended by the house, be passed. At some later time, after passage of the bill by both houses; a variation appeared in the language establishing senatorial district No. 15, notwithstanding the senate committee's report that the bill was correctly engrossed and enrolled. Unfortunately, in the engrossing of the bill the language relating to the city of Leawood was omitted, and the remaining language of the house amendment was such as to give no warning of the omission. The enrolled bill blindly followed the language of the engrossed bill, which was approved and signed by the governor on April 17, 1963.

With the undisputed legislative record in mind, let us examine the specific question before us. Is that statute void for the reason that the governor did not sign the bill passed by the legislature? The question requires an examination of our Constitution and previous decisions of this court as to its validity. The pertinent part of Article 2, Section 14, reads:

> Every bill and joint resolution passed by the house of representatives and senate shall, within two days thereafter, be signed by the presiding officers, and presented to the governor; if he approve, he shall sign it; but if not, he shall return it to the house of representatives, which shall enter the objections at large upon its journal and proceed to reconsider the same. . . .

Hence, it is important that we keep in mind the distinction between a bill and a law. A bill never becomes a law until the constitutional prerequisites respecting the manner of enactment have been fully complied with.

Another rule of long standing in this jurisdiction is that before an enrolled bill can be impeached successfully by the journals of the legislature, the latter must show affirmatively, clearly, conclusively and beyond all doubt that the bill as enrolled was not the bill passed. Also, that the records of the legislative journals import absolute verity and are conclusive as to the facts therein affirmatively shown.

Another rule requiring consideration is that it is the policy of the courts to uphold legislative intent rather than to defeat it, and if there is any reasonable way to construe legislation as constitutionally valid it will be so construed. Further, that doubts as to constitutionality always are resolved in favor of validity and statutes are not stricken down unless the infringement of the superior law is clear beyond substantial doubt.

Counsel for both parties assert that this court has not only the power but also the duty to sustain the constitutionality of the act by supplying the words "the city of Leawood in Johnson county, all of the territory in" as the same appears in line 49 of senate bill 440 and as passed by both houses but omitted therefrom when the bill was engrossed and enrolled. It is argued that in many cases of statutory construction the legislative intent can be derived only by inference or implication; that the present case is distinctly different in that speculation or reasoning as to the legislative intent need not and cannot be resorted to; that the record plainly shows the legislative intent and the action it took was to include Leawood in the 15th senatorial district and there is no room whatever for dispute of that fact. They further argue that while the general rule as to ambiguity applies in many cases, it is not always applicable, and that words may be inserted in or added to a statute in order to effectuate the legislative intent; that it is within the power of a court whenever necessary to effectuate legislative intent to supply language in construing an act, inserting such words and clauses as may reasonably appear to be called for; that words may be supplied in a statute in order to give it effect, or to avoid repugnancy or inconsistency with the legislative intent, or where omission is due to inadvertence, mistake, accident or clerical error, or where omission makes the statute absurd and that omissions may be supplied to prevent unconstitutionality. . . .

We have no quarrel with the authorities cited, but they are not authority for the proposition which is sought to be drawn from them, that is, where the legislature passes one bill and another bill is presented to and signed by the governor, the court may reach out and draw from the legislative records the omitted portion of a bill and insert by judicial construction the omitted portion into law. The parties candidly concede there is no ambiguity in that part of the bill which established senatorial district 15. What they ask this court to do is not to construe the statute, but in effect, enlarge it so that what was omitted by inadvertence or error, may be included within its scope. To supply the omissions under these circumstances would transcend the judicial function. This court has the power to declare a legislative act invalid when it infringes the superior law, but it has no power to correct or amend an act, or even construe it when expressed in plain and unambiguous language. The general rule is that where the statute is plain and unambiguous, there is no room left for judicial construction so as to change the language employed therein. In Russell v. Cogswell, it was said:

> . . . Errors plainly clerical in character, mere inadvertences of terminology, and other similar inaccuracies or deficiencies will be disregarded or corrected where the intention of the legislature is plain and unmistakable. But the court cannot delete vital provisions or supply vital omissions in a statute. No matter what the legislature may have really intended to do, *if it did not in fact do it — under any reasonable interpretation of the language used —* the defect is one which the legislature alone can correct. . . .

. . . [I]t was argued that where the legislative records clearly show the legislative intent and affirmatively show the action taken was to include the amendment — in the instant case to include that part of the original bill pertaining to the city of Leawood — the enrolled bill can be impeached successfully to show that it was the intention of both houses and the governor that the bill as passed by the legislature should be construed to be the effective bill, otherwise a clerical employee or printer can effectively thwart the purpose of the legislature and the governor and give to such errant and unknown clerk or printer the power to veto legislation.

The contention overlooks the fact that . . . a duly constituted committee of the legislature reported the bill . . . to be correctly engrossed and enrolled, when in truth and in fact they were not. Despite the fact that the mechanical work of engrossing bills is performed by clerical employees, the duly constituted committees of each body of the legislature cannot escape the responsibility of carefully examining all engrossed and enrolled bills. Had the committees done so in the *Robb* case and in the instant case, the omissions would have been discovered and timely corrected. . . .

We assume that the intention of both houses of the legislature and of the governor was to enact a law which gave adequate senatorial representation to every citizen of Kansas, including the residents of the city of Leawood.

No one questions that fact. But we are confronted with what was done, not what the legislature may have really intended to do. . . . The long and short of this case is that the bill passed by both houses of the legislature was not the bill approved and signed by the governor and this court has no authority to insert what was omitted. The requirements of Article 2, Section 14, are mandatory that the governor sign the same bill which passed the legislature. It follows that the enrolled bill the Governor signed (Laws 1963, Ch. 13) was not made into law in the form and manner prescribed, and is a void enactment.

Due to the nature of senate bill 440 and its importance to the people of the state, we have examined the question somewhat at length. It is to be deeply regretted that as important a law as this, covering a subject of great public interest, should, because of gross carelessness of someone, be wiped bodily from the statute book. But the court is not responsible for this; nor can it usurp the functions of the legislature or the governor, and, by shutting its eyes to the undisputed legislative record, declare a bill as passed by both houses of the legislature, which was never presented to the governor nor approved by him, to be a valid law. It is lamentable that error on the part of engrossing clerks and legislative committees should defeat the action of the legislature. But the strict rule calling for full compliance with constitutional requirements is, in the long run, a good one. In some cases it may work a hardship, but, by and large, it is beneficial to our republican form of government.

NOTES AND QUESTIONS

1. *A clear mistake without judicial remedy.* In this case, it is indisputable that there was a mistake. Why? It is also clear that the legislature intended the bill to include Leawood in the 15th Senatorial District. Given the certainty of the error and certainty of the remedy, why doesn't the court "fix" the statute? Do you think that the court in *National Bank of Oregon* (page 781 of this chapter) would have decided *Harris* differently?

2. *Passing and signing an identical bill.* Assume that the Governor signed the identical bill that the legislature enacted and that this bill excluded Leawood. Assume that the legislative history was silent on Leawood's place in the districting plan, but that, prior to this redistricting, Leawood had been in the 15th Senatorial District. What would the *Harris* court have done? What would you do as a member of the Kansas court?

3. *Adding legislative history.* Assume that you would have not remedied the problem above based on its record. Would any of the following pieces of legislative history make a difference in your decisionmaking? (a) Testimony expressing a desire that Leawood remain in the 15th Senatorial District by the Mayor of Leawood before the appropriate senate committee. (b) A statement noting pleasure in Leawood's continuation in the 15th

Senatorial District by its senator, on the floor prior to the bill's enactment. (c) A statement in the committee report of the appropriate senate committee that Leawood is intended to be part of the 15th Senatorial District.

C. PRIVATE RIGHTS OF ACTION

Through the two cases excerpted in this section, both decided in the same Supreme Court term, we explore the question of legislative silence and private rights of action. In each of these cases, the language of the statute is silent with respect to a private right of action, but the Court is asked to "find" one.

Cannon v. University of Chicago
441 U.S. 677 (1979)

Statute: 20 U.S.C. §1681 (Education Amendments of 1972, tit. IX, §901(a))
No person in the United States shall, on the basis of sex, be excluded from participation in, be denied the benefits of, or be subjected to discrimination under any education program or activity receiving Federal financial assistance. . . .

JUSTICE STEVENS delivered the opinion of the Court. [Internal citations have been omitted except where particularly relevant.]

Petitioner's complaints allege that her applications for admission to medical school were denied by the respondents because she is a woman. Accepting the truth of those allegations for the purpose of its decision, the Court of Appeals held that petitioner has no right of action against respondents that may be asserted in a federal court. . . .

Only two facts alleged in the complaints are relevant to our decision. First, petitioner was excluded from participation in the respondents' medical education programs because of her sex. Second, these education programs were receiving federal financial assistance at the time of her exclusion. These facts, admitted arguendo by respondents' motion to dismiss the complaints, establish a violation of §901(a) of Title IX of the Education Amendments of 1972 (hereinafter Title IX).

That section, in relevant part, provides:

> No person in the United States shall, on the basis of sex, be excluded from participation in, be denied the benefits of, or be subjected to discrimination under any education program or activity receiving Federal financial assistance. . . .

The statute does not, however, expressly authorize a private right of action by a person injured by a violation of §901. . . .

The Court of Appeals agreed that the statute did not contain an implied private remedy. Noting that §902 of Title IX establishes a procedure for the termination of federal financial support for institutions violating §901, the Court of Appeals concluded that Congress intended that remedy to be the exclusive means of enforcement.

After the Court of Appeals' decision was announced, Congress enacted the Civil Rights Attorney's Fees Awards Act of 1976, 90 Stat. 2641, which authorizes an award of fees to prevailing private parties in actions to enforce Title IX. The court therefore granted a petition for a rehearing to consider whether, in the light of that statute, its original interpretation of Title IX had been correct. . . . The court concluded that the 1976 Act was not intended to create a remedy that did not previously exist. . . .

I

First, the threshold question under [Cort v. Ash, 422 U.S. 66 (1975),] is whether the statute was enacted for the benefit of a special class of which the plaintiff is a member. That question is answered by looking to the language of the statute itself. . . .

The language in these statutes [Title IX and similar statutes] — which expressly identifies the class Congress intended to benefit — contrasts sharply with statutory language customarily found in criminal statutes . . . and other laws enacted for the protection of the general public. There would be far less reason to infer a private remedy in favor of individual persons if Congress, instead of drafting Title IX with an unmistakable focus on the benefited class, had written it simply as a ban on discriminatory conduct by recipients of federal funds or as a prohibition against the disbursement of public funds to educational institutions engaged in discriminatory practices.

Unquestionably, therefore, the first of the four factors identified in *Cort* favors the implication of a private cause of action. Title IX explicitly confers a benefit on persons discriminated against on the basis of sex, and petitioner is clearly a member of that class for whose special benefit the statute was enacted.

Second, the *Cort* analysis requires consideration of legislative history. We must recognize, however, that the legislative history of a statute that does not expressly create or deny a private remedy will typically be equally silent or ambiguous on the question. Therefore, in situations such as the present one "in which it is clear that federal law has granted a class of persons certain rights, it is not necessary to show an intention to *create* a private cause of action, although an explicit purpose to *deny* such cause of action would be controlling." *Cort,* 422 U.S., at 82 (emphasis in original).

But this is not the typical case. Far from evidencing any purpose to deny a private cause of action, the history of Title IX rather plainly indicates that Congress intended to create such a remedy.

Title IX was patterned after Title VI of the Civil Rights Act of 1964. Except for the substitution of the word "sex" in Title IX to replace the words "race, color, or national origin" in Title VI, the two statutes use identical language to describe the benefited class. Both statutes provide the same administrative mechanism for terminating federal financial support for institutions engaged in prohibited discrimination. Neither statute expressly mentions a private remedy for the person excluded from participation in a federally funded program. The drafters of Title IX explicitly assumed that it would be interpreted and applied as Title VI had been during the preceding eight years.

In 1972 when Title IX was enacted, the critical language in Title VI had already been construed as creating a private remedy. Most particularly, in 1967, a distinguished panel of the Court of Appeals for the Fifth Circuit squarely decided this issue in an opinion that was repeatedly cited with approval and never questioned during the ensuing five years. In addition, at least a dozen other federal courts reached similar conclusions in the same or related contexts during those years. It is always appropriate to assume that our elected representatives, like other citizens, know the law; in this case, because of their repeated references to Title VI and its modes of enforcement, we are especially justified in presuming both that those representatives were aware of the prior interpretation of Title VI and that that interpretation reflects their intent with respect to Title IX.

Moreover, in 1969, in Allen v. State Board of Elections, 393 U.S. 544, this Court had interpreted the comparable language in §5 of the Voting Rights Act as sufficient to authorize a private remedy. Indeed, during the period between the enactment of Title VI in 1964 and the enactment of Title IX in 1972, this Court had consistently found implied remedies — often in cases much less clear than this. It was after 1972 that this Court decided Cort v. Ash and the other cases cited by the Court of Appeals in support of its strict construction of the remedial aspect of the statute. We, of course, adhere to the strict approach followed in our recent cases, but our evaluation of congressional action in 1972 must take into account its contemporary legal context. In sum, it is not only appropriate but also realistic to presume that Congress was thoroughly familiar with these unusually important precedents from this and other federal courts and that it expected its enactment to be interpreted in conformity with them.

It is not, however, necessary to rely on these presumptions. The package of statutes of which Title IX is one part also contains a provision whose language and history demonstrate that Congress itself understood Title VI, and thus its companion, Title IX, as creating a private remedy. Section 718 of the Education Amendments authorizes federal courts to award attorney's fees to the prevailing parties, other than the United States, in private actions brought against public educational agencies to enforce Title VI in the context of elementary and secondary education. The language of this provision explicitly presumes the availability of private suits to enforce Title VI in the education context. For many such suits, no express cause of action was then available; hence Congress must have assumed that one could be implied under Title VI itself. That assumption was made explicit during the debates on §718 . . . and on Title IX itself, and is consistent with the Executive Branch's apparent understanding of Title VI at the time.

Finally, the very persistence — before 1972 and since, among judges and executive officials, as well as among litigants and their counsel, and even implicit in decisions of this Court — of the assumption that both Title VI and Title IX created a private right of action for the victims of illegal discrimination and the absence of legislative action to change that assumption provide further evidence that Congress at least acquiesces in, and apparently affirms, that assumption. . . . We have no doubt that Congress intended to create Title IX remedies comparable to those available under Title VI and that it understood Title VI as authorizing an implied private cause of action for victims of the prohibited discrimination.

Third, under *Cort,* a private remedy should not be implied if it would frustrate the underlying purpose of the legislative scheme. On the other hand, when that remedy is necessary or at least helpful to the accomplishment of the statutory purpose, the Court is decidedly receptive to its implication under the statute. Title IX, like its model Title VI, sought to accomplish two related, but nevertheless somewhat different, objectives. First, Congress wanted to avoid the use of federal resources to support discriminatory practices; second, it wanted to provide individual citizens effective protection against those practices. Both of these purposes were repeatedly identified in the debates on the two statutes. . . . The award of individual relief to a private litigant who has prosecuted her own suit is not only sensible but is also fully consistent with — and in some cases even necessary to — the orderly enforcement of the statute.

The Department of Health, Education, and Welfare . . . takes the unequivocal position that the individual remedy will provide effective assistance to achieving the statutory purposes. . . .

Fourth, the final inquiry suggested by *Cort* is whether implying a federal remedy is inappropriate because the subject matter involves an area basically of concern to the States. . . . It is the expenditure of federal funds that provides the justification for this particular statutory prohibition. There can be no question but that this aspect of the *Cort* analysis supports the implication of a private federal remedy. . . .

II

Respondents' principal argument against implying a cause of action under Title IX is that it is unwise to subject admissions decisions of universities to judicial scrutiny at the behest of disappointed applicants on a case-by-case basis. They argue that this kind of litigation is burdensome and inevitably will have an adverse effect on the independence of members of university committees.

III

This argument is not original to this litigation. It was forcefully advanced in both 1964 and 1972 by the congressional opponents of Title VI and Title IX, and squarely rejected by the congressional majorities that passed the two statutes. In short, respondents' principal contention is not a legal argument at all; it addresses a policy issue that Congress has already resolved. . . .

Respondents advance two other arguments that deserve brief mention. . . . But each of respondents' arguments is, in any event, unpersuasive.

The fact that other provisions of a complex statutory scheme create express remedies has not been accepted as a sufficient reason for refusing to imply an otherwise appropriate remedy under a separate section. . . . Rather, the Court has generally avoided this type of "excursion into extrapolation of legislative intent," . . . unless there is other, more convincing, evidence that Congress meant to exclude the remedy. . . .

The only excerpt relied upon by respondents that deals precisely with the question whether the victim of discrimination has a private remedy under Title VI was a comment by Senator Keating. In it, he expressed disappointment at the administration's failure to include his suggestion for an express remedy in its final proposed bill. Our analysis of the legislative history convinces us, however, that neither the administration's decision not to incorporate that suggestion expressly in its bill, nor Senator Keating's response to that decision, is indicative of a rejection of a private right of action against recipients of federal funds. Instead, the former appears to have been a compromise aimed at protecting individual rights without subjecting the Government to suits, while the latter is merely one Senator's isolated expression of a preference for an express private remedy. In short, neither is inconsistent with the implication of such a remedy. Nor is there any other indication in the legislative history that any Member of Congress voted in favor of the statute in reliance on an understanding that Title VI did not include a private remedy.

JUSTICE REHNQUIST with whom JUSTICE STEWART joins, concurring.

Having joined the Court's opinion in this case, my only purpose in writing separately is to make explicit what seems to me already implicit in that opinion. . . . The question of the existence of a private right of action is basically one of statutory construction. . . .

We do not write on an entirely clean slate, however, and the Court's opinion demonstrates that Congress, at least during the period of the enactment of the several Titles of the Civil Rights Act, tended to rely to a large extent on the courts to decide whether there should be a private right of action, rather than determining this question for itself. . . .

I fully agree with the Court's statement that "[when] Congress intends private litigants to have a cause of action to support their statutory rights, the far better course is for it to specify as much when it creates those rights." . . . It seems to me that the factors to which I have here briefly adverted apprise the lawmaking branch of the Federal Government that the ball, so to speak, may well now be in its court. Not only is it "far better" for Congress to so specify when it intends private litigants to have a cause of action, but for this very reason this Court in the future should be extremely reluctant to imply a cause of action absent such specificity on the part of the Legislative Branch.

JUSTICE WHITE with whom JUSTICE BLACKMUN joins, dissenting.

In avowedly seeking to provide an additional means to effectuate the broad purpose of §901 of the Education Amendments of 1972, 20 U.S.C. §1681, to end sex discrimination in federally funded educational programs, the Court fails to heed the concomitant legislative purpose not to create a new private remedy to implement this objective. . . .

I

The Court recognizes that because Title IX was explicitly patterned after Title VI of the Civil Rights Act of 1964 . . . it is difficult to infer a private cause of action in the former but not in the latter. I have set out once before my reasons for concluding that a new private cause of action to enforce Title VI should not be implied, University of California Regents v. Bakke, and I find nothing in the legislative materials reviewed by the Court that convinces me to the contrary. Rather, the legislative history, like the terms of Title VI itself, makes it abundantly clear that the Act was and is a mandate to federal agencies to eliminate discrimination in federally funded programs. Although there was no intention to cut back on private remedies existing under 42 U.S.C. §1983 to challenge discrimination occurring under color of state law, there is no basis for concluding that Congress contemplated the creation of private remedies either against private parties who previously had been subject to no constitutional or statutory obligation not to discriminate, or against federal officials or agencies involved in funding allegedly discriminatory programs. . . .

The Court argues that because funding termination, authorized by §602, 42 U.S.C. §2000d-1, is a drastic remedy, Congress must have contemplated private suits in order directly and less intrusively to terminate the discrimination allegedly being practiced by the recipient institutions. But the Court's conclusion does not follow from its premise because funding

termination was not contemplated as the only—or even the primary—
agency action to end discrimination. Rather, Congress considered termination of financial assistance to be a remedy of last resort, and expressly
obligated federal agencies to take measures to terminate discrimination
without resorting to termination of funding. . . .

Title VI was enacted on the proposition that it was contrary at least to the
"moral sense of the Nation" to expend federal funds in a racially discriminatory manner. . . . [C]ongress was plainly dissatisfied with agency efforts
to ensure the nondiscriminatory use of federal funds; and the predicate for
Title VI was the belief that "the time [had] come . . . to declare a broad
principle that is right and necessary, and to make it effective for every
Federal program involving financial assistance by grant, loan or contract."

Far from conferring new private authority to enforce the federal policy of
nondiscrimination, Title VI contemplated agency action to be the principal
mechanism for achieving this end. The proponents of Title VI stressed that
it did not "confer sweeping new authority, of undefined scope, to Federal
departments and agencies," but instead was intended to require the
exercise of existing authority to end discrimination by fund recipients,
and to furnish the procedure for this purpose. Thus, §601 states the federal
policy of nondiscrimination, and §602 mandates that the agencies achieve
compliance by refusing to grant or continue assistance or by "any other
means authorized by law." Under §602, cutting off funds is forbidden
unless the agency determines "that compliance cannot be secured by
voluntary means." . . .

II

The Court further concludes that even if it cannot be persuasively demonstrated that Title VI created a private right of action, nonetheless this
remedy should be inferred in Title IX because prior to its enactment several
lower courts had entertained private suits to enforce the prohibition on
racial discrimination in Title VI. . . . In the case the Court relies upon
most heavily, Bossier Parish School Board v. Lemon, . . . concluding that
plaintiffs could sue to enforce §601, the Court of Appeals expressed its view
that this prohibition merely repeated "the law as laid down in hundreds of
decisions, independent of the statute." Clearly, the defendant was in violation of "the law . . . independent of the statute" only because it was a state
entity, and the court was correct in concluding that §602 did not withdraw
the already existing right to sue to enforce this prohibition. However, to the
extent the court based its holding on the proposition that an individual
protected by a statute always has a right to enforce that statute, it was in
error; and an erroneous interpretation of Title VI should not be com-
pounded through importation into Title IX under the guise of effectuating
legislative intent. There is not one statement in the legislative history

indicating that the Congress that enacted Title IX was aware of the *Bossier* litigation, much less that it adopted the particular theory relied on to uphold plaintiffs' standing in that case.

The Court's reliance on §718 of the 1972 Act . . . is likewise misplaced. . . . Insofar as the provision refers to "discrimination . . . in violation of Title VI," one must strain to conclude that this was meant to encompass private suits against federal agencies whose mandate under Title VI was to enforce §601's nondiscrimination provision applicable to all recipients of federal funds. Rather, in referring to Title VI and the Fourteenth Amendment, §718 did no more than provide for fees in §1983 suits brought to end discrimination under color of state law.

III

The legislative intent not to create a new private remedy for enforcement of Title VI or Title IX cannot be ignored simply because in other cases involving analogous language the Court has recognized private remedies. The recent cases inferring a private right of action to enforce various civil rights statutes relied not merely upon the statutory language granting the right sought to be enforced, but also upon the clear compatibility, despite the absence of an explicit legislative mandate, between private enforcement and the legislative purpose demonstrated in the statute itself. . . .

Congress decided in Title IX, as it had in Title VI, to prohibit certain forms of discrimination by recipients of federal funds. Where those recipients were acting under color of state law, individuals could obtain redress in the federal courts for violation of these prohibitions. But, excepting post-Civil War enactments dealing with racial discrimination in specified situations, these forms of discrimination by private entities had not previously been subject to individual redress under federal law, and Congress decided to reach such discrimination not by creating a new remedy for individuals, but by relying on the authority of the Federal Government to enforce the terms under which federal assistance would be provided. Whatever may be the wisdom of this approach to the problem of private discrimination, it was Congress' choice, not to be overridden by this Court.

JUSTICE POWELL dissenting.

[A]s mounting evidence from the courts below suggests, and the decision of the Court today demonstrates, the mode of analysis we have applied in the recent past cannot be squared with the doctrine of the separation of powers. The time has come to reappraise our standards for the judicial implication of private causes of action.

Under Art. III, Congress alone has the responsibility for determining the jurisdiction of the lower federal courts. As the Legislative Branch, Congress also should determine when private parties are to be given causes of action under legislation it adopts. As countless statutes demonstrate, including Titles of the Civil Rights Act of 1964, Congress recognizes that the creation of private actions is a legislative function and frequently exercises it. When Congress chooses not to provide a private civil remedy, federal courts should not assume the legislative role of creating such a remedy and thereby enlarge their jurisdiction.

The facts of this case illustrate the undesirability of this assumption by the Judicial Branch of the legislative function. Whether every disappointed applicant for admission to a college or university receiving federal funds has the right to a civil-court remedy under Title IX is likely to be a matter of interest to many of the thousands of rejected applicants. It certainly is a question of vast importance to the entire higher educational community of this country. But quite apart from the interests of the persons and institutions affected, respect for our constitutional system dictates that the issue should have been resolved by the elected representatives in Congress after public hearings, debate, and legislative decision. It is not a question properly to be decided by relatively uninformed federal judges who are isolated from the political process. . . .

NOTES AND QUESTIONS

1. *Language and intent.* Title IX, enacted in 1972, contains no private right of action, except one for alleged discriminators whose funding the federal government has terminated. Yet the Court finds that there was a legislative intent to provide such a right. On what basis does the Court discern that the enacting Congress had such a purpose?

2. *Shifting the legislative burden?* According to the Court's analysis, the only way Congress could have assured that Title IX provided no private remedy was to have expressly stated that it did not. Do you agree with this statement? If not, what else could Congress have done? If you do agree, does this make any sense?

3. *The 1972 award for attorneys' fees.* At the time Title IX was being enacted, Congress adopted another bill that authorized a court to award attorneys' fees to prevailing private attorneys in certain Title VI actions. In referring to this provision the Court stated that, despite legislative silence about a private right of action, "Congress must have assumed that one could be implied under Title VI itself." Is the Court stating that this legislative "assumption" by the 1972 Congress evidences the intent of the 1964 Congress that enacted Title VI? If so, is this a rational conclusion about the legislative process? If not, on what basis does this "finding" support the Court's view that the enacting Congress intended Title IX to contain a private right of action?

4. *Judicial and legislative perspectives.* Consider the records on which the Court and Congress made their decisions. Before the Court is the evidence

that a female student has been denied admission to medical school on the basis of gender. The record before Congress, when it was considering Title IX, was one marked by evidence of broad discrimination against women. Despite this record, Congress did not expressly provide for a private remedy. Why do you think they did not? They did provide for an alternative remedy. How would you evaluate its impact? One aspect of the Court's analysis is its conclusion that implying a private right to sue is helpful, and in some cases necessary, to the statutory scheme. Is this a statement of judicial willfulness or of legislative intent?

Touche Ross & Co. v. Redington
442 U.S. 560 (1979)

Statute: 15 U.S.C. §78q(a) (Securities Exchange Act of 1934, §17a(a))

Every national securities exchange, every member thereof, . . . and every broker or dealer registered pursuant to . . . this title, shall make, keep, and preserve for such periods, such accounts, correspondence, . . . and other records, and make such reports, as the Commission by its rules and regulations may prescribe as necessary or appropriate in the public interest or for the protection of investors.

Justice Rehnquist delivered the opinion of the Court. Justice Powell took no part in the consideration or decision of the case.

Once again, we are called upon to decide whether a private remedy is implicit in a statute not expressly providing one. During this Term alone, we have been asked to undertake this task no fewer than five times in cases in which we have granted certiorari. Here we decide whether customers of securities brokerage firms that are required to file certain financial reports with regulatory authorities by §17(a) of the Securities Exchange Act of 1934 (1934 Act), 48 Stat. 897, as amended, 15 U.S.C. §78q(a), have an implied cause of action for damages under §17(a) against accountants who audit such reports, based on misstatements contained in the reports.

I

Petitioner Touche Ross & Co. is a firm of certified public accountants. Weis Securities, Inc. (Weis), a securities brokerage firm registered as a broker-dealer with the Securities and Exchange Commission (Commission) and a member of the New York Stock Exchange (Exchange), retained Touche Ross to serve as Weis' independent certified public accountant from 1969 to 1973. In this capacity, Touche Ross conducted audits of Weis' books and records and prepared for filing with the Commission the annual reports of financial condition required by §17(a) of the 1934 Act,

15 U.S.C. §78q(a). . . . Touche Ross also prepared for Weis responses to financial questionnaires required by the Exchange of its member firms.

This case arises out of the insolvency and liquidation of Weis. In 1973, the Commission and the Exchange learned of Weis' precarious financial condition and of possible violations of the 1934 Act by Weis and its officers. In May 1973, the Commission sought and was granted an injunction barring Weis . . . from conducting business in violation of the 1934 Act. At the same time, the Securities Investor Protection Corporation (SIPC) . . . applied in the United States District Court for the Southern District of New York for a decree adjudging that Weis' customers were in need of the protection afforded by the Securities Investor Protection Act of 1970 (SIPA). The District Court . . . appointed respondent, Redington (Trustee) to act as trustee in the liquidation of the Weis business under SIPA.

During the liquidation, Weis' cash and securities on hand appeared to be insufficient to make whole those customers who had left assets or deposits with Weis. Accordingly, pursuant to SIPA, SIPC advanced the Trustee $14 million to satisfy, up to specified statutory limits, the claims of the approximately 34,000 Weis customers and certain other creditors of Weis. Despite the advance of $14 million by SIPC, there apparently remain several million dollars of unsatisfied customer claims.

In 1976, SIPC and the Trustee filed this action for damages against Touche Ross in the District Court for the Southern District of New York. . . . SIPC and the Trustee seek to impose liability upon Touche Ross by reason of its allegedly improper audit and certification of the 1972 Weis financial statements and preparation of answers to the Exchange financial questionnaire. The federal claims are based on §17(a) of the 1934 Act. . . .

II

The question of the existence of a statutory cause of action is, of course, one of statutory construction. Cannon v. University of Chicago. . . . [O]ur task is limited solely to determining whether Congress intended to create the private right of action asserted by SIPC and the Trustee. And as with any case involving the interpretation of a statute, our analysis must begin with the language of the statute itself.

At the time pertinent to the case before us, §17(a) read, in relevant part, as follows:

> Every national securities exchange, every member thereof, . . . and every broker or dealer registered pursuant to . . . this title, shall make, keep, and preserve for such periods, such accounts, correspondence, . . . and other records, and make such reports, as the Commission by its rules and regulations may prescribe as necessary or appropriate in the public interest or for the protection of investors.

15 U.S.C. §78q(a) (1970 ed.). In terms, §17(a) simply requires broker-dealers and others to keep such records and file such reports as the Commission may prescribe. It does not, by its terms, purport to create a private cause of action in favor of anyone. It is true that in the past our cases have held that in certain circumstances a private right of action may be implied in a statute not expressly providing one. But in those cases finding such implied private remedies, the statute in question at least prohibited certain conduct or created federal rights in favor of private parties. E.g., Cannon v. University of Chicago. By contrast, §17(a) neither confers rights on private parties nor proscribes any conduct as unlawful.

The intent of §17(a) is evident from its face. Section 17(a) is like provisions in countless other statutes that simply require certain regulated businesses to keep records and file periodic reports to enable the relevant governmental authorities to perform their regulatory functions. The reports and records provide the regulatory authorities with the necessary information to oversee compliance with and enforce the various statutes and regulations with which they are concerned. In this case, the §17(a) reports, along with inspections and other information, enable the Commission and the Exchange to ensure compliance with the "net capital rule," the principal regulatory tool by which the Commission and the Exchange monitor the financial health of brokerage firms and protect customers from the risks involved in leaving their cash and securities with broker-dealers. . . . But §17(a) does not by any stretch of its language purport to confer private damages rights or, indeed, any remedy in the event the regulatory authorities are unsuccessful in achieving their objectives and the broker becomes insolvent before corrective steps can be taken. By its terms, §17(a) is forward-looking, not retrospective; it seeks to forestall insolvency, not to provide recompense after it has occurred. In short, there is no basis in the language of §17(a) for inferring that a civil cause of action for damages lay in favor of anyone.

. . . [T]he legislative history of the 1934 Act is entirely silent on the question whether a private right of action for damages should or should not be available under §17(a) in the circumstances of this case. SIPC and the Trustee nevertheless argue that because Congress did not express an intent to deny a private cause of action under §17(a), this Court should infer one. But implying a private right of action on the basis of congressional silence is a hazardous enterprise, at best. And where, as here, the plain language of the provision weighs against implication of a private remedy, the fact that there is no suggestion whatsoever in the legislative history that §17(a) may give rise to suits for damages reinforces our decision not to find such a right of action implicit within the section.

Further justification for our decision not to imply the private remedy that SIPC and the Trustee seek to establish may be found in the statutory scheme of which §17(a) is a part. First, §17(a) is flanked by provisions of the 1934 Act that explicitly grant private causes of action. . . . Obviously, then, when Congress wished to provide a private damages remedy, it knew how to do so and did so expressly. . . .

Second, §18(a) creates a private cause of action against persons, such as accountants, who "make or cause to be made" materially misleading statements in any reports or other documents filed with the Commission, although the cause of action is limited to persons who, in reliance on the statements, purchased or sold a security whose price was affected by the statements. Since SIPC and the Trustee do not allege that the Weis customers purchased or sold securities in reliance on the §17(a) reports at issue, they cannot sue Touche Ross under §18(a). Instead, their claim is that the Weis customers did not get the enforcement action they would have received if the §17(a) reports had been accurate. SIPC and the Trustee argue that §18(a) cannot provide the exclusive remedy for misstatements made in §17(a) reports because the cause of action created by §18(a) is expressly limited to purchasers and sellers. They assert that Congress could not have intended in §18(a) to deprive customers, such as those whom they seek to represent, of a cause of action for misstatements contained in §17(a) reports.

There is evidence to support the view that §18(a) was intended to provide the exclusive remedy for misstatements contained in any reports filed with the Commission, including those filed pursuant to §17(a). Certainly, SIPC and the Trustee have pointed to no evidence of a legislative intent to except §17(a) reports from §18(a)'s purview. . . . But we need not decide whether Congress expressly intended §18(a) to provide the exclusive remedy for misstatements contained in §17(a) reports. For where the principal express civil remedy for misstatements in reports created by Congress contemporaneously with the passage of §17(a) is by its terms limited to purchasers and sellers of securities, we are extremely reluctant to imply a cause of action in §17(a) that is significantly broader than the remedy that Congress chose to provide.

SIPC and the Trustee urge, and the Court of Appeals agreed, that the analysis should not stop here. Relying on the factors set forth in Cort v. Ash, they assert that we also must consider whether an implied private remedy is necessary to "effectuate the purpose of the section" and whether the cause of action is one traditionally relegated to state law. SIPC and the Trustee contend that implication of a private remedy is essential to the goals of §17(a) and that enforcement of §17(a) is properly a matter of federal, not state, concern. We need not reach the merits of the arguments concerning the "necessity" of implying a private remedy and the proper forum for enforcement of the rights asserted by SIPC and the Trustee, for we believe such inquiries have little relevance to the decision of this case. It is true that in Cort v. Ash, the Court set forth four factors that it considered "relevant" in determining whether a private remedy is implicit in a statute not expressly providing one. But the Court did not decide that each of these factors is entitled to equal weight. The central inquiry remains whether

Congress intended to create, either expressly or by implication, a private cause of action. Indeed, the first three factors discussed in *Cort* — the language and focus of the statute, its legislative history, and its purpose — are ones traditionally relied upon in determining legislative intent. Here, the statute by its terms grants no private rights to any identifiable class and proscribes no conduct as unlawful. And the parties as well as the Court of Appeals agree that the legislative history of the 1934 Act simply does not speak to the issue of private remedies under §17(a). At least in such a case as this, the inquiry ends there: The question whether Congress, either expressly or by implication, intended to create a private right of action, has been definitely answered in the negative. . . .

The invocation of the "remedial purposes" of the 1934 Act is similarly unavailing. . . . Certainly, the mere fact that §17(a) was designed to provide protection for brokers' customers does not require the implication of a private damages action in their behalf. Cannon v. University of Chicago. . . . The ultimate question is one of congressional intent, not one of whether this Court thinks that it can improve upon the statutory scheme that Congress enacted into law.

III

SIPC and the Trustee contend that the result we reach sanctions injustice. But even if that were the case, the argument is made in the wrong forum, for we are not at liberty to legislate. If there is to be a federal damages remedy under these circumstances, Congress must provide it. "[It] is not for us to fill any hiatus Congress has left in this area." Wheeldin v. Wheeler, 373 U.S. 647, 652 (1963). Obviously, nothing we have said prevents Congress from creating a private right of action on behalf of brokerage firm customers for losses arising from misstatements contained in §17(a) reports. But if Congress intends those customers to have such a federal right of action, it is well aware of how it may effectuate that intent.

The judgment of the Court of Appeals is reversed, and the case is remanded for further proceedings consistent with this opinion.

Justice Brennan filed a concurring opinion [omitted].

Justice Marshall, dissenting.

In determining whether to imply a private cause of action for damages under a statute that does not expressly authorize such a remedy, this Court has considered four factors: [the *Cort* factors]. . . .

Applying these factors, I believe respondents are entitled to bring an action against accountants who have allegedly breached duties imposed under §17(a) of the Securities Exchange Act of 1934. . . .

NOTES AND QUESTIONS

1. *Cannon and Redington.* In *Cannon,* the Supreme Court finds an implied individual cause of action. In *Redington,* it doesn't. Both were decided in the same Supreme Court term. On what basis does the Court arrive at different decisions? Is Justice Scalia correct when he observes in a 1992 concurrence, "We have abandoned the expansive rights-creating approach exemplified by *Cannon,* see Touche Ross & Co. v. Redington"? Franklin v. Gwinnett County Public Schools, 503 U.S. 60, 77 (1992).

2. *Legislative intent.* In both cases the Court focused on the intent of Congress in enacting the particular statute. In one, it found an intent to enact the right of private action; in the other, it did not. What does the term "legislative intent" mean in each decision? In answering this question, consider the comments of Justice Scalia in his concurrence in Thompson v. Thompson, 484 U.S. 174 (1988):

> I agree that the Parental Kidnaping Prevention Act, 28 U.S.C. §1738A, does not create a private right of action in federal court to determine which of two conflicting child custody decrees is valid. I disagree, however, with the portion of the Court's analysis that flows from the following statement: "Our focus on congressional intent does not mean that we require evidence that Members of Congress, in enacting the statute, actually had in mind the creation of a private cause of action." [Id.], at 179.
>
> I am at a loss to imagine what congressional intent to create a private right of action might mean, if it does not mean that Congress had in mind the creation of a private right of action. Our precedents, moreover, give no indication of a secret meaning, but to the contrary seem to use "intent" to mean "intent." . . . We have said, to be sure, that the existence of intent may be inferred from various indicia; but that is worlds apart from today's Delphic pronouncement that intent is required but need not really exist.

Would Justice Scalia extend such criticism to *Cannon* or *Redington?*

3. *Thurmond and Ginsburg.* As the following exchange between Senator Thurmond and Justice (then nominee) Ruth Bader Ginsburg at her confirmation hearing illustrates, this issue remains a continuing source of concern between the legislature and the judiciary.

> Senator THURMOND. Judge Ginsburg, one very important area of the law is the question of whether courts exceed their authority by creating rights of action for private litigants under Federal statutes where Congress did not expressly provide such rights of action. . . .
>
> Judge GINSBURG. I think that Congress should express itself plainly on the question of private rights of action. I think that judges would welcome that with great enthusiasm. Judges do not lightly imply private rights of action. In some areas of the law, securities law, for example, where private rights of action have been understood by the courts to be the legislature's intention, and that is always what the court is trying to divine, it appears that

the legislature has been content with those implications. It has left them alone now for in some cases even decades.

But I think the judges have said often enough in opinions, we are going to try to find out and try to determine as best we can whether Congress intended there to be a private right of action. We wish that Congress would speak clearly to this question, because, as you said, Senator, the existence of a private right of action or not is for Congress to say.

Isn't Justice Ginsburg's criticism of Congress better addressed to the judiciary for creating the problem of "statutes" by implication? Is it Congress' responsibility to state affirmatively in a statute that there shall be no private right of action?

4. *Legislative silence.* Legislatures do not set forth remedies (or other provisions) in a statute for the following reasons: (1) They don't want to. (2) They forget to. (3) They didn't think to. (4) They can't reach a consensus to. Do you think a court ever ought to supply a remedy? If so, in which cases?

D.   LEGISLATIVE HISTORY

Conroy v. Aniskoff
507 U.S. 511 (1993)

Statute: 50 U.S.C. App. §525 (Soldiers' and Sailors' Relief Act of 1940, §525)

The period of military service shall not be included in computing any period now or hereafter to be limited by any law, regulation, or order for the bringing of any action or proceeding in any court, board, bureau, commission, department, or other agency of government by or against any person in military service or by or against his heirs, executors, administrators, or assigns, whether such cause of action or the right or privilege to institute such action or proceeding shall have accrued prior to or during the period of such service, nor shall any part of such period which occurs after the date of enactment of the Soldiers' and Sailors' Civil Relief Act Amendments of 1942 be included in computing any period now or hereafter provided by any law for the redemption of real property sold or forfeited to enforce any obligation, tax, or assessment.

JUSTICE STEVENS delivered the opinion of the Court. [Internal citations have been omitted except where particularly relevant.]

The Soldiers' and Sailors' Civil Relief Act of 1940, 54 Stat. 1178, as amended, 50 U.S.C. App. §501 et seq. (Act), suspends various civil liabilities of persons in military service. At issue in this case is the provision in §525 that the "period of military service shall not be included in computing any period . . . provided by any law for the redemption of real property sold or forfeited to enforce any obligation, tax, or assessment." The question presented is whether a member of the Armed Services must show that his military service prejudiced his ability to redeem title to property before he can qualify for the statutory suspension of time.

I

Petitioner is an officer in the United States Army. He was on active duty continuously from 1966 until the time of trial. In 1973 he purchased a parcel of vacant land in the town of Danforth, Maine. He paid taxes on the property for 10 years, but failed to pay the 1984, 1985, and 1986 local real estate taxes. In 1986, following the Maine statutory procedures that authorize it to acquire tax-delinquent real estate, the town sold the property. . . .

II

The statutory command in §525 is unambiguous, unequivocal, and unlimited. It states that the period of military service "shall not be included" in the computation of "any period now or hereafter provided by any law for the redemption of real property. . . ." Respondents do not dispute the plain meaning of this text. Rather, they argue that when §525 is read in the context of the entire statute, it implicitly conditions its protection on a demonstration of hardship or prejudice resulting from military service. They make three points in support of this argument: that the history of the Act reveals an intent to provide protection only to those whose lives have been temporarily disrupted by military service; that other provisions of the Act are expressly conditioned on a showing of prejudice; and that a literal interpretation produces illogical and absurd results. Neither separately nor in combination do these points justify a departure from the unambiguous statutory text.

Respondents correctly describe the immediate cause for the statute's enactment in 1940, the year before our entry into World War II. Congress stated its purpose to "expedite the national defense under the emergent conditions which are threatening the peace and security of the United States. . . ." 50 U.S.C. App. §510. That purpose undoubtedly contemplated the special hardship that military duty imposed on those suddenly drafted into service by the national emergency. Neither that emergency, nor a particular legislative interest in easing sudden transfers from civilian to military status, however, justifies the conclusion that Congress did not intend all members of the Armed Forces, including career personnel, to receive the Act's protections. Indeed, because Congress extended the life of the Act indefinitely in 1948, well after the end of World War II, the complete legislative history confirms a congressional intent to protect all military personnel on active duty, just as the statutory language provides.

Respondents also correctly remind us to "follow the cardinal rule that a statute is to be read as a whole, since the meaning of statutory language, plain or not, depends on context." But . . . the context of this statute actually supports the conclusion that Congress meant what §525 says. Several provisions of the statute condition the protection they offer on a showing that military service adversely affected the ability to assert or protect a legal right. To choose one of many examples, §5332(2) authorizes a stay of enforcement of secured obligations unless "the ability of the defendant to comply with the terms of the obligation is not materially affected by reason of his military service." The comprehensive character of the entire statute indicates that Congress included a prejudice requirement whenever it considered it appropriate to do so, and that its omission of any such requirement in §525 was deliberate. . . .

Finally, both the history of this carefully reticulated statute, and our history of interpreting it, refute any argument that a literal construction of §525 is so absurd or illogical that Congress could not have intended it. . . .

Legislative history confirms that assumption. Since the enactment of the 1918 Act, Congress has expressed its understanding that absolute exemptions might save time or money for service members only at the cost of injuring their own credit, their family's credit, and the domestic economy; it presumably required a showing of prejudice only when it seemed necessary to confer on the service member a genuine benefit. By distinguishing sharply between the two types of protections, Congress unquestionably contemplated the ways that either type of protection would affect both military debtors and their civilian creditors.

The long and consistent history and the structure of this legislation therefore lead us to conclude that—just as the language of §525 suggests—Congress made a deliberate policy judgment placing a higher value on firmly protecting the service member's redemption rights than on occasionally burdening the tax collection process. Given the limited number of situations in which this precisely structured statute offers such absolute protection, we cannot say that Congress would have found our straightforward interpretation and application of its words either absurd or illogical. If the consequences of that interpretation had been—or prove to be—as unjust as respondents contend, we are confident that Congress would have corrected the injustice—or will do so in the future.

The judgment of the Supreme Judicial Court of Maine is reversed. . . .

Justice Scalia, concurring in the judgment.

The Court begins its analysis with the observation: "The statutory command in §525 is unambiguous, unequivocal, and unlimited." In my view, discussion of that point is where the remainder of the analysis should have ended. Instead, however, the Court feels compelled to demonstrate that its holding is consonant with legislative history, including some dating back to 1917 — a full quarter century before the provision at issue was enacted. That is not merely a waste of research time and ink; it is a false and disruptive lesson in the law. It says to the bar that even an "unambiguous [and] unequivocal" statute can never be dispositive; that, presumably under penalty of malpractice liability, the oracles of legislative history, far into the dimmy past, must always be consulted. This undermines the clarity of law, and condemns litigants (who, unlike us, must pay for it out of their own pockets) to subsidizing historical research by lawyers.

The greatest defect of legislative history is its illegitimacy. We are governed by laws, not by the intentions of legislators. As the Court said in 1844: "The law as it passed is the will of the majority of both houses, and the only mode in which that will is spoken is in the act itself. . . ." But not the least of the defects of legislative history is its indeterminacy. If one were to search for an interpretive technique that, on the whole, was more likely to confuse than to clarify, one could hardly find a more promising candidate than legislative history. And the present case nicely proves that point.

Judge Harold Leventhal used to describe the use of legislative history as the equivalent of entering a crowded cocktail party and looking over the heads of the guests for one's friends. If I may pursue that metaphor: The legislative history of §205 [codified as §525] of the Soldiers' and Sailors' Civil Relief Act contains a variety of diverse personages, a selected few of whom — its "friends" — the Court has introduced to us in support of its result. But there are many other faces in the crowd, most of which, I think, are set against today's result.

I will limit my exposition of the legislative history to the enactment of four statutes:

1. The Soldiers' and Sailors' Civil Relief Act of 1918 (1918 Act), 40 Stat. 440;
2. The Soldiers' and Sailors' Civil Relief Act of 1940 (1940 Act or Act), 54 Stat. 1178;
3. The Soldiers' and Sailors' Civil Relief Act Amendments of 1942 (1942 Amendments), 56 Stat. 769;
4. The Selective Service Act of 1948, 62 Stat. 604.

That, of course, cannot be said to be the "complete legislative history" relevant to this provision. . . . One of the problems with legislative history is that it is inherently open-ended. In this case, for example, one could go back further in time to examine the Civil War-era relief Acts, many of which are in fact set forth in an appendix to the House Report on the 1918 Act (hereinafter 1917 House Report). Or one could extend the search abroad and consider the various foreign statutes that were mentioned in that same House Report. Those additional statutes might be of questionable relevance, but then so too are the 1918 Act and the 1940 Act, neither of which contained a provision governing redemption periods. Nevertheless, I will limit my legislative history inquiry to those four statutes for the simple reason that that is the scope chosen by the Court.

The 1918 Act appears to have been the first comprehensive national soldiers' relief Act. The legislative history reveals that Congress intended that it serve the same vital purpose — providing "protection against suit to men in military service" — as various state statutes had served during the Civil War. Congress intended, however, that the 1918 Act should differ from the Civil War statutes "in two material respects." . . . [I]t is the second difference which has particular relevance to the Court's ruling today:

> The next material difference between this law and the various State laws is this, and in this I think you will find the chief excellence of the bill which we propose: Instead of the bill we are now considering being arbitrary, inelastic, inflexible, the discretion as to dealing out even-handed justice between the creditor and the soldier, taking into consideration the fact that the soldier has been called to his country's cause, rests largely, and in some cases entirely, in the breast of the judge who tries the case.

(Statement of Rep. Webb.) This comment cannot be dismissed as the passing remark of an insignificant Member, since the speaker was the Chairman of the House Judiciary Committee, the committee that reported the bill to the House floor. Moreover, his remarks merely echoed the House Report, which barely a page into its text stated: "We cannot point out too soon, or too emphatically, that the bill is not an inflexible stay of all claims against persons in military service." Congress intended to depart from the "arbitrary and rigid protection" that had been provided under the Civil War-era stay laws, which could give protection to men "who can and should pay their obligations in full," id., at 3. It is clear, therefore, that in the 1918 Act Congress intended to create flexible rules that would permit denial of protection to members of the military who could show no hardship.

The 1918 Act expired by its own terms six months after the end of the First World War. See 1918 Act, §603, 40 Stat. 449. The 1940 Act was adopted as the Nation prepared for its coming participation in the Second World War. Both the House and Senate Reports described it as being, "in substance, identical with the [1918 Act]." Moreover, in Boone v. Lightner, we acknowledged that the 1940 Act was "a substantial reenactment" of the 1918 Act, and looked to the legislative history of the 1918 Act for indications of congressional intent with respect to the 1940 Act. Relying on that legislative history, we found that "the very heart of the policy of the Act" was to provide "judicial discretion . . . instead of rigid and undiscriminating suspension of civil proceedings."

Although the Court never mentions this fact, it is clear that under the 1918 and 1940 Acts a redemption period would not be tolled during the period of military service. In both enactments, §205 governed only statutes of limitations and did not mention redemption periods. Moreover, in Ebert v. Poston, this Court held that neither §205 nor §302, which provides protection from foreclosures, conferred on a court any power to extend a statutory redemption period. Congress overturned the rule of *Ebert* in the 1942 Amendments, a central part of the legislative history that the Court curiously fails to discuss. Section 5 of those amendments rewrote §205 of the Act to place it in its current form, which directly addresses the redemption periods. The crucial question in the present case (if one believes in legislative history) is whether Congress intended this amendment to be consistent with the "heart of the policy of the Act"—conferring judicial discretion—or rather intended it to confer an unqualified right to extend the period of redemption. Both the House and Senate Reports state that, under the amended §205, "the running of the statutory period during which real property may be redeemed after sale to enforce any obligation, tax, or assessment is likewise tolled during the part of such period which occurs after enactment of the [1942 Amendments]." The Reports also state that "although the tolling of such periods is now within the spirit of the law, it has not been held to be within the letter thereof" (citing *Ebert*). These statements surely indicate an intention to provide a tolling period for redemptions similar to that already provided for statutes of limitations—which, on the basis of the legislative history I have described, can be considered discretionary rather than rigid. The existence of discretionary authority to suspend the tolling is also suggested by the House floor debates. Responding to questions, Representative Sparkman (who submitted the Report on behalf of the House Committee on Military Affairs) agreed that, while the bill "pertains to all persons in the armed forces," a man "serving in the armed forces for more money than he got in civil life . . . is not entitled to any of the benefits of the provisions of this bill." In response to that last comment, another representative inquired further whether "this is to take care of the men who are handicapped because of their military service." Representative Sparkman answered affirmatively. He confirmed that Congress did not intend to abandon the discretionary nature of the scheme: "With reference to all these matters we have tried to make the law flexible by lodging discretion within the courts to do or not to do as justice and equity may require." And finally, at a later point in the debates, Representative Brooks made clear that the Act was intended to remedy the prejudice resulting from compelled military service: "We feel that the normal obligations of the man contracted prior to service induction should be suspended as far as practicable during this tour of duty, and that the soldier should be protected from default in his obligations due to his inability to pay caused by reduction in income due to service."

The final component of the legislative history that I shall treat is the extension of the 1940 Act in the Selective Service Act of 1948. The Court misconstrues Congress's intent in this enactment in two respects. First, it asserts that "because Congress extended the life of the Act indefinitely in 1948, well after the end of World War II, the complete legislative history confirms a congressional intent to protect all military personnel on active duty, just as the statutory language provides." It is true enough that the War was over; but the draft was not. The extension of the 1940 Act was contained in the Selective Service Act of 1948, which required military service from citizens. And it would appear to have been contemplated that the "life of the Act" would be extended not "indefinitely," as the Court says, but for the duration of the draft. See H.R. Rep. No. 1881, 80th Cong., 2d Sess., 12 (1948) (extension was intended to "continue the Soldiers' and Sailors' Civil Relief Act of 1940 in its application to the personnel inducted or entering the armed forces during the life of this act"). The legislative history states that Congress intended to extend the provisions of the 1940 Act "to persons serving in the armed forces pursuant to this act." Career members of the military such as petitioner would not have been serving "pursuant to" the Selective Service Act, since they were expressly excepted from its service requirement. . . . In this focus upon draftees, the legislative history of the 1948 extension merely replicates that of the 1940 Act and the 1942 Amendments. The former was enacted on the heels of the Selective Training and Service Act of 1940, and was introduced on the Senate floor with the explanation that it would provide "relief . . . to those who are to be inducted into the military service for training under [the Selective Training and Service Act of 1940]." 86 Cong. Rec. 10292 (1940) (statement of Rep. Overton). In the debate on the 1942 Amendments, Representative Sparkman noted that "hundreds of thousands, and even millions, have been called" into military service since the enactment of the 1940 Act, and admonished his colleagues to "keep uppermost in your mind at all times the fact that the primary purpose of this legislation is to give relief to the boy that is called into service." In other words, the legislative history of the 1948 extension, like that of the Act itself and of the 1942 Amendments, suggests an intent to protect those who were prejudiced by military service, as many who were drafted would be.

The Court also errs in mistaking the probable effect of Congress's presumed awareness of our earlier opinions in *Ebert* and *Boone*. In *Boone*, we stated that the Act "is always to be liberally construed to protect those who have been obliged to drop their own affairs and take up the burdens of the nation," but that discretion was vested in the courts to insure that the immunities of the Act are not put to "unworthy use," since "the very heart of the policy of the Act" was to provide "judicial discretion . . . instead of rigid and undiscriminating suspension of civil proceedings." Awareness of *Boone* would likely have caused Congress to assume that the courts would vindicate "the very heart of the policy of the Act" by requiring a showing of prejudice. The Court argues, however, that Congress would also have been aware that *Ebert* recognized the "carefully segregated arrangement of the various provisions" of the Act. It is already an extension of the normal convention to assume that Congress was aware of the precise reasoning (as opposed to the holding) of earlier judicial opinions; but it goes much further to assume that Congress not only knew, but expected the courts would continue to follow, the reasoning of a case (*Ebert*) whose holding Congress had repudiated six years earlier. In any event, the Court seeks to use *Ebert* only to establish that Congress was aware that this Court was aware of the "carefully segregated arrangement" of the Act. That adds little, if anything, to direct reliance upon the plain language of the statute.

After reading the above described legislative history, one might well conclude that the result reached by the Court today, though faithful to law, betrays the congressional intent. Many have done so. Indeed, as far as I am aware, every court that has chosen to interpret §205 in light of its legislative history rather than on the basis of its plain text has found that Congress did not intend §205 to apply to career members of the military who cannot show prejudice or hardship. The only scholarly commentary I am aware of addressing this issue concludes: "An examination of the legislative history of the Act shows that the prevailing interpretation of section 205 [i.e., the Court's interpretation] is not consistent with congressional intent." Finally, even the Government itself, which successfully urged in this case the position we have adopted, until recently believed, on the basis of legislative history, the contrary.

I confess that I have not personally investigated the entire legislative history — or even that portion of it which relates to the four statutes listed above. The excerpts I have examined and quoted were unearthed by a hapless law clerk to whom I assigned the task. The other Justices have, in the aggregate, many more law clerks than I, and it is quite possible that if they all were unleashed upon this enterprise they would discover, in the legislative materials dating back to 1917 or earlier, many faces friendly to the Court's holding. Whether they would or not makes no difference to me — and evidently makes no difference to the Court, which gives lipservice to legislative history but does not trouble to set forth and discuss the foregoing material that others found so persuasive. In my view, that is as it should be, except for the lipservice. The language of the statute is entirely clear, and if that is not what Congress meant then Congress has made a mistake and Congress will have to correct it. We should not pretend to care about legislative intent (as opposed to the meaning of the law), lest we impose upon the practicing bar and their clients obligations that we do not ourselves take seriously.

NOTES AND QUESTIONS

1. *Language and intent.* In consideration of the applicability of this statute, there is no argument over the clarity of the legislative prescription.

The decision of the Maine court, reversed by this decision, also found the statute clear, but believed that outcome of its application in this case would have been inconsistent with legislative intent. What is important about this case is the review of legislative history by the Court, notwithstanding the clarity of the statute and Justice Scalia's argument against this endeavor. In Tennessee Valley Authority v. Hill, the Court makes reference to the legislative history of the endangered species legislation. With respect to the use of legislative history, the Court writes in footnote 29:

> When confronted with a statute which is plain and unambiguous on its face, we ordinarily do not look to legislative history as a guide to its meaning. Here it is not necessary to look beyond the words of the statute. We have undertaken such an analysis only to meet Justice Powell's suggestion that the "absurd" result reached in this case is not in accord with congressional intent.

Despite this statement, the Court, in *Conroy*, looks to the legislative history. Why did it do this? In responding, consider the following remarks of Judge Patricia Wald:

> As we conscientiously embark on our duty to ascertain what the words mean in the context of the statute's aims and purposes, we are almost inevitably drawn to the historical record of what the men and women who proposed and sponsored the legislation intended to enact. We feel better when their words confirm our reading of the text; we worry more when it contradicts the text. This does not mean, as the textualist Justices accuse, that we "transform" every "snippet of analysis" in congressional reports into "the law of the land" or "elevate to the level of statutory text a phrase taken from the legislative history." It does mean, however, that we think again when we face a contradiction between text and history and we should. That, in a nutshell, explains why we still resort to legislative history even when we label the meaning of a statutory provision "plain" or "clear."

Patricia M. Wald, The Sizzling Sleeper: The Use of Legislative History in Construing Statutes in the 1988-89 Term of the United States Supreme Court, 39 Am. U. L. Rev. 277, 301 (1990). For an example of Judge Wald following this course, see Georgetown University Hospital v. Bowen, 862 F.2d 323 (D.C. Cir. 1988): "Our 'plain meaning' reading of the statutory provision . . . is consistent with the available legislative history." Id. at 328. In concurrence, Judge Mikva wrote: "I concur in the decision and excellent opinion of the Chief Judge, except for the expendable discussion of legislative history. I believe that when the plain meaning of a statute is found, it is unnecessary and unwise to delve further." Id. at 330.

An important question raised by Judge Wald's approach is what to do if the legislative history suggests an answer contrary to the language. Isn't this Justice Scalia's point? Based on his analysis, would you dissent from the majority opinion? For a case in which legislative history trumps legislative language, see Train v. Colorado Public Interest Research Group, which follows these Notes and Questions.

2. *A canon of construction.* The Court in its analysis makes favorable reference to a canon of construction that it characterizes as "the cardinal rule that a statute is to be read as a whole, since the meaning of statutory language, plain or not, depends on content." How does the Court use this canon, and what does it mean? Do you think it is a reasonable presumption about the legislative enactment process?

3. *The Scalia view and the Court's response.* Note carefully the arguments Justice Scalia makes against the use of legislative history, at least in the case of clear statutes. What are the bases on which he opposes the Court's use of legislative history in this case? The Court responds to Justice Scalia's criticism in footnote 12 of its decision:

> In his . . . opinion concurring in the judgment, Justice Scalia suggests that our response to respondent's reliance on legislative history "is not merely a waste of research time and ink," but also "a false and disruptive lesson in the law." His "hapless law clerk" has found a good deal of evidence in the legislative history that many provisions of this statute were intended to confer discretion on trial judges. That, of course, is precisely our point: it is reasonable to conclude that Congress intended to authorize such discretion when it expressly provided for it and to deny such discretion when it did not. A jurisprudence that confines a court's inquiry to the "law as it is passed," and is wholly unconcerned about "the intentions of legislators," would enforce an unambiguous statutory text even when it produces manifestly unintended and profoundly unwise consequences. Respondent has argued that this is such a case. We disagree. Justice Scalia, however, is apparently willing to assume that this is such a case, but would nevertheless conclude that we have a duty to enforce the statute as written even if fully convinced that every Member of the enacting Congress, as well as the President who signed the Act, intended a different result. Again, we disagree.

What do you think of Justice Scalia's argument and the Court's response?

Train v. Colorado Public Interest Research Group
426 U.S. 1 (1976)

Statute: 33 U.S.C. §§1311, 1342, 1362 (Federal Water Pollution Control Act)

33 U.S.C. §1311. Except as in compliance with this section and section . . . 1342 . . . of this title, the discharge of any pollutants by any person shall be unlawful.

33 U.S.C. §1342. (1) [T]he Administrator may . . . issue a permit for the discharge of any pollutant . . . notwithstanding section 1311(a) of this title. . . .

33 U.S.C. §1362. . . . (6) The term "pollutant" means . . . radioactive materials. . . .

(19) The term "discharge" when used without qualification includes a discharge of a pollutant, and a discharge of pollutants.

JUSTICE MARSHALL delivered the opinion of the Court, in which all Members joined except JUSTICE STEVENS, who took no part in the consideration or decision of the case. [Internal citations have been omitted except where particularly relevant.] . . .

I

Respondents are Colorado-based organizations and Colorado residents who claim potential harm from the discharge of radioactive effluents from two nuclear plants. . . . These facilities are operated in conformity with radioactive effluent standards imposed by the AEC pursuant to the Atomic Energy Act. The dispute in this case arises because the EPA has disclaimed any authority under the FWPCA [Federal Water Pollution Control Act] to set standards of its own to govern the discharge of radioactive materials subject to regulation under the AEA. . . .

II

Since 1946, when the first Atomic Energy Act was passed, the Federal Government has exercised control over the production and use of atomic energy through the AEC — replaced since the commencement of this litigation by the Nuclear Regulatory Commission (NRC) and the Energy Research and Development Administration (ERDA). . . .

The comprehensive regulatory scheme created by the AEA embraces the production, possession, and use of three types of radioactive materials — source material, special nuclear material, and byproduct material. In carrying out its regulatory duties under the AEA, the AEC is authorized to establish "such standards . . . as [it] may deem necessary or desirable . . . to protect health or to minimize danger to life or property." 42 U.S.C. §2201(b). Pursuant to this authority, the AEC (NRC) has established by regulation maximum permissible releases of source, byproduct, and special nuclear materials into the environment by licensees. . . .

The FWPCA established a regulatory program to control and abate water pollution, stating as its ultimate objective the elimination of all discharges of "pollutants" into the navigable waters by 1985. In furtherance of this objective, the FWPCA calls for the achievement of effluent limitations that require applications of the "best practicable control technology currently available" by July 1, 1977, and the "best available technology economically achievable" by July 1, 1983. 33 U.S.C. §1311(b) (1970 ed., Supp. IV). These effluent limitations are enforced through a permit program. The discharge of "pollutants" into water is unlawful without a permit issued by the Administrator of the EPA or, if a State has developed a program that complies with the FWPCA, by the State. 33 U.S.C. §§1311(a), 1342 (1970 ed., Supp. IV).

The term "pollutant" is defined by the FWPCA to include, inter alia, "radioactive materials." But when the Administrator of the EPA adopted regulations governing the permit program, he specifically excluded source, byproduct, and special nuclear materials — those covered by the AEA — from the program upon his understanding of the relevant legislative history of the FWPCA:

> The legislative history of the Act reflects that the term "radioactive materials" as included within the definition of "pollutant" in section 502 of the Act covers only radioactive materials which are not encompassed in the definition of source, byproduct, or special nuclear materials as defined by the Atomic Energy Act of 1954, as amended, and regulated pursuant to the latter Act. Examples of radioactive materials not covered by the Atomic Energy Act and, therefore, included within the term "pollutant" are radium and accelerator produced isotopes. . . .

III

The Court of Appeals resolved the question exclusively by reference to the language of the statute. It observed that the FWPCA defines "pollution" as "the man-made or man-induced alteration of the chemical, physical, biological, and radiological integrity of water." 33 U.S.C. §1362(19) (1970 ed., Supp. IV). And it noted that the reference to "radioactive materials" in the definition of "pollutant" was without express qualification or exception, despite the fact that the overall definition of "pollutant" does contain two explicit exceptions. The court concluded from this analysis of the language that by the reference to "radioactive materials" Congress meant all radioactive materials. The court explained:

> In our view, then, the statute is plain and unambiguous and should be given its obvious meaning. Such being the case . . . we need not here concern ourselves with the legislative history of the 1972 Amendments. In this regard we would note parenthetically that in our view the legislative history of the 1972 Amendments is conflicting and inconclusive. Be that as it may, in the case before us there is no need to address ourselves to the ofttimes difficult task of ascertaining legislative intent through legislative history. Here, the legislative intent is clearly manifested in the language of the statute itself, and we need not resort to legislative history.

To the extent that the Court of Appeals excluded reference to the legislative history of the FWPCA in discerning its meaning, the court was in error. As we have noted before: "When aid to construction of the meaning of words, as used in the statute, is available, there certainly can be no 'rule of law' which forbids its use, however clear the words may appear on 'superficial examination.' " United States v. American Trucking Assns., 310 U.S. 534, 543-44 (1940). In this case, as we shall see, the legislative history sheds considerable light on the question before the Court. . . .

IV

The legislative history of the FWPCA speaks with force to the question whether source, byproduct, and special nuclear materials are "pollutants" subject to the Act's permit program. The House Committee Report was quite explicit on the subject:

> The term "pollutant" as defined in the bill includes "radioactive materials." *These materials are those not encompassed in the definition of source, byproduct, or special nuclear materials as defined by the Atomic Energy Act of 1954, as amended, and regulated pursuant to that Act. "Radioactive materials" encompassed by this bill are those beyond the jurisdiction of the Atomic Energy Commission.* Examples of radioactive material not covered by the Atomic Energy Act, and, therefore, included within the term "pollutant," are radium and accelerator produced isotopes.

(Emphasis added.)

The definition of "pollutant" in the House version of the bill contained the same broad reference to "radioactive materials" as did the definition in the Senate bill, and the bill ultimately enacted as the FWPCA; for our purposes the definitions are identical. Moreover, the House version of the bill contained the provision now codified as §1311(f), banning the discharge of radiological warfare agents and high-level radioactive waste "[n]otwitstanding any other provisions of this Act." Thus, the House Committee, describing the import of the precise statutory language with which we are concerned, cautioned that the definition of "pollutant" did not include those radioactive materials subject to regulation under the AEA.

Respondents claim to find in the Senate Committee Report an indication that the statutory definition of "pollutant" embraces radioactive materials subject to AEA regulation. Section 306 of the Senate bill, which corresponds to 33 U.S.C. §1316 (1970 ed., Supp. IV), required that the EPA Administrator establish "standards of performance" with respect to the discharge of pollutants from specified categories of sources, to be revised from time to time by the Administrator. The Senate Committee Report noted that nuclear fuels processing plants were not included, because the EPA did not then have "the technical capability to establish controls for such plants."

The Report then observed that the Committee "expects that EPA will develop the capability," and continued:

> The Bureau of Radiological Health, which was transferred to the Environmental Protection Agency, should have the capacity to determine those levels of control which can be achieved for nuclear fuels processing plants. If they do not, such a capability should be developed and this particular source should be added to the list of new sources as soon as possible.

Petitioners assert that this statement by the Committee has no bearing on the question before the Court. The statement, petitioners suggest, reflects no more than a recognition, shared by them, that the plants referred to were not intended to be wholly excluded from the reach of the FWPCA—a recognition that in their view means that the EPA can control the discharge from such plants of polluting materials other than source, byproduct, and special nuclear materials. In short, petitioners contend that the statement sheds no light on the question whether source, byproduct, and special nuclear materials are pollutants under the FWPCA.

We agree with the petitioners that the Senate Committee statement is addressed to the inclusion of nuclear fuels processing plants in the category of sources subject to the EPA's control, not to the inclusion of any particular materials within the definition of "pollutant." It is true that the reference to the development of control levels by the Bureau of Radiological Health does permit the inference that the Committee was contemplating controls over the discharge of AEA-regulated radioactive materials. Still, we are not prepared to attribute greater significance to this inference than to the more explicit statement contained in the House Committee Report, a statement that, as we shall see, is amply supported by the discussion on the floors of the House and the Senate.

A colloquy on the Senate floor between Senator Pastore, the Chairman of the Joint Committee on Atomic Energy, and Senator Muskie, the FWPCA's primary author, provides a strong indication that Congress did not intend the FWPCA to alter the AEC's control over the discharge of source, byproduct, and special nuclear materials. Senator Pastore, referring to the need to define what materials are "subject to control requirements" under the FWPCA, noted that the definition of "pollutant" included the words "radioactive materials." The following exchange then took place:

> Mr. PASTORE. . . .
> My question is this: Does this measure that has been reported by the committee in any way affect the existing law, that is, the existing Atomic Energy Act of 1954, insofar as the regulatory powers of the AEC are concerned with reference to radioactive material?
> Mr. MUSKIE.   It does not; and it is not the intent of this act to affect the 1954 legislation.

Mr. PASTORE.   In other words, this bill does not change that feature of the Atomic Energy Act in any regard?

Mr. MUSKIE.   That is correct. . . .

Respondents contend that this colloquy "merely reiterates that the FWPCA does not alter the regulatory authority of the AEC" over source, byproduct, and special nuclear materials. The exchange, they assert, says nothing about the EPA's authority to regulate the same materials. The discussion is consistent, they claim, with their position that the AEC must defer to the EPA in the setting of effluent limitations for AEA-regulated materials — that, for example, NRC licenses must conform to permits issued under the FWPCA. We disagree.

The thrust of Senator Muskie's assurances that the FWPCA would not "in any way affect" the regulatory powers of the AEC was, we think, that the AEC was to retain full authority to regulate the materials covered by the AEA, unaltered by the exercise of regulatory authority by any agency under the FWPCA. . . .

In the course of the House's consideration of the FWPCA, an unsuccessful attempt was made to alter the AEA's scheme for regulating the discharge of the radioactive materials involved in this case. Representative Wolff proposed to amend what is now 33 U.S.C. §1370 (1970 ed., Supp. IV), which gives States the authority to set more stringent limits on the discharge of pollutants, by adding a paragraph giving the States the authority to regulate the discharge of radioactive wastes from nuclear power plants. The debate on that amendment and its defeat by a 3-to-1 vote provide solid support for the conclusion that the FWPCA's grant of regulatory authority to the EPA and the States did not encompass the control of AEA-regulated materials.

The Wolff amendment, according to its author, would "give the States a voice in deciding what kinds and amounts of such radioactive wastes may be discharged into their waters." In explaining the need for such an amendment, Representative Wolff noted that the time had come "to seriously consider standards more stringent than those promulgated by the AEC." . . .

The opponents of the Wolff Amendment voiced strong opposition to the transfer of the AEC's regulatory authority to the States or to the EPA. Representative Stanton, a Member of the House Committee on Public Works, which reported the House bill, stated:

> The amendment presents the House with a very complex and difficult proposition. It proposes to take authority for the setting of pollution control standards from the AEC and place it in the hands of EPA. For normal operations involving pollution, that control properly belongs under EPA. But atomic energy is a peculiar field. To date, the operation of the atomic energy program has been under the control of the Commission itself. Eventually, such control will be delegated to the States as more and more knowledgeable

people at the State level become involved in the atomic energy program. That time, however, has not yet arrived. Until we reach that stage it is obvious that the control of which we speak should remain with the Atomic Energy Commission itself, as the committee points out on page 131 of House Report 92-911 which accompanies this bill. For this reason, I would oppose the amendment offered by my distinguished colleague.

Representative Price, Vice Chairman of the Joint Committee on Atomic Energy, argued against the amendment as follows:

The bill as reported establishes a program of effluent limitations and standards, and section 510 clearly provides that the States may set more restrictive standards should they so desire. The proposed amendment is aimed at two so-called pollutants — radioactive materials and thermal discharges — and seeks to collaterally amend any statute enacted by the Congress relative to them without any specific reference to the statutes that might be affected. As to radioactive materials, the target of the amendment is obvious. It seeks to reverse the decisions of the courts which have held that the Atomic Energy Act of 1954 preempted to the Federal Government, acting through the Atomic Energy Commission, the exclusive jurisdiction to regulate most radioactive materials. Clearly, if such is the will of the House, it should be undertaken only after a thorough examination of the impact of such a decision and it should be done directly by amending the statute involved — the Atomic Energy Act — not collaterally through this legislation. If this amendment had been proposed as a piece of original legislation, it would have been referred to the appropriate committee for hearings and evaluation of all the pertinent factors involved in such a decision. I could go on with the explanation of those factors, but this is not the time nor the place for such a consideration in the first instance. This bill is not the appropriate vehicle for amending a major piece of legislation, thoroughly considered in committee and by the Congress, which established at the direction of the Congress a thorough and pervasive regulatory program relative to radioactive materials.

Representative McCormack, a Member of the House Committee on Public Works and Chairman of the House Science and Astronautics Committee's Task Force on Energy Research and Development, urged the amendment's defeat in similar terms. After noting the inadvisability of "throwing away" the AEC's "meticulous work" in the area of safety in favor of state regulation, he concluded:

[I]t is obvious from the report by the House Committee on Public Works for this bill, and from the committee report from the other body that this bill does not impact directly upon the Atomic Energy Act of 1954. This bill applies only to radioactive materials not covered by the Atomic Energy Act of 1954 and, as such, the amendment is not relevant to this bill at all.

Respondents urge that the Wolff amendment was addressed only to the question of the States' regulatory authority, and that its defeat did not reflect any intent to foreclose regulation of source, byproduct, and special nuclear materials by the EPA. We do not agree that the House's consideration of the Wolff amendment leaves room for EPA regulation. Several of the opponents of the amendment were quite explicit in their reliance upon the House Committee Report's statement that radioactive materials subject to AEA regulation were excluded from the coverage of the FWPCA. Neither Representative Wolff nor Representative Frenzel took issue with that interpretation in the course of the debate on their amendment, and indeed it is arguable that their amendment was premised on the assumption that source, byproduct, and special nuclear materials were wholly beyond the scope of the FWPCA. If these materials were covered by the Act—that is, if they were "pollutants"—the amendment was wholly superfluous, for the unamended provision that is now 33 U.S.C. §1370 (1970 ed., Supp. IV) would permit the States to regulate their discharge. But regardless of the underlying assumptions of the sponsors of the Wolff amendment, the interpretation respondents would place upon its defeat is unacceptable. As respondents would have it, the House expressed an intent to permit EPA regulation of the materials in question, but to preclude state regulation of the same materials under the FWPCA. That result could find no basis in the language of the Act. In our view, then, the House's consideration and rejection of the Wolff amendment offers additional support for the interpretation stated in the House Committee Report that source, byproduct, and special nuclear materials are beyond the reach of the FWPCA.

The House's rather explicit statement of intent to exclude AEA-regulated materials from the FWPCA was unchallenged by the Conference Committee, which simply retained the same reference to "radioactive materials" contained in both the House and Senate bills. Representative Harsha, a ranking member of the Conference Committee, explained the import of the Conference Committee action as follows:

> The conference report does not change the original intent as it was made clear in the colloquy between Senators Muskie and Pastore in the course of the debate in the other body. I also note that an amendment to H.R. 11896 was offered on March 28, 1972, which would have overturned the Northern States Power against Minnesota case.
>
> The distinguished gentleman from California (Mr. Holifield) spoke in opposition to the amendment and pointed out the necessity of not changing the careful division of authority between the States and the Federal Government over nuclear materials and facilities as enunciated in the Northern States case. The amendment was defeated by a 3-to-1 vote of the House.
>
> I can say to the gentleman from Illinois that the managers in no way detracted from the intent of the language in H.R. 11896. I also note that the Committee on Public Works in its report on H.R. 11896 stated on page 131 that the term "pollutant" as defined in the bill includes "radioactive materials." These materials are not those encompassed in the definition of

source, byproduct, or special nuclear materials as defined by the Atomic Energy Act of 1954, as amended, and regulated pursuant to that act. "Radioactive materials" encompassed by this bill are those beyond the jurisdiction of the Atomic Energy Commission. Examples of radioactive materials not covered by the Atomic Energy Act, and, therefore, included within the term "pollutant" are radium and accelerator produced isotopes. This language adequately reflects the intent of the managers of the conference report.

With no one expressing a different view of the Conference action, the House proceeded to agree to the Conference Report.

V

If it was not clear at the outset, we think it abundantly clear after a review of the legislative materials that reliance on the "plain meaning" of the words "radioactive materials" contained in the definition of "pollutant" in the FWPCA contributes little to our understanding of whether Congress intended the Act to encompass the regulation of source, byproduct, and special nuclear materials. To have included these materials under the FWPCA would have marked a significant alteration of the pervasive regulatory scheme embodied in the AEA. Far from containing the clear indication of legislative intent that we might expect before recognizing such a change in policy, the legislative history reflects, on balance, an intention to preserve the pre-existing regulatory plan.

We conclude, therefore, that the "pollutants" subject to regulation under the FWPCA do not include source, byproduct, and special nuclear materials, and that the EPA Administrator has acted in accordance with his statutory mandate in declining to regulate the discharge of such materials. The judgment of the Court of Appeals is reversed. . . .

NOTES AND QUESTIONS

1. *Language and intent.* This decision is an example of legislative history trumping the statutory text. How does the Court rationalize this action? Do you think the application of the statute according to its clear meaning would lead to an absurd result?

2. *Legislative history.* Consider the use of legislative history in this decision. How probative of the Court's view is each piece of legislative history referenced? How probative are the pieces of legislative history referred to by the respondent? Are you convinced that the Court is correct that the legislative history demonstrates that the enacting Congress did not intend to cover pollutants subject to the Atomic Energy Act in provisions of the Federal Water Pollution Act?

CHAPTER 12

Resolving Ambiguities

In Section B of Chapter 10, we introduced the problem of applying ambiguous statutes. Revisit the introductory problem in Chapter 10. Assume that the controlling law is Amendment 3, which provides:

Amendment 3: When a sentence of imprisonment is pronounced . . . the defendant must, as soon as is practical, be committed to the custody of the appropriate public servant and detained until the sentence is complied with.

Each of the parties argues that the statute supports his or her position; that is why they are in court. But it is the judge who must make the decision. As Professor Jones has noted: "The case must be decided, one way or the other. Unlike the pure social scientist, the judge cannot withhold his action until all the returns are in. There is no hiding place from the political and moral obligation to decide." Harry W. Jones, An Invitation to Jurisprudence, 74 Colum. L. Rev. 1023, 1041 (1974). How is a court to make such a decision, when the language is unclear?

In this chapter, we will examine this question through reading a number of cases. All of the cases fall under the rubric of applying ambiguous statutes, but, for different points of emphasis, we divide them into four separate sections: those in which the ambiguity arises from the application of general language; those in which the ambiguity is the product of a compromise; those in which the ambiguity is impossible to resolve through traditional analysis — the so-called showdown questions; and those involving the *Chevron* doctrine (see Chapter 10, Section C).

Several of these cases will be familiar, or at least the statute they are applying will be. Section A is composed of cases applying the Voting Rights Act, including a portion of Thornburg v. Gingles, which was explored earlier in Chapter 6. The generality of its language and the poignancy of its politics make the Voting Rights Act an especially good statute for studying judicial construction. Also, considering the number of times we have used the statute to illustrate aspects of the legislative process, its use here completes the story. In Section B is Landgraf v. USI Film Products, the case that answers the question, discussed in Chapter 2, about the retroactivity of the Civil Rights Act of 1991.

A. AMBIGUITIES FROM THE USE OF GENERAL LANGUAGE

Thornburg v. Gingles
478 U.S. 30 (1986)

Statute: §2 of the Voting Rights Act of 1965, as amended
SEC. 2. (a) No voting qualification or prerequisite to voting or standard, practice, or procedure shall be imposed or applied by any State or political subdivision in a manner which results in a denial or abridgement of the right of any citizen of the United States to vote on account of race or color, or in contravention of the guarantees set forth in section 4(f)(2), as provided in subsection (b).

(b) A violation of subsection (a) is established if, based on the totality of circumstances, it is shown that the political processes leading to nomination or election in the State or political subdivision are not equally open to participation by members of a class of citizens protected by subsection (a) in that its members have less opportunity than other members of the electorate to participate in the political process and to elect representatives of their choice. The extent to which members of a protected class have been elected to office in the State or political subdivision is one circumstance which may be considered: Provided, That nothing in this section establishes a right to have members of a protected class elected in numbers equal to their proportion in the population.

This case requires that we construe for the first time §2 of the Voting Rights Act of 1965, as amended June 29, 1982. . . .

I. Background

In April 1982, the North Carolina General Assembly enacted a legislative redistricting plan for the State's Senate and House of Representatives.

Appellees, black citizens of North Carolina who are registered to vote, challenged seven districts, one single-member and six multimember districts, alleging that the redistricting scheme impaired black citizens' ability to elect representatives of their choice in violation of the Fourteenth and Fifteenth Amendments to the United States Constitution and of §2 of the Voting Rights Act.

After appellees brought suit, but before trial, Congress amended §2. The amendment was largely a response to this Court's plurality opinion in Mobile v. Bolden. . . . Congress substantially revised §2 to make clear that a violation could be proved by showing discriminatory effect alone and to establish as the relevant legal standard the "results test," applied by this Court in White v. Regester. . . .

The Senate Judiciary Committee majority Report accompanying the bill that amended §2 elaborates on the circumstances that might be probative of a §2 violation, noting the following "typical factors":

   1. the extent of any history of official discrimination in the state or political subdivision that touched the right of the members of the minority group to register, to vote, or otherwise to participate in the democratic process;
   2. the extent to which voting in the elections of the state or political subdivision is racially polarized;
   3. the extent to which the state or political subdivision has used unusually large election districts, majority vote requirements, anti–single shot provisions, or other voting practices or procedures that may enhance the opportunity for discrimination against the minority group;
   4. if there is a candidate slating process, whether the members of the minority group have been denied access to that process;
   5. the extent to which members of the minority group in the state or political subdivision bear the effects of discrimination in such areas as education, employment and health, which hinder their ability to participate effectively in the political process;
   6. whether political campaigns have been characterized by overt or subtle racial appeals;
   7. the extent to which members of the minority group have been elected to public office in the jurisdiction.
   Additional factors that in some cases have had probative value as part of plaintiffs' evidence to establish a violation are:
   whether there is a significant lack of responsiveness on the part of elected officials to the particularized needs of the members of the minority group.
   whether the policy underlying the state or political subdivision's use of such voting qualification, prerequisite to voting, or standard, practice or procedure is tenuous.

The District Court applied the "totality of the circumstances" test set forth in §2(b) to appellees' statutory claim, and, relying principally on the factors outlined in the Senate Report, held that the redistricting scheme violated §2 because it resulted in the dilution of black citizens' votes in all seven disputed districts. . . .

II.   Section 2 and Vote Dilution Through Use of
Multimember Districts . . .

A.   Section 2 and Its Legislative History . . .

The Senate Report which accompanied the 1982 amendments elaborates on the nature of §2 violations and on the proof required to establish these violations. . . . The "right" question, as the report emphasizes repeatedly, is whether "as a result of the challenged practice or structure plaintiffs do not have an equal opportunity to participate in the political processes and to elect candidates of their choice."

In order to answer this question, a court must assess the impact of the contested structure or practice on minority electoral opportunities "on the basis of objective factors." The Senate Report specifies factors which typically may be relevant to a §2 claim. . . . The Report stresses, however, that this list of typical factors is neither comprehensive nor exclusive. While the enumerated factors will often be pertinent to certain types of §2 violations, particularly to vote dilution claims, other factors may also be relevant and may be considered. Furthermore, the Senate Committee observed that "there is no requirement that any particular number of factors be proved, or that a majority of them point one way or the other." Rather, the Committee determined that "the question whether the political processes are 'equally open' depends upon a searching practical evaluation of the 'past and present reality,'" and on a "functional" view of the political process.

Although the Senate Report espouses a flexible, fact-intensive test for §2 violations, it limits the circumstances under which §2 violations may be proved in three ways. First, electoral devices, such as at-large elections, may not be considered per se violative of §2. Plaintiffs must demonstrate that, under the totality of the circumstances, the devices result in unequal access to the electoral process. Second, the conjunction of an allegedly dilutive electoral mechanism and the lack of proportional representation alone does not establish a violation. Third, the results test does not assume the existence of racial bloc voting; plaintiffs must prove it.

B.   Vote Dilution Through the Use of
Multimember Districts

Appellees contend that the legislative decision to employ multimember, rather than single-member, districts in the contested jurisdictions dilutes their votes by submerging them in a white majority, thus impairing their ability to elect representatives of their choice.

The essence of a §2 claim is that a certain electoral law, practice, or structure interacts with social and historical conditions to cause an inequality in the opportunities enjoyed by black and white voters to elect their preferred representatives. This Court has long recognized that multimember districts and at-large voting schemes may "'operate to minimize or cancel out the voting strength of racial [minorities in] the voting population.'" The theoretical basis for this type of impairment is that where minority and majority voters consistently prefer different candidates, the majority, by virtue of its numerical superiority, will regularly defeat the choices of minority voters. Minority voters who contend that the multimember form of districting violates §2 must prove that the use of a multimember electoral structure operates to minimize or cancel out their ability to elect their preferred candidates.

While many or all of the factors listed in the Senate Report may be relevant to a claim of vote dilution through submergence in multimember districts, unless there is a conjunction of the following circumstances, the use of multimember districts generally will not impede the ability of minority voters to elect representatives of their choice. Stated succinctly, a bloc voting majority must usually be able to defeat candidates supported by a politically cohesive, geographically insular minority group. These circumstances are necessary preconditions for multimember districts to operate to impair minority voters' ability to elect representatives of their choice for the following reasons. First, the minority group must be able to demonstrate that it is sufficiently large and geographically compact to constitute a majority in a single-member district. If it is not, as would be the case in a substantially integrated district, the multimember form of the district cannot be responsible for minority voters' inability to elect its candidates. Second, the minority group must be able to show that it is politically cohesive. If the minority group is not politically cohesive, it cannot be said that the selection of a multimember electoral structure thwarts distinctive minority group interests. Third, the minority must be able to demonstrate that the white majority votes sufficiently as a bloc to enable it — in the absence of special circumstances, such as the minority candidate running unopposed — usually to defeat the minority's preferred candidate. In establishing this last circumstance, the minority group demonstrates that submergence in a white multimember district impedes its ability to elect its chosen representatives.

Finally, we observe that the usual predictability of the majority's success distinguishes structural dilution from the mere loss of an occasional election. . . .

NOTES AND QUESTIONS

Thornburg redux. In Chapter 6, we focused on the details and significance of the *Thornburg* decision. In the following selection, we revisit the decision to examine the Court's approach to statutory construction. Can you discern from the language of the statute whether a redistricting plan is subject to its coverage? Assuming such coverage, can you determine from the statutory language the standards that are to be applied to determine whether a particular plan diminishes the opportunities for protected groups to participate in the political process? The Court does not deal with the first question. It will be discussed in Holder v. Hall later in this chapter. How does the Court answer the second question? How faithful is the Court to the Senate Report? How would Justice Scalia, given his stand against the use of legislative history, approach the question? If you were a member of the Court, would you turn to the report for aid? If not, what would you do? (Internal citations have been omitted except where particularly relevant.)

Chisom v. Roemer
501 U.S. 380 (1991)

Statute: §2 of the Voting Rights Act of 1965, as Amended

SEC. 2. (a) No voting qualification or prerequisite to voting or standard, practice, or procedure shall be imposed or applied by any State or political subdivision in a manner which results in a denial or abridgement of the right of any citizen of the United States to vote on account of race or color, or in contravention of the guarantees set forth in section 4(f)(2), as provided in subsection (b).

(b) A violation of subsection (a) is established if, based on the totality of circumstances, it is shown that the political processes leading to nomination or election in the State or political subdivision are not equally open to participation by members of a class of citizens protected by subsection (a) in that its members have less opportunity than other members of the electorate to participate in the political process and to elect representatives of their choice. The extent to which members of a protected class have been elected to office in the State or political subdivision is one circumstance which may be considered: Provided, That nothing in this section establishes a right to have members of a protected class elected in numbers equal to their proportion in the population.

JUSTICE STEVENS delivered the opinion of the Court. . . .

I

Petitioners . . . represent a class of approximately 135,000 black registered voters in Orleans Parish, Louisiana. They brought this action against the Governor and other state officials (respondents) to challenge the method of electing justices of the Louisiana Supreme Court from the New Orleans area. . . .

The Louisiana Supreme Court consists of seven justices, five of whom are elected from five single-member Supreme Court Districts, and two of whom are elected from one multimember Supreme Court District. Each of the seven members of the court must be a resident of the district from which he or she is elected and must have resided there for at least two years prior to election. Each of the justices on the Louisiana Supreme Court serves a term of 10 years. The one multimember district, the First Supreme Court District, consists of the parishes of Orleans, St. Bernard, Plaquemines, and Jefferson. Orleans Parish contains about half of the population of the First Supreme Court District and about half of the registered voters in that district. More than one-half of the registered voters of Orleans Parish are black, whereas more than three-fourths of the registered voters in the other three parishes are white.

Petitioners allege that "the present method of electing two justices to the Louisiana Supreme Court at-large from the New Orleans area impermissibly dilutes minority voting strength" in violation of §2 of the Voting Rights Act. . . . Petitioners seek a remedy that would divide the First District into two districts, one for Orleans Parish and the second for the other three parishes. If this remedy were adopted, the seven members of the Louisiana Supreme Court would each represent a separate single-member judicial district, and each of the two new districts would have approximately the same population. According to petitioners, the new Orleans Parish district would also have a majority black population and majority black voter registration.

II . . .

It is . . . undisputed that §2 applied to judicial elections prior to the 1982 amendment, and that §5 of the amended statute continues to apply to judicial elections. Moreover, there is no question that the terms "standard, practice, or procedure" are broad enough to encompass the use of multi-member districts to minimize a racial minority's ability to influence the outcome of an election covered by §2. The only matter in dispute is whether the test for determining the legality of such a practice, which was added to the statute in 1982, applies in judicial elections as well as in other elections.

III

The text of §2 of the Voting Rights Act as originally enacted read as follows:

SEC. 2. No voting qualification or prerequisite to voting, or standard, practice, or procedure shall be imposed or applied by any State or political subdivision to deny or abridge the right of any citizen of the United States to vote on account of race or color.

The terms "vote" and "voting" were defined elsewhere in the Act to include "all action necessary to make a vote effective in any primary, special, or general election." The statute further defined vote and voting as "votes cast with respect to candidates for public or party office and propositions for which votes are received in an election." . . .

Under the amended statute, proof of intent is no longer required to prove a §2 violation. Now plaintiffs can prevail under §2 by demonstrating that a challenged election practice has resulted in the denial or abridgement of the right to vote based on color or race. Congress not only incorporated the results test in the paragraph that formerly constituted the entire §2, but also designated that paragraph as subsection (a) and added a new subsection (b) to make clear that an application of the results test requires an inquiry into "the totality of the circumstances." . . .

The two purposes of the amendment are apparent from its text. Subsection 2(a) adopts a results test, thus providing that proof of discriminatory intent is no longer necessary to establish any violation of the section. Subsection 2(b) provides guidance about how the results test is to be applied.

Respondents contend . . . that Congress' choice of the word "representatives" in the phrase "have less opportunity than other members of the electorate to participate in the political process and to elect representatives of their choice" in subsection 2(b) is evidence of congressional intent to exclude vote dilution claims involving judicial elections from the coverage of §2. We reject that construction because we are convinced that if Congress had such an intent, Congress would have made it explicit in the statute, or at least some of the Members would have identified or mentioned it at some point in the unusually extensive legislative history of the 1982 amendment. Our conclusion is confirmed when we review the justifications offered by the *LULAC* [League of United Latin American Citizens Council No. 4434 v. Clements (holding that judicial elections were not covered under §2)] majority and respondents in support of their construction of the statute. . . .

IV

The *LULAC* majority assumed that §2 provides two distinct types of protection for minority voters — it protects their opportunity "to participate in the political process" and their opportunity "to elect representatives of their choice." Although the majority interpreted "representatives" as a word of limitation, it assumed that the word eliminated judicial elections only from the latter protection, without affecting the former. In other words, a standard, practice, or procedure in a judicial election, such as a limit on the times that polls are open, which has a disparate impact on black voters' opportunity to cast their ballots under §2, may be challenged even if a different practice that merely affects their opportunity to elect representatives of their choice to a judicial office may not. This reading of §2, however, is foreclosed by the statutory text and by our prior cases.

Any abridgement of the opportunity of members of a protected class to participate in the political process inevitably impairs their ability to influence the outcome of an election. As the statute is written, however, the inability to elect representatives of their choice is not sufficient to establish a violation unless, under the totality of the circumstances, it can also be said that the members of the protected class have less opportunity to participate in the political process. The statute does not create two separate and distinct rights. Subsection (a) covers every application of a qualification, standard, practice, or procedure that results in a denial or abridgement of "the right" to vote. The singular form is also used in subsection (b) when referring to an injury to members of the protected class who have less "opportunity" than others "to participate in the political process and to elect representatives of their choice." It would distort the plain meaning of the sentence to substitute the word "or" for the word "and." Such radical surgery would be required to separate the opportunity to participate from the opportunity to elect. . . .

V

Both respondents and the *LULAC* majority place their principal reliance on Congress' use of the word "representatives" instead of "legislators" in the phrase "to participate in the political process and to elect representatives of their choice." When Congress borrowed the phrase from White v. Regester, it replaced "legislators" with "representatives." This substitution indicates, at the very least, that Congress intended the amendment to cover more than legislative elections. Respondents argue, and the majority agreed, that the term "representatives" was used to extend §2 coverage to executive officials, but not to judges. We think, however, that the better reading of the word "representatives" describes the winners of representative, popular elections. If executive officers, such as prosecutors, sheriffs, state attorneys general, and state treasurers, can be considered "representatives" simply because they are chosen by popular election, then the same reasoning should apply to elected judges.

Respondents suggest that if Congress had intended to have the statute's prohibition against vote dilution apply to the election of judges, it would have used the word "candidates" instead of "representatives." But that confuses the ordinary meaning of the words. The word "representative" refers to someone who has prevailed in a popular election, whereas the word "candidate" refers to someone who is seeking an office. Thus, a candidate is nominated, not elected. When Congress used "candidate" in other parts of the statute, it did so precisely because it was referring to people who were aspirants for an office. . . .

The *LULAC* majority was, of course, entirely correct in observing that "judges need not be elected at all," and that ideally public opinion should be irrelevant to the judge's role because the judge is often called upon to disregard, or even to defy, popular sentiment. The Framers of the Constitution had a similar understanding of the judicial role, and as a consequence, they established that Article III judges would be appointed, rather than elected, and would be sheltered from public opinion by receiving life tenure and salary protection. Indeed, these views were generally shared by the States during the early years of the Republic. Louisiana, however, has chosen a different course. It has decided to elect its judges and to compel judicial candidates to vie for popular support just as other political candidates do.

The fundamental tension between the ideal character of the judicial office and the real world of electoral politics cannot be resolved by crediting judges with total indifference to the popular will while simultaneously requiring them to run for elected office. When each of several members of a court must be a resident of a separate district, and must be elected by the voters of that district, it seems both reasonable and realistic to characterize the winners as representatives of that district. Indeed, at one time the Louisiana Bar Association characterized the members of the Louisiana Supreme Court as representatives for that reason: "Each justice and judge now in office shall be considered as a representative of the judicial district within which is situated the parish of his residence at the time of his election." . . .

VII

Congress enacted the Voting Rights Act of 1965 for the broad remedial purpose of "ridding the country of racial discrimination in voting." South Carolina v. Katzenbach. In Allen v. State Board of Elections, we said that the Act should be interpreted in a manner that provides "the broadest possible scope" in combatting racial discrimination. Congress amended the Act in 1982 in order to relieve plaintiffs of the burden of proving discriminatory intent, after a plurality of this Court had concluded that the original Act, like the Fifteenth Amendment, contained such a requirement. Thus, Congress made clear that a violation of §2 could be established by proof of discriminatory results alone. It is difficult to believe that Congress, in an express effort to broaden the protection afforded by the Voting Rights Act, withdrew, without comment, an important category of elections from that protection. . . .

JUSTICE SCALIA, with whom THE CHIEF JUSTICE and JUSTICE KENNEDY join, dissenting.

Section 2 of the Voting Rights Act is not some all-purpose weapon for well-intentioned judges to wield as they please in the battle against discrimination. It is a statute. I thought we had adopted a regular method for interpreting the meaning of language in a statute: first, find the ordinary meaning of the language in its textual context; and second, using established canons of construction, ask whether there is any clear indication that some permissible meaning other than the ordinary one applies. If not — and especially if a good reason for the ordinary meaning appears plain — we apply that ordinary meaning. . . .

Today, however, the Court adopts a method quite out of accord with that usual practice. It begins not with what the statute says, but with an expectation about what the statute must mean absent particular phenomena ("we are convinced that if Congress had . . . an intent [to exclude judges] Congress would have made it explicit in the statute, or at least some of the Members would have identified or mentioned it at some point in the unusually extensive legislative history") and the Court then interprets the words of the statute to fulfill its expectation. Finding nothing in the legislative history affirming that judges were excluded from the coverage of §2, the Court gives the phrase "to elect representatives" the quite extraordinary meaning that covers the election of judges.

As method, this is just backwards, and however much we may be attracted by the result it produces in a particular case, we should in every case resist it. Our job begins with a text that Congress has passed and the President has signed. We are to read the words of that text as any ordinary Member of Congress would have read them, and apply the meaning so determined. In my view, that reading reveals that §2 extends to vote dilution claims for the elections of representatives only, and judges are not representatives.

I . . .

The 1982 amendments . . . radically transformed the Act. As currently written, the statute proscribes intentional discrimination only if it has a discriminatory effect, but proscribes practices with discriminatory effect whether or not intentional. This new "results" criterion provides a powerful, albeit sometimes blunt, weapon with which to attack even the most subtle forms of discrimination. The question we confront here is how broadly the new remedy applies. The foundation of the Court's analysis, the itinerary for its journey in the wrong direction, is the following statement: "It is difficult to believe that Congress, in an express effort to broaden the protection afforded by the Voting Rights Act, withdrew, without comment, an important category of elections from that protection."

There are two things wrong with this. First is the notion that Congress cannot be credited with having achieved anything of major importance by simply saying it, in ordinary language, in the text of a statute, "without comment" in the legislative history. As the Court colorfully puts it, if the dog of legislative history has not barked nothing of great significance can have transpired. . . . We are here to apply the statute, not legislative history, and certainly not the absence of legislative history. Statutes are the law though sleeping dogs lie. . . .

The more important error in the Court's starting-point, however, is the assumption that the effect of excluding judges from the revised §2 would be to "withdraw . . . an important category of elections from [the] protection [of the Voting Rights Act]." There is absolutely no question here of withdrawing protection. Since the pre-1982 content of §2 was coextensive with the Fifteenth Amendment, the entirety of that protection subsisted in the Constitution, and could be enforced through the other provisions of the Voting Rights Act. Nothing was lost from the prior coverage; all of the new "results" protection was an add-on. The issue is not, therefore, as the Court would have it, whether Congress has cut back on the coverage of the Voting Rights Act; the issue is how far it has extended it. Thus, even if a court's expectations were a proper basis for interpreting the text of a statute, while there would be reason to expect that Congress was not "withdrawing" protection, there is no particular reason to expect that the supplemental protection it provided was any more extensive than the text of the statute said. . . .

The Court . . . [has] labored mightily to establish that there is a meaning of "representatives" that would include judges, and no doubt there is. But our job is not to scavenge the world of English usage to discover whether there is any possible meaning of "representatives" which suits our preconception that the statute includes judges; our job is to determine whether the ordinary meaning includes them, and if it does not, to ask whether there is any solid indication in the text or structure of the statute that something other than ordinary meaning was intended.

There is little doubt that the ordinary meaning of "representatives" does not include judges, see Webster's Second New International Dictionary 2114 (1950). The Court's feeble argument to the contrary is that "representatives" means those who "are chosen by popular election." On that hypothesis, the fan-elected members of the baseball All-Star teams are "representatives" — hardly a common, if even a permissible, usage. Surely the word "representative" connotes one who is not only elected by the people, but who also, at a minimum, acts on behalf of the people. Judges do that in a sense — but not in the ordinary sense. As the captions of the pleadings in some States still display, it is the prosecutor who represents "the People"; the judge represents the Law — which often requires him to rule against the People. It is precisely because we do not ordinarily conceive of judges as representatives that we held judges not within the

Fourteenth Amendment's requirement of "one person, one vote." Wells v. Edwards. The point is not that a State could not make judges in some senses representative, or that all judges must be conceived of in the Article III mold, but rather, that giving "representatives" its ordinary meaning, the ordinary speaker in 1982 would not have applied the word to judges. It remains only to ask whether there is good indication that ordinary meaning does not apply.

. . . [W]e tacitly rejected a "plain statement" rule as applied to the una-mended §2 in City of Rome v. United States, though arguably that was before the rule had developed the significance it currently has. I am content to dispense with the "plain statement" rule in the present case . . . but it says something about the Court's approach to today's decision that the possibility of applying that rule never crossed its mind.

While the "plain statement" rule may not be applicable, there is assuredly nothing whatever that points in the opposite direction, indicat-ing that the ordinary meaning here should not be applied. Far from that, in my view the ordinary meaning of "representatives" gives clear purpose to congressional action that otherwise would seem pointless. As an initial matter, it is evident that Congress paid particular attention to the scope of elections covered by the "to elect" language. As the Court suggests, that language for the most part tracked this Court's opinions in White v. Regester and Whitcomb v. Chavis, but the word "legislators" was not copied. Significantly, it was replaced not with the more general term "can-didates" used repeatedly elsewhere in the Act, but with the term "repre-sentatives," which appears nowhere else in the Act (except as a proper noun referring to Members of the federal lower House, or designees of the Attorney General). The normal meaning of this term is broader than "legislators" (it includes, for example, school boards and city councils as well as senators and representatives) but narrower than "candidates."

The Court says that the seemingly significant refusal to use the term "candidate" and selection of the distinctive term "representative" are really inconsequential, because "candidate" could not have been used. According to the Court, since "candidate" refers to one who has been nominated but not yet elected, the phrase "to elect candidates" would be a contradiction in terms. The only flaw in this argument is that it is not true, as repeated usage of the formulation "to elect candidates" by this Court itself amply demon-strates. . . . In other words, far from being an impermissible choice, "can-didates" would have been the natural choice, even if it had not been used repeatedly elsewhere in the statute. It is quite absurd to think that Congress went out of its way to replace that term with "representatives," in order to convey what "candidates" naturally suggests (viz., coverage of all elec-tions) and what "representatives" naturally does not.

A second consideration confirms that "representatives" in §2 was meant in its ordinary sense. When given its ordinary meaning, it causes the statute to reproduce an established, eminently logical and perhaps practically indispensable limitation upon the availability of vote dilution claims. Whatever other requirements may be applicable to elections for "representatives" (in the sense of those who are not only elected by but act on behalf of the electorate), those elections, unlike elections for all office-holders, must be conducted in accordance with the equal-protection principle of "one person, one vote." And it so happens — more than coincidentally, I think — that in every case in which, prior to the amendment of §2, we recognized the possibility of a vote dilution claim, the principle of "one person, one vote" was applicable. . . . Indeed, it is the principle of "one person, one vote" that gives meaning to the concept of "dilution." One's vote is diluted if it is not, as it should be, of the same practical effect as everyone else's. Of course the mere fact that an election practice satisfies the constitutional requirement of "one person, one vote" does not establish that there has been no vote dilution for Voting Rights Act purposes, since that looks not merely to equality of individual votes but also to equality of minority blocs of votes. . . . But "one person, one vote" has been the premise and the necessary condition of a vote dilution claim, since it establishes the baseline for computing the voting strength that the minority bloc ought to have. . . .

Well before Congress amended §2, we had held that the principle of "one person, one vote" does not apply to the election of judges. If Congress was (through use of the extremely inapt word "representatives") making vote dilution claims available with respect to the election of judges, it was, for the first time, extending that remedy to a context in which "one person, one vote" did not apply. That would have been a significant change in the law, and given the need to identify some other baseline for computing "dilution," that is a matter which those who believe in barking dogs should be astounded to find unmentioned in the legislative history. If "representatives" is given its normal meaning, on the other hand, there is no change in the law (except elimination of the intent requirement) and the silence is entirely understandable.

I frankly find it very difficult to conceive how it is to be determined whether "dilution" has occurred, once one has eliminated both the requirement of actual intent to disfavor minorities, and the principle that 10,000 minority votes throughout the State should have as much practical "electability" effect as 10,000 non-minority votes. How does one begin to decide, in such a system, how much elective strength a minority bloc ought to have? I do not assert that it is utterly impossible to impose "vote dilution" restrictions upon an electoral regime that is not based on the "one person, one vote" principle. Congress can define "vote dilution" to be whatever it will, within constitutional bounds. But my point is that "one person, one vote" is inherent in the normal concept of "vote dilution," and was an essential element of the pre-existing, judicially crafted definition under §2; that Congress did not adopt any new definition; that creating a new definition is a seemingly standardless task; and that the word Congress selected ("representative") seems specifically designed to avoid these problems. . . .

Finally, the Court suggests that there is something "anomalous" about extending coverage under §5 of the Voting Rights Act to the election of judges, while not extending coverage under §2 to the same elections. This simply misconceives the different roles of §2 and §5. The latter requires certain jurisdictions to preclear changes in election methods before those changes are implemented; it is a means of assuring in advance the absence of all electoral illegality, not only that which violates the Voting Rights Act but that which violates the Constitution as well. In my view, judges are within the scope of §2 for nondilution claims, and thus for those claims, §5 preclearance would enforce the Voting Rights Act with respect to judges. Moreover, intentional discrimination in the election of judges, whatever its form, is constitutionally prohibited, and the preclearance provision of §5 gives the government a method by which to prevent that. The scheme makes entire sense without the need to bring judges within the "to elect" provision.

All this is enough to convince me that there is sense to the ordinary meaning of "representative" in §2(b) — that there is reason to Congress's choice — and since there is, then, under our normal presumption, that ordinary meaning prevails. I would read §2 as extending vote dilution claims to elections for "representatives," but not to elections for judges. For other claims under §2, however — those resting on the "to participate in the political process" provision rather than the "to elect" provision — no similar restriction would apply. Since the claims here are exclusively claims of dilution, I would affirm the judgment of the Fifth Circuit. . . .

NOTES AND QUESTIONS

1. *Ambiguity and intent.* Referring strictly to the words of the statute, what conclusion would you draw about whether elected judges are representatives? On what evidence of legislative intent did the Court rely to reach its conclusion?

2. *The silence of legislative history.* On what basis does the Court consider legislative silence determinative of a legislative intention to include elected judges within the definition of "representatives"? Is this a sensible presumption to make about the process leading up to the enactment of the amendment? Does the legislature in the enactment process have an obligation to bark to warn that change is afoot?

Assume that as part of the Senate report that accompanied the amendment the following passage was contained in the dissenting views of the bill's opponents: ". . . While we continue to oppose the bill because we believe it will lead to quotas, we are pleased to see that the majority has at least limited the most troublesome part of the bill to legislators through use of the term 'representatives.' " Would such a comment have made a difference to the Court or to you? Would it have made a difference to Justice Scalia?

3. *Judges as representatives.* How does the Court define the term "representative"? Is the Court drawing a difference between elected and appointed judges, other than that one group is elected while the other is appointed? Do elected judges have different decisionmaking responsibilities from those of appointed ones? Is this decision a judicial finding that all judges have policy-making powers? If so, does this mean that the statute can be read to cover a committee established by a U.S. senator to screen candidates for nomination to the federal district courts of that senator's state?

4. *A problem for a legislative counsel.* Assume that, as a result of the *Roemer* decision, the leadership of your state legislature decides to change their judicial selection process from an elected to appointed model. Would such a change, whether by statute or constitutional amendment, be subject to a §2 action?

5. *Justice Scalia's dissent.* Justice Scalia concedes the ambiguity of the statute and applies a canon of construction to resolve the issue. What is the canon? How well does it reflect the legislative process in general or in this case?

6. *Intentionalism and textualism.* The majority finds that it was the intent of the enacting Congress to include elected judges within the term "representative." Justice Scalia argues that the text of the statute, although not plain, precludes this coverage. Which view is more faithful to the legislative efforts, and why?

Assume that during a floor debate on this bill, a supporter of the bill offered an amendment to include judges specifically within its language. In response to this proposed amendment, one of the bill's sponsors stated: "This amendment would not change §2's existing coverage." Would this statement influence your view?

Holder v. Hall
512 U.S. 874 (1994)

Statute: §2 of the Voting Rights Act of 1965, as amended

SEC. 2. (a) No voting qualification or prerequisite to voting or standard, practice, or procedure shall be imposed or applied by any State or political subdivision in a manner which results in a denial or abridgement of the right of any citizen of the United States to vote on account of race or color, or in contravention of the guarantees set forth in section 4(f)(2), as provided in subsection (b).

(b) A violation of subsection (a) is established if, based on the totality of circumstances, it is shown that the political processes leading to nomination or election in the State or political subdivision are not equally open to participation by members of a class of citizens protected by subsection (a) in that its members have less opportunity than other members of the electorate to participate in the political process and to elect representatives of their choice. The extent to which members of a protected class have been elected to office in the State or political subdivision is one circumstance which may be considered: Provided, That nothing in this section establishes a right to have members of a protected class elected in numbers equal to their proportion in the population.

Judges: KENNEDY, J., announced the judgment of the Court and delivered an opinion, in which REHNQUIST, C.J., joined, and in all but Part II-B of which O'CONNOR, J., joined. O'CONNOR, J., filed an opinion concurring in part and concurring in the judgment. THOMAS, J., filed an opinion concurring in the judgment, in which SCALIA, J., joined. BLACKMUN, J., filed a dissenting opinion, in which STEVENS, SOUTER, and GINSBURG, JJ., joined. GINSBURG, J., filed a dissenting opinion. STEVENS, J., filed a separate opinion, in which BLACKMUN, SOUTER, and GINSBURG, JJ., joined. [Internal citations have been omitted except where particularly relevant.]

This case presents the question whether the size of a governing authority is subject to a vote dilution challenge under §2 of the Voting Rights Act of 1965, 42 U.S.C. §1973.

I

The State of Georgia has 159 counties, one of which is Bleckley County, a rural county in central Georgia. Black persons make up nearly 20% of the eligible voting population in Bleckley County. Since its creation in 1912, the county has had a single-commissioner form of government for the exercise of "county governing authority." Under this system, the Bleckley County Commissioner performs all of the executive and legislative functions of the county government, including the levying of general and special taxes, the directing and controlling of all county property, and the settling of all claims. In addition to Bleckley County, about 10 other Georgia counties use the single-commissioner system; the rest have multimember commissions.

In 1985, the Georgia Legislature authorized Bleckley County to adopt a multimember commission consisting of five commissioners elected from single-member districts and a single chairman elected at large. In a referendum held in 1986, however, the electorate did not adopt the change to a multimember commission. (In a similar referendum four years earlier, county voters had approved a five-member district plan for the election of the county school board.) . . .

II

A

Section 2 of the Voting Rights Act of 1965 provides that "no voting qualification or prerequisite to voting, or standard, practice, or procedure shall be imposed or applied by any State or political subdivision in a manner which results in a denial or abridgement of the right of any citizen of the United States to vote on account of race or color." In a §2 vote dilution suit, along with determining whether the *Gingles* preconditions are met and whether the totality of the circumstances supports a finding of liability, a court must find a reasonable alternative practice as a benchmark against which to measure the existing voting practice. . . .

In certain cases, the benchmark for comparison in a §2 dilution suit is obvious. The effect of an anti-single-shot voting rule, for instance, can be evaluated by comparing the system with that rule to the system without that rule. But where there is no objective and workable standard for choosing a reasonable benchmark by which to evaluate a challenged voting practice, it follows that the voting practice cannot be challenged as dilutive under §2. . . .

As the facts of this case well illustrate, the search for a benchmark is quite problematic when a §2 dilution challenge is brought to the size of a government body. There is no principled reason why one size should be picked over another as the benchmark for comparison. Respondents here argue that we should compare Bleckley County's sole commissioner system to a hypothetical five-member commission in order to determine whether the current system is dilutive. Respondents and the United States as amicus curiae give three reasons why the single commissioner structure should be compared to a five-member commission (instead of, say, a 3-, 10-, or 15-member body): (1) because the five-member commission is a common form of governing authority in the State; (2) because the state legislature had authorized Bleckley County to adopt a five-member commission, if it so chose (it did not); and (3) because the county had moved from a single superintendent of education to a school board with five members elected from single-member districts.

These referents do not bear upon dilution. It does not matter, for instance, how popular the single-member commission system is in Georgia in determining whether it dilutes the vote of a minority racial group in Bleckley County. That the single-member commission is uncommon in the State of Georgia, or that a five-member commission is quite common, tells us nothing about its effects on a minority group's voting strength. The sole commissioner system has the same impact regardless of whether it is shared by none, or by all, of the other counties in Georgia. It makes little sense to say (as do respondents and the United States) that the sole

commissioner system should be subject to a dilution challenge if it is rare —
but immune if it is common.

That Bleckley County was authorized by the State to expand its
commission, and that it adopted a five-member school board, are likewise
irrelevant considerations in the dilution inquiry. At most, those facts indicate that Bleckley County could change the size of its commission with
minimal disruption. But the county's failure to do so says nothing about
the effects the sole commissioner system has on the voting power of
Bleckley County's citizens. Surely a minority group's voting strength
would be no more or less diluted had the State not authorized the county
to alter the size of its commission, or had the county not enlarged its
school board. One gets the sense that respondents and the United States
have chosen a benchmark for the sake of having a benchmark. But it is one
thing to say that a benchmark can be found, quite another to give a convincing reason for finding it in the first place.

B

To bolster their argument, respondents point out that our §5 cases may
be interpreted to indicate that covered jurisdictions may not change the size
of their government bodies without obtaining preclearance from the Attorney General or the federal courts. Respondents contend that these §5 cases,
together with the similarity in language between §§2 and 5 of the Act,
compel the conclusion that the size of a government body must be subject
to a dilution challenge under §2. . . .

To be sure, if the structure and purpose of §2 mirrored that of §5, then the
case for interpreting §§2 and 5 to have the same application in all cases
would be convincing. But the two sections differ in structure, purpose,
and application. Section 5 applies only in certain jurisdictions specified
by Congress and "only to proposed changes in voting procedures." In
those covered jurisdictions, a proposed change in a voting practice must
be approved in advance by the Attorney General or the federal courts.
§1973c. . . . The baseline for comparison is present by definition; it is the
existing status. . . .

III

With respect to challenges to the size of a governing authority, respondents fail to explain where the search for reasonable alternative bench-
marks should begin and end, and they provide no acceptable principles
for deciding future cases. The wide range of possibilities makes the choice
"inherently standardless," and we therefore conclude that a plaintiff cannot

maintain a §2 challenge to the size of a government body, such as the Bleckley County Commission. . . .

Justice O'Connor, concurring in part and concurring in the judgment. . . .

[W]e have consistently said that a change in size is a "standard, practice, or procedure with respect to voting" that is subject to §5 preclearance. And though our cases involving size have concerned §5, I do not think it possible to read the terms of §2 more narrowly than the terms of §5. Section 2 covers any "standard, practice, or procedure," while §5 covers any "standard, practice, or procedure with respect to voting." As a textual matter, I cannot see how a practice can be a "standard, practice, or procedure with respect to voting," yet not be a "standard, practice, or procedure." . . .

But determining the threshold scope of coverage does not end the inquiry, at least so far as §2 dilution challenges are concerned. As Justices Kennedy and Blackmun agree, the fact that the size of a governing authority is a "standard, practice, or procedure" does not answer the question whether respondents may maintain a §2 vote dilution challenge. Section 2 vote dilution plaintiffs must establish that the challenged practice is dilutive. In order for an electoral system to dilute a minority group's voting power, there must be an alternative system that would provide greater electoral opportunity to minority voters. . . .

Accordingly, to determine whether voters possess the potential to elect representatives of choice in the absence of the challenged structure, courts must choose an objectively reasonable alternative practice as a benchmark for the dilution comparison. . . . We require preclearance of changes in size under §5, because in a §5 case the question of an alternative benchmark never arises — the benchmark is simply the former practice employed by the jurisdiction seeking approval of a change.

But §2 dilution challenges raise more difficult questions. This case presents the question whether, in a §2 dilution challenge to size, there can ever be an objective alternative benchmark for comparison. And I agree . . . that there cannot be. . . .

In a dilution challenge to the size of a governing authority, choosing the alternative for comparison — a hypothetical larger (or smaller) governing authority — is extremely problematic. The wide range of possibilities makes the choice inherently standardless. Here, for example, respondents argued that the single-member commission structure was dilutive in comparison to a five-member structure, in which African-Americans would probably have been able to elect one representative of their choice. Some groups, however, will not be able to constitute a majority in one of five districts. Once a court accepts respondents' reasoning, it will have to allow a plaintiff group insufficiently large or geographically compact to form a majority in one of five districts to argue that the jurisdiction's failure to establish a 10-, 15-, or 25-commissioner structure is dilutive.

JUSTICE THOMAS, with whom JUSTICE SCALIA joins, concurring in the judgment.

We are asked in this case to determine whether the size of a local governing body is subject to challenge under §2 of the Voting Rights Act as a "dilutive" practice. . . .

While the practical concerns Justices Kennedy and O'Connor point out can inform a proper construction of the Act, I would explicitly anchor analysis in this case in the statutory text. Only a "voting qualification or prerequisite to voting or standard, practice, or procedure" can be challenged under §2. I would hold that the size of a governing body is not a "standard, practice, or procedure" within the terms of the Act. In my view, however, the only principle limiting the scope of the terms "standard, practice, or procedure" that can be derived from the text of the Act would exclude, not only the challenge to size advanced today, but also challenges to allegedly dilutive election methods that we have considered within the scope of the Act in the past.

I believe that a systematic reassessment of our interpretation of §2 is required in this case. The broad reach we have given the section might suggest that the size of a governing body, like an election method that has the potential for diluting the vote of a minority group, should come within the terms of the Act. But the gloss we have placed on the words "standard, practice, or procedure" in cases alleging dilution is at odds with the terms of the statute and has proved utterly unworkable in practice. A review of the current state of our cases shows that by construing the Act to cover potentially dilutive electoral mechanisms, we have immersed the federal courts in a hopeless project of weighing questions of political theory — questions judges must confront to establish a benchmark concept of an "undiluted" vote. Worse, in pursuing the ideal measure of voting strength, we have devised a remedial mechanism that encourages federal courts to segregate voters into racially designated districts to ensure minority electoral success. In doing so, we have collaborated in what may aptly be termed the racial "balkanization" of the Nation. . . .

I

If one surveys the history of the Voting Rights Act, 42 U.S.C. §1973 et seq., one can only be struck by the sea change that has occurred in the application and enforcement of the Act since it was passed in 1965. The statute was originally perceived as a remedial provision directed specifically at eradicating discriminatory practices that restricted blacks' ability to register and vote in the segregated South. Now, the Act has grown into something entirely different. In construing the Act to cover claims of vote dilution, we have converted the Act into a device for regulating, rationing, and apportioning political power among racial and ethnic groups. In the process, we have read the Act essentially as a grant of authority to the federal judiciary to develop theories on basic principles of representative government, for it is only a resort to political theory that can enable a court to determine which electoral systems provide the "fairest" levels of representation or the most "effective" or "undiluted" votes to minorities.

... An examination of the current state of our decisions should make obvious a simple fact that for far too long has gone unmentioned: vote dilution cases have required the federal courts to make decisions based on highly political judgments—judgments that courts are inherently ill-equipped to make. A clear understanding of the destructive assumptions that have developed to guide vote dilution decisions and the role we have given the federal courts in redrawing the political landscape of the Nation should make clear the pressing need for us to reassess our interpretation of the Act.

A

As it was enforced in the years immediately following its enactment, the Voting Rights Act of 1965 was perceived primarily as legislation directed at eliminating literacy tests and similar devices that had been used to prevent black voter registration in the segregated South. ...

The Court's decision in Allen v. State Bd. of Elections, however, marked a fundamental shift in the focal point of the Act. In an opinion dealing with four companion cases, the *Allen* Court determined that the Act should be given "the broadest possible scope." ...

As a consequence, *Allen* also ensured that courts would be required to confront a number of complex and essentially political questions in assessing claims of vote dilution under the Voting Rights Act. The central difficulty in any vote dilution case, of course, is determining a point of comparison against which dilution can be measured. ... But in setting the benchmark of what "undiluted" or fully "effective" voting strength should be, a court must necessarily make some judgments based purely on an assessment of principles of political theory. As Justice Harlan pointed out in his dissent in *Allen*, the Voting Rights Act supplies no rule for a court to rely upon in deciding, for example, whether a multimember at-large system of election is to be preferred to a single-member district system; that is, whether one provides a more "effective" vote than another. ...

Perhaps the most prominent feature of the philosophy that has emerged in vote dilution decisions since *Allen* has been the Court's preference for single-member districting schemes, both as a benchmark for measuring undiluted minority voting strength and as a remedial mechanism for guaranteeing minorities undiluted voting power. ...

It should be apparent, however, that there is no principle inherent in our constitutional system, or even in the history of the Nation's electoral practices, that makes single-member districts the "proper" mechanism for electing representatives to governmental bodies or for giving "undiluted" effect to the votes of a numerical minority. On the contrary, from the earliest days of the Republic, multimember districts were a common feature of our political systems. The Framers left unanswered in the Constitution the question whether congressional delegations from the several States should be elected on a general ticket from each State as a whole or under a districting scheme and left that matter to be resolved by the States or by Congress. . . .

The obvious advantage the Court has perceived in single-member districts, of course, is their tendency to enhance the ability of any numerical minority in the electorate to gain control of seats in a representative body. . . . But in choosing single-member districting as a benchmark electoral plan on that basis the Court has made a political decision and, indeed, a decision that itself depends on a prior political choice made in answer to Justice Harlan's question in *Allen*. Justice Harlan asked whether a group's votes should be considered to be more "effective" when they provide influence over a greater number of seats, or control over a lesser number of seats. In answering that query, the Court has determined that the purpose of the vote—or of the fully "effective" vote—is controlling seats. In other words, in an effort to develop standards for assessing claims of dilution, the Court has adopted the view that members of any numerically significant minority are denied a fully effective use of the franchise unless they are able to control seats in an elected body. Under this theory, votes that do not control a representative are essentially wasted; those who cast them go unrepresented and are just as surely disenfranchised as if they had been barred from registering. Such conclusions, of course, depend upon a certain theory of the "effective" vote, a theory that is not inherent in the concept of representative democracy itself.

In fact, it should be clear that the assumptions that have guided the Court reflect only one possible understanding of effective exercise of the franchise, an understanding based on the view that voters are "represented" only when they choose a delegate who will mirror their views in the legislative halls. But it is certainly possible to construct a theory of effective political participation that would accord greater importance to voters' ability to influence, rather than control, elections. And especially in a two-party system such as ours, the influence of a potential "swing" group of voters composing 10%-20% of the electorate in a given district can be considerable. Even such a focus on practical influence, however, is not a necessary component of the definition of the "effective" vote. Some conceptions of representative government may primarily emphasize the formal value of the vote as a mechanism for participation in the electoral process, whether it results in control of a seat or not. Under such a theory, minorities unable to control elected posts would not be considered essentially without a vote; rather, a vote duly cast and counted would be deemed just as "effective" as any other. If a minority group is unable to control seats, that result may plausibly be attributed to the inescapable fact that, in a majoritarian system, numerical minorities lose elections.

But the political choices the Court has had to make do not end with the determination that the primary purpose of the "effective" vote is controlling seats or with the selection of single-member districting as the mechanism for providing that control. In one sense, these were not even the most critical decisions to be made in devising standards for assessing claims of dilution, for in itself, the selection of single-member districting as a benchmark election plan will tell a judge little about the number of minority districts to create. Single-member districting tells a court "how" members of a minority are to control seats, but not "how many" seats they should be allowed to control.

But "how many" is the critical issue. Once one accepts the proposition that the effectiveness of votes is measured in terms of the control of seats, the core of any vote dilution claim is an assertion that the group in question is unable to control the "proper" number of seats — that is, the number of seats that the minority's percentage of the population would enable it to control in the benchmark "fair" system. The claim is inherently based on ratios between the numbers of the minority in the population and the numbers of seats controlled. . . .

The ratio for which this Court has opted, and thus the mathematical principle driving the results in our cases, is undoubtedly direct proportionality. Indeed, four Members of the Court candidly recognized in *Gingles* that the Court had adopted a rule of roughly proportional representation, at least to the extent proportionality was possible given the geographic dispersion of minority populations.

B

The dabbling in political theory that dilution cases have prompted, however, is hardly the worst aspect of our vote dilution jurisprudence. Far more pernicious has been the Court's willingness to accept the one underlying premise that must inform every minority vote dilution claim: the assumption that the group asserting dilution is not merely a racial or ethnic group, but a group having distinct political interests as well. Of necessity, in resolving vote dilution actions we have given credence to the view that race defines political interest. We have acted on the implicit assumption that members of racial and ethnic groups must all think alike on important matters of public policy and must have their own "minority preferred" representatives holding seats in elected bodies if they are to be considered represented at all.

It is true that in *Gingles* we stated that whether a racial group is "politically cohesive" may not be assumed, but rather must be proved in each case. But the standards we have employed for determining political cohesion have proved so insubstantial that this "precondition" does not present much of a barrier to the assertion of vote dilution claims on behalf of any racial group. Moreover, it provides no test—indeed, it is not designed to provide a test—of whether race itself determines a distinctive political community of interest. According to the rule adopted in *Gingles*, plaintiffs must show simply that members of a racial group tend to prefer the same candidates. There is no set standard defining how strong the correlation must be, and an inquiry into the cause for the correlation (to determine, for example, whether it might be the product of similar socio-economic interests rather than some other factor related to race) is unnecessary. Thus, whenever similarities in political preferences along racial lines exist, we proclaim that the cause of the correlation is irrelevant, but we effectively rely on the fact of the correlation to assume that racial groups have unique political interests.

As a result, *Gingles'* requirement of proof of political cohesiveness, as practically applied, has proved little different from a working assumption that racial groups can be conceived of largely as political interest groups. And operating under that assumption, we have assigned federal courts the task of ensuring that minorities are assured their "just" share of seats in elected bodies throughout the Nation.

To achieve that result through the currently fashionable mechanism of drawing majority-minority single-member districts, we have embarked upon what has been aptly characterized as a process of "creating racially 'safe boroughs.'"

The assumptions upon which our vote dilution decisions have been based should be repugnant to any nation that strives for the ideal of a color-blind Constitution. "The principle of equality is at war with the notion that District A must be represented by a Negro, as it is with the notion that District B must be represented by a Caucasian, District C by a Jew, District D by a Catholic, and so on." . . . Under our jurisprudence, rather than requiring registration on racial rolls and dividing power purely on a population basis, we have simply resorted to the somewhat less precise expedient of drawing geographic district lines to capture minority populations and to ensure the existence of the "appropriate" number of "safe minority seats." . . .

As a practical political matter, our drive to segregate political districts by race can only serve to deepen racial divisions by destroying any need for voters or candidates to build bridges between racial groups or to form voting coalitions. "Black-preferred" candidates are assured election in "safe black districts"; white-preferred candidates are assured election in "safe white districts." Neither group needs to draw on support from the other's constituency to win on election day. . . .

As this description suggests, the system we have instituted affirmatively encourages a racially based understanding of the representative function. The clear premise of the system is that geographic districts are merely a device to be manipulated to establish "black representatives" whose real constituencies are defined, not in terms of the voters who populate their districts, but in terms of race. The "black representative's" function, in other words, is to represent the "black interest." . . .

C

While the results we have already achieved under the Voting Rights Act might seem bad enough, we should recognize that our approach to splintering the electorate into racially designated single-member districts does not by any means mark a limit on the authority federal judges may wield to rework electoral systems under our Voting Rights Act jurisprudence. On the contrary, in relying on single-member districting schemes as a touchstone, our cases so far have been somewhat arbitrarily limited to addressing the interests of minority voters who are sufficiently geographically compact to form a majority in a single-member district. There is no reason a priori, however, that our focus should be so constrained. The decision to rely on single-member geographic districts as a mechanism for conducting elections is merely a political choice — and one that we might reconsider in the future. Indeed, it is a choice that has undoubtedly been influenced by the adversary process: in the cases that have come before us, plaintiffs have focused largely upon attacking multimember districts and have offered single-member schemes as the benchmark of an "undiluted" alternative.

But as the destructive effects of our current penchant for majority-minority districts become more apparent, courts will undoubtedly be called upon to reconsider adherence to geographic districting as a method for ensuring minority voting power. Already, some advocates have criticized the current strategy of creating majority-minority districts and have urged the adoption of other voting mechanisms — for example, cumulative voting. . . .

Such changes may seem radical departures from the electoral systems with which we are most familiar. Indeed, they may be unwanted by the people in the several States who purposely have adopted districting systems in their electoral laws. But nothing in our present understanding of the Voting Rights Act places a principled limit on the authority of federal courts that would prevent them from instituting a system of cumulative voting as a remedy under §2, or even from establishing a more elaborate mechanism for securing proportional representation based on transferable votes. . . .

D

Such is the current state of our understanding of the Voting Rights Act. That our reading of the Act has assigned the federal judiciary the task of making the decisions I have described above should suggest to the Members of this Court that something in our jurisprudence has gone awry. We would be mighty Platonic guardians indeed if Congress had granted us the authority to determine the best form of local government for every county, city, village, and town in America. But under our constitutional system, this Court is not a centralized politburo appointed for life to dictate to the provinces the "correct" theories of democratic representation, the "best" electoral systems for securing truly "representative" government, the "fairest" proportions of minority political influence, or, as respondents would have us hold today, the "proper" sizes for local governing bodies. We should be cautious in interpreting any Act of Congress to grant us power to make such determinations. . . .

II

Section 2(a) of the Voting Rights Act provides that "no voting qualification or prerequisite to voting or standard, practice, or procedure shall be imposed or applied by any State or political subdivision in a manner which results in a denial or abridgement of the right of any citizen of the United States to vote" on account of race, color, or membership in one of the language minority groups defined in the Act. Respondents contend that the terms "standard, practice, or procedure" should extend to cover the size of a governmental body. An examination of the text of §2 makes it clear, however, that the terms of the Act do not reach that far; indeed, the terms of the Act do not allow many of the challenges to electoral mechanisms that we have permitted in the past. Properly understood, the terms "standard, practice, or procedure" in §2(a) refer only to practices that affect minority citizens' access to the ballot. Districting systems and electoral mechanisms that may affect the "weight" given to a ballot duly cast and counted are simply beyond the purview of the Act.

A

In determining the scope of §2(a), as when interpreting any statute, we should begin with the statutory language. Under the plain terms of the Act, §2(a) covers only a defined category of state actions. Only "voting qualifications," "prerequisites to voting," or "standards, practices, or procedures" are subject to challenge under the Act. The first two items in this list clearly refer to conditions or tests applied to regulate citizens' access to the ballot. They would cover, for example, any form of test or requirement imposed as a condition on registration or on the process of voting on election day.

Taken in isolation, the last grouping of terms — "standard, practice, or procedure" — may seem somewhat less precise. If we give the words their ordinary meanings, however — for they have no technical significance and are not defined in the Act — they would not normally be understood to include the size of a local governing body. Common sense indicates that the size of a governing body and other aspects of government structure do not comfortably fit within the terms "standard, practice, or procedure." Moreover, we need not simply treat the terms in isolation; indeed, it would be a mistake to do so. Reading the words in context strongly suggests that §2(a) must be understood as referring to any standard, practice, or procedure with respect to voting. And thus understood, the terms of the section would not extend to the size of a governmental body; we would not usually describe the size or form of a governing authority as a "practice" or "procedure" concerning voting.

But under our precedents, we have already stretched the terms "standard, practice, or procedure" beyond the limits of ordinary meaning. We have concluded, for example, that the choice of a certain set of district lines is a "procedure," or perhaps a "practice," concerning voting subject to challenge under the Act, even though the drawing of a given set of district lines has nothing to do with the basic process of allowing a citizen to vote — that is, the process of registering, casting a ballot, and having it counted. Similarly, we have determined that the use of multimember districts, rather than single-member districts, can be challenged under the Act. Undoubtedly, one of the critical reasons we have read §2 to reach such districting decisions is that the choice of one districting system over another can affect a minority group's power to control seats in the elected body. In that respect, however, the districting practices we have treated as subject to challenge under the Act are essentially similar to choices concerning the size of a governing authority. Just as drawing district lines one way rather than another, or using one type of districting system rather than another, can affect the ability of a minority group to control seats, so can restricting the number of seats that are available. And if how districts are drawn is a "practice" concerning voting, why not conclude that how many districts are drawn is a "practice" as well? . . .

If we return to the Act to reexamine the terms setting out the actions regulated by §2, a careful reading of the statutory text will reveal a good deal more about the limitations on the scope of the section than suggested above. The terms "standard, practice, or procedure" appear to have been included in §2 as a sort of catch-all provision. They seem phrased with an eye to eliminating the possibility of evasion. Nevertheless, they are catch-all terms that round out a list, and a sensible and long-established maxim of construction limits the way we should understand such general words appended to an enumeration of more specific items. The principle of ejusdem generis suggests that such general terms should be understood to refer to items belonging to the same class that is defined by the more specific terms in the list.

Here, the specific items described in §2(a) ("voting qualifications" and "prerequisites to voting") indicate that Congress was concerned in this section with any procedure, however it might be denominated, that regulates citizens' access to the ballot — that is, any procedure that might erect a barrier to prevent the potential voter from casting his vote. In describing the laws that would be subject to §2, Congress focused attention upon provisions regulating the interaction between the individual voter and the voting process — on hurdles the citizen might have to cross in the form of "prerequisites" or "qualifications." The general terms in the section are most naturally understood, therefore, to refer to any methods for conducting a part of the voting process that might similarly be used to interfere with a citizen's ability to cast his vote, and they are undoubtedly intended to ensure that the entire voting process — a process that begins with registration and includes the casting of a ballot and having the ballot counted — is covered by the Act. Simply by including general terms in §2(a) to ensure the efficacy of the restriction imposed, Congress should not be understood to have expanded the scope of the restriction beyond the logical limits implied in the specific terms of the statute.

Moreover, it is not only in the terms describing the practices regulated under the Act that §2(a) focuses on the individual voter. The section also speaks only in the singular of the right of "any citizen" to vote. Giving the terms "standard, practice, or procedure" an expansive interpretation to reach potentially dilutive practices, however, would distort that focus on the individual, for a vote dilution claim necessarily depends on the assertion of a group right. . . .

Of course, the scope of the right that is protected under the Act can provide further guidance concerning the meaning of the terms "standard, practice, or procedure." Under the terms of the Act, only a "standard, practice, or procedure" that may result in the "denial or abridgement of the right . . . to vote" is within the reach of §2(a). But nothing in the language used in §2(a) to describe the protection provided by the Act suggests that in protecting the "right to vote," the section was meant to incorporate a concept of voting that encompasses a concern for the "weight" or "influence" of votes. On the contrary, the definition of the terms "vote" and "voting" in §14(c)(1) of Act focuses precisely on access to the ballot. Thus, §14(c)(1) provides that the terms "vote" and "voting" shall encompass any measures necessary to ensure "registration" and any "other action required by law prerequisite to voting, casting a ballot, and having such ballot counted properly and included in the appropriate totals of votes cast."

It is true that §14(c)(1) also states that the term "voting" "includes all action necessary to make a vote effective," and the Court has seized on this language as an indication that Congress intended the Act to reach claims of vote dilution. But if the word "effective" is not plucked out of context, the rest of §14(c)(1) makes clear that the actions Congress deemed necessary to make a vote "effective" were precisely the actions listed above: registering, satisfying other voting prerequisites, casting a ballot, and having it included in the final tally of votes cast. These actions are described in the section only as examples of the steps necessary to make a vote effective. See 42 U.S.C. §1973(c)(1). And while the list of such actions is not exclusive, the nature of all the examples that are provided demonstrates that as far as the Act is concerned, an "effective" vote is merely one that has been cast and fairly counted. . . .

While the terms of §2(a) thus indicate that the section focuses only on securing access to the ballot, it might be argued that reenactment of §2 in 1982 should be understood as an endorsement of the interpretation contained in cases such as *Allen* that the terms "standard, practice, or procedure" were meant to reach potentially dilutive practices. It is true that we generally will assume that reenactment of specific statutory language is intended to include a "settled judicial interpretation" of that language. And while §2 was amended in 1982, the amended section did retain the same language that had appeared in the original Act regulating "standards, practices, or procedures." But it was hardly well settled in 1982 that *Allen*'s broad reading of the terms "standard, practice, or procedure" in §5 would set the scope of §2 as a provision reaching claims of vote dilution.

On the contrary, in 1980 in Mobile v. Bolden, a plurality of the Court construed §2 in a manner flatly inconsistent with the understanding that those terms were meant to reach dilutive practices. Emphasizing that the section tracked the language of the Fifteenth Amendment by prohibiting the use of practices that might "deny or abridge the right . . . to vote," the *Bolden* plurality determined that §2 was "intended to have an effect no different from that of the Fifteenth Amendment itself." In the plurality's view, however, the Fifteenth Amendment did not extend to reach dilution claims; its protections were satisfied as long as members of racial minorities could "'register and vote without hindrance.'" . . .

Finally, as our cases have shown, reading §2(a) to reach beyond laws that regulate in some way citizens' access to the ballot turns the section into a command for courts to evaluate abstract principles of political theory in order to develop rules for deciding which votes are "diluted" and which are not. Common sense would suggest that we should not lightly interpret the Act to require courts to address such matters so far outside the normal bounds of judicial competence, and the mere use of three more general terms at the end of the list of regulated practices in §2(a) cannot properly be understood to incorporate such an expansive command into the Act. . . .

Of course, this interpretation of the terms "standard, practice, or procedure" effectively means that §2(a) does not provide for any claims of what we have called vote "dilution." But that is precisely the result suggested by the text of the statute. Section 2(a) nowhere uses the term "vote dilution" or suggests that its goal is to ensure that votes are given their proper "weight." And an examination of §2(b) does not suggest any different result. . . .

But the mere adoption of a "results" test, rather than an "intent" test, says nothing about the type of state laws that may be challenged using that test.

On the contrary, the type of state law that may be challenged under §2 is addressed explicitly in §2(a). As we noted in Chisom v. Roemer, §§2(a) and 2(b) address distinct issues. While §2(a) defines and explicitly limits the type of voting practice that may be challenged under the Act, §2(b) provides only "the test for determining the legality of such a practice." . . .

Even putting that concern aside for the moment, it should be apparent that the incorporation of a results test into the amended section does not necessarily suggest that Congress intended to allow claims of vote dilution under §2. A results test is useful to plaintiffs whether they are challenging laws that restrict access to the ballot or laws that accomplish some diminution in the "proper weight" of a group's vote. Nothing about the test itself suggests that it is inherently tied to vote dilution claims. A law, for example, limiting the times and places at which registration can occur might be adopted with the purpose of limiting black voter registration, but it could be extremely difficult to prove the discriminatory intent behind such a facially neutral law. The results test would allow plaintiffs to mount a successful challenge to the law under §2 without such proof.

Moreover, nothing in the language §2(b) uses to describe the results test particularly indicates that the test was intended to be used under the Act for assessing claims of dilution. Section 2(b) directs courts to consider whether, under the "totality of circumstances," members of a minority group "have less opportunity than other members of the electorate to participate in the political process and to elect representatives of their choice." The most natural reading of that language would suggest that citizens have an equal "opportunity" to participate in the electoral process and an equal "opportunity" to elect representatives when they have been given the same free and open access to the ballot as other citizens and their votes have been properly counted. The section speaks in terms of an opportunity — a chance — to participate and to elect, not an assured ability to attain any particular result. And since the ballot provides the formal mechanism for obtaining access to the political process and for electing representatives, it would seem that one who has had the same chance as others to register and to cast his ballot has had an equal opportunity to participate and to elect, whether or not any of the candidates he chooses is ultimately successful. . . .

It is true that one factor courts may consider under the results test might fit more comfortably with an interpretation of the Act that reaches vote dilution claims. Section 2(b) provides that "one circumstance" that may be considered in assessing the results test is the "extent to which members of a protected class have been elected to office." Obviously, electoral outcomes would be relevant to claims of vote dilution (assuming, of course, that control of seats has been selected as the measure of effective voting). But in some circumstances, results in recent elections might also be relevant for demonstrating that a particular practice concerning registration or polling has served to suppress minority voting. Better factors to consider would be figures for voter registration or turnout at the last election, broken down according to race. But where such data is not readily available, election results may certainly be "one circumstance" to consider in determining whether a challenged practice has resulted in denying a minority group access to the political process. The Act merely directs courts not to ignore such evidence of electoral outcomes altogether.

Moreover, the language providing that electoral outcomes may be considered as "one circumstance" in the results test is explicitly qualified by the provision in §2(b) that most directly speaks to the question whether §2 was meant to reach claims of vote dilution — and which suggests that dilution claims are not covered by the section. The last clause in the subsection states in unmistakable terms that "nothing in this section establishes a right to have members of a protected class elected in numbers equal to their proportion in the population." As four Members of the Court observed in *Gingles*, there is "an inherent tension" between this disclaimer of proportional representation and an interpretation of §2 that encompasses vote dilution claims. As I explained above, dilution claims, by their very nature, depend upon a mathematical principle. The heart of the claim is an assertion that the plaintiff group does not hold the "proper" number of seats. As a result, the principle for deciding the case must be supplied by an arithmetic ratio. Either the group has attained the "proper" number of seats under the current election system, or it has not.

By declaring that the section provides no right to proportional representation, §2(b) necessarily commands that the existence or absence of proportional electoral results should not become the deciding factor in assessing §2 claims. But in doing so, §2(b) removes from consideration the most logical ratio for assessing a claim of vote dilution. To resolve a dilution claim under §2, therefore, a court either must arbitrarily select a different ratio to represent the "undiluted" norm, a ratio that would have less intuitive appeal than direct proportionality, or it must effectively apply a proportionality test in direct contravention of the text of the Act — hence the "inherent tension" between the text of the Act and vote dilution claims. Given that §2 nowhere speaks in terms of "dilution," an explicit disclaimer removing from the field of play the most natural deciding principle in dilution cases is surely a strong signal that such claims do not fall within the ambit of the Act.

It is true that the terms "standard, practice, or procedure" in §5 of the Act have been construed to reach districting systems and other potentially dilutive electoral mechanisms, and Congress has reenacted §5 subsequent to our decisions adopting that expansive interpretation. Nevertheless, the text of the section suggests precisely the same focus on measures that relate to access to the ballot that appears in §2. Section 5 requires covered jurisdictions to obtain preclearance for a change in "any voting qualification or prerequisite to voting, or standard, practice, or procedure with respect to voting." As in §2, the specific terms in the list of regulated state actions describe only laws that would limit access to the ballot. Moreover, §5 makes the focus on the individual voter and access to the voting booth even more apparent as the section goes on to state that "no person shall be denied the right to vote for failure to comply with such qualification, prerequisite, standard, practice, or procedure." . . . But it should be obvious that a districting system, or any other potentially dilutive mechanism for that matter, is not something with which a voter can comply. As is the case with §2, §5's description of the terms "standard, practice, or procedure" thus suggests a focus on rules that regulate the individual voter's ability to register and cast a ballot, not a more abstract concern with the effect that various electoral systems might have on the "weight" of the votes cast by a group that constitutes a numerical minority in the electorate.

In my view, the tension between the terms of the Act and the construction we have placed on §5 at the very least suggests that our interpretation of §5 should not be adopted wholesale to supply the meaning of the terms "standard, practice, or procedure" under §2. An expansive construction of §5 was well established in 1980, yet a plurality of the Court in *Bolden*, after focusing on the terms of the Act, did not adopt a similarly expansive construction of §2. Rather, the *Bolden* plurality concluded that §2 should be strictly limited to have the same reach as the Fifteenth Amendment, which the plurality interpreted as addressing only matters relating to access to the ballot. I would reach a similar result here. Where a careful reading of the language of §2 dictates a narrow interpretation of the section, there is no reason for transplanting our interpretation of the terms of §5 — an interpretation that I believe is in tension with the text of §5 itself — to another section of the Act.

B

. . . One might wonder, then, why we have consistently concluded that "we know that Congress intended to allow vote dilution claims to be brought under §2." The juxtaposition of the two statements surely makes the result in our cases appear extraordinary, since it suggests a sort of statutory construction through divination that has allowed us to determine that Congress "really meant" to enact a statute about vote dilution even though Congress did not do so explicitly. In truth, our method of construing §2 has been only little better than that, for the only source we have relied upon for the expansive meaning we have given §2 has been the legislative history of the Act.

We first considered the amended §2 in Thornburg v. Gingles. Although the precise scope of the terms "standard, practice, or procedure" was not specifically addressed in that case, *Gingles* nevertheless established our current interpretation of the amended section as a provision that addresses vote dilution, and in particular it fixed our understanding that the results test in §2(b) is intended to measure vote dilution in terms of electoral outcomes. . . .

In approaching §2, the *Gingles* Court, based on little more than a bald assertion that "the authoritative source for legislative intent lies in the Committee Reports on the bill," bypassed a consideration of the text of the Act and proceeded to interpret the section based almost exclusively on its legislative history. It was from the legislative history that the Court culled its understanding that §2 is a provision encompassing claims that an electoral system has diluted a minority group's vote and its understanding that claims of dilution are to be evaluated based upon how closely electoral outcomes under a given system approximate the outcomes that would obtain under an alternative, undiluted norm.

Contrary to the remarkable "legislative history first" method of statutory construction pursued in *Gingles*, however, I had thought it firmly established that the "authoritative source" for legislative intent was the text of the statute passed by both houses of Congress and presented to the President, not a series of partisan statements about purposes and objectives collected by congressional staffers and packaged into a Committee Report. . . .

Moreover, the legislative history of §2 itself, and the Court's use of it in *Gingles*, aptly illustrate that legislative history is often used by this Court as "a forensic rather than an interpretive device," and is read selectively to support the result the Court intends to achieve. It is well documented in the history of the 1982 amendments to the Act that §2 was passed only after a compromise was reached through the addition of the provision in §2(b) disclaiming any right to proportional representation. But the views of the author of that compromise, Senator Dole, hardly coincide with the gloss the Court has placed on §2.

According to Senator Dole, amended §2 would "absolutely not" provide any redress to a group of voters challenging electoral mechanisms in a jurisdiction "if the process is open, if there is equal access, if there are no barriers, direct or indirect, thrown up to keep someone from voting or having their vote counted, or registering, whatever the process may include." Contrary to the Court's interpretation of the section in *Gingles*, Senator Dole viewed §2 as a provision more narrowly focused on access to the processes surrounding the casting of a ballot, not a provision concerned with ensuring electoral outcomes in accordance with some "undiluted" norm. The legislative history thus hardly provided unambiguous support for the Court's interpretation; indeed, it seems that the Court used what was helpful to its interpretation in the legislative history and ignored what was not. . . .

Remarkably, thanks to our reliance on legislative history, we have interpreted §2 in such a way that four Members of this Court at one time candidly admitted that "there is an inherent tension [in §2] between what Congress wished to do and what it wished to avoid." But our understanding of what Congress purportedly "wished to do" — that is, to allow claims of vote "dilution" — depends solely on a selective reading of legislative history, whereas Congress' statement of what it "wished to avoid" appears explicitly in §2(b)'s disclaimer of a right to proportional representation. I can see no logical reason to import the "inherent tension" between these two imperatives into the Act, when on its face the statute incorporates only one of two potentially contradictory commands. I would have thought the key to resolving any such conflict between the text and the legislative history obvious: the text of the statute must control, and the text of §2 does not extend the Act to claims of dilution.

C

"Stare decisis is not an inexorable command." Indeed, "when governing decisions are unworkable or are badly reasoned, this Court has never felt constrained to follow precedent." The discussion above should make clear that our decision in *Gingles* interpreting the scope of §2 was badly reasoned; it wholly substituted reliance on legislative history for analysis of statutory text. In doing so, it produced a far more expansive interpretation of §2 than a careful reading of the language of the statute would allow. . . .

In my view, our current practice should not continue. Not for another Term, not until the next case, not for another day. The disastrous implications of the policies we have adopted under the Act are too grave; the dissembling in our approach to the Act too damaging to the credibility of the federal judiciary. The "inherent tension" — indeed, I would call it an irreconcilable conflict — between the standards we have adopted for evaluating vote dilution claims and the text of the Voting Rights Act would itself be sufficient in my view to warrant overruling the interpretation of §2 set out in *Gingles*. When that obvious conflict is combined with the destructive effects our expansive reading of the Act has had in involving the federal judiciary in the project of dividing the Nation into racially segregated electoral districts, I can see no reasonable alternative to abandoning our current unfortunate understanding of the Act.

Stare decisis is a powerful concern, especially in the field of statutory construction. Stare decisis should not bind the Court to an interpretation of the Voting Rights Act that was based on a flawed method of statutory construction from its inception and that in every day of its continued existence involves the federal judiciary in attempts to obscure the conflict between our cases and the explicit commands of the Act. . . .

III

For the foregoing reasons, I agree with the Court's conclusion that the size of a governing body is not subject to challenge under §2 of the Voting Rights Act. . . .

JUSTICE BLACKMUN, with whom JUSTICE STEVENS, JUSTICE SOUTER, and JUSTICE GINSBURG join, dissenting.

Five Justices today agree that the size of a governing body is a "standard, practice, or procedure" under §2 of the Voting Rights Act. . . . A different five Justices decide, under three separate theories, that voting rights plaintiffs cannot bring §2 dilution challenges based on size. I, however, believe that the Act, its history, and our own precedent require us to conclude not only that the size of a governing body is a "standard, practice, or procedure" under §2, but also that minority voters may challenge the dilutive effects of this practice by demonstrating their potential to elect representatives under an objectively reasonable alternative practice. Accordingly, I dissent from the Court's decision that minority voters cannot bring §2 vote dilution challenges based on the size of an existing government body.

I . . .

Nearly 30 years of precedent admonish us that the Act, which was adopted "for the broad remedial purpose of 'ridding the country of racial discrimination in voting,'" should be given "the broadest possible scope." Because "the Act itself nowhere amplifies the meaning of the phrase 'standard, practice, or procedure with respect to voting,'" the Court "has sought guidance from the history and purpose of the Act."

Consistent with the Act's remedial purposes, this Court has held that a wide variety of election- and voting-related practices fit within the term "standard, practice, or procedure." . . .

Specifically, this Court long has treated a change in the size of a governing authority as a change in a "standard, practice, or procedure with respect to voting." . . .

And, as the Court recognized . . . , a change in the size of a governing authority is a "standard, practice, or procedure with respect to voting" because the change "increases or diminishes the number of officials for whom the electorate may vote"; this change bears "on the substance of voting power" and has "a direct relation to voting and the election process."

To date, our precedent has dealt with §5 challenges to a change in the size of a governing authority, rather than §2 challenges to the existing size of a governing body. I agree . . . that, as a textual matter, "standard, practice, or procedure" under §2 is at least as broad as "standard, practice, or procedure with respect to voting" under §5. In fact, because of the "close connection" between §2 and §5, we interpret them similarly.

Congress repeatedly has endorsed the broad construction this Court has given the Act in general and §5 in particular. Significantly, when Congress considered the 1982 amendments to the Voting Rights Act, it made no effort to curtail the application of §5 to changes in size, in the face of the longstanding practice of submitting such changes for preclearance, and on the heels of this Court's recognition just two years earlier that it was "not disputed" that a change in the size of a governing body was covered under §5. Similarly, the Attorney General, whose construction of the Act "is entitled to considerable deference," for years has required §5 preclearance of the expansion or reduction of a governing body. It is not surprising that no party to this case argued that the size of a governing authority is not a "standard, practice, or procedure."

In light of this consistent and expansive interpretation of the Act by this Court, Congress, and the Attorney General, the Act's "all-inclusive" definition of "standard, practice, or procedure," cannot be read to exclude threshold coverage of challenges to the size of a governing authority. As five members of the Court today agree, the size of a governing authority is a "standard, practice, or procedure" with respect to voting for purposes of §2 as well as §5 of the Voting Rights Act.

II

Although five Justices agree that the size of a governing body is a "standard, practice, or procedure" under §2, a like number of Justices conclude, under varying rationales, that Voting Rights plaintiffs nonetheless cannot bring size challenges under §2. This conclusion is inconsistent with our precedent giving the Act" 'the broadest possible scope' in combatting racial discrimination," and with the vote-dilution analysis prescribed in Thornburg v. Gingles. . . .

By all objective measures, the proposed five-member Bleckley County Commission presents a reasonable, workable benchmark against which to measure the practice of electing a sole commissioner. First, the Georgia Legislature specifically authorized a five-member commission for Bleckley County. Moreover, a five-member commission is the most common form of governing authority in Georgia. Finally, the county itself has moved from a single superintendent of education to a school board with five members elected from single-member districts, providing a workable and readily available model for commission districts. Thus, the proposed five-member baseline is reasonable and workable.

In this case, identifying an appropriate baseline against which to measure dilution is not difficult. In other cases, it may be harder. But the need to make difficult judgments does not "justify a judicially created limitation on the coverage of the broadly worded statute, as enacted and amended by Congress." Vote dilution is inherently a relative concept, requiring a highly "flexible, fact-intensive" inquiry and calling for an exercise of the "court's overall judgment, based on the totality of the circumstances and guided by those relevant factors in the particular case," as mandated by Congress. Certainly judges who engage in the complex task of evaluating reapportionment plans and examining district lines will be able to determine whether a proposed baseline is an appropriate one against which to measure a claim of vote dilution based on the size of a county commission. . . .

Separate opinion of JUSTICE STEVENS, in which JUSTICE BLACKMUN, JUSTICE SOUTER, and JUSTICE GINSBURG join. . . .

Justice Thomas' narrow interpretation of the words "voting qualification . . . standard, practice, or procedure," if adopted, would require us to overrule *Allen* and the cases that have adhered to its reading of the critical statutory language. . . .

The large number of decisions that we would have to overrule or reconsider, as well as the congressional reenactments discussed above, suggests that Justice Thomas' radical reinterpretation of the Voting Rights Act is barred by the well-established principle that stare decisis has special force in the statutory arena.

Justice Thomas attempts to minimize the radical implications of his interpretation of the phrase "voting qualification . . . standard, practice, or procedure" by noting that this case involves only the interpretation of §2 of the Voting Rights Act. Section 5, he hints, might be interpreted differently. Even limiting the reinterpretation to §2 cases, however, would require overruling a sizable number of this Court's precedents. In addition, a distinction between §2 and §5 is difficult to square with the language of the statute. Sections 2 and 5 contain exactly the same words: "voting qualification . . . standard, practice, or procedure." If anything, the wording of §5 is narrower, because it adds the limiting phrase "with respect to voting" after the word "procedure." Moreover, when Congress amended the Voting Rights Act in 1982 in response to *Bolden*, it amended §2. As noted above, in those amendments Congress clearly endorsed the application of the Voting Rights Act to vote dilution claims. While a distinction between §2 and §5 might be supportable on policy grounds, it is an odd distinction for devotees of "plain language" interpretation.

Throughout his opinion, Justice Thomas argues that this case is an exception to stare decisis, because *Allen* and its progeny have "immersed the federal courts in a hopeless project of weighing questions of political theory." There is no question that the Voting Rights Act has required the courts to resolve difficult questions, but that is no reason to deviate from an interpretation that Congress has thrice approved. Statutes frequently require courts to make policy judgments. The Sherman Act, for example, requires courts to delve deeply into the theory of economic organization. Similarly, Title VII of the Civil Rights Act has required the courts to formulate a theory of equal opportunity. Our work would certainly be much easier if every case could be resolved by consulting a dictionary, but when Congress has legislated in general terms, judges may not invoke judicial modesty to avoid difficult questions.

III

When a statute has been authoritatively, repeatedly, and consistently construed for more than a quarter century, and when Congress has reenacted and extended the statute several times with full awareness of that construction, judges have an especially clear obligation to obey settled law. Whether Justice Thomas is correct that the Court's settled construction of the Voting Rights Act has been "a disastrous misadventure" should not affect the decision in this case. It is therefore inappropriate for me to comment on the portions of his opinion that are best described as an argument that the statute be repealed or amended in important respects. . . .

NOTES AND QUESTIONS

1. *The typical problem of general statutes.* From one perspective, this case represents the common problem of applying broad, general statutory language to a particular set of facts. From this perspective, the case is not much different from *Thornburg* and *Roemer*. The question for the Court is whether a "benchmark" is needed in a §2 dilution case. Excluding Justices Thomas and Scalia, on what basis do the remaining Justices answer the question?

2. *Justice Thomas' concurrence—the political vision.* What makes this case particularly interesting is Justice Thomas' concurrence. Joined by Justice Scalia, Justice Thomas undertakes a frontal assault on what he characterizes as a judicial conversion of the Voting Rights Act from a narrowly defined prohibition against certain practices to a "grant of authority to the federal judiciary to develop theories on basic principles of representative government." His aim is not on the size of governmental authorities (which, of course, the Court rejects as subject to §2), but the vote dilution cases that have been the mainstay of voting rights jurisprudence. Recall the debate over the Voting Rights Act found in Chapter 6. Where does Justice Thomas fit in this debate? What are the basic principles of representative government that Justice Thomas believes the Court has decided, and are these judicial determinations inconsistent with the Voting Rights Act of 1965, as amended? Is Justice Thomas' dispute in the first instance with the Court or Congress?

3. *Justice Thomas' concurrence—the approach to interpretation.* According to Justice Thomas, his criticism of the Court's voting rights jurisprudence is textually based. In other words, he argues that his view reflects statutory deference and those of his colleagues, excluding Justice Scalia, judicial willfulness. His argument revolves around the position that the phrase "standard, practice, and procedure" does not include redistricting plans (let alone the size of governmental authorities). On what basis does he argue that the text supports his narrow view of the Voting Rights Act?

4. *Several canons.* Three canons play a role in this decision. The first, employed by Justice Thomas, is ejusdem generis. What is the presumption behind this canon, how well does it reflect legislative procedure, and how well is it applied in this case? The second canon is "the reenactment of specific statutory language by a legislative body is the reenactment of settled judicial interpretation of that language." How well does this canon reflect the legislative process? How is it applied by the various Justices who discuss it? Finally, the dissent turns to the canon "remedial statute should be read broadly." As was discussed in Chapter 11, this canon is clearly not well anchored in the legislative process, which tends toward compromise, particularly in the making of substantial legislative changes. A better canon might be "remedial statutes should be read moderately." The canon's applicability is rejected here.

5. *A problem raised by Justice Thomas.* Assume your state legislature is bicameral, legislators in both houses being chosen from single-member districts. In your state, protected minorities constitute 20 percent of the population, but in no place in the state are they congregated enough to form a majority of any single district. Assume that no minority representative has been elected to the state legislature, although several have been candidates. In those cases, minorities have tended to vote for minorities and whites have tended to vote for whites. Members of the minority groups bring an action challenging the districting plan, arguing that it ought to be replaced by a cumulative-voting county-based model. Under this model, the total number of legislators to be elected would be divided by counties (assume all counties are basically the same size) and would run on an at-large basis from each county. In other words, if the population of your county supported five legislators, they would each run county-wide. Each voter of that county would then be able to cast five votes but would be able to cast all five for one candidate or split them in any way he or she wished. This form of voting would allow minority group members to elect a candidate of their choice if enough of them concentrated their votes for the chosen candidate. Do you think a court could impose this plan on your state legislature backed by §2 of the Voting Rights Act?

6. *Stare decisis.* As part of its decision process, the Court engages in a debate over the significance of stare decisis in the interpretation of statutes. What are the various views expressed in this debate?

7. *An exercise in theory.* Assume that each of the Justices who authored an opinion in this case had as his or her approach to statutory construction Professor Eskridge's theory of dynamic statutory construction (Chapter 10, page 710). How would each of them have decided this case? Similarly, assume that each of these Justices adopted Judge Easterbrook's approach (Chapter 10, page 708). How would each of them have decided this case?

B.   AMBIGUITIES FROM COMPROMISES

Landgraf v. USI Film Products
511 U.S. 244 (1994)

Statute: §§402(a) and (b), 109(c) of the Civil Rights Act of 1991

SECTION 402. (a) Except as otherwise specifically provided, this Act and the amendments made by this Act shall take effect upon enactment.

(b) Notwithstanding any other provision of this Act, nothing in this Act shall apply to any disparate impact case for which a complaint was filed before March 1, 1975, and for which an initial decision was rendered after October 30, 1983.

SECTION 109. (c) [Part of the section extending Title VII to overseas employers.] The amendments made by this section shall not apply with respect to conduct occurring before the date of the enactment of this Act.

JUSTICE STEVENS delivered the opinion of the Court. [Citations and footnotes have been omitted except where particularly relevant.]

The Civil Rights Act of 1991 (1991 Act or Act) creates a right to recover compensatory and punitive damages for certain violations of Title VII of the Civil Rights Act of 1964. The Act further provides that any party may demand a trial by jury if such damages are sought. We granted certiorari to decide whether these provisions apply to a Title VII case that was pending on appeal when the statute was enacted. We hold that they do not.

I

From September 4, 1984, through January 17, 1986, petitioner Barbara Landgraf was employed in the USI Film Products (USI) plant in Tyler, Texas. She worked the 11 P.M. to 7 A.M. shift operating a machine that produced plastic bags. A fellow employee named John Williams repeatedly harassed her with inappropriate remarks and physical contact. Petitioner's complaints to her immediate supervisor brought her no relief, but when she reported the incidents to the personnel manager, he conducted an investigation, reprimanded Williams, and transferred him to another department. Four days later petitioner quit her job. . . .

On July 21, 1989, petitioner commenced this action against USI, its corporate owner, and that company's successor-in-interest. After a bench trial, the District Court found that Williams had sexually harassed petitioner causing her to suffer mental anguish. However, the court concluded that she had not been constructively discharged. . . .

Because the court found that petitioner's employment was not terminated in violation of Title VII, she was not entitled to equitable relief, and because Title VII did not then authorize any other form of relief, the court dismissed her complaint.

On November 21, 1991, while petitioner's appeal was pending, the President signed into law the Civil Rights Act of 1991. . . .

II

Petitioner's primary submission is that the text of the 1991 Act requires that it be applied to cases pending on its enactment. Her argument, if accepted, would make the entire Act (with two narrow exceptions) applicable to conduct that occurred, and to cases that were filed, before the Act's effective date. Although only §102 is at issue in this case, we therefore preface our analysis with a brief description of the scope of the 1991 Act.

The Civil Rights Act of 1991 is in large part a response to a series of decisions of this Court interpreting the Civil Rights Acts of 1866 and 1964. Section 3(4) expressly identifies as one of the Act's purposes "to respond to recent decisions of the Supreme Court by expanding the scope of relevant civil rights statutes in order to provide adequate protection to victims of discrimination." . . .

A number of important provisions in the Act, however, were not responses to Supreme Court decisions. . . . Among the provisions that did not directly respond to any Supreme Court decision is the one at issue in this case, §102. . . .

Section 102 significantly expands the monetary relief potentially available to plaintiffs who would have been entitled to backpay under prior law. . . . Under §102, however, a Title VII plaintiff who wins a backpay award may also seek compensatory damages for "future pecuniary losses, emotional pain, suffering, inconvenience, mental anguish, loss of enjoyment of life, and other nonpecuniary losses." §102(b)(3). In addition, when it is shown that the employer acted "with malice or with reckless indifference to the [plaintiff's] federally protected rights," §102(b)(1), a plaintiff may recover punitive damages. . . .

In 1990, a comprehensive civil rights bill passed both Houses of Congress. Although similar to the 1991 Act in many other respects, the 1990 bill differed in that it contained language expressly calling for application of many of its provisions, including the section providing for damages in cases of intentional employment discrimination, to cases arising before its (expected) enactment. The President vetoed the 1990 legislation, however, citing the bill's "unfair retroactivity rules" as one reason for his disapproval. Congress narrowly failed to override the veto (66-34 Senate vote in favor of override).

The absence of comparable language in the 1991 Act cannot realistically be attributed to oversight or to unawareness of the retroactivity issue. Rather, it seems likely that one of the compromises that made it possible to enact the 1991 version was an agreement not to include the kind of explicit retroactivity command found in the 1990 bill.

The omission of the elaborate retroactivity provision of the 1990 bill — which was by no means the only source of political controversy over that legislation — is not dispositive because it does not tell us precisely where the compromise was struck in the 1991 Act. The Legislature might, for example, have settled in 1991 on a less expansive form of retroactivity that, unlike the 1990 bill, did not reach cases already finally decided. A decision to reach only cases still pending might explain Congress' failure to provide in the 1991 Act, as it had in 1990, that certain sections would apply to proceedings pending on specific preenactment dates. Our first question, then, is whether the statutory text on which petitioner relies manifests an intent that the 1991 Act should be applied to cases that arose and went to trial before its enactment.

III

Petitioner's textual argument relies on three provisions of the 1991 Act: §§402(a), 402(b), and 109(c). Section 402(a), the only provision of the Act that speaks directly to the question before us, states:

> Except as otherwise specifically provided, this Act and the amendments made by this Act shall take effect upon enactment.

That language does not, by itself, resolve the question before us. A statement that a statute will become effective on a certain date does not even arguably suggest that it has any application to conduct that occurred at an earlier date. Petitioner does not argue otherwise. Rather, she contends that the introductory clause of §402(a) would be superfluous unless it refers to §§402(b) and 109(c), which provide for prospective application in limited contexts.

The parties agree that §402(b) was intended to exempt a single disparate impact lawsuit against the Wards Cove Packing Company. Section 402(b) provides:

> (b) Certain Disparate Impact Cases. — Notwithstanding any other provision of this Act, nothing in this Act shall apply to any disparate impact case for which a complaint was filed before March 1, 1975, and for which an initial decision was rendered after October 30, 1983.

Section 109(c), part of the section extending Title VII to overseas employers, states:

> (c) Application of Amendments. — The amendments made by this section shall not apply with respect to conduct occurring before the date of the enactment of this Act.

According to petitioner, these two subsections are the "other provisions" contemplated in the first clause of §402(a), and together create a strong negative inference that all sections of the Act not specifically declared prospective apply to pending cases that arose before November 21, 1991.

Before addressing the particulars of petitioner's argument, we observe that she places extraordinary weight on two comparatively minor and narrow provisions in a long and complex statute. Applying the entire Act to cases arising from preenactment conduct would have important consequences, including the possibility that trials completed before its enactment would need to be retried and the possibility that employers would be liable for punitive damages for conduct antedating the Act's enactment. Purely prospective application, on the other hand, would prolong the life of a remedial scheme, and of judicial constructions of civil rights statutes, that Congress obviously found wanting. Given the high stakes of the retroactivity question, the broad coverage of the statute, and the prominent and specific retroactivity provisions in the 1990 bill, it would be surprising for Congress to have chosen to resolve that question through negative inferences drawn from two provisions of quite limited effect.

Petitioner, however, invokes the canon that a court should give effect to every provision of a statute and thus avoid redundancy among different provisions. Unless the word "otherwise" in §402(a) refers to either §402(b) or §109(c), she contends, the first five words in §402(a) are entirely superfluous. Moreover, relying on the canon "expressio unius est exclusio alterius," petitioner argues that because Congress provided specifically for prospectivity in two places (§§109(c) and 402(b)), we should infer that it intended the opposite for the remainder of the statute.

Petitioner emphasizes that §402(a) begins: "Except as otherwise specifically provided." A scan of the statute for other "specific provisions" concerning effective dates reveals that §§402(b) and 109(c) are the most likely candidates. Since those provisions decree prospectivity, and since §402(a) tells us that the specific provisions are exceptions, §402(b) should be considered as prescribing a general rule of retroactivity. Petitioner's argument has some force, but we find it most unlikely that Congress intended the introductory clause to carry the critically important meaning petitioner assigns it. Had Congress wished §402(a) to have such a determinate meaning, it surely would have used language comparable to its reference to the predecessor Title VII damages provisions in the 1990 legislation: that the new provisions "shall apply to all proceedings pending on or commenced after the date of enactment of this Act."

It is entirely possible that Congress inserted the "otherwise specifically provided" language not because it understood the "takes effect" clause to establish a rule of retroactivity to which only two "other specific provisions" would be exceptions, but instead to assure that any specific timing provisions in the Act would prevail over the general "take effect on enactment" command. The drafters of a complicated piece of legislation containing more than 50 separate sections may well have inserted the "except as otherwise provided" language merely to avoid the risk of an inadvertent conflict in the statute. If the introductory clause of §402(a) was intended to refer specifically to §§402(b), 109(c), or both, it is difficult to understand why the drafters chose the word "otherwise" rather than either or both of the appropriate section numbers.

We are also unpersuaded by petitioner's argument that both §§402(b) and 109(c) merely duplicate the "take effect upon enactment" command of §402(a) unless all other provisions, including the damages provisions of §102, apply to pending cases. That argument depends on the assumption that all those other provisions must be treated uniformly for purposes of their application to pending cases based on preenactment conduct. That thesis, however, is by no means an inevitable one. It is entirely possible — indeed, highly probable — that, because it was unable to resolve the retroactivity issue with the clarity of the 1990 legislation, Congress viewed the matter as an open issue to be resolved by the courts. Our precedents on retroactivity left doubts about what default rule would apply in the absence of congressional guidance, and suggested that some provisions might apply to cases arising before enactment while others might not. The only matters Congress did not leave to the courts were set out with specificity in §§109(c) and 402(b). Congressional doubt concerning judicial retroactivity doctrine, coupled with the likelihood that the routine "take effect upon enactment" language would require courts to fall back upon that doctrine, provide a plausible explanation for both §§402(b) and 109(c) that makes neither provision redundant.

Turning to the text of §402(b), it seems unlikely that the introductory phrase ("Notwithstanding any other provision of this Act") was meant to refer to the immediately preceding subsection. Since petitioner does not contend that any other provision speaks to the general effective date issue, the logic of her argument requires us to interpret that phrase to mean nothing more than "Notwithstanding §402(a)." Petitioner's textual argument assumes that the drafters selected the indefinite word "otherwise" in §402(a) to identify two specific subsections and the even more indefinite term "any other provision" in §402(b) to refer to nothing more than §402(b)'s next-door neighbor — §402(a). Here again, petitioner's statutory argument would require us to assume that Congress chose a surprisingly

874 Chapter 12 Resolving Ambiguities

indirect route to convey an important and easily expressed message concerning the Act's effect on pending cases.

The relevant legislative history of the 1991 Act reinforces our conclusion that §§402(a), 109(c) and 402(b) cannot bear the weight petitioner places upon them. The 1991 bill as originally introduced in the House contained explicit retroactivity provisions similar to those found in the 1990 bill. However, the Senate substitute that was agreed upon omitted those explicit retroactivity provisions. The legislative history discloses some frankly partisan statements about the meaning of the final effective date language, but those statements cannot plausibly be read as reflecting any general agreement. [See Chapter 2, Section B.10.] The history reveals no evidence that Members believed that an agreement had been tacitly struck on the controversial retroactivity issue, and little to suggest that Congress understood or intended the interplay of §§402(a), 402(b) and 109(c) to have the decisive effect petitioner assigns them. Instead, the history of the 1991 Act conveys the impression that legislators agreed to disagree about whether and to what extent the Act would apply to preenactment conduct.

Although the passage of the 1990 bill may indicate that a majority of the 1991 Congress also favored retroactive application, even the will of the majority does not become law unless it follows the path charted in Article I, §7, cl. 2 of the Constitution. See INS v. Chadha. In the absence of the kind of unambiguous directive found in §15 of the 1990 bill, we must look elsewhere for guidance on whether §102 applies to this case.

IV

It is not uncommon to find "apparent tension" between different canons of statutory construction. As Professor Llewellyn famously illustrated, many of the traditional canons have equal opposites. In order to resolve the question left open by the 1991 Act, federal courts have labored to reconcile two seemingly contradictory statements found in our decisions concerning the effect of intervening changes in the law. Each statement is framed as a generally applicable rule for interpreting statutes that do not specify their temporal reach. The first is the rule that "a court is to apply the law in effect at the time it renders its decision," Bradley [v. Richmond School Bd.]. The second is the axiom that "retroactivity is not favored in the law," and its interpretive corollary that "congressional enactments and administrative rules will not be construed to have retroactive effect unless their language requires this result." Bowen [v. Georgetown Univ. Hospital]. . . .

[W]e turn to the "apparent tension" between the two canons mindful of another canon of unquestionable vitality, the "maxim not to be disregarded that general expressions, in every opinion, are to be taken in connection with the case in which those expressions are used."

A

As Justice Scalia has demonstrated, the presumption against retroactive legislation is deeply rooted in our jurisprudence, and embodies a legal doctrine centuries older than our Republic. Elementary considerations of fairness dictate that individuals should have an opportunity to know what the law is and to conform their conduct accordingly; settled expectations should not be lightly disrupted. For that reason, the "principle that the legal effect of conduct should ordinarily be assessed under the law that existed when the conduct took place has timeless and universal appeal." In a free, dynamic society, creativity in both commercial and artistic endeavors is fostered by a rule of law that gives people confidence about the legal consequences of their actions.

It is therefore not surprising that the antiretroactivity principle finds expression in several provisions of our Constitution. The Ex Post Facto Clause flatly prohibits retroactive application of penal legislation. Article I, §10, cl. 1 prohibits States from passing another type of retroactive legislation, laws "impairing the Obligation of Contracts." The Fifth Amendment's Takings Clause prevents the Legislature (and other government actors) from depriving private persons of vested property rights except for a "public use" and upon payment of "just compensation." The prohibitions on "Bills of Attainder" in Art. I, §§9–10, prohibit legislatures from singling out disfavored persons and meting out summary punishment for past conduct. The Due Process Clause also protects the interests in fair notice and repose that may be compromised by retroactive legislation; a justification sufficient to validate a statute's prospective application under the Clause "may not suffice" to warrant its retroactive application.

These provisions demonstrate that retroactive statutes raise particular concerns. The Legislature's unmatched powers allow it to sweep away settled expectations suddenly and without individualized consideration. Its responsivity to political pressures poses a risk that it may be tempted to use retroactive legislation as a means of retribution against unpopular groups or individuals. . . .

The Constitution's restrictions, of course, are of limited scope. Absent a violation of one of those specific provisions, the potential unfairness of retroactive civil legislation is not a sufficient reason for a court to fail to give a statute its intended scope. Retroactivity provisions often serve entirely benign and legitimate purposes, whether to respond to emergencies, to correct mistakes, to prevent circumvention of a new statute in the interval immediately preceding its passage, or simply to give comprehensive effect to a new law Congress considers salutary. However, a requirement that Congress first make its intention clear helps ensure that Congress itself has determined that the benefits of retroactivity outweigh the potential for disruption or unfairness.

While statutory retroactivity has long been disfavored, deciding when a statute operates "retroactively" is not always a simple or mechanical task. . . .

A statute does not operate [retroactively] . . . merely because it is applied in a case arising from conduct antedating the statute's enactment or upsets expectations based in prior law. Rather, the court must ask whether the new provision attaches new legal consequences to events completed before its enactment. The conclusion that a particular rule operates "retroactively" comes at the end of a process of judgment concerning the nature and extent of the change in the law and the degree of connection between the operation of the new rule and a relevant past event. Any test of retroactivity will leave room for disagreement in hard cases, and is unlikely to classify the enormous variety of legal changes with perfect philosophical clarity. However, retroactivity is a matter on which judges tend to have "sound . . . instincts," and familiar considerations of fair notice, reasonable reliance, and settled expectations offer sound guidance.

Since the early days of this Court, we have declined to give retroactive effect to statutes burdening private rights unless Congress had made clear its intent. . . .

The presumption against statutory retroactivity had special force in the era in which courts tended to view legislative interference with property and contract rights circumspectly. In this century, legislation has come to supply the dominant means of legal ordering, and circumspection has given way to greater deference to legislative judgments. But while the constitutional impediments to retroactive civil legislation are now modest, prospectivity remains the appropriate default rule. Because it accords with widely held intuitions about how statutes ordinarily operate, a presumption against retroactivity will generally coincide with legislative and public expectations. Requiring clear intent assures that Congress itself has affirmatively considered the potential unfairness of retroactive application and determined that it is an acceptable price to pay for the countervailing benefits. Such a requirement allocates to Congress responsibility for fundamental policy judgments concerning the proper temporal reach of statutes, and has the additional virtue of giving legislators a predictable background rule against which to legislate.

B

Although we have long embraced a presumption against statutory retroactivity, for just as long we have recognized that, in many situations, a court should "apply the law in effect at the time it renders its decision," even though that law was enacted after the events that gave rise to the suit. . . .

When a case implicates a federal statute enacted after the events in suit, the court's first task is to determine whether Congress has expressly prescribed the statute's proper reach. If Congress has done so, of course, there is no need to resort to judicial default rules. When, however, the statute contains no such express command, the court must determine whether the new statute would have retroactive effect, i.e., whether it would impair rights a party possessed when he acted, increase a party's liability for past conduct, or impose new duties with respect to transactions already completed. If the statute would operate retroactively, our traditional presumption teaches that it does not govern absent clear congressional intent favoring such a result.

V

We now ask whether, given the absence of guiding instructions from Congress, §102 of the Civil Rights Act of 1991 is the type of provision that should govern cases arising before its enactment. As we observed, there is no special reason to think that all the diverse provisions of the Act must be treated uniformly for such purposes. To the contrary, we understand the instruction that the provisions are to "take effect upon enactment" to mean that courts should evaluate each provision of the Act in light of ordinary judicial principles concerning the application of new rules to pending cases and preenactment conduct.

Two provisions of §102 may be readily classified according to these principles. The jury trial right set out in §102(c)(1) is plainly a procedural change of the sort that would ordinarily govern in trials conducted after its effective date. If §102 did no more than introduce a right to jury trial in Title VII cases, the provision would presumably apply to cases tried after November 21, 1991, regardless of when the underlying conduct occurred. However, because §102(c) makes a jury trial available only "if a complaining party seeks compensatory or punitive damages," the jury trial option must stand or fall with the attached damages provisions.

Section 102(b)(1) is clearly on the other side of the line. That subsection authorizes punitive damages if the plaintiff shows that the defendant "engaged in a discriminatory practice or discriminatory practices with malice or with reckless indifference to the federally protected rights of an aggrieved individual." The very labels given "punitive" or "exemplary" damages, as well as the rationales that support them, demonstrate that they share key characteristics of criminal sanctions. Retroactive imposition of punitive damages would raise a serious constitutional question. . . .

The provision of §102(a)(1) authorizing the recovery of compensatory damages is not easily classified. It does not make unlawful conduct that was lawful when it occurred; as we have noted, §102 only reaches discriminatory conduct already prohibited by Title VII. Concerns about a lack of fair notice are further muted by the fact that such discrimination was in many cases (although not this one) already subject to monetary liability in the form of backpay. Nor could anyone seriously contend that the compensatory damages provisions smack of a "retributive" or other suspect legislative purpose. Section 102 reflects Congress' desire to afford victims of discrimination more complete redress for violations of rules established more than a generation ago in the Civil Rights Act of 1964. At least with respect to its compensatory damages provisions, then, §102 is not in a category in which objections to retroactive application on grounds of fairness have their greatest force.

Nonetheless, the new compensatory damages provision would operate "retrospectively" if it were applied to conduct occurring before November 21, 1991. Unlike certain other forms of relief, compensatory damages are quintessentially backward-looking. Compensatory damages may be intended less to sanction wrongdoers than to make victims whole, but they do so by a mechanism that affects the liabilities of defendants. They do not "compensate" by distributing funds from the public coffers, but by requiring particular employers to pay for harms they caused. The introduction of a right to compensatory damages is also the type of legal change that would have an impact on private parties' planning. In this case, the event to which the new damages provision relates is the discriminatory conduct of respondents' agent John Williams; if applied here, that provision would attach an important new legal burden to that conduct. The new damages remedy in §102, we conclude, is the kind of provision that does not apply to events antedating its enactment in the absence of clear congressional intent.

In cases like this one, in which prior law afforded no relief, §102 can be seen as creating a new cause of action, and its impact on parties' rights is especially pronounced. Section 102 confers a new right to monetary relief on persons like petitioner who were victims of a hostile work environment but were not constructively discharged, and the novel prospect of damages liability for their employers. Because Title VII previously authorized recovery of backpay in some cases, and because compensatory damages under §102(a) are in addition to any backpay recoverable, the new provision also resembles a statute increasing the amount of damages available under a preestablished cause of action. Even under that view, however, the provision would, if applied in cases arising before the Act's effective date, undoubtedly impose on employers found liable a "new disability" in respect to past events.

It will frequently be true, as petitioner . . . forcefully argue[s] here, that retroactive application of a new statute would vindicate its purpose more fully. That consideration, however, is not sufficient to rebut the presumption against retroactivity. Statutes are seldom crafted to pursue a single goal, and compromises necessary to their enactment may require adopting means other than those that would most effectively pursue the main goal. A legislator who supported a prospective statute might reasonably oppose retroactive application of the same statute. Indeed, there is reason to believe that the omission of the 1990 version's express retroactivity provisions was a factor in the passage of the 1991 bill. Section 102 is plainly not the sort of provision that must be understood to operate retroactively because a contrary reading would render it ineffective.

The presumption against statutory retroactivity is founded upon sound considerations of general policy and practice, and accords with long held and widely shared expectations about the usual operation of legislation. We are satisfied that it applies to §102. Because we have found no clear evidence of congressional intent that §102 of the Civil Rights Act of 1991 should apply to cases arising before its enactment, we conclude that the judgment of the Court of Appeals must be affirmed. . . .

JUSTICE SCALIA, with whom JUSTICE KENNEDY and JUSTICE THOMAS join, concurring in the judgments.

I

I of course agree with the Court that there exists a judicial presumption, of great antiquity, that a legislative enactment affecting substantive rights does not apply retroactively absent clear statement to the contrary. The Court, however, is willing to let that clear statement be supplied, not by the text of the law in question, but by individual legislators who participated in the enactment of the law, and even legislators in an earlier Congress which tried and failed to enact a similar law. For the Court not only combs the floor debate and committee reports of the statute at issue . . . but also reviews the procedural history of an earlier, unsuccessful, attempt by a different Congress to enact similar legislation, the Civil Rights Act of 1990.

This effectively converts the "clear statement" rule into a "discernible legislative intent" rule—and even that understates the difference. The Court's rejection of the floor statements of certain Senators because they are "frankly partisan" and "cannot plausibly be read as reflecting any general agreement" reads like any other exercise in the soft science of legislative historicizing, undisciplined by any distinctive "clear statement" requirement. If it is a "clear statement" we are seeking, surely it is not enough to insist that the statement can "plausibly be read as reflecting general agreement"; the statement must clearly reflect general agreement. No legislative history can do that, of course, but only the text of the statute itself. . . .

The 1991 Act does not expressly state that it operates retroactively, but petitioner contends that its specification of prospective only application for two sections, §§109(c) and 402(b), implies that its other provisions are retroactive. More precisely, petitioner argues that since §402(a) states that "except as otherwise specifically provided, [the 1991 Act] shall take effect upon enactment" and since §§109(c) and 402(b) specifically provide that those sections shall operate only prospectively; the term "shall take effect upon enactment" in §402(a) must mean retroactive effect. The short response to this refined and subtle argument is that refinement and subtlety are no substitute for clear statement. "Shall take effect upon enactment" is presumed to mean "shall have prospective effect upon enactment," and that presumption is too strong to be overcome by any negative inference derived from §§109(c) and 402(b). . . .

III

My last, and most significant, disagreement with the Court's analysis of this case pertains to the meaning of retroactivity. The Court adopts as its own the definition crafted by Justice Story in a case involving a provision of the New Hampshire Constitution that prohibited "retrospective" laws: a law is retroactive only if it "takes away or impairs vested rights acquired under existing laws, or creates a new obligation, imposes a new duty, or attaches a new disability, in respect to transactions or considerations already past."

One might expect from this "vested rights" focus that the Court would hold all changes in rules of procedure (as opposed to matters of substance) to apply retroactively. And one would draw the same conclusion from the Court's formulation of the test as being "whether the new provision attaches new legal consequences to events completed before its enactment"—a test borrowed directly from our ex post facto Clause jurisprudence, where we have adopted a substantive-procedural line. In fact, however, the Court shrinks from faithfully applying the test that it has announced. It first seemingly defends the procedural-substantive distinction that a "vested rights" theory entails. But it soon acknowledges a broad and ill defined (indeed, utterly undefined) exception: "Whether a new rule of trial procedure applies will generally depend upon the posture of the case in question." Under this exception, "a new rule concerning the filing of complaints would not govern an action in which the complaint had already been filed," and "the promulgation of a new jury trial rule would ordinarily not warrant retrial of cases that had previously been tried to a judge." It is hard to see how either of these refusals to allow retroactive application preserves any "vested right." "'No one has a vested right in any given mode of procedure.'"

The seemingly random exceptions to the Court's "vested rights" (substance-vs.-procedure) criterion must be made, I suggest, because that criterion is fundamentally wrong. It may well be that the upsetting of "vested substantive rights" was the proper touchstone for interpretation of New Hampshire's constitutional prohibition, as it is for interpretation of the United States Constitution's ex post facto Clauses. But I doubt that it has anything to do with the more mundane question before us here: absent clear statement to the contrary, what is the presumed temporal application of a statute? For purposes of that question, a procedural change should no more be presumed to be retroactive than a substantive one. The critical issue, I think, is not whether the rule affects "vested rights," or governs substance or procedure, but rather what is the relevant activity that the rule regulates. Absent clear statement otherwise, only such relevant activity which occurs after the effective date of the statute is covered. Most statutes are meant to regulate primary conduct, and hence will not be applied in trials involving conduct that occurred before their effective date. But other statutes have a different purpose and therefore a different relevant retroactivity event. A new rule of evidence governing expert testimony, for example, is aimed at regulating the conduct of trial, and the event relevant to retroactivity of the rule is introduction of the testimony. Even though it is a procedural rule, it would unquestionably not be applied to testimony already taken—reversing a case on appeal, for example, because the new rule had not been applied at a trial which antedated the statute.

The inadequacy of the Court's "vested rights" approach becomes apparent when a change in one of the incidents of trial alters substantive entitlements. The opinion classifies attorney's fees provisions as procedural and permits "retroactive" application (in the sense of application to cases involving pre-enactment conduct). It seems to me, however, that holding a person liable for attorney's fees affects a "substantive right" no less than holding him liable for compensatory or punitive damages, which the Court treats as affecting a vested right. If attorney's fees can be awarded in a suit involving conduct that antedated the fee-authorizing statute, it is because the purpose of the fee award is not to affect that conduct, but to encourage suit for the vindication of certain rights—so that the retroactivity event is the filing of suit, whereafter encouragement is no longer needed. Or perhaps because the purpose of the fee award is to facilitate suit—so that the retroactivity event is the termination of suit, whereafter facilitation can no longer be achieved.

The "vested rights" test does not square with our consistent practice of giving immediate effect to statutes that alter a court's jurisdiction. . . . The Court explains this aspect of our retroactivity jurisprudence by noting that "a new jurisdictional rule will often not involve 'retroactivity' in Justice Story's sense because it 'takes away no substantive right but simply changes the tribunal that is to hear the case.'" That may be true sometimes, but surely not always. A jurisdictional rule can deny a litigant a forum for his claim entirely, or may leave him with an alternate forum that will deny relief for some collateral reason (e.g., a statute of limitations bar). Our jurisdiction cases are explained, I think, by the fact that the purpose of provisions conferring or eliminating jurisdiction is to permit or forbid the exercise of judicial power—so that the relevant event for retroactivity purposes is the moment at which that power is sought to be exercised. Thus, applying a jurisdiction-eliminating statute to undo past judicial action would be applying it retroactively; but applying it to prevent any judicial action after the statute takes effect is applying it prospectively.

Finally, statutes eliminating previously available forms of prospective relief provide another challenge to the Court's approach. Courts traditionally withhold requested injunctions that are not authorized by then-current law, even if they were authorized at the time suit commenced and at the time the primary conduct sought to be enjoined was first engaged in. . . . The reason, which has nothing to do with whether it is possible to have a vested right to prospective relief, is that "obviously, this form of relief operates only in futuro." Since the purpose of prospective relief is to affect the future rather than remedy the past, the relevant time for judging its retroactivity is the very moment at which it is ordered.

I do not maintain that it will always be easy to determine, from the statute's purpose, the relevant event for assessing its retroactivity. As I have suggested, for example, a statutory provision for attorney's fees presents a difficult case. Ordinarily, however, the answer is clear—as it is in both *Landgraf* and *Rivers.* Unlike the Court, I do not think that any of the provisions at issue is "not easily classified." They are all directed at the regulation of primary conduct, and the occurrence of the primary conduct is the relevant event.

JUSTICE BLACKMUN, dissenting.

Perhaps from an eagerness to resolve the "apparent tension" between Bradley v. Richmond School Bd. and Bowen v. Georgetown University Hospital, the Court rejects the "most logical reading" of the Civil Rights Act of 1991 and resorts to a presumption against retroactivity. This approach seems to me to pay insufficient fidelity to the settled principle that the "starting point for interpretation of a statute 'is the language of the statute itself,' " and extends the presumption against retroactive legislation beyond its historical reach and purpose.

A straightforward textual analysis of the Act indicates that §102's provision of compensatory damages and its attendant right to a jury trial apply to cases pending on appeal on the date of enactment. This analysis begins with §402(a) of the Act: "Except as otherwise specifically provided, this Act and the amendments made by this Act shall take effect upon enactment." Under the "settled rule that a statute must, if possible, be construed in such fashion that every word has operative effect," §402(a)'s qualifying clause, "except as otherwise specifically provided," cannot be dismissed as mere surplusage or an "insurance policy" against future judicial interpretation. Instead, it most logically refers to the Act's two sections "specifically providing" that the statute does not apply to cases pending on the date of enactment: (a) §402(b), which provides, in effect, that the Act did not apply to the then pending case of Wards Cove Packing Co. v. Atonio, and (b) §109(c) which states that the Act's protections of overseas employment "shall not apply with respect to conduct occurring before the date of the enactment of this Act." Self-evidently, if the entire Act were inapplicable to pending cases, §§402(b) and 109(c) would be "entirely redundant." Thus, the clear implication is that, while §402(b) and §109(c) do not apply to pending cases, other provisions — including §102 — do. "'Absent a clearly expressed legislative intention to the contrary, [this] language must . . . be regarded as conclusive.'" The legislative history of the Act, featuring a welter of conflicting and "some frankly partisan" floor statements, but no committee report, evinces no such contrary legislative intent. Thus, I see no reason to dismiss as "unlikely" the most natural reading of the statute, in order to embrace some other reading that is also "possible."

Even if the language of the statute did not answer the retroactivity question, it would be appropriate under our precedents to apply §102 to pending cases. The well-established presumption against retroactive legislation, which serves to protect settled expectations, is grounded in a respect for vested rights. This presumption need not be applied to remedial legislation, such as §102, that does not proscribe any conduct that was previously legal.

At no time within the last generation has an employer had a vested right to engage in or to permit sexual harassment; "'there is no such thing as a vested right to do wrong.'" Section 102 of the Act expands the remedies available for acts of intentional discrimination, but does not alter the scope of the employee's basic right to be free from discrimination or the employer's corresponding legal duty. There is nothing unjust about holding an employer responsible for injuries caused by conduct that has been illegal for almost 30 years.

NOTES AND QUESTIONS

1. *The presumption of prospectivity.* In establishing the retroactivity of a statute, the Court states that a proponent of retroactivity must overcome a presumption of prospectivity. What is the source of this canon? How can a legislative body overcome its effect?

2. *The ambiguity.* In Chapter 2, we discussed the ambiguity of the effective date provision of the Civil Rights Act of 1991. Congress was aware of this ambiguity and chose not to resolve it. Yet language in the statute supports an argument in favor of the statute's retroactivity. On what basis does the Court dismiss this language and find the statute not retroactive in this case? Why does Justice Scalia, the Court's preeminent textualist, join the majority and ignore Justice Blackmun's call for textualism? Why is dissenting Justice Blackmun, one of the Court's leading purposivists, calling for a textual approach?

3. *The application of theory.* Review again the theories of Judge Easterbrook and Professor Eskridge found in Chapter 10, pages 708-711. How would each of them have decided this case?

4. *What-ifs.* The Court draws a distinction between sections of the statute that relate to its prior decisions and sections that do not. The section in question in this case does not. What if it did? Would it lead to a different decision in this case? This case applies to an action commenced prior to enactment of the statute. What if the action had been commenced subsequent to the enactment of the statute, but the event had occurred prior to its enactment?

5. *Overrun with canons.* This case illustrates both of the problems with canons: first, that they are frequently in conflict with each other; and second, that they are often wrong as presumptions about the legislative process. On the first point, consider the countervailing canons about retro-activity. To resolve them, the Court embraces another canon, an anti-canon canon: "general expressions, in every opinion, are to be taken in connect-ion with the case in which those expressions are used." What does this canon mean? On the second point, consider the argument of the petitioner that "a court must give effect to every provision of a statute and avoid redundancy." How reflective of the legislative process generally and the particular enactment process for the Civil Rights Act of 1991 is that canon?

6. *The beat goes on.* Despite the declaration of a rule regarding retroactivity in *Landgraf*, the question of a statute's retroactivity can still provide a hot interpretive contest. In Lindh v. Murphy, 521 U.S. 320 (1997), a divided court (5-4) declared §2254(d) of the Antiterrorism and Effective Death Pen-alty Act of 1996 (110 Stat. 1214) not applicable to pending cases on the basis of applying normal rules of construction to the question of whether a provision would produce a retroactive effect and in determining a statute's temporal reach.

C. SHOWDOWN QUESTIONS

In Chapter 10, we introduced the issue of "showdown" cases, in which the meaning of a statute in the context of a particular case cannot be found through reference to the statute's text or to the legislative process. The cases in this section are intended to provide examples of judicial approaches to resolving such ambiguities.

United States v. Thompson/Center Arms Co.
504 U.S. 505 (1992)

Statute: 26 U.S.C. §5845(i) (National Firearms Act)
The term "make," and the various derivatives of such word, shall include manufacturing (other than by one qualified to engage in such

business under this chapter), putting together, altering, any combination of these, or otherwise producing a firearm.

JUSTICE SOUTER announced the judgment of the Court and delivered an opinion in which THE CHIEF JUSTICE and JUSTICE O'CONNOR join. [Internal citations have been omitted except where particularly relevant.]

Section 5821 of the National Firearms Act (NFA or Act) levies a tax of $200 per unit upon anyone "making" a "firearm" as that term is defined in the Act. Neither pistols nor rifles with barrels 16 inches long or longer are firearms within the NFA definition, but rifles with barrels less than 16 inches long, known as short-barreled rifles, are. This case presents the question whether a gun manufacturer "makes" a short-barreled rifle when it packages as a unit a pistol together with a kit containing a shoulder stock and a 21-inch barrel, permitting the pistol's conversion into an unregulated long-barreled rifle, or, if the pistol's barrel is left on the gun, a short-barreled rifle that is regulated. We hold that the statutory language may not be construed to require payment of the tax under these facts.

I

The word "firearm" is used as a term of art in the NFA. It means, among other things, "a rifle having a barrel or barrels of less than 16 inches in length. . . ." "The term 'rifle' means a weapon designed or redesigned, made or remade, and intended to be fired from the shoulder and designed or redesigned and made or remade to use the energy of the explosive in a fixed cartridge to fire only a single projectile through a rifled bore for each single pull of the trigger, and shall include any such weapon which may be readily restored to fire a fixed cartridge."

The consequences of being the maker of a firearm are serious. Section 5821 (a) imposes a tax of $200 "for each firearm made," which "shall be paid by the person making the firearm." Before one may make a firearm, one must obtain the approval of the Secretary of the Treasury, and §5841 requires that the "manufacturer, importer, and maker . . . register each firearm he manufactures, imports, or makes" in a central registry maintained by the Secretary of the Treasury. A maker who fails to comply with the NFA's provisions is subject to criminal penalties of up to 10 years' imprisonment and a fine of up to $10,000, or both, which may be imposed without proof of willfulness or knowledge.

Respondent Thompson/Center Arms Company manufactures a single-shot pistol called the "Contender," designed so that its handle and barrel can be removed from its "receiver," the metal frame housing the trigger, hammer and firing mechanism. For a short time in 1985 Thompson/Center also manufactured a carbine-conversion kit consisting of a 21-inch barrel, a rifle stock, and a wooden fore-end. If one joins the receiver with the conversion kit's rifle stock, the 21-inch barrel, and the rifle fore-end, the product is a carbine rifle with a 21-inch barrel. If, however, the shorter, pistol-length barrel is not removed from the receiver when the rifle stock is added, one is left with a 10-inch or "short-barreled" carbine rifle. . . .

II

The NFA provides that "the term 'make,' and the various derivatives of such word, shall include manufacturing (other than by one qualified to engage in such business under this chapter), putting together, altering, any combination of these, or otherwise producing a firearm." But the provision does not expressly address the question whether a short-barreled rifle can be "made" by the aggregation of finished parts that can readily be assembled into one. The Government contends that assembly is not necessary; Thompson/Center argues that it is.

A

The Government urges us to view the shipment of the pistol with the kit just as we would the shipment of a bicycle that requires some home assembly. "The fact that a short-barrel rifle, or any other 'firearm,' is possessed or sold in a partially unassembled state does not remove it from regulation under the Act."

The Government's analogy of the partially assembled bicycle to the packaged pistol and conversion kit is not, of course, exact. While each example includes some unassembled parts, the crated bicycle parts can be assembled into nothing but a bicycle, whereas the contents of Thompson/Center's package can constitute a pistol, a long-barreled rifle, or a short-barreled version. These distinctions, however, do define the issues raised by the Government's argument, the first of which is whether the aggregation and segregation of separate parts that can be assembled only into a short-barreled rifle and are sufficient for that purpose amount to "making" that firearm, or whether the firearm is not "made" until the moment of final assembly. This is the issue on which the Federal and Seventh Circuits are divided.

We think the language of the statute provides a clear answer on this point. The definition of "make" includes not only "putting together," but also "manufacturing . . . or otherwise producing a firearm." If, as Thompson/Center submits, a firearm were only made at the time of final assembly (the moment the firearm was "put together"), the additional language would be redundant. Congress must, then, have understood "making" to cover more than final assembly, and some disassembled aggregation of parts must be included. Since the narrowest example of a combination of parts that might be included is a set of parts that could be used to make nothing but a short-barreled rifle, the aggregation of such a set of parts, at the very least, must fall within the definition of "making" such a rifle. . . .

We also think that a firearm is "made" on facts one step removed from the paradigm of the aggregated parts that can be used for nothing except assembling a firearm. Two courts to our knowledge have dealt in some way with claims that when a gun other than a firearm was placed together with a further part or parts that would have had no use in association with the gun except to convert it into a firearm, a firearm was produced. . . . Here it is true, of course, that some of the parts could be used without ever assembling a firearm, but the likelihood of that is belied by the utter uselessness of placing the converting parts with the others except for just such a conversion. Where the evidence in a given case supports a finding of such uselessness, the case falls within the fair intendment of "otherwise producing a firearm."

B

Here, however, we are not dealing with an aggregation of parts that can serve no useful purpose except the assembly of a firearm, or with an aggregation having no ostensible utility except to convert a gun into such a weapon. There is, to be sure, one resemblance to the latter example in the sale of the Contender with the converter kit, for packaging the two has no apparent object except to convert the pistol into something else at some point. But the resemblance ends with the fact that the unregulated Contender pistol can be converted not only into a short-barreled rifle, which is a regulated firearm, but also into a long-barreled rifle, which is not. The packaging of pistol and kit has an obvious utility for those who want both a pistol and a regular rifle, and the question is whether the mere possibility of their use to assemble a regulated firearm is enough to place their combined packaging within the scope of "making" one.

1

Neither the statute's language, nor its structure provides any definitive guidance. Thompson/Center suggests guidance may be found in some subsections of the statute governing other types of weapons by language that expressly covers combinations of parts. The definition of "machine-gun," for example, was amended by the Gun Control Act of 1968 to read that "the term shall also include . . . any combination of parts from which a machinegun can be assembled if such parts are in the possession or under the control of a person." In 1986, the definition of "silencer" was amended by the Firearm Owners' Protection Act to "include any combination of parts, designed or redesigned, and intended for use in assembling or fabricating a firearm silencer. . . ."

Thompson/Center stresses the contrast between these references to "any combination of parts" and the silence about parts in the definition of rifle, in arguing that no aggregation of parts can suffice to make the regulated rifle. This argument is subject to a number of answers, however. First, it sweeps so broadly as to conflict with the statutory definition of "make," applicable to all firearms, which implies that a firearm may be "made" even where not fully "put together." If this were all, of course, the conflict might well be resolved in Thompson/Center's favor. We do not, however, read the machinegun and silencer definitions as contrasting with the definition of rifle in such a way as to raise a conflict with the broad concept of "making."

The definition of "silencer" is now included in the NFA only by reference, whereas its text appears only at 18 U.S.C. §921(a)(24), in a statute that itself contains no definition of "make." Prior to 1986, the definition of "firearm" in the NFA included "a muffler or a silencer for any firearm whether or not such firearm is included within this definition." Two Courts of Appeals held this language to include unassembled silencers that could be readily and easily assembled.

In 1986, Congress replaced that language with "any silencer." . . . The language defining silencer that was added to 18 U.S.C. §921 at that same time reads: "The terms 'firearm silencer' and 'firearm muffler' mean any device for silencing, muffling, or diminishing the report of a portable firearm, including any combination of parts, designed or redesigned, and intended for use in assembling or fabricating a firearm silencer or firearm muffler, and any part intended only for use in such assembly or fabrication."

Thompson/Center argues that if, even before the amendment, a combination of parts was already "made" into a firearm, the "any combination of parts" language would be redundant. While such a conclusion of redundancy could suggest that Congress assumed that "make" in the NFA did not cover unassembled parts, the suggestion (and the implied conflict with our reading of "make") is proven false by evidence that Congress actually understood redundancy to result from its new silencer definition. Congress apparently assumed that the statute reached complete parts kits even without the "combination" language, and understood the net effect of the new definition as expanding the coverage of the Act beyond complete parts kits. "The definition of silencer is amended to include any part designed or redesigned and intended to be used as a silencer for a firearm. This will help to control the sale of incomplete silencer kits that now circumvent the prohibition on selling complete kits." H.R. Rep. No. 99-495, p. 21 (1986). Because the addition of the "combination of parts" language to the definition of silencer does not, therefore, bear the implication

Thompson/Center would put on it, that definition cannot give us much guidance in answering the question before us.

We get no more help from analyzing the machinegun definition's reference to parts. It speaks of "any combination" of them in the possession or control of any one person. Here the definition sweeps broader than the aggregation of parts clearly covered by "making" a rifle. The machinegun parts need not even be in any particular proximity to each other. There is thus no conflict between definitions, but neither is much light shed on the limits of "making" a short-barreled rifle. We can only say that the notion of an unassembled machinegun is probably broader than that of an unassembled rifle. But just where the line is to be drawn on short-barreled rifles is not demonstrated by textual considerations.

2

Thompson/Center also looks for the answer in the purpose and history of the NFA, arguing that the congressional purpose behind the NFA, of regulating weapons useful for criminal purposes, should caution against drawing the line in such a way as to apply the Act to the Contender pistol and carbine kit (the adoption of the original definition of rifle was intended to preclude coverage of antique guns held by collectors, "in pursuance of the clearly indicated congressional intent to cover under the National Firearms Act only such modern and lethal weapons, except pistols and revolvers, as could be used readily and efficiently by criminals or gangsters").

It is of course clear from the face of the Act that the NFA's object was to regulate certain weapons likely to be used for criminal purposes, just as the regulation of short-barreled rifles, for example, addresses a concealable weapon likely to be so used. But when Thompson/Center urges us to recognize that "the Contender pistol and carbine kit is not a criminal-type weapon," it does not really address the issue of where the line should be drawn in deciding what combinations of parts are "made" into short-barreled rifles. Its argument goes to the quite different issue whether the single-shot Contender should be treated as a firearm within the meaning of the Act even when assembled with a rifle stock.

Since Thompson/Center's observations on this extraneous issue shed no light on the limits of unassembled "making" under the Act, we will say no more about congressional purpose. Nor are we helped by the NFA's legislative history, in which we find nothing to support a conclusion one way or the other about the narrow issue presented here.

III

After applying the ordinary rules of statutory construction, then, we are left with an ambiguous statute. The key to resolving the ambiguity lies in recognizing that although it is a tax statute that we construe now in a civil setting, the NFA has criminal applications that carry no additional requirement of willfulness. Making a firearm without approval may be subject to criminal sanction, as is possession of an unregistered firearm and failure to pay the tax on one. It is proper, therefore, to apply the rule of lenity and resolve the ambiguity in Thompson/Center's favor. Accordingly, we conclude that the Contender pistol and carbine kit when packaged together by Thompson/Center have not been "made" into a short-barreled rifle for purposes of the NFA. . . .

JUSTICE SCALIA joined by JUSTICE THOMAS, concurring in the judgment.

I agree with the plurality that the application of the National Firearms Act (NFA) to Thompson/Center's pistol and conversion kit is sufficiently ambiguous to trigger the rule of lenity, leading to the conclusion that the kit is not covered. I disagree with the plurality, however, over where the ambiguity lies — a point that makes no difference to the outcome here, but will make considerable difference in future cases. The plurality thinks the ambiguity pertains to whether the making of a regulated firearm includes (i) the manufacture of parts kits that can possibly be used to assemble a regulated firearm, or rather includes only (ii) the manufacture of parts kits that serve no useful purpose except assembly, of a regulated firearm. I think the ambiguity pertains to the much more fundamental point of whether the making of a regulated firearm includes the manufacture, without assembly, of component parts where the definition of the particular firearm does not so indicate.

As Justice White points out, the choice the plurality worries about is nowhere suggested by the language of the statute: §5845 simply makes no reference to the "utility" of aggregable parts. It does, however, conspicuously combine references to "combination of parts" in the definitions of regulated silencers, machineguns, and destructive devices with the absence of any such reference in the definition of regulated rifles. This, rather than the utility or not of a given part in a given parts assemblage, convinces me that the provision does not encompass Thompson/Center's pistol and conversion kit, or at least does not do so unambiguously.

The plurality reaches its textually uncharted destination by determining that the statutory definition of "make," the derivative of which appears as an operative word in 26 U.S.C. §5821 ("There shall be levied, collected, and paid upon the making of a firearm a tax at the rate of $200 for each firearm made"), covers the making of parts that, assembled, are firearms. Noting that the "definition of 'make' includes not only 'putting together,' but also 'manufacturing . . . or otherwise producing a firearm,'" the plurality reasons that if "a firearm were only made at the time of final assembly (the moment the firearm was 'put together'), the additional language would be redundant."

This reasoning seems to me mistaken. I do not think that if "making" requires "putting together," other language of the definition section ("manufacturing" and "otherwise producing") becomes redundant. "Manufacturing" is qualified by the parenthetical phrase "(other than by one qualified to engage in such business under this chapter)," whereas "putting together" is not. Thus, one who assembles a firearm and also engages in the prior activity of producing the component parts can be immunized from being considered to be making firearms by demonstrating the relevant qualification, whereas one who merely assembles parts manufactured by others cannot. Recognition of this distinction is alone enough to explain the separate inclusion of "putting together," even though "manufacturing" itself includes assembly. As for the phrase "otherwise producing," that may well be redundant, but such residual provisions often are. They are often meant for insurance, to cover anything the draftsman might inadvertently have omitted in the antecedent catalog; and if the draftsman is good enough, he will have omitted nothing at all. They are a prime example of provisions in which "iteration is obviously afoot," and for which an inflexible rule of avoiding redundancy will produce disaster. In any event, the plurality's own interpretation (whereby "manufacturing" a firearm does not require assembling it, and "putting together" is an entirely separate category of "making") renders it not a bit easier to conceive of a nonredundant application for "otherwise producing."

The plurality struggles to explain why its interpretation ("making" does not require assembly of component parts) does not itself render redundant the "combination of parts" language found elsewhere in 26 U.S.C. §5845, in the definitions of machinegun and destructive device, §§5845(b) and (f), and in the incorporated-by-reference definition of silencer, §5845(a)(7) (referring to 18 U.S.C. §921). I do not find its explanations persuasive, particularly that with respect to silencer, which resorts to that last hope of lost interpretive causes, that St. Jude of the hagiology of statutory construction, legislative history. As I have said before, reliance on that source is particularly inappropriate in determining the meaning of a statute with criminal application.

There is another reason why the plurality's interpretation is incorrect: it determines what constitutes a regulated "firearm" via an operative provision of the National Firearms Act (here §5821, the making tax) rather than by way of §5845, which defines firearms covered by the chapter. With respect to the definitions of machineguns, destructive devices, and silencers, for instance, the reference to "combination of parts" causes parts aggregations to be firearms whenever those nouns are used, and not just when they are used in conjunction with the verb "make" and its derivatives. Thus, the restrictions of §5844, which regulate the importation of "firearms" (a term defined to include "machineguns," see §5845(a)(6)) apply to a "combination of parts from which a machinegun can be assembled" (because that is part of the definition of machinegun) even though the word "make" and its derivatives do not appear in §5844. This demonstrates, I say, the error of the plurality's interpretation, because it makes no sense to have the firearms regulated by the National Firearms Act bear one identity (which includes components of rifles and shotguns) when they are the object of the verb "make," and a different identity (excluding such components) when they are not. Subsection 5842(a), for example, requires anyone "making" a firearm to identify it with a serial number that may not be readily removed; subsection 5842(b) requires any person who "possesses" a firearm lacking the requisite serial number to identify it with one assigned by the Secretary of the Treasury. Under the plurality's interpretation, all the firearms covered by (a) are not covered by (b), since a person who "possesses" the components for a rifle or shotgun does not possess a firearm, even though a person who "makes" the components for a rifle or shotgun makes a firearm. For similar reasons, the tax imposed on "the making of a firearm" by §5821 would apply to the making of components for rifles and shotguns, but the tax imposed on "firearms transferred" by §5811 would not apply to the transfer of such components. This cannot possibly be right.

Finally, even if it were the case that unassembled parts could constitute a rifle, I do not think it was established in this case that respondent manufactured (assembled or not) a rifle "having a barrel or barrels of less than 16 inches in length," which is what the definition of "firearm" requires, §5845(a)(3). For the definition of "rifle" requires that it be "intended to be fired from the shoulder," §5845(c), and the only combination of parts so intended, as far as respondent is concerned (and the record contains no indication of anyone else's intent), is the combination that forms a rifle with a 21-inch barrel. The kit's instructions emphasized that legal sanctions attached to the unauthorized making of a short-barreled rifle, and there was even carved into the shoulder stock itself the following: "WARNING. FEDERAL LAW PROHIBITS USE WITH BARREL LESS THAN 16 INCHES."

Since I agree (for a different reason) that the rule of lenity prevents these kits from being considered firearms within the meaning of the NFA, I concur in the judgment of the Court.

JUSTICE WHITE, joined by JUSTICE BLACKMUN, JUSTICE STEVENS, and JUSTICE KENNEDY, dissenting.

The Court of Appeals for the Federal Circuit concluded that, to meet the definition of "firearm" under the National Firearms Act (NFA), "a short-barreled rifle actually must be assembled." I agree with the majority that this pinched interpretation of the statute would fail to accord the term "make" its full meaning as that term is defined, §5845(i), and used in the definition of the term "rifle," §5845(c). Because one "makes" a firearm not only in the actual "putting together" of the parts, but also by "manufacturing . . . or otherwise producing a firearm," Congress clearly intended that the "making" include a "disassembled aggregation of parts," where the assemblage of such parts results in a firearm. In short, when the components necessary to assemble a rifle are produced and held in conjunction with one another, a "rifle" is, not surprisingly, the result.

This was the difficult issue presented by this case, and its resolution, for me, is dispositive, as respondent Thompson/Center concedes that it manufactures and distributes together a collection of parts that may be readily assembled into a short-barreled rifle. Indeed, Thompson/Center's argument concerning statutory construction, as well as its appeal to the rule of lenity, does not suggest, nor does any case brought to our attention, that one may escape the tax and registration requirements the NFA imposes on those who "make" regulated rifles simply by distributing as part of the package other interchangeable pieces of sufficient design to avoid the regulated definition. The majority nevertheless draws an artificial line between, on the one hand, those parts that "can serve no useful purpose except the assembly of a firearm" or that have "no ostensible utility except to convert a gun into such a weapon," and, on the other hand, those parts that have "an obvious utility for those who want both a pistol and a regular rifle."

I cannot agree. Certainly the statute makes no distinction based on the "utility" of the extra parts. While the majority prefers to view this silence as creating ambiguity, I find it only to signal that such distinctions are irrelevant. To conclude otherwise is to resort to " 'ingenuity to create ambiguity' " that simply does not exist in this statute. As noted by the Government, when a weapon comes within the scope of the "firearm" definition, the fact that it may also have a nonregulated form provides no basis for failing to comply with the requirements of the NFA.

The Court today thus closes one loophole—one cannot circumvent the NFA simply by offering an unassembled collection of parts—only to open another of equal dimension—one can circumvent the NFA by offering a collection of parts that can be made either into a "firearm" or an unregulated rifle. I respectfully dissent.

JUSTICE STEVENS, dissenting.

If this were a criminal case in which the defendant did not have adequate notice of the Government's interpretation of an ambiguous statute, then it would be entirely appropriate to apply the rule of lenity. I am persuaded, however, that the Court has misapplied that rule to this quite different case.

I agree with Justice White, and also with the Court, that respondent has made a firearm even though it has not assembled its constituent parts. I also agree with Justice White that that should be the end of the case, and therefore, I join his opinion. I add this comment, however, because I am persuaded that the Government should prevail even if the statute were ambiguous.

The main function of the rule of lenity is to protect citizens from the unfair application of ambiguous punitive statutes. Obviously, citizens should not be subject to punishment without fair notice that their conduct is prohibited by law. The risk that this respondent would be the victim of such unfairness, is, however, extremely remote. In 1985, the Government properly advised respondent of its reading of the statute and gave it ample opportunity to challenge that reading in litigation in which nothing more than tax liability of $200 was at stake. Moreover, a proper construction of the statute in this case would entirely remove the risk of criminal liability in the future.

The Court, after acknowledging that this case involves "a tax statute" and its construction "in a civil setting," nevertheless proceeds to treat the case as though it were a criminal prosecution. In my view, the Court should approach this case like any other civil case testing the Government's interpretation of an important regulatory statute. This statute serves the critical objective of regulating the manufacture and distribution of concealable firearms — dangerous weapons that are a leading cause of countless crimes that occur every day throughout the Nation. This is a field that has long been subject to pervasive governmental regulation because of the dangerous nature of the product and the public interest in having that danger controlled. The public interest in carrying out the purposes that motivated the enactment of this statute is, in my judgment and on this record, far more compelling than a mechanical application of the rule of lenity.

Accordingly, for this reason, as well as for the reasons stated by Justice White, I respectfully dissent.

NOTES AND QUESTIONS

1. *The ambiguity?* The plurality and the concurrence agree that there is an ambiguity in applying the statute in this case, but disagree on what it is. What are their respective views on this point? How does each arrive at its position? What is the view of the dissent on this issue? What is your view over whether there is an ambiguity and what it is?

2. *A redundancy of redundancies.* The plurality and the concurrence criticize each other's construction of the statute as violating the canon of reading statutes to avoid redundancies (although Justice Scalia, as discussed in the following note, also criticizes this canon). What are the redundancies each finds, how does each deal with them, and how satisfactory do you consider their responses?

3. *Justice Scalia's new canon.* The statute defines the term "make" to include "manufacturing . . . or otherwise producing a firearm." To the plurality such words cover an unassembled collection of parts. Justice Scalia,

evidencing the wisdom of Professor Llewellyn's observations about the use of canons (Chapter 10, pages 689-693), comments:

> As for the phrase "otherwise producing," that may well be redundant, but such residual provisions often are. They are often meant for insurance, to cover anything the draftsman might inadvertently have omitted in the antecedent catalog; and if the draftsman is good enough he will have omitted nothing at all. They are a prime example of provisions . . . for which an inflexible rule of avoiding redundancy will produce disaster.

What is the source of the claim that such provisions are "often meant for insurance": the legislative process in general, the legislative history of this particular statute, or judicial willfulness? Is this claim by Justice Scalia more reliable as a basis for reading the statute narrowly, compared with the Court's dependence on legislative history to read the statute more broadly?

4. *Reading statutes narrowly.* Notice in the two voting rights cases in Section A of this chapter, in the civil rights case in Section B, and in this case how Justice Scalia's approach to construction leads to narrowing of the statute's coverage. Recall the observation of Judge Posner (Chapter 10, page 712) that "[i]nterpretation is not foundational; it sits uneasily on shifting political foundations." Does it have any application in this case? Is Justice Scalia attempting to establish a mega-canon, such as "all statutes should be read narrowly"? Recall Judge Easterbrook's mega-canon discussion in Chapter 10, pages 708-709. How do these two canons compare?

5. *Applying theory.* Revisit the writings of Professor Dworkin, Judge Easterbrook, and Professor Eskridge in Chapter 10, Section C.7. How would each resolve the question in this case? How do you think the enacting Congress would have resolved this question, presented to them squarely? Is this last question a reasonable approach to resolving "showdown" questions? Is this the approach the dissent is following?

6. *The rule of lenity.* Like the rule in favor of prospectivity, the rule of lenity is a Constitution-based canon of construction. It favors lenity, at least, in a criminal statute because "'a fair warning should be given to the world in language that the common world will understand, of what the law intends to do if a certain line is passed'" and because "of the seriousness of criminal penalties, and because criminal punishment usually represents the moral condemnation of the community, [and therefore] legislatures and not courts should define criminal activity." United States v. Bass, 404 U.S. 336, 348 (1971). Is it being applied more broadly in this case?

7. *Amending the statute—a drafting problem for legislative counsel.* Assume you are the counsel to a legislator. After reading the decision in *Thompson/Center,* you want to amend the law to reflect the view of the dissent. Draft such an amendment.

Braschi v. Stahl Associates
543 N.E.2d 49 (N.Y. 1989)

Statute: 9 N.Y.C.R.R. §2204.6(d)

No occupant of housing accommodations shall be evicted under this section where the occupant is either the surviving spouse or some other member of the deceased tenant's family who has been living with the tenant.

This regulation of the New York State Division of Housing and Community Renewal was adopted by the New York State Legislature Laws of 1983, Chapter 403, §28.

Judges KAYE and ALEXANDER concur with Judge TITONE; Judge BELLACOSA concurs in a separate opinion; Judge SIMONS dissents and votes to affirm in another opinion in which Judge HANCOCK, JR., concurs; CHIEF JUDGE WACHTLER taking no part. [Internal citations and footnotes have been omitted except where particularly relevant.]

In this dispute over occupancy rights to a rent-controlled apartment, the central question to be resolved . . . is whether appellant has demonstrated a likelihood of success on the merits by showing that, as a matter of law, he is entitled to seek protection from eviction under New York City Rent and Eviction Regulations, 9 N.Y.C.R.R. §2204.6(d). . . . That regulation provides that upon the death of a rent-control tenant, the landlord may not dispossess "either the surviving spouse of the deceased tenant or some other member of the deceased tenant's *family* who has been living with the tenant" (emphasis supplied). Resolution of this question requires this court to determine the meaning of the term "family" as it is used in this context.

I

Appellant, Miguel Braschi, was living with Leslie Blanchard in a rent-controlled apartment located at 405 East 54th Street from the summer of 1975 until Blanchard's death in September of 1986. In November of 1986, respondent, Stahl Associates Company, the owner of the apartment building, served a notice to cure on appellant contending that he was a mere licensee with no right to occupy the apartment since only Blanchard was the tenant of record. In December of 1986 respondent served appellant with a notice to terminate informing appellant that he had one month to vacate the apartment and that, if the apartment was not vacated, respondent would commence summary proceedings to evict him.

. . . After examining the nature of the relationship between the two men, Supreme Court concluded that appellant was a "family member" within the meaning of the regulation. . . .

The Appellate Division reversed, concluding that section 2204.6(d) provides noneviction protection only to "family members within traditional, legally recognized familial relationship." . . . We now reverse.

III

It is fundamental that in construing the words of a statute "[the] legislative intent is the great and controlling principle." Indeed, "the general purpose is a more important aid to the meaning than any rule which grammar or formal logic may lay down." Statutes are ordinarily interpreted so as to avoid objectionable consequences and to prevent hardship or injustice. Hence, where doubt exists as to the meaning of a term, and a choice between two constructions is afforded, the consequences that may result from the different interpretations should be considered. In addition, since rent-control laws are remedial in nature and designed to promote the public good, their provisions should be interpreted broadly to effectuate their purposes. Finally, where a problem as to the meaning of a given term arises, a court's role is not to delve into the minds of legislators, but rather to effectuate the statute by carrying out the purpose of the statute as it is embodied in the words chosen by the Legislature.

The present dispute arises because the term "family" is not defined in the rent-control code and the legislative history is devoid of any specific reference to the noneviction provision. All that is known is the legislative purpose underlying the enactment of the rent-control laws as a whole.

Rent control was enacted to address a "serious public emergency" created by "an acute shortage in dwellings," which resulted in "speculative, unwarranted and abnormal increases in rents." These measures were designed to regulate and control the housing market so as to "prevent exactions of unjust, unreasonable and oppressive rents and rental agreements and to forestall profiteering, speculation and other disruptive practices tending to produce threats to the public health . . . [and] to prevent uncertainty, hardship and dislocation." Although initially designed as an emergency measure to alleviate the housing shortage attributable to the end of World War II, "a serious public emergency continues to exist in the housing of a considerable number of persons." Consequently, the Legislature has found it necessary to continually reenact the rent-control laws, thereby providing continued protection to tenants.

To accomplish its goals, the Legislature recognized that not only would rents have to be controlled, but that evictions would have to be regulated and controlled as well. Hence, section 2204.6 of the New York City Rent and Eviction Regulations, which authorizes the issuance of a certificate for the eviction of persons occupying a rent-controlled apartment after the death of the named tenant, provides, in subdivision (d), noneviction protection to those occupants who are either the "surviving spouse of the deceased tenant or some other member of the deceased tenant's family who has been living with the tenant [of record]." The manifest intent of this section is to restrict the landowners' ability to evict a narrow class of occupants other than the tenant of record. . . . Juxtaposed against this intent favoring the protection of tenants, is the over-all objective of a gradual "transition from regulation to a normal market of free bargaining between landlord and tenant." . . .

We conclude that the term family, as used in 9 N.Y.C.R.R. §2204.6(d), should not be rigidly restricted to those people who have formalized their relationship by obtaining, for instance, a marriage certificate or an adoption order. The intended protection against sudden eviction should not rest on fictitious legal distinctions or genetic history, but instead should find its foundation in the reality of family life. In the context of eviction, a more realistic, and certainly equally valid, view of a family includes two adult lifetime partners whose relationship is long term and characterized by an emotional and financial commitment and interdependence. This view comports both with our society's traditional concept of "family" and with the expectations of individuals who live in such nuclear units. In fact, Webster's Dictionary defines "family" first as "a group of people united by certain convictions or common affiliation" (Webster's Ninth New Collegiate Dictionary 448 [1984]; see, Ballantine's Law Dictionary 456 [3d ed. 1969] ["family" defined as "(p)rimarily, the collective body of persons who live in one house and under one head or management"]; Black's Law Dictionary 543 [Special Deluxe 5th ed. 1979]). Hence, it is reasonable to conclude that, in using the term "family," the Legislature intended to extend protection to those who reside in households having all of the normal familial characteristics. Appellant Braschi should therefore be afforded the opportunity to prove that he and Blanchard had such a household.

This definition of "family" is consistent with both of the competing purposes of the rent-control laws: the protection of individuals from sudden dislocation and the gradual transition to a free market system. Family members, whether or not related by blood or law, who have always treated the apartment as their family home will be protected against the hardship of eviction following the death of the named tenant, thereby furthering the Legislature's goals of preventing dislocation and preserving family units which might otherwise be broken apart upon eviction. This approach will foster the transition from rent control to rent stabilization by drawing a distinction between those individuals who are, in fact, genuine family members, and those who are mere roommates or newly discovered relatives hoping to inherit the rent-controlled apartment after the existing tenant's death.

The determination as to whether an individual is entitled to noneviction protection should be based upon an objective examination of the relationship of the parties. . . .

Appellant and Blanchard lived together as permanent life partners for more than 10 years. They regarded one another, and were regarded by friends and family, as spouses. The two men's families were aware of the nature of the relationship, and they regularly visited each other's families and attended family functions together, as a couple. Even today, appellant continues to maintain a relationship with Blanchard's niece, who considers him an uncle.

In addition to their interwoven social lives, appellant clearly considered the apartment his home. He lists the apartment as his address on his driver's license and passport, and receives all his mail at the apartment address. Moreover, appellant's tenancy was known to the building's superintendent and doormen, who viewed the two men as a couple.

Financially, the two men shared all obligations including a household budget. The two were authorized signatories of three safe-deposit boxes, they maintained joint checking and savings accounts, and joint credit cards. In fact, rent was often paid with a check from their joint checking account. Additionally, Blanchard executed a power of attorney in appellant's favor so that appellant could make necessary decisions — financial, medical and personal — for him during his illness. Finally, appellant was the named beneficiary of Blanchard's life insurance policy, as well as the primary legatee and coexecutor of Blanchard's estate. Hence, a court examining these facts could reasonably conclude that these men were much more than mere roommates. . . .

BELLACOSA, J. (concurring). My vote to reverse and remit rests on a narrower view of what must be decided in this case than the plurality and dissenting opinions deem necessary.

The issue is solely whether petitioner qualifies as a member of a "family," as that generic and broadly embracive word is used in the anti-eviction regulation of the rent-control apparatus. The particular anti-eviction public policy enactment is fulfilled by affording the remedial protection to this petitioner on the facts advanced on this record at this preliminary injunction stage. The competing public policy of eventually restoring rent-controlled apartments to decontrol, to stabilization and even to arm's length market relationships is eclipsed in this instance, in my view, by the more pertinently expressed and clearly applicable anti-eviction policy.

Courts, in circumstances as are presented here where legislative intent is completely indecipherable (Division of Housing and Community Renewal, the agency charged with administering the policy, is equally silent in this case and on this issue), are not empowered or expected to expand or to constrict the meaning of the legislatively chosen word "family," which could have been and still can be qualified or defined by the duly constituted enacting body in satisfying its separate branch responsibility and prerogative. Construing a regulation does not allow substitution of judicial views or preferences for those of the enacting body when the latter either fails or is unable or deliberately refuses to specify criteria or definitional limits for its selected umbrella word, "family," especially where the societal, governmental, policy and fiscal implications are so sweeping. . . .

The plurality opinion favors the petitioner's side by invoking the nomenclature of "nuclear"/"normal"/"genuine" family versus the "traditional"/ "legally recognizable" family selected by the dissenting opinion in favor of the landlord. I eschew both polar camps because I see no valid reason for deciding so broadly; indeed, there are cogent reasons not to yaw towards either end of the spectrum.

The application of the governing word and statute to reach a decision in this case can be accomplished on a narrow and legitimate jurisprudential track. The enacting body has selected an unqualified word for a socially remedial statute, intended as a protection against one of the harshest decrees known to the law — eviction from one's home. Traditionally, in such circumstances, generous construction is favored. Petitioner has made his shared home in the affected apartment for 10 years. The only other occupant of that rent-controlled apartment over that same extended period of time was the tenant-in-law who has now died, precipitating this battle for the apartment. The best guidance available to the regulatory agency for correctly applying the rule in such circumstances is that it would be irrational not to include this petitioner and it is a more reasonable reflection of the intention behind the regulation to protect a person such as petitioner as within the regulation's class of "family." In that respect, he qualifies as a tenant in fact for purposes of the interlocking provisions and policies of the rent-control law. . . .

The reasons for my position in this case are as plain as the inappropriate criticism of the dissent that I have engaged in *ipse dixit* decision making. It should not be that difficult to appreciate my view that no more need be decided or said in this case under the traditional discipline of the judicial process. Interstitial adjudication, when a court cannot institutionally fashion a majoritarian rule of law either because it is fragmented or because it is not omnipotent, is quite respectable jurisprudence. We just do not know the answers or implications for an exponential number of varied fact situations, so we should do what courts are in the business of doing — deciding cases as best they fallibly can. Applying the unvarnished regulatory word, "family," as written, to the facts so far presented falls within a well-respected and long-accepted judicial method.

Simons, J. (dissenting). I would affirm. The plurality has adopted a definition of family which extends the language of the regulation well beyond the implication of the words used in it. In doing so, it has expanded the class indefinitely to include anyone who can satisfy an administrator that he or she had an emotional and financial "commitment" to the statutory tenant. Its interpretation is inconsistent with the legislative scheme underlying rent regulation, goes well beyond the intended purposes of 9 N.Y.C.R.R. §2204.6(d), and produces an unworkable test that is subject to abuse. The concurring opinion fails to address the problem. It merely decides, *ipse dixit*, that plaintiff should win.

Preliminarily, it will be helpful to briefly look at the legislative scheme underlying rent regulation.

Rent regulation in New York is implemented by rent control and rent stabilization. Rent control is the stricter of the two programs. In 1946 the first of many "temporary" rent-control measures was enacted to address a public emergency created by the shortage of residential accommodations after World War II. That statute, and the statutes and regulations which followed it, were designed to monitor the housing market to prevent unreasonable and oppressive rents. These laws regulate the terms and conditions of rent-controlled tenancies exclusively; owners can evict tenants or occupants only on limited specified grounds and only with the permission of the administrative agency.

The rent-stabilization system originated in 1969. It is a less onerous regulatory scheme, conceived as a compromise solution to permit regulation of an additional 400,000 previously uncontrolled properties but also to allow landlords reasonable latitude in controlling the use of the newly regulated properties. One of its principal purposes was to encourage new construction. As both the Rent Control Law and the Rent Stabilization Law make clear, the Legislature contemplated that eventually rent control would end as rent-controlled tenancies terminated, and thereafter became subject to rent stabilization. These programs were adopted notwithstanding the Legislature's expressed sentiment that the "ultimate objective of state policy" was the "normal market of free bargaining between a landlord and tenant." Manifestly, judicial decisions which permit the indefinite extension of rent-controlled tenancies run counter to the legislative goal of eventually eliminating rent control while maintaining some measure of stability in the residential housing market.

A limited exception to the general rule that rent-controlled properties, when vacated, become subject to rent stabilization is found in section 2204.6(d). It provides that:

> (d) No occupant of housing accommodations shall be evicted under this section where the occupant is either the *surviving spouse of the deceased tenant or some other member of the deceased tenant's family* who has been living with the tenant.

[Emphasis added.]

Occupants who come within the terms of the section obtain a new statutory rent-controlled tenancy. Those eligible are identified by the italicized phrase but nowhere in the regulations or in the rent-control statutes is the phrase or the word "family" defined. Notably, however, family is linked with spouse, a word of clearly defined legal content. Thus, one would assume that the draftsman intended family to be given its ordinary and commonly accepted meaning related in some way to customary legal relationships established by birth, marriage or adoption. The plurality, however, holds that the exception provided in the regulation includes relationships outside the traditional family. In my view, it does not.

Analysis starts with the familiar rule that a validly enacted regulation has "the force and effect of law"; it should be interpreted no differently than a statute. As such, the regulation should not be extended by construction beyond its express terms or the reasonable implications of its language and absent further definition in the regulation or enabling statutes, the words of the section are to be construed according to their ordinary and popular significance.

Central to any interpretation of the regulatory language is a determination of its purpose. There can be little doubt that the purpose of section 2204.6(d) was to create succession rights to a possessory interest in real property where the tenant of record has died or vacated the apartment. . . . The State concerns underlying this provision include the orderly and just succession of property interests (which includes protecting a deceased's spouse and family from loss of their longtime home) and the professed State objective that there be a gradual transition from government regulation to a normal market of free bargaining between landlord and tenant. Those objectives require a weighing of the interests of certain individuals living with the tenant of record at his or her death and the interests of the landlord in regaining possession of its property and rerenting it under the less onerous rent-stabilization laws. The interests are properly balanced if the regulation's exception is applied by using objectively verifiable relationships based on blood, marriage and adoption, as the State has historically done in the estate succession laws, family court acts and similar legislation. The distinction is warranted because members of families, so defined, assume certain legal obligations to each other and to third persons, such as creditors, which are not imposed on unrelated individuals and this legal interdependency is worthy of consideration in determining which individuals are entitled to succeed to the interest of the statutory tenant in rent-controlled premises. Moreover, such an interpretation promotes certainty and consistency in the law and obviates the need for drawn out hearings and litigation focusing on such intangibles as the strength and duration of the relationship and the extent of the emotional and financial interdependency. So limited, the regulation may be viewed as a tempered response, balancing the rights of landlords with those of the tenant. To come within that protected class, individuals must comply with State laws relating to marriage or adoption. Plaintiff cannot avail himself of these institutions, of course, but that only points up the need for a legislative solution, not a judicial one.

Aside from these general considerations, the language itself suggests the regulation should be construed along traditional lines. Significantly, although the problem of unrelated persons living with tenants in rent-controlled apartments has existed for as long as rent control, there has been no effort by the State Legislature, the New York City Council or the agency charged with enforcing the statutes to define the word "family" contained in 9 N.Y.C.R.R. §2204.6(d) and its predecessors and we have no direct evidence of the term's intended scope. The plurality's response to this problem is to turn to the dictionary and select one definition, from the several found there, which gives the regulation the desired expansive construction. I would search for the intended meaning by looking at what the Legislature and the Division of Housing and Community Renewal (DHCR), the agency charged with implementing rent control, have done in related areas. These sources produce persuasive evidence that both bodies intend the word family to be interpreted in the traditional sense.

The legislative view may be found in the "roommate" law enacted in 1983. That statute granted rights to persons living with, but unrelated to, the tenant of record. The statute was a response to our unanimous decision in Hudson View Props. v. Weiss. In *Hudson View* the landlord, by a provision in the lease, limited occupancy to the tenant of record and the tenant's "immediate family." When the landlord tried to evict the unmarried heterosexual partner of the named tenant of record, she defended the proceeding by claiming that the restrictive covenant in the lease violated provisions of the State and City Human Rights Laws prohibiting discrimination on the basis of marital status. We held that the exclusion had nothing to do with the tenants' unmarried status but depended on the lease's restriction of occupancy to the tenant and the tenant's "immediate family." Implicitly, we decided that the term "immediate family" did not include individuals who were unrelated by blood, marriage or adoption, notwithstanding "the close and loving relationship" of the parties.

The Legislature's response to *Weiss* was measured. It enacted Real Property Law, which provides that occupants of rent-controlled accommodations, whether related to the tenant of record or not, can continue living in rent-controlled and rent-stabilized apartments as long as the tenant of record continues to reside there. Lease provisions to the contrary are rendered void as against public policy. Significantly, the statute provides that no unrelated occupant "shall . . . acquire any right to continued occupancy in the event the tenant vacates the premises or acquire any other rights of tenancy." Read against this background, the statute is evidence the Legislature does not contemplate that individuals unrelated to the tenant of record by blood, marriage or adoption should enjoy a right to remain in rent-controlled apartments after the death of the tenant.

There is similar evidence of how DHCR intends the section to operate. Manifestly, rent stabilization and rent control are closely related in purpose. Both recognize that, because of the serious ongoing public emergency with respect to housing in the City of New York, restrictions must be placed on residential housing. The DHCR promulgates the regulations for both rent-regulation systems, and the eviction regulations in rent control and the exceptions to them share a common purpose with the renewal requirements contained in the Rent Stabilization Code. In the Rent Stabilization Code, DHCR has made it unmistakably clear that the definition of family includes only persons related by blood, marriage or adoption. Since the two statutes and the two regulations share a common purpose, it is appropriate to conclude that the definition of family in the rent-control regulations should be of similar scope.

Specifically, the rent-stabilization regulations provide under similar circumstances that the landlord must offer a renewal lease to "any member of such tenant's family . . . who has resided in the housing accommodation as a primary resident from the inception of the tenancy or commencement of the relationship." Family for purposes of these two provisions is defined in section 2520.6(o) as: "A husband, wife, son, daughter, stepson, stepdaughter, father, mother, stepfather, stepmother, brother, sister, nephew, niece, uncle, aunt, grandfather, grandmother, grandson, granddaughter, father-in-law, mother-in-law, son-in-law, or daughter-in-law of the tenant or permanent tenant."

All the enumerated relationships are traditional, legally recognized relationships based on blood, marriage or adoption. That being so, it would be anomalous, to say the least, were we to hold that the agency, having intentionally limited succession rights in rent-stabilized accommodations to those related by blood, marriage or adoption, intended a different result for rent-controlled accommodations; especially so when it is recognized that rent control was intended to give way to rent stabilization and that the broader the definition of family adopted, the longer rent-controlled tenancies will be perpetuated by sequentially created family members entitled to new tenancies. These expressions by the Legislature and the DHCR are far more probative of the regulation's intended meaning than the majority's selective use of a favored dictionary definition. . . .

Rent control generally and section 2204.6, in particular, are in substantial derogation of property owners' rights. The court should not reach out and devise an expansive definition in this policy-laden area based upon limited experience and knowledge of the problems. The evidence available suggests that such a definition was not intended and that the ordinary and popular meaning of family in the traditional sense should be applied. If that construction is not favored, the Legislature or the agency can alter it. . . .

NOTES AND QUESTIONS

1. *A classic showdown question—"indecipherable legislative intent."* This case presents a unique question of statutory construction. The language

in question was, prior to 1983, part of the regulations of a New York City agency charged with administering New York City rent control. In 1983, New York State enacted legislation to transfer the administration of rent control from the New York City agency to the State Division of Housing and Community Renewal. As part of the statute effecting this transfer, the state legislature provided that "all rules, regulations . . . shall continue in force . . . until duly modified or abrogated by the division of housing and community renewal [DHCR]." Laws 1983, c. 403, §28. One of the authors, Professor Lane, who was involved in the enactment of this statute, recalls that the focus of legislative attention was on the state takeover, and no attention was paid to the substance of any of the rules or regulations that were being "enacted" by the statute. In fact, this was a legislative "understanding," because if the agency's multitudinous regulations had been open to legislative consideration, the takeover might not have been accomplished. Judge Bellacosa's characterization of the legislative intent, regarding a definition for the term "family," as "indecipherable" certainly hits the mark. But a decision must be made on whether the tenant is a member of the deceased's family. If he is, he can have the apartment. If he isn't, he will be dispossessed. What approach does each of the opinions take toward the resolution of this showdown question? What is the difference between the views of Judge Titone and Judge Bellacosa? How would you apply the statute in this case?

2. *The application of theory.* Revisit the approaches offered by Professor Dworkin, Professor Eskridge, and Judge Easterbrook in Chapter 10, Section C.7. How would each of them have decided this case? What do you think the enacting legislature might have done if faced with this question? How do you think Justice Scalia would have analyzed this case?

Subsequent to this decision, DHCR promulgated a definition of family that included relationships such as the one described in this situation.

3. *Awash in canons.* Consider the variety of canons used by Judge Titone in his opinion. How well does any of them reflect the legislative process? How relevant are they to his opinion?

D. *CHEVRON* AND AMBIGUITIES

Sweet Home Chapter of Communities for a Great Oregon v. Babbitt
1 F.3d 1 (1993)

Statute: 16 U.S.C. §§1538(a)(1)(B), 1532(19) (Endangered Species Act)
16 U.S.C. §1538(a)(1)(B). Except as provided . . . with respect to any endangered species of fish or wildlife . . . it is unlawful for any person

subject to the jurisdiction of the United States to . . . take any such species within the United States. . . .

16 U.S.C. §1532(19). The term "take" means to harass, harm, pursue, hunt, shoot, wound, kill, trap, capture, or collect, or to attempt to engage in any such conduct.

Before MIKVA, Chief Judge; WILLIAMS and SENTELLE, Circuit Judges. Opinion for the Court filed by Chief Judge MIKVA, except section II(A)(1), which is filed per curiam. Opinion concurring in section II(A)(1) filed by Chief Judge MIKVA. Opinion concurring in section II(A)(1) filed by Circuit Judge WILLIAMS. Dissenting opinion filed by Circuit Judge SENTELLE.

MIKVA, CHIEF JUDGE: Appellants, a group of non-profit citizens' groups, lumber companies, and lumber trade associations, oppose two regulations promulgated by the Fish and Wildlife Service ("FWS" or "agency") under the Endangered Species Act ("ESA"), 16 U.S.C. §§1531-1544. . . .

I. Background

The Endangered Species Act of 1973 is a multifaceted and comprehensive law directed toward halting the extinction of species. It is implemented primarily by the Fish and Wildlife Service, an agency of the Department of the Interior. . . .

This appeal focuses largely on the prohibition against "taking" an endangered species. . . .

The ESA defines "take" as follows: "To harass, harm, pursue, hunt, shoot, wound, kill, trap, capture, or collect, or to attempt to engage in any such conduct." 16 U.S.C. §1532(19). Much of the controversy surrounding this definition has concerned the meaning of "harm" and the degree to which this term encompasses damage to habitats. One of the FWS regulations challenged by appellants states:

> Harm in the definition of "take" in the Act means an act which actually kills or injures wildlife. Such act may include significant habitat modification or degradation where it actually kills or injures wildlife by significantly impairing essential behavioral patterns, including breeding, feeding, or sheltering.

50 C.F.R. §17.3 (as amended in 1981). Appellants contend that this regulation's inclusion of habitat modification within the meaning of "take" violates the ESA. . . .

II. Analysis

A. The "Harm" Regulation

1. Compliance with the Endangered Species Act

Appellants argue that the "harm" regulation, 50 C.F.R. §17.3, violates the ESA, because the statute excludes habitat modification from the types of forbidden actions that qualify as "takings" of species. They assert that the ESA's language and structure, as well as its legislative history, clearly demonstrate that Congress did not intend to prohibit habitat modification when it defined "take" to include "harm" to an endangered species. 16 U.S.C. §1532(19). They claim that the meaning of harm should therefore be limited to direct physical injury to an identifiable member of a listed wildlife species.

We hold, per curiam, that the "harm" regulation does not violate the ESA by including actions that modify habitat among prohibited "takings." ...

MIKVA, CHIEF JUDGE, concurring in Section II(A)(1) of the opinion: I write separately in order to articulate fully my reasons for rejecting appellants' argument that we should set aside the "harm" regulation as violative of the ESA.

When we review an agency's construction of a statute that it is entrusted to administer, we follow the deferential approach set out by Chevron U.S.A. Inc. v. Natural Resources Defense Council, Inc. [see Chapter 10, page 715]. "If the statute is clear and unambiguous that is the end of the matter, for the court, as well as the agency, must give effect to the unambiguously expressed intent of Congress." K Mart Corp. v. Cartier, Inc. If, however, "the statute is silent or ambiguous with respect to the specific issue, the question for the court is whether the agency's answer is based on a permissible construction of the statute." *Chevron.* "In such a case, a court may not substitute its own construction of a statutory provision for a reasonable interpretation made by the administrator of an agency." Id.

Appellants contend that Congress clearly intended to exclude habitat modification from the types of takings prohibited by the ESA and that this Court thus owes no deference to the FWS "harm" regulation. I disagree. In my view, the "harm" regulation conflicts with neither the ESA itself nor its ambiguous legislative history and is unquestionably a permissible and reasonable construction of the statute. ...

It is hard to construct a legislative scenario in which Congress would have avoided the problem of habitat modification when it crafted the ESA. ...

Appellants acknowledge that Congress intended to halt injurious habitat modification when it passed the ESA. They contend only that Congress did not mean to combat habitat degradation on private lands through the prohibition against takings in 16 U.S.C. §1538. They argue that Congress intended to combat this problem solely through §1534's provision for federal land acquisition.

According to appellants, the legislative history of the "take" provision establishes that Congress did not mean for that term to encompass habitat modification. They note that the original bill that was referred to the Senate Committee on Commerce, S. 1983, defined "take" to include "destruction, modification, or curtailment of [an endangered species'] habitat or range." The bill reported out of committee, however, did not refer to habitat modification in the definition of "take." This omission, appellants argue, evinces Congress' intent not to include habitat modification within the scope of prohibited "takings."

Appellants maintain that Congress intended instead to address the problem of habitat modification caused by private actions on private lands exclusively through land acquisition by the federal government.... Appellants point to various statements in the legislative history that suggest that some members of Congress may have wanted land acquisition, not the prohibition of land uses, to be the ESA's sole weapon against habitat modification on private lands. Appellants further argue that Congress logically must have intended land acquisition to be the exclusive mechanism for preventing such habitat modification. Otherwise, they contend, agency officials would always choose the free alternative of prohibiting a damaging land use under the "take" provision, rather than paying to acquire the affected land.

I find the legislative history to be most ambiguous regarding whether Congress intended to include habitat modification within the meaning of "take." It is true that the Senate Committee chose not to use the S. 1983 definition of "take," which specifically encompassed habitat modification. Instead, the Committee adopted a definition from the other bill under consideration, S. 1592, which did not explicitly include habitat modification. But as the district court noted, there is no indication in the legislative history as to why the Committee selected one definition over the other.

There is nothing to suggest that Congress chose the definition it did in order to exclude habitat modification. The Committee may have rejected the S. 1983 definition only because it apparently would have made habitat modification a per se violation of the ESA. It is certainly possible that the Committee did not intend to foreclose an administrative regulation prohibiting habitat modification — so long as that prohibition was accompanied by limitations, such as those contained in the FWS regulation under review, requiring that there be actual injury or death to the species. In any case, Congress manifested no clear intent to exclude habitat modification from the "take" definition. Indeed, the Senate Committee Report states that "'Take' is defined ... in the broadest possible manner to include every conceivable way in which a person can 'take' or attempt to 'take' any fish or wildlife."

Appellants' contention that Congress intended land acquisition to be the exclusive instrument for curbing habitat modification on private lands is similarly speculative. Nothing in the language of 16 U.S.C. §1534 or in the legislative history establishes that Congress meant land acquisition to be the only mechanism for habitat protection on private lands. The only evidence appellants can garner in support of their assertion to the contrary is a few isolated and ambiguous remarks by members of Congress on the floor. The general rule is that "debates in Congress expressive of the views and motives of individual members are not a safe guide . . . in ascertaining the meaning and purpose of the law-making body." Duplex Printing Press Co. v. Deering. In any case, these statements do not establish that even the speakers themselves intended land acquisition to be the exclusive protective mechanism for habitats on private lands.

There is also little force behind appellants' claim that including habitat modification within the meaning of "take" renders the land acquisition provision of §1534 a nullity. Appellants suggest that agency officials will not pay to acquire land if they can accomplish the same habitat preservation objective without cost by banning the offending land use. But there are in fact many reasons why, in its effort to protect endangered and threatened species, the government might choose to acquire land rather than simply forbid damaging activity. Federal wildlife managers can surely do more to help such species on government-owned and controlled preserves than they could ever accomplish on private lands. Indeed, §1534 land acquisition is explicitly designed to facilitate "conservation programs," a phrase that suggests a type of intervention more complex and proactive than simply forbidding certain activities on private lands.

Appellants argue that the agency must interpret the word "harm" narrowly so as not to include habitat modification because none of the other "take" terms — "harass, . . . pursue, hunt, shoot, wound, kill, trap, capture, [and] collect" — represents a land use action that injures wildlife only indirectly. They argue that under the principle of statutory construction known as *noscitur a sociis*, a general term in a list should be interpreted narrowly "to avoid the giving of unintended breadth to the Acts of Congress." Jarecki v. G. D. Searle & Co.

Despite appellants' suggestions, however, the other prohibitions can limit a private landowner's use of his land in a rather broad manner. In particular, the prohibition against "harassment" can be used to suppress activities that are in no way intended to injure an endangered species. The House Report stated:

> [Take] includes harassment, whether intentional or not. This would allow, for example, the Secretary to regulate or prohibit the activities of birdwatchers where the effect of those activities might disturb the birds and make it difficult for them to hatch or raise their young.

Indeed, the FWS has defined "harass" in a way that is almost as broad as the "harm" definition:

> Harass in the definition of "take" in the Act means an intentional or negligent act or omission which creates the likelihood of injury to wildlife by annoying it to such an extent as to significantly disrupt normal behavioral patterns which include, but are not limited to, breeding, feeding, or sheltering.

50 C.F.R. §17.3. Appellants have not challenged this definition.

Noscitur a sociis means, literally, that a word is known by the company it keeps. In the definition of "take," the term "harm" is accompanied by an assortment of words ranging from the precise and narrow "shoot" to the vague and expansive "harass." Consequently, even if I were willing to find an agency's construction of a statute to be impermissible based solely on a seldom-used and indeterminate principle of statutory construction, I would not do so in the present case.

Although the ESA is generally ambiguous as to whether the "take" prohibition forbids habitat modification, there is at least one feature of the statute that strongly suggests that Congress did in fact intend to include habitat modification within the meaning of "take." In 1982, Congress amended the ESA to include a provision authorizing the FWS to issue a permit allowing "any taking otherwise prohibited by section 1538(a)(1)(B) of this title if such taking is incidental to, and not the purpose of, the carrying out of an otherwise lawful activity." 16 U.S.C. §1539(a)(1)(B).

By allowing the agency, at its discretion, to permit "incidental takings," Congress implicitly confirmed that incidental takings were otherwise forbidden by the Act. And it is hard to imagine what "incidental takings" might be other than habitat modification. Indeed, the legislative history of the 1982 amendments reveals that habitat modification was precisely what Congress had in mind. The House Report states, "This provision is modeled after a habitat conservation plan that has been developed by three Northern California cities. . . . [It] will . . . provide the institutional framework to permit cooperation between the public and private sectors in the interest of endangered species and habitat conservation."

Overall, there is nothing in the ESA itself or in its legislative history that unambiguously demonstrates that the term "take" does not encompass habitat modification. Indeed, as I noted in my discussion of the 1982 amendments, there is evidence to the contrary. *Chevron* commands that unless it is absolutely clear that an agency's interpretation of a statute, entrusted to it to administer, is contrary to the will of Congress, courts must defer to that interpretation so long as it is reasonable.

In upholding the challenged regulation, we join the Ninth Circuit, which has similarly held that the agency's inclusion of habitat destruction in the definition of "harm" is a permissible interpretation of the ESA. That Circuit has stated that "the Secretary's inclusion of habitat destruction that could result in extinction follows the plain language of the statute because it serves the overall purpose of the Act. . . ."

WILLIAMS, J., concurring in Section II(A)(1) of the opinion: I agree that the "harm" regulation, 50 C.R.F. §17.3, complies with the Endangered Species Act — but only because of the 1982 amendments to the ESA. Those amendments, which authorize the FWS to issue permits for "any taking otherwise prohibited by section 1538(a)(1)(B) of this title if such taking is incidental to, and not the purpose of, the carrying out of an otherwise lawful activity," 16 U.S.C. §1539(a)(1)(B), support the inference that the ESA otherwise forbids some such incidental takings, including some habitat modification. But for the 1982 amendments, I would find Judge Sentelle's analysis highly persuasive — including his discussion of the *noscitur a sociis* canon. . . .

SENTELLE, J., dissenting: As we have observed, "some will find ambiguity even in a 'No Smoking' sign." In the present case the Fish and Wildlife Service has established that it would not only find such ambiguity, but would deem a congressional authorization for the erection of "No Smoking" signs to authorize the adoption of regulations against chewing and spitting.

As Chief Judge Mikva notes, this case is governed by *Chevron.* . . . That decision mandates a two-step analysis. At the first step "we inquire into whether Congress has directly spoken to the precise question at issue. If we can come to the unmistakable conclusion that Congress had an intention on the precise question at issue, our inquiry ends there." [Internal quotation marks omitted.] At the second step "if the statute . . . is silent or ambiguous with respect to the specific issue before us . . . we defer to the agency's interpretation of the statute if it is reasonable and consistent with the statute's purpose." [Internal quotation marks omitted.] While I am willing to concede the possibility that some ambiguity may remain in the unusually specific recitation by Congress of its intent in defining the term "take," I cannot cram the agency's huge regulatory definition into the tiny crack of ambiguity Congress left. . . .

In the present case, I see no reasonable way that the term "take" can be defined to include "significant habitat modification or degradation" as it is defined in 50 C.F.R. §17.3. I have in my time seen a great many farmers modifying habitat. They modify by plowing, by tilling, by clearing, and in a thousand other ways. At no point when I have seen a farmer so engaged has it occurred to me that he is taking game. Nor do I think it would occur to anyone else that he was taking wildlife. He may be doing something harmful to wildlife, but he is not "taking" it. . . .

As my colleague observes, there is an ancient "principle of statutory construction known as *noscitur a sociis*, a general word in a list should be interpreted narrowly." . . . In the present statute, all the other terms among which "harm" finds itself keeping company relate to an act which a specifically acting human does to a specific individual representative of a wildlife species. In fact, they are the sorts of things an individual human commonly does when he intends to "take" an animal. Otherwise put, if I were intent on taking a rabbit, a squirrel, or a deer, as the term "take" is used in common English parlance, I would go forth with my dogs or my guns or my snares and proceed to "harass, . . . pursue, hunt, shoot, wound, kill, trap, capture, or collect" one of the target species. 16 U.S.C. §1532(19). If I succeeded in that endeavor, I would certainly have "taken" the beast. If I failed, I would at least have "attempted to engage in . . . such conduct." Id.

All this falls neatly within a reasonable construction of "take," just as puffing a pipe falls neatly within the definition of smoking, and I would not dare to do such in front of a "No Smoking" sign. However, I would think it most unreasonable if a regulator told me that I could not chew nicotine gum in front of the same sign because the agency had decided that it was harmful and therefore constituted smoking. It appears to me that the Fish and Wildlife Service has engaged in a similarly unreasonable expansion of terms in the present case.

I do not find the unreasonableness of the Service's construction to be in any way alleviated by the Senate Committee Report stating that "'take' is defined . . . in the broadest possible manner to include every conceivable way in which a person can 'take' or attempt to 'take' any fish or wildlife." Should one committee of the anti-smoking Congress have included in its discussion of the "No Smoking" sign authorization language to the effect that "'smoking' is defined in the broadest possible manner to include every conceivable way in which a person can 'smoke' or attempt to 'smoke' any form of tobacco," that still would not convince me that the term could be defined to include chewing. Nor does the majority's reliance on that same sort of legislative history convince me that Congress, by mandating the broadest possible manner of definition, intended to deprive the definition of any bounds whatsoever and turn the word into a free form concept inclusive of anything an agency might wish it to cover.

I am bolstered in my conviction by another rule of statutory construction: that is, the presumption against surplusage. "We are hesitant to adopt an interpretation of a congressional enactment which renders superfluous another portion of that same law." The construction placed upon the word "harm" by the agency and adopted by the court today renders superfluous everything else in the definition of "take." If "harm" means any "act which actually kills or injures wildlife," including "habitat modification or degradation," I can see no reason why Congress also included in the definition of "take" the terms "harass, . . . pursue, hunt, shoot, wound, kill, trap, capture, [and] collect." 16 U.S.C. §1532(19). Every single one of those acts, particularly when coupled with further language of the congressional definition which includes "to attempt to engage in any such conduct," id., falls within the definition of "harm" as understood by the agency. I am unwilling to believe that Congress deliberately wasted the considerable ink and paper devoted to the many copies of this legislation containing all the other words in section 1532(19). I am, therefore, unwilling to accept the Service's definition in the present case, no matter how well intended. . . .

Sweet Home Chapter of Communities for a Great Oregon v. Babbitt
17 F.3d 1463 (1994)

Statute: 16 U.S.C. §§1538(a)(1)(B), 1532(19) (Endangered Species Act)

16 U.S.C. §1538(a)(1)(B). Except as provided in . . . with respect to any endangered species of fish or wildlife . . . it is unlawful for any person subject to the jurisdiction of the United States to . . . take any such species within the United States. . . .

16 U.S.C. §1532(19). The term "take" means to harass, harm, pursue, hunt, shoot, wound, kill, trap, capture, or collect, or to attempt to engage in any such conduct.

Before MIKVA, Chief Judge, WILLIAMS and SENTELLE, Circuit Judges. Opinion for the Court filed by Circuit Judge WILLIAMS. Concurring opinion filed by Circuit Judge SENTELLE. Dissenting opinion filed by Chief Judge MIKVA.

WILLIAMS, J.: . . . The issue that split the court involved the scope of the Act's prohibition of the "taking" of endangered species. On petition for rehearing, and after securing a response from the government, we alter our view on that issue. . . .

We find that the Service's definition of "harm" was neither clearly authorized by Congress nor a "reasonable interpretation" of the statute, see Chevron U.S.A. Inc. v. Natural Resources Defense Council and we find that no later action of Congress supplied the missing authority.

The Language, Structure and Legislative History of the 1973 Act

The Fish & Wildlife Service found habitat modification within the idea of "harm," the most elastic of the words Congress used to define the acts that §9 of the ESA forbids private individuals to commit. The potential breadth of the word "harm" is indisputable. . . . As a matter of pure linguistic possibility one can easily recast any withholding of a benefit as an infliction of harm. In one sense of the word, we "harm" the people of Somalia to the extent that we refrain from providing humanitarian aid, and we harm the people of Bosnia to the extent that we fail to stop "ethnic cleansing." By the same token, it is linguistically possible to read "harm" as referring to a landowner's withholding of the benefits of a habitat that is beneficial to a species. A farmer who harvests crops or trees on which a species may depend harms it in the sense of withdrawing a benefit; if the benefit withdrawn be important, then the Service's regulation sweeps up the farmer's decision.

The immediate context of the word, however, argues strongly against any such broad reading. With the single exception of the word "harm," the words of the definition contemplate the perpetrator's direct application of force against the animal taken: "harass, harm, pursue, hunt, shoot, wound, kill, trap, capture, or collect." The forbidden acts fit, in ordinary language, the basic model "A hit B."

For some of the words, to be sure, the application of force may not be instantaneous or immediate, and the force may not involve a bullet or blade. In the case of "pursue," the perpetrator does not necessarily catch or destroy the animal, but pursuit would always or almost always be a step toward deliberate capture or destruction, and so would be picked up by §1532(19)'s reference to "attempts." While one may, "trap" an animal without being physically present, the perpetrator, will have previously arranged for release of the energy that directly captures the animal. And one may under some circumstances "harass" an animal by aiming sound or light in its direction, but the waves and particles are themselves physical forces launched by the perpetrator. . . .

Thus the gulf between the Service's habitat modification concept of "harm" and the other words of the statutory definition, and the implications in terms of the resulting extinction of private rights, counsel application of the maxim *noscitur a sociis*. The maxim, that a word is known by the company it keeps, while not an inescapable rule, is often wisely applied where a word is capable of many meanings in order "to avoid the giving of unintended breadth to the Acts of Congress." The Service's interpretation appears to yield precisely the "unintended breadth" that use of the maxim properly prevents.

The structure and history of the Act confirm this reading. . . . [O]n a specific segment of society, the federal government, the Act imposes very broad burdens, including the avoidance of adverse habitat modifications; on a broad segment, every person, it imposes relatively narrow ones.

The legislative history reflects this balance, and confirms the intention to assign the primary task of habitat preservation to the government. Explaining the land acquisition program, Senator Tunney, the Senate floor manager for the ESA, stated: "Through these land acquisition provisions, we will be able to conserve habitats necessary to protect fish and wildlife from further destruction."

Representative Sullivan, the floor manager for H.R. 37—the House version of the bill—confirmed this approach:

> For the most part, the principal threat to animals stems from the destruction of their habitat. The destruction may be intentional, as would be the case in clearing of fields and forests for development of resource extraction, or it may be unintentional, as in the case of the spread of pesticides beyond their target area. Whether it is intentional or not, however, the result is unfortunate for the species of animals that depend on that habitat, most of whom are already living on the edge of survival. H.R. 37 will meet this problem by providing funds for acquisition of critical habitat through the use of the land and water conservation fund. It will also enable the Department of Agriculture to cooperate with willing landowners who desire to assist in the protection of endangered species, but who are understandably unwilling to do so at excessive cost to themselves.

. . . For habitat modification, then, Representative Sullivan saw the Act as providing duties for the government, with private persons acting only in the form of "willing landowners" assisted by the Department of Agriculture.

The floor managers differentiated loss of habitat from the hazard that was the target of the "taking" ban and the other prohibitions of §9. After the passage quoted, Representative Sullivan went on to identify "another hazard to endangered species" which "arises from those who would capture or kill them for pleasure or profit. There is no way that the Congress can make it less pleasurable for a person to take an animal, but we can certainly make it less profitable for them to do so." Id. Senator Tunney drew the same line:

> Although most endangered species are threatened primarily by the destruction of their natural habitats, a significant portion of these animals are subject to predation by man for commercial, sport, consumption, or other purposes. The provisions in S. 1983 would prohibit the commerce in or the importation, exportation, or taking of endangered species except where permitted by the Secretary.

Congress's deliberate deletion of habitat modification from the definition of "take" strengthens our conclusion. As introduced before the Senate Commerce Committee, S. 1983 defined "take" as including "the destruction, modification, or curtailment of [a species'] habitat or range." A number of persons appearing before the Subcommittee on Environment explicitly endorsed this language and stressed its importance. . . . Senators made the same point. . . . But the "take" definition of the version of S. 1983 submitted to the Senate omitted any reference to habitat modification, defining "take" to mean "harass, pursue, hunt, shoot, wound, kill, trap, capture, or collect, or to attempt to engage in any such conduct."

In rejecting the Service's understanding of "take" to encompass habitat modification, "we are mindful that Congress had before it, but failed to pass, just such a scheme." John Hancock Mutual Life Insurance Co. v. Harris Trust & Savings Bank.

The Effect of the 1982 Amendments

Congress amended the Act in 1982, with two possible implications. First, one might argue that one of the amendments so altered the context of the definition of "take" as to render the Service's interpretation reasonable, or even, conceivably, to reflect express congressional adoption of that view. Second, one might argue that the process of amendment, which brought the Service's regulation and a judicial endorsement to the attention of a congressional subcommittee, constituted a ratification of the regulation. We reject both theories.

1. The only legislative act from which the government claims support is the addition of ESA §10(a)(1)(B), 16 U.S.C. §1539(a)(1)(B), which authorizes the FWS to issue permits for "any taking otherwise prohibited by section 1538(a)(1)(B) of this title if such taking is incidental to, and not the purpose of, the carrying out of an otherwise lawful activity." This language clearly implies that some prohibited takings are "incidental" to otherwise lawful activities. It does not follow, however, that such incidental takings include the habitat modifications embraced by the Service's definition of "harm." Harms involving the direct applications of force that characterize the nine other verbs of §1532(19) pose the problem of incidental takings. The trapping of a nonendangered animal, for example, may incidentally trap an endangered species.

In fact, the key example of the sort of problem to be corrected by §10(a)(1)(B) involved the immediate destruction of animals that would be trapped by a human enterprise. Northeast Utilities reported that it had sought to construct a nuclear plant on the Connecticut River. Dr. John P. Cagnetta explained on behalf of Northeast that the "EPA had concluded that Section 9 of the Act constituted a 'zero taking' rule which would prohibit the entrainment or impingement of any Shortnose Sturgeon eggs, larvae or adults by the Montague intake structure." The "entrainment" and "impingement" of sturgeon eggs involve the crushing or capture of the eggs as a direct result of a human enterprise, just as would nets that catch fish driven in their way by the tides.

The sort of advance conservation plan authorized by §10(a) makes complete sense for the kind of incidental taking exemplified by Northeast's dilemma. Dr. Cagnetta expressed concern that after the firm had invested $2 billion in the proposed plant, it might be subject to closure by injunction granted at the behest of a private person. Section 10(a) provides procedural means by which to improve the trade-off between protecting endangered species and permitting normal development. Firms whose activities might incidentally "take" members of an endangered species can get advance protection from legal liability, but only if they convince the Secretary that the plan uses the maximum devices possible to mitigate and minimize species loss, and that the resulting losses will not unduly harm the species.

Thus, adoption of §10(a)'s permit plan, at least as evidenced by Northeast's instigating role, arose from interpretive assumptions about the meaning of "taking" — namely the EPA's views (1) that the perpetrator need not have intended to take the creature in question, and (2) that even the slightest taking would violate the Act (the "zero taking" rule). We need not explore the possible impact of these assumptions on the interpretation of "take"; a member of Congress might have supported the permit system on a completely agnostic premise about those interpretations. . . . Normally, erroneous legislative assumptions about the meaning of an existing statute, even when they serve as the premise of an amendment, do not alter the meaning of unamended provisions. . . . Here, however, the matter is even easier, as the amendment involved no assumptions supporting the Service's position on habitat modification. So far as the creation of the permit plan is concerned, the implicit assumptions simply do not embrace the idea that "take" included any significant habitat modification injurious to wildlife.

2. For its ratification theory, the government invokes (besides the §10(a)(2) amendment itself) (a) language in the Conference on the 1982 amendments; (b) notice to a House subcommittee of the Service's habitat modification regulation and of a decision upholding it; and (c) the decision of a senator not to offer an amendment. We first examine these and then consider the cases on ratification of mistaken interpretations, on the basis of congressional awareness and peripheral action.

(a) The Conference Report. The government highlights some observations of H.R. Rep. No. 835, 97th Cong., 2d Sess. (1982) ("Conference Report"), speaking of the innovation made by §10(a):

> This provision is modeled after a habitat conservation plan that has been developed by three Northern California cities, the County of San Mateo, and private landowners and developers to provide for the conservation of the habitat of three endangered species and other unlisted species of concern within the San Bruno Mountain area of San Mateo County.
>
> This provision will measurably reduce conflicts under the Act and will provide the institutional framework to permit cooperation between the public and private sectors in the interest of endangered species and habitat conservation.
>
> The terms of this provision require a unique partnership between the public and private sectors in the interest of species and habitat conservation. . . .

Although the passage thrice uses the phrase "habitat conservation," the first reference simply describes the particular plan on which the provision was modeled, while the second and third couple the phrase with, respectively, "the interest of endangered species" and "the interest of species." The focus is on the flexibility of the relief offered. The expectation that relief under the §10(a) permit scheme would include habitat conservation does not imply an assumption that takings encompass habitat modification. Thus, if a nuclear plant will "entrain" and "impinge" sturgeon eggs, the area where this occurs will certainly not be hospitable for the sturgeon, and mitigation measures invited by §10(a) might well include provision of alternative habitat. Similarly, although §10(a) relief contemplates advancing "the interest of endangered species," it does not follow that every act detrimental to an endangered species constitutes a forbidden taking.

(b) Notice of the regulation. The Subcommittee on Fisheries and Wildlife Conservation and the Environment of the House Committee on Merchant Marine and Fisheries had notice of the regulation. In addition, speakers brought a decision of the 9th Circuit upholding the application of the ESA to habitat modification, Palila v. Hawaii Dep't of Land & Natural Resources, to the attention of subcommittee members in attendance (expressions of conflicting views on validity of interpretation of "harm" to encompass habitat modification). So far as appears, no congressional awareness of the Service's regulation or of *Palila* reached the floor of either House.

(c) The withdrawn amendment. The government says that Senator Garn proposed an amendment to change the definition of "take" but "withdrew it voluntarily because he realized it did not have enough support for passage." This falsely suggests a focus on "habitat modification" that was simply not there. In fact, the amendment that Senator Garn withdrew was not an isolated redefinition of the term "take," but a wholesale "rewrite" of the ESA — the reading of which was dispensed with on the Senate floor, and the text of which took 16 dense pages of legislative history. . . .

Similarly, where Congress adopts amendments on the basis of a misconception as to the meaning of a prior statute's related provisions, the later act does not turn the misconception into law. . . .

A variant on this theme is TVA v. Hill, involving claims that Congress's several appropriations for the Tellico Dam, made with full awareness of its risks to the snail darter and with express statements in various House and Senate Appropriations Committees' reports that the ESA was not meant to apply to this project, effectively exempted the dam from §7 of the Act. Despite Congress's endorsement of the disputed project with the ultimate accolade — hard cash — the Court refused to find any exemption. The Court underscored the proposition that only congressional committees had expressed the understanding of §7 that contradicted the Court's reading.

Our own decision in State of Ohio v. U.S. Department of the Interior . . . considered a situation where Congress had amended the key sections being construed and had reenacted the entire statute. . . . Although the court evidently understood congressional inaction to stem from a belief that the statute had been "clear all along" (against the administrative interpretation), the ambiguity we pinpointed is relevant more broadly. Congressional inaction may indicate no more than the press of other business. As inaction is inadequate to repeal a law, it should be inadequate to modify a law. Yet modification is required to sustain an interpretation that is invalid as against the original legislation. Professor Tribe has pointed out that judicial reliance on congressional silence generates an elaborate buck-passing. The courts pass the buck to Congress by invoking the congressional inaction, and individual members of Congress can freely pass the buck back by pointing to the courts' action.

We do not pretend that the Court's treatment of this issue has been absolutely uniform. There are cases indicating some readiness to infer ratification merely from amendment of related provisions (coupled with acute congressional focus on outstanding interpretations), and even from mere notice followed by inaction. . . .

These cases may ultimately not be fully reconcilable. We note, however, that the cases drawing inferences from inaction typically fail to address the serious jurisprudential problems of doing so — especially those captured in Judge Wald's observation that there are plenty of statutes "on the books for which no congressional majority could presently be garnered either to reenact or to repeal." It hardly seems consistent to enforce such statutes yet to accept non-amendment of an interpretation as the equivalent of congressional endorsement.

If the 1982 Congress had reenacted the pertinent sections of the ESA and "voiced its approval" of the FWS's interpretation, it might be appropriate to treat the reenactment as an adoption of that interpretation. Here, however, Congress neither reenacted the sections having to do with "take," nor "voiced its approval" of the harm regulation. As we have seen, its creation of the permit scheme is fully consistent with the meaning of "take" as enacted in 1973; the other developments show no more than awareness of the Service's view, its survival in *Palila*, and the absence of any action to endorse or repudiate those developments. . . .

MIKVA, CHIEF JUDGE, dissenting. . . .

The statute's purpose and legislative history provide equally insufficient grounds for rejecting the agency's interpretation. The majority, adopting the view of the appellants in this case, acknowledges that Congress intended to halt injurious habitat modification when it passed the ESA. It contends that Congress intended to combat this problem solely through §1534's provision for federal land acquisition, and not through §1538's prohibition of private takings.

According to the majority, the legislative history of the "take" provision establishes that Congress did not mean for that term to encompass habitat modification. . . .

I find the legislative history to be most ambiguous regarding whether Congress intended to include habitat modification within the meaning of "take." It is true that the Senate Committee chose not to use the S. 1983 definition of "take," which specifically encompassed habitat modification. Instead, the Committee adopted a definition from the other bill under consideration, S. 1592, which did not explicitly include habitat modification. But as the district court noted, there is no indication in the legislative history as to why the Committee selected one definition over the other. And, in any event, the crucial word "harm" was never voted on by the Committee but was added later on the floor of the Senate. It might well have been intended to cover the entire landscape originally contemplated by the S. 1983 definition (Statement of Sen. Tunney) ("The amendments will help to achieve the purposes of the bill and will clarify some confusion caused by language remaining in the bill from earlier drafts or omitted from earlier drafts which went unnoticed during the final committee markup").

Most importantly for our *Chevron* inquiry, there is nothing to suggest that Congress chose the definition it did in order to exclude habitat modification. . . .

[T]he agency's interpretation draws support from a subsequent amendment to the ESA. In 1982, Congress amended the ESA to include a provision authorizing the FWS to issue a permit allowing "any taking otherwise prohibited by section 1538(a)(1)(B) of this title if such taking is incidental to, and not the purpose of, the carrying out of an otherwise lawful activity." 16 U.S.C. §1539(a)(1)(B). By negative inference, this provision demonstrates that Congress thought at least some "incidental takings" must be prohibited by §1538(a)(1)(B) in the first instance. The majority speculates on what Congress could have meant by "incidental takings," but the evidence quite clearly suggests that Congress meant habitat modification. . . .

Moreover, the 1982 amendments came after the Secretary promulgated the present definition of "harm" at issue in this case. But instead of using the amendments as an occasion to overrule the Secretary's interpretation, Congress chose to allow the definition of "take" to stand, while amending another section of the statute—making clear in the process that it knew habitat modification could be (and was being) prohibited under the ESA. . . .

Judge Williams devotes a large portion of his majority opinion to a refutation of this argument. I presume the reason for this emphasis is that he concurred in the initial panel opinion in this case solely on the ground that the 1982 amendments "support the inference" that the prohibition of takings includes a prohibition of some habitat modification. Having placed all of his eggs in that basket, he understandably finds it necessary to explain his error at length now that he has changed his mind.

I agree that Judge Williams was wrong the first time. He was wrong to rely solely on the 1982 amendments for his decision; I agree that they do not alone support its weight. They indicate that Congress in 1982 probably believed that habitat modification was properly covered by the prohibition on takings. Admittedly, the 1982 amendments prove little about Congress's intent in 1973, and had Congress in 1973 specifically stated that "take" does not include habitat modification the 1982 amendments would not save the FWS regulation. But Congress did no such thing in 1973; it was silent on the question. Consequently, the 1982 amendments do lend some weight to the reasonableness of the agency's definition—if Congress in 1982 believed the definition was reasonable, and the agency believed it was reasonable, then *Chevron* demands that we uphold the regulation unless we find solid evidence to the contrary. No such evidence exists. . . .

NOTES AND QUESTIONS

1. *Reading the statute.* Does the language of the statute, without reference to any legislative history or to the agency's interpretation, answer for you the question of whether or not the use of private land can trigger the statute's protection of endangered species? Now add the legislative history, again without reference to the administrative rule. What is your view and on what specifically is it based?

2. *Adding* Chevron *to the mix.* These cases provide another good illustration of the struggles to establish the meaning of an ambiguous statute. What distinguishes them from earlier cases in this chapter is the presence of an administrative rule (of the Fish and Wildlife Service) that interprets the same language of the statute that the courts are being asked to interpret. Under the Supreme Court's *Chevron* doctrine (see Chapter 10, page 715), courts are required to give deference to administrative interpretations of ambiguous statutes. Each of the judges states his agreement with *Chevron's* doctrinal rendering. On what points do they disagree over the application of *Chevron?*

3. *The canon* noscitur a sociis. Judge Williams, in the first *Sweet* decision, states that, but for the 1982 amendments, he would have agreed with Judge Sentelle's view of the statute, specifically because of the *noscitur a sociis* canon. How applicable is this canon as a reflection of legislative intent? How sensible is its application in this case?

4. *The 1982 amendment.* In 1982 Congress amended the Endangered Species Act of 1973 to allow the FWS to authorize incidental "takings." What, if any, is the significance to each of the judges of this amendment to the question of whether the 1973 statute authorized the contested agency rule? What do you think of their views? Is it on the basis of this amendment that Judge Williams reversed himself in the second *Sweet* decision, and, if so, what about that amendment changed his mind? The rule in question in the case was in effect at the time of the 1982 amendment. What is the significance of this fact to each of the judges? What do you think of their views?

5. *The Senate bill.* When sent to committee in 1973, the Senate version of the Endangered Species Act contained language that, if enacted, would have barred the FWS from promulgating the contested rule. That bill did not contain the term "harm." The committee reported a bill without the limitation and "harm" was added on the Senate floor. How do the various judges weigh each of these facts? What is your take on them?

6. *The view of the Supreme Court.* In 1995 the Supreme Court resolved the debate among members of the Court of Appeals of the District of Columbia and among various other courts of appeals over the meaning of "harm" in the Endangered Species Act of 1973. Supporting the view of Judge Mikva in the first *Sweet* decision (page 906 in this chapter), the Court wrote:

> First, an ordinary understanding of the word "harm" supports it [the Secretary's broad interpretation of the statutory provision]. The dictionary definition of the verb form of "harm" is "to cause hurt or damage to; injure." In the context of the ESA, that definition naturally encompasses habitat modification that results in actual injury or death to members of an endangered species. . . .
>
> . . . [T]he dictionary definition does not include the word "directly" or suggest in any way that only direct or willful action that leads to injury constitutes "harm." Moreover, unless the statutory term "harm" encompasses indirect as well as direct injuries, the word has no meaning that does not duplicate the meaning of other words that §3 uses to define "take." A reluctance to treat statutory terms as surplusage supports the reasonableness of the Secretary's interpretation.
>
> Second, the broad purpose of the ESA supports the Secretary's decision to extend protection against activities that cause the precise harms Congress enacted the statute to avoid. . . . As stated in §2 of the Act, among its central purposes is "to provide a means whereby the ecosystems upon which endangered species and threatened species depend may be conserved. . . ."
>
> Third, the fact that Congress in 1982 authorized the Secretary to issue permits for takings that §9(a)(1)(B) would otherwise prohibit, "if such taking is incidental to, and not the purpose of, the carrying out of an otherwise lawful activity," strongly suggests that Congress understood §9(a)(1)(B) to prohibit indirect as well as deliberate takings. . . . No one could seriously request an "incidental" take permit to avert §9 liability for direct, deliberate action against a member of an endangered or threatened species, but respondents would read "harm" so narrowly that the permit procedure would have little more than that absurd purpose. "When Congress acts to amend a statute, we presume it intends its amendment to have real and substantial effect."

Babbitt v. Sweet Home Chapter of Communities for a Great Oregon, 515 U.S. 687, 693-94 (1995) (internal citations omitted).

Table of Cases

923

Bibliography

Advocacy Institute, The Elements of a Successful Public Interest Advocacy
    Campaign 11-12 (1990)
Alexander, Financing Politics (3d ed. 1984)
Alexander, Financing Politics (4th ed. 1992)
Ayres, State Term Limits are Transforming the Legislatures (1997)

Bach, The Nature of Congressional Rules, 5 J.L. & Pol. 725 (1989)
Bach and Smith, Managing Uncertainty in the House of Representatives
    (1988)
Baker, The History of Congressional Ethics, in Representation and
    Responsibility (1985)
Barone and Ujifusa, Almanac of American Politics 356 (1994)
Barry, The Ambition and the Power (1989)
Barry, The Ambition and the Power 98 (1990)
Bell, Jr., The Referendum: Democracy's Barrier to Racial Equality, 54 Wash. L.
    Rev. 1 (1978)
Blackstone, Commentaries an the Laws of England (5th ed. 1773)
Blatt, The History of Statutory Interpretation: A Study in Form and Substance,
    6 Cardozo L. Rev. 799 (1985)
Bonfield, State Administrative Rule Making (1986)
Brennan and Buchanan, Is Public Choice Immoral? The Case for the "Nobel"
    Lie, 74 Va. L. Rev. 179 (1988)
Breyer, On the Uses of Legislative History in Interpreting Statutes, 65 S. Cal. L.
    Rev., 845, 870 (1992)
Briffault, Distrust of Democracy (1985)
Briffault, The Item Veto, 2 Emerging Issues in State Constitutional Law 85,
    90-91 (1989)

Calabresi, A Common Law for the Age of Statutes (1982)
California Ballot Pamphlet: The Pros and Cons of Proposition 140, reprinted in
    Limiting Legislative Terms (Gerald Benjamin and Michael J. Malbin eds.
    1992)
Cardozo, The Nature of the Judicial Process 21 (1921)
Chappie and Kane, Gift Cases Often Favor Members, Roll Call

Charlow, Judicial Review, Equal Protection and the Problem with Plebiscites (1994)
Cigler and Loomis, Introduction, Interest Group Politics 2, 3-5, 7 (3d ed. 1991)
Cloud, Cong. Q. Week. Rep. 2854 (1993)
Clymer, One Bill's Detour on the Way to the White House (1995)
Congressional Quarterly, Congressional Campaign Finances (1992)
Congressional Quarterly, Congressional Ethics (1992)
Congressional Quarterly, Guide to Congress (3d ed. 1982)
Congressional Quarterly, Guide to Congress (4th ed. 1991)
Conable, Jr., Congress and the Income Tax (1989)
Congressional Government 303 (1885)
Congressional Record, 48th Congress
Costello, Average Voting Members and Other "Benign Fictions": The Relative Reliability of Committee Reports, Floor Debates, and Other Sources of Legislative History (1990)
Council on Governmental Ethics Law, The Blue Book: A Compilation of Campaign, Ethics, and Lobbying Reform Laws (1988)
Cox, Executive Privilege, 122 U. Pa. L. Rev. 1383 (1974)
Cronin, Direct Democracy 224-232 (1989)
Cutler, To Form a Government, Foreign Aff. 126 (1980)

DeTocqueville, Democracy in America 106-107 (Vol II) (Alfred A. Knopf 1980)
Dickerson, The Fundamentals of Legal Drafting (2d ed. 1986)
Dickerson, The Interpretation and Application of Statutes 144 (1975)
Dillard, The Amendatory Veto Revisited: How Far Can the Governor's Magic Constitutional Pen Reach? 111. B.J. (July 1988)
Donovan, Democrats May Punish Chairmen Who Defied Clinton on Vote, Cong. Q. 1411 (June 5, 1993)
Donovan, Maverick Chairmen Forgiven as Clinton Reworks Bill, 51 Cong. Q. 1451 (June 12, 1993)
Dwarris, A General Treatise on Statutes 121 (1885)
Dworkin, A Matter of Principle 328-329 (1985)
Dworkin, The Curse of American Politics (1996)
Dworkin, How to Read the Civil Rights Act, The New York Review, Dec. 20, 1979
Dworkin, Law's Empire 352 (1986)

Easterbrook, Statutes' Domain, 50 U. Chi. L. Rev. 533, 544-52 (1983)
Eskridge, Jr., Dynamic Statutory Interpretation, 135 U. Pa. L. Rev: 1479, 1484 (1987)
Eskridge, Jr., Spinning Legislative Supremacy, 78 Geo. L.J. 319, 334-337 (1989)
Eskridge, Jr. and Frickey, Cases and Materials of Legislation 630 (1988)
Eule, Judicial Review of Direct Democracy, 99 Yale L.J. 1503, 1550-1551 (1990)
Evans, A History of the Australian Ballot in the United States (1917)
Everson, The Impact of Term Limitations on the States: Cutting the Underbrush or Chopping Down the Tall Timber, in Limiting Legislative Terms (Gerald Benjamin & Michael J. Malbin eds., 1992)

Farber, Statutory Interpretation and Legislative Supremacy, 78 Geo. L.J. 281, 289 (1989)
Farber and Frickey, The Jurisprudence of Public Choice, 65 Tex. L. Rev. 873 (1987)
Farina, Statutory Interpretation and the Balance of Power in the Administrative State, 89 Colum. L. Rev. 452 (1989)
Federalist No. 10 (J. Madison) (Jacob E. Cooke ed. 1961)
Federalist No. 14 (J. Madison) (Jacob E. Cooke ed. 1961)
Federalist No. 22 (J. Madison) (Jacob E. Cooke ed. 1961)

Federalist No. 30 (A. Hamilton) (Jacob E. Cooke ed. 1961)
Federalist No. 39 (J. Madison) (Jacob E. Cooke ed. 1961)
Federalist No. 51 (J. Madison) (Jacob E. Cooke ed. 1961)
Federalist No. 52 (J. Madison) (Jacob E. Cooke ed. 1961)
Federalist No. 57 (J. Madison) (Jacob E. Cooke ed. 1961)
Federalist No. 58 (J. Madison) (Jacob E. Cooke ed. 1961)
Federalist No. 62 (J. Madison) (Jacob E. Cooke ed. 1961)
Federalist No. 73 (A. Hamilton) (Jacob E. Cooke ed. 1961)
Federalist No. 78 (Jacob E. Cooke ed. 1961)
Feingold, Special Interest and Soft Money (1998)
Fenno, Jr., Congressmen in Committees (1973)
Filson, The Legislative Drafter's Desk Reference (1992)
Fink, in the Modern New York State Legislature (Gerald Benjamin and Robert T. Nakamura eds. 1991)
Fiorina, The Decline of Collective Responsibility in American Politics (1980)
Fisher, American Legal Realism (1993)
Fisher, The Politics of Shared Power (3d ed. 1993)
Fisher and Devins, How Successfully Can the States' Item Veto Be Transferred to the President? 75 Geo. L.J. 159, 178-195 (1986)
Fordham and Leach, Interpretation of Statutes in Derogation of the Common Law, 3 Vand. L. Rev. 438 (1950)
Fountaine, Note, Lousy Lawmaking: Questioning the Desirability and Constitutionality of Legislating by Initiative, 61 So. Cal. L. Rev. 733, 760 (1988)
Frank, Courts on Trial (1950)
Frickey, From the Big Sleep to the Big Heat: The Revival of Theory in Statutory Interpretation, 77 Minn. L. Rev. 241, 247 (1992)
Friedman, History of American Law (1985)

Gaines, A Gathering of Old Men (1987)
Garrett, Term Limitation and the Myth of the Citizen-Legislator (1996)
Garrow, Protest at Selma (1978)
Gay, Congressional Term Limits: Good Government or Minority Vote Dilution? 141 U. Pa. L. Rev. 2311 (1983)
Gilmore, The Ages of American Law (1977)
Gottlieb, The Dilemma of Election Campaign Finance Reform, 18 Hofstra L. Rev. 213 (1989)
Government Ethics Reform for the 1990s (Bruce A. Green ed. 1991)
Grad, The Ascendancy of Legislation: Legal Problem Solving in Our Time, 9 Dalhousie L.J. 228 (1985)
Grad, The State Constitution: Its Function and Form for Our Time, 54 Va. L. Rev. 928 (1968)
Guinier, The Triumph of Tokenism: The Voting Rights Act and the Theory of Black Electoral Success, 89 Mich. L. Rev. 1077 (1991)
Gutmann and Thompson, The Theory of Legislative Ethics, in Representation and Responsibility (Bruce Jennings and David Callahan eds. 1985)

Hall, The Magic Mirror (1989)
Hart, Jr. and Sacks, The Legal Process: Basic Problems in the Making and Application of Law 1395, 1396 (1958)
Hastings Center, Revising the United States Senate Code of Ethics (1981)
Hedlund, Lobbying and Legislative Ethics, in Representation and Responsibility (Bruce Jennings and David Callahan eds., 1985)
Holmes, The Path of the Law, 10 Harv. L. Rev. 457, 468-469 (1897)
Horowitz, The Transformation of American Law (1977)
House Committee on Standards of Official Conduct, Report of the Special Outside Counsel (Feb. 21, 1989)

Hurst, Dealing with Statutes (1982)
Hurst, The Growth of American Law, in The Law Makers (1950)

Issacharoff, Polarized Voting and the Political-Process: The Transformation of
    Voting Rights Jurisprudence, 90 Mich. L. Rev. 1833 (1992)

Jackson, Problems of Statutory Interpretation (1948)
Jacobson, The Politics of Congressional Elections (2d ed. 1987)
Jacobson, Running Scared: Elections and Congressional Politics in the 1980s, in
    Congress: Structure and Policy (Matthew D. McCubbins and Terry Sullivan
    eds., 1987)
Jacoby, The Newly Registered Lobbyists: "Coalitions" (1996)
Jones, An Invitation to Jurisprudence, 74 Colum. L. Rev. 1023, 1041 (1974)
Jones, Statute Law Making in the United States (1912)

Kaye, State Courts at the Dawn of a New Century: Common Law Courts Reading
    Statutes and Constitutions (1995)
Keefe, The Functions and Powers of the State Legislature, in State Legislatures in
    American Politics (Alexander Heard ed. 1966)
Kingdon, Congressmen's Voting Decisions (3d ed. 1989)

Lane, Albany's Travesty of Democracy (1997)
Lane, How to Read a Statute in New York: A Response to Judge Kaye and
    Some More (1999)
Lane, Legislative Process and Its Judicial Renderings: A Study in Contrast, 48
    U. Pitt. L. Rev. 639, 648-649 (1987)
Letter from Daniel Webster to Nicholas Biddle (Dec. 21, 1833), reprinted in 2
    The Papers of Daniel Webster, Legal Papers (1983)
Letter from James Madison to W. T Barby, August 4, 1822; in Writings of James
    Madison 103, (Hunt ed. 1910)
Levin, Advocacy, Congressional Ethics and Constituent Advocacy in an Age of
    Distrust (1996)
Levmore, Bicameralism: When Are Two Decisions Better than One, 12 Intl. Rev.
    of Law & Econ. 143 (1992)
Linde, Due Process of Lawmaking, 55 Neb. L. Rev. 197 (1976)
Linde, When Initiative Lawmaking Is Not "Republican Government": The
    Campaign Against Homosexuality, 72 Or. L. Rev. 19, 24 (1993)
Llewellyn, Remarks on the Theory of Appellate Decision and the Rules or
    Canons About How Statutes Are to Be Construed, 3 Vand. L. Rev. 395, 399
    (1950)
Longley and Oleszek, Bicameral Politics and the Conference Committees 21-24
    (1989)
Lowi, The End of Liberalism 296 (1969)
Luneburg and the ABA Section of Administrative Law and Regulatory Practice,
    Lobbying Manual (1998)

MacCallum, Jr., Legislative Intent, 75 Yale L.J. 754, 763 (1966)
Macey and Miller, The Canons of Statutory Construction and Judicial
    Preferences, 45 Vand. L. Rev. 647 (1992)
Magleby, Direct Legislation 181-188 (1984)
Malbin and Benjamin, Legislatures after Term Limits, in Limiting Legislative
    Terms (Gerald Benjamin and Michael J. Malbin eds., 1992)
Mandelker et al., State and Local Government in a Federal System (3d. ed.
    1990)
Marshall, The Canons of Statutory Construction and Judicial Constraints:
    A Response to Matey and Miller, 45 Vand. L. Rev. (1992)

Mayhew, The Electoral Connection and Congress, reprinted in Congress: Structure and Policy (Matthew D. McCubbins and Terry Sullivan eds., 1987)

Meltzer, The *Weber Case:* The Judicial Abrogation of the Antidiscrimination Standard in Employment, 47 U. Chi. L. Rev. 423, 456-458 (1980)

Mikva, A Reply to Judge Starr's Observations, 1987 Duke L.J. 380, 384

Mikva, The Changing Role of Judicial Review, 38 Admin. L. Rev. 115, 117 (1986)

Mikva, Congress: The Purse, the Purpose, and the Power, 21 Ga. L. Rev. 1 (1986)

Mikva, Foreword to Symposium on the Theory of Public Choice, 74 Va. L. Rev. 167 (1988)

Mikva, Interest Representation in Congress: The Social Responsibilities of the Washington Lawyer, 38 Geo. Wash. L. Rev. 651, 661, 667 (1970)

Mikva, Reading and Writing Statutes, 48 U. Pitt. L. Rev. 627, 632 (1987)

Mikva, The Shifting Sands of Legal Topography, 96 Harv. L. Rev. 534, 540-543 (1982)

Mikva and Lane, The Muzak of Justice Scalia's Revolutionary Call to Read Unclear Statutes Narrowly (2000)

Mikva and Saris, The American Congress (1983)

Mitchell, A New Form of Lobbying Puts Public Face on Private Interest (1998)

National Conference of State Legislatures, Legislative Review of Administrative Rules & Regulations (1990)

Oleszek, Congressional Procedures and the Policy Process (1989)

Pertschuk, Giant Killers 151-178 (1986).

Petracca, Rotation in Office: The History of an Idea, in Limiting Legislative Terms (Gerald Benjamin and Michael J. Malbin eds. 1992)

Pitkin, The Concept of Representation 212 (1967)

Pollock, Essays in Jurisprudence and Ethics 85 (1882)

Posner, The Problems of Jurisprudence 271 (1990)

Posner, Statutory Interpretation—in the Classroom and in the Courtroom, 50 U. Chi. L. Rev. 800, 806 (1983)

Pound, Common Law and Legislation, 21 Harv. L. Rev. 383 (1908)

Pound, Law in Books and Law in Action, 44 Am. L. Rev. 12 (1910)

Radin, Statutory Interpretation, 43 Harv. L. Rev. 863, 870 (1929-1930)

Rawls, A Theory of Justice (1971)

Rosenbaum, I'll Sleep on the Idea, But Must I Vote on It? (1995)

Rosenthal, Legislative Life (1981)

Rosenthal, The Third House 6, 155 (1993)

Ross, Where Have You Gone Karl Llewellyn? Should Congress Turn Its Lonely Eyes to You? 45 Vand. L. Rev. 561, 563 (1992)

Rudd, No Law Shall Embrace More Than One Subject, 42 Minn. L. Rev. 389 (1958)

Salant and Sammon, Cong. Q. Weekly, Rep. 2238 (1995)

Schacter, The Pursuit of "Popular Intent": Interpretive Dilemmas in Direct Democracy (1995)

Sedler, The Negative Commerce Clause as a Restriction on State Regulation and Taxation, 31 Wayne L. Rev. 885 (1985).

Sencer, Note, Read My Lips: Examining the Legal Implications of Knowingly False Campaign Promises, 90 Mich. L. Rev. 428 (1991)

Sherman, A Citizen of New Haven (1788)

Smist, Congress Oversees the United States Intelligence Community, 1947-1989 (1990)

Smith, Faulty Assumptions and Undemocratic Consequences of Campaign Finance Reform (1996)

Smith, Old-Breed Lobbying, New-Breed Lobbying, American Politics, Classic & Contemporary Readings 370 (Cigler and Loomis eds. 1989)

Sourauf, Inside Campaign Finance (1992)

Starr, Observations About the Use of Legislative History, 1987 Duke L.J. 371, 375

Stein, Ethics in the States: The Laboratories of Reform, in Representation and Responsibility (Bruce Jennings and Daniel Callahan eds. 1985)

Stern, Ethics in the States: In Representation and Responsibility 243 (Bruce Jennings and Daniel Callahan eds. 1985)

Story, Constitution §§840, 841

Story, The Constitution of the United States 117-118 (Regnery Gateway Bicentennial ed. 1986)

Story, A Familiar Exposition of the Constitution of the United States, 70-71 (1986)

Strauss, When the Judge Is Not the Primary Official with Responsibility to Read: Agency Interpretation and the Problem of Legislative History, 66 Chi.-Kent L. Rev. 321, 335 (1990)

Sundquist, Constitutional Reform and Effective Government (1986)

Sundquist The Decline and Resurgence of Congress (1981)

Sunstein, After the Rights Revolution (1990)

Sunstein, Interpreting Statutes in the Regulatory State, 103 Harv. L. Rev. 405, 412 (1989)

Sunstein, Law and Administration after *Chevron*, 90 Colum. L. Rev. 2071 (1990)

Thernstrom, Whose Vote Counts? (1987)

Thompson, Political Ethics arid Public Office (1987)

Tiefer, Congressional Practice and Procedure (1989)

Tiefer, The Reconceptualization of Legislative History in the Supreme Court (2000)

Turner, The Significance of the Frontier in American History (1893)

Use of Congressional Staff in Election Campaigning, 82 Colum. L. Rev. 998 (1982)

U.S. Department of Justice, Office of Legal Policy, Using and Misusing Legislative History: A Re-evaluation of the Status of Legislative History in Statutory Interpretation, 6-20 (1989)

Veto Power and *Kennedy v. Sampson:* Burning a Hole in the President's Pocket, 69 Nw. U. L. Rev. 587 (1985)

Wald, The Sizzling Sleeper: The Use of Legislative History in Construing Statutes in the 1988-89 Term of the United States Supreme Court, 39 Am. U. L. Rev. 277, 281 (1990)

Wald, Some Observations on the Use of Legislative History in the 1981 Supreme Court Term, 68 Iowa L. Rev. 195 (1982)

Wang, Note: Legislative History in Washington, 7 U. Puget Sound L. Rev. 751 (1984)

Warren, The Making of the Constitution 158-159 (reprinted 1967)

Williams, J., Eyes on the Prize (Blackside ed., 1987)

Williams, R., State Constitutional Law Processes, 24 Wm. & Mary L. Rev. 169 (1983)

Williams, R.F., State Constitutional Limits on Legislative Procedure: Legislative Compliance and Judicial Enforcement, 48 U. Pitt. L. Rev. 797 (1987)

Williams, R.F., Statutory Law in Legal Education: Still Second Class After All
    These Years, 35 Mercer L. Rev. 803 (1984)
Williamson, American Suffrage from Property to Democracy (1960)
Wilson, Congressional Government (Johns Hopkins ed. 1981)
Wood, The Creation of the American Republic, 1776-1787 (1969)

Index